JUDICIAL POLITICS
Readings from *Judicature*

Elliot E. Slotnick, Editor

The Ohio State University

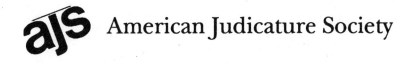
American Judicature Society

COVER ILLUSTRATION
Hans A. Mattes
Bench And Bar
acrylic, 18" x 20"
The West Collection
Copyright 1977, West Publishing Company

The American Judicature Society is grateful to the contributors to this volume for granting permission to use their articles, and to West Publishing Company for permission to use artwork from its collection on the cover.

Library of Congress Catalog Card Number 92-70682
Copyright: American Judicature Society, 1992
ISBN 0-938870-56-4

American Judicature Society
25 E. Washington, Suite 1600
Chicago, IL 60602
(312) 558-6900

For information about ordering, contact:
Nelson-Hall Publishers
111 N. Canal St.
Chicago, IL 60606

Contents

Preface

Editing this volume has been, from the outset, a labor of love. Instructors of courses on judicial politics have recognized for quite some time that some of the most important, interesting, current, and accessible research in our domain has appeared in the pages of *Judicature*. Several of us have, over the years, hoped that an anthology of *Judicature* articles could be made available for classroom use and, indeed, several of us have suggested such a volume at various times to the folks at the American Judicature Society. I was fortunate when in the spring of 1990 the stars and the planets were correctly aligned, AJS had the resources to pursue this project, and I was offered the opportunity to edit it.

In a very real sense the volume before you represents the results of a collaborative effort. Early on, we designed a questionnaire soliciting suggestions about topical coverage and structure for the reader. Over 100 colleagues responded to our questionnaire, and we are indebted to them for their valuable input. Subsequently, several colleagues offered their thoughts on the "first cut" table of contents for the collection. I know that the shape of the current volume reflects the ideas of many people, and the scope of topical coverage is both broader and stronger than it would have been had I been working on the volume alone.

My gratitude is owed to many individuals. At Ohio State my colleagues Larry Baum and Greg Caldeira were, as always, excellent sounding boards and sources of sensible advice. Donna Rogers provided excellent work in her preparation of the manuscript. My graduate assistant, Jeffrey Beatty, was invaluable during the early stages of the project, preparing memos and preliminary recommendations on literally hundreds of articles being considered for inclusion in the volume. At the American Judicature Society much advice, editorial guidance, and support came throughout the project from David Richert, Frances Zemans, and Kate Sampson. In particular, they were most helpful when my own biases "kicked in" and, as a result of their gentle prodding, this anthology has greater depth and breadth. Stan Kowalski did an excellent job of typesetting the book. Finally, in the later stages of this project, our debts extended to friends in commercial publishing houses, most particularly Cindy Stormer of Brooks/Cole and Lauren Silverman of Harper Collins who gave freely of their thoughts and their time in answering questions from a fledgling textbook publishing operation.

The ultimate test of this volume's success will, of course, be determined by its utility in the classroom. I must confess that my hardest task has been to "keep a lid" on things; there were a seemingly infinite number of pieces warranting inclusion and each new issue of *Judicature* that was published during my work on the anthology offered new possibilities. Inevitably, I have made errors of inclusion and exclusion. Looking to the future and the hope that this collection will enjoy many revisions, I urge colleagues and students to drop me a note about those selections that have been working well and those (hopefully few) that have been less successful. I would also welcome suggestions about pieces that are not in this volume that were published during the past decade or so in *Judicature* and that warrant a "sober second look." Perhaps most important, I look forward to hearing from colleagues as we collectively monitor future editions of *Judicature* with an eye towards articles we would like our students to read in the years to come. In this sense, the responsibility is ours to continue the kind of scholarly work that, under David Richert's editorial direction, has contributed to *Judicature*'s excellence.

At bottom, this book has been prepared for our students. They can learn a great deal, relatively painlessly, if they digest what is in this collection. They will also be given a great deal to think about regarding our system of justice. With that in mind, this book is dedicated to our students—past, present, and future—and their efforts to improve that system.

The American Constitutional System and the Role of the Supreme Court in the American Polity

INTRODUCTION   In every society some mechanism is established for adjudicating disputes and performing a judicial function. In the United States the American judiciary is uniquely powerful from a policy-making perspective. Much of the unusual authority of American courts stems from their exercise of the power of judicial review, the ability to invalidate the acts and actions of other governmental entities because of their failure to meet the guidelines set by the U.S. Constitution, the fundamental charter of American government. While judicial review may give American courts the "final" say in legitimating policy choices made elsewhere, it is a power that has always been exercised amid great controversy. Indeed, considerable historical scholarship exists that debates the fundamental question of whether judicial review was "intended" by the framers of the Constitution since this potentially awesome power is not explicitly mentioned within the written document itself.

Our first section of readings examines several facets of the dilemma of judicial review and judicial authority within the fabric of American democracy. In "The place of judicial review in the American tradition," Elliot Slotnick takes the reviewing power as a "given" and examines why the American political context was a uniquely hospitable one for such an extraordinary judicial prerogative to take hold.

In addition to underlying concerns about the historical legitimacy of judicial review and its place in the American scheme of things, analysts have always debated the question of judicial review's consistency with democracy. After all, critics have contended, isn't there something fundamentally undemocratic when a group of nine justices, appointed for life and largely unaccountable, invalidate (sometimes by a 5-4 vote), the will of popular majorities enacted into law by representative legislative bodies? Others are quick to respond, however, that American democracy means more than simply majority rule and, in fact, is equally concerned about questions of minority rights. For such analysts judicial review can serve as a bulwark for democracy in the protection of minority rights. In "Judicial review: The usurpation and democracy questions," puzzles such as these are explored by Albert Melone and George Mace. The authors recognize that one cannot turn back the clock and that judicial review is a fact of American life. Further, they argue, concern over whether judicial review is democratic or undemocratic begs an equally important question, the compatibility of judicial review with a "good" democracy, one that "operates to guard against threats to liberty and human happiness."

While scholarly questions about the legitimacy of judicial review and its relationship to democracy are interesting and important ones, their exploration does not "solve" the problem faced by American judges who must come to grips with their reviewing authority and make decisions about the scope of its exercise. In "Interpreting the Constitution," opposing perspectives are offered in companion articles by federal Judge J. Clifford Wallace and law professor Jeffrey Shaman. Wallace's article presents, "The case for judicial restraint," premised on the judge's reliance on "'interpretivism,'...the principle that judges, in resolving constitutional questions, should rely on the express provisions of the Constitution or upon those norms that are clearly implicit in its text." Shaman's answer, however, in "The Supreme Court's proper and historic function," is that such interpretivism is both impossible and unwise. Indeed, "The Court's role, when all is said and done, is to create meaning for a Constitution that otherwise would be a hollow document."

In reading the articles in this section, one is struck by the frequent use of terms such as "strict construction," "interpretivism," "non-interpretivism," "judicial restraint," "judicial activism," and others in the parlance of authors making a case for the "appropriate" exercise of judicial power. In much writing about the judiciary, such terms are ill-defined or, even worse, not defined at all. Rounding out this section of readings is Bradley Canon's attempt at "Defining the dimensions of judicial activism." Canon's effort brings an analytical structure to a concept which, like several others utilized throughout this section's readings, is often treated elsewhere with ideological overtones resulting in polemical writing lacking analytical rigor and clarity.

The place of judicial review in the American tradition: the emergence of an eclectic power

Whether judicial review was "intended" by the framers or not, it developed as a pragmatic response to the American experience, consistent with main currents of our political history.

by Elliot E. Slotnick

Traditionally, historical analyses of the American doctrine of judicial review have gone through a series of elaborate manipulations of memoirs and documents in an effort to decide whether judicial review was "intended" by the framers of the Constitution. The question of whether such "intentions" existed could be viewed as a peripheral one having little contemporary importance, except for the reality that emerges whenever there is any discussion of the role of the Supreme Court. As one scholar has noted:

A doubt that the whole package of present judicial power was legitimately conferred . . . lurks in the background of American politics and emerges to help convert grievance into passion when any sector of the population is greatly disappointed with the behavior of the Supreme Court in Constitutional cases.[1]

The question of the validity of judicial review has not been solely academically inspired, but was a great concern of many of the Constitution's framers and their contemporaries. The precedent for judicial review was established in the landmark case of *Marbury v. Madison* in an opinion by Chief Justice John Marshall. Yet the precedent was not, in reality, actively supported by all or even the great majority of his contemporaries. Thomas Jefferson raised what has since become a common argument against the judiciary's "proud preeminence."

. . . Yet this case of Marbury and Madison is continually cited by bench and bar as if it were settled law without any animadversion on its being merely an *obiter* dissertation of the Chief Justice.[2]

Despite the arguments of Jefferson and others,

judicial review was here to stay. The inability of its critics to eliminate judicial review has traditionally been traced to two major factors: the contemporary political situation, and Marshall's judicial craftsmanship. While establishing a precedent for judicial review in *Marbury v. Madison*, Marshall did, in fact, decide the case as the Jeffersonians wanted. What better means of obtaining acquiescence in the *entire* decision? While the Jeffersonians won the case, the price they paid was substantially greater than they had anticipated.

. . . This decision bears many of the earmarks of a deliberate partisan coup. The court was bent on reading the President a lecture on his legal and moral duty to recent Federalist appointees to judicial office, whose commissions the last Administration had not had time to deliver, but at the same time hesitated to (initiate opposition) by actually asserting jurisdiction of the matter. It therefore took the engaging position of declining to exercise power which the Constitution withheld from it by making the occasion an opportunity to assert a far more transcendent power.[3]

The role of Marshall in this coup has rarely been underestimated.

The problem was given no answer by the Constitution. A hole was left where the Court might drive in the peg of judicial supremacy if it could. And this is what John Marshall did. He drove it in, so firmly that no one yet has been able to pull it out.[4]

While the question of whether judicial review was "provided" for by the framers is an interesting one, our verdict shall not be added to the countless others already in. Rather, for the most part, the existence of judicial review will be accepted as a "given." Beginning with the existence of judicial review, we shall attempt to relate what was a peculiarly American phenomenon to a number of undercurrents in American political thought.

Several facets of the American political experience are, at least, consistent with the Court's review power. Among these factors we shall examine the following: precedents relating to judicial review, colonial notions about the "common law," colonial notions about "natural law," limited government and constitutionalism, American pragmatism and the fear of legislative omnipotence, and the prevalence of "magical" conceptions of the judicial function and the role of justices.

Finally, we shall attempt to relate the ambivalence of many of these factors to the emergence of an American tradition of "judicial self-restraint." In essence, we shall attempt to view judicial review as a "composite" power and take an eclectic approach. Judicial review may be seen as consistent with a number of modes of constitutional thought which otherwise have not been seen as consistent with each other. Although Hamilton and Jefferson stood on opposite sides of the judicial review question, there was no inherent reason why both Hamiltonians and Jeffersonians could not support the power. The foundations of judicial review were simply that broad.

The primary principles formulated as a basis for the American doctrine were: first, that a written Constitution is fundamental and paramount and therefore superior to common and statutory law; second, that the powers of the legislature are limited, a written constitution being in the nature of a commission to the legislature by which its powers are delegated and its limitations defined; third, that judges are the special guardians of the provisions of written constitutions which are in the nature of mandatory instructions to the judges, who must uphold these provisions and refuse to enforce any legislative enactment in conflict therewith. To understand the nature of these principles it is necessary to examine the notion of a higher law ... During the seventeenth and eighteenth centuries this idea of a higher law became the basis in England and France for laws which were held to be fundamental and unalterable and for a theory of the supremacy of courts.[5]

It is to a consideration of these and other themes and their relationship to judicial review that the bulk of this article will be addressed. First, we shall consider some of the precedents pointed to by the "headcounters" of the Constitutional Convention as evidence of the "intention" of the framers.

Not a new doctrine

The enunciations of the doctrine of judicial review by Marshall in *Marbury v. Madison* was not the first time that America was confronted with its existence. The review power had previously been recognized numerous times by colonial and state practices, debates held in the Constitutional and state conventions, and by specific clauses in state constitutions. Clearly, the notion of judicial review was not foreign to the American ear. Jefferson, it may be asserted, opposed judicial review, but he clearly recognized its existence in states other than his native Virginia.

In Virginia, where a great proportion of the legislature considers the constitution but as other acts of legislation, laws have been frequently passed which controlled its effects. I have not heard that in the other states they have ever infringed their Constitutions, and I suppose they have not done it, as the judges would consider any law void which was contrary to the Constitution.[6]

Jefferson is attesting to the existence of conceptions of judicial review in states other than his own. Yet, for an earlier period, there even exists evidence of judicial review in Jefferson's Virginia.

In Virginia . . . the Supreme Court of the colony, having been put the question, early in 1766, whether officers of the law would incur a penalty if they did not use stamped paper in conformance with the prescription of the Stamp Act, answered that the act did not bind the inhabitants of Virginia, "inasmuch as they conceived" it "to be unconstitutional."[7]

Similar words were used in many of the state courts and courts of the colonies. On the very eve of the Declaration of Independence, Judge Cushing, later one of the original members of the Supreme Court of the United States, charged a Massachusetts jury to ignore certain acts of Parliament as "void" and "inoperative."[8] Further, it is interesting to note that many of the opponents of the federal Constitution, and particularly its provisions relating to the judiciary, were critics simply because they felt that the power of judicial review, exercised so well by the state courts, would be weakened by the new system. Patrick Henry's remarks stand out.

The honorable gentleman did our judiciary honor in saying that they had the firmness to counteract the legislature in some cases. Yes, sir, our judges opposed the acts of the legislature. We have this landmark to guide us. They had fortitude to declare that they were the judiciary, and would oppose unconstitutional acts. Are you sure that your federal judiciary will act thus?[9]

It is obvious that the framers knew of precedents for courts exercising an authority analogous to judicial review. There even exists a great deal of evidence to support the view that many people felt that judicial review had, in fact, been *included* in the federal Constitution. The Convention spent much time on a proposal for a Council of Revision that would review constitutionality. When discussing the court's role in such a council, there was a general fear of giving the courts a *double* power.

It is clear, then, that one of the reasons why the Council of Revision proposal was rejected was that some of the members assumed that the courts would exercise the power of judicial review, and they doubted the wisdom of conferring any further power of a similar character upon the judiciary.[10]

And, discussing the Council of Revision, Elbridge Gerry expressed his doubts.

... Whether the Judiciary ought to form a part of it, as they will have a sufficient check against encroachments ... by their exposition of the laws which involved a power of deciding on their constitutionality.[11]

Other pronouncements by various Framers can also serve as further evidence for the fact that judicial review, in their eyes, was not unprecedented. Rufus King simply stated in the Convention that, "... Judges will have the expounding of those Laws when they come before them, and they will, no doubt, stop the operation of such as shall appear repugnant to the Constitution."[12] Similar remarks were made at state ratifying conventions. When George Nicholas was asked in the Virginia convention who would determine the extent of legislative powers, he replied directly, "... the same power which, in all well-regulated communities determines the extent of legislative powers. If they exceed these powers, the judiciary will declare it void."[13]

Similarly, in the Massachusetts convention, Samuel Adams said that, "any law ... beyond the power granted by the proposed constitution ... (will be) adjudged by the courts of law to be void." Oliver Ellsworth told the Connecticut convention that if the general legislature should at any time overleap their limits, the judicial department is a constitutional check; "a law which the constitution does not authorize is 'void,' and the judges 'will declare it to be void.' " Similar statements were made by Wilson in Pennsylvania and by John Marshall in Virginia.[14]

A few remarks made by Wilson can serve to illustrate the extent to which judicial review, in some minds, was regarded as an integral part of the judicial function. When the suggestion arose in the Pennsylvania ratification convention that judges might be impeached if they were to "decide against the law," Wilson retorted, "The judges are to be impeached because they decide an act null and void, that was made in defiance of the Constitution! What House of Representatives would dare to impeach, or Senate to commit, judges for performance of their duty?"[15]

Supporters of judicial review often relied on more than simply their word as evidence of its existence. Specifically, two clauses in the Constitution, the "arising under" clause and the "supremacy clause" were cited as "proof" of the framers' intentions. Admittedly, these clauses do not, in and of themselves, furnish undeniable proof of the intended existence of judicial review. But our purpose in this survey of precedents is not to "prove" the "intention" of the framers but, rather, to show that, at worst, the power was not unheard of and inconceivable. To a certain extent, we can readily endorse Corwin's view of *Marbury v. Madison* as a logical culmination of events preceding it in the American experience.

Upon the latent talent the problem of the time acted as incentive and stimulant, eliciting from it suggestion after suggestion which it needed but the ripe occasion to erect into institutions composing a harmonious whole.[16]

Common law and Coke

In discussing the relationship between judicial review and the American experience we may take as a starting point the American conception of the English common law and our particular reverence of the juridical philosophy of Sir Edward Coke. In part, Coke's doctrine, pronounced in the *Dr. Bonham's Case*, was seen as a precedent of judicial review; in part, it served as inspiration for it. In Coke's view, adjudication was a very special function, with the common law courts standing above all else, including the Crown, in matters of law. According to Haines, Coke sought "to erect the judges into a tribunal of arbitration between the king and the nation."[17] At bottom, Coke attempted to revive what he conceived were the limits imposed upon all authority by the Magna Carta. In his view, sovereignty had little meaning in England because "Magna Carta is such a fellow that he will

precedent for judicial review ... infl. by Coke

have no sovereign." As a result, parliamentary acts that were "contrary to common right and reason" were to be declared "void."[18] The common law, however, and "common right and reason" were the peculiar province of judges.[19]

Coke's conception of judicial function as pronounced in *Dr. Bonham's Case* would be echoed in almost identical form in many arguments raised by American colonial judges. As early as 1688, during the short reign of the Stuart despotism, there is evidence that "the men of Massachusetts ... did much quote Lord Coke."[20] In 1761, allegedly on Coke's authority, James Otis at Boston—in the Writs of Assistance case—plunged at once into the most fundamental issues. His argument was, that whether such writs were warranted by Act of Parliament or not, was a matter of indifference, since such Act of Parliament would be "against the Constitution" and "against natural equity" and therefore "void."[21]

Others followed Coke even more closely.

Governor Hutchinson, referring to the opposition to the Stamp Act, wrote, "The prevailing reason at this time is that the Act of Parliament is against Magna Carta, and the natural rights of Englishmen, and therefore according to Lord Coke, null and void." As late, indeed, as 1766, Judge Cushing, who was destined to become 20 years later a member of the first bench of the United States Supreme Court, charged a Massachusetts jury to ignore certain acts of Parliament as void and inoperative, and was felicitated by John Adams for his courage in doing so.[22]

Coke's doctrine had quite a different status in England than it did in the colonies, and this is the source of an interesting paradox related to the American readiness to accept judicial review. "The conception of a fundamental law as a rule to guide common law courts whose duty it is to keep both King and Parliament within bounds seems to have existed, so far as England is concerned, chiefly in the mind of Coke and a few of his very willing followers."[23]

Yet acceptance of Coke in America could be seen as a pragmatic coup; a means of accepting the common law and at the same time rejecting Great Britain. As Carr notes,

Coke's thesis was never really accepted in England, ... but the *Dr. Bonham Case* was known in the American colonies ... Accordingly, when in the second half of the 18th century the great controversy between the colonies and England began, and became centered in opposition in Parliament, Americans could not resist the tempta-

tion to use Coke's reasoning in the *Dr. Bonham's Case* ... Thus, on the eve of the writing of the American constitution, and long after England had repudiated the idea of a legislature's dependence upon a higher law enforced by the Courts, the idea was known and accepted in this country, in part at least, for a very practical reason.[24]

What better method could the colonies employ than invoking a doctrine which had had its birth in the mother country? No argument was likely to be as persuasive for the colonies as the accusation that England no longer subscribed to limitations she, herself, had formulated. Unquestionably, "At the moment when Americans were beginning to lay about them for weapons with which to resist the pretensions of Parliament," Coke's doctrine "met with a degree of success—enough at least to make it a permanent memory with the men of the time."[25] It would be difficult for a country professedly founded in idealism not to adopt this doctrine as its own.

A reductionist view

The relationship between Coke's doctrine and American development has even been extended into a reductionist explanation of the American revolution itself. Such a view goes far beyond merely using Coke to justify opposition to Britain. According to Boudin, the theory is "nothing less than the assertion that the American Revolution was but a lawyers' revolution, designed to revive and perpetuate in America Lord Coke's doctrine of Judicial Power which seems to have fallen upon evil days in England just about that time." The theory "first took definite form in the special committee appointed by the New York State Bar Association." As stated in the Committee Report, "In short, the American Revolution was a lawyer's revolution to enforce Lord Coke's theory of the invalidity of Acts of Parliament in derogation of common right and the rights of Englishmen."[26]

We need not accept such an obviously incomplete and simplistic explanation of the Revolution to assert simply that the views held of Coke's jurisprudence in America were consistent with the development of the power of judicial review in this country. When Perry Miller speaks of the "ambivalence" in the American experience towards the common law, to a certain extent this ambivalence may be viewed simply as an acceptance of Coke (who was rejected in Britain) and a xenophobia towards and rejection of things that were British. This corresponds to the paradox already noted.

Indeed, it is fascinating to consider how, during these and subsequent decades, the ambivalence persisted between hostility to the intricacy of the Common Law and at the same time reluctance to abandon it as constituting the bulwark of rights and liberties.[27]

Miller's "ambivalence" seems less of a paradox, and is more understandable when we trace back our acceptance of the "bulwark of rights and liberties" to Coke, and our rejection of the remaining intricacies of the common law to our xenophobia towards basically British accoutrements.

Natural law thinking

A second factor which may be seen as totally consistent with the American doctrine of judicial review and as related to our conception of the common law is the prevalence of natural law thinking in America at the time of the country's founding. Natural law reasoning, in fact, emerges as the basic argument for why judicial review was consistent with Jeffersonian thought and could be supported by his followers even while Jefferson himself opposed the doctrine. The natural law thinking of the era was not, in any sense, a contemporary invention, but reverted back to an earlier mode of thought. "The enthusiasm which manifested itself in the fight for human rights on both sides of the Atlantic gave new life and vigor to the Roman and medieval conception of a law of nature."[28] According to this regeneration of natural law thought, there were certain things which even government could not do, and the judiciary would serve as an overseer to guard against unwarranted governmental usurpation. Thus, according to Corwin, the idea of a "universally valid code of justice which is knowable to all men in the form given it in seventeenth century England by Locke and others, of a code of individual rights prior to government and available against it, this idea is basic to all ... conceptions of judicial review."[29]

There is much evidence that serves to link natural law thinking with judicial review, including even the somewhat questionable assertion that the very reasoning used by Marshall in *Marbury v. Madison* stemmed from ideas about natural law.

Like Marshall in *Marbury v. Madison*, (Gouverneur) Morris believed that judicial authority to void such legislation was "derived from higher authority than this Constitution. They derive it from the Constitution of man, from the nature of things, from the necessary progress of human affairs."[30]

Perhaps Dewey does stretch a point unnecessarily when he cites Morris to make an assertion about Marshall. Nevertheless, we are satisfied by the notion that judicial review (or some form of review) was, indeed, linked by some with natural law thinking. Further, this linkage was by no means limited to Morris.

The influence of the notion of an overruling law of nature is clearly apparent at an early period in the American colonies ... George Mason in a Virginia case argued: "The laws of nature are the laws of God, whose authority can be superseded by no power on earth ... All human constitutions which contradict his laws we are in conscience bound to disobey." Basing its judgement on a similar doctrine, a Connecticut court said: "The fundamental law which God and nature have given to the people cannot be infringed ..." The analytical theory which deems positive law an independent of moral consideration and as based on a sovereign will, was not accepted at the time; in fact the colonies were so impressed with the idea of an overruling law of nature that the laws of God and so-called natural laws were regarded "As the true law, and all temporal legislation was to be considered binding only insofar as it was an expression of this natural law."[31]

Natural law doctrine did not simply appeal to the Americans on an intellectual level, but was also used from a pragmatic standpoint, sometimes serving to bring an end to troublesome debates. As Perry Miller notes, "it was in order that the first efforts to manufacture a doctrine of American law after the Revolution should devote long sections to the law of nature, particularly because in 1790 ... there was so little accurate information about what constituted law in America."[32] It is unnecessary to assert that all justices or adherents of judicial review justified it on the basis of natural law, yet such an argument could and did certainly aid in adding a mystical aura to the function which removed it, to a certain degree, from reproach.

In reality, strict natural law doctrine was in no sense the major thrust of specific judicial review arguments, but natural law did serve to bolster judicial review in the abstract. Essentially, natural law arguments were used most often in the formative stages of the development and ascendance of judicial review, and served to make the judicial power a bit more palatable to a wider spectrum of citizens. As Haines notes, "The idea of rejecting laws contrary to natural justice or as infractions of the law of nature though frequently repeated by justices was, in the beginning of judicial review, seldom regarded as sufficient grounds to declare legislative acts void."[53] Nevertheless, natural law did place a cloak of idealism over the judicial function, and could serve as ample incentive to mobilize one line of support for judicial review.

Other justifications

Closely linked to natural law thought supporting judicial review were various strands of thought centering upon constitutionalism and limited government as the justification for the doctrine.

It may be remarked here that the doctrine of declaring legislative Acts void as being contrary to the Constitution was probably helped into existence by a theory . . . that Courts might disregard such acts if they were contrary to the fundamental maxims of morality, or . . . the laws of nature.[54]

Arguments for judicial review based on constitutionalism and limited government would appeal to a somewhat different segment of the population than did assertions based solely on the "mystical" natural law. The Constitution loomed as something more concrete than the heavens and the soul of man.

One of the most important principles which led to the acceptance of the American doctrine was the theory that a Constitution is a fundamental or paramount enactment. At the same time that the idea of a superior law of nature was prevalent the conception that a written constitution is a fundamental act was acquiring new meaning . . . in America.[55]

At the same time, however, judicial review's natural law constituency remained enticed by the apparent congruence between natural law, limited government, and constitutionalism.

Many historians have felt that in favoring judicial review the men of the Convention were influenced by a strong belief in certain fundamental principles . . . Accordingly they established a written constitution as the fundamental law and authorized judges to act as guardians of this Constitution by enforcing it against the improper laws which the legislature might enact.[56]

Written constitutions were alleged to be reflections of the natural law and, consequently, were viewed as fundamental, fixed, immutable, and permanent. Linking natural law with constitutionalism we are faced with, in Cahn's terms, "A change from higher-than-positive law to higher, positive law."

This, of course, is the very change that Marshall consummated in *Marbury v. Madison*; by legitimizing the appeal to the Courts he presumedly bastardized any possible "appeal to heaven" . . . "Appeal to heaven" having served its historic purpose, had nothing to offer toward meeting the need of a new era, i.e., the day to day enforcement of a written constitution.[57]

Once constitutions replace natural law, upholding the documents becomes as serious a task as meeting the earlier moral code.

It is easy to smile at the vagaries of ancient political practice, and to reflect with pleasure on modern superiority—but perhaps not wholly justified. For we are about to see a strange phenomenon: the typical political theorist of seventeenth century England proceeds in a sensible fashion to secularize and naturalize the process of drafting a fundamental law; he transmutes the obsolete supernatural code into a product of human ingenuity and intellect; yet—the moment the draft has been formulated—incontinently he assumes the prostrate attitude of the ancients, invests the document with the same reverential awe he declares for its source, and declares . . . that every part and the whole of it shall remain immutable forever and in perpetuity![58]

The general notion of written constitutions as a reflection of basic fundamental law can be traced to several threads in the American fabric. Haines attributes such a notion primarily to the French, and to the English conception of Magna Carta. Even in the very early American experience we have evidence of the theme repeatedly; it appears in Puritan writings where, perhaps, notions of the primacy or importance of secular law would be expected to be muted. Winthrop writes, however,

The deputies having conceived great danger to our State, we regard that our magistrates, for want of positive laws, in many cases, might proceed according to their discretions, it was agreed that some men should be appointed to frame a body of grounds of laws, in resemblance to a Magna Carta, which, being allowed by some of the ministers, and the general Court, should be received for fundamental laws.[39]

Thus, charters were written in the early Pilgrim settlements and these served as useful precedents for the American colonies. The courts were to play a significant role in elucidating the charters.

These charters were in the strict sense written law: As their restraints upon the colonial legislatures were enforced by the English Courts of last resort, so might they be enforced through the colonial courts, by disregarding as null what went counter to them.[40]

These charters were also significant in that they

were self-imposed by "the people." What greater reason could exist for treating them as "fundamental?"

... there was no longer an external sovereign. Our conception now was that "the people" took his place ... So far as existing institutions were left untouched they were construed by translating the name and style of the English sovereign into that of our new rules—ourselves, the People. After this the charters, and still more obviously the new constitutions, were not so many orders from without, backed by an organized outside government, which simply performed an ordinary function enforcing them; they were precepts from the people themselves who were to be governed, addressed ... especially to those who were charged with the duty of conducting the government.[41]

Thus, judicial review emerges as being consistent with theories of constitutionalism aimed at establishing the rule of law over the rule of men. "The basic antithesis ... remains substantially what it was in the period between Coke and Locke, that is, the antithesis between ... legal precept and executive prerogative, between wise rules and exercise of wide discretion ..."[42]

The link between judicial review and constitutionalism only maintains clarity and consistency if, somehow, judges are a different breed than executives and legislators, and adjudication does not imply wide discretion and the "rule of men," but, rather, reinforces a rule of law. We will return to this point later but, for the moment, can conclude with Andrew McLaughlin that judicial review was consistent with and was an extension of American views on constitutionalism and limited government.

The doctrine of what is now called "judicial review" is the last word, logically and historically speaking, in the attempt of a free people to establish and maintain a non-autocratic government. It is the culmination of the essentials of Revolutionary thinking and, indeed, of the thinking of those who a hundred years or more before the Revolution called for a government of laws and not men.[43]

John Marshall incorporated these views of constitutionalism in *Marbury v. Madison*. Between the lines one can read of "the Constitution" as "fundamental" law, but there remains a sense of linkage with natural law as well. Marshall, like McLaughlin, skirts the issue of why judges alone can "know" the Constitution and, as will be developed, this becomes a crucial point in the American genesis of judicial review.

Between the alternatives there is no middle ground. The constitution is either a superior paramount law, unchangeable by ordinary means, or it is on a level with ordinary legislative acts, and, like other acts, is alterable when the legislature shall please to alter it. If the former part of the alternative be true, then a legislative act, contrary to the Constitution, is not law; if the latter part be true then written constitutions are absurd attempts on the part of the people to limit a power, in its own nature, illimitable. Certainly, all those who have framed written constitutions contemplate them as forming the fundamental and paramount law of the nation, and consequently, the theory of every such government must be, that an act of the legislature, repugnant to the Constitution is void.[44]

The fear of legislative omnipotence has been a major part of the American political tradition, and this is another crucial area where judicial review served as a doctrine which could be supported by both Federalists and Jeffersonians. While the followers of Hamilton and Jefferson were rarely found on the same side of basic constitutional questions, it is crucial to an understanding of the place of judicial review in the American tradition to see how politically antagonistic groups could support the same doctrine for essentially diametrically opposed reasons. Thus, it can be demonstrated that the Hamiltonian Federalists feared that the popularly elected legislatures might not respect the prerogatives of property rights; the Jeffersonian conception, on the other hand, stressed the threat of legislatures to other minorities with the assertion that a multitude of despots were as bad as one. Approaching the problem of legislative omnipotence from different perspectives, it is instructive that judicial review was a doctrine that could serve several masters. According to Haines, "The right of the judiciary to declare law invalid, and thus to check the rapacity of legislative assemblies, was in the opinion of many to be the chief cornerstone of a governmental structure planned with particular reference to preserving property rights inviolate and to assuring special sanction for individual liberties."[45] In its utility for the preservation of property rights, judicial review became a primary Federalist doctrine; similarly, the stress on individual liberties made it acceptable to the Jeffersonians.

State legislative power

Federalist support for the doctrine of judicial review and fear of the legislature grew out of two closely related phenomena observable under the Articles of Confederation: the vast scope of state legislative power, and the use of that power against the interests of private property rights. In their framework for a new federal government, the Federalist's view of state legislatures would be instrumental in the call for both a separation and a division of powers emphasizing a new balance. Clearly, their view of the state legislatures was not a benevolent one. As Corwin notes of the "constitutional reaction" culminating in the formation of a new government, "The reaction embraced two phases, that of nationalism against State sovereignty, that of private rights against uncontrolled legislative power; but the point of attack in both instances was the State legislature."[46]

Suspicion of the post-1776 legislatures arose, in large part, as a result of their nearly unlimited powers. With virtually unchecked power in their possession, abuses followed and, as Madison noted, "Experience in all the States had evinced a powerful tendency in the Legislature to absorb all power into its real vortex. This was the real source of danger to the American Constitution, and suggested the necessity of giving every defensive authority to the other departments that was consistent with republican principles."[47] Hamilton raises a similar argument in *Federalist 78* in presenting his rationale for the judicial power.

The complete independence of the courts of justice is peculiarly essential in a limited constitution. By a limited constitution I understand one which contains certain specified exceptions to the legislative authority; . . . Limitations of this kind can be preserved in practice no other way than through the medium of courts of justice, whose duty it must be to declare all acts contrary to the manifest tenor of the Constitution void. Without this, all the reservations of particular rights or privileges would amount to nothing.[48]

The insistence upon further checks on Congress became the rallying cry of the Constitutional Convention for many Federalists. Yet by and large the checks they sought were not to protect the populace but, rather, to seek protection *from* the popularly elected legislatures. Much of this argument is articulated in the work of Charles Beard.

This very system of checks and balances, which is undeniably the essential element of the Constitution, is built upon the doctrine that the popular branch of the government cannot be allowed full sway, and least of all in the enactment of laws touching the rights of property.[49]

In seeking to avert "legislative tyranny" the Federalists sought a judiciary which would be the bastion of property, in Gouverneur Morris' words, "aristocracy, men who from pride will support consistency and permanency . . . Such an aristocratic body will keep down the turbulence of democracy."[50] Thus, as Paul notes, "The right wing Federalists . . . led by Hamilton and later by Marshall, had early regarded the judiciary as potentially the key bulwark of conservative defense."[51] Yet just as judicial review could serve the propertied Federalist interests, the doctrine could also be found in the arguments of anti-Federalists. Fear of legislatures was clearly a two-edged sword.

One who would understand the significance of judicial review for the Founders does well to start from the fact that in 1787 there was widespread fear of oppression by a remote federal government centered largely in dread of 'legislative despotism.'[52]

Jeffersonian support

Support for judicial review by Jeffersonians can trace its roots to the existence of natural law doctrine and its espousal by the Puritans as seen in the work of Winthrop. Winthrop notes the deficiencies of positive law as pronounced by *legislatures*.

Those who make laws . . . are also men subjecte to Temptations, and may also miscarrye through Ignorance, headlessnesse, or sinister respects: And it is not hard, to prove, that the Lawe makers, in all States, have Committed more and more pernitious errors than the Judges.[53]

Winthrop's characterization of the unique features of the judiciary are central to any understanding of judicial review in the American political tradition, and while Jefferson himself did not support judicial review, he often echoed the bulk of Winthrop's argument.

All of the powers of government, legislative, executive and judiciary, result to the legislative body. The concentrating of these in the same hands is precisely the definition of despotic government. It will be no alleviation that these powers will be exercised by a plurality of hands . . . 173 despots would surely be as oppressive as one . . . An elective despotism was not the government we fought for.[54]

To the extent that Jeffersonians could subscribe to Winthrop's conception of the nature of judicial power, judicial review could serve as a means to avert despotic government. Clearly Jefferson himself was not "mystified" by the judicial robes, yet "judicial magic" did serve to ingratiate judicial review to many Jeffersonians. Thus, the doctrine created strange bedfellows, serving as a rallying cry for both Federalists and Jeffersonians; the former supporting the doctrine as a protection from the excesses of mass democracy, and the latter supporting it as the very means by which to maintain such a mass democracy. *Reasons for each grp. to support jud. review.*

concerned w/ practice rather than theory

Pragmatic support

That judicial review could serve so many masters attests to the underlying pragmatic nature of support for the doctrine. Such "pragmatism" may, in fact, be seen as a manifestation of the seemingly "theoretical" American approach to politics, particularly as demonstrated during the formative years of our constitutional development. The basic pragmatism inherent in the doctrine of judicial review follows directly from the consequences of possible judge-made errors as compared to the much more severe societal consequences of legislative errors. Thus, John Winthrop noted,

If a Judge should sometymes erre in his Sentence; through misprision, or Temptation; the error or fault is his owne: and the injurye or damage extends not farr: but an error in the Lawe resteth upon the Ordinance it selfe, and the hurt of it may reache far, even to posteritye, there is more unrighteousness, and dishonor, in one unjust Lawe than in many unjust Sentences.[55]

an absolute ruler

Further, it was legislative despotism the founders feared, and not necessarily the despotism of courts. The work of Charles Beard becomes instructive in viewing judicial review as a pragmatic, nondoctrinaire response to the need the founders saw for a firmly founded, economically based government. In Beard's formulation, judicial review was just one of several bulwarks against populism. In a similar vein, Corwin notes that "judicial review was expedient, since the judiciary had control of neither the purse nor the sword; it was the substitute offered by political wisdom for the destructive right of revolution."[56] Some authoritative organ was clearly needed to interpret the meaning of the vague formulations of the Constitution and, in large measure, judicial review can be seen as a "peculiarly" pragmatic, non-ideological American response to a glaring need.

What is the basis of this power . . . of . . . no limit save self-restraint? Why did the country let the court—let it?— insist that it should have this power? What is the magic? There is no magic. It is the most commonplace of situations. When a great people finds that there are certain things they want done, and no one specifically

appointed to do the work, a job to be done and no one named to do it, they look around. When an applicant appears, shovel on his shoulder, they take him. He proves quiet, industrious, and discreet. What if he does go on a drunk now and then? He sobers off and goes to work again. Before you know it, John is a fixture. He likes his job. He is a good worker. He's a member of the family. No one else seems to know how to do the work so well.[57]

Curtis aptly portrays the importance of tradition and the basic pragmatism inherent in delineating a constitutional system out of a largely unspecified constitutional framework. Yet pragmatism cannot be the whole answer, for pragmatic men could have looked elsewhere to delegate a reviewing authority in governmental affairs. Such was, in fact, the reasoning behind demands for a Council of Revision in the original constitutional convention. While Chief Justice Marshall argued against the wisdom of allowing the legislature to be limited by limits they set for themselves, Bickel has noted that the Constitution limits "the power of the Courts as well, and it may be equally absurd, therefore, to allow the courts to set the limits."[58]

We are finally ready to address the question, then, of why *judicial* review? To this point we have attempted to demonstrate that review of some sort followed in the tradition of several different strands of American political thought. Yet to more fully understand the implications of and for *judicial* review, we must begin to view the peculiar role played by courts, judges, and the gloss of legality in American political thought.

A necessary principle

The principle of fundamental and superior constitutions, as well as defined and limited legislative powers, was necessary but not sufficient for the establishment of the American doctrine of judicial review. The role of "judicial magic" and the American conception of "the people" were both crucial to the assertion of the judicial review power in America. For the origin of the review power and its special relationship with the judiciary we may return again to the common law view of courts as outlined by Lord Coke. In his doctrine, the source of judicial power was not strictly based on or limited by constitutionalism but, rather, was inherent in the judicial office itself. "Common right and reason" were talents peculiarly held by judges and enforceable by them. That law was the special province of judges went far towards legitimizing judicial review.

As the law derives a semblance of eternal stability from this idea of Coke's that the law is over all government, so tradition lends a feeling of ancient stability to the Court. As the laws we enact are felt to be only a part of Law itself, so the Court feels that it belongs in a judicial lineage that is far older than the Constitution which it is interpreting and expounding. The Court, in fact, was already sitting and had been sitting for centuries before the Constitution was entrusted to its keeping, and Marshall's announcement of the doctrine of judicial review was, in one sense, the most natural thing in the world.[59]

Behind the common law conception of the judicial function there often lay an implicit intricate interrelationship between the role of the judge, and his position on earth as a representative of God; this corresponds to the natural law input of the common law. As early as the work of John Winthrop in America we get a clear portrayal of the place of the judiciary. Winthrop writes of special "parts and gifts, as the word of God requires in a judge,"[60] and implores, "... may we not ... trust him (God) to give ... muche wisdom ... to such Judges as he shall sett up after us?"[61] While American legality is not simply the reflection of the common law, as we have argued, it is clear that the "religious" nature of the judicial calling survived well beyond the era of our Constitution's framing, and served for many as sufficient justification for the legitimacy of judicial review. Thus, Perry Miller notes of the legal profession in general that it "operated under a religious sanction, even when engaged in the most hairsplitting disputation."[62]

For some, the connection between religion and adjudication has been quite a direct link. Theodore Dwight Woolsey, an ex-President of Yale, said in the post-Civil War period that, "Judges ... are in no sense representatives of the people or the king, or of any will whatever ... In a higher sense they are not representatives of the community nor of its chief magistrates, but of justice and of God! ... They are in fact more immediately servants of God than any other men who manage the affairs of a country."[63] Similarly, Perry Miller cites the words of Jesse Bledsoe in 1827. "An able and upright judge does, among men, perform the office of God's viceregent. The ministers of religion, as is their duty, may show the divine anathema pointed against crime and unrighteousness; but it is the sword of law, wielded by the judge, which, from its nearness and immediate effect, operates most

strongly to deter from their commission."[64]

We need not assert that all of America saw judges as the representatives of God on earth to make the more important and general point that judges have been viewed, in a sense, as a special breed of men. The "high priest" status of members of the Bar may, in part, be traced to the use of complex legalisms and "mystical" Latin phraseologies by judges and lawyers. While not accepting the "divine" element of judging, most Americans have at least been willing to grant the judicial process a peculiarly nonpolitical status.

This is a country that has most emphatically rejected the divine origin of government ... To tell the truth, this leaves a void, which we seek somehow to fill, disguising what we are doing under different names ... Likewise the Court's power seems to be more than can rationally be ascribed to its competence in its work. There seems to be some undisclosed factor in the equation, and its presence is indicated by excessive admiration.[65]

In the American conception, "men" were viewed as subject to acts that were arbitrary and capricious, yet "law" was seen as stable and enduring. "'Equal Justice Under Law,' we read as we enter the ... home of the United States Supreme Court ... In our minds takes shape a picture of impartial, impersonal judges applying traditional and immutable principles of law so as to render absolute justice to all men. Here there is no uncertainty, no mere whim or caprice, no arbitrary edict by man over man."[66] We need not look very far before seeing countless instances of the "peculiar" role of the American judiciary in our system of government.

Hamilton, for example, asserts in *Federalist 78* that the Court, "may truly be said to have neither Force nor Will, but merely judgment."[67] Similarly, Madison stated in the Virginia convention, "Were I to select a power which might be given with confidence, it would be the judicial power."[68] Largely due to a mysticism of their own making, judges and lawyers were able to take a unique place in the American scheme of things. As Miller notes, "The figure of John Marshall loomed as the paragon of reason, as vivid a symbol to the American imagination as Natty Bumppo."[69]

Miller also notes that:

Again and again the lawyers impressed upon the democracy the idea that to attain distinction at the Bar required so severe an intellectual discipline that few could ever even hope to measure up to it. They devised a litany in which the awesome terms were regularly flung out.

The law "demands the energies of the most powerful minds, and exhausts all the stores of learning." The profession is allied to every department of human knowledge: it must with the metaphysician explore the mysterious powers of the mind, with the logician it must master the rules of evidence, with the moral philosophers ascertain the duties and obligations of men, with the artisan it must learn methods and processes. In short, said Warren Dutton, "it calls to its aid all that the wisdom and experience of past times has recorded, and, in its highest exercises, becomes a model of all that is captivating or powerful in eloquence."[70]

In the landmark case of *Marbury v. Madison* Chief Justice Marshall asserted that it was "emphatically the province and duty of the judicial department to say what the law is,"[71] and we may cite with great understanding John Randolph's reaction to another of Marshall's opinions: "All wrong, all wrong, but no man in the United States can tell why or wherein."[72]

Thus, in large part, the acceptance of judicial review and the unique potential of America for the development of the doctrine rested upon "an act of faith" that judges alone "knew" the law. As evidence that this was indeed the case Americans relied upon a myriad of diverse authorities from the common law to the founding fathers themselves.

Says Montesquieu: "Judges are no more than the mouth that pronounces the words of the Law." Mr. Pope in his article in the Harvard Law Review . . . insists upon the belief in 1787 that judges knew the law, while others had only opinions on it.[73]

Further, as Daniel Webster noted:

The president may say a law is unconstitutional, but he is not the judge . . . If it were otherwise, then there would be not a government of law, but we should all live under the government, the rule, the caprices of individuals.[74]

And, finally, we return to Hamilton in *Federalist 22*: "Laws are a dead letter without Courts to expound and define their true meaning and operation."[75]

The final link

Only one more link remains to be established to answer the question, why *judicial* review? While we have demonstrated that judges were invested by the populace with God-like qualities, it would be oversimplistic to equate them directly with God's will on earth. (Although this reasoning process was practiced by some.) The "missing link" may be found in the place of "the people" in American political thought and the acceptance of the judi-

ciary as the representative not necessarily of God on earth but, perhaps more importantly, as the surrogate for "the people." Like so many other constructs, the importance of "the people" in the American system may be traced to the common law whose very name notes the locus of sovereignty in lawmaking. Sovereignty in America was identified with "the people" who were viewed both as the source of, as well as the location of, ultimate governing power. When Jefferson critiques judicial review, the role of "the people" becomes his primary argument. "But the Chief Justice says, 'there must be an ultimate arbiter somewhere.' True, there must, but does that prove it is either party? The ultimate arbiter is the people of the Union . . ."[76] Yet in his opposition to judicial review, Jefferson fails to take note of the ultimate coup which the Court has accomplished; that is, the identification of its pronouncements with the will of "the people." Bickel notes the apparent paradox involved.

The root difficulty is that judicial review is a countermajoritarian force in our system. There are various ways of sliding over this ineluctable reality. Marshall did so when he spoke of enforcing, in behalf of "the people," the limits that they have ordained for the institution of a limited government.[77]

Marshall, and several other justices, simply exercised the potential of the mystique that contemporary attitudes toward the judiciary afforded them. He disavowed any desire for judicial supremacy nor, alternatively did he support legislative supremacy. Rather, the will of "the people" was superior to both and the judges were the "oracles" of this "will." This theme is not unique to Marshall, but was widely echoed in the constitutional era and has reappeared with regularity ever since. Bryce states, "the Supreme Court is the living voice of the Constitution . . . that is, of the will of the people expressed in the fundamental law they have enacted."[78] The argument was stated most precisely in its pre-*Marbury v. Madison* form by Hamilton in *Federalist 78*.

It is not . . . to be supposed that the Constitution could intend to enable the representatives of the people to substitute their will to that of their constituents. It is far more rational to suppose that the Courts were designed to be an intermediate body between the people and the legislature, in order, among other things, to keep the latter within the limits assigned to their authority. The interpretation of the laws is the proper and peculiar province of the courts. A Constitution is, in fact, and

[handwritten marginal note:] Judges say what the law is

must be regarded by the judges as a fundamental law . . . That which has superior obligation and validity ought, of course, to be preferred . . . The Constitution ought to be preferred to the statute. The intention of the people to the intention of their agents. Nor does this conclusion by any means suppose a superiority of the judicial to the legislative power. It only supposes that the power of the People is superior to both; and that when the will of the legislature, declared in its statutes, stands in opposition to that of the people, declared in the Constitution, the judges ought to be governed by the latter rather than the former.[79]

Hamilton's argument, and its virtual repetition by Marshall in *Marbury v. Madison,* successfully performed an admirable "sleight of hand." Until their pronouncements, the representatives of the people were, by and large, viewed as "the people." Yet as the judicial version of the Constitution became accepted as "the Constitution," likewise did the judiciary substitute itself as "the people." Alpheus T. Mason succinctly states the essence of the "judicial magic" through which the Court interposed itself as the representatives of "the people" of 1789, a position which it apparently still holds in the eyes of many Americans.

The fiction is that constitutional interpretation consists in finding meanings that can be clear only to judges. To them the purport of the Constitution is obvious; to the President and Congress, its meaning is hidden and obscure. The only final and authoritative voice of the Constitution is a majority of the Supreme Court, and its every version, gleaned from a sort of brooding omnipresence, has the special virtue of never mangling, distorting, or changing the original instrument. The continuing myth is that the Court does not govern, nor does it affect those who do. What really controls is the immortal, unchanging instrument of 1789.[80]

In the final analysis, the American concept of the judicial function was and is a somewhat more "acceptable" version of the earlier Puritan conception. "The Puritan covenant had been that of God with his elect; the American covenant was an act of the people" speaking with their original, collective voice.[81] For the Puritans, "Judges are Gods upon earthe: Therefore, in the Administrations, they are to holde forthe the wisdome and mercye of God."[82] While not necessarily the manifestation of God on earth, early on the American judiciary interposed itself between "the people" who had ratified the American covenant and the current government. In such a way the judiciary became the living voice of "the people." In asserting this role, opposition to the judicial branch strong enough to deny it its

coup could never be mounted. Largely, this could be credited to the unique position that judges were able to command in the American mind, traceable to the Common Law, the Puritans, and the trappings of legality in early American society. The consequences of this for the American doctrine of judicial review are telling, as the doctrine could be more readily accepted, and more easily legitimized and justified when the substantial powers were held by a body lacking both "force" and "will."

A continuing role

We have demonstrated that American pragmatism played a key part in the genesis of the doctrine of judicial review. Such pragmatism has also played a critical role in the doctrine's exercise and continued legitimacy. In a government based on separation of powers and checks and balances, the need arises for checking the potentially awesome power of judicial review. Yet any external check on this aspect of judicial power would fly in the face of the entire rationale for the legitimacy of judicial review. If justices were a "peculiar" breed of men how could an external check be justified? American pragmatism again supplies what has proven to be, at most times, a workable answer. In balancing the checks, the Court must simply check itself. As Justice Iredell stated, "That such a power in the Judge may be abused is very certain; that it will be, is not very probable."[83]

Advocates of "judicial supremacy" have often criticized the Court for what they feel is excessive exercise of judicial self-restraint. Such arguments stress that it is the Constitution, and not the questionable statute that should be given the benefit of the doubt. Some have gone so far as to say that judicial self-restraint is, "Plainly a betrayal of the very basis on which the whole doctrine of judicial review has been based. A betrayal of the rights of the litigant, and the judicial duty owed him by the Court."[84] Nevertheless, it is essential to any discussion of judicial review to recognize that judicial self-restraint has had a long and honored history, and to the extent that judicial review was, and has been legitimized, its limits have always been implicitly recognized.

An essential maneuver in the exquisite strategy by which the Courts maintained their cause, despite the rising tide of democracy, was a prolongation of their advocacy of the Common Law into fervent adherence to the principle of judicial restraint. As long as they insisted upon this self-limitation, who could attack them?[85]

In the very next breath, after advocates had argued for the necessity of judicial review, they argued coincidingly for judicial self-restraint. Indeed, Hamilton himself, for example, stressed the importance of precedents for the courts, the very touchstone of judicial self-restraint.

To avoid an arbitrary discretion in the Courts, it is indispensable that they should be bound down by strict rules and precedents which serve to define and point out their duty in every particular case that comes before them.[86]

The same theme was continually sounded by a majority of the early members of the American judiciary.

Justice Iredell said in 1798 that because the authority to declare a legislative act, federal or state, "void, is of a delicate and awful nature, the Court will never resort to that authority but in a clear and unjust case." "A very clear case," said Justice Chase. In *McCulloch v. Maryland*, Marshall indicated that something like a "bold and plain usurpation, to which the Constitution gave no countenance," was required to invoke the exercise of judicial annulment. In *Fletcher v. Peck* . . . Marshall said, "The question whether a law be void for its repugnancy to the Constitution, is, at all times, a question of much delicacy which ought seldom, if ever, to be decided in the affirmative, in a doubtful case . . . The opposition between the Constitution and the law should be such that the judge feels a clear and strong conviction of their incompatibility with each other." This attitude carried over, as is evidenced by the remark of Justice Bushrod Washington in 1827, "It is but a decent respect due to the wisdom, the integrity, and the patriotism of the legislative body by which any law is passed to presume in favor of its validity until its violation of the Constitution is proved beyond all reasonable doubt." (*Ogden v. Saunders*)[87]

What is demonstrated by the above statements is the final pragmatic thrust at making the doctrine of judicial review a palatable one. In essence, the logic of the doctrine itself has been turned around and the ultimate question being addressed becomes one not of ascertaining the "true" meaning of the Constitution, but rather of deciding whether specific legislation can be sustained. Judicial review when aligned with the doctrine of judicial self-restraint becomes primarily a "negative" and/or defensive power, as opposed to a much more problematical and less acceptable positive initiating power. When viewed from this perspective, the review power can be seen as amenable to several opposing schools of governmental philosophy in America.

Marbury v. Madison has proved to be one of those very special occurrences that mark an epoch in the life of the republic. Culminating the great achievements of the Constitutional Period, it accomplished the transition from perpetuity to efficacy, from immutability to adaptation, and from heavenly to judicial sanction. Finally, it introduced an unending colloquy between the Supreme Court and the people of the United States, in which the Court continually asserts, "You live under a Constitution but the Constitution is what we say it is," and the people incessantly reply, "As long as your version of the Constitution enables us to live with pride in what we consider a free and just society, you may continue exercising this august, awesome and altogether revocable authority."[88]

These remarks are instructive in emphasizing the crucial interrelationship between judicial review and judicial self-restraint. We need only casually scan the periods during which the most severe Court curbing activity has occurred (i.e., the New Deal period, post-*Brown* decision Warren Court, etc.) to recognize that such efforts have coincided with periods during which a philosophical commitment to judicial self-restraint, even on the most abstract level, has been abandoned by the Court. Indeed, historical perspective helps us to understand the contemporary controversies about the appropriate scope of the judicial role as played out in the contemporary dialogue between the William Brennan and Edwin Meese jurisprudential camps.

Conclusion

We have attempted to demonstrate that judicial review was able to develop in America as a consequence of several distinct facets of American political thought which, while often in opposition to each other, were mutually amenable to and supportive of judicial review. This is not to say that all Americans of every persuasion welcomed the doctrine with open arms and gave it full sway. Rather, we have argued that the doctrine itself is such a multifaceted one that virtually all in America could support it because of at least one of its facets or, at worst, that a significant and vigorous opposition to the doctrine could not be mustered. Corwin has most completely captured the eclectic nature of the American experience which led to the ability of the landmark case of *Marbury v. Madison* to serve as the culmination of several distinct trends.

Upon this latent talent the problems of the times acted as incentive and stimulant, eliciting from it suggestion after suggestion which it needed but the ripe occasion to erect into institutions composing a harmonious whole ...

1. from Massachusetts and New Hampshire came the idea of this ordered and regular procedure for making constitutions, with the result ... of furthering the idea ... of the legal character of the constitution.

2. from New Jersey, Connecticut, Virginia, Rhode Island and perhaps New Hampshire came the idea of judicial review, partly on the basis of the doctrine of the right of revolution and partly on the basis of the doctrine of certain principles fundamental to the Common Law that had found recognition in the State constitutions.

3. from North Carolina ... came the idea of judicial review based squarely on the written constitution and the principle of the separation of powers.

4. from various sources came the idea that legislative power, instead of being governmental power in general, is a peculiar kind of power.

5. from various sources came the idea that judicial power exercised as it habitually was under the guiding influence of Common Law principles was naturally conservative of private rights.

6. from various sources came the idea that the judiciary must be put in a position to defend its prerogative against the legislative tendency to absorb all powers, and this idea was connected with the idea of judicial review both in the relation of means and of ends.

7. from the Congress of the Confederation came the idea that the Articles of Confederation and treatises made under them were rightfully to be regarded as part and parcel of the law of every State paramount, moreover, to conflicting acts of the State legislatures and enforceable by the State Courts.

Probably no one public man of the time shared all these ideas when the Philadelphia Convention met. But the able membership of that famous body was in a position to compare views drawn from every section of the country. Slowly, by a process of discussion and conservation, these men ... discovered the intrinsic harmony of the ideas just passed in review; discovered, in other words, that the acceptance of the others also, that each implied a system embracing all.[89]

Perhaps Corwin has overidealized the "intrinsic harmony" of the American experience in a misplaced effort to prove that the American outcome was, somehow, "natural." Such an approach is not really necessary and is, to some extent, misleading. In examining the peculiar American phenomenon of judicial review we have chosen to emphasize its eclectic nature. Post-revolutionary America was the site of numerous conflicts which often became serious points of contention in the general and ongoing Federalist/Democratic-Republican debate.

We have argued, however, that several facets of the judicial review doctrine enabled *all* people to at least *accept*, if not actually support the power. While Jefferson clearly opposed judicial review, it seems equally clear that a Jeffersonian could, in good conscience, support the doctrine because of its natural law and limited government orientation. Staunch Federalists, on the other hand, could support the doctrine for distinctly different reasons; namely its alleged tendency to control popular majorities. Two further tendencies served to make the doctrine acceptable in the American context. First was the entire dimension of "judicial magic" whereby all aspects of legalism possessed a mystique allowing the doctrine of judicial review to appear both less dangerous and more "natural." Judges, after all, were not "creating" the law, but were simply "midwives" lacking "force" and "will." Yet despite all of this, the American experience was a particularly pragmatic one, and "judicial magic" only appears to be functional when the judiciary has adhered to narrow limits self-imposed on judicial review, the adherence to judicial self-restraint.

We have argued that in addressing the seemingly unanswerable question of whether judicial review was part of the framers' "intentions" an equally important question has been largely ignored. We have attempted to demonstrate not that judicial review was "intended," but, rather, that it is clearly consistent with several facets of American political thought and that it emerged in America, whether strictly "intended" or not, in a peculiarly amenable and ripe environment.

NOTES

This article originally appeared in Volume 71, Number 2, August-September 1987, pages 68-79. It is dedicated to Alpheus T. Mason whom I had the good fortune to serve as a Graduate Teaching Assistant a decade and a half ago. His love for and deep commitment to American constitutionalism kindled my interests and the legacy of his scholarship well informs our bicentennial celebration.

1. Hyneman, THE SUPREME COURT ON TRIAL 114 (New York: Atherton Press, 1964).

2. Dumbauld, editor, THE POLITICAL WRITING OF THOMAS JEFFERSON 147 (New York: Liberal Arts Press, 1955).

3. Corwin, THE DOCTRINE OF JUDICIAL REVIEW 9 (Princeton: Princeton University Press, 1914).

4. Curtis, LIONS UNDER THE THRONE 12 (Boston: Houghton Mifflin Co., 1947).

5. Haines, THE AMERICAN DOCTRINE OF JUDICIAL SUPREMACY 18 (New York: Macmillan Company, 1914).

6. Dumbauld, *supra* n. 2, at 107.

7. Corwin, *supra* n. 3, at 31-32.

8. *Id.* at 32.

9. Berger, CONGRESS V. THE SUPREME COURT 251 (Cambridge: Harvard University Press, 1969).

10. Carr, THE SUPREME COURT AND JUDICIAL REVIEW 45 (New York: Holt, Rinehart and Winston, 1942).

11. Berger, *supra* n. 9, at 50.

12. *Id.* at 53.

13. *Id.* at 15-16.
14. *Id.* at 15-16.
15. *Id.* at 43.
16. Corwin, *supra* n. 3, at 38.
17. Haines, *supra* n. 5, at 27.
18. Corwin, *supra* n. 3, at 18-19.
19. Berger, *supra* n. 9, at 182.
20. Corwin, COURT OVER CONSTITUTION 22 (Princeton: Princeton University Press, 1938).
21. Corwin, *supra* n. 3, at 29-30.
22. Corwin, *supra* n. 20, at 22-23.
23. Haines, *supra* n. 5, at 34.
24. Carr, *supra* n. 10, at 41-43.
25. Corwin, *supra* n. 3, at 29-31.
26. Boudin, GOVERNMENT BY JUDICIARY, volume 1, 11-12 (New York: WIlliam Goodwin, Inc., 1932).
27. Miller, THE LIFE OF THE MIND IN AMERICA 241 (New York: Harcourt, Brace, and World, Inc., 1965).
28. Haines, *supra* n. 5, at 21.
29. Corwin, *supra* n. 20, at 5.
30. Dewey, MARSHALL VERSUS JEFFERSON: THE POLITICAL BACKGROUND OF MARBURY V. MADISON 65 (New York: Alfred A. Knopf, 1970).
31. Haines, *supra* n. 5, at 23-24.
32. Miller, *supra* n. 27, at 165.
33. Haines, *supra* n. 5, at 177.
34. Levy, (ed.), JUDICIAL REVIEW AND THE SUPREME COURT 46 (New York: Harper Torchbooks, 1967).
35. Haines, *supra* n. 5, at 24.
36. Carr, *supra* n. 10, at 47.
37. Cahn, (ed.), SUPREME COURT AND SUPREME LAW 16 (New York: New York University Press, 1954).
38. *Id.* at 4.
39. Morgan, PURITAN POLITICAL MAN 101 (New York: Bobbs-Merrill Company, Inc., 1965).
40. Levy, *supra* n. 34, at 44-45.
41. *Id.* at 45.
42. Cahn, *supra* n. 37, at 2.
43. Carr, *supra* n. 10, at 48.
44. Marbury v. Madison, 1 Cranch 137 (1803).
45. Carr, *supra* n. 10, at 49.
46. Corwin, *supra* n. 3, at 37.
47. Berger, *supra* n. 9, at 72.
48. Fairfield, (ed.), THE FEDERALIST PAPERS 228 (New York: Doubleday and Company, Inc., 1961).
49. Beard, THE SUPREME COURT AND THE CONSTITUTION 95 (New York: The Macmillan Company, 1916).
50. *Id.* at 91.
51. Paul, CONSERVATIVE CRISIS AND THE RULE OF LAW 231 (Ithaca: Cornell University Press, 1960).
52. Berger, *supra* n. 9, at 8.
53. Morgan, *supra* n. 39, at 156.
54. Dumbauld, *supra* n. 2, at 222-224.
55. Morgan, *supra* n. 39, at 157.
56. Corwin, *supra* n. 3, at 59.
57. Curtis, *supra* n. 4, at 46.
58. Berger, *supra* n. 9, at 183.
59. Curtis, *supra* n. 4, at 64.
60. Morgan, *supra* n. 9, at 123.
61. *Id.* at 153.
62. Miller, *supra* n. 27, at 186.
63. Curtis, *supra* n. 4, at 53-54.
64. Miller, *supra* n. 27, at 186.
65. Curtis, *supra* n. 4, at 53-54.
66. Carr, *supra* n. 10, at 1-2.
67. Fairfield, *supra* n. 48, at 227.
68. Berger, *supra* n. 9, at 185.
69. Miller, *supra* n. 27, at 119-120.
70. *Id.* at 136.
71. Marbury v. Madison, *supra* n. 44.
72. Rostow, THE SOVEREIGN PREROGATIVE: THE SUPREME COURT AND THE QUEST FOR LAW 87 (New Haven: Yale University Press, 1962).
73. Corwin, *supra* n. 3, at 63-64.
74. *Id.* at 22.
75. Fairfield, *supra* n. 48, at 55.
76. Dumbauld, *supra* n. 2, at 148.
77. Bickel, THE LEAST DANGEROUS BRANCH 16 (New York: Bobbs-Merrill Company, 1962).
78. Rostow, *supra* n. 73, at 122-123.
79. Fairfield, *supra* n. 48, at 229.
80. Mason and Beaney, AMERICAN CONSTITUTIONAL LAW, 4th edition, 18 (Englewood Cliffs: Prentice-Hall, Inc., 1968).
81. Miller, *supra* n. 27, at 217.
82. Morgan, *supra* n. 39, at 152.
83. Haines, *supra* n. 5, at 181.
84. Curtis, *supra* n. 4, at 25.
85. Miller, *supra* n. 27, at 236.
86. Fairfield, *supra* n. 48, at 232-233.
87. Berger, *supra* n. 9, at 338-339.
88. Cahn, *supra* n. 37, at 25.
89. Corwin, *supra* n. 3, at 38-41.

[handwritten: to take a power/position by force]

Judicial review: the usurpation and democracy questions

Whatever its origins, judicial review is a fact of political life. Debate continues, however, as to whether or not it is consistent with the spirit and form of democratic government.

by Albert P. Melone and George Mace

It is emphatically the province and duty of the judicial department, to say what the law is . . .
—John Marshall in *Marbury v. Madison*

[handwritten margin note: no mention of Jud. Review in Constitution]

Although it may be inferred, there is no explicit mention of judicial review in the Constitution. The only "express wording" that supports that power is the oath of office, the same oath taken by other members of the national government.[1] Therefore, the justification for judicial review requires more than an inspection of the wording of the basic document. Indeed, the justification in *Marbury v. Madison* (1803)[2] rests not only upon an *interpretation* of words, but equally upon an interpretation of a much more nebulous *intent* of the entire document.

The first issue explored in this article concerns the establishment of judicial review, which has been questioned from Jefferson's time by many who insist that the Court usurped power when claiming this function. For them, there is no constitutional justification—implicit or explicit. They insist that the founding fathers never intended to invest the judiciary with such power. Thus, we will seek to answer the question best phrased by historian Charles A. Beard: "The Supreme Court—'Usurper or Grantee?' "[3]

The second part of this article concerns the matter of Court rulings which, in the final analysis, seem to be legislative mandates emanating from *lawmakers* who are not directly accountable through the electoral process. This has led some to charge that such a power wielded by the judiciary is not consistent with the spirit and form of democratic government.

These two problems are closely linked. Those who believe judicial review is not democratic portray the judiciary, not as the unambiguous spokespersons of the Constitution, but as so many individuals who express their own personal attitudes or group interests. To them, the judiciary is little more than an outrageous oligarchy masquerading in the black robes of constitutional impartiality. The history of these issues forms the foundation for the analysis that follows.

Those interested in other issues such as the judicial capacity[4] and interpretivism[5] debates necessarily must face the fundamental questions explored in this article. If the federal judiciary may not legitimately exercise review and if that power is incompatible with democracy, then no amount of interpretation, selective use of power or its carefully considered timing may excuse its exercise.

The usurpation question

Judge John B. Gibson's 1825 dissenting opinion in the Pennsylvania Supreme Court case of *Eakin v. Raub*[6] is the classic statement addressing the usurpation of power issue. It is considered by many the most effective answer given to John Marshall's famous arguments in support of judicial review.[7] Judge Gibson weaves at least six related points.

First, he states that the ordinary and essential powers of the judiciary do not extend to the annulling of an act of the legislature.[8] In other words, the everyday duty of courts is to interpret the meaning of laws. Today, we would call this the duty of statutory interpretation; and indeed, courts spend considerable time and effort in deciding what the legislature meant when it enacted a given piece of legislation, and how the legislation should be interpreted, given the facts of the particular case or controversy before it. This task, argues Gibson, is the ordinary and essential aspect of judicial power.

Secondly, Judge Gibson argues that what is good for one co-equal branch of the government should be good for the others. He claims that it would be viewed as a usurpation of judicial power if the legislature should attempt to reverse a Supreme Court decision. Yet, it is not regarded as a usurpation of legislative power when the judiciary holds a statute unconstitutional.[9] This argument is all the more cogent in the light of twentieth century experience. Interest groups have attempted, and sometimes succeeded, in reversing controversial Supreme Court decisions by proposing the rewriting of statutes to avoid previously held unconstitutional provisions, removing appellate jurisdiction or even campaigning for constitutional amendments. Defenders of Court decisions will often appeal to a sense of deep commitment to the Court as the guardian of the Constitution.[10] Though reason may require equal regard for the authority of the legislative branch, as Gibson points out, the judiciary occupies a special status within the governmental system, unaffected by the rules of logic.

Third, Gibson argues that the concept of checks and balances does not include the idea of a judicial veto. Within the legislative branch itself, a proposal must pass through two legislative chambers. If the framers intended to impose the judiciary as an additional barrier, they would have explicitly granted to the judges the power, instead of leaving the matter in doubt.[11]

Fourth, Gibson takes up the matter of the oath, which John Marshall regarded as a high moral duty. For Gibson, the oath of office taken by judicial officers, or for that matter any government official, extends only to supporting the Constitution as far as it extends to official conduct. If one's duty does not entail excursions into the legislative realm, neither does one's oath.[12] This conclusion gives rise to a rhetorical question that we may treat as Gibson's fifth point.

Does a judge violate the Constitution when he permits an unconstitutional legislative act to stand? "No!" Gibson says. The enactment and the interpretation of a legislative act are not concurrent. In other words, the judge does not adopt unconstitutional legislation as his own simply because he interprets it. Members of the legislative branch enact legislation, not the judiciary.[13]

The sixth major point states that if the legislature enacts an unconstitutional law, the people may petition their elected representatives to repeal it. If the judiciary makes a mistake, then a constitutional amendment is needed. The former remedy is clearly preferable to the latter one, given the relatively drastic and cumbersome process of amending a constitution.[14]

The remainder of Gibson's famous dissent is an exposition of the authority of state courts under the Constitution. However, what is of lasting value is his contribution to the debate over judicial review. Interestingly, Gibson later recanted his bold view because the Pennsylvania legislature had "sanctioned the pretensions of the courts to deal freely with the acts of the legislature, and from experience of the necessity of the case."[15]

Judicial self-restraint

Forty years after Gibson's death, James B. Thayer stood before the Congress on Jurisprudence and Law Reform on August 9, 1893, to read one of the most influential papers ever delivered on the subject of judicial review.[16] After noting with favor Judge Gibson's dissent, he went on to argue for the view he had adopted early in life. If the Supreme Court exercised judicial review at all, he said, it must be with great restraint; it may declare acts void only when their constitutionality was beyond all reasonable doubt.

The Harvard law professor reviewed carefully the historical antecedents to the establishment of judicial review. He came to the skeptical conclusion: "[t]he judiciary may well reflect that if they had been regarded by the people as the chief protection against legislative violation of the constitution, they would not have been allowed . . . incidental and postponed control."[17] Yet, Thayer accepts judicial review as a legitimate judicial function, and not a per se usurpation of legislative power. What is unacceptable is the employment of judicial review in those instances in which reasonable persons may disagree. Judicial review should be reserved for those cases where there is no "reasonable doubt" that the legislature enacted an unconstitutional law.[18]

Thayer counsels for judicial self-restraint because the very independence of the judiciary may be jeopardized without it. He argues that repeated and unnecessary use of the judicial veto could excite institutional jealousy and diminish public reverence for the laws. He acknowledges that judges are part of the political process and therefore should "... apply methods and principles that befit their task."[19] It is this view of the Court's relationship with the other branches of government that clearly distinguishes advocates of judicial self-restraint from others—whether these be mechanistic rule-oriented absolutists on the one hand, or, on the other hand, activist judges committed to using courts to right the many wrongs abroad in the land in the manor of a superlegislature.

This famous essay is the foundation on which Justices Holmes, Brandeis and Frankfurter constructed their judicial philosophies. All three were associated with Harvard and connected with Thayer as faculty member or student. All three acknowledged the intellectual impact of Thayerism upon their own thinking. The three justices represent the most articulate spokespersons for judicial self-restraint from 1902 to 1962. While all three made unique contributions to constitutional law, reading the judicial opinions of each provides scholar and practitioner alike with the finest primer available in any form on the doctrine of judicial self-restraint. Consider the dissent from the Supreme Court's social Darwinist activist era at the turn of the century through the mid-1930s. Also reflect on the opposition to the writing of the Bill of Rights into the Constitution as a prohibition against state power through the 1950s and early 1960s and beyond. The legacy of Holmes, Brandeis and Frankfurter is unmistakable.[20]

The timelessness of the Thayer article is evident when considering contemporary criticisms of the Supreme Court. The charge that the Supreme Court has become a policy-making institution, with little regard for popular opinion and proper deference toward the legislature, is one that modern conservative ideologues, including those in the Reagan administration, have trumpeted with great resonance. Yet, the political noise directed against the Court is not limited to this age. The same arguments were directed against the Court by liberals in an earlier age who opposed the Court's tendency to strike down social and economic legislation designed to protect the masses against economic wealth and power.

Without intending undue cynicism, we must point out from a historical perspective that positions on judicial activism versus restraint often turn on whose ox is being gored. Yesterday's liberals often criticized the Court for is activism; today, it is the conservatives who condemn the Court for the same sin. Though this fact does not alter the validity, if any, of Professor Thayer's views, it nonetheless reinforces his basic underlying assumption of the Supreme Court as a political institution.

Judicial review as obligation

In the face of rising controversy surrounding the Court's activism in apparent opposition to government regulation of the economy, Associate Justice Horace H. Lurton in 1911 defended the institution against its critics.[21] Few men were more suitable for the task, whether from conviction or deed.

Justice Lurton argues that public opinion and the oath of office are not sufficient guarantees insuring that legislators will stay within constitutional boundaries when promulgating laws. Lurton proceeds from the premises first enunciated by Montesquieu in *The Spirit of the Laws* (1748). The great French scholar of the eighteenth century concluded that liberty could not be maintained without a separation of powers between the legislative, executive and judicial functions. Lurton argues that American history supports the contention that the exercise of judicial review is an obligation of the judiciary as a guarantor of liberty.[22]

Not only is early case law presented in support of judicial review, but Lurton asserts also that its practice was accepted by the people in the early years of the republic. Unfortunately, however, the enormous mass of new immigrants, "unaccustomed to democratic government," consider the judicial veto as a usurpation of legislative authority.[23] Justice Lurton then proceeds to instruct that in a government of laws there is no such thing as unlimited power. Rather, all power is delegated.

Thus, when courts exercise judicial review they are not legislating or employing uncontrolled political power; they are applying the elementary principle that "... the acts of an agent in excess of his authority do not bind his principal." Judges in such instances have no choice but to "... enforce the constitution as the law of highest obligation."[24]

There is an unstated premise in Lurton's argument. It is that law and politics are somehow separate and distinct; the judges' role is simply to find the law, not to make it. Indeed, the widespread belief that legal rules are superior to individual choice is the genesis of the phrase: a nation of laws, not of men. The ideology of legalism summarized in this phrase has as much attraction today as it did when Lurton wrote his article over three-quarters of a century ago. The search for neutral principles of law and objectivity in decision making is a recurring theme in American law. The current so-called interpretivism or intentionalism debate championed by Attorney General Edwin Meese and Robert Bork, among others, is but the latest variation on an old theme. As long as humans believe that their decisions should be based upon principles transcending self-interest and subjectivity, essays such as Lurton's will be written. Yet, how we believe we ought to behave is not always how we *in fact* behave. The confusion of a value prescription for a factual description is as common to judges as it is to ordinary mortals.

Rebutting judicial review

Justice Lurton's vigorous defense of judicial review was answered contemporaneously with an equally spirited essay. Louis Boudin, a New York labor lawyer and prominent member of the American Labor Party during the early part of this century, challenged Lurton's arguments.[25] The debate reached well beyond cloistered academic halls. The fact is the Supreme Court deployed constitutional concepts, such as substantive due process and liberty of contract, to strike down legislation designed to protect working persons. Organized labor and progressives viewed the Supreme Court at the turn of the century as an important force of reaction and opposition.

Boudin sets out to make two major points. First, he presents evidence to discredit Justice Lurton's claim that judicial review was intended by the framers of the Constitution. Second, he argues that as a matter of fact, the power of judicial review as exercised by the turn of the century Supreme Court is nothing less than revolutionary.

The author maintains that judicial review was not a recognized power at the time of the American revolution. He argues that the authority was not recognized in England, and that Lurton's reliance on the writings of Montesquieu is misplaced. The failure of John Marshall to cite so-called existing precedents from state courts was wise because, according to Boudin, the "precedents" do not demonstrate opinion in favor of judicial review, but its very opposite.[26]

Boudin examines evidence concerning the framers' intent. He concludes that although some who gathered at Philadelphia favored judicial review, given their explicit silence on the subject, ". . . the great majority of the Framers never suspected a general power of the judiciary to control legislation could be interpreted into the new constitution."[27]

Citing Judge Gibson's dissent approvingly, Marshall's decision in *Marbury v. Madison* is characterized by Boudin in the first instance as "amazing."[28] Boudin also makes two additional points worthy of consideration. First, the *Marbury* decision related particularly to judicial power, and not to general legislation. It is one thing for the Supreme Court to defend the judicial branch against legislative encroachment; it is quite another to claim the Court is the sole and binding interpreter of the Constitution. Second, Jefferson won the immediate battle because Marbury was denied the commission he sought. Thus, the unpopular Federalist attempt to stack the judiciary with the party faithful was spoiled. The decision in *Marbury* provoked no extended public debate because it had no practical importance. The lack of a huge public outcry should therefore not be interpreted as acceptance of judicial review.[29]

If one line of reasoning fails to convince judge and jury, try another. This is true even if the two arguments proceed from different premises. This typical lawyer tactic is employed by Boudin in his "brief" against the then contemporary Supreme Court. He first makes the case that there is nothing in the pre-convention history, court precedents, intent of the framers and Supreme Court decisions to justify judicial review. Boudin then argues, in essence, that if all the arguments just presented are rejected, and one accepts the exercise of judicial review as a legitimate authority, the contemporary Court has nonetheless employed the power improperly.[30] In short, a posture of self-restraint is prescribed. Let the policy judgments of the legislatures stand, Boudin says. If the legislative branch violates the Constitution, the best protection against such abuse is the people, not the courts. At this point in the essay, Boudin reads very much like Thayer.

Boudin ends his argument with a consideration of how the Supreme Court abused its power in a number of important recent cases. Boudin argues that the Court's conservative majority substituted their personal policy views for that of legislatures. The Court's famous decisions in *Lochner v. New York* (1905), *Adair v. United States* (1908), and others are pointed to as proof that there are not "plain and simple" rules of constitutional interpretation as claimed by Justice Lurton. "On the contrary, there are now practically no rules at all,"[31] said Boudin. Once again, we are reminded of contemporary criticism. The principal difference is that since the mid-1950s, the critical voices come from the political right, instead of the political left.

The intent of the framers

Mr. Boudin's accusations and those of his fellow doubters did not pass unnoticed. A popular Columbia University professor, later to become president of both the American Historical Association and the American Political Science Association, answered the complaint.[32] Through an examination of the direct and indirect declarations of certain members of the Philadelphia Convention and the "general purpose and spirit of the federal Constitution," Charles A. Beard concludes that judicial review was not usurped; it was intended by the framers. The evidence adduced in support of his conclusion, and the assumptions underlying his research methodology, not only shed light upon the usurpation question, but also point to the many difficulties inherent in constitutional interpretation.

Beard begins his argument by conceding that the delegates to the Constitutional Convention did not consider a proposition to grant the judicial branch veto power over legislative acts. In fact, none was submitted. A council of revision was proposed that would have joined a number of judges with the executive to revise laws passed by Congress.[33] According to Beard, however, that is a different proposition from judicial review. It may be legitimately asked whether this difference is sufficiently dissimilar to sustain Beard's point. Later in the article, Beard cites the apparent support of certain delegates for the revisionary council proposition as persuasive evidence of their belief in judicial review. Logic militates against arguing on the one hand that judicial review and the revisionary proposition were not the same; and then, on the other hand, suggesting that if a delegate favored the revisionary proposition, he probably also favored judicial review. In any event, Beard claims the "question of judicial control . . . did not come

squarely before the Convention, in such form that a vote could be taken."[34]

The bulk of Beard's article is devoted to the difficult question of what the framers intended. He prefaces this research approach with the caution that any such inquiry must be incomplete because new research could uncover additional information. However, the search for intent is fraught with even greater difficulties, not the least of which are its underlying assumptions. These are succinctly outlined by Professors Walter Murphy and C. Herman Pritchett in their standard modern text.[35]

The first assumption is that future generations should be bound by the specific intentions of the framers, not the general principles that guided their actions. If the assumption is accepted, then Americans will be constitutionally mired in the eighteenth century. In this view, the Constitution must be interpreted as a set of rules that can be clearly understood as articulated by the framers. In fairness, both Beard and his intellectual antagonist, Boudin, silently accept this questionable assumption. Yet given the nature of the argument, it is reasonable for Beard to search for specific intent. It is Boudin and others who claim that, because the framers were silent on the matter of judicial review, they could not have intended to make it a part of the Constitution. Beard uses evidence of the specific intent of the individual framers to counter this point.

The second assumption underlying the search for the framers' intent is more difficult to defend. It is that the framers had a single intention. In fact, it is probable that they had many different, sometimes contradictory and even irreconcilable "intentions." Indeed, the Philadelphia Convention was not an exercise in ascertaining the "general will" or Confucian harmony. Rather, it was a matter of compromise, logrolling and negotiation about matters that do not lend themselves to simple solutions. The politics of such a setting renders the ascertainment of a solid and unified group intention difficult at best.

Beard mitigates the problem of intent by breaking the group down into its constituent parts, namely, each individual delegate. He does this by examining the debates at the Convention, public comments made after Philadelphia, congressional votes and the letters and private documents of many of the delegates.

He does not examine the views of all 55 delegates

to the Philadelphia Convention. Rather, Beard first investigates the views of what he calls the leading or the most influential members of the Convention.[36] He concludes that, of these, not less than 13 believed that judicial power extended to the nullification of an act of Congress. He adds four more delegates to his total by virtue of their subsequent votes in support of the Judiciary Act of 1789.[37] Of the less influential delegates, six either expressed themselves in favor of judicial review or approved of it by virtue of their votes on the 1789 act.[38] [Beard's reference to the Judiciary Act is to that part of the law dealing with federal-state relations under the Constitution's Supremacy Clause. The argument supposes that favoring judicial review of state actions is the equivalent of support for judicial control over congressional acts. Though the two are related, one should consider whether it is reasonable to support the federalism principle without favoring third branch veto over congressional enactments. Finally, with respect to the Judiciary Act, it must be pointed out that the methodological problems inherent in ascertaining legislative intent are, in principle, similar to those met when studying constitutional intent.]

We are not persuaded that the evidence presented for each delegate's position on judicial review is clear and convincing. Beard's best case argument does not add up to even a majority of the delegates favoring judicial review. He finds that 23 were for judicial review, 5 were against review, and the views of the remaining 27 are unknown. Edward S. Corwin, whose authority ranks with that of Beard's, found only 17 in favor of judicial review.[39] Nevertheless, both scholars insist that the framers intended judicial review. It is troublesome nonetheless that as influential as the 23 or 17 delegates may have been, it requires considerable faith in their leadership abilities to conclude that all, most, or even a majority of the delegates would have voted for judicial review if the proposition were presented squarely to them.

However, as one progresses through Beard's presentation, it is discovered that numbers are not everything. Beard's fall back position is clear enough: ". . . the Constitution was not designed to be perfectly explicit on all points and to embody definitely the opinions of a majority of the Convention . . . ."[40] If this is true, then why did Beard make the case for the specific intent of as many convention delegates as he could? Beard does not rest his

case with the submission of evidence on the framers' intentions. He continues the "brief" against Boudin and other named and unnamed opposing counsels by addressing the remaining usurpation charges and evidence.

Constitutions are not only framed, they are also ratified. Beard presents admittedly fragmentary evidence on this point. He offers information from the debates in 4 of 13 state ratifying conventions in support of his argument that those who ratified the Constitution favored judicial review.[41] Beard is also unimpressed by arguments that state judicial opinions do not serve as adequate precedents for judicial review.[42] Finally, Beard defends John Marshall against the charge that he created judicial review out of whole cloth. Beard points out that the concept was known within legal circles at the time of the founding; indeed, before the decision in *Marbury*, the Supreme Court had alluded to judicial review in a number of decisions.[43]

Reasonable persons may disagree on the usurpation question. It may be true, as former Chief Justice Warren Burger has stated, "[i]t is now accepted that the original assertion of the power was not judicial usurpation as Jefferson considered it."[44] However, whether that acceptance is based upon reasoned analysis or political reality is another matter altogether.

The compatibility question

Behind the usurpation of power question lurks the equally difficult issue of the compatibility of judicial review with democratic values. Democratic sensibilities are offended by nine persons voiding acts of popularly selected representatives of the people. Moreover, the judiciary is independent of the people and their elected representatives. The result is a third branch free from popular control. Is judicial review a menace to popular democracy? Alternatively, is review a way to perfect democratic government? In essence, is there any way to reconcile the practice of judicial review with democratic theory?

We first consider the arguments of Robert Yates, a leading opponent of the ratification of the proposed constitution crafted at Philadelphia. Yates, Alexander Hamilton and John Lansing had composed the New York delegation to the Constitutional Convention. Yates and Lansing walked out on the Convention some two and one-half months before its work was completed. The two joined other Americans in making speeches, writing pamphlets, essays and letters. Collectively, they came to be called Antifederalists. The other side of the debate was represented successfully by the Federalists.

As is often the case for winners and losers, much is widely known about Federalist thought, but little is understood about Antifederalist thinking. Fundamentally, this loosely knitted group believed the great choice facing humankind was either despotism or republicanism. The latter is based on consent of the governed or self-government, and the former is insured by force. Antifederalists believed the proposed constitution granted too much power to the people's representatives without providing an effective counter check. They reasoned that privileged people would benefit from the proposed constitution at the expense of ordinary people. Unless restrictions could be placed on all three constitutional branches of the central government, they feared, the potential for despotism would become a reality. Though they lost the ratification debate, Antifederalist ideology was largely responsible for the addition of the Bill of Rights to our constitutional structure.[45]

Writing under the pseudonym of "Brutus," Robert Yates, then a judge of the New York Supreme Court, makes the case against the excesses of Article III. In the process of showing why the new government would prove destructive of political happiness, he argues that due to the nature of judicial review, members of the Court have such overwhelming power they could ". . . mould the government into almost any shape they please."[46]

For the most part, this follows from two facts. First, there was no limit to the amount of power the Court could imply from the Constitution since interpretation would not be restricted to the "letter" of the Constitution, that is, to the "words in their common acception." Thus, the Court could build through implication from nebulous "spirit" and "intent" of the document. Second, and even more to be feared, the Court was not held accountable to either the people or their representatives. As such, the Court constituted a will, independent of society, which could be "controlled" only by an appeal to the sword.[47]

Yates was one delegate to the Philadelphia Convention who had no doubt the proposed constitution contained within its meaning the power of judicial review. He finds it particularly alarming because the judges are ". . . rendered totally inde-

pendent, both of the people and the legislature, both with respect to their offices and salaries. No errors they may commit can be corrected by any person above them, if any such power there be . . . ."[48]

The probable impact of the federal judiciary upon the States' rights was central to Antifederalist republican principles and concerns. Every enlargement of national power will restrict state power, Yates believed. This will happen, he said, because the necessary and proper clause of Article I, section 8, may be interpreted by the federal judiciary to permit the Congress to do ". . . which in their best judgement is best."[49] To be sure, the employment of the "elastic clause" has been a source of continuing controversy over the 200-year history of the Constitution.

Though Yates approves of judicial independence, he argues that the type of independence contained in the proposed constitution was unknown anywhere in the world, including England. Judges in both England and under the proposed constitution hold office during good behavior and possess fixed salaries. In England, Parliament may override judicial decisions but no such analogous power was contemplated for the would-be Congress of the United States.[50]

Yates' interpretation of history is important. English judges were given life tenure and salary guarantees so that the king would no longer influence them to support royal claims to the detriment of the liberties of the people. The great difference is that in the United States, there is no hereditary monarch with a vested interest in maintaining power at the expense of liberty. Government officials are elected in this country by the people and are consequently controlled by them. There is no need, according to Yates, to create uncontrolled power unless the goal is autonomy, not from a despotic king, but from the democratic tendencies of a free people.[51] Alexander Hamilton addresses this very point.

The Federalist papers

As with the Antifederalists, ratification proponents of the proposed constitution published their arguments. These appeared in New York newspapers from October 27, 1787, to August 16, 1788. Alexander Hamilton, James Madison and John Jay, writing under the name "Publius," prepared 85 short essays referred to as *The Federalist*.

[handwritten margin note: Antifederalists → Const. gave too much pwr. Resp. for Bill of Rights to Reps; Const. gave too much pwr.]

The influential constitutional scholar Edward S. Corwin noted:

Hamilton's later argument in Federalist 78 and 81 seems to have been inspired by the effort of Yates, an opponent of the Constitution to inflate judicial review to the dimensions of a bugaboo, and thereby convert the case for it into an argument against the constitution.[52]

This seems all the more apparent when we look to *Federalist* 29, published in the *Daily Advertiser* on January 19, 1778, coincidently with the Brutus letters. Hamilton observed:

In reading many of the publications against the Constitution, a man is apt to imagine that he is perusing some ill-written tale or romance, which, instead of natural and aggreable images, exhibits to the mind nothing but frightful and distorted shapes—
"Gorgons, hydras, and chimeras dire"; discoloring and disfiguring whatever it represents, and transforming everything it touches into a monster.

Returning to this theme in *Federalist* 78, Hamilton wrote of his constitutional adversaries', ". . . rage for objection, which disorders their imaginations and judgments." He proposed, nevertheless, to discuss those unreasoned objections in the light of constitutional provision for the appointment and tenure of judges, the partition of authority to various courts and the relation of those courts to one another. Of all these, the major objection was ". . . the tenure by which the judges are to hold their places: this chiefly concerns their duration in office; the provisions for their support; and the precautions for their responsibility."

The crux of the matter lay in the constitutional provision for responsibility. Hamilton's argument is precisely what we would expect it not to be. Rather than showing the accountability of the judiciary to the people or how their will is not insulated from or independent of society, Hamilton instead showed a lack of direct responsibility, and why this should be celebrated and not dreaded. The reason, as Madison had observed in *Federalist* 48, is that tyranny should be feared from the legislative branch more than any other, due to our form of government. The sort of despotism most likely in a democratic republic would follow from ". . . the encroachments and oppressions of the representative body."

If it were most likely that tyranny were to stem from the branch of government most responsible to the very source of that tyranny, the people, then it would hardly seem wise to make the judiciary responsible to that tyrannical majority when its purpose is to check it. Thus, the criticism in "Brutus" is well-founded; judicial power may be used to check the will of the people's elected representatives.

It should be understood that Hamilton is reflecting in part the views of the commercial class in America. During the preceding decade (1777-1787), they experienced to their horror and detriment the practice of state legislatures giving in to the demands of the debtor classes. The excesses of the majority were at least one reason for scrapping the Articles of Confederation in favor of the Philadelphia proposal. Though clearly admitting that the judiciary may not be accountable to the elected representatives of the people, Hamilton argued there is no cause for alarm since the judiciary has ". . . neither FORCE nor WILL, but merely judgment; and must ultimately depend upon the executive arm even for the efficacy of its judgments."[53]

It can be discerned why the judiciary lacks force. Obviously, the judiciary must depend upon the executive branch for enforcement of its will. However, it is not so easy to understand why judicial will is only "judgment" and therefore not will. After all, if the judiciary is to check the legislative branch, it must have a will of its own, regardless of whether the success of that check depends upon executive cooperation. What Hamilton means is, insofar as the judiciary must depend upon the executive, the federal courts have no *meaningful will*.

The Court's will is not enforced unless it is also the will of the executive. Thus, while the Court and its determination of will remain independent of society in terms of responsibility, the application of that will is never independent since it occurs through the executive who is accountable. Though the judiciary can at times have a will independent of society, which differs from the will of the executive, it may not be applied, and thus is not to be feared.

Federalist 81 reinforces the view expressed in *Federalist* 78. Hamilton answers the charge ". . . the errors and usurpations of the Supreme Court . . . will be uncontrollable and remediless."

First, it is argued that the powers of the federal judiciary are no different in principle from those enjoyed by the state judiciaries. The power of courts to limit legislative acts stems from the general theory of limited government, and does not follow directly from a novel authority granted to the federal bench in the proposed constitution. Second, it is not true, as some have claimed, that state legislatures or the English Parliament may correct an undesirable court decision. In this sense, the federal judiciary under the proposed constitution would be no more uncontrollable than those in Britain and the states. The final point is a reiteration of the least dangerous branch argument made in *Federalist* 78, with an additional point. Hamilton doubts whether judicial encroachment upon legislative prerogatives would ever become extensive. If, per chance, it does, the impeachment power can be employed: "[t]his alone is a complete security." Whatever might be the merits of Hamilton's first two arguments, historical experience points to the dubious quality of the last.

Neither Robert Yates nor Alexander Hamilton believed judicial review is democratic. Yates condemned it for that reason, while Hamilton applauded it as a necessary check on the majority. There is a third view. It is best expressed by former Yale Law School Dean Eugene V. Rostow. He argues judicial review is in fact democratic.[54]

Judicial review as democratic

It is not surprising that Rostow prefaces his seminal 1952 article by acknowledging widespread "uneasiness, and even guilt" about judicial review.[55] Certainly by the end of World War II the activist posture of the Supreme Court, which resulted in striking down state and federal government economic regulation during the first third of the twentieth century, was thoroughly discredited. Judicial self-restraint had become part of the liberal credo. However, by the late 1940s and early 1950s the difficult issues reaching the Supreme Court were no longer government regulation of the economy. Rather, issues such as First Amendment questions involving communist control, religious freedom, minority rights and the application of the Bill of Rights to the states through the Due Process Clause of the Fourteenth Amendment became salient. The liberal impulse is to come to the aid of the political minority and under-represented in society. But how could the Supreme Court justify its intervention without renouncing the lessons of the past? Rostow attempts to show the way.

Rostow maintains that it is erroneous to define democracy solely in terms of people voting directly on every issue. The real task is to assure that both elected and appointed officials are ultimately responsible to the people for their acts. Moreover,

Supreme Court justices are not the only governmental officers not held accountable through the electoral process. Other unelected officials such as admirals, generals and members of the independent regulatory agencies are not perceived to be acting undemocratically. Why then should Court justices be considered undemocratic?

Besides, Rostow continues,

... the final responsibility of the people is appropriately guaranteed by the provisions for amending the Constitution itself, and by the benign influence of time, which changes the personnel of courts. Given the possibility of constitutional amendment, there is nothing undemocratic in having responsible and independent judges act as important constitutional mediators.[56]

Article V of the Constitution, the amendment provision, requires a two-thirds and three-fourths vote depending upon the procedures employed; and thus, Rostow has not so subtly substituted simple majority rule with extraordinary majority rule. Also note that most recent U.S. presidents have usually appointed no more than two justices to the nine-member high court, thereby requiring special patience and faith in the "benign influence of time."

For the sake of argument, one may concede Rostow's point that the Supreme Court is ultimately responsible to the people. However, this proves only that our governmental system is based on popular sovereignty. It does not prove that the Supreme Court's use of judicial review to strike down acts of representative bodies is democratic.

Among the most important ideas contributed by Rostow to the judicial review debate is the notion that the Supreme Court may contribute to democracy by helping maintain a pluralistic equilibrium in society. It can mediate conflict between political institutions to insure the maintenance of rights for all citizens.[57] One way to judge how democratic institutions may be is to study what they do. That is, the substance of decisions may be at least as important as the procedures employed to make those decisions. Rostow attacks what he regards as the over-reliance upon judicial self-restraint as a failure to ensure the democratic character of U.S. society.[58]

Thus, democracy entails more than procedural majority rule; it also entails the protection of minority rights. Indeed, for Rostow, judicial review is not only compatible with democracy, it is, in fact, democratic.

Rostow would have been more correct had he written of the compatibility of the Supreme Court's exercise of judicial review with democracy, rather than "The Democratic Character of Judicial Review." Judicial review is neither democratic nor undemocratic; rather, it is anti-democratic.

Ironically, it is precisely the anti-democratic character of judicial review that imparts a major and beneficial contribution to the democratic system of which it is a part. In Aristotelian terms, judicial review contributes to our "good democracy."

The classic distinction between bad and good democracies is crucial to a justification of judicial review. To be sure, process plays a central role in any democracy. However, it is not the whole of the matter. A good democracy is directed to the interests of the whole people, including both majorities. The Supreme Court must resist the other branches or divisions of government when they act tyrannically, whether against majorities or minorities. When the Court exercises a check against a tyrannical majority it acts in an anti-democratic fashion. But it is precisely this anti-democratic feature, known as judicial review, that makes our governmental system a good democracy.[59]

Conclusion

The exercise of judicial review has often placed the court at the heart of political controversies, and this has resulted in the posing of serious questions concerning that role.

The first concerns the origins of judicial review. Many have insisted the Court usurped law-making power when claiming this function. The writings of Judge Gibson and Louis Boudin are illustrative of this viewpoint. Others, including Justice Lurton and Charles Beard, argue there is sufficient justification to support the conclusion that the Constitution framers intended judicial review and, together with other historical evidence, point to the conclusion that it is a desirable feature of our governmental system. Still others, such as James B. Thayer, accept judicial review as an authority properly possessed, but nonetheless, counsel restraint in its employment.

It is difficult to make a case one way or the other with absolute certitude. However, judicial review is a fact of political life, usurpation or not! The Supreme Court has exercised the authority and has gotten away with it. Albeit, the use of the judicial veto has from time to time in U.S. history generated serious opposition for the Court. Yet through it all, the high bench has been able to maintain its extraordinary authority, a power masterfully seized by John Marshall in *Marbury v. Madison.*

There is a second great and difficult query surrounding the exercise of judicial review; is judicial review compatible with democracy? Unlike the first question, the answer is less doubtful, though far from definitive and unqualified.

It is significant that both Robert Yates and Alexander Hamilton agreed that judicial review is inconsistent with the democratic principle that government ought to be accountable to the people. Yet, of course, they each came to different conclusions about its desirability. Yates, the Antifederalist, argued against the proposed constitution and judicial review because the Court would constitute a will independent of society. Hamilton applauds review because the Court's independence of society would serve as a safeguard against tyranny inflicted by the elected representatives of the people.

A third view is best expressed by Eugene Rostow. It is an argument positively proclaiming the democratic character of judicial review. According to this view, the judiciary is accountable to the people for its decisions. Further, judicial review must not be assessed solely in procedural terms; it also most be judged in terms of the ends it serves. Therefore, to the extent judicial review protects precious rights and liberties, it is consistent with democratic theory, and the justices of the Supreme Court should feel no guilt about its use.

There is at least one additional view. Judicial review is neither democratic nor undemocratic. Rather, it is anti-democratic. Because it is anti-democratic, it is consistent with the Aristotelian notion of a "good democracy." Therefore, we applaud judicial review as a functional tool in the service of important democratic values. While review is anti-democratic, it is nonetheless compatible with democracy; it operates to guard against threats to liberty and human happiness.

Whatever the legitimacy of its origins, judicial review may be justified in terms of democratic theory. It is also clear that many proponents of judicial supremacy find it difficult to defend. This is especially true when Court decisions seem removed from prevailing public opinion. Obviously, not all exercises of judicial review have placed the Court under severe attack. The justices themselves have attempted to protect the Court from attack through the exercise of judicial self-restraint. However, rational political calculation is not the only explanation for this behavior. No doubt, as Eugene Rostow explained, there is a sense of guilt surrounding the use of the judicial veto. It is an uneasiness that does not seem to disappear, despite repeated usage and the passing of time.

Supreme Court justices, judges of other courts, constitutional scholars, bar association representatives, members of Congress, the executive branch and others, have felt compelled to justify the Court's power. Though no responsible public figure has in recent years called for the end to judicial review, there have been forcefully presented criticisms of its uses and alleged misuses.

Contemporary conservatives such as Chief Justice William Rehnquist and Judge Robert Bork have written and spoken about the importance of exercising judicial self-restraint. Justice William Brennan and Judge Frank Johnson, who many would characterize as liberals, are representative of those arguing for the importance of an activist posture. Courts must function to articulate and protect valuable constitutional rights, so goes the refrain. President Ronald Reagan's Justice Department speaks of the Jurisprudence of Original Intention when interpreting constitutional provisions.[60] At the same time, there have been recurrent calls for Court curbing, including the introduction of legislation that would remove appellate jurisdiction from the Supreme Court to hear cases involving certain controversial issues.[61]

We believe the recurring debate about the Court's role is traceable to the fundamental question of legitimacy centering around the usurpation and compatibility issues. However, what is rarely acknowledged, and will be denied by many, is an underlying uncertainty about whether ordinary Americans can understand the intellectual justification for judicial review without coming to a conclusion that may contribute to the instability of the political system. A recently reported empirical study found that public confidence in the incumbents of the Court is related to judicial activism. The conventional wisdom that the Court skates on thin ice when it invalidates federal statutes is substantiated by the data.[62] However, confidence in particular justices of the Supreme Court is probably different from support for the Court as an institution. Empirical studies demonstrate that while specific support for Court decisions may wane from time to time, diffuse support for the Supreme Court remains relatively high and favorable.[63] It is also true that political elites have a tendency to come to the aid of the Court when direct institutional attacks are made upon its authority.[64] We do not have convincing empirical evidence linking a diminution of public confidence in Supreme Court justices or in the exercise of judicial review with a drastic decline in diffuse support. Nevertheless, it is conceivable that at some point public acquiescence may turn to intolerance, resulting in the removal of the deep reservoir of public support necessary for the Court to continue its historic role in U.S. politics.

Paradoxically, because the judicial review debate refuses to disappear, the use of that power is made more secure. Proponents and opponents of the judicial veto are compelled to carefully assess and reassess its costs against its benefits. The debate serves as a reminder to all that in a democratic society all power must be limited.

NOTES

This article originally appeared in Volume 71, Number 4, December-January 1988, pages 202-210. It is based on the authors' book, JUDICIAL REVIEW AND AMERICAN DEMOCRACY, published by Iowa State University Press.

1. *See* Judge Gibson's argument in Eakin v. Raub, 12 S.&R. 330 (Pa. 1825).

2. 5 U.S. (Cranch) 137, 2 L. Ed. 60.

3. Beard, *The Supreme Court—Usurper or Grantee?*, 27 POL. SCI. Q. 1 (1912).

4. Horwitz, THE COURTS AND SOCIAL POLICY (Washington, DC: Brookings Institution, 1977).

5. Grey, *Do We Have an Unwritten Constitution?*, 27 STAN. L. REV. 703-18 (1975); Berger, GOVERNMENT BY JUDICIARY: THE TRANSFORMATION OF THE FOURTEENTH AMENDMENT (Cambridge, MA: Harvard University Press, 1977); Ely, DEMOCRACY AND DISTRUST (Cambridge, MA: Harvard University Press, 1981); The Federalist Society, THE GREAT DEBATE: INTERPRETING OUR WRITTEN CONSTITUTION (Washington, DC: The Federalist Society, 1986).

6. 12 S.&R. at 343-81 (Pa. 1825).

7. Mason, Beaney and Stephenson, AMERICAN CONSTITUTIONAL LAW: INTRODUCTORY ESSAYS AND SELECTED CASES, 7th Ed. 50 (Englewood Cliffs, NJ: Prentice-Hall, Inc., 1983).

8. Eakin v. Raub, 12 S.&R. at 346.

9. *Id.* at 347.

10. Melone, SYSTEM SUPPORT POLITICS AND THE CONGRESSIONAL COURT OF APPEALS, 51 N.D.L. REV. 597-613 (1975); also see special issue of 69 JUDICATURE (October 1981).

11. Eakin v. Raub, 12 S.&R. at 351-52.

12. *Id.* at 352-53.

13. *Id.* at 353-54.

14. *Id.* at 354-55.

15. Mason, Beaney and Stephenson, *supra* n. 7.

16. Published as: Thayer, *The Origin and Scope of the American Doctrine of Constitutional Law*, 7 HARV. L. REV. 129-56 (1896).

17. *Id.* at 136.

18. *Id.* at 151.

19. *Id.* at 152.

20. Mendelson, SUPREME COURT STATECRAFT: THE RULE OF LAW AND MEN 5-17 (Ames, IA: Iowa State University Press, 1985).

21. Lurton, *A Government of Law Or A Government of Men?*, 193 N. AM. REV. 9-25 (1911).

22. *Id.* at 13.

23. *Id.* at 17.

24. *Id.* at 19.

25. Boudin, *Government by Judiciary*, 26 POL. SCI. Q. 238-70 (1911).

26. *Id.* at 243-47.

27. *Id.* at 248.

28. *Id.* at 253.

29. *Id.* at 254-56.

30. *Id.* at 264.

31. *Id.* at 267.

32. Beard, *supra* n. 3.

33. *Id.* at 3.

34. *Id.*

35. COURTS, JUDGES, & POLITICS, 4th Ed., 485-86 (New York: Random House, 1986).

36. Beard, *supra* n. 3, at 3-4.

37. *Id.* at 19.

38. *Id.*

39. THE DOCTRINE OF JUDICIAL REVIEW 11 (Gloucester, MA: Peter Smith, 1963).

40. Beard, *supra* n. 3, at 24.

41. *Id.* at 24-28.

42. *Id.* at 22.

43. *Id.* at 32-34.

44. Berger, *The Doctrine of Judicial Review: Mr. Marshall, Mr. Jefferson and Mr. Marbury*, in Cannon and O'Brien (eds.), VIEWS FROM THE BENCH: THE JUDICIARY AND CONSTITUTIONAL POLITICS 8 (Chatham, NJ: Chatham House, Inc., 1985).

45. Allen and Lloyds, eds., THE ESSENTIAL ANTI-FEDERALIST viii-xiv (Washington, DC: University Press of America, 1985).

46. BRUTUS XI.

47. *Id.*

48. BRUTUS XII.

49. *Id.*

50. BRUTUS XV.

51. *Id.*

52. COURT OVER CONSTITUTION 45-46 (Glouster, MA: Peter Smith, 1957).

53. FEDERALIST 78.

54. Rostow, *The Democratic Character of Judicial Review*, 66 HARV. L. REV. 193-224 (1952).

55. *Id.* at 193.

56. *Id.* at 197.

57. *Id.* at 203-10.

58. *Id.* at 210-23.

59. Mace, *The Anti-Democratic Character of Judicial Review*, 60 CAL. L. REV. 1140-49 (1972).

60. For a convenient compilation of recent speeches, see: THE GREAT DEBATE, *supra* n. 5, especially speeches by Attorney General Edwin Meese and Justice William J. Brennan, Jr.

61. *Supra* n. 10.

62. Caldeira, *Neither the Purse Nor the Sword: Dynamics of Public Confidence in the Supreme Court*, 80 AM. POL. SCI. REV. 1222 (1986).

63. Murphy and Tanenhaus, *Public Opinion and the United States Supreme Court: A Preliminary Mapping of Some Prerequisites for Court Legitimation of Regime Changes*, 2 L. & SOC'Y REV. 357-382 (1968); Murphy, Tanenhaus and Kastner, PUBLIC EVALUATIONS OF CONSTITUTIONAL COURTS: ALTERNATIVE EXPLANATIONS (Beverly Hills, CA: Sage Publications, 1973); Tanenhaus and Murphy, *Patterns of Public Support for the Supreme Court: A Panel Study*, 43 J. OF POL. 24-39 (1981).

64. Melone, *supra* n. 10.

Interpreting the Constitution: the case for judicial restraint

Our constitutional plan was never meant to allow judges to impose their values instead of the original intent of the framers.

by J. Clifford Wallace

This year we celebrate the 200th anniversary of our Constitution. This remarkable document has structured our government and secured our liberty as we have developed from 13 fledgling colonies into a mature and strong democracy. Without doubt, the Constitution is one of the grandest political achievements of the modern world.

In spite of this marvelous record, we will celebrate our nation's charter in the midst of a hotly contested debate on the continuing role that it should have in our society. Two schools of constitutional jurisprudence are engaged in a long-running battle. Some contend that the outcome of this conflict may well determine whether the Constitution remains our vital organic document or whether it instead becomes a curious historical relic. The competing positions in this constitutional battle are often summarized by a variety of labels: judicial restraint versus judicial activism, strict construction versus loose construction, positivism versus natural law, conservative versus liberal, interpretivism versus noninterpretivism.

In large measure, these labels alone are of little assistance in analyzing a complex problem. Ultimately, what is at stake is what Constitution will govern this country. Will it be the written document drafted by the framers, ratified by the people, and passed down, with amendments, to us? Or will it be an illusive parchment upon which modern-day judges may freely engrave their own political and sociological preferences?

In this article, I intend to outline and defend a constitutional jurisprudence of judicial restraint.[1] My primary thesis is that a key principle of judicial restraint—namely, interpretivism—is required by our constitutional plan. I will also explore how practitioners of judicial restraint should resolve the tension that can arise in our current state of constitutional law between interpretivism and a second important principle, respect for judicial precedent.

Interpretivism vs. noninterpretivism

What is the difference between "interpretivism" and "noninterpretivism"? This question is important because I believe interpretivism to be the cornerstone of a constitutional jurisprudence of judicial restraint. By "interpretivism," I mean the principle that judges, in resolving constitutional questions, should rely on the express provisions of the Constitution or upon those norms that are clearly implicit in its text.[2] Under an interpretivist approach, the original intention of the framers is the controlling guide for constitutional interpretation. This does not mean, of course, that judges may apply a constitutional provision only to situations specifically contemplated by the framers. Rather, it simply requires that when considering whether to invalidate the work of the political branches, the judges do so from a starting point fairly discoverable in the Constitution.[3] By contrast, under noninterpretive review, judges may freely rest their decisions on value judgments that admittedly are not supported by, and may even contravene, the text of the Constitution and the intent of the framers.[4]

Interpretivist review

I believe that the Constitution itself envisions and

requires interpretivist review. To explore this thesis, we should first examine the Constitution as a political and historical document.

As people read the Constitution, many are struck by how procedural and technical its provisions are. Perhaps on first reading it may be something of a disappointment. In contrast to the fiery eloquence of the Declaration of Independence, the Constitution may seem dry or even dull. This difference in style, of course, reflects the very different functions of the two documents. The Declaration of Independence is an indictment of the reign of King George III. In a flamboyant tone, it is brilliantly crafted to persuade the world of the justice of our fight for independence. The Constitution, by contrast, establishes the basic set of rules for the nation. Its genius lies deeper, in its skillful design of a government structure that would best ensure liberty and democracy.

The primary mechanism by which the Constitution aims to protect liberty and democracy is the dispersion of government power. Recognizing that concentrated power poses the threat of tyranny, the framers divided authority between the states and the federal government. In addition, they created three separate and co-equal branches of the federal government in a system of checks and balances.

The framers were also aware, of course, that liberty and democracy can come into conflict. The Constitution, therefore, strikes a careful balance between democratic rule and minority rights. Its republican, representative features are designed to channel and refine cruder majoritarian impulses. In addition, the Constitution's specific individual protections, particularly in the Bill of Rights, guarantee against certain majority intrusions. Beyond these guarantees, the Constitution places its trust in the democratic process—the voice of the people expressed through their freely elected representatives.

Raoul Berger argues persuasively in *Government by Judiciary* that the Constitution "was written against a background of interpretive presuppositions that assured the Framers their design would be effectuated."[5] The importance of that statement may escape us today, when it is easy to take for granted that the Constitution is a written document. But for the framers, the fact that the Constitution was in writing was not merely incidental. They recognized that a written constitution provides the most stable basis for the rule of law, upon which liberty and justice ultimately depend.

As Thomas Jefferson observed, "Our peculiar security is in the possession of a written constitution. Let us not make it a blank paper by construction."[6] Chief Justice John Marshall, in *Marbury v. Madison*, the very case establishing the power of judicial review, emphasized the constraints imposed by the written text and the judicial duty to respect these constraints in all cases raising constitutional questions.[7]

Moreover, the framers recognized the importance of interpreting the Constitution according to their original intent. In Madison's words, if "the sense in which the Constitution was accepted and ratified by the Nation . . . be not the guide in expounding it, there can be no security for a consistent and stable government, [nor] for a faithful exercise of its powers."[8] Similarly, Jefferson as president acknowledged his duty to administer the Constitution "according to the safe and honest meaning contemplated by the plain understanding of the people at the time of its adoption—a meaning to be found in the explanations of those who advocated . . . it."[9] It seems clear, therefore, that the leading framers were interpretivists and believed that constitutional questions should be reviewed by that approach.

Next, I would like to consider whether interpretivism is necessary to effectuate the constitutional plan. The essential starting point is that the Constitution established a separation of powers to protect our freedom. Because freedom is fundamental, so too is the separation of powers. But separation of powers becomes a meaningless slogan if judges may confer constitutional status on whichever rights they happen to deem important, regardless of textual basis. In effect, under noninterpretive review, the judiciary functions as a superlegislature beyond the check of the other two branches. Noninterpretivist review also disregards the Constitution's careful allocation of most decisions to the democratic process, allowing the legislature to make decisions deemed best for society. Ultimately, noninterpretivist review reduces our written Constitution to insignificance and threatens to impose a tyranny of the judiciary.

Prudential considerations

Important prudential considerations also weigh heavily in favor of interpretivist review. The rule of law is fundamental in our society. To be effective,

interpretivist = Const. to the letter
noninterpretivist = Const. varies by concepts.

it cannot be tossed to and fro by each new sociological wind. Because it is rooted in written text, interpretivist review promotes the stability and predictability essential to the rule of law. By contrast, noninterpretivist review presents an infinitely variable array of possibilities. The Constitution would vary with each judge's conception of what is important. To demonstrate the wide variety of tests that could be applied, let us briefly look at the writings of legal academics who advocate noninterpretivism.

Assume each is a judge deciding the same constitutional issue. One professor seeks to "cement[] a union between the distributional patterns of the modern welfare state and the federal constitution." Another "would guarantee a whole range of nontextually based rights against government to ensure 'the dignity of full membership in society.' " A third argues that the courts should give "concrete meaning and application" to those values that "give our society an identity and inner coherence [and] its distinctive public morality." Yet another professor sees the court as having a "prophetic" role in developing moral standards in a "dialectical relationship" with Congress, from which he sees emerging a "more mature" political morality. One professor even urges that the court apply the contractarian moral theory of Professor Rawls' *A Theory of Justice* to constitutional questions.[10] One can easily see the fatal vagueness and subjectivity of this approach: each judge would apply his or her own separate and diverse personal values in interpreting the same constitutional question. Without anchor, we drift at sea.

Another prudential argument against noninterpretivism is that judges are not particularly well-suited to make judgments of broad social policy. We judges decide cases on the basis of a limited record that largely represents the efforts of the parties to the litigation. Legislators, with their committees, hearings, and more direct role in the political process, are much better equipped institutionally to decide what is best for society.

Noninterpretivist arguments

But are there arguments in favor of non–interpretivism? Let us consider several assertions commonly put forth by proponents. One argument asserts that certain constitutional provisions invite judges to import into the constitutional decision process value judgments derived from outside the Constitution. Most commonly, advocates of

this view rely on the due process clause of the Fifth and Fourteenth Amendments. It is true that courts have interpreted the due process clause to authorize broad review of the substantive merits of legislation. But is that what the draftsmen had in mind? Some constitutional scholars make a strong argument that the clause, consistent with its plain language, was intended to have a limited procedural meaning.[11]

A second argument asserts that the meaning of the constitutional text and the intention of the framers cannot be ascertained with sufficient precision to guide constitutional decision making. I readily acknowledge that interpretivism will not always provide easy answers to difficult constitutional questions. The judicial role will always involve the exercise of discretion. The strength of interpretivism is that it channels and constrains this discretion in a manner consistent with the Constitution. While it does not necessarily ensure a correct result, it does exclude from consideration entire ranges of improper judicial responses.

Third, some have suggested that the Fourteenth Amendment effected such a fundamental revision in the nature of our government that the intentions of the original framers are scarcely relevant any longer. It is, of course, true that federal judges have seized upon the Fourteenth Amendment as a vehicle to restructure federal/state relations. The argument, however, is not one-sided. Berger, for example, persuasively demonstrates that the framers of the Fourteenth Amendment sought much more limited objectives.[12] In addition, one reasonable interpretation of the history of the amendment demonstrates that its framers, rather than intending an expanded role for the federal courts, meant for Congress (under section 5 of the amendment) to play the primary role in enforcing its provisions.[13] Thus, it can be argued that to the extent that the Fourteenth Amendment represented an innovation in the constitutional role of the judiciary, it was by limiting the courts' traditional role in enforcing constitutional rights and by providing added responsibility for the Congress.

Advocates of noninterpretivism also contend that we should have a "living Constitution" rather than be bound by "the dead hand of the framers." These slogans prove nothing. An interpretivist approach would not constrict government processes; on the contrary, it would ensure that issues are freely subject to the workings of the democratic process. Moreover, to the extent that the Constitution might profit from revision, the amendment process of Article V provides the only constitutional means. Judicial amendment under a noninterpretivist approach is simply an unconstitutional usurpation.

Almost certainly, the greatest support for a noninterpretive approach derives from its perceived capacity to achieve just results. Why quibble over the Constitution, after all, if judges who disregard it nevertheless "do justice"? Such a view is dangerously shortsighted and naive. In the first place, one has no cause to believe that the results of noninterpretivism will generally be "right." Individual judges have widely varying conceptions of what values are important. Noninterpretists spawned the "conservative" substantive economic due process of the 1930s as well as the "liberal" decisions of the Warren Court. There is no principled result in noninterpretivism.

But even if the judge would always be right, the process would be wrong. A benevolent judicial tyranny is nonetheless a tyranny. Our Constitution rests on the faith that democracy is intrinsically valuable. From an instrumental perspective, democracy might at times produce results that are not as desirable as platonic guardians might produce. But the democratic process—our participation in a system of self-government—has transcendental value. Moreover, one must consider the very real danger that an activist judiciary stunts the development of a responsible democracy by removing from it the duty to make difficult decisions. If we are to remain faithful to the values of democracy and liberty, we must insist that courts respect the Constitution's allocation of social decision making to the political branches.

Respect for precedent

I emphasized earlier the importance of stability to the rule of law. I return to that theme now to consider a second principle of judicial restraint: respect for precedent. Respect for precedent is a principle widely accepted, even if not always faithfully followed. It requires simply that a judge follow prior case law in deciding legal questions. Respect for precedent promotes predictability and uniformity. It constrains a judge's discretion and satisfies the reasonable expectations of the parties. Through its application, citizens can have a better understanding of what the law is and act accordingly.

Unfortunately, in the present state of constitutional law, the two principles of judicial restraint that I have outlined can come into conflict. While much of constitutional law is consistent with the principle of interpretivism, a significant portion is not. This raises the question how a practitioner of judicial restraint should act in circumstances where respecting precedent would require acceptance of law developed under a noninterpretivist approach.

The answer is easy for a judge in my position, and, indeed, for any judge below the United States Supreme Court. As a judge on the Ninth Circuit Court of Appeals, I am bound to follow Supreme Court and Ninth Circuit precedent even when I believe it to be wrong. There is a distinction, however, between following precedent and extending it. Where existing precedent does not fairly govern a legal question, the principle of interpretivism should guide a judge.

For Supreme Court justices, the issue is more complex. The Supreme Court obviously is not infallible. Throughout its history, the Court has at times rejected its own precedents. Because the Supreme Court has the ultimate judicial say on what the Constitution means, its justices have a special responsibility to ensure that they are properly expounding constitutional law as well as fostering stability and predictability.

Must Supreme Court advocates of judicial restraint passively accept the errors of activist predecessors? There is little rational basis for doing so. Periodic activist inroads could emasculate fundamental doctrines and undermine the separation of powers. Nevertheless, the values of predictability and uniformity that respect for precedent promotes demand caution in overturning precedent. In my view, a justice should consider overturning a prior decision only when the decision is clearly wrong, has significant effects, and would otherwise be difficult to remedy.

Significantly, constitutional decisions based on a noninterpretivist approach may satisfy these three criteria. When judges confer constitutional status on their own value judgments without support in the language of the Constitution and the original intention of the framers, they commit clear error. Because constitutional errors frequently affect the institutional structure of government and the allocation of decisions to the democratic process, they are likely to have important effects. And because constitutional decisions, unlike statutory decisions,

cannot be set aside through normal political channels, they will generally meet the third requirement. In sum, then, despite the prudential interests furthered by respect for precedent, advocates
of judicial restraint may be justified in seeking to
overturn noninterpretivist precedent.

Conclusion

It is obvious that courts employing interpretivist
review cannot solve many of the social and political
problems facing America, indeed, even some very
important problems. The interpretivist would respond that the Constitution did not place the
responsibility for solving those problems with the
courts. The courts were not meant to govern the
core of our political and social life—Article I gave
that duty, for national issues, to the Congress. It is
through our democratically elected representatives that we legitimately develop this fabric of our
life. Interpretivism encourages that process. It is,
therefore, closer to the constitutional plan of governance than is noninterpretivist review.

After 200 years, the Constitution is not "broke"—
we need not fix it—just apply it.

NOTES

This article originally appeared in Volume 71, Number 2,
August-September 1987, pages 81-84. It is adapted from an
address given at Hillsdale College, Hillsdale, Michigan, on
March 5, 1986.

1. I have elsewhere presented various aspects of this jurispru-
dence. *See, e.g.*, Wallace, *A Two Hundred Year Old Constitution in
Modern Society*, 61 TEX. L. REV. 1575 (1983); Wallace, *The
Jurisprudence of Judicial Restraint: A Return to the Moorings*, 50
GEO. WASH. L. REV. 1 (1981).

2. Wallace, *A Two Hundred Year Old Constitution, supra* n. 1;
Ely, DEMOCRACY AND DISTRUST 1 (Cambridge, MA: Harvard
University Press, 1980).

3. Ely, *supra* n. 2, at 2.

4. *See id.* at 43-72.

5. Berger, GOVERNMENT BY JUDICIARY 366 (Cambridge, MA:
Harvard University Press, 1977).

6. *Id.* at 364, *quoting* Letter of Wilson Cary Nicholas (Sept. 7,
1803).

7. Marbury v. Madison, 5 U.S. (1 Cranch) 137, 176-80
(1803).

8. Berger, *supra* n. 5, at 364, *quoting* THE WRITINGS OF JAMES
MADISON 191 (G. Hunt ed. 1900-1910).

9. *Id.* at 366-67, *citing* 4 Elliot, DEBATES IN THE SEVERAL STATE
CONVENTIONS ON THE ADOPTION OF THE FEDERAL CONSTITUTION 446
(1836).

10. Monaghan, *Our Perfect Constitution*, 56 N.Y.U. L. REV. 353,
358-60 (1981) (summarizing theories of noninterpretivists).

11. *See, e.g.*, Berger, *supra* n. 5, at 193-220.

12. *See id.*

13. *See id.* at 220-29.

Interpreting the Constitution: the Supreme Court's proper and historic function

The Court's role, when all is said and done, is, and always has been, to create meaning for a Constitution that would otherwise be a hollow document.

by Jeffrey M. Shaman

Considerable criticism, frequently quite sharp, has recently been directed at the Supreme Court for the way it has gone about its historic function of interpreting the Constitution. In particular, Edwin Meese, the current Attorney General of the United States, has accused the Court of exceeding its lawful authority by failing to adhere strictly to the words of the Constitution and the intentions of the framers who drafted those words.[1]

The attorney general's attack upon the Court echoes a similar one made by Richard Nixon, who, campaigning for the presidency in 1968, denounced Supreme Court justices who, he claimed, twisted and bent the Constitution according to their personal predilections. If elected president, Nixon promised to appoint to the Court strict constructionists whose decisions would conform to the text of the Constitution and the intent of the framers. (Ironically, it is some of the Nixon appointees to the Court that Meese now accuses of twisting and bending the Constitution.)

I hasten to add that it is not only politicians who sing the praises of strict constructionism; there are judges and lawyers, as well as some scholars, who join the song. Among legal scholars, though, the response to strict constructionism has been overwhelmingly negative. There are legal scholars, for instance, who describe strict constructionism as a "misconceived quest,"[2] an "impossibility,"[3] and even a "fraud."[4]

Those who criticize the Court point to rulings during the tenure of Chief Justice Burger, most notably the decision in *Roe v. Wade*[5] legalizing abortion, as examples of illegitimate revision or amendment of the Constitution based upon the personal beliefs of the justices. Some years ago, similar charges were leveled at the Warren Court for its ruling requiring reapportionment along the lines of one person-one vote,[6] its decision striking down school prayer,[7] and other rulings, even including the one in *Brown v. Board of Education* outlawing school segregation.[8]

It should not be supposed, however, that strict constructionism is always on the side of conservative political values. In the 1930s it was the liberals who claimed that the Supreme Court was not strictly construing the Constitution when the justices repeatedly held that minimum wage, maximum hour, and other protective legislation violated the Fourteenth Amendment.[9] As the liberals then saw it, the conservative justices on the Court were illegitimately incorporating their personal values into the Fourteenth Amendment, which had been meant to abolish racial discrimination, not to protect the prerogatives of employers.

History lessons

The lesson of this bit of history seems to be that, whether liberal or conservative or somewhere in between, whoever has an ox that is being gored at the time has a tendency to yell "foul." Whenever the Supreme Court renders a decision that someone doesn't like, apparently it is not enough to disagree with the decision; there also has to be an accusation that the Court's decision was illegitimate, being based upon the justice's personal views and not the words of the Constitution or the intent of the framers.

We can go back much further in history than the 1930s to find the Supreme Court being accused of illegitimacy. In 1810, for instance, Thomas Jefferson condemned Chief Justice John Marshall for "twistifying" the Constitution according to his "personal biases."[10]

History also reveals something else extremely significant about the Court, which is that from its earliest days, the Court has found it necessary in interpreting the Constitution to look beyond the language of the document and the intent of the framers. In the words of Stanford Law Professor Thomas Grey, it is "a matter of unarguable historical fact" that over the years the Court has developed a large body of constitutional law that derives neither from the text of the document nor the intent of the framers.[11]

Moreover, this has been so from the court's very beginning. Consider, for example, a case entitled *Hylton v. United States*,[12] which was decided in 1796 during the term of the Court's first Chief Justice, John Jay. The *Hylton* case involved a tax ranging from $1.00 to $10.00 that had been levied by Congress on carriages. Mr. Hylton, who was in the carriage trade and owned 125 carriages, understandably was unhappy about the tax, and went to court to challenge it. He claimed that the tax violated section 2 of Article I of the Constitution, which provides that direct taxes shall be apportioned among the several states according to their populations. Hylton argued that this tax was a direct one, and therefore unconstitutional because it had not been apportioned among the states by population. This, of course, was years before the enactment of the Sixteenth Amendment in 1913, authorizing a federal income tax. Prior to that, Article I prohibited a federal income tax, but what about a tax on the use or ownership of carriages— was that the sort of "direct" tax that was only permissible under Article I if apportioned among the states by population?

The Supreme Court, with several justices filing separate opinions in the case (which was customary at that time), upheld the tax as constitutional on the ground that it was not direct, and therefore not required to be apportioned. What is most significant about the *Hylton* case is how the Court went about making its decision. As described by Professor David Currie of the University of Chicago Law School, the court in *Hylton* "paid little heed to the Constitution's words," and "policy considerations dominated all three opinions" filed by the justices.[13] In fact, each of the opinions asserted that apportioning a carriage tax among the states would be unfair, because a person in a state with fewer carriages would have to pay a higher tax. While this may or may not be unfair, the justices pointed to nothing in the Constitution itself or the intent of the framers to support their personal views of fairness. Moreover, one of the justices, Justice Patterson, went so far in his opinion as to assert that the constitutional requirement of apportioning direct taxes was "radically wrong," and therefore should not be extended to this case. In other words, he based his decision, at least in part, upon his antipathy to a constitutional provision.

While Justice Patterson went too far in that respect, he and his colleagues on the Court could hardly have made a decision in the case by looking to the text of the Constitution or the intent of the framers. The language of the document simply does not provide an answer to the constitutional issue raised by the situation in *Hylton*. The text of the document merely refers to "direct" taxes and provides no definition of what is meant by a direct tax. Furthermore, as Professor Currie points out, the records of the debates at the Constitutional Convention show that "the Framers had no clear idea of what they meant by direct taxes."[14] Thus, to fulfill their responsibility to decide the case and interpret the law, the justices found it necessary to create meaning for the Constitution.

Creating meaning

Indeed, it is often necessary for the Supreme Court to create meaning for the Constitution. This is so because the Constitution, being a document designed (in the words of John Marshall) to "endure for ages,"[15] is rife with general and abstract language. Those two great sources of liberty in the Constitution, the due process and equal protection clauses, are obviously examples of abstract constitutional language that must be invested with meaning. The Fourth Amendment uses extremely general language in prohibiting "unreasonable" searches and seizures, and the Eighth Amendment is similarly general in disallowing "cruel and unusual" punishment.

Even many of the more specific provisions of the Constitution need to be supplied with meaning that simply cannot be found within the four corners of the document. The First Amendment, for instance, states that Congress shall not abridge freedom of speech—but does that mean that the government may not regulate obscene, slanderous, or deceptive speech? The First Amendment also says that Congress shall not abridge the free exercise of religion—does that mean that the government may not prohibit polygamy or child labor when dictated by religious belief? These questions—which, by the way, all arose in actual cases—and, in fact, the vast majority of constitutional questions presented to the Supreme Court, cannot be resolved by mere linguistic analysis of the Constitution. In reality there is no choice but to look beyond the text of the document to provide meaning for the Constitution.

There are those, such as Attorney General Meese, who would hope to find meaning for the Constitution from its authors, the beloved and hallowed framers of the sacred text. By reputation, these fellows are considered saints and geniuses; in actuality, they were politicians motivated significantly by self-interest.

Theoretical drawbacks

But even if the framers do deserve the awe that they inspire, reliance on their intentions to find meaning for the Constitution still has serious theoretical drawbacks. In the first place, why should we be concerned only with the intentions of the 55 individuals who drafted the Constitution and not the intentions of the people throughout the nation who ratified it, not to mention the intentions of the succeeding generations who retain the Constitution? After all, even when finally framed, the Constitution remained a legal nullity until ratified by the people, and would be a legal nullity again if revoked by the people. The framers wrote the Constitution, but it is the people who enacted and retain the Constitution; so if anything, it is the people's intent about the document that would seem to be the relevant inquiry.

Moreover, there are considerable difficulties in discerning what in fact the framers intended. The *Journal of the Constitutional Convention,* which is the primary record of the framers' intent, is neither complete nor entirely accurate. The notes for the *Journal* were carelessly kept, and have been shown to contain several mistakes.[16]

Even when the record cannot be faulted, it is not always possible to ascertain the framers' intent. As might be expected, the framers did not express an intention about every constitutional issue that would arise after the document was drafted and adopted. No group of people, regardless of its members' ability, enjoys that sort of prescience. When the framers did address particular problems, often only a few of them spoke out. What frequently is taken to be the intent of the framers as a group turns out to be the intent of merely a few or even only one of the framers.

There are also constitutional issues about which the framers expressed conflicting intentions. A collective body of 55 individuals, the framers embraced a widely diverse and frequently inconsistent set of views. The two principal architects of the Constitution, James Madison and Alexander Hamilton, for instance, had extremely divergent political views. Madison also on occasion differed with George Washington over the meaning of the Constitution. When Washington, who had presided over the Constitutional Convention, became president, he claimed that the underlying intent of the Constitution gave him the sole authority as president to proclaim neutrality and to withhold treaty papers from Congress. Madison, who had been a leader at the Constitutional Convention, disagreed vehemently. And so, the man who would come to be known as the father of this nation and the man who would come to be known as the father of the Constitution had opposing views of what the framers intended.[17]

These examples demonstrate that it simply makes no sense to suppose that a multi-member group of human beings such as the framers shared a unitary intent about the kind of controversial political issues addressed in our Constitution. We can see, then, that, at best, the so-called framers' intent is inadequately documented, ambiguous, and inconclusive; at worst, it is nonexistent, an illusion.

Even if these insurmountable obstacles could be surmounted, there are other serious problems with trying to follow the path laid down by the framers. The framers formed their intentions in the context of a past reality and in accordance with past attitudes, both of which have changed considerably since the days when the Constitution was drafted. To transfer those intentions, fashioned as they were under past conditions and views, to contemporary situations may produce sorry consequences that even the framers would have abhorred had they been able to foresee them. Blindly following intentions formulated in response to past conditions and attitudes is not likely to be an effective means of dealing with the needs of contemporary society.

Locked to the past

Some scholars take this line of reasoning one step further by maintaining that the framers' intent is inextricably locked to the past and has no meaning at all for the present.[18] In other words, because the framers formed their intentions with reference to a reality and attitudes that no longer exist, their intentions cannot be transplanted to the present day. What the framers intended for their time is not what they may have intended for ours. Life constantly changes, and the reality and ideas that surrounded the framers are long since gone.

The futility of looking to the framers' intent to resolve modern constitutional issues can be illustrated by several cases that have arisen under the Fourth and Fifth Amendments. The Fourth Amendment prohibits unreasonable searches and seizures, and further requires that no search warrants be issued unless there is probable cause that a crime has been committed. Are bugging and other electronic surveillance devices "unreasonable searches?" May they be used by the police without a warrant based on probable cause? What about the current practice of some law enforcement agencies of using airplanes to fly over a suspect's property to take pictures with a telescopic camera—is that an "unreasonable search?" The Fifth Amendment states that no person shall be compelled to be a witness against himself. What about forcing a suspect to take a breathalyzer test, or a blood test, or to have his or her stomach pumped—do those procedures amount to self-incrimination that violates the Fifth Amendment?

Whatever you may think should be the answers to these questions, you cannot find the answers by looking to the framers' intent. The framers had no intent at all about electronic surveillance, airplanes, telescopic cameras, breathalyzer tests, or stomach pumping, for the simple reason that none of those things existed until well after the days of the framers. Not even Benjamin Franklin, for all his inventiveness, was able to foresee that in the 20th century constables would zip around in flying machines taking snapshots of criminal suspects through a telescopic lens.

Many of the difficulties in attempting to resolve constitutional issues by turning to the framers are illustrated by the school prayer cases.[19] The religious beliefs of the framers ranged from theism to atheism, and among even the more devout framers there was a wide diversity of opinion concerning the proper relationship between church and state. Moreover, as often happens when human beings ponder complex issues, the views of individual framers about church and state did not remain the same over time. As a member of Congress, James Madison, for example, once voted to approve a chaplain for the House of Representatives, but later decided that the appointment of the chaplain had been unconstitutional.[20] Insofar as school prayer specifically was concerned, the framers expressed virtually no opinion on the matter, for the simple reason that at the time public schools were extremely rare. Thus, the framers had no intention, either pro or con, about prayer in public schools.

Given the theoretical deficiencies of trying to decide constitutional questions by looking to the framers' intent, it should come as no surprise that this approach has been a failure when attempted by the Supreme Court. Scholars who have closely studied the Court's use of this approach commonly agree that it has not been a satisfactory method of constitutional decision making, because the Court ends up manipulating, revising, or even creating history under the guise of following the framers' intent.[21] The fact of the matter is that neither the framers' intent nor the words of the document are capable of providing much constitutional meaning.

Bare bones

What we are left with, then, are the bare bones of a Constitution, the meaning of which must be augmented by the justices of the Supreme Court. And that is exactly what the justices have been doing since the Court was first established. The overwhelming evidence of history shows that the meaning of the Constitution has undergone constant change and evolution at the hands of the Supreme Court. Through the continual interpretation and reinterpretation of the text of the document, the court perpetually creates new meaning for the document. Although it is formally correct that we, unlike the citizens of Great Britain, have a written Constitution, its words have been defined and redefined to the extent that for the most part we, like the citizens of Great Britain, have an unwritten Constitution, the meaning of which originates with the Supreme Court.

Strict constructionists argue that it is undemocratic for Supreme Court justices—unelected officials who are unaccountable to the populace—to create meaning for the Constitution. Of course, using the framers' intent to interpret the Constitution also is undemocratic; following the will of the 55 persons who supposedly framed the Constitution or the smaller group of them who actually participated in the framing is hardly an exercise in democracy.

When strict constructionists cry that the Court is undemocratic, they are ignoring that our government is not (and was not intended by the framers) to be a pure democracy. Rather, it is a limited or constitutional democracy. What this means is that there are constitutional limits to what the majority may do. The majority may not, for example, engage in racial discrimination, even if it votes to do so in overwhelming numbers. The majority may not abridge freedom of speech or the free exercise of religion or other constitutional rights guaranteed to every individual.

Article III of the Constitution states that there shall be a Supreme Court, and, in combination with Article II, decrees the court's independence from the electorate. By its very terms, the Constitution establishes a counter-majoritarian branch of government, the Supreme Court, in juxtaposition to the more democratic executive and legislative branches. This scheme reflects one of the guiding principles that underlies the Constitution—the principle of separate powers that check and balance one another. The Supreme Court's constitutionally mandated independence functions as a check and balance upon the more majoritarian branches of federal and state governments. It thereby provides a means of maintaining constitutional boundaries on majoritarian rule.

The role of the Supreme Court is to enforce constitutional requirements upon the majoritarian branches of government, which otherwise would be completely unbridled. As dictated by the Constitution, majority control should be the predominant feature of our government, but subject to constitutional limits.

Moreover, the Supreme Court is not quite as undemocratic as the strict constructionists sometimes like to portray it to be. While it is true that the justices who sit on the Court are appointed rather than elected and that they may be removed from

office only for improper behavior, it is also true that they are appointed by a popularly elected president, and their appointments must be confirmed by a popularly elected Senate. Turnover of the Court's personnel, which sometimes occurs frequently, enhances popular control of the Court. Additionally, the Court's constitutional rulings may be overruled by the people through constitutional amendment, which, though a difficult procedure, has been accomplished on four occasions.[22] Thus, while the Court is not directly answerable to the public, it is not entirely immune from popular control.

The ultimate authority

The people also have the ultimate authority to abolish the Supreme Court. That they have not done so during our two centuries of experience indicates popular acceptance of the Court's role. Admittedly, there are particular decisions rendered by the Court that have aroused considerable public outcry, but given the many controversial issues that the Court must decide, this is inevitable. More telling about the public attitude toward the Court is that the people have taken no action to curtail the Court's authority to interpret the Constitution. Indeed, the public has shown little, if any, inclination toward abolishing the Court or even restricting its powers. Despite Franklin Delano Roosevelt's overwhelming popularity, his "court-packing plan" was a dismal failure;[23] the proposal to establish a "Court of the Union" composed of state court justices which would have the power to overrule the Supreme Court evoked such widespread public disapproval that it was quickly abandoned;[24] the campaigns to impeach Justices Earl Warren and William O. Douglas never got off the ground;[25] and although various members of Congress often propose bills threatening to restrict the Court's jurisdiction, the full Congress always rebuffs those threats.[26] These experiences suggest that even in the face of controversial constitutional decisions, there has been abiding public consent to the role of the Supreme Court in our scheme of government.

The Court's role, when all is said and done, is to create meaning for a Constitution that otherwise would be a hollow document. It is perfectly appropriate for anyone to disagree with Supreme Court decisions, and to criticize the Court on that basis. But it is not appropriate to attack the court's decisions as illegitimate on the ground that they do not follow the framers' intent. Pretending to use the framers' intent to impugn the legitimacy of the Supreme Court is a spurious enterprise. The Court's legitimate function is, and always has been, to provide meaning for the Constitution.

NOTES

This article originally appeared in Volume 71, Number 2, August-September 1987, pages 80, 84-87, 122.

1. Address by Attorney General Edwin Meese, III, before the American Bar Association, Washington, DC (July 9, 1985); *Q and A with the Attorney General*, 81 A.B.A. J. 44 (July, 1985).

2. Brest, *The Misconceived Quest for the Original Understanding*, 60 B.U. L. REV. 204 (1980).

3. Ely, *Constitutional Interpretation: Its Allure and Impossibility*, 53 IND. L. J. 399 (1978).

4. Nowak, *Realism, Nihilism, and the Supreme Court: Do the Emperors Have Nothing But Robes?*, 22 WASHBURN L. J. 246, 257 (1983).

5. 410 U.S. 113 (1973).

6. Reynolds v. Sims, 377 U.S. 533 (1964).

7. Engle v. Vitale, 370 U.S. 421 (1962); Abington School Dist. v. Schempp, 374 U.S. 203 (1963).

8. 347 U.S. 483 (1954).

9. See, e.g., Boudin, GOVERNMENT BY JUDICIARY 433-34 (New York: W. Goodwin, 1932); Haines, THE AMERICAN DOCTRINE OF JUDICIAL SUPREMACY (Berkeley, CA: University of California Press, 1932).

10. Ford (ed.) 9 WRITINGS OF THOMAS JEFFERSON 275-76 (1902).

11. Grey, *Origins of the Unwritten Constitution: Fundamental Law in American Revolutionary Thought*, 30 STAN. L. REV. 843, 844 (1978).

12. 3 U.S. (3 Dall.) 171 (1796).

13. Currie, THE CONSTITUTION IN THE SUPREME COURT 1789-1888, 34 (Chicago: University of Chicago Press, 1985).

14. *Id.* at 36.

15. McCulloch v. Maryland, 17 U.S. (4 Wheat.) 316, 414 (1819).

16. *See*, Rohde & Spaeth, SUPREME COURT DECISION MAKING 41 (1976); 1 THE RECORDS OF THE FEDERAL CONVENTION OF 1787 xii-xiv (Farrand ed. San Francisco: W.H. Freeman, 1937).

17. Burns, THE VINEYARD OF LIBERTY 101-04 (New York: Knopf, 1982).

18. Wofford, *The Blinding Light: The Uses of History in Constitutional Interpretation*, 21 U. CHI. L. REV. 502 (1964).

19. *Supra* n. 7.

20. Stokes & Pfeffer, CHURCH AND STATE IN THE UNITED STATES 481-82 (Colorado Springs: Shepard's, 1975).

21. *See, e.g.*, tenBrock, *Uses by the United States Supreme Court of Extrinsic Aids in Constitutional Construction*, 27 CALIF. L. REV. 399, 404 (1939); Kelly, *Clio and the Court: An Illicit Love Affair*, 1965 SUP. CT. REV. 119, 122-25; Alfange, *On Judicial Policymaking and Constitutional Change: Another Look at the "Original Intent" Theory of Constitutional Interpretation*, 5 HASTINGS CONST. L. Q. 603, 617 (1978).

22. The Eleventh Amendment overruled the holding of Chisholm v. Georgia, 2 U.S. (2 Dall.) 419 (1793); the Fourteenth Amendment nullified, in part, the decision in Dred Scott v. Sandford, 60 U.S. (19 How.) 393 (1857); the Sixteenth Amendment nullified the holding of Pollock v. Farmers' Loan and Trust Co., 157 U.S. 429 (1895); the Twenty-sixth Amendment neutralized Oregon v. Mitchell, 400 U.S. 112 (1970).

23. "Not all the influence of a master politician in the prime of his popularity was quite enough to carry a program that would impair judicial review," McCloskey, THE AMERICAN SUPREME COURT 177 (Chicago: University of Chicago Press, 1960).

The plan was rejected vehemently by the Senate Judiciary Committee. See SENATE COMM. ON THE JUDICIARY, REORGANIZATION OF THE FED. JUDICIARY, ADVERSE REPORT, S. Rep. No. 711, 75th Cong., 1st Sess. 23 (1937).

24. Pfeffer, THIS HONORABLE COURT 424-25 (Boston: Beacon Press, 1965).

25. Those who campaigned for Chief Justice Warren's impeachment were unable to have impeachment proceedings initiated against him. While impeachment proceedings were instituted against Justice Douglas, they never got beyond the subcommittee stage and were eventually forsaken. See SPECIAL SUBCOMM. ON H. RES. 920 OF THE HOUSE COMM. ON THE JUDICIARY, 91 Cong., 2d Sess., Final Report, Associate Justice William O. Douglas (Comm. Print 1970).

26. "In the fifteen years between 1953 and 1968, over sixty bills were introduced in Congress to eliminate the jurisdiction of the federal courts over a variety of specific subjects; none of these became law." Bator, Mishkin, Shapiro & Wechsler, HART & WECHSLER'S THE FEDERAL COURTS AND THE FEDERAL SYSTEM 360 (Mineola, NY: Foundation Press, 2d ed. 1973).

Defining the dimensions of judicial activism

Discussions of judicial activism usually leave the term ill-defined. But this author identifies six specific elements that give general structure to the concept.

by Bradley C. Canon

Discussions of judicial activism seldom address the basic question of what constitutes judicial activism itself. In 1972 a book came out that illustrated well this point.[1] The contributors were 18 judges and scholars, including such prominent ones as justices Robert Jackson and the younger John Marshall Harlan, judges Learned Hand and J. Skelly Wright, and professors Alexander Bickel, Philip Kurland, and Herbert Wechsler. With one exception, none of the authors even tried to define judicial activism precisely.[2] At best readers could infer only a general conception of it without any framework or boundaries. Most recent essays into judicial activism suffer similarly: the term judicial activism is used without clarity. Moreover, even when someone does define it, the effort is usually ignored by all other commentators.

Much of the discussion about judicial activism is implicitly ideological, and that is a problem. Judicial activism is often equated with political liberalism, and restraint with conservatism. The Warren Court is widely equated with both activist jurisprudence and liberal results. The critics who have called for restraints on the federal courts have almost always been conservatives. But it was not always this way.

Classic discussion of activism focused on the nullification of liberal legislation by conservative justices, or on the invention or contortion of common law principles to protect wealth from severe damage judgments. In the constitutional crisis of 1936-1937, it was the New Deal liberals who argued for judicial restraint and the Old Guard conservatives who championed the role of the federal courts in shaping public policy. Today the ideological shift may be coming full circle. Currently some

liberals accuse the Burger Court of activism by blunting or dismantling many of the holdings of the Warren Court.[3] Laissez-faire critics of the post-1937 Court engaged in essentially the same shift.

More importantly, however, many commentators have considerably different concerns when they discuss judicial activism, concerns that often reflect whatever the courts are doing at the time. Thus in the New Deal era Attorney General (and later Justice) Robert Jackson and historian Henry Steele Commager focused on the judicial usurpation of majority rule in their analysis of activism.[4] A similar but narrower focus prevailed in the 1940s and 1950s as the Supreme Court followed the "preferred position" doctrine (broad construction of the First and Fourteenth Amendments) in the wake of Justice Harlan F. Stone's famous *Carolene Products* footnote.[5] Justice Felix Frankfurter, Judge Learned Hand, and scholar Wallace Mendelson aimed their criticisms at this so-called "libertarian activism."[6]

When the Warren Court began overruling longstanding legal doctrines or important precedents, criticism of activism shifted again. The Court's unwillingness to maintain continuity, precedent, or "neutral principles" was criticized.[7] Similarly, contemporary critics such as Raoul Berger, echoed by Justice William Rehnquist and in his own way by the late Justice Hugo Black, have reacted to the Supreme Court's expanded substantive interpretation of such constitutional provisions as the First and Fourteenth Amendment by equating activism with the Court's failure to abide by the words of these provisions or the intentions of their drafters.[8]

Also in recent years scholars such as Donald Horowitz and Nathan Glazer have challenged the

Court's initiation of complicated and often far-reaching policy changes, which sometimes involve the virtual day-to-day supervision of school systems, prisons, hospitals, and other institutions.[9] Their version of activism exists when courts act beyond their capacities and expertise. Finally, some decry the courts' politicization. Legal scholars such as Bickel and Kurland argue in terms of both comity and capacity that the courts should refrain from resolving disputes in those issues areas where the other branches of government have the authority and ability to do so.[10]

Two factors undergird this variety of approaches. First, judicial activism is often seen as a significant *court-generated change* in public policy. The court is literally active in public policy. When a court strikes down laws or overrules precedents or institutes cross-town busing or prison reforms, it by definition changes public policy. The second factor is *illegitimacy*. An activist decision is one perceived as illegitimate in terms of one or more commonly articulated beliefs about the proper role of the judiciary, and especially the Supreme Court, in the American constitutional system.

If commentators have numerous and disparate concepts of activism and do not articulate them very well, serious general use of the term becomes difficult if not meaningless. Overall, we receive little more than a babel of loosely connected discussion; the utility of any particular idea is limited. Those wanting to understand the discussion are left pretty much to their own devices.

I will not presume to propose a definitive meaning of judicial activism. I doubt that I could fashion one that would include in a meaningful way all of the focuses noted above. What I will do is try to give some general structure to the concept. I have identified and elaborated on six separate dimensions of judicial activism. These dimensions correspond roughly with the focuses noted above. I have derived them from a review of both the polemical and evaluative literature pertaining to judicial activism, including some literature that does not use the term itself, but in which the underlying factors of policy change or illegitimate authority are clearly evident.[11]

Six dimensions of activism

The six dimensions are described very briefly here and will be spelled out in detail below.

(1) Majoritarianism—the degree to which poli-cies adopted through democratic processes are judicially negated.

(2) Interpretive Stability—the degree to which earlier court decisions, doctrines, or interpretations are altered.

(3) Interpretive Fidelity—the degree to which constitutional provisions are interpreted contrary to the clear intentions of their drafters or the clear implications of the language used.

(4) Substance/Democratic Process Distinction—the degree to which judicial decisions make substantive policy rather than affect the preservation of democratic political processes.

(5) Specificity of Policy—the degree to which a judicial decision establishes policy itself as opposed to leaving discretion to other agencies or individuals.

(6) Availability of an Alternative Policymaker—the degree to which a judicial decision supersedes serious consideration of the same problem by other governmental agencies.

In developing these dimensions I tried to impose some objective boundaries so that particular cases can be described as either activist or non-activist under each dimension's criteria. Obviously, there are limits to this in practice. Not everyone will agree with all my illustrative classifications. The important thing, I think, is not to agree completely on how every case should be classified, but to agree on the essential nature of the approaches to activism.

Also, I have made no effort to control for what might be called the intensity of activism on any of these dimensions. For example, a decision wiping out laws prohibiting abortion throughout the nation will generate more frequent and intense discussion than will one striking down a law in one state that mandates license plate mottoes. But both are equally activist in the sense that they overturn policies adopted by legislative majorities. I have made no formal attempt to differentiate them.[12]

A word of caution here. More often than not, activism is a pejorative term. The norm in our system is that courts do not make policy, but rather that they merely implement policies inherent in the Constitution and statutes. We all realize that strict adherence to this norm is virtually impossible, but the norm's existence itself makes the concept of judicial activism suspect. Thus, only a few judges, such as Skelly Wright, admit to being activists.[13] From Justice Owen Roberts to Judge Frank Johnson, most simply insist they are applying a clear constitutional mandate to the situation at hand.[14] Legal scholars are much more open about the existence of activism. For many of them, however, activist decisions are an inviting target for critical analysis. Articles supportive of admittedly activist decisions usually take on a defensive or even apologetic tone. In this essay, however, I do not treat activism as a pathology. I neither condemn nor defend it. It is simply a fact of judicial life.

I limit the ensuing discussion of the six dimensions to the activism of the U.S. Supreme Court in its development of constitutional law. While the concept of activism certainly applies to the construction of statutes, the development of common law, and other judicial doctrines, constitutional law lies at the heart of the controversy and produces the sharpest and most memorable colloquy.

Majoritarianism

Majoritarianism is probably the most frequent criterion used in assessing Supreme Court activism. It suggests that when the Court exercises judicial review, it substitutes another public policy for that enacted by elected representatives in Congress, state legislatures, or city councils. Such action is often seen as illegitimate from the perspective of democratic theory.

The violation of majoritarianism is most pronounced when the Court declares an act of Congress unconstitutional. Elected from throughout the nation, Congress constitutes a coordinate branch of the federal government. The justices have voided congressional legislation an average of once a year since the Civil War, with the average approaching twice a year in the last two decades. Some such decisions strike down provisions having only local application or ones of little real importance, but numerous major congressional policies have also been voided. *Dred Scott*[15] and the several decisions striking down New Deal policies of the 1930s provoked constitutional crises of the first magnitude. Three judicial overrulings generated amendments to the Constitution.[16] Two others induced a serious attempt to write an overruling amendment into the Constitution.[17] Beyond these cases, it is easy to point to a number of others that have voided acts of Congress and that subsequently received widespread public and scholarly criticism.

The majoritarian dimension also includes Supreme Court nullification of state laws, state constitutional provisions, and local ordinances. Such voidings arguably are less offensive in principle. A federal system requires some mechanism for reviewing local legislation in order to retain federal supremacy in specified areas. The U.S. judiciary does this, and it is too late in the game to rethink that selection. Nonetheless, the nullification of local laws arguably violates our commitments to majority rule and federalism, especially when the laws involved are not patently unconstitutional. Further, striking down some state laws can have a profound national impact. Criticism following *Abington Township v. Schempp,* on school prayer,[18] or *Roe v. Wade*[19] has far exceeded that from any recent nullification of any federal law and has generated strong and continuing efforts to amend the Constitution.

Interpretive stability

This dimension measures the degree to which a Supreme Court decision either retains or abandons precedent or existing judicial doctrine. Interpretive stability is an important element in the debate over the merits of activism, although it is often unrecognized as such and its components are often poorly articulated. Discussions of the Warren Court's activism probably focused more on the frequency and scope of its radical alterations of prior jurisprudence than on the anti-majoritarian nature of its decisions. Many of its most memorable cases, *Mapp v. Ohio,*[20] *Miranda v. Arizona,*[21] and *New York Times v. Sullivan,*[22] to name a few, nullified no statute or ordinance but simply overturned precedent, common law doctrine, or old understandings about the Constitution. Moreover, some decisions that voided legislation faced even greater criticism because they also overruled precedent: *Baker v. Carr*[23] and *Brown v. Board of Education,*[24] are cases in point. Nor is the Warren Court the sole exemplar of interpretive instability. The Burger Court is sometimes similarly criticized for its decisions restricting or overturning Warren Court doctrines, for example, *National League of Cities v. Usery.*[25] And the post-1937 Court was seen as activist by many for its decisions legitimizing New Deal legislation, which sometimes overruled or emasculated the doctrines of freedom of contract, substantive due process, and dual federalism.

The most visible and dramatic instance of interpretive instability comes when the Court explicitly overrules one of its own earlier decisions. Usually the Court is straightforward about it, for example, "Our conclusion is that the case of *Adkins v. Children's*

Hospital, supra, should be, and it is, overruled."[26] Occasionally it is indirect, as in the *Brown v. Board* phrasing, "any language in *Plessy v. Ferguson* contrary to this finding is rejected."[27] Few failed, however, to appreciate that *Plessy* had been overruled.

The Court can also drastically weaken a precedent without formally overruling it. Of course, over time we expect that future decisions may put some limits on a precedent's applicability. The clarification and development of precedent are the woof and warp of judicial business and such cases hardly constitute activism. But when a precedent is drastically weakened by a single subsequent decision that greatly restricts its scope or seriously compromises its logic, the ideal of interpretive stability is weakened. For example, *Gertz v. Welch*[28] significantly altered the concept of a "public person" as set forth in *Rosenbloom v. Metromedia*,[29] and the *Reidel*[30] and *Twelve Reels*[31] cases almost totally undermined the logic and practical utility of *Stanley v. Georgia*,[32] protecting private possession of pornography.

Precedent can be enhanced as well as restricted. Again, some growth in scope and reasoning naturally occurs. However, on occasion the Court will expand precedent by a virtual quantum leap—by applying it to a new legal area or giving it hitherto unforeseen or rejected implications, for example, *Frontiero's*[33] reliance on *Bolling v. Sharpe*,[34] or *Collector v. Day*[35] as a new application of *McCulloch v. Maryland*.[36]

Interpretive stability need not be measured against precedent. Another baseline is what I will call "ongoing interpretation" of the Constitution. Ongoing interpretation is an inferential interpretation of constitutional meaning drawn from longstanding and/or widespread laws or practices. No specific Supreme Court precedents directly support such an interpretation, although such support may exist at other levels. For instance, from 1791 forward virtually everyone assumed that obscenity was not protected by the First Amendment and acted accordingly; the assumption that tax exemptions for ecclesiastically owned property did not violate the establishment clause is similarly ancient. Only after a century and a half of ongoing interpretation did the Court affirm these assumptions.[37] However, the constitutionality of such practice is not always affirmed. Recently the Court has deemed unconstitutional some longstanding practices such as the "spoils system"[38] and state-enforced restrictions on advertising by professionals,[39] to say nothing of its decisions in *Abington Township v. Schempp*, concerning school prayer, and *Roe v. Wade*.

Interpretive fidelity

This dimension measures the Court's actual or inferential construction of provisions of the Constitution. Activism occurs when an interpretation does not accord with the ordinary meaning of wording of the provision and/or with the known, consensual intentions or goals of its drafters.

If the Supreme Court has primary responsibility for interpreting the Constitution's provisions, how then, we might wonder, can the Court misconstrue that document? It is analogous to asking whether the Pope can espouse heresy. This is not the place for a lengthy discussion of the rights and wrongs of Supreme Court discretion in interpreting constitutional provisions. But it is the place to note that there are judges and scholars who to a greater or lesser degree believe it is possible to measure the interpretive fidelity of some Court decisions.[40] Words and phrases, after all, do have some meaning, and drafters of constitutional provisions did have intentions and goals. When these appear to be transgressed, dissenting justices and legal scholars often protest vigorously and engage in considerable semantic analysis or historical research. Sometimes the issue is hard to resolve, but sometimes interpretive hindsight condemns "interpretive infidelity," as in the cases where the Court upheld the constitutionality of relocating Japanese Americans during World War II, an action now almost universally acknowledged to have violated their constitutional rights.[41]

While conceding the necessity for discretion in applying vague phrases to particular situations, critics of activism on this dimension argue that *the* Constitution is not *a* constitution if it can be significantly altered at the will of nine or five justices in the course of a lawsuit. Although it is a "Constitution intended to endure for ages to come,"[42] it does not follow that the Court can ignore the very words of the document. Article V provides an amending process if particular provisions prove unpopular or dysfunctional.

Supporters of activism here argue that the Court's main function is the smooth application of an Eighteenth Century document to Twentieth Century problems, which may require new meanings for old provisions. It is the spirit of the document, they argue, rather than the exact wording or the framers' time-bound intentions that is important. At any rate, interpretive fidelity is clearly a dimension of judicial activism and warrants discussion in any overall treatment of the phenomena.

Let me discuss the two considerations separately. With regard to wording, I think it is fair to call activist any decision that appears to clearly contradict any constitutional provision in terms of the ordinary meaning of its wording, or any decision that is contrary to the logical implications of two or more provisions considered together. The Minnesota moratorium case[43] is illustrative. The Court upheld a state law impairing contracts despite the explicit prohibition against such legislation found in Article I, Section 10.

The *Harper*[44] decision, which declared state poll taxes unconstitutional, provides a more complex example. The Twenty-fourth Amendment, adopted two years earlier, banned poll taxes in federal elections but said nothing about poll taxes in state elections. It is unclear why the latter were omitted. Perhaps Congress would not pass or the states would not ratify an amendment barring poll taxes in state elections. Perhaps it was a matter of strategy, with the elimination of poll taxes in federal elections helping to eliminate them in state elections. Nonetheless, the Court, although it did not discuss the Twenty-fourth Amendment in deciding *Harper*, amended the Constitution in a manner that Congress and the states had refrained from just two years earlier.

Also activist are those decisions that effectively create new constitutional provisions by finding them, through a strained or illogical interpretation of language, in pre-existing provisions. A prime example is creation of the "equal protection component" of the Fifth Amendment.[45] It is difficult to derive such an interpretation from an ordinary reading of the words "nor shall any person . . . be deprived of life, liberty or property without the due process of law." Moreover, if the words had been historically understood to convey such a meaning, the equal protection clause of the Fourteenth Amendment would have been unnecessary as that amendment already contained a due process clause.

Constitutional history contains other important "additions." For instance, the method by which the Court extended the Fourteenth Amendment's due process clause from persons to corporations is perhaps well known but hardly well reasoned.[46]

And the transformation of the same clause to constrain state "establishment" of religion—for example, aid to parochial schools—is neither well known nor well understood.[47]

As an aside, it is interesting to note that many such "amendments" generate little controversy. Apparently these actions "go with the flow." It would be anomalous to forbid states from engaging in racial discrimination, but to have the federal government doing so. Corporations were the obvious progenitors of economic progress in the late Nineteenth Century and the contract clause did not provide sufficient protection against potentially devastating government regulation. In sum, many Court "amendments" are welcome ones, but they are no less activist for that.

I also categorize as activist those decisions interpreting a provision contrary to the reasonably clear and consensual intentions of its writers. It is also fair to place in this category those decisions applying a provision to a situation existing at the time of the provision's adoption to which it is clear the drafters did not intend for it to apply. Decisions flying in the face of the framers' intentions are infrequent, but do occur. Again the Minnesota moratorium case comes to mind. The clear purpose of the contract clause was to prevent states from altering repayment schedules, as some had done in the hard times of the 1780s. Yet this was exactly what the Minnesota law did and the Court upheld it.

Decisions applying constitutional provisions to situations where the drafters did not anticipate application are more common. The Founding Fathers, for instance, would have been (and a few were) quite surprised to learn that the contract clause forbade states from altering the terms of corporate charters they granted, as *Dartmouth College v. Woodward*[48] held. Anti-abortion laws were prevalent when the Fourteenth Amendment was adopted, but no one suggested that the due process clause would render them unconstitutional.

It should be emphasized that because of inadequate discussion, poor records or conflict in the evidence, it is by no means always easy to ascertain the intentions of the framers. In such cases, the justices cannot be faulted for adopting an interpretation for which there is a reasonable evidentiary basis. Indeed, in cases such as the desegregation decision where historical evidence concerning intentions can be adduced to support both sides of the coin (not necessarily in equal proportions), the Court would be damned to activism no matter which way it decided. The essence of the drafters' intentions criterion is that the intentions have substantial clarity.

Substance/democratic process distinction

It is often argued that there is greater justification in some areas for court policy making than in others. In footnote four of the *Caroline Products* case Justice Stone offered the classic identification of those preferred areas: "legislation which restricts those political processes which can ordinarily be expected to bring about repeal of undesirable legislation" and "[legislation] which tends seriously to curtail the operation of those political processes ordinarily to be relied upon to protect [discrete and insular minorities]."[49]

In the wake of this famous footnote, the Court for about a decade followed the "preferred position" doctrine, which subjected laws impinging on the political process to greater judicial scrutiny. While the Court has since abandoned "preferred position" as formal doctrine, it still uses reasoning and rhetoric reminiscent of it, and many civil libertarians continue to harken to it as a rationale for heightened judicial scrutiny in the area of their primary interest.[50] Not all agree, of course; many see little distinction between Court policy making concerning freedom of expression and that affecting more substantive policy areas. It is this dispute that renders the substance/process distinction an important element in a discussion of activism. Thus, the footnote four philosophy serves as the genesis of the substance/democratic process distinction.

The crucial distinction is between those Court decisions relating to the integrity of the democratic political processes and those that do not affect them. It is a fundamental tenet of our constitutional system that political minorities have an opportunity through open communication and democratic political processes to become a majority. Court decisions protecting or enhancing this tenet can be accounted as more justified than decisions affecting other types of public policy.

According to this logic, decisions developing or altering policies affecting the political processes are not activist. Basically, these involve freedom of expression, the franchise, conduct of elections, and the nature of representation. Such decisions do not directly affect substantive policies. Rather

they relate to citizens' opportunities for input into the policy-making system. The high Court has made many such decisions upholding, widening, and equalizing these opportunities in the past half century.

Activist decisions on this dimension are those that make economic policy, regulate the non-political-process activities of institutions or groups, or impinge people's careers, lifestyles, morals, or religious values. Obviously the scope of this category is broad. It includes the "substantive due process" decisions so common to the first 40 years of this century as well as the "new due process" coming in the wake of the *Griswold v. Connecticut*[51] birth control decision. (Note, however, that I am not defining as activist those decisions that uphold legislation regulating the economy, lifestyles, etc. Only when the Court negates other agencies' policies or makes such policy itself is it being activist.)

Brown v. Board and many subsequent desegregation decisions (but not those involving the right to vote or the legality of sit-ins or other forms of protest) occupy something of a middle ground on this dimension. Blacks clearly constitute a "discrete and insular minority." However, many race related decisions also have substantive aspects in that they directly affect people's lifestyles or values.

Specificity of policy

Traditionally, courts stepped into public policy only to nullify laws. Such a decision often left legislators or administrators free to pursue other approaches to a problem. While nullification is still common, in recent years courts have increasingly become positive policymakers as well. That is, they have begun to command government agencies to undertake certain policies, sometimes in minute detail. In some celebrated cases, courts have virtually taken over the management of school systems, prisons, and hospitals. Positive policy making by the judiciary could be the wave of the future, but it will not arrive without considerable criticism.

Courts may have the right to nullify unconstitutional policies, critics argue, but they have no warrant to behave like a legislative or administrative body. Proponents of positive policy making reply that the Constitution contains commands as well as prohibitions and that courts are obligated to enforce the former when other agencies cannot or will not. I will designate this emergent facet of the debate on activism the Specificity of Policy dimension.

The key to activism on this dimension is positive policy making by the Court. This includes those decisions that, in effect, declare or develop new policy, sometimes with attention to detail, or that specify particular behavior government agencies need to follow in pursuit of an existing policy. Examples are not hard to find. *Roe v. Wade* did more than strike down state abortion laws; it rewrote them in chapter and verse. In *Miller v. California*[52] an explicit obscenity code was developed. *Miranda* dictated to the police what officers must do prior to interrogating a suspect.

Some positive Court decisions possess aspects of negative and/or permissive types of policy. Common sense and context will have to be applied to their classification. The abortion case and *Miller v. California*, for instance, have a permissive component: states are free to have no laws whatsoever governing abortion or obscenity. However, few states have chosen this option and, moreover, the options's existence was not crucial to the Court's decision in either case. *Roe v. Wade* also has a negative component in that it rendered unconstitutional then-existing laws prohibiting or severely limiting abortions. Had that been all the Court did, a negative classification would have been appropriate; however, the Court's promulgation of its own trimester policy warrants a positive classification for the case.

Availability of an alternate policy maker

"Courts," Justice Stone noted in 1936, "are not the only agency of government that must be presumed to have the capacity to govern."[53] This is a frequently echoed theme: the Supreme Court must exercise self-restraint in the face of other agencies' attempts to develop policies for pressing problems. Such protest usually takes into account how well courts are equipped vis-a-vis a legislature or an administrative agency to make intelligent policy in any given area.

Thus the final dimension pertains to what I will call the Availability of an Alternative Policy Maker.[54] The central question here is: to what extent could another agency make policy similar to that found in the Court's decision? Two factors shape the answer: First, does another agency have the authority to make policy and, if so, is it politically or practically feasible for it to do so? Second, does another agency have more expertise and access to information to make policy than the Supreme Court?

Sometimes Court decisions or ongoing interpretation will leave a potential alternate policymaker uncertain of its legal authority. In the era of substantive due process and dual federalism, Congress was often inhibited in its regulation of labor conditions around the nation. Similarly, even integrationists mistrusted Congress' authority to desegregate schools before 1954 because the Court's *Plessy* decision had explicitly upheld the constitutionality of separate facilities. More often, however, lack of authority is not the inhibiting factor. Legislatures have always had the authority to pass laws prohibiting prayers in schools, require busing for the achievement of racial balance in schools or even mandate *Miranda*-like warnings before the interrogation of suspects. The crucial question is usually the political or practical likelihood of another agency taking such action.

The phrase "political or practical likelihood" of action does not mean that the alternate policymaker necessarily has to arrive at the same policy as that embodied in the Court's decision. This would imply the inevitability or absolute correctness of the policy, in which case it would make little difference who promulgated it. Policy making is a matter of choice. But it is to some extent a reasoned and genuine choice—one where two or more policies (one encompassing the Court's decision) are possible or probable outcomes of debate and political pressure. In short, there does have to be a reasonable likelihood that an alternate policymaker could have come to the Court's position.

Quite often this is not the case. Occasionally, the decisional structure effectively precludes such a choice. It would be quixotic to expect rurally dominated legislatures in urban states to reapportion themselves along the one-man-one-vote line commanded by the Court. More often, intense political pressures make any real consideration of alternative policies unlikely. The word "intense" here is intended to delineate a situation going beyond mere majority opposition to the Court's policy. It implies a communal divisiveness or a strong antipathy toward minority political, religious, or cultural positions. During the 1950s, for example, no one would have expected Southern legislatures to enact desegregation laws and few legislative bodies of any region or level could resist proposed anticommunist laws.

Judges can lay claim to no particular expertise in substantive policy areas. Few have acquired any specialized knowledge through prior legislative concentration or administrative service, and judicial dockets are always broad in scope. More important, judges lack a specialized staff for in-depth research on the non-legal aspects of the issues posed in many cases. By comparison to other agencies, courts have virtually no staff at all.

Moreover, the information processing system accompanying judicial decision making is not generally conducive to informed policy making. The case can stem from a particular event or situation that may or may not represent the policy dilemma generally. Briefs and oral arguments are developed by lawyers schooled in and encouraged to stress precedent and analogy rather than facts illuminating the social consequences of alternate policy choices. While social science data are occasionally included in briefs or opinions, more often lawyers and judges give little systematic attention to a decision's impact.[55]

Not all judicial decisions, however, call for expertise or complex data. Sometimes the information needed is simple and the crucial question is one of values. Judges are as competent as anyone else to make such choices. Statistical analyses might inform the details of a reapportionment decision, but they are irrelevant to the fundamental philosophical issue. Impact analyses would do little to enlighten a decision about the constitutional wisdom of prayers in the public schools. Indeed, where the focus is on a facet of the judicial process itself (e.g., did the appellant receive due process?) the judges' expertise is paramount.

Activism on this dimension consists of decisions that (a) establish policy where there is a reasonable likelihood that an alternative policy-making agency would have adopted a similar policy in the foreseeable future, and/or (b) the nature of the policy is such that choices are better informed by data or expertise not normally available in the judicial process. Again *Roe v. Wade* serves as an illustration. The policy at issue was—as Justice Blackmun's opinion conceded—illuminated by physiology and medical technology, subjects normally beyond the ken of jurists. Moreover, several state legislatures had already adopted policies similar in spirit if not detail to the Court's, and public opinion polls showed majority support for liberalized abortion policies. *Bell v. Maryland*[56] where the Court deferred consideration of the constitutional question surrounding the public accommodations issue while

Congress was considering the Civil Rights Act of 1964 is an example of judicial restraint on this dimension.

Gideon v. Wainwright[57] is an example of (a) but not (b). There was considerable discussion of the merits and logistics of providing counsel for indigent felony defendants at the time of the decision and many legislatures had taken steps to that effect. However, judges were certainly as knowledgeable as legislators in making policy so close to their own realm of experience. *Aptheker v. Secretary of State*[58] illustrates (b) but not (a). Congress and the State Department certainly knew more about the national security implications of overseas travel by members of the Communist Party, but given the temper of the times, the passport provisions of the McCarren Act were not likely to be repealed.

Conclusion

Judicial activism is a central, if not well understood, feature of the American political system. As such, it has long been subject to both polemical and scholarly analyses, although sometimes it is not easy to separate the two. Most such attention, however, has been ad hoc or at least without a general approach to the phenomena. Thus, for most of us, the concept of judicial activism has little common structure or meaning.

My purpose here has been to give the concept some structure and meaning. I have done this by developing out of the literature six distinct dimensions of what has been termed judicial activism. I have tried to remove or minimize the ideological components or motivations found in the literature. On my dimensions, judicial activism is a multi-directional phenomenon. It can be liberal or conservative, libertarian or statist, politically necessary or unnecessary, or, for that matter, unrelated to ideology and politics at all. I hope that these dimensions will prove useful to understanding judicial activism, and that they will sharpen discussions and analyses of it.

NOTES

This article originally appeared in Volume 66, Number 6, December-January 1983, pages 236-246. Portions of it are excerpted by permission of the publisher from the author's work, *A Framework for the Analysis of Judicial Activism,* in Halpern and Lamb, SUPREME COURT ACTIVISM AND RESTRAINT (Lexington, MA: Lexington Books, 1982).

Work on this article was supported by a Minor Grant from Project '87, for which I am grateful.

1. Forte, ed., THE SUPEME COURT IN AMERICAN POLITICS: JUDICIAL

ACTIVISM VS. JUDICIAL RESTRAINT (Lexington, MA: D.C. Heath, 1972).

2. Political scientist Glendon Schubert said, "The Court is activist when its decisions conflict with those of other political policymakers." *Id.* at 17.

3. Goldman, *In Defense of Justice*, 29 J. POL. 148-158 (1977).

4. Jackson, THE STRUGGLE FOR JUDICIAL SUPREMACY (New York: Knopf, 1941); Commager, MAJORITY RULE AND MINORITY RIGHTS (New York: Oxford University Press, 1943).

5. United States v. Carolene Prods. 304 U.S. 144, at 152-53 (1938).

6. *See* Frankfurter's dissent in West Virginia Bd. of Educ. v. Barnette, 319 U.S. 624 (1943); Hand, THE BILL OF RIGHTS (Cambridge, MA: Harvard University Press, 1958); Mendelson, THE SUPREME COURT: LAW AND DISCRETION (Indianapolis, IN: Bobbs-Merrill, 1967).

7. Wechsler, *Toward Neutral Principles of Constitutional Law,* 73 HARV. L. REV. 1-35 (1959); and Henkin, *Some Reflections on Current Constitutional Controversies,* 109 U. PA. L. REV. 637-662 (1961).

8. Berger, GOVERNMENT BY JUDICIARY (Cambridge, MA: Harvard University Press, 1977); Rehnquist, *The Notion of a Living Constitution,* 54 TEX. L. REV. 693-709 (1976). *See* Justice Black's dissent in Katz v. United States, 389 U.S. 347 (1967).

9. Horwitz, THE COURTS AND SOCIAL POLICY (Washington, DC: The Brookings Institute, 1977); Glazer, *Should Judges Administer Social Services,* 50 PUB. INTEREST 64-80 (1979).

10. Bickel, THE SUPREME COURT AND THE IDEA OF PROGRESS (New York: Harper & Row, 1970), and THE MORALITY OF CONSENT (New Haven: Yale University Press, 1975); Kurland, POLITICS, THE CONSTITUTION AND THE WARREN COURT (Chicago: University of Chicago Press, 1970).

11. *Supra* n. 6-10.

12. I do differentiate levels of activism in a longer work, *A Framework for the Analysis of Judicial Activism,* in Halpern and Lamb, eds., SUPREME COURT ACTIVISM AND RESTRAINT 385-419 (Lexington, MA: Lexington Books, 1982).

13. Wright, *The Role of the Supreme Court in a Democratic Society—Judicial Activism or Restraint,* 54 CORNELL L. REV. 1-28 (1968).

14. *See* Justice Roberts' famous "squaring" statement in United States v. Butler, 297 U.S. 1, at 62-63 (1936). Johnson, *The Role of the Judiciary With Respect to the Other Branches of Government,* in Murphy and Pritchett, eds., COURTS, JUDGES AND POLITICS, 3rd ed., 66-71 (New York: Random House, 1979).

15. Dred Scott v. Sanford, 19 How. 393 (1857).

16. *Dred Scott* was repudiated by the Fourteenth Amendment; Pollock v. Farmers' Loan and Trust Co., 157 U.S. 429 (1895), was overturned by the Sixteenth Amendment; and Oregon v. Mitchell, 400 U.S. 112 (1970), led to the Twenty-sixth Amendment, setting the minimum voting age at 18.

17. Hammer v. Dagenhart, 247 U.S. 251 (1918), and Bailey v. Drexel Furniture Co., 259 U.S. 20 (1922), led Congress to pass the Child Labor Amendment in 1924, but it was never ratified by three-fourths of the states.

18. 374 U.S. 203 (1963).

19. 410 U.S. 113 (1973).

20. 367 U.S. 643 (1962).

21. 384 U.S. 436 (1966).

22. 376 U.S. 254 (1964).

23. 369 U.S. 186 (1962).

24. 347 U.S. 483 (1954).

25. 426 U.S. 833 (1976). *Usury* also overturned congressional legislation, a 1974 amendment to the Fair Labor Standards Act extending the minimum wage to state and municipal employees.

26. West Cost Hotel Co. v. Parrish, 300 U.S. 379, at 400 (1937).

27. 347 U.S. 483, at 494-95 (1954). Plessy v. Ferguson, 163 U.S. 537 (1896) was overruled.

28. 418 U.S. 323 (1974).

29. 403 U.S. 29 (1971).

30. United States v. Reidel, 402 U.S. 351 (1971).

31. United States v. Twelve 200-Foot Reels, 413 U.S. 123 (1973).

32. 394 U.S. 557 (1969).

33. Frontiero v. Richardson, 411 U.S. 677 (1973).

34. 347 U.S. 497 (1954).

35. 11 Wall. 113 (1871).

36. 4 Wheat. 316 (1819).

37. Roth v. U.S., 354 U.S. 476 (1957), and Walz v. Tax Comm'n, 397 U.S. 664 (1970), respectively.

38. Elrod v. Burns, 427 U.S. 347 (1976).

39. Bates v. State Bar of Ariz., 433 U.S. 350 (1977).

40. Berger, *supra* n. 8, is the classic example of such a scholar. Justice Black is the classic example of such a judge. *See, for example,* his dissents in Barenblatt v. United States, 360 U.S. 109 (1959), and Smith v. California, 361 U.S. 147 (1959). More generally, *see* John Hart Ely's discussion of this philosophy, which he calls "interpretivism," in DEMOCRACY AND DISTRUST: A THEORY OF JUDICIAL REVIEW, chs. 1, 2 (Cambridge, MA: Harvard University Press, 1980).

41. Hirabayashi v. United States, 320 U.S. 81 (1943), and Korematsu v. United States, 323 U.S. 214 (1944).

42. McCulloch v. Maryland, 4 Wheat. 316, at 408, 415 (1819).

43. Home Bldg. and Loan Ass'n v. Blaisdell, 290 U.S. 3908 (1934).

44. Harper v. Virginia Bd. of Elections, 383 U.S. 663 (1966).

45. Bolling v. Sharpe, 347 U.S. 497 (1954); Frontiero v. Richardson, *supra* n. 33.

46. Santa Clara County v. Southern Pacific R. Co., 118 U.S. 394 (1886). At the beginning of the case, Chief Justice Waite announced that the Court did not wish to hear argument on the question as all justices were of the opinion that the Fourteenth Amendment applied to corporations.

47. The first such case is Everson v. Board of Educ. of Ewing Township, 330 U.S. 1 (1947).

48. Dartmouth College v. Woodward, 4 Wheat. 518 (1819).

49. *Supra* n. 5.

50. Recently John Hart Ely and Jesse Choper have advanced this basic position in sophisticated book-length arguments. Ely, *supra* n. 40, and Choper, JUDICIAL REVIEW AND THE NATIONAL POLITICAL PROCESS: A FUNCTIONAL RECONSIDERATION OF THE ROLE OF THE SUPREME COURT (Chicago: University of Chicago Press, 1980).

51. 381 U.S. 479 (1965).

52. 413 U.S. 15 (1973).

53. United States v. Butler, 297 U.S. 1, at 87 (1936) (dissenting opinion).

54. I have borrowed the term from Carter, *When Courts Should Make Policy: An Institutional Approach,* in Gardiner, ed., PUBLIC LAW AND PUBLIC POLICY (New York: Praeger, 1977).

55. For discussions of the information problem *see* Miller and Barron, *The Supreme Court, the Adversary System and the Flow of Information to the Justices,* 62 VA. L. REV. 1187-1245 (1975); and Lamb, *Judicial Policy-Making and Information Flow to the Supreme Court,* 29 VAND. L. REV. 45-124 (1976).

56. 378 U.S. 226 (1964).

57. 372 U.S. 355 (1963).

58. 378 U.S. 500 (1964).

Actors in the Judicial Process
Judges: Judicial Selection Systems and Their Consequences

INTRODUCTION

Among all the actors in the American judicial process it is the judge who often emerges as the focal point, the participant at the heart of the courtroom who controls and directs an unfolding legal drama and often decides its outcome. The issue of judicial selection, how judges obtain their positions, is one that frequently has engaged analysts because it is felt by many that the nature of selection processes has implications for the kinds of people chosen and, ultimately, for the decisions reached by the chosen few. There are numerous judicial selection systems operative in the United States, including appointment for the three levels of the federal bench and elective, appointive and hybrid selection systems (which can incorporate elements of election, appointment and/or merit panel processes) spread throughout the American states. In some states, fundamentally different selection procedures are used to choose judges for different levels of the judiciary. Indeed, given the reality of 50 distinct state judiciaries and a three tiered federal judicial system the possibilities for important nuances of difference among judicial selection procedures in the United States is staggering. The articles in this section attempt to come to grips with alternative approaches to judicial selection and some of their consequences.

At the outset, Larry Berkson's piece, "Judicial selection in the United States," offers the reader a lay of the land surveying the history and rationales for the emergence of alternative approaches to choosing judges in America. Berkson underlines that "the combination of schemes used to select judges is almost endless. Almost no two states are alike, and few employ the same method for choosing judges at all levels of the judiciary."

One of the selection systems outlined by Berkson is the merit selection model in which nominating commissions generate a limited number of judicial candidates who, following appointment to a limited judicial term, generally must run on an unopposed retention ballot by which they are simply retained in office or defeated. In some states retention is accomplished through review by a commission.

Such selection systems have developed as a means of trying to balance the conflicting goals of judicial independence and accountability and their operation has served as the subject of considerable scholarly inquiry. In "What twenty years of judicial retention elections have told us," William Hall and Larry Aspin report on the empirical patterns observed in the results of nearly 1,900 retention elections for major trial court judgeships conducted in 10 states over a 20-year period. The study examines retention elections in both merit selection states and those where judges initially gained their seats through competitive partisan elections. It reveals, in the aggregate, extraordinarily high affirmative voting in retention elections, which are generally characterized by low voter turnout, the absence of voting cues, and low levels of voter information.

Hall & Aspin — retention of seats

While Hall and Aspin's study lends credence to the criticism that retention elections actually serve to insulate judges from popular control, this should not be taken to mean that under no circumstances will a judge standing for retention be defeated. Indeed, in "The defeat of the California justices," John Wold and John Culver present a case study of the kinds of circumstances that can and did lead to defeat for three California Supreme Court justices in a highly publicized 1986 judicial retention election. (It should be noted that supreme court justices in California receive their seats initially through appointment by the governor. Subsequently, they are subject to retention elections analogous to those operative in the very different merit selection systems of other states. Merit selection, of course, includes utilization of nominating commissions, which are not employed in the appointment of supreme court justices in California.) Ironically, while Hall and Aspin's study raises questions about the value of retention elections in which almost all judges are retained, Wold and Culver's analysis raises the issue of what standard of accountability voters employ in those rare instances when judges fail to be retained. If that standard is the content of decisions, as appears to have been the case in California where segments of the public were unhappy with the substantive rulings rendered by the defeated justices, the spectre is raised of a public removing the ultimate power of interpreting the law from the courts. Thus the possibility of a "chilling effect" of retention elections on judges' decisions cannot be discounted.

Wold & Culver — defeat in retention elections

In "The electoral fates of incumbent judges in the Ohio Court of Common Pleas," Lawrence Baum turns our attention away from the retention election setting to a state's trial court elections that, at least on the surface, are structured as non-partisan and competitive. Utilizing a large data set of nearly 20 years of Ohio elections, Baum examines the advantages of incumbency in differing competitive contexts. The research underlines the important long-term role that governors play in states where they enjoy the power to appoint "interim" judges to fill out the terms of vacated judgeships prior to a subsequent election. More generally, Baum demonstrates that while a competitive electoral setting is "more dangerous for incumbents than are retention elections under 'merit selection' systems, . . . the similarities are more striking than the differences."

The next three articles in this section focus on federal judicial selection. As with the other panel discussions reprinted in this anthology, "The federal judiciary: what role politics?" does not present the reader with definitive answers. Rather, it explores numerous perspectives on important and vexing issues, in this instance the processes and criteria for selection of federal judges. Sheldon Goldman's "The Bush imprint on the judiciary" examines the processes utilized and the outcomes achieved by George Bush in making judicial appointments during his first two years in office and compares and contrasts the processes and outcomes with those of Presidents Johnson through Reagan. The article underlines the importance of judicial recruitment in a president's domestic policy making agenda and the ability of a presidency to "live on" through its lifetime judicial appointments. Indeed, Goldman writes that, "Just as the Roosevelt and Truman appointees carried through the constitutionalization of the New Deal . . . so too the Reagan and Bush appointees will be likely to constitutionalize the Reagan-Bush social agenda, which means institutionalizing judicial restraint in matters of governmental civil liberties and civil rights policy making. Rights and liberties may be subjected to majority rule in each state and in the nation to an extent not seen in almost sixty years."

In Henry Abraham's "A bench happily filled," our attention is turned to the appointment process to the U.S. Supreme Court. Abraham explores the motivations for presidential nominations as well as for the confirmation behavior of the Senate. Four historical illustrations of specific appointments are offered that underline the complexities and nuances of the Supreme Court appointment process.

The final selection in this section, Senator Howell Heflin's "The impeachment process: modernizing an archaic system," explores the problems of the federal system's constitutional procedures for removing judges from office. As a participant in recent impeachment proceedings in the Senate, Heflin argues that existing procedures fail to give adequate attention to the substantive charges under examination while also failing to provide the accused due process. Heflin suggests a constitutional amendment that would allow Congress to utilize impeachment procedures modelled along the lines of other more efficient systems he points to for removing judges in many states. The Senate has been engaged in several impeachment proceedings since Heflin's article was written, while no constitutional alterations have taken place. Nevertheless, the issues of discipline and removal of judges in the federal and state systems remain the focus of considerable contemporary debate.

Judicial selection in the United States: a special report

by Larry C. Berkson

[handwritten marginalia: not content of conf. exec. cuz Too wide of power. not complete control of judiciary]

Historically there has been considerable controversy about how American judges should be chosen. During the colonial era, they were selected by the king, but his intolerably wide powers over them was one of the abuses that the colonists attacked in the Declaration of Independence. After the Revolution, the states continued to select judges by appointment, but the new processes prevented the chief executive from controlling the judiciary.[1]

Gradually, however, states began to adopt popular election as a means of choosing judges. For example, as early as 1812 Georgia amended its constitution to provide that judges of inferior courts be popularly elected. In 1816, Indiana entered the Union with a constitution that provided for the election of associate judges of the circuit court. Sixteen years later, Mississippi became the first state in which all judges were popularly elected. Michigan held elections for trial judges in 1836.

By that time the appointive system had come under serious attack. People resented the fact that property owners controlled the judiciary.[2] They were determined to end this privilege of the upper class and to ensure the popular sovereignty we describe as Jacksonian Democracy.

During the next decade, there was little opposition to those who advocated popular elections. For example, in the New York Constitutional Convention of 1846 there was not even a lengthy discussion of the subject. As one writer has stated:

The debates on an elective judiciary were brief; there was apparently little need to discuss the abuses of the appointive system, or its failures, or why election would be better. A few delegates argued cogently for the retention of the old system, and indeed forecast the possible evils if the judiciary fell under political domination . . . . But the spirit of reform carried the day.[3]

New York's adoption of an electoral system signaled the beginning of this trend. By the time of the Civil War, 24 of 34 states had established an elected judiciary with seven states adopting the system in 1850 alone.[4] As new states were admitted to the Union, all of them adopted popular election of some or all judges until the admission of Alaska in 1959.

No panacea

Within a short time, however, it became apparent that this new system was no panacea, and the need for reform again was recognized. For example, as early as 1853 delegates to the Massachusetts Constitutional Convention viewed the popular election of judges in New York as a failure and refused to adopt the system. One delegate claimed that it had "fallen hopelessly into the great cistern" and quoted an article in the *Evening Post* that illustrated that judges had become enmeshed in the "political mill."[5] By 1867, the subject was a matter of great debate in New York, and in 1873 a proposed amendment to return to the appointive system gained strong support at the general election.[6]

One of the main concerns during this period was that judges were almost invariably selected by political machines and controlled by them. Judges were often perceived as corrupt and incompetent. The notion of a judiciary uncontrolled by special interests had simply not been realized. It was in this context that the concept of nonpartisan elections began to emerge.

The idea of judicial candidates appearing on the ballot without party label was used as early as 1873 in Cook County [Chicago], Illinois. Interestingly, it was the judges themselves who decided to run on a nonpartisan ballot rather than doing so pursuant to a statute or some other authority. Subsequent elections in 1885 and 1893 were also nonpartisan. By the turn of the century the idea of nonpartisan judicial elections had gained strength, and several states had adopted the idea. By 1927, 12 states employed the nonpartisan idea.[7]

Once again, criticism of nonpartisan elections arose almost as soon as such elections began. As early as 1908 members of the South Dakota Bar Association indicated dissatisfaction with how the idea was working in their state. By 1927, Iowa, Kansas, and Pennsylvania had already tried the plan and abandoned it.[8] The major objection was that there was still no real public choice. New candidates for judgeships were regularly selected by party leaders and thrust upon an unknowledgeable electorate, which, without the guidance of party labels, was not able to make reasoned choices.

The rise of commission plans

While others attacked nonpartisan elections, a number of well-known scholars, judges and concerned citizens began assailing all elective systems as failures. One of the most outspoken critics, Roscoe Pound, delivered a now classic address to the American Bar Association in 1906 on "The Causes of Popular Dissatisfaction with the Administration of Justice." He claimed that "putting courts into politics, and compelling judges to become politicians in many jurisdictions . . . [had] almost destroyed the traditional respect for the bench."[9]

Several years later in a speech before the Cincinnati Bar Association, William Howard Taft claimed that it was "disgraceful" to see men campaigning for the state supreme court on the ground that their decisions would have a particular class flavor. It was "so shocking, and so out of keeping with the fixedness of moral principles," he said, that it ought to be "condemned."[10]

Reformers claimed that the worst features of partisan politics could be eliminated through what they called a "merit plan" for selecting judges. The plan would expand the pool of candidates to include persons other than friends of politicians. Selectors would not consider inappropriate partisan factors such as an individual's party affiliation, party service, or friendship with an appointing executive so the most distinguished members of the bar, regardless of party, could be elevated to the bench.[11]

Origins of the plan are usually traced to Albert M. Kales, one of the founders of the American Judicature Society. Versions of his proposal were introduced in state legislatures throughout the 1930s. The American Bar Association endorsed a merit plan in 1937, and in 1940 Missouri became the first state to put one into effect. Today it is variously known as the Kales plan, Missouri plan, merit plan, or commission plan.

Almost none of the state plans is identical, but they do share common features. Most include a permanent, nonpartisan commission composed of lawyers and nonlawyers (appointed by a variety of public and private officials) who actively recruit and screen prospective candidates. The commission then forwards a list of three to five qualified individuals to the executive, who must make an appointment from the list.

Usually the judge serves a one-year probationary period, after which he must run unopposed on a retention ballot. The sole question on which the electorate votes is: "Shall Judge __ be retained in office?" A judge must win a majority of the vote in order to serve a full term.

Judicial selection today

Today the combination of schemes used to select judges is almost endless. Almost no two states are alike, and few employ the same method for choosing judges at all levels of their judiciary. It is possible, however, to classify the states in two categories: those that appoint their judges and those that elect them. The two groups turn out to be fairly equal in number.

Appointment: Thirty-three states use commission plans to aid the governor in selecting judges (22 states and the District of Columbia use panels for initial selection, and 11 others use them only for vacancies). Since 1980, 15 states adopted or extended their commission plan.

In five states—California, Maine, New Hampshire, Rhode Island, and New Jersey—the governor appoints judges *without* using a nominating commission (subject to senatorial confirmation in Maine, New Jersey, and Rhode Island, and a five-member elected council in New Hampshire). In Hawaii, Louisiana, and Illinois, judges themselves appoint some of their colleagues. In South Carolina and Virginia the legislature appoints or elects most, if not all, of the judges, and in Rhode Island the legislators elect supreme court justices.

Elections: Partisan elections are held to select most or all judges in eight states and some judges in five other states. Nonpartisan elections are held to select most or all judges in 13 states and some judges in four states. Thus, 30 states choose most or all of their judges by elections.

Another way to examine how judges are chosen is to group the states by the plans they use for each level in their court system. Again, the states are fairly evenly divided between those that elect and those that appoint their judges.

Supreme courts: Twenty-two states hold elections for judges on courts of last resort: nine are partisan, and 13 are nonpartisan. In 21 states and the District of Columbia, nominating commissions help governors appoint these judges; in four states, the governor acts on his own. Legislatures elect or appoint court of last resort judges in three states.

Appellate courts: Seventeen states (out of the 37 that have intermediate appellate courts) elect judges to these courts: six use partisan elections, and 11 use nonpartisan elections. In 16 of the other 20 states, governors utilize nominating commissions to help appoint these judges. In California and New Jersey, the governor makes appointments without the help of a commission; in South Carolina and Virginia the legislature elects or appoints appellate judges.

Trial courts: Forty-six states have a single court of general jurisdiction, and four states have two courts of general jurisdiction (Indiana, Louisiana, Maryland, Michigan).[12] Ten states hold partisan elections, and 16 hold nonpartisan elections to *initially* select judges for these courts. Thirteen states and the District of Columbia use a nominating commission to aid the governor in appointing these judges. In four states (Maine, New Hampshire, New Jersey, and Rhode Island), the governor alone makes the choice. The legislature appoints or elects these officials in two states (South Carolina and Virginia).

NOTES

This article originally appeared in Volume 64, Number 4, October 1980, pages 176-193, and was updated in January 1992. It is condensed from a larger study, JUDICIAL SELECTION IN THE UNITED STATES: A COMPENDIUM OF PROVISIONS (Chicago: American Judicature Society, 1980).

1. Eight of the original 13 states vested the appointment power in one or both houses of legislature. Two allowed appointment by the governor and his council, and three vested appointment authority in the governor but required him to obtain consent of the council. Escovitz, JUDICIAL SELECTION AND TENURE 4 (Chicago: American Judicature Society, 1975).

2. Niles, *The Popular Election of Judges in Historical Perspective*, THE RECORD OF THE ASSOCIATION OF THE BAR OF THE CITY OF NEW YORK 523 (November, 1966).

3. *Id.* at 526.

4. Escovitz, *supra* n. 1, at 6.

5. Niles, *supra* n. 2, at 528.

6. *Id.* at 535, n. 46.

7. Aumann, *Selection, Tenure, Retirement and Compensation of Judges in Ohio*, 5 U. CIN. L. REV. 412, n. 11 (1931).

8. *Id.*

9. Pound, *The Causes of Popular Dissatisfaction With the Administration of Justice*, 20 J. AM. JUD. SOC'Y 178 (February, 1937).

10. Taft, *The Selection and Tenure of Judges*, 38 A.B.A. REP. 418 (1913).

11. Kales, UNPOPULAR GOVERNMENT IN THE UNITED STATES Chap. 17 (Chicago: University of Chicago Press, 1914). *See also* Harley, *Taking Judges Out of Politics*, in PUBLIC ADMINISTRATION AND POLITICS (Philadelphia: The American Academy of Political and Social Science, 1916); and Winters, *Judicial Selection and Tenure*, in Winters (ed.), SELECTED READINGS: JUDICIAL SELECTION AND TENURE (Chicago: American Judicature Society, 1973).

12. Courts of general jurisdiction are defined as having unlimited civil and criminal jurisdiction. In each of the four states, the initial method of selection for both courts is the same, although retention is different for the two courts in Indiana. Because judges in several states are selected by more than one method to serve on the same court, the following figures do not total to 50.

What twenty years of judicial retention elections have told us

Because voters in retention elections have little information on which to base their decisions, their level of trust in political institutions in the nation as a whole may be more important than characteristics of individual judges.

by William K. Hall and Larry T. Aspin

This is a study of judicial retention elections for major trial court judges. Judicial retention elections are a fascinating topic for examination because they differ from the more traditional partisan and non-partisan elections in several important respects. Retention elections are devoid of traditional voting cues, including party labels, issues, candidate appeals and campaigns. Judicial retention elections are a symbol of the ongoing struggle between those who favor a judiciary that is held accountable to the public and those who seek a judicial system that provides for an independent judiciary.

Although judicial retention elections were first proposed 70 years ago, they were used sparingly until a spate of adoptions in the 1960s and '70s. Thus, it is only now that there is a substantial base of election results that can be used to study and evaluate judicial retention elections.

Surprisingly, there are few multi-state, multi-year studies of judicial retention elections. Most studies have been either single-state[1] or single-election studies.[2] Of the few multi-state studies, most are of appellate courts.[3] Partially filling this void, this study sheds some light on judicial retention elections and their attendant controversies by reporting the empirical patterns observed in a study of almost 1,900 judicial retention elections at the major trial court level.

We have chosen to focus on trial courts because more than 90 per cent of all court business takes place in the state trial courts of the nation. A very small percentage of cases is appealed and reviewed by higher courts. For that reason, trial court judges have been called "America's judicial foot-soldiers" and the "tribunes and guardians of everyday American justice."[4]

Judicial retention elections

Almost from the very moment the idea was first proposed in 1914, the concept of judicial retention elections, as well as the mechanism, has been under constant and continuous attack. Some of these attacks are based on a misunderstanding of the basic purposes of retention plebiscites. Reformers who proposed the concept of retention elections sought to steer a course through narrow and sometimes treacherous political straits. As the 20th century dawned, the nation's state judiciaries were held in low esteem. Judges appointed to the bench were thought to have gained appointment because they were "in the pocket" of the dominant political machine boss, while judges who gained office by election were not regarded much more highly because the elections were considered "rubber-stamp confirmations of the machine's slate."[5] Determined to restore the public's confidence in the judiciary, reformers sought new ways of judicial selection, ways that would break the grip of the political machines on judicial selection.

Many of the reformers wanted to propose a selection system that had as its chief goal keeping judges on the bench for extended periods of time. Unlike many political reformers, however, they realized that political realities would sooner or later intrude and play a major role in shaping their proposals. They were especially cognizant of the forces and the popular appeal of the progressive movement then sweeping across the land.

The progressives—who were interested in reining in the powerful and corrupt political machines—concentrated their efforts at strengthening the public's direct control over officeholders. To that end, the progressives pushed for direct primaries, nonpartisan elections, the sort ballot, voting rights for women, as well as the initiative, the recall and the referendum. All of these proposals, which were designed to increase public accountability of public officials, were popular. The public favored the popular selection of numerous public officials, including judges. It seemed clear that any proposal advanced by the reformers would have to include some mechanism that would insure accountability to the people.

Long service on the bench was not the only goal of the reformers. They also sought to create politically independent state judiciaries. Out of these conflicting goals would come the commission (later known as the merit selection) plan for selecting judges. A nominating commission would nominate candidates for a judicial position and the governor would then make the appointment from the list of nominees.

In order to placate the progressives and to gain their much-needed support in the state legislatures and in efforts to amend the judicial article in state constitutions, the mechanism of the judicial retention election was proposed as a part of the plan. Citizens would be asked to determine—by means of a retention election—whether a judge should remain on the bench. The retention ballot did not require a judge to run against an opponent, but only on the record compiled in office. If a judge was not retained, the selection process was begun anew.

The merit selection plan, as it was ultimately known, was seen as a practical, workable compromise. It was an attempt to enjoy a system of rule of law presumed possible with an "independent" judiciary[6] while at the same time reaping the benefits associated with popular government presumed possible with a publicly accountable judiciary.[7]

Criticisms of the plan

As the merit selection plan, with its judicial retention election mechanism, has spread, debate over the benefits of judicial retention elections has intensified. There are essentially five significant criticisms of the judicial retention election mechanism. All stem from a concern over the suitability of the mechanism to hold judges publicly accountable.

First, it is claimed that judicial retention elections serve to insulate judges from popular control.[8] because fewer than 50 trial court judges have been defeated in retention bids over a span of nearly 50 years, critics claim the public is not able to exert any meaningful control. Because a judge faces no opponent in such an election, as a judge would have to do in partisan and nonpartisan elections, the public is allegedly denied an effective choice.

Second, judicial retention elections are generally characterized by low voter turnout. Many voters choose to opt out of judicial retention elections.[9] Some voters do not vote in judicial retention elections because they lack enough information to cast an informed vote. Some do not vote because the mechanism is noncompetitive and there is no choice. Still others do not vote for one of a variety of other reasons. Whatever the reason, judicial retention elections attract the smallest turnout of all the types of judicial elections.[10]

Third, judicial retention elections are criticized because they tend to be issueless and lackluster when compared to many competitive two-candidate contests. These retention elections are often so low-key that they do not generate the amount of publicity necessary to help inform the public about the judges seeking retention. The level of public knowledge about judges and judicial retention elections is appallingly low.[11]

Fourth, it is said that judicial retention elections fail to provide the cues most voters need to cast their ballots. The most important of these missing cues is the party label. Without the labels, "a larger portion of voters find themselves with no meaningful guide to voting and thus fail to participate."[12] For most citizens, party identification is the major organizing device in their political lives, the cue card that allows them to make the multiple decisions they face on election day.[13]

Other familiar cues are also absent. In most judicial retention elections there are no campaigns. This is crucial, because election campaigns are known to play an important role in providing information for voters.[14] Because a judge does not face a live opponent but instead runs on his/her record, there are no "combative personal confrontations" as often occur in other types of political campaigns.

If the voting cues of partisanship, issues, and candidate appeal are unavailable, voters will be forced to look to other cues for guidance. Candidates' surnames provide ethnic cues that are important to some voters.[15] Other voters key on the use of a nickname on the ballot or on the sex of the candidate.[16] Others weigh the relative ballot position of the various candidates.[17] Most of these cues are far more appropriate to partisan or nonpartisan contests fought between competing candidates, however, than to the plebiscitory retention elections.

One of the few meaningful guides in retention elections is the rating provided by bar associations. Although it is clear that bar association polls can provide voters with useful information,[18] studies are not of one mind in assessing their importance.[19] There is no agreement about the effectiveness of bar polls in providing useful information to voters. The lack of effectiveness may be due to the way bar associations disseminate their results and recommendations.

In a national study of bar polling practices, Guterman and Meidinger[20] discovered two different models of bar association recommendations. The first they labeled the "public service approach." According to this model, bar associations provide recommendations (bar poll results) to the media and the public, but that is all. The second model is the "special interest approach" according to which, in addition to providing recommendations to the media and the public, bar associations try to secure a particular election result. Even without agreement on the effectiveness of bar polls, there is considerable evidence to suggest that if voters are provided with information on judicial candidates from legal sources, they would make use of such information.[21]

Fifth, opponents claim that judicial retention elections have resulted in life-tenured judges.[22] Although it is not the focus of this study, our preliminary research indicates that judges are not staying on the states' trial court benches for life, but that they are leaving the bench for reasons other than being defeated in retention bids. Slightly more than 1 per cent of those judges seeking retention have been defeated in retention bids. With that statistic in mind, we were surprised by the turnover in judges at the major trial court level.

Election data set

While valuable, most prior studies of judicial reten-tion at the major trial court level have been confined to a single state or a single election. However, the comprehensive data set from a recent project on judicial retention elections is not so constrained. Analysis of these data not only confirms some prior empirical findings, but also uncovers new patterns that enhance our understanding of judicial retention elections and evaluation of contending arguments.

By 1976, 12 states had adopted the merit selection plan coupled with retention elections for selecting all or a portion of their major trial court judges. In addition, two other states (Illinois and Pennsylvania) coupled in an "incongruous joinder"[23] the retention election part of the merit selection plan with partisan elections for the initial selection of trial court judges.

The data set provides an excellent opportunity to examine the phenomenon of affirmative voting in judicial retention elections. It contains each of the retention elections held in 10 of the 14 states that use retention elections for major trial court judges. These ten states—Alaska, Arizona, Colorado, Illinois, Indiana, Iowa, Kansas, Missouri, Nebraska, and Wyoming—are the only states that hold retention elections for major trial court judges at the same time, at the even-numbered years' fall general elections (i.e., 1976, 1978, 1980, etc.).[24]

Three states—Idaho, Montana and Utah—were excluded because they use "qualified" retention elections. That is, if a sitting judge is challenged, a nonpartisan election between the incumbent and the challenger is held. Only if unchallenged does a judge stand in an uncontested retention election.

The time period 1964-1984 was selected because before 1964 only Missouri featured judicial retention elections for major trial court judges, and then in only two of the state's 114 counties. First used in 1942, fewer than 60 major trial court retention elections were held in Missouri between 1942 and 1962. Beginning with the election of 1964, three states—Illinois, Iowa,[25] and Nebraska—joined Missouri in using judicial retention elections at the trial court level. The other six states began using judicial retention elections at the major trial court level in the 1970s.

Findings

The presentation of findings begins with the defeated judges and then reports the observed patterns when the elections are grouped by year, state, judicial district, and individual judge. Finally, ob-

Table 1   Defeated major trial court judges, 1964-1984

| | State | District | Year | N[1] | Election in which judge was defeated | | | | Prior election affirmative vote | |
| | | | | | Affirmative vote | | Rolloff | | | |
					Judge	District[2]	Judge	District[3]	Judge	District[4]
Judge A	AL	3	82	7	45.5	55.6	17.9	18.4	67.1	60.7
Judge B	AL	3	82	7	42.3	55.6	18.3	18.4	—	60.7
Judge C	AZ	1	78	19	45.9	72.5	26.6	33.9	—	76.9
Judge D	CO	1	78	4	44.5	68.6	15.1	18.1	60.3	78.1
Judge E	CO	3	78	1	42.7	—	22.1	—	70.5	67.7
Judge F	CO	10	72	3	39.0	63.0	29.4	32.2	—	65.0
Judge G	CO	15	82	1	40.6	—	18.5	—	58.4	76.9
Judge H	IL	3	80	3	59.1	62.0	32.7	33.3	—	83.0
Judge I	IL	3	80	3	53.8	62.0	30.5	34.4	—	83.0
Judge J	IL	4	78	6	58.4	65.3	48.5	49.3	61.4	73.0
Judge K	IL	10	78	6	59.8	68.3	35.3	34.0	79.5	83.0
Judge L	IL	10	78	6	50.9	68.3	31.4	34.8	82.8	83.0
Judge M	IL	17	80	3	43.6	71.7	25.0	21.4	—	84.1
Judge N	IL	25	74	25	59.8	73.2	59.1	59.4	—	80.0
Judge O	IL	25	76	32	58.9	75.1	49.0	55.1	87.5	73.2
Judge P	IL	25	78	24	59.1	72.0	56.6	59.0	72.2	75.1
Judge Q	IL	25	82	68	56.3	73.6	51.9	52.7	—	72.7
Judge R	IN	2	78	1	38.6	—	59.9	—	—	—
Judge S	KA	5	80	1	25.4	—	4.8	—	78.3	78.3
Judge T	NE	8	84	1	25.8	—	3.4	—	69.5	69.5
Judge U	WY	4	74	1	44.2	—	10.4	—	—	—
Judge V	WY	6	84	1	43.4	—	3.8	—	77.2	77.3

1. Number of judges up for retention in the district.
2. Mean affirmative vote for retained judges in the district.
3. Mean rolloff for retained judges in the district.
4. Mean affirmative vote for all other judges in the district.

served patterns for rolloff are set forth.

Affirmative vote and the defeated judges. In terms of general findings, our data confirm the high mean affirmative vote totals for major trial courts judges in retention elections found in other studies.[26] For the 1,864 elections, the mean affirmative vote was 77.2 per cent. In only 45 of 1,864 elections was the mean affirmative vote below 60 per cent. Table 1 lists the 22 judges who were defeated. Nine of the ten defeated judges in Illinois would still be on the bench, but for Illinois having a 60 per cent minimum instead of the 50 per cent minimum affirmative vote used in all other states.

One noteworthy trend in Table 1 is that defeated judges do not significantly reduce the affirmative vote for other judges running for retention on the same ballot. Even in those elections in which two judges from the same district were defeated, that did not spell defeat for other judges in the district. When, in 1982, Judges A and B were defeated in Alaska's Third District, five other judges were retained. Voters were clearly discriminating between judges, but as will be reported shortly, this discrimination among judges appears to be atypical.

Only 22 defeats in 1,864 elections supports the conclusion that judges are insulated from the public; however, two things in Table 1 suggest that the defeat of a judge does not involve a slow erosion of support across a series of retention elections. Ten

of the judges were defeated the first time they stood for retention. Of the 12 defeated judges who had previously survived retention elections, only Judge J had previously come close to losing a retention bid. The other 11 defeated judges suffered major declines in support from their previous retention successes. This decline ranged from a loss of 10 per cent affirmative vote to a loss of 73 per cent.

In addition to the 77.2 per cent mean affirmative vote and the small number of defeated judges, there are other interesting patterns of variation in the votes, not all of which can be explained. These patterns can be seen by breaking the 1,864 elections into groups by year, state, judicial district, and individual judge.

Election year. One of the more interesting findings to emerge from this study is the fact that the mean affirmative vote declined over this 20-year period. For each of the first three retention elections held in the 1960s, the mean affirmative vote exceeded 85 per cent. Then, beginning in 1970, the mean affirmative vote dropped steadily for the next eight years to a low of 73.8 per cent in 1978. Over the three elections of the 1980s, however, the mean affirmative vote climbed almost three per cent.

The research indicates that one plausible explanation of the variation in the mean affirmative vote is that political trust is a major cue in judicial

Table 2 Judges receiving 80 per cent or more affirmative votes

Year	1964	1966	1968	1970	1972	1974	1976	1978	1980	1982	1984
Per cent	92.9	80.9	84.6	64.7	50.9	17.0	27.9	16.6	24.4	24.9	26.4

retention voting.[27] Although the match is not perfect, the national trends in political trust and those in the mean affirmative vote of judicial retention elections are very similar. The correlation[28] between trust and the mean affirmative vote is .95 for the 11 election years. The correlation between change in political trust and change in the mean affirmative vote is .57. Both correlations are statistically significant.[29]

For the 1964-1984 period, there are numerous points of similarity in the trends. Both fall from initial high levels to the 1978-1982 floor and then both are again rising by 1984. When we also consider that the decline in trust from the 1964 levels occurred for all major American institutions,[30] it is difficult not to believe the changes in the mean affirmative vote are due—in part—to changes in the levels of political trust.

The decline in the mean affirmative vote can be viewed from another perspective. As the data in Table 2 indicate, the number of judges receiving affirmative vote totals of 80 per cent or more has decreased significantly.

Another election year finding is the small difference (1.6 per cent) between the mean affirmative vote for elections held in presidential years (77.9 per cent) and the mean affirmative vote for elections held in non-presidential election years (76.3 per cent). Why are voters in presidential election years slightly more likely to vote in favor of retention? As studies have shown, there is a "surge" of voters to the polls during presidential elections.[31] The surge comes when a large number of "peripheral voters" join the "core voters" in the voting booths.[32] In the off-years, the peripherals stay at home, causing a decline in voter turnout.

Surprisingly, the peripheral voters may be just as likely to vote in judicial retention elections as the core voters, for there is no significant difference between presidential and non-presidential years when it comes to voter rolloff. However, the peripheral voter may be slightly more inclined to vote yes in the judicial retention election than the core voter because of lower levels of information. Several studies find a negative relationship between information/knowledge levels and support of the courts.[33]

State variables. There is a difference of more than 10 per cent between the state with the highest mean affirmative vote and the state with the lowest. Table 3 presents the mean affirmative vote by state and election year.

Our efforts to determine whether this variation from state to state is due to state-level variables such as state population, degree of urbanness, political culture, or type of ballot, or whether these state differences are simply the result of aggregating the differential effects of district-level variables, has

Table 3 Mean affirmative vote for major trial courts, 1964-1984

	1964	1966	1968	1970	1972	1974	1976	1978	1980	1982	1984	Mean
Alaska	—	—	—	76.7	75.3	70.4	70.6	68.3	59.0	61.3	67.8	69.3
				(12)	(6)	(10)	(6)	(7)	(4)	(11)	(5)	(61)
Arizona	—	—	—	—	—	—	76.7	73.8	81.3	79.9	81.2	78.3
							(14)	(31)	(16)	(35)	(19)	(115)
Colorado	—	—	—	75.5	73.6	75.7	73.8	70.6	71.7	72.1	74.3	73.2
				(26)	(36)	(14)	(32)	(41)	(25)	(34)	(36)	(244)
Illinois	85.5	87.4	86.4	84.4	79.4	74.1	76.7	72.7	73.4	74.4	77.2	78.3
	(72)	(28)	(19)	(71)	(146)	(33)	(65)	(90)	(57)	(109)	(96)	(785)
Indiana	—	—	—	—	7.19	72.0	—	64.7	68.6	66.4	74.2	68.7
					(5)	(3)		(9)	(6)	(3)	(3)	(29)
Iowa	—	—	—	—	—	—	—	78.4	78.3	78.2	77.4	78.1
								(41)	(31)	(34)	(38)	(144)
Kansas	—	—	—	—	—	—	81.1	79.9	76.5	82.5	82.7	80.4
							(29)	(18)	(25)	(17)	(21)	(110)
Missouri	82.5	81.0	83.1	78.9	79.5	77.4	77.6	74.0	71.9	70.0	73.2	76.2
	(12)	(17)	(7)	(20)	(22)	(17)	(16)	(27)	(25)	(22)	(25)	(210)
Nebraska	87.3	86.5	—	83.4	83.4	81.3	77.7	77.4	77.7	79.2	73.4	81.0
	(29)	(2)		(21)	(3)	(12)	(13)	(8)	(16)	(15)	(13)	(132)
Wyoming	—	—	—	—	—	66.1	81.2	79.5	76.3	73.4	74.1	75.6
						(5)	(8)	(5)	(4)	(6)	(6)	(34)
Mean	85.7	85.1	85.5	81.4	78.2	75.0	77.0	73.8	74.7	75.0	76.7	77.2
	(113)	(47)	(26)	(150)	(218)	(94)	(183)	(277)	(209)	(285)	(262)	(1,864)

Table 4   Mean affirmative vote by district within each state

District	Alaska	Arizona[1]	Colorado	Illinois[2]	Indiana[3]	Iowa[4]	Kansas	Missouri	Nebraska	Wyoming
1	74.7 (14)	77.3 (80)	73.1 (18)	72.6 (25)	69.8 (14)	72.4 (6)	76.4 (5)	—	80.3 (4)	78.7 (5)
2	84.5 (2)	80.3 (35)	76.0 (47)	71.3 (36)	38.6 (1)	78.4 (10)	83.3 (3)	—	79.5 (5)	78.6 (6)
3	66.4 (30)		66.0 (6)	76.4 (15)	67.4 (9)	77.5 (8)	83.6 (16)	—	85.5 (11)	81.5 (3)
4	68.1 (15)		70.0 (27)	70.5 (30)	73.8 (5)	79.9 (17)	79.0 (5)	—	83.7 (35)	59.0 (3)
5			73.3 (4)	79.5 (25)		82.0 (7)	63.2 (3)	—	83.2 (6)	74.7 (5)
6			74.6 (6)	82.6 (30)		79.2 (9)	79.3 (2)	75.1 (3)	80.6 (5)	66.0 (3)
7			72.1 (6)	81.4 (18)		75.4 (7)	85.1 (5)	73.4 (8)	77.2 (4)	78.0 (4)
8			76.9 (9)	80.1 (26)		77.4 (28)	84.7 (5)	—	68.0 (4)	82.7 (2)
9			73.9 (7)	80.1 (25)		79.6 (7)	89.4 (3)	—	84.1 (7)	78.6 (3)
10			70.4 (14)	79.9 (26)		78.8 (17)	83.3 (16)	—	82.2 (8)	
11			71.0 (7)	82.4 (20)		75.4 (13)	74.9 (8)	—	76.1 (6)	
12			71.3 (4)	78.0 (22)		77.7 (9)	82.5 (3)	—	83.2 (3)	
13			73.1 (10)	81.2 (15)		81.2 (6)	—	—	77.1 (4)	
14			72.8 (4)	81.7 (21)			81.0 (2)	—	85.4 (4)	
15			65.0 (5)	83.7 (17)			59.1 (1)	—	76.3 (3)	
16			71.8 (5)	77.2 (22)			—	75.2 (65)	74.6 (5)	
17			71.2 (15)	80.0 (16)			81.7 (1)	—	78.1 (5)	
18			76.4 (20)	78.8 (18)			—	—	82.2 (3)	
19			74.4 (10)	79.3 (17)			81.4 (3)	—	79.1 (4)	
20			76.6 (11)	77.6 (28)			—	—	77.1 (4)	
21			72.4 (7)	78.3 (333)			85.0 (4)	73.6 (50)	76.4 (2)	
22			66.3 (2)				79.3 (1)	78.8 (84)		
23							77.5 (2)			
25							81.7 (2)			

Except for Arizona, Indiana, and Iowa, the number listed in the district column is the judicial district number.
1. (1) Maricopa Co. (2) Pima Co.
2. (21) is Cook Co.
3. (1) Allen Co. (2) Lake Co. (3) St. Joseph Co. (4) Vanderburg Co.
4. Districts labels changed from 1A, 1B, 2A, 2B, etc. to 1, 2, 3, 4, etc.

met with little success. It has been very difficult to verify the importance of state-level variables. This may be quite natural, as judicial retention elections for trial court judges take place in substate districts.

Judicial district variables. Our data reveal significant intrastate differences in the mean affirmative vote. Table 4 presents the mean affirmative vote by district for each state. Seven of the ten states have district variations of 10 per cent or more. Although it can be stated that the interstate variation remains even after the defeated judges are excluded from the calculations, the variation remains to be ex-

plained. We found no significant correlation between district population and mean affirmative vote. Nor did we find a significant correlation between number of counties in the judicial district and the mean affirmative vote. This was tested both by using the number of counties and by dichotomizing the districts into single-county districts and multi-county districts.

In addition to the interdistrict variation reported in Table 4, prior research has also reported significant intradistrict variation.[34] The voters in the home county of a judge vote more heavily either for or

Table 5   Dispersion of affirmative vote about district/year means[1]

	Average absolute deviation[2] from district/year mean			Distribution of deviations from district/year mean		
	Average	**Number[3]**		**Deviation**	**Frequency**	**Per cent**
Alaska	4.68	(27)		0-1%	400	37.8%
Arizona	3.74	(109)		1%-2%	257	62.8
Colorado	3.36	(73)		2-3	141	75.5
Illinois	2.40	(519)		3-4	76	82.7
Indiana	1.77	(5)		4-5	55	87.9
Iowa	1.91	(68)		5-6	39	91.6
Kansas	1.04	(27)		6-7	21	93.6
Missouri	1.51	(192)		7-8	13	94.8
Nebraska	1.75	(37)		8-9	9	95.6
Wyoming	—	—		>9	46	100.0
Total	2.41	(1,057)			1,057	

1. District/year mean is the average of all elections held in a district in one year.
2. Absolute deviations are in percentage points.
3. Only those elections where four or more judges appeared on the same ballot are included.

against the judge than do the non-home county voters. The non-home county voters tend to treat all judges in the district the same.

Individual judges. One of the clearest patterns to emerge from our data is that voters do not differentiate much between judges. Simply put, judges in the same district are winding up with very similar affirmative vote percentages. This apparent lack of differentiation cannot be completely seen when comparing elections from different districts because there is clear variation between the districts. Likewise, variation from election to election also hides the lack of differentiation among the judges. The lack of variation among individual judges is thus most evident when examining the districts where multiple judges were on the ballot in the same election.

To systematically examine this lack of differentiation among the judges, we first selected the 1,057 elections where four or more judges stood for retention on the same ballot in the same election. For each electoral district the mean percentage voting yes was calculated for each election year (i.e., the district/year mean). This district/year mean represents the typical affirmative vote received by the judges in the district. Then, the absolute deviation (i.e., the absolute difference) of each judge's affirmative vote from the appropriate district/year mean was calculated. This absolute deviation indicates the amount of difference between the affirmative vote for an individual judge and the typical affirmative vote in his/her district that year. If in an election year voters are treating all judges in a district the same, then the absolute deviations should be very small.

Table 5 presents two aspects of the absolute deviations from the district/year means. On the left is the average absolute deviation from the district/year means presented by state and for all 1,057 elections. Although there is some variation by state, for all 1,057 elections the average deviation is only 2.41 percentage points. Even more important is the distribution of the absolute deviations, which is presented in the right side of Table 5.

Of the 1,057 elections, 75.5 per cent are within three percentage points of the mean and 91.6 per cent are within six percentage points of the district/year mean. This finding strongly suggests that many voters are casting retention votes on the basis of cues other than those peculiar to individual judges (information on performance on the bench, decisions rendered, surname, ethnicity, sex, ballot position, etc.). This reinforces our conviction that political trust is a major voting cue.

Ballot rolloff. Given the controversy surrounding judicial retention elections, it is necessary to consider rolloff as well as the actual vote. The average rolloff (i.e., the percentage of voters who cast ballots for the lead partisan office on the ballot, but fail to vote in the judicial retention election) is 36.2 per cent for the 1,864 elections. Like the mean affirmative vote, there is variation by year, state, judicial district, and individual judge. However, in contrast to the mean affirmative vote, rolloff is not a function of political trust. Rolloff is a positive function of district population.[35]

Rolloff apparently can be reduced by reducing the size of the judicial districts; however, there is no indication that such an action would affect the actual vote. While critics may bemoan the high rates of rolloff, the degree of rolloff is unrelated to the vote.

No matter what unit of analysis was employed, we found no relationship between rolloff and the affirmative vote—with one exception. For the 22 judges not retained by the voters, there is a correlation of .69 between the affirmative retention vote and voter rolloff. For the 45 judges who polled less than 60 per cent affirmative votes (including the 22 who were defeated), the correlation is .38.

These correlations confirm the findings of another study[36] that there are some retention elections in which negative information or campaigns have stimulated more voters to vote in the judicial retention election. In that study, 58 per cent of those judges (at all levels) who were defeated in retention bids from 1942-1978 were the subjects of public campaigns to remove them from office.[37] The rolloff for the 45 judges polling less than 60 per cent of the vote is 27.6 per cent, whereas it is 36.2 per cent for all 1,864 judges.

What about those judges who received the highest percentage of affirmative votes? Is it possible that positive information or campaigns also made these elections more visible, with a resulting lower rolloff? In this case, the answer is maybe. For neither the 11 judges polling an affirmative vote over 90 per cent nor the 233 judges polling over 85 per cent is there a significant correlation between rolloff and the affirmative vote. However, this lack of a relationship may be an artifact of the sample, for these high affirmative votes, in sharp contrast to the affirmative votes of the unretained judges, are very similar to one another. Thus, it may be noteworthy that the rolloff for the 11 judges polling over 90 per cent is 24.5 per cent and the rolloff for the 233 judges polling over 85 per cent is 31.2 per cent. Rolloff for both groups of judges is lower than the 36.2 per cent rolloff for all 1,864 judges.

A final note on rolloff is the apparent remarkable voter persistence in finishing the judicial retention election section of the ballot. When the number of judges on the ballot is controlled, the percentages of voters voting on each judge are almost identical. This was the case even where there were dozens of judges on the ballot and/or where one or more of the judges was defeated (e.g., see the rolloff values in Table 1). Ballot fatigue did not occur in the former case and voters attracted to the retention election because of publicity surrounding a particular judge apparently voted on all of the other judges as well.

Conclusion

A large number of studies have been devoted to analyzing judicial retention elections. This study set out to analyze affirmative voting in 10 states for the period 1964-1984. We found that three out of four voters in these states generally voted to retain a judge. For the 1,864 elections analyzed, the mean affirmative vote was 77.2 per cent.

One of the most important findings is that political trust is a major cue in retention voting. The national trends in trust and those in the mean affirmative vote were quite similar. As Americans' political trust declined, the mean affirmative vote dipped. As Americans became more trusting, the mean affirmative vote for judges went up.

We found few differences in voting in presidential years compared to voting in non-presidential years. Peripheral voters tended to behave just like core voters. Although we found substantial interstate and intrastate variations in the mean affirmative vote, we could find few satisfactory explanations of these variations.

One of the clearest patterns was that voters do not generally differentiate much between judges. Judges running in the same district tended to end up with similar affirmative vote percentages. On only a very few occasions did voters single out judges for defeat. Importantly, when voters did single out judges for defeat or for extraordinarily high affirmative vote percentages, voter interest increased and rolloff decreased.

What have we learned about judicial retention elections from this study? First, those who maintain that retention elections serve to insulate judges from popular control seem to be correct. Only 22 judges (1.2 per cent) were defeated in retention bids in these 10 states over the 20-year period. Only 45 judges (including the 22 defeated judges) polled less than 60 per cent affirmative votes. As the founders of retention elections had hoped, few judges were removed from the bench by the public.

Second, judicial retention elections are generally characterized by low voter turnout. We found that at least one-third of the voters passed up the opportunity to vote in retention elections. However, all else being equal, there are no indications that the outcomes would be significantly different had all voters cast ballots in the judicial retention elections.

Third, judicial retention elections fail to provide cues to help voters in the voting booth. With the customary cues missing, we found voters relying on other cues such as trust in the political system.

Because judges running in the same district generally received similar affirmative vote totals, voters did not seem willing or able to differentiate among them.

NOTES

This article originally appeared in Volume 70, Number 6, April-May 1987, pages 340-347.

1. Stookey and Watson, *Merit retention elections: can the bar influence voters?*, 64 JUDICATURE 234 (1980); Jacob, *Courts*, in Gray, Jacob, and Vines (eds.), POLITICS IN THE AMERICAN STATES: A COMPARATIVE ANALYSIS (4th ed., New York: Little, Brown & Co., 1983).

2. Jenkins, *Retention elections: who wins when no one loses?*, 61 JUDICATURE 79 (1977).

3. Adamany and Dubois, *Electing State Judges*, 3 WIS. L. REV. 731 (1976); Dubois, *The Significance of Voting Cues in State Supreme Court Elections*, 13 LAW AND SOC'Y REV. 757 (1979); Dubois, FROM BALLOT TO BENCH: JUDICIAL ELECTIONS AND THE QUEST FOR ACCOUNTABILITY (Austin: University of Texas Press, 1980); Dubois, *Public Participation in Trial Court Elections*, 2 LAW AND POL'Y Q. 133 (1980).

4. Jackson, JUDGES (New York: Atheneum, 1974).

5. Carbon and Berkson, JUDICIAL RETENTION ELECTIONS IN THE UNITED STATES, Appendix A (Chicago: American Judicature Society, 1980).

6. Dubois, *The Significance of Voting Cues*, supra n. 3; Stookey and Watson, supra n. 1; Carbon and Berkson, supra n. 5; and Lovrich and Sheldon, *Voters in Contested, Nonpartisan Judicial Elections: A Responsible Electorate or a Problematic Public?*, 36 W. POL. Q. 241 (1983).

7. Lovrich and Sheldon, supra n. 6; Lovrich and Sheldon, *Assessing Judicial Elections: Effects upon the Electorate of High and Low Articulation Systems*, 38 W. POL. Q. 276 (1985); Dubois, *The Significance of Voting Cues*, supra n. 3; Carbon and Berkson, supra n. 5; Jenkins, supra n. 2; Jacob, supra n. 1.

8. Carbon, *Judicial retention elections: are they serving their intended purpose?*, 64 JUDICATURE 210 (1980); Moran, *Method of Selecting Judges*, 32 FLA. B. J. 471 (1958); Jenkins, supra n. 2.

9. Hall and Aspin, *Voter Rolloff in Judicial Retention Elections*, 24 SOC. SCI. J. (1987).

10. Dubois, *Voter Turnout in State Judicial Elections: An Analysis of the Tail on the Electoral Kite*, 41 J. OF POL. 865 (1979); Beechen, *Can judicial elections express the people's choice?*, 57 JUDICATURE 242 (1974); Hall, JUDICIAL RETENTION ELECTIONS: DO BAR ASSOCIATION POLLS INCREASE VOTER AWARENESS? (Urbana, IL: Institute of Government and Public Affairs, 1985).

11. Klots, *The Selection of Judges and the Short Ballot*, 38 J. OF THE AM. JUDICATURE SOC'Y 134 (1955); Johnson et al., *The Salience of Judicial Candidates and Elections*, 59 SOC. SCI. Q. 371 (1978); Adamany and Dubois, supra n. 3; McKnight et al., *Choosing judges: do the voters know what they're doing?*, 62 JUDICATURE 94 (1978); Griffin and Horan, *Merit retention elections: what influences the voters?*, 63 JUDICATURE 78 (1979); Lovrich and Sheldon, supra n. 6; THE PUBLIC IMAGE OF COURTS (Williamsburg: National Center for State Courts, 1978).

12. Dubois, *Public Participation in Trial Court Elections*, supra n. 3, at 133, 135.

13. Campbell et al., THE AMERICAN VOTER (New York: John Wiley & Sons, 1960).

14. *Id.*; Goldstein, *Bar poll ratings as the leading influence on a non-partisan judicial election*, 63 JUDICATURE 377 (1980); Becker and Dunwoody, *Media Use, Public Affairs Knowledge and Voting in a Local Election*, 59 JOURNALISM Q. 212 (1982).

15. Byrne and Pueschel, *But Who Should I Vote for For County Coroner?*, 36 J. OF POL. 778 (1974); Dubois, *Public Participation*

in *Trial Court Elections*, supra n. 3; Nagel, COMPARING ELECTED AND APPOINTED JUDICIAL SYSTEMS (Beverly Hills: Sage Professional Papers in American Politics, 1973).

16. Byrne and Pueschel, supra n. 15.

17. Byrne and Pueschel, supra n. 15; Bain and Hecock, BALLOT POSITION AND VOTER'S CHOICE: THE ARRANGEMENT OF NAMES ON THE BALLOT AND ITS EFFECT ON THE VOTER (Westport, CT: Greenwood Press, 1957); Volcansek, *An Exploration of the Judicial Election Process*, 34 W. POL. Q. 572 (1981).

18. Goldstein, supra n. 14; Stookey and Watson, supra n. 1; Hall, supra n. 10; Maddi, JUDICIAL PERFORMANCE POLLS (Chicago: American Bar Foundation, 1977); Johnson et al., supra n. 11; Sheldon, *Influencing the Selection of Judges: The Variety and Effectiveness of State Bar Activities*, 30 W. POL. Q. 397 (1977).

19. Carbon and Berkson, supra n. 5; Goldstein, supra n. 14; Griffin and Horan, supra n. 11; Guterman and Meidinger, IN THE OPINION OF THE BAR: A NATIONAL SURVEY OF BAR POLLING PRACTICES (Chicago: American Judicature Society, 1977); Hall, supra n. 10; Johnson, et al., supra n. 11; Lovrich and Sheldon, supra n. 6; Maddi, supra n. 18; McKnight, et al., supra n. 11; Sheldon, supra n. 18; Stookey and Watson, supra n. 1.

20. Guterman and Meidinger, supra n. 19.

21. Johnson et al., supra n. 11.

22. Carbon, supra n. 8, at 218.

23. Cohn, TO JUDGE WITH JUSTICE: HISTORY AND POLITICS OF ILLINOIS JUDICIAL REFORM 148 (Urbana: University of Illinois Press, 1973).

24. Pennsylvania uses retention elections for major trial court judges, but it is excluded because the retention elections are held in odd-numbered years (i.e., 1977, 1979, 1981, etc.).

25. Election data for judicial retention elections prior to 1978 are not available.

26. Watson and Downing, THE POLITICS OF THE BENCH AND BAR: JUDICIAL SELECTION UNDER THE MISSOURI NONPARTISAN COURT PLAN (New York: John Wiley & Sons, 1969); Jenkins, supra n. 2; Adamany and Dubois, supra n. 3.

27. Aspin and Hall, *Judicial Retention Elections: A Vote of Trust*, forthcoming, 1987.

28. Although simply referred to as the correlation in the text, the Pearson product-moment correlation coefficient measures the strength and direction of the relationship between two variables. It ranges from -1.00 (a perfect negative relationship) through zero (no relationship) to +1.00 (a perfect positive relationship). The square of the correlation represents the amount of variation in one variable which can be accounted for by knowledge of the other variable.

29. The .05 level of significance is employed throughout the paper. This means there is one chance in 20 that there is no relationship and the correlation occurred by chance alone.

30. Lipset and Schneider, THE CONFIDENCE GAP: BUSINESS, LABOR AND GOVERNMENT (New York: The Free Press, 1983).

31. Campbell, *Surge and Decline: A Study of Electoral Change*, in Campbell et al., (eds.) ELECTIONS AND THE POLITICAL ORDER 40-62 (New York: John Wiley & Sons, 1966).

32. *Id.*

33. THE PUBLIC IMAGE OF COURTS, supra n. 11; Dolbeare, *The Public Views the Supreme Court*, in Jacob, (ed.), LAW, POLITICS AND THE FEDERAL COURTS (Boston: Little, Brown & Co., 1967); Walker et al., *Contact and Support: An Empirical Assessment of Public Attitudes Toward the Police and Courts*, 51 N. C. L. REV. 43 (1972).

34. Aspin and Hall, *The "Friends and Neighbors Effect" in Judicial Retention Elections*, 40 W. POL. Q. (1987).

35. Hall and Aspin, supra n. 9.

36. Jenkins, supra n. 2.

37. *Id.*

The defeat of the California justices: the campaign, the electorate, and the issue of judicial accountability

The 1986 election results in California indicate that normal voter indifference to judicial elections can be dispelled by publicizing decisions that arouse attention and hostility. Whether that will have a chilling effect on future judges' decisions remains to be seen.

by John T. Wold and John H. Culver

In our pre-election article on the background to the controversy over Chief Justice Rose Bird of the California Supreme Court, we noted the comments of Bill Roberts, a veteran campaign manager and head of a prominent anti-Bird organization: "The only question is can we make it so the other two are gone, too. There's nothing that's going to save her. She is going to be slam dunked out of business."[1] Roberts' remarks were accurate, though hardly startling, since it had long been apparent to most observers that Bird had no realistic chance of surviving the November, 1986, retention election. The question Roberts posed as to the fate of the "other two" was also settled by the voters on election day. For the first time since retention elections were adopted for the state's appellate justices in 1934, the public not only rejected a chief justice, but defeated two other justices, Cruz Reynoso and Joseph Grodin, as well. In renouncing the three jurists, the voters in one stroke removed from the high court three of the four remaining appointees of former Governor Edmund G. (Jerry) Brown, Jr.

We shall focus in this article upon several aspects of the judicial election in California. We shall discuss first the preelection campaigns for and against the retention of Justices Bird, Reynoso, and Grodin. Second, we shall compare the election results with historical trends nationwide in judicial retention elections. Next we shall explore the general issue of standards of accountability that might guide voters in judicial retention elections. Fourth, we shall examine data from public opinion polls, in search of clues as to standards actually employed by

California voters in rejecting the three justices. Finally, we shall explore the implications of our findings for the California high court and for future retention elections.

The campaign

In an unusual set of circumstances, six of the seven justices on the California supreme court were on the retention ballot in 1986.[2] Allen Broussard, the only remaining appointee of Jerry Brown on the court, was the only justice not required to face reelection. There was no controversy regarding the retention of two other justices, Malcolm Lucas and Edward Panelli, both of whom were appointed to the bench by Brown's successor as governor, George Deukmejian.

Justice Stanley Mosk was also on the ballot. A former state attorney general, Mosk had been appointed to the court by Governor Edmund G. (Pat) Brown, Sr., in 1964 and was the senior member of the court. (We shall refer to the two Browns by their nicknames, in order to avoid confusing Brown, Sr., with his son, who also served two terms as governor of California.) Mosk had been targeted for defeat by the organized opposition in early 1986, but had been deleted as a target later that year when the two major anti-Bird groups, Californians to Defeat Rose Bird, and Crime Victims for Court Reform, joined ranks under the Crime Victims banner. Mosk was a highly respected justice who had authored many significant decisions during his 22 years on the court.[3] Although Mosk had voted to overturn death sentences in the past, he had also voted to uphold the sentences in 14 of the 15 capital cases decided between December 1985 and October 1986. According to Mosk, his death penalty decisions had not "changed significantly" over the years, but rather "the bugs and flaws in the 1978 death penalty law" had gradually been eliminated by the court, thereby making it easier to affirm capital sentences.[4]

In late August 1986, Governor Deukmejian publicly indicated that he would vote to retain Mosk. At the same news conference, he also announced that he would oppose Justices Grodin and Reynoso, in addition to Bird, because their votes and opinions on death penalty cases "indicate a lack of impartiality and objectivity."[5]

Opposition to Bird, Reynoso and Grodin came from a variety of sources. Governor Deukmejian, other Republican incumbents and challengers, Crime Victims for Court Reform, and a coalition of state and local prosecutors (the Prosecutors' Working Group),[6] all actively campaigned against the three. Most law enforcement organizations also opposed them.

Only a few Democrats publicly supported the justices. Others, such as Mayor Tom Bradley of Los Angeles and Senator Alan Cranston, refused to state their positions concerning Bird. Because they took a neutral stance, they were portrayed by Republicans as in effect supporting her.[7]

Until mid-summer, Bird's own Committee to Conserve the Courts did not mount any effort on her behalf. Moreover, it was never made clear whether the Committee to Conserve the Courts was to speak for just Bird, or for Reynoso and Grodin, or for all six of the justices on the ballot.[8] Bird contracted with a Santa Monica political consulting firm in 1985 to manage the campaign, but she disagreed with the firm's strategy and severed ties with the organization several months later. She then engaged John Law, a Washington political consultant, but that relationship ended several months later as well.[9] In both instances, the terminations resulted from Bird's refusal to consider running negative campaign ads and her reluctance to engage in large-scale fundraising.[10]

To credit the Committee to Conserve the Courts with a campaign strategy is to be charitable. Two television ads were run, which Bird wrote and appeared in, stressing the traditional independence of the judiciary. In one ad, Bird spoke of a "court system with the courage to protect our form of government," i.e., a government in which freedoms of speech, religion and press were upheld, in contrast to their suppression in the Soviet Union and South Africa. In the second, she addressed the cultural, racial and religious diversity of California: "Our diversity of ideas and viewpoints makes us stronger. In California, we have a Supreme Court that reflects that diversity. That's a California tradition to be proud of."[11] Both ads showed Bird, wearing a dark blue dress rather than her judicial robes, seated in her Los Angeles chambers with an open book in front of her and law books filling the shelves behind her.

According to Bill Zimmerman, the first consultant Bird retained, her emphasis upon judicial independence ran directly counter to the approach he felt would be the most effective, such as emphasizing the court's environmental record or focusing upon her detractors as corporate special interests. Essentially, Bird's opponents charged her with being soft on criminal matters, especially the death penalty, and Bird's response focused on judicial independence rather than a defense of the court's overall record in criminal cases. In a post-election essay, Zimmerman succinctly articulated the problems with her "remarkably inept" campaign: "she had no campaign manager, no political consultant, no advertising agency, no pollster, no steering committee and no fundraising coordinator . . . . And although polling indicated that judicial independence was the one message that would *not* work, she adopted it as the sole basis of her campaign."[12]

Former Governor Pat Brown tried to breathe new life into the pro-Bird effort by establishing the Independent Citizens' Committee to Keep Politics Out of the Courts. The elder Brown and Shirley Hufstedler, former U.S. Secretary of Education, served as co-chairs. This committee drew some support, primarily from Democratic activists in labor, ethnic, environmental and women's organizations. The organizations supported retention of all six justices on the ballot. In one of the letters sent to prospective financial contributors, Brown and Hufstedler linked the effort to unseat Bird to "the Moral Majority and the rest of the radical right." (In literature sent out by Californians to Defeat Rose Bird, references had been made to the fact that Bird was supported by Tom Hayden and Jane Fonda—e.g., "Do you want a Supreme Court that will be dominated by the extremist left-wing philosophy of Jerry Brown, Tom Hayden and Jane

Fonda? . . .") With specific references to several conservative California lawmakers, the letter added, "If these home-grown California fanatics are successful in defeating Rose Bird and other targeted Supreme Court Justices in November, it will send an unmistakable message to every judge in every county in California who has ever drawn the line between Church and State or tried to protect and enhance our civil rights: either do what the radical right says, or we'll be coming after you." Aside from showing the flag for Bird, the Committee did not generate much publicity in the state's media, at least in part because the group was formed only four months before the election.

The state's major newspapers split in their endorsements of the justices. The *Los Angeles Times, San Jose Mercury*, and *Sacramento Bee* endorsed all six justices. The *San Diego Tribune* opposed Bird and Reynoso, while the *San Francisco Chronicle* and *San Francisco Examiner* recommended the ouster of Bird, Reynoso and Grodin.

The voters in any event had firmly linked Reynoso and Grodin with Bird by election day. Bird received a positive vote of only 34 per cent, Reynoso tallied 40 per cent, and Grodin 43 per cent. Voters in only two counties (Alameda and San Francisco) supported all three justices; Reynoso carried a third (Marin), which Grodin also won along with two others (Santa Clara and Santa Cruz). All of these counties are in the San Francisco Bay area. The pattern of voting for the justices in these counties mirrored the statewide vote in terms of Grodin's receiving the most votes to confirm, Reynoso's occupying the middle ground, and Bird's finishing last.

Fundraising and decision making

Even by California standards, the amount of money raised and spent by the pro- and anti-Bird factions was phenomenally high—an estimated seven and one-half million dollars.[13] The amount may prove to be closer to eight million dollars when all financial disclosure forms relating to the campaign are filed with the California secretary of state. Analysis of these data will reveal the extent to which interest groups financed the contest. Throughout the campaign, some Bird supporters charged that special interests had contributed large amounts to the anti-Bird groups. In response, Crime Victims for Court Reform claimed that the majority of its contributions were from private citizens in amounts of $100 or less. Quarterly campaign statements re-

vealed that sizable contributions to anti-Bird organizations were from oil and gas, agribusiness, auto dealers, and real estate interests, while contributions in support of the chief justice included the California Trial Lawyers Association, which contributed more than $200,000, and four Los Angeles personal-injury firms, which added another $217,000 to her cause.[14] Collectively, Bird, Reynoso and Grodin spent about two million dollars, in contrast to the five and one-half million expended by their opponents. The other three justices spent nothing beyond the filing fee.

As Schotland has noted, changes in partisan electoral politics have had an impact upon the judiciary. Judicial contests that were once "personal, quiet, and inexpensive, have now become noisier, nastier and costlier."[15] Whether multimillion dollar campaigns will be waged subsequently against California justices remains to be seen. However, it is not unreasonable to forecast less expensive but nevertheless well-organized challenges against individual justices in the future.

Justices who frequently hand down controversial decisions may invariably be faced with challenges to their retention. They could respond by mounting a campaign against the challengers, as Chief Justice Bird did. Another approach would be to ignore the potential opposition. Such was the response of Justice Mosk when targeted for defeat by anti-Bird groups in early 1986. He chose not to react, perhaps concluding that after 22 years on the court, and as a former attorney general, his legal qualifications were beyond reproach.

A third possible response would be for justices to alter their positions on controversial issues when faced with hostile public opinion. To do so, of course, would be to compromise to some degree the concept of an independent judiciary. The point may be illustrated by citing the comments of former Justice Otto Kaus. Kaus, a Jerry Brown appointee to the high court, has revealed that his then-upcoming appearance on the November, 1982, ballot might have influenced his decision regarding the constitutionality of the Victim's Bill of Rights, a popular initiative passed by the voters in June of the same year. Kaus voted with the 4-3 majority to uphold the initiative. As he said in 1986, "I decided the case [the initiative] the way I saw it. But to this day, I don't know to what extent I was subliminally motivated by the thing you could not forget—that it might do you some good politically to vote one way or the other.''[16]

The defeat of the three California justices may well prove to be a historical aberration, but few justices in the future should be able to ignore the 1986 results altogether when contemplating their own chances for retention. More frequently than in the past, jurists will probably calculate, if only privately, the potential reactions to their decisions of affected interest groups and the public at large.

Some historical comparisons

The ability to cashier judges has been a prerogative rarely exercised by the electorate in retention elections. Nationwide, few jurists have been rejected at the polls. According to Carbon, from 1934 to 1980, only 33 judges were not retained; and from 1972 to 1978, of 1,499 judges on retention ballots in 20 states, a minuscule 1.6 per cent were not retained (n=24).[17] The voters typically have not only retained sitting jurists, but have done so by wide margins.[18]

Compared with historical patterns, the California election of 1986 was an obvious aberration. Among the anomalies was the defeat of several members of a multimember court. Never before had the voters of any state rejected more than a single judge of an appellate tribunal in any particular election.[19] California voters not only rejected three justices, but defeated all three decisively (see Table 1).

Another anomaly was the apparent absence of "voter fatigue" or "voter rolloff," i.e., the tendency of many voters to leave unmarked the portion of their ballots dealing with the judiciary.[20] Scholars have attributed "voter fatigue" to the customary low salience of judicial elections. In fact, exit polling revealed that, far from being uninterested in the judicial section of the ballot, voters in California had actually been drawn to the voting booth on November 4, 1986, by the opportunity to vote on Bird's confirmation. Voting on Bird was second only to voting in the gubernatorial race among reasons given for casting ballots on election day.[21] The difference between the number of ballots cast in the governor's race and for or against the retention of Bird, Reynoso and Grodin was only 9.5 per cent. Interestingly, many voters who marked their ballots on the three targeted justices actually refrained from voting on the other three jurists on the ballot. The difference between the number of ballots cast in the governor's race and the average

Table 1   Election results: California Supreme Court, November 4, 1986

	Confirm (%)	Reject (%)
Rose Elizabeth Bird	2,369,063 (34%)	4,622,066 (66%)
Cruz Reynoso	2,536,114 (40)	3,874,601 (60)
Joseph R. Grodin	2,741,962 (43)	3,570,569 (57)
Stanley Mosk	4,472,678 (74)	1,604,806 (26)
Edward A. Panelli	4,648,505 (79)	1,260,385 (21)
Malcolm M. Lucas	4,692,329 (79)	1,211,013 (21)

number on the retention of Mosk, Panelli, and Lucas was 18 per cent.

Prior studies have also indicated that judicial campaigns and elections are typically low-visibility affairs.[22] In contrast, the issue of Bird's retention was a prominent, if not the *most* prominent, issue of the entire 1986 California campaign. One needed only to be exposed to televised campaign spots to appreciate the extent to which candidates for partisan state offices vied with one another as to the degree of their opposition to Bird.[23]

Bird was also not the unknown quantity that appellate jurists in most states have been.[24] In fact, her professional qualifications, personality, and record as a justice had been long-term issues in California. Much of the controversy surrounding Bird dated back virtually to the time of her elevation to the high court.[25]

Conventional wisdom likewise suggests that an officeholder's incumbency benefits him or her at election time. And, as Kingdon observed: ". . . incumbents have an opportunity through the years to build up quite an advantage, not only in exposure to the public, but also popular confidence in the job they are doing."[26] Bird, Reynoso and Grodin nonetheless proved to be exceptions to Kingdon's generalization. Despite a tenure on the supreme court of more than nine, four, and four years, respectively, all three were overwhelmingly defeated by the California voters.

Chief Justice Bird's fate did bear out Abramowitz's comment that a jurist's visibility does not assure popularity.[27] Similarly, as others have noted, negative press attention (such as that often received by Bird) can be highly detrimental to an incumbent judge.[28]

Standards of accountability

What is the proper balance between judicial independence and accountability? Should the public insulate judges altogether from direct popular accountability, or require that jurists periodically face the voters? And if the public opts for an

ppl. voting was at almost same amt. voting for gov. "voter rolloff" occured w/ the other 3 judges but not w/ Bird, Reynoso, & Grodin.

Figure 1 Continuum of accountability

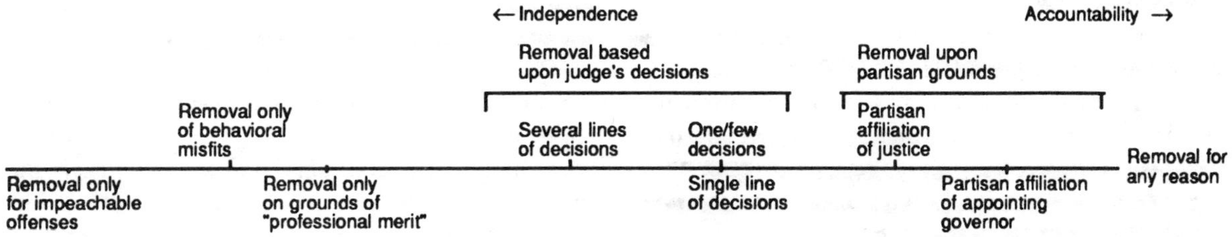

elective system, what standards should guide the conscientious voter?

These questions, touching ultimately upon the issue of the proper role of courts and judges in American society, have been discussed extensively in the literature.[29] The "solution" embraced by the framers of the United States Constitution was of course to maximize judicial independence. Federal jurists enjoy *de facto* lifetime tenure, subject only to a requirement of "good behavior."[30]

Most states have rejected the federal model.[31] The states typically have instead required their judges to stand for reelection on partisan, nonpartisan and/or retention ballots.[32] Elections inherently emphasize the accountability of judges to the public. California is among the states employing nonpartisan retention elections for members of its court of last resort.[33]

One may contrast the federal with the state system in another way. Judges in the federal courts may be replaced only in the event of a jurist's death, resignation, retirement, or removal via the impeachment process.[34] A federal judge thus may not be removed directly by the voters merely because he or she, for whatever reason, has aroused the anger of the public. In contrast, state elective systems permit the voters directly to remove jurists with whom they are dissatisfied, and to do so at fixed intervals.

What standards might the individual voter employ in "judging judges" in retention elections? The possible positions may be arrayed along a continuum[35] (see Figure 1). The positions range from those maximizing judicial independence to those maximizing judicial accountability. The reader should note that each standard implicitly also permits the removal of judges under each of the standards more protective of judicial independence, i.e., to its left, on the continuum.

Our intent is to present the various basic positions that individual voters *might* choose with respect to the retention of state judges. We shall not

attempt to determine whether those standards are in any normative sense defensible or "correct," or whether the positions are even reasonable. Indeed, we recognize that one of the potential weaknesses of existing systems of judicial election is the complete freedom they give the electorate to retain or reject sitting jurists for any reason the voters deem fit.

Most supportive of independence would be a standard under which the voter viewed himself as constrained to retain all judges except those who have committed impeachable offenses. If employed by a majority of the electorate, such an approach effectively would extend to state jurists the same type of tenure historically enjoyed by federal judges.[36]

A standard somewhat less supportive of judicial independence would be one under which the voter also believed it legitimate to remove "behavioral misfits": judges who are, e.g., alcoholic, abusive, or mentally ill. This standard would in effect duplicate other formal mechanisms available in all states.[37]

Under a third standard the voter would, in addition, consider it acceptable to remove jurists on the basis of a criterion of "professional merit," i.e., in terms of the quality of a judge's written opinions. This position has perhaps best been articulated by Robert S. Thompson, a retired California appellate justice. According to Thompson, judges deserve to be retained as long as they reach decisions through a process which "disciplines their decisions impartially," a process Thompson termed "discipline impartiality."[38] He also added: "The judge who has followed [California's late chief justice] Robert Traynor's admonition and truly 'wrestled with the devil' to produce the writing which justifies the result reached has satisfied the discipline of a judge."[39]

None of the foregoing approaches would permit an individual to vote against a judge because of the jurist's vote in particular cases. In contrast, the voter's adoption of the next position on the continuum would allow him to cast a ballot against a *ideological consider.*

judge simply because the voter disagreed with the judge's decisions. That is, under the next approach, the voter would consider it legitimate to evaluate the *substance* of a judge's decisions, not merely his or her personal behavior or the process used in arriving at decisions.[40] This approach would include voting based upon ideological considerations, e.g., upon the perceived "liberalism" or "conservatism" of a jurist's decisions.

Most restrictive within this standard would be a requirement that the judge had engaged in an "excessive" number of what the voter perceived as "incorrect" or offensive decisions in more than one area of the law. Less restrictive requirements would permit the voter to cast a negative vote on the basis of decreasing numbers of decisions. The approaches would thus range from a single line of decisions, to several particular decisions, and ultimately to a single unpopular decision.

Near the end-point of our continuum is a position based upon partisan considerations. This standard would permit the voter to cast a negative ballot for such reasons as the party affiliation of either a particular judge or the governor who had appointed the jurist.

Some voters may also consider it acceptable to vote against a judge for reasons having little or nothing to do with the jurist's performance in office. These reasons might include aversion to a judge's personality, "style," religion, racial or ethnic background, personal appearance, gender, and any other factor. Such an approach would in effect obliterate all distinctions between the elections of judges and those of executive officers, legislators, or other public officials. While the standard is one that the voter might adopt, it lies beyond the range of our continuum, and is in any event a position we would expect few adherents to espouse openly.

The voters' standards

Upon what standards did California voters base their ouster of Justices Bird, Reynoso, and Grodin? To attempt to answer this question, we examined relevant data collected by the California (Field) Poll between 1972 and 1986. Our examination led us to conclude that a majority of the California electorate employed an exclusively *decisional* standard of accountability in 1986. The voters appeared to have been particularly exercised by two lines of decisions handed down by the state court. Of apparent primary concern was the three jurists' perceived opposition to the death penalty; of secondary concern, the justices' perceived leniency toward criminal defendants generally.

One month before the election, for example, the reasons most frequently cited by potential voters for opposing Bird were that she "opposes the death penalty" (45 per cent of respondents) and that she was "too lenient, soft on criminals/she lets killers go free" (26 per cent). Another four per cent claimed that the chief justice "ignores the rights of victims." These three sets of responses together constituted 54 per cent of all the reasons voiced by Bird's opponents for opposing her retention.[41]

Other comments cited in the same survey may also have reflected voters' concerns about crime and the death penalty. For instance, 15 per cent of those interviewed remarked that they did not "like [Bird's] positions, where she stands on the issues." Another 15 per cent claimed that Bird had not "held up the will of the people [or] enforce[d] the law."[42]

Voters who desired the defeat of Reynoso and Grodin, in addition to the removal of the chief justice, expressed views similar to those voiced against Bird individually. Nineteen per cent of these respondents claimed that the three justices were not enforcing the death penalty, and an equivalent number asserted that the jurists were too lenient on criminals. Three per cent, echoing comments leveled at Bird separately, stated that the justices "were not fair to victims and their families." These three categories of responses together comprised 40 per cent of the reasons given for opposing the collective retention of the three justices.[43]

The data from earlier surveys reinforced the conclusion that voters were almost exclusively concerned with the perceived trend of decisions in the Bird Court. For example, as far back as May, 1985 voters emphasized Bird's decisions, her asserted leniency on crime, and her alleged opposition to the death penalty as the primary reasons for opposing her retention.[44]

Voters also had long been overwhelmingly critical of what they viewed as either Bird's or the supreme court's leniency toward "murderers" and criminal defendants generally. For instance, the foremost criticism of the high court voiced in May 1985—an opinion held by 67 per cent of respondents—was that the court had "gone too far in protecting the rights of convicted murderers."[45] Seventy-two per cent expressed a similar complaint three months later.[46] And in August 1986, interviewees agreed by a margin of 35 percentage points (62 per cent to 27 per cent) with the statement that Chief Justice Bird had "gone too far in protecting criminal defendants." Likewise, voters agreed by a similar margin (61 per cent to 25 per cent) with the statement that Bird "allows her own opposition to the death penalty to affect her decisions."[47]

The public also had long held two other related sets of attitudes. One concerned the death penalty itself. Survey data indicated a consistent and increasing level of support for capital punishment over time. By April 1985, retention of the death penalty as a punishment for serious crimes was reportedly favored by 83 per cent of California voters, an all-time high.[48]

Another set of attitudes concerned the issue of crime. As early as 1973, and as recently as 1985, a plurality of Californians (35 per cent and 24 per cent, respectively) had expressed the opinion that crime/law enforcement was the most pressing problem facing the community and the state.[49]

In sum, survey data gathered by the California Poll strongly suggested that voter opposition to Bird, and ultimately to two other liberal members of the California court, was animated by two basic attitudes. One view was that the court had persistently been too lenient toward criminal defendants generally and convicted murderers in particular; the other was that the justices had repeatedly exhibited hostility toward capital punishment. As the Field Institute itself concluded shortly before the election: "The public's strong support for the death penalty and the belief that the Chief Justice is personally opposed to it are directly linked to the desire to have Bird removed from the high court."[50]

Standards not employed

Californians opposing Rose Bird's retention obviously rejected the view that citizens should restrict themselves to standards that enhance judicial *independence* over accountability. For instance, voters clearly rejected the concept that they should retain all justices except those guilty of impeachable offenses, or those who were "behavioral misfits," or those they deemed unqualified in terms of professional ability. In fact, public attitudes were apparently quite favorable toward Bird from a "professional" standpoint. Three months before the election, respondents expressed disagreement by a wide margin (52 per cent to 33 per cent) with the

view that the chief justice was "not qualified to be a justice of the California supreme court."[51]

Opponents of Bird, Reynoso, and Grodin nonetheless also appeared to reject extreme concepts of judicial *accountability*. For example, the survey data indicated that voters did not base their opposition to the three justices upon merely a few unpopular decisions, or only a single decision, that the jurists had handed down. Also, opposition to and support for Bird were apparently not primarily based upon partisan or ideological considerations. Although Democrats and political liberals in fact tended to support her retention, the disposition to vote *against* the chief justice cut across many demographic, partisan and ideological lines.[52]

Respondents likewise only rarely suggested that it was legitimate to remove judges for merely "personal" or idiosyncratic reasons. For instance, just 7 per cent of those opposed to Bird did so because of her "personality" or "style."[53] Voters also apparently did not oppose Bird because of her gender. By a margin of 61 per cent to 31 per cent, respondents to one survey disagreed with the view that the attacks on the chief justice stemmed partly from the fact that she was the first woman on the state high court.[54]

In sum, opposition to Bird, Reynoso, and Grodin appears to have been galvanized by a series of decisions involving the death penalty and other criminal cases. There is little evidence, however, that voters were willing to oust judges for "nonjudicial" factors such as the judge's gender, religious affiliation, racial or ethnic background, or other "personal" characteristics. The California vote suggests that, although a majority of the electorate spurned standards that stress judicial independence, they also were not motivated, at least in the 1986 election, by extreme concepts of judicial accountability or by concepts extraneous to judicial performance.

Implications

What do our findings imply with respect to future judicial retention elections? One implication is that, although voter indifference to judicial elections may be the historical norm, such indifference can be dispelled by a pattern of highly publicized judicial decisions. In other words, lines of decisions that arouse voter attention *and* hostility can become influential factors in retention elections. Likewise, despite historical patterns throughout the nation, judicial retention campaigns *can* become highly visible phenomena.

Another implication is that voters may not uninterruptedly permit interpretation of the law to be solely the province of the courts. In the 1986 election a majority of California voters apparently believed it legitimate to reject jurists on the basis of lines of judicial decisions that did not comport with what voters thought the law *should* be.

Last, and probably not surprisingly, the California results suggest that voters in state retention elections do not necessarily view themselves as bound by standards similar to those protecting federal judges. A state judge's *decisions*, and not merely his or her adherence to accepted norms concerning personal and professional behavior, may be considered by the public a legitimate basis for voting the jurist out of office.

One obvious result of the defeat of the three justices was the opportunity it provided Governor Deukmejian to place three additional nominees to sit with his previous two appointees to the high court. These appointments will collectively produce a conservative majority for the first time in several decades. The dramatic change in the composition of the court will undoubtedly alter judicial policies. For instance, California's 20-year moratorium on the implementation of the death penalty should end within the next several years. Also, the new court should be less protective of the rights of suspects than the Bird court. Among the criteria mentioned by Governor Deukmejian for selecting nominees to replace the defeated justices was that they "have an overriding concern for public safety."[55]

The controversy over Rose Bird and the results of the 1986 election have fueled discussion regarding possible institutional changes concerning the high court. One state senator had proposed limiting the justices to a single 12 year term, with a two-thirds vote required of the state senate to confirm before appointment.[56] An alternative plan, suggested by Kaus, would abolish retention elections and give justices life tenure. Kaus's proposal also calls for enlarging the three-member commission that has the initial responsibility for confirming or rejecting gubernatorial nominees to the appellate bench. Kaus rejects the notion of the state legislature as a confirming body; in his view such an arrangement would "let in through the back door what we are trying to get rid of up front: the politicization of the judiciary."[57]

It is unlikely, in our judgment, that any sweeping changes, such as life tenure or confirmation by the legislature, will occur as a result of the controversy over Bird. The composition of the Commission on Judicial Appointments may well change within the next several years, although past criticisms of that body have not resulted in any alterations of it.[58] However, one change that is likely to be implemented concerns the method of selecting judges to sit temporarily on the high court. Under the present procedure, the chief justice has complete discretion with respect to their selection. Bird was criticized by some for allegedly selecting *pro tem* justices who shared her activist philosophy.[59] In order to eliminate any hint of court packing, the change would probably have temporary justices chosen randomly or by the court collectively.

Conclusion

One can only speculate on whether the ire of the voters and organized opposition to justices will surface in subsequent retention elections.[60] Bird repeatedly emphasized in her campaign speeches that judicial independence requires judges to set aside their personal views concerning issues before the court. There is no evidence to indicate that voters disagreed with Bird's view. To the contrary, they clearly felt that Bird *had* injected her personal views into her decisions regarding litigation and court administration. Should they ultimately perceive any of Deukmejian's nominees as having likewise personalized the law, the voters might react in future elections much as they did in 1986. Thus far, however, Deukmejian has appointed experienced and respected jurists to the bench. His appointees appear to adhere to the philosophy of judicial self-restraint, and not to be "activists" or either the "right" or the "left."[61]

Do the election results of 1986 augur a long-term assault by California voters upon the basic independence of their high court? It is impossible at this early juncture to foretell. On the one hand, the 1986 election may prove to have been a historical aberration, reflecting a profound public concern with specific lines of decisions handed down by the justices over several years. Even if jurists were to be defeated upon a similar decisional basis in the future, their removal might not seriously infringe upon judicial independence. On the other hand, the California voters may prove willing in the future to defeat justices upon grounds much more tenuous than those that apparently motivated the electorate in 1986. Likewise, last year's results may also prove to have had a chilling effect upon the willingness of California judges to hand down potentially unpopular decisions, even when jurists deem such decisions to be legally "correct." Should either of the latter eventualities occur, judicial accountability will have been enhanced, but at a considerable, and possibly unacceptable, price in terms of judicial independence.

jud. accountability compromises jud. independence

NOTES

This article originally appeared in Volume 70, Number 6, April-May 1987, pages 348-355.

The authors gratefully acknowledge the assistance of David Thelen.

1. Culver and Wold, *Rose Bird and the politics of judicial accountability in California*, 70 JUDICATURE 81, 87 (1986).

2. This was the first time since retention elections for appellate justices were introduced in California in 1934 that so many supreme court justices appeared on the ballot. The term of office for justices is 12 years. However, when a vacancy occurs, the newly appointed justice must face the voters at the next gubernatorial election. The justice must face the electorate again when the balance of the term of his or her predecessor expires. Under this system Bird was initially appointed to the bench in 1977, appeared on the ballot in 1978, and was on the ballot again in 1986 when the 12-year term of her predecessor, Chief Justice Donald Wright, expired. Had Bird been retained in 1986, then she would have served a full term before facing the voters again. See, Smith, *The California Method of Selecting Judges*, 3 STAN. L. REV. 510 (July, 1951).

3. See the articles in tribute to Mosk in 12 HASTINGS CONST. L. Q. 365-461 (1985); *esp. see*, Goldberg, *Stanley Mosk: A Federalist for the 1980s, id.* at 395-420.

4. LOS ANGELES TIMES, Oct. 21, 1986, at I:3.

5. See the full text of Gov. Deukmejian's statement in LOS ANGELES DAILY JOURNAL, Aug. 8, 1986, at 22.

6. LOS ANGELES TIMES, Aug. 14, 1985, at I:3.

7. For example, in his unsuccessful campaign to unseat U.S. Senator Alan Cranston, Republican Ed Zschau portrayed Cranston in television ads as comparable to Bird: "It's hard to tell the difference between the two. They both ignore the will of the people and they both oppose the death penalty."

8. Neither Mosk, Panelli nor Lucas engaged in any campaigning. In late summer 1986, Grodin and Reynoso each ran several television ads that focused on their individual records.

9. LOS ANGELES TIMES, Dec. 17, 1985, at I:3.

10. LOS ANGELES TIMES, Nov. 9, at 1986, at V:1.

11. See the full text of both ads reprinted in the LOS ANGELES DAILY JOURNAL, August 26, 1986, at 22.

12. LOS ANGELES TIMES, Nov. 9, 1986, at V:1.

13. LOS ANGELES DAILY JOURNAL, Oct. 24, 1986, at 1.

14. *See*, LOS ANGELES TIMES, Aug. 4, 1986, at I:3; SAN FRANCISCO CHRONICLE, Sept. 10, 1986, at 11; LOS ANGELES DAILY JOURNAL, Oct. 21, 1986, at 2; and LOS ANGELES DAILY JOURNAL, Oct. 24, 1986, at 1.

15. Schotland, *Elective Judges' Campaign Financing: Are State Judges' Robes the Emperor's Clothes of American Democracy?*, 2 J. OF L. & POL. 76 (Spring, 1985).

16. LOS ANGELES TIMES, Sept. 28, 1986, at I:3.

17. Carbon, *Judicial retention elections: are they serving their intended purpose?*, 64 JUDICATURE 221-223 (1980). *See, also,* Jenkins,

Retention elections: who wins when no one loses?, 61 JUDICATURE 79 (1977); Griffin and Horan, *Patterns of voting behavior in judicial retention elections for supreme court justices in Wyoming*, 67 JUDICATURE 68 (1983); Hall and Aspin, *What twenty years of judicial retention elections have told us*, 70 JUDICATURE 340 (1987).

18. *See, e.g.,* Jenkins, *supra* n. 17, at 80; Griffin and Horan, *Merit retention elections: what influences the voters?*, 63 JUDICATURE 78, 83 (1979).

19. Carbon, *supra* n. 17, at 222.

20. *See*, Dubois, *Voter Turnout in State Judicial Elections: An Analysis of the Tail on the Electoral Kite*, 41 J. OF POL. 865 (1979); Griffin and Horan, *supra* n. 18, at 83.

21. LOS ANGELES TIMES, Nov. 6, 1986, at I:3.

22. *See, e.g.,* Johnson, Schaefer, and McKnight, *The Salience of Judicial Candidates and Elections*, 59 SOC. SCI. Q. 371, 374 (1978).

23. See the example, *supra* n. 7; in the race for state controller, Bill Campbell's printed mailers said of Democrat Gray Davis that "Gray Davis was so close to Rose Bird that she performed Gray Davis's wedding ceremony! Davis is Bird's close, personal friend, admirer and chief supporter." (Campbell nonetheless lost the race.)

24. *See*, Johnson, Schaefer and McKnight, *supra* n. 22, at 374-376; Griffin and Horan, *supra* n. 18, at 85. *But cf.* Sheldon and Lovrich, *Knowledge and judicial voting: the Oregon and Washington experience*, 67 JUDICATURE 234, 236-237 (1983).

25. See the survey data gathered since 1978 by the Field Institute. THE CALIFORNIA POLL, Oct. 11, 1978; Feb. 19, 1985; Oct. 9, 1985. See also Culver and Wold, *supra* n. 1, at 83-85.

26. Kingdon, CANDIDATES FOR OFFICE: BELIEFS AND STRATEGIES 110 (New York: Random House, 1968). But see also Volcansek, *An Exploration of the Judicial Election Process*, 34 W. POL. Q. 572, 575 (1981). By August, 1986, 94 per cent of registered voters in California claimed that they had seen or heard some news stories about Bird "in recent months." THE CALIFORNIA POLL, Aug. 12, 1986, at 1.

27. Abramowitz, *Name Familiarity, Reputation, and the Incumbency Effect in a Congressional Election*, 28 W. POL. Q. 668, 684 (1975).

28. Volcansek, *supra* n. 26, at 577. Among those who had been exposed to news stories concerning Bird, 55 per cent perceived the coverage to have been mostly negative, while only three per cent viewed coverage to have been mostly positive. THE CALIFORNIA POLL, Aug. 12, 1986, at 2.

29. *See, e.g.,* Adamany and Dubois, *Electing State Judges*, WIS. L. REV. 731 (1976); Ladinsky and Silver, *Popular Democracy and Judicial Independence: Electorate and Elite Reactions to Two Wisconsin Supreme Court Elections*, WIS. L. REV. 128 (1967); Sheldon and Lovrich, *Judicial accountability vs. responsibility: balancing the views of voters and judges*, 65 JUDICATURE 470 (1982); White, THE AMERICAN JUDICIAL TRADITION (New York: Oxford University Press, 1976).

30. U.S. Const., art III, sec. 1. *See*, Berkson and Tesitor, *Holding federal judges accountable*, 61 JUDICATURE 442 (1978).

31. Glick and Vines, STATE COURT SYSTEMS 37-38 (Englewood Cliffs, NJ: Prentice Hall, 1973).

32. *Id.* at 39-46. All of the states have mechanisms for dealing with judges who are incompetent, physically or mentally disabled, or otherwise unfit for the bench; *See*, Tesitor and Sinks, JUDICIAL CONDUCT ORGANIZATIONS, 2nd Ed. (Chicago: American Judicature Society, 1980).

33. California has six intermediate appellate courts, the justices of which also face retention elections. The election of the state's trial judges may be contested by other candidates. As of 1980, 20 states had adopted retention elections for at least some of their courts. Carbon, *supra* n. 17, at 211-215.

34. The impeachment process has resulted historically in the removal of only five federal jurists, all of whom were district judges.

35. Although we believe that the following discussion includes the major positions that the voter might adopt, we of course do not claim that our list exhausts the entire range of possible options. *Cf., e.g.*, the "responsibility-accountability continuum" developed in Sheldon and Lovrich, *supra* n. 29, at 477.

36. See the qualified endorsement of the standard by Mendelson, *Problems of Judicial Independence and Accountability*, 53 FLA. BAR J. 138 (1979). See also the position taken by attorney Vanderet, who, while not explicitly adopting the impeachment standard, strongly supported the insulation of courts from "current political passions." LOS ANGELES TIMES, Oct. 30, 1986, at II:7. Likewise, see the discussion of the "impeachment model" by Uelman, "Standards for Judicial Retention Elections in California," paper presented at the Chief Justice Donald R. Wright Memorial Symposium on the California Judiciary, Univ. of So. Calif. (Nov. 21-22, 1985), at 2-3.

37. This approach resembles the "sanctions" function described by Sheldon and Lovrich, *supra* n. 29, at 477. See the discussion in Uelman, *supra* n. 36, at 8-10; See also Culver and Wold, *supra* n. 1, at 82, and the sources there cited.

38. Thompson, 59 So. CAL. L. REV. 809, 831 (1986).

39. *Id.* at 838. The "professional-merit" standard would probably not attract a large proportion of voters, given the relatively esoteric knowledge it requires, and its implicit requirement that the voter rely upon legal "experts" for voting cues.

40. *See, e.g.*, Kanner's argument that judges of state supreme courts should be judged by the voters on the basis of the substance of their decisions, particularly when the jurists "enter avowedly the area of pure social policy making." Kanner, "Standards for Judging Judges: There is No Such Thing as a Free Lunch," paper presented at the Chief Justice Donald R. Wright Memorial Symposium on the California Judiciary, Univ. of So. Calif. (Nov. 21-22, 1985), at 9, 13, 15.

41. THE CALIFORNIA POLL, Oct. 19, 1986, at 2.

42. *Id.*

43. *Id.* at 6. We note also that voters most frequently responded that they did not "like Rose Bird and her court/their performances in office" (26 per cent). Likewise, 18 per cent asserted that the three justices were "not carrying out the laws/will of the people/the constitution."

44. THE CALIFORNIA POLL, May 22, 1985, at 2.

45. THE CALIFORNIA POLL, May 7, 1985, at 1.

46. THE CALIFORNIA POLL, Aug. 20, 1985, at 2.

47. THE CALIFORNIA POLL, Aug. 12, 1986, at 3.

48. THE CALIFORNIA POLL, Apr. 3, 1985, at 1.

49. THE CALIFORNIA POLL, Mar. 22, 1973, at 1; Mar. 6, 1985, at 3.

50. THE CALIFORNIA POLL, Aug. 12, 1986, at 3.

51. *Id.*

52. THE CALIFORNIA POLL, Oct. 9, 1985, at 4.

53. *Id.* at 2.

54. THE CALIFORNIA POLL, Aug. 12, 1986, at 3.

55. LOS ANGELES TIMES, Dec. 14, 1986, at I:3.

56. LOS ANGELES TIMES, Nov. 12, 1986, at II:5.

57. LOS ANGELES TIMES, Nov. 13, 1986, at II:7.

58. *See*, Culver, *Politics and the California plan for choosing appellate judges*, 66 JUDICATURE 151 (1982).

59. *See*, Barnett and Rubinfeld, *The Assignment of Temporary Justices in the California Supreme Court*, 17 PAC. L. J. 1045 (1986). The authors argued that Bird and several of her predecessors selected replacement judges whose views reflected their own. However, for a different conclusion, see Wildman and Whitehead, *A Study of Justice Pro Tempore Assignments in the California Supreme Court*, 20 U.S. F. L. REV. 1 (1985).

60. In addition to Malcolm Lucas, the new chief justice of the California Supreme Court, four other Deukmejian high court appointees will be on the 1990 ballot.

61. For excellent discussions of the historical controversy over activism and restraint, see the readings in Halpern and Lamb (eds.), SUPREME COURT ACTIVISM AND RESTRAINT (Lexington, MA: Lexington Books, 1982). See especially, regarding "conservative" and "liberal" activism, Lamb, *Judicial Restraint on the Supreme Court, id.* at 7-36.

The electoral fates of incumbent judges in the Ohio Court of Common Pleas

Since incumbent judges are seldom voted out of office, Ohio's judicial elections may not be all that different from retention votes in other states.

by Lawrence Baum

E lection has been the most common system for the selection of state judges.[1] For this reason debates over methods of judicial selection tend to focus on the merits and demerits of elective systems.[2] Unfortunately, analysis of these merits and demerits has often been speculative rather than empirical. The growing body of empirical studies of judicial elections has provided a better basis for realistic evaluation of elective systems,[3] but the answers to many questions about these systems remain unclear.

The purpose of this article is to provide more information on one major question about judicial elections—the fate of judges who run for re-election. An elective system might operate in such a way that incumbent judges face regular challenges and suffer frequent defeats; alternatively, most judges might run unopposed, with defeat a very uncommon outcome. Which of these situations is preferable depends upon one's premises, but, in any case, meaningful evaluation of elective systems requires an understanding of how incumbent judges fare.

Empirical studies of elections have provided important evidence,[4] but our picture of incumbency in judicial election systems remains incomplete, in part because most studies take broader views of the election process. The study reported here attempts to provide additional information about judicial incumbency by in-depth examination of one set of courts.[5] It focuses on four issues:

• What is the general pattern of results for previously elected judges who run for re-election?

• What is the comparable pattern for appointed judges facing their first election?

• How are these patterns affected by the population size and urbanism of the county that judges serve?

• How are the fates of incumbents affected by the balance of electoral strength between political parties in their counties, and by partisan tides in particular years?

The subject of study is elections for Ohio common pleas judgeships from 1962 though 1980. The Court of Common Pleas is the trial court of general jurisdiction in Ohio, organized at the county level.[6] Like other Ohio judges, its members are elected to six-year terms through a "hybrid" system of partisan primary elections and nonpartisan general elections.[7] The governor fills vacancies in judgeships though appointments, with interim elections for the remainder of the term held at the next general election.

As a subject of study the Ohio Common Pleas court has some advantages. Findings on the fates of its incumbents can be compared with those obtained by Kathleen Barber for the Ohio Supreme Court,[8] in order to learn about differences in the functioning of an elective system at the trial and supreme court level. Additionally, the hybrid system makes investigation of the role of partisan forces particularly interesting. But an in-depth study of *any* set of trial courts would be useful as a means to more fully understand the situation of judicial incumbents.

The advantage of incumbency

Incumbency ordinarily aids candidates in winning

office by giving them name recognition and the opportunity to develop a favorable image with the voters.[9] Those advantages are reflected in the high proportions of public officials who win re-election.[10] But the rate of success for incumbents varies considerably among offices, based upon differences in the factors that affect voters' choices and in other relevant conditions.

The advantage of incumbent judges is strengthened by the low visibility of judicial elections. Judgeship campaigns usually receive little publicity, and their issue content is severely limited by the Code of Judicial Conduct.[11] As a result, most voters attain a low level of knowledge about judicial candidates.[12] In such an election, a challenger generally finds it difficult to provide voters with a reason to oppose the incumbent. But this strength is accompanied by a weakness; incumbent judges are generally limited in their ability to become known and to develop positive images with the voters. The low visibility of elections, and of the courts themselves, should provide, however, a net advantage to incumbent judges—an advantage that is reinforced by a special reluctance of potential opponents to challenge sitting judges. Indeed, most studies of judicial elections have indicated a low rate of opposition and defeat for incumbent judges.[13]

The general advantage of judicial incumbency should be greater for lower courts than for higher courts. A race for the state supreme court is likely to be relatively visible. If this is the case, the challenger gains a relatively good opportunity to mount an effective attack against the incumbent. Moreover, seats on the supreme court are attractive, and potential challengers (and, where relevant, political parties) have an incentive to contest supreme court races. In contrast, trial judgeships are less attractive, and the campaigns are less visible. As a result, efforts to defeat incumbent trial judges should be less frequent and less successful than similar efforts at the supreme court level. Studies of judicial elections provide some evidence that supports this view.[14]

Additionally, the incumbency advantage in general elections should be greater in states with nonpartisan general elections than in states with partisan elections.[15] The partisan ballot gives voters an important cue that competes with incumbency by bringing voters' party loyalties into play. The significance of this cue is suggested by Philip Dubois' analysis of county-level correlations between vot-

ing for supreme court justices and for state executive offices. In states with partisan judicial ballots Dubois found a strong tendency for a party's judicial candidates to have the same strong and weak counties as their party colleagues running for executive offices.[16]

Because of the party cue, an incumbent in a state with partisan elections can be defeated under unfavorable conditions, such as an adverse partisan tide in a particular election. Where party affiliations are not disclosed by the ballot, such unfavorable conditions are less likely to have that effect. This difference is illustrated by the record of incumbent defeats in state supreme court elections from 1948 through 1974: 12 in 11 nonpartisan states, 24 in eight partisan states.[17]

Ohio is difficult to categorize in these terms because of its combination of a partisan primary and a nonpartisan general election ballot. Races for the supreme court have a fairly strong partisan tinge because party organizations are actively involved and campaign publicity links candidates to their parties.[18] The result is a meaningful correlation between party voting for justices and for executive officials on a county-by-county basis, though it is weaker than in any state with a partisan ballot.[19] The partisanship of races is reflected in a notable record: ten supreme court incumbents were defeated in general elections in the 1948-74 period, four more than in any other state.[20]

Below the supreme court level, races in Ohio seem to take more of a nonpartisan character, primarily because the party organizations generally play relatively limited roles. Indeed, one study found little relationship between party voting for the courts of appeals and for partisan nonjudicial offices.[21] We might expect party to have an equally limited effect on trial court voting. If so, the combination of low-visibility races and limited partisanship should give incumbents a high rate of success. This expectation may be tested with a look at the results in elections from 1962 through 1980.

Previously elected incumbents

The overall pattern of results for incumbents who have previously won elections is a simple one. Incumbents face limited competition, and when competition does arise it usually is unsuccessful.

The data for the 1962-80 period are shown in Table 1. In the primary election, 95 per cent of all incumbents ran unopposed. Clearly, the primary is

Table 1 Outcomes for previously elected common pleas incumbents, primary and general elections, 1962-1980

Outcome	Primary	General
Unopposed	95.1%	73.1%
Won by more than 2 to 1	1.3	11.5
Won by less than 2 to 1	1.6	10.9
Defeated	2.0	4.5
(N)	*(637)*	*(644)*

Table 2 Outcomes for appointed incumbents, primary and general elections

Outcome	Primary	General
Unopposed	93.3%	44.4%
Won by more than 2 to 1	2.7	11.1
Won by less than 2 to 1	3.3	30.7
Defeated	0.7	13.8
(N)	*(150)*	*(189)*

not a significant hurdle for incumbents as a group. When an incumbent was opposed in the primary, however, the leading opponent usually was strong enough to produce a meaningful race. Indeed, in 42 per cent of the contested races (13 of 31), the incumbent was defeated. These results suggest that challengers within the incumbent's party seldom enter races except when the incumbent is unusually vulnerable.

The level of competition in the general election was somewhat higher than in the primary, but even in the general election 73 per cent of all incumbents were unopposed. Indeed, 71 per cent of all incumbents did not face opposition in either the primary or the general election. Though opposition was more common in the general election, it was less likely to be successful; only 17 per cent of all opposed incumbents were defeated, and 43 per cent won by a margin of greater than 2-1.

The total number of incumbents who were defeated in the primary or general election was 42 (6 per cent of the number who ran for re-election). By almost any standard, this represents a high rate of success for incumbents. In comparison, during about the same period, approximately 15 per cent of all incumbent candidates for the Ohio House were defeated.[22]

Appointed incumbents

In the period from 1961 though 1980, 207 common pleas judges were appointed by the governor. Altogether, about 40 per cent of the common pleas judges in that period reached the office through appointment. The comparable proportion for the Ohio appellate courts during that period was only 16 per cent.[23]

Examining the fates of these judges in their first election[24] is useful in understanding the impact of incumbency and the operation of the selection system. If appointees nearly always win elections, then the system in practice has a very strong element of gubernatorial influence. If appointees lose their elections a high proportion of the time, the governor's

role can be characterized as fairly limited.

The electoral success of gubernatorial appointees in elective systems has been studied at the supreme court level in some detail. One study of the period from 1948 through 1974 found that the partisan ballot made a fundamental difference, at least in nonsouthern states.[25] In nonpartisan states nearly half the appointees were unopposed, and more than 95 per cent were elected. In the partisan states the great majority of judges were opposed, and almost 30 per cent were defeated. The states with hybrid systems such as Ohio resembled those with the partisan ballot. Indeed, Ohio ranked ahead of any other state in the number of appointees defeated—seven. In the 1960-80 period, 55 per cent of all Ohio supreme court appointees suffered defeat. This striking record reflected the extreme electoral difficulties of Democratic appointees during that period.[26]

We can expect common pleas appointees to be more successful than those appointed to the supreme court, because of the differences between the two courts that were discussed earlier. But appointees should be considerably less successful than previously elected incumbents, because an appointee who was not already well known may have too little time to develop name recognition, and because appointees in counties where their party is weak may be vulnerable to a party-based challenge.

The actual patterns of success for Ohio common pleas appointees are shown in Table 2. In the primary,[27] appointees were only slightly more likely to attract opposition than were elected incumbents; one in 15 was opposed. Appointees were even less likely than other incumbents to be defeated. In the 20-year period that was studied, only one appointee lost a primary.

In the general election appointees did distinctly less well than did elected incumbents. More than 55 per cent faced opposition, and 80 per cent of the challengers either lost by less than a 2-1 margin or won. Of the appointees who were opposed, 25 per

Table 3 Outcomes for previously elected incumbents, primary and general elections, by county population

Group	Unopposed	Won	Lost
Primary election			
Largest *(N=200)*	96.5%	3.0%	0.5%
2d group *(N=116)*	97.4	0.9	1.7
3d group *(N=135)*	95.6	2.2	2.2
Smallest *(N=186)*	91.9	4.3	3.8
General election			
Largest *(N=206)*	54.9%	40.8%	4.4%
2d group *(N=119)*	73.1	22.7	4.2
3d group *(N=133)*	85.0	10.5	4.5
Smallest *(N=186)*	84.9	10.2	4.8

Table 4 Outcomes for appointed incumbents, primary and general elections, by county population

Group	Unopposed	Won	Lost
Primary election			
Largest *(N=61)*	95.1%	4.9%	0.0%
2d group *(N=27)*	92.6	7.4	0.0
3d group *(N=30)*	96.7	3.3	0.0
Smallest *(N=32)*	87.5	9.4	3.1
General election			
Largest *(N=81)*	24.7%	59.3%	16.0%
2d group *(N=31)*	35.5	48.4	16.1
3d group *(N=36)*	52.8	30.6	16.7
Smallest *(N=41)*	82.9	12.2	4.9

cent were defeated (versus 17 per cent of the previously elected incumbents). Of all appointees who ran in the general election, 14 per cent were defeated. This rate was more than three times as high as that for elected incumbents.

Still, only one-seventh of the appointees were defeated in either election. Indeed, 43 per cent faced no opposition in either the primary or the general election. Clearly the appointment power allows the governor to staff the judiciary for something more than the interim period prior to the next general election.

Population and incumbent success

As in other states, Ohio counties vary tremendously in population; in the 1980 census, the largest county housed more than one hundred times as many people as the smallest. Because land area of counties varies far less, population is also a fairly good indicator of population density and urbanism.

There are reasons to expect differences in the situations of incumbents between populous urban counties and low-population rural counties, but these reasons conflict. Incumbents might face more competition in larger counties because of the larger pool of attorneys who are potential candidates and because of higher general levels of political competition.[28] On the other hand, in smaller counties it may be easier to mount an effective challenge against an incumbent through direct contact with voters.[29] Because of these contradictory expectations, the relationship between population and incumbent success is particularly worthy of investigation.

For purposes of analysis, the counties have been divided into four groups on the basis of their 1970 population: (A) "Largest"—the six largest counties, each with population greater than 400,000;[30] (B) "Second"—the next 13 counties, with population between 100,000 and 400,000; (C) "Third"—

24 counties with population between 50,000 and 100,000; (D) "Smallest"—45 counties with population less than 50,000.

The pattern of competition faced by previously elected incumbents is broken down into these four categories in Table 3. The results for the primary and general elections differed. In the primary election, no set of counties diverged from the general rule of low competition. In each of the four groups, more than 90 per cent of the incumbents were unopposed and more than 95 per cent won nomination. There was a weak but steady relationship between county population and proportion of defeats: incumbents were less vulnerable in large counties. This difference suggests that small population facilitates communication about candidates, allowing challenges to incumbents.

In the general election, the proportion of opposed incumbents increased substantially with county population, but the proportion of incumbent defeats hardly varied at all. In the largest counties interparty opposition occurred even in a good many races that appeared to have been hopeless: in these counties, more than half of the candidates who ran against incumbents lost by margins of more than 2-1. Even so, fewer than half the incumbents in these counties faced any opposition in the general election. In the two smallest groups of counties people were less likely to run against incumbents in lost causes, and 31 per cent of all the general election challengers were victorious.

Table 4 provides comparable information for appointees who were facing their first electoral test. In the primary election population made little difference; appointees were unlikely to face opposition anywhere. As in the primaries for elected incumbents, however, opposition was most common in the least populous counties.

In the general election opposition increased with each rise in county population. Indeed, the

Table 5   Outcomes for previously elected incumbents, general elections, by incumbent's party and county's party strength

Group	Unopposed	Won	Lost
Republican incumbents			
35 most Dem. counties* (N=150)	70.0%	27.3%	2.7%
53 most Rep. counties** (N=231)	73.2	23.4	3.5
Democratic incumbents			
35 most Dem. counties* (N=174)	79.3%	19.5%	1.1%
53 most Rep. counties** (N=78)	65.4	17.9	16.7

*Mean proportion Democratic of the two-party vote in gubernatorial elections 1962-78 ranged from 57.0% to 41.9% in these counties.

**Mean proportion Democratic of the two-party vote in gubernatorial elections 1962-78 ranged from 41.7% to 29.4% in these counties.

increase was quite substantial, much greater than the increase for elected incumbents. The proportion of appointees who actually were defeated was fairly uniform except in the smallest counties, where more than 95 per cent of the appointees were elected. Among the judges who faced opposition, the proportion of defeats also was fairly uniform among the four groups of counties.

The impact of population size, then, is not entirely consistent. Nor, in most respects, is it particularly dramatic. In the analyzed period the main effect of large population was to increase the likelihood than an incumbent would face an opponent in the general election. The proportions of judges who actually suffered defeat, on the other hand, varied only moderately by population. Most important, there were no startling deviations from the general pattern of incumbent success. Neither in urbanized, politically competitive counties nor in rural counties with personalized politics were incumbents highly vulnerable to defeat.

The impact of partisan forces

The role of political parties in judicial elections was discussed in the section on the incumbency advantage. That discussion noted the relatively nonpartisan character of Ohio common pleas elections, a trait that would seem to favor incumbents. The high rate of success enjoyed by common pleas incumbents suggests that party activity and partisan voting do not cause large numbers of judges to suffer defeat. But the impact of partisanship in common pleas elections requires a more direct examination.

The general issue is how much the fates of common pleas judges are affected by the relative positions of the two major parties. More specifically, I will look at two forms of impact for partisan forces: the effect of long-term patterns of party strength in particular counties on the re-election success of the

two parties' incumbents in those counties, and the impact of statewide partisan tides on incumbents.

As in other states, Ohio counties differ a good deal in patterns of party strength.[31] The Democrats are the majority party in several counties, including most of the more populous ones. Another set of counties is closely competitive. The largest group, primarily rural, features strong Republican dominance. We need to determine whether the safety of incumbents increases with the long-term strength of their party in their county.

To address this question, the 88 counties were ranked according to the mean Democratic vote in the five gubernatorial elections from 1962 through 1978. For analytic purposes the counties were then divided into five groups of nearly equal size, from the most Democratic quintile to the most Republican. Judges were identified as Republican or Democratic, primarily on the basis of the primary elections in which they ran. The affiliations of a few judges could not be identified, and several ran as independents; both sets were excluded from this part of the analysis. For the remaining judges, the success of each party's incumbents was then compared across the five groups of counties.

The pattern for previously elected incumbents is shown in Table 5. For purposes of presentation, the five groups of counties have been collapsed into two. (As the notes to the table show, the two groups are not mirror images of each other in party strength; indeed, the appropriate labels for them might be "competitive" and "Republican.") The data indicate that the impact of county party strength differed by the incumbent's party. For Republican incumbents, the balance between the parties seemed to have little effect. Opposition in the general election was most common in the most Democratic quintile, but even in those counties nearly 60 per cent of the Republican incumbents were unopposed. More importantly, there was essentially no relationship between party strength and the likelihood of defeat.

For Democratic incumbents party strength clearly made a difference. In the relatively favorable counties Democratic incumbents almost never lost. In the Republican-inclined counties one in six was defeated, and nearly half of those who faced general election challenges lost their seats. The significance of this latter finding should not be exaggerated, because it undoubtedly reflects the disinclination to make futile challenges that we found in

Table 6 Outcomes for appointed incumbents, general elections, by incumbent's party and county's party strength

Group	Unopposed	Won	Lost
Republican incumbents			
35 most Dem. counties *(N=66)*	25.8%	53.0%	21.2%
53 most Rep. counties *(N=57)*	54.4	40.4	5.3
Democratic incumbents			
35 most Dem. counties *(N=34)*	55.9%	41.2%	2.9%
53 most Rep. counties *(N=22)*	54.5	31.8	13.6

Table 7 Proportions of defeats for incumbent judges, general elections, by incumbent's party and year *(Opposed and unopposed incumbents included)*

Years	Previously elected (N)	Previously elected %	Appointed (N)	Appointed %
Republican incumbents				
"Democratic" years (1964, 1970)	40	2.5	24	16.7
"Middle" years	220	3.2	65	13.8
"Republican" years (1966, 1972)	121	3.3	34	11.8
Democratic incumbents				
"Democratic" years	32	0.0	8	0.0
"Middle" years	131	6.9	37	8.1
"Republican" years	89	6.7	11	9.1

less populous counties. But the overall difference between the two sets of counties is striking.

Table 6 shows the pattern for appointed incumbents. Both Democratic and Republican appointees were about four times as likely to be defeated in the other party's stronger counties than in their own party's stronger counties. For Republicans, but not for Democrats, party strength also was related to the likelihood of opposition. These findings make it clear that county party strength affects Republican judges as well as Democrats, though specific effects differed by party.

The analysis thus far might be misleading because of the relationship between party strength and county population. As noted earlier, Democratic counties tend to be relatively large in population, Republican counties relatively small. To gauge the effects of party strength alone, it is necessary to control for population size. Accordingly, the relationship between party strength and incumbent success was analyzed separately for the two larger groups of counties and for the two smaller groups. The results of this reanalysis differed only marginally from those of the original analysis. Thus the original results are not misleading.

A remaining limitation of this analysis is that it does not take into account variation over time in the balance between the parties. The long-term party positions in a county may be disturbed by partisan tides in particular years. It is very difficult to probe the effects of these tides at the county level, but we can do so at the statewide level by comparing the outcomes of judicial elections in different years. On the basis of the division of the Ohio vote for president and governor, 1964 and 1970 were particularly good Democratic years, while 1966 and 1972 were particularly good Republican years. In those years, did common pleas judges on the same ballots as the presidential and gubernatorial candidates feel an effect?

The findings in Table 7 show that there was only

a limited and inconsistent effect. In the best Democratic years Democratic judges seemed to benefit, but they did not suffer in the best Republican years. (The findings for Democratic appointees should be interpreted very cautiously because of the limited numbers of judges in particular categories.) Republican appointees did best in their party's good years and worst in its bad years, but the differences are too small to be meaningful. Previously elected Republicans felt no effects at all. The most important finding is that weakness at the head of the ticket did not make judges particularly vulnerable to defeat. In this respect running in an unfavorable county seemed to entail far more risk than running in an unfavorable year. Even in unfavorable counties, however, we found that large majorities of judges won re-election.

Research implications

Incumbents are highly successful in winning common pleas elections in Ohio. Overall, both previously elected and appointed incumbents do very well. During the 1962-80 period only 8 per cent of the campaigns to retain common pleas judgeships resulted in primary or general election defeats. Because of this high rate of success, defeat of incumbents accounts for a fairly small proportion of the accessions of the new judges—13 per cent in the period from 1962 through 1980. New judges come to office primarily through appointments by the governor and elections to open seats.

Not all the success of incumbents can be ascribed to incumbency as such. A favorable pattern of party strength or an absence of other attorneys interested in judicial office can help to make the incumbent's position secure. Yet it is striking that incumbents are rather successful even under the most unfavorable circumstance, minority party status in large counties.

The advantage of incumbency is reflected in both the frequency with which incumbents run unopposed and in the high rates of incumbent success in contested races. There are several bases for these two phenomena. But for the most part they undoubtedly arise from a common source, the difficulty of defeating a sitting judge.

A high rate of success for incumbents, of course, is not unique to the courts of common pleas. But common pleas incumbents are somewhat more successful than are incumbents in many other positions. As expected, common pleas judges were less likely to face opposition or to suffer defeat than were members of the Ohio Supreme Court; in a comparable period uncontested races for the supreme court were rare and incumbent justices running for election lost 30 per cent of the contested races.[32]

This study's findings on the incumbency advantage are consistent with those of other studies of trial court elections, though too few states have been analyzed to allow strong generalizations. Standing by themselves, what implications do the findings on Ohio have for the debate over elective systems for judges?

In some respects the findings should reduce the concerns of those who oppose judicial election. That opposition is based in part on fears about the effects of periodic electoral tests on sitting judges.[33] But most sitting common pleas judges obtain new terms without facing any such tests, and a very small percentage actually lose their positions. Common pleas elections are more dangerous for incumbents than are retention elections under "merit selection" systems,[34] but the similarities are more striking than the differences.

At the same time, opponents of election may retain concerns about the circumstances under which incumbents suffer defeats. This study has indicated little about those circumstances, and it is not at all clear that the least able judges are the ones who lose. The limited impact of short-term partisan tides on incumbents may be reassuring. On the other hand, in most categories of judges incumbents are more likely to lose where their party is weak electorally, and many observers—though not all—would regard this tendency as unfortunate.[35]

For those who are sympathetic toward the elective system, the implications of this study may be even more obscure. Judicial elections have the potential virtue of providing accountability for sitting judges. Whether such accountability exists in practice depends upon the conditions under which challenges to and defeats of incumbents occur. As noted above, this study offers little information on those questions beyond some broad patterns.

This kind of research, then, represents only the first step in assessing the operation of judicial elections. Determination of the outcome for incumbents in general, and in particular kinds of settings, is necessary as a means to understand the basic contours of the elective system. A useful second step is to examine the cases in which judges face strong electoral competition and particularly the cases in which they lose to challengers.[36]

On one matter the implications of this study are quite clear. The strength of appointed incumbents means that the governor plays a central role in the selection of common pleas judges; the governor's appointees are not temporary stand-ins but constitute a large minority of the permanent judiciary. Because Ohio governors typically have relied heavily on county party organizations to recommend appointees, the governor's power extends to the political parties.

The importance of the appointment power in most nominally elective systems is well understood, and this study simply reinforces the findings of previous research. But it is worth emphasizing that the power of interim appointment must be seen as an integral feature of the systems in which it exists. Some apparent characteristics of elective systems actually are characteristics of election-plus-appointment. Ironically, gubernatorial appointment decisions remain, perhaps, the least understood feature of judicial selection systems. In the effort to learn more about how state judges are chosen, we cannot afford to ignore the appointment process.

At several points I have noted differences between the Ohio Supreme Court and the Courts of Common Pleas in the operation of the elective system. Though the formal system for the two courts is identical, the system operates quite differently in practice. Most importantly, elections to the supreme court are more competitive, and appointment plays a larger role in staffing the common pleas bench. These and other differences can be ascribed to factors such as the relative attractiveness of the supreme court and the higher level of party competition at the statewide level than in most counties.

The differences between the two levels underline the need for sensitivity to the context in which selection systems operate. A particular system may vary in its workings not only among states but within them—between higher and lower courts, between urban and rural counties. The existence of so many sources of potential variation means that conclusions about judicial election as a system should not be based on a limited investigation of its operation.

More generally, our limited knowledge on the workings of the elective system should counsel against hasty judgments about its merits. The certainty of many commentators' conclusions about judicial election seems unjustified in light of the uncertainties that remain. If the selection of judges is an important issue—as it certainly is—we need to learn more about the methods of selection from which we must choose.

NOTES

This article originally appeared in Volume 66, Number 9, April 1983, pages 420-430.

The author would like to thank Herbert Asher, Kathleen Barber, Elliot Slotnick, and an anonymous reviewer for their comments on an earlier version of this paper.

1. On the state selection systems, *see* Berkson, Beller, and Grimaldi, JUDICIAL SELECTION IN THE UNITED STATES: A COMPENDIUM OF PROVISIONS (Chicago: American Judicature Society, 1981).

2. *See* Winters, ed., SELECTED READINGS: JUDICIAL SELECTION AND TENURE (Chicago: American Judicature Society, rev. ed. 1973).

3. *See, e.g.,* Dubois, FROM BALLOT TO BENCH (Austin: University of Texas Press, 1980); Hannah, *Competition in Michigan's Judicial Elections: Democratic Ideals vs. Judicial Realities,* 24 WAYNE ST. L. REV. 1267 (1978); Henderson and Sinclair, *The Selection of Judges in Texas,* 5 HOUS. L. REV. (1968); Johnson, Shaefer, and McKnight, *The Salience of Judicial Candidates and Elections,* 59 SOC. SCI. Q. 371 (1978); Ladinsky and Silver, *Popular Democracy and Judicial Independence: Electorate and Elite Reactions to Two Wisconsin Supreme Court Elections,* 1967 WIS. L. REV. 128; and Barber, *Ohio Judicial Elections—Nonpartisan Premises with Partisan Results,* 32 OHIO ST. L. J. 762 (1971).

4. Dubois, *supra* n. 3, at 108-137; Barber, *supra* n. 3; Hannah, *supra* n. 3.

5. The empirical analysis is based on data in publications and records of the Ohio Secretary of State. The primary sources were Ohio Secretary of State, OHIO ELECTION STATISTICS (1962-80); and Ohio Secretary of State, OFFICIAL ROSTER—FEDERAL, STATE, COUNTY OFFICERS AND DEPARTMENTAL INFORMATION (1961/62-1979/80).

6. OHIO CONST. art. IV, sec. 4. The common pleas courts handle "major" criminal and civil cases as well as three areas of special responsibility (probate, juvenile, and domestic relations). In most counties one or more of these special areas are dealt with by judges specifically assigned to them. All common pleas judges, whatever their responsibilities, are included in this study.

7. Provisions for the selection of Ohio judges are compiled in Berkson, Beller, and Grimaldi, *supra* n. 1, at 137-139. The history of judicial selection in Ohio is described in Aumann, *The Selection, Tenure, Retirement and Compensation of Judges in Ohio,* 5 U. CIN. L. REV. 408 (1931).

8. Barber, *supra* n. 3; Barber, "Nonpartisan Ballots and Voter Confusion in Judicial Elections," 1982 (unpublished paper presented at meeting of the Midwest Political Science Association).

9. The discussion in this section draws from Hinckley, Hofstetter and Kessel, *Information and the Vote: A Comparative Election Study,* 2 AM. POL. Q. 131 (1974); Mann and Wolfinger, *Candidates and Parties in Congressional Elections,* 74 AM. POL. SCI. REV. 617 (1980); Abramovitz, *A Comparison of Voting for U.S. Senator and Representative in 1978,* 74 AM. POL. SCI. REV. 633 (1980); Wright, ELECTORAL CHOICE IN AMERICA (Chapel Hill: University of North Carolina, 1974).

10. Incumbency as a source of re-election success often is reinforced by the strength of the incumbent's party. Jewell and Patterson, THE LEGISLATIVE PROCESS IN THE UNITED STATES 91-97 (New York: Random House, 3d ed. 1977).

11. American Bar Association, Code of Judicial Conduct, Canon 7(B)(1)(c) (1972).

12. Ladinsky and Silver, *supra* n. 3, at 161; *How Much Do Voters Know or Care About Judicial Candidates?,* 38 J. AM. JUD. SOC'Y 141 (1955); Johnson *et al., supra* n. 3, at 374.

13. Hannah, *supra* n. 3, at 1306; Henderson and Sinclair, *supra* n. 3, at 442; Jacob, *Judicial Insulation—Elections, Direct Participation, and Public Attention to the Courts in Wisconsin,* 1966 WIS. L. REV. 801, 806-808; Moos, *Judicial Elections and Partisan Endorsement of Judicial Candidates in Minnesota,* 35 AM. POL. SCI. REV. 69 (1941).

14. Hannah, *supra* n. 3, at 1306; Jacob, *supra* n. 13, at 807-808.

15. On nonpartisan elections, *see* Lee, THE POLITICS OF NONPARTISANSHIP (Berkeley: University of California Press, 1960); Adrian, *Some General Characteristics of Nonpartisan Elections,* 46 AM. POL. SCI. REV. 766 (1952); Mueller, *Choosing Among 133 Candidates,* 34 PUB. OPINION Q. 395 (1970).

16. Dubois, *supra* n. 3, at 70-79.

17. *Id.* at 112. The three states with "mixed" systems, including Ohio, are excluded; all southern states are excluded.

18. *See, e.g.,* Murray, *3 Ohio Supreme Court Seats Up for Election,* DAYTON DAILY NEWS, October 14, 1980, at 20; Ruth, *Court's Makeup Is Critical,* COLUMBUS DISPATCH, September 17, 1978, at B-3.

19. Dubois, *supra* n. 3, at 75, 81-85; Barber, *supra* n. 8, at 28.

20. Dubois, *supra* n. 3, at 109.

21. Barber, *supra* n. 3, at 781-782.

22. The period was 1960-76. However, in the last two elections of this period, the success rates for incumbents were 95 per cent and 97 per cent. Asher, "The Unintended Consequences of Legislative Professionalism," 1978 (unpublished paper presented at meeting of the American Political Science Association), at 23.

23. The proportion was 27 per cent for the supreme court, 13 per cent for the court of appeals. Barber, *supra* n. 8, at 17. In general large proportions of judges initially are appointed in states with elective systems. Winter, *One-Man Judicial Selection,* 45 J. AM JUD. SOC'Y 198 (1962); Herndon, *Appointment as a Means of Initial Accession to Elective State Courts of Last Resort,* 38 N.D. L. REV. 60 (1962); Dubois, *supra* n. 3, at 105-109.

24. Occasionally an appointee chooses not to run in the subsequent election. But well over 90 per cent of the appointees in the 1961-80 period did seek election.

25. Dubois, *supra* n. 3, at 101-143. *See also* Herndon, *supra* n. 23.

26. Barber, *supra* n. 8, at 17-18.

27. As the totals in Table 2 indicate, appointments frequently occur too late in an even-numbered year to hold a special primary election.

28. In general elections, competition in populous counties also is facilitated by the strength of many party organizations and the close competition between parties that is frequently absent in smaller counties. Primary election competition for state legislative seats also tends to be higher in urban areas. Jewell and Patterson, *supra* n. 10, at 90.

29. Notably, in California judicial elections Dubois found a higher rate of voter participation (relative to elections for other offices) in rural counties than in urban counties. This finding suggests a greater knowledge of candidates in the rural areas. Dubois, *Public Participation in Trial Court Elections*, 2 LAW & POLICY Q. 133 (1980).

30. These also are the six counties that contained cities with populations of more than 200,000. The six largest counties in order of population, with their largest cities, were Cuyahoga (Cleveland), Hamilton (Cincinnati), Franklin (Columbus), Montgomery (Dayton), Summit (Akron), and Lucas (Toledo).

31. On this variation and its sources, *see* Fenton, MIDWEST POLITICS 117-154 (New York: Holt, Rinehart and Winston, 1966); Flinn, *The Outline of Ohio's Politics*, 13 WEST. POL. Q. 702 (1960); Eulau, *The Ecological Basis of Party Systems: The Case of Ohio*, 1 MIDWEST J. POL. SCI. 125 (1957).

32. Barber, *supra* n. 8, at 24-30.

33. *See* Dyer, *State Trial Courts from a Federal Viewpoint*, 54 JUDICATURE 372, 373-374 (1971); Dubois, *supra* n. 3, at 21-22.

34. The proportions of judges who lose retention elections under the "merit selection" system are small, about 1.6 per cent in the 1972-78 period. Carbon, *Judicial Retention Elections: Are They Serving Their Intended Purpose?* 64 JUDICATURE 210, 221 (1980).

35. For the contrary argument, *see* Dubois, *supra* n. 3, at 245-246.

36. Susan Carbon's analysis of defeats in retention elections is a good model for such examinations. Carbon, *supra* n. 34.

The federal judiciary: what role politics?

At the mid-year meeting of the American Judicature Society on February 16, 1985, in Detroit, Fred W. Friendly led a panel of 15 lawyers, judges, journalists, public officials and others in an examination of the federal judicial selection process . . . . Here is an edited transcript of the panel's dialogue on the selection of a new Supreme Court justice.

Fred W. Friendly: Let's make it the year 1989. The most aged member of the court is 88 years old. His name is Oliver Brandeis Vision. Judge Vision is everything that a Supreme Court justice should be. He's a great patriot. He combines all the values of all the people.

The participants on the panel

Moderator: **Fred W. Friendly,** Edward R. Murrow Professor Emeritus, Columbia University Graduate School of Journalism. Participants: **William J. Bauer,** Judge, U.S. Court of Appeals for the Seventh Circuit; **Benjamin R. Civiletti,** Former U.S. attorney general; **Charles Halpern,** Dean, CUNY—Queens School of Law; **Charles W. Joiner,** Judge, U.S. District Court for the Eastern District of Michigan; **Elaine R. Jones,** NAACP Legal Defense Fund; **Wade H. McCree, Jr.,** University of Michigan Law School and former judge, U.S. Court of Appeals for the Sixth Circuit; **Robert B. McKay,** president, Association of the Bar of the City of New York, and former dean, N.Y.U. School of Law; **Robert D. Raven,** Former Chairman, ABA Standing Committee on Federal Judiciary; **Jonathan E. Rose,** Former Assistant attorney general, Office of Legal Policy, U.S. Department of Justice; **Maurice Rosenberg,** Columbia University Law School; **Edward C. Schmults,** Former U.S. Deputy attorney general; **Elliot E. Slotnick,** Professor of Political Science, Ohio State University; **Augustine T. Smythe,** Esquire, South Carolina; **Joseph Tybor,** *Chicago Tribune;* **Stephen Wermiel,** *Wall Street Journal.*

One day Judge Vision is at a reception at the White House and as he's about to leave, he says to the President of the United States, Mr. McKay, "Mr. President, could Bessie and I stay for a few minutes afterward. We'd like to chat with you." Would you let him stay?

Robert McKay: Of course.

Friendly: Then you go into the Lincoln bedroom and sit before the fireplace and he tells you that he is thinking of retiring. You say all the appropriate things and he says, "but I haven't quite decided to do it yet." I haven't told you by the way that he's black—he's the third black member of the Supreme Court of the United States, and he says, "I will retire on my next birthday, which is in five weeks. But, Mr. President, I would like a promise from you that you will appoint a distinguished black jurist to take my place on the Supreme Court of the United States. This conversation is just between you and me. Do we have a deal?"

McKay: The answer is I could make no such deal. I would certainly take it into consideration, but measuring the qualifications of the individual you have in mind against all others, I would have to think about that.

Friendly: I have no individual in mind. I just want a promise from you that there will be a black seat. There's been one since the days of Lyndon Johnson who appointed Thurgood Marshall. I want a promise from you that there will be a black member of the Supreme Court.

McKay: I would be very sensitive to the need to have black representation on the Court.

Friendly: Are you saying the answer is yes?

McKay: No sir. Not a guarantee.

* * * *

Friendly: How does a judge retire? Does he write the president? Does he write to Mr. Civiletti? Does he write to Mr. Schmults? What's the process?

Charles W. Joiner: My understanding is he writes a letter to the president saying that he retires.

Friendly: You write the president. What does he do? Is he the first one to see it?

Benjamin Civiletti: It depends. Of course the letter is the formal act but sometimes I understand messages have been sent or carried in such a scenario as you proposed to alert the president or attorney general that there is a potential or an expectation of retirement within a certain period of time. The first thing I think the president does, if there has been no preadvice, is to call the attorney general and probably the White House counsel and have a meeting about the process of selecting an alternative.

Friendly: You've got a letter delivered by hand, and it's sent to the President of the United States and it says, "As of the first of January I wish to announce my retirement. I hope you will remember our conversation about appointing a black to the Court; it's very important that we have this representation in our day and age." You call in your attorney general and your deputy attorney general?

McKay: I would think so.

Friendly: What do you say to them?

McKay: I say, "We now have, as you perhaps are already aware, a potential vacancy on the Court. This is one of the most important appointments that a president can make and so I want you to make an immediate investigation of all those who have been recommended."

Friendly: Well nobody has recommended anybody, have they, because there's no vacancy? Do people go along all the time making recommendations in limbo?

McKay: They do indeed.

Friendly: Really?

McKay: There is always a list of candidates for the Supreme Court of the United States.

Friendly: All right. So how does this conversation conclude? "Go get me the best person?"

McKay: Not necessarily the best person, but get the recommendations that come from responsible sources from around the country and look at them and begin screening them through the American Bar Association. When you have a narrower list, come back to me.

Friendly: What do you mean the American Bar Association? They have a big prior restraint on this?

McKay: The ABA helps in the screening by making an investigation throughout the country.

Friendly: This early? Mr. Raven, you're an expert on this. Is that the way it works?

Robert Raven: Well, the last time two names were sent to the committee.

Friendly: By the American Bar Association?

Raven: No, by the president through the attorney general.

Friendly: But does the Bar Association send in names?

Raven: No. The Standing Committee of the ABA has never sponsored anyone. In fact, the few times it's been asked to, it made it very clear that that's not its function. It's not in the selection process at all. It's merely in the evaluation process for the attorney general.

Friendly: Professor Slotnick, would it ever be proper for the head of the ABA to write a personal letter to the president and say, "In considering candidates for this vacancy, why don't you think of so and so?"

Elliot Slotnick: I don't think it would be proper and I'm sure the ABA Committee would never try to do it because it would really alter their institutional role in the process.

Friendly: So they're more of a screening device to look at people after the event.

Slotnick: Right.

Friendly: Do you agree with that Dean Halpern?

Charles Halpern: It seems to me the president of the ABA—who is not part of the screening process—could quite appropriately send in suggestions to the president.

Friendly: Do you agree with that Professor Rosenberg?

Maurice Rosenberg: I guess he could. It's a free country and the First Amendment applies to him, but I think he'd be ill-advised to do it.

Friendly: Why would he be ill-advised?

Rosenberg: It seems to me that there are so many other sources of information and I'm not sure that we have yet quite gotten the process started the way it should be started.

Friendly: How should it be started?

Rosenberg: I think that in this conversation the president is having with the attorney general and others they would talk about some other things besides who.

Friendly: Like what?

Rosenberg: What sort of person do we want?

Friendly: What kind of person do we want?

Rosenberg: What term is the president in—first or second?

Friendly: He's just begun. This is his first term.

Rosenberg: He's just begun; in 1989 he's in his first term. The appointment of a person of one gender or one racial background or another would reflect upon his political chances.

Friendly: Did you notice that the president did not mention anything about the conversation with the justice about appointing a black? Did you think that was a purposeful omission by President McKay?

Rosenberg: Well I think that the president was going directly to the who question and not the what. I'd start with a question of what kind of person are we looking for.

I do think that the question of what the Court looks like when the pictures of the nine justices appear is a very important symbolic question.

Friendly: There's no black on the Court once Judge Vision retires. Is that important?

Rosenberg: I think so.

Friendly: Why? One hundred and fifty years after *Dred Scott* we still have to have a black seat?

Rosenberg: I don't say that we have to have a black seat. What we have to do is think of the implications of having a very well qualified—perhaps as well qualified as anybody else who could be found—person who's black sitting on the Court instead of someone else.

* * * *

Wade H. McCree, Jr.: May I interject at this point. I think that we're moving too rapidly in the process. What the president should do if the letter of resignation indicates a date of resignation is go public with the letter. The fact that he has written a letter indicating his intention to take senior status or retired status January 1st would lock the vacancy in. Some great problems could result from a president getting a letter like this. I submit my retirement effective upon the appointment and qualification of my successor. Now you're in trouble because the justice then can control that process. If he doesn't like the name that comes up, he can produce mischief.

Friendly: How does he do that?

McCree: Well he can indicate that he had an understanding with the president and that this was not in fulfillment of it. But if the letter said January 1st, I think he goes public with that to lock in the retirement and then he proceeds into the nomination process.

Friendly: All right. Thanks for the advice. I'm going to pull the curtain on this little epilogue just

for a moment and I'm going to move along to the fact that the team of Civiletti, Schmults, Rose, Rosenberg have come up with three names. They've talked to all the people, all the bar associations. They've looked at all the letters, they talked to the chairman of the Judiciary Committee, Senator Smythe . . . did they talk to the chief justice by the way? Is that permissible, Mr. Civiletti?

Civiletti: Permissible, but not necessarily advisable.

Friendly: Why is it not advisable? Who would know better?

Civiletti: Because he doesn't have a role in the appointment process ordinarily, and if you're inviting him in then he will take the opportunity to exercise his judgment.

Friendly: He doesn't have First Amendment rights?

Civiletti: You'll have enough problems dealing with the chairman of the Senate Judiciary Committee, the majority leader of the House, and other congressional leaders that I don't think you will want to get the chief justice involved in the selection process.

Friendly: You're not suggesting that in the last eight or nine appointments to the Supreme Court chief justices haven't been consulted and listened to?

Civiletti: Yes, but that's after the selection generally.

Friendly: Is it true, Attorney General Schmults, that the chief justice is not generally consulted until after the appointment?

Schmults: I would say that was right—the ones I'm aware of. I think what is far more likely is the chief justice would come and talk to you.

Joiner: I don't think the chief justice should go to the president unless he's asked. I think the president has the power and he should initiate all of the inquiries that he thinks are appropriate.

Rosenberg: It seems to me that some preliminary decision might have been made by the president and his close advisors as to who they want to take into consideration. If they want to take into consideration judges of the courts of appeals, for example, then they might want to find out who knows them and the chief justice might be a likely source.

Friendly: Is there anything wrong with the chief justice going over and saying, "Mr. President, I have watched all these judges. We go to these circuit meetings. I know them better than anybody in the country. I have three names I want to give you and I'd like to see you tomorrow at a time convenient with you or any time in the next week or so." Anything wrong with that, Mr. McKay?

McKay: I think it's absolutely proper. If the American Bar Association and the attorney general and the Senate and everybody around the country is going to advise the president, why not the chief justice? That's my view.

Elaine R. Jones: I would really disagree with the notion that as a matter of course the chief justice, or any other sitting justice on the Supreme Court, should inform the president as to his or her choices for that Court without having first been asked.

Friendly: Why?

Jones: I think when the chief justice and justices of the Supreme Court interject themselves into the nomination process whether it's at the court of appeals level, the district court level, or the Supreme Court level, you have an institutional problem. The president knows well that the chief justice is the chief justice, and knows the workings and operations of the Court, and if he wants that advice, he knows where to get it.

Friendly: So it's up to the president.

Jones: I think so.

Friendly: All right. Interesting difference of opinion. Curtains down on that.

We've got three names agreed to by our committee. Mr. President, here are three names. The first is a male court of appeals judge from X circuit— been on the circuit for 12 years, written a lot of great opinions, all the right material and everything else—couldn't go wrong with him. We have a black male. He was a state trial judge in criminal courts in a big metropolitan city like Chicago, New York, St. Louis, Los Angeles, was appointed to fill a vacancy to the Senate, and a year and a half later was elected. So he is a Senator, former state judge, on the Judiciary Committee—very well thought of, member of the right political party, and has a judicial mind. He is black. He's a close friend of Judge Vision. Third is a woman—white. Was the dean of a law school in the sun belt and is now a member of the court of appeals.

So we have three people. White female, white male, black male. I want you to be my committee. You're changing roles, now. You're going to be my advisors. I'm the president. I may ask one or two of you to be president before we're through. Who do you vote for, Ms. Jones?

Jones: Well the bottom line is that all of these

people are qualified. And I assume the court consists of eight white males.

Friendly: It's seven white males, Ms. O'Connor, and a vacancy.

Jones: There's no black on the court and we do have an interest in diversity of judgment. My vote is for the black.

Schmults: I'd like to know which candidate is closest to the president in political and judicial philosophy.

Friendly: How are you gonna find that out? You're going to invite these three people for a meeting?

Schmults: Actually, you would have done a lot of other things before this. You would have read all the decisions.

Friendly: You've done all that and they're all pretty much your kind of person. I'll be the white male. There we are, we're having a drink together at 5:00 in the afternoon. What do you want to know?

Schmults: I would like to discuss with you how you see the role of courts in our governmental system.

Friendly: I see it as it is said in the Constitution. We are a court of appeal, we've decided ever since 1801 (*Marbury v. Madison*) that we will be the referee with the striped shirt, we will make these decisions. I believe in judicial review but I'm not an activist judge. I'm your kind of judge, Mr. President, the kind you spoke about when you accepted the nomination. Any other questions?

Schmults: No. It sounds like we know what your judicial philosophy is.

Friendly: What else do you want to know? Anything you want to know about any big cases coming up?

Schmults: No, I wouldn't want to know about any big cases.

Friendly: But you know in the platform they said, "that on gun control and abortion we will appoint no one to the Supreme Court who does not believe as our party believes." Aren't you going to honor your party's commitment to that?

Schmults: No, I think what you do is determine whether the people on your list have the same view of the role of the courts in our system as the president and I do not think you would ask them how they would decide specific cases. That would be demeaning to the candidates and to the president.

Friendly: Well why don't you try a candidate? Why don't you ask Judge Bauer how he feels about abortion laws? That's what the party said. You ran on that platform. Don't you believe in it?

Schmults: I do believe in the platform—that's what I ran on. Presumably that's my platform but I don't have to apply it specifically in this way by asking judicial candidates questions how they would decide specific cases. I think I should determine whether the person I'm going to appoint has my general outlook about the role of the courts, judicial/political philosophy, view of the nation; but as to how you would decide a specific case, I really think that would be inappropriate. I would not ask the candidate that. First of all the facts and circumstances are changed at the time the case comes up.

Friendly: You remember that *Roe v. Wade* case back in 1972 or '73, if that were tried tomorrow, same set of facts except we know a lot more about medical science now and we can preserve a life from the second week on—wouldn't you ask Judge Bauer/Judge Joiner how they'd feel about that case if it were argued tomorrow?

Schmults: Well I think that is a good point. I think you might well ask them about a case like *Roe v. Wade* that perhaps, in the discussion of that case, would bring out the candidates' view of the courts and the Court's role in applying the law.

Friendly: Why don't you ask Judge Bauer?

Schmults: I'd be interested in your analysis of *Roe v. Wade.* Do you think that the way that case was decided, and the principles that were enunciated was consistent with your views as to what the courts ought to be doing in our system of government?

Bauer: I'm not in the position at the moment, Mr. President, to totally criticize the opinion. On the other hand there have been a lot of changes in facts, additional things that must be brought to the attention of the Court or could be brought to the attention of the Court, and I'd certainly be willing to give it a second look in view of new knowledge.

Schmults: I'm really not asking you about an abortion decision as such.

Bauer: You're asking about *Roe v. Wade?*

Schmults: Yes, I was asking about *Roe v. Wade* but I'm not really asking you about what you think about abortion. Really what I'm trying to get at is your view as to whether the courts ought to pay considerable deference to Congress and the legislatures or should courts be looking for ways to reach out by deciding questions that are very controversial in our society.

Bauer: Mr. President, the courts are frequently forced into deciding controversial questions present in our society because of an absence of action by either the Congress or the executive branch of government.

Schmults: So it's your view that courts should step into vacuums where the likely accountable branches don't act.

Bauer: Mr. President, you and I both know that the Court never steps into a vacuum. The vacuum is brought to them and thrust upon them.

Friendly: Come on, answer the question, judge.

Bauer: I've just answered the question. I do not think that courts should seek out solutions for problems that have not been brought to their attention, but I don't think they can avoid problems that are forced upon them.

Friendly: Do you have a better way to answer the question, Mr. Civiletti?

Civiletti: I wouldn't be asking those questions in the first place. I'd be looking for intellectual capacity first and exploring that . . . and making a very close analysis of the opinions. Beyond capacity, the ability to be creative in the law—to understand and apply the law.

Friendly: But you're using all kinds of fancy words to duck the issue.

Civiletti: No, no, no. Third, I'd want to look for fairness among these three last candidates. I think those three qualities make a great chief justice or a great justice, and from my point of view as attorney general, not as a president who has said I'm not going to have anybody on the Court who's going to decide things contrary to my political philosophy. You can't control a justice anyway once they're on the Court. There's been a lot of disappointments between what the president thought he was getting when he appointed a justice and what he actually got.

* * * *

Friendly: We're back to our three candidates. Who are you going to be for, Mr. Slotnick?

Slotnick: I think there was something you said in the hypothetical that made it even more apparent that the black judge makes sense, and that was that he was on the Senate Judiciary Committee and was in the majority. He would just sail through the Senate.

Friendly: Is that a consideration?

Slotnick: Oh, I think it should be for a president.

Friendly: You mean the President of the United States under Article II selects judges and under

Section III for life, and he is going to do it on the basis of how quickly they're going to be confirmed.

Slotnick: Not on the basis of that, but you're saying they're all good.

Friendly: But that's why you're going to do it—because he's on that committee?

Slotnick: I think having the black candidate when you have no black members of the Court combined with the fact that this is an individual who is on the Judiciary Committee in the majority means everything is coming up right for this particular person.

Friendly: He's the perfect candidate politically.

McCree: I think I'd go with the black male. I understand that he is a member of the Senate of the United States and he's on the Judiciary Committee. As president I can only appoint someone by and with the advice and consent of the Senate. And here I have someone coming from the Senate who's going to have an easier path through it. Plus another point. Abner Mikva, who used to sit in the Congress and is now a judge of the Court of Appeals for the District of Columbia, has written recently about the absence of someone on the Court who has knowledge of the legislative process. Much of the Court's business today, most of it, is interpreting statutes. It's not the Constitution, it's not the common law, it's congressional statutes.

Friendly: You want a legislator because that's what the Supreme Court does is legislate?

McCree: No, I didn't say that. What the Supreme Court does is interpret statutes.

Friendly: Which is another way of saying it legislates.

McCree: If you prefer it. But I prefer to say that they interpret statutes. There hasn't been anyone since Hugo Black with any legislative experience. If we talk about the Court as being representative of the country, here you get a black male who is also a legislator.

Friendly: Who are you going to put on the Court, Dean McKay?

McKay: Well if everything is truly equal, I would put the black male on, but you haven't adequately put in one of the factors that I think the president would take into account.

Friendly: What's that?

McKay: Which of the candidates most closely adheres to the views that the president personally espouses for the Court.

Friendly: If you push me to the limit, it's the white male. He is the carbon copy of the president of the United States.

McKay: Then I think the president—and I don't necessarily speak as myself—I think the president would probably choose the white male as the one who would be most reliable.

Friendly: And you're going to not have a black on the Court for the first time since 1963?

McKay: The one who will most likely espouse the views that I think are appropriate for the courts is the one that I would choose.

Friendly: But it's a political decision you're making.

McKay: Of course. It's a political situation.

Friendly: You're willing to admit it. I've heard all the stuff about substance, point of view; you want somebody who agrees with you on *Roe v. Wade.*

McKay: Very closely. Very closely. I don't think we should have a black seat, or a Catholic seat, or a Jewish seat, or a female seat. We might want more than one of each of those at various times.

Friendly: We're going to get the Court up to 50 members.

Bauer: I think that the reason that the country follows what the Supreme Court says, and remember the Supreme Court has no militia, no troops or anything like that, is because we accept the Supreme Court. If we don't appoint that black male to replace the black male, we're going to bring to a large segment of the population an idea, true or false, that they have been disenfranchised somehow, and cheated, and I would not perpetrate that upon the American public. I would, therefore, vote for the black male. But I would tell him why I was doing it.

Schmults: One of the things I'd like to do is know the context. How many more appointments am I going to have?

Friendly: Who knows? How many did President Carter have to the Supreme Court? Zip! . . . .

NOTE

This transcript originally appeared in Volume 68, Numbers 9-10, April-May 1985, pages 330-336.

The Bush imprint on the judiciary: carrying on a tradition

The judges appointed by President Bush so far bear many similarities to the Reagan judicial appointees. By 1993, about two-thirds of the federal judiciary will have been selected by these two presidents.

by Sheldon Goldman

On March 25, 1969, just about two months after the start of the Nixon presidency, White House aide Tom Charles Huston wrote a memorandum for the president in which he argued:

Through his judicial appointments, a President has the opportunity to influence the course of national affairs for a quarter of a century after he leaves office . . . . [I]t is necessary to remember that the decision as to who will make the decisions affects what decisions will be made . . . . [T]he President [can] establish precise guidelines as to the type of man [sic] he wishes to appoint—his professional competence, his political disposition, his understanding of the judicial function—and establish a White House review procedure to assure that each prospective nominee recommended by the Attorney General meets the guidelines . . . . He [the President] may insist that some evidence exists as to the attitude of the prospective judge toward the role of the court. He may insist upon a man who has a passion for judicial restraint . . . . The criteria he can establish are as varied as the views held in different political, social, and legal circles today. But if he establishes *his* criteria and establishes his machinery for insuring that the criteria are met, the appointments he makes will be his, in fact, as in theory.[1]

The president read the memo and on the cover sheet handwrote:

"To Kliendienst [Deputy Attorney General]: RN *agrees*—Have this analysis in mind in making judicial nominations."[2]

If the Nixon administration had the desire to attempt a systematic philosophical screening process for prospective appointments to the lower federal courts, it was left to the Reagan administration to implement what Huston and Nixon envi-

sioned.[3] The Bush administration, by continuing the screening process, has institutionalized it and in this sense can be seen as carrying on a tradition. In terms of the demographic portrait of Bush appointees, we shall see shortly the extent to which the administration has maintained tradition.

This article examines the first two years of appointments by President George Bush of lifetime judgeships to courts of general jurisdiction. The pattern established is of special significance in light of the Federal Judgeships Act of 1990 that created 85 new federal judgeships, which along with current and future vacancies will enable the Bush administration to leave its imprint on the judiciary.

Judicial selection overview

George Bush was elected to the presidency on November 8, 1988, by an electoral college landslide and by a comfortable but not overwhelming popular vote majority. At the same time the nation elected a Republican president for the fifth of the last six presidential elections, it also elected a Democratic Party controlled House and Senate.

The Senate Judiciary Committee during the first two years of Bush's presidency (coinciding with the 101st Congress) remained (and remains) under the leadership of Democratic Senator Joseph Biden. The potential for partisan confrontation over judgeships was present but generally did not occur as Democrats and the Bush administration exercised restraint.

In total, President Bush appointed 48 district court and 18 appeals court judges and one Supreme Court justice, for a total of 9.2 per cent of the permanent Article III judgeships on courts of general jurisdiction.[4] When the 101st Congress ended, only two district court nominees and one appeals court nominee had not been acted upon. This contrasts with the last two years of the Reagan presidency in which three district court and two appeals court nominations were withdrawn and nine district court and six appeals court nominees were not acted upon (some as a result of the Democrats' decision to wait until after the presidential election and some because the nominees were controversial).

Dick Thornburgh, who had been appointed attorney general in August of 1988 during the last six months of Reagan's presidency, was retained by Bush. Thornburgh was not as controversial as his predecessor, Edwin Meese III, and gave the impression of wanting to change the image of the Justice Department from a confrontational to a more quietly professional one.

The move away from controversy is reflected, in part, by the decision not to renominate four of the nine Reagan district court and three of the six Reagan appeals court nominees whose nominations were not acted upon by the end of the 100th Congress.[5] It is also reflected in part by Thornburgh's decision to end the Office of Legal Policy, which had been the center of judicial selection activity in the Justice Department, and to create a new office in the Justice Department, the Office of Policy Development, to handle non-judicial legal policy matters.

Thornburgh planned to bring in Robert B. Fiske, Jr., a prominent establishment lawyer and conservative Republican, to be deputy attorney general and to transfer judicial selection activity to the deputy's office as had typically been done before the Reagan administration. However, right-wing Republicans objected to Fiske because he had been chairman of the ABA Standing Committee on Federal Judiciary. To right-wing conservative groups the ABA committee, or some members of it, improperly used political or ideological criteria to assess the professional qualifications of nominees. Most grating were the four minority votes on the 15-member ABA committee finding Robert Bork not qualified for a seat on the Supreme Court.

Perhaps to defuse the opposition to Fiske as well as to recognize the importance of right-wing political support for the administration and the merits of

the complaint against the ABA, Thornburgh asked the ABA to disavow taking into consideration the political or ideological views of judicial nominees when undertaking the ABA rating process. The ABA, however, maintained the position that it did not consider such views of prospective nominees as part of the rating process unless those views had a bearing on professional qualifications such as judicial temperament, competence, and integrity. That response was unsatisfactory to the attorney general who declared that the administration would no longer consult with the ABA committee unless it reversed itself on this issue. Finally, the attorney general and the ABA committee came to an agreement that included an explicit disavowal by the ABA committee of any consideration of a nominee's political or ideological views in the rating process.[6]

Members of the Senate Judiciary Committee were dissatisfied with the ABA's role in judicial selection, the committee's rating system, and the committee's secretive processes. On June 2, 1989, the Senate Judiciary Committee held a hearing on the ABA committee's role, at which time the president of the ABA testified that in deference to the concerns of the Senate Judiciary Committee and the attorney general the ABA would eliminate the "Exceptionally Well Qualified" rating, leaving only the "Well Qualified," "Qualified," and "Not Qualified" ratings.[7] Starting in early summer, the Bush Justice Department, for the first time since Bush took office, provided the ABA with the names of intended nominees for rating purposes.

Even after the disagreement with the ABA was resolved, some key conservative senators continued to oppose Fiske. Although it appeared that were Fiske to have been formally nominated he would likely have been confirmed, the White House delayed submitting the nomination apparently to avoid a fight with some conservative Republican senators.[8] Finally, on July 6, 1989, after it was clear that the White House was reluctant to support Fiske, he asked that his name be withdrawn from consideration. By this time, judicial selection activity had been moved directly to the attorney general's office and Thornburgh's longtime aide Murray G. Dickman, assistant to the attorney general, was given responsibility for coordinating judicial selection in the Justice Department.

After the withdrawal of Fiske, the attorney general decided that judicial selection should remain centered in his office.[9] However, as a by-product of the restructuring of judicial selection within the Justice Department, the dispute with the ABA, and the attempt to appoint Fiske, only two nominations to the appeals courts and three to the district courts were sent to the Senate during the first six months of 1989 (and all the nominees had previously been nominated by Reagan). In the entire year of 1989 only a total of 22 district and appeals court nominations were sent to the Senate, while in 1990 there were more than twice that number.

Another highlight of judicial selection activity during the first two years of the Bush administration was, of course, the selection of David H. Souter to replace retiring Justice William J. Brennan, Jr. Filling the vacancy was a potential minefield because of the abortion issue, but the administration avoided a contentious confrontation battle by choosing a low-profile, non-doctrinaire, conservative judge with no public position on abortion rights. After a tour-de-force performance before the Senate Judiciary Committee, Souter was confirmed on October 2, 1990, by a vote of 90 to 9.

Another general point of note concerning the selection process is the increasing activity of interest groups in the selection process. The Alliance for Justice along with People for the American Way, both civil liberties oriented groups, began issuing annual reports on lower court nominations and distributing them to the media. Other liberal as well as conservative groups paid close attention to who was nominated. These groups communicated their views to the Justice Department and to senators, particularly those on the Senate Judiciary Committee.

At the start of the Bush administration there were a number of questions about how judicial selection would proceed and what would be the Bush imprint on the judiciary.[10] After two years of the Bush administration the answers to those questions are taking shape. We will next examine in greater detail the judicial selection process under Bush. This will be followed by the professional, demographic, and attribute profiles of the Bush appointees compared to those of previous Republican Presidents Reagan, Ford, and Nixon and Democratic Presidents Carter and Johnson. The final portions of this article will consider whether there is already a Bush imprint on the judiciary as well as speculate on future judicial selection developments during the next two years and what the likely shape of the judiciary will be after the administration has filled the 85 newly created judgeships

along with current and expected vacancies.

Principal data sources for Tables 1 and 2 included the questionnaires completed by the judicial nominees and submitted to the Senate Judiciary Committee, transcripts of confirmation hearings, personal interviews, certain biographical directories,[11] and answers by nominees to queries from this author. Occasionally, newspaper stories from the appointee's home state contained relevant data. The data appearing in the tables are for those confirmed by the 101st Congress to lifetime appointments on courts of general jurisdiction.

Selection under Bush

Two major judicial selection innovations of the Reagan administration—the systematic screening process emphasizing judicial philosophy and including extensive personal interviews of the major candidates, and the creation of the President's Committee on Federal Judicial Selection—were continued by the Bush administration. The interviewing of prospective nominees is done essentially within the Justice Department. The leading candidates for appeals court and district court judgeships are invited to Washington at their own expense (federal law prohibits reimbursement) and are interviewed by various Justice Department officials, including the deputy attorney general and the solicitor general. The interviews are for the purpose of allowing Justice officials to gain a first-hand understanding of the candidate's judicial philosophy as well as his/her intellectual ability. Candidates are *not* asked, just as they were not asked during the Reagan administration, how they would decide particular cases or whether they favor overturning such Supreme Court precedents as *Roe v. Wade*.[12]

As part of the screening process, Justice officials analyze a candidate's judicial record if the candidate has one. Analysis of the judicial record is also undertaken in the White House Counsel's office. Assistant White House Counsel Lee Liberman, in particular, analyzes judicial opinions and focuses on how candidates think about legal problems and arrive at judicial solutions.

The President's Committee on Federal Judicial Selection meets weekly at the White House, usually for two to three hours. The agenda is distributed in advance and the committee is chaired by White House Counsel C. Boyden Gray. The meetings themselves are run informally. Membership on the committee is somewhat different than during the Reagan administration. The Assistant Attorney General for Policy Development, the successor to the Office of Legal Policy, no longer handles judicial selection and, therefore, is not a member of the committee. Murray Dickman, assistant to the attorney general who coordinates judicial selection in the Justice Department, is, as one would expect, a member of the committee. So is Assistant White House Counsel Lee Liberman, who focuses on judicial nominations and whose office processes the nominations for the president's signature.

Like the committee during the Reagan administration, the committee during the Bush administration also consists of the attorney general, the deputy attorney general, the assistant to the president for personnel, and the assistant to the president for legislative affairs. The White House Chief of Staff, just as during the Reagan administration, is a member of the committee and also just as during the Reagan administration is usually too preoccupied with other matters and attends meetings infrequently.

For district court appointments, the Justice Department asks Republican senators to submit three names for Department consideration. There has been some resistance on the part of some senators, but the administration is not sympathetic to senators who submit one name and insist that person be named. However, the Justice Department will consider one candidate at a time provided that if the person proposed is not satisfactory to Justice, the senator will submit another name until a suitable candidate is found.

Bush has told those in the administration handling judicial nominations to keep in mind four points: (1) that he wants to name highly qualified persons who are philosophically conservative; (2) that he is looking for persons sensitive to the separation of powers under the Constitution; (3) that recruitment of judges should be opened up to provide greater access for qualified people than achieved under old-boy networks; and (4) that recruitment should be expanded to search out appropriately qualified women and minorities.[13] Although points 3 and 4 are similar to recruitment objectives of the Carter administration, the Bush administration did not embrace the selection commission method favored by Carter that, in fact, did objectively open up access to the judiciary.[14] It is difficult to determine just how successful the Bush

administration has been in opening the process beyond what appears to be the willingness of Justice officials to consider highly qualified persons without strong party connections. As for the Bush record of women and minority appointments, Tables 1 and 2, as discussed shortly, reveal the extent of their success.

Another feature of the Bush selection process is what appears to be an even more subtle shift to the White House in terms of the process of determining who is to be nominated. During the Carter administration, the White House counsel's office tried to promote affirmative action candidacies, but was at a disadvantage as the Justice Department maintained effective control of the nomination process. The Reagan administration effectuated a formal White House role with the establishment of the President's Committee on Federal Judicial Selection that met regularly at the White House and which produced shared control of the nomination process. Now the Bush administration has not only continued the committee and maintained shared control, but appears to have expanded the role of the White House counsel's office in the nomination process. It is perhaps significant to note that outgoing Assistant Attorney General for Legal Policy Stephen J. Markman not only briefed Assistant to the Attorney General Murray Dickman as to the selection process, he also briefed Assistant White House Counsel Lee Liberman.

White House Counsel C. Boyden Gray ordinarily consults with and briefs the president on judicial nomination matters. When the president has thoughts concerning judicial selection, the chain of communication is typically from the president to the White House counsel to the attorney general. This, of course, does not suggest any strain in relationship between the Justice Department and the White House. Indeed, all the evidence suggests a close day-to-day working relationship between the attorney general's office and the White House counsel's office. The evidence also suggests that there is a consensus between the Bush Justice Department and the White House in evaluating candidacies and applying the criteria set by the president. But the stage may be set for some future administration employing the same institutional arrangement to assert the supremacy of the Office of the White House Counsel over the Justice Department in deciding whom to nominate. If in some future administration the White House is more concerned with patronage considerations than professional merit and the reverse is true for the Justice Department, the end result could have a considerable impact on the judiciary.

After the initial strain in relations with the ABA Committee was resolved, the Justice Department resumed submitting names of likely nominees to the committee. One name, and not several, is given for each vacancy. Thus far, no one with a majority rating of *Not Qualified* has been nominated. However, seven nominees received a split majority *Qualified*/minority *Not Qualified* rating. No doubt, this was as unwelcome for the Bush administration as similar split ratings were for the Reagan administration, despite the ABA's assurance that a majority *Qualified* rating means that the individual receiving it is fully qualified for judicial office. The ABA Committee continues its policy of not explaining individual ratings and not revealing the raw vote totals. Its meetings continue to be closed to the public, a practice upheld by the Supreme Court in 1989 in *Public Citizen v. U.S. Dept. of Justice.*[15] Indeed, the Court's decision on June 21, 1989, ended the uncertainty concerning the committee's operations that threatened to remove it from the selection process.

District court appointments

In Table 1 we find selected backgrounds and attributes of the 48 Bush appointees to the federal district courts confirmed by the 101st Congress in 1989 and 1990 as compared to the federal district court appointees of Bush's five predecessors.

Occupation. The figures for occupation at time of appointment suggest that the proportion of appointees recruited from the largest law firms was approximately the same as that of the Reagan appointees, which in turn was higher than that of previous administrations. This is particularly true for the proportion recruited from the superfirms (100 or more partners/associates). Overall, however, the proportion of Bush appointees drawn from private practice was lower than that for the Reagan administration.

Close to half of the Bush appointees were recruited directly from the judiciary, and this was the highest proportion of all six administrations. These figures lend support to the suggestion that the administration was more concerned with recruiting highly qualified, philosophically compatible persons (with judicial records that could be scruti-

nized) than with recruiting those whose most prominent qualifications were their political activism.

Unlike the Reagan administration that drew in excess of 10 per cent of its appointees from the U.S. attorney's office, the Bush administration proportion was about 6 per cent. Of the six administrations, the only one with a lower proportion was the Carter administration. Like the Reagan administration, however, the proportion of law professors appointed to the district courts was lower than that of the Carter, Nixon, and Johnson administrations. Because Republican senators play an important role in judicial selection and also because the number of Bush appointees is relatively low, these findings should be kept in perspective.

Experience. Half the Bush appointees had previous judicial experience with all but one of them a sitting judge at the time of appointment. In terms of judicial experience, only the Carter appointees exceeded Bush's. As for prosecutorial experience, the Bush proportion was lower than that for the Reagan appointees and the lowest of all six administrations. Similarly, the proportion of Bush appointees with neither judicial nor prosecutorial experience was also the lowest of all six administrations.

Starting with the Carter administration, there was a tendency for the appointees to have more judicial than prosecutorial experience. Previously, it was the other way around. A judicial record, of course, can be evaluated to determine the judge's philosophical orientation, judicial temperament, and dispositional tendencies. We know that these were concerns of the Bush administration. Additionally, by promoting state judges or federal magistrates or bankruptcy judges to the federal district bench, the concept of a professionalized career judiciary was reinforced.[16]

Education. If socioeconomic differences between the Republican and Democratic parties are reflected in the backgrounds of judicial appointees, they are likely to show up in the type of education of the appointees. The findings in Table 1 for undergraduate education do seem to hint at such differences. Only a minority of the appointees of Democratic presidents Johnson and Carter had a private undergraduate school experience, whereas the majority of the appointees of Republicans Nixon, Ford, Reagan, and Bush received a private school education.

When law school education is examined, the

Table 1   How Bush's appointees to the district courts compare to the appointees of Reagan, Carter, Ford, Nixon, and Johnson

	Bush % N	Reagan % N	Carter % N	Ford % N	Nixon % N	Johnson % N
Occupation						
Politics/gov't	10.4%	12.8%	4.4%	21.2%	10.6%	21.3%
	5	37	9	11	19	26
Judiciary	47.9%	37.2%	44.6%	34.6%	28.5%	31.1%
	23	108	90	18	51	38
Large law firm						
100+ members	6.2%	5.9%	2.0%	1.9%	0.6%	0.8%
	3	17	4	1	1	1
50-99	4.2%	5.2%	6.0%	3.9%	0.6%	1.6%
	2	15	12	2	1	2
25-49	6.2%	6.6%	6.0%	3.9%	10.1%	—
	3	19	12	2	18	—
Moderate size firm						
10-24 members	10.4%	10.3%	9.4%	7.7%	8.9%	12.3%
	5	30	19	4	16	15
5-9	8.3%	9.0%	10.4%	17.3%	19.0%	6.6%
	4	26	21	9	34	8
Small firm						
2-4	4.2%	7.6%	11.4%	7.7%	14.5%	11.5%
	2	22	23	4	26	14
Solo	—	2.8%	2.5%	1.9%	4.5%	11.5%
	—	8	5	1	8	14
Professor of law	2.1%	2.1%	3.0%	—	2.8%	3.3%
	1	6	6	—	5	4
Other	—	0.7%	0.5%	—	—	—
	—	2	1	—	—	—
Experience						
Judicial	50.0%	46.6%	54.5%	42.3%	35.2%	34.4%
	24	135	110	22	63	42
Prosecutorial	37.5%	44.1%	38.6%	50.0%	41.9%	45.9%
	18	128	78	26	75	56
Neither one	27.1%	28.3%	28.2%	30.8%	36.3%	33.6%
	13	82	57	16	65	41
Undergraduate education						
Public	41.7%	35.5%	57.4%	48.1%	41.3%	38.5%
	20	103	116	25	74	47
Private	50.0%	50.3%	32.7%	34.6%	38.5%	31.1%
	24	146	66	18	69	38
Ivy League	8.3%	14.1%	9.9%	17.3%	19.6%	16.4%
	4	41	20	9	35	20
None indicated	—	—	—	—	0.6%	13.9%
	—	—	—	—	1	17
Law school education						
Public	47.9%	42.4%	50.5%	44.2%	41.9%	40.2%*
	23	123	102	23	75	49
Private	39.6%	45.5%	32.2%	38.5%	36.9%	36.9%
	19	132	65	20	66	45
Ivy League	12.5%	12.1%	17.3%	17.3%	21.2%	21.3%
	6	35	35	9	38	26

proportion of Bush appointees with a prestigious Ivy League law school education is about the same as that of the Reagan appointees, and the proportions of both sets of appointees were lower than that of the Carter, Ford, Nixon, and Johnson appointees. Including such prestigious non-Ivy League law schools as Berkeley, Duke, Georgetown, Northwestern, Stanford, Texas, and Virginia raises the proportion of Bush appointees with a prestige legal education to about 42 per cent.

Affirmative action. The record of the Bush administration of selecting qualified women to the district courts is better proportionately than the Reagan administration's record. Indeed, it surpasses all previous administrations with the exception of Carter's. The record of black-American appointments, however, matches the low proportion of appointments by Reagan, which was the worst record since Eisenhower. The proportion of Hispanic-American appointments is also low and is less than half the Reagan proportion. No Asian-Americans received appointments for the first time since the Nixon administration.

ABA Ratings. As recounted earlier, the Bush administration's dispute with the ABA Committee on Federal Judiciary was resolved, in part, by the

Table 1 (continued)

	Bush % N	Reagan % N	Carter % N	Ford % N	Nixon % N	Johnson % N
Gender						
Male	89.6%	91.7%	85.6%	98.1%	99.4%	98.4%
	43	266	173	51	178	120
Female	10.4%	8.3%	14.4%	1.9%	0.6%	1.6%
	5	24	29	1	1	2
Ethnicity or race						
White	95.8%	92.4%	78.7%	88.5%	95.5%	93.4%
	46	268	159	46	171	114
Black	2.1%	2.1%	13.9%	5.8%	3.4%	4.1%
	1	6	28	3	6	5
Hispanic	2.1%	4.8%	6.9%	1.9%	1.1%	2.5%
	1	14	14	1	2	3
Asian	—	0.7%	0.5%	3.9%	—	—
	—	2	1	2	—	—
A.B.A. Ratings						
EWQ/WQ	58.3%	54.1%	50.9%	46.1%	45.3%	48.4%
	28	157	103	24	81	59
Qualified	41.7%	45.9%	47.5%	53.8%	54.8%	49.2%
	20	133	96	28	98	60
Not Qualified	—	—	1.5%	—	—	2.5%
	—	—	3	—	—	3
Party						
Democratic	4.2%	4.8%	92.6%	21.2%	7.3%	94.3%
	2	14	187	11	13	115
Republican	93.8%	93.1%	4.4%	78.8%	92.7%	5.7%
	45	270	9	41	166	7
Independent	2.1%	2.1%	2.9%	—	—	—
	1	6	6	—	—	—
Past Party Activism	62.5%	58.6%	60.9%	50.0%	48.6%	49.2%
	30	170	123	26	87	60
Religious origin or affiliation						
Protestant	64.6%	60.3%**	60.4%	73.1%	73.2%	58.2%
	31	175	122	38	131	71
Catholic	22.9%	30.0%	27.7%	17.3%	18.4%	31.1%
	11	87	56	9	33	38
Jewish	12.5%	9.3%	11.9%	9.6%	8.4%	10.7%
	6	27	24	5	15	13
Net Worth						
Under $200,000	6.2%	17.6%	35.8%***	NA	NA	NA
	3	51	53			
200-499,999	29.2%	37.6%	41.2%	NA	NA	NA
	14	109	61			
500-999,999	31.2%	21.7%	18.9%	NA	NA	NA
	15	63	28			
1+million	33.3%	23.1%	4.0%	NA	NA	NA
	16	67	6			
Total number of appointees	48	290	202	52	179	122
Average age at nomination	49.6	48.7	49.7	49.2	49.1	51.4

*Two Johnson appointees (1.6%) did not attend law school.

**There was one Reagan district court appointee self-classified as non-denominational.

***These figures are for appointees confirmed by the 96th Congress. Professor Elliot Slotnick of Ohio State University generously provided the net worth figures for all but six Carter district court appointees for whom no data were available.

committee's agreement to eliminate the *Exceptionally Well Qualified* rating. Now the highest rating is *Well Qualified*. Table 1 merges the *Exceptionally Well Qualified* and the *Well Qualified* ratings for the Reagan, Carter, Ford, Nixon, and Johnson appointees so as to enable a comparison to the Bush appointees. When that comparison is made, it appears that the Bush appointees have the highest ABA ratings of all six administrations. If the ABA ratings are taken as fair representations of legal ability, the Bush appointees as a group have the largest proportion of appointees with the highest

ABA ratings since the Kennedy administration.[17]

Despite the unprecedented proportion of those with the highest ABA ratings, 30 per cent of those with the *Qualified* rating received a split *Qualified/ Not Qualified* rating which meant that an unspecified number of members of the ABA committee, although not in the majority, perhaps even only one member, rated the appointee to be *Not Qualified*. This was a higher proportion than that of the Reagan second-term appointees (about 25 per cent). This lack of consensus within the committee may suggest that some less-than-first-class lawyers are coming to the bench. Without a majority and minority report justifying the basis for each rating, it is difficult to know precisely why some appointees met with a less than unanimous seal of committee approval. However, it should be stressed that the official committee position is that any appointee receiving a *Qualified* rating is considered to be fully qualified for judicial office whether or not the committee is unanimous.[18]

Other considerations. As expected, President Bush appointed an overwhelming proportion of Republicans to the district courts, a proportion about the same as that of Reagan's. Table 1 also presents figures for party activism that show over 62 per cent of the Bush appointees with a history of party activism. This is an even higher proportion than that of the Reagan administration and proportionally is the highest of all six administrations. These figures, however, seem to undermine the observation made earlier that the Bush administration may be placing *less* emphasis on party activity than previous administrations. The explanation for this contradiction lies simply in the fact that an appointee was classified as being a party activist if at any time (including college and law school years) the appointee was politically active. Much of the Bush appointees' party activism was not recent involvement in national politics or even necessarily close political ties with Republican senators. Thus the high proportion for the Bush appointees does not signal that party activism was an unusually important criterion in the selection process.

The religious origins or religious affiliations of the appointees is shown in Table 1.[19] Before the Reagan administration, Democratic administrations appointed larger proportions of Catholics than Republican administrations, reflecting the large proportion of Catholics affiliated with the Democratic party and represented in the pool from which the judiciary is drawn. But Catholic political allegiances shifted significantly towards the Republican party particularly in the 1980s. Indeed, the proportion of Catholics appointed by Reagan exceeded Carter's and about equaled Johnson's. The proportion of Catholics appointed by Bush, however, appears to have declined somewhat although it is higher than Nixon's and Ford's. The proportion of Jewish appointees by Bush was the highest of all six administrations, but the relatively small numbers involved requires us to treat this finding as no more than highly tentative. It

appears that religion is not a factor in the selection process.

Table 1 also presents the net worth of the Bush, Reagan, and Carter appointees. In 1989, the previous analysis of judicial appointments contained the observation that: "Without a more competitive pay scale, we can expect an increase in the number of wealthy individuals who become judges as some non-wealthy highly qualified lawyers will not be able to afford a pay cut to go on the bench."[20] That expectation was borne out as the proportion of millionaires appointed by Bush reached one-third, an increase over the proportion for the Reagan appointees, which, in turn, had been a dramatic increase over the Carter proportion of millionaires. However, effective January 1, 1991, judicial salaries increased by 28.6 per cent (which includes a one-time 25 per cent salary increase and 3.6 per cent cost of living adjustment). Although the new judicial salaries still are not at the level recommended by the Commission on Executive, Legislative and Judicial Salaries in 1988, they come close.[21] It will be of interest to see two years from now whether proportionately more people of more modest means are becoming judges now that the salaries are somewhat more attractive.

If the Bush administration is seeking to recruit younger judges, much like it appeared during Reagan's second term,[22] that is not necessarily reflected in the finding reported in Table 1. The average age at time of nomination of the Bush appointees was higher than that for the Nixon, Ford, and Reagan appointees. During the Reagan administration the proportion of those appointed under the age of 40 was about 7 per cent for the first term and about 12 per cent for the second term. The proportion for the Bush appointees was about 8 per cent. For the Reagan appointees the proportion *under* the age of 45 was 26 per cent in the first term and 37 per cent in the second term. For the Bush appointees the proportion was about 31 per cent.

Appeals court appointments

Table 2 reveals the findings regarding the Bush administration's 18 appointees to the courts of appeals. The relatively low number of Bush appointees as well as the low number of Ford appointees requires that percentage differences be treated cautiously.

Occupation and experience. When examining

Table 2, we note that the proportion of appeals court appointees drawn by Bush from the sitting judiciary was about the same as that of the Reagan, Nixon, and Johnson administrations. But whereas about one in four Reagan appointees came from private law practice and one in eight from law schools, about one in three Bush appointees came from private practice and none from the law schools. About one in eight Bush and Reagan appointees came from large law firms. It is possible that the Reagan administration exhausted the supply of prominent conservative law professors and that no obvious academic bright light was there to be chosen by Bush in the geographic areas in which there were appeals court vacancies. It is also possible that the lack of appointing law professors was more a matter of finding the right academic for the right vacancy. If the latter reflects the reality, we can expect law professors to be selected; but it is uncertain whether Bush will match the relatively high proportions of law professors appointed by Reagan and Carter.

The proportion of Bush appointed appeals judges with neither previous judicial nor prosecutorial experience was similar to that for the Reagan and Carter administrations. For these administrations, lack of such experience apparently posed no serious obstacles to appointment.

Education and affirmative action. Like the Reagan and Carter appointees, the large majority of Bush appointees were educated as undergraduates and law school students in non-public schools. The Bush appointees had the lowest proportion of all six administrations of those educated at a publicly supported law school. The proportion of Bush appointees with an Ivy League law school education was higher than that of the Reagan appointees. However, when prestige non-Ivy League law schools such as those mentioned in the discussion of district court appointees are included, the proportion of both the Bush and Reagan appointees is approximately the same—about 45 per cent.

The Bush record of appointment of women is proportionately the second best in our history, exceeding that of the Reagan administration. Because the total number of Bush appeals court appointees is low, it cannot be said with certainty that this reflects either a trend or an appointment priority. However, taken in conjunction with the larger proportion (than achieved by the Reagan administration) of women district court appoin-

tees, it is plausible to argue that this proportion can be seen as demonstrating a Bush administration commitment to the recruitment of qualified women.

Only one African-American and one Hispanic-American received appointments by the Bush administration. No Asian-American received an appointment. Greater efforts by the administration will be needed to bring to fruition the president's stated desire to open the door of opportunity to qualified minorities.

ABA ratings. About three out of four Bush appointees received the highest ABA ratings compared to the Reagan record of three out of five. Only one Bush appointee received a split *Qualified/ Not Qualified* rating, but that split rating went for the first time to a sitting federal district judge. Because the ABA committee does not offer reasons for its ratings there is no basis for knowing what moved the minority of the committee to a rating of *Not Qualified.* Before the Bush administration, the ABA ratings of U.S. district judges nominated for elevation were typically *Well Qualified* or *Exceptionally Well Qualified.* It is possible that political-ideological considerations were behind the elevation of this judge. It is also possible that political-ideological considerations motivated the minority *Not Qualified* rating. Alternatively, this appointee may in fact be only marginally qualified. Nevertheless, on balance, if the ABA ratings are considered a measure of professional quality, none of the previous five administrations exceeded the Bush record in appointing highly qualified people. In general, then, the Bush appointees can be considered to be among the best qualified judges to assume the appellate bench.

Other considerations. Like the Reagan administration before it, the Bush administration failed to name even one Democrat to the appeals courts. Before the Reagan administration, it was the Kennedy administration that provided an instance of a president failing to find even one member of the opposition party worthy of a position on an appeals court. Also like the Reagan appointees, about two out of three appointees had some background of party activism. Only the Carter appointees had a higher proportion of appointees with a background of prior partisan activism.

The relatively small number of Bush appointees means that comparisons of proportions of the Bush appointees to those of previous administrations must not place too much emphasis on some-

Table 2 How Bush's appointees to the appeals courts compare to the appointees of Reagan, Carter, Ford, Nixon, and Johnson

	Bush % N	Reagan % N	Carter % N	Ford % N	Nixon % N	Johnson % N
Occupation						
Politics/gov't	11.1% 2	6.4% 5	5.4% 3	8.3% 1	4.4% 2	10.0% 4
Judiciary	55.6% 10	55.1% 43	46.4% 26	75.0% 9	53.3% 24	57.5% 23
Large law firm						
100+ members	5.6% 1	3.9% 3	1.8% 1	— —	— —	— —
50-99	11.1% 2	2.6% 2	5.4% 3	8.3% 1	2.2% 1	2.5% 1
25-49	— —	6.4% 5	3.6% 2	— —	2.2% 1	2.5% 1
Moderate size firm						
10-24 members	16.7% 3	3.9% 3	14.3% 8	— —	11.1% 5	7.5% 3
5-9	— —	6.4% 5	1.8% 1	8.3% 1	11.1% 5	10.0% 4
Small firm						
2-4 members	— —	1.3% 1	3.6% 2	— —	6.7% 3	2.5% 1
Solo	— —	— —	1.8% 1	— —	— —	5.0% 2
Professor of law	— —	12.8% 10	14.3% 8	— —	2.2% 1	2.5% 1
Other	— —	1.3% 1	1.8% 1	— —	6.7% 3	— —
Experience						
Judicial	55.6% 10	60.3% 47	53.6% 30	75.0% 9	57.8% 26	65.0% 26
Prosecutorial	33.3% 6	28.2% 22	32.1% 18	25.0% 3	46.7% 21	47.5% 19
Neither one	38.9% 7	34.6% 27	37.5% 21	25.0% 3	17.8% 8	20.0% 8
Undergraduate education						
Public	33.3% 6	24.4% 19	30.4% 17	50.0% 6	40.0% 18	32.5% 13
Private	50.0% 9	51.3% 40	50.0% 28	41.7% 5	35.6% 16	40.0% 16
Ivy League	16.7% 3	24.4% 19	19.6% 11	8.3% 1	20.0% 9	17.5% 7
None indicated	— —	— —	— —	— —	4.4% 2	10.0% 4
Law school education						
Public	22.2% 4	39.7% 31	39.3% 22	50.0% 6	37.8% 17	40.0% 16
Private	44.4% 8	37.2% 29	19.6% 11	25.0% 3	26.7% 12	32.5% 13
Ivy League	33.3% 6	23.1% 18	41.1% 23	25.0% 3	35.6% 16	27.5% 11

what small percentage differences. Nevertheless, it appears from Table 2 that the Bush administration exceeded the Reagan administration in the proportion of Catholics appointed to the appeals courts, a proportion that appears to be the highest of all six administrations. Once again, this may be a manifestation of the changing composition of the Republican party, and also it may be indicative of the total eradication of religious discrimination of the most subtle kind in judicial recruitment.

The net worth of the Bush appointees is presented in Table 2 and reveals that just as with Bush's district court appointees about one out of three appeals court appointees were millionaires. There was a lower proportion of Reagan appointees who were millionaires and a much lower proportion for the Carter appointees. The reasons offered in the discussion of the Bush district court appointees are applicable here. It will be of interest to see whether the new salary scale of the federal judiciary will broaden the socio-economic backgrounds of the appointees. Of course, the Republican party tends to attract larger proportions of the upper-income electorate than does the Democratic party, thus the relationship between salary scale and net worth may not be able to be tested until there is a Demo-

Table 2 (continued)

	Bush % N	Reagan % N	Carter % N	Ford % N	Nixon % N	Johnson % N
Occupation						
Male	88.9%	94.9%	80.4%	100.0%	100.0%	97.5%
	16	74	45	12	45	39
Female	11.1%	5.1%	19.6%	—	—	2.5%
	2	4	11	—	—	1
Ethnicity or race						
White	88.9%	97.4%	78.6%	100.0%	97.8%	95.0%
	16	76	44	12	44	38
Black	5.6%	1.3%	16.1%	—	—	5.0%
	1	1	9	—	—	2
Hispanic	5.6%	1.3%	3.6%	—	—	—
	1	1	2	—	—	—
Asian	—	—	1.8%	—	2.2%	—
	—	—	1	—	1	—
A.B.A. Ratings						
EWQ/WQ	77.8%	59.0%	75.0%	58.3%	73.3%	75.0%*
	14	46	42	7	33	30
Qualified	22.2%	41.0%	25.0%	33.3%	26.7%	20.0%
	4	32	14	4	12	8
Not Qualified	—	—	—	8.3%	—	2.5%
	—	—	—	1	—	1
Party						
Democratic	—	—	82.1%	8.3%	6.7%	95.0%
	—	—	46	1	3	38
Republican	94.4%	97.4%	7.1%	91.7%	93.3%	5.0%
	17	76	4	11	42	2
Independent	5.6%	1.3%	10.7%	—	—	—
	1	1	6	—	—	—
Other	—	1.3%	—	—	—	—
	—	1	—	—	—	—
Past Party Activism	66.7%	69.2%	73.2%	58.3%	60.0%	57.5%
	12	54	41	7	27	23
Religious origin or affiliation						
Protestant	55.6%	55.1%	60.7%	58.3%	75.6%	60.0%
	10	43	34	7	34	24
Catholic	38.9%	30.8%	23.2%	33.3%	15.6%	25.0%
	7	24	13	4	7	10
Jewish	5.6%	14.1%	16.1%	8.3%	8.9%	15.0%
	1	11	9	1	4	6
Net Worth						
Under $200,000	5.6%	15.6%**	33.3%***	NA	NA	NA
	1	12	13	NA	NA	NA
200-499,999	33.3%	32.5%	38.5%	NA	NA	NA
	6	25	15	NA	NA	NA
500-999,999	22.2%	33.8%	17.9%	NA	NA	NA
	4	26	7	NA	NA	NA
1+ million	38.9%	18.2%	10.3%	NA	NA	NA
	7	14	4	NA	NA	NA
Total number of appointees	18	78	56	12	45	40
Average age at nomination	48.5	50.0	51.9	52.1	53.8	52.2

*There was one Johnson appointee for whom no ABA rating was requested.

**Net worth was unavailable for one appointee.

***Net worth only for Carter appointees confirmed by the 96th Congress with the exception of five appointees for whom net worth was unavailable.

cratic administration in the White House appointing federal judges.

In contrast to the findings concerning average age at time of nomination for Bush's district court judges, the findings for the Bush appeals court appointees show them to have the youngest average age of all six administrations. The average age was 1.5 years younger than that for the Reagan appointees, almost 3.5 years younger than the Carter appointees, and over 5 years younger than the Nixon appointees.[23] Administrations, of course, have more leeway over appeals court appointments than district court appointments, and these findings for age may indeed reflect a deliberate attempt on the part of the administration to select younger rather than older people so as to extend the Bush legacy.

The Bush imprint?

Has there been a Bush imprint on the judiciary?

The answer, of course, is how can there not be. More to the point, however, is the nature of that imprint. It is obvious that the full portrait of the Bush judiciary can only be drawn when the Bush administration has appointed its final judge. But the sketch we can see (and have seen) has lines extending back to the Reagan and also to previous administrations.

There was no more important decision that George Bush made with import for judicial selection than was his decision to retain Dick Thornburgh as attorney general. Thornburgh had begun service as attorney general in August of 1988 following Edwin Meese's resignation after being cleared of alleged criminal wrongdoings. Thornburgh, thus, was first a Reagan appointee. For the Bush administration, continuity with Reagan was seen as politically important in order to cement Reagan's following to the Republican party. But when Thornburgh first became attorney general, he faced a Justice Department that had its public image tarnished and one in which internal strains had taken their toll. Insofar as judicial selection was concerned, the administration had clashed frequently with the Democratic-controlled Senate Judiciary Committee, perhaps because the Reagan Justice Department had not fully grasped the political import of the Democrats assuming control of the Senate in 1987 for the first time during Reagan's presidency. Thornburgh, apparently, appreciated the new political reality and his task of rebuilding the Justice Department and its public image. It is significant that Thornburgh moved judicial selection to his office, thus assuring his continual oversight in this ongoing and sensitive task. During the first two years of Bush's presidency, Thornburgh, with only few exceptions, avoided controversial nominations . . . . Yet the profile of the Bush appointees, as we have seen, bears many similarities to the Reagan appointees.

Equally significant for judicial recruitment was George Bush's decision to continue the Reagan-initiated President's Committee on Federal Judicial Selection and to entrust its chairmanship to his close friend, White House Counsel C. Boyden Gray. Bush's insistence on naming those who shared a conservative judicial philosophy assured not only a continuation of the Reagan-initiated screening process, including extensive interviewing, but placed a parallel screening process (without the personal interviewing) at the White House level.

There has been some evidence suggesting that there has been a decisional impact of the Reagan appointees that has moved the federal courts and federal law decidedly to the right of the philosophical spectrum.[24] It is too soon to be able to gauge the decisional impact of the Bush appointees, but it is likely to be similar. It is not insignificant to note that of the 10 Bush appointments of sitting judges to the courts of appeals, nine were elevations of federal district court judges, *all* of whom had been Reagan district court appointees.

The Bush imprint, thus far, seems to include a commitment to recruit qualified women. But, in terms of results thus far, it is difficult to say the same for blacks and other ethnic minorities.

The next two years

Despite the relatively low numbers of appointees thus far, there are some trends that appear to have emerged. When the Bush administration fills the 74 new federal district and 11 new federal appeals court positions created by the Federal Judgeships Act of 1990, along with other vacancies,[25] the shape of the Bush judiciary will be considerably clearer. Nevertheless, we can safely predict that the overwhelming proportion of appointees will continue to be middle-aged, well-to-do white male Republicans. It is also likely that at least 10 per cent of the appointments will be women. We can also expect that the emphasis on judicial experience will continue since a judicial track record provides the best evidence of a judge's judicial philosophy. There will likely be efforts to recruit black-Americans and other minorities, but it is uncertain whether the Bush administration will improve upon the Reagan administration's poor record.

If there is a Supreme Court vacancy during 1991 or 1992, national attention, of course, will be centered on judicial selection. If the Souter appointment is a guide to how the administration will manage judicial selection for the highest court, we can expect a deliberate attempt to avoid controversy. This would be a particularly wise strategy to follow as the chances for presidential defeat of a Supreme Court nomination increase the closer the nomination is to a presidential election year.[26] If Justice Thurgood Marshall decides to retire from the Court, the administration will surely replace him with an African-American (to do otherwise would suggest that there is no African-American in the entire United States qualified to sit on the

Supreme Court, a position that at the least would be awkward to take for a president running for reelection). Clarence Thomas, although only 42 years old, has been mentioned by Court watchers as a possibility,[27] but it is uncertain how controversial his nomination would be (much would likely depend upon his record on the D.C. Circuit). Another possibility whose name has been mentioned is 53-year-old Judge Amalya Kearse, a highly regarded Second Circuit jurist who has served on that court since 1979.[28]

Even without another Supreme Court appointment, by 1993 George Bush will likely have named over 200 lower federal court judges, itself a major accomplishment. Added to the over 325 Reagan appointees remaining on the bench, about two-thirds of the judiciary will have been appointed by Reagan and Bush alone. By 1993, Democrats will account for only about 25 per cent of the federal bench, an imbalance exceeded only after the 20 years of appointments by Roosevelt and Truman. Just as the Roosevelt and Truman appointees carried through the constitutionalization of the New Deal, which meant institutionalizing judicial restraint in matters of governmental economic policy making, so too the Reagan and Bush appointees will be likely to constitutionalize the Reagan-Bush social agenda, which means institutionalizing judicial restraint in matters of governmental civil liberties and civil rights policy making. Rights and liberties may be subjected to majority rule in each state and in the nation to an extent not seen in almost 60 years. Whether this bodes well or ill for the nation will be a subject for continuing and vigorous debate.

NOTES

This article originally appeared in Volume 74, Number 6, April-May 1991, pages 294-306.

I would like to thank the Research Council and Dean Samuel F. Conti of the Graduate School of the University of Massachusetts at Amherst for a Faculty Fellowship Award which enabled me to conduct this research. I am also grateful to Senator Joseph Biden's staff at the Senate Judiciary Committee for their great help and cooperation and to Assistant to the Attorney General Murray G. Dickman and Deputy White House Counsel Lee Liberman for their gracious assistance. All errors of fact and interpretation are mine alone.

1. Emphasis is in the original. So is the blatant sexism. The original copy of the memorandum, with written comments by President Nixon, was withdrawn from the president's papers at Nixon's direction. However, I found a copy of the memorandum in White House Central Files, FG 50, Box 1, Folder WHCF ExFG50 The Judicial Branch [1969-1970], Nixon Presidential Materials Project.

2. I am grateful to Professor John Anthony Maltese of the University of Georgia for providing me a copy of the cover sheet with Nixon's handwritten directive and for alerting me to the existence of the Huston memo. Also see, Maltese, *The selling of Clement Haynsworth: politics and the confirmation of Supreme Court justices*, 72 JUDICATURE 338 at 343 n. 29 (1989).

3. *See* Goldman, *Reagan's judicial appointments at mid-term: shaping the bench in his own image*, 66 JUDICATURE 334 (1983); *Reaganizing the judiciary: the first term appointments*, 68 JUDICATURE 313 (1985); *Reagan's second term judicial appointments: the battle at midway*, 70 JUDICATURE 324 (1987); and *Reagan's judicial legacy: completing the puzzle and summing up*, 72 JUDICATURE 318 (1989). Also see Murphy, *Reagan's Judicial Strategy*, in Berman (ed.), LOOKING BACK ON THE REAGAN PRESIDENCY 207 (Baltimore: The Johns Hopkins University Press, 1990).

4. The 9.2 per cent figure is based on the total number of permanent lifetime judgeships excluding the newly created judgeships in the Federal Judgeships Act of 1990. Not included in this study are appointees to such specialized courts as the Court of International Trade, the U.S. Court of Appeals for the Federal Circuit, and the local courts of the District of Columbia. Article III courts of general jurisdiction consider a wide range of constitutional and statutory law issues and are therefore more politically important than the specialized courts. These courts also hold special interest for students of the judiciary and of the presidency.

5. Not all the Reagan nominees not resubmitted by Bush were controversial.

6. The committee added to its rules: "Political or ideological philosophy are not considered." See Lavelle, . . . *And the Role of the ABA*, NATIONAL LAW JOURNAL, August 6, 1990, at 43.

7. For an account of the unpublished June 2 hearing, see Biskupic, *Justice Department and ABA Settle Their Differences*, 47 CONGRESSIONAL QUARTERLY WEEKLY REPORT 1327 (June 3, 1989). At the hearing, the attorney general reported on the agreement with the ABA. The hearing was held at the urging of five Republican senators who were members of the Senate Judiciary Committee. For an account of senatorial views leading up to the hearing, see Biskupic, *ABA's Role Under Scrutiny*, 47 CONGRESSIONAL QUARTERLY WEEKLY REPORT, 896 (April 22, 1989).

8. *See* Wines, *Thornburgh Abandons Choice for Top Justice Post*, NEW YORK TIMES, July 7, 1989, at A-1, A-11.

9. Interview with Murray G. Dickman, assistant to the attorney general, January 7, 1991. Note that it was reported that in an effort to make Fiske acceptable to conservative senators, Thornburgh said that Fiske would not handle judicial selection. NEW YORK TIMES, *supra* n. 8.

10. *See, for example*, the questions raised in Goldman, *Reagan's judicial legacy*, *supra* n. 3, at 330.

11. The various directories include THE AMERICAN BENCH (5th edition), MARTINDALE-HUBBELL LAW DIRECTORY, and WHO'S WHO (national and regional editions).

12. 410 U.S. 113 (1973).

13. Interview with Lee Liberman, Deputy White House Counsel, January 9, 1991. President Bush, in a November 30, 1990, letter to Senate Minority Leader Bob Dole asked for the help of Republican senators in finding qualified women and minority district court candidates that also met the other criteria. *See* Biskupic, *Bush Boosts Bench Strength of Conservative Judges*, 49 CONGRESSIONAL QUARTERLY WEEKLY REPORT 171 (January 19, 1991).

14. For an assessment of the selection commissions during the years of Carter's presidency, see Berkson and Carbon, THE UNITED STATES CIRCUIT JUDGE NOMINATING COMMISSION: ITS MEMBERS, PROCEDURES AND CANDIDATES (Chicago: American Judicature Society, 1980) and Neff, THE UNITED STATES DISTRICT JUDGE NOMINATING COMMISSIONS: THEIR MEMBERS, PROCEDURES AND CANDIDATES (Chicago: American Judicature Society, 1981).

15. 109 S.Ct. 2558 (1989).

16. *See* Smith, *Former U.S. magistrates as district judges: the possibilities and consequences of promotion within the federal judiciary,* 73 JUDICATURE 268 (1990).

17. For the ABA ratings of the Eisenhower and Kennedy appointees, see Grossman, LAWYERS AND JUDGES 198 (New York: Wiley, 1965).

18. In general, see Slotnick, *The ABA Standing Committee on Federal Judiciary: A contemporary assessment,* 66 JUDICATURE 348, 385 (1983).

19. This has now become a difficult attribute to determine if it is not mentioned in the questionnaires or standard biographical sources. *See* the discussion in Goldman, *Reagan's second term judicial appointments, supra* n. 3, at 330. Many Bush appointees were willing to respond to my queries concerning religious affiliation or origin, but a few indicated they considered such a query offensive and irrelevant.

20. *Reagan's judicial legacy, supra* n. 3 at 323.

21. The new salaries that became effective January 1, 1991 were: for federal district judges—$125,100; for federal circuit court judges—$132,700; for associate justices of the Supreme Court—$153,600; and for the Chief Justice of the United States—$160,600. The original recommendations of the Commission on Executive, Legislative and Judicial Salaries were that the salaries of federal district judges be raised to $135,000, federal circuit court judges to $140,000, associate justices on the Supreme Court to $165,000, and the Chief Justice of the United States to $175,000. President Reagan accepted these recommendations that were supposed to become effective on February 8, 1989, but they were tied to unpopular congressional pay increases and the entire package was disapproved by both houses of Congress. The resolution of disapproval was signed by President Bush preventing the increases from going into effect. Eventually Congress enacted the Ethics Reform Act of 1989 which authorized the judicial pay increases that became effective at the start of 1991.

22. *Reagan's judicial legacy, supra* n. 3 at 323-324, 326-327.

23. About 16 per cent of Reagan's first term appeals court appointees were under the age of 45. In 1985-1986 that proportion jumped to over one-third (34.4 per cent), but in the last two years of Reagan's presidency declined to 13.3 per cent. In contrast, for the first two years of the Bush administration the proportion of appeals court appointees under the age of 45 was 22.2 per cent. In general, *see* Goldman, *The Age of Judges: Reagan's Second Term Appeals Court Appointees Compared to the Appointees of Presidents Since 1891,* 73 A.B.A.J. 94 (1987).

24. See the discussion of the studies in Goldman, *Reagan's second term judicial appointments, supra* n. 3, at 335-338. Also see Tomasi and Velma, *All the President's Men? A Study of Ronald Reagan's Appointments to the U.S. Courts of Appeals,* 87 COLUM. L. REV. 766 (1987); H. Schwartz, PACKING THE COURTS: THE CONSERVATIVE CAMPAIGN TO REWRITE THE CONSTITUTION (New York: Charles Scribner's Sons, 1988); B. Schwartz, THE NEW RIGHT AND THE CONSTITUTION: TURNING BACK THE LEGAL CLOCK (Boston: Northeastern University Press, 1990); Smith, *Polarization and change in the federal courts: en banc decisions in the U.S. courts of appeals,* 74 JUDICATURE 133 (1990); Alumbaugh and Rowland, *The links between platform-based appointment criteria and trial judges' abortion judgments,* 74 JUDICATURE 153 (1990).

25. At the beginning of the 102nd Congress the total number of vacancies, including the newly created positions, was 124 (18 to the courts of appeals and 106 to the district courts).

26. See Cameron, Cover, and Segal, *Senate Voting on Supreme Court Nominees: A Neoinstitutional Model,* 84 AM. POL. SCI. REV. 525 (1990) and Segal and Spaeth, *If a Supreme Court vacancy occurs, will the Senate confirm a Reagan nominee?,* 69 JUDICATURE 186 (1986).

27. *See, for example,* Lewis, *Panel Backs Appeals Court Nominee,* NEW YORK TIMES, February 23, 1990, at A-16.

28. Of course there are many other African-Americans qualified to sit on the Supreme Court.

"A bench happily filled:" some historical reflections on the Supreme Court appointment process

Politics and "balancing representation" may play a major role in the selection of Supreme Court justices, but the quality of those appointed has been consistently high.

by Henry Abraham

A total of only 102 individuals have served to date on the Supreme Court of the United States, evincing an average longevity exceeded only by symphony orchestra conductors. I cannot speak to the latter, but what of the former's quantifiable characteristics?[1] The 101 men and the one woman were nominated by 35 presidents, with three—W. H. Harrison, Taylor, and Carter—having no opportunity to choose anyone at all, and one, Andrew Johnson, seeing his efforts frustrated by a hostile Senate. Not counting a mere refusal to act on nominations—of which there were several—that constitutional partner in the appointment process has so far formally rejected 26 presidential nominations to the Court, all but four of these (namely, lower federal court judges Parker, Haynsworth, and Carswell, and the aborted promotion of Justice Fortas to chief justice) coming in the nineteenth century.

The total rejection figure comprises a remarkable but contemporary unthinkable 23 per cent! Why were so many rejected by the Senate? Among the reasons, seven seem to be most compelling:

• Opposition to the nominating President, not necessarily the nominee—e.g., President John Quincy Adams' nomination of sometime United States Senator from Kentucky, John J. Crittenden, in 1828.

• The nominee's involvement with a visible or contentious issue of public policy—e.g., President George Washington's nomination of South Carolina's then Chief Justice, John Rutledge, as Chief Justice of the United States in 1795, because of the outspoken nominee's vigorous opposition to the Jay Treaty of 1794.

• Senatorial opposition to the record of the incumbent Court which the nominee seemed to support—e.g., President Ulysses S. Grant's selection of his own Attorney General, Ebenezer R. Hoar, in 1870.

• Senatorial courtesy, closely linked to the presumed consultative nominating process—e.g., President Grover Cleveland's choices of William B. Hornblower and Wheeler S. Peckham in 1893 and 1894, respectively, both ardently opposed by their fellow New Yorker, Democratic Senator David B. Hill.

• A perceived "political unreliability" of the nominee—e.g., another unsuccessful Grant nomination, this one of his one-time Attorney General Caleb Cushing, to the chief justiceship in 1874.

• An alleged lack of qualification or limited ability on the nominee's part—e.g., President James Madison's selection of Connecticut attorney and ex-United States Collector of Customs, Alexander Wolcott, in 1811.

• Powerful opposition to an otherwise patently qualified nominee by special issue interest or pressure groups—e.g., President Herbert Hoover's attempted promotion of United States District Court Judge John R. Parker of North Carolina in 1930.

Not at all infrequently, more than one of these seven reasons has combined to bring about an individual's rejection. The unenviable record of having more nominees rejected than any other President (five) is held by John Tyler.

The successful appointees

The 102 successful lawyer-appointees have come

from 10 major professional sub-groups, with 22 each from three of these, i.e., the lower federal judiciary, the state judiciary, and from diverse posts in the federal executive/administrative branch. Upon ascending to the high bench they resided in 31 different states, headed by 15 from New York, nine from Ohio, eight from Massachusetts, and seven from Virginia; 10 states have sent one; 19 none at all. The latter fact of political life prompted Republican Senator William ("Wild Bill") Langer of North Dakota, then a senior member of the Senate's Committee on the Judiciary, to commence in 1953 a campaign of opposition to any and all presidential nominees to the Court until his home state received a Supreme Court nomination. He went to his grave in 1959, his wish still unrealized—as it is to this day.

The acknowledged religious preferences of the 102 individual jurists fall into 12 different groups, the only ones in "double-digit-figures" being 27 Episcopalians, 25 avowedly unspecified Protestants, and 17 Presbyterians; there have been six Roman Catholics, five Jews, and the balance have been specified other Protestant adherents. Five professed political party designations characterize the successful nominees, including one Whig, one Independent, 12 Federalists, 40 Republicans, and 48 Democrats—hence, it is difficult to categorize an overwhelming partisan flavor to the bench.

Such a flavor unmistakably, however, has informed the selection of nominees in terms of their political affiliation in concord with that of the nominating president: the lowest partisan percentage to date—and now necessarily counting *all* federal judges—having been earned by President Ford (81.2 per cent Republican), the highest by President Washington (100 per cent Federalist). The lowest partisan-correlation nomination percentage in this century for all federal judges is still President Ford's aforementioned 81.2 (President Taft's 82.2 being a close second), the highest that by the sole Ph.D. in political science so far to occupy the White House, Woodrow Wilson, who amassed a near perfect 98.6 per cent score of Democratic appointees. More or less tied for the second highest correlative slot are presidents Carter and Harding, with 97.8 Democratic and 97.7 Republican identifications, respectively.

Indubitably the profile and statistics just cited point to a broad-gauged commitment to a "representative" philosophy for judicial appointments.

Whether that is wise may be put aside for the moment in favor of an examination of the intention of the Founding Fathers on that always so lively controversial issue. The conclusion is as crystal clear as it is inevitable that "representativeness" was not even considered, let alone advocated. Merit was the sole criterion on the mind of the delegates, "representativeness" being reserved to the legislature.

Methodology, not qualifications

Monday, May 14, 1787, was the date agreed upon for the opening of the Federal Constitutional Convention in the Old Independence Hall, called the State House, down on Fifth and Chestnut Streets in Philadelphia. But since only two states—Virginia and Pennsylvania—were represented on that historic day, the Convention was compelled to adjourn for lack of a quorum. This procedure continued daily, until Friday, May 25, at last saw the requisite majority of the 13 constituent states in their seats. Some five months later, on Tuesday, September 17, 1787, the Convention adjourned, having signed the historic document, the nascent Constitution of the United States, on the preceding day, highlighted by Dr. Franklin's magnificent closing address to the assemblage (which was read for him by his fellow-Pennsylvanian, James Wilson). As the most authoritative accounts, records, and interpretations of the events of that historic period demonstrate reliably—for example, James Madison's *Notes of Debates in the Federal Convention of 1787*;[2] *The Federalist*;[3] Charles Warren's *The Making of the Constitution*;[4] and Joseph P. Harris' *The Advice and Consent of the Senate*[5]—while the question of the methodology to be employed for judicial appointments was subjected to intensive floor debate during 12 days in June, July, August and September, *criteria* for such appointments were neither debated nor did they appear to loom as a matter of either significance or puzzlement.

Those few delegates who vocalized the issue of *criteria* at all did so by assuming *viva voce* and *sub silentio* that *merit*, as opposed to favoritism, should, and indeed would, govern naturally. The central issue *cum* controversy concerned the degree of power to be vested in the executive and/or the degree of legislative participation. The provision finally agreed upon as a result of debates on September 6, 7, and 15 represented a compromise between those who, like Benjamin Franklin, James Madison, and John Rutledge, feared "monarchical" tendencies in strong solo executive prerogatives on the issue and called for a potent legislative role; and those who, like James Wilson, Alexander Hamilton, and Gouverneur Morris favored broadly independent executive appointive powers. It was the latter group that did most of the compromising, resulting in the largely James Madison-fashioned ultimate adoption of Article II, Section 2, as we know that provision today.[6]

If it may be validly considered as having been raised at all, the issue of judicial qualifications was addressed, however briefly, on June 5 by Doctor Franklin in pointing to the Scottish mode of appointment "in which the nomination proceeded from the lawyers, who always selected the ablest of the profession in order to get rid of him, and share his practice among themselves."[7] If any concern about qualifications was subsequently expressed by delegates, it came all but inevitably in connection with the controversy over the role of the participatory political branch, ultimately the agreed-upon senatorial one, about which James Madison, for one, notwithstanding his support of the legislative input, raised questions of "partiality." Delegates simply assumed, perhaps a mite naively, albeit quite understandably, that those selected as federal jurists would be chosen on the basis of merit. Period.

It is thus clear—with convenient 20/20 hindsight—that the Founding Fathers did not foresee the role political parties would soon come to play in the appointment process. Only John Adams among the notable contemporary statesmen—and he, of course, was not a member of the Constitutional Convention—visualized clearly the future rise of political parties and, as Harris put it well, "that partisan considerations rather than the fitness of nominees would often be the controlling consideration of the Senate in passing on nominations."[8]

Merit over politics

Little attention was given to the matter of judicial appointments in the debates surrounding the ensuing state ratifying conventions. It was assumed as a matter of course that merit would govern. Alexander Hamilton did address the appointment power in *The Federalist, Nos. 66, 72, 76,* and *77,* which render patently evident that even that supreme political cognoscenti verily championed merit. Thus, in his *No. 66,* he expressed full confidence that the Senate, whatever its stance on a particular nominee might be, would be guided by a candidate's *merit.*[9] In

his famed *No. 76,* in which he so trenchantly and approbatively elucidated the judicial function, he lauded the Senate's putative role as "an excellent check upon a spirit of favoritism in the President . . . [one that] would tend greatly to prevent the appointment of unfit characters from State prejudice, from family connection, from personal attachment, or from a view of popularity."[10]

And his *No. 77* assumed without self-doubt—and, of course, quite erroneously—that individual senators would not exert influence on presidential nominations. For he, too, quite unlike Adams, failed to foresee the influence that political parties would exert on appointments; the leverage they would provide thereby to an assertive chief executive; and the prominent role senators would soon play in dictating nominations.[11] In sum, and notwithstanding Hamilton's interest and concerns, the debates in the state constitutional conventions paid but passing heed, if any, to the appointive arrangements, in general, and judicial ones, in particular. Engaged by issues of far more moment to them in their crucial decision whether or not to ratify the handiwork of the Founding Fathers, they assumed that those appointed to the bench would be qualified. Merit was assumed; "representativeness" did not even surface as an academic question.

Representativeness as an issue

Yet if it was not an issue then, it has assuredly become one—and increasingly so in modern mold. Indeed, it has become a demonstrable fact of the life of government and politics that so-called "equitable considerations" in the selection and nominations to the bench are not only omnipresent, but arguably omnipotent, in the decisional processes leading to selection, nomination, and appointment. And whereas initially these commitments were perhaps confined largely to the components of political persuasion and geography, the passing parade of the century in which we live has witnessed the insistent adoption and adaption of such additional expectations and requirements as contemporarily inform the "representation" of race, gender, religion, and perhaps even age. Whatever the framers' ascertainable intentions may have been, the notion of the entitlement to a "peer model" has become all but pervasive in judicial staffing today.

If, as the great Holmes insisted so warmly, a page of history is truly worth more than a volume of logic, one might have little difficulty in arriving at history's verdict on the conundrum of "representativeness" in the appointment process. The past, however, is prologue as well as history. It may thus be argued with some cogency that the "equitable components enumerated above operate currently in a setting of our democratic polity that is naturally quite at variance with that of the late eighteenth century—in moral, in philosophical, and in political terms. It is a setting that would be demonstrably puzzling or foreign to the Founding Fathers, whose fledgling Republic enjoyed a degree of homogeneity never again to be equaled in this land's ensuing history. Nonetheless, even granting the imperatives of the polity's dramatic transformation, one may well still pose the troubling question that underlies these painful ruminations: Is the nation, is the citizenry, served better, served more appropriately, if "representativeness" is rendered a prolegomenum for judicial selection, nomination, and appointment?

The attempted answer has evoked lively, often bitter, debate for close to half-a-century now, reaching a crescendo during the past generation. [My 91-year-old friend, Dumas Malone, tells me that Mr. Jefferson's definition of "generation" encompassed 20 years. Needless to say that I would never challenge my old teacher—and assuredly not on matters Jeffersonian!] I suspect that the verdict is in: if something can be "more or less" *res judicata,* it is obvious that the political branches have embraced "representativeness." That the pages of history demonstrate beyond any shadow of a doubt that the Founding Fathers did not ponder the issue does not necessarily determine its wisdom or desirability. But it is on those frontiers that an opinion opting for the sole criterion of *merit* as *the* irreducible imperative basic threshold requirement may be respectfully submitted, joined to the plea *cum* conviction that any "plus" considerations in behalf of "representativeness" must be wholly dependent upon the demonstrable presence of merit at the threshold.

The concept of merit

The concept, the phenomenon, of merit unfortunately defies universal definition; it is neither axiom nor theorem. It may even lie entirely in the eye and mind of the beholder—but it need not do so. It is possible to suggest a merit model, and I should like to suggest one—eschewing any claim to originality.

A sextet, the model comprises the following self-evident components (in no particular order of significance):

One: demonstrated judicial temperament.
Two: professional expertise and competence.
Three: absolute personal as well as professional integrity.
Four: an able, agile, lucid mind.
Five: appropriate professional educational background or training.
Six: the ability to communicate clearly, both orally and in writing, especially the latter.

Not only are these attainable components, but the history of our Supreme Court has demonstrated their presence amply. If the Holmesian tongue-in-cheek aphorism that the job of a jurist requires a "combination of Justinian, Jesus Christ, and John Marshall"[12] may not always have been attainable—it is apposite to note that with one possible exception even that trio may not have been perfect! If political party affiliation has almost always played a role—well, there are but nine positions on the highest bench, and there are unquestionably just as many qualified Republicans as there are qualified Democrats, and as many qualified Democrats as there are qualified Republicans. Nor is there any gainsaying a nominator's resolve to select a nominee with whom he is ideologically and jurisprudentially comfortable. You would, and I would, act similarly, always assuming the presence of threshold merit.

At any rate, as president after president has found out, without any particular degree of amusement, if there is anything certain about his nominees' on-bench performance in jurisprudential terms, it is that it is hardly predictable with accuracy, let alone certainty—which, to a very considerable degree, is a comforting fact of the judicial process. "You shoot an arrow into a far-distant future," wrote Alexander M. Bickel not long before his untimely death, "when you appoint a justice and not the man himself can tell you what he will think about some of the problems he will face."[13]

That is, of course, why such wise politicians as that All-American boy President Theodore Roosevelt, in a famed exchange with Connecticut's United States Senator Henry Cabot Lodge regarding the potential candidacy of Democrat Horace H. Lurton in 1906, wrote his objecting fellow-Republican that "the nominal politics of the man has nothing to do with his actions on the bench. His *real* politics are important . . . ." And T.R. lauded Lurton's position on sundry policies "in which you and I believe."[14] Lodge concurred in substance, but replied that he saw no reason "why Republicans cannot be found who hold these opinions as well as Democrats."[15] And he urged the appointment of the incumbent attorney general, William H. Moody, whom T.R. then sent to the Court.

Interestingly, but three years later Lurton was appointed by Roosevelt's successor, William Howard Taft—and precisely because of those "real politics" with which Taft was comfortable. Incidentally, it was Taft, our only president to date who would also serve as Chief Justice of the United States, who appointed the largest number of "other Party" members—three of his six—to the Supreme Court. How Chief Justice Taft loved his post—infinitely more so than being president! He regarded his chief justiceship as ". . . next to my wife and children . . . the nearest thing to my heart in life."[16] When President Harding nominated him in 1921, Taft exulted: "I love judges and I love courts. They are my ideals on earth of what we shall meet afterward in Heaven under a just God."[17] When fatal illness truncated his career nine years later, he formally resigned in tears on February 3, 1930. On his bedside table lay a touching message from his eight colleagues: "We call you Chief Justice still, for we cannot quickly give up the title by which we have known you for all these later years and which you have made so dear to us."[18]

Yet the moving finger of time wrote rapidly: within five hours of Taft's resignation, President Hoover would nominate—with Taft's advance blessings—another giant to the center chair: ex-Associate Justice of the Supreme Court, ex-Governor of New York, one time (and almost successful) candidate for the presidency, and ex-Secretary of State, Charles Evans Hughes. Yet, notwithstanding the selectee's indubitably outstanding qualifications for the post, 26 senators voted against his confirmation and 18 abstained—whereas but four had cast "nay" votes against his predecessor. Like his predecessor, he would grace the institution that Madison had so devoutly prayed to become "happily filled."

Reasons for selection

While there has been a trickle-increase in biographical studies of Supreme Court justices, my recent involvement in researching just what has been done must render the regrettable judgment of "not nearly enough." There are many good reasons that account for that fact, among them the delicate and difficult problem of the existence and availability of the papers of justices, plus the dearth of biographical craftsmen of the stature of Alpheus Thomas Mason. Yet there are enough data to permit an annotated catalogue of the major ascertainable decisional reasons or motivations for the presidential selection of members of the bench. In rendering such judgments, one must acknowledge concurrently that only the president really knows why he either selected a nominee to the Court or gave the nod to others, in effect, to select for him.

History does demonstrate, however, that an identifiable quartet of such reasons or motivations has governed the selection process—a quartet that, were I a quantifyer or "behavioralist," might well lend itself to at least a measure of statistical proof. The quartet of criteria are: (1) objective merit; (2) personal and political friendship; (3) balancing "representation" on the Court; and (4) "real" political and ideological compatibility. Obviously, more than one of these factors was present in most of the nominations and in some all four were. Yet it is not impossible to point to one as the overriding one. My necessarily few examples endeavor to do so while minding the Jeffersonian-Malonian generational definition by doubling it and thus utilizing only illustrations that inform appointments more than 40 years ago—in any event, none made by any president after the one who had more opportunities than any other save George Washington, namely Franklin Delano Roosevelt.

1. Objective merit

A classic example of presidential selection based purely on the first category, objective merit, *qua* merit, is that of Democrat Benjamin Nathan Cardozo by Republican Herbert Hoover to succeed Justice Holmes early in 1932. The two were neither personal nor professional friends: they were hardly, not even arguably, politically or ideologically compatible; and there was no question of "balancing representation." If anything, as Hoover would soon make clear, his reluctance to appoint the long-time, great New York appellate jurist was at least partly due to the fact that two other distinguished New Yorkers already were ornaments of the bench, namely Justices Stone and

Hughes, and Cardozo's religious faith—he was a Sephardic Jew—was "represented" by Justice Brandeis. Yet if ever a nomination was forced upon a president by all but unanimous public and private acclaim, this was it.

On January 15, 1932, Oliver Wendell Holmes, Jr., now almost 91 but still alert and cheerful, had bowed to old age and precarious health and resigned. More than three decades of an incredibly productive and towering judicial career thus came to an end. How to replace the "judicial philosopher of the age"? Hoover, striking out on his own, let it be known that he would like to see a "noncontroversial western Republican" as the Old Yankee's successor. But almost at once the chairman of the Senate's Judiciary Committee, George W. Norris, made it plain to the president that he and his fellow committeemen, largely Democrats and Progressive Republicans, would insist on a judicial liberal in the Holmes mold.

Others were rather more specific: the entire faculty of the Law School of the University of Chicago urged Hoover to nominate Benjamin Nathan Cardozo, Chief Justice of the New York Court of Appeals—a man widely regarded as one of America's most brilliant jurists, one who might already have been on the U.S. Supreme Court had it not been for Chief Justice Taft's sustained opposition to him during the 1920s. The deans of the schools of law of Harvard, Yale, and Columbia universities joined in a similar strongly worded plea. Labor as well as business leaders, liberals as well as conservatives, advocates of judicial self-restraint as well as judicial activists, all participated in a uniquely unified appeal on behalf of a candidate to the Court—so strong an impression had Cardozo made, so splendid a record had he achieved during his 18 years as associate judge and chief judge on New York's highest tribunal, then probably the country's busiest and most distinguished appellate state court.

The president could hardly have been unaware of the clamor for Cardozo's nomination! The now 62-year-old bachelor had not only made his mark as a jurist, but his stylistically beautiful and scholarly publications, such as the still-seminal *The Nature of the Judicial Process*,[19] had won him universal praise. His lucid, cogent opinions, his realistic approach to law and democratic society, his love of his land and its Constitution stamped him as Holmes' logical successor. But Hoover continued to demur; he

really did not want to appoint a man, no matter how superbly and uniquely qualified he might be, from a state that already had two eminent such "representatives" whom, incidentally, he had sent there himself—and whose religion would assuredly cause Justice McReynolds to act up again (it did). No, Herbert Hoover would look elsewhere, even though Justice Stone had told him he would be willing to resign from the Court so that the nation might have Cardozo.[20]

Now, however, the powerful chairman of the Senate Foreign Relations Committee, Republican William E. Borah of Idaho, whose support Hoover needed on other fronts, became involved and loudly and repeatedly called for Cardozo's designation. No particular friend of Easterners, especially New Yorkers, Borah, like Norris, recognized Cardozo's rare merit. Twenty-four hours before Hoover had indicated he would announce his candidate publicly, he called for Borah.

In an often-told, dramatic confrontation between two proud men, the president, after discussing the vacancy generally, suddenly handed Borah a list on which he had ranked those individuals he was considering for the nomination in descending order of preference. The name at the bottom was that of Benjamin N. Cardozo. Borah glanced at it and replied: "Your list is all right, but you handed it to me upside down." Hoover protested at first: there was the geographical question to be considered and he had to take "religious or sectarian repercussions" into account. Senator Borah sharply retorted that "Cardozo belongs as much to Idaho as to New York" and that geography should no more bar the judge than the presence of two Virginians—John Blair and Bushrod Washington—should have kept President Adams from naming John Marshall to be Chief Justice." And, he added sternly, "anyone who raises the question of race (sic) is unfit to advise you concerning so important a matter."[21]

Hoover at last bowed to what he now regarded as the inevitable. His memoirs simply state: ". . . On February 15, 1932 . . . I nominated Chief Justice Benjamin N. Cardozo of the New York Court of Appeals, a Democrat. The appointment met with Senate approval."[22] Indeed it did, instantly and unanimously, and without discussion or roll call when the nomination reached the floor of the Senate a few days later. In finally appointing Cardozo, commented Zechariah Chafee, "Hoover ignored geography and made history."[23]

Cardozo's brethren on the Court were delighted: "Hope you come soon," Stone wrote him on the very day of his official nomination. "We have been saving up some interesting cases for you."[24] Accurately *The New York Times* commented that "seldom, if ever, in the history of the Court has an appointment been so universally commended."[25] But fate would allow Cardozo a scant six years on the high bench—during which he penned more than 100 expertly crafted, stylistically beautiful opinions, including the 1937 *Social Security Cases*[26] and, of course, the seminal *Palko v. Connecticut.*[27]

Cardozo's friend and fellow judicial stylist and craftsman, Learned Hand, movingly eulogized the gentle spirit shortly after his death in 1938, concluding:

In this America of ours when the passion for publicity is a disease, and where swarms of foolish, tawdry moths dash with rapture into its consuming fire, it was a rare good fortune that brought to such eminence a man so reserved, so unassuming, so retiring, so gracious to high and low, and so serene. He is gone, and while the west is still lighted with his radiance, it is well for us to pause and take count of our own coarser selves. He had a lesson to teach us if we care to stop and learn; a lesson at variance of most that we practice, and much that we profess.[28]

2. Personal and political friendship

Examples that point to personal and political friendship as the overriding causation for presidential choice are legion—although in most instances other considerations loomed as contributory, if perhaps either as buttressing or subsidiary reasons. One of the several illustrations that quickly come to mind, and that unquestionably were characterized by the threshold presence of merit, is President Andrew Jackson's selection—or, more accurately, selections—of Roger Brooke Taney upon the resignation from the Court of the octogenarian Justice Gabriel Duval of Maryland.

The worst apprehensions of contemporary Whigs and Calhounians were promptly confirmed when Jackson nominated his close friend, long-time loyal adviser and supporter, to the seat. Taney, now 58, had successfully navigated the political shoals from the localism of Maryland politics to national prominence, having served as chairman of the Jackson Central Committee of Maryland in 1828, as Jackson's attorney general and, on a recess appointment, as secretary of the treasury after the Cabinet reorgani-

zation of 1832.

It was in the latter post that Taney had incurred the undying enmity of the Whig-Calhounian political axis: he had fully approved of and complied with Jackson's order that all government deposits be removed from the Bank of the United States—the major controversy of the time. The enraged opposition struck back at Jackson and Taney by rejecting the latter's formal appointment as secretary of the treasury, thus forcing him to resign. Jackson vowed revenge, and in a letter to Taney that left little doubt that his political opponents had not heard the last of the matter, he wrote: "For the prompt and distinterested aid thus afforded me, at the risk of personal sacrifice which were then probable and which has now been realized, I feel that I owe you a debt of gratitude and regard which I have not the power to discharge . . . ."[29] Duval's resignation gave Jackson his first opportunity to discharge that debt of gratitude. The Senate thwarted him by "postponing" the nomination on the last day of its session—but not before it had voted to do away with the vacant seat entirely, a maneuver that failed of enactment, however, in the House of Representatives.

Enraged, Jackson refused to make another nomination and resolved to try Taney again. Fate played into his hands. On July 6, 1835, after almost 35 years on the bench, Mr. Chief Justice John Marshall died in Philadelphia. Jackson now had two vacancies to fill. That one of them would go to Taney was a foregone conclusion. But the president bided his time; he appeared to be considering a host of candidates for both the associate and chief justice vacancies. All attention focused on his choice for chief justice, of course. A strong possibility was the brilliant Justice James Story, but Jackson was not about to promote the man whose record out-Marshalled Marshall. There was wide advocacy of Daniel Webster, but he, too, personified the old Federalist team. A good many urged the promotion of John McLean, but he had already incurred the displeasure of the president and most Democrats by his iconoclastic behavior on the Court. Jackson kept his counsel until the end of December and then proposed Maryland's Taney to succeed John Marshall of Virginia and Philip P. Barbour of Virginia to succeed Gabriel Duval of Maryland. Even-steven geographically—and, "Senate of the United States, here we go again," Jackson might well have chuckled.

"Judge Story thinks the Supreme Court is gone, and I think so too," Daniel Webster had written on hearing of Taney's selection.[30] The remarkable chief justiceship of Taney would prove both men wrong, indeed. But first Jackson's favorite nominee would have to run the gauntlet of a hostile and powerful group of senators. For close to three months the battle raged in the upper house, but when the vote finally came it was not nearly so close as the bitter debates had led the country to believe. Taney won the nomination by a 14-vote margin, 29-15, opposed to the last by such powerful and influential Senate leaders as Calhoun, Clay, and Webster, who later would come to respect the superb performance of the man they had so ardently opposed.

Taney, whom history and the experts have justly accorded the mark of greatness, was resolved to enhance the role of the states as governmental and philosophical entities. But shrewd political tactician and skillful leader that he was, Taney knew how to exercise judicial self-restraint. Not a devotee of overt manifestations of power, he guided his Court along pathways of conciliation and compromise virtually devoid of dogmatism and ploys. Thus, not only were the Court's actions accepted by the majority of political leaders of the time, but its position as the logical ultimate, and fair-minded, arbiter of the Constitution was fully secured as well. Far from assaulting the Marshall-built fortress of judicial power, the Taney Court secured it and did so with all but general approbation.

Even the *Dred Scott* decision,[31] monumental aberration though it was, could not destroy the institution that Taney and Marshall had fashioned. It is a pity that Taney is so often remembered by that case rather than by his supreme accomplishments in achieving governmental concord and constitutional understanding. On October 12, 1864, he died at 87, having served in the center chair for three decades. Alone, tired, and disillusioned, when the end came, he did not recognize how much he had meant to his government and his people. Together, he and Marshall had presided over the Court for 65 years!

3. Balancing representation

Although demonstrated professional merit was indubitably present, a case of presidential choice committed patently to what I have categorized as the balancing of "representation," and in this instance that of *geography*, was F.D.R.'s early 1943 selection of Wiley Blount Rutledge of Iowa. Roosevelt had appointed eight justices in less than four years between 1937 and 1941. Barring unforeseeable illness or resignations, that certainly would presumably be the end of the line. Yet in October 1942 came Justice Byrne's resignation from the Court and the ninth vacancy! This time there was no obvious successor, no obvious political debt to be paid. Such major New Deal supporters as Messrs. Black, Reed, Frankfurter, Douglas, Murphy, Jackson, and Byrnes had been sent to the Court; others, such as Attorney General Francis Biddle, were not interested. At last F.D.R. might indulge his repeatedly expressed desire to nominate someone from west of the Mississippi.

There was no rush as far as he was concerned, and he asked Biddle to look around carefully for a likely candidate. The ultimate nominee, pressed on the administration by Biddle as well as by such allies as Senator Norris of Nebraska, Justices Murphy and Douglas—Frankfurter and Stone still asked for Learned Hand—and particularly by the influential *Des Moines Register* and *Chicago Sun* journalist Irving Brant, was perhaps a rather "marginal" Westerner, but with identifiable claims to that region: 49-year-old Judge Wiley Rutledge of the United States Court of Appeals for the District of Columbia. Rutledge would be the only Roosevelt appointee with federal judicial experience (four years) and one of only three with any judicial background—the other two being Black and Murphy. F.D.R. was not personally acquainted with Rutledge, but after chatting with him at the White House, and being assured by Biddle that the candidate was a bona fide libertarian, an early and solid New Dealer who ardently championed the Court-packing plan, and a judge whose opinions demonstrated a solid commitment to the presidential philosophy, he nominated him in February 1943. "Wiley, you have geography," F.D.R. beamed at his happy selectee.[32] Confirmation came readily without a formal roll call by the Senate.

Born in Kentucky, brought up there and in North Carolina and Tennessee, schooled in Tennessee and Wisconsin, Rutledge had taught and worked in the public school systems in Colorado, Indiana, and New Mexico before becoming professor of law at the University of Colorado, professor of law and dean at Washington University in St. Louis, and dean at the University of Iowa's School of Law. Once he attained the bench, Rutledge—

who genuinely loved people of all walks of life—demonstrated his libertarian commitments. Indeed, his score in behalf of individual claims against alleged violations by government was higher than any of his colleagues (followed closely by Murphy's). Thus it was Rutledge who joined Murphy's broad-gauged extensions of civil liberty safeguards beyond the Constitution's verbiage when he concurred in the latter's famed dissenting opinion in *Adamson v. California* in 1947.[33]

During his scant six and a half years on the bench Rutledge's scholarship, his mastery of law, his articulate explication of difficult issues, and his prodigious workmanship combined to establish him as an all but universally respected jurist. He left a proud record, highlighted by some celebrated dissenting opinions, such as those for *In re Yamashita*[34] and *Everson v. Board of Education of Ewing Township.*[35] The former decision upheld, 7-2, Japanese General Tomoyuki Yamashita's summary military commission conviction for violating the rules of war. The latter sanctioned, 5-4, state-subsidized transportation of parochial as well as public school students. Rutledge regarded these opinions as his best. Thus he admonished the Chief Justice Stone-led majority in *Yamashita* that it "is not in our tradition for anyone to be charged with crime which is defined after his conduct, alleged to be criminal, has taken place; or in language not sufficient to inform him of the nature of the offense or to enable him to make defense. Mass guilt we do not impute to individuals . . . ."[36] And, in *Everson*, before appending Madison's "Memorial and Remonstrance Against Religious Assessment," Rutledge warned the Justice Black-authored majority:

Like St. Paul's freedom, religious liberty with a great price must be bought. And for those who exercise it most fully, by insisting upon religious education for their children mixed with secular by the terms of our Constitution the price is greater than for others.[37]

When he succumbed to a cerebral hemorrhage at 55 while vacationing in Maine in September, 1949, an era had come to an end. Justice Rutledge—for whom Justice John Paul Stevens would clerk in 1947-48—had been the last of the nine Roosevelt appointees.

4. Political/ideological compatibility

The last of my suggested quartet of historically demonstrable major motivations in the presidential selection process of future justices of the Su-

preme Court is that of "real" political and ideological compatibility. My chosen example again points to the salutary fact that, notwithstanding the identifiable commitment to one or more of the quartet, threshold merit is prolegomenum or accompanist. Thus, it was patently true, too, of President Harding's Chief Justice Taft-inspired selection of George Sutherland of Utah in 1922.

That September 4, Justice John Hessin Clarke of Ohio had resigned after less than six years of service. The following day the president nominated the then 60-year-old Sutherland, and the Senate confirmed its two-term ex-fellow senator on the very same day, thereby establishing a speed record in the appointment process. Seldom in the history of the Court had, or indeed has, a successor-candidate been so universally obvious: a close personal and political ally of the president, Sutherland was insistently and enthusiastically backed by Taft, who earlier had written to the nominee: "I look forward to having you on the bench with me. I know, as you do, that the president intends to put you there."[38] Sutherland was the first (and to date the only) Supreme Court justice from Utah and one of the very few of foreign birth (England) to reach the Court.

Sutherland came to it with a wealth of legal and governmental experience: a leading expert in constitutional law and an active member of the Utah and U.S. Supreme Court bars for many years, he had served in the Utah Senate and the U.S. House of Representatives as well as the U.S. Senate. His friendship with Harding began when the two served together in the upper house, the association culminating in the role of brain truster to the president. He could have had any position in the Harding administration he desired; but he preferred to accept spot and trouble-shooting assignments in Washington and abroad—in frank anticipation of a vacancy on the Court.

Once he attained the high tribunal, George Sutherland demonstrated that the evaluation of his supporters had been entirely correct: he not only proved himself to be the judicial conservative everyone knew him to be, but he soon became the lucid and articulate spokesman for the Court's so-called Darwin-Spencer wing (also consisting of his colleagues Van Devanter, McReynolds, and Butler). The jurist whom his biographer characterized aptly as "A Man Against the State"[39] spent 16 years on the Court as the personification of those against whom Holmes had railed in his anguished *Lochner* dissent, exclaiming that "The Fourteenth Amendment does not enact Mr. Herbert Spencer's Social Statics."[40] Yet to Sutherland, the Fourteenth Amendment meant "Keep-your-hands-off, government!" and in the libertarian as well as the proprietarian sense. Thus it was he who in 1932 wrote the 7-2 majority opinion in the landmark "Scottsboro Case," *Powell v. Alabama*,[41] which became the bellwether in the gradually developing application of procedural safeguards in the Bill of Rights to the states by way of interpretation of the due process of law clause of the Fourteenth Amendment.

As the intellectual leader of the so-called "Four Horsemen" and their allies, Sutherland proved himself a worthy successor of the Field-Brewer-Peckham wing of the Fuller Court era. In the 1930s he became the scourge of the New Deal, heading a majority that struck down more than a dozen pieces of domestic legislation fundamental to the New Deal in 1935-36.[42] Yet he was not blindly opposed to the exercise of governmental power, particularly in the realm of foreign relations. One of the most significant opinions in support of presidential authority, *United States v. Curtiss-Wright Export Corporation*, was from his pen. It is only just that no matter how many of them have disapproved of his philosophical imperatives, leading students of the Court have never hesitated to accord him the high regard and rating history has so deservedly bestowed upon him.

* * *

The four illustrations selected almost at random, as well as the numerous others alluded to with affection and admiration throughout these reflections, testify to the rich mine of giants that have served so remarkably well on the Court in its now almost two centuries of life. They provide proof positive of promises fulfilled and achievements rendered. Indeed, notwithstanding the often tiresome, and not infrequently self-serving—albeit exasperating—sniping that has characterized the Court's existence, sniping that has regrettably, although not surprisingly, emanated most loudly from prestigious centers of learning located near bodies of water on both the East and West Coasts, it has, I submit with conviction, truly been, in James Madison's words, a "bench happily filled." His wish *cum* plea, expressed in 1787, has stood the test of time admirably.

NOTES

This article originally appeared in Volume 66, Number 7, February 1983, pages 282-295. It was adapted from the "Annual Lecture" presented to The Supreme Court Historical Society on April 30, 1982 in the restored Supreme Court Chamber in the U.S. Capitol.

1. The following statistical information is taken from Abraham, JUSTICES AND PRESIDENTS: A POLITICAL HISTORY OF APPOINTMENTS TO THE SUPREME COURT, esp. Chs. 2 and 3 (New York: Oxford University Press, 1974 and Penguin Press, 1975).

2. Madison, NOTES OF DEBATES IN THE FEDERAL CONVENTION OF 1787; Introduction by Adrienne Koch (Athens, OH: Ohio University Press, 1966).

3. Lodge (ed.), THE FEDERALIST (New York: G.P. Putnam's Sons, 1888).

4. Warren, THE MAKING OF THE CONSTITUTION (Boston: Little, Brown and Company, 1937).

5. Harris, THE ADVICE AND CONSENT OF THE SENATE (Berkeley and Los Angeles: University of California Press, 1953).

6. Madison, *supra* n. 2, at 67-68; 112-113; 314-317; 343-346; 517; 527; 575.

7. *Id.* at 67-68.

8. Harris, *supra* n. 5, at 28-30; 34.

9. THE FEDERALIST, *supra* n. 3, at 416-417.

10. *Id.* at 474-475.

11. *Id.* at 476-480.

12. As quoted by Judge Irving R. Kaufman, *Charting a Judicial Pedigree*, THE NEW YORK TIMES, January 24, 1981, at 23.

13. TIME MAGAZINE, May 23, 1969, at 24.

14. Abraham, *supra* n. 1, at 276, n. 7.

15. *Id.* at 229.

16. *Id.* at 174.

17. *Id.* at 175.

18. *Id.* at 187.

19. Cardozo, THE NATURE OF THE JUDICIAL PROCESS (New Haven: Yale University Press, 1921).

20. Mason, HARLAN FISKE STONE: PILLAR OF THE LAW 336 (New York: Viking Press, 1956).

21. Johnson, BORAH OF IDAHO 452 (New York: Longmans, Green & Co., 1936).

22. Hoover, THE MEMOIRS OF HERBERT HOOVER: THE CABINET AND THE PRESIDENT, 1920-1933, Vol. II, 269 (New York: The Macmillan Co., 1952).

23. Chafee, *Mr. Justice Cardozo*, HARPER'S MAGAZINE, June 1932, at 34.

24. Mason, *supra* n. 20, at 337.

25. THE NEW YORK TIMES, February 15, 1932, at 1.

26. Steward Machine Co. v. Davis, 301 U.S. 548, and Helvering v. Davis, 301 U.S. 619.

27. 302 U.S. 319 (1937).

28. As requoted in *The Talk of the Town*, THE NEW YORKER, April 4, 1970, at 33.

29. Taylor, ROGER BROOKE TANEY 233 (Baltimore: John Murphy and Co., 1872).

30. Warren, THE SUPREME COURT IN UNITED STATES HISTORY, Vol. II, 10 (Boston: Little, Brown and Company, 1926).

31. Dred Scott v. Sandford, 19 Howard 393 (1857).

32. As quoted by David Fellman (letter to author, August 13, 1974).

33. 332 U.S. 46.

34. 327 U.S. 1 (1946).

35. 330 U.S. 1 (1947).

36. 327 U.S. 1 (1946), at 43.

37. 330 U.S. 1 (1947), at 59.

38. Paschal, MR. JUSTICE SUTHERLAND: A MAN AGAINST THE STATE 113 (Princeton: Princeton University Press, 1951).

39. *Id.* (The biography's subtitle.)

40. Lochner v. New York, 198 U.S. 45 (1905), at 74.

41. 287 U.S. 45.

42. *See* Abraham, *supra* n. 1, at Ch. 7, n. 60.

The impeachment process: modernizing an archaic system

The process of removing federal judges set up by the Constitution's framers is unworkable today. What's needed is a constitutional amendment establishing a new procedure similar to that used by many states.

by Howell T. Heflin

I recently introduced a resolution in the United States Senate calling for a constitutional amendment to give the Congress the authority to provide for alternative procedures for the removal from office of federal judges who are serving pursuant to Article III of the Constitution.

The impetus for my proposal stems from my participation in the first impeachment trial to occur in the United States Senate in 50 years. As a result of serving on the 12 member Impeachment Committee and participating in the Senate floor impeachment proceedings against Judge Harry Claiborne of Nevada, I have concluded that our current impeachment rules were written for an era that has passed and a Congress that has changed. In light of these recent impeachment proceedings and in view of the fact that similar proceedings are entirely possible in the near future, I feel it is important for the Congress to reexamine our current federal impeachment system.

The United States Constitution provides in Article 1, Section 2, Clause 5 that "[t]he House of Representatives shall . . . have the sole power of impeachment" and Article 1, Section 3, Clause 6 provides that "[t]he Senate shall have the sole power to try all impeachments." By these words, the Constitution requires the Senate to conduct an impeachment trial, in which the Senate functions both as judge and jury. In order to carry out such a weighty responsibility, a senator must necessarily be acutely aware of all the facts of any such case. Where the facts are in dispute, the actual observation of witnesses under cross examination is

uniquely important. I believe the full Senate is no longer structurally able to carry out such a responsibility because of the time and attention necessary for such a proceeding.

Since the adoption of our Constitution almost 200 years ago, there have been only 13 impeachments by the House of Representatives. As a result of those 13 impeachments the Senate has conducted 11 impeachment trials, only four of which ended in convictions. It seems apparent that the framers of the Constitution intended that the Senate conduct a full judicial trial on the Senate floor. In effect, this is how the Senate conducted impeachment trials until 1986. But as I noted previously, times have changed. The Congress is not the same institution it was 200 years ago, or even 50 years ago. While I will address primarily the Senate's role in the impeachment process in this article, I believe many of the institutional problems herein are equally applicable to the House of Representatives.

The United States Senate no longer has just 26 members as it did when the Constitution was ratified, but is made up of 100 individuals. The Senate's work schedule is much more intense and varied than it was in the late 18th, 19th or early 20th centuries. Furthermore, the role of a United States Senator has changed substantially over the past 200 years. In 1936, the United States Senate took notice of some of the changes that had occurred during the Republic's first 150 years and tried to alleviate these problems by adopting Senate Rule 11, providing for the formation of an Impeachment Committee. But, while it adopted this rule, the Senate did not utilize the Impeachment Committee during the 1936 impeachment of Judge Willis Ritter.

The Claiborne trial

impeach mt Committee

In the Claiborne impeachment trial, the Senate made the historic decision to establish a 12-person Impeachment Committee to receive evidence and take testimony prior to any trial on the Senate floor. The Senate leadership felt that the use of the Impeachment Committee would allow the full Senate to continue to perform its legislative responsibilities while simultaneously preserving the rights of the impeached individual. While I believe that the Committee functioned effectively in its limited role during the Claiborne impeachment, I do not believe the overriding problems inherent in the impeachment process were resolved.

The impeachment trial of Judge Harry Claiborne presented some unique problems. In addition to being the first impeachment trial in 50 years, one of its most unique features was the fact that Judge Claiborne had already been convicted by a court of law and was serving time in a federal prison. The American people were rightfully outraged that a federal judge could be drawing his judicial salary while serving time in prison. Based on the above facts, the House of Representatives voted unanimously to impeach Judge Claiborne on July 22, 1986.

The House's view was that the prior conviction should govern and a new trial in the Senate was not necessary. Some senators shared the views of the House of Representatives, but both the Committee and the Senate leadership determined that Judge Claiborne should receive an appropriate hearing. In my judgment, an impeachment trial should always be considered separate and distinct from a trial in a federal or state court.

Attendance at the Committee's hearings by all 12 senators was good by usual Senate committee attendance standards and a quorum of seven senators was always present. However, when compared to jury attendance standards, it was unacceptable. As any attorney knows, if a juror is absent without an alternate, the trial is stopped.

The Senate Impeachment Committee's role was extremely limited. During Judge Claiborne's impeachment hearing, senators on the Committee were able to listen to most of the witnesses, including Judge Claiborne, and cross examine them. But, under Senate Rule 11, the Committee was prohibited from making any recommendation regarding Judge Claiborne's guilt or innocence. It should be noted that serious constitutional questions would have been raised had the Committee exercised powers beyond its limited scope.

The 12 senators who comprised the Impeachment Committee were well aware of the facts and issues involved. However, the other 88 members of the Senate did not have the advantage of hearing the testimony and arguments by counsel. The transcript of the hearing on Judge Claiborne's impeachment totaled over 3,500 pages. Therefore, it is highly improbable that any senator had the time to thoroughly review this material. Few senators other than the 12 members of the Impeachment Committee were familiar with all of the elements of the case.

After the Impeachment Committee concluded its work and a record of its hearings were published, the full Senate began consideration of the matter. Yet this consideration was limited. The Senate decided not to rehear witnesses that the Committee had heard, but, rather, to allow only the House Managers and Judge Claiborne's attorney to make closing statements. Further, during Judge Claiborne's closing statement approximately 40 senators were not present in the chamber to hear any of his statement. Indeed, I would guess that at least 35 senators were never present on the floor for any of the presentations by either the prosecution or the defense. It is possible that some of these members heard part of the proceedings on the Senate's radio or television station. Nevertheless, I believe that this fact illustrates the central problem: How can a United States Senator carry out his constitutionally mandated impeachment responsibilities if he does not participate in either the committee hearing or have an opportunity to gain knowledge of the case from a full trial on the Senate floor?

I have concluded that the current impeachment process no longer functions effectively. I question whether these recent proceedings were in accordance with the due process clause of the Fifth Amendment. Therefore, I feel that we must find a better way of removing federal judges from the bench.

A better way

On April 9, 1987, along with Senators Shelby, Stevens, and Sanford, I introduced S.J. Res. 113, a joint resolution proposing an amendment to the Constitution with respect to the impeachment of Article III judges. The resolution states that "[t]he Congress shall have the power to provide procedures for the removal from office of Federal judges serving pursuant to Article III of the Constitution, found to have committed treason, bribery, or other high crimes and misdemeanors." I consider this resolution a starting point for an examination of our current impeachment process. This proposed amendment only applies to Article III federal judges and not to any other civil officer of the United States.

First, I believe that such a constitutional amendment is the correct manner in which to proceed. My view is that the Constitution provides for one, and only one, method of removing federal judges—impeachment by the House of Representatives and trial by the Senate. Therefore, if we want to alter this procedure we must do it by constitutional amendment. Secondly, the amendment I am proposing will in no way alter the reasons for which a federal judge may be removed from office. The causes for removal stated in my resolution are drawn directly from the Constitution.

The Senate Judiciary Committee's Subcommittee on Courts and Administrative Practice, which I chair, plans to hold hearings on this resolution in the near future. During the hearing process the Committee, hopefully, will thoroughly examine the relationship between Article III, Section 1, which provides that "[t]he judges, both of the supreme and inferior courts, shall hold their offices during good behavior . . ." and Article II, Section 4, which provides that "[t]he president, vice-president and all civil officers of the United States, shall be removed from office on impeachment for, and conviction of, treason, bribery, or other high crimes and misdemeanors."

The relationship between these two provisions has been the subject of much controversy. Through the hearing process, the Subcommittee will examine such questions as whether impeachment lies only for indictable offenses, or whether the "misbehavior" clause provides a basis for removal in addition to those established by Article II, Section 4. Some scholars have argued for a broad interpretation of the above two sections, saying that, in addition to treason, bribery, or other high crimes and misdemeanors, as opposed to other civil officers, Article III judges may be impeached for misbe-

havior. Also, it has been argued that misbehavior is included within "high crimes and misdemeanors." Other scholars have argued in favor of a more narrow interpretation.

Another question to be addressed is what the framers meant by the words "high crimes and misdemeanors" and judicial "good behavior." Many have questioned whether actions such as habitual drunkenness or chronic gambling fit within the definition of misbehavior and, as such, constitute impeachable offenses. Broadly speaking, some legal scholars have argued that the Constitution leaves the definition of these words to Congress and places no restriction on the impeachment power—except to limit its punishment to removal from office and disqualification from holding future office.

The states' example

I believe the Congress would do well to examine the various ways in which the states remove judges. The states have developed a variety of methods for removing judges, but one of the most common is the so-called "bifurcated" system. Under such a system, there is usually a body called the Judicial Inquiry Commission, which is composed of individuals appointed by the state judiciary, governor, and state bar. The Commission investigates, receives or initiates complaints concerning judges. These complaints are then filed with a body called the Court of the Judiciary, which is comprised of members of the state judiciary and state bar. The Court usually has the authority to remove, suspend, censure or otherwise discipline judges in the state. The decision of the Court of the Judiciary is reviewable by the state supreme court. The State of Alabama has such a system and it has worked extremely well.

Another method, which is probably the more common, also makes use of a Judicial Inquiry Commission. Under this system, the Commission makes recommendations directly to the state supreme court, which is empowered to remove or otherwise discipline state judges directly.

I am currently in the process of drawing up legislation to implement my proposed constitutional amendment. This legislation would create a Judicial Inquiry Commission and a Court of the Judiciary. The membership of the seven member Judicial Inquiry Commission would include two United States district court judges and one United

States court of appeals judge appointed by the Chief Justice of the United States Supreme Court. The Speaker of the House of Representatives and the President Pro Tempore of the Senate would each nominate one attorney who must be a member of the United States Supreme Court bar. Lastly, the president would nominate two non-lawyers. This Commission, like similar commissions in the states, would be empowered to receive and initiate all complaints concerning federal judges. If a majority of the members of the Commission finds that a reasonable basis exists to charge a judge with misconduct in office, then the Commission would file a complaint with the Court of the Judiciary.

The Court of the Judiciary would also be composed of seven members. The Chief Justice of the United States Supreme Court would select two United States district court judges and one United States court of appeals judge. The Speaker of the House of Representatives and the President Pro Tempore of the Senate would each appoint one member from among the members of the United States Supreme Court bar. The president of the United States would appoint two members who are non-lawyers. Additionally, the judge selected from the United States court of appeals would serve as the chief judge of the Court.

The Court of the Judiciary would have the power, after notice and a public hearing, to adjudicate all cases brought before it. A judge could appeal a decision of the Court of the Judiciary to the United States Supreme Court. While this proposed impeachment system is still in the planning stage, I firmly believe that the Congress would do well to closely examine the methods which the states have developed for removing judges. I feel confident that many members of Congress, as well as the public, will conclude that the states have superior impeachment systems to our current federal impeachment scheme.

While I believe that the impeachment process should be changed, I want to emphasize that one of the overriding considerations in this area should be that of maintaining judicial independence. No federal judge should ever be challenged because of his decisions or opinions.

The need for change

Finally, some have argued that since impeachments occur so infrequently, the Senate should not alter the manner in which it conducts impeach-

ment trials. In my opinion, these individuals fail to realize that our federal judiciary is in the midst of a monumental change. The number of federal judges and the volume of litigation are growing at an unbelievable rate. Congress has authorized 575 district court judgeships and 168 court of appeals judgeships. The Judicial Conference proposed that we create 26 new federal district court judgeships in 1986. If accepted by Congress, this would bring the number of federal district judges to 601. Unfortunately, it is likely that as the number of our federal judges increases, we will have more cases of judicial misconduct. There are currently two possible impeachment trials on the horizon. It is entirely possible that, in the coming years, impeachment proceedings could become more than a rarity, and the Senate could be faced with a number of impeachment trials that could severely inhibit its ability to perform its legislative functions.

The time to act is now. We must look at both statutory and constitutional solutions that would make our impeachment process function more effectively in today's world. There is no rule that requires Congress to act only in response to a crisis. This issue demands a reasoned and deliberative approach. In this case, Congress should act, instead of reacting.

NOTE

This article originally appeared in Volume 71, Number 2, August-September 1987, pages 123-125.

Actors in the Judicial Process
Magistrates and Clerks

INTRODUCTION   While a great deal has been written about judges and their role in judicial politics, such is not the case with other functionaries in the American judiciary such as U.S. magistrate judges and law clerks, the subjects of the two articles in this section of readings. U.S. magistrate judges (known simply as U.S. magistrates prior to 1990) are critically important yet largely invisible actors in the federal judiciary. Indeed, as Christopher Smith reveals in "Who are the U.S. magistrates?," they "perform a wide range of duties, including sentencing misdemeanants; supervising civil discovery; reviewing social security disability benefit appeals; writing published opinions that contribute to the development of case law; and even conducting full civil trials with the consent of litigants." Smith's article adds a great deal to our limited knowledge of who magistrates are, how they get there, and what they do.

In "Law clerks: their roles and relationships with their judges," David Crump explores the benefits and liabilities of the necessary clerking system in the judicial process. The article underlines the considerable diversity in what clerks do and examines their potential for influence in judicial decision making. Throughout the article Crump broadly addresses the issue of how clerks ought to be used by their judges.

Who are the U.S. magistrates?

Although U.S. magistrates are highly influential judicial decision makers, little is known about their backgrounds or about how they get selected. This study begins to fill in the gaps in our knowledge.

by Christopher E. Smith

Congress created the position of U.S. magistrate in 1968 to assist district judges with their judicial duties.[1] In establishing the magistrate system to replace the U.S. commissioners, the legislation mandated specific legal qualifications for this new tier of federal judicial officers and granted the magistrates broader authority than the limited petty offense and criminal warrant activities of the commissioners.[2] In response to several factors, including legal challenges to the magistrates' authority,[3] diverse practices in the utilization of magistrates that had developed in various district courts,[4] and increasing caseload pressures,[5] Congress clarified and expanded the authority of magistrates in 1976 and 1979.[6]

Magistrates now perform a wide range of duties, including sentencing misdemeanants; supervising civil discovery; reviewing social security disability benefit appeals; writing published opinions that contribute to the development of case law;[7] and even conducting full civil trials with the consent of litigants.[8] Magistrates are undertaking, under specified conditions and controls, virtually all tasks performed by federal district judges except trying and sentencing felony defendants.[9] In 1986 magistrates handled 445,575 matters for the federal courts including 984 actual civil trials.[10]

According to the October 1986 roster of magistrates at the Administrative Office of the U.S. Courts, there are 266 full-time and 183 part-time magistrates throughout the country, with the number growing each year as vacancies are filled and additional positions are authorized.[11]

The important and significant judicial power exercised by magistrates was recently illuminated by the Supreme Court's decision[12] recognizing the constitutionality of the Bail Reform Act of 1984.[13] Under that Act, a federal judicial officer may order a criminal defendant to be detained without bail until trial if there is clear and convincing evidence that no combination of pretrial release conditions can assure the safety of the community and reasonably assure the defendant's presence at trial.[14] The Act was challenged as violative of the Excessive Bail Clause of the Eighth Amendment and the constitutional due process guarantees against deprivation of liberty. Although the Supreme Court upheld the Act, it recognized the importance of the judicial officer's detention decision because "[i]n our society liberty is the norm, and detention prior to trial or without trial is the carefully limited exception."[15]

The federal judicial officers primarily responsible for generating this front-page constitutional controversy[16] were U.S. magistrates. In impliedly criticizing the Supreme Court decision, a national newsmagazine placed a spotlight upon the authority and actions of magistrates:

[The magistrate] sent . . . a janitor with eight kids, to jail until the case could go to trial. But those that the gods would humble, they first make magistrates. A federal jury took just 25 minutes to find that [the defendant], who had exculpatory alibis, was not guilty. By then this innocent man had spent 71 days in jail.[17]

Magistrates are called upon frequently to make difficult decisions affecting individuals' liberty and rights. In 1986 magistrates conducted 9,444 detention hearings.[18]

The importance of magistrates is evident in many ways, including the statistics compiled by the Administrative Office showing that magistrates are responsible for a multitude of judicial tasks,[19] observers' characterizations of magistrates as "integral"[20] and "essential"[21] to the federal judiciary, and magistrates' important decisions affecting personal liberty and constitutional rights. Despite this evidence, these judicial officials have received relatively little attention from scholars, the press, and the public. There is a wealth of literature describing and discussing the characteristics and selection of federal judges who must go through the public process of presidential nomination and Senate confirmation.[22] By contrast, magistrates are selected by judges within each district through a less visible process that is not accessible to scholarly or public scrutiny.

Based upon interviews with magistrates, judges, and magistrate selection committee members in nine diverse districts,[23] and data obtained from the Administrative Office, this article will discuss the characteristics and selection of these important judicial officers in the lower tier of the federal courts. This initial marshalling of descriptive data about magistrates pales in comparison to the detailed monitoring and rich analysis of federal judges' characteristics.[24] However, even with the limited data available on magistrates, it is possible to gain a general picture of their backgrounds and experiences. The data on magistrates also illuminate the results of alternative judicial selection methods within a specific context because magistrates have been appointed through two different methods: direct appointment by district judges and a merit selection process. Although the merit selection process for magistrates takes a particular form, namely having appointment ultimately determined by judges rather than a merit committee or elected officials, the magistrates provide one example of a merit selection process in action.

Selection procedures

When the magistrate system was first implemented, district judges directly appointed attorneys for the eight-year terms of full-time magistrates and the four-year terms of part-time positions. From 1970 to 1979 the number of authorized full-time positions increased from 61 to 201.[25] The judges in the districts receiving new magistrates or replacing retiring magistrates agreed by consensus on the individuals to be appointed. In some districts the judges rotated the prerogative of recommending an individual for appointment. Except for a bar

membership requirement for appointees, there were no statutory or regulatory requirements mandating a search process or otherwise guiding the judges' selection methods.

The selection of magistrates directly by district judges led to the appointments of many individuals who were close to the judges, especially former law clerks and former assistant U.S. attorneys. For example, in the districts studied, one former assistant U.S. attorney was recruited by the district's chief judge; another magistrate was tapped by a judge with whom he had co-authored a book; a former law clerk was appointed when his mentor-judge outmaneuvered another judge seeking the position for a different law clerk; and another former assistant U.S. attorney was asked to take the position by two district judges with whom he had long been acquainted.

In appointing magistrates, Congress assumed that judges "will be anxious to obtain the best-qualified lawyer to fill the vacancy."[26] The creation of a new judicial position, however, inevitably creates uncertainty about exactly what role the new judicial officer is to play. Without a clear conception of what these new magistrates were to do, the judges within districts could not agree among themselves on precisely what criteria defined the "best-qualified lawyer." As a result, many judges appointed individuals with whom they had already established a comfortable working relationship rather than aggressively seeking to test the market for possible candidates. Thus judges tended to appoint their former law clerks who, in several cases, were only one or two years out of law school and therefore lacked knowledge and expertise in litigation and court procedures.

In some districts, the appointment of former law clerks reflected and reinforced the judges' conception and use of magistrates primarily in law clerk functions, such as reviewing social security appeals and prisoner petitions. This limited use of magistrates did not meet the legislative desire to add "a new level of flexibility and creativity to the Federal court system."[27] Although some districts continue to use magistrates as specialists for social security and prisoner cases, most follow a broader range of statutorily-authorized judicial tasks.[28]

The direct selection method fostered several problems in addition to the appointment of some inexperienced law clerks and the reinforcement of the new judicial officer's role as that of permanent law clerk. Direct selection created the appearance and possibility of impropriety in granting district judges an opportunity for political patronage appointments. Although judges would clearly do themselves and the courts a disservice by appointing unqualified individuals, during interviews several judges referred to specific magistrates appointed prior to the start of merit selection as "political hack[s]" or "political appointment[s]." One magistrate singled out by several judges was reported to have received an initial appointment through family connections with several powerful politicians and judges.[29]

In addition to the possibility of political patronage in appointments, another criticism of direct selection focused on the lack of women and minority group members appointed. In 1979 women comprised less than 9 per cent of the full-time magistrates and minority group members constituted only 5 per cent.[30] Although these percentages exceeded and continue to exceed representation figures for federal judges, with the exception of Carter-era appointees,[31] in the late 1970s members of Congress viewed the magistrate system as providing an opportunity to redress the persistent fact that "women and minorities are under-represented in the Federal judiciary relative to the population at large."[32]

Congress recognized that "not all [magistrate] appointees evidenced the same high quality" because judges "did not fully-appreciate the full range of duties that a magistrate could perform."[33] This uneven quality of appointees, as well as concerns about the appearance of possible patronage in judges' selections and the lack of representativeness in appointments, led to the initiation of legislation in Congress to reform the selection procedures.

Merit selection

When magistrates' authority was expanded in 1979 to enable them to supervise entire civil trials, Congress acted simultaneously to standardize selection procedures and upgrade the quality of appointees. The new methods were advocated as part of the Carter Administration's judicial selection reforms. According to one witness at the Senate hearings on the 1979 Magistrates Act, the merit selection procedure for magistrates was designed to "conform to President Carter's policies regarding Federal judicial selection, namely an open process, full public participation, and the policy objective of integrating the Federal courts in terms of gender and race."[34] The new procedure requires district judges to appoint merit selection panels that will advertise vacancies, evaluate candidates, and submit a list of five nominees to the district's judges.

The magistrate is selected by a majority of the active judges, although in some districts the opinions of judges on senior status are also solicited and considered. The judges retain the power to select the magistrate, but the merit process is intended to publicize openings and widen the pool of applicants. The regulations promulgated by the Judicial Conference to govern the merit selection process,[35] following from the legislative intent of the 1979 Magistrates Act, specifically instruct committee members to "make an affirmative effort to identify and give due consideration to all qualified candidates including women and members of minority groups."[36]

The Judicial Conference did not specifically instruct the district judges on how to select the merit selection committee members. The regulations require only that "[t]he panel shall be composed of a chairman and other members appointed by a majority vote of the active judges of the district court. The panel shall have no fewer than six members [and] ... shall consist of lawyers and other members of the community."[37] In addition, the Administrative Office recommends that the selection board have an odd number of members and include at least two nonlawyers.[38] The district judges can either maintain the same committee for all appointment and reappointment procedures or constitute a new panel for each occasion when the selection process is needed. For selection of some part-time magistrates, the committee may be comprised of fewer than six members and may also include judges.[39]

At the same time that the merit selection process was established, the Magistrates Act also upgraded qualifications for magistrates by requiring five years of legal experience in addition to bar membership. This requirement did not preclude the appointment of former law clerks, but it halted the previous practice of law clerks becoming magistrates immediately upon leaving employment in the judge's chambers.

Data on magistrates

Biographical data on magistrates were obtained from information sheets at the Magistrates Division of the Administrative Office of the U.S. Courts. All 402 available data sheets on magistrates serving during October 1986 were examined to gain information on magistrates' employment backgrounds, legal education, and age.[40] The information sheets are voluntarily submitted to the Administrative Office by the magistrates. Some magistrates did not submit a biographical data sheet and others omitted information, particularly concerning employment background. Survey forms were sent by the author to 19 full-time magistrates who provided no biographical information to the Administrative Office. Twelve forms were returned, although not all of these contained complete information. Thus the tables accompanying this article have slightly different numbers of magistrates for each information category. The tables contain at least some information about 97.4 per cent of the full-time and 84.7 per cent of the part-time magistrates serving during October 1986.

Additional information on the gender and racial composition of the magistrates system was obtained from the Administrative Office. Unfortunately, however, 1981 was the "first reporting year for the Judicial Equal Employment Opportunity Program."[41] Therefore, other sources have been used in an attempt to determine the effects of the implementation of merit selection in 1980 upon representation of women and minority groups among the magistrate appointees. The data from the Administrative Office are supplemented by information gained in the interviews in nine districts.

Employment background

One of the purposes of the merit selection process was to eliminate the appearance of patronage that resulted from judges directly appointing former law clerks and other court personnel to magistrate positions. Table 1 shows that the pattern of appointment for people with close connections to the federal court continues even after the implementation of the merit committee selection process. The category labeled "Federal court personnel" includes former law clerks, assistant U.S. attorneys, U.S. attorneys, federal defenders, clerks of court, bankruptcy judges, and federal probation officers. Ninety-three per cent of the magistrates in that category are either former law clerks or former assistant U.S. attorneys.

Virtually the same percentage of former court personnel have been appointed since the start of

Table 1 Employment backgrounds of full-time magistrates by selection process (includes more than one employment category per magistrate)

	Total full-time magistrates [N=259]	Selected Pre-merit [N=132]	Post-merit [N=127]
Federal court personnel	59.5%	59.1%	59.8%
	[154]	[78]	[76]
Private practice	69.3	60.6	70.1
	[169]	[80]	[89]
Local prosecution	13.9	11.4	16.5
	[36]	[15]	[21]
Federal government	13.9	13.6	14.2
	[36]	[18]	[18]
State government	12.7	11.4	14.2
	[33]	[15]	[18]
Teaching	8.9	6.1	11.8
	[23]	[8]	[15]
State judge	7.7	4.5	11.0
	[20]	[6]	[14]
Legal aid/services	4.6	3.8	5.5
	[12]	[5]	[7]
State law clerk	4.2	3.8	4.7
	[11]	[5]	[6]
Public defender	3.1	2.3	3.9
	[8]	[3]	[5]
City government	3.1	4.5	1.6
	[8]	[6]	[2]
Corporation	1.9	0.8	3.1
	[5]	[1]	[4]

merit selection as were appointed through the previous direct selection method—at least among individuals who continue to serve as full-time magistrates. The work of the merit panels dilutes the appearance of patronage because the magistrate vacancies are now publicly advertised and applications are accepted and screened by panel members. For some reason, the previous appointment pattern persists.

There are several reasons presented by magistrates, judges, and selection board members for the significant numbers of law clerks and other former court personnel appointed. First, law clerks and assistant U.S. attorneys tend to have outstanding academic records, strong intellectual abilities, and impressive writing skills. These are among the qualities that merit committees and judges seek in magistrate appointees. Second, law clerks and other court personnel often possess a commitment to public service careers and an interest in federal law that lead them to apply for magistrate positions. Third, unlike successful lawyers in private practice who would be forced to accept substantial pay cuts in order to become magistrates, law clerks and assistant U.S. attorneys are accustomed to public sector salaries so that the magistrate's salary would not be unattractive.

One court official, referring to the first year of the magistrates' existence, attributed the appointments of court personnel to the low salary of $22,000 that the first magistrates received. That explanation, however, is less forceful now since magistrates' salaries have more than tripled within a relatively brief 15 year period and would now be attractive to a larger group of outside lawyers who can submit applications in the open selection process. In sum, magistrates and judges argue that law clerks and other court personnel tend to be precisely the kinds of interested, qualified people who are attracted to the magistrate position and whose credentials make them desirable to merit panels and district judges.

All of the preceding arguments are true, but the essential characteristics of the merit selection process make other factors important too. The judges ultimately make appointments. No matter what the merit committee decides about the finalists, the judges are likely to be best acquainted with a nominee who was previously a law clerk, assistant U.S. attorney, or other close member of that federal court's working community. The judges inevitably rely upon their own personal knowledge and assessments of the finalist in making appointments. Thus, former court personnel are in an advantageous position by virtue of the judges' familiarity with them. Moreover, if the former law clerk or assistant U.S. attorney is a protege of a sitting district judge, the judges may have even more reason to appoint that person.

The judges are firmly in control of the selection process. They appoint the committee members and they have the power to reject all nominees put forward and thereby force the merit committee to produce a new list of finalists.[42] Interviews with judges and merit committee members indicate that judges communicate criteria and preferences to the panel members during the search process. In some districts, judges closely monitor the search process and even veto the consideration of specific applicants before the panel has submitted the list of finalists.[43] Most panel members stated forthrightly in interviews that throughout the search process they were concerned with pleasing the district's judges with the list of nominees. The judges' power over the selection process enhances prospects for former court personnel because merit panel members are influenced by perceptions of what the judges want and by a desire to please

them.[44] In creating a list of recommended finalists, panelists may, therefore, tend to select former court personnel whom the panelists believe are favored by the judges.

Does the continued pattern of appointments for court personnel in the judge-dominated merit selection process mean that the legislative goals of the new procedure have failed to be attained? Not necessarily. The merit process has opened up applications to the entire legal community. Judges now have the opportunity to consider candidates who might have remained unknown under the old system of quickly appointing a known individual from the federal courthouse. The merit panel evaluates candidates and files a detailed report on the selection process and the ranking of candidates—activities which busy district judges may not have either the time or the inclination to do on their own in a direct selection procedure. In addition, the statutory requirement of five years legal experience has now precluded the selection of inexperienced law clerks. These aspects of the new selection procedures have given judges the opportunity to consider a broader array of candidates. Although judges continue to appoint many individuals with similar backgrounds, we will never know how many more former law clerks and other court personnel might have been appointed perfunctorily if the merit procedures had not interposed the activities of a selection committee to counteract the previous appearance of possible patronage.

Arguably, the limited power of the merit panels in the judge-dominated process has not cleansed the appearance of patronage from the selection procedures because the pattern of appointments for federal court personnel continues. However, even if one questions the propriety of the selection methods and results, other purposes underlie the congressional decision to leave the selection of magistrates under the control of the judges. Most importantly, the constitutional issues surrounding a tier of limited tenure, non-Article III officials undertaking judicial tasks raise questions about the maintenance of independent judicial power and separation of powers. The appointment and control of magistrates by district judges was regarded as one of the "three pillars" underlying the constitutionality of magistrates undertaking judicial tasks as adjuncts to independent Article III judges.[45] According to the leading case on magistrates' constitutional authority, judicial independence is maintained in the magistrate system because vesting selection and retention powers in district judges prevents magistrates from being "directly dependent upon loyalty to officers in either of the political branches."[46] Thus the merit process designed by Congress, with limited power granted to the selection panel, attempts to advance specific goals for magistrate appointments without jeopardizing the constitutionality of the entire magistrate system.

One notable development in appointments after the implementation of the merit process is an increase in the number of former state judges and law professors selected to be magistrates. Several judges stated in interviews that the ideal magistrate would be a former state judge who could step right in and handle civil litigation matters and trials. The increases may indicate that merit selection panels are heeding or agreeing with the views of judges who seek appointees with well-developed expertise.

By the very nature of the position, part-time magistrates tend to be individuals who have positions with the flexibility to mix career responsibilities . . . .[47] Busy, successful law practices and salaried corporate positions may not provide the needed flexibility. As one full-time magistrate wrote on a survey form concerning prior experience as a part-time magistrate, "[m]y private practice during those two years declined to virtually none."

Age at appointment

The average age at time of appointment was nearly identical for full- and part-time magistrates. For full-time magistrates it was 42.1 years and for part-time it was 41.0 years. The average age for graduation from law school within the sample fell between 26 and 27 so that the appointment age indicates that magistrates have an average of approximately 15 years of legal experience prior to appointment. This average disguises the fact . . . that there are tremendous age and experience ranges for new appointees as part-time and full-time magistrates. Age at first appointment ranged from 27 to 70 for current full-time magistrates and from 27 to 66 for part-time magistrates. Consequently, years of legal experience prior to appointment ranged from 2 to 46 for full-time magistrates and 1 to 40 for part-time magistrates.

Interviews with judges and magistrates revealed that the diversity of age and experience reflects the different ways in which district court judges con-

Table 2   Legal education of full-time magistrates by selection process

	Total full-time magistrates [N=254]	Selected Pre-merit [N=128]	Selected Post-merit [N=126]
Elite	15.7% [40]	12.5% [16]	19.0% [24]
Public (non-elite)	47.2 [120]	51.6 [66]	42.9 [54]
Private (non-elite)	37.0 [94]	35.9 [46]	38.1 [48]

ceptualized the magistrate's role. The very youthful appointees under the old direct selection method show the inclination of some judges to view magistrates as permanent law clerks who perform very limited task assignments.[48] The requirement of five years legal experience in the Magistrates Act has eliminated the appointment of any individuals under 30 years of age during the merit selection era . . . .

Legal education

The legal education of judges has frequently been studied and the analyses employed have often been the subject of disagreement.[49] Graduation from a law school of only local or regional reputation does not imply the acquisition of an inferior legal education. However, graduation from a state-funded law school may indicate something about one's financial background because these schools are generally less expensive. Attendance at an "Ivy League" private law school can reflect the historical links between those schools and the top socioeconomic stratum of society.[50] Arguably, an additional reason to examine law school background is that attendance at an elite law school reflects high academic achievement and consequently, a broad array of lucrative employment opportunities. Thus, for example, the recruitment and selection of magistrates from elite law schools, while not implying that these are the most qualified individuals, has implications for the manner in which the prestige, authority, and salary of the magistrate are viewed relative to the complete range of legal career possibilities.

In Tables 2 and 3 "Elite" law schools are defined as Ivy League law schools plus Chicago, Stanford, Michigan, and California/Berkeley as a rough approximation of the top nine schools by reputation. As indicated in the tables, there are differences in the legal education backgrounds of full- and part-time magistrates. Greater percentages of full-time magistrates graduated from elite and private law

Table 3 Legal education of part-time magistrates by selection process

	Total part-time magistrates [N=153]	Selected Pre-merit [N=93]	Selected Post-merit [N=60]
Elite	6.5% [10]	5.4% [5]	8.3% [5]
Public (non-elite)	65.4 [100]	66.7 [62]	63.3 [38]
Private (non-elite)	28.1 [43]	28.0 [26]	28.3 [17]

Table 4 Full-time magistrates, women and minority representation

	Total full-time magistrates	Women	Minority
1979 Prior to merit selection	174	15 (8.6%)	9 (5.2%)
1981 After merit selection, one year	200	16 (8.0%)	12 (6.0%)
1986 After merit selection, six years	287*	39 (13.6%)	24 (8.4%)
October 1986 roster	266	42 (15.8%)	

*Includes all persons who served as full-time magistrates at any time during June 1985 to June 1986.

schools, while public school graduates comprise a greater percentage of the part-time magistrates. Assuming the elite and private law school graduates have the widest range of career options due to the prestige of their degrees in the eyes of employers, the data bear out that full-time magistrate positions are more desirable than part-time positions.

This conclusion comports with the differences in authority, salary, and prestige for the positions. Full-time magistrates are paid $72,500 annually while part-time magistrates are paid from $2,015 to half of the full-time salary depending upon the number of hours required for the position. In addition, full-time magistrates in many districts preside over civil trials and undertake a wide range of judicial responsibilities, while many part-time magistrates handle primarily petty offenses in national parks. The percentages for part-time magistrates are additionally skewed in favor of public school graduates due to the location of part-time positions. Many national parks and concomitant part-time magistrate positions are located in less populous Western states. The local attorneys who are potential applicants for magistrate positions in sparsely populated Western states, such as Montana and Wyoming, tend to be produced by their own state universities, which provide the only law schools within the state.

When looking solely at full-time positions, it appears that elite and private law school graduates may have a competitive edge in the eyes of judges and merit committees that make selection decisions. This may in part reflect the fact that elite and private educations are strongly represented among the selectors themselves.[51]

Women and minorities

The merit selection process for magistrates was established in 1979, in part because the Carter administration was pushing for such procedures to be widely applied in the federal judiciary. The

magistrate selection legislation and implementing regulations share the Carter administration's goal of appointing members of underrepresented groups to judicial office. Under the new process, as with the Carter-era appointments to the federal bench,[52] an increased number of women and minority magistrates have been appointed. As indicated in Tables 4 and 5, the number of magistrates from these groups has increased both in absolute numbers and as a percentage of total magistrates.[53]

The specific regulatory instructions to seek a broader applicant pool had the intent of encouraging judges and merit committees to consider candidates from underrepresented groups. Interviews indicated that district judges can guide merit panels toward consideration of underrepresented group members by showing the strength of the judges' commitment to broad recruiting during the initial communications between the district judges and the committee. For example, one panel member described being encouraged by a chief judge to "give extra consideration to selecting a woman." Although district judges ultimately determine if women and minority candidates will be selected, the merit panel can greatly assist the judges by seeking a wide range of applicants.

The great increase in authorized full-time magistrate positions over the past 15 years has helped to facilitate the addition of women and minority magistrates because incumbents did not have to be replaced in order to increase representativeness within the magistrate system. Women and minority group members could be appointed to newly created positions without waiting for the original magistrates to retire or resign.

Table 5   Part-time magistrates, women and minority representation

	Total part-time magistrates	Women	Minority
1981 After merit selection, one year	236	4 (1.7%)	4 (1.7%)
1986 After merit selection, six years	183	8 (4.8%)	5 (2.7%)

Conclusion

The ties between persons appointed to magistrate positions and the federal courts, as evidenced by the significant proportions of former court personnel appointed both prior to and after the advent of merit selection, seem indicative of the power wielded by district judges over the magistrate system. The evidence of judges' influence may be viewed in a positive light if regarded, as Congress and the federal courts have generally viewed it, as a component of Article III judicial independence. By permitting Article III district judges to control the selection and work of magistrates, the lower tier of limited tenure judicial officers can properly perform tasks for the judiciary without being influenced by the legislative or executive branches, and thus avoid separation of powers problems under our constitutional system.[54] The power of the judges, while not without its problems in the early selection and conceptualization of magistrates according to a law clerk model, serves as one element that permits magistrates to assist the federal courts as Article III adjuncts.

Progress has been made toward the legislative goals underlying the implementation of merit selection in the Magistrates Act. The representation of women and minority group members among magistrates may be attributable, at least in part, to the merit procedures of advertising vacancies, soliciting applications from a broad array of candidates, and giving due consideration to "all qualified candidates including women and members of minority groups."[55]

The U.S. magistrates continue to play an important role in the processing of cases within the federal courts. This preliminary examination of available data presents a general picture of the characteristics of these relatively invisible but highly influential judicial decisionmakers. As more dis-

tricts utilize magistrates for civil trials and other judicial tasks that fit within magistrates' broad statutory authority,[56] the characteristics and activities of this tier of judicial officers will deserve continued scrutiny and analysis.

NOTES

This article originally appeared in Volume 71, Number 3, October-November 1987, pages 142-150.

I would like to thank the Magistrates Division of the Administrative Office of the U.S. Courts for permitting access to biographical data; George F. Cole, C. Neal Tate, and anonymous reviewers for helpful comments on earlier versions of this article; and Charlotte J. Smith for invaluable research assistance.

1. Federal Magistrates Act codified as amended at 28 U.S.C. §§631-639.

2. Unlike the U.S. commissioners, many of whom had no legal training, the new magistrates were required to be members of the bar—except that a part-time lay magistrate could be appointed if no qualified members of the bar were available at a specific location. Magistrates could be assigned duties that were not normally undertaken by the commissioners. As explained by the House report on the 1968 Magistrates Act, "[t]hese additional duties may include, but are not limited to, service as special masters, supervision of pretrial or discovery proceedings, and preliminary consideration of petitions for postconviction relief." H.R. REP. No. 1629, Federal Magistrates Act, U.S. CODE CONG. & ADMIN. NEWS 4252, 4254 (1968). *See also* Spaniol, *The Federal Magistrates Act: History and Development*, ARIZ. ST. L. J. 566 (1974).

3. The 1976 amendments to the Federal Magistrates Act expressly counteracted the Supreme Court's decision in *Wingo v. Wedding*, 418 U.S. 461 (1974), by authorizing magistrates to conduct evidentiary hearings in habeas corpus cases.

4. The 1979 amendments authorized magistrates to handle civil trials with the consent of litigants. At the time the legislation was passed by Congress, 36 districts were already permitting magistrates to handle trials without explicit statutory authorization. H.R. REP No. 1364, 95th Cong., 2d Sess. 4 (1978).

5. According to the Senate report accompanying the 1979 Act, "[In 1967] there were 340 authorized district judgeships with . . . a total caseload of 303 cases per judgeship[]. [In 1979] there are 516 district judgeships . . . [with] an average caseload of 323 cases per judgeship . . . . It is clear that the growing complement of district judges have a continuing need for the assistance of magistrates in the disposition of their caseloads." S. REP. No. 74, Federal Magistrate Act of 1979, U.S. CODE CONG. & ADMIN. NEWS 1469, 1470 (1979).

6. The 1976 Act clarified the magistrates' powers, especially with regard to evidentiary hearings for habeas corpus cases. The 1979 Act granted magistrates the power to conduct complete civil trials by consent of the litigants as well as creating a new method for selecting magistrates. *See* McCabe, *The Federal Magistrate Act of 1979*, 16 HARV. J. ON LEGIS. 341 (1979).

7. Magistrates' opinions may be published in Federal Supplement if they are adopted verbatim by district judges and appear as the judges' decisions. Magistrates' opinions on procedural matters appear in their own names in reporters concerned with such issues. *See, e.g.*, William v. Keenan, 106 F.R.D. 565 (D. Mass. 1985); Hoffman v. Owens-Illinois Glass Co., 107 F.R.D. 793 (D. Mass. 1985).

8. Under the statute, "[u]pon the consent of the parties, a full-time United States magistrate or a part-time United States magistrate who serves as a full-time judicial officer may con-

duct any or all proceedings in a jury or nonjury civil matter and order the entry of judgment in the case, when specially designated to exercise such jurisdiction by the district court or courts he serves." 28 U.S.C. §636(C)(1).

9. Magistrates have a broad range of authority under the statute. *See* Aug, *Magistrate Act of 1979: From a Magistrate's Perspective*, 49 CIN. L. REV. 363 (1980); Streepy, *The Developing Role of the Magistrate in the Federal Courts*, 29 CLEV. ST. L. REV. 81 (1980). Although broad authority exists, it is not utilized in every district. Many districts limit the tasks assigned to magistrates. For example, magistrates seldom or never conduct trials in some districts. *See* Seron, THE ROLES OF MAGISTRATES: NINE CASE STUDIES (Washington, DC: The Federal Judicial Center, 1985).

10. ANNUAL REPORT OF THE DIRECTOR OF THE ADMINISTRATIVE OFFICE OF THE UNITED STATES COURTS 37-38 (Washington, DC: U.S. Government Printing Office, 1986).

11. According to the statute, "[The Judicial Conference of the United States] shall determine, in the light of the recommendations of the Director [of the Administrative Office of the U.S. Courts], the district courts, and the [circuit] councils, the number of full-time United States magistrates and part-time United States magistrates, the location at which they shall serve, and their respective salaries," 28 U.S.C. §633(b). According to the most recent annual report from the Judicial Conference and the Administrative Office, "[t]he Judicial Conference authorized creation of . . . additional full-time positions . . . expanding the number of full-time positions . . . to 280 . . . the number of part-time positions to 177 . . . and the number of combination clerk of court/magistrate positions to 10." Administrative office, *supra* n. 10, at 65.

12. United States v. Salerno and Cafaro, 55 U.S.L.W. 4663 (1987).

13. 18 U.S.C. §3141 et seq.

14. *See* Sinclair, PRACTICE BEFORE FEDERAL MAGISTRATES 4-19-4-26.1 (New York: Matthew Bender, 1987).

15. United States v. Salerno and Cafaro at 4668.

16. *See, e.g., Court upholds pretrial jailing*, BOSTON GLOBE, May 27, 1987, at 1.

17. *First Jail, Then a Trial*, NEWSWEEK, June 8, 1987, at 19.

18. Administrative Office, *supra* n. 10, at 36.

19. *Id.* at 40.

20. Goodale, *Federal Magistrates Play Major Role in U.S. District Court*, 13 MASS. L. WEEKLY 561 (1985).

21. Letter from former member of Congress to author (March 7, 1986) (discussing member's opposition to 1968 Magistrates Act and subsequent support for the magistrate system).

22. *See, e.g.*, Slotnick, *Lowering the Bench or Raising it Higher?: Affirmative Action and Judicial Selection During the Carter Administration*, 1 YALE L. & POL'Y REV. 270 (1983); Fowler, *Judicial selection under Reagan and Carter: a comparison of their initial recommendation procedures*, 67 JUDICATURE 265 (1984); Walker and Barrow, *The Diversification of the Federal Bench: Policy and Process Ramifications*, 47 J. POL. 598 (1985); Davis, *President Carter's Selection Reforms and Judicial Policymaking*, 14 AM. POL. Q. 328 (1986).

23. Not-for-attribution interviews ranging in length from 30 minutes to three and one half hours were conducted with 15 district judges, 21 magistrates, and nine magistrate selection committee members in nine districts in the First, Second, Sixth, and Seventh Circuits. The average length of each interview was approximately one hour. Two of the districts had one full-time magistrate and two active district judges located in a single courthouse. One district had one full-time and one part-time magistrate split between two courthouses which each housed one active judge. Three districts had two to four magistrates and three to six judges divided between two or

three courthouses. Two districts had five full-time magistrates and 11 active judges split between two or three locations. Each of these districts contained a large urban courthouse with three or four magistrates and seven to ten judges in one location. One district contained eight full-time magistrates and 14 active judges. There were four different courthouses, but the large, urban court housed five of the magistrates and 11 of the judges. The interviews were conducted between March 1986 and July 1987.

24. For an example of monitoring and detailed description, see Goldman, *Reagan's second term judicial appointments: the battle at midway*, 70 JUDICATURE 324 (1987). For an example of detailed analysis, see Tate, *Personal Attribute Models of the Voting Behavior of U.S. Supreme Court Justices: Liberalism in Civil Liberties and Economics Decisions, 1946-1978*, 75 AM. POL. SCI. REV. 355 (1981).

25. Seron, THE ROLE OF MAGISTRATES IN THE FEDERAL DISTRICT COURTS 11 (Washington, DC: The Federal Judicial Center, 1983).

26. S. REP NO. 74, *supra* n. 5, at 1477.

27. *The Federal Magistrate Act of 1979: Hearings on S. 237 Before a Subcommittee of the Senate Committee on the Judiciary*, 96th Cong., 1st Sess. 18 (1979) (statement of the Hon. Otto Skopil).

28. *See* Seron, *supra* n. 9; Seron, *supra* n. 25; Administrative Office, *supra* n. 10, at 358-378.

29. Evidence of overt political partisanship affecting appointments appeared in several interviews. In one district magistrates mentioned the involvement of United States senators in lobbying judges for the appointment of particular individuals as magistrates. In another district a merit selection committee member reported that "important, influential people" contacted panel members to urge the nomination of particular individuals.

30. McCabe, *supra* n. 6, at 395.

31. "One thing, however, does remain clear. Recruitment outcomes during the Carter Administration resulted in a more 'representative' bench than ever existed, if the concept of representation is assessed by the sheer number and percentage of appointees who were *not* white males. Of Carter's 262 district and appeals court appointees 40 were women, 38 were black, and 16 were Hispanics (7 of the black and 1 of the 16 nominees were women). This constituted a greater number of non-traditional appointees than had been designated over the course of the nation's entire history and, clearly, was an obvious departure from the selection behavior of recent presidents. As noted by Goldman, 'By the end of the Carter Administration the proportion of women judges on the federal bench has risen from one per cent to close to seven per cent and, for blacks, from four per cent to close to nine per cent.' "Slotnick, *supra* n. 22, at 280 [quoting Goldman, *Carter's judicial appointments: a lasting legacy*, 64 JUDICATURE 344, 349 (1981)].

32. H.R. REP. NO. 1364, *supra* n. 4, at 17.

33. S. REP NO. 74, *supra* n. 5, at 1478.

34. Hearings on S. 237, *supra* n. 27, at 56 (statement of Charles Halpern).

35. The statute provides that the "[magistrate] is selected pursuant to standards and procedures promulgated by the Judicial Conference of the United States. Such standards shall contain provision for public notice of all vacancies in magistrate positions and for the establishment by the district courts of merit selection panels, composed of residents of the individual judicial districts, to assist the courts in identifying the recommending persons who are best qualified to fill such positions." 28 U.S.C. §631(b)(5).

36. Administrative Office of the U.S. Courts, THE SELECTION AND APPOINTMENT OF UNITED STATES MAGISTRATES 14 (February 1981).

37. *Id.* at 43-44.

38. *Id.* at 5.

39. The alternative selection procedures apply to the selection and appointment of a part-time magistrate "whose authorized annual salary is less than one-third of the maximum salary authorized for a full-time magistrate." *Id.* at 45.

40. An additional 64 data sheets were contained in the files at the Administrative Office. These sheets were also examined but it was subsequently determined that these individuals were no longer serving as magistrates in October 1986.

41. Letter from the Director of Equal Employment Opportunity at the Administrative Office of the U.S. Courts to the author (December 8, 1986) (explaining the lack of statistical information over the history of the magistrate system).

42. According to the regulations promulgated by the Judicial Conference, "a district court may, by majority vote, reject the first list submitted by the panel. If such list is rejected, the panel shall submit a second list from which the district court shall then select its magistrate." Administrative Office, *supra* n. 36, at 44-45.

43. In a national survey of chief district judges being undertaken by the author to examine the magistrate selection process, at least 15 chief judges have indicated that the names of applicants were given to the judges before the merit panel began to develop its list of finalists. In one of the interview districts, panel members acknowledged that judges actually eliminated applicants that they found personally unacceptable even before the panel began to evaluate all of the applicants.

44. For example, in one interview district the merit panel members were very aware that they could make one judge particularly happy by nominating that judge's former law clerk.

45. The other two "pillars" are that "both parties must consent to trial before a magistrate" and "in all instances an appeal from a magistrate's decision lies in an Article III court." H.R. REP NO. 1364, *supra* n. 4, at 11.

46. Pacemaker Diagnostic Clinic of America v. Instromedix, 725 F.2d 537, 545 (9th Cir. 1984) (en banc) cert. denied 469 U.S. 824 (1984).

47. Part-time magistrates are often lawyers in private practice who perform limited judicial duties for the federal courts as a sideline. Frequently their duties are limited to handling petty offenses on federal lands, such as national parks. In many ways they are an extension of the old U.S. commissioners who were replaced by the magistrate system, and indeed a number of the part-time magistrates are former commissioners.

48. Seron, *supra* n. 9, has characterized some magistrates as "specialists" in social security and prisoner cases. These magistrates are primarily limited to writing reports and recommendations for judges based upon case filings in these limited categories of cases. This activity is similar to the tasks performed for judges by law clerks, and in fact, in those districts in which magistrates do not have limited tasks, the judges' law clerks often undertake the drafting of decisional memoranda on social security or prisoner cases. Interviews with judges reveal that particular conceptualizations of the magistrate's role, such as regarding the magistrate as a permanent law clerk in regard to task assignments, were often established with the first magistrates selected and then are perpetuated in the district even as individual magistrates and judges retire and are replaced.

49. *See, e.g.*, Grimit, *More important judicial qualities*, 70 JUDICATURE 141 (1986) (letter to the editor).

50. Goldman, *Reagan's judicial appointments at mid-term: shaping the bench in his own image*, 66 JUDICATURE 334, 338-340 (1983).

51. For example, there is a significant representation of individuals with elite and private law school educations among the district judges appointed during the last four presidential administrations. *Id.* at 338. During Reagan's second term, 60 per cent of district judges came from elite and private law schools. Goldman, *supra* n. 24, at 328.

52. *See, e.g.*, Berkson, Carbon & Neff, *A study of the U.S. Circuit Judge Nominating Commission* 63 JUDICATURE 104 (1979).

53. Data on the composition of the magistrate system are drawn from McCabe, *supra* n. 6, at 395; Administrative Office of the U.S. Courts, ANNUAL REPORT ON THE JUDICIARY EQUAL EMPLOYMENT OPPORTUNITY PROGRAM FOR THE TWELVE-MONTH PERIOD ENDED JUNE 30, 1981, 25 (Washington, DC: U.S. Government Printing Office, 1981); Administrative Office of the U.S. Courts, ANNUAL REPORT ON THE JUDICIARY EQUAL EMPLOYMENT OPPORTUNITY PROGRAM FOR THE TWELVE-MONTH PERIOD ENDED JUNE 30, 1986); and the October 1986 roster of magistrates obtained from the Administrative Office.

54. For additional discussion of the constitutionality of the magistrate system, see, e.g., McCabe, *supra* n. 6, at 369-374; Silberman, *Masters and Magistrates Part II: The American Analogue*, 50 N.Y.U.L. REV. 1297 (1975); Note, *Article III Constraints and the Expanding Civil Jurisdiction of Federal Magistrates: A Dissenting View*, 88 YALE L. J. 1023 (1979).

55. Administrative Office, *supra* n. 36, at 44.

56. For example, from 1985 to 1986 the number of civil cases in which litigants consented to have their cases handled by a magistrate increased 33.4 per cent from 3,717 to 4,960. Administrative Office, *supra* n. 10, at 37.

Law clerks: their roles and relationships with their judges

Although nearly everyone agrees that law clerks are necessary, there is considerable disagreement as to what their role should be.

by David Crump

To some people, law clerks are part of a long and noble tradition. To a few others, they are 25-year-old Svengalis influencing the judicial process toward views inculcated into them by a phalanx of activist law professors.

In any event, nearly everyone views law clerks as necessary. Justice John Paul Stevens has said that the Supreme Court is "too busy to decide whether there [is] anything we could do about the problem of being too busy."[1] And United States District Court Judge Norman Black, whose docket is roughly double the national average and who has managed, through hard work, only to hold down the amount of its annual increase, says simply: "I couldn't function without them."[2]

For the law clerk, the experience is likely to be a high point in his or her legal career. "It was wonderful," says Sal Levatino, a former law clerk to a federal district judge in Austin, Texas. "It really ought to be at the end of your career, rather than at the beginning."[3] In fact, law clerks speak of "law clerk letdown" when they begin practicing law. The clerkship represented a "pure" experience with the law, constantly exciting—and without the risk of failure.[4]

In contrast, the practice of law itself involves clients with unrealistic expectations, cases or transaction that don't turn very fast, and work that is more often tedious than exciting. To the law clerk's surprise, the possibilities of missing time deadlines, failing to get evidence admitted, or making any one of a variety of similar mistakes aren't something that happens to lesser practitioners. They are very real dangers for the inexperienced—such as a

lawyer fresh from a judicial clerkship.

The clerk's duties

The functions of law clerks vary tremendously. A few judges use them as research assistants only. For other judges they may perform a screening function: summarizing the contents of papers filed by the parties in the manner of an honest broker. Still others—and these are clearly the majority—use law clerks as preliminary drafters of opinions or orders. The amount of direction supplied to a clerk drafting an opinion varies enormously from judge to judge.

In a trial court, as Judge Black points out, more than 90 per cent of cases are typically settled.[5] A federal district judge may well find that he can use his clerks most effectively in motion practice, because prompt, simple rulings on motions make the cases settle faster, more cheaply, and more fairly. A typical district judge may assign each of his clerks half the docket by odd and even numbers, having them coordinate with the district clerk's office to study each motion as soon as possible after its submission date.[6]

Screening of each motion for complexity and for the need for a hearing is the typical first step. As the judge considers each motion, informal discussion with the law clerk—or a memorandum prepared by the clerk, probably with a recommendation—highlights the issues (the practice varies). The judge may then orally outline the chosen disposition and discuss the general content of the order or memorandum the clerk is to prepare. If the motion does require a hearing or a conference, the assigned law clerk is likely to be made responsible for coordinating with the district clerk's office to see that it is properly scheduled. At trial, a law clerk's functions may range from assistance in charge preparation to on-the-spot research on evidence questions. And if an opinion results, the first draft will probably be written by the law clerk.

In appellate courts, law clerks' time is often largely occupied in preparing pre-argument memoranda and writing initial drafts of opinions. In courts of last resort with discretionary review, clerks often have significant (some would say, excessive) functions in deciding which cases will be heard.

The influence of clerks

There is no question among former law clerks now practicing law that the decision of their own cases can be influenced or even determined by the judgments of law clerks. Should a lawyer use different tactics if he is trying a case before a trial judge with a full complement of clerks? Former Supreme Court clerk John O'Neill says that if the judge relies heavily on his clerks, "It's important to appeal to *their* imagination."[7] In that endeavor, says O'Neill, "You'd make more academic and policy arguments."[8] Before a judge without clerks, the lawyer might do well to put more emphasis on explaining the case law. Former state appellate law clerk Rob Johnson says, "You'd play to the sympathies of the person who's really" going to report on the case.[9] Following his law school training, the law clerk may be more likely than the judge to see the case as controlled by social policy.

But Mike Kuhn,[10] a former Fifth Circuit clerk, disagrees. "There are too many variables," he says. "I don't think I'd stress public policy just because the judge has law clerks; the clerk himself might be more interested in *stare decisis*." Besides, he points out, it's risky to "play to the clerks" when the judge is still the one who makes the final decision.[11]

But whether the law clerk performs a research function, a screening or "filtering" function, or a drafting or recommending function, the judgment factor is there. And even though the judge "is the judge," and remains so, the judgment of the law clerk is frequently an ingredient in the decision.

To some observers, this "leavening effect" is a positive thing. "In our ideal form," writes John B. Oakley, a former law clerk to a judge of the Supreme Court of California, "the law clerk is meant to fiddle with the law, to advocate innovation, to introduce to its inner sanctums the views of those outside."[12] Oakley's work, *Law Clerks and the Judicial Process* (co-authored with Robert S. Thompson), is the most comprehensive recent work on the subject. The law clerk "gives the law needed capacity for change,"[13] Oakley and Thompson write. "[T]he fabric of the law has been woven from the warp of the judiciary and the woof of their law clerks."[14] This metaphor depicts the judge as the lengthwise thread (or warp) in the weave of the law and the clerk as its crosswise thread (or woof). If there are to be "passing variations in texture and elasticity," says Oakley and Thompson, "they must be woven into the fabric by means of the woof."[15] And in what they correctly acknowledge is a very bad pun, Oakley and Thompson argue that the law clerk should be "a fiddler in the woof."[16]

In a written opinion, the Fifth Circuit has provided some support for this model. "The association with law clerks is also valuable to the judge; in addition to relieving him of many clerical and administrative chores, law clerks may serve as sounding boards for new ideas, often affording a different perspective . . . .," said the court in *Fredonia Broadcasting Corporation v. RCA Corporation.*[17] Judge Frank M. Coffin, in his book *The Ways of a Judge*, adds that law clerks "bring to chambers their recent exposure to excellent professors in demanding schools of law from all parts of the country. They are questioning, articulate, idealistic." As a result, they "provide the judge with a continuing seminar that cannot fail to keep his mind open and his mental juices flowing."[18]

Oakley and Thompson point out that the historical ideal of the law clerk fits the warp-and-woof metaphor too.[19] Felix Frankfurter was given to lengthy substantive discussions with his law clerks, in which "[a]nger, scorn, sarcasm, [and] humor buttressed straightforward argument."[20] The law clerk was placed "on an equal footing" with the judge in the "ecstasy of combat."[21]

Oakley and Thompson recognize that the judge must make the final decisions. But this result, they argue, will flow from "the judge's natural resistance to the influence of a young and fleeting law clerk."[22] In fact, Oakley and Thompson conclude, a greater problem may be that the judge's thinking wins out merely because of his position and tenure. For that reason, they say, the law clerk will have a proper incentive to "fight the judge for every inch of fair ground."[23]

A different view

But to others, this "ideal" is not so attractive. They point out that the law clerk is not appointed by the president, is not confirmed by the Senate, and has not been qualified under the Constitution to perform judicial functions.

Oakley and Thompson's statement that law clerks are innovators who fiddle with the law and provide it with capacity for change is hotly disputed by most former law clerks interviewed for this article. "That's so naive," says O'Neill.[24] He points out that most activist judges do not need the intervention of law clerks to make them into innovators. "What about Mr. Justice Douglas?" he asks. "The function of the law clerk ought to be to find what the law is," he says. "And a lawyer who's practiced a long time [*i.e.*, the judge] ought to make the policy decisions."[25]

Rob Johnson, who was the single clerk for a state appellate court with three judges back in the days when "I'm not sure we even had an electric typewriter," is more blunt. "I don't like the idea of wild-eyed 24- and 25-year-olds, who come right out of law school, tinkering with the law in a way that might affect my life," he says.[26] And Judge Black (who teaches in law school himself) disagrees with the notion that a judge's chambers are "an ivory tower" that needs a recently graduated lawyer to provide "a pipeline to reality."[27] Judge Black has a simple answer to the model of the law clerk as "innovator:" "I've seen the argument made," he says. "I've never seen it put into effect."[28]

In addition to the law clerk's lack of constitutional authority, there are at least two other reasons for opposing a decision-making role. One is the effect of the law clerk's education. Harvard law student Alexander Troy describes his first year torts class (which, it is to be hoped, was atypical) as "a desultory survey of economics, epistemology and social psychology, but the professor also found time to address the issue of the limits of a court's power in a democratic society."[29] That issue, according to Troy, was resolved by the professor's conclusion that "[j]udicial decisions are substantively indistinguishable from legislative ones." Thus the "inference left for students to draw is that there is little a court cannot do."[30] Many judges may feel a need to counteract the pronouncements of some of Troy's professors who, he says, were critical of judicial restraint as a general principle.[31]

The merit of this view is not really the issue; the point is that, for the judge himself, presidential appointment and Senate hearings—or election, in a state system—provide an acceptable filtering process as well as a reminder of the separation of powers. But as Rob Johnson says: "A law clerk, all he's done is get good grades in law school."[32]

The second reason against the law clerk as decisionmaker is experience, both in law and in life. Law clerks are less likely to have had mortgages—or children whom they must decide to send to either public or private school. "They don't see the tugs and pulls; they don't see the results down at the end of the line," says Johnson.[33] He points out that "school cases just look different when you haven't got school-age kids and neither do any of your close friends. So does freedom of speech when you don't have a home that might have an x-rated movie across from it."[34] What is more, a 25-year-old may not realize that such experiences are likely to mature his outlook. The "fiddler in the woof" viewpoint might regard this inexperience as a net plus, characterizing it as a fresh approach; a less positive view would see the lack of self-knowledge as a negative factor.

And in the law itself, lack of experience is likely to reflect itself in harmful naivete. The difficulty of preserving error for appeal, of maintaining a trial schedule, and even of presenting the bodies of one's witnesses physically at the trial may be unknown to law clerks. The proposition that an error-free criminal trial is unusual may be differently perceived by those who have seen trials firsthand and those who have seen them only in law school casebooks, through what Mr. Justice Fortas once called the "remote knothole" of appellate decisions.[35]

As Levatino puts it, even the law clerk's job itself is "somewhat deceptive."[36] As a law clerk, one might draft an opinion in a case presented by attorneys, "And you say, 'hey, this is easy.' " But "it's harder to have clients come into your office and dump something on your desk and ask if there's something you can do, when you can't even tell if it's a securities case, or a labor matter, or what." As a result, says Levatino, "If I went back now, 13 years later, I'd have a whole lot more empathy for the attorneys."[37]

The difference between the "fiddler and innovator" argument, and the opposing view (as expressed by Johnson) that the law clerk's job "is to do what he's told to," can easily be exaggerated.[38] Most law clerks acknowledge that delegation by judges to clerks of the task of writing a first draft of an opinion is common. If the judge handles the delegation properly, and deals adequately with the result, the judge remains the decisionmaker.

And former Fifth Circuit law clerk Michael Kuhn, although not himself in favor of judicial activism, defends the law clerk's prerogative. "A law clerk has a right and a duty to express his views," he says. "If you think your judge has missed a point, if he's off base, it's your job to say, 'Judge, you're deciding this case as though it were a rule-of-reason case and it's not; it's a per se violation.' "[39] Other law clerks give examples of occasions, in fact, in which law clerks have restrained judicial activism (or even prevented unfortunate displays of anger by judges with hair-trigger tempers).

The other side of the coin, says Kuhn, is that the law clerk "shouldn't be offended if his recommendation isn't adopted." If the judge replies, "I don't care; I think the rule of reason is the better way to decide this case," Kuhn concludes that the law clerk ought to draft a good, sound opinion—"using the rule of reason, as the judge said."[40]

Using law clerks well

Since law clerks are here to stay, the real question concerns the way a judge ought to go about using them. Lawyers and law clerks have a variety of opinions on the subject.

The number of law clerks. Each United States Supreme Court justice presides over a law firm of four clerks. Each federal court of appeals judge has three, and California's chief justice has an astounding 14 (although many of their duties are performed for the court as a whole or for other justices).

The suspicion arises that a plethora of law clerks dilutes the judge's ability to make the important decisions. Former district court clerk Tom Houghton thinks even a lawyer who is a good manager "can't personally supervise more than three or four associates."[41] And if he is not a good manager, he may supervise one law clerk poorly. With numbers like 14, intermediate managers are required, says Houghton. In such a situation, asks Johnson, "Does the judge write any opinions at all? It sounds as though they wouldn't have time. They'd be reading reams of paper from their law clerks."[42]

But busy judges without adequate assistance from clerks draw criticism too. As Levatino says, a conscientious judge working alone in a complex case "may not even have time to read all of the briefs."[43]

Length of opinions. One consequence of the number of law clerks is an opinion explosion. United States Supreme Court Reports have gone from 2133 pages in the 1960 October Term to 4269 in the 1983 Term, not so much because of workload as because of the length of individual opinions. "When the opinions start looking like law review articles, you know you're in trouble," says one former law clerk.

The result is an increase in complexity—a proliferation of conflicting opinions—all without the benefit of the consistency and certainty that are the apparent aim. While it is desirable that judges express the reasons for their decisions as a means of encouraging rational decision making, there is little utility in a district court summary judgment opinion that contains a treatise on Rule 56. Former trial court clerk Levatino says flatly, "most trial level cases don't require opinions."[44] Findings and conclusions would be preferable from a functional standpoint. And Houghton points out that the great appellate judges of the past—Hand, Cardozo and Holmes—wrote long opinions when it was necessary, "but most of their opinions are a page and a half in the reporter system."[45]

The types of opinions law clerks may produce is also a matter of concern. Dan Peterson, a former law clerk on the Iowa Supreme Court, suspects that law clerks left to their own devices might draft "opinions that are full of global statements that you don't need to support the holding and don't apply as globally as they're written." These statements "muddle things in the next case and have to be distinguished."[46] A judge's experience, Peterson thinks, would help him avoid that sort of writing and eliminate it from a law clerk's preliminary draft.

Discretionary review. In courts of last resort or other courts with discretionary review, there is heavy reliance on law clerks in the selection of cases for decision. For example, it is an open secret (reported in the newspapers) that at least six Supreme Court justices rely on one designated law clerk to summarize each certiorari petition. "I do not even look at the papers in over 80 per cent of the cases that are filed," Justice Stevens has publicly stated.[47]

Former Supreme Court clerk O'Neill points out that when law clerks perform such a task, "they may reflect values learned in law school, not over a career." Hence the problems they may find significant are "the ones they've been taught about, not the great practical ones that you'd identify over 10 years of practice."[48] Issues that O'Neill calls "interstitial"—crucial issues in energy, finance, or similar areas that determine the fate of the nation just as surely as do constitutional questions—may not commend themselves to a law clerk's imagination simply because they are not the subject of any law school course.[49]

It is probably inevitable that discretionary review will prompt heavy reliance on clerks, because the task is tedious. The supreme courts of Texas and California also rely heavily upon law clerk involvement. Anonymously poring over reams of dross to discover one case for review is obviously less satisfying than crafting a signed opinion, and a judge may not regard it as the most productive use of his time.

But because they are more experienced lawyers, with longer memories for recurring issues, judges can provide a corrective to the syndrome of selection by law school course content. The judge can do so by express direction to his clerk, by discussions exposing "law clerk's bias" to the law clerk himself, or by a final review in which the judge consciously tries to counteract the fact that he is, to a degree, the prisoner of his law clerk's education.

Guidance, supervision, and orientation. A good many law clerks learn about office policies of the judge through trial and error. A few judges have had success in the use of office manuals or memoranda explaining the job to new arrivals. Given the planned turnover of clerks, such a practice might be a good management tool. In a district court, identification of various procedures (different kinds of motions, jury charge preparation, etc.) and the approach the judge uses on each would shorten the learning curve—and not incidentally, would help the judge to promulgate his own decisions. In appellate courts, a written explanation of standards for the court's summary docket, methodology in handling motions, and like matters would be just as helpful.

There is, in fact, a "Law Clerk Handbook," published by the Federal Judicial Center; certain states have published similar aids. Ranging from the general to the specific, the Handbook covers such topics as the history of law clerks (the tradition was begun at the Supreme Court by Justice Horace Gray in 1882 and continued by his successor, Oliver Wendell Holmes) to telephone etiquette ("If the judge is . . . unavailable, you should inquire, 'May I take a message?' ").[50] Its coverage of procedure,

drafting tips, and organization appears quite useful. It is necessarily general, and its usefulness would be enhanced if individual judges rewrote it to reflect their own practices (having their law clerks, of course, do the drafting!).

There are early limits to the usefulness of this idea; many practices in a court are "not suitable for a memorandum," as former district court clerk Tom Houghton puts it.[51] "What it takes is treatment of the clerk the way a senior lawyer uses an associate," with individual day-to-day attention recognizing that the law clerk needs supervision.[52]

Another suggestion is that law schools might provide courses in their curricula for future law clerks. For example, a one-hour course based upon the "Law Clerk Handbook" (and other materials) is under active consideration at the South Texas College of Law, which in 1985 supplied more clerks to the Texas Supreme Court than any other school. There is some question, however, whether it is feasible thus to prepare clerks for such diverse environments as federal trial courts and state appellate courts—and for an infinite variety of individual judges' preferences. Furthermore, some academics doubt that a law school's resources should be expended in a way that will guide so few students for such a brief period in their careers. Still, the proposal is worth trying because of its possible public benefits. An alternative suggestion of a national orientation program, perhaps conducted by the Federal Judicial Center, might offer some benefits, but they are not likely to justify the costs.

Management styles. Many former clerks are skeptical of proposals for periodic staff meetings, believing them to be ineffective in a small office handling highly individualized problems. But if the office handles a large volume of matters—a district court with a large backlog, for example, or a court of last resort that has a considerable discretionary docket—staff meetings in which the status of each case is reviewed may make dispositions more efficient. Similarly, if the judge has more than three or four law clerks, staff meetings may be necessary to reinforce the policies the judge wants followed.

Both judges and clerks seem to regard a one-on-one relationship as preferable. A "committee" or "intermediate manager" approach may be necessary in a larger office, however, and the trial of a larger case may require the services of more than one clerk. In normal operations, most judges and clerks view direct supervision of the clerk by the judge as more efficient. It also seems clear that this management style is best for reasons unrelated to efficiency: it maximizes control of actual decision making by the judge, and it avoids the dilution of his personal responsibility for each case.

Confidentiality and the appearance of propriety. Most law clerks probably recognize that public identification of the law clerk as a decisionmaker is undesirable. Most probably come to the task with an appreciation that what they see and hear is privileged. "I'm their client," says Judge Black. "They're my lawyers."[53] The "Law Clerk Handbook" is explicit and eloquent on the subject: "If judges wish to publish their jurisprudential, economic or social views, they know how to do so."[54]

But unfortunately, the available evidence indicates that understanding of these concepts is neither innate nor universal among law clerks. Furthermore, says Houghton, "the judge needs to emphasize that the need for circumspection goes on after the clerkship is over." "*The Brethren*[55] is inexcusable," he says.[56] Such disclosures come about because law clerks "sometimes come out of clerkships with bloated heads" and with a need to expand upon their roles in major decisions.[57] (It might be added that if one has doubt that the maturity of law clerks is a real concern, one might consider *The Brethren*—and the hemorrhage of confidential disclosures it reflects—a strong piece of evidence to that effect.)

One trial lawyer tells a related story that is equally disconcerting. While interviewing a prospective new associate, he mentioned a case he had recently tried. "Oh," said the interviewee, "That was John Smith's case." John Smith (a fictitious name) was the judge's law clerk; he had drafted the opinion. The interviewee, a former clerk himself, was apparently unaware that such disclosures do not serve the judge who trusted his circumspection. To the trial lawyer (who, of course, thought it was *his* case), it meant a more jaundiced view of the court. This was especially so since John Smith hadn't been in the courtroom when the case was orally argued, leaving the lawyer to conclude that, if the case was indeed "John Smith's," his arguments were not heard.

The subject is difficult, because courts are a part of the government. And a blanket prohibition upon law clerks talking to reporters would be inap-propriate, for the same reason that it would be inappropriate to impose a gag upon personnel in other governmental offices. The important issue is one of confidentiality and deference to the judge.

A personal relationship

There is another side to the law clerk issue. Judges benefit personally from relationships with their law clerks, and not just because they need clerks' research skills. The job of a judge, strictly defined, is solitary and remote. If we are to attract good judges, perhaps we must consider the need that lawyers and judges have in common with most of the human race: the need for a collegial atmosphere, in which one's work is shared with other people.

For the best of the profession—the sort of lawyers we would like to attract to the judiciary—the job doesn't pay well in comparison to private practice. And as Judge Black points out, "Making decisions is hard work."[58] For that reason, Judge Black points out, emotional and mental maturity in a law clerk applicant is a primary qualification; there's "nothing to assure you," as he puts it, "that a person with a 98.5 grade average will be a good law clerk."[59]

The old adage holds that a federal judge is just a lawyer who knows a senator. But as far as almost every law clerk is concerned, *his* judge is extraordinary. Talking to Judge Black, one senses immediately that the affection is usually mutual—and that relationships with law clerks can sometimes go a long way toward filling the compensation gap. As Judge Coffin puts it, "[T]he pleasure of their company is one of a judge's most refreshing fringe benefits."[60]

NOTES

This article originally appeared in Volume 69, Number 4, December-January 1986, pages 236-240.

1. Middleton, *High Court's Case Load too Heavy: Three Justices*, 68 A.B.A. J. 1201 (October, 1982).

2. Interview with Judge Norman Black, United States District Court, in Houston, Texas (December 1, 1982).

3. Telephone interview with Sal Levantino, former law clerk (October 21, 1982).

4. *Id.*

5. Interview Black, *supra* n. 2.

6. *Id.*

7. Interview with John O'Neill, former law clerk, in Houston, Texas (October 21, 1982).

8. *Id.*

9. Interview with Rob Johnson, former law clerk, in Houston, Texas (October 21, 1982).

10. Interview with Mike Kuhn, former law clerk, in Houston, Texas (October 21, 1982).

11. *Id.*

12. Oakley and Thompson, LAW CLERKS AND THE JUDICIAL PROCESS 138 (Berkeley, CA: University of California Press, 1980).

13. *Id.*

14. *Id.*

15. *Id.*

16. *Id.*

17. Fredonia Broadcasting Corp. v. RCA Corp., 569 F.2d 251, 255-256 (5th Cir. 1978).

18. Coffin, THE WAYS OF A JUDGE 72 (Boston: Houghton Mifflin Co., 1980).

19. Oakley and Thompson, *supra* n. 12, at 138.

20. Sacks, *Felix Frankfurter,* in 3 THE JUSTICES OF THE UNITED STATES SUPREME COURT 1789-1969, 2403-2404 (New York: Chelsea House in association with Bowker Company, 1969).

21. *Id.*

22. Oakley and Thompson, *supra* n. 12, at 38.

23. *Id.*

24. Interview O'Neill, *supra* n. 7.

25. *Id.*

26. Interview Johnson, *supra* n. 9.

27. Interview Black, *supra* n. 2.

28. *Id.*

29. Troy, *Learning the Law at Harvard,* WALL ST. J., August 6, 1982, at 14 col. 2.

30. *Id.*

31. *Id.* at col. 3.

32. Interview Johnson, *supra* n. 9.

33. *Id.*

34. *Id.*

35. Time Inc. v. Hill, 385 U.S. 374 (1967).

36. Interview Levatino, *supra* n. 3.

37. *Id.*

38. Interview Johnson, *supra* n. 9.

39. Interview Kuhn, *supra* n. 10.

40. *Id.*

41. Interview with Tom Houghton, former law clerk, in Houston, Texas (October 27, 1982).

42. Interview Johnson, *supra* n. 9.

43. Interview Levatino, *supra* n. 3.

44. *Id.*

45. Interview Houghton, *supra* n. 41.

46. Interview with Dan Peterson, former law clerk, in Houston, Texas (October 21, 1982).

47. Middleton, *supra* n. 1, at 1201.

48. Interview O'Neill, *supra* n. 7.

49. *Id.*

50. Dileo and Rubin, LAW CLERK HANDBOOK: A HANDBOOK FOR FEDERAL DISTRICT AND APPELLATE COURT LAW CLERKS (Washington, D.C.: Federal Judicial Center, 1977).

51. Interview Houghton, *supra* n. 41.

52. *Id.*

53. Interview Black, *supra* n. 2.

54. Dileo and Rubin, *supra* n. 50.

55. Woodward and Armstrong, THE BRETHREN: INSIDE THE SUPREME COURT (New York: Simon and Schuster, 1979).

56. Interview Houghton, *supra* n. 41.

57. *Id.*

58. Interview Black, *supra* n. 2.

59. *Id.*

60. Coffin, *supra* n. 18, at 71.

Actors in the Judicial Process
Lawyers and Legal Practices

INTRODUCTION   The role of lawyers in the American judicial process has been romanticized and glamorized through accounts of the exploits, both real and fictional, of the Daniel Websters, Clarence Darrows, Perry Masons, and Michael Kuzaks of courtrooms past and present. Naturally, pursuit of the profession of law entails many tasks, roles, and job possibilities that would be quite foreign to our folklore's most famous litigators. Indeed, a great many lawyers never try a case and many never see the inside of a courtroom. The articles in this section address several facets of the legal profession and the diverse types of practice it may entail.

We begin with Nathan Posner's query, "Truth, justice and the client's interest: Can the lawyer serve all three?" Posner explores many ethical dilemmas faced by advocates whose clients' personal interests may conflict with the ideals of truth and justice that the lawyer must also serve. Posner is "convinced that our adversary system in its present form endorses various techniques that at best avoid the truth and at worst make a mockery of 'justice.'"

Posner writes on a small palette in which he examines the problems faced by individual practitioners in their relationships with their clients. In "The legal profession: a critical evaluation," Arlin Adams utilizes broader brushstrokes in developing his concerns about the contemporary practice of law. Adams' critique is an important one that raises fundamental questions regarding the profession's commitment to pursuing its mission in the wake of the great "professional metamorphosis" of the past decades. Adams documents important changes in the law as well as fundamental changes in lawyering that have caused problems for the judicial process and "the disappearance of the individual legal personality." Adams feels that professionalism has given way to commercialism and that those civic values lawyers historically possessed while serving as the nation's "secular ministry" have eroded. Adams' sobering account ends with a call for lawyers to reassert the values of service to the community, legal craftsmanship, and professional devotion he associates with earlier generations of his colleagues.

One of the problems alluded to in Adams' critique of the legal profession is the decline in the ability of most lawyers to serve as generalists who can handle skillfully the day to day problems confronted by individuals seeking help with their mundane legal concerns. Basic questions about legal competency have been raised with frequency in recent years, particularly in the wake of former Chief Justice Burger's long-term focus on his concern about the quality of legal advocacy he often saw in the Supreme Court's oral argumentation. In "Ensuring legal competency: the South Carolina approach," Bruce Littlejohn offers a case study of what one state has done in an effort to induce law students to seek more practical legal training while encouraging law schools to provide more clinically-relevant educational experience.

Finally, in "Legal services before the Supreme Court," Susan Lawrence examines the operation of a non-traditional form of legal practice, the Legal Services Program established by the Johnson administration, which was aimed at providing indigents with greater access to the civil justice system. While the Legal Services Program was discontinued in 1974, Lawrence argues that its litigation activism was a success that "reduced the poor's de facto exclusion from the judicial processes which culminate in the U.S. Supreme Court." The article examines the success of the Legal Services Program's advocacy before the Court.

Truth, justice, and the client's interest: Can the lawyer serve all three?

by Nathan L. Posner

Our changing society confronts the lawyer with a serious problem: can there be a truly rational administration of justice unless *all* relevant facts are accurately determined? The lawyer usually satisfies himself with the belief that the adversary system is the proper and best means for dispensing justice. I would like to adopt such a philosophy, but I am convinced that our adversary system in its present form endorses various techniques that at best avoid the truth and at worst make a mockery of "justice." Adversary procedures must be amended and altered if we seek a better determination of where the truth lies in any issue.

A lawyer's traditional obligation is to seek justice and truth. This duty must be invulnerable to attack, because the lawyer is an officer of the court and a pillar of the system of the administration of justice. A lawyer has a professional obligation to seek the truth in every instance.

The adversary system reveals one of its major weaknesses when a skillful, well-prepared lawyer opposes an incompetent or unprepared lawyer. It is questionable whether the system enhances the cause of justice in such a case, and whether the verdict is a dispensation of justice or merely the product of competence versus incompetence. On occasion, the effect of incompetence is minimized because of the safeguards provided by the judge and jury in their respective functions of determining the law and finding the facts. Therefore, some may argue, after proper instructions from the court concerning the weight of the evidence and its credibility, the verdict rendered must be fair and proper. Nevertheless, the administration of justice in such instances has been hampered, and the adversary system has impeded rather than aided our democratic approach to the administration of justice.

Much has been written concerning lawyers' ethics in the adversary system. Some suggest that the lawyer's devotion to the success of the client's cause regardless of means and expedience overrules the requirement of decency and the search for truth. Such zealous advocates hold that the lawyer, because of his confidential relationship with the client, may not disclose the truth, and, even when the lawyer has learned the truth from sources other than the client, may not bring it to the knowledge of the authorities because it might adversely affect the client.

More to the point, despite expressly contrary prohibitions contained in the Code of Professional Responsibility,[1] some theorists argue that when the client or a witness commits perjury in the offering of testimony, the lawyer may not protest, withdraw from the case, or in any other fashion divulge the fact that perjury has been committed. I cannot agree that zealous advocacy embraces the ignoring of obvious perjury. Such behavior is equivalent to subornation.

No one would suggest that, in a case in which the life or personal liberty of one accused of a crime is at stake, there should be any diminution of the many safeguards provided by the Constitution and Rules of Criminal Procedure. The constitutional rights of a defendant charged with crime must be resistant to all attacks, and it is the duty of the lawyer to protect those rights. It is because of this principle of law that all those who advocate the lawyer's obligation to effect the cause of the client, regardless of truth and justice, feel justified in maintaining their obligation as paramount.

But let us for the moment dismiss from our minds the criminal law and the constitutional privileges of criminal defendants and view the matter of ethics and the adversary system in the context of the civil courts. There, weighty considerations of constitutional rights, which concern the members of the criminal bar who champion the client's cause above all else, are less important. In the civil courts it is largely monetary benefits and property rights that are at stake.

Even in the criminal adversary system, there has been recognition of the principle of full disclosure; the prosecutor's primary duty is to seek justice rather than simply to win cases and achieve convictions. Accordingly, he or she should attempt[2] during the course of his investigation to ferret out *all* relevant evidence even if it detracts from his case or tends to exonerate the defendant; and, at trial, should disclose *all* relevant evidence, again without regard to which side evidence favors. It is also presently recognized that the lawyer representing the government in a civil adversary proceeding should seek justice by developing a full and fair record, and should not use the power of the government and the procedural rules to harass opposing parties.[3]

Why should this responsibility not be extended to all lawyers engaged in the trial of civil cases? Such a duty would complement the existing admonition to all lawyers in all types of cases[4] to disclose to the tribunal all law applicable to the litigation, including the existence of precedents or statutes adverse to the legal positions of their clients. Once the facts and the law have been presented in this manner, the lawyers are free to zealously advocate the inferences and conclusions to be drawn from them in a light most favorable to their clients, and may challenge the applicability or the soundness of any unfavorable law. The likelihood of a truly just result is much greater under this system than under a system of trial by concealment, half-truth and subterfuge.

No one is prepared to venture an opinion concerning what perjury or subornation is committed in a typical civil case. However, it is sure that exaggerations and half-truths abound. A few examples should serve to highlight the problem.

• The adversary system is stultified when a lawyer suggests that a witness avoid certain statements because they might influence a jury against the cause of the client. I consider a lawyer in violation of his oath when he dares suggest to a witness prior to trial: "If the facts in this case are what I have been led to believe, then the proper answer to this question should be . . . ."

• I question the ethics of a lawyer who, during the preparation of a tort case, reads to the client various decisions of the appellate courts dealing with distances and car lengths, emphasizing that the appellate courts affirmed a finding of contributory negligence where the distance between the two cars was less than the certain quoted number of yards, and that therefore recovery was denied. He then asks the client, "And how many yards away were you when you first saw the other car?" Conceding that the lawyer may be properly disturbed with certain arbitrary rules that would preclude recovery to the client, has he the right to make suggestions that will give the right of recovery to his client based on "induced" testimony? Is he seeking justice and truth, or is he seeking to win the case for his client no matter what?

• Then there is a theory known as "selective ignorance." This refers to the lawyer who tells the client during their first meeting, "Don't say anything that will hurt your case." Not having been told, the lawyer can proceed with the case as he sees it on the information supplied to him after the warning. This lawyer does not recognize his responsibility to society, and does not serve the cause for which he became a lawyer. He is merely trying to justify his conduct by his rationalization of "service to the client," which unfortunately, in most instances, involves substantial fees.

Similar problems arise with respect to documentary evidence. A letter or memorandum that was never received by one party and which purports to confirm an oral agreement made by him, which in fact was never made, will appear as evidence in his opponent's case. Conversely, some clients have heeded the "message" conveyed by their lawyer when he suggests at the outset that "all those old accounting records, which you are not legally required to keep and which would be helpful evidence to your adversary, must take up a lot of filing space. Many businesses like yours dispose of their outdated records so that they can use their filing space for more current material."

• Finally, I do not believe it is ethical for a lawyer to seek delay in a matter because of the client's inability to make payment on a judgment that will be secured unless a defense is interposed.[5] There have been instances where rules have been used against parties, and technicalities raised in pleadings, in order that more time could be accorded the defendant before the inevitable judgment would be entered against him. When a lawyer is aware that there is no defense to an action, and that his sole obligation to the client's cause is to "buy" time, he is breaching the Code of Professional Responsibility. The "justice" that he seeks is one-sided and brings prejudice to others involved.

Other areas of the civil practice removed from the trial of cases have readily adopted and followed the suggested higher standards of full disclosure. For example, a lawyer representing a corporation that desires to sell its securities to the public must be certain that all relevant facts are fully and accurately represented in the documents filed with the Securities and Exchange Commission, including the prospectus that is to be distributed to the investing public in connection with the offer and sale of the securities.

Such a lawyer may not merely accept the client's description of the facts but must make his own independent investigation, using due diligence to assure himself that the client's records support the factual representations being made, that the various assets of the client are fully and accurately described in the documents, and that all financial information is correct and not misleading. If the lawyer finds a mistake, an omission of a fact, or an adverse fact, he must insist that the client make the appropriate disclosure.

These same principles are applicable to the lawyer retained to prepare the periodic reports required to be filed by public companies. Some even contend that such a lawyer, should he fail to convince the client to make the necessary full disclosure, has the obligation to report the client's failure to the appropriate regulatory agency. In the practice of decedents' estates and trusts as well, the lawyer's responsibility to disclose all assets subject to tax has long been recognized and unquestioned. Should the civil litigation system settle for lower standards?

A true lawyer must realize that he is an administrator of justice as well as an advocate on behalf of his client. Each lawyer must know and seek to inform those who are training to become lawyers of the positive responsibility on the part of every member of the profession to nurture and encourage justice and truth. The accomplishment of that goal transcends the obligation of advocacy.

NOTES

This article originally appeared in Volume 60, Number 3, October 1976, pages 111-113.

1. DR 7-102. See also EC 7-6 and EC 7-26.
2. EC 7-13.
3. EC 7-14.
4. EC 7-23.
5. *See* EC 7-4, EC 7-9, and DR 7-102 A(1) and (2).

The legal profession: a critical evaluation

The legal profession and the practice of law have undergone a drastic transformation in recent years, and the changes have not been for the better. Members of the profession must regain a sense of their individual legal personality and faith in the ultimate mission of their calling.

by Arlin M. Adams

All professions, especially one as central to American life as the legal profession, should undergo a continuing process of examination and self-evaluation. Any group that does not engage in such an exercise loses much that makes it a profession: a shared set of principles and customs that transcend self-interest and speak to the essential nature of the particular calling or trade.

There are greater reasons beyond periodic examination, however, that make this topic most compelling. In recent years, the legal profession has undergone fundamental changes that threaten to sever it from its traditional moorings. A qualitative revolution has occurred within the legal community to the extent that the practice which existed 40 years ago is hardly recognizable today.

No calling has occupied a more important and undeviating role in the emergence and development of American society. The practice of law, almost by definition, should establish and promote the common good and bring forth the advancement and betterment of society. As a profession, however, we have departed from the practice as it has been envisioned from the early days of the Republic. This dramatic change has strong overtones for the future. Although many authors have chronicled the recent transition of the legal profession, few are willing to argue that these developments have evolved for the betterment of society.

The sources causing the changes in the legal profession are both external and internal. The external pressures arise from great movements in the body of substantive law and in the types of services that lawyers are now required to perform. The changes in what constitute the practice of law,

in turn, have transformed who constitutes the practitioners of law. From an internal standpoint, the profession has undergone as drastic a transformation as the substantive law that governs us. I shall attempt to address these two antecedents of professional metamorphosis.

Changes in the law

Just a few decades ago the rules governing society were almost entirely of the common law variety. Under the common law system, the recognized doctrines of law originated from historic precedent and were gradually forged by lawyers and judges as society advanced and matured. In recent years, however, the proliferation of statutory and regulatory law has relegated the common law to a far less prominent position.

The common law system was designed to adjudicate disputes between two relatively equal parties according to well-established principles. The former common law practitioner drew on diverse and traditional doctrines regarding the relationship between government and property, whereas the modern day practice consists primarily of various statutory, regulatory, and administrative specialties. A great share of litigation today entails large and complicated breach of contract suits, complex real estate transactions, intricate corporate matters, and financial maneuvering in the international capital markets. The substance and function of the types of matters the law addresses has shifted from the small scale of the common law to the large scope of a practice dominated by extensive financial concerns.

The second source of change in the law is the

burgeoning areas of practice relating to government. The rise of the administrative state—the so-called headless fourth branch of government—has been sweeping. The establishment of quasi-judicial authorities and agencies, such as the Federal Communications Commission, the Occupational Safety and Health Administration, and the Environmental Protection Agency, has accelerated continuously since World War II, and shows little sign of abating. The number of federal agencies alone has increased from 20 to well over 70, many with narrow, sometimes overlapping purposes.

Furthermore, in the coming months additional federal bodies governing the closing of industrial facilities and merger-and-acquisition transactions undoubtedly will be established. The proliferation of federal administrative agencies has been matched by a parallel expansion of state and local bodies. As expected, a government of greater size and scope has necessarily increased the share of legal work devoted to relatively novel, specialized administrative areas.

A third and perhaps most significant development in the law in the past few decades is the emergence of several new forms of legal actions. The number of class action suits and other types of multiparty litigation has grown substantially. This phenomenon has led to the introduction of "public" issues into the private litigation setting. Public issues are generally defined as those involving societal concerns and numerous parties, and are thus arguably more appropriate for legislative consideration. In contrast, private controversies are those amenable to judicial resolution between two discrete parties.

The distinction between public and private issues serves as a point of comparison between the past and the present era. Matters that once were clearly within the realm of public affairs now routinely appear before courts. There has been a clear departure in the perceived role of the judiciary. Litigation encompassing environmental and public health issues, products liability, industrial and nuclear safety, civil rights, and other litigation involving nontraditional plaintiffs is a relatively new development, which reflects this departure.

Much of the expansion in public interest litigation can be attributed to the characteristics of our latter-day economy. Mass producers of consumer goods, environmental polluters, and other large industrial aggregations now possess the ability to affect or injure large classes of citizens. Whether the radical innovations in the conduct of judicial affairs are a reflection of a change in the prevailing notions of the law or of greater economic forces, however, is not the issue at hand. The question whether law is a product of economic determinism or whether law shapes the path of economic change is a subject worthy of its own discrete forum.

In either event, the effect of these innovations on the profession is undeniable. The characteristic of gradualism—the belief that law originated from natural truths and was fashioned, through time, to accommodate newly developing human relationships—was the foundation of our common law history. Around this basic orientation, ethical norms and mores developed that fostered the evolution of the common law. Taken as a whole these practices emerged into a philosophy of legal professionalism. This concept of gradual change through reasoned treatment, however, is subjugated, or at least strained, in a legal climate of rapid and drastic transformation.

Changes in lawyering

The decline in professionalism as it relates to the law has occurred, at least in part, because of a diminution in the defining element of gradualism. Change in the law necessarily causes change in the profession. The great emphasis in today's practice on large transactional matters at the expense of individual client service particularly tends to undermine the values that define professionalism. The results of this transformation are readily apparent in how the typical law practice has changed.

A few year ago, single practitioners and small groups of lawyers dominated the practice. A firm with 20 attorneys was considered large. Today, firms with over 200 lawyers are not unusual, and a partnership of 20 is generally limited to handling small matters. In 1975, there were only four firms with over 200 lawyers in the United States, and they were viewed with great skepticism. In contrast, a recent survey reported well over 150 firms with more than 200 attorneys and there is far less reservation about the wisdom of the large firm as a legal institution. Indeed, last year, one of these firms celebrated the hiring of its 1,000th lawyer.

The advent of megafirms has substantially altered law practice. It is not unusual now to have firms with offices throughout the nation and even in major cities abroad. Moreover, a firm in Philadelphia attempting to hire students from Harvard, Yale, or Stanford will likely have to bid against firms from New York, Los Angeles, Chicago, and Denver. Thus, the marketplace for legal services and the marketplace for attorneys has grown national, sometimes international, in scope.

The small-town practitioner with intimate ties only to his local community is becoming a vanishing figure. Industry analysts predict that the growth in firm size will continue and will lead to a shakeout where the giant conglomerates will be the principal survivors. Indeed, proposals have been made in many state bars that would allow non-lawyers to own and control law firms so that they may operate more like business corporations. If this trend continues, there may be no place left for the individual practitioner or the small group of practitioners.

The expansion in the large, institutionalized practice has been made possible, I believe, by three developments in the way lawyers are trained and work. Taken as a whole, these elements—the new labor economies of the practice—constitute the changing internal climate of the profession.

The first development is the proliferation of law schools and lawyers. The number of lawyers in the United States has doubled since 1970 and is now well over 700,000, far and away the most lawyers for any nation in the world. The students fueling this expanding army are being trained at a growing number of law schools and in larger entering classes. The elite schools such as Harvard, Yale, and Pennsylvania have attempted to maintain the same number of students. Other law schools, however, especially state university law schools, have greatly expanded their enrollments.

A second factor allowing the progression of larger and larger firms is the fees for services that these firms now charge. This development is especially pertinent to the transactional nature of the practice. Forty years ago, the cost and time spent on legal services were a negligible part of business decisions. Today, the consideration of legal fees is a major factor in many of these transactions.

The rise of large legal fees has had other significant effects. Many have read about the $75,000 starting salaries and $10,000 bonuses given to graduating students, but even these numbers do not reflect the magnitude of the factor of money in large firm practice. *The American Lawyer*, a publication devoted to glamorizing big firms, now publishes annual financial data on such firms. Recent figures show firms realizing over $1,000,000 per year in revenues per lawyer; $1,000,000 in profit per partner; and one New York firm approaching $300,000,000 in total revenues.[1] Under headlines that blare: "Generating Revenue: The Key to The Bottom Line,"[2] the editors assure that faltering local economies will not affect business,[3] and warn that excessive pro bono work may lower a firm's profitability.[4]

Concentration on profit-maximization provides less and less time for lawyers to spend on public and professional activities. Obligations to the community and to the profession are subordinated when constant attention must be given to monetary aspects. Consequently, these vital elements undergirding the ideal of the principled, public-minded practitioner of old are victims of the recent preoccupation with fees, firm profits, and inordinate salaries.

The third element permitting the growth of large institutional firms is the level of specialization now required in the legal profession. At one time a lawyer may have dealt with a number of different types of matters in any particular period. Today's young attorneys, however, are required to specialize almost immediately. Sizable firms generally are organized into departments practicing one type of law. Differentiation of the legal labor force is essential to sustain these large organizations. The necessity to develop "instant expertise" is particularly troublesome, I believe, as it is inconsistent with the traditional vision of legal practice as a diverse and liberal endeavor. Excessive specialization inevitably detracts from the rich and full legacy of the profession.

The strained judicial process

With a clearer understanding of what the changing legal environment encompasses, we can now focus on its implications for the historic mission of the practitioner in our society. It is appropriate to ask what effect the confluence of these pressures has had on the judicial system that attempts to adjust to them. The structure of our system of courts and judges was shaped, essentially, for the common law practice of yesteryear. Consequently, just like any other infrastructure designed to accommodate traffic, be it an interstate highway or a shopping mall, the addition of greater and greater amounts of traffic creates a strain and hinders the ability of the system to function efficiently.

The exponential growth in litigation in recent

years has imposed such a tension on our legal infrastructure. The number of lawsuits filed in both state and federal courts is unprecedented. Heavier caseloads and the growing percentage of complex multiparty actions create a burden that courts are not institutionally equipped to handle. As a result, the level of procedural excess and abuse of pretrial procedures has risen as well. That our judicial system, which is charged in large part with the development of substantive law and the efficient administration of justice, must now endure a constant state of procedural impasse is without precedent and is a poor reflection on the state of the profession. A pivotal role of an advocate in our adversarial system is the public duty to advance the edification of the courts and to assist in their efficient administration. Abuse of the discovery process and dilatory tactics abridge this duty and diminish yet another public aspect of the profession.

The political response to the judicial crisis caused by the changing legal atmosphere has been primarily to add more judges to an already overburdened system. Thus, in 1945 there were 100 federal judges; today there are more than 700. To a lesser extent, the response has been to hire court administrators and to install high-tech equipment. The emergence of court administrators, whose jobs are primarily to facilitate the operation of the courts, is illustrative of the continuing need simply to keep traffic moving. The question then arises as to what effect a constant preoccupation with the quantity of judicial output has on the qualitative aspects of that product.

The destruction and replacement of historic doctrines of the law, I believe, is at least a partial result. The introduction of public issues into a judicial setting and increased use of class action methodologies are directly attributable to and symptomatic of justice dispensed in wholesale fashion. In a larger sense, the role of judges in this type of environment has changed. The gradualism and intellectual spirit of the common law, where the judge performed the passive roles of preserving legal doctrine and pursuing thoughtful objectivity, are often lost in today's courtrooms.

In recent years, there has been a robust debate within the legal community as to whether judges should follow a path of judicial activism or restraint. In many ways, this debate embraces a non-issue. The distinction between active and passive interpretation is, I believe, tenuous and better

given to philosophical consideration. It is significant, however, that such a debate even exists. Whether a judge should engage in aggressive intervention in disputes departs from the ideal of the neutral and objective arbitrator. Nonetheless, many judges are now known for their predisposition to engage in activism by creating new causes of action rather than the traditional qualities of consistent thoughtful deliberation. This new emphasis in the judicial process is a direct function of what is perceived as the changing legal profession.

Disappearance of legal personality

A second, more noteworthy, consequence of the shift in the profession is the disappearance of what may be characterized as the individual legal personality. Just as increased traffic flow means that one is unlikely to be acquainted with the person driving the automobile next to yours, the increased traffic within the profession creates its own type of anonymity. Legal relationships, whether lawyer-client or among lawyers, have become far less personal in the past few decades. Practice in a large law firm has a tendency to mechanize the relationship between counsel.

At one time, admission into the bar meant passage into a sort of egalitarian fraternity. The large law firm of today, however, imposes both explicit and implicit hierarchical arrangements among its attorneys. Under these circumstances, professional alienation can flourish. A lawyer who is required, even before graduation, to focus on a specialty can easily view himself more as a technician and less as a servant of the profession itself and its role in the larger community. Since practice in a sizable firm necessarily involves large, institutionalized clients, the real sense of inclusion and obligation to the broader community is often lost.

The idea that a lawyer's day-to-day experience can be so divorced from actual contact or knowledge of his or her clients was virtually unknown just a few short years ago. Yet an attorney working for a substantial institutional client can have very little, if any, relationship with his client on a personal basis. Deprived of this type of gratifying professional satisfaction, more and more attorneys must find an external reason, whether individual enjoyment or money, to gain a sense of purpose.

Although there are numerous and diverse opportunities for an attorney to obtain satisfaction through public interest or pro bono work, those relationships too have taken on a distinct institutional flavor. Large organized programs are now required to provide pro bono services. It is most unfortunate that a graduating law student, because of the demands of time and money, has so little opportunity to secure a personal sense of reward by using his or her skills to assist an indigent individual.

Perhaps even more significant than the mechanism of lawyer-client relations is the loss of personal community among lawyers themselves. It is not unusual, in fact it is quite likely, that lawyers in a typical firm are practically strangers. This fact alone is not startling because any large organization, be it a university, a hospital, or a bank, must be operated on an impersonal, organizational level. The case of the large, urban law firm is particularly disturbing, however, because of what must be subordinated to organizational structure.

The collegiality and democratic spirit that once governed relations within a firm have been replaced by bureaucratic forms of control and frequently a somewhat oppressive "up-or-out" mentality. The sense of individual legal personality is sacrificed to the concept of firm identity. Moreover, the sense of professionalism and professional identity among lawyers is often replaced by the commercial exigencies of large firm competition.

Lawyers have historically provided a wellspring of governmental and political leadership to the nation. The common law was an incomparable incubator for developing the qualities and dedication that we ascribe to sound, progressive, and energetic civil leadership. Scholarship, broad vision, and equanimity—elements that marked a successful common law practitioner—also defined the hallmarks of a dedicated public servant.

The disappearance of the individual legal personality threatens to disrupt the profession's important role in preparing public servants. I question whether apprenticeship in a large firm today can be a measure of the training that the common law practice provided. Can the specialized, institutional experience of a large firm become the equivalent of development through individual common law practice in the selection of our next generation of governors, judges, mayors, and other officials? These questions should be quite high in the pantheon of considerations for the continuing mission of our profession as large legal entities capture the most promising legal talent available.

Regrettably, the answers to these questions appear to be in the negative. The large firms of today are simply not producing this type of leadership. Last year, of the nearly 11,000 students graduating from the top law schools, only 243 chose to begin their careers in some type of public interest work.[5] Plucked directly from school and dropped into well-paying positions that demand enormous commitments of time and energy, it is not surprising that these young attorneys might view public service as secondary and unrewarding.

The law firms themselves, however, must also share responsibility for not contributing to the leadership of their communities. As a young attorney, I was encouraged to enter public life by the senior partner of my firm as an opportunity to serve the public. Today, the structural and financial necessities of maintaining a large firm create pressures that, in turn, deter young lawyers from entering public service. Within the business mindset of large firms, it simply is not profitable to lend talent to the community at large.

Commercialization of law and practice

The third, and perhaps most pervasive, manifestation of the change in the legal climate is the decline of professionalism and its replacement with commercialism. If one general theme could encompass the many changes in our legal environment, it would be the adoption of the mores and manners of the marketplace at the expense of expressions of professional affiliation. One might legitimately ask: "What is wrong with this?" After all, lawyering is like any other calling; young people still choose to go into law primarily for monetary reasons and, more often than not, are rewarded for that choice. I suppose that one would be hard-pressed to persuade the general public, whether on a street corner in New York City or Davenport, Iowa, that what the practice of law is all about is not money. But the real danger lies when those within the profession are convinced that what it is all about is material success.

The profession occupies a key role in a democratically organized society. Americans tend to divide the dimensions of public life into two general spheres. One half is the business or economic realm. An economy based on capitalism and the institution of private property is the source of this culture. Economic freedom, efficiency, and material reward are its basic values. The other half of what constitutes our public affairs is the political or civil culture. The highest virtues here are political freedom, equality, and justice. Its institutional foundations are the free-functioning political process and the unbiased administration of justice.

Each culture or set of values must be allowed to flourish; that is what, to a considerable extent, constitutes the genius of the American polity. Furthermore, it is important that neither should grow to dominate the other. A correct balance between the influences of our civil government and the business marketplace is the perpetual challenge of democracy. Given this challenge, it is the proper role of the lawyer to stabilize the social equilibrium of the forces and counterforces of a dynamic society. The law is an affirmation or expression of the structure of our government and our consensual beliefs. Lawyers must operate as its vigilant defenders. Just as the true entrepreneur may be viewed as the paradigm of the business culture, each lawyer should represent the epitome of the values and virtues of the civic culture.

When the legal profession adopts too many of the commercial aspects of business, the civic values that lawyers should represent are in danger of being eroded. It is for this reason that mourning the decline in professionalism is not merely an exercise in sentimentality. We must not permit the practice of law to become just another white-collar industry. Nor must we permit lawyers to be viewed as economic units of production and their work product to be seen as "widgets." Such a mercantilistic vision would be tantamount to an admission that our civic heritage is quantifiable and can be exchanged, and that what was once self-evident and inalienable is no longer so.

Yet, evidence of this development can be found in several respects. The one that is perhaps most representative, and coincidentally the one I personally find quite troubling, although probably necessary, is the timesheets that lawyers are required to have nearby throughout the working day. Aside from being a continuous distraction, these instruments are a repeated reminder that everything a lawyer does can and should be quantified for payment. In large cities, some firms have begun billing based on one-twelfth of an hour. That means that every action that a lawyer performs, whether opening mail or answering a short telephone call, will be recorded and billed to the client.

The commercialization of the profession, however, runs far deeper than timesheets or expense accounts. The decline in professionalism has deprived an entire generation of practitioners of suitable role models. At the risk of sounding nostalgic, I believe that the profession has lost its grasp of the big picture and of the aspects and aspirations of the higher calling of this secular ministry.

Lawyers that are perceived as most successful today, or at least the ones gaining the most remuneration, are those who specialize in merger and acquisition work. This development is particularly illustrative of the overall commercialization of practice, in that elaborate takeover schemes in large part involve the reorganization of interests while adding little value to society. Seldom in these complex, money-changing arrangements is there room for consideration of the public interest or societal consequences. The ideal of the lawyer as vindicator of the rights vested in our civic culture is lost. Just as the inventor of the hula hoop or bikini once gained the greatest reward in the business culture, the lawyer specializing in junk bonds is the new example of success in the legal firmament.

Nor is commercialization of the civic culture lost on the general public. One astute social observer remarked recently that members of our society are no longer referred to as "citizens" but instead are simply grouped into the class known as "consumers." When the philosophy of every free person possessing an equal franchise in our democratic society is lost, and citizens are best recognized for their position in the macroeconomy, our civic heritage has been seriously compromised.

Just as we might despair over the loss of the true entrepreneur in society, the decline of professionalism in legal practice should invite equal consternation. The public perception of the profession is now gained more through avenues such as *The People's Court, L.A. Law,* or television and telephone book ads for attorneys, rather than from the practice of the profession. What could be more discouraging than a generation of individuals receiving their understanding of their civic rights and obligations through these vistas?

Equally distressing is the prospect of members of the profession *affirmatively accepting* this commercialized vision of themselves. Law schools, which should be the bulwark of the loftiest ideals of the profession, are frequently more hospitable to various hucksters or personalities of law rather than to the great role models of yesteryear. It is a melancholy commentary that the inventor of a heart valve frequently will labor in obscurity while the promoter of some new patent medicine, whether a baldness cure or weight loss miracle, will gain immediate attention and riches. But the decline in the professionalism of the legal practice and the rise of the poor substitute of commercial manners, is an equally regrettable indictment of our society. When the giants of legal history are relegated to the back of the classroom or the rear of a bar association meeting, it is important to consider who is moving to the front.

Conclusion

We must be on guard to assure that my assessment of the state of our profession is not merely the product of an affection for days past. In this regard, I am reminded that in 1905, Louis Brandeis, later a Supreme Court Justice, remarked that the profession at that time caused him much concern. He was alarmed at the progressive encroachment of material influences on the great and beloved principles of the law. A year later, Roscoe Pound, soon to be Dean of Harvard Law School, in a seminal address entitled ''Causes of Popular Dissatisfaction with the Administration of Justice,'' criticized the prevailing legal institutions as not being able to serve a nation on the verge of realizing its destiny. Pound noted the absence of any encompassing ''Philosophy of the Law'' that would allow the profession to guide the nation through the challenges of the new century.

Even if what I have said thus far can be attributed to generational politics, and I concede that the thrust of my comments parallels to some extent those of Brandeis and Pound, there still remains the constant necessity to reexamine the ideals and premises of the profession. Even if we are not in the last days of the principled practice of law, the current developments, as I have sought to describe them, deserve careful attention. The quest for Pound's ''Philosophy of the Law'' must continue if our profession is to lead society once again into the potentials of a new century that soon will be upon us.

Assuming that the state of the practice deserves the scrutiny of both the legal and non-legal communities, it is customary for the commentator to point out the obvious but unchosen answer. If there exists such an answer or path to be pursued, however, it will not be found in these remarks. The most compelling reason for this is simply that I am not in possession of any such remedy.

If there is an answer to the renewal of the professional ethic in the legal community, I do not believe it will come from any technical adjustment in the rules. The dramatic forces at work in the profession, both internally and externally, will not recede through administrative tinkering. That type of technocratic answer does not exist and, even if we could discover it, it recalls a solution more representative of the business culture. There simply is no quick antidote to materialism.

Rather, if a reassertion of professional faith is to occur, it must arise from a reaffirmation of our civic heritage. Members of the profession, the lawyers and the judges, must again possess a sense of their individual legal personality and faith in the ultimate mission of their calling. Additional bar programs or law school requirements may help, but by themselves they will not recapture the passion and dedication of elapsed faith. The role of the lawyer has not changed. The members of the profession must be willing to reassume it, and to do so with necessary vigor.

On the occasion of the 200th anniversary of our Constitution, I outlined the aspects of what I view as the unchanged role of the practitioner.[6] These basic qualities, I submit, merit reiteration. The first is service to the community. Lawyers must again recognize that they have been entrusted with a great privilege, and that obligations to the community go with that privilege. Attorneys have occupied a singular role in service to our society from the framing of our Constitution to the Civil Rights Movement. Members of the profession must once again accept the responsibility of formulating theories and rules to allow the various elements of the public to expand the ability of a nation to serve its citizens. Any enduring philosophy regarding legal practice must be rooted in the belief that lawyers receive their license and are empowered by the greater society, and must therefore labor to insure its progress. The idea of the practice of law as a completely private exercise of private ends is contrary to this conviction.

A second characteristic is dedication to what Justice Holmes called the ''craftsmanship'' of lawyering. There must be a renewed sense of pride in the work that lawyers do, not merely for its value in the marketplace, but for its historic function of vindicating the rights of citizens.

The third characteristic is devotion to the profession itself. The changing face of the law demands that lawyers reassert their professional ties and responsibilities. Members of the bar have traditionally recognized the importance of supporting their bar associations and continuing an active role in legal education. Profit must not become our dominant ethic. Nor must profit become the primary engine for professional change. A renewal in the faith of professionalism must originate from within and reverse our troubling path. Only when such a new direction is pursued will good sense and professional virtue prevail.

Despite the sobering tone of my remarks, I am not completely discouraged. Although many of us have halting doubts about recent developments in the profession, I believe it can still fulfill what is highest in the yearnings of the human spirit. Our history has been replete with inspiring figures: John Marshall, Oliver Wendell Holmes, Benjamin Cardozo, and Learned Hand, to name a few. Each can serve as a beacon.

As Judge Hand eloquently put it in addressing the conflict that is normal in a pluralistic society:

For it is always dawn. Day breaks forever, and above the eastern horizon the sun is now about to peep. Full light of day? No, perhaps not ever. But yet it grows lighter, and the paths that were frequently so blind will, if one watches sharply enough, become hourly plainer. We shall learn to walk straighter. Yes, it is always dawn.[7]

NOTES

This article originally appeared in Volume 74, Number 2, August-September 1990, pages 77-83. It was adapted from DICKINSON LAW REVIEW Vol. 93, No. 4, Summer 1989, copyright 1989 by Dickinson School of Law and was originally delivered as the Tresolini Lecture at Lehigh University on November 10, 1988.

1. *The Am Law 100 Report*, THE AMERICAN LAWYER, July/August, 1988.

2. *Id.* at 34

3. *Id.* at 58.

4. *Id.* at 20.

5. Kaplan, *Out of 11,000, 243 Went into Public Interest*, NAT'L L.J., Aug. 8, 1988, at 1, col. 1.

6. Adams, Remarks at the "We the People 200" Convocation with the Supreme Court Justices at the Arch Street Friends Society (Oct. 2, 1987).

7. Hand, THE SPIRIT OF LIBERTY: PAPERS AND ADDRESSES OF LEARNED HAND 101 (I. Dillard, 3d ed., 1974).

Ensuring lawyer competency: the South Carolina approach

by Bruce Littlejohn

For more than 10 years, Chief Justice Warren E. Burger has been calling to the attention of the bench, the bar, and the public the fact that legal educators are providing students with less than the practical training they need to begin a career in law.[1] As a result of his intense concern, we have seen several related activities and actions: (1) the Devitt committee study, (2) the Indiana Admissions Rules, (3) the experimental program at Northeastern University Law School, and (4) the report of the Task Force on "Lawyer Competency and the Role of the Law Schools" by the A.B.A. Section of Legal Education and Admissions to the Bar, and (5) clinical programs promoted by the Council on Legal Education for Professional Responsibility.[2]

In South Carolina, too, the Supreme Court became increasingly concerned with the fact that young lawyers handling cases at both the trial and appellate levels appeared to have less than adequate training.[3] Because of its concern, the court appointed a committee in 1977 to study its Rules of Admission to the Bar, with a view toward recommending changes that would inspire students to seek more practical training and encourage law schools to provide it.[4] The committee study lasted about 18 months and sought the advice and thinking of many groups.[5]

The subject all were asked was: "If the law school you attended failed to give you any training you have come to feel you need, what would you say it was?" The overwhelming consensus of opinion was that law schools concentrated too much on theory and failed to give that practical training necessary for the practice of law. There was too little empha-

sis on trial advocacy.

The old system

Teaching methods at the law schools have changed little since the day of Langdell (about 1873). Law school faculty members have status; their resistance to any proposed reform is substantial. Professor Kevin M. Clermont, of the Cornell University Law School faculty, said:

As a teacher one learns early on that the curriculum is the law schools' immovable object. Too many vested interests and too many jaded spirits abound. 'What about my course?' and 'Haven't we been through all this before?' are all that one hears.[6]

Early in our research, we realized that the bench and bar know little of what goes on at the law schools. For example, lawyers and judges in South Carolina seemed amazed to learn that our own law school did not require courses in such basic subjects as evidence, equity, insurance, and taxation. It was hard for them to believe that the law school bulletin for 1977-78 listed 109 courses, a substantial portion of which bore little relation to the everyday practice of law in the state that the law school was created to serve.

It is unfortunate that students know so little about what courses they should pursue, and it is not without precedent that students are urged to take certain courses because the professor needs a quorum to justify his teaching the subject. At the same time, students may be denied the right to take subjects that they need because the course is "closed"—which means the maximum number of students allowed have already signed up.

A needed change

In our committee study, it soon became apparent that, if the court was to carry out its constitutional duty of seeing that persons admitted to practice law are competent, a rule change would be necessary. Professor Clermont was right. The law school curriculum doesn't change as rapidly as the needs of the practitioner. It was with much reluctance that the court came to concern itself with legal education, but the duty of the law schools to provide competent training and the constitutional duty of the court to see that only competent persons are permitted to practice law cannot be completely divorced.

Our Admissions Study Committee also found that the problem of inadequate law school training was not only a South Carolina problem but a national one. We discovered that Indiana had pioneered in the field of requiring more practical training for admission to the bar. Chief Justice Richard M. Givan and Dean William F. Harvey of the Indiana School of Law at Indianapolis were extremely helpful to us. In the last analysis, we followed and attempted to emulate a rule that has been in effect in that state for several years. Both Chief Justice Givan and Dean Harvey verify that the rule has worked well and has been beneficial.[7]

When it became apparent that the supreme court was going to promulgate a rule to require applicants for admission to the bar to have more practical training, the dean of our law school requested a hearing so that opponents could express their views. The president of the university, the chairman of the board of trustees and several members attended and spoke, along with faculty members and other interested parties. These included undergraduate school faculty members.[8]

All were generally opposed to the supreme court taking any action that might directly or indirectly affect the training provided at any law school. Their opposition can be summarized in a single expression: "Academic freedom must be preserved." There seemed to be more interest in preserving academic freedom than in providing students that training which the court knows every lawyer should have before offering his services to the public.

Undergraduate preparation

Our committee decided, and the supreme court agreed, that preparation for a career at the law should be logically commenced at the undergraduate level. Students have been known to take "crip courses" in college in order to build up a good grade point average to enhance their chances of being accepted at law school. But if lawyers should have a background in such subjects as public speaking, English composition, United States history, economics, and accounting, it is a disservice to let them spend four years getting bachelor's degrees without alerting them to the fact that study of these areas would be advantageous. This is consistent with medical school requirements that certain basic subjects be taken at the undergraduate level prior to admission to medical school. For some reason, which legal educators cannot satisfactorily explain, no prelaw courses are required, or even greatly encouraged.

In order to alert students, the committee recommended, and the court passed, a rule requiring the clerk of the supreme court to advise all of the undergraduate school prelaw advisors in the state that the supreme court considers the study of certain courses "highly beneficial" and that students expecting to practice law in this state are encouraged to take as many of the recommended courses as possible. Those courses are English composition, public speaking, United States history, accounting, economics, logic, literature, political science, and philosophy.

While there was substantial thinking on the committee, and on the court that at least a portion of these subjects should be absolutely required as a prerequisite to standing the bar examination, a majority preferred to leave it in the status of a strong recommendation. Hopefully, the rule will serve the purpose of persuading prelaw students to begin preparing for a career at the law at the undergraduate level.

Required courses

There is a tendency throughout the law school world to allow students more and more electives. The contention that some law schools are teaching some subjects more appropriate to a liberal arts education is not entirely without merit. The court adopted, in large measure, Indiana's Rule 13, which sets forth as a prerequisite to standing the bar the study of certain basic subjects. The South Carolina rule now requires an applicant to pursue these subjects: business law, civil procedure, criminal law, constitutional law, contracts, equity, evidence, legal writing and research, professional responsibility, property, taxation, torts, and trial advocacy.

The study of these courses requires approximately two years, leaving each student one full year to pursue electives. The adoption of this rule encountered the same resistance experienced in Indiana; many law school deans throughout the country wrote letters of dismay and disdain. The rule is not a rigid one and allows for substantial flexibility. For example, any one of several designated courses may meet the business law requirement.

Trial experience

The third facet of our rule deals with what we refer to as trial experiences. Perhaps the inspiration for this rule comes from the fact that 9 of the 11 law clerks the writer has had, in as many years, stated that they had never seen an entire trial of a case. One said that he had never even been in a courtroom. All had graduated from an accredited law school, passed the state bar examination, and were admitted to practice and authorized to try cases.

Our rule requires that every new admittee to the bar must have 11 trial experiences before he may appear in the trial of a case alone. The experiences may be gained by participating in full trials with an older lawyer, or by observation of entire contested testimonial-type hearings. The 11 trial experiences are as follows: three civil jury trials, three criminal jury trials, three trials in family court, one trial in equity court, and one trial before an administrative officer. The presiding officer must certify in each instance that the admittee complied with the rule.

It must be admitted that these three rules will not make of every young lawyer an effective advocate, but it is a step in the right direction. The committee is now studying the advisability of encouraging, if not requiring, some form of internship. New graduates might be expected to work with a practicing attorney before they would be admitted to the bar.

As a result of the interest created in South Carolina in more practical training, Chief Justice Woodrow Lewis and former Dean Richard Day agreed upon a plan whereby court is held at the University of South Carolina Law School so that students may conveniently sit in on trials. For the time being, only nonjury trials are being scheduled. Hopefully, facilities for holding jury trials may be developed. This is akin to the system of trials inaugurated by Judge Marvin E. Aspen, of Chicago, at Northwestern University.[9] The students are enthu-

siastic at the prospect of learning by observation.

No single solution

A steadily increasing number of lawyers, judges, and law school teachers are beginning to agree with Chief Justice Burger's contention that more practical training should be provided by all law schools. But after that initial agreement, the thinking of law school people on the one hand, and the bench and bar on the other, begin to diverge. We disagree about the *method* of providing the needed practical training. Certainly, there is no short, quick solution to the problem.

Our new rule, in effect now for more than a year, has received high praise from lawyers, judges, and lay people in both South Carolina and throughout the country. It has also developed substantial support among law school people. Students have been enthusiastic and generally support the new requirements for admission to the bar. They have come to realize that their stay at the law school should result in practical, as well as theoretical, training. There is now a greater demand for trial advocacy type courses, and less demand for the many courses that bear little relation to the actual practice of law.[10]

Judges and admissions boards throughout the country have shown an interest in the new requirements. In several states, new admissions requirements are being studied. There is much interest in the matter of providing internships.

While neither the committee nor the court is satisfied that our rule is the overall solution to providing the public with a more competent lawyer, we are confident that it is accomplishing much to assure the consuming public that the persons admitted to practice in South Carolina will provide adequate representation.

NOTES

This article originally appeared in Volume 64, Number 3, September 1980, pages 109-113.

1. "The shortcoming of today's graduate lies not in a deficient knowledge of law but that he has little, if any, training in dealing with the *facts*—the stuff of which *cases* are made. It is a rare law graduate, for example, who knows how to ask questions—simple, single questions, one at a time, in order to develop facts in evidence. And a lawyer who cannot do that cannot do his tasks properly." Keynote address of Warren E. Burger, Annual Conference of Phi Alpha Delta Fraternity, Mayflower Hotel, August 28, 1968.

2. On the Devitt Committee's work, *see* Bagg, *What the Devitt Committee recommends to improve advocacy in federal courts*, 63 JUDICATURE 309 (February 1980).

On the Indiana Admissions rule, *see* Rule 13 of Rules for Admission to Practice Law in Indiana.

On the Northeastern University program, see NORTHEASTERN TODAY ALUMNI MAGAZINE, Volume 3, Number 3, November 1979.

On the Task Force report, *see* REPORT AND RECOMMENDATIONS OF THE TASK FORCE ON LAWYER COMPETENCY: THE ROLE OF THE LAW SCHOOLS (Chicago: ABA, 1979).

On the clinical program, *see* Council on Legal Education for Professional Responsibility Newsletters, Volume VIII-XII (1976-1980) (now collected in a single volume). The newsletters are available free from the Council on Legal Education for Professional Responsibility, 36 W. 44th Street, New York, New York 10036.

3. The South Carolina Constitution imposes upon the supreme court the duty of admitting qualified persons to the practice of law. The court carries out this duty with the aid of a board of examiners that gives an examination twice each year. About 90 per cent of the applicants are graduates of the University of South Carolina Law School. The court has nothing to do with the operation of any law school.

4. The committee is composed of this writer, as chairman, Frank Mood, Chairman of the Board of Examiners, Professor John Freeman of the University of South Carolina Law School, Frank Lyles, general practitioner, and Morris Rosen, a general practitioner who recently served as president of the South Carolina State Bar.

5. We were especially interested in the views of young lawyers. Testimony was taken at length from two trial judges of general jurisdiction, the president and vice president of the Student Bar Association of the University of South Carolina, a public defender, a representative of the attorney general's office, the president and the chairman of the Young Lawyer Division of the State Bar, a representative of the South Carolina Trial Lawyers' Association (a plaintiffs' group), a representative of the Defense Lawyers' Association, and representatives of the faculty of the University of South Carolina Law School.

6. CORNELL LAW FORUM, February 1979.

7. Givan, *Indiana's Rule 13—It Doesn't Invite Conformity: It Compels Competency,* LEARNING AND THE LAW, Vol. 3, No. 2 (Summer 1976), page 16.

8. We considered dozens of letters from law school deans from many states. These were in opposition to our rule and were obviously inspired by the Association of American Law Schools.

9. Aspen, *Bring Your Court into Law School,* 17 THE JUDGES' JOURNAL 36 (Summer 1978).

10. Many law schools have developed clinic programs designed to give students practical training, but such programs are not looked upon by the law school faculty with great enthusiasm. President William Pincus, of the Council on Legal Education for Professional Responsibility, speaking to the Conference of Chief Justices, said: "Clinic courses are not integrated with the rest of the law school curriculum or with each other. There is no clinical curriculum built on an ordered arrangement of clinic experience. Clinic teachers and supervisors are considered second class citizens in the law school faculties, and their working conditions and remuneration are inferior to those given to classroom teachers. In short, clinical education has gotten its foot inside the door but is far from becoming part of the family in legal education." Address of William Pincus, president of the Council on Legal Education for Professional Responsibility, to the Conference of Chief Justices, Atlanta, Georgia, February 12, 1979. The address was recently published in Pincus, CLINICAL EDUCATION FOR LAW STUDENTS: ESSAYS BY WILLIAM PINCUS 415 (New York: Meilen Press, Inc., 1980).

Legal services before the Supreme Court

Viewed not as an interest group pursuing widespread reform, but as a mechanism by which a new class of litigants was able to place its civil claims before the Supreme Court, the Legal Services Program can be characterized a success.

by Susan E. Lawrence

The establishment of the Legal Services Program in 1965 signaled a new national commitment to providing indigents with access to civil courts. Like many Great Society programs, the Office of Economic Opportunity (OEO) Legal Services Program (LSP) was aimed at both service and reform. After much internal debate, LSP decided that its attorneys should handle routine civil casework *and* seek to bring about social and economic change through appellate advocacy.[1] This reformist orientation and substantial federal funding marked a significant break from the traditions of the pre-existing legal aid societies. Set up as a federal grant-dispensing organization, by 1973 the national LSP had funded more than 250 local legal services projects with more than 2,600 attorneys. Between 1965 and 1971, funding for civil legal assistance increased ten-fold. Volume increased as well. In 1959, local legal aid societies handled 426,457 cases annually. In 1971, LSP attorneys processed 1,237,275 applications for legal assistance, about three times legal aid's annual rate.[2]

More importantly, LSP attorneys brought a new philosophy to their work.[3] Legal aid lawyers did not challenge the justice of existing law; they emphasized the routine processing of individual client claims.[4] LSP attorneys adopted a more active posture, litigating 17 per cent of their clients' cases compared to the 6 per cent litigated by legal aid societies before 1965.[5] Legal aid societies had rarely pursued appeals at any level and never took their clients' claims to the U.S. Supreme Court.[6] In remarkable contrast, during its nine-year tenure, 1965 through 1974, LSP attorneys brought 164 cases to the Supreme Court on behalf of the poor,

199 of which were accepted for review.

LSP's appellate litigation precipitated considerable political controversy. As a result, the Program was replaced with the Legal Services Corporation in 1975 which, though more insulated from politics, still de-emphasized appellate advocacy.[7] Those who had hoped for widespread reform of the welfare system and the creation of a constitutional right to the necessities of life concluded that the Program's short-lived law reform efforts had failed.[8] But, those ambitious goals were not shared by all LSP supporters. Broader support for the Program rested on normative beliefs in equal access to justice.

In this article, LSP is viewed as a mechanism that enfranchised the poor in the halls of justice. By providing counsel and encouraging appellate challenges, LSP reduced the poor's *de facto* exclusion from the judicial processes that culminate in the U.S. Supreme Court. To assess the effect of LSP's enfranchisement of the poor, this article examines LSP's participation in the Supreme Court's docket and the court's response to these cases during the 1966 through 1974 October terms. It evaluates and explains LSP's success before the U.S. Supreme Court.

LSP and appellate advocacy

When LSP was established in 1965, there was no consensus on the Program's mission beyond "helping poor people." To a large extent, for the first two years LSP operated within the standard OEO rhetoric of decentralization and local control. On March 17, 1967, law reform formally was announced as the Program's "priority management goal."[9] The national LSP adopted appellate litigation as its primary method of promoting social and economic change. Test cases seemed to be a way to respond to the flood of clients at local projects and to help those turned away because the need outstripped the Program's resources. The organized bar viewed appellate advocacy as a proper part of a lawyer's role. It responded to both those who wanted LSP to serve individual clients, the old legal aid proponents, and those who wanted it to promote social and economic change, the initiators of the national program.[10] All the local projects were required to both handle routine casework and pursue clients' claims in the appellate courts, although compliance with the latter requirement varied. LSP resolved, in practice, the often alleged tension between the service and reform goals.

The Program's appellate challenges were a result of attorneys' casework, not of a strategy to bring about specific policy changes. LSP's appellate caseload was determined by the client's financial eligibility for legal services, rather than by congruence between case issues and pre-existing policy goals. Through the patterns LSP lawyers saw in their casework, they discovered problems the poor repeatedly faced that could be diminished by Supreme Court rulings.

Unlike the National Association for the Advancement of Colored People Legal Defense Fund, which served as the prototype,[11] LSP never had a grand litigation strategy. It pursued the nebulous goal of helping poor people. Only in the welfare area was there a definite strategy, designed by Edward Sparer at the Columbia Center for Social Welfare Policy,[12] but it is questionable how much of that strategy was ever implemented.[13] While many of Sparer's critiques of the welfare system were addressed by the Supreme Court in LSP cases, the cases were brought to the Court idiosyncratically by individual LSP attorneys. The litigation was not coordinated; cases were brought out of sequence and several involved unfavorable fact patterns.

The commitment to appellate advocacy varied greatly among projects. During the Program's operation, students of the Program concluded it had failed to promote law reform.[14] In fact, at the Supreme Court level the Program was quite active. LSP attorneys from 116 of the 265 local LSP projects participated in at least one Supreme Court appeal, either as counsel or by filing an amicus curiae brief. However, LSP attorneys' activity in the Supreme Court was often the result of their individual attempts to give meaning to their work and provide full representation to their clients, rather than their desire to comply with Program policy.[15] Decisions to appeal were discrete and insular. Control remained with the individual lawyer or local project. As a result, the cases appealed to the Court reflected the heterogeneous concerns of individual poor clients as translated into legal controversies by their LSP lawyers.[16] The LSP's Supreme Court docket was not the result of the kind of orchestrated litigation strategy that is associated with group success before the Court. Rather, it was a serendipitous outgrowth of the Program's immersion in casework.

Data

All LSP-sponsored Supreme Court cases decided during the 1966 through 1974 October terms are examined. The Court heard its first LSP case, *Thorpe v. Housing Authority of the City of Durham*,[17] during the 1966 October term. The 1974 October term coincides with the year between the passage of the Legal Services Corporation Act, replacing the LSP, and the Corporation's first board of directors meeting. While the national LSP had actively advocated appellate challenges, the Corporation was, at best, lukewarm on the notion.[18]

The LSP's Supreme Court "litigation strategy," or lack thereof, and the operation of the Program was investigated through 24 interviews with former Program personnel and affiliates, a survey of the extensive materials published during the operation of the Program and the subsequent studies of its attorneys.

LSP kept no consistent records of its appellate cases. A list of the Program's Supreme Court litigation was compiled by surveying all issues of *Clearinghouse Review* published between its inception in September 1967 through 1976.[19] This list of cases decided during the 1966 through 1974 terms (i.e., Court denied review or reached a decision-on-the merits) and the organizational affiliation of counsel was cross-checked against a list of all LSP-funded projects. This procedure yielded a list of 164 LSP-sponsored appeals to the U.S. Supreme Court, 119 of which were accepted for review.[20] Each of these cases was coded for a variety of characteristics or variables. In some instances, comparable data for the Court's entire docket during this era was compiled from *Harvard Law Review's* annual statistical report. Patterns of judicial support for the LSP's claims were drawn from the justices' votes in these cases.

The cases

Although all LSP's Supreme Court participation was precipitated by representation of indigent clients, there is great variety in its cases. The Program's 164 Supreme Court cases involved 26 subject areas. Contrary to the common notion that poverty law is welfare law, only 40 per cent of these cases involved redistributive programs. In 84 per cent of the cases, LSP attorneys invoked over 20 constitutional issues, though new Fourteenth Amendment equal protection or due process claims were the most common. Sixty-seven per cent of the time the Supreme Court was asked to review lower federal court decisions; the remaining 33 per cent were requests to review state court decisions. However, 79 per cent of the LSP's Supreme Court cases were challenges to state or local laws, and in 74 per cent of the cases, state or local governments were the opposing party.

LSP attorneys represented the petitioner in two-thirds of the 164 cases (see Table 1). In 84 per cent of cases in which the LSP was the respondent, state governments were challenging the Program's lower court victories. Even when the LSP represented the respondent, its law reform work was the necessary prerequisite for Supreme Court action. If LSP attorneys had not gone to trial and participated in lower court appeals, the opposing party would not have had the opportunity to appeal to the Supreme Court. As one LSP attorney said: "The important thing was that there was a lawyer there at all that could file an appeal. [For example,] before the LSP was established there was only one [appellate] case in which residence requirements were discussed, *Heydenreich v. Lyons.*[21] By the time *Shapiro*[22] got to the Supreme Court, cases challenging residency requirements had been filed in 15 or 20 jurisdictions."

Getting on the agenda

Obviously, that Legal Services represented indigents in 164 petitions or appeals to the Supreme Court was no guarantee that the justices would address the concerns of the poor. Conceivably, all 164 could have been denied review as over 27,000 other cases were between 1966 and 1974. Had the acceptance rate in LSP-sponsored cases corresponded to overall review rates, the Court only would have decided about 64 LSP cases, giving plenary consideration to 24.[23] In fact, LSP fared remarkably well in the Court's case selection process. The Court granted review in 199 LSP cases, issuing written

Table 1 The LSP's participation in the Supreme Court docket, 1966-1974 terms

LSP	Review rate %	Success rate in reviewed cases %
Petitioner	63.9	60.9
	(N=108)	(N=69)
Respondent	89.3	64.0
	(N=56)	(N=50)
Total	72.6	62.2
	(N=164)	(N=119)

opinions in 80.[24] As the petitioner in 108 cases, LSP enjoyed a 64 per cent acceptance rate. The LSP's opponents enjoyed an 89 per cent acceptance rate in 56 cases (see Table 1). These unusually high acceptance rates for both classes of petitioners suggest that the issues presented were more important than the identity of the petitioner in the justices' case selections.

The Court's willingness to review LSP-sponsored cases was not merely business as usual. For example, Tanenhaus has demonstrated that there is a correlation between review grants and certain "cues," such as federal government favors review, presence of civil liberties issues and dissension in the court below.[25] Subsequent studies have redefined and refined these cues and confirmed the correlation between review grants and cues.[26] If we avoid the disputes over exactly how these cues should be defined and make assumptions that would be most likely to confirm that the review rate in LSP cases was simply a function of the Court's usual response to cued cases, we find that, even under the most generous assumptions, LSP's review rate exceeds those predicted by cue theory. Tanenhaus predicted a 45 to 80 per cent review rate in cases in which the solicitor general favored review, depending upon the presence of the civil liberties and dissension cues.[27] In LSP cases, the Court granted review in 91 per cent of the 22 cases in which the solicitor general favored *or* opposed review.[28] Tanenhaus predicted an 18 to 43 per cent review rate in cases which contained only civil liberties and/or dissension cues.[29] In LSP cases, the Court granted review in 70 per cent of the remaining 141 cases that could have contained only civil liberties and/or dissension cues.

Of course, as Provine confirmed, judicial conceptions of the importance of the subject matter and the proper work of the Court also influence case selection decisions.[30] To the extent political climate affects these judicial views, perhaps the Court's

Table 2   LSP success rates by presence of a constitutional issue

	n	Wins N	%
Constitutional issue	60	102	58.8
No constitutional issue	14	17	82.4
Total	74	119	62.2

Yule's Q = -0.53.

willingness to review LSP cases is not quite so startling. Poverty and equality concerns were dominant items on the national agenda during this era.[31]

Court's response on-the-merits

LSP attorneys won 62 per cent of their 119 Supreme Court cases, whether decided summarily or with written opinions.[32] In terms of the entire work of the Court during the 1966 through 1974 terms, 7 per cent of all written opinions were responses to LSP cases; 4 per cent were pro- LSP opinions. The LSP's appellate advocacy and the Court's review of its cases gave the poor a voice in the Supreme Court's policy making and doctrinal development.

The LSP was considerably more successful than suggested predictions, based on the justices' treatment of its civil docket as a whole. Breaking from its usual habit of reversing two-thirds of the cases it reviews,[33] the Court only reversed 36 per cent of the cases in which the LSP argued for an affirmance. When the LSP argued for a reversal, the Court returned to its usual pattern, reversing the lower court in 61 per cent of the 69 LSP requests (see Table 1).

Contrary to usual patterns and hypotheses, measures of association between case outcome and case characteristic variables (government as the opposing party, presence of experienced and expert counsel and filing of amicus curiae briefs) were not statistically significant.[34] Although statistical measures indicate a random association, LSP was more successful in opposing governmental units than most other parties. Between 1966 and 1974, the Court ruled against the federal government in only 28 per cent of its civil cases and against state governments in 56 per cent of their civil cases. In LSP cases, the federal government lost 47 per cent of its 13 cases and state governments lost 67 per cent of their 90 cases.

Measures of association between case outcome and type of lower court, appeal or certiorari jurisdiction, level and type of rule challenged, subject, type of consideration and basis of decision were not

Table 3   Ranking of LSP support scores and Spaeth's equality ranking

	Judicial support for LSP* N	%	Spaeth's equality ranking**
Douglas	80	81.3	Douglas
Marshall	98	76.5	Fortas
Brennan	98	72.6	Warren
Fortas	6	66.7	Brennan
Warren	8	66.7	Marshall
White	113	59.3	White
Stewart	105	57.6	Stewart
Blackmun	90	57.3	Powell
Powell	62	53.7	Blackmun
Harlan	39	52.4	Harlan
Rehnquist	56	45.5	Burger
Burger	90	45.4	Black
Black	25	45.2	Rehnquist

*Support scores were computed as the number of times the justice voted for the LSP's position divided by the number of LSP cases the justice participated in.
**Spaeth, *Supreme Court Policy Making: Explanation and Prediction*, 135 (1979).

statistically significant.[35] Only one variable, absence of a constitutional issue, had a moderate association with case outcome (see Table 2). Such cases only account for 19 per cent of the Program's victories. The LSP's 62 per cent success rate does not conform to usual patterns of Supreme Court decision making, nor is it the result of multiple favorable decisions in similar cases. The poor, through the LSP, presented the Court with a heterogeneous mix of cases.

Further, the Program's success does not appear to be tied to a particular configuration of liberal justices. During the nine terms LSP participated in the Supreme Court's docket, the personnel of the Court was in flux. LSP began its work with the Warren Court firmly in place; by the time the Program ended, Nixon had appointed four justices and the Burger Court era was in full swing. We would expect a liberal Court, such as the Warren Court, to be more supportive of the poor's claims than a more conservative Court, such as the Burger Court. Although there are year-by-year and Court-by-Court fluctuations in the Program's success rate, it remained over 60 per cent after 1971 when all four Nixon appointees were sitting.[36]

Not surprisingly, the traditionally liberal justices were the most supportive of the LSP: Douglas, Marshall, Brennan, Fortas and Warren. The conservative justices and most of the Nixon appointees were less so: Harlan, Burger, Powell and Rehnquist. The three moderates, White, Stewart and Blackmun, had LSP support scores just under the LSP's win rate (see Table 3).[37] Blackmun and White voted

Table 4 Vote divisions in LSP cases

LSP wins (N=73)*

Majority	Minority 0	1	2	3	4
9	38				9
8	2	5			
7	2	0	4		
6		1	4	6	
5			2	5	2
4				2	

One vote decisions = 4 (5.5%)

LSP losses (N=45)

Majority	Minority 0	1	2	3	4
	17				9
8	0	4			
7	1	1	2		
6		1	3	10	
5				2	4
4					

One vote decisions = 4 (8.9%)

All LSP cases (N=118)*

Majority	Minority 0	1	2	3	4
	55				
8	2	9			
7	3	1	6		
6		2	7	16	
5			2	7	6
4				2	

One vote decisions = 8 (6.8%)
*Excluding one application for an injunction decided by Justice Black.

Table 5 Difference between agreement rates of LSP cases and the Court's docket, 1966-1974 terms*

Pair	Value	Pair	Value
Douglas-Rehnquist	+24.8	Marshall-Powell	+8.6
Brennan-Rehnquist	+21.6	Brennan-White	+8.4
Blackmun-Douglas	+20.8	Douglas-Stewart	+8.3
Blackmun-Brennan	+19.5	Rehnquist-White	+8.1
Brennan-Powell	+18.6	Blackmun-Stewart	+7.9
Douglas-Powell	+18.5	Brennan-Douglas	+6.8
Blackmun-Marshall	+18.2	Harlan-Marshall	+6.7
Blackmun-Harlan	+17.9	Brennan-Stewart	+6.3
Black-Burger	+15.7	Burger-Douglas	+5.4
Blackmun-Stewart	+14.9	Douglas-Harlan	+5.1
Stewart-White	+14.9	Harlan-Stewart	+4.4
Harlan-White	+14.6	Brennan-Marshall	+4.2
Brennan-Harlan	+14.4	Burger-Marshall	+3.5
Marshall-Rehnquist	+14.2	Marshall-Stewart	+2.8
Blackmun-White	+13.3	Black-Marshall	+2.8
Powell-Rehnquist	+12.7	Burger-White	+2.4
Rehnquist-Stewart	+12.5	Black-Harlan	+1.1
Burger-Stewart	+11.2	Burger-Powell	+0.3
Powell-White	+11.0	Blackmun-Burger	-0.3
Douglas-White	+10.7	Burger-Rehnquist	-0.5
Blackmun-Powell	+10.4	Burger-Harlan	-2.0
Douglas-Marshall	+10.2	Black-Blackmun	-3.2
Marshall-White	+10.2	Black-Brennan	-6.7
Powell-Stewart	+9.5	Black-White	-13.9
Brennan-Burger	+9.0	Black-Douglas	-15.4

*(+) Indicates a higher agreement rate in LSP cases
(-) Indicates a lower agreement rate in LSP cases
Justices participating in less than ten LSP cases are omitted here.
Agreement rates on the Court's entire docket were compiled from "The Supreme Court, 19xx Term: The Statistics," *Harvard Law Review* (1967-1975).

with the majority 94 per cent and 96 per cent of the time, respectively, in LSP cases, suggesting that they provided swing votes in these cases.

An examination of vote divisions in LSP cases reveals that LSP's success was not simply the result of liberal justices attracting one or two additional votes. Less than 6 per cent of the LSP's victories and 9 per cent of its losses were decided by a single vote. Furthermore, 58 per cent of the LSP's wins were unanimous. In contrast, only 40 per cent of its losses were unanimous, which corresponds to the Court's usual unanimity rate during this period (see Table 4).[38]

LSP's cases provoked consensus among almost all the justices, except Black. Liberal and conservative justices agreed more often in LSP cases than in the Court's docket as a whole.[39] Table 5 lists the pairs of justices in rank order based on the difference between their agreement rates in LSP cases and in the entire work of the Court during the 1966 through 1974 terms.[40] Only 14 per cent of the pairs agreed less often in LSP cases.[41] Among this 14 per cent there are no liberal/conservative pairs. The lowest scoring liberal/conservative pair, Douglas and Harlan, agreed 5 per cent more often in LSP cases than in the entire docket. The top of the ranking is dominated by liberal/conservative pairs, indicating that they agreed much more often in LSP cases than usual.

Indeed, the top two pairs are Rehnquist with Douglas and Brennan agreeing over 20 per cent more often in LSP cases than in the docket as a whole. They are followed by Blackmun with Douglas and Brennan agreeing about 20 per cent more often in LSP cases, and Powell with Douglas and Brennan agreeing about 19 per cent more often. Rehnquist, Blackmun and Powell voted with Douglas over 54 per cent of the time in LSP cases, but on the entire docket none of them voted with Douglas more than 40 per cent of the time. Rehnquist, Blackmun and Powell voted with Brennan over 65 per cent of the time in LSP cases, but on the entire docket none of them voted with Brennan more than 55 per cent of the time.[42] There was more consensus on LSP cases than on the Court's docket generally and the Court was unusually inclined to unanimously support the LSP's claims.

Evaluating the success

The common wisdom is that the justices were

ultimately unresponsive to LSP's litigation and poverty issues.[43] Most accounts focus on the Program's welfare litigation. The chroniclers begin with the early big victories. The most frequently cited cases are *Shapiro v. Thompson*,[44] holding that state residency requirements for the receipt of AFDC unconstitutionally burden the right to travel, and *Goldberg v. Kelly*,[45] holding that due process guarantees adhere to statutory entitlements such as welfare. The Court's clear focus on poverty in holding filing fees in divorce actions unconstitutional as applied to indigents usually merits the inclusion of *Boddie v. Connecticut*[46] in a litany of the LSP's early victories.

Commentators then turn to the big defeats. The Court's failure to establish a right to the necessities of life or find maximum family welfare grants in violation of the Equal Protection Clause in *Dandridge v. Williams*,[47] and the Court's unwillingness to find a violation of the equal protection clause in district property tax based financing of public schools in *San Antonio v. Rodriguez*[48] are read as sounding the death knell for poverty litigation. The Court's unwillingness to extend the combined rationales of *Goldberg* and *Boddie* in challenges to filing fees for appellate review of welfare administrative hearings or in bankruptcy proceedings[49] and its failure to extend the spirit of its earlier decisions in cases such as *Wyman v. James*[50] are cited as final logs on the funeral pyre.

This view of the Program's litigation comes from assessing LSP as an interest group pursuing widespread reform of the welfare system and attempting to create a constitutional right to the necessities of life. Judged from this perspective, LSP's litigation fell short of achieving its goals.

On the other hand, if LSP is viewed as a mechanism by which a new class of litigants was able to place its civil claims before the Supreme Court and influence the policy decisions emanating from that institution, LSP can be characterized as a success. First, the Program was instrumental in getting the poor's claims to the Supreme Court's jurisdictional agenda. Second, although some cases with major policy implications were lost on-the-merits, 62 per cent of the clients LSP attorneys represented before the Court won their cases.[51] In 42 cases, or 61 per cent of the attempts, lower court defeats were overturned and in 32 cases, or 64 per cent of the challenges, lower court victories were affirmed. Though these victories were not inconsequential,

many are often overlooked because they are not directly related to the welfare system or poverty per se. Indeed, about half of LSP cases given plenary consideration involved issues that could affect the middle class, as well as the poor.[52]

The catalog of LSP victories includes a number of noted cases that are not generally associated with the Program. For example, in *Stanley v. Illinois*[53] the Court required that unwed fathers be assured of a hearing before deprivation of custody of their illegitimate children. The Social Security Act's classifications of illegitimate children for the purpose of determining a parent's disability insurance benefits was held to violate the Equal Protection Clause in *Jiminez v. Weinberger*.[54] In *Vlandis v. Kline*,[55] the Court disallowed a statutory presumption of nonresidence for the purpose of determining tuition at state colleges. The Court required public schools to establish programs to deal with non-English speaking students in *Lau v. Nichols*.[56] In *Goss v. Lopez*,[57] the Court required that suspension from public school be preceded by notice and hearing. The Court cast a critical eye towards replevin laws that allowed a seizure of goods by a creditor prior to the possessor's opportunity to be heard in *Fuentes v. Shevin*.[58] The Court struck down New York's barring of aliens from competitive civil service positions in *Sugarman v. Dougall*.[59] LSP attorneys scored victories for their indigent clients in these cases, even though the issues are not directly related to poverty.

Further, LSP's cases were important components in the Court's development of its due process and equal protection doctrines. LSP's cases provided vehicles for the elimination of the right-privilege distinction[60] and early hints of its replacement with an entitlement test along with a growing flexibility in determinations of what process was due when.[61] The justices flirted with establishment of an irrebuttable presumptions doctrine under the due process clause in LSP cases.[62] Access to the civil courts was expanded for some in cases that provided early indications of the Burger Court's continued attention to family law.[63] LSP cases were vehicles for the addition of alienage to suspect class analysis[64] and the right to travel to fundamental rights analysis under the Equal Protection Clause.[65] The poor were clearly excluded from the list of suspect classes,[66] and education and welfare, or the basic necessities of life, were excluded from the list of fundamental rights that trigger strict scrutiny under the Court's equal protection jurisprudence.[67] Some of LSP's equal protection cases divided the justices and appeared to encourage shifting levels of scrutiny under the Court's multi-tiered approach.[68] The Legal Services Program's cases provided the beginning, and sometimes the whole, of new constitutional configurations that limited some governmental actions while allowing others. No account of the Supreme Court's due process and equal protection jurisprudence can ignore the justices' response to the poor's claims.

Hence, if LSP is evaluated in terms of its representation of poor clients and its influence on the development of Supreme Court doctrine and policy, it fares much better than if evaluated in terms of the achievement of the particular policy goals often ascribed to it. Poor clients represented by LSP attorneys shaped the judicial landscape and affected the policy outcomes and doctrinal development of this era.

Conclusion

LSP's poor clients provided the Supreme Court with a new set of claims that the justices embraced. The Court agreed to review 72 per cent of the 164 LSP cases and issued favorable decisions in 62 per cent of the reviewed cases. Seven per cent of all written opinions handed down by the high court during the 1966-1974 terms were responses to LSP cases. The justices' attention to these cases suggests that litigant claims are an important part of the calculus that determines judicial policy and doctrinal developments.

The LSP's appellate agenda was an outgrowth of its casework, rather than being a separate enterprise. The Program was never able to orchestrate and implement a coherent litigation strategy directed toward specific policy change. The LSP lacked several of the resources considered critical for the success of interest group litigation efforts: longevity, a cohesive legal staff experienced in Supreme Court litigation,[69] frequent support of the solicitor general,[70] and substantial support from like-minded groups.[71] Of course, the LSP enjoyed funding levels far surpassing those of even the most solvent litigation-oriented interest groups, but the majority of the money supported the Program's casework. The flood of clients at the local projects provided some restraints comparable to the fiscal limitations many groups suffer. Further, as interest groups must constantly seek contributions and

foundation support, LSP was constantly faced with bureaucratic and political battles both in and out of Congress.[72]

The one resource for success that LSP clearly did enjoy was "extra-legal publicity" and a favorable political climate.[73] While many groups turn to litigation because they believe that the political branches are unreceptive to their goals,[74] some of their greatest successes coincided with substantial elite support or emerging public favor.[75] Unlike many groups, the LSP did not initially face hostility from the national political branches. Rather, the Program itself was the result of legislation, The Office of Economic Opportunity Act of 1964, favorable to its clients and clientele. To the extent there was political opposition to the decisions in LSP cases, it came largely from state and local government officials and was directed toward the Program, not the Court.[76]

Legal bases for favorable decisions in LSP cases had been developed in earlier due process and equal protection cases and such issues were increasingly gaining the Court's attention.[77] Perhaps most importantly, the central applications of the Due Process Clause to criminal proceedings and the Equal Protection Clause to racial discrimination had already been achieved, easing expansion of the scope of those guarantees in some LSP cases. During the early 1960s, articles developing doctrinal justifications for decisions favorable to the poor began to appear in leading publications such as *Harvard Law Review* and *Yale Law Journal.*[78] Indeed, Krislov has suggested that LSP's failure to convince the Court to declare a right to the necessities of life in *Dandridge v. Williams*[79] is partly attributable to the lack of such extra-Court development of supportive legal arguments.[80]

LSP began bringing cases to the Supreme Court at a time when the justices had already evinced some concern with the plight of the poor in the American system. In 1963, they reached out to review *Gideon v. Wainwright*[81] and later they struck down some financial barriers to the electoral process.[82] To the extent that the political environment plays a role in determining what issues the justices believe compel their attention, LSP was fortunate to be litigating in an era when poverty and equality concerns were prominent themes on the executive and legislative agenda.[83] Given the setting, perhaps LSP's achievements are not very surprising.

However, focusing on LSP's success rates may

obscure the broader importance of Legal Services' expansion of access to the judicial forum. In a liberal democratic regime committed to the rule of law, it is particularly important that all classes be able to set the law in motion. Without citizen access to courts, law violations by government may remain unchecked.[84] In an era when the courts are increasingly involved in making policy and enforcing the public policies of the other branches, any measure of the democracy of our system must include an assessment of the citizens' access to the courts.[85] Through the LSP, the poor were enfranchised in the judicial policy process.

NOTES

This article originally appeared in Volume 72, Number 5, February-March 1989, pages 266-273.

The author wishes to thank The Brookings Institution, the American Judicature Society and the Rutgers University Research Council for the financial support they provided for the larger project upon which this article draws.

1. Johnson, JUSTICE AND REFORM: THE FORMATIVE YEARS OF THE AMERICAN LEGAL SERVICES PROGRAM 105-134 (New Brunswick, NJ: Transaction Books, 1978).

2. *Id.* at xxix, 18, 188-190.

3. Katz, POOR PEOPLE'S LAWYERS IN TRANSITION (New Brunswick, NJ: Rutgers University Press, 1982).

4. Carlin and Howard, *Legal Representation and Class Justice,* 12 UCLA L. REV. 381 (1965); Johnson, *supra* n. 1, at 3-19; Brownell, LEGAL AID IN THE UNITED STATES, SUPPLEMENT (Rochester, NY: The Lawyers Co-operative Publishing Co., 1961).

5. The remaining 83 per cent of the LSP's cases were settled, or disposed of through advice or referral. Johnson, *supra* n. 1, at 293; Brownell, *supra* n. 4, at 44.

6. Johnson, *supra* n. 1, at 13, 337-338. Of course, there is a long tradition of interest groups representing clients who are unable to secure private counsel, often for financial as well as political reasons. However, in contrast to the LSP, these groups generally only provide representation when the case provides an opportunity for advancement of the group's policy goals.

7. Failinger and May, *Litigating Against Poverty: Legal Services and Group Representation,* 45 OHIO STATE L. J. 1 (1984); George, *Development of the Legal Services Corporation,* 61 CORNELL L. REV. 681 (1976).

8. Rosenblatt, *Legal Entitlements and Welfare Benefits,* in Kairys, ed., THE POLITICS OF LAW (New York: Pantheon Books, 1982); Krislov, *The OEO Lawyers Fail to Constitutionalize a Right to Welfare: A Study in the Uses and Limits of the Judicial Process,* 58 MINN. L. REV. 211 (1973).

9. Johnson, *supra* n. 1, at 105-134; Hannon, *Law Enforcement at the Local Level: A Legal Services Case Study,* 19 J. OF PUB. LAW 13 (1970); Johnson, *Refutation and Endorsement: A Reaction to Hannon's Analysis of the Murphy Amendment and the Bar,* 28 LEGAL AID BRIEFCASE 257 (1970).

10. Johnson, *supra* n. 1, at 131. For a more current discussion of the continuing debate between proponents of client casework and those favoring law reform, see Failinger and May, *supra* n. 7; Abel, *Informalism: A Tactical Equivalent to Law?* 19 CLEARINGHOUSE REVIEW 375 (1985).

11. Handler, Hollingsworth and Erlanger, LAWYERS AND THE PURSUIT OF LEGAL RIGHTS 23 (New York: Academic Press, 1978).

12. Sparer, *The Role of the Welfare Client's Lawyer,* 12 UCLA L. REV. 361 (1964); Sparer, *Social Welfare Law Testing,* 12 THE

PRACTICAL LAWYER 12 (1966).

13. Krislov, *supra* n. 8; Greenberg, *Litigation for Social Change: Methods, Limits, and Role in Democracy,* 29 RECORD OF THE BAR ASSOC. OF THE CITY OF N.Y. 320 (1974).

14. Champagne, *The Internal Operation of OEO Legal Services Projects,* 51 J. OF URBAN L. 649 (1974); Finman, *OEO Legal Services Programs and the Pursuit of Social Change: The Relationship Between Program Ideology and Program Performance,* 1971 WISC. L. REV. 1001 (1971); Hannon, *supra* n. 9; Pious, *Policy and Public Administration: The Legal Services Program and the War on Poverty,* 1 POL. AND SOC'Y 365 (1971).

15. *See* Katz, *supra* n. 3, at 105-122.

16. Regarding the accuracy of such translation processes in the context of social welfare litigation, see Olson, CLIENTS AND LAWYERS: SECURING THE RIGHTS OF DISABLED PERSONS 21-39, 109-167 (Westport, CT: Greenwood Press, 1984) and sources cited therein.

17. 386 U.S. 670 (1967).

18. The first board of directors meeting was July 25, 1975. The official transfer from the LSP to the Corporation occurred 90 days later, on October 12, 1975. *See* George, *supra* n. 7; Handler, et al., *supra* n. 11, at 155-195.

19. Each issue of CLEARINGHOUSE REVIEW, an LSP publication, contains a section entitled "Poverty Law Developments" composed of summaries of appellate litigation (at all stages) brought by LSP attorneys across the country. Some poverty cases that were not brought by LSP attorneys were also reported. They are not included in my LSP figures. Johnson's figures are somewhat higher than mine because he includes all Supreme Court cases reported in POVERTY LAW REPORTER, including those not sponsored by the LSP. Johnson, *supra* n. 1, at 189.

20. In addition, 24 cases in which the LSP participated only through the filing of amicus curiae briefs on-the-merits were located. These cases are not included in the figures presented here.

21. 394 Ill. 557, 30 NE2d 46 (1940).

22. Shapiro v. Thompson, 394 U.S. 618 (1969).

23. These figures are based on the Court's acceptance rates for certiorari and appeal cases during this period compiled from *The Supreme Court, 19xx Term: The Statistics,* HARV. L. REV. (1967-1975); Stern and Gressman, SUPREME COURT PRACTICE, 4th ed. (Washington, D.C.: Bureau of National Affairs, 1969). The predictions are 58 appeals and six certiorari petitions granted review with only 20 appeals and four certiorari petitions given plenary review.

24. The Court accepted 81 appeals and 38 certiorari petitions, giving plenary consideration to 52 appeals and 28 certiorari petitions.

25. Tanenhaus, Schick, Muraskin, and Rosen, *The Supreme Court's Certiorari Jurisdiction: Cue Theory,* in Goldman and Sarat, eds., AMERICAN COURT SYSTEMS: READINGS IN JUDICIAL PROCESS AND BEHAVIOR (San Francisco: W.H. Freeman and Co., 1978).

26. Ulmer, *The Supreme Court's Certiorari Decisions: Conflict as a Predictive Variable,* 78 AM. POL. SCI. REV. 901 (1984); Teger and Kosinski, *The Cue Theory of Supreme Court Certiorari Jurisdiction: A Reconsideration,* 42 J. OF POL. 834 (1980). But see, Provine, CASE SELECTION IN THE UNITED STATES SUPREME COURT 78-83 (Chicago: University of Chicago Press, 1980).

27. Tanenhaus, et al., *supra* n. 25, at 143. On the importance of the solicitor general in case selection, see also Perry, "Deciding to Decide: Agenda Setting in the United States Supreme Court," 354-361, Ph.D. Dissertation, University of Michigan, 1987.

28. Including all cases in which the solicitor general participated avoids the problem of determining the strength or weakness of his opposition. Formally, the solicitor general participated as the petitioner in nine cases, all of which were

reviewed, and as the respondent in 13 cases, 11 of which were reviewed.

29. Tanenhaus, et al., *supra* n. 25, at 143.

30. Provine, *supra* n. 26, at 104-130.

31. Patterson, AMERICA'S STRUGGLE AGAINST POVERTY, 1900-1985 (Cambridge: Harvard University Press, 1986).

32. Remanded cases were read and substantively analyzed, then coded as an LSP win or loss. The LSP won 74 cases, 23 of which were remanded. It lost 45 cases, 9 of which were remanded.

33. Brenner, *The New Certiorari Game*, 41 J. OF POL. 649 (1979).

34. None of the associations yielded a Gamma or Yule's cue greater than + or -0.25. Back-up center sponsorship and/or co-sponsorship by another interest group such as the NAACP LDF or ACLU was used as a measure of presence of experienced and expert counsel.

35. None of the associations yielded a Gamma or Yule's cue greater than + or -0.3.

36. The LSP won 61.7 per cent of the 47 cases the Court decided in 1967 through 1971. It won 62.5 per cent of the 72 cases the Court decided in 1972, the first year when all four Nixon appointees were sitting, through the end of the 1974 Term.

37. Spaeth's equality scale is adopted here for purposes of comparison. Spaeth, SUPREME COURT POLICY MAKING: EXPLANATION AND PREDICTION 135 (San Francisco: W.H. Freeman and Co., 1979). Of the available ranking scales the equality scale seems to include more of the types of claims brought by the LSP than the other scales.

38. During this time 42.2 per cent of all the Court's decisions were unanimous. Compiled from HARV. L. REV., *supra* n. 23.

39. By comparing agreement rates between pairs of justices in LSP cases and the Court's entire docket during the same time period, other factors that effect judicial voting behavior on collegial courts, such as small group interaction, especially as manifested in the "freshman effect," are controlled for. The newness of these cases would lead us to expect lower agreement rates in LSP cases as all the justices were in the process of developing their own positions on these issues, a situation that would create considerable flux in the coalitions. See Murphy, ELEMENTS OF JUDICIAL STRATEGY 37-90 (Chicago: The University of Chicago Press, 1964); Howard, *On the Fluidity of Judicial Choice*, 62 AM. POL. SCI. REV. 43 (1968).

40. Justices Clark, Fortas and Warren, who only participated in one, six and nine LSP cases, respectively, are omitted in the analysis of differences in agreement rates.

41. Four of these seven negative pairs include Black who showed an amazing propensity to disagree with all his Brethren during this time. His agreement rates ranged from 43 per cent (Marshall) to 63 per cent (Warren) during this era. His dissenting opinions in LSP victories suggest that, though he was sympathetic to the poor's claims, he felt constrained by his view of the judicial role.

42. We would not expect that LSP cases tapped a particular value dimension upon which traditionally liberal and traditionally conservative justices were likely to agree. Indeed, it is unclear what such a value dimension would be. Further, these characterizations of the justices' value positions subsume both ideological policy preferences and judicial role conceptions. *See* Baum, THE SUPREME COURT, 2d ed., 143-145 (Washington, D.C.: Congressional Quarterly Press, 1985); Spaeth, *supra* n. 37, at 109-139.

43. Bennett, *The Burger Court and the Poor*, in Blasi, ed., THE BURGER COURT: THE COUNTER-REVOLUTION THAT WASN'T (New Haven: Yale University Press, 1983); Krislov, *supra* n. 8; Rosenblatt, *supra* n. 8.

44. *Supra* n. 22.

45. 397 U.S. 254 (1970).

46. 401 U.S. 371 (1971).

47. 397 U.S. 471 (1970).

48. 411 U.S. 1 (1973).

49. Ortwein v. Schwab, 410 U.S. 656 (1973); U.S. v. Kras, 409 U.S. 434 (1973).

50. 400 U.S. 309 (1971). Fourth Amendment does not prohibit warrantless searches by welfare case workers.

51. Of course, both the Program's victories and its losses affected many people besides the individual clients. Generally, the losses allowed government to proceed as it wished rather than preventing innovative programs as the Court had earlier in such cases as Lochner v. New York, 198 U.S. 45 (1905) and Adkins v. Children's Hospital, 261 U.S. 525 (1923).

52. There is no significant difference between the Program's success rate in these two groups of cases, winning over 60 per cent in each.

53. 405 U.S. 645 (1972).

54. 417 U.S. 628 (1974).

55. 412 U.S. 441 (1973).

56. 414 U.S. 563 (1974).

57. 419 U.S. 565 (1975).

58. 407 U.S. 67 (1972). The Court backed off its Fuentes decision two years later in another LSP case, Mitchell v. W.T. Grant Co., 416 U.S. 600 (1974). Indeed, two concurring justices expressed the view that Mitchell overruled Fuentes.

59. 413 U.S. 634 (1972).

60. Goldberg v. Kelly, *supra* n. 45; Wheeler v. Montgomery, 397 U.S. 280 (1970); Fuentes v. Shevin, *supra* n. 58.

61. Mitchell v. W.T. Grant Co., *supra* n. 58; Goss v. Lopez, *supra* n. 57; Jackson v. Metropolitan Edison Co., 419 U.S. 345 (1974).

62. Vlandis v. Kline, *supra* n. 55; Mourning v. Family Publications Service, 411 U.S. 356 (1973); Weinburger v. Salfi, 422 U.S. 749 (1975).

63. Boddie v. Connecticut, *supra* n. 46; Lindsey v. Normet, 405 U.S. 56 (1972); Stanley v. Illinois, *supra* n. 53. But see, Ortwein v. Schwab, *supra* n. 49; U.S. v. Kras, *supra* n. 49; Wyman v. James, *supra* n. 50.

64. Graham v. Richardson, 403 U.S. 365 (1971); Sugarman v. Dougall, *supra* n. 59.

65. Shapiro v. Thompson, *supra* n. 22; Pease v. Hansen, 404 U.S. 70 (1971).

66. U.S. v. Kras, *supra* n. 49; San Antonio v. Rodriguez, *supra* n. 48; James v. Valtierra, 402 U.S. 137 (1971); Jefferson v. Hackney, 406 U.S. 535 (1972).

67. San Antonio v. Rodriguez, *supra* n. 48; Goss v. Lopez, *supra* n. 57; Dandridge v. Williams, *supra* n. 47; Jefferson v. Hackney, *supra* n. 66; Geduldig v. Aiello, 417 U.S. 484 (1974); Weinberger v. Salfi, *supra* n. 62. *But see*, U.S. Dept. of Agriculture v. Moreno, 413 U.S. 528 (1973); Jiminez v. Weinberger, *supra* n. 54.

68. *See especially*, Justice Marshall's dissents in Dandridge v. Williams, *supra* n. 47; Lindsey v. Normet, *supra* n. 63; San Antonio v. Rodriguez, *supra* n. 48.

69. Local attorneys from 116 different projects participated in the LSP's Supreme Court docket. The specialized LSP funded back-up centers formally participated in only 25 of the 119 cases decided on-the-merits. There is no significant association between back-up center participation and case outcome. Further, my interviews indicated that cases often proceeded without even informal participation by the centers. *See also* Johnson, *supra* n. 1, at 274. Hander, et al. have also found that LSP attorneys were a fairly representative sample of the bar, though generally a bit younger. Handler et al., *supra* n. 11.

70. The solicitor general was co-counsel with the LSP in only two reviewed cases, both of which they won, and he filed amicus briefs in support of the LSP in only eight reviewed

cases, five of which they won.

71. Epstein, CONSERVATIVES IN COURT 12-14 (Knoxville: The University of Tennessee Press, 1985) and sources cited therein. Other groups such as the NAACP LDF and ACLU co-sponsored 15 decided cases with the LSP, 7 of which they won. Groups filed amicus curiae briefs in support of the LSP in 54 reviewed cases. The LSP won 59 per cent of these cases compared to its success in 65 per cent of the 65 reviewed cases that proceeded without amicus support. There is not a statistically significant relationship between the filing of pro- LSP amicus briefs and case outcome.

72. Johnson, *supra* n. 1, at 105-184; Pious, *Congress, The Organized Bar, and the Legal Services Program,* 1972 WISC. L. REV. 418 (1972).

73. Epstein, *supra* n. 71, at 13.

74. Cortner, *Strategies and Tactics of Litigants in Constitutional Cases,* 17 J. OF PUB. L. 287 (1968).

75. *See* Greenberg, *supra* n. 13, at 333-334; Sorauf, THE WALL OF SEPARATION: THE CONSTITUTIONAL POLITICS OF CHURCH AND STATE 333-334 (Princeton: Princeton University Press, 1976); O'Connor and Epstein, *Beyond legislative lobbying: women's rights groups and the Supreme Court,* 67 JUDICATURE 134 (1983).

76. George, *supra* n. 7; Johnson, *supra* n. 1, at 193-194; Cramton, *Promise and Reality in Legal Services,* 61 CORNELL L. REV. 670 (1976).

77. Pacelle, "The Supreme Court and the Growth of Civil Liberties: The Process and Dynamics of Agenda Change," paper delivered at the annual meetings of the American Political Science Association, Chicago, September 1987.

78. For example, Justice Brennan cited Reich, *The New Property,* 73 YALE L.J. 733 (1964) and Reich, *Individual Rights and Social Welfare: The Emerging Legal Issues,* 74 YALE L.J. 1245 (1965), in his majority opinion in Goldberg v. Kelly, *supra* n. 45.

79. *Supra* n. 47.

80. Krislov, *supra* n. 8, at 245.

81. 372 U.S. 335 (1963).

82. Harper v. Virginia Board of Elections, 383 U.S. 663 (1966); Bullock v. Carter, 405 U.S. 134 (1972); Lubin v. Panish, 415 U.S. 709 (1974).

83. Patterson, *supra* n. 31.

84. For example, 18 LSP cases given plenary consideration involved a claim that a state law was in conflict with a federal statute.

85. *See* Zemans, *Legal Mobilization: The Neglected Role of the Law in the Political System,* 77 AM. POL. SCI. REV. 690 (1983).

Actors in the Judicial Process
Litigants and Interest Groups

INTRODUCTION   Unlike the legislative process where a governmental institution may address a problem simply as a matter of choice, courts are responsive bodies and can only deal with cases brought before them by litigants engaged in an adversarial proceeding. Governmental litigants are the chief users of the American judiciary and, indeed, every criminal case is pursued by the government on behalf of "the people." Individual litigants may be brought to court by the government or they may initiate cases in civil proceedings.

At a surface level, litigation often appears to resemble an effort to redress individual concerns. It is important to recognize, however, that litigation can have significant policy consequences for society extending far beyond the importance of a case for the individual litigants of the moment. Indeed, the judicial process can be the most efficient means by which interest groups may seek to pursue their preferred policy ends either through the filing of an amicus curiae brief or, alternatively, by making the larger commitment of sponsoring a "test case." While we do not know a great deal about individual litigants in a systematic way (except, perhaps, for our knowledge about criminal defendants as a class of litigants brought to court by the government against their will), we continue to learn much about the role of interest groups in the judicial process. This section of readings examines several facets of group participation in the American judiciary.

In "Civil rights litigation by organizations: constraints and choices," Stephen Wasby examines the real world operation of "planned" litigation in which a group attempts to pursue societal change through the courts. Wasby's specific focus is on the NAACP's efforts in the civil rights arena, and he demonstrates convincingly that much group behavior regarding litigation is not conducive to tight organizational control. Rather, litigation seeking social change "is often reflexive and far from completely planned with many constraints . . . many detours along the road to organizational goals, and much flexibility of action by both the litigating organizations and individual staff attorneys."

In "Beyond legislative lobbying: women's rights groups and the

Supreme Court," Karen O'Connor and Lee Epstein examine the relative merits and the comparative success of group efforts to advance women's rights in legislative and judicial settings. The article demonstrates the alternative approaches (amicus preparation versus test case sponsorship) favored by different women's rights advocates such as NOW and the ACLU while exploring the groups' strategic concerns. The Supreme Court emerges from this study as a uniquely receptive arena for the pursuit of women's rights claims.

Perhaps the most graphic example of interest group participation in Supreme Court litigation occurred in *Webster v. Reproductive Health Services* (1989), a case dealing with state legislation regulating abortions that was perceived by many analysts as the instrument through which the Court might overturn *Roe v. Wade* (1973), the seminal precedent enhancing freedom of choice. Susan Behuniak-Long's article, "Friendly fire: amici curiae and *Webster v. Reproductive Health Services*," offers a detailed case study of group participation in *Webster*. Behuniak-Long's analysis examines who filed amicus briefs and what arguments were raised. It also explores the impact of briefs on the justices' diverse opinions by amicus participants and the possible reasons for differences in behavior between groups on the pro-life and freedom of choice sides of the case.

In "The amicus curiae role of the U.S. solicitor general in Supreme Court litigation," Karen O'Connor underlines one way in which the U.S. government serves as the most active "group" seeking its preferred policy ends in Supreme Court cases. In comparing and contrasting the amicus brief writing behavior of solicitor generals Griswold, Bork, and McCree from 1967 through 1981, O'Connor demonstrates that changes in the legal posture of the government in policy-oriented litigation are responsive to changes in presidential administrations as well as in the identity of the solicitors general. Important differences existed in the types of cases each solicitor general participated in as well as the positions that they took.

Finally, it is useful to note, groups can be important participants in the judicial process beyond their role in litigation per se. Thus, for example, they may be active players in judicial selection, as demonstrated by Elliot Slotnick's study, "The ABA Standing Committee on Federal Judiciary: a contemporary assessment." Slotnick's analysis details the ABA committee's operation, raises questions about its "most favored" status in federal judicial recruitment, and examines empirically the committee's evaluation of judicial nominees.

Civil rights litigation by organizations: constraints and choices

Litigation for social change is far from completely planned. Numerous external and internal factors affect both the planning and execution of a campaign.

by **Stephen L. Wasby**

Organized groups have long made use of the courts in their efforts to produce—or retard—social change. Despite claims that "social policy" litigation, which courts are said to lack the capacity to handle,[1] is new, such litigation has long taken place. In the 1930s, for example, conservative groups went to court to challenge New Deal legislation. In terms of litigation systematically brought by interest groups—a litigation "campaign" or "planned" litigation—the efforts to overturn school segregation, resulting in *Brown v. Board of Education*,[2] are most likely to come to mind. These efforts by the NAACP Legal Defense Fund (LDF) have become the model for planned litigation, followed both by those seeking civil rights for other segments of society, for example, women, and those litigating outside the civil rights field, such as environmental groups like the Sierra Club and the Natural Resources Defense Council.[3] The growth of public interest law firms, both liberal and conservative, indicates the use of the model across the political spectrum.[4]

Not all litigation aimed at producing social change is "planned" litigation or takes the form of litigation campaigns. Nor are all test cases instances of planned litigation. For example, it was only recently that the American Civil Liberties Union (ACLU), which we associate with test case litigation, began to undertake systematic litigation in particular areas of the law through "projects" staffed by particular attorneys, instead of litigating primarily against "targets of opportunity."[5]

Mounting a litigation campaign is no easy task. It requires attention not only to strategy in particular cases but also to larger strategy, including choosing areas of law in which to litigate, choosing cases within those areas of law, and developing the resources necessary to undertake the litigation.

Planning any individual case, such as a large antitrust case, a class action toxic injury case or a drug case like the DES litigation, poses many problems for the lawyers involved. Yet when an organization, such as a civil rights group like LDF, contemplates undertaking a litigation "campaign" in a particular area of the law,[6] matters become even more difficult: the organization must worry not simply about individual cases but about a number of them.

In an effort to cast more light on "planned" litigation, particularly in the area of civil rights, this article explores some aspects of civil rights litigation undertaken by interest groups and the lawyers associated with them, emphasizing cases on school desegregation, employment discrimination (primarily cases under Title VII of the Civil Rights Act of 1964), and housing discrimination. After a look at some possible effects of litigation campaigns on the work of courts, we turn our attention to lawyers' perspectives on the role of interest groups in planned litigation, with particular attention to organizations' choices of areas of law in which to litigate and of cases to pursue, and to the internal dynamics of those cases. Then we will examine relations between staff attorneys and "cooperating" attorneys and interorganizational relationships affecting litigation.

Primary attention is paid to the work of the National Association for the Advancement of Colored People (NAACP) and the NAACP Legal Defense and Educational Fund, Inc. (LDF) from the late 1960s through the early 1980s. This period was chosen because it was an "age of complexity" for race relations interest group litigators. The environment in which the litigators functioned became increasingly complex; in addition to having to attend to judicial rulings, they had to focus on statutes and implementing regulations as well. Moreover, pubic opinion concerning civil rights became more conservative than it had been in the early and mid-1960s. Congress also became less supportive of civil rights, as did the executive branch, in the transitions both from the Johnson to Nixon presidencies and later, from the Carter to Reagan administrations.

Litigation itself became more complex; school cases were no longer a matter of attacking segregation statutes but required considerable resources both to prove violations and then to develop and implement remedies or involved challenges to "second-generation" discrimination within schools. In employment discrimination, the most blatant forms of discrimination had been replaced by more subtle forms, varying from industry to industry, which also required considerable resources to demonstrate.

This article is based primarily on interviews with more than 40 attorneys who are or were associated with the NAACP, the LDF, or other active organizational participants in race relations litigation (e.g., the Lawyers Committee for Civil Rights Under Law, the National Committee Against Discrimination in Housing, the Center for National Policy Review, and the Center for Law and Education). Among those interviewed were the senior attorneys for these organizations; several lawyers closely involved in organizations' litigation planning, although they did not serve as staff attorneys; and many "cooperating attorneys" in major race relations cases. The cooperating attorneys include some who were expert in a particular type of litigation such as school desegregation, some who tried cases across the country, and others involved in cases in their own states and communities.

The interviews, based primarily on open-ended questions, were structured but allowed respondents to discuss matters they thought especially salient. Among matters covered were organizations' choices of areas of law in which to litigate, choices of particular cases, organizations' use of cooperating attorneys, relations between litigating organizations, and the effect and importance of factors that might affect the litigation in which the respondents or their organization had been involved. Aspects of the particular cases in which the cooperating attorneys had been involved were explored in interviews with these individuals.

Litigation campaigns and the courts

Although interest groups attempt to use the courts to achieve social change, such litigation does not *necessarily* add significantly to the courts' work. Particularly when precedent is an organization's goal, a litigation campaign may involve bringing a number of cases so that the organization has several appropriate cases reach the appellate courts in the appropriate sequence, with allowance being made for some cases being settled and some "washing out" for other reasons. Nonetheless, the number of cases may be no greater than if individual plaintiffs asserted their rights in separate cases. Whether or not a litigation campaign was under way to achieve school desegregation, suits would have had to be filed against many school districts, and many Title VII lawsuits would have been necessary to resolve complaints of employment discrimination even if the LDF had not decided to proceed systematically.[7]

Without the efforts of the NAACP and the LDF, fewer school desegregation or employment discrimination cases would have been brought, but that is primarily because those organizations provided resources—staff attorneys, cooperating attorneys, and expenses—not otherwise available to many prospective plaintiffs. It is thus the interest groups' efforts and injection of resources, not that these efforts took the form of planned litigation, that may have produced more cases for the courts, just as governmental actions with respect to schools, or action by private entities concerning employment, often prompted the litigation.

Litigation campaigns may in a way have *reduced* the number of cases with which the courts had to contend because class action suits combining many claims were major vehicles in the LDF Title VII campaign. Without the class action suits, there might have been more individual plaintiffs' suits. As it was, there were many of those, brought by attorneys using materials made available by organizational litigators. The class action suits, however, were more complex and thus took more time to litigate, just as northern school desegregation suits involved significant problems of proof. Civil rights litigation often took the form of "public law" cases—polycentric controversies involving multiple parties and entailing detailed and continuing relief, and thus requiring prolonged involvement by the judge hearing the case[8]—or "structural lawsuits" with "an array of competing interests and perspectives organized around a number of issues and a single decisional agency, the judge."[9]

The growing complexity of cases can affect case outcomes in a number of ways. Litigators' needs for substantial resources may mean that they may not be able to pursue some complaints or that some complaints once commenced must be abandoned. Principal civil rights litigating organizations concentrating only on the "big," potentially precedent-setting cases have fewer resources to devote to "small," individual-plaintiff cases, which must be pursued, if at all, by local counsel. Judicial standards, requiring proof of intent to discriminate, not merely of disparate effects,[10] not only require civil rights lawyers to put on a more elaborate case but also make it less likely that civil rights plaintiffs will prevail.

The courts have themselves contributed to the complexity of civil rights litigation—and thus to their own workload. One way is through the just-noted requirement of proof of intent to discriminate. Courts also affect litigation in other ways, for example, by their receptivity to certain arguments and, because of groups' need for financial resources for civil rights litigation, their willingness to grant attorneys fees under the Civil Rights Attorneys Fees Awards Act of 1976. The Supreme Court's willingness to grant review to cases in certain areas of the law and its disinclination to hear cases in other areas affect litigators' pursuit of cases to that level. For example, the Court's not having previously granted certiorari in restrictive covenant cases made the NAACP pay particular attention to framing cases so that the Court would grant review[11] and the Court's unwillingness to hear claims of discrimination in public housing and urban renewal cases "depressed the market" for such cases.[12]

The Court's procedural rulings, such as those on the standing of parties to sue, have important effects as well: *Warth v. Seldin*[13] is said to have had a devastating effect on the campaign against exclusionary zoning. And of course the Court's substantive rulings are crucial. An example is the decision in *San Antonio School District v. Rodriguez*,[14] which shut off federal court challenges to the property tax basis for financing public education. That case led civil rights lawyers to redirect their efforts to state courts, an indication of the effect of judicial decisions on litigators' choice of federal or state forum. The abortive campaign to reform the welfare system through litigation provides another example.[15] Although the Court issued favorable rulings in benefit termination cases on due process grounds,[16] when it handed down adverse rulings on benefit levels[17] the campaign came to an end.

Planned litigation

To write about litigators' perspectives on "planned litigation" is to assume that such litigation exists.[18] We must, however, be careful not to assume that all litigation to which some attach the label "planned" is thoroughly or fully planned, with litigators in control of the areas of law in which they focus their efforts, of particular cases, or of sequence of cases. To use the term is to say, at the least, that some make efforts at planned litigation; it is not to say how thorough or successful those efforts are.

If the conventional wisdom is that civil rights litigation of the 1940s and early 1950s consisted of planned, organized campaigns to produce social change, the picture presented here of the more recent period is quite different. Even in the litigation leading to *Brown v. Board of Education*, we get a picture rather different from Kluger's portrayal in *Simple Justice*, which Mark Tushnet has properly criticized as being one of "essentially unproblematic success."[19] Instead, there was "a tremendous amount of matter extraneous to policy which determined whether a case was brought in one state rather than another or one place rather than another," and policy was made primarily "around Thurgood Marshall's desk," with a "lot of improvisation."[20]

Recent civil rights litigation certainly contains elements of planning, and much of the litigation is undertaken systematically. However, much about that litigation is problematic, in part because it is quite complex and much is unplanned, so that to a considerable degree even principal civil rights lawyers do not fully control it. Particularly in point is the observation by a major civil rights litigator, "The vagaries of litigation are such that if you bring a case solely to go the Supreme Court, there are 100 ways not to get there, and if you try to play cute in order to stay away, you end up there."

Nor do all those who have participated in

"planned litigation" share a view of the activity as derived from a blueprint. Litigation, said one lawyer, is a "responsive posture" inhibiting one from doing anything. Litigation provided "some room for maneuver," but was "not a strategic tool." Civil rights lawyers—lawyers with definite goals, working for organizations which have clear statements of purpose—frequently volunteered comments about the unplanned nature of their enterprise and unhesitatingly stressed the difficulties of keeping litigation strategy under control. In particular, one must keep in mind one litigator's acerbic comment, "Retrospective analyses that discern grand (and not so grand) strategies are often piffle. Many initiatives are impromptu." Furthermore, in general "the nature of the business prevents it from being a grand design:" "Whatever gets done, gets done, rather than by design."

Control of litigation

At the heart of planned litigation is *control*.[21] This includes the ability to "influence the development and sequence of cases," so that lawyers can "produce cases which presented the issues they wanted decided, where and when they wanted them,"[22] something "far from automatic and not subject to tight control."[23] Among the many matters not subject to control are, in the words of one LDF lawyer, "the chance occurrences of any lawsuit, the defection of the plaintiffs or capitulation of defendants, disagreement among counsel, unanticipated precedents, and the effect of public sentiment and political currents on adjudication."[24] Litigators might be able to exercise control at the level of the individual case and might also be able to choose areas of law in which to litigate and to establish priorities among those areas. Within any area of law, however, there is a less tidy picture; lawyers' ability to control the flow of cases and thus to choose cases decreases because there are more problems "whenever you clutter the landscape with litigation." Many decisions are made *inductively* (or responsively), a result of pressure, circumstance, and the flow of cases to litigators, rather than *deductively*, following logically from certain established criteria.

That an organization does more than respond idiosyncratically to cases cannot be taken for granted. Even when organizations bring test cases—the quintessence of planned litigation—they may not have done so as a result of broad litigation planning.

Instead they may have responded to "fortuitous events." Even where an organization has undertaken a planned litigation campaign, such as LDF's Title VII litigation, some cases have been taken reflexively, in response to client and membership pressure. Thus even when an organization does attempt to plan litigation, its activities may not result from strategy. Although an organization may be capable of developing "offensive" strategies, "circumstances control." Thus it has been difficult for the NAACP "to control priorities and time expenditures," making it "reflective and responsive to events and developments." If at times it seemed "as if there was a grand strategy applied from New York, the opposite was true:" matters "arose in the countryside" and then moved to the national level. Moreover, when there is a plan, flexibility—essential to success—will result in departures from it. The speed with which cases arise may also make it difficult for litigators to control litigation.

Strategy sessions can be an important element of "planning" in planned litigation.[25] However, observers believe that efforts to get lawyers together to plan strategy have seldom produced "grand strategizing;" they produce "petty strategizing if anything." When six people were brought together in a hotel room to plan, "not much came out of any of that type of activity," because what results from "sitting around" is "too abstract" for use in actual situations. Even where strategy has been planned, the presence of a larger number of litigators increases the likelihood that "another actor will enter the fray and set matters back several years." Indeed, "too many people are doing too many things for planned litigation to be more than a myth. If you are going to bring up cases A, B, C, and D, before you can, 12 others bring it up." That forces you to "move when you can where you can," with litigation more like "secret warfare."

Choosing areas of law

If planning involves choice, what do we find about interest group litigators' choices?[26] The choice of particular areas of law in which to focus litigation activities is a crucial part of planned litigation. Certain areas in which organizations litigate, for example, Title VII and capital punishment by LDF, are chosen with some care, with constraints imposed mostly by limited resources. School desegregation, the "most programmatically developed" area of NAACP litigation, has been that organization's primary litigation focus, taking up "90 per cent of the conscious effort" in litigation. The NAACP has also been active in the fight against employment discrimination, but that area of law did not receive the same attention by the group's legal department. Indeed, as a result of a request from the NAACP's labor director, highly involved for many years in battling job discrimination, the LDF did the "biggest piece" of the NAACP cases; the lack of NAACP resources meant the organization had to "funnel" many Title VII cases to the LDF, with "the strategy [being] LDF strategy."

Litigation in some other areas of the law evolves because many cases on a topic come to an organization, such as the sit-in and demonstration cases of the early 1960s.[27] Other areas are said "simply [to] arise naturally." To the extent staff attorneys can "free-wheel" and pursue cases that fall outside the organization's basic litigation agenda, its litigation focus will become more diffuse.

Among the elements entering into the choice of areas of law for attention is an organizational one; the NAACP "had to consider that other organizations were considering some issues." The branches' "significant input" is an important intra-organizational fact, with the size and strength of a branch a relevant factor. Resolutions by the board of directors are also relevant, but board votes don't translate directly into litigation campaigns because of the "interplay" between board votes and the views of the general counsel, who has considerable autonomy to pursue his own interests, subject to his having to deal with the organization's own "bureaucratic" problems and having to serve as NAACP's house counsel. Staff lawyers play an important role, "orchestrating, certainly in tactical matters," and their views predominate, particularly when NAACP branches do not have lawyers among their officers. As with any litigating organization, resources are a crucial matter, indeed a "primary consideration" in NAACP's choice of areas of law.

The mid-1960s enactment of new civil rights statutes provided a "natural dividing line" in LDF's litigation efforts. Its focused litigation campaign, the most significant of private efforts to enforce Title VII, came about in part because job discrimination was an issue with substantial, immediate, and visible economic ramifications for minorities. This indicates that pressures on a nonmembership "public interest law firm" like LDF may be similar to those on the membership-based NAACP. Pressure may not be felt directly by LDF, but it is felt through clients coming to cooperating attorneys, from whom LDF gets most of its cases. Indeed, although neither the LDF nor the NAACP preferred having "ad hoc" cases, both had some. "Given the nature of the [NAACP] organization," that is, its membership base, the NAACP did "have to have some ad hoc cases" and has had more than has LDF.

Funding—particularly foundation funding—has been said to particularly influence the areas in which LDF has litigated. LDF has also been thought quite persuasive in getting foundations to support what LDF wanted to do. In short, LDF "solicits for specific issues," and "to the extent the funds are earmarked, [LDF staff] play a part in the earmarking."

Choosing cases

Once cases are channeled to an organization, decisions must be made as to which ones to pursue. Choosing areas of law and choosing cases are closely related. Decisions about the former help channel certain types of cases to the litigators. At least equally important, and reinforcement for the "inductive" or responsive view of "planned" litigation, is that decisions about areas of law in which to concentrate are influenced by the flow of cases to an organization. This makes how cases come to a litigating organization quite important. With cooperating attorneys the primary source of cases, organizational control of litigation planning may be reduced unless cooperating attorneys' choices are influenced by national organizational criteria. Nor do litigating organizations enter all cases from the beginning, which would facilitate control; they may become involved in some cases already initiated by others—sometimes defensively to prevent "bad" precedent or avoid rulings not in line with organizational strategy. This is a clear indication of the limits on organizations' ability to plan their litigation and control implementation of their strategy.

Lawyers associated with civil rights groups identify a variety of criteria used to select cases, but there is no clear consensus on the criteria used; moreover, constraints and organizational politics affect attempts to apply the criteria. NAACP decisions to take cases were based on several factors, including the significance of the case (those with broad impact were preferred) and the importance of the branch that initiated a case.

The NAACP took some cases because people in a particular community "had started to do the right thing" and one "had to help them." The NAACP also took cases because governments took actions that were "affronts [that] had to be challenged," giving the organization "no choice" but to get involved even if the cases did not fit with litigation strategy. However, the NAACP preferred not to fund a case unless the organization and its lawyers controlled the case and the case was "consistent with organizational policy." Particularly when a case had already been started, the NAACP would enter it only if it could "exercise significant direction" over the case. The view is "that general counsel and the New York staff will control litigation in which the organization is involved." Thus "if a branch went off with inconsistent litigation, or hadn't precleared the case, there would be hell to pay."

A number of observers felt, however, that case selection did not function according to prescribed procedures or on the basis of criteria related to litigation strategy. Indeed, the process by which cases came to NAACP has been called "helter-skelter," with the NAACP having "no sense of direction" and "jumping into cases without an idea of the factors or what the costs will be." At times the NAACP got involved in cases because its attorneys focused on the particular case rather than on the "larger picture." Some staff lawyers did not consider themselves "social engineers" and thus were not firm believers in planned litigation for social change. Not able to "tell what the effects of precedent will be," they focused on racial problems in individual cases. And because the organization was "relatively flexible internally as to lawyers' choices," at times it was up to the individual lawyer to decide whether to take a case.

The received tradition about LDF's planned litigation would lead one to expect case selection to be governed by a highly developed set of regularly applied criteria. Instead, LDF was criticized by lawyers associated with it for not having done more to "institutionalize" its process for deciding which cases to take and for not developing criteria for the purpose. Moreover, the process for choosing cases was "not organized, it's organic." "Greater organizational sophistication," a result of experience and organizational growth, did mean, however, "an ability to deal with the brush fires" with which the organization had to contend.

Once brought to LDF's attention, a case was evaluated to determine its "strength" in terms of cost, the quality of the cooperating attorney, "other cases doing the same thing," the state of the law, and "the likelihood of winning." LDF's criteria seemed better developed in Title VII litigation, perhaps because of the focused litigation campaign within that area of the law, leading to special attention in choosing the industries and geographical areas in which to focus litigation. In general, however, lawyers' views were that at LDF "you assess cases as they come to you," with a focus on "how to get the job done in the case."

Thus "LDF didn't make policy in the abstract; it made it through cases." The situation was "not the National Security Council with a weekly sitting-down." Instead, "by sitting in the doctor's office, you get a view of the world." There was attention to issues, "but on a day-to-day basis, you pick the best cases." One reason was that the importance of a case was not always clear when the case was initiated. More than one case had to be picked because "cases drop out for any number of reasons," including settlements offered "which you can't refuse"—although in addition to recommending taking the settlement, the lawyer "might also point out that we took the case to develop the law." In short, there was no "unified legal theory in the civil tradition" from which LDF operated; LDF took "individual cases, from which legal theory was deduced."

LDF made an "enormous commitment to initiating cases" but, while "we prefer to be in from the beginning," LDF entered other cases, particularly if it could play no other role or a cooperating attorney had handled the case, because it was "good at putting cases on the record." LDF would also enter a case after its initiation if the case was seen to have a potentially significant precedential effect. Although there are "obvious problems if you'd not had a part in planning and developing a case," some of these cases were actually viewed favorably because developments in the case provided more information than LDF would otherwise have at the case-selection stage, giving the organization a clearer picture of what it might be facing.

Case dynamics

The internal dynamics of cases also affect—and can frustrate—attempts to plan litigation. Day-to-day litigation matters often get in the way of litigation planning; lawyers "don't plan that far ahead; they deal with immediate issues." For example, lawyers are "concerned with the violation" in school cases and are "not planning ahead to the remedy stage."[28] Decisions from the Supreme Court coming in mid-litigation—likely because of the extended nature of planned civil rights litigation—can undermine the theory at the heart of a litigant's case. The effects of the Supreme Court's ruling on the welfare litigation campaign were noted previously, as were the effects of the Court's adverse ruling on standing to challenge exclusionary zoning.[29]

Although, to be successful, litigators must be responsive to changes in judicial doctrine, momentum or inertia, the *absence* of dynamics also limits planning in litigation by hindering groups from responding to changes in their environment. For example, Derrick Bell has argued that lawyers have persisted in seeking racially balanced schools despite changes in judicial outlook, "reverses in the school desegregation campaign," and "membership demands for more attention to quality education."[30] Continuing success in litigation, like the Warren Court's expansion of civil rights, is quite likely to kindle a spirit propelling a group to continue litigation and thus to limit shifts in litigation strategy. Apart from success, however, many lawyers believe in the "myth of rights," the idea that litigation can produce positive statements of rights as well as the implementation of those rights. The hold of this myth helps explain why lawyers continued to turn to the courts in pursuit of their clients' rights, even when earlier "ground-breaking" rulings had not been implemented.[31]

Closely related is the fact that victorious litigants do not wish to give up, or be seen as giving up, what they had pressed hard to achieve; altering legal theories in mid-litigation may be thought to be particularly inappropriate. Success thus reinforces what has been called lawyers' general conservatism in planned litigation. "People tend to repeat lessons from the past; lawyers trying to win a case will use what's worked." Moreover, the pace of litigation makes litigation "not a process giving one time to think," further limiting one's ability to respond to changes in one's legal environment.

The presence of other litigators, who may get to the appellate courts first—and "on a worse record"—also serves to press litigators to continue to take cases to those appellate courts even when favorable rulings are not expected. (There are, of course, other reasons, such as the belief that per-

haps a limited victory might be obtained or "damage control" achieved.) This helps explain why the talk by civil rights and civil liberties lawyers of avoiding the Burger Court was not matched by a significant decrease in "going to the High Court." After all, said one lawyer, "It's the only Supreme Court we've got." Moreover, in cases where lower court rulings have favored civil rights claims, a conservative high tribunal will be more likely to accept appeals from defeated defendants—extremely evident in recent criminal procedure cases—thus removing from the hands of civil rights litigators the choice not to pursue the case further.

Cooperating attorneys

The prescribed method by which an organization obtains cases may indicate a relatively highly centralized relationship between the organization and cooperating attorneys;[32] this is particularly the case if one looks at the formal process by which cases are supposed to come to the NAACP. However, use of cooperating attorneys means decentralization of the organization's work. An important aspect of that decentralization is whether and to what extent an organization's local units and their goals, as well as the goals of cooperating attorneys, are guided by the goals of the organization at the national level.[33]

One way to assure that cooperating attorneys act within the scope of national policy is to transmit that policy to the local level; providing assistance to the cooperating attorneys also helps achieve this goal.[34] Otherwise, decentralization can cut against a group's national strategy and local membership pressure can dominate determination of the cases to which cooperating attorneys give greatest attention. This is particularly likely when local affiliates initiate cases[35] or when lawyers act independently.[36] At times, national staff attorneys may be "lead counsel" only nominally, with local lawyers handling much of the case and planning much of the strategy and tactics. Lawyers who share a national organization's "world view" may be allowed to "fine-tune or even make major changes in litigation," and may be allowed to run the case instead of being given marching orders. However, with cases becoming more complex, local attorneys are more likely to need assistance, thus binding them more closely to the national organization.

Attorneys' roles

The processes by which cases come to national

litigating organizations, and the ways in which the organizations involve cooperating attorneys in their work, serve to define cooperating attorneys' varying roles. In some situations, national staff attorneys handle all trial work, with the cooperating attorney playing a clearly "subordinate role," gathering information and filing papers, serving as required local counsel, and acting principally as liaison between national staff lawyers and the local community. In short, cooperating attorneys may seem like little more than "water carriers" for the staff attorneys, although such a role may be assumed without complaint, particularly when local counsel have their own practices to attend to and realize they can't "carry" a major case.

In another role relationship, an organization's national staff lawyers develop new theories of litigation, with cooperating attorneys applying those theories. In still other situations, cooperating attorneys, who may have generated the cases themselves, serve as "lead counsel." Having greater familiarity with state court rules, local attorneys may be used for state cases, with staff attorneys handling federal litigation.

Roles are also affected by the *availability* of cooperating attorneys to pursue cases. Here race enters the picture. The use of white counsel rather than black counsel in cases brought by the NAACP or LDF is a question of long standing, although black lawyers have long handled civil rights cases. In cases originated locally, especially in the South, one occasionally found an especially courageous white lawyer or a local black lawyer who needed even more courage. The question of who was preferred by the national organizations was complicated when local black attorneys took the initiative in bringing test cases and adopted a position the national NAACP would have preferred not be pursued.[37] In the South, NAACP branch cases were often undertaken by white attorneys, who also "bore the principal burden of the national office's legal activity." White attorneys also handled many Northern cases because the law practices of many Northern black attorneys were not focused on civil rights and constitutional law, making "their usefulness to the . . . NAACP . . . limited."[38]

One thus found the predominant use of prestigious—and often conservative—white lawyers until the 1930s, which marked "a decisive turning point" toward greater use of black attorneys as a result of "pressure . . . from a small but growing elite of brilliant young Negroes educated in ivy league law schools" in the mid-1920s[39] and the National Bar Association's criticism of civil rights organizations for not using black attorneys. However, even when lawyers like Charles Houston and William Hastie were brought into NAACP cases,[40] there was not an adequate pool of black attorneys—nor of cooperating attorneys of any race—to handle Southern cases. This led to programs to prepare civil rights lawyers. The LDF's intern program is the best known and has been a notable success: Julius Chambers, the newly-named director-counsel of LDF, was one of LDF's first two interns, and other Southern attorneys who are "graduates" of that program are now judges. The number of available cooperating attorneys, both in solo practice and in large prestigious law firms, "recruited" by the Lawyers Committee for Civil Rights Under Law (LCCRUL), also increased because of the possibility of attorneys' fees, which provide an incentive for large law firms to handle civil rights cases.

Attorneys' views

How does the staff attorney-cooperating attorney relationship look to the attorneys? Lawyers associated with LDF suggest that there has been little change in recent years in LDF's use of cooperating attorneys, although the intern program "expanded the base" of those with whom the organization could work. The organization found itself, because of its work in poverty law and the campaign against the death penalty, in contact with attorneys with whom it had not been previously involved, altering the "relatively small and ethnically homogeneous group" with which LDF had worked. Those changes affected LDF staff attorneys' relations with cooperating attorneys.

Overall relations between staff and cooperating attorneys are "remarkably cooperative and supportive," with "remarkably little competition" between the two sets of lawyers. They work well together in part because they have a "recognized common enemy" and a common purpose. The skills of each are recognized by the other, with relationships adjusted to be appropriate to attorneys' backgrounds and case issues. When a cooperating attorney is experienced, staff might be able to help simply by providing briefs developed for other cases, which the cooperating attorney would know how to use; indeed, the staff attorneys prefer to work with those who do much work but only "need support and help."

Staff attorneys don't appreciate it when a cooperating attorney "tries to dump all the work on the staff." Indeed, they try to "keep to a minimum" cases handled solely by staff, although in some categories (e.g., Title VII for LDF), and particularly in new areas of the law, staff attorneys may do "virtually all the work." It should also be remembered that they wish to leave their own mark on a case, which can lead to a situation in which cooperating attorneys feel they are not being allowed to do very much.

Staff attorneys acknowledge the value of having cooperating attorneys who know the community from which a case comes; the cooperating attorneys "tend to know local people and problems better, and are not regarded as outsiders;" they understand the judges and the local courthouse. They may well provide a balance to the idealism and naivete of the young staff lawyers. They can also help those lawyers from New York City obtain the trust of local clients, and can provide a buffer between the organization and its clients so that client contact does not eat up a great deal of staff attorney time.

One should note that there are differences between organizations in the relations between staff and cooperating attorneys. NAACP's posture toward local attorneys seems more directive than is true at LDF, which may not need to exert pressure because cooperating attorneys who have been through the LDF internship program are well socialized in LDF values and procedures. NAACP does not appear to hesitate to assign lead counsel from outside the community, justifying this practice as being done to "protect local lawyers from pressure." The NAACP may also remove local counsel from a case if there is disagreement on how the case should be handled. NAACP staff attorneys shrug off "negative publicity" from such intervention, but there is some criticism of NAACP's willingness to engage in such "strongarm" tactics.

Interorganizational relations

Litigation is affected by the number of litigating groups. In recent years, more groups have been litigating, and, as a result, intergroup relations have become more confused. Prior to *Brown v. Board of Education*, there really was only one national civil rights litigating entity: the NAACP and

LDF were functionally one organization, but now the two are fully separate and indeed have been involved in litigation against each other. There are also many other civil rights litigating units in crucial, if less central, roles. Proliferation of litigators has led to a loss of control by any single litigator and thus has decreased the ability to pursue a concerted strategy.[41] Further dispersion has been produced by the feeling of some that instead of "total coordination," a "decentralized, multi-faceted approach" was preferable.

Dispersion and competition *and* convergence and cooperation characterize intergroup relations affecting litigation. Cooperation between groups is most likely to take the form of information exchange, which is important for control of cases as well as for more efficient resource allocation; such cooperation is likely to continue despite friction between organizations. At times more than information exchange occurs. Sessions are held among litigating groups, organizational representatives, and other attorneys to discuss issues and plan litigation,[42] and there are efforts to enlist other groups as companion plaintiffs or as amicus curiae participants in litigation.

In the latter situation, groups do make efforts to coordinate their briefs. Despite difficulties, civil rights lawyers on the whole felt—perhaps because of their frequent interactions—that coordination was not particularly difficult and that they were successful in achieving it. An attorney for a group contemplating filing an amicus brief in another group's case might "feed arguments" to the sponsoring group's attorney for those briefs; indeed, potential amici may help regular counsel develop their principal arguments. Likewise, attorneys for the parties would indicate to attorneys for groups contemplating filing an amicus brief "the general direction of their briefs." This would not, however, be a matter of "orchestrating" the other organization's amicus participation; a staff lawyer simply "would try to make them assist his case." Such attempts at coordination were not always appreciated, however, and there was a "problem of having to send a brief around" to everyone. As one lawyer put it, "writing briefs by committee doesn't work very well," leading the organization to allow others to join its brief but without attempting to coordinate with other groups.

In general, groups did not want to be associated with another organization through amicus participation unless they had input into the brief. This effort to "try to have some substantive input" was fairly general. That didn't mean civil rights litigators were always stand-offish about amicus participation even when concerned about protecting their own reputation: "It's to one's advantage to work with" some groups, said one lawyer, because "there are first-rate lawyers" working with those groups. Nonetheless, "ecumenical amicus briefs" (where everyone signed on) were generally to be avoided and a number of lawyers quoted former federal judge Marvin Frankel: "If you want to file a petition, go to Congress."

Although "some civil rights lawyers are . . . ideologically opposed to national coordination," as can be seen from the looseness of the "campaign" against exclusionary zoning,[43] a partial convergence of perspectives develops among lawyers in the generally small and relatively cohesive "civil rights bar." This convergence leads members of this "civil rights bar" to assist each other regardless of their organizations' formal positions. The civil rights bar is thus part of the "glue" that serves to hold the pieces of civil rights litigation together at both the national and local levels. Cooperation here is also more likely than in litigation that has a "commercialized purpose" because the civil rights lawyers "shared a real enemy" and "shared a conception of that enemy." This allows them to work together even when their organizational superiors are at odds, an instance of captains doing more talking to each other than the commanders-in-chief.

We also find dispersion and competition. That groups interested in a particular area of the law have similar views does not necessarily mean that they will participate conjointly in activity; instead they may decide to go separate ways as long as one of their number is stating their basic position on a particular case. This differentiation—or "comparative advantage"—allows each group to focus its efforts most effectively; some groups will concentrate on certain subjects or activities while others focus their efforts elsewhere *because* of the former's efforts. For example, at the national level, LDF did not initially direct its resources to the campaign against exclusionary zoning because other national groups already were investing their efforts there.[44] The local level also provides instances of division of labor. For example, in Mississippi, the LDF handled school desegregation cases while the Lawyers Committee for Civil Rights Under

Law undertook criminal defense work, and the Lawyers Constitutional Defense Committee dealt with both criminal defense work and police and prison brutality matters.[45]

Division of labor is less likely to be the result of explicit agreement than to be implicit, to be more a matter of "we saw what they were doing" and of groups "trying to stay out of each other's way" than of explicitly "carving up the territory." This can be seen in a number of areas of race relations law. One is school desegregation, where the LDF focused on the South and the NAACP dealt with the North—in part because they used divergent theories on which to base their cases, and in part because LDF made a "tactical choice as to where to get mileage" and felt it could do so in Southern and border states rather than in Northern cases which others, particularly the NAACP, were litigating.

Examination of these instances suggests that the litigation pie is not neatly and completely divided as a result of intergroup interaction. However, clear patterns develop, thus decreasing the considerable "potential for legal chaos" possible when a number of groups are litigating issues in a major area of the law; the picture is *not* one of "fragmentation." Because of the LDF's litigating predominance, NAACP's major involvement, and the regular presence of specialized litigating entities, there is some "order and stability" with respect to the areas of law in which litigation is carried out.[46]

Conclusion

Perhaps the most important generalization to be drawn from recent interest group civil rights litigation is that much of it is responsive and reflexive, and not subject to organizational control. Thus organizational litigators definitely do not dominate the domain in which they seek to operate.

Litigators make clear that each of the major civil rights litigation organizations have intentionally focused their energies in certain areas of the law, and each also has other designated interests, such as welfare for LDF a decade ago and voting rights for both NAACP and LDF more recently; criminal justice concerns have come to occupy a major place in race relations litigation as a result of LDF and NAACP efforts. NAACP and LDF have differed in the degree to which they focused their efforts and mounted resources for concentrated litigation "campaigns." However, not even for LDF, whose work is the "model" for "planned litigation for social change," were all areas of law in which the organization became involved subjects of litigation campaigns.

Among principal factors affecting organizational attention to specific areas of law have been resources, including the availability of foundation money, and the views of staff lawyers, also a major element in determining which cases to pursue. The goal of eliminating discrimination and concern for the well-being of minorities help explain why both the membership-based NAACP and the non-membership LDF focus on employment discrimination and, more recently, on the administration of criminal justice. In addition to such overlap, there also has been an implicit division of labor, leading the two groups to emphasize differing subjects or different geographical areas within a subject. This serves to spread overall litigation resources further than if the choices of the two organizations converged fully and thus duplicated each other.

Litigators' perspectives on organizations' choices of cases indicate rather clearly that the process of choosing cases has been far more diffuse than the term "planned litigation" might suggest, with case-selection decisions inductive and much affected by the flow of cases, rather than being deduced from a firm application of previously selected criteria. Litigating organizations' legal staffs, which operate in a flexible and "noninstitutionalized" way, seem to play a larger role in choice of cases than do organizational processes on "the books."

Some selection criteria are noted by most litigators, and seem likely to be taken into account in many cases. However, identification of other criteria seems largely a post hoc process. There is also agreement that criteria are not applied systematically or uniformly, in part because events require that certain cases be pursued, with civil rights litigators entering cases even when control, identified as crucial to planned litigation for social change, is not likely. Cooperating attorneys serve as the principal source of cases for litigators, with organizations taking the experience, credibility and competence of cooperating attorneys into account in choosing cases. LDF's socialization of cooperating attorneys has facilitated organizational control of cases, and has meant that LDF's case selection is not as likely as NAACP's to be diffuse.

Not surprisingly, we have found some differences in perspectives about civil rights litigation.

The world looks somewhat different from a staff position at an organization's national headquarters than it does to a cooperating attorney in the field. However, there is probably more diversity of perspectives *among* cooperating attorneys than *between* them on the one hand and staff attorneys on the other. This is largely the result of the varying roles played by cooperating attorneys. Some of the divergence of perspectives noted here is organizationally-based; NAACP lawyers and LDF attorneys tend to see the world of race relations somewhat differently. However, in the larger view of things, differences in perspectives among principal litigating organizations and other lawyers laboring in the civil rights vineyard are limited. There are also similarities in perspectives stemming from litigating experience and the cohesiveness resulting from the presence of a "civil rights bar" sharing commitment to a particular goal. Litigation for social change, then, is often reflexive and far from completely planned, with many constraints on the planning of litigation campaigns, many detours along the road to organizational goals, and much flexibility of action by both the litigating organizations and individual staff attorneys.

NOTES

This article originally appeared in Volume 68, Numbers 9-10, April-May 1985, pages 337-352.

I wish to express particular appreciation to Dr. Hubert Locke, Director, William O. Douglas Institute, for prompting the study from which this article is taken. For research support I am indebted to the Institute, the Johnson Research Fund of American Philosophical Society, and the Office of Research and the Graduate School of Public Affairs, State University of New York at Albany. I also wish to thank colleagues who have contributed useful comments at various stages of this process and two anonymous reviewers for this journal and David Richert, its editor, for their observations.

This article is dedicated to the memory of the late Clement Vose, who died in January, 1985. His presence and work stimulated the study of interest group litigation.

1. Horowitz, THE COURTS AND SOCIAL POLICY (Washington, D.C.: The Brookings Institution, 1977). *But see* Wasby, *Arrogation of power or accountability: "judicial imperialism" revisited,* 65 JUDICATURE 209 (1981).

2. 347 U.S. 483 (1954); Kluger, SIMPLE JUSTICE: THE HISTORY OF BROWN v. BOARD OF EDUCATION AND BLACK AMERICA'S STRUGGLE FOR EQUALITY (New York: Alfred Knopf, 1976). *See also* Vose, CAUCASIANS ONLY: THE SUPREME COURT, THE NAACP AND THE RESTRICTIVE COVENANT CASES (Berkeley: University of California Press, 1959).

3. O'Connor, WOMEN'S ORGANIZATIONS' USE OF THE COURTS (Lexington, MA: Lexington Books, 1980); Melnick, REGULATION AND THE COURTS: THE CASE OF THE CLEAN AIR ACT (Washington, D.C.: The Brookings Institution, 1983).

4. *See* Weisbrod et al., PUBLIC INTEREST LAW: AN ECONOMIC AND INSTITUTIONAL ANALYSIS (Berkeley: University of California Press, 1978); O'Connor and Epstein, *The Rise of Conservative Interest Group Litigation,* 45 J. OF POL. 479 (1983).

5. Scheingold, THE POLITICS OF RIGHTS: LAWYERS, PUBLIC POLICY, AND POLITICAL CHANGE 5 (New Haven: Yale University Press, 1974). *See also* Rabin, *Lawyers for Social Change: Perspectives on Public Interest Law*, 28 STAN. L. REV. 207, at 221 (1976).

6. Belton, *A Comparative Review of Public and Private Enforcement of Title VII and the Civil Rights Act of 1964*, 31 VAND. L. REV.905 (1978); Meltsner, CRUEL AND UNUSUAL: THE SUPREME COURT AND CAPITAL PUNISHMENT (New York: Random House, 1973).

7. Belton, *supra* n. 6.

8. Chayes, *The Role of the Judge in Public Law Litigation*, 89 HARV. L. REV. 1281, at 1284 (1976).

9. Fiss, *The Social and Political Foundations of Adjudication*, 6 LAW AND HUM. BEHAV. 121 at 123 (1982); *see also* Fiss, *Foreword: The Forms of Justice*, 93 HARV. L. REV. 1 (1979).

10. *See* City of Mobile v. Bolden, 446 U.S. 55 (1980) (Sec. 2 of Voting Rights Act); Washington v. Davis, 426 U.S. 299 (1976) (employment cases under 14th Amendment).

11. Vose, *supra* n. 2, at 155-158.

12. Wasby, D'Amato, and Metrailer, DESEGREGATION FROM BROWN TO ALEXANDER: AN EXPLORATION OF SUPREME COURT STRATEGIES 228-235 (Carbondale, IL: Southern Illinois University Press, 1977); Ulmer, *The Longitudinal Behavior of Hugo L. Black: Parabolic Support for Civil Liberties, 1937-1971*, 1 FLA. ST. U. L. REV. 131, at 149 (1973).

13. 422 U.S. 490 (1975).

14. 411 U.S. 1 (1973).

15. *See* Greenberg, "Litigation for Social Change: Methods, Limits and Role in Democracy" (Cardozo Lecture), Association of the Bar of the City of New York (1973).

16. Goldberg v. Kelly, 397 U.S. 254 (1970) and Wheeler v. Montgomery, 397 U.S. 280 (1970).

17. For example, Dandridge v. Williams, 397 U.S. 471 (1970).

18. This and the following sections are based on Wasby, *How Planned is "Planned Litigation"?*, 1984 A. B. F. RES. J. 83.

19. Tushnet, "Organizational Structure and Legal Strategy: The NAACP's Campaign Against Segregated Education, 1929-1950," unpublished ms. (1980), at I-1 to I-2.

20. Material which appears in quotation marks without attribution is drawn from interviews conducted by the author.

21. *See* O'Connor, *supra* n. 3, at 87-88, 144-145.

22. Greenberg, *supra* n. 15, at 20.

23. *Id.*

24. Belton, *supra* n. 6, at 943.

25. *See* Sorauf, THE WALL OF SEPARATION: THE CONSTITUTIONAL POLITICS OF CHURCH AND STATE 84 (Princeton, NJ: Princeton University Press, 1976); Vose, *supra* n. 2, at 58, 151; and Meltsner, *supra* n. 6, at 114, 238-239.

26. This section draws on Wasby, "The Multi-Faceted Elephant: Litigator Perspectives on Planned Litigation for Social Change," paper presented to Law & Society Association, Denver, Colorado, June 1983.

27. Grossman, *A Model for Judicial Policy Analysis: The Supreme Court and the Sit-In Cases*, in Grossman and Tanenhaus, eds., FRONTIERS OF JUDICIAL RESEARCH (New York: John Wiley, 1969).

28. Leubsdorf, *Completing the Desegregation Remedy*, 57 B.U.L. REV. 34, at 94 (1977).

29. *See* Danielson, THE POLITICS OF EXCLUSION 168 (New York: Columbia University Press, 1976).

30. Bell, *Serving Two Masters: Integration Ideals and Client Interests in School Desegregation Litigation*, 85 YALE L. J. 470, at 428, 487, 492 (1976).

31. Scheingold, *supra* n. 5, at 5, 95, 151, 197.

32. This section and the next two draw on Wasby, "Some Horizontal and Vertical Dynamics of Civil Rights Litigation: Litigator Perspectives," paper presented to Southern Political Science Association, Birmingham, Alabama, November 1983.

33. *See* Vose, CONSTITUTOINAL CHANGE: AMENDMENT POLITICS AND SUPREME COURT LITIGATION SINCE 1900, 321 (Lexington, MA: Lexington Books, 1972).

34. Casper, LAWYERS BEFORE THE WARREN COURT: CIVIL LIBERTIES AND CIVIL RIGHTS, 1957-66, 142-143 (Urbana: University of Illinois Press, 1972).

35. Orfield, MUST WE BUS? SEGREGATED SCHOOLS AND NATIONAL POLICY 371 (Washington, D.C.: The Brookings Institution, 1978); Rabin, *supra* n. 5, at 212-213 (1976).

36. For examples, see Vose, *supra* n. 2, at 157; Vose, *supra* n. 33, at 315.

37. See Vose, *supra* n. 33, at 315.

38. Meier and Rudwick, *Attorneys Black and White: A Case Study of Race Relations Within the NAACP*, 62 J. OF AM. HIST. 913, 915-916 (1976).

39. *Id.* at 930, 933.

40. Note that "the first case in which the NAACP had employed exclusively black counsel before the U.S. Supreme Court" was Hillins v. Oklahoma, 295 U.S. 394 (1935), in which an Oklahoma black man had been sentenced to death for rape. McNeil, GROUNDWORK: CHARLES HAMILTON HOUSTON AND THE STRUGGLE FOR CIVIL RIGHTS 121-122 (Philadelphia: University of Pennsylvania Press, 1983).

41. O'Connor, *supra* n. 3, at 145.

42. *See* n. 25, *supra*.

43. Orfield, *supra* n. 34, at 372; Shields and Spector, *Opening Up the Suburbs: Notes on a Movement for Social Change*, 2 YALE REV. OF L. AND SOCIAL ORDER 300 (1972).

44. Shields and Spector, *supra* n. 43.

45. *See* Heck and Stewart, *Ensuring Access to Justice: the Role of Interest Group Lawyers in the 60s Campaign for Civil Rights*, 66 JUDICATURE 84 (1982); Stewart and Heck, *The Day-to-Day Activities of Interest Group Lawyers*, 64 SOC. SCI. Q. 173 (1983).

46. For intergroup relations in church-state litigation, see Sorauf, *supra* n. 25, at 81.

Beyond legislative lobbying: women's rights groups and the Supreme Court

While women's rights groups often have been frustrated in legislative forums, the Supreme Court has served as a source of expanded women's rights.

by Karen O'Connor and Lee Epstein

While women's rights groups[1] have been able to attain some of their goals in the legislative sphere,[2] their inability to secure ratification of highly visible objectives including the Equal Rights Amendment[3] and other important "rights" legislation through conventional lobbying,[4] allows them to be classified as "disadvantaged."[5] According to Richard C. Cortner, "disadvantaged" groups are wise to pursue their goals through judicial lobbying. The National Association for the Advancement of Colored People (NAACP), for example, initially used the courts to achieve its objectives.[6] In contrast, women's rights groups generally have relied heavily on legislative as opposed to judicial lobbying to achieve their goals,[7] even though the Burger Court is receptive to claims of gender-based discrimination.[8]

To assess whether litigation may provide an additional political strategy, this article examines the results of gender-based discrimination cases brought by women's rights groups in the 1970s. More specifically, we examine all 63 gender-based cases decided during the 1969 to 1980 terms of the United States Supreme Court and the groups that participated in those cases.[9]

Disadvantaged groups and the court

Writing in 1968, Cortner claimed there were numerous disadvantaged groups that:

are highly dependent upon the judicial process as a means of pursuing their policy interests, usually because they are temporarily, or even permanently, disadvantaged in terms of their abilities to attain successfully their goals in the electoral process, within the elected political institutions or in the bureaucracy. If they are to succeed at all in the pursuit of their goals they are almost compelled to resort to litigation.[10]

Notable and well studied examples of disadvantaged groups that have relied on litigation include the NAACP and the independent NAACP Legal Defense Fund (LDF),[11] the Jehovah's Witnesses[12] and the American Jewish Congress.[13]

Additionally, while many scholars have agreed on the utility of litigation, they have also offered similar reasons for the success of these groups. For example, control over the course of litigation, generally in the form of group sponsorship of test cases— facilitated by the presence of only one major organization—often has been noted as critical to the NAACP LDF's victories in several issue areas.[14]

Support from and cooperation with other groups is another factor offered for the success of disadvantaged litigators. This kind of assistance, generally in the form of "compatible" amicus curiae briefs, is welcomed by most disadvantaged groups. In fact, David Manwaring noted that, "(I)ndeed, without massive interest group backing, neither side of the Gobitis (flag salute) litigation could have stayed in court for long."[15]

Another factor that played a role in the successes of disadvantaged groups including the NAACP LDF and the Jehovah's Witnesses was the relative absence of organized opposition. While individual and loosely organized groups opposed their various efforts, no major interest groups appeared to challenge their respective arguments in Court.[16]

Thus, for most disadvantaged groups, control of litigation, cooperation with other groups and absence of organized opposition played a major role in their successes. Most important, however, was their initial recognition of the utility of litigation as a political mechanism.

Women's groups and litigation

As has been noted, however, women's rights organizations did not initially rely heavily on litigation.[17] While most groups recognized the potential importance of litigation,[18] initial efforts to lobby the courts in a systematic fashion were fraught with internal organizational problems and intergroup conflicts. For example, although the National Organization for Women (NOW), the first major women's rights organization, tried to model itself after the NAACP as early as 1966,[19] it was unable to create a working legal defense fund until 1977.[20]

NOW's initial litigation efforts were hampered by several factors: first, internal dissension over the conduct of employment discrimination cases led some NOW attorneys to found their own group, Human Rights for Women (HRW).[21] This defection left NOW without experienced litigators. Second, NOW's leadership was divided as to the form a legal defense fund should take.[22] Third, the battle for the ERA and other types of anti-discrimination legislation led NOW to concentrate its efforts in those areas—to the detriment of litigation. Finally, by 1972, other groups, particularly the American Civil Liberties Union (ACLU), were beginning to attack gender-based discrimination through litigation.

In 1972, the ACLU created a Women's Rights Project (WRP) to fill the void it perceived in gender-based litigation.[23] By this time, the Women's Equity Action League (WEAL) had also begun negotiations with the Ford Foundation to secure funding for its own legal defense fund.[24] Thus, during the early 1970s, numerous other groups interested in litigation allowed NOW to concentrate its efforts in the legislative forum.[25]

In the wake of the recent defeat of the ERA, many women's rights groups now are reevaluating their strategies,[26] and many are considering increased resort to litigation. Given the kinds of problems that have traditionally hampered women's rights groups in the legislative sphere, litigation may, in fact, provide a more expedient political mechanism for the expansion of women's rights as it has also done for other disadvantaged groups.

Women's groups and the Court

To assess how litigation may be used by women's

rights groups in the future, we examine their past performance in the U.S. Supreme Court. More specifically, we address the following questions:

• Which groups have been involved;
• What strategies have they employed;
• What kind of external opposition have they faced; and,
• How successful have women's rights groups been?

To address these questions, we identified 63 cases that the Supreme Court decided between its 1969 to 1980 terms, which involved gender-based discrimination. Gender-based cases were defined as those that had ramifications on women's rights including those where reproductive freedom issues were at stake. A women's rights issue, however, did not have to be the primary issue presented to the Court to be included in this analysis.

Only full opinion cases were considered because accurate information concerning group participation in those cases are available on microfiche. Group participation was identified by reading briefs of direct sponsors and amicus curiae in all 63 cases. Women's rights groups participated in 73 per cent (n=46) of these cases.

Participation

As revealed in Figure 1, several women's rights groups participated in Supreme Court litigation. The ACLU, however, clearly emerged as "the" representative of women before the Court, with NOW, WEAL, and the Women's Legal Defense Fund (WLDF) entering more than 20 per cent of the cases in which at least one women's group participated.[27] Additionally, the Center for Constitutional Rights (CCR), a New York-based radical public interest law firm, whose female attorneys are specifically interested in women's rights, participated in nine cases.[28]

The ACLU's early commitment to gender-based discrimination litigation increased throughout the decade as indicated in Figure 2. Over the 12-term period, it participated in 66 per cent (n=42) of the 63 gender-based discrimination cases decided by the Supreme Court. In fact, it was involved in all but four of the cases in which at least one women's rights organization was present. It is interesting to note that even though the remarkably linear trend of the ACLU was somewhat disturbed when the other groups became more active, the aggregated level of its activity still increased.

Figure 1   Women's groups' participation in Supreme Court litigation, 1969-1980

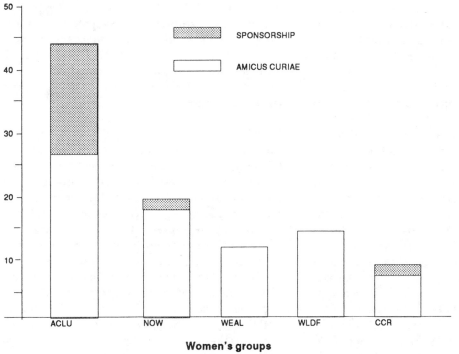

Women's groups

Figure 2   Participation of women's groups in Supreme Court litigation

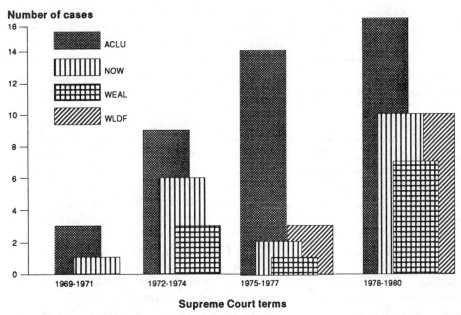

Its continued commitment to litigation can be attributed to several factors: first, the Women's Rights Project (WRP)[29] and later the Reproductive Freedom Project (RFP)[30] were established at a time when ACLU leaders recognized that the Court was willing to expand interpretation of the Constitution. Thus, the ACLU acted quickly to take full advantage of a favorable judicial climate. Second, establishment of the projects allowed lawyers to specialize in gender-based discrimination litigation and to develop their expertise.[31] Third, while funds for women's rights litigation were scarce, the ACLU could draw upon its own resources and its own experience in seeking outside funding.[32] By the mid-1970s, then, most groups were willing to defer to the expertise of the ACLU. Consequently, the ACLU's prominence in this area has gone unchallenged.

While the ACLU's dominance cannot be disputed, other groups, particularly since the late 1970s, also have litigated for expanded rights. As indicated in Figure 2, NOW, WEAL, and WLDF have played increasingly important roles in gender-based discrimination litigation. Although NOW participated in seven cases during the 1969 to 1977 terms, its participation was largely reactive, and not part of a planned strategy. For example, while NOW co-sponsored *Pittsburgh Press v. Pittsburgh Commission on Human Relations*[33] at the Supreme Court level, it did so at the request of the city attorney, who took primary responsibility for preparation of the brief.[34] Beginning in 1977, however, NOW began to turn to the courts in a more systematic fashion. At that time, funds finally were allocated for a lawyer, whose addition to the staff allowed NOW belatedly to initiate litigation, or at least to be sufficiently informed to file important amicus curiae briefs.[35]

WEAL also began participating before the Supreme Court with greater frequency in the late 1970s. While it created a legal defense fund in 1972, funding problems hampered its own litigation activities. Additionally, in 1974 the Center for Law and Social Policy's Women's Rights Project began to handle cases on WEAL's behalf.

In contrast to NOW and WEAL, which created special funds to litigate, WLDF initially was created in 1971 to "provide *pro bono* legal assistance to women,"[36] particularly to those who had suffered employment discrimination. Since 1978, WLDF has played an increasingly visible role in gender-based discrimination litigation, often soliciting the participation of, or representing, other women's rights groups before the U.S. Supreme Court.

While other groups have participated in gender-based discrimination litigation, these four organizations—ACLU, NOW, WEAL, WLDF—have been the major women's rights participants in this area.[37] Collectively, they have been involved in 73 per cent (n=46) of the 63 cases.

Strategies

Interest group participation in U.S. Supreme Court litigation can take several forms, with direct sponsorship or submission of amicus curiae briefs among the most common. As indicated in Figure 1, only one women's rights group has regularly sponsored litigation at the Supreme Court level. The ACLU sponsored 25.4 per cent (n=16) of the 63 gender-based cases. Its greatest concentration, however, occurred in cases involving challenges to facially discriminatory governmental programs or laws. For example, in *Reed v. Reed*,[38] *Frontiero v. Richardson*,[39] and *Weinberger v. Wiesenfeld*,[40] the ACLU represented parties claiming that gender-based discrimination violated constitutional principles of equal protection or due process. During the 1970s, the ACLU also sponsored test cases dealing with expanded abortion rights and jury discrimination. Thus, like other disadvantaged groups, ACLU attorneys saw the utility in controlling litigation, particularly when constitutional issues were involved.[41]

In contrast, NOW, WEAL, WLDF, and CCR have generally limited their participation to that of amicus curiae, as also indicated in Figure 1. While NOW and CCR each sponsored one case, women's groups' limited resources and deference to the ACLU have led them to opt for the amicus curiae strategy.[42]

The amicus curiae can be a particularly effective strategy when used in cooperation with direct sponsors or with other amicus curiae.[43] As indicated by Table 1, several women's groups regularly supported each other's efforts.[44] For example, NOW regularly supported the ACLU. In 78.9 per cent of the cases in which NOW participated, it either filed an amicus curiae brief with or in support of the ACLU. Most women's rights groups, in fact, revealed very high support for the ACLU.

The support that most groups lent to the ACLU, however, was not uniformly revealed in their support of other women's rights groups. For example,

Table 1   **Intergroup support**

Group	Support for the ACLU	Directional support
NOW	.789	NOW .421 → WEAL ← .727
WEAL	.636	NOW .578 → WLDF ← .846
WLDF	.538	NOW .210 → CCR ← .444
CCR	.777	WEAL .545 → WLDF ← .461
		WEAL .090 → CCR ← .111
		WLDF .230 → CCR ← .333

CCR, the most radical of these groups, and WEAL, generally regarded as somewhat traditional in nature,[45] have little in common.[46] Not surprisingly, therefore, they were not supportive of each other's litigation activities.

In general, though, women's groups' litigation efforts reveal a high degree of intergroup support. The average support score between any two groups was .483. More specifically, most groups support the ACLU through submission of amicus curiae briefs.

External opposition

When women's rights groups lobby state or national legislatures they face opposition from several sources including other women's groups, business interests, and conservative organizations.[47] While women's rights groups' legislative lobbying efforts generally have attracted opposition across issue areas, their judicial lobbying efforts have not met consistent opposition. In general, women's rights groups faced organized third party opposition in 58.6 per cent (n=27) of their cases. Similar to the opposition faced in the legislative arena, opposition in Court came from women's groups, business interests, and conservative organizations. Yet, the intensity, the scope and the sources of this opposition varied considerably by the nature of the issue(s) at stake.

For example, women's rights groups faced substantial opposition when discriminatory employ-

ment practices were alleged. In the 13 employment discrimination cases in which a women's rights group participated, they faced third party opposition in 69.2 per cent (n=9) with conservative groups and business interests accounting for 100 per cent.[48] Yet, no women's group challenged the claims of women's rights organizations seeking expanded employment rights. This finding is not surprising given the near unanimous agreement among women about the importance of equal job opportunity.[49] Thus, women's rights groups have faced vigorous opposition from business interests, but those interests have an economic stake in the outcome of the cases and are not necessarily opposed to expanded women's rights *per se.*

Opposition to women's rights claims also was evident in cases involving reproductive freedom. In the 12 reproductive freedom cases in which women's rights groups participated, they faced opposition from organized anti-abortion or religious groups in 75 per cent (n=9). Like groups involved in employment discrimination cases, organizations including Americans United for Life and the United States Catholic Conference opposed expanded abortion rights based on moral grounds and *not* upon general opposition to equality for women.[50] In contrast to cases involving employment discrimination, however, some women's groups opposed expanded abortion rights. In three cases, women's groups, including Feminists for Life and Women for the Unborn, filed amicus curiae briefs urging the Court to uphold the constitutionality of restrictive state abortion or consent laws. Thus, similar to legislatures, the Court has been the target of competing women's groups. But, the intensity of this opposition has been far less emotional and extensive than women's rights groups encountered in the legislative sphere.[51]

In contrast to litigation involving abortion or employment discrimination, cases alleging discrimination in the distribution of or qualifications for government benefits generated minimal opposition to women's rights groups' claims. In only one case, *McCarty v. McCarty,*[52] involving a divorced woman's claim to a share of her former husband's military pension, did any organized group oppose her claims.[53]

The absence of opposition from other organized interests, especially from conservative women, is exceptionally interesting given the nature of the cases in this area. Many involved challenges to traditional assumptions about women's roles in society. When the same kinds of changes are proposed in the legislative sphere—alimony, child support or custody, for example—conservative women's groups turn out in large numbers to lobby against any proposed changes in the traditional family relationship.[54] When these same issues are addressed through litigation, no conservative women's groups appeared. Litigation in this area then may be particularly attractive and amenable to the purposes of women's rights groups because of the absence of opposition.

Thus, unlike the situation in the legislative sphere, conservative women's groups generally *do not* oppose expanded rights for women before the U.S. Supreme Court. Almost all the opposition that women's rights groups have faced has come from pro-business interests that have an economic stake in the outcome of the litigation or from anti-abortion groups that are morally opposed to expanded abortion rights. Therefore, particularly in cases involving the distribution of benefits, the absence of opposition makes the Court an attractive forum for women's rights groups to use to attain expanded rights.

Success

Whether participating as direct sponsors or as amicus curiae, women's rights organizations were successful. They won 63 per cent (n=29) of their 46 cases. A major reason for this high success rate has been the consistent efforts of the ACLU. In fact, the ACLU's presence in a case increased the chances of success for a gender-based claim by 16 per cent.[55]

Even when the ACLU's participation met with only mixed results, its presence before the Court tended to minimize losses—which can be considered another facet of success. For example, in *Dothard v. Rawlinson*[56] its amicus curiae brief provided the Court with a fall back position if the Court was to uphold Alabama's refusal to hire women as prison guards. In noting that the state's prisons were among the worst in the nation, the ACLU gave the Court the "out" to construe narrowly the bona fide occupational qualification exception to Title VII.[57]

While the ACLU is a very successful litigator, its initial efforts might have been even more successful if it had been supported by other women's groups. For example, *Kahn v. Shevin*,[58] a case sponsored by the ACLU, resulted in a major doctrinal loss when a majority of the Court upheld the constitutionality of benign discrimination. In *Kahn*, no women's rights groups filed amicus curiae briefs in support of the ACLU; amicus curiae briefs could have shown the Court that women were uniformly opposed to such benign forms of discrimination. Thus, the absence of support in this and other cases may have made crucial differences in the outcome of litigation.[59]

In recent years, then, the increased interest of women's rights groups in litigation, as illustrated by Figure 2, has undoubtedly aided the cause of equal rights. For example, in *County of Washington v. Gunther*,[60] a case that few commentators predicted would result in such a resounding victory for women's rights forces,[61] the Court adopted the position advocated by 16 women's rights groups.[62] This was particularly significant given the tremendous business opposition to the concept of equal pay for comparable work and the potential ramifications of *Gunther*. Thus, while women's rights groups generally have been successful, greater cooperation and participation could have a positive impact on the Court's disposition of future cases.

Conclusion

Women's rights groups have been unable to secure all or even most of their goals in the legislative forum. To assess whether women's rights groups, like other disadvantaged groups, would be better served by increased reliance on litigation, we examined their efforts in the Supreme Court during the 1970s. More specifically, we analyzed four aspects of that activity. First, we found that the ACLU was a major participant. Other women's rights groups have only recently begun to use litigation in a systematic fashion. Second, we discovered that while the ACLU prefers the direct sponsorship tactic, other women's rights groups often appear as amicus curiae. Most of those amicus curiae efforts, however, have been in support of ACLU arguments. Third, we discovered that both the intensity and the sources of opposition to women's rights groups' claims differed from those in the legislative forum. In general, groups opposed women's rights groups claims on economic or moral grounds and not because they opposed the expansion of women's rights, *per se*. Finally, we found that women's rights groups have been very successful before the United States Supreme Court.

Thus, we conclude that women's rights groups, like other disadvantaged groups, may continue to find that the Court is receptive to their arguments because thus far, unlike the legislative forum, women have faced relatively minimal opposition in Court. And, the nature of this opposition, given the constraints of the judicial forum, is less emotional and less highly charged than the opposition in the legislative forum. Perhaps more important, however, the ACLU's emergence as "the" spokesperson of women's interests has influenced the Court, particularly when its efforts have been supported by other groups.

Thus, while women's groups' efforts often have been frustrated in legislative forums, the Supreme Court has served as a source of expanded women's rights. Women's rights groups have used this forum effectively in the past. Based on this study, continued efforts in this forum would appear likely to result in further success.

NOTES

This article originally appeared in Volume 67, Number 3, September 1983, pages 134-142.

The authors would like to thank Thomas G. Walker and the anonymous reviewers for their numerous helpful comments on an earlier draft of this manuscript.

1. For the purposes of this paper, the term women's rights groups includes organizations founded by women to achieve expanded rights, groups that have established specific projects to litigate on behalf of women, or those that specialize in women's rights litigation.

2. Boneparth, WOMEN, POWER AND PUBLIC POLICY (New York: Pergamon Press, 1982); Gelb and Palley, WOMEN AND PUBLIC POLICIES (Princeton: Princeton University Press, 1982); Freeman, THE POLITICS OF WOMEN'S LIBERATION (New York: David McKay, 1975); and Murphy, PUBLIC POLICY ON THE STATUS OF WOMEN (Lexington, MA: Lexington Books, 1973).

3. Boles, THE POLITICS OF THE EQUAL RIGHTS AMENDMENT (New York: Longman, 1979) and *Building Support for the ERA: A Case of 'Too Much, Too Late'*, XV PS 572-577 (Fall 1982).

4. Andre, HOMEMAKERS: THE FORGOTTEN WORKERS (Chicago: University of Chicago Press, 1981) and Rubin, ABORTION, POLITICS AND COURTS (Westport, CT: Greenwood Press, 1982).

5. Cortner, *Strategies and Tactics of Litigants in Constitutional Cases*, 17 J. PUB. L. 287-307 (1968).

6. Vose, CAUCASIANS ONLY (Berkeley: University of California Press, 1959) and Greenberg, JUDICIAL PROCESS AND SOCIAL CHANGE (St. Paul, MN: West Publishing Co., 1977).

7. Freeman, *supra* n. 2 and Gelb and Palley, *Women and Interest Group Politics*, 5 AM. POL. Q. 331-352 (July 1977).

8. O'Connor and Epstein, *Sex and the Supreme Court: An Analysis of Judicial Support for Gender Based Claims*, 64 SOC. SCI. Q. (June 1983).

9. A list of these cases is available from the authors.

10. Cortner, *supra* n. 5, at 287.

11. Vose, *supra* n. 6; Kluger, SIMPLE JUSTICE: THE HISTORY OF BROWN V. BOARD OF EDUCATION AND BLACK AMERICANS' STRUGGLE FOR EQUALITY (New York: Alfred A. Knopf, 1976); Shields and Spector, *Opening Up the Suburbs: Notes on a Movement for Social Change*, 2 YALE REV. OF L. AND SOC. ACTION 300-333 (1972); Belton, *A Comparative Review of Public and Private Enforcement of Title VII of the Civil Rights Act of 1964*, 31 VAND. L. REV. 905

(1978); Wasby, *Interest Groups in Court: Race Relations Litigation*, in Cigler and Loomis, eds., INTEREST GROUP POLITICS (Washington, DC: Congressional Quarterly Press, 1983); and Meltsner, CRUEL AND UNUSUAL: THE SUPREME COURT AND CAPITAL PUNISHMENT (New York: Random House, 1973).

12. Manwaring, RENDER UNTO CAESAR (Chicago: University of Chicago Press, 1962).

13. Sorauf, THE WALL OF SEPARATION (Princeton: Princeton University Press, 1976); and Pfeffer, *Amici in Church-State Litigation*, 44 LAW & CONTEMP. PROBS. 83-110 (1981).

14. Belton, *supra* n. 11; Westin, *Someone Has to Translate Rights into Realities*, 2 CIV. LIBERTIES REV. 104-128 (1975); and Wasby, *supra* n. 11.

15. Manwaring, *supra* n. 12, at 249.

16. Vose, *supra* n. 6.

17. O'Connor, WOMEN'S ORGANIZATIONS' USE OF THE COURTS (Lexington, MA: Lexington Books, 1980).

18. Freeman, *supra* n. 2, at 181.

19. Papachristou, WOMEN TOGETHER: A HISTORY IN DOCUMENTS OF THE WOMEN'S MOVEMENT IN THE UNITED STATES 220 (New York: Alfred A. Knopf, 1976).

20. O'Connor, *supra* n. 17, at 103-104.

21. Freeman, *supra* n. 2, at 155.

22. Greenwald, "Litigation for Social Change," unpublished manuscript.

23. Cortner, THE SUPREME COURT AND CIVIL LIBERTIES POLICY 183-212 (Palo Alto, CA: Mayfield Publishing Co., 1975), and Cowan, *Women's Rights Through Litigation: An Examination of the American Civil Liberties Union Women's Rights Project, 1971-1976*, 8 COLUM. HUM. RTS. L. REV. 373-412 (1976).

24. Later, an internal WEAL dispute led to the founding of the Women's Law Fund, which like the NOW-HRW split earlier, hampered WEAL's initial attempts to litigate. O'Connor, *supra* n. 17, at 106-107.

25. Yet, many of these efforts were unsuccessful. For example, the U.S. Congress has yet to enact numerous pieces of legislation supported by NOW including the Homemakers' Bill of Rights, additional federal funding of day care centers, and many of the provisions contained in the Women's Economic Equity Act. On the state level, NOW also has attempted to secure bills specifically outlawing domestic violence and the revision of criminal laws to recognize the problems of battered women.

26. NOW, for example, has created several political action committees to support candidates for national and state offices who back NOW's positions.

27. The National League of Women Voters participated in five cases. The American Association of University Women, Equal Rights Advocates, Federally Employed Women, the National Federation of Business and Professional Women's Clubs, the National Women's Political Caucus and Universalist Unitarian Women each participated in four cases. Human Rights for Women, the National Women's Conference of the American Ethical Union, the Women's Law Fund and the Women's Law Project each appeared in three cases. Participating twice were the American Nurses Association, Association for Women in Psychology, Center for Women's Policy Studies, Coalition of Labor Union Women, Federation of Organizations for Professional Women, National Center on Women and Family Law, National Women's Health Network, National Women's Rights Organization, Professional Women's Caucus, Rural American Women, Women's Rights Litigation Clinic, and the Young Women's Christian Association.

Action for Former Military Wives, Antioch Women's Rights Clinic, Association of Women in Science, Coalition of Medical Rights for Women, Comparable Worth Project, Department of Church Women, Elizabeth Blackwell Health Center for Women, Institute for Women Today, Mexican-American Women's

National Association, Michigan Women's Group, National Coalition of American Nurses, National Council of Jewish Women, National Federation of Temple Sisterhood, National Hook-up of Black Women, National Women's Student Group, North West Women's Center, Older Women's League, Organization for Pan Asian American Women, Rochester Women Against Violence Against Women, Sociologists for Women, Union Wage, Wisconsin Women's Network, Women Employed, Women Lawyer's Bar Association, Women Lawyers of Los Angeles, Women in Mathematics, Women's Action Alliance, Women's Bar Association of the District of Columbia, Women's Health Services, Women's Justice Center, Women's Lawyers of Santa Barbara, Women's Lobby, and the Women's Network each participated in only one case.

28. O'Connor, *supra* n. 17, at 111-112.

29. Cowan, *supra* n. 23.

30. Epstein, "Interest Groups, Controversy and the Court: An Analysis of Abortion Litigation," unpublished M.A. Thesis, Emory University, 1982.

31. Cowan, *supra* n. 23.

32. Berger, "Litigation on Behalf of Women: An Assessment," (New York: Ford Foundation) mimeo (1979) and O'Connor, *supra* n. 17, at 123-131.

33. 413 U.S. 376 (1973).

34. O'Connor, *supra* n. 17, at 104-105.

35. Greenwald, *supra* n. 22.

36. Brief Amicus Curiae submitted by the American Civil Liberties Union in *County of Washington v. Gunther*, 1981.

37. Other groups that have participated on behalf of women's rights although they are not included in our definition of women's rights groups include the International Union of Electrical, Radio and Machine Workers (IUE) (n=7), the NAACP LDF (n=4), and the Southern Poverty Law Center (n=4).

38. 400 U.S. 71 (1971).

39. 411 U.S. 677 (1973).

40. 420 U.S. 636 (1975).

41. Cowan, *supra* n. 23.

42. NOW co-sponsored *Pittsburgh Press v. Pittsburgh Commission on Human Relations*, 413 U.S. 375 (1973). CCR co-sponsored *Harris v. McRae*, 448 U.S. 297 (1981) with Planned Parenthood and the ACLU. In addition, the Women's Law Fund sponsored *Cleveland Board of Education v. LaFleur*, 414 U.S. 632 (1973).

43. Peltason, FEDERAL COURTS IN THE POLITICAL PROCESS (New York: Random House, 1955).

44. Support was conceptually defined either as a women's rights group filing an amicus curiae brief in support of another women's group or two or more women's groups submitting a joint amicus brief. Support was operationally defined as: support = $\frac{\text{n of supportive cases}}{\text{total cases entered}}$

45. Costain, *The Struggle for a National Women's Lobby: Organizing A Diffuse Interest*, 33 W. POL. Q. 476-491 (1980) and Freeman, *supra* n. 2.

46. Given CCR's heavy involvement in abortion litigation, this lack of support between it and WEAL is not surprising. WEAL, in fact, was organized by several NOW members who were in disagreement with NOW's public support of reproductive freedom.

47. Brady and Tedin, *Ladies in Pink: Religion and Political Ideology in the Anti-ERA Movement*, 56 SOC. SCI. Q. 564-575 (1976); Crowell, *Four Days in Houston*, 10 CIV. LIBERTIES DIG. 2-13 (1978); Babcock, et al., SEX DISCRIMINATIN AND THE LAW 181-184 (Boston: Little, Brown and Co., 1975); Murphy, *supra* n. 2; Boles, *supra* n. 3; and Freeman, *supra* n. 2, at 220-221.

48. *See generally*, Greenwald, "Women's Rights, Courts and Congress: Conflict Over Pregnancy Disability Compensation Policies," paper delivered at the annual meeting of the Ameri-can Political Science Association, New York City, September 1978. Two organizations, in particular, the Chamber of Commerce of the United States of America and the Equal Employment Advisory Council, regularly filed amicus curiae briefs urging the Court to rule in favor of employer interests. Large businesses and corporations also regularly opposed women's claims. For example, in *General Electric Co. v. Gilbert* (1976), 22 airlines filed a joint amicus curiae brief urging the Court to rule that pregnancy-related disabilities did not have to be covered by employer health benefit plans.

49. Felsenthal, THE SWEETHEART OF THE SILENT MAJORITY—THE BIOGRAPHY OF PHYLLIS SCHLAFLY (Garden City, NY: Doubleday & Co., 1981).

50. Balides, et al., *The Abortion Issue: Major Groups, Organizations and Funding Sources*, in Osofsky and Osofsky, eds. THE ABORTION EXPERIENCE (Hagerstown, MD: Harper and Row, 1973).

51. *See generally*, Merton, ENEMIES OF CHOICE (Boston: Beacon Press, 1981) and Rubin, *supra* n. 4.

52. 453 U.S. 210 (1981).

53. In McCarty, seven servicemen's organizations urged the Court not to award any part of McCarty's pension to his ex-wife.

54. Andre, *supra* n. 4, at 164-287 and McGlen and O'Connor, WOMEN'S RIGHTS (New York: Praeger, 1983).

55. Of the 63 cases, 66 per cent were held for the women's rights' position when the ACLU participated, whereas only 50 per cent were decided similarly when the ACLU chose not to participate.

56. 433 U.S. 321 (1977).

57. O'Connor, *supra* n. 17, at 113-114.

58. 416 U.S. 351 (1974).

59. Another case in which support may have helped the ACLU was Matthews v. de Castro, 429 U.S. 181 (1976). While the Women's Rights Litigation Clinic at Rutgers University co-sponsored the case along with the ACLU, no women's rights groups participated as amicus curiae.

60. 452 U.S. 161 (1981).

61. *See, for example*, Wermeil, *Business Starts Pushing More at High Court*, WALL STREET JOURNAL, April 23, 1982, sec. 2, p. 29.

62. These groups were: ACLU, NOW, WLDF, League of Women Voters, Women Employed, Comparable Worth Project, American Nurses Association, Wisconsin Women's Network, Women's Network, National Hook-up of Black Women, Federally Employed Women, Antioch Women's Rights Clinic, National Women's Political Caucus, Coalition of Labor Union Women, WEAL and the Women's Bar Association of the District of Columbia.

Friendly fire: amici curiae and *Webster v. Reproductive Health Services*

With Roe v. Wade *in the balance, the unprecedented 78 amicus briefs filed in Webster played an important role in helping to inform and shape the Court's debate over abortion.*

by Susan Behuniak-Long

The unprecedented number of amicus curiae briefs filed in *Webster v. Reproductive Health Services*[1] signaled not only the intensity of the abortion battle, but also the extent of interest group politics before the United States Supreme Court. If the response of 57 amicus briefs to *Regents of the University of California v. Bakke*[2] was unusual, the response to Webster was extraordinary. A total of 78 amicus briefs were filed; 46 on behalf of the appellants and 32 on behalf of the appellees. With over 400 organizations signing on as cosponsors, and thousands of individuals joining as signatories, *Webster*, though not a typical case, demonstrates the importance of interest group politics before the Court.

With the 1988 appointment of Justice Anthony Kennedy to fill the vacancy left by Justice Lewis Powell, a reversal of *Roe v. Wade*[3] was possible. Court watchers tallied a 4-1-4 line-up. Expected to support Roe were Justices Harry Blackmun, William Brennan, Thurgood Marshall and John Paul Stevens. The original dissenters in *Roe*, Justices William Rehnquist and Byron White were expected to be joined by Justices Antonin Scalia and Kennedy. With Justice Sandra Day O'Connor viewed as the swing vote, *Roe* was now subject to a 5-4 reversal. When the Court agreed to hear *Webster* during its 1988 term, the time was ripe for a major abortion decision. Such anticipation led to the unprecedented number of amicus briefs.

At issue in *Webster* was a Missouri statute which contained: (1) a preamble stating that "the life of each human being begins at conception,"[4] (2) sections restricting public facilities and employees

from performing or assisting in an abortion (except to save the mother's life), (3) sections prohibiting the use of public funds, employees or hospitals from encouraging or counseling a woman to have an abortion (again, with the maternal life preservation exception), and (4) sections requiring that when a physician believes a woman to be 20 or more weeks pregnant, viability will be tested by performance of "such medical examinations and tests as are necessary to make a finding of the gestational age, weight, and lung maturity of the unborn child."[5]

Because of the number of briefs filed and the fact that all the briefs were spawned by the same constitutional issue, the *Webster* amicus briefs offer a unique opportunity to study this particular form of interest group litigation and to examine how the public debate over abortion is carried out in a legal arena. In focusing on these amicus briefs, several questions will frame the study: who submitted the briefs, what was argued in the briefs, and what impact did the briefs have on the outcome of the case? These questions are asked with two goals in mind. First, what do the amicus briefs demonstrate regarding this type of interest group activity? Second, what do the amicus briefs reveal concerning the nature of the two movements involved in the struggle over abortion rights?[6]

Who filed?

Table 1 provides a list of the names of the first group or individual listed as a sponsor hereinafter called "first sponsors" for each of the amicus briefs filed on behalf of the appellants, and Table 2 lists

Table 1   46 briefs in support of appellants

First sponsors of amicus briefs	Total sponsors
1. Agudeth Israel of America	1
2. Alabama Lawyers for Unborn Children, Inc.	1
3. Edward Allen	1
4. American Academy of Medical Ethics	1
5. American Assoc. of Pro-Life Obst. and Gynecol. and The American Assoc. of Pro-Life Pediatricians	2
6. American Collegians for Life, Inc. and Catholic League for Religious & Civil Rights	2
7. American Family Association, Inc.	1
8. American Life League, Inc.	1
9. Association for Public Justice and The Value of Life Committee, Inc.	2
10. Attorneys General of Louisiana, Arizona, Idaho, Pennsylvania, and Wisconsin	1
11. Birthright, Inc.	1
12. Catholic Health Association of the US	1
13. Catholic Lawyers Guild of the Archdiocese of Boston, Inc.	1
14. Catholics United for Life, et al. (10)	11
15. Center for Judicial Studies and Certain Members of Congress (56)	2
16. Certain American State Legislators (over 250)	1
17. Certain Members of the General Assembly of PA (69)	1
18. Christian Advocates Serving Evangelism	1
19. Covenant House and Good Counsel, Inc.	2
20. Doctors for Life, et al. (4)	5
21. Feminists for Life of America, et al. (4)	5
22. Focus on Family and Family Research Council of America	2
23. Free Speech Advocates	1
24. Holy Orthodox Church	1
25. Human Life International	1
26. International Right to Life Federation	1
27. Larry Joyce	1
28. Knights of Columbus	1
29. Lutheran Church-Missouri Synod, et al. (2)	3
30. James Joseph Lynch, Jr.	1
31. Paul Marx	1
32. 127 Members of the Missouri General Assembly	1
33. Missouri Catholic Conference	1
34. Bernard Nathanson, M.D.	1
35. National Legal Foundation	1
36. National Right to Life Committee	1
37. New England Christian Action Council, Inc.	1
38. Right to Life Advocates, Inc.	1
39. Right to Life League of Southern California, Inc.	1
40. Rutherford Institute, et al. (18)	19
41. Hon. Christopher H. Smith, et al. (9 Senators, 44 Representatives)	1
42. Southern Center for Law and Ethics	1
43. Southwest Life and Law Center, Inc.	1
44. United States	1
45. US Catholic Conference	1
46. Austin Vaughn and Crusade for Life, Inc.	1
Totals: 85 organizations + 5 single individuals =	90

Table 2   32 briefs in support of appellees

First sponsors of amicus briefs	Total sponsors
1. American Civil Liberties Union, et al. (5)	6
2. 281 American Historians	1
3. American Jewish Congress, et al. (35)	36
4. American Library Assoc. and Freedom to Read Foundation	2
5. American Medical Assoc., et al. (7)	8
6. American Nurses Assoc. and The Nurses' Assoc. of the Amer. College of Obstet. and Gynec.	2
7. American Public Health Assoc., et al. (8 & inds.)	9
8. American Psychological Assoc.	1
9. Americans for Democratic Action, et al. (4)	5
10. Americans United for Separation of Church and State	1
11. Assoc. of Reproductive Health Professionals, et al. (7 & inds.)	8
12. Attorneys General of California, Colorado, Massachusetts, New York, Texas, and Vermont	1
13. Bioethicists for Privacy	1
14. California National Org. for Women, et al. (2 & inds.)	3
15. Canadian Women's Orgs. (4)	4
16. Catholics for a Free Choice, et al. (3 & inds.)	4
17. Center for Population Options, et al. (3)	4
18. Certain Members of the Congress of the US (25 Senators, 115 Representatives)	1
19. Committees on Civil Rights, Medicine & Law, Sex & Law of the Assoc. of the Bar of the City of New York, et al. (6)	7
20. 167 Distinguished Scientists and Physicians Including 11 Nobel Laureates	1
21. Group of American Law Professors	1
22. International Women's Health Organizations (22)	22
23. National Assoc. of Public Hospitals	1
24. National Assoc. of Women Lawyers and National Conference of Women's Bar Associates	2
25. National Coalition Against Domestic Violence	1
26. National Council of Negro Women, Inc., et al. (114 & inds.)	115
27. National Family Planning and Reproductive Health Assoc.	1
28. National Organization for Women	1
29. 77 Organizations Committed to Women's Equality	77
30. Population-Environmental Balance, et al. (6)	7
31. 608 State Legislators from 32 States	1
32. Women Who Have Had Abortions (2887) and Friends (627)	1
Totals:	335

the first sponsors of those filed on behalf of the appellees.[7] When there are two organizations jointly filing a brief, both names are listed. When there are more than two organizations, only the first sponsor is named followed by "et al." (indicating that there are other filers), followed by a number enclosed in parentheses to indicate how many. If the individuals who signed a brief were not united under an organizational title (either permanent or ad hoc), the abbreviation "ind." also appears within the parentheses. At the right of both tables is the total number of organizational sponsors for each brief.

Coalition Building. Tables 1 and 2 show that 85

organizations filed on behalf of appellants, while 335 filed on behalf of appellees. The percentage of briefs with a single sponsor was 76 per cent for the appellants and 44 per cent for the appellees. The number of appellants' sponsors per brief ranged from 1 to 19 (the high being the 19 branches of the Rutherford Institute), while the number of the appellees' filers per brief ranged from 1 to 115 (the high being the brief submitted by the National Council of Negro Women and 114 others). Using rough averages, appellants had 2 sponsors per brief, while appellees had 10 sponsors per brief. What these numbers suggest is that the two sides differed concerning the value of coalition building.

Clearly, the appellees acted as if the number of sponsors was more important than the number of briefs filed, while the appellants favored the strategy of filing the most briefs (46 to 32). This raises the question of which is a more effective strategy, to file as many individual briefs as possible or to gather a larger total number of cosponsoring organizations? Caldeira and Wright have observed that there "is a general absence of large coalitions of groups on individual briefs," and that this implies that those who make the decision about filing the amicus believe "it is the number of briefs, not the number of organizations listed on each brief, that impresses the justices."[8]

So why did the appellees appear to reject this general belief? There are several possible explanations: (1) the desire to save money, (2) the belief that the justices are susceptible to the democratic principle that the majority should rule, (3) the fact that only a finite number of arguments can be made, (4) a difference between multi-issue interest groups and single-issue interest groups concerning the need to file independently, and (5) adoption of a strategy that valued impact of the collection over the number of briefs filed.

First, while the amicus brief offers groups that are limited in time and resources the access to influence litigation without assuming the financial and time burdens required of a full-fledged party,[9] there is no question that even the filing of an amicus makes demands upon the organization. In Caldeira and Wright's study of the amicus briefs filed during the Court's 1982 term, the cost of preparing and filing a brief ranged from $500 to $50,000 with a mean slightly above $8,000.[10] For some groups, the cost of filing an amicus is prohibitive. Caldeira and Wright note, "The litigation budgets of most organizations are quite modest, and most do not have sufficient in-house manpower and legal expertise to prepare briefs on their own."[11] Many of the appellees' cosponsoring groups would appear to fit this profile. For them, cosponsorship allowed participation in the *Webster* case without the financial hardship involved in preparing an individual brief.

Second, the appellees seemed to act on the democratic belief that the justices would be swayed by the numbers associated with the abortion rights position. Indeed, several of their briefs resembled petitions as they included lists of individuals as signatories.[12] Collectively, the appellees' briefs signaled to the Court that their position has the support of the majority of the population and that a reversal of *Roe* would place the Court in the uncomfortable position of fighting against the mainstream. However, reliance on the democratic argument also poses risks. Justices may take offense

at being pressured to defer to majority rule.[13] Another risk of assembling petition briefs is that coalition building may work to limit the number of arguments presented to the Court by decreasing the number of amicus briefs.

The appellees, however, seemed to minimize both risks. While the democratic argument was implicit in the number of sponsors and signatories, this claim was not explicitly made by the appellees. Instead, appellees let the numbers speak for themselves, thereby avoiding reliance on the democratic argument while at the same time signaling to the Court in a not-so-subtle way where the majority of the population stood on the issue. The second risk was overcome by the filing of a significant number of briefs. While 14 less than the number submitted by the appellants, 32 briefs is by any measure a considerable number. Therefore, the appellees' coalitions did not come at the price of sacrificing the number of arguments presented. In sum, the appellees' strategy of garnering the support of several hundred cosponsors was intended to add weight to the already numerous briefs.

A third explanation of the appellees' coalition building is that since there is a finite number of legal arguments to be made on any issue, too many briefs lead to repetition and perhaps even work to irritate the justices. In light of charges that amicus briefs are a waste of time, "repetitious at best and emotional explosions at worst,"[14] and that a large number would increase the already heavy burden on the justices, the appellees may have opted to limit the number of briefs even though they knew that the appellants would file more.

Fourth, an examination of multi-issue interest groups versus single-issue interest groups may explain the different values appellants and appellees attributed to coalition building. Appellees' base of support was largely multi-issue interest groups while single-issue interest groups were more prevalent among the amici of the appellants. [This fact will be discussed in greater detail below.] Multi-issue interest groups enjoy more of a choice in determining whether or not to file an amicus brief than do single-issue interest groups. "The broader a group's political interests, the less intense its attachment to a particular interest . . . . Focus is crucial to intensity."[15] Single-issue interest groups must react when there is a direct threat to their membership's interests. Within this context, the appellants' pro-life organizations were compelled to file independent

Table 3 First sponsors categorized

	Appellants*	Totals	Appellees**	Totals
Individual	3, 27, 30, 31, 34	5		0
Citizen groups	1, 6, 7, 8, 9, 11, 14, 21, 22, 24, 25,		1, 3, 7, 9, 10, 14, 15, 16, 17, 22, 26,	
	26, 28, 29, 33, 36, 37, 38, 39, 45, 46	21	28, 29, 30, 32	15
Professional	2, 4, 5, 13, 20	5	2, 5, 6, 8, 11, 13, 19, 20, 21, 24	10
Public interest law	15, 18, 23, 35, 40, 42, 43	7		0
Government	10, 16, 17, 32, 41, 44	6	12, 18, 31	3
Peak organizations	12	1	4, 23, 25, 27	4
Other	19	1		0
		46		32

* Numbers refer to sponsors in Table 1.
** Numbers refer to sponsors in Table 2.

briefs. In contrast, the multi-issue interest groups of the appellees could meet internal demands through coalitional activity rather than as independent sponsors.

Finally, the appellees' amici were organized according to a strategy that favored impact over the number of briefs. Kathryn Kolbert, who worked on behalf of the American Civil Liberties Union and Planned Parenthood Federation to coordinate all of the amicus briefs, attempted to discourage duplication among the briefs and to encourage coalition building among amici with similar interests.[16] It was believed that overlapping arguments would work to "dilute the overall impact of the collection,"[17] so groups who shared interests were encouraged to form a coalition. Coalitions were organized so that each argued points most appropriate to their interests and expertise. This contrasted with appellants who appeared to strive for a large number of briefs at the expense of repetition. For example, attorney Robert L. Sassone filed six separate briefs on behalf of clients with very similar interests rather than one brief with six sponsors.[18]

Diversity. An attempt was also made to look closer at the groups who filed in order to determine the level of diversity among the first sponsors of the 78 briefs. Seven of the 14 membership categories developed by Caldeira and Wright were used to distinguish the groups: individuals, citizen-based interest groups, professional organizations (where members share the same occupation), public interest law firms or research groups, government sponsors, peak organizations (an organization consisting of groups), and other.[19] Table 3 lists the seven categories and refers to each first sponsor according to the number assigned to it in Tables 1 and 2. Table 4 compares the percentage of briefs filed by groups of each of the seven categories.

Study of Table 4 reveals that both appellants and appellees drew the most support from briefs filed by citizen-based groups, 45.7 per cent and 46.8 per cent, respectively. Of all seven categories employed, the citizen-based groups category contains the most diversity in ideology, membership numbers, prestige, goals, and resources. For instance, The American Civil Liberties Union, Population-Environmental Balance, American Life League, and Agudeth Israel of America are all classified as citizen-based groups.

Next in order of frequency for the appellants were briefs filed by: public interest law firms (15.2 per cent), government sponsors (13 per cent), professional groups and individuals (both with 10.9 per cent), then peak organizations, and other (both with 2.2 per cent). Appellees had no briefs filed by individuals, public interest law firms or other. After the citizen-based groups, the order of frequency were briefs filed by: professional groups (31.3 per cent), peak organizations (12.5 per cent), and government sponsors (9.4 per cent).

One drawback of the seven divisions is that they hide three types of groups relevant to the abortion controversy—the religious groups associated with the pro-life position, the feminist groups aligned with the pro-choice cause, and the single-issue interest groups present in both movements.[20] To remedy this problem, Table 5 was constructed to identify these three types of groups. While these three categories are not mutually exclusive, they reveal some interesting trends concerning the nature of the groups who participated as amici on both sides of *Webster*.

Table 5 confirms some expectations concerning the role feminist and religious groups play in each movement. The appellants drew great support from religiously oriented groups (16 sponsors), but also drew support from one feminist sponsor (Feminists for Life). There were nine feminist sponsors for the appellee side, but also two from religious groups. Altogether, these 28 religious and feminist

Table 4 First sponsors percentages

	Appellants	Appellees	Totals
Individual	5 (10.9%)	0 (0%)	6.4%
Citizen groups	21 (45.7%)	15 (46.9%)	46.2
Professional	5 (10.9%)	10 (31.3%)	19.2
Public interest law	7 (15.2%)	0 (0%)	9
Government	6 (13.0%)	3 (9.4%)	11.5
Peak organizations	1 (2.2%)	4 (12.5%)	6.4
Other	1 (2.2%)	0 (0%)	1.3
	46 (100.1%)*	32 (100.1%)*	78 (100.0%)

* Figure over 100% due to rounding.

sponsors account for only about 36 per cent of the amicus briefs filed. Clearly, the abortion issue was of great concern to organizations whose memberships did not fit either description.

Indeed, as Table 5 reveals, single-issue interest groups played an important role in this case. In order to study the abortion issue here, a single-issue interest group is defined as an organization that is formed to advocate a position on the abortion rights question. While it is admittedly arguable whether a pro-life group has an agenda that is broader than the abortion issue, or whether NOW is more a single-issue than a multi-issue interest group, an initial appraisal of the groups indicates that about 70 per cent of the first sponsors on behalf of the appellants were single-issue interest groups, while about 40 per cent of the appellees' first sponsors were single-issue interest groups. When these single-issue interest groups are compared, it becomes evident that there was a difference in the nature of the permanency of the groups. Appellants drew support from permanent single-issue organizations, while appellees' single-issue organizations tended to be ad hoc groups of professional individuals or peak organizations.

Some tentative conclusions can be drawn from this information concerning the nature of the two movements. Overall, the appellants' amici appear to be more singular in purpose. The public interest law firms, the individuals, the governmental coalitions, and even the professional groups were united in that most were specifically formed either to oppose abortion rights or already had religious tenets supportive of such a political posture. With the exception of the government coalitions, these were permanent groups. In contrast, the appellees relied heavily on the support of professional groups with multiple interests, five of which were ad hoc organizations formed in order to file a brief. These observations suggest that the appellants had a more single-mindedly committed and more permanent group of amici, while the

appellees relied on the support of amici who joined together temporarily and who distributed their resources over a range of issues. The question of whether diversity or homogeneity translated into unity will be examined below.

In sum, the question of who filed these 78 briefs has revealed differences in coalition building and a diversity of interests among the sponsoring groups. It is expected that these organizations employed an assortment of strategies as well as provided the Court with a variety of information. The next question to be examined, therefore, is what was argued in the briefs. Did the diversity among the sponsors translate into a richness of resources for the Court?

What was argued?

Both Webster and the Reproductive Health Services had to launch an offensive campaign while maintaining a defensive posture. The appellants had to defend the Missouri statute while attacking the legal doctrines set down in *Roe*. The appellees guarded *Roe* as precedent while they took aim at the restrictive law. The strategies of the sides and the roles left to the amicus briefs are best informed by an examination of the party briefs. The party briefs carry the burden of presenting the legal arguments for the litigants and, therefore, form a good basis for comparison of the two sides as well as the 78 amicus briefs.

The appellants' brief first summarized the case and then opened its argument by attacking *Roe*, criticizing the "viability" dividing point as arbitrary and calling for the Court to overrule *Roe*. This offensive took only four pages. The rest of the party brief, approximately 28 pages, was a point-by-point defense of the Missouri law. In contrast, the appellees' brief, which omitted a reconstruction of the case, began by defending *Roe* as a fundamental constitutional right and supporting the viability concept as both legally and medically sound. This defense occupied 17 pages. The next 32 pages challenged the Missouri law section by section. For both sides, then, *Roe* was of primary concern. It was only once this precedent was either challenged or defended that a discussion of the state law could begin.

Arguments. Turning to the amicus briefs and referring to the "List of amici arguments," pages 202-203, it can be seen that when the major arguments for the amici are compared, a point and counterpoint pattern emerges. There were six main

Table 5 Special interests of first sponsors

	Appellants*	Totals	Appellees**	Totals
Feminist	21	1/46	14, 15, 22, 24, 25, 26, 28, 29, 32	9/32
Religious	1, 6, 7, 9, 12, 13, 14, 18, 22, 24, 28, 29, 33, 37, 45, 46	16/46	3, 16	2/32
Single-issue	2, 3, 4, 5, 6, 7, 8, 9, 10, 11, 14, 16, 17, 20, 21, 22, 23, 25, 26, 27, 30, 31, 32, 34, 36, 37, 38, 39, 40, 41, 43, 46	32/46	2, 12, 13, 15, 16, 18, 20, 21, 22, 27, 29, 31, 32	13/32

* Numbers refer to sponsors in Table 1.
** Numbers refer to sponsors in Table 2.

points of contention concerning *Roe*: (1) fetal vs. women's rights, (2) if a constitutional basis for a right to abortion exists, (3) whether the trimester scheme is of utility, (4) how abortion fits within the context of American history and tradition, (5) the applicability of the doctrine of *stare decisis*, and (6) the consequences of overturning or following *Roe* as precedent. There were also six main disputes regarding the Missouri statute: (1) whether the state had the power to restrict abortion through its democratic process, or whether the Court must act to prevent the violation of constitutional rights, (2) the rational basis test vs. strict scrutiny as the appropriate standard of review, (3) if the statute's preamble was prefatory or of substance, (4) the constitutionality (or mootness) of the ban on funding abortion counseling, (5) the constitutionality of the ban on abortions in public facilities, and (6) the constitutionality of the viability tests requirement.

Amid the noise of these debated issues, silence is also instructive. Some of the arguments presented by the amici were not present in the party briefs. Referring again to the "List of arguments," a "*" sign indicates those arguments that were employed by both the party brief and at least one amicus. Therefore, absent from the appellants' party brief were arguments that: fetuses are constitutionally protected persons; abortion has harmful effects on women and on society; the law would not involve criminal prosecutions; and the states are better suited than the courts to decide such a politically charged issue. On the appellee side, there was a greater overlap between the party and amicus briefs. Only two major points made by amici were not present in the party brief: the freedom of religion argument and an examination of the consequences of a *Roe* reversal. The latter, nonlegal point constituted an important focus for many of the appellee amicus briefs.

Strategies. The differences between party and amicus argumentation suggest that appellants and appellees adopted different strategies. Once again

the 4-1-4 Court configuration must be appreciated. Litigants had to hold together their four-person coalition while vying for O'Connor's vote. The two sides divided the workload in different ways. O'Connor appears to be the main target of the appellants' party brief while appellees seem to make a bid for her vote through the filing of amicus briefs which focus on her central concerns.

The appellants' party brief is striking in its avoidance of any "pro-life" rhetoric or argumentation. It carefully sidesteps any discussion of the rights of the "preborn," the sacredness of human life, or the uncertain basis for the right to privacy (discussing it in terms of a liberty interest instead). The party brief challenges Roe in terms that would most appeal to O'Connor. It questions the textual, historical, and doctrinal basis of *Roe* and challenges the trimester approach by citing O'Connor's dissent in *Akron v. Akron Center for Reproductive Health*.[21] The brief also argues that should the Court uphold *Roe*, then it should apply the "undue burden" test (favored by O'Connor) to uphold the Missouri regulations. This moderate approach, then, appears to be crafted for O'Connor. However, this strategy was not universally applied as some of the amici did include language and claims from the pro-life movement.[22] The more controversial arguments on behalf of fetal rights and a ban on abortion were voiced not by the parties but by the amici. It was the amici who urged Rehnquist, White, Scalia, and Kennedy to go further than the party brief suggested and to make abortions illegal by recognizing constitutionally protected fetal rights.

The division of labor helps to explain why the appellant briefs, sponsored by organizations more homogeneous than those of the appellees, had more conflicts, inconsistencies, and contradictions. One trouble undoubtedly arose from the fact that the party brief appeared willing to "give" on two important points within the abortion debate. First, it did not call for a total ban on abortion, instead arguing that should the Court overturn *Roe*, the law should once again allow the states to determine abortion policy (presumably either way). Second, it did not assert that a fetus is a constitutionally protected person. Since these were concessions that not all the 46 amici could accept, why would the parties risk such conflict? Again, the answer seems to be the effort to capture O'Connor's vote while hoping that the arguments presented by the amici might persuade all five justices to recognize fetal rights.

In contrast, the appellees appeared to assign the amici the task of capturing O'Connor's vote. There were at least two routes to her. One was to challenge O'Connor to use her test of whether the abortion restrictions in question posed an "undue burden" on women exercising their constitutional right.[23] The amicus briefs presented her with technical information regarding the dire impact of a *Roe* reversal. In fact, the brief from the National Council of Negro Women, citing the disproportionate impact on women of color, the poor, and the young, was crafted especially for O'Connor and her test.[24] A second strategy was to challenge her statement in *Akron* that *Roe* is "on a collision course with itself."[25] O'Connor had used scientific sources to conclude that the point of "viability" would shift forward as medical technology improved. The Brief by 167 Scientists and Physicians not only refuted her argument, but included the signatures of some of the authors on whom she had relied in *Akron*.[26]

What may seem surprising is that the more diverse appellee side produced the more internally consistent argument. This can be explained in two ways. First, the parties and all the amici were aware of how the Court had already chipped away at the right to abortion. All understood that there was no room for concessions without jeopardizing the right itself. Second, this consistency was yet another payoff of organization and coalition building. Kathryn Kolbert, the coordinator of the briefs, helped groups identify what was at issue in *Webster* and how they could best contribute to the case.[27] What emerged was a collection of evidence startling in its singularity of purpose.

Roles. While it is difficult to accurately assess the roles adopted by each interest group, the amici do appear to serve three general purposes.[28] First, there are the endorsement briefs that either repeat the party's position or offer a variation. These briefs may recount all the party's arguments or may center and expand on one point alone. Second are the

technical briefs that offer the Court specialized knowledge that is predominantly nonlegalistic in nature. Third are the risk takers. These briefs range from those who undertake an unconventional legal argument to those who shun the legal elements of the case in favor of an emotional appeal. Among the *Webster* briefs, all three types of briefs were present on each side. Some examples illustrate the different roles and strategies that amici can assume.

The endorsement briefs allow interest groups to throw their prestige behind a party. While these briefs are often repetitive, Barker argues that "this very repetition reflects the 'group combat' flavor of the briefs."[29] This was true with the briefs on behalf of appellants filed by the United States, National Right to Life Association, and the Center for Judicial Studies and on behalf of appellees filed by Members of Congress, NOW, and 77 Organizations Committed to Women's Equality. These briefs presented legal arguments already present in the party briefs, although they usually focused on one element and expanded on it.

The technical briefs concentrated on providing information concerning history and medical science. Many focused on the questions of whether abortion is a part of the American social tradition, how the medical and social sciences contribute to our understanding of fetal life, and what impact legal versus illegal abortion has on women. For the appellants, the Association for Public Justice and Certain American State Legislators argued against abortion being an acceptable part of American society. Briefs filed by the American Association of Pro-life Obstetricians and Gynecologists, Doctors for Life, Paul Marx, and Bernard Nathanson argued that the "preborn" are persons. For the appellees, refutations of these arguments were offered by 281 American Historians, the American Medical Association, 167 Distinguished Scientists, and the Association of Reproductive Health Professionals. The National Council of Negro Women (with 114 other groups) offered both statistical and anecdotal information illustrating the disproportionately severe impact that a reversal of *Roe* would have on poor women and women of color.

The risk takers offered the most unusual arguments. On the appellants' side, the Free Speech Advocates took a confrontational approach, arguing that the abortion cases were "shams" and that the Court "has grown to accept fawning over all its errors."[30] James Joseph Lynch, Jr. contradicted the party brief's assurance that preambles are without legal effect by asserting that the fetus is protected by the reference to "posterity" made in the United States Constitution's preamble. Agudeth Israel also challenged the party line by insisting that the Missouri preamble be struck down as a violation of religious freedom. American Collegians adopted an argument sometimes used by abortion rights advocates that the Ninth and Tenth Amendments are substantive in that they reserve rights that are not listed in the Constitution's text to the states and citizens. Birthright admitted that its brief contained "very little legal precedent," and instead

relied on "logic, common sense, reasoning, intelligence, and conclusions in accord with what is best for all the people of this nation."[31]

The risk takers on behalf of the appellees argued that there was a right to be free from government imposed harm to health (American Public Health Association), that a denial of abortion rights would violate the equal protection clause (National Coalition against Domestic Violence), and that religious freedom demanded that women be free to choose (Catholics for a Free Choice). An emotional appeal made by Women Who Have Had Abortions took the form of a petition-like brief

List of amici arguments

Roe: offense and defense

Issue 1: Rights

Appellants: The preborn are constitutionally protected persons under the 14th Amendment. This fact is supported by scientific data which shows that life begins at conception. The Court has erred before in denying personhood to blacks and American Indians.

*Appellees: Medical evidence is not clear when life begins. Constitutional rights are only bestowed upon live birth. Therefore, there is no comparison between the history of slaves and Indians, and the rights of fetuses. To rule otherwise will threaten not only abortion, but birth control methods as well.

Issue 2: The Constitution

Appellants: *Roe* lacks a sound constitutional basis. The right to privacy was a judicial construct, and there is no constitutional right to abortion.

*Appellees: The constitutional right to privacy is fundamental and includes the right to abortion. This right is supported by the 14th's liberty guarantee as well as the concept of equality.

Issue 3: The Trimester Scheme

*Appellants: *Roe's* trimester scheme is arbitrary, incoherent, and unworkable. Due to medical technology, the viability point shifts and is too uncertain to serve as a marker for dividing the second from the third trimester.

*Appellees: Viability is a reliable cutoff point between the second and third trimesters. Medical technology has not caused the point to shift.

Issue 4: History

*Appellants: A right must be supported by the nation's history and tradition. Abortion conflicts

with the American tradition in that it was restricted by the states throughout most of American history.

*Appellees: American history demonstrates an acceptance of abortion until the 1820s. Then, restrictions were for the sake of the mother's health, not to protect the fetus.

Issue 5: Stare Decisis

*Appellants: Because *Roe* is a Court created error, *stare decisis* should not stand in the Court's way in overruling this precedent.

*Appellees: *Stare decisis* requires adherence to the *Roe* precedent.

Issue 6: Consequences

Appellants: Overturning *Roe* will not lead to criminal prosecutions. It will, however, end the exploitation of women at the hands of abortionists and will prevent women from the harmful physical and emotional effects of having had an abortion.

Appellees: Overturning *Roe* will have dire consequences for women's rights, with a disproportionate impact on the lives of the poor, teenagers, and women of color. Ending abortion rights would be a violation of the 13th Amendment's prohibition on servitude. Legalized abortion is safe, and there is no evidence of harmful psychological impact. Illegal abortions will force women to obtain abortions from backalley butchers. A reversal of *Roe* has international consequences for population control.

The Missouri Statute: offense and defense

Issue 1: States' Rights vs. Constitutional Rights

*Appellants: The states are the appropriate forum for resolving political issues. The majority should rule in these issues, not the undemocratic containing letters of testimony.

This survey of the three types of amici suggests that certain types of groups tend to gravitate to a specific amicus role. The most obvious connection is that between professional organizations and technical briefs. A professional organization has the knowledge and expertise necessary to provide the Court with information outside of the legal realm. There also seems to be a relationship between single-issue interest groups and the role of risk taker. Since these groups enjoy a unified constituency that is devoted to promoting a particular issue, these groups may have more freedom in speaking from a perspective outside the mainstream. They can assume a challenging voice without losing their constituents. The endorsement briefs are sponsored by a variety of groups, but tend to gain the support of multi-issue interest groups. These groups tend to have less of a stake in the interest at issue, and they have to hold together a diversified constituency. Multi-issue interest groups can satisfy organizational demands by merely endorsing the party brief.

This analysis would explain why the appellants had more amici act as risk takers while the appellees had more amici submit technical briefs. Since single-

---

Court. The states retain powers under the 9th and 10th Amendments to protect their citizens from harm.

*Appellees: When rights are violated, the Court has a duty to step in and void the offending state law. Rights are not subject to majority rule. The state of Missouri's law violates the constitutionally protected rights of privacy, speech [and religion— amici only].

Issue 2: Standard of Review

*Appellants: The Court should use the rational basis test in evaluating the Missouri law. This level of scrutiny is appropriate since no fundamental right is at stake and in order to protect the state's rights.

*Appellees: Strict scrutiny is required in evaluating this statute since it threatens fundamental rights. Rights cannot be balanced, they must be protected.

Issue 3: The Preamble

*Appellants: The preamble should be allowed to stand since it is a prefatory statement without legal effect.

*Appellees: The preamble should be struck down since it contradicts *Roe*, violates the Missouri Constitution, and will be used as a guide to interpreting the statute.

Issue 4: Ban on Funding Abortion Counseling

*Appellants: This section does not obstruct privacy rights. Neither is it vague nor a violation of the 1st Amendment. There is no obligation to subsidize constitutional rights.

*Appellees: There is no longer a case or controversy regarding the public funds provision. The state has not contested the District Court's ruling declaring these restrictions unconstitutional. If there is a case or controversy, then the provision is unconstitutional.

Issue 5: Ban on Abortions in Public Facilities

*Appellants: This restriction does not constitute an undue burden on the woman in obtaining an abortion. The Court held in *Poelker v. Doe* (1977) that a public hospital is not obliged to provide abortion services.

*Appellees: This provision goes beyond the restrictions upheld in *Poelker* as it bans the performance of abortions in public hospitals even when no public funds or public employees are involved. It therefore unconstitutionally interferes with wholly private medical treatment.

Issue 6: Viability Testing

*Appellants: The state has a compelling interest in determining viability in order to exert its power to protect fetal life. The *Colautti v. Franklin* (1979) precedent does not apply here since not one but three factors are used to determine viability. The law does not require that all three tests be performed, but that the physician performs such tests as are necessary to make the viability determination.

*Appellees: Under any standard of review, the viability testing is unconstitutional. The required tests are expensive and dangerous and of little use in determining viability until the 28th week. The law should be read to indicate that the three tests are required in order to make specific findings regarding viability.

---

*Argument cited in party brief as well.

issue interest groups were more prevalent among appellants' amici, it could be expected that appellants would have more amici who assumed the role of risk taker. In contrast, since professional organizations were three-to-one behind the appellees, it was predictable that this side would submit more technical briefs.

Together these three types of briefs offered the Court not only an abundance of information concerning abortion, but a sense of the urgency and complexity of this political issue as well. The Court saw briefs which towed the party line, others which offered specialized information, and still others that challenged the Court to break new legal ground. While many perspectives were present, the next question is how many were heard?

What impact?

While the main purpose of an amicus brief is to persuade the Court to rule on behalf of a particular litigant, the impact of amici is not limited to this result alone. Interest groups may also claim success if the Court adopts the language or perspective of the brief, or if the litigant's argument is strengthened by the endorsement of the amicus.[32] In filing an amicus, an interest group may gain publicity, an opportunity to refine and articulate its position, and experience in the judicial system.[33] Such third-party involvement also allows groups to feel as though they have participated in the decisional process.[34] Some of the impact of amici may not be apparent until future cases emerge which reflect the information, argument, or concerns of the earlier amici.

Impact is of course most readily identifiable in terms of the winners and losers of a case. However, such an approach is obviously limited for a case like *Webster* where the Court lineup was 4-1-4 from the start. With this in mind, the discussion here will also include a content analysis of which briefs were cited by the justices in the decision, and a study of how some of the arguments made by the amici seemed to sway certain justices.

In a 5-4 vote with two concurrences and two dissenting opinions, the *Webster* decision upheld the sections restricting public employees and facilities from performing or assisting in abortions, and the sections requiring viability testing. While the Court did not rule on the constitutionality of the statute's preamble, it declared the counseling section moot. In the course of deciding these issues,

the Court also began to dismantle the principles of *Roe*, the trimester scheme in particular. Chief Justice William Rehnquist, with Justices Byron White and Anthony Kennedy, attacked the "rigid trimester analysis" as inconsistent with the Constitution.[35] He argued, "We do not see why the State's interest in protecting human life should come into existence only at the point of viability . . . ."[36] Justice Antonin Scalia concurred stating that Rehnquist's argument would effectively overrule *Roe*, but that he would do so more explicitly.[37] Justice Sandra Day O'Connor agreed with the constitutionality of the Missouri statute, but not with the need to unravel *Roe*. She relied instead on *Roe* and its progeny to uphold the Missouri law.[38] The four dissenting justices, Harry Blackmun, William Brennan, Thurgood Marshall, and John Paul Stevens, would have used *Roe* to void the Missouri statute.

Therefore, when speaking strictly in terms of win versus lose, the appellants emerged as the victors in this case. The Missouri law was upheld, the Court signaled its willingness to uphold restrictive state abortion policies, and four justices indicated a willingness to overturn *Roe*. Within these terms, appellees could claim only that *Roe* survived—for now. Yet, measuring impact in this way assumes that the win is due to arguments set forth by amici. It also ignores the fact that amici on the losing side have impact as well. Therefore, it is important to consider as well two other indicators: the amici cited by the Court, and evidence that the Court accepted arguments advanced only by the amici.

The counting of citations demonstrates that the justices considered the arguments set forth by the amici.[39] This is not to say, of course, that the only briefs which had impact were the ones cited, but the data is useful as a "blunt indicator" of how the Court used the briefs.[40] Table 6 presents the results of counting each direct reference to a brief made by one of the five justices who wrote an opinion in the *Webster* case. References to the appellants' party briefs totaled six while the appellees' party briefs were cited eight times. Excluding party briefs, amicus briefs were cited 29 times. Twelve different amicus briefs, six from each side, were cited at least once. Appellants' amici were cited 12 times while appellees' amici were cited 17 times. The amicus briefs cited tended to be those that contained either religious arguments or which provided technical information on medicine or on the law. Be-

Table 6 Briefs cited by the justices

	Rehnquist	Majority O'Connor	Scalia	Minority Blackmun	Stevens	Total
Appellants' brief	4	—	—	—	2	6
Agudeth Israel	—	—	—	—	1	1
American Assoc. of Pro-Life Obstetricians	—	3	—	—	—	3
Holy Orthodox Church	—	—	—	—	2	2
Lutheran Church	—	—	—	—	2	2
Missouri Catholic Conference	—	—	—	—	1	1
United States	1	—	—	2	—	3
subtotals	5	3	—	2	8	18
Appellees' brief	5	3	—	—	—	8
American Medical Association	—	2	—	2	—	4
Americans United for Separation of Church & State	—	—	—	—	2	2
Association of Reproductive Health Professionals	—	1	—	1	4	6
Catholics for a Free Choice	—	—	—	—	2	2
Group of American Law Profs.	—	—	—	1	—	1
National Association of Public Hospitals	—	1	—	1	—	2
subtotals	5	7	—	5	8	25
total amici alone	1	7	—	7	14	29
total briefs	10	10	—	7	16	43

sides the direct references to the amicus briefs, Justices Blackmun and Stevens together cited seven different published articles: three which were largely scientific, two commenting on religious issues, one on the impact of illegal abortions, and one on the law.

Rehnquist, writing for the majority, cited the appellants' brief four times and the appellees' brief five times. The only amicus to which he referred was that of the United States. In O'Connor's concurring opinion, she cited the appellees' brief three times, and referred to the four amicus briefs containing medical and scientific information, again indicating her struggle with the viability issue. Scalia's concurrence made no direct references to briefs or outside sources. The dissents of Justices Blackmun and Stevens did not cite the party briefs of either side. These justices referred instead to the amicus briefs for a total of 29 citations. As with O'Connor, most of Blackmun's references came from the technical medical briefs. In contrast, Stevens cited mostly the religiously oriented briefs.

Yet, briefs can be cited and then rejected. Did the briefs have any real influence on the justices in constructing their decision? It is suggested that the answer is yes. Consider again the role of the amici. The appellants' amici seemed to urge their coalition of four justices to overturn *Roe*. The appellees' amici appeared to focus on convincing O'Connor to cast the fifth vote to protect *Roe*. The amici on both sides enjoyed some success.

The victory enjoyed by the appellants was not of the parties' making alone. The Court went further than the parties had urged, surging ahead on the path marked by the appellants' amici. When the Court accepts an argument that was advanced only by an amicus brief, it is an indication of influence.[41] Again, the party brief had devoted only four pages to challenging *Roe* and the viability point. It was instead the amici who supplied both the technical and legal information which subverted the *Roe* trimester scheme.

There are signs that the appellees' amici had influence as well. Again, their target was O'Connor and the two routes to her were to have her apply her "undue burden" test to strike down the Missouri statute, and to have her retreat from her criticism of *Roe's* trimester scheme. While the amici were unsuccessful concerning the first point, there are signs that they made some progress concerning the second.

It is not what O'Connor's *Webster* opinion says but what it does not say that is important.[42] Considering her *Akron* dissent in which she argued that the trimester approach was "completely unworkable"[43] and on a "collision course with itself,"[44] and that she adhered to this position three years later in *Thornburgh v. American College of Obstetricians and Gynecologists*,[45] it is curious that in *Webster*—a case that brings the viability issue to the forefront and causes four other justices to voice concerns that the trimester framework is indeed unworkable—O'Connor remarks only that she continues to regard the trimester approach as "problematic."[46] She cites her *Akron* dissent not to repudiate the trimester scheme, but to illustrate how to apply the "undue burden" test. If indeed O'Connor is retreating from her *Akron* critique, the appellees' amici may be responsible for planting the seed of doubt in her mind.

Conclusion

The 78 *Webster* amici produced an uncomparable collection of information on the abortion rights issue. While *Webster* is certainly not a typical case, nor was the response of interest groups usual, it does serve to magnify the amicus curiae role. Interest groups can lobby the Court concerning an issue even as politicized as abortion if they enter the Court through the open door extended to amici. In working to present their arguments before the Court, the pro-life and pro-choice movements also revealed something about themselves. The briefs reflected the composition of their constituencies, their legal strategies, and their core values. The study of amici, then, is not only instructive for court watching but for monitoring interest group politics as well.

The writing and organization of 78 briefs was a monumental undertaking, but it was not a wasted effort. It appears that the amici on both sides made inroads with the Court. The briefs were not only read; they also had impact. Their arguments and information helped to shape the terms of the Court debate. Whether the justices refuted the briefs, modified an argument because of them, or accepted and integrated their points, the amici mattered. Through the presentation of the briefs, the battle over abortion rights was waged before the Court. It is no surprise, then, that in the midst of this friendly fire, some of the justices were struck.

NOTES

This article originally appeared in Volume 74, Number 5, February-March 1991, pages 261-270.

I would like to thank Lee Epstein and Gregory Caldeira for sharing their research and ideas, and the anonymous reviewer who provided a list of insightful comments. Special thanks to Catherine Bell Fleming of the National Abortion Rights Action League for providing me with all the appellees' amicus briefs.

An earlier version of this article was presented at the Annual Meeting of the Northeastern Political Science Association, Philadelphia, PA, November 9-11, 1989.

1. 492 U.S. __; 109 S.Ct. 3040 (1989).
2. 438 U.S. 265 (1978).
3. 410 U.S. 113 (1973).
4. 109 S.Ct. 3040, 3041 (1989).
5. *Id.*, at 3047.
6. While I have framed the controversy in terms of abortion rights, throughout this article I refer to the two movements as "pro-life" and "pro-choice." While these labels cloud the actual legal issue, they represent not only how the popular

media refer to the movements but also how the movements refer to themselves.

7. While focusing on the first sponsor may not accurately reflect the organization that assumed the bulk of the legal work, it usually illustrates the character and role of the brief. For example, although the Center for Constitutional Rights constructed the brief for which the National Council of Negro Women appears as the first sponsor, the NCNW is representative of the nature of the brief since it speaks of the impact that restrictive abortion policy will have on women of color.

8. Caldeira and Wright, *Amici Curiae Before the Supreme Court: Who Participates, When and How Much?*, Forthcoming 18 J. POL. (1990).

9. O'Connor and Epstein, *Amicus Curiae Participation in U.S. Supreme Court Litigation: An Appraisal of Hakman's "Folklore"*, 16 LAW & SOC'Y REV. 313 (1981-82).

10. Caldeira and Wright, "Why Organized Interests Participate as Amici Curiae in the U.S. Supreme Court," paper presented at the 1989 Annual Meeting of the American Political Science Association, Atlanta, Georgia, page 11.

11. *Id.*

12. *See,* Brief for Women Who Have Had Abortions (2887 signatures and 627 signatures of friends); Brief for 608 State Legislators from 32 States; Brief for Group of American Law Professors (885 signatures); 281 American Historians; Brief for 167 Distinguished Scientists and Physicians; Brief for Certain Members of the Congress of the United States; Brief for Catholics for a Free Choice; Brief for Bioethicists for Privacy.

13. In fact, Justice Scalia's *Webster* opinion did object to the belief of interest groups that unelected and life-tenured justices should weigh popular opinion. *See,* Scalia's dissent at 3065-66.

14. Harper and Etherington, *Lobbyists Before the Court,* 101 U. PA L. REV. 1172 (1953).

15. Kobylka, *A Court-Created Contest for Group Litigation: Libertarian Groups and Obscenity,* 49 J. POL. 1073 (1987).

16. Telephone interview with Kathryn Kolbert, attorney-consultant to the ACLU Reproductive Freedom Project, November 30, 1990; Kolbert, *Webster v. Reproductive Health Services: Reproductive Freedom Hanging by a Thread,* 11 WOMEN'S RIGHTS L. REP. 153, 156 (1989).

17. Kolbert, *supra* n. 16, at 157.

18. Brief for Edward Allen, Brief for Human Life International, Brief for Paul Marx, Brief for Bernard Nathanson, Brief for Right to Life League of Southern California, and Brief for Austin Vaughn and Crusade for Life, Inc.

19. Caldeira and Wright, *supra* n. 5.

20. Alternative typologies were considered and rejected. Dividing the groups according to their purpose (governmental, religious, advocate, and multi-interest) did not provide enough detail to gain a sense of the diversity among the groups. More substantive divisions, such as religious, medical, feminist, and academic, did not provide mutually exclusive categories. An ideological divide of liberal versus conservative would essentially divide the amici into the already existing appellant versus appellee lineup. *See,* O'Connor and Epstein, *The Rise of Conservative Interest Group Litigation,* 45 J. POL. 479-489 (1983). O'Neill's typology of oligarchic, democratic, and managerial groups was designed more to study the structures of the groups themselves than the nature of Court politics. *See* O'Neill, BAKKE AND THE POLITICS OF EQUALITY: FRIENDS AND FOES IN THE CLASSROOM OF LITIGATION (Middletown, CT: Wesleyan University Press, 1985). Bradley and Gardner's underdog versus upperdog distinction provides only two divisions and appears to be designed for studying diverse cases over a period of time. *See,* Bradley and Gardner, *Underdogs, Upperdogs and the Use of the Amicus Brief: Trends and Explanations,* 10 JUST. SYS. J. 78-96, (1985).

21. 462 U.S. 416, 452 (1983).

22. *See,* Brief for Alabama Lawyers for Unborn Children, Inc.; Brief for Edward Allen; Brief for Attorneys General from Five States; Brief for Catholics United for Life; Brief for Alan Ernest; Brief for Free Speech Advocates; Brief for The Holy Orthodox Church; Brief for Human Life International; Brief for International Right to Life Federation; Brief for Larry Joyce; Brief for the Knights of Columbus; Brief for James Joseph Lynch, Jr.; Brief for Paul Marx; Brief for Bernard Nathanson; Brief for the Right to Life League of Southern California; Brief for the Southwest Life and Law Center, Inc.; Brief for Austin Vaughn and Crusade for Life, Inc.

23. *See,* Akron, *supra* n. 21, at 453.

24. Kolbert, *supra* n. 16.

25. Akron, *supra* n. 21, at 458.

26. Kolbert, *supra* n. 16.

27. *Id.*

28. Krislov, *The Amicus Brief: From Friendship to Advocacy,* 72 YALE L. J. 694-721, (1963).

29. Barker, *Third Parties in Litigation: A Systemic View of the Judicial Function,* 29 J. POL. 62, (1967).

30. Brief for Free Speech Advocates, at 6, 23.

31. Brief for Birthright, at 17.

32. O'Connor, WOMEN'S ORGANIZATIONS' USE OF THE COURTS 146 (Lexington, MA: Lexington Books, 1980).

33. *Id.*

34. Krislov, *supra* n. 28, at 721.

35. Webster, *supra* n. 1, at 3056.

36. *Id.* at 3057.

37. *Id.* at 3064.

38. *Id.* at 3060.

39. Angell, *The Amicus Curiae: American Development of English Institutions,* 16 INT'L & COMP. L. Q. 1036-1044 (1967).

40. O'Connor and Epstein, *Court Rules and Workload: A Case Study of Rules Governing Amicus Curiae Participation,* 8 JUS. SYS. J. 43 (1983).

41. Angell, *supra* n. 39, at 1036.

42. This point was brought to my attention by Kathryn Kolbert; interview, *supra* n. 16.

43. Akron, *supra* n. 21, at 454.

44. *Id.* at 458.

45. 476 U.S. 747, at 814 (1986).

46. Webster, *supra* n. 1, at 3063.

The amicus curiae role of the U.S. solicitor general in Supreme Court litigation

Although there is little public scrutiny of the office, the solicitor general can and does significantly affect public policy, this study shows.

by Karen O'Connor

Since 1870 the U.S. solicitor general has represented the United States government in Supreme Court litigation. Whether participating as a direct party or as an amicus curiae, the solicitor general is the most frequent litigator before the Court, generally playing some role in more than half of the cases argued annually. (See Table 1.)

Despite the significant role played by the solicitor general in Supreme Court litigation, little research has been conducted on the office or its occupants. Several scholars have examined the solicitor general's high success rates[1] or the types of issues that the government most frequently joins in as amicus curiae.[2] However, there has been no systematic attempt to determine whether differences exist in the litigation activities of specific solicitors general.

This article examines the amicus curiae participation of three U.S. solicitors general who completed terms during the Burger Court era: Erwin N. Griswold (1967-1973), Robert H. Bork (1973-1977), and Wade H. McCree, Jr. (1977-1981). Their participation across three issue areas is studied for any differences in the nature and extent of their involvement as amicus curiae. Although each solicitor general also represented the United States when it was a direct party to a suit, only amicus submission is studied here because the solicitors generally enjoy substantial personal discretion over this type of activity.[3]

Solicitors Griswold, Bork, and McCree

Congress created the position of solicitor general in 1870 to provide "an officer, learned in the law to assist the Attorney General in the performance of his duties."[4] "Learned in the law" is an apt characterization of all of the subjects of this study.[5] Erwin N. Griswold graduated from Harvard Law School where he was on the law review staff.[6] After a short stint in the U.S. solicitor general's office, Griswold became a professor and later dean of the Harvard Law School. Lyndon Johnson appointed him solicitor general in 1967, and he continued in this position during the Nixon administration until resigning in 1972.

As the author of several books and article, Griswold's scholarly reputation long has been widely respected. He is a frequent advocate of judicial restraint, and in fact, shortly after his resignation from government service, he told members of The Association of the Bar of the City of New York, "(A)ctivism that carries us beyond the proper exercise of the judicial function is not legitimately called activism."[7]

Solicitor General Robert H. Bork also advocated judicial restraint, but often in a more controversial manner. He was a Phi Beta Kappa graduate of the University of Chicago[8] and an antitrust lawyer before he joined the Yale Law School faculty in 1962. Characterizing himself as a "classic liberal,"[9] Bork regularly criticized modern liberals in general, and the Warren Court's decisions in particular, in both scholarly articles and popular journals, noting that the Warren Court "represent(s) a sharp challenge to the traditional relationship of the judiciary to the process of democratic government."[10] His philosophy led to public support for Richard Nixon's re-election, and testimony before Congress in favor

Table 1 Office of Solicitor General participation in cases argued before the U.S. Supreme Court, 1970-1979

	1970	1971	1972	1973	1974	1975	1976	1977	1978	1979
All cases	151 100%	173 100%	177 100%	170 100%	173 100%	179 100%	176 100%	164 100%	168 100%	156 100%
Government participating as direct party	63 42	62 36	75 42	67 39	89 51	76 42	65 37	75 46	63 38	78 50
Government participating as amicus curiae	26 19	16 9	28 15	26 15	22 13	45 25	34 19	22 13	36 21	30 19
No government participation	62 41	95 55	74 42	77 45	62 36	58 32	77 44	67 41	69 41	48 31

Source: Annual Reports of the Attorney General of the United States, 1976 and 1980.

of the Nixon administration's anti-busing proposals prior to his appointment as solicitor general by Nixon in 1973.

Unlike Griswold and Bork, McCree had significant judicial experience before becoming solicitor general. An early black graduate of Harvard Law School,[11] McCree practiced law in Detroit before his appointment in 1954, and subsequent election, to the Michigan Circuit Court in 1955. He held that position until John F. Kennedy appointed him to the U.S. district court in 1961. In 1966 President Johnson elevated McCree to the U.S. Court of Appeals for the Sixth Circuit, where he served for 11 years until his appointment as solicitor general by Jimmy Carter in 1977.

Although McCree's education, legal training and experience, like Griswold's and Bork's, were in conservative, business-oriented environments, his opinions as a federal judge reflected a strong concern with individual liberties.[12] And while McCree declined to label himself an activist judge, at the time of his appointment as solicitor general one of his law clerks noted his tendency "to come down more on the side of the defendant than some other judges on this circuit."[13]

Functions of the office

The solicitor general's office performs four major functions: first, it screens prospective federal cases for possible appeal to the U.S. Supreme Court.[14] Each solicitor has approached this task somewhat differently. Bork, for example, early on noted his concern that he might "have to abandon the longstanding tradition that the solicitor general reads every word of every pleading that goes to the Supreme Court" because of the increasing volume of government litigation.[15] McCree, however, said that he "personally review(ed)" the files of all cases that came to the office.[16]

While the solicitors varied in their personal approach to these appeals, each recognized the importance of thorough screening. In fact, it is through this screening process that the solicitors general maintain their prestige with the Court.[17] Given the potentially large number of appealable cases that could be used to develop legal doctrine favorable to the overall interest of the solicitor general's office and the U.S. government, the solicitor general carefully weeds out all but the "best" cases. As a rule cases are not appealed unless they have good facts, can potentially make good law, and present issues that the justices appear willing to address.[18] For example, former Solicitor General Griswold has commented that

. . . he tries to take to the Court only cases which, based upon his close observation of the work of the Court, he thinks that the Court will accept.[19]

Thus solicitors appeal or seek writs of certiorari in only a small portion of potentially appealable cases.

The solicitor general's second function is the filing of petitions for writ of certiorari for or against acceptance of cases not involving the United States as a party. Former Solicitor General Charles Fahy believed that the filing of briefs in opposition to grants of certiorari in private conflicts was the "principal aid the solicitor general affords the Court."[20] Through the filing of such petitions the solicitor offers the justices a wider perspective on the issues at hand. This may prevent the Court from accepting a case that does not present the best possible facts to resolve a potentially larger legal issue.

By paying attention to the kinds of issues the justices seem ready to address, the solicitor general's office has been a very successful party, as well as amicus curiae. This attention has reinforced the institutional bond between the Court and the office, fostering a special relationship between each solicitor general and the Supreme Court. This relationship has been noted by many former solicitors general,[21] scholars,[22] and justices of the court.[23]

One author has even referred to the solicitor general as the "Court's 'ninth and a half' member."[24]

The third function the solicitor general performs comes through his submission of well-crafted briefs. In formulating these arguments, each solicitor general remains mindful of the special relationship he has with the Court. Former Solicitor Bork has written that the solicitor general

owes (the Court) complete candor even when that impairs his efficacy as an advocate. The Court and its function are far more important than a government victory in any given case.[25]

In addition, briefs submitted by the solicitor general's office generally are quite scholarly and at times present facts not available to the other parties to the litigation, such as data from private governmental reports. Solicitors' briefs may also deal with the potential policy ramifications of the justices' decision; information not generally addressed by private parties concerned with an immediate outcome.[26]

The fourth function the solicitor general performs is via his role as amicus curiae. As an amicus curiae the solicitor can inform the Court of the ramifications of the position urged by each party and can apprise the justices of his opinions, which are given great weight. The solicitor's contribution as amicus is particularly useful when one or both parties to the lawsuit are inexperienced yet present the justices with an important case.[27]

While some commentators have claimed that government amicus briefs are "neutral," during the Carter administration at least one division head of the Justice Department departed from the "neutralist" approach. Drew Days, III, a former NAACP Legal Defense Fund attorney, during his tenure as head of the Civil Rights Division of the Justice Department included Supreme Court "amicus participation (as) an important and integral part of the (Civil Rights) division enforcement program."[28] Days was responsible for recommending that the solicitor general file amicus briefs in cases affecting civil rights. He also encouraged attorneys in his division to maintain contacts with private civil rights organizations so as better to identify cases for potential support.[29]

The solicitor's extraordinary influence

Whether government amicus curiae briefs are drafted to assist a party or interest group, the high regard the Court has for these briefs is reflected in its rules. The solicitor general is exempt from the standard requirement that parties wishing to participate as amicus curiae must obtain the consent of both parties or receive special permission from the Court. The Court also occasionally asks the solicitor general to file an amicus brief, particularly in cases of potential constitutional importance. At times, the solicitor general even appears as an amicus curiae to argue his position orally before the Court.

Studies evaluating the solicitor general's office as a party or amicus curiae reveal that the government's participation has a positive impact on case outcomes.[30] In fact, the solicitor general's success rate as amicus curiae surpasses the high win-loss ratio that the government enjoys as a party to a suit. For example, in the race discrimination employment area, from 1970 to 1981, the solicitor general's office won 81.6 per cent (N=16) of cases in which it filed amicus curiae briefs, compared to its rate of 70 per cent (N=10) when it was an actual party to the suit.[31] These figures closely approximate those found by Scigliano for 1943, 1944, 1963, and 1965 terms of the Court. In those years, the solicitor general enjoyed an overall amicus success rate of 87 per cent.[32]

Given the high success rate associated with the solicitor general's amicus briefs, Scigliano questioned the "fairness of the government's trying to get a favored litigant into Court."[33] He noted that:

this behavior smacks too much of partisanship; it subjects the solicitor general to strong pressures from organizations and individual litigants . . .[34]

This kind of group pressure and in particular the opposition of women's rights groups to the government's amicus brief in *Personnel Administrator of Massachusetts v. Feeney*,[35] a challenge to a statutory veteran's preference scheme, caused Attorney General Griffin Bell to institute a policy requiring the solicitor to give notice to Bell of all cases involving policy issues. This policy permitted Bell to examine the matter, and if necessary, consult with the president *before* the solicitor's brief was written.[36]

Even prior to the *Feeney* controversy, civil rights groups had been upset when a draft of the government's amicus brief in *Regents of the University of California v. Bakke*[37] was leaked to the press, purporting to side with Alan Bakke. Then-HEW Secretary Joseph Califano urged several civil rights groups to contact the solicitor general to urge him to change his position regarding affirmative action.[58]

These examples of political pressures on the solicitor general highlight the importance of the office. Whether or not political or personal reasons enter into the solicitor general's filing of amicus curiae briefs, scholars and former occupants of the office have noted the generally wide latitude that each solicitor general typically has in this area. Thus, given the discretionary nature of this highly influential activity, it is of particular importance to study the activities of individual solicitors general.

The study: data and method

I attempted to answer two questions concerning the three solicitors' general participation as amicus curiae in Supreme Court litigation: first, do particular solicitors general affect the types of issues the government enters? and second, does the direction of this participation vary according to who occupies that office?

To answer these questions, I noted first each case in which one of the three solicitors general participated as an amicus curiae during the 1967 to 1979 terms of the Court.[39] Cases resulting in written opinions then were divided into three categories and coded as follows: (1) personal liberties,[40] (2) civil equality,[41] and (3) criminal rights.[42]

After each case was categorized, the participating solicitor general was identified. In addition, the nature of that participation, as adjudged to be pro- or anti- the "rights" position, also was recorded. For example, if the solicitor general filed a brief in support of a criminal defendant who alleged that his constitutional rights were violated by state police officers, the solicitor's action was coded as "pro" criminal defendant's rights.

As Table 2 indicates, the overall differences in the kinds of cases in which each solicitor general participated as an amicus curiae are statistically significant. Since this study concerns a period of substantial activism, however, it should be noted that each solicitor was met with a changing mix of cases that were eligible for selection for amicus action. Thus some difference in issue concentration may be due to this phenomenon. Solicitor General Bork tended to participate in proportionately fewer civil equalities cases than either solicitors Griswold or McCree. While Griswold and McCree focused their amicus curiae participation on the civil equalities area, Bork divided his partici-

Table 2 Solicitor general participation as amicus curiae in three issue areas

	Griswold	Bork	McCree
Personal liberties	8.0%	7.0%	9.3%
	(N=4)	(N=3)	(N=4)
Civil equality	76.0	48.8	74.4
	(N=38)	(N=21)	(N=32)
Criminal rights	16.0	44.2	16.3
	(N=8)	(N=19)	(N=7)
Totals	100.0	100.0	100.0
(N)	(50)	(43)	(43)

$X^2 = 12.48$
$p = .014$

pation almost equally between criminal rights and civil equalities cases. In contrast, Griswold and McCree participated in few of the criminal rights cases. Thus, the only issue area that reveals similar rates of participation by the respective solicitors general is the personal liberties category.

An examination of the position taken by each solicitor general, i.e., whether they submitted an amicus brief for or against personal liberties, civil equality, or criminal rights claims also reveals interesting differences among the three solicitors general. While Griswold and McCree took decidedly more pronounced "pro-rights" positions than did Bork, the two solicitors who served during Republican administrations[43] adopted "anti-rights" positions more frequently than McCree. As revealed in Table 3, both Griswold and Bork filed "pro-rights" amicus curiae briefs in proportionately fewer cases than did McCree. In fact, McCree filed "pro-rights" amicus curiae briefs twice as often as his immediate predecessor.

The anti-rights position taken by Bork, while not surprising given his restraintist philosophies, is interesting because of the differences between him and Griswold, who also served under President Nixon. Bork's frequent submission of anti-rights briefs also stands in contrast to the conclusions of scholars who have examined the solicitor general's office more generally. In fact, several researchers have concluded that when the government acts as amicus curiae before the U.S. Supreme Court, the solicitor general usually advocates a liberal position.[44] However, Bork filed amicus briefs against the "liberal" (or "pro-rights") position 59.5 per cent (N=25) of the time.

An analysis of each solicitor general's participation in the three issue areas was conducted to investigate further the differences in direction indicated in Table 3. Table 3 also indicates the variation in each solicitor's support of parties advancing

Table 3   The nature of each solicitor general's amicus curiae participation

	Griswold	Bork	McCree
"Pro rights" amicus in general[1]	62.0% (N=31/50)	40.5% (N=17/42)[2]	79.0% (N=34/43)
"Pro rights" amicus in personal liberties claims[3]	25.0 (N=1/4)	33.3 (N=1/3)	75.0 (N=3/4)
"Pro rights" amicus in civil equality claims[4]	76.3 (N=29/38)	76.2 (N=16/21)	87.5 (N=28/32)
"Pro rights" amicus in criminal cases[5]	12.5 (N=1/8)	0.0 (N=0/18)	42.9 (N=3/7)

1. X^2=13.32, p=.001
2. One of Solicitor Bork's amicus briefs could not be readily categorized as pro or anti criminal defendants rights. This brief was excluded from the remaining analysis. *See* note 59.
3. X^2=2.26, p=.322
4. X^2=1.68, p=.4385
5. X^2=8.69, p=.013

a personal liberties claim. McCree and Griswold, who showed similarities in terms of the nature and direction of their participation (see Table 2 and 3) reveal differences when their positions in the personal liberties area are isolated.

Griswold and Bork each adopted a "pro-rights" stance as amicus curiae only once in the personal liberties area. Griswold's lone support of a personal liberties claim occurred in *Pittsburgh Press v. Pittsburgh Commission on Human Relations*,[45] involving sex-discrimination and free press claims. There, the U.S. government argued that discriminatory, sex-segregated job advertisements were not protected from challenge by the First Amendment.[46]

Solicitor General Bork's lone "pro rights" amicus curiae brief also involved commercial speech. In *Bates v. State Bar of Arizona*, he supported Bates' claims that the Arizona bar's refusal to allow most forms of lawyer advertising violated the First Amendment.[47] Solicitor General McCree also supported expanded personal liberties claims, but did so on a more regular basis than his predecessors. For example, in *Pruneyard Shopping Center v. Robins*,[48] McCree argued that California could guarantee its citizens expansive free speech rights even where they were alleged to conflict with private property claims. However, while McCree clearly adopted the pro-rights position more frequently than his two predecessors, the very small number of cases involving these kinds of claims make it difficult to draw any meaningful comparisons.

The pursuit of civil equality

In contrast, all three solicitors general participated much more frequently in cases involving civil equalities claims. As indicated in Table 3, Solicitor General McCree advanced a pro-civil equalities claim in a slightly higher percentage of his amicus briefs than either solicitors Griswold or Bork. All these solicitors, however, filed "pro-rights" briefs over 75 per cent of the time. Given both Griswold's and Bork's public disapproval of judicial activism, their high pro-rights stances here are interesting. And, while they were somewhat less supportive of civil equality issues than McCree, each solicitor general's highest "pro rights" participation occurred in this area (see Table 3).

It should be noted, though, that at least two of Griswold's anti-rights positions resulted from the apparent instructions of the White House. Prior to the filing of government briefs in *Swann v. Charlotte-Mecklenberg Board of Education*[49] and *Davis v. Board of School Commissioners*,[50] President Nixon publicly announced that his administration would no longer support forced busing to achieve integration. Prior to that time, however, Griswold had consistently argued against all forms of segregation. For example, Griswold opposed freedom of choice plans,[51] transfer plans,[52] and housing discrimination.[53]

While McCree's strong support of civil equalities claims meshes with his philosophy as a jurist, as well as those of the Carter administration generally, Griswold's and, to a greater extent, Bork's support is somewhat surprising. Bork, for example, regularly sided with employees alleging sex[54] or race[55] discrimination in employment. Thus, consistent with conventional wisdom, all solicitors generally adopted a pro-civil equalities position.

The solicitors' positions concerning criminal rights, however, stand in sharp contrast. The most striking dissimilarities in the direction of each solicitor general's participation are indicated in Table 3. While McCree submitted amicus curiae briefs *supporting* criminal rights 42.9 per cent of the time, Griswold and McCree argued *against* defendant's rights in a vast majority of the cases heard by the Court during their terms as solicitor. Griswold and Bork's "anti-rights" position was probably rooted in the Nixon administration's strong law and order stance. This position is most clearly reflected in Bork's uniform opposition to criminal defendant's claims. For example, even in his first amicus submission involving criminal defendant's rights, Bork argued that pre-Miranda interrogations were at times constitutionally permissible.[56] He also consistently argued against right to counsel claims[57] and for the constitutionality of the death penalty.[58]

McCree's submission of amicus curiae briefs against criminal defendants was less expected. His minimal support for criminal rights claims, however, may be a function of the relatively low number of cases in which he participated. However, it is fair to say that no administration or solicitor general was generally favorable toward expanded criminal rights.

Conclusion

The U.S. solicitor general, while a critical actor in Supreme Court litigation, has been the subject of only minimal scholarly attention. To add to our knowledge of that office and its occupants, this article addressed two questions concerning particular solicitor generals' participation before the Court. First, this study asked whether there are significant differences in the kinds of cases in which the office of solicitor general participated during the terms of Bork, Griswold, and McCree. In general, Bork participated as amicus curiae in a disproportionately high number of criminal rights cases when compared with either Griswold or McCree. In contrast, Griswold and McCree filed a majority of their briefs in cases with civil equalities issues.

This article also asked whether there were differences in the legal positions advocated by each of the solicitors. Generally, Griswold and McCree advocated pro-rights positions more frequently than Mr. Bork. This general difference can be explained by substantial variation among the solicitors in their pursuit of civil equalities and by more dramatic distinctions in cases involving criminal rights. Bork,[59] for example, never advocated a pro criminal rights decision in an amicus curiae brief.

Thus, these findings are significant. Other research has documented the success of the solicitor general's office and the role it plays in determining cases to be appealed. The data analyzed here indicate that the "government's position" on issues may change, not only because of changes in administrations, but also by *each* solicitor general. In effect, a subtle, though substantial change in public policy may occur at a level where there is little public scrutiny.

NOTES

This article originally appeared in Volume 66, Number 6, December-January 1983, pages 256-264.

This research was funded by a faculty grant from Emory University. An earlier version of this article was delivered at the 1981 annual meeting of the American Political Science Association. The author would like to thank Lee Epstein for her invaluable assistance in collecting and analyzing this data. William Dixon also made several useful suggestions concerning presentation of the data. They, and Thomas Walker, Allen McDonogh and Stephen Wasby, read an earlier draft of this paper and made extensive comments and criticisms.

1. Puro, "The Role of the Amicus Curiae in the United States Supreme Court: 1920-1966," unpublished Ph.D. dissertation, SUNY Buffalo (1971); Puro, *The United States as Amicus Curiae* in Ulmer, ed., COURTS, LAW, AND JUDICIAL PROCESSES (New York: The Free Press, 1981); and Scigliano, THE SUPREME COURT AND THE PRESIDENCY (New York: The Free Press, 1971).

2. Puro, "The Role of the Amicus Curiae," *supra* n. 1; Krislov, *The Roles of the Attorney General as Amicus Curiae* in Huston, ed., ROLES OF THE ATTORNEY GENERAL OF THE UNITED STATES (Washington, D.C.: American Enterprise Institute, 1968).

3. Note, *The Solicitor General and Intragovernmental Conflict*, 76 MICH. L. REV. 327 (1977); Note, *Government Litigation in the Supreme Court: the Roles of the Solicitor General*, 78 YALE L. J. 1475 (1969).

4. Judiciary Act of 1870, ch. 150 §2, 16 Stat 162.

5. Rex E. Lee, the former Dean of the Brigham Young University Law School, was appointed by Ronald Reagan to succeed McCree.

6. LL.B. 1928, S.J.D. 1929.

7. Griswold, THE JUDICIAL PROCESS 22 (New York: Association of the Bar of the City of New York, 1973).

8. B.A. 1948, J.D. 1953.

9. Oelsner, *Government's Advocate*, N.Y. TIMES, July 18, 1981, sec. 1 at 9.

10. *Id.*

11. B.A. Fisk 1941, LL.B., 1948.

12. Scott, *Bell's Solicitor General-Designate Is a Precedent Setter*, THE WASHINGTON POST, Feb. 2, 1977, at D-2.

13. *Id.*

14. *See generally*, Brigman, "The Office of the Solicitor General of the United States," unpublished Ph.D. dissertation, University of North Carolina at Chapel Hill (1966).

15. Bork, *The Problems and Pleasures of Being Solicitor General*, 42 ANTITRUST L. J. 704 (1972-1973).

16. Interview with Solicitor General Wade H. McCree, Jr., 12 THIRD BRANCH 3 (August 1980).

17. In essence, the solicitor general is a classic "repeat player," Galanter, *Why the 'Haves' Come Out Ahead*, 9 L. & SOC'Y REV. 95 (1974).

18. Note, *Government Litigation*, *supra* n. 3; Note, *The Solicitor General*, *supra* n. 3; Sobeloff, *Attorney for the Government: the Work of the Solicitor General's Office*, 41 A.B.A. J. 229 (1955).

19. Griswold, *Rationing Justice—the Supreme Court's Caseload and What the Court Does Not Do*, 75 CORNELL L. REV. 344 (1975).

20. Fahy, *The Office of the Solicitor General*, 28 A.B.A. J. 22 (1942).

21. Thatcher, *Genesis and Present Duties of the Office of Solicitor General*, 17 A.B.A. J. 519 (1931); Sobeloff, *supra* n. 18; and Bork, *supra* n. 15.

22. Krislov, *supra* n. 2, at 89-92; Puro, "The Role of the Amicus Curiae,"; *supra* n. 1; Scigliano, *supra* n. 1.

23. According to one former attorney general, Justice Burger purported to speak on behalf of the entire Court when he noted the solicitor general's "highly important role in the selection of cases to be brought here." Bell, *The Attorney General: the Federal Government's Chief Lawyer and Chief Litigator, or One Among Many?* 46 FORDHAM L. REV. 1060-1061 (1978).

24. Werdegar, *The Solicitor General and Administrative Due Process*, GEO. WASH. L. REV. 482 (1967-68).

25. Bork, *supra* n. 15, at 705.

26. Puro, *The United States as Amicus Curiae, supra* n. 1, at 221.

27. Puro, "The Role of the Amicus Curiae," *supra* n. 1, at 143. Days, "Memo to Holders of U.S. Attorneys Manuals" (updates U.S. Attorneys Manual Title 8—Civil Rights Division) at 2 (May 23, 1980).

Charles J. Bonaparte was the first solicitor general (1906-1909) to use " amicus curiae briefs in an attempt to effect major social changes and implement broad public policies." [Quoted in Krislov, *supra* n. 2, at 80.]

Succeeding solicitors general believed that their briefs represented interests that had not already been heard. In addition, each, or at least those studied by Steven Puro, has felt his brief "to be supporting 'a positive civil liberties climate' or 'the public interest'." [Puro, "The Role of the Amicus Curiae," *supra* n. 1, at 247.]

28. Days, *supra* n. 27, at 1.

29. *Id.* at 2.

30. Scigliano, *supra* n. 1, at 180. O'Connor and Epstein, "An Overview of Interest Group Participation in Gender- and Racially-Based Employment Discrimination," paper delivered at the 1981 annual meeting of the Law and Society Association.

31. *Id.*

32. Scigliano, *supra* n. 1, at 180.

33. *Id.*

34. *Id.*

35. 442 U.S. 269 (1979).

36. Bell, *Office of Attorney General's Client Relationship*, 36 BUSINESS LAWYER 94-95 (1981).

37. 438 U.S. 265 (1978).

38. Califano, GOVERNING AMERICA: AN INSIDER'S REPORT FROM THE WHITE HOUSE 235-242 (New York: Simon and Schuster, 1981).

39. Per curiam cases were excluded from analysis. Although all cases were examined, only those involving an aspect of personal liberties, civil equality or criminal rights were included in this analysis. If more than one issue was contained in a case, i.e., both a civil equality and a criminal rights claim were present, the case was placed in the issue area which was stressed in the solicitor's brief.

40. This category includes all First Amendment claims, including free speech, conscientious objection and obscenity cases.

41. This category includes race- and gender-based discrimination claims, including school desegregation and employment discrimination cases.

42. This category includes Fourth, Fifth, Sixth, Seventh, and Eighth Amendment claims.

43. Although Griswold was appointed by Johnson, Puro notes that Griswold took cues from Nixon concerning what the solicitor's position should be. Puro, "Presidential Relationships with the Solicitors General of the United States: Political Research at Presidential Libraries," paper presented to Missouri and Kansas Political Science Association, at 5 (1978).

44. Scigliano, *supra* n. 1, at 186-187; Pritchett, THE ROOSEVELT COURT: A STUDY IN JUDICIAL POLITICS AND VALUES 207-208, 254 (New York: Times Books, 1948). *See contra*, however, Howard, COURTS OF APPEALS IN THE FEDERAL JUDICIAL SYSTEM: A STUDY OF THE SECOND, FIFTH AND DISTRICT OF COLUMBIA CIRCUITS 64 (Princeton, NJ: Princeton University Press, 1981).

45. 413 U.S. 376 (1973).

46. This case, while having both civil equalities and personal liberties overtones, was coded as a personal liberties claim because of the commercial speech aspect.

47. 433 U.S. 350 (1977).

48. 447 U.S. 74 (1980).

49. 402 U.S. 1 (1971).

50. 402 U.S. 33 (1971).

51. Greene v. Co. School Board of New Kent, 391 U.S. 430 (1968); Raney v. Board of Education of the Gould School District, 391 U.S. 450 (1968).

52. Monroe v. Board of Comm'r of the City of Jackson, 391 U.S. 450 (1968).

53. Jones v. Mayer, 392 U.S. 409 (1968).

54. Cleveland Board of Education v. LaFleur, 414 U.S. 632 (1973); General Electric Co. v. Gilbert, 429 U.S. 125 (1976).

55. Alexander-Gardner v. Denver, 415 U.S. 36 (1974); Johnson v. Ry. Express Agency, Inc., 421 U.S. 454 (1975); McDonald v. Santa Fe Trail Trans. Co., 427 U.S. 273 (1976).

56. Michigan v. Tucker, 417 U.S. 433 (1976).

57. Weatherford v. Bursey, 429 U.S. 545 (1977).

58. Profitt v. Florida, 428 U.S. 242 (1976); Gregg v. Georgia, 428 U.S. 153 (1976); Woodson v. North Carolina, 428 U.S. 280 (1976).

59. In *Brown v. Illinois*, 422 U.S. 590 (1975), the Memorandum for the United States as Amicus Curiae submitted by Bork urged the Court to remand the case for additional evidentiary materials before undertaking to resolve such a complex problem of Miranda warnings as was presented in the instant case. Thus, this amicus brief was not coded as pro- or anti-criminal defendants rights.

The ABA Standing Committee on Federal Judiciary: a contemporary assessment

The ABA's Standing Committee on Federal Judiciary is a major—and controversial—actor in the judicial selection process. How it plays its role is crucial to the quality of the bench.

by Elliot E. Slotnick

The changes instituted in the federal judicial selection process during the Carter years and the apparent return to "normalcy" during the Reagan administration have been the subject of considerable research, analysis, and debate.[1] Studies have focused on changes in the president's role in judicial selection, on the behavior of individual senators who created nominating panels in their states, and on the advice and consent role of the institution of the Senate as a whole. Scholars have looked at the processes of the panels that searched out candidates for most judgeships during the Carter years and some candidates during the Reagan administration.[2] And analysts are studying the outcome of the judicial selection process closely: the legacy of 258 federal judges appointed by Jimmy Carter largely as a consequence of the Omnibus Judgeship Act (OJA), and the 77 appointments President Reagan made in his first 20 months in office.[3]

Curiously, one major institutionalized actor in the judicial selection process has remained "underexamined" in recent years—the American Bar Association's Standing Committee on Federal Judiciary. The committee advises the president through his representatives in the Justice Department and makes its views known to the Senate and, most particularly, to the Senate Judiciary Committee. Unlike the nominating panels, the ABA committee does not generate names for judgeship vacancies, but at the request of the president or the Judiciary Committee, it evaluates the qualifications of nominees and of those being considered for nomination.

The lack of detailed analyses of the ABA committee's role in recent years is surprising in light of the controversy surrounding the committee. At the first public hearing of the Senate Judiciary Committee on judicial selection during the 96th Congress, for example, several senators and hearing witnesses were quick to criticize the committee's role and its operation. Speaking for the Judicial Selection Project, a broad-based interest group that monitored judicial recruitment activity, Charles Halpern asserted:

We object . . . to the quasi-official status that is sometimes given to that committee and to its recommendations . . . . We were troubled by the testimony of Attorney General Bell which seemed to think that the success of a judicial selection process could be measured by how many of the names submitted to the Senate have been [given a] very well qualified or exceptionally well qualified ABA imprimatur.[4]

Similarly, Senator Patrick Leahy (D-Vermont) noted,

[W]ith all due respect to the American Bar Association, there have been some . . . who have suggested that their very significant role in determining the qualifications of judges has been on some occasions like Jack the Ripper determining the qualifications of surgeons in 18th century England.[5]

More recently, in commenting on the Senate Judiciary Committee's willingness to make recommendations to the Senate in direct opposition to the ABA's findings, one reporter noted that the ABA committee was suffering from "the latest in a succession of attacks that have sent the committee's prestige plummeting to the lowest point in a decade."[6]

The workings of the ABA committee deserve fresh study in part because the existing literature is outdated,[7] and, more importantly, because the scope of the committee's task and the nature of its role have not been immune from the changes that resulted from the Omnibus Judgeship Act of 1978 and the 152 new federal judgeships it created. How did the ABA committee respond to the many changes in federal judicial recruitment processes and, ultimately, how have recent judicial recruitment reforms affected the role the ABA committee plays in judicial selection today?

In this analysis, we will not attempt to do an exhaustive historical examination of the ABA committee's operation or its evaluation processes. Rather, our aim—a less ambitious one—is to examine the least visible—and most controversial—aspects of the ABA committee's functioning. Our inquiry, based on interviews with the former chairperson and current chairperson of the committee, will be focused primarily on four broad concerns.

• First, we shall examine how the committee responded to the changing judicial selection environment of recent years.

• Second, we shall examine several aspects of the committee's decisional processes.

• Third, we shall attempt a broad, overall assessment of the committee's role in contemporary federal judicial selection processes.

• Finally, we shall move beyond this largely descriptive view of the ABA committee and examine empirically whether candidates who possess specific characteristics (males or graduates of elite law schools, for example) are more likely to receive a higher evaluation from the committee.

The changing environment

The Omnibus Judgeship Act of 1978 created an unprecedented workload for the ABA committee. In an "average" year, the committee evaluates about 40 potential lower federal court nominees; the OJA created 152 such vacancies at one time. It does not appear, however, that any fundamental changes occurred in the committee's traditional evaluation processes except for minor adjustments accomplished by re-activating some former committee chairs or temporarily transferring some current committee members to help alleviate burdens in circuits where the most judgeships were added. While the committee had contingency plans to add additional members to the body, the plans were never put into effect.

In short, the committee response to an incredible increase in workload was analogous to the responses of the federal judiciary to heavily concentrated caseloads in specific lower courts. "The simplest answer is that a lot of people worked harder than ever before," said Robert Raven, the former chairperson of the committee (1978-1980). "There was a larger commitment of time by those who served." Said the current chairperson, Brooksley Born:

We didn't change the committee structure or the nature of the investigation, although we did distribute the work somewhat differently. On the Fifth Circuit, for example, we allocated some of the heavy workload to other members or former chairmen or other former members of the committee.

In some respects, the committee's workload was not increased as drastically as the sheer numbers of the OJA might suggest. In the past, the names of several potential nominees might have been submitted to the committee for evaluation for a judicial vacancy, but the new nominating commissions structured and limited the president's options to fewer candidates, usually three to five. Subsequently, during the Carter years the ABA committee generally found itself evaluating the one candidate the president favored for each judicial post.

The ABA committee was quite conscious of the need to work efficiently and smoothly so that it would not be criticized for delaying the appointment process. On that score, Robert Raven asserted, "We have not been the bottleneck. We've always been ahead of the Senate Judiciary Committee . . . we were concerned . . . about a potential overload problem. We vowed that we wouldn't be the bottleneck."

More cooperation

But if the committee's internal operating processes did not change, the committee's relationship with the executive and with the Senate Judiciary Committee did change during the Carter years. From the perspective of the committee, all the changes were perceived to be beneficial as it began to work more closely with the governmental actors in the selection arena. When "problems" emerged during the investigation of potential nominees, the committee met early with the attorney general in an effort to avoid confrontations with the executive branch later in the selection process. The committee also developed a closer working relationship with the Senate Judiciary Committee; in one case, Senator Dennis DeConcini (D-Arizona) "arranged a meeting where we were asked to confer more with senators and their staffs," former chairperson Raven reported. The current chairperson, Brooksley Born, added, "To some extent there was a broader feed-in by us to the Judiciary Committee on the 'not qualifieds' earlier in the process."

Both ABA chairpersons felt that the independent investigatory arm established by the Judiciary Committee under Senator Edward M. Kennedy (D-Massachusetts) had a positive impact on the ABA-Senate relationship. "We're very much in favor of the committee's investigatory function. They can develop a record, under oath, that we can't," said Raven. "There grew a tendency for the investigators to come to us to ask for details and check further into some of our findings," said Born. The investigatory functions of the Senate and ABA bodies were "complementary," both ABA leaders said. The increased interaction during the Carter years continued during the most active periods of judicial recruitment of the Reagan presidency. Said Born:

I think part of the reason for the increased interaction during the Carter administration was the great number of people being appointed. The level of interaction remained high during the most active appointment period of the Reagan administration. Now, there are fewer appointments so the [overall] interaction has tailed off. Basically, the level of interaction has remained about the same.

Most favored status

In addition to the great increase in judgeships under the Omnibus Judgeship Act, the ABA committee worked in an environment during the Carter years characterized by the widespread participation of new groups and actors in the judicial selection arena and much greater publicity surrounding the selection process. Both Raven and Born applauded these efforts. "The more the merrier. With numerous concerns active the spotlight has really helped." Born noted that the narrow scope of the ABA's inquiry made participation of other interests desirable and beneficial. Other groups, however, faced great difficulties in matching the resources invested by the ABA committee in its investigatory process, she said. "You need a very supportive institution. There are a lot of people I can hand my work to [at Arnold and Porter, her law firm in Washington, D.C.]."

Thus, while encouraging other participants in the process, the ABA representatives agreed that they had a "most favored status" among participants and that this status was justifiable. According to Born, "It's historically based, and we put in more energy and resources and time . . . . The National Bar Association and the Federation of Women Lawyers try to do a much more limited investigation. For that reason, their reports do not carry the same amount of weight."

While President Reagan has significantly reduced the role of such groups in the recruitment process, Born contended that the reemergence of the ABA's monopoly of direct access to the selection process has not basically changed the committee's status or role.

I don't think that the role of the committee has changed; I think the role of other groups has changed. During the Carter Administration, we still had a 'most favored status' based on the amount of work we put in. During the Reagan Administration, the Justice Department has told the National Bar Association and the Federation of Women Lawyers that they would not deal with them directly as was the case during the Carter presidency. They were encouraged to give their views to our committee.

But this wasn't really a change, said Born, since the ABA committee always solicited the views of such groups, even during the Carter years.

The commissions and the ABA

Perhaps the most fundamental change in the environment in recent years was the proliferation of nominating commissions from 1977 to 1980 to aid President Carter and U.S. senators, most of them from his party, in designating nominees for federal judgeships. Though Robert Raven suggested that the creation of commissions was not as significant for the ABA role as, for example, the increased committee give-and-take with the executive branch and the Senate Judiciary Committee, one could argue that the nominating panels cut at the heart of the ABA committee's credibility if it opposed a nominee the panels had approved. In effect, the president could fall back on the commission's recommendation and remain insulated from the negative impact of a poor ABA rating. The president held an advantage in any disagreement with the ABA's findings since his panels were representative and included several attorneys from the region where an appointment was being made while the ABA's depended on an investigation predominately run by a single attorney from the region.[8]

While not agreeing with the logic behind this argument, both ABA committee chairpersons found its implications troublesome, particularly since it sometimes seemed to hold true in cases like that of Donald O'Brien, who was confirmed with relative ease to a federal judgeship in Iowa in 1978 despite vigorous ABA opposition.[9] According to Born:

There has been some tendency to say, where we have found a candidate 'not qualified' and a commission has been involved, that the commission has done an adequate job and how can we dare suggest that the candidate is not qualified—as in the O'Brien case. That attitude, which can be politically motivated, misses the point that the commissions cannot do as thorough a job with many candidates that we can do with one.

But, Born said, some changes in the ABA committee role could be traced to the commissions.

In the past, we were used more often as a screening commission. Now the nominating commissions do that. We now are a post-selection check. We continue to play a significant role in the in-depth investigations that the nominating commissions cannot do.

In discussing the ABA's "defeat" in the O'Brien case, Raven said that any damage to the committee from the incident flowed from a misunderstanding of its role.

The experience in the O'Brien hearing is one that is worrisome . . . . [W]e really perform a different function than most people think. People asked, 'How could the ABA find O'Brien unqualified?' The failure to appreciate our much different function gave us some trouble there. It would be similar to our finding someone qualified and the FBI then finding the individual unqualified. We view a different picture.

Despite the unhappy experience in the O'Brien case, Raven saw the commissions as a good and improving component of the recruitment process.

They have been successful in their primary function of bringing people forward who never before would have been considered, and this does not only refer to minorities . . . . The more independent the selection commissions become and the more they are perfected, the less difficult our job and everyone else's downstream in the process will become.

The representativeness of the judiciary

Perhaps the greatest controversy surrounding the ABA committee's operation in the context of con-temporary judicial selection has been the implications of its functioning for efforts aimed at increasing the representativeness of the federal bench on dimensions such as the race, gender, professional background, and age of those appointed to judgeships. Historically, critics have always said that the ABA committee favors appointees cast in its own image over non-traditional prospects. Thus, for example, Senator Philip Hart (D-Michigan) once complained at a congressional hearing to former ABA committee chair Bernard Segal about the committee's composition:

It does not include anyone very much younger than I am and I regret to say that is not very young, and it certainly does not include anybody whose color is different from mine. It represents the men who have demonstrated excellence in the practice of what you and I were prepared for when we were in law school—when a course on poverty law would have sounded like something that was suggested by somebody just arriving from the moon.[10]

In the wake of the Omnibus Judgeship Act, the question of the committee's representativeness returned to the fore.

At the beginning, the committee was top-heavy with corporate lawyers. Rigid standards—including lengthy trial experience for district court nominees—assured that the most lauded candidates fit the white, male, middle-aged mold of the committee itself. But the 1978 Omnibus Judgeship Act . . . provided a prod that . . . has forced the committee to deal with more disparate judicial nominees.[11]

Clearly, the committee has not enjoyed a good reputation among those concerned with increasing the ranks of the underrepresented on the federal bench and, indeed, the head of the predominantly black National Bar Association recently noted, "Blacks have long suspected that the ABA's rating of blacks has not been fair and is used primarily as a tool for maintaining segregated courts and for keeping strong black civil rights lawyers from becoming federal judges."[12]

A more representative committee

The committee's representativeness does concern Raven, though he argues that the committee is becoming more representative and that safeguards protect non-traditional candidates involved in the process. Brooksley Born, for example, is the first woman to chair the ABA committee—but she is also the only woman on the committee of 14. The committee also includes two black members and one Hispanic member. Raven admitted it was difficult for the committee to obtain all of the views it would ideally like to consider.

We're constantly working towards getting more representative views. The concern that too many of us are white, older, etc., is a real one. We want to change that if we can and are working hard at it. I know from experience how difficult this is to do. There's going to be difficulty in getting solo practitioners. We try to help out with the overload the job creates. Should there be an ABA subsidy? That's one thing we have to examine. Getting young people is also a problem.

But it isn't easy to achieve a committee both diverse and well-known among lawyers, Raven said.

The core of our process is trust in our committee members out there in the community. We need members who have a reputation in the legal community. When I first got on, a lot of lawyers didn't know me. That's one of the problems we're up against in bringing together a more diverse committee.

One reason that diversity is not easy to obtain is that committee members are required to perform a time-consuming service for the bar without pay while earning a living. Attorneys from large and lucrative practices can afford to participate—and these "traditional" attorneys give the committee immediate credibility in the field. It's harder for younger attorneys in a less traditional practice to sacrifice so much time.

But if the committee's representativeness is a problem, Raven denied any suggestion of institutionalized bias or racism in the committee's evaluations. At a Senate confirmation hearing where the issue was raised, he was quick to respond. "I don't mind getting beat about everytime we come down here," he said, "but I do mind being called racist."[13]

To make the committee more representative, reformers suggest that the ABA elect committee members instead of having them appointed by the ABA president. Raven did not favor such a change.

I wouldn't advocate electoral choice. Pretty soon you'd have bar politics into it . . . and there's not very much involved in it at this time. The most critical thing is to be sure that you're getting a good cross section of the community. And that has changed a lot. If you get good, decent people, then the system will work.

The ABA and affirmative action

What is the ABA committee's position on affirmative action in the judicial recruitment process? Did the committee evaluate prospective nominees from underrepresented groups differently from white males and, particularly during the Carter years, did the committee alter its standards to accommodate the president's avowed affirmative action effort?[14] According to Raven,

Judge Bell made it clear that he and the president had an affirmative action program. We'd like to think that we apply the same standards consistently, but I think that we have stretched a little, giving the benefit of the doubt with regard to minorities and women. Not a lot, but a little . . . . No points are given for race or sex . . . . We'll look for trial equivalent a little harder in women, for example, than we would in white males.

Born elaborated a bit on this effort:

We were quite concerned about criteria not having been met by women and/or minorities because of the realities of professional discrimination . . . . There were a number of women and minority candidates that we found 'qualified' despite the lack of 12 years at the bar. Less experience was sufficient in some women, but not for some white males.

Indeed, Born pointed out, 11 out of 13 Carter nominees with less than 12 years of legal experience were rated "qualified" or better by the ABA committee; the 11 included two white males, three white females, two black males, one black female, and three Hispanic males. The two candidates with less than 12 years of experience who were rated not qualified were a white male and a black male.

At bottom, Born asserted, the committee's actions were consistent with the guidelines spelled out in print by the ABA.

In evaluating experience, the committee recognizes that women and members of certain minority groups have entered the profession in large numbers only in recent years and that their opportunities for advancement in the profession may have been limited.[15]

The committee guidelines, however, do emphasize "that political activity and public service are valuable experiences, but that such activity and service are not a substitute for significant experience in the practice of law."[16]

A discriminatory impact?

When Raven was told that the ABA ratings during the Carter years were considerably lower in the aggregate for women and minorities than for white males, he noted that this had not been the case in the initial rounds of appointments. During that period, "The ratings for minorities stacked up well or better, [but] that hasn't been true since." His explanation was simple.

When you look at the universe or pool, there really isn't one for blacks, women, or Hispanics. The Administration has been going to younger people, which is the right way to go. Yet they're lighter on trial experience and breadth of experience. Consequently, they often come up with some awful good people who come out 'qualified' rather than 'well qualified.' In a few years they'd be 'well qualified.'

In effect, faced with a choice between less experienced minority and women jurists who had greater potential than more experienced minority and women attorneys in the pool, Raven supported the Carter administration's strategy of favoring potential, despite the fact that it meant those appointees would rate lower ABA ratings today.

Because of the alleged discriminatory impact of the committee's minimum experience and maximum age criteria, critics have called for change and the committee has considered reform. By 1980, the criterion of 12-15 years of legal experience (which had once been 15 years) had been softened to "at least 12 years."[17] Further, the committee was willing to *evaluate* a candidate without reference to his or her age—although it would still *judge* a candidate "not qualified by reason of age."[18] Aware of pragmatic and political realities, Mr. Raven noted, the president can make exceptions on candidates rated "not qualified by reason of age" and he has done so.[19] "They're in a better position to know the supply of good candidates, the state of an individual's health, etc."

Indeed, late in 1980, the ABA abandoned its rating of not qualified by reason of age. Born explained the reasons for the change.

It was a whole series of factors.
• First, the attitudes in society towards the elderly had changed a lot as evidenced, in part, by legislation not directly applicable to our work.
• Second, there was a joint resolution in Congress calling on us to abandon our age guideline.
• Third, we had always used those guidelines at the request of the administration, and our guidelines have always been reflections of theirs. President Reagan had said that he did not plan to have age guidelines for the selection of judges.
• Fourth, many [in the ABA] have felt that the age guidelines were not an appropriate standard for us to be applying. We characterize our activity as measuring candidates solely on professional standards . . . . [T]he age criterion was not necessarily consistent with our goal.

Committee processes

Perhaps the least analyzed area of the ABA committee's functioning is the processes through which it rates judgeship candidates as exceptionally well qualified, well qualified, qualified, or not qualified. Indeed, the most developed documentation of how the committee works is a pamphlet published by the American Bar Association itself.[20]

The ABA pictures the process this way. First, the attorney general sends the names of the prospective nominees (or of a single prospective nominee) to the chair of the ABA committee, who generally assigns the investigation to the committee member from the circuit with the vacancy. Once the prospective nominee returns an ABA-designed personal data questionnaire (PDQ) sent by the attorney general, the ABA committee initiates its independent investigation.

Utilizing data from the PDQ, the principal ABA investigator examines the legal writings of the candidate and conducts confidential interviews with judges, attorneys, law professors, and others who can offer an informed evaluation of the candidate. It should be noted that the ABA mandates a *representative* inquiry.

The circuit member interviews a representative sample of the profession in the community, including attorneys from different sized offices . . . who practice in different fields of law . . . legal services and public interest attorneys, women attorneys and attorneys who are members of various minority groups. Spokespersons of professional organizations including those representing women and minorities are also contacted . . . .[21]

If a "clear pattern" emerges from these steps, the investigation is brought to a quick conclusion. If questions remain unanswered or if disagreement about the candidate's merits arise, however, the investigation probes the problem area to reach a "fair and accurate assessment." The primary investigator, sometimes aided by another committee member, will meet with the candidate to pose any remaining questions or discuss ongoing problem areas.

At the conclusion of this process, the investigator or member prepares a written informal report for the committee chairperson, including a summary of the investigation and a recommended rating from the principal investigator. The chairperson then makes an informal report to the attorney general, passing on the substance of the ABA's findings and offering a tentative evaluation of the rating likely to result if a formal ABA report is requested.

If the attorney general wishes to proceed and requests a formal report, the primary investigator finishes the inquiry and prepares the document. The formal report and the PDQ are sent to all members of the ABA committee and each member informs the chairperson of his or her vote. If committee members raise questions at this stage, there may be a conference call or a committee meeting. When the committee reaches closure, the chairperson confidentially reports the rating to the attorney general and tells him whether it was reached "unanimously," by a "substantial majority," or by a "majority" of the committee.

Voting mechanisms

On paper, the process appears simple and well institutionalized. But several important issues deserve further study, including the actual voting mechanisms employed and their implications, possible switching in the ABA's ratings, and the safeguards it adopts to protect it from problems of an investigation generally dominated by one individual.

As noted above, the attorney general first discusses substantive information about a candidate with the ABA committee chairperson during the informal stage of the ABA process before the committee votes. It is not until a formal report is requested that the entire ABA committee becomes involved. Before the Omnibus Judgeship Act, the ABA committee members submitted each vote in writing, but as the workload increased, Robert Raven reported, "The influx of nominations led to phone-in calls of the votes to the ABA secretary in my office, with a written confirmation following." Raven recognized that the way the vote was reported could cause some confusion for the public.

A majority vote determines the rating. Quite often, the report will indicate to the attorney general or the Judiciary Committee, 'a substantial majority' which is 10 or more, or 'a minority found . . . .' That could be one person.

When asked why the report does not simply give the actual vote, Raven responded, "Maybe we should just use numbers. Now the Judiciary Committee wants the numbers on dissents, and they call me and I give it to them. I'm one of those who would do it by vote, so it's hard for me to make the other argument. We do make known what the areas of

debate were."

On the same issue, Born added:

We'll report pretty much what the numbers say . . . . The rationale for not reporting numbers is the undue pressure this could place on individual members of the committee. Both the attorney general and the Senate Judiciary Committee know what our system means in terms of votes. We may also get a call asking about the reasons offered by the minority and how many [minority votes] there were.

Despite the slower pace of judicial recruitment during the Reagan presidency, the committee still employs the phone-in voting procedure. "We found that was very efficient and allowed us to report our results to the Justice Department earlier," Born said.

Changing ratings in midstream

Closely related to questions of the committee's voting mechanism is the issue of whether the committee's rating changes between the informal and formal reports.[22] Bernard Segal, a former ABA Committee chairperson, indicated in a Senate Judiciary Committee hearing that fluctuation in the ABA rating was infrequent. Of the informal report, Segal stated, "It binds nobody, but it has proved to be a pretty good indication of the ultimate result . . . In 95 per cent of the cases (I'm guessing), the eventual rating in the full committee's formal report is the same as the preliminary informal report."[23] In his classic study of judicial selection, based on his first hand view of two years of recruitment during the Kennedy Administration, Harold Chase differed with Segal, contending that Segal's "guess was not very accurate." Said Chase:

In short, in the give and take of discussion, something happened in nearly 30 per cent of the cases, usually resulting in an upgrading. Of course, the informal report was never intended to be a finished product and perhaps the changes were not the consequence of persuasion by the men at Justice. But observation leads to the conclusion that a good part of them were.[24]

When they were told that Chase estimated 30 per cent of the votes changed between the informal and formal stages, both Raven and Born said Segal's estimate (95 per cent unchanged) was better. According to Raven:

I can't say about the past, but no, that's not the case today. That's not to say that it doesn't happen occasionally. That's one good thing about working closely with the Judiciary Committee and the attorney general. We get different points of view and might get into things much more in depth. Now, we can even go down on a recommendation. In no way, however, does any of that occur 30 per cent of the time. In the five years that I've been on the committee it hasn't happened one per cent of the time.

Born agreed that switching never amounted to 30 per cent, but she said discussions between the committee and the attorney general between the informal and formal reports have led to some switching.

There have been instances, particularly on minority candidates and women where there was much interaction with the attorney general and the White House. Much of the discussion focused on how standards should be applied, and we discussed standards in rather general terms. On one case, the attorney general asked for a reconsideration. We did a new investigation and got a new rating of 'qualified.'

Reliance on a single investigator

Perhaps the most frequent criticism of the ABA investigation process centers on its heavy reliance on the initial efforts of a single prime investigator. Critics argue that the process lacks sufficient safeguards. For example, Senator Howard Metzenbaum (D-Ohio) voiced his unhappiness to Robert Raven at a Judiciary Committee hearing.

One person from each circuit. That one person really does all of this investigation . . . . That one individual talks to everybody and then writes up the report. If that person has a preconceived idea, isn't there an element of subjectivity in that person, in that kind of an investigation? Don't we all hear what we want to hear and reject that which we don't want to hear? How do you assure yourself that the individual that has all the limitations that each of us has doesn't inject into the matter his own reaction as a practicing lawyer? . . . How do you protect yourself against that?

I must tell you that I practiced law all the time until I came to this body . . . . To this moment I haven't the slightest idea of who the individual is, nor did I ever know who the individual was that represented the American Bar Association in the Circuit in which I lived.[25]

Partly as a consequence of this investigatory process, the ABA committee encounters heavy criticism each time it finds a judicial candidate "not qualified"—and often the now tarnished candidate leads the attack. During the Carter Administration, Fred Gray, a black Alabama attorney who was found "not qualified," told the Senate Judiciary Committee at his nomination hearing that the allegations in the ABA report were based on "hearsay, conjecture,

surmise, and innuendos."[26] The president of the predominantly black National Bar Association raised the issue of racism. According to the *National Law Journal*, "NBA President Robert Harris called the Clemon-Gray reports a compilation of anonymous accusations, hearsay evidence and newspaper clippings that conclusively exposed the ABA techniques as an 'evaluation process that violated fundamental due process.' "[27]

Several of our questions focused on these kinds of concerns. We asked, for example, whether, in view of the committee's investigatory process, two hypothetical nominees identical in every respect could be given two different ABA ratings depending on the question of where the nominee was from. Yes, Raven agreed, but infrequently and only under certain circumstances.

I am quite confident that one could not be found 'qualified' versus 'unqualified.' The committee members raise questions about these distinctions. I could not tell you whether from time to time it has made a difference between 'qualified' and 'well qualified.' There's less focus on these distinctions and my function is to try and keep that as uniform as possible. It wouldn't happen on 'exceptionally well qualified' and 'well qualified' either.

Born echoed the view that the committee chairperson plays a central role in assuring consistency in the committee ratings. Admitting that the hypothetical scenario we presented "is theoretically possible," she added, "We do, however, have safeguards against it. All reports come to me first and are in depth. The role that the chair plays is really one of quality control. Have the right people been contacted? Is the recommendation proper based on the data?"

Better safeguards

Ultimately, both Raven and Born believe that the very nature of the committee membership and their methods of performing the task provided the best safeguards. Said Raven:

I think that the way we do our reports is a safeguard. Committee members must put down as completely as possible their full interview . . . . We've recently gone more and more, whenever there's a problem, to having two interviews with the candidate. Sometimes I've had three teams of interviewers: first, two lawyers from the committee; then some former chairmen; and finally, two more lawyers to interview the candidate. We think that the people on the committee are not going to lie.

Now that we go to additional interviewers, however,

we think it will give us more credibility. It's like any institution. Procedures improve over time, and our reports are much better now than earlier ones. In the past, there were no lengthy conclusions where committee members laid bare their souls. Now they do that. Now our members are, effectively, writing a brief.

Born, too, placed great importance on the nature of the committee's members and the way they operated to assure committee integrity.

[A] safeguard comes from the nature of the committee and the independent-mindedness of its members. Sometimes, in fact, a majority will vote against the recommendation in the initial report. Thirdly, all members feel free to pursue their doubts. Members call and question each other, there are exchanges of correspondence, etc. Finally, there is the most important check of all. When we find it beginning to appear as if things are moving towards a 'not qualified,' we bring other members of the committee into the investigatory process.

The role of the ABA committee

Assessing the role of the ABA's Standing Committee on Federal Judiciary in the federal judicial selection process is clearly not easy. It is oversimplistic and sensational to assert, as Joseph Goulden did, that, "Put most simply, the ABA wants to exercise professional birth control over the judiciary, but not take full responsibility for doing so."[28] It is equally overdrawn and inaccurate to call the committee chairman "The Judge Maker," as Goulden did, and to argue that if a lawyer is found not qualified under standards set by the ABA committee, "the President will not nominate him for office."[29]

But presidents greatly desire smooth sailing for their judgeship candidates before the ABA committee, and it is unusual for candidates to be nominated and appointed over ABA opposition.[30] Just how often have the ABA committee's rating and findings led the president to abort a prospective nomination? "It's hard to estimate," said Born. "Most of it happens when we don't even hear about it." Raven added, "That's a touchy thing. We can't talk about them as specific matters and, at least in the past, we didn't keep records of the thing. It's not a high percentage figure, although that's where we do our best work."

Of course, the ABA's ratings are a two-edged sword for the appointing authorities and the committee is sometimes "used" by senators and the president as a scapegoat for a nomination that simply will not fly but which, for political reasons,

must be floated. In effect, the official pays a political debt in a currency that cannot be collected on—through no fault of the debtor. Born commented:

I have a feeling that the president and the attorney general have used our committee and its standards as a grounds for telling senators that a nominee won't make it . . . . That is our function. It's one of the reasons we come in for criticism. We can be the fall guy or the excuse for a senator.

The ABA committee does not exercise an iron-clad veto over judicial appointments, but critics argue the bar would prefer such power. Should the ABA be granted a veto power? Raven and Born thought that such a policy would be inappropriate. Should an ABA finding of "not qualified" be a sufficient basis for the president to end consideration of a candidate or for the Senate to reject one? Raven said no, "not in and of itself."

We feel first that we need a good explanation. Then they have to satisfy themselves. We're relying on the facts and we think that they'll do so as well. We can be wrong and we don't feel that we're the one infallible institution on earth. We also appreciate that there can be political considerations which are none of our affair. We appreciate that in the whole process what we look at—competency, integrity, judicial temperament—is not the whole thing. The issue of whether a nominee should be appointed is a much larger question.

Born further underlined the multifaceted and inherently political nature of appointment transactions which were not factors entering the committee's calculus.

The president and the Senate have the selection role. They're the political bodies which have the constitutional role. They should take our report into consideration. Obviously, they have other considerations. On the U.W. Clemon case, it was legitimate, as a senator, to weigh the problems with the appointment against the enormous need to have a black judge in Alabama. The Senate must make an evaluative judgment of whether to take appointment risks. We make fairly narrow judgments and report on that.

Yet while eschewing any desire for an absolute veto, Raven and Born recognized that the ABA committee enjoys a "most favored status" among interests active in the process, and they thought such a position was quite justifiable. Said Raven:

It's justifiable in one area we purport to cover. We're a conduit for the perspective of the legal community back to the president and the Senate Judiciary Committee on the competency, integrity, and best guess on judicial temperament. In that area, we do get and deserve to get a high degree of credibility.

Since the ABA committee's rankings are so important in the judicial selection process, it would make sense to assess the performance of federal judges in light of their ABA ratings. "Somebody ought to look at that, but it shouldn't be us," said Raven. "One, we haven't got the time and, secondly, people that do the rating shouldn't evaluate how they did. It would be a tremendous project. We'd have to give some cooperation to give information from our committee investigations."

While clearly a difficult task, a project aimed at evaluating the ABA's evaluations would not face intractable problems—if researchers could develop an acceptable gauge of judicial performance. The project, however, should constitute a high priority for future research in this area.

The committee's performance

Almost since the ABA Standing Committee on Federal Judiciary was established in 1946, critics have argued that it tends to bias its rankings in favor of the dominant groups in the bar, the successful "elites" who possess the credentials the committee (consciously or unconsciously) looks for.[31] No one has systematically investigated these allegations of bias, however, largely because it has been difficult to gather the personal data about federal judicial candidates needed to substantiate such charges.[32] Thus, it has not been clear to what extent specific background characteristics (attending a high status law school, for example) are correlated with a higher ABA ranking. (This, of course, is a separate concern from the question of whether specific characteristics *should* be correlated with that ranking.)

As a result of the major reforms in judicial recruitment and judicial selection initiated by the president and others during the Carter Administration, that comparison is now possible. During the 96th Congress (1979-80), the Senate Judiciary Committee, in the context of the Omnibus Judgeship Act and the 152 new federal judgeships it created, required nominees to complete extensive Personal Data Questionnaires (PDQs) before a nomination hearing was held on a candidate. The analysis that follows relies on the completed questionnaire responses of 213 judgeship candidates.[33]

The detailed questionnaires contain a wealth of comparable data of a kind previously difficult or impossible to obtain. The questionnaires are likely to be valid since they constituted a record, submitted under oath, on which members of the judiciary committee, the Senate, the press, other interested parties and the general public would scrutinize a nominee.

This kind of investigation is important in light of recent developments in judicial selection. President Carter nominated more non-traditional candidates during his presidency than any other president—40 women, 38 blacks, and 16 Hispanics and members of other minority groups.[34] He had instructed the newly-created circuit judge nominating commission to take affirmative action to recruit qualified women and minority candidates for the bench, and he encouraged senators to do the same, whether or not they employed nominating commissions to help generate names for district court vacancies.[35]

By studying the characteristics of the different candidates chosen under this new system, we can perhaps see more distinctly the differing qualities of the traditional and "non-traditional" candidates—measured in terms of what might be called "establishment" values. This comparison may help us understand why groups which have not generally shared the opportunity to achieve the qualifications embodied in those norms (attendance at a high status law school, for example) expect the ABA to look beyond traditional values when it evaluates them, since they were largely excluded from competing for many of the "honors" by which traditional candidates are judged.

Further, the extent to which the quality of non-traditional candidates does not emerge clearly on the ABA's metric is a strong indication of the glaring need for nominating authorities to develop evaluative mechanisms which are more sensitive to the legal experiences and professional backgrounds such candidates have to offer.

Demographic characteristics

Our study first examined the relationship between the nominee's rating and his or her age, political party affiliation, race, religion, place of birth, sex, and income.[36] Political party and religion were not related to the nominees' ABA rankings, but all of the other demographic variables were significantly related to the ABA designation.

• Candidates who were born in the district or circuit of their appointment, for example, tended to earn a higher ABA rating than those who were

Table 1   ABA ratings and candidate income

	Under $20,000 N=3	$20-40,000 N=29	$40-60,000 N=61	$60-80,000 N=43	$80-100,000 N=17	Over $100,000 N=37
Exceptionally well qualified	—%	7%	7%	5%	6%	14%
Well qualified	—	38	46	42	59	57
Qualified	100	52	48	49	35	30
Not qualified	—	3	—	5	—	—

Tau C = -0.14, significance = 0.01

Table 2A   ABA ratings and sex, race, and candidate status

	Sex		Race		Candidate status	
	Male N=179	Female N=34	White N=163	Non-white N=50	Non-traditional N=77	White-male N=136
Exceptionally well qualified	8%	3%	9%	2%	3%	10%
Well qualified	51	18	52	24	22	59
Qualified	40	79	39	70	73	31
Not qualified	2	—	1	4	3	1

Sex: Tau C = 0.20, significance = 0.00
Race: Tau C = 0.26, significance = 0.00
Candidate status: Tau C = -0.41, significance = 0.00

not. (Tau C = 0.11)[37]

• ABA ratings were related to the candidate's income for the five-year period before the judicial nomination (Table 1). Over two-thirds of those earning over $80,000 per year received one of the two highest ABA designations; only 48 per cent of those earning under $80,000 received such ratings.

• Males were nearly three times more likely than females to receive one of the ABA's two highest designations, and whites were three times more likely to win such ratings than non-white judgeship candidates (Table 2A).

When we combine the race and sex variables to see what happens with the non-traditional appointee (those who are not white males), the correlation of candidates and ratings was even more graphic. Nearly 10 per cent of the white male designates received exceptionally well qualified ratings, and over two-thirds of the white males received one of the ABA's two highest recommendations. But only three per cent of non-traditional candidates received the highest rating, and only one-fourth of those candidates earned one of the two highest designations.

Is there a relationship between age and ABA rankings, as critics contend? Table 2B dramatically reveals that candidate rankings do improve, in the aggregate, as the chronological age of candidates increases. Perhaps this correlation reflects, in part, the fact that professional experiences and success also improve with age. Clearly, however, finding a candidate unqualified by reason of age was not

tantamount to a poor ABA ranking of a candidate's professional credentials.[38] Indeed, nearly all (87 per cent) of the candidates in the 60-69 age group received a rating in the ABA's two highest categories, but only 28 per cent of the 30-39 age group earned a well-qualified rating, and none of them was found exceptionally well qualified.

The strong relationships between several demographic characteristics of nominees and their ABA rankings must be interpreted cautiously. It is possible that the relationships are spurious and reflect professional qualifications and experiences which, presumably, translate more directly into measures of a nominee's qualifications and which disproportionately characterize identifiable racial, sexual, income, and age groups among nominees. Many of these variables will be explored below and several of them correlate with ABA ratings as well.

It should be underlined, however, as research reported elsewhere has shown, that "quality" insofar as that concept is tapped by some of the variables under analysis, is not monopolized by one racial or sexual group among judicial candidates.[39] To argue that race or sex, for example, are merely summary variables which can serve as surrogates for the nature of the candidates' legal training and experiences simply will not wash. Put bluntly, race and sex do not distinguish the more qualified candidates from the less qualified ones.

ABA ratings and education

Several of our variables measured facets of the

Table 2B   ABA ratings and candidate age

	30-39 N=22	40-49 N=75	50-59 N=96	60-69 N=15
Exceptionally well qualified	—%	5%	6%	3%
Well qualified	27	35	58	53
Qualified	68	59	35	7
Not qualified	5	1	—	7

Tau B = -0.32, significance = 0.00

Table 3   ABA ratings and law school attended

	'Elite' N=86	Non-elite N=122
Exceptionally well qualified	12%	4%
Well qualified	48	45
Qualified	40	49
Not qualified	1	2

Tau C = 0.13, significance = 0.03

Table 4   ABA ratings of district judge candidates and legal aid experience

	Legal aid experience N=45	No legal aid experience N=117
Exceptionally well qualified	4%	3%
Well qualified	27	50
Qualified	67	45
Not qualified	2	2

Tau C = -0.16, significance = 0.01

Table 5   ABA ratings and candidate clerking experience

	No experience N=164	Experience N=44
Exceptionally well qualified	4%	20%
Well qualified	47	43
Qualified	48	36
Not qualified	2	—

Tau C = -0.14, significance = 0.01

judicial candidates' educational training and background, including the type of college and law school the candidate attended (public, private, or Ivy League), the location of the law school (within or outside the state or circuit of the candidate's appointment), the honors the candidate received during his or her legal training, and the "elite" status of the law school.

For the most part, the relationships we found were insignificant and insubstantial. We saw no relationship whatsoever between the public, private or Ivy status of the candidate's college and law school or its location and ABA designation. In other words, the committee does not give better ratings to graduates of schools in the home region or any other region.

Recipients of law school honors were slightly more likely, however, to receive higher ABA ratings (61 per cent of these candidates were rated well or exceptionally well qualified compared to 50 per cent of the candidates without law school honors),[40] but this relationship was not statistically significant (Tau C = 0.10, Significance = 0.06).

The only statistically significant relationship between an educational variable and ABA ratings was that graduates of "elite" law schools were more likely to receive higher ABA designations.[41] In fact, alumni of elite law schools were nearly three times more likely to receive the ABA's highest recommendation than candidates graduated from other institutions (Table 3).

Admittedly, our measures of educational training and backgrounds do not include all the factors contributing to the quality of an attorney's formal legal training but it does appear that the *nature* of

the law school a candidate attended and the strength of his or her law school performance are related, albeit moderately, to the ABA ratings.

Political activity of nominees

Throughout the years, the ABA committee had steadfastly maintained that political considerations do not enter into its evaluations of candidates; it is guided solely by professional concerns. Commentators have pointed out that politics certainly affect the *president's* final nominee; President Carter, for example, appointed Democrats in 86 per cent of his judicial nominations.[42] But do politically active nominees receive higher (or lower) ABA ratings?

The judiciary committee questionnaires measured the frequency of speechmaking by the candidate and the candidate's service as a public official, as a candidate for elective non-judicial office, or in a significant role in a political campaign. We found no statistically significant relationship between any of these variables and a candidate's ABA rating. In short, the political activity of a nominee, as we measured it, was not a factor in the ABA evaluation of candidates.

The legal career of nominees

The legal and litigation experience of judgeship candidates should putatively be most strongly associated with ABA rankings. Our data measured a candidate's legal career in terms of his or her last job prior to nomination to the bench, years at bar, prosecutorial experience, judicial experience, legal aid experience, clerkship experience, publica-

Table 6 ABA ratings and candidate publication record

	No publications N=83	1-10 publications N=102	More than 10 N=21
Exceptionally well qualified	6%	6%	19%
Well qualified	36	51	62
Qualified	57	41	19
Not qualified	1	2	—

Tau C = -0.18, significance = 0.00

Table 7 ABA ratings and highest court before which a candidate has been admitted to practice

	State court N=7	Federal district N=40	Federal circuit N=48	U.S. Supreme Court N=111
Exceptionally well qualified	—%	3%	4%	11%
Well qualified	43	28	52	50
Qualified	57	70	42	39
Not qualified	—	—	2	2

Tau B = -0.19, significance = 0.00

tion record, and the highest court before which a candidate was admitted to practice. The correlation between these legal career variables and ABA ratings varied greatly.

A candidate's last job prior to nomination was *not* related to the ABA rating received, and a candidate's possession (or lack) of prosecutorial experience was also not related to the ABA designation. Perhaps of greater interest (and surprise) we found that judicial experience was not related to the ABA rating. Other legal career variables, however, demonstrated more robust relationships with the ABA rankings.

Though not statistically significant in the aggregate, candidates who had legal aid experience in their background tended to receive lower ABA ratings (Tau C = 0.10, Significance = 0.07). As Table 4 reveals, this relationship is strong and statistically significant when we analyze district judge nominees separately. Fewer than one-third of the district candidates with legal aid experience were rated well qualified or exceptionally well qualified, but half the candidates who did not count substantial legal aid experience in their professional backgrounds received one of those designations.

Table 5 reveals that prestigious clerkships with federal judges or state supreme court justices were positively associated with one's ABA ranking. Candidates with clerking experience were nearly six times more likely to attain the ABA committee's highest endorsement. Presumably, the factors which make an attorney an attractive candidate for a high status clerkship also render him or her a more

attractive candidate for a judgeship.

Similarly, candidates with professional publication records and those who have been admitted to practice before higher level courts also tend to earn higher ABA designations (Tables 6 and 7). Indeed, over 80 per cent of the candidates with extensive publication records received a well qualified or better rating, and over 60 per cent of those admitted to practice before the U.S. Supreme Court were similarly ranked.

The most dramatic relationship in this area that we found was that high ABA ratings were associated with the length of one's legal experience—years at bar. As Table 8 shows, no candidate received an exceptionally well qualified rating with less than 16 years of legal experience; more than half of those receiving this rating had over 25 years of legal experience, and nearly half had over 30. Indeed, over 80 per cent of those with more than 30 years of legal experience were rated well qualified or exceptionally well qualified.

Taken together, the relationship between legal experience variables and ABA ratings presents somewhat of a mixed bag. Judicial experience by itself did not appear to upgrade the ABA committee's view of a candidacy, but clerkships, professional publications, and admission to practice before higher courts were associated with positive ABA evaluations. The somewhat conservative bent of the ABA's evaluation of candidates' legal careers is best revealed by the negative relationship (particularly for trial court candidates) between ABA rat-

Table 8 ABA ratings and legal experience

	6-10 yrs. N=2	11-15 yrs. N=24	16-20 yrs. N=33	21-25 yrs. N=51	26-30 yrs. N=50	More than 30 N=48
Exceptionally well qualified	—%	—%	2%	8%	4%	15%
Well qualified	—	17	42	39	52	67
Qualified	100	79	52	53	40	19
Not qualified	—	4	—	—	4	—

Tau C = -0.28, significance = 0.00

Table 9A   ABA ratings and nominees' federal litigation workload

	0-10% N=83	11-50% N=63	51-89% N=37	90-100% N=15
Exceptionally well qualified	2%	8%	14%	13%
Well qualified	43	54	51	33
Qualified	53	37	32	53
Not qualified	1	2	3	—

Tau B = -0.14, significance = 0.02

Table 9B   ABA ratings and nominees' state litigation workload

	0-10% N=15	11-50% N=55	51-89% N=74	90-100% N=55
Exceptionally well qualified	7%	13%	7%	2%
Well qualified	40	49	50	44
Qualified	53	36	42	53
Not qualified	—	2	1	2

Tau B = 0.10, significance = 0.05

Table 9C   ABA ratings and nominees' civil litigation workload

	0-10% N=5	11-50% N=27	51-89% N=64	90-100% N=102
Exceptionally well qualified	—%	11%	9%	5%
Well qualified	20	37	38	58
Qualified	80	52	50	36
Not qualified	—	—	3	1

Tau B = -0.12, significance = 0.03

ings and legal aid experience, a "non-traditional" professional pursuit, particularly when we juxtapose that result with the strong association between ABA ratings and years at bar.

Litigation experience

We measured the litigating experience of the nominees through nominees' estimates of the frequency of their court appearance, the percentage of their litigation in federal, state, or other courts, and the percentage of their litigation that involved civil matters versus criminal concerns. Since candidates provided detailed case studies of the 10 most significant legal matters that they, in their view, had handled during their careers, we decided to code each case on a number of variables for each nominee. We then measured the percentage of the case studies arising in the federal courts, the percentage involving civil law, and the percentage involving appellate courts. Each case study was also coded according to its subject matter so we could operationalize the concept of a "non-traditional" legal practice in terms of the subject matter of all the cases together.[43]

The data revealed that a nominee's frequency of litigation experience was not related to his or her ABA rating. As Tables 9A, 9B and 9C demonstrate, however, the nature and mix of one's litigating experience was significantly (albeit moderately) related to the ABA rating received. Thus, the ABA ratings of candidates tended to be somewhat higher as their relative federal litigation load increased (Table 9A), as their state litigation load decreased (Table 9B), and as their civil litigation load increased (Table 9C).

In the 10 case studies volunteered by the nominees, our results were mixed. We found no apparent relationship between the amount of federal or civil litigations selected by nominees as among their most important cases and the ABA rating they received. However, ABA ratings did tend to increase as the percentage of appellate litigation identified by respondents increased (Table 10). And in terms of the subject matter of the candidate's 10 case studies, nominees with "traditional" legal practices fared better than appointees characterized as being engaged in a "non-traditional" legal practice (Table 11). Indeed, slightly more than half of the nominees whose legal practices were characterized as nontraditional received the ABA's two lesser rankings, and all of the candidates found not qualified by the ABA were characterized as pursuing a non-traditional legal practice based on their case studies.

Clearly, the strongest relationship between ABA ratings and a career variable emerged on our mea-

Table 10   ABA ratings and appellate matters included in a nominee's 10 case studies

	No appellate matters N=15	10-30% N=42	40-60% N=57	70-90% N=44	All appellate N=8
Exceptionally well qualified	—%	—%	9%	16%	—%
Well qualified	20	48	58	45	50
Qualified	80	52	32	34	50
Not qualified	—	—	2	5	—

Tau C = -0.15, significance = 0.00

Table 11   ABA ratings and subject matter of nominee case studies

	Traditional practice N=93	Non-traditional practice N=78
Exceptionally well qualified	6%	8%
Well qualified	57	40
Qualified	37	49
Not qualified	—	4

Tau C = 0.15, significance = 0.03

sure of the years of legal experience that a nominee possessed. The larger picture emerges of a rating system that tends to give the highest rankings to candidates whose legal careers have followed the well-worn paths of those who have successfully traveled the road before them.

Conclusions

For the most part, the variables that were most associated with ABA rankings tended to be demographic and legal career variables, not education or political activity. Despite ABA assertions that committee judgments are based entirely on professional considerations, it is noteworthy that some of the demographic measures tended to be associated even more strongly with ABA ratings than were some professional concerns. Indeed, the strongest possible relationship that emerged in our analysis was that between the ABA rating and the candidate's white male status. In addition, very strong positive relationships were also found among ABA rankings, chronological age, and legal experience.

More moderate, albeit statistically significant, relationships were found among several other variables. For example, the ABA tended to give higher marks to identifiable subgroups under each of our variables, including:

• those who were admitted to practice before the Supreme Court, and those who practiced predominantly before federal and appellate tribunals;

• those who practiced predominantly in civil litigation and in the traditional subject areas of the law;

• those who were born in the jurisdiction of their appointment;

• those who attended elite law schools;

• those who had at one time achieved a prestigious legal clerkship; and

• those who earned relatively higher incomes than other candidates.

Surely the aggregate data do not in any sense

establish with perfect symmetry that specific traits invariably lead to higher ABA ratings for judgeship candidates. The correlations do demonstrate convincingly, however, that the ABA and its Standing Committee on Federal Judiciary do not approach the judicial selection process in a political vacuum. Rather, like all groups active in the political process, the ABA and its standing committee are composed of individuals responding to political events from a value structure and perceptions of self and societal interests not necessarily shared by all interested parties in the political arena.

So long as we understand the perspective the ABA brings to judicial selection, so long as we realize that it tends to favor traditional candidates, we can respect its efforts to offer guidance to the president and the Senate. But we must also recognize the importance of allowing other groups to have an institutionalized voice and to bring their values, values that are equally relevant, to the selection process. If we truly intend to make the judiciary more representative and more sensitive and responsive to the complexities of contemporary litigation, several prescriptions appear to be warranted.

Clearly, the ABA committee must redouble its already considerable efforts to represent the diversity of the constituency it speaks on behalf of—the organized bar. More to the point, committee members of every stripe must recognize that non-traditional judgeship candidates, in the aggregate, will not present the same credentials as their white male counterparts, but this difference does not necessarily render the non-traditional candidates inferior choices for judgeships.

Most importantly, we must not seek a remedy for the narrowness of perspectives that nominating authorities receive on judgeships solely by altering the nature of the ABA committee composition or its evaluative standards and processes. Like all interests in the American political process, the ABA committee ultimately retains both the right and the responsibility to press for its own views and values. That we must expect and accept.

The paramount problem, however, is that the ABA committee holds a monopoly as an institutionalized, nongovernmental voice in the federal judicial selection process. Important ameliorative steps were taken during the Carter administration to expand the scope of interests whose evaluative perspectives were sought out in assessing the merit of judgeship candidates. Thus, for example, both the predominantly black National Bar Association and the Federation of Women Lawyers submitted their evaluations directly to the Justice Department during the Carter years.

With the Reagan administration's return to "business as usual," however, the ABA committee possesses not only its "most favored status" but a virtual exclusivity in the right to participate in the selection process. Such monopolization of access is not appropriate if we truly would like to see the federal bench become as diverse in composition as the nation it serves.

NOTES

This article originally appeared in two issues—Volume 66, Number 8, March 1983, pages 348-362, and Volume 66, Number 9, April 1983, pages 385-393.

The author wishes to thank the Graduate School of The Ohio State University for its generous support of his research. He also wishes to thank Robert Raven, former chairperson of the ABA Standing Committee on Federal Judiciary, and Brooksley Born, the current chairperson, for their time and their candidness in his interviews with them.

1. For the most comprehensive studies of the Carter reforms, see Berkson and Carbon, THE UNITED STATES CIRCUIT JUDGE NOMINATING COMMISSION: ITS MEMBERS, PROCEDURES, AND CANDIDATES (Chicago: American Judicature Society, 1980); and Neff, THE UNITED STATES DISTRICT JUDGE NOMINATING COMMISSIONS: THEIR MEMBERS, PROCEDURES, AND CANDIDATES (Chicago: American Judicature Society, 1981).

2. President Reagan abolished the U.S. Circuit Judge Nominating Commission on May 4, 1981, in an Executive Order. See Stiegler, U.S. Circuit Judge Nominating Commission abolished by Reagan, 65 JUDICATURE 44 (1981). In about 15 states, Republican senators (and some Democrats) have now established nominating panels to help them choose U.S. district judges for the districts in their states. See Fowler, Judicial Selection Under Reagan and Carter: A Comparison of Initial Recommendation Procedures, YALE L. & POL. REV. (Spring 1983). President Reagan has encouraged the use of such panels. See Stiegler, Selecting federal judges during the Reagan Administration, 64 JUDICATURE 427 (1981). At the height of these commissions in 1979, Democratic and some Republican senators had created such panels in 29 states. See Neff, supra n. 1.

3. See, e.g., Goldman, Reagan's judicial appointments at midterm: shaping the bench in his own image, 66 JUDICATURE 334 (1983); Collins, Reagan naming fewer minorities, women to bench, USA TODAY, November 19, 1982, at 8A; Cohodas, Reagan's Judicial Selections Draw Differing Assessments, 41 CONG. Q. 83 (January 15, 1983); and Cohodas, Reagan Slow in Appointing Women, Blacks, Hispanics to Federal Judiciary Seats, 39 CONG. Q. 2559 (December 26, 1981).

4. Testimony of Charles Halpern before the Senate Judiciary Committee on Selection and Confirmation of Federal Judges, 96th Cong., 1st Sess., January 25, 1979, Serial No. 96-21. See also Slotnick, The changing role of the Senate Judiciary Committee in judicial selection, 62 JUDICATURE 508 (1979).

5. Id.

6. Klement, Blacks, ABA Spar Over Judges, NATIONAL LAW JOURNAL, August 4, 1980, at 3.

7. For a representative cross section of the literature focusing on the ABA committee and its role in federal judicial selection processes, see Grossman, LAWYERS AND JUDGES (New York: John Wiley and Sons, 1965); Chase, FEDERAL JUDGES: THE APPOINTING PROCESS (Minneapolis: University of Minnesota Press, 1972); and Goulden, THE BENCHWARMERS (New York: Weybright and Talley, 1974).

8. For further development of this point, see Slotnick, The U.S. Circuit Judge Nominating Commission, 1 LAW POL'Y Q. 491-492 (1979).

9. See, e.g., The politics of merit (editorial), THE WALL STREET JOURNAL, October 23, 1978, at 24.

10. Goulden, supra n. 7, at 43.

11. Klement, supra n. 6, at 46.

12. Id. at 45.

13. Id.

14. President Carter urged his U.S. Circuit Judge Nominating Commission "to make special efforts to seek out and identify well-qualified women and members of minority groups as potential nominees." Executive Order 12059, May 11, 1978. He urged the district judge panels which senators were creating to give "public notice" of vacancies and to make "an affirmative effort . . . to identify qualified candidates, including women and members of minority groups." Executive Order 12097, November 8, 1978.

For a discussion of Carter's affirmative action program, see Lipshutz and Huron, Achieving a more representative federal judiciary, 62 JUDICATURE 483 (1980). See also Berkson and Carbon, supra n. 1; Neff, supra n. 1; and Slotnick, "Affirmative Action and Judicial Selection During the Carter Administration," paper delivered at the annual meeting of the American Political Science Association, Denver, Colorado, September 2-5, 1982.

15. American Bar Association, STANDING COMMITTEE ON FEDERAL JUDICIARY: WHAT IT IS AND HOW IT WORKS 3 (Chicago: ABA, 1980).

16. Id. at 4.

17. The Senate had passed (97-0) Senate Resolution 374 on April 1, 1980, urging the ABA to end discrimination against potential federal judges on the basis of arbitrary age barriers. The House passed a similar resolution (House Resolution 693) by a vote of 341-19 on November 17, 1980.

At the Mid-Winter meeting of the ABA, February 1981, the Standing Committee announced in its "Report to the House of Delegates" that it was discontinuing the use of its age guidelines and the rating "Not Qualified by Reason of Age."

18. Supra n. 15, at 6.

19. One example of an older candidate whom a president appointed despite her age is Sara Hughes, chosen by President Kennedy in 1961 at the age of 65. See Goulden, supra n. 7, at 61, 62.

Of course, presidents sometimes reject candidates ostensibly on the basis of their age, but in reality for other reasons. President Carter, for example, would not nominate Archibald Cox for a vacancy in the first circuit, though Cox was the Commission's first choice, largely because Carter wanted to punish Cox's chief proponent, Senator Kennedy, who was running against Carter in the primaries. See Healy, Carter won't name Cox to federal judgeship, BOSTON GLOBE, August 3, 1979, at 1.

20. Supra n. 15, at 6-8.

21. Id. at 6.

22. One publicly-known example of switching involved the case of Charles Winberry, Jr. The Senate Judiciary Committee rejected his nomination on March 4, 1980—the first time it had rejected a federal judicial nominee in 42 years. The ABA committee had first found Winberry qualified, but it reversed its position later and found him unqualified. See Senate Panel Rejects Winberry Nomination, 38 CONG. Q. 674 (March 8, 1980).

23. Chase, supra n. 7, at 135.

24. Id.

25. Testimony of Senate Howard Metzenbaum before the Hearing of the Judiciary Committee of the U.S. Senate on the Selection and Confirmation of Federal Judges, 96th Cong., 1st Sess., January 25, 1979, Serial No. 96-21.

26. *Federal Jude Nominee Disputes ABA Criticism*, THE WASHINGTON POST, May 29, 1980.

27. Klement, *supra* n. 6, at 46.

28. Goulden, *supra* n. 7, at 40.

29. *Id.* at 39.

30. In the period we studied, only three persons received Senate confirmation despite ABA ratings of "not qualified." Donald E. O'Brien of Iowa, a white male, and U.W. Clemon of Alabama, a black male, were rated "not qualified." W.M. Kidd of West Virginia, a 64-year-old white male, was rated "Not Qualified by Reason of Age." *See* Neff, *supra* n. 1, at 44, 50 n. 50.

31. *See, e.g.*, Slotnick, *supra* n. 4; Klement, *supra* n. 6; Goulden, *supra* n. 7; and *Federal Judge Nominee Disputes ABA Criticism*, THE WASHINGTON POST, May 29, 1980.

32. Goldman has examined the judicial appointments of the last six presidents on several demographic dimensions, but his purpose was to compare the types of candidates different presidents have chosen, not to compare the different ABA ratings among subgroups of a president's nominations, as we do here. *See, e.g.*, Goldman, *supra* n. 3; and Goldman, *Profile of Carter's judicial nominees*, 62 JUDICATURE 246 (1978), especially note 1, where Goldman cites his earlier work.

See also Cohodas, *Merit Selection Diversified Federal Bench*, 37 CONG. Q. 2418 (October 27, 1979); Collins, *supra* n. 3; and Cohodas, *supra* n. 3.

33. Questionnaire data were supplemented by additional variables graciously provided by Professor Sheldon Goldman. These variables included measures of the nominees' partisan identification, ethnicity, religion, and ABA ratings.

The 213 candidates in the study constituted almost all the candidates nominated by the president during the 96th Congress. The study omits only a few candidates who were nominated during the "lame duck" period of the Carter administration, and whose names were later withdrawn.

34. Cohodas, *supra* n. 3.

35. *See* Executive Orders 12059 and 12097, *supra* n. 14.

Senators in 29 states actually established district judge nominating commissions. *See* Neff, *supra* n. 1.

36. In our presentation of data, we generally aggregate district and appellate nominees. But when we see substantively meaningful differences between the two groups, we report district and appellate nominees separately.

37. We generally consider a relationship to be statistically significant at $p \leq 0.05$. We utilized contingency coefficients in the few instances where variables were measured at the nominal level. For ordinally measured variables, we utilized Tau B for "square" tables with equal numbers of rows and columns, and Tau C for "rectangular" tables with unequal numbers of rows and columns.

38. During the four years of the Carter administration, the ABA Standing Committee on Federal Judiciary followed age guidelines which made it difficult for older attorneys to reach the bench. "An individual sixty years of age or older is 'Not Qualified by Reason of Age' for an initial appointment to a lifetime federal judgeship unless in excellent health and unless evaluated as 'Well Qualified' or 'Exceptionally Well Qualified,' " said the ABA. "In no event are persons sixty-four years of age or older found qualified for initial appointment.

"In considering District Judges sixty years of age or older for possible elevation to the Courts of Appeals, the Committee finds such a person 'Not Qualified by Reason of Age' unless evaluated as 'Well Qualified' or 'Exceptionally Well Qualified.' District Judges sixty-eight years of age or older are in no event found qualified for such elevation."

But at the Mid-Winter Meeting of the ABA in February of 1981, the standing committee announced that it had "decided to discontinue the use of its age guidelines as stated in the committee's brochure . . . . The Committee's primary function is to evaluate federal judicial candidates in terms of professional qualifications—professional competence, judicial temperament and character.

"The committee intends to continue to consider age as a factor [only] if it affects professional qualifications—for example, if age were to affect a candidate's competence, temperament, or ability to work the long hours required of a federal judge." American Bar Association Standing Committee on Federal Judiciary, "Report to the House of Delegates, Mid-Winter Meeting, 1981" (unpublished report), page 2. See also *Rating Older Judges*, 1980 CQ ALMANAC 407 and the text of this article at footnote 17.

39. For a comparison of white with non-white, male with female, and white male with non-traditional judgeship candidates on all of the demographic, educational, politicization, legal career, and litigation variables utilized in this study, *see* Slotnick, *Affirmative Action and Judicial Selection During the Carter Administration*, 1 YALE L. & POL'Y REV. (1983).

40. Law school honors were defined as attaining membership on the school's law review or law journal, earning Order of the Coif distinction, graduating at the top of one's class, competing in national moot court competition, etc.

41. A law school was considered to be "elite" if it was included on three of the following six measures: The Fourman Report (14 "distinguished" law schools); Barron's Guide "Group 1" law schools (14 "high resource" law schools); Blau-Margulies Report (top nine law schools); Cartter Report (top 15 law schools); Ladd-Lipset Report (top eight law schools); and *Juris Doctor* magazine (top 13 law schools). In all, 15 law schools appear on three of these measures.

42. Berkson and Carbon, *supra* n. 1, at 146.

43. We used 11 subject matter codes to categorize the case studies: Business Organization and Management; Contracts; Real Property; Torts; Personal Finances, Family and Estate; Criminal; and four Public Law categories (Governmental Regulatory Powers, Prisoner and Defendant Rights, Equal Protection, and Abuse of Governmental Authority).

We characterized an attorney's legal practice as "non-traditional" if four of the 10 most significant cases he or she submitted were in the areas of criminal defense, public law plaintiff (or defendant against governmental regulatory activity), tort plaintiff, personal finances, and family law.

Actors in the Judicial Process
Juries

INTRODUCTION   Juries have been at once the most romanticized and most vilified actors in the American judicial process. They are, at times, credited with being the public's guarantor of fairness and equity in court, while they are also heavily criticized for reaching arbitrary judgments that do not reflect the dictates of the law. Both extremes probably accurately tap the behavior of some juries some of the time. It is also important to note that jury trials are a rarity since most legal problems are resolved by settlement prior to trial or by a "bench trial" in which a judge renders the verdict. Nevertheless, dramatic jury trials remain the mythical view of judicial processes held by most Americans, and their potential use in most trial settings does render them important actors warranting our consideration. Unfortunately, scholarly attention to juries has been limited by lack of direct access to jury deliberations and the inherent difficulties of jury research based on simulation and post-hoc interviewing techniques.

Peter Sperlich's article "...And then there were six: the decline of the American jury" portrays the decline in the usage of juries and the changes in their nature brought about by a series of Supreme Court holdings that allowed for reductions in jury size and less than unanimous verdicts. Sperlich argues that the Court's rulings were ill-considered and endanger the very rights juries were fashioned to protect.

Jurors' demographic characteristics are thought to influence their decisions. In the second piece in this section, Carol Mills and Wayne Bohannon report on an empirical study that examined "Juror characteristics: to what extent are they related to jury verdicts?" Utilizing interview data, the authors investigate the relationship between variables such as the jurors' sex, race, and education and their verdict. Mills and Bohannon demonstrate that the relationships they seek are complex ones and that it is dangerous to view a single variable in isolation when trying to understand jury behavior.

If identifiable juror characteristics are related to specific juror dispositions, it then becomes possible and desirable for attorneys to try to structure juries to produce favorable results. The "state of the art" regarding this possibility is explored by Shari Seidman Diamond in "Scientific jury selection: what social scientists know and do not know." Diamond's argument is a sobering one for critics who contend that with enough money and social science know-how congenial outcomes from jury trials can be assured for a litigant. She cautions that anyone considering the use of a consultant to help develop a desired juror profile "needs to be a vigilant and critical consumer of the services that are offered."

One of the most frequent criticisms of the contemporary role of American juries focuses on the reality that the jury's basic fact-finding function has not changed through time, while litigation has grown exceedingly complex, far surpassing a lay jury's level of competence. "Helping juries handle complex cases" is a "thinkpiece" in which David Strawn and G. Thomas Munsterman suggest several procedural changes in trials that, they argue, would facilitate the jury's task. The reforms the authors suggest and the implications they could have for the American judicial system are clearly worthy of the reader's consideration.

. . . And then there were six: the decline of the American jury

In the last 10 years, the Supreme Court has allowed states to reduce the jury's size and abolish the unanimous verdict. But the Court generally ignored social science evidence that shows the importance of both these factors to the jury in performing its traditional role.

by Peter W. Sperlich

The 1970s may well be remembered as the decade in which we almost lost the jury. The institution of *trial by jury* came to this continent as part of the general transfer of the English legal system to the colonies. For nearly 400 years, Americans have regarded the common law trial jury as one of the bulwarks of their liberty, and for nearly 400 years, there was no essential disagreement that trial by jury meant a body of 12 deciding unanimously.

No institution is without critics, of course. In recent years, a number of judges adopted the position that the jury was no longer needed, that judges could be entrusted with the liberties of the people, and that, in any case, the jury was an inefficient and expensive instrument of dispute resolution, one that no longer could be afforded.[1] Nevertheless, the American jury seemed secure, particularly because the U.S. Supreme Court always was one of the common law jury's strong supporters. As late as 1968, the Court extended the Sixth Amendment right to trial by jury to defendants accused of serious crimes in state courts.[2]

But then came *Williams v. Florida*[3] in 1970. *Williams* was the first act in what turned out to be a major reorientation of the Court's approach to the trial jury. The *Williams* ruling, permitting state criminal juries of six, came unexpected and sent a shock through the legal and scholarly community. Given the open-ended nature of the ruling (six was not necessarily to be the lower limit), the very survival of the jury seemed in doubt. Had the Court begun to side with the abolitionist minority? Was this the beginning of the end of lay participation in

the American judicial process? Hans Zeisel, an observer not given to panic, expressed these concerns in the very title of his *Williams* review: ". . . And Then There Were None."[4]

The title of this article is somewhat less despairing, reflecting two recent decisions (*Ballew* and *Burch, infra*), which indicate that the American jury will survive the 1970s. But the jury that has survived is not the jury of 10 years ago. Except for some state experimentations, the American criminal and civil trial jury at that time was the jury at common law, 12 persons deciding unanimously. As the decade ends, juries of 12 are no longer required in federal civil trials or in state criminal trials. Majority verdicts have been held to be constitutionally adequate in state criminal trials. Majority verdicts in federal criminal trials have been averted (so far) by the vote of a single justice.

What the future will bring we cannot know. But it is clear that what remains of the American jury at the end of the decade is less than firmly planted. It is possible that American developments will replicate English legal history, leading to an almost complete abrogation of trial by jury.[5] It is also possible that the worst is over. The vigorous defense of the jury that followed *Williams* and the other jury-diminishing decisions may have persuaded the Court of the error of the *Williams* approach.

I. The revolution in jury law

The U.S. Supreme Court changed the American trial jury in a sequence of six cases, spanning the full decade from 1970 to 1979. The first four served to diminish the jury: *Williams v. Florida, Johnson v. Louisiana,*[6] *Apodaca v. Oregon,*[7] and *Colgrove v. Battin.*[8] The last two indicate the current limits of jury diminution: *Ballew v. Georgia*[9] and *Burch v. Louisiana.*[10]

In *Williams,* the Supreme Court ruled that the U.S. Constitution does not require a jury of 12, and that a state may use a jury of six in criminal trials even when the sentence is as severe as life imprisonment. The decision applied only to state criminal juries, but the opinion of Justice White clearly signaled what was to come: "In sweeping language, the Court removed the constitutional obstacles to decreasing the size of federal and state juries in both civil and criminal cases."[11]

Federal judges quickly took the hint. In 1972, a year before *Colgrove,* a majority of the federal district courts already had adopted six-person civil juries. *Colgrove* legitimated this change. The Court formally ruled that the U.S. Constitution does not require 12-person civil juries, and that six-person federal civil juries are constitutionally adequate. *Johnson* and *Apodaca,* finally, produced the ruling that majority verdicts are constitutionally permissible in state criminal trials.[12]

The four cases amounted to no less than a revolution in American jury law.[13] But not only was this revolution unexpected, it also was uncompelled. There were no irresistible forces of legal or societal development to which the justices were forced to pay homage. Indeed, to achieve the goal of smaller and nonunanimous juries, the Court had to do considerable violence to legal history and empirical evidence. Not surprisingly, it reaped sharp criticism in the scholarly community.[14] Support for the decisions came largely from the same judges who had advocated jury slicing all along.[15]

The casualties of *Williams*
Williams signaled the transformation of the American trial jury and established the pattern of judicial reasoning in support of the change. The reasoning, as noted, left much to be desired, and three specific areas were short-changed: history, the American constitutional tradition, and empirical evidence.

History suffered the first blow. For nearly seven centuries, the common law jury of England and, thus, of the United States, had been a body of 12. It is not known how that size became standardized at 12 in 14th-century England; perhaps the number could equally well have been 11 or 13. It is not likely that the number could just as well have been five, or six, or seven.

The Court, however, took the position that unless it could discover a rational justification in history for the number 12, then that number could be regarded as an accident. As could have been predicted, no such justification was to be found. The Court concluded that the number 12 "appears to have been a historical accident, unrelated to the great purposes which gave rise to the jury in the first place."[16]

At least three objections must be raised to the Court's historical scholarship. The first is epistemological: the failure to discover a reason is not proof of its nonexistence. The second regards the conversion of quantitative into qualitative changes: as noted, the choice between 12 and 11 may not be of much consequence, but a change from 12 to six involves fundamental differences. The third objection involves objectivity of analysis and validity of inference: the Court only looked for reasons *for* removing the requirement of 12; it did not look for reasons *against* such a removal.[17]

The second blow was struck against an American constitutional tradition. While the Court had not explicitly ruled that the American trial jury was a body of 12 deciding unanimously, all the Court's statements and dicta had supported this position.[18] Firm tradition and invariate interpretations, however, had little power to protect the jury. The Court decided to treat the issue of jury size as open and unresolved, asking in leading language whether "this accidental feature of the jury has been immutably codified into our Constitution."[19] The answer, of course, was *no.* The Court revealed that all its prior interpretations were in error because they had assumed "that if a given feature existed in a jury at common law in 1789, then it was necessarily preserved in the Constitution."[20]

The third casualty of *Williams* was empirical evidence. The Court took the position that the six-person criminal jury would satisfy the requirements of the Sixth Amendment of "trial by an impartial jury" if it could be shown to be *functionally equivalent* to a 12-person jury: "The relevant inquiry, as we see it, must be the function that the particular feature [size] performs and its relations to the purposes of the jury trial."[21] The purpose of the jury trial "is to prevent oppression by the Government," and its essential feature is the "interposition between the accused and his accuser of the common-sense judgment of a group of laymen, and . . . the community participation and shared responsibility that results from that group's determination of guilt or innocence.''[22] The Court examined the evidence and came to the conclusion that ''[t]he performance of this role is not a function of the particular number of the body that makes up the jury . . . . And, certainly the reliability of the jury as a factfinder hardly seems likely to be a function of its size.''[23] As will be seen, the facts do *not* support these conclusions.

Other jury-size cases

Colgrove v. Battin is the second jury-size case, legitimating the six-person civil jury in the federal courts. In substance and style, *Colgrove* was pure *Williams*. Historical, constitutional, and empirical reasoning was flawed. *Colgrove* was particularly difficult to justify on constitutional grounds since the Seventh Amendment (in contrast to the Sixth Amendment in *Williams*) explicitly refers to the common law.

The Court overcame this obstacle by announcing that the size of the common law jury was not part of the real ''substance'' of the common law right of trial by jury, but was a ''mere matter of form or procedure.''[24] What remained, as in *Williams*, was the question of functional equivalence, ''whether jury performance is a function of jury size.''[25] The Court inspected the evidence and ruled that performance is not a function of size. Unfortunately, once again the facts fail to support the conclusion, as we will see later.

Ballew v. Georgia,[26] the third jury-size case, was a decision of the greatest importance. It was the first indication that the diminution of the jury had come to a halt. The Court decided that Georgia's criminal trial jury of five was constitutionally inadequate, that state criminal juries must consist of at least six. *Ballew* also was the first indication that the vigorous scholarly defense of the jury, mounted in the post-*Williams* years, had met with some success.

As will be seen below, the success was far from complete. The Court still did not refrain from using empirical evidence in questionable ways. But there were signs of a new spirit. The Court concluded ''that the purpose and functioning of the jury in a criminal trial is seriously impaired, and to a constitutional degree, by a reduction in size below six members.''[27] And Justice Blackmun was explicit that the empirical studies play a major role

in the development of this conclusion:

> But the assembled data raise substantial doubt about the reliability and appropriate representation of panels smaller than six. Because of the fundamental importance of the jury trial to the American system of criminal justice, any further reduction that promotes inaccurate and possibly biased decisionmaking, that causes untoward differences in verdicts, and that prevents juries from truly representing their communities, attains constitutional significance.[28]

The decision-rule cases

Johnson v. Louisiana and *Apodaca v. Oregon* were decided on the same day, May 22, 1972; both belong to the set of four cases that diminished the American trial jury.[29] *Johnson* permitted a 9/12 and *Apodaca* a 10/12 majority verdict in state criminal trials. *Johnson* and *Apodaca* moved along similar tracks as *Williams* and *Colgrove*. Once more, the keystone was the assertion of functional equivalence:

> Our inquiry must focus upon the function served by the jury . . . As we said in *Duncan*, the purpose of trial by jury is to prevent oppression by the Government . . . In terms of this function we perceive no difference between juries required to act unanimously and those permitted to convict or acquit by votes of 10 to two or 11 to one.[30]

For this claim the Court offered no evidence at all.[31] Instead, it was satisfied to rely upon its ''longstanding perceptions about jury behavior.''[32] The Court did not reveal how these ''perceptions'' were gathered, or what kind of systematic comparisons were made between unanimous and majority-verdict juries. Nor did the Court dispute the fact that jury deliberations are secret and not easily perceived. It is unlikely that the ''longstanding perceptions'' are more than an exercise of judicial creativity, throwing a cloak over the uncomfortable sight of an empirical issue having been decided without reference to empirical evidence.[33]

After *Johnson* and *Apodaca* joined *Williams* and *Colgrove*, a deep and widespread concern developed for the jury's future. No end was in sight to reductions in size (*Ballew* was not decided until 1978). And combinations of smaller size and majority rule could be expected to be legitimated next. *Burch v. Louisiana*, as *Ballew*, halted the diminution of the jury this year. The Court decided in *Burch* that ''conviction by a nonunanimous six-member jury in a state criminal trial for a nonpetty offense deprives the accused of his constitutional right to trial by jury.''[34]

It remains to be seen, of course, whether such

combinations as 6/7 or 5/8 will be found constitutionally inadequate. At least the worst fears have been set aside by *Burch*. In the foreseeable future the American trial jury will not be a body of three, deciding with a majority of two. As in the other decision-rule cases, it should be noted, the Court offered no empirical evidence for its ruling on the functional equivalence issue in *Burch*.

II. 'Functional equivalence' of juries

The major issue that emerges from the six jury decisions is the functional equivalence or non-equivalence of juries of different size and decision rules. The issue is closely related to the general question of the use of scientific evidence in the legal process. (See Sperlich, "Social science evidence in the courts: reaching beyond the adversary process," 63 *Judicature* 280 (1980)). Of course, important questions also can be raised about the Court's treatment of legal history and constitutional law. However, since the Court decides what the Constitution requires and what has been "immutably codified into our Constitution," little is to be gained by disputing with the Court about such matters as "the intent of the framers."

The U.S. Supreme Court, however, is not the highest authority on matters of fact. The case facts (adjudicative facts) must be determined by the trier of the facts, the trial judge or the trial jury. Wisely, the appellate courts have adopted a bearing of great restraint regarding case facts and generally refuse to second-guess the trier of the facts. Such well-placed restraint, unfortunately, has been less common in respect to the social facts relevant to the case in question.[35]

There is a tendency to rely on common sense and personal experience, and to take "judicial notice" of "common knowledge" rather than to obtain the required information from the appropriate expert sources, the relevant scientific disciplines. Untrained in scientific methods and isolated from the world of scientific investigations, judges seem to come quite easily to the view that judicial horse-sense is a more dependable guide to valid knowledge than scientific expertise.

Common knowledge and judicial intuition are notoriously unreliable paths to empirical fact. More often than not they lead into blind alleys and embarrassing retreats. Just as theological wisdom and common observation could not, in the long run, prevail against the expertise of scientific as-

tronomers, so judicial wisdom and common sense could not prevail against scientific expertise in ballistics.[36] The Court reasonably can maintain its interpretation of the Constitution against the views of other constitutional experts. The Court cannot maintain its own view of social facts and scientific principles against the testimony of the experts from the relevant sciences—at least it cannot do so without being seen as willful and incompetent.[37]

In the jury decisions of the 1970s it was indeed appropriate for the justices to determine upon which principle the rulings should be based, i.e., functional equivalence. It was not appropriate, however, for the justices to assume the role of competent determiners of the facts of equivalence or nonequivalence. It is disturbing when justices decide issues of social fact by relying upon their "longstanding perceptions about jury behavior." Nor will it do for justices to complain about "reliance on numerology,"[38] when after years of erroneous determination of the facts, reliable scientific investigations finally are being used.[39]

At this time in history, of course, and perhaps for a long time to come, there are many questions to which the sciences, particularly the social sciences, cannot give unequivocal answers. Not all details have been filled out in the studies of jury behavior.[40] There is much that is not known about just how different juries differ. This much, however, is well-established: Juries of different sizes and decision rules are *not* functionally equivalent. The protections offered by smaller and majority-rule juries are not the same as those offered by the traditional common law jury—12 persons deciding unanimously.

As noted earlier, *Johnson, Apodaca*, and *Burch* decided on the equivalence/nonequivalence of different decision rules *without any reference* to empirical evidence, relying instead on mysterious "longstanding judicial perceptions." *Williams, Colgrove*, and *Ballew*, the jury size cases, do refer to empirical evidence. The relevance and validity of that evidence, thus, can be examined.

Relevance and validity of evidence

Given the path-setting nature of the *Williams* decision and the continuing dominance of the *Williams* doctrine (6=12), it is of considerable interest to see how the claim of functional equivalence was established. The Court cited six "experiments" to support its contentions.[41] This was the substance of the evidence: (1) an unsupported claim that "it could be argued that there would be no differences''; (2) the unsupported statement of a judge that he found five-person juries quite satisfactory; (3) an unsupported report that one court clerk and three attorneys had said that they could not detect any difference in the verdicts of 12- and six-person juries as these had been used on an experimental basis in a Massachusetts court; (4) another report of the same opinions as recounted in the previous item; (5) a notice, without any evaluation, that a court has experimented with a six-person jury in a civil negligence case; (6) a judge's thoughts on the economic advantages of smaller juries.[42]

Williams' notion of "empirical evidence" was of embarrassing incompetence,[43] and the reviews did not spare the Court. Zeisel concluded that the six items were "scant evidence by any standards," and pointed out how and where better evidence could have been obtained.[44] Saks noted that the scholarship displayed in *Williams* would not win a passing grade in high school.[45] Walbert chided the Court for its errors of interpretation and for its failure to make use of available competent evidence.[46] And Wick charged that "[t]he willingness of the Court to be persuaded by such flimsy evidence lays bare its lack of concern for the institution of jury trial."[47] *Williams* did not demonstrate that juries of six and of 12 are functionally equivalent. By its own chosen standard, the Court had rendered a constitutionally invalid decision.[48] The error still awaits correction.

It may appear difficult to do worse than *Williams.* Yet *Colgrove*, the next jury-size decision, in some ways did worse indeed. The Court showed itself supremely scornful of the scholarly criticisms and suggestions that had followed *Williams.* Not only did the Court not change its general approach to empirical evidence, it even returned for support to some of the *Williams* items, the inadequacy of which had clearly been demonstrated.[49]

The Court refused to show doubt regarding *Williams.* To the contrary, it practically taunted its critics. There was the bold restatement of the false claim that the *Williams* decision rested on actual jury "studies." And there was the pointed comment that the critical literature generated by *Williams* was "nonpersuasive." Said the *Colgrove* court:

We had no difficulty reaching the conclusion in *Williams* that a jury of six would guarantee an accused the trial by jury secured by Art. III and the Sixth Amendment. Significantly, our determination that there was 'no discernible difference between the results reached by the

two different-sized juries' . . . drew largely upon the results of studies of the operations of juries of six in civil cases. Since then, much has been written about the six-member jury, but nothing that persuades us to depart from the conclusion reached in *Williams.*[50]

The flaws in *Colgrove*

In addition to resurrecting the deficient items of *Williams, Colgrove* sought to present new support for the functional equivalence assertion, reporting that "four very recent studies have provided convincing empirical evidence of the correctness of the *Williams* conclusion."[51] Far from providing "convincing empirical evidence," however, the new items were entirely incapable to support the Court's contentions. The flaws can be stated briefly:[52]

• One situation permitted attorneys to choose a jury of 12 rather than six. The choices of the larger jury did not occur at random but reflected the nature and complexity of the case.

• The second new item also reported a procedure in which the litigants had a choice between six- and 12-person juries. The choices, again, were not random.

• The next study used a before-and-after design to take advantage of a recent change from 12- to six-person juries. Other changes, however, occurred at the same time (mediation board, discovery of insurance). None of these three items permitted valid comparisons of the behavior and verdicts of larger and smaller juries.

• The final study used videotaped mock trials with student subjects. The study contained serious errors, such as a wholly one-sided case presentation and faulty computations.[53]

Again, there were many critical reviews. Zeisel and Diamond wrote that *Colgrove's* handling of evidence presented a "disconcerting picture,"[54] and suggested that it was one of the cases where the intent of references to empirical evidence is not to shed light on the facts, but "merely to ornament an already determined result."[55] Regarding the functional equivalence assertions, Zeisel wrote elsewhere that "[w]ith all due respect to the judges who composed the majority of the Court in these cases—on this point they were simply wrong. The Court's so-called evidence proved nothing of the sort."[56] Referring to *Colgrove's* "convincing empirical evidence," Wick wrote that "[t]he only conviction which emerges from examination of these four studies is that the majority of the Court was pre-disposed to be convinced."[57]

The *Williams-Johnson-Apodaca-Colgrove* sequence of opinions furnishes one of the more depressing sets of readings to emerge from the pens of U.S. Supreme Court justices. One aspect is technical: the uncritical and incompetent treatment of empirical evidence. The other is substantive: the continuous slicing away at the traditional common law jury and, thus, the continuing reduction in the protective function of trial by jury. The second was worrisome all the more because of strong signs that the Court would legitimate trial juries even smaller than six,[58] and majorities even smaller than *Johnson*'s nine-to-three division.[59] Indeed, there was reason to be concerned that the two methods of jury reduction would be legitimated in a combined format.[60]

Partial remedies

Eight years after *Williams* and five years after *Colgrove* the Court decided *Ballew v. Georgia* and at least partially remedied the inadequacies of the earlier cases. As *Williams* is the milestone marking the beginning of the decline of the American jury, so *Ballew* may well be the milestone marking the onset of recovery.[61] The *Ballew* Court ruled[62] that Georgia's criminal jury of five was constitutionally inadequate because it did not meet the Court's test of functional equivalence.

For the first time in the jury decisions of the 1970s, the Court correctly used empirical evidence to establish a social fact: deliberative bodies of five and of 12 are *not* equivalent. Criminal juries of five do not offer the same protection to the accused as those of 12. The irony of *Ballew* is that the evidence used to deny five just as much condemns six. The scientific investigations cited in *Ballew* were designed to test the *Williams* doctrine of 6=12. The findings exposed the error of that doctrine. Yet *Ballew* includes an explicit affirmation of *Williams*.[63] *Ballew*, thus, is only a partial redress for the Court's past failings.

Justice Blackmun noted many functional inequalities between larger and smaller juries. He arranged them in five major groups:

(1) **Effectiveness of group deliberation.** The quality of group performance and group productivity is higher in larger groups.[64] Reduction in the size of the group leads to impaired fact-finding and common-sense application. Members of smaller groups are less likely to contribute to the solution of the problem, and (collectively) are less likely to

overcome the biases of their members.[65]

(2) **Accuracy, consistency, and reliability of deliberation results.** Smaller panels produce a larger proportion of conviction errors, i.e., convicting innocent persons. (Increases in panel size increase the opposite error: not convicting guilty persons.)[66] Smaller panels show more verdict inconsistency and produce less reliable decisions.[67]

(3) **Detriment to the defense.** The functional difference between smaller and larger panels is not neutral in criminal trials. Smaller panels are detrimental to the defense. The number of hung juries is substantially reduced with smaller panels, largely because of less support for the juror holding the minority viewpoint.[68]

(4) **Community participation and representativeness.** Smaller panels reduce the representativeness of the jury and allow less participation of the minority groups in the community.[69]

(5) **Substantial effects of small differences.** Some studies have found that larger and smaller juries would produce different verdicts in only a relatively small proportion of the cases, e.g., 14 per cent. These small percentages, however, mask a very large number of cases. Furthermore, it is precisely in those cases of disagreement, when the evidence is not clear-cut, that the jury system is of greatest value. A similar point applies to the small percentage differences often found between jury verdicts and judge verdicts. Aggregate comparisons mask the true extent of differences. Case-by-case comparisons show higher rates of disagreement.[70]

Having noted all these differences, Justice Blackmun wrote that these studies "lead us to conclude that the purpose and functioning of the jury in a criminal trial is seriously impaired, and to a constitutional degree, by a reduction in size to below six members."[71]

It is ironic that one of the best listings of evidence to refute the *Williams* doctrine should be found in a decision that explicitly affirms that doctrine.[72] The assembly of empirical evidence in *Ballew* is particularly impressive[73] when it is recognized that the litigants brought to the attention of the Court only a small part.[74] Additional literature, however, could have been drawn upon.

Saari, for example, has pointed out that from some perspectives six is not even one-half of 12. One of the crucial issues in the jury-size controversy is the interaction of the jurors. The evidence is that both quality and quantity differ. Saari points to the interesting fact that juries of 12 have 261,624 potential relational patterns, but juries of six only have 301 (about 1/10 of 1 per cent).[75] Missing from *Ballew* are references to the extensive work of Gelfand and Solomon,[76] Grofman,[77] Buckhout,[78] and Snortum et al.,[79] as well as to the partially unpublished but well-known study of Padawer-Singer & Barton.[80] A recent review of the jury literature by Davis et al. also would have been a useful addition.[81] It is important to emphasize, however, that the inclusion of these items would not have changed any of the findings of *Ballew* regarding the functional non-equivalence of five- and 12-person juries, though, again, the real message was the non-equivalence of six and 12.

A halt to jury reduction

Burch v. Louisiana is the final case in this decade's sequence of jury decisions. *Burch* stands in the same relationship to *Johnson* and *Apodaca* as *Ballew* to *Williams* and *Colgrove*. *Burch* ruled that conviction by a nonunanimous six-person jury for a nonpetty offense violates the right to trial by jury as guaranteed by the Sixth and Fourteenth Amendments.[82] While *Burch* resembled *Ballew* in putting a halt to the further diminution of the American trial jury, it greatly differs from *Ballew* in its treatment of evidence.

Burch makes no reference to empirical evidence,[83] except for an allusion to the "reasons that led us in *Ballew* to decide that use of a five-member jury threatened the fairness of the proceeding and the proper role of the jury."[84] Justice Rehnquist, the author of the *Burch* opinion, had associated himself with the Powell complaint about *Ballew*'s "reliance on numerology" (*cf* note 38 *supra*), seemingly having less use for science as a source of social facts than Justice Blackmun.

In addition to references to *Ballew* (but no analysis of the *Ballew* evidence for its relevance to *Burch*), Justice Rehnquist sought to support the *Burch* decision by taking note of current practice:

We are buttressed in this view by the current jury practices of the several States. It appears that of those States that utilize six-member juries in trials of nonpetty offenses, only two, including Louisiana, also allow nonunanimous verdicts. We think that this near uniform judgment of the Nation provides a useful guide in delimiting the line between those jury practices that are constitutionally permissible and those that are not.[85]

Justice Rehnquist also found it profitable to resurrect and reaffirm once more the functional equivalence error of the *Williams* court "that a jury of 12 was neither more reliable as a factfinder, more advantageous to the defendant, nor more representative of the variety of viewpoints in the community than a jury of six."[86]

What Justice Rehnquist failed to do was to examine relevant and competent evidence. The Court's self-chosen test in all of the jury cases is that of the functional equivalence of different juries. The question of functional equivalence is an empirical question. It can be answered only by the examination of empirical evidence. It cannot be answered by an audit of current court practices. Nor can the question of the functional equivalence of different decision rules be answered by referring to the Court's reasoning in the jury-size cases, particularly given the less than competent treatment of evidence in these cases.

The reasoning of *Burch* is sorely deficient. Nevertheless, the decision is welcome to those who have an interest in preserving trial by jury in the courts of this nation. As *Ballew* before it, *Burch* creates an important obstacle against the additional diminution of the jury.

III. Hidden agendas?

It has been argued that the Court's use of empirical evidence is "real," if occasionally faulty. But the view that the Court also refers to empirical evidence to ornament and to camouflage has considerable prevalence.[87] Short of judicial disclosure, there seems to be no clear way to verify such propositions, and judicial denial may not convince everyone.

The matter must be approached with care. We do not need another conspiracy theory. Yet, the problem cannot be ignored.[88] The conclusion that the Court ornaments and camouflages is almost inescapable when confronted with "evidence" of the nature and quality used in *Williams* to justify a jury of six.[89] The jury cases and their context suggest the possible existence of four hidden agendas: jury cost, court delay, judicial power, and law and order.

Jury cost

Five of the six jury cases are silent on the issue of jury cost, and *Ballew* rejects Georgia's argument of an overriding state interest in "savings in court time and in financial costs."[90] Yet the jury reduction literature[91] of recent decades has placed such strong emphasis on the savings to be realized by smaller juries that it is difficult to dismiss the thought altogether that the Court may have wanted to reduce the cost of justice as well as to permit jury diversity in deciding these cases. The thought is particularly hard to dismiss because *Williams* justified the six-person jury by relying, *inter alia*, on Judge Phillips' article, which is a purely economic argument for reduction,[92] and because of Chief Justice Burger's remarkable media and lecture circuit activism in the cause of court reform, more than once linking economic considerations and jury size.[93]

The jury reform/reduction literature almost without exception presents expected financial savings as a justification for reducing the size of the jury. The savings are said to occur for several reasons, including the claims that: (a) fewer panelists are required for the jury venire,[94] (b) less time is needed for the voir dire of the prospective jurors,[95] (c) less time is required for courtroom proceedings,[96] (d) jury deliberation time is shorter,[97] (e) juror fees and expenses are reduced.[98] Some of the assertions, especially (a) and (e) are quite plausible; the others are more questionable.[99] There actually appears to be rather little saving in voir dire time and trial proceedings, and, thus, in judicial time and court cost.[100]

Juror fees probably are the item in which the largest savings can be achieved by reducing the size of the trial jury. Since juror fees are notoriously low,[101] however, and since juror fees consitute a miniscule part of a court's budget,[102] the actual amount is not all that large. Even the figures presented by proponents are not particularly impressive. Bogue and Fritz write:

Minnehaha County [spent] $27,164.50 for juror fees in 1971. There are an estimated 95,000 people living in Minnehaha County. Divide $27,164.50 into 95,000 people and it will be ascertained that it cost [sic] each person in Minnehaha County about 35¢ plus for the cost of trial by jury.[103]

This, it should be noted, is an argument *for* reducing the jury to six members. If the six-person jury saves about half the amount, it means that each resident of Minnehaha County could enjoy the full benefits and protections of the common law jury for about 18¢ extra per year.

Judge Devitt offers a nationwide figure:

The saving in jury expenses if the six-man rule were in effect nation-wide is impressive. In fiscal year 1970, 3,371 civil jury trials were conducted in the federal court system. These cases took 10,701 trial days and, with twelve-person juries, a total of 128,512 juror days. If this figure is cut in half and multiplied by $25, the approximate saving effected by employing a jury of six, rather than twelve, could exceed $1,600,000.[104]

Assuming even a cost of $2 million, given a population of about 200 million, the saving per person per year is about *one cent*. Zeisel and Diamond have estimated a saving of $4 million annually if all federal juries consisted of six rather than 12 persons (as the civil juries now largely do). This still works out to only two cents of savings per person per year.[105]

Savings of $4 million must also be seen in the context of other expenditures, such as annual outlays of $631 million for golf equipment.[106] While, of course, no one argues in favor of waste in the judicial system, the cost of the traditional common law jury seems bearable.[107] But if savings must be achieved, there are other court reforms we can undertake, such as the elimination of the continuous presence of a newspaper-reading bailiff in all non-jury civil and in many non-jury criminal trials, and a more efficient administration of the jury system itself.[108]

Delay

This is not a topic in any of the six jury cases either. Yet there are some grounds for suspecting that this issue may also have been on the Court's mind. The chief justice has frequently spoken about the need to eliminate delay and has clearly linked the use of the jury to the existence of trial delay.[109] And the jury-reduction literature is just as emphatic that delay can be cured by jury reform,[110] as it is on the point that much money can be saved. Particularly the civil jury is seen as cause of delay. Judge Devitt, for example, writes:

I think it is fair to say that the backlog of cases in the federal courts, particularly in the metropolitan centers, is caused largely by the number of civil jury trials required by the Seventh Amendment.[111]

This type of analysis tends to be based more on wishful thinking than on fact. Inferences often are drawn from judge/jury comparisons, without full recognition of the differences in the types of cases that are submitted to bench and to jury trials. Courts without juries, it should be noted, also experience substantial delay. "The New York Court of Claims, dealing with cases against the State of New York, is almost two years behind on its calendar, yet does not use the jury system."[112]

It has been pointed out that delay is caused by some administrative practices of the courts, and that much of the delay can be cured by the addition of rather small increments in judicial work-time or judicial position.[113] While delay in court can damage the cause of justice and should indeed be cured, smaller juries, majority juries, and reduced use of jury trials do not seem to be the cure. What little *systematic* analysis exists does not identify trial by jury as the cause of delay.[114]

Judicial power

The jury reduction literature contains some interesting hints about the desirability of increasing the power of the judges. American legal history can be read as a struggle between judge and jury, between the professional and the lay element. It is evident that professional judges are in ascendance. The power of the jury to decide on the law has largely been taken away, at least as a matter of right.[115] In effect, juries still have the power to set aside laws that are perceived to be unjust (in general or in application to the case at hand). But when they exercise this power, they are regarded as "runaway" or "lawless."[116]

The argument for smaller juries sometimes is stated in the terms that this will make the court more "businesslike."[117] Often the language is stronger. Gleisser, for example, argues that the trial judge should be the "master of his own courtroom," and that he should be "free to comment in any way he wishes on the evidence," including "which witnesses are to be believed."[118] In jurisdictions where this is not currently permissible, what can this mean but a greater judicial influence on the fact decision of the jury?[119] It should be noted, however, that studies show that the majority of trial judges favors trial by jury, even in civil trials.[120] It cannot be guessed, of course, whether the Court saw increased judicial power as one of the benefits of smaller juries and resulting reductions in the use of juries.[121]

Law-and-order

The smaller criminal jury works to the disadvantage of the defendant.[122] This fact, not acknowledged by the Court until *Ballew*, and even then applied only to the five-person issue, underlies the speculation that an increase in the rate of criminal convictions was one of the hidden agendas of the jury cases.

The 1960s saw a strong public concern with law-and-order. It was a strong factor in the election of President Nixon, and, as political pundits say, the Court follows the election returns. More importantly, the Nixon appointees to the Court were selected to at least some degree because of their position on the law-and-order issue.[123] While presidents tend to have little luck in appointing justices who will carry forward the judicial philosophy that made them attractive, it cannot be denied that the Burger Court has produced some fairly "Nixonian" rulings in respect to such matters as freedom of the press, search and seizure, admission of evidence, self-incrimination, and right to counsel.[124] Some of these decisions point in the same direction as the smaller and the majority jury: an increase in the rate of criminal convictions, reflecting a general climate of punitiveness. Zeisel has raised the issue in this way:

One wonders what is behind this new zeal for cutting into the jury. The ostensible argument is reducing costs and delay . . . . There is obviously more to this concerted drive at this point in time.

Unconsciously, perhaps, the motives are likely to be similar to those that went into the rewriting of the military code of procedure; not only more efficiency, but also less tolerance toward a dissenting minority.[125]

And again Zeisel:

One must see the reduction of the jury size in civil cases in the federal courts as but one move in a major attack on the jury system that began in the 'law-and-order days,' when it was thought that the jury, as we have known it since the founding of the Republic, might stand in the way of law enforcement.[126]

Speculating about hidden agendas, unstated reasons, and concealed motivations is to skate on thin ice. While some inferences may be plausible, little can be proven, yet the matter cannot be avoided. The true reasons and motivations producing the Court's decisions are among the most important facts of judicial policy analysis, constitutional law, and the planning of litigation. When, as in the jury cases, the Court's cited evidence does not support the decisions, and when the Court persists in affirming demonstrably false doctrines, speculation about hidden agendas inescapably will emerge.

IV. A role for ordinary citizens

The Declaration of Independence (1776) set forth a series of complaints against the King to justify the revolution. One of the key complaints was "For depriving us in many cases, of the benefits of Trial by jury." It can be argued that the Court's jury decisions of this decade have caused a similar deprivation. In the Virginia Ratification Convention the Wythe Committee declared that "the ancient trial by jury is one of the greatest securities to the rights of the people, and is to remain sacred and inviolable."[127] And until *Williams*, essentially, it did. It does no longer. The evidence is clear: six does not equal 12, and 75 per cent does not equal 100 per cent.

How will the Court decide future jury cases? *Ballew* and *Burch* indicate that the worst may be over. Yet majority verdicts for the federal criminal jury were avoided by only a single vote, and it remains undetermined what type of majority rule for less-than-12-person state criminal juries will be legitimated. *Ballew* and *Burch* are no cause for leaving the ramparts. Trial by jury is likely to survive only through vigorous efforts on its behalf.

It is unclear what combination of reasons and motivations produced *Williams* and the subsequent decisions. To the degree that empirical evidence played an important role—however mistakenly used—extraordinary scholarly efforts will be required to provide the Court with social facts, to educate the Court in the use of scientific findings, and to help the legal profession in developing new institutions and processes by which the flow of scientific evidence to the Court can be improved, while preserving principles of procedural fairness.[128]

To the degree that hidden agendas were instrumental in the decisions, scholarly and political efforts will be required. The Court needs more information about just how much (how little) time and money will be saved by smaller juries and non-unanimous decisions. In addition, however, the political process will have to carry the message to the Court that the jury shall not be destroyed to save pennies or to increase the rate of criminal convictions, and that the people will not trust the professional judges with their liberties,[129] but that ordinary citizens shall retain their role in the American judicial process.

The task of preventing any further decline of trial by jury does not appear hopeless. Indeed, over time it may even be possible to persuade the Court to acknowledge the error of the functional equivalence doctrine and to reverse itself. Stare decisis is not the only principle in law. There is no *final word*, even from the U.S. Supreme Court.

NOTES

This article originally appeared in Volume 63, Number 6, December-January 1980, pages 262-279.

I am indebted to William Zinn for criticism of the first draft, to Karin Carmin and Coronet Galloway for finding some of the economic data, and to the Institute of Governmental Studies of the University of California for various forms of assistance and typing of the manuscript.

1. "When the Declaration of Independence was adopted and the Constitution drafted, we had every reason to be concerned about citizen-juror protection from King George's judges. But King George is long gone, and so are his judges. We have our own now, and they are competent, experienced, fair, and well qualified to decide law and fact issues in civil cases." Devitt, *Federal Civil Jury Trials Should be Abolished*, 60 A.B.A. J. 570, 572 (1974).

For a sampling of judicial criticism of the jury, from the mid-1950s to the mid-1970s, *see* Augelli, *Six-Member Juries in Civil Actions in the Federal Judicial System*, 3 SETON HALL L. REV. 281 (1972), Lumbard, *Let the Jury Be—But Modified*, 7 TRIAL 17 (Nov.-Dec. 1971), Tamm, *A Proposal for Five-Member Civil Juries in the Federal Courts*, 50 A.B.A. J. 162 (1964), Thompson, *Six Will Do*, 10 TRIAL 12 (Nov.-Dec. 1974), and Wiehl, *The Six Man Jury*, 4 GONZAGA L. REV. 35 (1968).

Summaries of criticisms can be found in: Comment, *With Love in Their Hearts but Reform on Their Minds: How Trial Judges View the Civil Jury*, 4 COLUM. J. L. SOC. PROBL. 178 (1968), James, CRISIS IN THE COURTS 193-199 (New York: David McKay, rev. ed., 1971), and Powell, *Reducing the Size of Juries*, 5 U. MICH. J. L. REF. 87 (1971). The most comprehensive attack on the jury system still is Frank, COURTS ON TRIAL (Princeton: Princeton University Press, 1949).

Views supportive of the traditional common law jury can be found in: Avakian, *Trial by Jury: Is It Worth the Ordeal?*, 2 LITIGATION 8 (Winter 1976), Baum, *The Six-Man Jury—The Cross Section Aborted*, 12 JUDGE'S J. 12 (1973), Hogan, *Some Thoughts on Juries in Civil Cases*, 50 A.B.A. J. 752 (1964), Kalven, *The Dignity of the Civil Jury*, 50 VA. L. REV. 1055 (1964), Nunnelly, *When a Trial by Jury?*, in Winters, THE JURY 25 (Chicago: American Judicature Society, 1971), Summers, *Some Merits of Civil Jury Trials*, 39 TUL. L. REV. 3 (1964), and Zeisel, *The Jury and Court Delay*, 328 ANNALS 46 (March 1960).

2. Duncan v. Louisiana, 391 U.S. 145 (1968). The Court extended the Sixth Amendment right of trial by jury in criminal cases to the states by way of the Fourteenth Amendment.

3. 399 U.S. 78 (1970).

4. Zeisel, . . . *And Then There Were None: The Diminution of the Federal Jury*, 38 U. CHI. L. REV. 710 (1971).

5. Trial by jury has fared better in the U.S. than in the home country. Beginning in 1854, England reduced the use of the civil jury in a series of steps from complete usage (in non-equity cases) to about 2 per cent of current cases. The use of the criminal jury also has been greatly reduced (employed in less than 10 per cent of current cases). The grand jury (an endangered American institution not discussed in this essay) was abolished in England in 1933.

For discussions of English jury abolition and diminution see Abraham, THE JUDICIAL PROCESS 245 (New York: Oxford University Press, third ed., 1975), Clark, THE GRAND JURY 104 (New York: Quadrangle, 1972), Devlin, TRIAL BY JURY 129-133 (London: Stevens and Sous, 1966), Ehrmann, COMPARATIVE LEGAL

CULTURES 97-100 (Englewood Cliffs: Prentice Hall, 1976), and Zander, *The Jury in England: Decline and Fall?*, in Annual Chief Justice Earl Warren Conference on Advocacy in the United States, THE AMERICAN JURY SYSTEM 29-34 (Cambridge, MA: American Trial Lawyers Foundation, 1977).

6. 406 U.S. 356 (1972).

7. 406 U.S. 404 (1972).

8. 413 U.S. 149 (1973).

9. 435 U.S. 223 (1978).

10. 47 L.W. 4393 (1979).

11. Zeisel, *supra* n. 4, at 712.

12. The legitimation of majority verdicts in federal criminal trials was averted by a single vote. Justice Powell interpreted the Sixth Amendment to require unanimous jury verdicts. He was unwilling, however, to extend this requirement to the states through the Fourteenth Amendment.

13. The discussion of the cases must be brief. For a more detailed treatment, *see* Sperlich, *Trial by Jury: It May Have a Future*, SUPREME COURT REVIEW 191, 195-209, 218-222 (1979).

14. For some of the major criticisms, *see*, for *Williams*: Beiser and Varrin, *Six-Member Juries in the Federal Court*, 58 JUDICATURE 424 (1975), Stevens, *Defendant's Right to a Jury Trial: Is Six Enough?*, 59 KY. L. J. 996 (1971), Walbert, *The Effect of Jury Size on the Probability of Conviction*, 22 CASE W. RES. L. REV. 529 (1971), Zeisel, *The Waning of the American Jury*, 58 A.B.A. J. 367 (1972), and Zeisel, *supra* n. 4.

For *Colgrove*: Diamond, *A Jury Experiment Reanalyzed*, 7 U. MICH. J. L. REF. 520 (1973), and Zeisel and Diamond, *Convincing Empirical Evidence on the Six Member Jury*, 41 U. CHI. L. REV. 281 (1974).

For *Williams* and *Colgrove*: Lempert, *Uncovering "Nondiscernible" Differences: Empirical Research and the Jury-Size Cases*, 73 MICH. L. REV. 643 (1975), Saks, *Ignorance of Science Is No Excuse*, 10 TRIAL 18 (Nov.-Dec. 1974), and Wick, *The Half-Filled Jury Box: Is Half Loaf Better Than None?*, 2 LITIGATION 11 (Winter 1976).

For *Johnson* and *Apodaca*: Buckhout, *Unanimous vs Majority Verdicts in Jury Deliberations*, 4 SOC. ACTION & THE L. 15 (Sept. 1977).

For *Williams, Johnson,* and *Apodaca*: Padawer-Singer, *Justice or Judgments?*, in Annual Chief Justice Earl Warren Conference on Advocacy in the United States, THE AMERICAN JURY SYSTEM, *supra* n. 5, at 45, Padawer-Singer and Barton, "Interim Report: Experimental Study of Decision-Making in the 12- Versus 6-Man Jury Under Unanimous Versus Non-Unanimous Decisions," Columbia University, Bureau of Applied Social Research (1975), and Saks, JURY VERDICTS: THE ROLE OF GROUP SIZE AND SOCIAL DECISION RULE (New York: Lexington, 1977).

For all four cases: Buckhout et al., JURY VERDICTS: COMPARISON OF SIX VS. 12 PERSON JURIES AND UNANIMOUS VS. MAJORITY DECISION RULE IN A MURDER TRIAL, Report No. CR-12 (New York: Center for Responsive Psychology, 1977).

15. *Cf. supra* n. 1.

16. 399 U.S. at 89-90.

17. *Cf.* Stevens, *supra* n. 14, at 1000-1001, and Zeisel, *supra* n. 4, at 712.

18. The leading statements are found in Thompson v. Utah, 170 U.S. 343 (1898), Maxwell v. Dow, 176 U.S. 581 (1900), Rasmussen v. United States, 197 U.S. 516 (1905), Patton v. United States, 281 U.S. 276 (1930), and Capital Traction Co. v. Hof, 174 U.S. 1 (1899), a civil action.

19. 399 U.S. at 90.

20. *Id.* at 92-93.

21. *Id.* at 99-100.

22. *Id.* at 100.

23. *Id.* at 100-101.

24. 413 U.S. at 156.

25. *Id.* at 157.

26. The facts of *Ballew* can be stated briefly. (A more detailed discussion is found in Sperlich, *supra* n. 13, at 191-193.) The petitioner, Claude Davis Ballew, manager of a movie theatre, was convicted by a jury of five on a two-count misdemeanor charge for knowingly exhibiting obscene materials. In various motions and appeals, Ballew raised a number of issues regarding the constitutionality of his trial and conviction. The U.S. Supreme Court decided the case entirely on the issue of the constitutional adequacy of a state criminal jury of five. The other issues were not reached.

27. 435 U.S. at 239.

28. *Id.*

29. It may seem at first glance that a change in decision rule does not as such constitute a case of jury diminution. But a 12-person ten-to-two jury is equivalent to a ten-person jury. "The important element to observe is that the abandonment of the unanimity rule is but another way of reducing the size of the jury. But it is reduction with a vengeance, for a majority verdict is far more effective in nullifying the potency of minority viewpoints than is the out-right reduction of a jury to a size equivalent to the majority that is allowed to agree on a verdict." Zeisel, *supra* n. 4, at 772.

30. 406 U.S. at 410-411.

31. Justice White, nevertheless, did not shrink from complaining that the petitioner (Johnson) did not provide empirical evidence to support the claim that jury deliberations are not the same under unanimity and majority rule. The matter is particularly astonishing since by this complaint Justice White shifts the burden of proof from the State of Louisiana, seeking to change a constitutional tradition, to the petitioner, pleading for his customary rights. *Cf.* 406 U.S. at 362.

32. *Id.*

33. Some, of course, would argue that empirical evidence had rather little to do with the decision on the functional equivalency issue in the four cases that diminished the trial jury. The notion is prevalent that the Court used empirical evidence not so much to reach decisions, but to dress them up after they have been made. *Cf.* Zeisel and Diamond speaking of decisions "merely ornamented by the 'facts'," *supra* n. 14, at 281.

34. 47 L.W. at 4394.

35. Legal scholars and judges have not yet agreed on a standard terminology to refer to various types of facts and evidence. "Legislative facts," "social facts," "situation sense," and other terms are used in a variety of meanings. *Cf.* Davis, 2 ADMINISTRATIVE LAW TREATISE 353 (St. Paul, MN: West, 1958), and Louisell and Mueller, 1 FEDERAL EVIDENCE 395 (San Francisco: Bancroft-Whitney, 1977), as well as Horowitz, THE COURTS AND SOCIAL POLICY 274-284 (Washington, DC: Brookings Institute, 1977), Marvell, APPELLATE COURTS AND LAWYERS 149-153 (Westport, MA: Greenwood Press, 1978), and Rosen, THE SUPREME COURT AND SOCIAL SCIENCE 53-54 (Urbana: University of Illinois Press, 1972).

In this essay, *case fact* refers to the question: did this apple fall from the defendant's tree and hit the plaintiff on the head? *Social fact* is used to refer to relevant scientific principles, i.e., the law of gravity: do apples normally move up, down, or sideways when breaking off the stem?

36. Even a "hard" science, such as ballistics, has not been immune from judicial know-it-all. In People v. Berkman, 307 Ill. 492, 501, 139 N.E. 91, 94 (1923), "the court characterized offered testimony concerning ballistics as 'preposterous,' a denunciation tacitly withdrawn only seven years later in People v. Fisher, 340 Ill. 216, 172 N.E. 743 (1930)." Strong, *Questions Affecting the Admissibility of Scientific Evidence*, 1970 U. ILL. L. FORUM 1, 10, note 31 (1970).

37. Courts, of course, are put into a most difficult position when experts disagree. The problematic nature of psychiatric

testimony readily comes to mind. Disagreement among competent scientific studies was not, however, the cause of the Court's inept handling of social fact issues in the jury decisions.

38. 435 U.S. at 246. Opinion of Justice Powell, joined by Justices Burger and Rehnquist.

39. Nor is it particularly gracious to refer to the investigations of the academic experts on jury behavior as "merely . . . [the] findings of persons interested in the jury system." *Id.*

40. To a large extent, the lack of knowledge about jurors and juries is due to the non-cooperation of the courts. To a smaller degree it is due to congressional opposition. *Cf.* Sperlich, *supra* n. 13, at 201, note 38.

41. 399 U.S. at 101, note 48.

42. For a detailed review of the six items, *see* Zeisel, *supra* n. 4, at 714-715.

43. The Court not only relied on incompetent items, but misinterpreted the evidence presented in competent studies. Zeisel was forced to complain that "[i]n *Williams* the Court cites the studies conducted in connection with The American Jury to support its proposition that 'jurors in the minority on the first ballot are likely to be influenced by the proportional size of the majority aligned against them.' It is only fair to point out that the findings were quite different." *Id.* at 719.

44. *Id.* at 715. In the circumstance, "scant evidence" is a mild rebuke. As Lempert has pointed out: "Zeisel is gentle with the Court; he never emphasizes the majority's extreme disingenuousness in citing these reports as experiments and in relying on them as evidence . . ." Lempert, *supra* n. 14, at 645.

45. Saks, *Ignorance . . . , supra* n. 14, at 18.

46. Walbert, *supra* n. 14, at 535.

47. Wick, *supra* n. 14, at 14.

48. "The test laid down in *Williams* indicates that the reduced jury is unconstitutional if the smaller size impairs its performance. Consequently, a correct application of the Court's test would hold that a jury of six persons is unconstitutional." Walbert, *supra* n. 14, at 554.

49. In his review of *Williams*, Zeisel noted the spurious nature of the first of the six items, the Court's reference to Judge Wiehl's comments on the six-person jury: "Judge Wiehl approvingly cites Joiner's Civil Justice and the Jury, in which Joiner somewhat disingenuously states that 'it could easily be argued that a six-man jury would deliberate equally as well as one of twelve.' Since Joiner had no evidence for his conclusion, Judge Wiehl also does not have any." (*Supra* n. 4, at 714) The *Colgrove* Court was well aware of Zeisel's criticism. (413 U.S. at 159, note 15) Nevertheless, Joiner's opinion is included in the list of items offered by *Colgrove* in support of the functional equivalence assertion. (*Id.*)

50. 413 U.S. at 158-159.

51. *Id.* at 159, note 15.

52. For detailed discussions, *see* Zeisel & Diamond, *supra* n. 14, at 282-290, and Diamond, *supra* n. 14.

53. It must be acknowledged that some of the flaws contained in the four studies were not immediately obvious and required a certain amount of methodological understanding for their detection. This, however, does not permit the inference that the justices were victimized by inadequate science. First, the Court has consistently failed to take notice of deficiencies in the evidence that were well within the competence of the justices to discover (e.g., that an unsupported opinion that there would be no differences cannot validate a claim that there are none).

Second, the degree of methological expertise required to spot the inadequacies of the *Williams* and *Colgrove* items actually was very modest (*Cf.* Saks, *Ignorance . . . , supra* n. 14, at 20, and Zeisel & Diamond, *supra* n. 14, at 292).

Third, the Court had the ability to call for advice on specific technical questions, without having to return the case to the trial courts. Fourth, reading the Court's opinions raises substantial doubt that the "empirical evidence" actually decided these cases. The suspicion is not easily dismissed that the empirical references served "merely to ornament an already determined result" (Zeisel & Diamond, *supra* n. 14, at 281).

54. Zeisel & Diamond, *supra* n. 14, at 290.

55. *Id.* at 281.

56. Zeisel, *Twelve is Just*, 10 Trial 13 (Nov.-Dec. 1974).

57. Wick, *supra* n. 14, at 14.

58. *Williams* included this sentence: "We have no occasion in this case to determine what minimum number can still constitute a 'jury,' but we do not doubt that six is above the minimum." (399 U.S. at 91, note 28) As the State of Georgia would correctly but unsuccessfully argue in *Ballew*, if six is above the minimum, five cannot be below it, given that juries cannot consist of five and one-half persons.

59. This possibility was considered by Justice Blackmun in his concurring opinion to *Johnson*, writing that "a system employing a 7-5 standard, rather than a 9-3 or 75 per cent minimum, would afford me great difficulty." (406 U.S. at 366).

60. Reducing the proportion of jurors required to convict decreases the effective size of the jury. Indeed, it may be a more severe reduction in jury size than a direct decrease in the number of jurors. *Cf.* Zeisel, *supra* n. 29.

61. If not signaling recovery, *Ballew* (and *Burch*) indicate at least that there is a limit to the Court's favorable view of state experimentation with the trial jury.

62. It is of interest to note that *Ballew* does not have a majority opinion. Justice Blackmun's opinion for the Court was joined by Justice Stevens. Justices Blackmun, Powell, Rehnquist, Stevens, White, and the chief justice concurred in the judgment. Justices Brennan, Marshall, and Stewart concurred in the holding, but disagreed that the petitioner should be subjected to a new trial.

63. 435 U.S. at 239.

64. The relationships reported here do not have infinite linear extensions, of course. The quality of performance is not likely to be greater in a group of 2,000 than in a group of six. The smaller/larger comparisons in this context refer only to the 6/12 or 5/12 contrast.

65. 435 U.S. at 232-234. The findings were secured by references to Kelley & Thibaut, *Group Problem Solving* in 4 Lindsey & Aronson, Handbook of Social Psychology 29 (Reading, MA: Addison-Wesley, 2d ed., 1969); Lempert, *supra* n. 14; Saks, Jury Verdicts, *supra* n. 14; and, by way of Lempert, Barnlund, *A Comparative Study of Individual, Majority, and Group Judgment*, 58 J. Ab. & Soc. Psych. 55 (1959), Faust, *Group versus Individual Problem-Solving*, 59 J. Ab. & Soc. Psych. 68 (1959), and Thomas & Fink, *Effects of Group Size*, 60 Psych. Bull. 371 (1963).

66. Justice Blackmun's analysis of the empirical materials, *as it regards the five person issue*, stands in marked contrast to the treatment of "evidence" in the earlier decisions. The specific items are fair selections from the relevant literature, though a number of items could usefully have been added (*Cf. infra*).

The treatment of the selected items is competent, if not without weaknesses. The most important error occurs in the treatment of Nagel & Neef's modeling effort, which seems to have been regarded as an inductive-empirical study, without adequate attention to the dependence of the conclusions on the highly speculative assumptions made by the model. The justice relied on Nagel & Neef for the inference that the optimal jury size was between six and eight. (435 U.S. at 234) It can equally well be concluded from the model that the ideal jury size is 23. *See* Sperlich, *supra* n. 13, at 216, note 107.

67. 435 U.S. at 234-235. The findings were secured by

references to Friedman, *Trial by Jury*, 27 AM. STAT. 21 (1972); Lempert, *supra* n. 14; Nagel & Neef, *Deductive Modeling to Determine an Optimum of Jury Size and Fraction Required to Convict*, 1975 WASH. U.L.Q. 933 (1975); Saks, JURY VERDICTS, *supra* n. 14; Walbert (Note), *supra* n. 14; and, by way of Nagel & Neef, Kalven & Zeisel, THE AMERICAN JURY (Boston: Little, Brown, 1966).

68. 435 U.S. at 236. The findings were secured by reference to Lempert, *supra* n. 14; Zeisel, *supra* n. 4; and, by way of Lempert, Asch, *Effects of Group Pressure upon the Modification and Distortion of Judgments*, in Cartwright & Zander, GROUP DYNAMICS 189 (New York: Row, Peterson, 2d ed., 1960).

69. 435 U.S. at 236-237. The findings were secured by references to Lempert, *supra* n. 14; and Saks, JURY VERDICTS, *supra* n. 14.

70. 435 U.S. at 237-239. The findings were secured by references to Diamond, *supra* n. 14; Kalven & Zeisel, *supra* n. 67; Lempert, *supra* n. 14; Nagel & Neef, *supra* n. 67; Saks, *Ignorance . . .*, *supra* n. 14; Saks, JURY VERDICTS, *supra* n. 14; Walbert (Note), *supra* n. 14; and Zeisel & Diamond, *supra* n. 14.

71. 435 U.S. at 239.

72. Justice Blackmun's opinion becomes tortured when it affirms that six equals 12, while denying that five equals 12, all of this based on evidence that does not even consider the issue five, but clearly demonstrates the falsity of 6=12. It is inconceivable that the justice was oblivious to the situation. One might speculate that the explanation lies in the political realities of Supreme Court decision making, i.e., that the votes to strike down *five* were available only at the price of affirming *six*.

73. In addition to the items referred to in the preceding paragraph, Justice Blackmun took note of a number of other studies. *See* 435 U.S. at 231, note 10.

74. The State of Georgia was satisfied to dig out one of Judge Tamm's articles of questionable relevance: *The Five-Man Civil Jury: A Proposed Constitutional Amendment*, 51 GEO. L.J. 120 (1962). The attorneys for the petitioner utilized a total of six items. *Cf.* Sperlich, *supra* n. 13, at 217, note 111.

75. Saari, *The Criminal Jury Faces Future Shock*, 57 JUDICATURE 12, 14 (June-July 1973).

76. For example, Gelfand, *A Statistical Case for the 12-Member Jury*, 13 TRIAL 41 (Feb. 1977), and Gelfand & Solomon, *Analyzing the Decision-Making Process of the American Jury*, 70 J. AM. STAT. ASSOC. 305 (1975).

77. For example, Grofman, *Jury Decision-Making Models*, in Nagel, MODELING THE CRIMINAL JUSTICE SYSTEM 191 (Beverly Hills, CA: Sage, 1977).

78. For example, Buckhout, "The U.S. Supreme Court vs. Social Science: The Jury" (unpublished manuscript, 1977), as well as the many items published in SOCIAL ACTION & THE LAW.

79. Snortum et al., *The Impact of an Aggressive Juror in Six-and Twelve-Member Juries*, 3 CRIM. JUSTICE & BEHAV. 255 (1976).

80. Padawer-Singer & Barton, "Interim Report," *supra* n. 14.

81. Davis et al., *The Empirical Study of Decision Processes in Juries: A Critical Review*, in Tapp & Levine, LAW, JUSTICE, AND THE INDIVIDUAL IN SOCIETY 326 (New York: Holt, Rinehart and Winston, 1977).

82. 47 L.W. at 4393.

83. Many of the items cited in *Ballew*, as well as almost all of those suggested as additions in the preceding paragraph, offer evidence on the decision-rule issue. For purposes of *Burch*, it would also have been useful to direct attention to the work of Nemeth; for example, *Interactions Between Jurors as a Function of Majority vs. Unanimity Decision Rules*, 7 J. APPL. SOC. PSYCH. 38 (1977).

The various decision-rule studies lead to the same conclusion: different decision rules are not functionally equivalent. They also show quite clearly that unanimity differs not only

from *Burch's* 5/6 majority rule, but also from the fractions of *Johnson* and *Apodaca*. Not critically reviewing empirical evidence, Justice Rehnquist, of course, had no opportunity to doubt the wisdom of the earlier two decisions.

84. 47 L.W. at 4395.

85. *Id.*

86. *Id.* at 4394, note 7.

87. *Cf. supra* n. 33. *See also* Horowitz, *supra* n. 35, at 279, Lempert, personal communication, as quote by Grofman, *supra* n. 77, at 6, Lochner, *Some Limits on the Application of Social Science Research in the Legal Process*, 197 L. & SOC. ORDER 815, 835-836 (1973), and Rosenblum, *A Place for Social Science Along the Judiciary's Constitutional Law Frontier*, 66 NW. U.L. REV. 459 (1971). The notion also has adherents that judicial camouflaging extends far beyond the use of references to empirical evidence. "The judicial process is overwhelmingly a means of rationalizing preferred ends." Levy, AGAINST THE LAW 36 (New York: Harper and Row, 1974).

88. False information has consequences. If the real basis of a decision is not known, parties cannot effectively respond to it, which undermines the adversary process. Camouflage also is likely to mislead constitutional scholarship, lead counsel into faulty argument, and create erroneous expectations among litigants.

89. *Cf.* pp. 240-241 *supra*.

90. 435 U.S. at 243.

91. *Cf. supra* n. 1.

92. Phillips, *A Jury of Six in All Cases*, 30 CONN. BAR J. 354 (1956).

93. As examples, *see* Burger, *Report on the State of the Federal Judiciary*, 6 SUFFOLK U.L. REV. 776, 781 (1972), and *Interview with Chief Justice Warren E. Burger*, 69 U.S. NEWS & WORLD REPORT (Dec. 14, 1970) at 32, 39.

94. Augelli, *supra* n. 1, at 292, Tamm, *supra* n. 74, at 134, Thompson, *supra* n. 1, at 14, Wiehl, *supra* n. 1, at 292, and Institute of Judicial Administration, A COMPARISON OF SIX- AND TWELVE-MEMBER CIVIL JURIES IN THE NEW JERSEY SUPERIOR AND COUNTY COURTS 19 (New York: 1972).

95. Augelli, *supra* n. 1, at 291-292, Comment, *With Love . . .*, *supra* n. 1, at 192, Institute of Judicial Administration, *supra* n. 94, at 27-28, 33-34, Phillips, *supra* n. 92, at 356, Powell, *supra* n. 1, at 96-97, Tamm, *supra* n. 74, at 131-132, Thompson, *supra* n. 1, at 14, and Wiehl, *supra* n. 1, at 40.

96. Augelli, *supra* n. 1, at 292, Institute of Judicial Administration, *supra* n. 94, at 24-26, Phillips, *supra* n. 92, at 356-357, Powell, *supra* n. 1, at 97, Tamm, *supra* n. 74, at 132, Thompson, *supra* n. 1, at 14, Wiehgl, *supra* n. 1, at 40, Bogue and Fritz, *The Six-Man Jury*, 17 S.D. L. REV. 285, 288 (1972), and Devitt, *The Six-Man Jury in the Federal Courts*, 53 F.R.D. 273, 275 (1971).

97. Augelli, *supra* n. 1, at 292, Comment, *With Love . . .*, *supra* n. 1, at 192, Devitt, *supra* n. 96, at 276, Institute for Judicial Administration, *supra* n. 94, at 28-32, Phillips, *supra* n. 92, at 357, Powell, *supra* n. 1, at 97, 101, Tamm, *supra* n. 74, at 132, Thompson, *supra* n. 1, at 14, and Wiehl, *supra* n. 1, at 40.

98. Augelli, *supra* n. 1, at 291, Bogue & Fritz, *supra* n. 96, at 288-289, Devitt, *supra* n. 96, at 276-277, Phillips, *supra* n. 92, at 357-358, Powell, *supra* n. 1, at 98, Tamm, *supra* n. 74, at 133, Thompson, *supra* n. 1, at 14, and Zimmerman, *Evaluating the Six Member Jury*, 36 SOC. SCIENCE 45, 46 (1961).

99. Some of the claims are amusing, showing a rather desperate desire to justify smaller juries by appealing to thrift and fiscal responsibility. One learns, for example, that fewer jurors can move in and out of the jury box in a shorter time than a larger number. Devitt, *supra* n. 96, at 275, and Phillips, *supra* n. 92, at 357. One also learns that smaller juries can do with smaller jury boxes and smaller jury rooms. Thompson, *supra* n. 1, at 14.

It is astonishing to see that judges are capable of arguing that in deciding the fate of the jury we should take into account the few seconds saved in the movement of the jurors, and the few square feet of courtroom space saved by a smaller jury box. Besides, most American courtrooms serve a variety of trials, some of which will still require juries of 12, so that the larger jury box has to be preserved. Furthermore, most existing jury rooms are so small to begin with, that cutting them in half to create two smaller rooms would have juries deliberate in spaces resembling cells or closets.

100. For studies and discussions, *see* Baum, *supra* n. 1, at 128, Padawer-Singer, *supra* n. 14, at 50, Zeisel, *supra* n. 4, at 771-772, Zeisel, *supra* n. 56, at 13-15, Zeisel & Diamond, *supra* n. 14, at 294, Bloomstein, VERDICT: THE JURY SYSTEM 128 (New York: Dodd, Mead, 1972), Broeder, *The University of Chicago Jury Project,* 38 NEBRASKA L. REV. 744, 747 (1959), Pabst, *Statistical Studies of the Costs of Six-Man Versus Twelve-Man Juries,* 14 WILLIAM & MARY L. REV. 326 (1972), and Pabst, *What Do Six-Member Juries Really Save?,* 57 JUDICATURE 6 (1973).

101. Daily juror fees range from zero to about $20, and some courts pay a fee only when a juror actually serves on a jury, not when he waits to be chosen. For an overview of fees paid, *see* Pabst & Munsterman, *The Economic Hardship of Jury Duty,* 58 JUDICATURE 495 (1975).

102. For example, the total 1975-76 budget of New York City was $12.3 billion, of which $200 million, or 1.6 per cent, was allocated to the city's courts. Juror fees can be estimated to have been $2 million, that is, less than one-tenth of one per cent of the total city budget, one per cent of the budget of the city courts, and approximately 25¢ per resident, per year. Looking at a state, juror fees constituted one-tenth of one per cent of the Connecticut budget for 1976-77. Annual Chief Justice Earl Warren Conference on Advocacy, THE AMERICAN JURY SYSTEM, *supra* n. 5, at 8-9.

103. Bogue & Fritz, *supra* n. 96, at 289.

104. Devitt, *Six-Member Civil Juries Gain Backing,* 57 A.B.A. J. 1111, 1112 (1971).

105. Zeisel & Diamond, *supra* n. 14, at 294.

106. Multi-million dollar savings become less impressive when it is remembered that this country spends millions of dollars each year on such products as pet rocks, animal jewelry, and white walls for tires, as well as about $156 million for nail polish, $500 million for recreational outboard motors, $2 billion for movie tickets, $17 billion for tobacco products, and uncounted billions for alcoholic beverages, drugs and gambling.

107. With the "Spirit of Proposition 13" in the country, it is particularly important to examine the relative cost of the jury system, and the actual savings that could be realized by reducing or even abolishing the trial jury. A candidate, looking for issues, might even run for president by opposing "the waste of the jury system."

108. Substantial savings, for example, can be gained by eliminating the wasteful practice of calling much larger numbers of jurors than needed to court each day. *See* Pabst, *An End to Juror Waiting,* 55 JUDICATURE 277 (1972), and Note, *D.C. Court Achieves Jury Economies,* 43 JUDICATURE 171 (1960).

109. *See, for example,* Burger, *Report . . . , supra* n. 93, at 781.

110. Comment, *With Love . . . , supra* n. 1, at 180, 189, Lumbard, *supra* n. 1, at 17, Phillips, *supra* n. 92, at 354 *et seq.,* Tamm, *supra* n. 74, at 120 *et seq.,* Thompson, *supra* n. 1, at 12, Wiehl, *supra* n. 1, at 35 *et seq.,* Bullivant, *Abolition of Jury Trial in Civil Cases,* 5 OREGON L. REV. 185, 192 (1926), Gleisser, JURIES AND JUSTICE 203, 205 (New York: Barnes, 1968), Kaufman, *Harbingers of Jury Reform,* 58 A.B.A. J. 695 (1972); *see also* three articles reprinted in Winters, THE JURY: SELECTED READINGS (Chicago: American Judicature Society, 1971): Desmond, *Juries in Civil Cases—Yes or No?,* 17-19, Kronzer & O'Quinn, *Let's Return to Majority Rule in Civil Jury Cases,* 71-73, and Landis, *Jury*

Trials and the Delay of Justice, 20-21.

111. Devitt, *supra* n. 1, at 570.

112. Bloomstein, *supra* n. 100, at 128. Appellate courts function without juries, it should further be noted, but experience delay.

113. *See* Zeisel, Kalven & Buchholz, DELAY IN COURT 83-86 (Boston: Little, Brown, 1959), Kalven, *supra* n. 1, at 1058-1061, Zeisel, *supra* n. 4, at 711, Pabst, *Statistical Studies . . . , supra* n. 100, at 330, and Flynn, *Public Preference for the Jury,* 32 N.Y. STATE BAR BULL. 103, 108-109 (1960).

114. In a recent study of urban criminal courts, Levin found that delay has a variety of sources, including the *benefit* of delay to some of the parties: One of the "most striking counterintuitive findings is that, in the five criminal courts analyzed, delay did not seem to be an external phenomenon thrust upon unwilling participants. Rather, it was primarily associated with the voluntary behavior of the judges, defense attorneys, and prosecutors as they pursued their own interests. This differs from the conventional causal explanations that stress the delays caused by large caseloads thrust upon mismanaged, inefficient courts," Levin, URBAN POLITICS AND THE CRIMINAL COURTS 3 (Chicago: University of Chicago Press, 1977).

115. "In American legal theory, jury power was enormous and subject to few controls. There was a maxim of law that the jury was judge both of law and of fact in criminal cases. This idea was particularly strong in the first, Revolutionary generation, when memories of royal injustice were fresh . . . . But the rule came under savage attack from some judges and other authorities," Friedman, A HISTORY OF AMERICAN LAW 251 (New York: Simon and Schuster, 1973). Broeder speaks of the process of the "judicial emasculation" of the jury. *The Functions of the Jury: Facts or Fictions?* 21 U. CHI. L. REV. 386, 403 (1954).

116. For discussions of current jury practice regarding law decisions, *see* Jacobsohn, *The Right to Disagree: Judges, Juries and the Administration of Criminal Justice in Maryland,* 1974 WASH. U.L.Q. 571 (1976), Jacobsohn, *Citizen Participation in Policy-Making: The Role of the Jury,* 39 J. OF POLITICS 73 (1977), Kadish & Kadish, DISCRETION TO DISOBEY: A STUDY OF LAWFUL DEPARTURES FROM LEGAL RULES, especially 46-66 (Stanford: Stanford University Press, 1973), and Scheflin, *Jury Nullification: The Right to Say No,* 45 SO. CAL. L. REV. 168 (1972).

117. Phillips, *supra* n. 92, at 357.

118. Gleisser, *supra* n. 110, at 309-310. Gleisser also believes that "the judges themselves would be performing a valued service to their courts if they would encourage the waiving of juries altogether . . ." *Id.* at 310.

119. Judge Lumbard, for one, wants to speed up trials, reduce the use of the jury, and give the trial judge greater control. Regarding voir dire, he advocates that all examinations of the jurors should be conducted by the judge, and writes in a singularly revealing phrase: "It should be enough that counsel be *permitted to suggest* questions to the judge." Lumbard, *supra* n. 1, at 17; emphasis added.

120. The majority of attorneys seems to favor the larger jury. The public, particularly former jurors, strongly favors trial by jury. For data regarding the views of the various groups, *see* Association of Trial Lawyers of America, *Judges and the Jury: A Distillation of a Survey,* in Annual Chief Justice Earl Warren Conference on Advocacy in the United States, THE AMERICAN JURY SYSTEM, *supra* n. 5, at 97-99, Comment, *With Love . . . , supra* n. 1, at 183-194, Flynn, *supra* n. 113, at 103-104, Institute of Judicial Administration, *supra* n. 94, at 5, 9-14 *et seq.,* Kalven, *supra* n. 1, at 1072-1074, and Joiner, CIVIL JUSTICE AND THE JURY, 201-205 (Englewood Cliffs: Prentice-Hall, 1962).

121. As Zeisel has pointed out: "If the jury size is reduced from twelve to six, [the lawyer's perception] of the approxi-

mate balance between jury and bench trial will be disturbed. Henceforth, the 'gamble' with a jury will be significantly greater than the 'gamble' with a judge and, as a result, more lawyers might waive their right to a jury, perhaps a consequence not unexpected by those who initiated the reform.'' Zeisel, *supra* n. 1, at 719.

122. *Cf.* p. 273 *supra.*

123. Levy, *supra* n. 87, at 12-36, 43-60.

124. *Id.*, especially Chapters 2-4.

125. Zeisel, *supra* n. 14, at 370.

126. Zeisel, *supra* n. 56, at 15.

127. Berger, GOVERNMENT BY JUDICIARY 399 (Cambridge, MA: Harvard University Press, 1977).

128. See, *Social science evidence in the courts: reaching beyond the adversary process,* 63 JUDICATURE 280 (Dec/Jan 1980) for a systematic examination of these matters.

129. *Cf. supra* n. 1.

Juror characteristics: to what extent are they related to jury verdicts?

In terms of sex, race, age, and education, jurors who vote to convict aren't very different as a group from jurors who vote to acquit, a new study suggests.

by Carol J. Mills and Wayne E. Bohannon

The degree to which jurors' decision-making is guided by issues of fact has been the subject of investigation for at least 50 years.[1] The results clearly indicate that jurors consider more than issues of fact, and often recognize values outside the official rules.[2] A number of juror social and personality characteristics have been implicated in both the individual's personal decision and the process through which the jury comes to its collective verdict.[3]

To what extent these "personal" decisions, as well as the process of reaching a consensus decision, are related to jurors' demographic characteristics is an empirical question that has recently attracted new interest within the research community.[4] Part of this interest may be attributed to the political trials of the late 1960s,[5] in which jury selection teams stressed consideration of the prospective juror's individual characteristics as determinants of jury behavior.[6]

Many studies have reported the relationship between jury decisions and such demographic variables as sex, race, age, and education.[7] A juror's sex is the variable most often correlated with his or her verdict; a juror is more likely to acquit (or find for) a litigant if the juror is the same sex as the litigant.[8] The dynamics underlying this relationship are complex. Females are considerably less assertive in jury deliberations than males,[9] thus leading to less preferential treatment for females. Furthermore, females are commonly considered more empathic and lenient, and thus less "conviction-prone" than males.[10]

Education, race, and age are also related to jury decisions. One study found that highly educated jurors participate in discussions more than jurors with less education, but seem to have no more influence than the less educated jurors.[11] Blacks favored acquittal more than whites,[12] but studies examining the effects of age on jury decisions have been inconclusive.[13]

Few studies have attempted to examine the relationships between variables or how interactions among demographic variables may affect specific aspects of jury behavior. Contradictory or inconclusive results found in the literature[14] may be caused by a failure to examine the interaction between the various demographic variables. In a modest attempt to remedy this situation, this study not only tested some specific predictions, but also undertook a descriptive investigation of existing relationships between jurors' sex, race, education, and age, and self-reports of verdict patterns and perceptions of the jury experience. In addition, an attempt was made to understand such relationships as they may exist.[15]

Since the results from using simulated or mock jury trials, especially with college students as subjects, are questionable,[16] this study examined persons who served on a jury during an actual trial. And since courts limit the information available on jurors' behavior and the methods used to collect such information,[17] this study relied exclusively on self-report data for jurors' perceptions of the jury experience and general verdict patterns. As a reliability check, however, the study obtained information on final verdicts—and demographic information for each juror—through court records.

Questions and predictions

Since the purpose of this study was to examine the relationship between demographic characteristics of jurors and jury decision-making, information was collected on the final product (decision reached), the juror's perception of his or her role in the jury process, the effectiveness (and influence) in that role, and, finally, the juror's attitude concerning the final outcome (see "Questionnaire sent to jury study participants").

Verdict was of primary interest since it is the purpose for, and culmination of, all that occurs in a jury trial. General verdict patterns, both individual and group decisions (questionnaire items 1, 2, and 3), were examined for each of the demographic classifications. There is some evidence that females and blacks are more lenient and less "conviction-prone" than males and whites.[18] Sex and race differences were thus predicted, as well as differential patterns depending upon the type of case involved as suggested by other investigators of jury behavior.[19]

Individual jurors' perceived effectiveness and influence in the jury process (questionnaire items 4, 5, and 6) were examined in order to understand the dynamics involved when 12 individuals attempt to reach a consensus and whether certain "types" (e.g., males, older individuals, more highly educated individuals) of jurors may be more influential or effective than others. Serving as jury foreman and a juror's perceived ability to influence another juror's decision were chosen as measures of effectiveness and influence.

The bulk of evidence suggests that men are more assertive and influential on juries,[20] and that men serve as foremen more often than women.[21] Given the evidence and prevailing sex biases in our society[22] concerning women in leadership roles, we expected to find both a smaller percentage of women as jury foremen, and women's self-perceived influence on other jurors to be less than that of men. In addition, racial differences were expected: black males and black females would probably be more similar to white females in self-perceived effectiveness. The role of education and age in this regard is less clear from existing research, but it was expected that older and more educated individuals would generally perceive themselves as more influential.

A juror's perception of his or her role or duty in the jury situation was examined, but no predictions

were made for any of the demographic categories. Influence on a juror's decision (questionnaire items 8 and 9) beyond the evidence in a case, such as the defendant's intentions (questionnaire item 8) and the judge's charge to the jury (questionnaire item 9), was ascertained.

A sex difference was anticipated for consideration of a defendant's intentions since it has been suggested that women are more empathic than men in jury situations.[23] Taking account of a defendant's intentions in addition to the facts in a trial could be interpreted as an empathic orientation to decision-making. Little evidence is available concerning the importance to the juror of the judge's charge, and we made no predictions for this factor. The juror's perception of the ease with which his or her decision was made (questionnaire item 10) and the satisfaction experienced with that decision (questionnaire item 11) were also of interest.

Who were the jurors?

Participants in the study consisted of 117 females and 80 males who responded to an original mailing of 226 males and 324 females randomly selected from the Baltimore jury panels. Panels are selected from voter registration lists for a six-month period. It is impossible to assess the potential systematic biases introduced into the present study due to data missing from nonresponders (36 per cent response rate). However, when we compared this group with demographic information from census records and court records on jurors' demographic characteristics, we found it was highly representative of both the general population and the Baltimore jury population.[24]

Percentages in each of the demographic categories (e.g., male vs. female) for the present sample as compared to the total pool of jury participants did not differ by more than 6 per cent, and the large majority of classifications differed by only 1-2 per cent. The sample then consisted of 117 females and 80 males between the ages of 18 and 77. The mean age was 43, with 8 per cent of the jurors between 18-25, 20 per cent between 26-35, 24 per cent between 36-49, 29 per cent between 50-64, and 9 per cent over 65. Educational level ranged from 7-17 years, with a mean of 11.9 years. The majority of jurors (41 per cent) had a high school education, 30 per cent had less than this, and 29 per cent of the jurors had attended college.

Subjects received by mail a packet containing (a) a

cover letter explaining the purpose of the study and instructions for completing the material; (b) a questionnaire dealing with the juror's perceptions of the trial experience and deliberations; (c) an answer sheet; and (d) a self-addressed, stamped envelope.

Analyzing the data

Data from each questionnaire item broken down by sex, race, education, and age were analyzed by computing chi-squares, a test of statistical significance. This statistic is used to determine whether a systematic relationship exists between two variables.[25] Multivariate analyses were done to examine the multiple contribution of the four demographic variables to the prediction of questionnaire data as well as the inter-relationships between the variables. A linear regression equation was computed for each of three types of cases (murder, rape, and robbery).[26]

A significant sex difference was found for initial decision (item 1),[27] with females reporting more initial verdicts of guilty. In fact, 67 per cent of all the guilty verdicts reached were by females. This was particularly true for rape and murder cases where females gave more initial guilty verdicts (78 per cent and 71 per cent, respectively) than males (53 per cent and 50 per cent).

In order to clarify this sex difference in verdict patterns, the data were further analyzed by race. The largest sex difference was found for blacks, with black females reporting a significantly higher percentage of initial (personal) guilty verdicts (73 per cent) than black males (50 per cent).[28] No significant difference between white males (61 per cent) and females (69 per cent) was found. These findings were the opposite of those expected for the sexes. The major contribution to this surprising finding was the significant difference between black males and females with black females reporting the highest percentage of initial guilty verdicts.

Since there is some evidence that females and blacks are less conviction-prone, this was somewhat puzzling. It is interesting that a study done in 1974[29] reports that young black females (in a Baltimore sample) had the *lowest* threshold for seriousness when rating crimes; i.e., being black, female, or both black and female lead to a generally higher seriousness rating over all crimes. It is highly pos-

---

Questionnaire sent to jury study participants

Directions: Please choose *one* case (trial) you served on as a juror and that you would like to answer questions about. Use that *one* to answer the following questions. Please give only one answer for each question.

1. What was your initial (personal) decision in the case? (circle one)

    Guilty   Not Guilty

2. What was the jury's final decision in the case? (circle one)*

    Guilty   Not Guilty   Hung Jury

3. If a verdict was reached for the case you are reporting, was your initial (personal) decision the same as the jury's final decision? (circle one)

    Yes   No

4. Were you the foreman in this case? (circle one)

    Yes   No

5. If you were *not* the foreman, was the foreman: (circle one)

    Male   Female

6. Were you personally responsible for changing other jurors' decisions? (circle one)

    Yes   No

7. Did you believe that it was better to reach *some* decision, even if you were unsure of the right decision? (circle one)

    Yes   No

8. Were the defendant's "intentions" behind his/her actions important in helping you make your decision? (circle one)

    Yes   No

9. Did the judge's "charge to the jury" help you in making your decision? (circle one)

    Yes   No

10. Was your personal decision in this case an easy one to make? (circle one)

    Yes   No

11. Were you, and are you now, satisfied with the decision reached? (circle one)

    Yes   No

---

*Analyses for final group verdict patterns in most instances utilized only the "guilty" and "not guilty" responses. Only nine respondents reported a "hung jury."

Figure 1
Percentage of guilty verdicts for males and females in five age groups

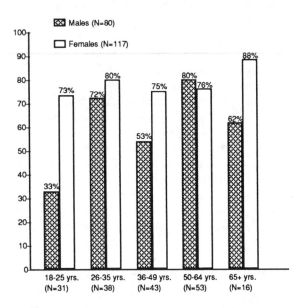

reported themselves to be less influential) than males on a jury.[32]

Effect of age and education

Jurors' guilty verdicts generally increased with age,[33] particularly for rape cases where the strongest relationship between age and number of guilty verdicts was found.[34] The relationship between verdict and age, however, was not the same for both sexes. Guilty verdicts remained high for females across all age levels (mean of 79 per cent), but increased with age for males (see Figure 1).[35] For males there were two peaks for guilty verdicts—between 26 and 35 years of age and between 50 and 64 years of age—with the lowest percentage occurring for males between 18 and 25 years of age.[36] Other researchers have reported a U-shaped relationship between age and verdicts.[37]

Level of education was also found to be related to jury voting patterns.[38] Contrary to Simon's findings that more educated jurors are more likely to convict,[39] this study found that, in general, as education level increased, so did acquittals. Again, this relationship was different for males and females (see Figure 2). Guilty verdicts remained relatively high across all educational levels for females (mean of 78 per cent), but decreased as educational level increased for males.[40] It appears that females are more conviction-prone across all education levels, whereas males with post-high school education are less likely to convict than males with less education.

Effectiveness and influence

In this sample, 65 per cent of jury foremen were males and 35 per cent females (items 4 and 5).[41] A similar ratio of males versus females serving as foremen has been found by other researchers of jury behavior.[42] Such a difference seems surprising for this sample considering the method employed for selecting foremen: the individual whose name is called first to serve on a jury is considered the foreman. Judges and attorneys, however, can affect this selection process by excusing the first listed juror and calling for the second. Selection as jury foreman did not differ by race, age, or education.

There was also a significant difference between the sexes in terms of the perception of their effectiveness within the jury experience (item 6).[43] As expected, fewer female jurors felt responsible for changing other jurors' decisions (26 per cent) than male jurors (43 per cent). This finding lends

sible that a lowered threshold for crime seriousness is associated with a propensity to convict the person accused of such crimes. Victimization rates of this subgroup (black females) of the population in large cities such as Baltimore may help to explain both of these findings.

Although the majority of jurors' personal decisions originally agreed with the final group decision, a significant sex difference was found for the amount of agreement between personal and group decisions (item 3).[30] The personal decision of 67.5 per cent of the males and 81 per cent of the females agreed with the final group decision. Only 5 per cent of the female jurors reported changing their initial decisions from not guilty to guilty, whereas 10 per cent of the male jurors did so.

In addition, if one examines only those cases where the *group* (or final) verdict was guilty, one finds that female jurors report a significantly higher percentage of initial guilty decisions than male jurors.[31] This suggests that women jurors were able to persuade other jurors to vote their way, or that they were more accurate in assessing how the group verdict would eventually turn out, particularly in the case of a guilty verdict. The first hypothesis seems untenable since the present study, as well as several other studies, found women less influential and assertive (at least in the present study they

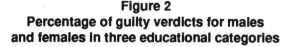

Figure 2
Percentage of guilty verdicts for males and females in three educational categories

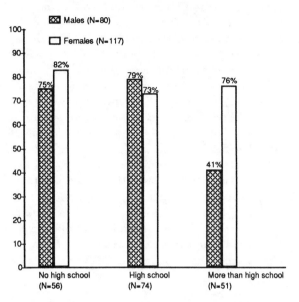

credence to the belief that female jurors are less assertive than male jurors (consistent with their role in society). Attorneys and jury selection teams, however, should keep in mind that the role of women in our society is undergoing great changes at the present time, and the impact of women as jurors should be reassessed in the near future.

When the races were separated, the above reported sex difference only held for white subjects[44] (white males=48 per cent; white females=29 per cent); black males perceived their effectiveness about the same as females overall (black males=36 per cent; black females=22 per cent). This difference between the races in terms of perceived influence and effectiveness was anticipated in view of the existing power structure in our society. Perceived effectiveness was also significantly related to level of education: more educated jurors felt greater personal responsibility for changing other jurors' minds.[45] Thus, individuals with more than a high school education reported more acquittal votes and greater perceived effectiveness than less educated individuals, and both of these relationships were greater for males than females.

Personal perceptions and influences

More males (19 per cent) than females (10 per

cent) believed that it was better to reach *some* decision, even if one were unsure of the right decision (item 7), but the difference was not significant. A majority of both males and females (86 per cent) said no decision was better than an uncertain one. Interestingly, however, 14 per cent of the jurors believed that their overriding "duty" was to reach a decision, regardless of their certainty about it. Perhaps juror education or orientation programs could address this issue more fully.

Over half of all subjects considered a defendant's intentions important in making their decision (item 8), but men and women did not differ on this variable, although we had anticipated that they would. Similarly, the judge's charge (item 9) did not influence males and females differently. Since consideration of a defendant's intentions can be seen as an empathic orientation to decision-making, the finding that women are no more likely to adopt this stance than men is consistent with the finding that women jurors in this study are more likely to give a vote of guilty than men jurors.

The races did not differ in their consideration of the defendant's intentions, but white jurors tended to consider the judge's charge to the jury more often than black jurors.[46] The race of the judge for each of the cases jurors were reporting on was not available, but it may affect this relationship. For male jurors only, level of education was related to the role that the defendant's intentions played in their making a decision[47]; intentions were least important for male jurors with some college, and most important for males with less than a high school education.

Jurors from both sexes and races and from all age and educational levels did not differ in their perception of the difficulty associated with their decision (item 10). Sex was the only demographic category in which jurors differed in their satisfaction with decision reached (item 11): women were more often satisfied than men.[48]

Multiple regression analyses

In order to examine the multiple contribution of the demographic variables, the relationships between the variables, and to separate out the differential patterns for different types of cases as suggested by other researchers,[49] we computed separate regression equations for murder, rape, and robbery cases (the Ns for drug cases [28] and civil cases [23] were too small to use in a meaningful

Table 1   Correlation coefficients and standardized
          regression coefficients* for demographic
          variables with verdict** for three types of
          cases

Demographic Variables	Type of Case		
	Murder (N=45)	Rape (N=56)	Robbery (N=45)
Sex[a]	-.11	-.04	-.35
	(-.12)	(-.03)	(-.23)
Race[b]	-.08	.01	-.07
	(-.02)	(.01)	(-.08)
Age	.28	-.31	.07
	(.28)	(-.12)	(.08)
Education	-.03	.28	-.15
	(.01)	(.23)	(-.07)
Intercept	1.42	.85	.89
R	.32	.38	.39

*Standardized regression coefficients are in parentheses ( ).
**Verdict was coded: Guilty=1, Not Guilty=2.
a Males=1, Females=2.
b Whites=1, Blacks=2.

Note: Correlations among the predictor variables were as follows:

	education	sex	race
sex	-.13		
race	-.07	.11	
age	-.25	-.07	-.14

regression equation). The independent variables of sex, race, age, and education were used to predict verdict.

Because we anticipated that the order of importance of the variables would differ for each type of case, we did not attempt to order the variables beforehand. The results of the regression analyses are shown in Table 1. As expected, the variables differed in terms of their relative predictive ability, depending upon the type of case involved. The multiple correlation coefficients shown in Table 1 indicate that from 10 per cent to 16 per cent (R^2) of the variance in verdict can be accounted for by a combination of the four demographic variables. An examination of the individual variables and the accompanying beta weights (in parentheses) shows that the four demographic variables differ widely in terms of importance, as well as direction (positive or negative sign) for each of the types of cases.

In most instances, only one or two of the demographic variables were correlated to any appreciable degree with the verdicts. Little predictive ability, therefore, was gained by a linear combination of all four demographic variables. The pattern of individual correlations, however, not only confirmed earlier reported relationships, but also illustrated the differing relationships between demographics and verdicts for various types of cases.

In only one kind of case was the sex of a juror strongly related to a particular verdict; in robbery cases, women were more likely to convict than men.

No relationship was found between race and verdict for any of the three types of cases. The important relationship, of course, was the interaction between sex and race, so that verdict patterns differed significantly for black males and females, but not for white males and females. This relationship cannot be seen with the multivariate analyses.

The relationship between age and verdict was in opposing directions for murder and rape cases. In rape cases, older people were more likely to convict (the same relationship as that reported for the total sample). For murder cases, however, older people were less likely to convict. Finally, less educated jurors were more likely to convict only in rape cases. In general, age was the best predictor of verdicts for murder cases; age and education (in opposing directions) for rape cases; and sex for robbery cases. The demographic variable that will be most salient is apparently related to the varying circumstances associated with different types of cases.

Some possible conclusions

Although demographic variables of a jury are clearly related to certain aspects of jury behavior, it is dangerous to consider the relationships between jury behavior and any variable in isolation. Sex and race interactions were particularly strong and prevalent with regard to almost all the reported findings. For instance, female jurors were found to be more conviction-prone than male jurors, but this difference applied only to black males and females. The sex and race differences reported in this study may reflect differing sexual and racial roles in our society, as well as differing sexual roles for blacks as compared to whites (i.e., within racial group, sex differences).

Age and education were related to verdict in opposing directions, but only for males. As the age of a male juror increases, he becomes more likely to convict; as his education increases, he becomes more likely to acquit. Multivariate analyses revealed that such relationships may depend on the type of case involved.

Not only did the sexes differ in regard to verdict patterns and interrelationships with other variables, but also in terms of effectiveness and influence within the deliberation process. Females did not perceive themselves as influential, and the odds of females serving as jury foreman (a position of some influence) were only half that of males. It is possible that the selection of jury foremen may be affected by sex role stereotypes.

Individuals involved with the court system should be cognizant of this possibility so that existing procedures can be examined and decisions made in the best interests of the justice system. In addition, changing roles in our society for women may have an effect on the future impact of women on juries. The perceived effectiveness of blacks was similar to that of women, presumably also a reflection of the existing social structure.

Contrary to expectations, women were not found to be more empathic than men in terms of guilty verdicts or in terms of considering a defendant's intentions. They were, however, more likely to agree with the decision of the jury and to express more satisfaction with the decision reached.

Multivariate analyses provided some clarification of the demographic variables by type of case interaction for verdict patterns. Little predictive ability was gained, however, by a linear combination of the variables. Rather, depending upon the type of case involved, one particular demographic variable was the primary predictor. In addition, the modifying effects of the various demographic variables on each other were more clearly seen with the chi-square analyses.

It must be kept in mind that this study was based on self-report data; it is thus subject to all the problems inherent in this type of data. A juror's unique (and often biased) perceptions of his or her role as juror, personal effectiveness in that role, decision reached, and effect associated with the outcome (decision) of his or her experience is, however, the essence of what this study set out to explore—particularly as these perceptions and feelings differed for the sex, race, age and educational categories.

Some aspects of the jury process can be validated (court records of verdict and confirming reports from other members of the jury), but others are too subjective to be validated (influences on a juror's decisions) and impossible to verify since one cannot watch juries in session. The authors were struck by the seriousness the jurors in this study exhibited toward the importance of the jury experience. The majority of jurors appeared to understand what was expected of them and most performed without undue influence from extraneous factors.

This study supports the utility of studying social characteristics as an aid in understanding juror

behavior. Since meaningful relationships emerged from the complex array of factors contained in the jury situation, and since some effects were attenuated as a result of the elimination of "extreme" types by the prosecution and defense attorneys during voir dire proceedings, we think further investigation of the relationship between demographic characteristics and jury behavior is warranted.

NOTES

This article originally appeared in Volume 64, Number 1, June-July 1980, pages 22-31.

The authors wish to thank Richard Christie, Robert Hogan, Milton Strauss, and Neil Vidmar for their helpful comments on an earlier version of this article, and Scotti Kaminer for her assistance in scoring and analyzing the data. The research was supported in part by a grant from the Spencer Foundation and the City of Baltimore. Special thanks go to Baltimore City Jury Commissioner Frank Sliwka and Dan Lipstein of the Mayor's Coordinating Council on Criminal Justice.

1. Marston, *Studies in Testimony*, 15 J. OF CRIM. L. AND CRIMINOLOGY 5 (1924).

2. Osborne, THE MIND OF THE JUROR AS JUDGE OF THE FACTS (Albany, NY: Boyd Printing Co., 1937); Kalven and Zeisel, THE AMERICAN JURY (Boston: Little, Brown, 1966); Kadish and Kadish, *The Institutionalization of Conflicts: Jury Acquittals*, 27 J. OF SOCIAL ISSUES 99 (1971); Tapp, *Psychology and the Law: An Overture*, 27 ANN. REV. OF PSYCH. 359 (1976).

3. Erlanger, *Jury Research in America: Its Past and Future*, 4 LAW & SOC'Y REV. 345 (1970).

4. Gerbasi, Zuckerman, and Reis, *Justice Needs a New Blindfold: A Review of Mock Jury Research*, 84 PSYCH. BULL. 323 (1977).

5. Simon, THE JURY SYSTEM IN AMERICA (Beverly Hills, CA: Sage, 1975).

6. Schulman, Shaver, Colman, Emrich, & Christie, *Recipe for a Jury*, 6 PSYCH. TODAY 37 (1973).

7. Simon, THE JURY AND THE DEFENSE OF INSANITY (Boston: Little, Brown, 1967); Kalven and Zeisel, *supra* n. 2; Sealy and Cornish, *Jurors and Their Verdicts*, 36 MODERN L. REV. 496 (1973).

8. Rose and Prell, *Does the Punishment Fit the Crime? A Study in Social Valuation*, 61 AM. J. OF SOC. 247 (1955); Nagel and Weitzman, *Women as Litigants*, 23 HASTINGS L. J. 171 (1971); Stephan, *Sex Prejudice in Jury Simulation*, 88 J. OF PSYCH. 305 (1974); Stephan and Tully, *The Influence of Physical Attractiveness as a Plaintiff on the Decisions of Simulated Jurors* in Simon, *supra* n. 5, at 100.

9. Strodtbeck and Mann, *Sex Role Differentiation in Jury Deliberations*, 19 SOCIOMETRY 3 (1956); Stephan, *supra* n. 8.

10. Stephan, *supra* n. 8.

11. James-Simon, *Status and Competence in Jury Deliberations*, 64 AM. J. OF SOC. 563 (1959).

12. Simon, *supra* n. 7; Broeder, *The University of Chicago Jury Project*, 38 NEB. L. REV. 744 (1959).

13. Stephan and Tully, *supra* n. 8.

14. Simon, *supra* n. 7.

15. Since sex appears to be basic for understanding jury behavior, interaction analyses in this study focused on this variable as it interacted with the variables of race, age, and education. In addition, multivariate analyses utilizing all four demographic variables to predict jury behavior were performed for various types of cases (e.g., murder, rape, robbery). Simon, *supra* n. 7.

16. Berman, McGuire, McKinley and Salo, *The Logic of Simulation in Jury Research*, 1 CRIM. JUST. AND BEHAVIOR 224

(1974); Miller, Fontes, Boster, Joseph, and Sunnafrank, "Methodological Issues in Jury Research: What Can Simulation Tell Us?", paper presented at the 85th annual convention of the American Psychological Association (1977).

17. Kalvin and Zeisel, *supra* n. 2.

18. Broder, *supra* n. 12; Simon, *supra* n. 7; Stephan, *supra* n. 8.

19. Simon, *supra* n. 7.

20. Strodtbeck and Mann, *supra* n. 9; Stephan, *supra* n. 8.

21. Strodtbeck, James and Hawkins, *Social Status in Jury Deliberations*, 22 AM. SOC. REV. 713 (1957); Beckham and Aronson, *Selection of Jury Foremen as a Measure of the Social Status of Women*, 43 PSYCH. REP. 475 (1978).

22. Broverman, Vogel, Broverman, Clarkson, and Rosenkrantz, *Sex Role Stereotypes: A Current Appraisal*, 28 J. OF SOC. ISSUES 59 (1972).

23. Stephan, *supra* n. 8.

24. A demographic comparison of the present sample with the population of the City of Baltimore and the Baltimore city jury population is available from the senior author.

25. This is done by computing the cell frequencies which would be expected if *no* relationship were present between the variables given the existing row and column totals (marginals). The expected cell frequencies are then compared to the actual values found. The greater the discrepancies between the expected and actual frequencies, the larger chi-square becomes. A large chi-square implies that a systematic relationship of some sort exists between the variables. For an introduction to the chi-square test of statistical significance, *see* Siegel, NON-PARAMETRIC STATISTICS (New York: McGraw-Hill, 1956).

26. Multiple regression analysis examines the linear association of one (dependent) variable (verdict) with several other (independent) variables (sex, race, age, and education); i.e., this analysis measures the strength of the association between verdict and the best fitting linear combination of the demographic variables. The multiple correlation coefficient that is generated is a direct generalization of the simple correlation coefficient "r." For a detailed discussion of regression analysis, *see* Kleinbaum and Kupper, APPLIED REGRESSION ANALYSIS AND OTHER MULTIVARIABLE METHODS (North Scituate, MA: Duxbury Press, 1978).

27. $X^2(1)=6.45$, $p<.01$.

28. $X^2(1)=4.23$, $p<.03$.

29. Rossi, Waite, Bose and Berk, *The Seriousness of Crimes: Normative Structure and Individual Differences*, 39 AM. SOC. REV. 224 (1974).

30. $X^2(1)=3.99$, $p<.05$.

31. $X^2(1)=6.49$, $p<.01$.

32. Strodtbeck and Mann, *supra* n. 9; Stephan, *supra* n. 8.

33. $X^2(4)=9.28$, $p<.05$.

34. $X^2(4)=9.73$, $p<.05$.

35. $X^2(4)=10.77$, $p<.05$.

36. One can speculate on why the youngest age group of male jurors was the least likely to convict. Perhaps this age group (18 to 25 years of age) is the least socialized and thus the least likely to uphold (by conviction) society's laws. It is also possible that this age group is more likely to identify with the large number of young male defendants accused of felonies in large cities.

37. Sealy and Cornish, *supra* n. 7.

38. $X^2(2)=10.22$, $p<.05$.

39. Simon, *supra* n. 7.

40. $X^2(2)=11.75$, $p<.02$.

41. $X^2(1)=24.17$, $p<.001$.

42. Strodtbeck et al., *supra* n. 21; Beckham and Aronson, *supra* n. 21.

43. $X^2(1)=5.23$, $p<.03$.

44. $X^2(1)=4.45$, $p<.05$.

45. $X^2(2)=15.78$, $p<.01$.

46. $X^2(1)=4.13$, $p<.06$.

47. $X^2(2)=18.59$, $p<.001$.

48. $X^2(1)=5.72$, $p<.04$.

49. Simon, *supra* n. 7.

Scientific jury selection: what social scientists know and do not know

The effects of scientific jury selection are modest at best. Social science consultants offer the most valuable aid when they help attorneys develop trial presentations that are clear and convincing.

by Shari Seidman Diamond

A jury is rarely unanimous when it takes its first vote,[1] but its final verdict is generally the decision initially favored by a majority of the jurors.[2] If the voir dire in a close case replaces only a few jurors who would favor one side with jurors who will favor the opposing side, jury selection can be critical. A voir dire that shifts the distribution of jurors to create a new majority can dramatically affect the probability of a favorable verdict.

The evidence presented at trial cannot account for initial disagreements among jurors: all jurors are exposed to the same evidence. The differences in juror reaction must stem from pre-existing differences among the jurors that affect juror responses to the evidence.[3] If 'scientific jury selection' (SJS) can help identify attributes of unfriendly jurors in advance, the attorney can exercise peremptory challenges to remove those jurors during voir dire. The prospect is enticing: what litigator faced with the uncertainties of trial would not appreciate a little assistance?

Before 1970, attorneys had to rely solely on their personal and trial experience with people and on their knowledge of their cases to develop voir dire questions and weed out unsympathetic jurors. The expert advice available from various trial specialists offered conflicting guidance.[4] A survey of litigators showed similarly inconsistent philosophies in jury selection.[5] Against this background of inconsistency, social scientists have offered their assistance, claiming a scientific basis for the advice they offer.

SJS began when the Berrigan brothers, two anti-war activist priests, were put on trial for conspiring to kidnap then Secretary of State Henry Kissinger.

Sociologist Jay Schulman and his colleagues assisted the defense in selecting the jury that hung 10 to 2 for acquittal. In the early days of SJS, the method was used largely in political criminal cases that involved substantial publicity. Prospective jurors in those cases often had strong preconceived notions about the defendants or the alleged offense. More recently, an active consulting industry has applied SJS to a wide variety of criminal and civil actions.

Methods of SJS

A primary research method used in SJS is a telephone survey in which members of the public who would be eligible to serve as jurors are asked three sets of questions. One set asks for the respondent's background characteristics (age, sex, occupation, prior jury service, prior experience as an accident victim if the case involves personal injury, etc.). The attorneys will be able to obtain this same information on each prospective juror during the voir dire.

The second set of questions on the survey may or may not be asked during voir dire. This set measures beliefs and attitudes that are likely to be associated with a favorable or unfavorable trial verdict (a dislike of oil companies or of the particular oil company which is the defendant; for a malpractice case, the belief that doctors generally do what is best for their patients).

The third set of questions directly attempts to assess which side the respondent would favor in the trial. A brief description of the case is read and the respondent is asked to vote as if on a jury deciding the case.

The jury consultant then analyzes the responses to the survey to determine which juror characteristics correlate with favorable attitudes and verdict preferences, and which attitudes and beliefs correlate with verdict preferences. This information is used to create juror profiles to guide jury selection.

Researchers may also develop selection profiles by testing respondents at research facilities. Respondents are shown opening statements or full mock trials. When they are brought into a testing facility respondents can be exposed to a better approximation of what the trial will actually involve and can be questioned more extensively than when they are tested in a telephone survey. To the extent that the simulation accurately portrays the crucial elements of the trial as it will unfold, the verdict preferences in the simulation will more accurately reflect juror reactions to the trial than the preferences expressed in the telephone survey.

The disadvantage of tests in a research facility is that a telephone survey can test a much larger and more representative sample at a much lower cost per respondent. One large jury consulting firm uses a facility for mock trials in a north suburb of Chicago. Respondents cannot easily get to the location without a car and, not surprisingly, inner city residents who appear on the jury rolls do not appear at this facility. While facilities for mock trials can be more carefully chosen, representativeness is easier to obtain in a telephone survey because more potential respondents are willing to answer a few questions over the phone than attend a testing facility. Because each method has disadvantages, SJS often relies on a combination of telephone surveys and mock trials.

The primary test of any jury selection technique is whether it can predict, based on information available before challenges must be exercised, how jurors will react to the evidence presented at trial. For SJS there is an additional test: assuming that SJS does have some predictive power, under what conditions does the 'scientific' method outperform the more intuitive method of jury selection traditionally used by the trial attorney?

There is significant disagreement in the legal and scientific communities about the answers to both of these questions. In this article, I analyze the evidence for and against the claims made for SJS. After concluding that the approach can have a modest effect at best and that it can *decrease* as well

as *increase* the probability of a favorable verdict, I outline some methods the trial attorney can use to test the value of the advice a consultant offers in a particular case. Finally, I suggest that the emphasis on SJS as the key social science tool in trial preparation is misplaced. The primary determinant of the jury's outcome is the evidence, and social science consultants offer the most valuable aid when they help the attorney to develop a trial presentation that is clear and convincing.

Effect of SJS

The consultants who offer selection advice are quick to point to cases in which the winning side used SJS techniques. While such victories are not unusual, no one has yet produced convincing evidence that advice on jury selection made the difference. The demands of the courtroom preclude a full controlled test of the technique in the courtroom setting. In the ideal test of SJS, a series of cases would be tried before multiple juries, some 'scientifically' selected and others traditionally chosen. A comparison of the verdicts rendered by the two types of juries would test the value of the method.[6] This direct test of SJS has not yet been done.

The early pioneers in SJS conducted some indirect tests. Schulman and his colleagues[7] interviewed jurors who were excused during voir dire or jury eligible community members who did not go through jury selection at all. They compared the verdict preferences of these potential jurors with those given by the jury that decided the case, that is, a jury selected with the help of SJS. The flaw in such tests is that only the real jurors have sat through the case and heard all of the evidence—those excused or never called have not. As nearly every study of jury decisionmaking indicates, the evidence presented at trial is the primary determinant of a jury verdict.[8] Accordingly, verdicts of the actual jury and the excused or never called jurors may differ, not because of the selection strategy, but because they are responses to different evidence.

In an interesting attempt to conduct a controlled test of the effects of SJS, Horowitz trained law students in either SJS or the traditional clinical approach to jury selection.[9] The law students then used the assigned technique to conduct a voir dire. Those trained to use SJS were given data from a survey of prospective jurors to guide their jury selection.

All of the prospective jurors, whether chosen or rejected, listened to the case and indicated their preferred verdicts. Horowitz then evaluated how well each method performed by examining the verdict preferences of the jurors selected by each method. On two of the four cases, the law students who used SJS made more accurate choices than those who used the traditional approach; on one case the students using the traditional approach were more accurate and on the remaining case there was no difference.

These results suggest that superior performance by SJS occurs in some, but not all, cases. The results, however, may not generalize beyond law student-attorneys. It is not clear whether the SJS method used in these cases fully replicated the range of questions used by other SJS practitioners; it is certainly clear that the law students lacked the training and experience of many trial attorneys.

SJS uses juror characteristics to predict verdict preferences and thus inform selection choices. Accordingly, a test of the foundations of SJS is the extent to which juror characteristics which predict juror verdicts can be identified. In one such study, Saks measured 461 Ohio jurors on 27 attitudes and background characteristics.[10] His respondents then watched a videotaped burglary trial and deliberated to a verdict. The best predictor of juror verdict preferences was whether a juror believed that crime was mainly the product of "bad people" or "bad social condition."[11] That question accounted for a modest 9 per cent of the variance in verdict preferences.[12] Only three other predictors improved the prediction—and together the four predictors accounted for less than 13 per cent of the variance in juror verdict preferences.

Penrod tested 367 Massachusetts jurors on 21 attitude and background characteristics and then had them indicate verdict preferences in three criminal cases and one civil case.[13] One predictor accounted for 7 per cent of the variance in verdict preferences on the rape case: jurors who favored conviction were more likely to agree that there should be evidence of physical resistance before a defendant is convicted of rape. The best predictors were able to account for about 14 per cent of the variance on the murder case, 16 per cent on the rape, under 10 per cent on the negligence case and under 5 per cent on the robbery. Juror verdict preferences on one case did not predict verdict preferences on any of the other three cases and the best predictors of verdict were not the same across the four cases.

Hastie et al. showed 828 jurors the videotaped reenactment of a real murder trial.[14] Four of the 12 background characteristics of the jurors were significant predictors of verdict preferences; they accounted for 3.2 per cent of the variance in verdicts. A sub-sample of 269 jurors was tested on a number of additional background characteristics and attitudes. With these additional predictors, Hastie et al. were able to explain 11 per cent of the variance in juror verdicts.

In an effort to predict juror verdicts in real trials, Moran and Comfort mailed questionnaires to jurors who just completed jury service.[15] They obtained responses from 319 jurors who reported what their verdict preferences had been when they began deliberating as jurors, answered questions on 11 background characteristics and filled out 13 opinion/personality scales. Two of the personality measures explained 11 per cent of the variation in verdict preferences for female jurors; no other variable increased the accuracy of the prediction. For males, only one measure was a significant predictor of verdict preference and it explained 6 per cent.

Other studies have shown similar or lower correlations between predictors and verdict preferences.[16] While each of the studies reviewed here suffers from some limitations, the pattern of results is consistent. The most important implication of this research is that claims for predicting juror responses to trial evidence should be modest indeed. The studies reviewed here report an ability to account for up to 15 per cent of the variation in juror verdict preferences.

It is, of course, possible that more powerful attitudinal measures can be developed, but there is good reason to be skeptical about the potential of SJS to improve selection decisions substantially. Assuming that more powerful attitudinal measures are available or can be developed, the measures will be valuable for jury selection only if they can be administered in court. The courtroom version of an attitude scale is a crude cousin to the sensitive measure that shows predictive power in the preparatory research. A reliable measure of attitude is generally composed of a set of questions which each respondent answers independently. In the courtroom, judges will not ask or permit attorneys to ask each potential juror the 17 questions that form the measure of empathy.[17] Even if jurors are questioned individually, they are exposed to the responses of other jurors to those same questions and their answers may be affected by those earlier responses. Moreover, courts do not permit voir dire questions unless they appear logically relevant to the case. For example, while juror support for the death penalty is consistently associated with a greater willingness to convict,[18] the question can only be asked in capital cases. Attorneys who use the results of SJS in the courtroom must thus decide which jurors to excuse based on abbreviated tests of attitudes distorted by the public arena in which they are expressed.

The national trend is toward a limited voir dire, often conducted almost entirely by the judge.[19] Under these conditions, the predictors from SJS that will be available to the attorney during jury selection will be confined to background characteristics that appear to offer limited predictive power. Even if the judge agrees to ask some of the additional questions proposed by the attorneys, the judge may change the wording so that they lose all predictive power.[20]

A second implication of the research on jury selection is that there is no profile of the good defense (or prosecution or plaintiff) juror that can be used across cases. Characteristics that emerge as predictors on one case do not show the same pattern on another case. Jurors who are most favorable to the defense in one trial will not necessarily make the best defense jurors in another trial. This is not particularly surprising. Psychologists have spent years trying to predict behavior and the results have revealed only modest levels of consistency across situations.[21] The jury consultant who provides a profile of the good defense juror suitable for all cases and applicable to all communities is offering the most blatant voodoo voir dire advice.

Finally, research on jury selection indicates that the survey efforts of SJS will not improve the accuracy of jury selection in every case. In some cases, a jury consultant may even be less accurate than the trial attorney operating without consultant advice. Statistical prediction is usually, but not always, more accurate than clinical prediction.[22] The trial attorney knows the evidence in the case, both on the client's and on the opposition's side, better than does the consultant. In addition, the attorney operating in a familiar court may be able to use the incidental information that emerges during voir dire (e.g., the strike at a local business where a prospective juror is employed). The attorney can eliminate some hostile jurors without

expert advice.[23] Accordingly, the attorney should accept advice from a survey formula for jury selection only when provided with hard evidence that the advice offers the genuine prospect of improved prediction.

Testing the consultant's advice

Consultants using SJS typically test the predictive power of a large battery of juror beliefs, attitudes and background characteristics that the consultants, the parties, and the attorneys think may be related to verdict preferences: publications read, frequency of watching the news, age, gender, number of children, occupation, marital status, income, prior jury service, attitudes toward big corporations, etc. Each of these possible predictors is compared with the juror's preferred verdict.[24] The juror characteristics that are statistically significant predictors of preferred verdicts are then included in the juror profile that will be used during jury selection.

As an example, a jury survey done in preparation for a personal injury case includes 40 potential predictors. The consultant analyzes the results of the survey and reports that males are significantly more likely to favor a verdict for the plaintiff than females; respondents who think that people generally get what they deserve are significantly more likely to favor the defense. Both relationships are significant at the traditional .05 probability level.[25] No other characteristics are significant predictors.

Any use of these results in selecting a jury would be like basing predictions on patterns in a roulette wheel. A relationship is statistically significant at the traditional .05 level if there is one chance in 20 that the result would occur in the absence of any relationship between the predictor and the verdict preference. Thus, if all 40 predictors were totally unrelated to verdict preferences, 1 in 20 or 2 of those predictors would show a significant relationship to verdict preference.[26]

Such explorations for relationships are often referred to as "fishing." They may disclose unexpected relationships between juror characteristics and verdict preferences; they may also turn up "relationships" that are simply due to chance and which will not exist when they are applied to the next set of jurors—the ones at trial. Fortunately, there are several ways to test before trial how likely it is that a relationship revealed in the survey is due to chance.[27]

First, if the number of significant predictors exceeds the number expected by chance, then the most powerful of these are likely to reflect reliable relationships.[28] Thus, if gender, age, and attitude toward oil companies are the three predictors out of 40 that are significant, it is likely that only one of the three is a dependable predictor. A consultant can easily produce the probability levels and effect sizes associated with each predictor to assess which predictor deserves attention.

Second, reliable prediction models should be reproducible on new samples. A consultant should be prepared to demonstrate that the prediction model produced from one half of the respondents in a survey can explain responses by the remaining respondents to the survey, or a new set of respondents if more than one survey is conducted. A statistical model that is based on the vagaries of sample selection or other chance elements will not produce robust results that explain the behavior or a new set of respondents. In one test of the reliability of a selection model, Baker[29] tested 18 potential predictors to produce a model with four predictors that explained 11 per cent of the variance on a measure of conviction. When tested on a new sample of respondents, respondents that the model predicted would be pro-conviction did not have higher conviction scores than those the model predicted would be anti-conviction. The model was a complete failure.

Finally, when mock juries or focus groups are held after the survey results are in, it is possible to test the consultant's model prospectively and compare it with the attorney's prediction.[30] A mock trial exposes simulated jurors to opening statements or abbreviated trial enactments. The jurors answer background questions before the mock trial takes place. They also fill out questionnaires during and after the evidence is presented. After the fact, it often seems obvious why particular jurors turned out to be pro-plaintiff or pro-defendant; the key is whether those predictions can be made before the juror's verdict preference is known. The attorney who plans to use the advice of a consultant can arrange a test in which both attorney and consultant make predictions about the likely responses of prospective jurors. If attorney and consultant use the juror background questionnaires to predict juror verdicts and the survey results do not guide the consultant to more favorable jurors, the attorney should seriously question the value of the consultant's advice in jury selection.[31]

The other role for social science

Some jury consultants are well aware of the weakness of much of their selection advice. Yet prospective clients are often eager to believe that consultants can reduce the uncertain prospect of a hostile jury and consultants are naturally reluctant to reject a friendly marketing opportunity. The result is that the client gets selection advice. In addition, however, the consultant may in the process provide other services that substantially enhance the client's position at trial. These include support for a motion for change of venue or expansive voir dire, and assistance in identifying arguments jurors will and will not find persuasive.

Change of venue. When, because of pretrial publicity or the identity of one of the parties, prospective jurors in the community may have strong preconceived notions about the facts of the case or deeply held biases towards one of the parties, a party may seek a change of venue. Evidence in the form of a community survey is one standard way to demonstrate the extent of community knowledge about the case and the prospects of a biased jury pool. It is crucial that the consultant used to conduct such a survey be able to testify competently that appropriate random sampling techniques were used to identify respondents for the survey, and that the responses were verified according to the usual survey standards.[32]

Even if the court denies a motion for a change of venue, evidence of potential prejudice may persuade the court to expand the questioning of prospective jurors during the voir dire, may convince the court that individual as opposed to group questioning is appropriate and may increase the willingness of the court to grant challenges for cause when a juror gives some sign of predisposition in the case.

Clarity and persuasiveness of the evidence. The focus on SJS neglects the key determinant of trial outcomes: the evidence. In studies that have measured the contributions of juror characteristics and trial testimony to jury verdicts, the trial testimony dominates. For example, Visher[33] studied the judgments of defendant guilt by 340 jurors in actual trials for sexual assault. She was able to explain nearly half the variation in the juror's judgments: evidence factors accounted for 34 per cent of the variance, victim and defendant characteristics accounted for an additional 8 per cent, and jurors' characteristics and attitudes accounted for only 2 per cent.[34]

The litigator has limited control over the potential evidence in a case, but litigation can involve massive amounts of potential evidence. No jury can absorb every piece of evidence that could be, or even is, presented at trial. The litigator must decide how to distill the mass of information and organize it in a framework that will be maximally intelligible and convincing. The structure provided in opening statements helps the jury organize the evidence and guides the jury's thinking during the trial.[35]

Experienced trial attorneys are skilled communicators, but they cannot see the themes of the dispute through the eyes of the juror. A pretrial test of juror reactions to the facts of the case and arguments that both sides are expected to make can provide a crucial warning that the message is unclear, that the theme initially selected is not plausible, that jurors will be bothered or unconvinced by parts of the message or that jurors are troubled by missing information that could be supplied.

By comparing the reactions of jurors to various versions of the opening statement, the consultant can help the attorney to construct the clearest and most persuasive statement of the client's position. For example, damages in the form of a firm's lost profits may be computed by showing past earnings and extrapolating into the future or by providing data on the profits of another comparable firm. A trial simulation compares jurors' reactions to the two damage models in order to determine which damage model should be emphasized at trial, and whether the presentation of both models undermines or increases the credibility of the damage estimate. Similar questions about issues like the ordering of witnesses and the best way to present statistical data can be explored before trial.

The consultant provides this feedback by selecting lay respondents representative of those who will serve as jurors in the trial, running the focus groups or trial simulations and designing appropriate questions and questionnaires to measure juror reactions. The consultant may also help prepare opening statements and trial presentation materials, ensuring in particular that the opposition's case is powerfully presented. The attorneys can watch the simulated juries as they deliberate or the focus groups as they are questioned, or they may get transcripts or videos of the juror's discussions and reports on their questionnaire responses.[36] Whether formal or informal, these "dry runs" are nearly always instructive for the attorneys. After all, aside from verdicts and an occasional question to the jurors after a verdict comes in, few attorneys have had the opportunity to get direct feedback on their courtroom attempts to persuade.

Conclusions

Attorneys are professional critics of evidence. Why then are they willing to accept the advice of consultants on jury selection so uncritically? For most attorneys, the jury is the unknown element in the trial process. The jury trial takes place precisely because the parties do not agree what the jury's verdict will be. And, unlike the judge, a jury has no reputation before the trial begins and has made no previous rulings in the case. Silent throughout the trial, the jury has the last word.[37]

The attorney preparing to select a jury at the beginning of a trial thus confronts an uncertain outcome. The active attorney, attempting to achieve control, culls his or her store of knowledge for useful counsel, some of it based on experience and logic, and some of it based on folklore, superstition, and magic.[38] Scientific magic in the form of SJS may reduce dysfunctional stress or simply appease a client who wants to be assured that every available tool has been used to prepare for trial. Significant harm is unlikely and there may be some improvement in the use of challenges if the attorney does not simply turn the decisionmaking responsibility over to the consultant or forget that evidence, far more than jury selection, determines trial outcomes.

If the effects of SJS are generally modest at best, what promise does the method offer for jury selection, apart from its value as a placebo to build litigant and attorney confidence? It is likely that SJS can in some cases affect the proportion of jurors who favor a particular verdict, just as in some cases the peremptory challenges exercised by attorneys can make a difference.[39] The difficulty is that we currently have no reliable way to identify which cases will be amenable to SJS, so that at this point we cannot be sure when the effort will justify the expense.[40] When enormous sums of money are at risk so that even a small increase in the probability of one more favorable juror represents a major achievement, a cost-benefit analysis may justify the investment in SJS despite the uncertainty. In most other cases, the uncertainty suggests a challenge for jury consultants: to demonstrate when and how their techniques are predictive. Until such documentation is provided, the attorney who considers hiring such a consultant needs to be a vigilant and critical consumer of the services that are offered.

NOTES

This article originally appeared in Volume 73, Number 4, December-January 1990, pages 178-183.

I am indebted to many people, for I have watched the development and practice of scientific jury selection as an academic psychologist, practicing attorney, and consultant. Among those who shared their views with me along the way (but are in no way responsible for mine) are Geraldine M. Alexis, Philip J. Crihfield, Reid Hastie, Richard Lempert, Henry L. Mason III, Thomas Munsterman, Arthur Patterson, Zick Rubin and Sarah Tanford. I am grateful for their insights and suggestions.

1. Kalven and Zeisel, THE AMERICAN JURY (Boston: Little Brown, 1966).

2. *Id.*; Zeisel and Diamond, *The Effect of Peremptory Challenges on Jury and Verdict: An Experiment in a Federal District Court,* 30 STAN. L. REV. 491 (1978); also see Davis, *Group Decision and Procedural Justice* in Fishbein (ed.) PROGRESS IN SOCIAL PSYCHOLOGY, VOL. 1 (Hillsdale, NJ: Erlbaum, 1980); Penrod and Hastie, *Models of Jury Decision Making: A Critical Review,* 86 PSY BULL. 462 (1979).

3. Diamond and Zeisel, *Jury Behavior* in ENCYCLOPEDIA OF CRIME AND JUSTICE (New York: Macmillan, 1983).

4. *E.g.,* Darrow (*Attorney for the Defense* May ESQUIRE MAGAZINE) counseled defense attorneys to avoid women jurors, while Katz (*The Twelve Man Jury,* 42 TRIAL 39 (1969-70)) considered women to be favorable defense jurors unless the defendant was a woman.

5. Kallen, *Peremptory Challenges Based upon Juror Background— A Rational Use?,* 13 TRIAL LAWYER'S GUIDE 37 (1969).

6. This research design was approximated in a test of the accuracy of traditional attorney jury selection (Diamond and Zeisel, *A Courtroom Experiment on Jury Selection and Decision-Making,* 1 PERSONALITY AND SOC. PSY. BULL. 276 (1974); Zeisel and Diamond, *supra* n. 2). In that study, the jurors excused by either side were retained to form a separate jury that stayed through the case and deliberated to a verdict. The results indicated that, using traditional selection methods, defense attorneys in some cases increased their odds of winning as a result of their choices during voir dire.

7. Schulman et al., *Recipe for a Jury,* PSYCHOLOGY TODAY 37 (June 1973); Kairys et al., THE JURY SYSTEM: NEW METHODS FOR REDUCING JURY PREJUDICE (Philadelphia: National Jury Project, 1975).

8. E.g., Lafree et al., *Jurors' Responses to Victims' Behavior and Legal Issues in Sexual Assault Trials,* 32 SOC. PROB. 389 (1985).

9. Horowitz, *Juror Selection: A Comparison of Two Methods in Several Criminal Cases,* 10 J. APP. PSY. 86 (1980).

10. Saks, JURY VERDICTS: THE ROLE OF GROUP SIZE AND SOCIAL DECISION RULE (Lexington, MA: Lexington, 1977).

11. Interestingly, people who believed that crime was primarily the product of bad social conditions were *more* likely to regard the defendant as guilty.

12. When jurors differ in their verdict preferences, the measure of that variability is referred to as 'variance'. If a juror characteristic or belief can help to predict jurors' verdict

preferences, it is said to explain part of the variance. The more powerful the predictor or set of predictors, the higher the proportion of the variance explained and the more accurate the prediction. Explained variation in principle can be as low as 0 or as high as 100 per cent.

13. Penrod, "Study of Attorney and 'Scientific' Jury Selection Models." Unpublished Doctoral Dissertation, Harvard University (1980).

14. Hastie et al., INSIDE THE JURY (Cambridge, MA: Harvard University Press, 1983).

15. Moran and Comfort, *Scientific Juror Selection: Sex as a Moderator of Demographic and Personality Predictors of Impaneled Felony Juror Behavior,* 43 J. PERS. SOC. PSY. 1052 (1982).

16. E.g., Simon, THE JURY AND THE DEFENSE OF INSANITY (Boston: Little Brown, 1967); Berg and Vidmar, *Authoritarianism and Recall of Evidence about Criminal Behavior,* 9 J. OF RESEARCH IN PERSONALITY 147 (1975); Buckhout et al., *Discretion in Jury Selection* in Abt and Stuart (eds.) SOCIAL PSYCHOLOGY AND DISCRETIONARY LAW (New York: Van Nostrand Reinhold, 1979); Bridgeman and Marlowe, *Jury Decisionmaking: An Empirical Study Based on Actual Felony Jury,* 64 J. OF APPLIED PSY. 91 (1979); Mills and Bohannon, *Juror characteristics: to what extent are they related to jury verdict?,* 64 JUDICATURE 23 (1980).

17. Moran and Comfort, *supra* n. 15.

18. *See, e.g.,* Cowan et al., *The Effects of Death Qualification on Jurors' Predisposition to Convict and on the Quality of Deliberation,* 8 LAW & HUM. BEHAV. 53 (1984).

19. Berman and Shapard, *The Voir Dire Examination: Juror Challenges and Adversary Advocacy* in Sales (ed.) PERSPECTIVES IN LAW AND PSYCHOLOGY, VOL. 2: THE TRIAL PROCESS (New York: Plenum, 1981); Van Dyke, JURY SELECTION PROCEDURES (Cambridge, MA: Ballinger, 1977). Some evidence indicates that jurors are less candid about their attitudes when a judge conducts the voir dire than when the attorneys conduct the voir dire (Jones, *Judge-Versus Attorney-Conducted Voir Dire: An Empirical Investigation of Juror Candor,* 11 LAW & HUM. BEHAV. 131 (1987). As a result, the trend toward judge-conducted voir dire should reduce the reliable information available to counsel during jury selection.

20. Some courts permit the parties to submit questions that the jurors answer in writing before selection begins. This procedure of course standardizes the questions and permits parallel analysis of the survey and the responses to the court questionnaire.

21. Mischel, PERSONALITY AND ASSESSMENT (New York: Wiley, 1968).

22. Meehl, *When Shall We Use Our Heads Instead of the Formula?,* 4 J. OF COUNSELING PSY. 268 (1957); Kleinmuntz, *Why We Still Use Our Heads Instead of Formulas: Toward an Integrative Approach,* PSYCHOLOGICAL BULLETIN. Human judges make systematic errors when they gather and combine information to make prediction (Dawes, *A Case Study of Graduate Admissions: Application of Three Principles of Human Decision Making,* 26 AM. PSYCHOLOGIST 180 (1971)); Dawes, *The Robust Beauty of Improper Linear Models in Decision Making,* 34 AM. PSYCHOLOGIST 571 (1979)), but even this imperfect decisionmaking can be superior to a computer model if the model omits predictors that the human decisionmaker can use.

23. Diamond and Zeisel, *supra* n. 6; Zeisel and Diamond, *supra* n. 2.

24. A proxy for the verdict preferences may be a factor score that summarizes a series of responses to questions that are expected to indicate which side the juror is likely to favor.

25. Scientific research generally accepts a difference between two groups on some measure (e.g., the verdict preferences of males versus females) as real if a difference as big as that shown in the research would occur less than five chances in a hundred if there was no real difference between the two

groups on that measure.

26. The same problem arises when multiple predictors are simultaneously tested in a multiple regression analysis and no adjustment is made in the explained variance or R^2. The probability of 'discovering' relationships due to chance is even greater when AID (automatic interaction detector) is used to test combinations of predictors (Berk et al., *The Vagaries and Vulgarities of Scientific Jury Selection: A Methodological Evaluation*, 1 EVALUATION Q. 143 (1977)). Moreover, unless sample sizes far exceed the usual 300-500 respondents typically tested in jury selection surveys, predictions about the behavior of jurors based on combinations of characteristics (e.g., female physicians) will be highly unreliable.

27. One of the reviewers suggested that no consultant would agree to cooperate with the tests proposed in this section. Markets and clients, however, determine what suppliers are willing to provide.

28. Berk et al., *supra* n. 26.

29. Baker, "Conviction Proneness as a Predictor of Sworn Jury Decisions." Unpublished Doctoral Dissertation, C.U.N.Y. (1984).

30. To adequately conduct such a test it is necessary to have a sufficient number of jurors participate in the mock trial. Even when SJS assists in selection, it only improves the odds. As a result, SJS may not appear to cause any increment in predictability in a test with a small sample, while in a large sample a genuine improvement could be detected.

31. It may be desirable to conduct a simulated voir dire before the trial simulation, but such an elaborate approach is costly in both attorney and juror time.

32. *See* National Jury Project, JURYWORK: SYSTEMATIC TECHNIQUES (New York: Clark Boardman, 1986), Chapter 7, for a good discussion of motions for change of venue.

33. Visher, *Juror Decision Making: The Importance of Evidence*, 11 LAW & HUM. BEHAV. 1 (1987).

34. *See* Saks & Hastie, SOCIAL PSYCHOLOGY IN COURT (New York: Van Nostrand Reinhold, 1978), chapter 3, for a review of research that demonstrates the dominant effect of evidence on jury verdicts.

35. Wrightsman and his colleagues have studied the way that the timing and content of opening statements can affect verdict preferences (Pyszczynski & Wrightman, *The Effects of Opening Statements on Mock Jurors' Verdicts in a Simulated Criminal Trial*, 11 J. OF APPLIED SOC. PSY. 301 (1981); Wells, Wrightsman & Miene, *The Timing of the Defense Opening Statement: Don't Wait Until the Evidence is in*, 15 J. OF APPLIED SOC. PSY. 758 (1985)). They suggest that an opening statement sets up a thematic framework that guides jurors in their processing and interpretation of subsequent testimony and evidence.

36. With little or no assistance from a consultant, an attorney can also obtain a low cost, informal reading on prospective juror reaction. Consultants generally sub-contract to field services in the city where the trial is to take place. The field service obtains respondents who are eligible for jury service according to the specifications of the consultant. Attorneys who, for example, want to try out an opening statement before a jury-eligible audience can use these same field services to obtain respondents. It may, however, be useful to use the services of a consultant to probe juror reactions.

37. The exception is that rare case in which the jury's verdict is so inconsistent with the evidence that the court sets it aside.

38. Saks, *Blaming the Jury*, 75 GEO. L. J. 693 (1986).

39. Diamond and Zeisel, *supra* n. 6; Zeisel and Diamond, *supra* n. 2.

40. Two requirements appear to be an opportunity for extensive voir dire and subject matter about which prospective jurors have substantial experience or strong opinions.

Helping juries handle complex cases

Procedural changes such as letting jurors ask questions and sequentially litigating cases could enable juries to do a better job.

by David U. Strawn and G. Thomas Munsterman

The jury trial evolved as a linear, chronological event during a leisurely time in our history. There was time to think and deliberate. Communities were small enough that jurors might know something about a subject being disputed. In fact, it was expected. Technology was far simpler, and it was reasonable to expect many men and women to understand all of the pertinent technology of the day.

The same institution today is being used without serious deliberate change in its procedures, in a culture that is intensively technological, and in which legal concepts and factual concerns have become far more refined and difficult. Obviously, the jury trial's inertia is straining against the new tides of a culture that it aided in creating, and is vital to preserving.

While the jury's factfinding function has not changed, the law has become more convoluted, and the facts-to-be-found more complex. When a complex cases arises—civil or criminal—judges are often specially selected by the bench, counsel are among the bar's finest, a special venire may be brought in (often warned of the probable length of the trial), experts on jury selection are consulted, voir dire is often done individually and at great length, pretrial is more intense and pretrial motions may challenge everything from jury selection to the jurisdiction of the court. Although *pre*trial procedures have become specialized for such complex cases, it is business as usual in the courtroom after selection of the jury. The trial proceeds much as it would have 100 years ago.

It is naive to think that the format for presentation of information that resolves a one-day burglary case can intelligently and defensibly resolve a three-month patent infringement or antitrust case. The jury that can recall all witnesses in the burglary case cannot be expected to resolve conflicts in the testimony of 100 witnesses in an antitrust case. The lawyers in this latter case may well be relying on computers to "remember" what they cannot be expected to recall as humans. Yet the jury may not even be permitted to take notes in many courtrooms.

We expect miraculous performances of today's juries in complex cases, but we don't need miracles. Instead, procedural changes could permit juries to continue to handle complex cases more effectively. Some possibilities are suggested in this article.

A step-by-step approach

Why do trials have to take place "all at once"? There is a hierarchy of decisions in every jury trial. Freshman law students learn this quickly in order to survive the onslaught of information from texts and faculty. They then learn to use the hierarchies in answering examination questions. Juries could do the same.

The most complex legal problem can be outlined, and an algorithm or "logic tree" created that will permit orderly discussion and resolution of the problem. For example, the first question in an algorithm for a burglary case might be, "Was the defendant in the store on the date and at the time of the burglary?" The "first question" to be answered by juries in more complex litigation will be nothing more than the first question the advocate knows he or she must answer in evaluating the litigation. Jury instructions using this sort of plain language algorithm have been successfully used, and have demonstrated that they do not alter outcomes while they do reduce deliberation times and increase jury focus on the evidence, showing a potential over traditional instructions for juror comprehension.[1]

The levels of decision suggested by these contemporary jury instructions may also suggest time dimensions for the judge's conduct of the case. For example, in a product liability case, where there are crossclaims and third party claims, the claims of the original plaintiff against the original array of defendants potentially liable to the plaintiff might be litigated first. By having a jury verdict returned on these issues alone, the necessity for all defendants to provide evidence and argument on the crossclaims and third party claims for indemnity or the like will possibly be eliminated or reduced by the verdict determining which defendants are liable to plaintiff. The jury's answers to special interrogatories will dictate any necessary further litigation between defendants and tiers of defendants.

Rather than litigating everything at once, the only matters litigated are those logically dictated by the order effects of the law. The same jury can serve throughout this progressive process in successive deliberations.

The idea of sequentially litigating issues has been applied in some courts.[2] For instance, in Seattle counsel asked the court to try the case issue by issue with the decision on the first issue given after presentation of evidence restricted to that issue.[3] Via this method, the parties hoped to narrow the discovery required. In addition, having the case terminated early by one of the first issue verdicts or by settlement would reduce the added expense to the clients, already high due to the complex nature of the case. When applied to the jury trial, there is the added potential of reduced counsel preparation time.

Expert panels and "how to" training

Since juror comprehension is considered the root of the problem in the complex case, why not have portions of the case requiring minor value judgments tried by the judge only, or expert panels, and other portions tried by the jury? For example, a suit involving patent violation in a complex process might have the engineering issues decided by a panel of experts or the court alone. If a violation is found, the balance of the case, including damages, would be decided by a jury.

Communication scientists and psychologists have long known that simple training exercises can greatly aid groups in avoiding deadlock and efficiently resolving conflicts. How about giving the jury some special training in how to be a jury? Such training could aid juries in avoiding "debate" and encourage "deliberation." Perhaps the jury selected for trial of a complex case should have instructions not only on the law but on the deliberation process. Simple training could help prepare them for the problems that groups predictably encounter in resolving conflicts. Very elementary rules have already been published and hang in many deliberation rooms.[4] For example, avoiding a "straw vote" [a commitment] before discussing the evidence.

Jury forepersons could be trained to aid the jury as facilitators of full deliberation. In those courts where the judge selects the foreperson, judges tend to look for persons having leadership qualities to strengthen deliberation. Perhaps the jury foreperson should receive special training, even if only concise written suggestions.

Videotaped testimony and instructions

Why don't we videotape testimony so that, instead of "reading back" with all of its inherent dullness and differences in communication from actual witnesses' testimony, the jury could call for and receive an actual recreation of the testimony of any witness, at any time, in the jury room. It is unnecessary to parade everyone into the courtroom to have a reporter flatly intone once-live testimony. The TV screen could be placed in the jury room to facilitate this.

We should also videotape the judge's instructions. This could be done quickly and easily in a simple courthouse studio. Before they are actually given to a jury, the judge could edit and correct any errors. Trial counsel would be given an opportunity to preview the instructions, although ideally a charge conference would have occurred before the taping. These instructions can be replayed by the jury as many times as necessary to assure comprehension of important legal points.

If we have an audio or video recording of the judge's instructions, why not create a written transcript of the soundtrack and give it to the jury? Research has demonstrated that juror comprehension of instructions for a burglary case increased by as much as 14 per cent by letting jurors read the instructions along with the judge, as opposed to merely listening to him.[5]

Judicious law giving

When instructions are given at the beginning of the trial or throughout the trial as is now done in some courts,[6] juror comprehension of legal ideas is enhanced. The inadequacy, in the complex case, of the traditional method of waiting until the end of the trial to tell the jurors what they should have been looking for throughout the trial is obvious. In complex cases, the judge's teaching function needs much greater emphasis. A day or two of judicially-conducted "classroom" instruction on the law, after jury selection but before the trial begins, should be the norm in complicated cases. This instruction should not be mistaken as day-long lectures on the lineage of the trial from the Magna Carta to the present, as some courts still feel is necessary.

Trial counsel's opening statements should be expanded to encourage use of visual aids and demonstrative devices. Judges should consider allowing counsel brief introductory statements to the jury before the testimony of expert witnesses to aid the jury in listening for those points counsel believes are vital. A "day's end" summary by counsel of the testimony and evidence produced that day should be encouraged. An appropriate time limit will discourage a series of "closing arguments" resulting from these procedures.

Communication science literature indicates that the first information obtained by the jury about the case is probably the information around which they will form their preliminary hypotheses. It is therefore desirable that the first information the jury hears about the law be from the judge, not from the lawyers during voir dire.

Lawyers protest that they cannot test for bias about the case unless jurors know about the case and the law's requirements. Why not have the judge instruct the *entire venire* about the law as the first event of the trial? Then, have counsel make opening statements, *at length*, to the entire venire. And, only then, proceed with voir dire. The likelihood of selection of a well-informed jury, capable of trying the complex case, should be greatly improved by these procedures.

Answering jurors' questions

If we are ever to learn what the jury understands and does not understand about the law and the issues in the case, it will only be from listening to jurors as they ask questions. What lawyer could imagine going through law school and never asking a question of a professor? And what judge can imagine a confident understanding of complex appellate arguments without an opportunity to question the attorneys?

We do not encourage feedback from jurors because we are frightened of "prejudice." Why don't we find a way to encourage juror questioning and therefore juror comprehension, avoiding prejudice at the same time? Several judges have found ways.[7] For example, a routine could be developed in which jurors would be encouraged to write their questions out as they have them, submit them to the bailiff at each recess or more often if they think the question is highly pertinent at the time. The bailiff will deliver the questions to the court, who will then determine an appropriate answer with the aid of counsel, or ask the witness the question. If the juror has asked an objectionable question, then the juror can be told simply that such evidence is not permissible in the case, and the case must be decided on the evidence that the law allows.

Experience indicates that jurors' questions do not, per se, transform the American trial process from its adversarial model to an inquisitorial one. It is still the adversaries who will provide information deemed necessary by the fact finder, where the evidence is admissible. If the evidence is not admissible, then it will be the judge's responsibility to explain this fact to the juror.

A tactic for making such explanations more palatable to the juror would be to explain in advance of trial the theory of the rules of evidence, such as using "hearsay" as an example of a "rule against rumors." Many judges who permit juror questioning tell the jury at the beginning of the trial that their questions will be considered as are questions from the attorneys, and the same standards will apply. The judge should also promise to explain the rejection or denial of any question after deliberations are completed to assure each juror that all will be clarified.

Conclusion

We offer these suggestions to show that means for aiding the American jury's continued evolution are at hand. Some are simple and demonstrated, others costly and in need of verification. The bench and bar should not assume that the jury cannot address the complex case. Trial procedure should now receive the attention and effort lavished upon pretrial procedures in the past three decades.

Rather than let the uninitiated examine the issue, a commission, including former jurors, appellate and trial judges, trial attorneys, social scientists, and experts in communications and information processing should study the problem. The commission would examine the ideas advanced in this article and elsewhere and other proposals that it would no doubt generate to provide unique perspectives about the proper presentation of complex cases to juries.

Current trial procedures do not help jurors comprehend and properly resolve complex cases. Many feel the jury is not being given a fair trial by the members of the bench and bar who would trim its importance. The American jury is the embodiment of much of our constitutional ideal. It has become an engine of our democratic republic—a focal point of participatory government. We should not be so easily persuaded to adopt the English way, after struggling so resolutely to be free of it and to be assured of participation in government through the jury.

NOTES

This article originally appeared in Volume 65, Numbers 8-9, March-April 1982, pages 444-447.

1. Strawn, Taylor and Buchannan, *Finding a Verdict Step by Step*, 60 JUDICATURE 383 (March, 1977); Pryor, Buchanan and Strawn, "Communication In The Courtroom: The Effect of Process Instructions on Jury Deliberation," paper presented at April 1978 meeting of the Southern Speech Communication Association.

Other research has demonstrated that careful attention to vocabulary and structure of jury instructions can yield significant gains in juror comprehension. *See*, Alfini, Elwork and Sales, *Juridic Decsion*, L. AND CONTEMP. PROB., 1979, and their article *Toward understandable jury instructions*, 65 JUDICATURE 432 (March-April 1982).

2. Withrow and Suggs, *Procedures for Improving Jury Trial of Complex Litigation*, 25 ANTITRUST BULL. 493 (Fall 1980).

3. Private communication with Judge James A. Noe, Seattle Superior Court, November 1980.

4. Center for Jury Studies Newsletter, No. 2-5, September 1980.

5. Strawn and Buchanan, *Jury Confusion, A Threat to Justice*, 59 JUDICATURE 478 (May 1976).

6. *Let's Learn to Instruct the Jury*, 18 JUDGE's J. 40 (Summer 1979).

7. Center for Jury Studies Newsletter, No. 3-1, January 1981.

The American Judiciary and the Politics of Representation

INTRODUCTION

Unlike legislatures, courts are not generally thought of as "representative" institutions. Nevertheless, most judges do "represent" well-defined geographical constituencies and many are, indeed, elected. To the degree that judges in a given judicial system carry unequal workloads or "service" different numbers of people, we may legitimately raise a concern about judicial "malapportionment." Further, inasmuch as juries are required to be chosen from a pool representative of the population, how great a leap is required before it is legitimate to voice concerns about a "representative" judicial branch? The issue of representation and the judiciary is a multifaceted one, and the articles in this section explore that issue in its diversity.

One major concern involving representation and the American courts centers on the relevance of the 1964 Voting Rights Act and its applicability to allegations of racial discrimination in numerous state judicial selection settings. This section of readings begins with companion pieces on "The Voting Rights Act and judicial elections litigation," in which Robert McDuff offers the plaintiff's perspective based on his experiences representing black voters, while Ronald Weber outlines the defendant's position based on his experience as an expert witness for the State of Louisiana. For McDuff, the American judiciary remains a largely segregated institution where important improvements can be brought about through rigorous enforcement of the Voting Rights Act. Weber counters by summarizing the major points put forward by the states, starting with the fundamental argument that the Voting Rights Act does not apply to judicial elections and ranging through less radical positions which, nevertheless, maximize state perogatives while creating difficulties for the plaintiffs.

For the moment, the debate between McDuff and Weber has been "settled" by a 1991 Supreme Court ruling in which the Voting Rights Act was held to be applicable to judicial elections at issue in Texas and Louisiana. The scope and full implications of the ruling will undoubtedly be defined in continued litigation. It should be noted, however, that the Court specifically excluded appointive systems from its holding. Further, it should be underlined, the Court's decision applying the Voting Rights Act to contested judicial elections was based on statutory interpretation. Consequently, future congressional action could alter the Court's ruling if legislators are unhappy with the justices' reading of congressional intent in the Voting Rights Act.

Sheldon Goldman's "Should there be affirmative action for the judiciary?" is an advocacy piece written during a time when considerable controversy existed over the Carter administration's efforts to increase the number of women, blacks, and other minorities on the federal bench. Goldman considers the litany of criticism levelled at affirmative action in judicial recruitment and offers his arguments for why none of these criticisms offer compelling indictments.

Barbara Luck Graham's study, "Judicial recruitment and racial diversity on state courts," is empirical in its orientation and presents an overview of the representation of blacks on the state bench. Graham's data are sobering and suggestive, underlining, for example, that while gains continue to be made, blacks have not achieved full parity, and their representation remains skewed towards lower status courts of limited jurisdiction.

"Different voices, different choices?" is a panel discussion that explores the consequences of the increased number of women lawyers and judges for the administration of justice in America. The discussion is wide ranging and the reading includes substantial and interesting data on women in the legal profession.

Finally, in "The paths to the federal bench: gender, race, and judicial recruitment variation," Elliot Slotnick explores empirically the different career paths through which "nontraditional" judgeship nominees (women and blacks) came to the federal bench. The data reveal that "nontraditional" candidates constitute a varied lot whose experiences and backgrounds reflect the social groups from which they came. Slotnick concludes that "representativeness in the judicial branch is difficult to come by and ... can only be realized by a commitment to a broad search for qualified candidates in nontraditional settings, thus overcoming the bias inherent in longstanding judicial selection norms and traditions."

The Voting Rights Act and judicial elections litigation: the plaintiffs' perspective

by Robert McDuff

When a lawsuit was filed in federal court in Mississippi in 1984 challenging at-large voting for state court judges, only one of the state's 100 trial court judges was black. In July 1989, five black judges were sworn into office as the result of special court-ordered elections from revised districts and voting systems, and it is possible more will be elected during the regular 1990 elections.

When a similar suit was filed in federal court in Louisiana in 1986, only six black citizens sat among the 233 judges of the state district courts, courts of appeal, and supreme court. This past July 5, the Louisiana legislature responded to a federal court order mandating changes by creating majority black voter registration districts covering 49 of those judgeships.

These are the first fruits of the proliferation of cases challenging the dilution of minority voting strength in judicial elections in a number of states around the country. Once the dust settles from all of the litigation, several state judiciaries will likely be much more racially integrated than now.

It has been a long time coming. The courts in this country are almost completely the enclave of white judges. Although the nation's population is over 18 per cent black and Hispanic according to the 1980 census, and is expected to be even higher under the 1990 count, less than 4 per cent of the judges are black and just over 1 per cent are Hispanic.[1]

This article is about the litigation over judicial election systems and its importance in desegregating state court judiciaries. It is written from my perspective as an attorney for black voters in the first two cases to go to trial, the challenge involving state trial judges in Mississippi[2] and the case dealing with state trial and appellate judges in Louisiana.[3]

Application of the Act

For nearly two decades now, minority citizens have challenged at-large elections for state legislative seats, city and county governing boards, and school boards under legal principles that prevent unfair dilution of minority voting strength. Many of the challenges have been successful, resulting in major increases in the number of black and Hispanic public officials in this country. But it is only recently that judgeships have become the target of similar lawsuits.

The question has been raised whether Section 2 of the federal Voting Rights Act, which is the primary basis for dilution lawsuits, even applies to the election of judges. Some of the states that have been sued say that the Act applies only to those public officials whose functions include representing the political interests of their constituents in specific policy decisions. Since judges are not supposed to "represent" the substantive political interests of the voters, goes the argument, the racial power-sharing principles behind the Voting Rights Act should not apply to judicial elections.

The fact that judges are not supposed to "represent" the substantive political concerns of the voters is irrelevant. The judicial districting litigation does not hinge on a theory that minority citizens should have greater political access to judges in order to affect particular judicial decisions. Instead, it is grounded in the notion that the process of electing judges—of choosing those who will sit on the bench—should be free of racial discrimination, and that minority voters should have a meaningful say in the choice just as white voters do.

The federal courts have resolved the dispute by holding that Section 2 does apply to judicial elections. The leading decision is *Chisom v. Edwards*,[4] where the United States Court of Appeals for the Fifth Circuit said this:

Where racial discrimination exists, it is not confined to elections for legislative and executive officials; in such instance, it extends throughout the entire electoral spectrum. Minorities may not be prevented from using Section 2 in their efforts to combat racial discrimination in the election of state judges; a contrary result would prohibit minorities from achieving an effective voice in choosing those individuals society elects to administer and interpret the law.[5]

The nature of the problem

Given that Section 2 applies, the next question is how to determine whether specific judicial districts violate Section 2. An answer to that question requires an understanding of the way at-large elections tend to discriminate against minority voters.

The major problem being challenged in the judicial districting litigation is the widespread use of at-large voting in multimember districts with a majority of white voters.[6] The Supreme Court noted in the recent voting rights case of *Thornburg v. Gingles*[7] that "multimember districts and at-large voting schemes may 'operate to minimize or cancel out the voting strength of racial [minorities in] the voting population.' "[8] The problem stems from the winner-take-all feature of at-large voting in multimember districts. Since every voter casts a ballot for each seat, white voters who constitute a majority in a district can control all of the seats in that district.

This becomes a particularly acute problem in light of the unfortunate and well-documented tendency of white voters in this country rarely to vote for minority candidates. For instance, between 1978 and 1987, black candidates ran against white candidates for judgeships in Louisiana on 54 different occasions, and in none of those elections did a majority, or even a plurality, of the white voters support a black candidate.[9] When that type of bloc voting is combined with the winner-take-all feature of at-large elections in districts with a majority of whites casting ballots, it is extremely difficult for minority candidates to be elected.

By contrast, changes can be made in the system to open it up so that minority voters have the power to elect candidates of their choice. For example, many at-large districts can be subdivided into smaller election districts, some of which would have black or Hispanic voting majorities. Instead of being virtually shut out from the opportunity to select judges, as in the at-large setting, minority voters would have sufficient voting power to choose some of the judges just as white voters choose judges. The practical result of this would be more minority judges, inasmuch as minority voters generally support minority candidates in the same way white voters usually vote for white candidates.

All of these factors come into play when courts are deciding whether particular at-large election districts transgress Section 2, which specifically prohibits election systems that cause minority voters to have less opportunity than white voters to elect candidates of their choice. The court have held that at-large elections are discriminatory, and Section 2 is violated, where (1) minority voters generally support minority candidates, (2) white voters generally support white candidates, with the result that minority candidates are usually defeated, and (3) an alternative system can be created by which minority voters could better elect candidates of their choice.[10] Although other factors are relevant, those are generally the core of a Section 2 violation.[11] This is true of judicial election cases as well as of legislative election cases, inasmuch as the analytical tools used to uncover discrimination in one are just as useful for detecting discrimination in the other.[12]

Designing the remedy

Once liability in particular districts has been found, the need arises to implement a remedy, a new system which cures the prior racial discrimination.

Probably the best remedial concept in most situations is that of dividing existing at-large districts into smaller subdistricts for the election of judges, with some of the subdistricts containing black or Hispanic majorities sufficient to elect candidates of choice. Indeed, subdistricts have been adopted as a remedial response in the only two cases to reach the remedial stage thus far. The subdistrict concept is discussed momentarily, as are two other systems which offer the potential to cure unlawful dilution—limited voting and cumulative voting. But first, it is important to set to rest the erroneous notion that Section 2 violations can be remedied easily by switching from elective to appointive systems.

The case against appointment

After liability was found in Louisiana for most trial and appellate court districts, the federal court gave the Louisiana legislature an opportunity to come up with a remedial proposal. Proponents of appointive judgeships attempted to persuade the legislature to change to an appointive system. The effort failed, but a similar push is underway in Texas, where Section 2 litigation is pending over existing at-large election districts.

However, appointive systems are not likely to be acceptable as a remedy for Section 2 violations in judicial elections. First of all, there is something rather sinister about taking away the power to vote for judges at the very time litigation under the Voting Rights Act promises that minority citizens will finally have their fair share of that power. States that find elective systems quite satisfactory during the years and decades when white voters control nearly all of the judicial seats ordinarily should not junk elections once it looks as though minority voters will elect judges to some of the seats as well. That kind of timing may well lead to disapproval by the federal courts of any change to appointment, or to objection by the U.S. Department of Justice in those states where the Justice Department's approval of voting changes is required under Section 5 of the Voting Rights Act.

Indeed, there are historical parallels. For instance, in 1966, just as black voters were becoming registered in Mississippi by virtue of the 1965 passage of the Voting Rights Act, the state legislature changed the method of choosing county school superintendents in a number of majority black counties from election to appointment. The Justice Department refused to approve the change under Section 5, concluding that it had the purpose and effect of diluting black voting strength.[13] A change to appointment of judges in the wake of voting rights litigation could well meet a similar fate.

Also, in a sense, appointive systems would not satisfy the key objective of Section 2 of the Voting Rights Act, which is to increase the opportunity of minority voters to elect candidates of their choice, be those candidates black, Hispanic, or white. It so happens that minority voters generally cast their ballots for minority candidates, and if a remedy increases the opportunity of minority voters to elect candidates of choice, it likely will increase the number of minority judges. But whatever candidates are chosen, the goal of the Voting Rights Act is to assure minorities a fair share of the power to choose those candidates, and that goal is not met

when elective power is taken away altogether and placed in the hands of an appointing authority such as the governor.

Even if the objective were conceived simply as increasing the number of minority judges—rather than giving minority voters a greater voice in the selection of judges—an appointive system in no way guarantees a fair number of minority judges. It depends entirely upon the discretion of the person or persons making the appointments. When a violation of the Voting Rights Act is found by a federal court, an effective remedy must be ensured by the court and not left to the discretion of a single state official.

The same uncertainties apply even where the governor's choices are limited to a list of names submitted by a nominating commission. It might help the situation to draw majority black and Hispanic nomination districts, with a requirement that the nominating commissions reflect the racial composition of the districts. Even then, however, several variables could prevent the appointment of a reasonable number of minority judges.

For all of these reasons, the efficacy of appointive systems as a Section 2 remedy is questionable. This is not to say, as a matter of general principle, that elective systems are better than appointive systems. It is only to say that a switch to an appointive system at the very time minority citizens are gaining, through voting rights litigation, a meaningful opportunity to elect some of the judges may not remedy any voting rights violations in a state's judicial election scheme. Years down the road, after a fair election system has been instituted and a state's judiciary is well integrated, it might make more sense to move to appointment of judges.

Election subdistricts

One of the best methods for remedying voting rights violations arising from multimember judicial election districts will be to divide those multimember districts into smaller subdistricts, with some having black or Hispanic voting majorities sufficient to elect candidates of choice. That is what has happened in the first two cases to proceed to the remedy stage, *Martin v. Mabus* in Mississippi and *Clark v. Roemer* in Louisiana.[14]

After the federal court in *Martin* found a violation of Section 2 in eight multimember judicial districts, no remedial action was taken by the Mississippi legislature, so the judge had to fashion the remedy. He carved the eight districts into single-member subdistricts, with judges being elected from the subdistricts yet continuing to serve the original district, and with case assignment among the judges allowed to proceed as before. No subdistrict residency requirement was imposed, and candidates were able to run from any subdistrict within their original district.[15] The plaintiffs had suggested, and were pleased with, the subdistrict concept, but contended that some of the court's subdistricts were not drawn in a way that would give black voters a fair shot at electing candidates of choice, particularly in the rural Mississippi Delta. Nevertheless, they agreed to a compromise with the state by which neither side would appeal, and court-ordered special elections went forward in the spring and summer of this year. More black trial judges were elected than ever before in Mississippi, although not as many as would have been elected under the plaintiffs' proposed subdistricts.

Meanwhile, in *Clark*, the Louisiana legislature heeded the call to devise a remedy after the federal court struck down most of the districts used to elect district and appellate court judges in the state. The new plan, passed on July 5, adopted subdistricts, many with substantial black majorities. The demographics required that some of the pre-existing districts be divided into single-member subdistricts in order to achieve sufficient black majorities, while others were divided into multimember subdistricts somewhat smaller than the original districts. Like the plan adopted by the federal court in Mississippi, the Louisiana legislature's proposal retains district-wide jurisdiction for judges elected from subdistricts, with case assignment to proceed as before, and imposes no subdistrict residency requirement. The Louisiana redistricting is linked to a state constitutional amendment which will be considered by the state's voters on October 7, 1989, and which also must be precleared by the U.S. attorney general under Section 5 of the Voting Rights Act and approved by the federal court hearing the Clark case before implementation.

Objections

A handful of objections have been raised to the subdistrict concept. Examined closely, they are meritless. Some say, for example, that it is improper to elect judges from districts that are not coterminous with the judges' geographic jurisdiction. However, no jurisprudential or constitutional principle prevents that. Indeed, it is done in several states, and repeatedly has been held to comply with the federal Constitution.[16]

Another objection to the subdistrict system is that citizens would not have an opportunity to vote on all judges who may end up hearing cases involving those citizens. Yet no right exists for litigants to vote on the particular judges who may hear their cases. As it is now, citizens are often in court in civil or criminal cases in jurisdictions where they do not live or vote, yet none has ever been able to challenge a judge's authority because the citizen had no opportunity to vote for that judge.

Some have raised the specter of corruption in the sense that judges may favor litigants from their own subdistrict over litigants from another subdistrict. If that is a problem, it is a problem as well under existing election systems inasmuch as judges frequently hear cases involving one litigant from the local judicial district and another from outside the district. Yet that has never been considered a disqualifying feature, and no one has demonstrated that any state's judiciary is rife with home-team favoritism. And no evidence exists to show that judges elected from subdistricts will be any less honest or diligent than those chosen under the current systems.

It has been suggested that subdistricts will intolerably exacerbate political pressures on judges because they would be smaller and contain fewer voters than the existing districts. This ignores the fact that most decisions made by state court judges have little political effect—they are important to the litigants and no others. To the extent that state judges do face, from time to time, controversial decisions whose outcome may sway the electorate, those decisions are usually of such notoriety that they would be as well-known, and would have as much political effect, in the pre-existing larger district as in the smaller subdistrict. Finally, even if some slight difference did exist in the political pressure coming from a subdistrict as opposed to a district election, judges are already expected to withstand that type of pressure, and such a slight difference is worth the price in order to cleanse the judicial election process of unlawful discrimination.

Limited and cumulative voting

Where the demographics make it difficult to create subdistricts with sufficiently high black or Hispanic percentages, or where other considerations suggest that subdistricts are not the way to go, other possible remedies include limited voting and cumulative voting. Briefly, the systems work this way.[17]

Under limited voting, voters have fewer votes than there are seats up for election, with the exact ratio being dependent upon the racial demographics of the district. All candidates continue to run at-large, but in a pool, and the highest number of vote getters equivalent to the number of open seats win the election. By keeping the number of ballots lower than the number of seats, limited voting minimizes the ability of white voters to sweep all of the seats and allows minority voters to concentrate their ballots behind minority candidates.

Cumulative voting is similar, except each voter has a like number of votes as there are contested seats, and each voter may cast all votes for a single candidate, or split the votes among a number of candidates. For instance, if four seats are up, a voter may cast four votes for a candidate, or three for one candidate and one for another, or one vote for each of four candidates, or any other combination. This system is much more complicated than subdistricts or limited voting, and requires a greater degree of political organization. But, it allows minority voters to concentrate their voting strength behind minority candidates and makes it unlikely that white ballots will be cast in such a way as to take all seats.

Both of these systems have been used in some jurisdictions to elect officials of local governments, with limited voting the more common of the two. They are also occasionally being adopted as remedies in local government voting rights cases.[18]

Conclusion

America's judiciary is fairly well segregated. Although that is not going to change overnight, the application of the Voting Rights Act to judicial elections will make some important inroads in several states. If the Act is applied vigorously, and strong remedies are implemented when violations are found, changes will come, and the changes will be for the better.

NOTES

This article originally appeared in Volume 73, Number 2, August-September 1989, pages 82-85.

1. The latest comprehensive statistics covering the state courts are from the 1985 publication of the Fund for Modern Courts, Inc., entitled *The Success of Women and Minorities In Achieving Judicial Office*.

2. Martin v. Allain, 658 F.Supp. 1183 (S.D. Miss. 1987) (on liability); Martin v. Mabus, 700 F.Supp. 327 (S.D. Miss. 1988)

(on remedy).

3. Clark v. Edwards, No. 86-435-A (M.D. La., unpublished opinions of August 15, 1988, and August 31, 1988).

4. 839 F.2d 1056 (5th Cir.), *cert. denied*, __ U.S. __ (1988).

5. *Id.* at 1065. *See also*, Mallory v. Eyrich, 839 F.2d 275 (6th Cir. 1988) (also holding that Section 2 applies to judicial elections).

6. In addition to contesting the use of at-large voting in particular districts, some of the lawsuits also complain about the actual drawing of lines between districts, contending that the lines fragment minority voting populations in a way that unfairly minimizes the number of majority black or Hispanic districts. In such lawsuits, the complaint is not only with the use of at-large voting within given districts, but also the placement of the lines which create the districts in the first place.

7. 478 U.S. 30 (1986).

8. *Id.* at 47, *quoting* Burns v. Richardson, 384 U.S. 73, 88 (1966).

9. The analysis of those 54 elections is documented by Professor Richard Engstrom, *When blacks run for judge: racial divisions in the candidate preferences of Louisiana voters*, 73 JUDICATURE 87 (August-September 1989).

10. Thornburg v. Gingles, 478 U.S. 30 (1986); Citizens For A Better Gretna v. City of Gretna, 834 F.2d 496 (5th Cir. 1987), *cert. denied*, __ U.S. __ (1989).

11. Thornburg v. Gingles, 478 U.S. at 48-49, n. 15, 50-51.

12. Martin v. Allain, 658 F.Supp. at 1204; Clark v. Edwards, unpublished opinion of August 15, 1988, at 38-39, and unpublished order of August 31, 1988, at 3-4; Rangel v. Mattox, No. B-88-053 (S.D. Tex., opinion of July 28, 1989), at 17-18, 20.

13. Section 5 objection letter of the Mississippi attorney general from the assistant attorney general, Civil Rights Division, U.S. Department of Justice, May 21, 1969, p. 2. *See also*, Allen v. Board of Elections, 393 U.S. 544, 570 (1969) (holding that any change from election to appointment of public officers in a covered jurisdiction must be precleared under Section 5 of the Voting Rights Act).

14. The cases originally were entitled Martin v. Allain and Clark v. Edwards, but by the time the cases reached the remedy stage, the names of the new governors were inserted as defendants, and the cases are now known as *Martin v. Mabus* and *Clark v. Roemer*.

15. Martin v. Mabus, 700 F.Supp. 327 (S.D. Miss. 1988).

16. For instance, supreme court justices in a number of states, including Louisiana and Mississippi, are elected from a portion of the state, yet hear cases from throughout the state. The same is true with some intermediate appellate court judges, whose jurisdiction is larger than their electoral district. On the trial court level, the non-record justice court judges in Mississippi (formerly justices of the peace) are elected from single-member districts within the county but have countywide jurisdiction. Certain city judges in New York City come from districts within the city but have citywide jurisdiction. Many trial judges from North Carolina are elected from areas different from their normal territorial jurisdiction, being chosen in statewide balloting but generally serving smaller districts, and until recently many trial judges in Georgia were chosen the same way. Systems such as these have been held to comply with the federal Constitution even though the jurisdiction of the judges is not geographically coterminous with their election districts. *See* Cox v. Katz, 241 N.E.2d 747 (Ct. App. N.Y. 1968), *affirming* 293 N.Y.S.2d 829 (App. Div. 1968), *cert. denied*, 394 U.S. 919 (1968); Stokes v. Fortson, 234 F.Supp. 575 (N.D. Ga. 1964) (three-judge court); Holshouser v. Scott, 335 F.Supp. 928 (M.D.N.C. 1971) (three-judge court), *summarily affirmed*, 409 U.S. 807 (1972).

17. For a fuller discussion, *see, e.g.*, Karlan, *Maps and Misreadings: The Role of Geographic Compactness in Racial Vote*

Dilution Litigation, 24 HARV. C.R.C.L. 173, 223-236 (1989); Still, *Alternatives to Single Member Districts* in Davidson, ed., MINORITY VOTE DILUTION 253 (1984).

    18. Karlan, *supra* n. 17, at 227-230, 233-235.

The Voting Rights Act and judicial elections litigation: the defendant states' perspective

by Ronald E. Weber

The electoral systems for selecting state judges are now under challenge in about 10 states by plaintiffs who allege that those systems dilute the opportunity of minority voters to elect judicial candidates of choice and hence, those systems violate Section 2 of the U.S. Voting Rights Act as amended in 1982. To date, the defendant states have employed a variety of approaches and defenses in trying to rebut the challenges of the plaintiffs. I will summarize the major approaches and defenses taken by the defendant states in responding to these voting rights suits.

The inapplicability of Section 2 of the Voting Rights Act to judicial elections

In the initial stage of each case, the state defendants have sought to show that Section 2 of the Voting Rights Act does not apply to judicial elections. They argue that judges are not "representatives" within the meaning of the word as used in Section 2 and that the U.S. Congress did not intend for Section 2 to apply to the judiciary. They further argue that since the U.S. Supreme Court has held that judicial districting plans are not subject to "one-person, one-vote" challenges under the Fourteenth Amendment to the U.S. Constitution because judges do not perform governmental functions, the Voting Rights Act adopted to carry out the Fourteenth Amendment does not apply to judicial elections. To date, all circuit and trial courts which have addressed this question have held that Section 2 does apply to judicial elections.[1]

Applicability of Section 2 requires use of "One-Person, One-Vote" criterion in proving violations

Once it is decided that Section 2 does apply to judicial elections, it is then the position of state defendants that the federal courts must employ the "one-person, one-vote" criterion in assessing whether or not judicial electoral systems are in violation of Section 2. State defendants argue that the plaintiffs must prove that the minority group is sufficiently large and geographically compact to be a majority in a single-member district. This argument suggests that a Section 2 claim cannot be proven by creating illustrative single-member districts that violate the "one-person, one-vote" criterion.

Judicial roles and judicial elections are sufficiently unique that the federal courts must exercise caution in applying the Voting Rights Act to judicial elections

The state defendants also argue that the judicial functions and roles are sufficiently different from those of the legislature and executive to warrant caution by the federal courts in applying the Voting Rights Act to the judiciary. They argue that elites and voters view the judiciary differently from other governmental institutions and hence bring different criteria to bear when making voting decisions in judicial elections. State defendants suggest that this point is borne out by evidence about the uniqueness of judicial elections. Studies of judicial elections show that, compared to elections for legislative and administrative offices, they are quite different. Judicial elections are distinguished by lower levels of turnout and voter roll-off, less competition and greater reliance by the voters on factors such as incumbency, previous judicial experience, and party affiliation in making choices among competing candidates. Thus, state defendants contend that the federal courts need to be cautious in reaching conclusions about voter polarization and dilution in judicial elections based on what they have learned before about elections for legislative and administrative offices.

The minority group must be sufficiently large and geographically compact to be a voter majority in an ungerrymandered single-member district

The state defendants contend that plaintiffs must prove clearly that the minority group is sufficiently large and geographically compact to be a voter majority in an ungerrymandered single-member judicial election district. This is a threshold requirement in Section 2 voting rights cases and if it is not met, the state defendants argue that the federal courts must dismiss the case. A simple population majority is not enough to prove the claim; instead, the plaintiffs must use voting age population or voter registration data to meet this threshold requirement.[2] Furthermore, because the minority group must be geographically compact, racially gerrymandered illustrative single-member districts cannot be employed to meet this test.

The methodologies and data used to estimate the turnout and voting preferences of racial groups must be valid and reliable

State defendants argue that estimates of turnout and voting preferences of racial groups in judicial elections are valid and reliable only under special circumstances. The analyses conducted by plaintiffs' experts should be given credibility by the courts when the analyses meet all the following tests: a) a sufficient number of cases, b) variation on both dependent and independent variables, c) contemporaneousness of election returns with the data on the racial composition of the voting age population, d) comparability of the geographical units (usually precincts) in the analysis, e) proper procedures to verify the data and f) a properly functioning statistical analysis program. Plaintiffs' experts bear the burden of showing that their analyses meet these criteria.

Racially polarized voting in judicial elections must be shown by analyzing all elections for judicial office

The state defendants also contend that it is inappropriate for plaintiffs to try to prove the presence of racially polarized voting by examining only those elections in which minority candidates have participated. In the absence of judicial elections with minority candidate participation, plaintiffs employ elections for nonjudicial offices with minority candidate participation as substitutes for the judicial

elections. State defendants' position is that elections for nonjudicial offices cannot be used to prove racially polarized voting for judicial offices. Instead, they argue that only recent judicial elections must be analyzed and that the analyses should not be limited to the subset of elections with minority candidates.

Vote dilution in judicial elections must be shown by proving that the majority bloc votes regularly in judicial elections to prevent the choices of minority bloc voters from being elected

State defendants also argue that the presence of racially polarized voting in judicial elections does not necessarily mean that vote dilution is occurring in those elections. It is their position that vote dilution occurs only when the majority bloc votes regularly to prevent the election of candidates supported by minority bloc voters. This regularity must include all elections for judicial office and not just those in which minority candidates have participated.

The failure of minority bloc supported candidates to win judicial elections may be accounted for by factors other than the race of the candidates

State defendants further contend that the federal courts must look into alternative explanations to explain why minority bloc supported candidates fail to win judicial elections. Whereas plaintiffs allege that it is the race of the candidates that provides the explanation for minority supported candidate failure, state defendants suggest that other factors may apply. Political party affiliation, incumbency, previous judicial experience, campaign spending, and voter mobilization efforts often will explain the lack of success by minority supported judicial candidates.

Remedies in judicial election voting rights cases may include the retention of multijudge election subdistricts, staggered terms, and place election systems

State defendants finally claim that the single-member election subdistrict remedy may not always be the best solution to vote dilution by at-large judicial election systems. They argue that multimember election subdistricts should be adopted if at all possible when the minority population is sufficiently large. They also suggest that staggered term and place election systems can be used when the election subdistricts are sufficiently homogeneous so those systems will not have the effect of acting as anti-single shot voting impediments to voting participation.

NOTES

This article originally appeared in Volume 73, Number 2, August-September 1989, pages 85-86, 118.

1. Martin v. Allain, 658 F.Supp. 1183 (S.D. Miss. 1987); Chisom v. Edwards, 839 F.2d 1056 (5th Cir. 1988); Mallory v. Eyrich, 839 F.2d 275 (6th Cir. 1988); Clark v. Edwards, No. 86-435-A (M.D. La., unpublished opinion of August 15, 1988); SCLC v. Siegelman, No. 88-D-0462-N (N.D. Ala., unpublished opinion of June 7, 1989).

2. Houston v. Haley, 869 F.2d 807 (5th Cir. 1989); Westwego Citizens for Better Government v. City of Westwego, 872 F.2d 1201 (5th Cir. 1989).

Should there be affirmative action for the judiciary?

Special efforts to find qualified women and minorities for the federal bench are not incompatible with merit selection because they ensure that we choose the "best" judges from among all possible candidates.

by Sheldon Goldman

The Carter administration jolted the legal community with its outspoken and widely publicized affirmative action policy of placing women and ethnic minorities on the federal bench. Many of the arguments raised against the implementation of affirmative action programs elsewhere are now being heard with regard to the judiciary along with arguments attuned to the special status of the federal bench. But after considering the nature of the administration's efforts and successes in implementing judicial affirmative action, I have concluded that the legal profession ought to applaud President Carter and Attorney General Bell.

As I see it, six major objections can be raised against an affirmative action approach to federal judicial selection. Each, I believe, can be persuasively answered. I would like to discuss these objections briefly and the rejoinders I find convincing.

1. The dangers of classifying people. Affirmative action inevitably leads government agencies to define race, critics argue, and it leads government officials to make judgments about racial characteristics. Is an individual with one black grandparent or great-grandparent (say, Homer Plessy) to be classified as black? What about someone with one black parent who was raised by white foster parents? Is an American-born individual with an American father and Mexican mother Hispanic? The argument, essentially, is that it is dangerous for government to make any racial classifications. Such activities stir memories of the racial laws of Nazi Germany and run counter to the value Americans have traditionally placed on treating individuals on the basis of their personal qualities and not their racial attributes.

Response: While many (including myself) are uncomfortable with government concern with race/ethnicity, I believe there is a crucial and fundamental distinction between America's official racial consciousness for purposes of affirmative action and the racial classifications of totalitarian regimes. America's purpose is to aid definable classes of persons who have historically suffered from official discrimination. Racial classifications in Nazi Germany were, of course, for ghastly purposes, and in more contemporary totalitarian societies ethnic designations on identity cards and other records form the basis for official discrimination.

The federal judiciary has been and still is an overwhelmingly white, male institution, for many reasons. America's long-standing racism and sexism, for example, have historically limited opportunities in the judiciary for women, blacks, and Hispanics. It does not seem unreasonable to make special efforts to recruit from these groupings of Americans for federal judgeships. Deliberate considerations of race and sex should not be given negative connotations so long as the government demonstrates positive, anti-racist, anti-sexist motives and purposes.

2. The threat of reverse discrimination. The real result of affirmative action, opponents argue, is reverse discrimination. Government selects a group or groups of persons for favored treatment, thereby putting all others at a disadvantage. This is reminiscent of George Orwell's *Animal Farm* where all animals are equal but some are more equal than others. On an individual basis this produces reverse discrimination; individuals are ruled out of consideration *because* they are the "wrong" race or sex. Furthermore, when it comes to judicial selection, those women, blacks, and Hispanics who are favored for judgeships are frequently from the same social class and similar backgrounds as competing white males, and their careers have not necessarily suffered from discrimination. Why then should they have an advantage?

Response: I cannot be persuaded that affirmative action is reverse discrimination—at least when the objective is *not* to give minorities a majority hold. I have not seen evidence that any affirmative action program of any kind in the United States has seriously threatened the majority status of white males in government, industry, the professions, or academia. Certainly the type of affirmative action that the Carter Administration is promoting for the judiciary in no way threatens the overwhelming majority status of white males.

Although the administration's efforts thus far to place women, blacks, and Hispanics on the federal bench have been spectacular when compared with the record of previous administrations, taken alone the results of the Carter administration's affirmative action policy are actually very modest. About 12 per cent of the Carter nominees have been black, and about the same proportion have been women.[1] In terms of the entire federal bench, the proportions of blacks and women are exceedingly small and for Hispanics almost non-existent.

At the individual level, the charge of reverse discrimination potentially can be more troublesome, as it was in the *Bakke* case. But we do not have to be concerned with this since judicial selection traditionally has involved numerous variables. The addition of racial/ethnic and sexual considerations is in no way inconsistent with the host of other considerations that have been involved in judicial selection, including geography, party affiliation, party activity, sponsorship by senators and other key politicians, professional connections, ideological or policy outlook, and so on. Race/ethnicity and sex are today politically relevant variables and they have been added to other political type variables in a selection process that historically has been political.

3. The error of focusing on group affiliation. No matter how worthy an objective it may be, critics say, affirmative action is inconsistent with the professional goal of merit selection, which many judicial reformers and the Carter administration itself espouse. How can one accept the principle that only the best qualified should be given judgeships and then decree that women, blacks, and Hispanics are to be given special preference? Merit selection emphasizes individual qualities; affirmative action stresses group affiliation.

Response: It does a disservice to women, blacks, and Hispanics to suggest that they do not ordinarily possess as strong a set of professional credentials as white males do, but I will not dwell on this obvious rejoinder. What I find persuasive is the fact that, based on my own extensive research and that of others,[2] we never had, we do not now have, and we probably never will have a judicial selection method based solely on professional merits. The professional credentials of candidates do play a part in judicial selection, but rarely have they been the determining factor. Of course, it is important to have qualified persons sitting on the bench, and there is no question in my mind that Attorney General Bell, under affirmative action, is recommending to the president only persons with the professional credentials essential to perform the job.

Ironically, affirmative action may provide a more potent push towards merit selection than anything else that has ever been done. By searching for well qualified women, blacks, and Hispanics, the administration and Democratic senators are downplaying party activity and political connections. This breaks with the past judges-as-patronage syndrome that historically characterized much of judicial selection.

Let me add for the record that the administration's so-called merit selection of appeals judges is not merit selection in fact. As recent issues of *Judicature* have shown,[3] mostly Democrats (including large numbers of Carter loyalists) have chosen mostly other Democrats for placement on the lists given the president. Other Democrats then lobby the Democratic president as to which Democrats to choose.

However, the selection process has become more open in large part due to institution of merit commissions and the affirmative action push. It is highly unrealistic to expect a civil service type merit approach to judicial selection ever to be established. Even assuming that an effective merit selection process could be instituted, I would have to be persuaded that the sorts of people chosen were better suited for the bench than the sorts of people chosen through our traditional political processes.

4. The need for government neutrality, not favoritism. Affirmative action is a remedy to right a proven constitutional wrong, critics emphasize. Even if it could be proven that racism and sexism served to exclude blacks, women, and Hispanics from the judiciary, that would not justify affirmative action in choosing the highest officials of the federal government. It would only justify efforts to ensure that these groups were no longer deliberately excluded.

Blacks prevented from voting were eventually protected by federal legislation and action to enable them to exercise the franchise, but they were not given the right to elect so many black congressmen or black state representatives. Women given the right to vote in 1920 were not given the right to have a specific number of women in high elective or appointive office. Isn't it sufficient that the judicial selection process be non-discriminatory? Isn't affirmative action inappropriate here?

Remedy: The racial and sexual make-up of the judiciary, past and present, speaks for itself. It is clear that all-pervasive societal attitudes toward women, blacks, Hispanics, and indeed other groups such as Asian-Americans and American Indians severely limited their opportunities in the law and that they were, in fact, routinely and systematically excluded from federal judgeships. Justice Department officials and senators were not necessarily themselves racist or sexist. It is simply that within the framework of political reality and racist and sexist belief systems in the larger society, appointments of women, blacks, and some other ethnic groups were impossible.

But leaving aside the difficult questions of proof, and, indeed, whether constitutional wrongs were committed in the past, it can be argued that government can serve as a teacher by setting a good example and structuring situations in which learning and personal growth can occur. Clearly, the widespread racist and sexist attitudes of the past and the discrimination so widely practiced were moral, if not constitutional, wrongs. We should seize this opportunity to correct them.

By seeking out and appointing to federal judgeships a visible number of qualified women and minorities, government is teaching the nation that racial and sexual stereotypes are invalid. Government is also teaching young women, young blacks, and young Hispanics that it no longer recognizes as political reality the racial and sexual biases of the past, and that individual accomplishment and achievement are more important than race and sex.

Yes, it is ironic that affirmative action that recognizes race and sex is necessary in order to hasten the time when race and sex will be irrelevant, and when racism and sexism are virtually non-existent. Perhaps most importantly, by voluntarily undertaking affirmative action, the government is practicing what it preaches (although, make no mistake about it, the Carter administration is responding to its own political needs and commitments). We ought to welcome any diminution of government hypocrisy.

5. The problem of quotas. Affirmative action in practice results in a quota system, opponents contend, and quotas are dysfunctional for the workings of American institutions. Quotas based on group affiliation and not individual merit can work grave hardship on well-qualified individuals who are in excess of their group's quota, and, in general, quotas tend to promote mediocrity. Quotas can exclude superior qualified persons who have the wrong sex, race, religion, or ethnic affiliation; they can include not only the marginally qualified, but even unqualified persons. Affirmative action is the first step on the road to the balkanization of America, and the courts—our prized palladiums of justice—should be the last place where this concept is imposed.

Response: Affirmative action programs have existed for close to a decade, and I am not persuaded that the parade of horrors suggested above has even begun to come about. I see no movement within the United States for each ethnic or religious grouping to claim a quota of public or private jobs. Most Americans accept individual merit as the proper basis for school admissions and employment opportunities.

Although the distinction may be fuzzy, I do see a difference between affirmative action and a quota system. Affirmative action does not have a rigid numerical goal; it retains flexibility yet is a good faith effort to widen the recruitment net, indeed to vigorously recruit, and pay particular attention to women and disadvantaged racial/ethnic groups. Affirmative action also means selecting the individual from the previously discriminated-against group when all else is approximately equal.

I have not heard or read the word "quota" in connection with the Carter administration's affirmative action objectives for judicial selection. I would oppose the use of a quota system as unnecessarily rigid and singularly inappropriate for the judiciary, but this is not at issue. The Carter administration itself, as I understand it, is making strenuous efforts to recruit, or have selection commissions and senators recruit, qualified women, blacks, and Hispanic candidates. The administration, as I also understand it, is quite concerned with the qualifications of minority and women candidates.

If the politics of federal judicial selection today makes it unlikely that incompetent white males will go on the bench, the politics of affirmative action requires that only competent minorities and women be appointed. The surest way to sabotage affirmative action is to link it with incompetency. The Carter Administration's record of minority and women appointments thus far has been excellent and there is every reason to believe that the concern with credentials of minority and women candidates will continue to yield well-qualified judges.

6. An inappropriate program for the judiciary. No matter what the merits of affirmative action may be for other spheres of American life, critics insist, it is highly inappropriate for the judicial branch. Even though merit may not actually be the sole criterion for judicial selection, it is recognized as ideally the basis for choosing judges, and leading professional groups have been working to make progress towards that goal. But if a criterion other than individual merit gains legitimacy, it becomes all the more difficult to assign to oblivion the "extraneous" political considerations that have traditionally "polluted" the process. And it becomes more difficult to win support for a partisan-free merit selection process.

Part of the justification for merit selection is that a federal judge must be highly skilled since the federal courts are the fastest legal tracks in town. We need the best people for the job; would we select a surgeon to perform a highly complex and delicate operation on any basis other than the best person available? Why should we do less with the judiciary? We need the best people on the bench regardless of race, sex or national origin. In the words of the president, "Why not the best?"

Response: This is a slippery argument to counter. To be sure, there must be highly competent judges to service the trial and appellate courts of the nation. Official recognition of race and sex does appear at first blush to detract from the goal of a non-discriminatory process for obtaining the best

qualified persons to serve. But a closer look at the job of federal judges should make it clear that our judges have always been involved in the major political controversies of the day. As Tocqueville so perceptively observed over 140 years ago, "Scarcely any political question arises in the United States that is not resolved, sooner or later, into a judicial question."[4]

Today, racial and sexual discrimination are major legal issues before the courts. A judge who is a member of a racial minority or a woman cannot help but bring to the bench a certain sensitivity—indeed, certain qualities of the heart and mind—that may be particularly helpful in dealing with these issues. This is not to say that white judges are necessarily insensitive to issues of racial discrimination or that male judges cannot cope with issues of sexual discrimination. But the presence on the bench in visible numbers of well qualified judges drawn from the minorities and women cannot help but add a new dimension of justice to our courts in most instances.

These judges cannot help but educate their colleagues by the example they set, by the creation of precedents, and by informal as well as formal interchange. They are likely the "best" people to fill certain of the vacancies and new judgeships.

Yes, we ought to aspire to obtaining the "best" people for our judiciary—but the "best" bench may be one composed of persons of all races and both sexes with diverse backgrounds and experiences and not necessarily only those who were editors of the Harvard and Yale law reviews. It is difficult to define—much less find—the "best." Despite occasional mistakes, the current selection process with its political sensitivity has served the nation well. But affirmative action of the sort advocated and being practiced by the Carter Administration should strengthen the federal bench. And perhaps most significantly, it may be that by searching for the best possible women and minority candidates, a precedent will be established for emphasizing the individual professional merits of all candidates for judgeships, regardless of race and sex.

NOTES

This article originally appeared in Volume 62, Number 10, May 1979, pages 488-494.

1. Goldman, *A profile of Carter's judicial nominees*, 62 JUDICATURE 246 (November 1978).

2. *See* the text and citations in Goldman and Jahnige, THE

FEDERAL COURTS AS A POLITICAL SYSTEM 47-78 (New York: Harper & Row, 1976, 2nd ed.).

3. Carbon, *The U.S. Circuit Judge Nominating Commission: a comparison of two of its panels*, 62 JUDICATURE 233 at 236 (November 1978); Slotnick, *What panelists are saying about the circuit judge nominating commission*, 62 JUDICATURE 320 (February 1979).

4. de Tocqueville, DEMOCRACY IN AMERICA 290 (New York: Random House, Vintage Books edition, vol. 1, 1945).

Judicial recruitment and racial diversity on state courts: an overview

Despite gains since the 1970s, blacks remain underrepresented on the state bench. Although affirmative action programs and judicial redistricting may enhance representation, the effects of institutional arrangements, political participation, and elite behavior need further exploration.

by Barbara Luck Graham

The informal and formal processes of determining who becomes a judge evoke intense interest and debate among various groups that seek to influence the nature, character, and policy outcomes of our nation's courts. Political parties, bar associations, political elites, and interest groups (business, union, environmental, or civil rights organizations, etc.) struggle to participate and influence the processes of judicial recruitment and selection at the national and state level with the desired goal of shaping judicial policy outcomes favorable to their interests. The political struggle over judicial recruitment and selection also raises the issue of diversity on the bench, whereby members of racial and ethnic minority groups and women seek representatives of their groups to serve on courts in order to insure that they have a voice in judicial decision making. Viewed in this context, judicial recruitment is an important area of study because it speaks to the broader theoretical issue of minority group elite recruitment and representation in the judicial arena.

The issue of racial diversity on courts is one that has been given uneven scholarly attention in the literature on judicial recruitment.[1] On one hand, considerable attention has been paid to minority group representation at the federal court level. For example, conventional wisdom now posits that representational criteria such as race, gender, and religious factors figure prominently for nomination to the U.S. Supreme Court and the lower federal courts.[2] To be sure, the determination of how much weight will be attached to representa-

tional factors varies among presidents and is usually dependent upon partisan and ideological considerations. Yet the literature seems to suggest that there is an expectation that diversity on the federal bench will continue to be an issue as long as the federal courts are accorded special status in our dual legal system.

Only recently, however, has similar attention been given to minority judicial recruitment at the state level. Recognizing the importance of state courts in the administration of justice and that most minority citizens are likely to come into contact with state, not federal courts, minority groups are now focusing on the extent to which state judicial systems provide opportunities to serve on the bench. Minority group efforts to penetrate access to the state bench become more problematic when we consider the existence of 50 state court systems accompanied with varied formal and informal judicial recruitment and selection processes to fill vacant seats on these courts. Whether states become and remain committed to a diverse bench will be a major challenge for minority groups and women in the 1990s.

An examination of the literature on judicial recruitment and black representation on the state bench reveals that additional research is necessary to address the important questions raised in this area. This study seeks to fill a major gap in the literature in its examination of minority judicial recruitment at the state level. The purpose of this article is to examine characteristics of judicial recruitment as it pertains to racial diversity on the state bench. It focuses on four major areas of concern. First, data are examined that explore the extent to which blacks are represented on state courts at all levels of the judicial hierarchy. Next, it looks at the structural and contextual explanations of black underrepresentation on state courts. Third, it examines two remedies for correcting the problem of black underrepresentation on the state bench. Finally, it considers the consequences and implications of the lack of racial diversity on the state bench for the administration of justice.

The research population under investigation is the universe of black judges presiding over state courts of general and limited jurisdiction in the United States. The data source for identifying black judges comes from a list of black judges in the United States compiled by the Joint Center for Political Studies (JCPS) and the Judicial Council of the National Bar Association.[3] This roster includes names, addresses, and indication of the court presided over by the judge as of July 1986. Attempts were made to verify the existence of the judges on the specified courts and to determine how they initially obtained their seats for the highest general jurisdiction and special jurisdiction courts (civil or criminal) in the states. These data collection efforts involved gathering information from state court clerks and administrators,[4] court biographical directories,[5] state reporters, and state official manuals. As a result, this study analyzes data on 714 state court judges covering 41 states for 1986. Several major developments compel a reexamination of how characteristics of judicial recruitment affect racial diversity on the state bench. Greater attention to the policymaking activities of state courts raises the issue of whether women and minorities will have the opportunity to influence outcomes at all levels of the state judiciary. This development comes at a time when the U.S. Supreme Court and the lower federal judiciary are becoming increasingly conservative on issues of civil liberties and civil rights. The importance of this research is also underscored in light of several states' reexamination of their methods of selecting state judges. A contemporary assessment of black representation on state courts is expected to reveal additional insights into the problem of minority judicial recruitment at the state level.

Are blacks underrepresented?

The few empirical studies that analyze black judi-

cial recruitment largely draw upon a data base in the early 1970s, a period in which there were extremely small numbers of black judges on state courts.[6] In 1972, Cook noted that one of the major research problems that occurs in an examination of black representation in the judiciary was identifying and locating black judges on state courts.[7] In order to assess the factors that affect black judicial recruitment, it is first necessary to offer a recent profile of black representation on state courts. In this section, two major issues are addressed. First, data are presented which show the nationwide distribution of black judges on state courts by level of court. In analyzing these data, I attempt to address the substantive question of whether blacks are actually underrepresented on state courts.

The JCPS publication identified 714 black judges presiding over state courts of general and limited jurisdiction and included a listing of quasi-judicial officials as of July 1986.[8] These data were coded and classified according to the distribution of black judges on the state bench by level of court and are presented in Table 1. The number of seats on states' major appellate and trial courts are also included. As of 1986, we find that 41 states had black representation on their major and minor courts. Specifically, the data in Table 1 reveal that nine states, Alaska, Hawaii, Maine, Montana, New Hampshire, North Dakota, South Dakota, Vermont, and Wyoming, lacked black representation on their state courts. One might argue that opportunities for recruitment would be increased or limited depending on the size of the black population in the state. If the percentage of the black voting age population in the state is used as a measure of black population size,[9] we find that among the nine states listed above, seven had a black voting age population of less than one-half of 1 per cent. Contrastingly, Idaho and Utah, states with less than one-half of 1 per cent black voting age population, had black representation on their state courts.

Table 1 also demonstrates that 41 per cent (N=293) of the black judges identified by the JCPS roster were classified as general jurisdiction judges and 59 per cent (N=421) were either limited jurisdiction judges or quasi-judicial officials. This finding indicates that black judges are more likely to be found on limited jurisdiction judges or quasi-judicial officials. This finding indicates that black judges are more likely to be found on limited jurisdiction courts such as municipal courts, small claims courts,

Table 1 Distribution of black judges on state bench by level of court, 1986

State	State supreme court	Intermediate appellate court	General trial court	Total major courts	Limited juris. courts	Total all
Alabama	1 (9)	— (8)	4 (124)	5	14	19
Arizona	— (5)	— (18)	1 (101)	1	1	2
Arkansas	— (7)	— (6)	— (62)	0	2	2
California	1 (7)	4 (77)	29 (724)	34	54	88
Colorado	— (7)	— (10)	3 (107)	3	2	5
Connecticut	— (7)	— (9)	7 (139)	7	—	7
Delaware	— (5)	*	1 (13)	1	4	5
Florida	1 (7)	1 (46)	7 (362)	9	7	16
Georgia	— (7)	1 (9)	4 (131)	5	15	20
Idaho	— (5)	— (3)	1 (33)	1	—	1
Illinois	— (7)	3 (34)	42 (780)	45	—	45
Indiana	— (5)	— (12)	2 (206)	2	3	5
Iowa	— (9)	— (6)	1 (153)	1	—	1
Kansas	— (7)	1 (10)	2 (215)	3	—	3
Kentucky	— (7)	— (14)	2 (91)	2	—	2
Louisiana	— (7)	1 (48)	5 (192)	6	27	33
Maryland	1 (7)	1 (13)	11 (109)	13	10	23
Massachusetts	— (7)	1 (10)	4 (61)	5	12	17
Michigan	1 (7)	2 (18)	22 (196)	25	44	69
Minnesota	— (7)	— (12)	4 (224)	4	—	4
Mississippi	1 (9)	*	1 (79)	2	31	33
Missouri	— (7)	1 (32)	6 (303)	7	4	11
Nebraska	— (7)	*	— (48)	0	1	1
Nevada	— (5)	*	2 (35)	2	—	2
New Jersey	— (7)	1 (28)	11 (321)	12	21	33
New Mexico	— (5)	— (7)	— (59)	0	1	1
New York	1 (7)	3 (47)	24 (484)	28	35	63
North Carolina	1 (7)	2 (12)	1 (72)	4	14	18
Ohio	— (7)	2 (53)	6 (330)	8	19	27
Oklahoma	— (12)**	— (12)	1 (143)	1	2	3
Oregon	— (7)	— (10)	1 (85)	1	1	2
Pennsylvania	1 (7)	1 (24)	24 (330)	26	10	36
Rhode Island	— (5)	*	— (19)	0	1	1
South Carolina	1 (5)	1 (6)	1 (31)	3	51	54
Tennessee ·	— (5)	— (21)	8 (125)	8	3	11
Texas	— (18)**	1 (80)	6 (374)	7	27	34
Utah	— (5)	— (7)	— (29)	0	1	1
Virginia	1 (7)	1 (10)	2 (122)	4	2	6
Washington	— (9)	— (16)	3 (133)	3	1	4
West Virginia	— (5)	*	2 (60)	2	1	3
Wisconsin	— (7)	— (13)	3 (197)	3	—	3
Total	11	28	254	293	421	714
	(289)	(741)	(7402)	(8432)		

( ) Number of seats on state courts. See Council of State Governments, *The Book of the States, 1988-89 Edition*, (Lexington, KY) 157-160 for a complete description of how these figures were derived.

— No black judges on court.

* Court does not exist in state.

Includes state supreme court and court of criminal appeals seats.

family courts, or justice of the peace courts. It is likely that limited jurisdiction courts serve as important access routes for black judgeships in the state judiciary and subsequently advancing through the judicial hierarchy.[10] An examination of biographical data on black judges serving on general jurisdiction courts indicates that many of them served on limited jurisdiction courts prior to their 1986 positions.

The fact that most black judges in the state judiciary are located on limited jurisdiction courts also suggests that they currently have limited opportunities to participate in judicial policy making at the trial and appellate levels. The data presented in Table 1 show that 87 per cent (N=254) of the black judges preside over trial courts of general jurisdiction and 13 per cent (N=39) preside over intermediate appellate courts and state supreme courts. General jurisdiction courts address a wide range of issues on matters such as criminal offenses, personal injury actions, divorce cases, and the overall important policymaking function of allocating resources (in terms of gains and losses) that affect millions of individuals. Moreover, issues of discrimination in a variety of contexts are frequently before state courts; thus minority judges may be able to bring additional sensitivity and insight in dealing with these issues. Without greater numbers of black judges at the major trial and appellate levels, one can argue that the black community is deprived of the minority perspective on legal matters and the development of the law at the state level.

The judicial recruitment literature also indicates the importance of region as a contextual factor in contributing to our understanding of the distribution of judicial selection systems throughout the country. An overview of the distribution of the five major selection systems indicates the nonrandom tendency of states to choose one selection system over another. For example, we find that elective systems (partisan and nonpartisan) dominate among southern states, merit systems are most often found in the midwest and western regions, and gubernatorial appointment systems are primarily found in the northeast. A breakdown of Table 1 by region indicates that the north central states have the highest number of general jurisdiction black judges (N=88), followed by the northeast (N=70), south (N=56) and the west (N=40).[11] These findings are somewhat striking given that 15 states make up the south as defined in this study and that the south has the highest black voting age population and the highest percentage of black elected officials compared with other regions of the country. This finding illustrates a wide disparity in regional distributions of general jurisdiction black judges. In contrast, the south leads the other regions for limited jurisdiction judges (N=210), followed by the northeast (N=79), north central (N=71), and the west (N=61). Region, then, is a useful contextual variable when examining recruitment patterns of blacks to the state bench.

Have black attorneys made progress in obtaining seats on state courts? The American Judicature Society reported in 1973 that slightly more than 1 per cent of judges on the state bench were black.[12] The trends presented in Table 2 indicate that progress has been made for obtaining general jurisdiction seats over time. What is significant about the figures presented in Table 2 is that a large percentage of black judges (46 per cent) for which data were available obtained their seats since 1980. If this trend continues, one can speculate that black attorneys will continue to make progress in obtaining seats on the state bench in the 1990s.

Against this background, are blacks underrepresented in the state judiciary? Of course, representation can be defined in several ways such as symbolic, substantive, and proportional.[13] Symbolic representation is exemplified by the presence of judges by identifiable members of their race or gender. Smith and Crockett have shown how black judges provide symbolic pride and inspiration and serve as a symbol of law and justice for members of their group.[14] Once on the bench, it is argued that black judges provide substantive representation by deciding cases in a manner that reduces the vestiges of racism in the legal system.[15] Empirical studies have shown that once on the bench, black judicial decision making increases equality of treatment among defenders.[16]

The most prevalent definition of representation found in the judicial recruitment literature is proportional representation; that is, the proportion of black judges should reflect the same proportion of blacks in the general population. Indeed, if this definition is used, unquestionably blacks are underrepresented on the state bench. Yet, using proportional representation as the yardstick is problematic since for a large majority of seats on state courts, only licensed attorneys are eligible to serve as judges. From another perspective then, an argument can be raised that the black attorney population is the most relevant population to measure against the proportion of black judges on the state bench.

Recent figures indicate that black judges make up approximately 3.8 per cent of all the full and part-time seats on the state bench.[17] Similarly, black attorneys constitute approximately 3 per cent of the legal profession. Tentatively, one could conclude from these figures that black judges are not underrepresented on the state bench since the proportion of judges on the state bench are roughly equal to the number of attorneys. On the other hand, we should consider the point that black attorneys are grossly underrepresented in the legal profession; figures indicate that there are about 25,000 black attorneys out of a total pool of 750,000.[18] From this perspective, using the proportion of black attorneys as the population to measure against is misleading for it does not take into account the small pool of available black attorneys to serve on the bench. In the following section, I will consider the utility of this contextual factor in explaining black representation on the state bench.

Explaining a homogeneous bench

What explains black underrepresentation on the

Table 2   Year general jurisdiction judges initially obtained seats*

Year	N	%
1957-1969	14	6%
1970-1974	40	17%
1975-1979	72	31%
1980-1986	109	46%
Total	235	100%

* The year the judge initially reached the bench could not be determined for 58 judges.

state bench? The judicial recruitment and selection literature advances two dominant approaches in accounting for the lack of racial diversity on the state bench: structural and contextual explanations. The theoretical underpinnings of the empirical research that highlights structural characteristics of judicial recruitment and selection are generally linked to elite recruitment in other political contexts. This view suggests that structural and systemic forces in the political environment affect the extent to which underrepresented groups gain access to positions at all levels of government. For example, the political participation literature has demonstrated that barriers to voting (e.g., vote dilution techniques and registration requirements) have enhanced black nonvoting and engenders the inability of black citizens to choose representatives of their choice. Drawing on this literature, studies have sought to determine whether judicial selection mechanisms are central to our understanding of recruitment outcomes for minority groups.

Contextual explanations have also emerged in explaining the paucity of black judges on the state bench. This approach suggests that other factors besides judicial selection affect the extent to which blacks will be represented on the state bench. The contextual variable that has received the most attention in the literature is the availability of black attorneys to serve on the state bench. The expectation is that the lack of black attorneys correlates with the lack of black judges on the bench. State statutory qualifications are likely to affect the size of the pool of available attorneys from which judges are selected. The primary ones include age, residency requirements, and legal qualifications such as being a member of the state bar or having practiced law for a certain period of time. These requirements[19] vary among the states, but because of the lack of nationwide data on black attorneys by state, it is difficult to assess the impact of these qualifications or the extent to which they affect the numbers of black attorneys to serve on the state bench.

Three early studies offer some insights on the effects of judicial selection and black representation on the state bench. Cook[20] found that in southern courts, electoral systems did not produce black judges on major courts, but a large majority of blacks served on rural courts of limited jurisdiction where in many instances a law degree was not a necessary qualification. Her examination of black representation on northern courts revealed that nonpartisan elections were more favorable in enhancing black representation on state courts, partisan elections were least favorable and that gubernatorial appointment tended to produce idiosyncratic results. In her study, Cook also demonstrated that the very low percentage of black lawyers correlated with the lack of black judges on both northern and southern courts, but this variable did not account entirely for the small number of black judges.

Smith examined black judicial attitudes toward recruitment and selection based on an early 1970s survey of 185 state and federal judges.[21] His study indicated that while 55 per cent of the judgeships were listed as elective, 77 per cent of the black jurists surveyed were appointed to the bench. His analysis also demonstrated that judicial elections tended to be less influential in the recruitment of black judges. Black voters, according to Smith, were less influential in getting blacks to judicial office than professional standing, political party, and friendship.

A 1973 American Judicature Society study revealed that black judges constituted approximately 1.3 per cent of the judiciary.[22] Despite the argument that black attorneys stand a better chance of acquiring judgeships through the elective rather than the appointive process, the study showed that most black jurists surveyed attained their positions through some form of appointment. The study found that the prime reason for the small proportion of black judges was the small number of black lawyers available to serve on the bench.

Recent attempts to address the question of whether different methods of judicial selection result in different degrees of access to the bench depending on such factors as gender and race include a 1985 study published by the Fund for Modern Courts.[23] In a nationwide survey, the study demonstrated that the success of women and minorities in achieving judicial office depends on methods of selection—that a higher percentage of women and minorities attained more judicial positions through appointment than an elective process.

When statistical controls were employed, Dubois found only minor differences between elective and appointive systems for female and nonwhite judges recruited to sit on the California trial court bench.[24] He attributed this finding to the under-representation of women and nonwhites in the legal profession. Utilizing the Fund for Modern Courts data, Alozie directly addressed the question of whether methods of formal judicial selection account for the differential distribution of black judges on state judiciaries.[25] He found that the percentage of black lawyers in the state was the most significant factor in explaining the degree of variation of black judges in the state, not formal methods of judicial selection.

In another study, Graham addressed the question of whether formal and informal methods of judicial selection predict the likelihood of a black or white attorney serving as a trial judge.[26] In an examination of individual level data collected on 3,823 black and white trial court judges in 36 states, Graham found that formal structures made little difference in black representation because black judges who were formally elected were actually appointed to the bench. Moreover, the study showed that informal methods to the bench, that is, actual routes, were significant. Specifically, gubernatorial appointment and legislative appointment systems seemed to increase black representation on the state trial bench. Overall, the study provided support for the contention that structural arrangements of state judicial selection are significant in accounting for black underrepresentation on the state bench.

A closer examination of these competing approaches in explaining black underrepresentation on the state bench might reveal that scholars have viewed the trees but not the forest in addressing this problem. The research that suggests that blacks will increase their judgeships by increasing the proportion of black lawyers does not adequately consider the extent to which structural forces in the political and legal environments not only effect the proportion of black judges, but also the availability of black attorneys. Walton's observation is noteworthy here, for he argues that "by barring blacks from the voting booths, the bar rosters and associations, law schools, and full participation in the political arena, states have determined to a great extent the parameters of the black judiciary."[27] Focusing on contextual factors alone does little to expand our substantive understanding of how state judicial recruitment affects outcomes for minority participants. What this literature does reveal is that we are only beginning to make advances in our understanding of the impact of structural characteristics of judicial recruitment for minority representation on state courts.

Patterns of accession

For descriptive purposes, the data presented in Table 1 were re-examined within the context of how black judges reach the state bench by the states' formal designation and by actual routes. The judicial selection literature identifies five major formal routes to the state bench: gubernatorial appointment, Missouri Plan, legislative appointment, partisan election, and nonpartisan election. As Berkson pointed out, almost no two states are alike in the methods used to select their judges and few states employ the same method for choosing judges at all levels of the state judiciary.[28] Table 3 presents the patterns of accession to the state bench by formal and actual routes for the general jurisdiction judges.

An examination of the formal route category shows that most black general jurisdiction judges preside over courts in states that formally use partisan and nonpartisan elections.[29] This was not an unexpected finding since 25 of the 36 states with black representation on their major courts formally use elective systems for all or some of their judgeships. When the actual routes to the major state court bench were determined, the figures presented in Table 3 indicate the prevalence of interim appointments in formal selection systems, primarily partisan and nonpartisan systems. With the exception of Illinois and Louisiana, all states with elective systems examined in this study permit the governor to fill vacancies occurring between elections. Most of the black judges in elective systems initially obtained their seats by gubernatorial appointment. Moreover, vacancy appointments were more common in nonpartisan systems than partisan systems. These findings are compatible with prior research that indicates that in elective systems, a considerable proportion of judges ini-

Table 3   How black judges reach the bench: formal and actual routes, 1986

Selection system	Formal route[1]	%	Actual route	%
Gubernatorial appointment	18	6.1	182	6.2
Missouri Plan	39	13.3	36[2]	12.4
Legislative appointment	14	4.8	12[3]	4.1
Partisan election	106	36.2	502	17.2
Nonpartisan election	97	33.1	242	8.2
Circuit court appointment	19	6.5	192	6.5
Supreme court appointment	—	—	142	4.8
Vacancy	—	—	1132	38.8
Court reorganization/consolidation	—	—	52	1.7
Total	293	100.0	291[4]	99.9

— not applicable

1. In some states, different formal selection systems may be used for trial and appellate courts. The figures for the formal designation category were derived by first calculating the total for trial and appellate courts separately and then collapsing both totals into one category. The coding for the formal routes is: appellate courts 1Xgubernatorial appointment (CA); 2XMissouri Plan (FL, KS, MD, MA, MO, NY); 3Xlegislative appointment (SC, VA); 4Xpartisan election (AL, IL, MS, NC, PA, TX) and 5Xnonpartisan election (GA, LA, MI, OH); trial courts 1Xgubernatorial appointment (NJ, NC special judges of superior courts in NC are appointed by governor); 2XMissouri Plan (AZ, CO, DE, IA, MD, MA, MO, IN); 3Xlegislative appointment (CT, SC, VA); 4Xpartisan election (AL, IL, IN, KS, MS, NY, PA, TN, TX, WV); 5Xnonpartisan election (CA, FL, GA, ID, KY, LA, MI, MN, NV, OH, OK, OR, WA, WI) and 6Xcircuit court appointment (IL-associate circuit court judges).

2. Excludes 3 judges who initially reached the bench through court reorganization.

3. Excludes 2 gubernatorial appointments in filling vacancies in Virginia and South Carolina.

4. The author was unable to identify how 1 Ohio judge and 1 Louisiana judge reached the bench.

tially reach the bench by executive appointment.[30]

The data presented in Table 3 are significant in that they demonstrate the importance of the politics of the appointing governor in determining the extent to which minorities will occupy seats on our nation's state courts, despite the formal method used to select judges. Glick observed that "governors usually pick individuals who have been involved in state politics and whose past activity either has been of personal benefit, or has benefited a political party or political allies."[31] He also acknowledged that governors make symbolic appointments to these positions in their attempt to satisfy several constituencies. This analysis suggests that greater attention to the appointment politics of governors might reveal important insights for understanding minority recruitment outcomes.

Remedies

What can be done to remedy the problem of the lack of racial diversity on the state bench? The two remedies discussed here seek to address the broad problem of a racially homogenous state bench. The first remedy involves the development of affirmative action policies to overcome past inequities in judicial recruitment and selection. Such efforts could be successfully implemented among appointive systems of judicial selection, including the filling of vacancies in elective systems. Since representational criteria are generally among the host of other factors in determining recruitment outcomes, affirmative action goals are clearly consistent with attracting legally qualified minority candidates to

the state bench. President Carter's innovations on the federal level in the creation of merit panels among the states serves as a model.[32] Carter's appointments of minorities and women to the federal bench during his single term in office was a dramatic departure from the appointment practices of previous presidential administrations.[33] In addition, various groups (civil rights organizations, women's groups, bar associations) will have to play a greater role in state judicial recruitment and selection in order to realize the goals of a diverse state bench.

Elective systems have structural components not found in appointive systems that are likely to affect the chances of minorities in obtaining seats on the state bench in greater numbers. Several states use at-large or multi-member boundaries as the geographic basis for electing judges.[34] Lawsuits have been filed by minorities challenging the use of at-large and multimember districts in state judicial elections because they have not been successful at the polls.[35] Lower federal court decisions have responded to black voters' claims by expanding the concept of minority vote dilution to judicial elections.[36] The Fifth and Sixth Circuit Courts of Appeals have subsequently applied Sections 2 and 5 of the Voting Rights Act of 1965 as amended to judicial elections.[37] In response to these decisions, several jurisdictions must redraw their judicial districts in order to insure that black voters will have the opportunity to elect judicial candidates of their choice. The immediate effect of these decisions will be felt in the south where much of the litigation originated. Consequently, judicial redistricting is expected to be successful in bringing minorities to the bench in those areas where there are a heavy concentration of minorities.[38]

Conclusion

The purpose of this article is to present an overview of the characteristics of judicial recruitment and selection as they contribute to our understanding of black representation on the state bench. Viewed in this context, this research has important implications about the ongoing debate with respect to who gets chosen to fill judgeships on the state bench. This study revealed that although black attorneys have made significant gains on the state bench since the 1970s, black underrepresentation still remains a problem. An examination of the literature that attempted to explain the problem demonstrates the need for systematic analyses of structural variables that might affect minority recruitment outcomes. It was also suggested that the application of affirmative action criteria and judicial redistricting were expected to enhance minority representation at the state level. This article has clear implications about the direction future research should take in addressing the problem of a racially homogenous state bench. Slotnick has argued that analyses of judicial recruitment have failed to take into account studies of elite recruitment in other political contexts.[39] Since this research suggests that minority representation is as important in the state judiciary as it is in other branches of government, perhaps future research should consider the extent to which institutional arrangements, political participation, and elite behavior reveal insights about judicial recruitment and selection.

NOTES

This article originally appeared in Volume 74, Number 1, June-July 1990, pages 28-34.

1. For an overview and annotated bibliography of this extensive literature, see Chinn and Berkson, LITERATURE ON JUDICIAL SELECTION (Chicago: American Judicature Society, 1980); Slotnick, *Review essay on judicial recruitment and selection*, 13 JUST SYS. J. 109 (1988).

2. See, for example, Abraham, THE JUDICIAL PROCESS (New York: Oxford University Press, 5th ed., 1986).

3. See Joint Center for Political Studies, BLACK JUDGES IN THE UNITED STATES (Washington, D.C.: 1986).

4. The author would like to thank the state court clerks and administrators for their assistance in the collection of the data.

5. Two directories are: THE AMERICAN BENCH: JUDGES OF THE NATION (Sacramento: Reginald Bishop Foster & Associates, Inc., 3rd ed., 1985/86); CALIFORNIA COURTS AND JUDGES (San Francisco: Law Book Service Co., 4th ed., 1985).

6. See Cook, *Black representation in the third branch*, 1 BLACK L. J. 260 (1972); Smith, RACE VERSUS ROBE (Port Washington, NY: Associated Faculty Press, 1983); American Judicature Society, *The black judge in America: a statistical profile*, 57 JUDICATURE 18 (1973). But see Alozie, *Black representation on state judiciaries*, 69 SOC. SCI. Q. 979 (1988).

7. Cook, supra n. 6, at 261.

8. "Quasi-judicial officials are defined as officers required to investigate facts, hold hearings, and recommend official actions on the basis of those facts." See Joint Center for Political Studes, supra n. 3, at 11.

9. See Joint Center for Political Studies, BLACK ELECTED OFFICIALS: A NATIONAL ROSTER (Washington, D.C., 16th ed., 1987).

10. See Smith, supra n. 6; Ryan et al., AMERICAN TRIAL JUDGES: THEIR WORK STYLES AND PERFORMANCE (New York: Free Press, 1980).

11. The geographic divisions used in this study are compatible with those found in JCPS, BLACK ELECTED OFFICIALS, supra n. 9. They are: south=MD, DE, WV, VA, KY, NC,SC, TN, GA, MS, AL, FL, TX, LA, OK AK DE; northeast=PA, NJ, NY, CT, MA, RI; north central=OH, IL, IN, WI, MO, MI, MN, IA, KS; west=CA, OR, WA, ID, AZ, CO, NM, UT, NV.

12. American Judicature Society, supra n. 6, at 18.

13. See Pitkin, ed., REPRESENTATION (New York: Atherton Press, 1969).

14. Smith, supra n. 6; Crockett, *Judicial selection and the black experience*, 58 JUDICATURE 438 (1971).

15. See Crockett, *Racism in the courts*, 20 J. OF PUB. L. 685 (1970).

16. See, for example Welch, Combs and Gruhl, *Do black judges make a difference?*, 32 AM. J. OF POL. SCI. 126 (1988).

17. Fund for Modern Courts, THE SUCCESS OF WOMEN AND MINORITIES IN ACHIEVING JUDICIAL OFFICE: THE SELECTION PROCESS 13 (New York: 1985).

18. These figures were supplied by the National Bar Association, Washington, D.C., January 22, 1990.

19. See National Center for State Courts, STATE COURT ORGANIZATION, 1987 (Williamsburg, VA: 1988) for a listing of state trial and appellate court qualifications to serve on the bench.

20. Cook, supra n. 6.

21. Smith, supra n. 6.

22. American Judicature Society, supra n. 6.

23. Fund for Modern Courts, supra n. 17.

24. Dubois, *The influence of selection system on the characteristics of a trial court bench: the case of California*, 8 JUST SYS. J. 59 (1983).

25. Alozie, supra n. 6.

26. Graham, *Do judicial selection systems matter? A study of black representation on state courts*, AM. POL. Q. (1990).

27. Walton, INVISIBLE POLITICS 224 (Albany: SUNY Press, 1985).

28. Berkson, *Judicial selection in the United States: a special report*, 64 JUDICATURE 179 (1980).

29. Data were not collected on the limited jurisdiction judges in this study because of the difficulty in obtaining biographical data for these judges and the fact that judicial selection mechanisms vary considerably among these judgeships and they frequently do not conform to the five major methods of judicial selection discussed in this article. See Berkson, supra n. 28.

30. See Herndon, *Appointment as a means of initial accession to elective state courts of last resort*, 38 N. DAK. L. REV. 60 (1962); Atkins and Glick, *Formal judicial recruitment and state supreme court decisions*, 2 AM. POL. Q. 427 (1974); Dubois, FROM BALLOT TO BENCH (Houston: University of Texas Press, 1980).

31. Glick, COURTS, POLITICS, AND JUSTICE 89 (New York: McGraw-Hill, 2nd ed., 1988).

32. See, for example Goldman, *Should there be affirmative action*

for the judiciary?, 62 JUDICATURE 488 (1979); Slotnick, *The U.S. Circuit Judge Nominating Commission*, 1 LAW & POL. Q. 465 (1979); Slotnick, *Federal appellate judge selection during the Carter administration: recruitment changes and unanswered questions*, 6 JUST SYS. J. 283 (1981).

33. *See* Goldman, *Reagan's judicial legacy: completing the puzzle and summing up*, 72 JUDICATURE 318 (1989) for a comparative analysis.

34. *See* National Center for State Courts, *supra* n. 19.

35. *See* American Judicature Society, *The Voting Rights Act and judicial elections: an update on current litigation*, 73 JUDICATURE 74 (1989).

36. *See* Davidson, ed., MINORITY VOTE DILUTION (Washington, D.C.: Howard University Press, 1984) for a discussion of this concept. *See also* Voter Information Project, Inc. v. City of Baton Rouge, 612 F.2d 208 (5th Cir. 1980).

37. *See* Haith v. Martin, 618 F.Supp. 410 (E.D.N.C. 1985), *aff'd* 477 U.S. 901 (1986); Mallory v. Eyrich, 839 F.2d 275 (6th Cir. 1988); Chisom v. Edwards, 839 F.2d 1056 (5th Cir. 1988), *cert. denied*, Roemer v. Chisom 109 S.Ct. 390 (1988).

38. For example, the first election after judicial redistricting in Mississippi produced two black winners in contested judicial elections—the first in the history of Mississippi elections. *See* Canerdy, *Black candidates appear to do poorly in judicial races*, THE CLARION-LEDGER, June 21, 1989, at 1, col. 1. *See also*, McDuff, *The Voting Rights Act and judicial elections litigation: the plaintiffs' perspective*, 73 JUDICATURE 82 (1989).

39. Slotnick, *supra* n. 1.

Different voices, different choices?
The impact of more women lawyers and judges on the justice system

An edited transcript of the panel at the American Judicature Society Annual Meeting, August 4, 1990.

Introduction

Our world has changed considerably since 1869, when the Illinois Supreme Court refused to license Myra Bradwell as an attorney, arguing that since she was a married woman, only her husband could contract on her behalf. Therefore, she would not be bound by the implied contract needed between lawyer and client. As recently as 1952, Sandra Day O'Connor was offered a job as a legal secretary after graduating at the top of her Stanford Law School graduating class.

But, like the proverbial camel's nose under the tent, once change came, it was dramatic. Significant growth in the number of women lawyers began in the 1970s, and by 1984, approximately 13 per cent of legal practitioners were women.

Participation of women on the bench followed the same pattern. Although women judicial officers had been appointed to limited jurisdiction courts beginning in 1870, it was not until 1921 that Florence Allen became the first woman judge elected to a general jurisdiction court, the Court of Common Pleas in Cuyahoga County, Ohio. By 1940, 21 states had women judges, and by 1950, 29. The best information now available suggests that women comprise approximately 6 to 8 per cent of state appellate and trial judges and about 9 per cent of federal appellate and trial judges.[1]

It is estimated that by the year 2000, women will constitute 35 to 40 per cent of the profession and a significantly increased proportion of the bench, a projection supported by the fact that 43 per cent of currently enrolled law students are women.[2]

What has been or will be the effect of these changes? As might be expected, researchers are beginning to address questions about the impact of increasing numbers of women lawyers and judges on the legal system.

In a recent article, law professor Carrie Menkel-Meadow of U.C.L.A. discusses several aspects of "feminization" of the legal profession, including (1) feminization simply in terms of increased participation of women; (2) feminization in terms of whether the profession will be changed or influenced by the increased participation of women; (3) feminization in terms of the incorporation of qualities traditionally described as feminine (e.g., empathy, nurturance, consensus-building) into the performance of legal tasks and functions; and (4) feminization in terms of changes in the practice of law, adaptations of work to family, for example, and in substantive areas such as employment discrimination, family law, and criminal law.[3]

Studies comparing men and women judges in an effort to find links between gender and decisional outcomes have resulted in mixed findings. One study found that women were slightly more liberal than men in voting on race and sex discrimination cases, but not on criminal issues.[4] However, another study found men to be slightly more liberal in their support of personal rights.[5] And two studies of sentencing decisions made by men and women judges found the only significant difference to be the tendency of male judges to give lesser sentences to female defendants.[6]

A very recent study suggests ways the different perspectives represented by women judges could affect their behavior as judges. The author speculates that those differences might influence such things as (1) decisional output, especially in sex discrimination cases; (2) conduct of courtroom business, especially as regards sexist behavior by litigators; (3) influence on sex-role attitudes held by their male colleagues, especially on appellate courts where decisions are collegial; (4) administrative behavior—in hiring women law clerks, for example; and (5) collective actions, through formal organizations, undertaken to heighten the judicial system's response to gender bias problems in both law and process.[7]

Clearly, we do not yet have hard data to document the impact of the increasing participation of women on the practice of law and the courts. However, scholars are studying the phenomena and thoughtful practitioners are speaking and writing about what changes we already have seen and what changes might emerge in the future.

At the 1990 annual meeting of AJS in Chicago, a panel of practitioners and scholars explored whether and how the growing number of women lawyers and women judges has affected and/or will affect the administration of justice. The panel incvcuded: Fern Schair Sussman, Esquire, Chief Administrative Officer, Association of the Bar of the City of New York as moderator, and panelists Jean Reed Haynes, Esquire, Kirkland & Ellis, New York; Professor D. Marie Provine, Syracuse University, Syracuse, New York; Honorable J. Brendan Ryan, Twenty-second Judicial Circuit Court, St. Louis, Missouri; Honorable Fern M. Smith, U.S. District Court for the Northern District of California, San Francisco; and Guy A. Zoghby, Vice President & General Counsel PPG Industries, Inc., Pittsburgh, Pennsylvania.

—*Kathleen Sampson*
Director of Information
and Program Services, AJS

Professor D. Marie Provine: My presentation is in two parts. The first part will give you some basic background statistics that provide kind of a base line. Then I would like to introduce some questions for our panelists, who come from many different backgrounds and bring different perspectives to these issues.

As shown in Table 1, there's a big leap between 1970 and 1980 in the percentage of female law school graduates (my own graduation was in 1971 so these statistics have a personal meaning to me.)

Table 1   Women as a per cent of all law school graduates

Year	Per cent
1870	.02
1900	1.31
1910	2.21
1930	5.41
1940	6.71
1950	3.41
1960	3.81
1970	8.61
1980	33.51
1982	35.01

Source: Cook, "The Path to the Bench: Ambitions and Attitudes of Women in the Law," 19 Trial 49-50 (1983).

Table 2   Proportion of women in the legal profession, 1890-1980

Year	Number	Percentage
1890	208	.02
1900	1,010	.08
1910	558	1.11
1920	1,738	1.41
1930	3,385	2.11
1940	4,447	2.41
1950	6,348	3.51
1960	7,543	3.31
1970	13,000	4.71
1980	62,000	12.81

Source: U.S. Department of Commerce, Bureau of the Census.

By 1985 (not shown), 38.5 per cent of law students were female, and in many of the elite law schools the class is over half female . . . . This is, I think, stark testimony to the end of the kind of ladies-day treatment that I and the other three women in my class experienced in law school.

Figure 1 is simply a graphical view of the same thing. I thought it might be helpful to us here because, as you can see, the increasing number of lawyers being produced in American society, beginning in about 1973, is not due to more and more men going to law school, but due to more and more women doing so.

Table 2 is a somewhat dated representation of women's absorption into the legal profession. It shows that when a previously excluded group comes onto the scene, their percentage in the profession is obviously a lot less than the percentage in law schools. This is a situation that we can expect to change. For example, by 1987, 19 per cent of the profession was female; by the year 2000 projections are that it will be 35 to 40 per cent, maybe even higher depending on how quickly males leave the profession and how determinedly women stay in it.

Table 3 looks at a pre-1971 cohort of women lawyers and a post-1971 cohort. The earlier group followed a somewhat different career path, a more

Figure 1: Yearly admissions by sex (1961-83)

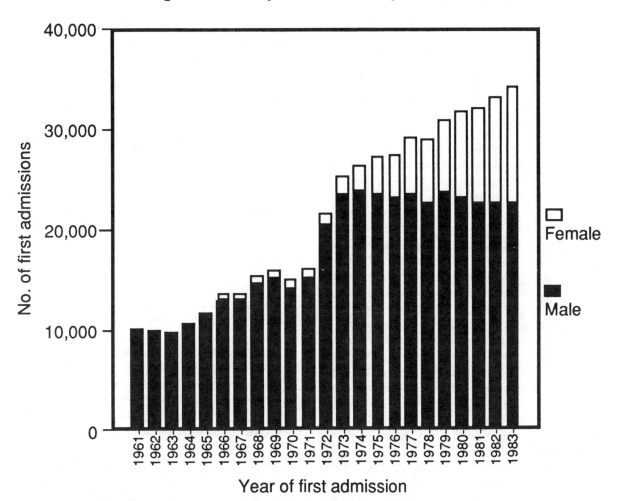

Source: Curran, *The Lawyer Statistical Report: A Statistical Profile of the U.S. Legal Profession in the 1980s*, 9 (Chicago: American Bar Foundation, 1985).

Table 3 Private practitioners by practice setting, sex, and admission cohort (1980)

| | Admitted pre-1971 | | Admitted 1971-79 | |
	Males N=204,696 %	**Females** N=5,623 %	**Males** N=140,816 %	**Females** N=18,967 %
Solo practice	48.9	67.9	47.1	51.9
2 lawyer firm	9.8	10.3	7.7	5.5
3 lawyer firm	6.6	3.9	5.9	2.9
4 lawyer firm	4.7	2.4	4.3	2.5
5 lawyer firm	3.3	1.6	3.1	2.1
6-10 lawyer firm	9.1	3.8	9.4	6.6
11-20 lawyer firm	6.2	2.8	7.1	6.8
21-50 lawyer firm	5.5	2.9	6.8	7.5
> 50 lawyer firm	5.9	4.4	8.6	14.2
Total	100.0	100.0	100.0	100.0

Source: Curran, The Lawyer Statistical Report: A Statistical Profile of the U.S. Legal Profession in the 1980s, 46 (Chicago: American Bar Foundation, 1985).

Table 4   Lawyers in judiciary by jurisdiction and sex (1980)

	Males N=17,507 %	Females N=1,653 %
Federal	12.9	21.1
State/local	87.1	78.9
Total	100.0	100.0

Source: Curran, The Lawyer Statistical Report: A Statistical Profile of the U.S. Legal Profession in the 1980s. 42 (Chicago: American Bar Foundation, 1985).

Table 5 Changing makeup of the professions, some comparative statistics

	1970 % women	1985 % women
Law-school enrollments	8.5	38.5
Practitioners	4.8	18.0[***]
Medical-school enrollments	9.1[*]	33.9
Physicians	9.0	17.2
Engineers	1.0	6.7
Full-time faculty	22.3[**]	27.1

[*] 1969
[**] 1972
[***] 1986

Source: Bannan, "Equality for Women in the Professions: Are We There Yet?" Paper presented at the New Mexico Women Studies Conference, Portales, New Mexico, October 23, 1987.

strikingly different career path than men. A much higher percentage of women than men were going into solo practice, so that the differences between the sexes were striking. If you look at the post-'71 cohort the career patterns are much more similar.

I also looked at the National Law Journal's latest survey of the 250 largest corporations and their top legal officers—it's a kind of who's who at the top of the pile in corporate law in distinction to the law firm statistics we just saw. I counted the number of current female chief legal officers in these largest corporations and came up with a striking statistic—only seven out of 250 top legal officers are women.

Moving on to the judiciary, Table 4 is a 1980 view of the state and federal judiciary by sex. In 1980, for example, 16 states had no female judges on courts of general jurisdiction. I was amazed by that; I don't think its any longer true but when we recall we have had only one female justice in the history of the United States Supreme Court—we need to think about just how much of a minority we remain even if we have more up-to-date statistics.

Table 5 provides a comparative view of labor force participation by sex and race, and by various professions. What you see in every case, from engineering and medicine to faculty in academia, is pretty much the same pattern of explosive growth between 1970 and the mid-1980s. Women are still, as you can see, less than 7 per cent of all working engineers, but in academia, where I never did think things were so terrific, we looked reasonably good compared to some of these other professional groups. In law, in terms of enrollment, it looks better than medicine so what we are seeing is a picture that's typical of American professions generally, with law somewhere in the middle or even at the high end in terms of women entering the profession.

Table 6 is a different slice on professional participation by men and women. It shows the primary person who does housework and essentially wor-

ries about the household—makes sure everybody gets their vaccinations and that the lights get fixed and that sort of thing. You can see that the difference between male and female and concerns in personal life is reasonably striking.

The differences

My final slide is about differences. It's a pair of blue footed boobies, one male, one female. They look virtually identical here except that the size of the pupil is slightly different in the male and the female. To the boobies, the differences between the sexes are everything, and I am sure they make life what it is for a blue footed boobie. But to us casual human viewers the males and the females are identical. I think you will see in our discussion that we keep coming back to the problem of how to evaluate how important the differences between male and female lawyers and judges are. The bottom line may be that it depends on what you're looking for and who's doing the looking.

What follows are essentially notes from the field on this important issue. Notes from the field are appropriate at this stage in our understanding of the impact of gender on legal practice. Our panelists were worried that they could not speak with sufficient generality. "We aren't statisticians," they said. Statistics can't give us all the answers either. All our panelists are very well placed to give us their first-hand observations, even though they are not what social scientists would call systematic observers. We will all bear in mind that we are talking about a fluid situation that is in the process of change; I think the statistics made that clear.

The basic question the panel is wrestling with is whether the acknowledged physical and experiential differences between men and women make a difference that we can see in the way men and

Table 6 Primary person who does housework and runs household in judges' families

	Judge personally	Judge's spouse	Judge/spouse equally	Hired help
Housework				
Men (n=84)	18.7%	72.5%	13.0%	14.5%
Women (n=30)	12.9%	13.2%	16.1%	67.7%
Runs household				
Men (n=84)	14.3%	82.1%	11.04%	—
Women (n=30)	59.4%	19.3%	12.5%	18.8%

Source: Martin, "Men and women on the bench: vive la difference?," 73 Judicature 206 (1990).

women approach their professional roles as lawyers and judges.

Feminist analysis starts from the proposition that context and history are relevant. I can think of three contextual differences that seem to be particularly pertinent to the law. One is the history of exclusion of women from law which is rather eloquently shown in statistics—women have been in the profession in small numbers, very small numbers, for a long time. The reality of exclusion even from being allowed to attend, for example, Columbia Law School in the '50s is part of the difference that men and woman have in their experience of law. The models of practice and law itself are male; women are newly arrived players in this professional world.

Another difference that is hard to know how to assess, but I think we would all agree is there, is in the socialization of boys and girls. We are raised differently with different expectations about our futures and different expectations about how we relate to other people. Research suggests the difference in treatment begins in the hospital nursery and continues throughout our lives.

And a third area is the physical fact of childbearing. Whatever we do with surrogacy and extra-vitro fertilization, the fact is women bear children and men never have. Although not all women bear children, it is a physical difference to which societies have historically attached much importance.

But how do we link such differences to judges and the practice of law? One answer is suggested by Carol Gilligan, whose book *In a Different Voice*, inspired the creation (and naming) of this panel. Gilligan studied the views of children about justice and fairness and made the argument, essentially, that boys and girls do differ in how they make moral choices. Whatever differences there are in the backgrounds of boys and girls do, in other words, translate into differences in beliefs about what's fair. She also suggests that the characteristically feminine viewpoint (which isn't shared by all women and isn't exclusive to the sex), is good and should be valued. So, Gilligan says, first, there are differences that can be seen, noted, and should be talked about, and second, the feminine perspective is one that we should value because it may be a better way of analyzing some problems.

This suggests a good point of departure for the panel and I am just about to turn it over to them. The way we've agreed to frame these issues is to ask whether traditionally feminine characteristics translate into differences in attitudes and behavior that can be observed by our panel. Let me give you an example of how gender might affect a judge's priorities and behavior.

Judge Shirley Abrahamson in Wisconsin has written about something she did when she was a new judge. She was concerned about whether the courts really are accessible to ordinary people. So on vacation, when she was in her t-shirt, wrap-around skirt, and sandals, she would visit various courts around Wisconsin and see how she was treated. She would ask questions such as "Can I sit in on your pretrial conferences?" "Tell me what's going on here today?" "What are these motions about?" She didn't say "I am Judge Shirley Abrahamson," she just said "I'm Shirley" and she looked like she might be a housewife. In general she wasn't given a particularly warm reception. Is it relevant that Judge Abrahamson is female? The concern for hospitality, assigned to women in our culture, suggests a connection. The ease with which she could pass for a non-powerful person is another gender aspect of this story.

Would a man assuming judicial office put on his golf clothes or his old baggy gardening shorts or whatever and go from court to court and see how he was received? And even if he did such a thing, could he pass himself off as just a kind of curious guy off the streets looking to see how the judicial branch works?

Questions

Let me ask five questions that will draw on these issues in a more specific way. The first question is whether you see men and women sorting themselves out or being sorted into masculine and feminine specialties? This is a demographic question—where are the men and where are the women and what does that mean? Second question, as women increase in numbers in the legal profession, are working relationships changing, as Gilligan would suggest, towards less hierarchy and more egalitarian relationships, towards a generally—to pick up a phrase of our president—"kinder, gentler" working environment? And, is the workplace itself becoming more humane as the realities of the fact that people live at home as well as at work must be confronted, and women do bring that to us because women don't have wives.

The third question concerns the adversary method of resolving disputes. On its surface it seems male, with its images drawn from war and sports—I'm always hearing about the level playing field, for example. Is the adversary approach to problem resolution going to change as women become litigators? Are women less adverserial than men in their orientation towards litigation? I'm sure our litigators on this panel will have something to say about that. My fourth question is more general: do differences in women's backgrounds translate into differences in professional judgment?

The last question returns us to the beginning of this session. We can see that the revolution has obviously only begun—women are entering the profession in such large numbers that it is going to be transformed to a degree that has not yet occurred. Is the growth of the number of females in the profession going to change what it means to be a lawyer, to be a legal professional? These are hard questions and I wish the panel good luck, but this is a tremendously talented panel so I'm not worried.

Fern Schair Sussman: Let's start with Jean Haynes from a law firm perspective.

Jean Reed Haynes: I'll try to do the questions in some order. As to whether men and women are sorting themselves into masculine and feminine roles within the profession, I'm not sure I have the perspective to answer that if you look at the profession as a whole. I think that we have statistics, and they may be among the ones that were shared with

you today, indicating that the number of women practicing, particularly at the partner level, in large firms is one of the smaller statistical representations of women. I am a firm believer that this will change over time, but I think we have to leave open the possibility that women may not be entering large law firm practices with the intent of making that a long-term, full-time career in the same percentages that men have in the past and indeed still may well be.

At least in the firm I know and speak about it is crystal clear to me that there is not a patterning by either force or by choice for women, for instance, to become trust and estate lawyers while men go off to become the litigators and do the big transactional deals. That's not happening at Kirkland & Ellis; others may have different experiences but I can only speak from mine. But then again I leave open the possibility that people who have chosen to come to a firm like ours have already made decisions as to what they want out of their career. I suggest that the choice may have been made before they ever think about Kirkland & Ellis, so our experience may not shed a tremendous amount of light on that question for the profession as a whole.

Of these questions the one I think I feel most strongly about is the second and it begins to blur in my mind into several of the others—the question of whether relationships are changing. I think in answering that there are a couple of caveats I want to make. First of all, it is totally wrong to think about these questions in terms of there being one type of behavior that we say is typical of men or one type that is typical of women. If I think about the partners with whom I work in any given week, I find a wide spectrum of approaches to dealing with any kind of interpersonal problem or any kind of relationship issue. Be it within the firm, with opposing counsel, with clients or whatever, these are not things that fall into easy categories.

I think we are talking to some extent, though, about whether taking the average woman as a whole or the average man as a whole you begin to see any difference, and I am a believer that women tend to be less hierarchial in their approaches to things. I certainly see as I've begun to grow into a position of having responsibility for working with and managing younger lawyers that in many ways my style is different, and I've talked to a lot of other women about this. I think there probably is a greater tendency on the part of women to have a participatory style of management and, on balance, some greater tendency on the part of men to have a hierarchial style.

What does that mean for us? What I believe it means is that there are indeed different ways of being effective. This is not a matter of one style being better than the other. I think that as women come into the profession, we are opening up additional options for behavior within our firms in dealing with our clients and if indeed Gilligan is right and I am right that they are equally effective, all we're really doing is increasing the ways in which we can be effective, the ways in which we can work together. There isn't a right or wrong. Hopefully though, and I think it's true that there are enough men and particularly young men who are interested in something of a participatory style, the fact that these options are perhaps somewhat more available in the work place will be beneficial to them and not leave us saying that the changes affect only women.

I'm not sure I view all of this as a question of it becoming a gentler workplace. Again, I don't think gentleness has anything to do with it. I think there are different styles, different ways one can be effective. On balance, perhaps women tend to be slightly different, but it's all just a question of degree.

More or less adversarial

Let me address the question which has to do with whether women are less adversarial. And I guess I bring the same kind of perspective to bear on that—what does it mean to be adversarial? If you focus this question as are women more or less likely to get up and scream and yell and pound the table and the like, I don't know that I have an answer. I think certainly in the days when women coming into the profession felt that part of their role was to be as much like men as possible—and indeed I do think that has been part of our history and believe and hope it is changing somewhat—but at that time I think you probably had a fair share of women who pounded on tables and yelled and screamed and you still may. My personal belief is that being a successful advocate, which I believe is what our role is whether we're litigators in court or whether we're representing our client in a transaction or whatever, being a successful advocate on behalf of our client is not necessarily best achieved by outward aggressive behaviors that we associate with yelling and screaming.

I think that women are absolutely as effective advocates as men. I think among the range of different styles you will have some who will tend more towards an "I'm in charge here" attitude and others who will tend to lean more towards a "let's work together, so that we come out with the result that is best for my client in the end." But I have no doubt that women are as adversarial and effective at it—although perhaps in different ways.

I want to sum up my initial remarks here by coming back to something I just alluded to. I am a firm believer that an important part of being a trial lawyer is becoming comfortable being yourself. You must deal with a set of technical rules, a set of skills, and a variety of settings that we most assuredly did not grow up with, but I have learned in the years that I have been doing this that the goal is to become myself within this profession. I think because I feel that so strongly, I truly believe that to the extent that there are differences between men and women, women will be the most effective lawyers they can be when they behave within the bounds and the propriety of the profession, with the instincts they bring to it, as opposed to saying, "I'm going to get up this morning and before I go to work put being a women aside and leave that at home," because then we're trying to be something that we aren't and I don't think you can be your best with one hand tied behind your back.

Sussman: Thank you, Jean. It seems clear that at least from Jean's perspective (and I wonder how some of you feel about it) having more women in the profession leads to more choices and more styles that one can have and still be effective. There is no more, as there used to be, a sense that there is one model to follow in the kind of practice you have and the way you relate to it: having more women is giving us more choices.

I'm going to turn to Guy Zogbhy now, who is also practicing law but with the additional obligation of dealing with a corporate law department and in a setting that is slightly different from the law firm setting. He's going to talk to you about not only his reactions to the questions but how in some ways the corporate law department differs from the other settings in the ability to deal with differences.

Guy Zogbhy: Let me start by saying Judge Ryan and I, as we went through getting ready for this panel, kind of learned what it felt like to be a minority. The point I'd like to make as we go through these questions is that I think where we have thought in the past there were differences we may find there are not differences at all.

I'd like to deal with the questions in a generalized way rather than one, two, three, four, five. First, women in the workplace. Second, humanity in the workplace, and third, different judgments from men and women, and finally, is there something of a synthesis occurring and can we see it as it's coming? First, women in the workplace.

I think very real change has occurred both in law firms and in corporate law departments. Jean did a super job on law firms so I'll talk about corporate law departments. Women were in the vanguard of the change, no question about that. In the past, if you had to stay home because of the plumber, the only acceptable explanation was you were sick or you were doing something else more important, not that you were doing something personal. I would say that has substantially changed. People now, certainly in the departments I am familiar with, are quite willing to understand a range of responsibilities that make a whole person.

In my experience as IBM's managing attorney, we dealt with a number of lawyers and in the first 10 years of a lawyer's career he or she was expected to move three times. Now, when you move a family three times, that is tough on the family; when you move a two-career family three times, that is doubly tough and one of the things we struggled with early on was should we continue to hire two-career families? If people are going to have two spouses working can we deal with that, is it something we can manage or must we say to them honestly up front "we don't think this is the kind of law career for you? You ought to work someplace else where you stay there." The decision probably was we weren't prepared to write off that many very good people. It became a talent question, and as we watched two careers become more the norm and less the exception, the only choice you had was to accommodate that or basically tell yourself you have excluded a very important part of the labor group. So it was not an altruistic decision, but simply a straightforward, sensible decision.

That accommodation took lots of forms. We lost early on a male lawyer whose spouse was a doctor and when she started her career he couldn't move anymore so he had to go. We have had situations where the other spouse is a minister and they move

churches from time to time and so you see if you can accommodate that and I will tell you that business is learning to accommodate it in very many and very direct ways. I would say that women brought that change to the workplace but it is a change that's not at all limited now. Two careers involve men and women and typically, those two careers involve accommodation and business is learning to do that because to fail to do it is simply to exclude an important part of the labor group.

When I think back 10 or 15 years, more women in corporate law departments tended to be in the labor law, human resources areas, less in the antitrust areas, more in the environmental areas today but less in the past as fewer women were going through chemistry and engineering and the hard sciences. Again, all that's changing. We're seeing more and more women committed to environmental law and in fact my own environmental law department has one man and three women. It could have been the other way around, that's just simply the people that we managed to attract at the time.

I don't believe there are different judgments, substantive judgments between men and women on legal questions, I don't think they have a different view of right and wrong. Everything that I have seen as to the way they work leads me to that conclusion but I think they may behave differently and they may raise different issues and they may come to problems in a different way.

This leads me to the final point that I'd like to make. Let me just read a quotation—this is from the Osgoode Hall Law Journal a few years ago, 1986: "one can imagine a time when parity is achieved between men and women in the legal profession and the particular contribution of women to the profession may simply wither away. As discrimination diminishes and women enter the profession in ever larger numbers those who imagine this time can contemplate an androgenous legal profession whatever shape that may take."

I believe that what's happened in the past 10, 15, 20 years is that women have brought more choice to the legal profession, not less, and it is not simply a question of different choices or different voices, it's a question of more choices and more voices and the options for dealing with legal problems perhaps are expanded. Corporate law departments will be forever changed by the way young people are addressing their careers and working together, and I think that corporate law departments and law firms will not have much choice but to follow, to recognize that reality and accommodate it rather than resist it.

Sussman: Something that neither of the first two panelists have touched on is the effect of some less enlightened law firms than Kirkland & Ellis, and their handling of the issues that we have been discussing. What effect might an inhospitable law firm environment have on other parts of the profession; do corporate law departments, for instance, have available more females, as well as some males, that have decided to make career shifts and are seeing their commitment to their professional lives differently? Judge Smith, will you take us into some of these issues?

Honorable Fern Smith: I have to be careful not to mimic too closely the comments that Jean made. We not only share gender, but our backgrounds are fairly similar in that both of us went to law school after having done other things, having had other life experiences. Jean is still in a large firm— I started in a large firm and practiced in one for 11 years before I went on the Superior Court in San Francisco and from there to the federal bench. I will try not to be repetitive, but much of what she said I must echo in my own way.

We have to start by accepting the fact that the legal and judicial systems are male institutions, basically derived by men, for male behavioral standards. It was never anticipated initially that women would play a role in those systems and, in fact, it was not until the mid-1970s that the last state finally agreed that women could serve as jurors let alone be lawyers or, perish the thought, judges. And so when many of us started in the legal profession there was no other model than the male model.

I think it is fair to say that men are comfortable with a hierarchy. They are used to it from team sports, from being in the military, and for a variety of reasons. I don't think it's biological, I don't think its genetic, it's simply a life experience. Women are less comfortable, however. When women started in the profession that was the model that existed. Yes, there were ranges of behavior among men as there are ranges of behavior among women, but in general, it was an authoritarian hierarchy that we were presented with. I think for women just starting out, especially women who had not had other careers or experiences, it was very difficult to have the self-confidence to breech that model and to engage in

a whole new mode of behavior that might be ridiculed, that might be unacceptable, for which there would be no positive reinforcement.

As an example, some of you may remember a book called *Dress for Success* that came out a while ago which aimed to teach women that if you had the right clothes you could make it to the top. The book was written by a man, and I think I can summarize by saying that the thesis was that if a women wore a little blue suit with a little white shirt with a little round collar with a little bow tie her success was assured. If she wore anything else, she was doomed to failure. I would hazard a guess that among my women professional friends, lawyers, judges, whatever, you could do a survey of their closets and find nary a blue suit or a little white shirt with a little bow tie. But it took a while for women to accept the fact that there might be another viewpoint.

Now again, I have personal bias because I entered the legal profession in my golden years, as it were, and so I had come from a different life experience, and while I didn't know what I was going to be as a lawyer, I knew pretty well what I was as a person. And Jean had done some other things and was more comfortable with herself. So I credit, in part, a contribution by some of the women who came into the profession from other areas as being able to establish new ways of doing things, new styles. Also, as more and more women entered the profession there were role models from whom to learn, from whom to gauge one's own comfort level. I echo Jean in saying that the most important thing in being effective as an advocate is being comfortable with your style and what works for you because, clearly, it is a profession of persuasion. Even for judges there are times that, while we have the authority to demand, it's much better to use a persuasive approach for a variety of reasons. Everyone is often better served when we do.

Do women look at fairness and justice differently? I don't think so. I don't think people see right and wrong differently because of their gender. I do think that ethnicity and race and socioeconomic status change people's perception of fairness and justice and that's a very important issue and one that bears considering, but I think that the presence of women expands the areas in which justice and fairness are now applied. There are causes of action and crimes and lawsuits that have come about not just because of women in the profession but because of women in the workplace. Ten years ago you didn't hear about date rape, you didn't hear about spousal rape, you didn't hear about sexual harassment. There are areas of inequality and problems in our society that have been brought to the level of people's consciousness by expanding the number of people who are in the workplace and in the profession. That is terribly important and I think that is a difference women have made and will continue to make.

"We are people"

I would like to touch on the whole idea of women leaving the profession as well and what Guy said about women coming into the corporate structure from law firms. The legal profession right now is in dire straits for a variety of reasons. The latest statistics that I've seen say that 41 per cent of associates with big firms leave their firm within the first two years of practice. Now, that's a very, very compelling and concerning statistic and what it says is that the law firms are spending a great deal of money recruiting people, and training people, who then leave. The law firms must ask the question "why are they leaving?" These are not all women lawyers, many are, but a lot of them are men, and I think the answer is that the profession as a whole is losing a great deal of its humanity in this constant, competitive race. It has become a business, law firms merge, law firms disappear overnight, partners leave, associates leave, and that has started a vicious cycle of raising associates' salaries with a concomitant raise in expectations. I think associates are saying, and partners are saying, "no more, we are not willing to do it anymore. We are people, we have lives, we have families, we have other interests."

These issues are often relegated to something called a "mommy track" and firms say, "well, these are women's concerns." But they aren't, it's much more widespread than that. The role of the women in the firms has been to bring those concerns to the surface, to make it legitimate to say "I have other responsibilities and I have other concerns. I want to be the best lawyer I can be but I am also a person." Because of that, more and more men are now willing to acknowledge the concerns they have for their family, for community activities, for other things. It is now legitimate to raise those issues and as more and more women come into the profession, new ways of looking at things will become more valid. A "human track" will be more valid

than a "mommy track." In the long run that will be a contribution to the profession, to the clients that we all serve and to the community. That's my main belief about what role women have played and will continue to play as we move along.

Sussman: Judge Smith, would you comment on something that you had mentioned earlier, which is the difference that you perceive in how women talk about justice?

Smith: I don't think women perceive justice differently but let me echo something else that has been said. Within male behavior there are all sorts of ranges, very aggressive men, and more soft-spoken men. There are also very aggressive women, and more soft-spoken women, but, as a generality, women are more willing to speak about humanistic things or in humanistic terms. Women are more willing to acknowledge emotions, women are more willing to acknowledge fears than men are and that provides a different atmosphere in a courtroom.

I am more participatory. With jurors I am less formal, I believe, than many of my male colleagues. I don't equate that with a loss of dignity of the court or a loss of competence, I am simply comfortable putting myself out there in an open, less autocratic fashion and I think many women also adopt that style.

Now part of it may have to do with the fact that I raised a family before I became a judge. I was giving a talk somewhere recently and somebody in the audience asked me if I had ever held anybody in contempt. I said "no, I had never found it necessary and I hoped I never would." He said "what do you do if you have a really obstreperous attorney and you really want to show your displeasure for his or her egregious behavior?" I said "I go like this a lot (shaking a finger)." It worked when I was raising my kids and so far it's stood me in pretty good stead in the courtroom, so until somebody comes along with something that works better for me I will probably continue to go like this (shaking a finger).

Honorable J. Brendan Ryan: When Judge Smith is considerate of the jurors in her courtroom, I don't think that's gender, I think that's common sense, I think that's experience. That may be something that is found more often in women judges, but I don't think so. So, I disagree a little that it's based upon gender. I've seen judges, male and female, who, when they got their robe, began to wonder who the hell they were. Again, I don't think that's gender, I think that's common sense and being a good judge.

Addressing some of the questions specifically, changing roles and sorting out of roles, remember that I've been on the bench a little more than 11 years and so I'm not that familiar anymore with law firms and how they do things. But I know this, in our area, and I can only speak from a midwestern background, when we have five women judges, five colleagues at the trial level in the city of St. Louis, we don't put them in juvenile or family court to stay there. We rotate deliberately to avoid the kind of thing we are talking about here today.

I don't see any difference based upon gender in the area of criminal law and I have a criminal assignment this year and roughly 35 per cent of the public defenders in our city are women, roughly 20 per cent of the prosecutors are women. I don't see any difference at all; they try the murder cases, they try the check cases, they do the whole scheme. The same thing is true in the family court situations.

The area that I see where women have not caught up, at least in our area, is in the area of civil litigation. You do not find in my area women handling the big lawsuits—personal injury or contract. They may second chair somebody but they are not the primary trial counsel. I am particularly struck by that because I spent a couple of years, 1987 and 1988, as presiding judge and part of my role as presiding judge was to hear all pre-trial civil motions and I heard between 20 and 30 motions every day trying to move cases along. That's when I first learned that maybe lawyers and judges have a different goal. Sounds strange, doesn't it? But, anyway, my idea was to keep moving these cases along and that's not necessarily the role of the attorney, and I'm not criticizing that, I'm just acknowledging a fact of life. But in any event, I would see generally younger members unless it was really a motion that was going to be dispositive of the lawsuit. I generally saw the newer counsel, the younger counsel and as a result of that many, many women attorneys would come into court for the first time, getting their experience handling motions. I know they are competent, and I know that they have the ability, it's just taken a little longer in that area. But that's the only area where I see that.

When you think about it, 15 or 20 years ago we wouldn't be having this panel. We're changing, not

as rapidly as some would like, maybe too rapidly for others. I see some gender differences, but not a whole lot. I see some, I'll call it sensitivity, but once again I'm not sure that's gender. What I do see is this. In my court—I'm speaking 300 miles from St. Louis and they'll never hear about this—I see a difference, and I'm right about in the middle, age-bracket wise, of my colleagues and there are 31 judges in the city of St. Louis and I can see a tremendous difference in the younger judges as opposed to—shall we say more experienced older judges and their role as activists if you will.

Things are changing. There are some gender differences, but I don't think traumatic gender differences any longer. We have some catching up to do and I definitely don't think we're less adversarial because we have women in the courtroom. I agree with Guy, I do not believe that men and women judges view the substantive issue of justice differently. There are some differences of style and Jean made a very good point followed up by Judge Smith—you gotta be yourself. What I'm saying is a good trial lawyer is a good trial lawyer. They're good because they are good and her point was, and I think it's well taken, while you can learn from them you can't imitate them because it doesn't come off. But you can take the good litigator and adopt what they do to your style and you become very, very effective.

Sussman: Nothing that's been said here so far explains why in many states females are still in the family courts and in the juvenile courts in large numbers. Maybe that's self-selection, maybe that's acceptance, maybe it's denial of access to other courts and maybe that needs to be considered as part of the larger subject that AJS and all of you have some interest in, which is how judges are selected and how does gender play into that or doesn't it?

We also didn't get into the issue of law firm or client expectations—are there still in this day and age expectations on the part of clients as to how males or females might handle a case that have any role in the assignment of cases? And the more difficult one that even the panel had some very diverse opinions about this morning, which is expectations on the part of law firms when a parent, male or female, and it is mostly female, decides to drop back and take a couple of years part-time. Does that mean they are less serious, does that mean they are off the track, whatever it is, to great success? All of these issues raise questions, perhaps to be explored in future panels.

NOTES

This transcript originally appeared in Volume 74, Number 5, October-November 1990, pages 138-146.

1. Figures supplied by the Federal Judicial Center and National Center for State Courts.

2. ABA Legal Education Division, telephone conversation June 1990; Berkson, *Women on the bench: a brief history*, 65 JUDICATURE 286, 291 (1982); Menkel-Meadow, *The Comparative Sociology of Women Lawyers: The 'Feminization' of the Legal Profession*, 24 OSGOODE HALL L. J. 897, 905 (1986).

3. Menkel-Meadow, *supra* n. 2, at 898-899.

4. Gottschall, *Carter's judicial appointments: the influence of affirmative action and merit selection on voting on the U.S. courts of appeals*, 67 JUDICATURE 165 (1983).

5. Walker and Barrow, *The Diversification of the Federal Bench: Policy and Process Ramifications*, 47 J. POL. 143 (1986).

6. Gruhl, Spohn and Welch, *Woman as Policymakers: The Case of Trial Judges*, 25 AM. J. POL. SCI. 308 (1981); Kritzer and Uhlman, *Sisterhood in the Courtroom*, 14 SOC. SCI. J. 77 (1977).

7. Martin, *Men and women on the bench: vive la difference?*, 73 JUDICATURE 204 (1990).

The paths to the federal bench: gender, race, and judicial recruitment variation

Paths to federal judgeships clearly differ for nonwhites and women. A recent study reveals that these "nontraditional" candidates reflect the socioeconomic and political roles played by such groups in American society and the opportunities available to them.

by Elliot E. Slotnick

For several decades judicial politics research has centered on the social backgrounds and career experiences of those recruited for judgeships.[1] Generally, research in this genre on federal judges has explored two primary questions. Above all, analysts have been concerned with the similarities and differences in the backgrounds of judicial appointees of different presidential administrations with an eye towards assessing the representativeness of recruitment outcomes.[2]

More ambitious studies have gone beyond the question of representativeness to the larger behavioral concern of how judicial backgrounds are related to a judge's decisional behavior.[3] But studies of "nontraditional" judges (those who are female and/or nonwhite)—the focus of this article—have, for the reasons explored below, been limited in scope and number.

Homogeneity, not diversity

Relating background characteristics to judicial decisionmaking has proven to be somewhat problematic for a number of reasons. For one, it has often been difficult to isolate variables and collect data that are sufficiently powerful in the aggregate to differentiate meaningfully among federal judges and their decisions. More to the point, a prime characteristic of the federal bench is its homogeneity and not its diversity. Consequently, as Grossman has argued, instead of seeking to understand decisional outcomes as a reflection of the differences among judges, analysis might be better served by focusing on the widespread consensus that marks

judicial decision making and trying to understand such consensus by examining judicial backgrounds.[4]

Such a cautionary perspective is well taken. Historically, the federal bench has been a bastion of white male dominance in American society and it has been quite evident that the path to federal judgeships has been a well worn one. Successful aspirants are generally well endowed with "traditional" measures of professional success including elite socioeconomic backgrounds and educational training, high status and high income legal careers and, perhaps, a partisan political background which helps create "access" to patronage oriented federal judgeships in the first place.

In view of these factors, studies of "nontraditional" judges have been few. As pointed out by Carbon, "Because the entry of women into the judiciary is so recent, it is not surprising to find little about them in professional journals. Indeed, until the past decade, their numbers were so small that . . . generalizations about women judges would have been almost meaningless."[5] These assertions are equally applicable to nonwhite judges, and, indeed, analyses of nontraditional judges have been virtually confined to studies of trial court judges in the lower levels of state and municipal court systems.[6] In these limited research settings, however, questions have been raised concerning whether significant differences of a substantively meaningful nature differentiate between the "nontraditional" judges and their white male colleagues on the bench. Thus, for example, Kritzer and Uhlman's data portray the woman judge as one who has successfully emerged from a man's world.

They all had served either as an assistant prosecuting attorney or as a deputy state attorney general (or both). All had been highly successful in the private practice of law. More than half had been part-time lecturers or instructors in law schools prior to judicial service. There is nothing to distinguish these careers from those of other successful attorneys . . . .[7]

Uhlman's research also documents the emergence of primarily "safe" black jurists on the Metro City trial bench:

Extremely "safe" blacks appear to have been the primary recruits to the Metro City bench while the broader spectrum and in large measure the richness of the black legal experience has been underrepresented. Quality black law school graduates, public defenders, community lawyers, and individual practitioners have much to offer. To date, they have not been afforded the judicial opportunity as the black bench in Metro City remains an extraordinary subset of the black legal fraternity.[8]

The need to understand variation

The importance of understanding race and gender variation in judicial recruitment is clear as "contrasting background and career attributes . . . may uncover criteria conducive to judicial selection and biases present in the recruitment process."[9] Such analyses would have great implications for those concerned with the representativeness of the American bench. Further, it could be argued, gender and race recruitment variation are suggestive of important differences in the decisional propensities of white male and nontraditional judges which could serve to alter the policies fashioned by American courts. Cook's research offers a cautionary note, however, on that score.

Acceptance of a woman judge depends upon her adherence to the inherited norms . . . There is little room even for the brilliant woman to effect major changes in procedures and policies. Her career security depends on her general acceptance of the old norms . . . Those identified as deviants in any way except gender are vulnerable to criticism and removal from power. Challenges to the culture are somewhat easier (although less likely) from those who fit the stereotype of ascriptions. Women judges probably can not make major changes in policy outputs . . . .[10]

It may, however, be instructive to differentiate between the isolated token selections of women and black judges who traditionally ascended to the bench and the more numerous nontraditional judges who have survived recruitment processes in recent years—particularly regarding selection to the federal bench during the Carter administration. Uhlman, for one, has alluded to such a distinction in his Metro City study.

A distinction has often been drawn between "traditional" and "second generation" black elites. A "traditional" black elite is viewed as a conservative, nonthreatening black leadership that adheres to white decisionmaking patterns . . . . This group is contrasted to a younger "second generation" of black leadership characterized as reform minded and activist in orientation, articulating the interests of the politically, economically and socially disadvantaged black Americans.[11]

A new impetus for study

At bottom, the literature on nontraditional judges has been quite exploratory, limited in scope, and somewhat inconclusive. In recent years, though, added impetus for such analysis has resulted from the Carter administration's recruitment of unprecedented numbers of women and nonwhite candidates who were appointed to the federal bench. Indeed, when President Carter took office in 1977 only 22 nonwhites and six women sat among the approximately 500 active federal jurists.[12] His administration's judicial selection opportunities were aided greatly by the passage of the Omnibus Judgeship Act of 1978 (OJA) which created 152 new federal judgeships (117 district and 35 appeals court positions). Following an avowed affirmative action program in the filling of the OJA vacancies as well as those additional vacancies created by normal attrition during his presidency through death and retirement, Carter was able to drastically alter the composition of the federal bench.[13]

Thus, of Carter's 258 district and appeals court appointees 40 were women and 54 were nonwhite (eight of the nonwhite nominees were women).[14] This constituted a greater number of nontraditional federal judgeship appointees than had been designated over the course of the nation's entire history. As noted by Goldman, "By the end of the Carter Administration the proportion of women judges on the federal bench had risen from 1 per cent to close to 7 per cent and, for blacks, from 4 per cent to close to 9 per cent."[15]

It is, perhaps, somewhat premature to analyze the importance of these nontraditional judges for judicial policy-making outcomes on the federal bench.[16] It is, however, possible to address in a more detailed and systematic fashion than previous research allowed the question of how, ultimately, the path to

Table 1 Political party, age, and birthplace by nominee status

Nominee status	Party[1]			Age[2]				Birthplace[3]	
	Democrat	Republican	Independent	30-39	40-49	50-59	60-69	In state or circuit	Outside of state or circuit
White male	130	9	0	10	43	72	12	103	33
	93.5%	6.5%	0.0%	7.3%	31.4%	52.6%	8.8%	75.7%	24.3%
Nonwhite male	42	0	1	6	16	16	3	28	11
	97.7%	0.0%	2.3%	14.6%	39.0%	39.0%	7.3%	71.8%	28.2%
White female	24	1	2	4	13	9	0	13	10
	88.9%	3.7%	7.4%	15.4%	50.0%	34.6%	0.0%	56.5%	43.5%
Nonwhite female	5	0	2	2	5	0	0	1	5
	71.4%	0.0%	28.6%	28.6%	71.4%	0.0%	0.0%	16.7%	83.3%

1. Contingency coefficient=0.35, S=0.00
2. Contingency coefficient=0.28, S=0.03
3. Contingency coefficient=0.24, S=0.01

the federal bench differs for white male and other judicial appointees? Throughout the remainder of this article this broad concern will be addressed utilizing data collected on all judicial nominees whose names were sent to the Senate Judiciary Committee for confirmation hearings during the 96th Congress. My analysis will compare white male, nonwhite male, white female, and nonwhite female nominees on several dimensions including their demographic profiles, educational achievement, level of politicization, legal career patterns, and litigation records.[17] On many variables meaningful differences will be apparent which differentiate between each of our four classes of nominees. In some instances, however, white male nominees will be found to differ consistently from all other nominees in the aggregate. This will be noted, and comparisons will be drawn between white male and "nontraditional" judgeship candidates.[18]

Demographic backgrounds

Substantively meaningful and statistically significant differences were found among virtually all of the demographic characteristics of the nominees except for their religious preferences, where no pattern was present. While not statistically significant (S=0.16), because of the large number of data cells and relatively few observations, there was a pronounced tendency for white male nominees to enjoy relatively higher incomes than each of the other categories of judgeship candidates (Contingency Coefficient=0.31). Thus, over one-third (35.5 per cent) of white male nominees earned more than $80,000 per year prior to their nomination while the corresponding figures for nonwhite males, white females, and nonwhite females were 12.8 per cent, 16.7 per cent, and 20.0 per cent respectively. Collapsing these data reveals that the income dis-

parities between white male and all other (i.e., all nontraditional) judgeship nominees were quite graphic (Tau C=0.21, S=0.00).

As Table 1 reveals, important differences among the four classes of nominees were also found to exist on measures of the nominees' political party preferences, age at appointment, and birthplace. While the vast majority of all nominees during the 96th Congress were Democrats, virtually all (9 out of 10) Republican nominees were found among white male candidates.

Two explanations might come into play here. For one, gender and/or racial "deviance" already constituted a burden which might work against the nontraditional candidate. Partisan deviance, under such circumstances, could prove to be a "fatal" blow to a judgeship candidacy already outside the mainstream. Perhaps more to the point, however, candidate pools for nonwhites and females are clearly more limited than those for white males. Under such circumstances qualified Republicans, particularly among nonwhites, might prove virtually impossible to find.

Our findings concerning the age and place of birth of the judgeship nominees can also be understood with reference to the nature of the candidate pools. Thus, nontraditional candidates emerged disproportionately from younger age groups (Tau C=0.24, S=0.00), with nonwhite females clearly the youngest nominees in the aggregate. Indeed, no nonwhite female judges were appointed who were over the age of 50, whereas over half (53.1 per cent) of all other nominees had passed that plateau. The data suggest that nonwhite females comprise the group which has most recently succeeded in gaining membership to law schools in significant numbers. Traditional patterns of discrimination preclude the presence of significant numbers of nonwhite females among age groupings where judgeship candidates have generally been found.

A similar pattern emerges when we consider the place of birth for our judgeship nominees. White males, in particular, are relatively plentiful and, in the aggregate, display the localism that traditionally characterizes the judicial recruitment process. Thus, 75.7 per cent were born in the state or circuit of their appointment. The pool of local non-traditional candidates is considerably reduced, however, and nominating authorities often have to look to candidates who were born outside the locality of the appointment (Tau B=0.15, S=0.02). This is especially the case regarding the nomination of women generally, and, most particularly nonwhite women, 83.3 per cent of whom were not locally born.

The data lend credence to the view that local roots could facilitate access to the federal bench. While the argument could be made that extended search efforts were necessary to locate suitable women nominees and often resulted in candidacies of non-local lineage, such an assertion fails to explain the relative absence of differences in the birthplace of whites and nonwhites where similar search is presumably needed.[19] We may speculate that the legal careers of the successful woman nominees evidenced greater geographic mobility than those of the white males since the women's careers may have been more intimately linked to the careers and geographic mobility of their spouses. Presumably, males could more easily pursue career opportunities closer to home and, therefore, would reveal the more dominant path to a judgeship.

In toto, our socioeconomic and demographic data revealed that the differences among white male, nonwhite male, white female and nonwhite female judicial nominees went well beyond the obvious racial and gender differences. The size of the candidate pools differed significantly for these groups, as did the paths through which nominees gained entree to eligibility for federal judgeships.

Educational backgrounds

Our data included several variables focusing on the educational backgrounds of nominees including measures of what kinds of colleges and law schools they attended (public, private, or Ivy), where they went to law school (in or out of the state or circuit of their appointment), whether or not they attended an "elite" law school, and whether or not

Table 2   Type of law school attended and nominee status

Nominee status	Elite	Not elite
White male	59	78
	43.1%	56.9%
Nonwhite male	12	29
	29.3%	70.7%
White female	14	12
	53.8%	46.2%
Nonwhite female	2	5
	28.6%	71.4%

Contingency coefficient=0.15, S=0.19

they received law school honors.[20] For the most part, statistically significant relationships did not emerge from our educational measures, although some patterns among groups of nominees are worthy of mention.

For example, women and, most particularly, white women were more likely to receive their college and law school degrees from private or Ivy institutions than other candidates. Further, different patterns of attendance regarding educational backgrounds and, presumably, opportunities among our categories of nominees are revealed in Table 2, which examines the "elite" versus "non-elite" status of the law school attended by a candidate. Clearly, white women were most likely, and the few black women appointees the least likely to graduate from such institutions. These findings appear consistent with what conventional wisdom about educational opportunity would lead one to expect. That is, it could be argued that the historical pattern of disadvantagedness and institutionalized discrimination against nonwhites in American educational institutions (and even more so, against nonwhite women) would be most evident in fewer graduates of elite institutions being found among nonwhite judgeship candidates. As noted by Uhlman, "Only in the mid-to-late 1960s did legal training at a predominantly white institution become a realistic possibility for American blacks."[21]

The elite educational background associated with white women nominees in the aggregate may also be understood from the perspective of educational opportunities. While American educational institutions have predominantly been training grounds for white males, females, generally, have not been absolutely barred from attendance as often or as recently as was the case for nonwhites.

Traditionally, however, it was the truly exceptional woman whose education proceeded beyond the level of a college degree. In the absence of an absolute bar to attendance, one would expect that

Table 3   Law school honors and nominee status

Nominee status	Yes	No
White male	50	87
	36.5%	63.5%
Nonwhite male	3	38
	7.3%	92.7%
White female	12	14
	46.2%	53.8%
Nonwhite female	4	3
	57.1%	42.9%

Contingency coefficient=0.27, S=0.00

among the relatively few "successful" women who did attend law school there would be a representative rate of enrollment in elite law programs. Further, attendance at such an institution could be a means by which a woman attorney attained a degree of professional prominence—particularly if her law degree did not necessarily open the door to the kinds of career opportunities traditionally enjoyed by successful white male attorneys. Indeed, perhaps attendance at an "elite" law school has been a threshold criterion for serious consideration of women for federal judgeship candidacies to a greater extent than is the case for other potential nominees. In a similar vein, one would expect that excellence in law school performance could be a means by which a woman attorney could gain some degree of professional prominence in a way that would positively affect her potential judgeship candidacy, whereas nominating authorities might seek other career-relevant attributes in recruiting white males to judgeships.

Table 3 reveals that the most graphic differences among our nominees on educational variables emerged on our measure of law school honors where women, in the aggregate, excelled.[22] Conversely, the data make it quite apparent that the emergence and recruitment of nonwhite male candidates for the bench does not come about as a consequence of locating candidates who attained an unusual degree of success in their law school careers. To characterize the path to a federal judgeship for nonwhite males, one must look elsewhere.

In sum, the educational background variables examined are difficult to characterize for our four classes of nominees. While few statistically significant relationships were found, it does appear that an "elite" law school training and excellence in law school can be factors which promote the judgeship candidacies of individuals who might not be identified by more conventional measures of professional success. Such appears to have been the case for women nominees in the aggregate and, most

particularly, white women candidates.

Politicization

Research on the federal judicial selection process has generally drawn much attention to the role that patronage plays in the emergence of judgeship candidacies. At times it has even been suggested that federal judges are simply attorneys who "knew" a senator and, indeed, it has traditionally been true that judgeships are, in part, a reward for political services rendered. Thus, partisan political activism has always been considered to be a great boon to a judgeship candidacy, and the question arises of whether this traditional path to a judgeship corresponds to the road taken by nontraditional judgeship candidates.

Our measures of political involvement are somewhat imperfect and clearly not inclusive. They should, however, collectively create a portrait of the level of political activity of the judicial nominees. The variables utilized included measures of whether the candidate had made any speeches during the past five years (of unspecified subject matter and, possibly, nonpolitical content) that they characterized as "significant," whether they had ever held (through appointment or election) a public office, whether they had ever played a significant role in a political campaign, and whether they had ever been a candidate for a nonjudicial, elective office.

The data demonstrate that systematic differences in politicization fell predominantly along gender lines, with females generally displaying lower levels of political activity than males. The one exception emerged on our measure of significant speechmaking where women were considerably more active than men. (Tau C=0.12, S=0.01). Thus, over three fourths of the women nominees (78.1 per cent) admitted to such speechmaking, with the corresponding figure for male candidates a considerably lower 59.7 per cent. Fully 80.8 per cent of white females had engaged in significant speechmaking.

Since women appear to be less politicized than men on all of our other measures, it is quite possible that a large portion of the significant speechmaking done by women is civically oriented yet nonpolitical in a partisan sense. If that is the case, Merritt's assertions about volunteer civic activism among women suggest that such activity could substitute for more blatant politicization as a means by which female candidates demonstrate

Table 4   Politicization and nominee status

Nominee status	Service as public official[1]		Political campaign role[2]		Elective candidate[3]	
	Yes	No	Yes	No	Yes	No
White male	116	21	64	72	59	78
	84.7%	15.3%	47.1%	52.9%	43.1%	56.9%
Nonwhite male	37	4	14	27	19	22
	90.2%	9.8%	34.1%	65.9%	46.3%	53.7%
White female	17	9	6	20	4	22
	65.4%	34.6%	23.1%	76.9%	15.4%	84.6%
Nonwhite female	4	3	2	5	0	7
	57.1%	42.9%	28.6%	71.4%	0.0%	100.0%

1. Contingency coefficient=0.28, S=0.01
2. Contingency coefficient=0.18, S=0.08
3. Contingency coefficient=0.24, S=0.01

their suitability for the federal bench. While such a linkage cannot be drawn with certainty given the nature of our variables, it is clearly a construction of the data which appears to make much sense. As Merritt has noted:

> . . . (W)omen have greater experience with nonpartisan political groups such as citizens' committees, community action groups, . . . or the League of Women Voters. It is possible that for women civic activism is . . . a key factor in political recruitment. Through volunteer activities women become knowledgeable about issues and acquainted with problem solving strategies; they sharpen their verbal and interpersonal skills; and they become known in the community, making connections with influentials and "proving themselves" as competent and serious both to their potential constituents and to themselves.[23]

In effect, as Merritt's analysis suggests, different "feeder" mechanisms may exist for advancing candidacies of women for public office than is the case for men. On that score, Stewart adds,

> "Findings . . . inevitably raise questions about alternative organizational settings for launching female public office holding careers. Perhaps organizations where women lay strong claim to experience, like the PTA, or where they constitute nearly the entire membership, like the League of Women Voters, provide more effective launching pads than do political parties . . . (E)xperience outside the conventional male feeder organizations may be a prerequisite for some women who ultimately gain public office."[24]

Our other measures of politicization, as portrayed in Table 4, clearly reveal that political backgrounds were enjoyed predominantly by male judgeship candidates. Thus, while a majority of candidates in all categories exhibited prior experience as a public official, such backgrounds were considerably more likely among males than females. (Tau B=0.21, S=0.00) Similarly, males were more likely than females to have played a significant role in a political campaign other than their own (Tau B=0.15, S=0.02), with white males, in particular, playing such a role.

Finally, it is quite apparent that male judgeship candidates were much more likely than females to have sought election to a nonjudicial political office. (Tau B=0.24, S=0.00) Indeed, nearly half (43.8 per cent) of the male judgeship candidates had run for such an office, whereas the corresponding figures for female candidates was a paltry 12.1 per cent—with *no* nonwhite female elective candidates.

In sum, the data clearly demonstrate that significant records of partisan political activity—generally considered prime paths to a federal judgeship—were predominantly associated with the more traditional male judgeship candidates. Political campaign activity, perhaps the greatest contribution which an individual could make to their party, was most associated with white male nominees. Gender differences existed on all of our politicization measures, and partisan political backgrounds did not appear to be a means by which female candidates were located for judgeship vacancies. There is some suggestion in our data, however, that significant speechmaking (possibly of a civic nature) was a route by which the potential candidacies of some women attorneys could become visible.

Our findings comport well with Goldman's assertion that while Carter's nominees were generally more active partisans than those appointed by Presidents Ford, Nixon, and Johnson, "women appointees were the major exception to this rule." As Goldman notes of Carter's circuit appointments, "In their quest to appoint well qualified women and blacks . . . Carter . . . departed from the political criteria that have traditionally played such an important role in the selection process (and still play a role for white males)."[25] While recognizing that the female appointees were not generally partisan activists, this is not necessarily to say that they

Table 5   ABA ratings and nominee status

Nominee status	Exceptionally well qualified	Well qualified	Qualified	Not qualified
White male	13	80	42	1
	9.6%	58.8%	30.9%	0.7%
Nonwhite male	1	11	29	2
	2.3%	25.6%	67.4%	4.7%
White female	1	5	21	0
	3.7%	18.5%	77.8%	0.0%
Nonwhite female	0	1	6	0
	0.0%	14.3%	85.7%	0.0%

Contingency coefficient=0.41, S=0.00

were, in any sense, apolitical. Here, our data is suggestive of the conclusions drawn by Martin.

If we redefine political activism from the traditional emphasis on holding party or public office and take into account the different patterns of political participation for women we see that our women judges are not politically passive . . . . Almost all have served on appointed blue ribbon citizen committees of some sort; most have served on several. Thus, they demonstrate an interest in and commitment to public service. Almost 90 per cent show a commitment to feminism, ranging from giving speeches to taking sex discrimination cases to being delegates to the International Women's Year Conference . . . . Thus, it appears that our women judges are political, but do not follow the same participation pattern as their male peers.[26]

Legal careers and litigation records

Perhaps the area in which the greatest differences would be expected to be found among our nominees would lie in their career patterns and litigation records. If, indeed, establishment values prevailed in the appointment process which resulted in the creation of a virtually exclusive white male bench in the past, it would be expected that nontraditional nominees would evidence alternate career paths to their judicial appointments. That this is the case is clearly suggested by the ABA Committee ratings earned by the judicial nominees as portrayed in Table 5.[27]

The ABA Committee, a group known for its mainstream evaluations of judicial candidates based largely upon criteria valued by the most successful elements in the bar, distinguished greatly between white male and all other candidates. (Tau C=0.41, S=0.00) Nearly four times as many white males (9.6 per cent) were designated "exceptionally well qualified" as compared with nonwhites and females (2.6 per cent), with 86.7 per cent of the ABA's highest designations going to white male candidates. Under one quarter (24.7 per cent) of the nontraditional candidates received one of the two highest ABA designations, while a substantial majority of white

males (68.4 per cent) enjoyed this distinction. Women candidates and, particularly, nonwhite women received the least favorable ratings from the ABA Committee. If, as it is contended, the ABA ratings are a reflection of the nature of a candidate's professional credentials, we should expect to find great differences in the career paths and litigation records of the categories of judicial nominees under analysis.

Our data included numerous indicators of the nature of the legal careers from which judgeship nominees emerged. Among them were measures of the following:

• Years at bar
• Highest court before which a nominee has been admitted to practice (state court, U.S. district or court of appeals, U.S. Supreme Court)
• Prior judicial experience
• Prior prosecutorial experience
• Clerking experience with state supreme court justice, U.S. district or appeals court judge, U.S. Supreme Court justice
• Legal aid or public defender experience
• Last job prior to nomination.

The data on years of legal experience and court admissions (presented in Tables 6 and 7) comported quite well with the ABA ratings. Clearly, white male judges enjoyed greater years of professional experience prior to their appointment than did nontraditional candidates. (Tau C=0.36, S=0.00) Indeed, only 19 per cent of the white male nominees had under 20 years to their credit in the legal profession while nearly half (46 per cent) of the nontraditional nominees fell into this category.

On the other side of the coin, 57.6 per cent of the white males had more than 25 years to their credit in the legal profession while the figure dropped dramatically to 27 per cent for nontraditional nominees. Women, in the aggregate, evidenced the least legal experience prior to their judicial appointment with only 24.2 per cent having served more

Table 6 Years at bar and nominee status

Nominee status	6-10	11-15	16-20	21-25	26.30	31+
White male	0	9	17	32	38	41
	0.0%	6.6%	12.4%	23.4%	27.7%	29.9%
Nonwhite male	1	5	9	14	8	4
	2.4%	12.2%	22.0%	34.1%	19.5%	9.8%
White female	1	8	4	5	4	4
	3.8%	30.8%	15.4%	19.2%	15.4%	15.4%
Nonwhite female	0	2	4	1	0	0
	0.0%	28.6%	57.1%	14.3%	0.0%	0.0%

Contingency coefficient=0.40, S=0.00

than 25 years in the legal profession while more than half (57.5 per cent) had under 20 years of professional experience.

Similarly, on another measure which could be related to professional prestige, albeit cautiously, white male candidates tended to have been admitted to practice before a "higher" level court than nonwhites and women. (Tau C=0.14, S=0.02) Indeed, 57.8 per cent of the white male nominees have been admitted to practice before the U.S. Supreme Court, and 81.5 per cent have been admitted to the federal bar at least as high as the circuit court level.

The corresponding figures for nontraditional candidates are 45.9 per cent and 68.9 per cent respectively, with women candidates, in particular, least likely to enjoy admission status before relatively higher level tribunals. It should be noted, however, that admission to practice before prestigious courts, such as the U.S. Supreme Court, is often largely honorific—requiring only a sponsor and the payment of a fee. Perhaps the data does reflect, however, the tendency of the nontraditional nominees not to share equally in the accouterments of status as defined by the established white male bar. Indeed, we would expect differences among our categories of nominees to be quite pronounced as we consider, in greater detail, specific facets of the nature of their legal experience.

Job immediately preceding appointment

One career variable of considerable interest in distinguishing among the paths to judgeships taken by different types of nominees focuses on the candidates' last job prior to their pending judicial appointment. The data presented in Table 8 reveals significant, substantively meaningful differences on this measure. Thus, the modal job from which white male candidates moved to the federal bench was the private practice of law—nearly half (49.6 per cent) of these candidates followed that route. Approximately half as many nontraditional

nominees (25.7 per cent) came to the federal bench from such positions, underlining the reality that prominent law practices of the kind that serve as incubators for federal judges are not widely staffed by nonwhite and female attorneys.[28] As Cook notes, "Social culture affects attitudes, roles, and resources of women, and legal culture affects attitudes, practices, and experiences that constrain the opportunities for women to become legal professionals and to hold law jobs."[29]

The modal job held by members of all categories of nontraditional nominees prior to their current appointment was another judgeship—with 59.5 per cent of the nontraditional nominees already sitting as judges as compared to only 39.4 per cent of the white males. In a similar vein, nearly twice as many nontraditional nominees (9.5 per cent) held law school professorships immediately prior to their appointment than white males (5.1 per cent).

These figures suggest that for the nontraditional nominees the prominence necessary to become a viable candidate for a federal judgeship often was not readily available through private law practices. Lower court judgeships could have had relatively greater appeal to nontraditional attorneys than to white males since "highly qualified men find it difficult to take the kind of salary cut the bench entails at their level of professional development."[30]

In particular, when nominating authorities sought nonwhite judicial candidates existing lower court judgeships became a fertile field in which to conduct their search. Indeed, judicial experience emerged as a substitute for the other credentials which black candidates may have lacked. Clearly, affirmative action concerns about the underrepresentation of blacks in the American judiciary predated concern about the dearth of women on the bench. Often, black judges were appointed to lower state tribunals for local political reasons. Thus, it is of some interest to note that of the white males who enjoyed judicial experience, 74.6 per cent gained such experience in service in state

Table 7 Highest court admission and nominee status

Nominee status	State court	United States district court	United States court of appeals	United States Supreme Court
White male	3	22	32	78
	2.2%	16.3%	23.7%	57.8%
Nonwhite male	0	11	10	20
	0.0%	26.8%	24.4%	48.8%
White female	4	6	4	12
	15.4%	23.1%	15.4%	46.2%
Nonwhite female	1	1	3	2
	14.3%	14.3%	42.9%	28.6%

Contingency coefficient=0.29, S=0.02

judicial systems. The corresponding figure for the nontraditional nominees was a somewhat more robust 83.3 per cent.

Also of note is the relatively large number of practicing academicians found among the white women gaining entree to the federal bench—over two times as great a proportion than evidenced by any other nominee grouping. Apparently with few women creating a pool for judgeship candidacies in private practices or on the bench, the search for females turned to the academy. The relatively large proportion of female academicians appointed to the bench suggests, as underlined by Martin, "that what the women lacked in political credentials, they compensated for by their professional scholarship." Further, "(w)omen judges have continued their intellectual interests, each publishing an average of 11 articles or books."[31]

These differences in the jobs our nominees held immediately prior to their federal judgeship appointments are suggestive of broader differences in their career backgrounds. In Table 9, several of these differences are examined including consideration of whether the nominees ever had gained judicial experience, prosecutorial experience, legal aid or public defender experience, or clerking experience with a state supreme court justice, U.S. district or appeals court judge, or Supreme Court justice.

Table 9 reveals that our finding that nontraditional candidates were relatively more likely to be appointed from sitting judgeships to the federal bench than was the case with white males can be extended to note that nontraditional candidates were considerably more likely to have served as a judge at some time during their careers than was the case with white males. (Tau B=0.17, S=0.01) Indeed, less than half of the white male nominees (48.9 per cent) as compared to approximately two thirds (66.2 per cent) of the nontraditional candidates had ever served as judges prior to their cur-

rent federal appointment.

As expected, nonwhite males (predominately blacks) were relatively most likely to have gained prior judicial experience, and such a credential appears to have been a basis for lending credibility to their candidacies. White males, on the other hand, were least likely to have previous service as a judge. As we have seen, however, several alternative aspects of their backgrounds could serve to render their candidacies prominent and accessible.

In the aggregate, there appeared to be little difference in the relative likelihood of nontraditional candidates and white males having prosecutorial experience (Tau B=0.06, S=0.20) and, in general, such job experience appeared to be somewhat conducive to federal judicial appointment. Women nominees, however, particularly white women, were quite unlikely to have served in a prosecutorial capacity and this was clearly not a major route to their federal judicial appointment.

On the other hand, while white male and all other nominees demonstrated no differences regarding their possession of law clerking experience (Tau B=0.08, S=0.11), white female candidates were the most likely to have served in a prestigious clerkship. Thus, as was the case regarding measures of their educational backgrounds, prominent clerkships may have been another means of bringing women's candidacies to the fore. Such clerkships were clearly not a basis for legitimizing candidacies of nonwhites, particularly nonwhite males.

Finally, it should be noted that more than twice as many nonwhite nominees (48.6 per cent) has served in a public defender/legal aid capacity than was the case among the white males (23.7 per cent). (Tau B=0.25, S=0.00) Indeed, more than half (53.7 per cent) of the nonwhite male candidates had such experience and, presumably, this was a career factor which was conducive to their identification, accessibility and, presumably, advancement.

Table 8   Last job prior to judicial appointment and nominee status

Nominee status	Politics-government legal	Politics-government other	Judiciary	Law practice	Law professor
White male	5	3	54	68	7
	3.6%	2.2%	39.4%	49.6%	5.1%
Nonwhite male	1	0	27	10	3
	2.4%	0.0%	65.9%	24.4%	7.3%
White female	1	0	14	7	4
	3.8%	0.0%	53.8%	26.9%	15.4%
Nonwhite female	2	0	3	2	0
	28.6%	0.0%	42.9%	28.6%	0.0%

Contingency coefficient=0.34, S=0.01

It is not surprising to learn that nontraditional attorneys whose legal careers had included what might be characterized as a "social work" component were identified as judgeship candidates. Thus, for example, regarding women attorneys, Epstein has noted that, "a 1970 study . . . suggested that law school gatekeepers held pervasive beliefs that women were motivated by desires . . . to help the poor and oppressed."[32] "Representing the poor and disadvantaged is one of the major areas of 'women's work' in the law. It is a realm in which women have found work in the past and in which they still tend to cluster."[33] Indeed, data cited by Epstein demonstrate that women disproportionately take "legal services" positions and, presumably, assertions such as those made above are equally applicable to all nontraditional attorneys.[34]

Litigating experience

Our data also included several measures focusing on the litigating experience of nominees. These included estimates of the frequency of their court appearances, the percentage of their litigation which occurred in federal, state, or other courts, and the percentage of their litigation which involved civil matters versus criminal concerns. Each candidate's Judiciary Committee questionnaire responses also provided detailed case studies of what were, in the candidate's view, the 10 most significant legal matters that they had personally handled during their careers.

Operating on the assumption that these case studies offered important evidence of how nominees perceived and characterized their own careers, each case was coded on a number of variables for each nominee. Summary variables were also created for each nominee based on aggregating the data obtained from the 10 case studies. Included were measures of the percentage of the case studies arising in the federal judiciary, involving

civil law and involving appellate courts. Finally, each case study was also coded according to its subject matter and an attempt was made to operationalize the concept of a "nontraditional" legal practice based on the summary aggregation of the subject matter of the case studies for each nominee.[35]

As Table 10 reveals, while all categories of judgeship candidates appeared to be heavily involved in litigation, this was even more the case regarding nonwhite and, most particularly, nonwhite males. The location of litigation differed somewhat for our categories of nominees, with women relatively more likely to litigate in federal courts than men and considerably less likely to litigate in state courts. Indeed, 68.4 per cent of the male nominees litigated the majority of their cases in state courts, with the corresponding figure of 42.9 per cent for women.

Further examination of the volunteered case studies outlining the most important cases the nominees had personally handled reveals that women designated at least 70 per cent federal cases 47.6 per cent of the time and all federal cases 19.0 per cent of the time. Male nominees, on the other hand, elected at least 70 per cent federal cases as among their most important only 20.6 per cent of the time and all federal cases just 4.5 per cent of the time. Thus, while our data may suggest that women, particularly white women, are relatively more likely to be recruited for judgeships from outside of legal practices and while they are not among the heaviest litigators examined, there is a significantly greater tendency for women nominees to have litigated predominantly in federal courts.[36]

Of greatest interest is the finding that it is the nature of the litigating experience and not simply its extent which helps to distinguish among our categories of nominees. In the aggregate, nontraditional nominees were more heavily in-

Table 9　Career experience and nominee status

Nominee status	Judicial experience[1]		Prosecutorial experience[2]		Clerkship experience[3]		Legal aid experience[4]	
	Yes	No	Yes	No	Yes	No	Yes	No
White male	67	70	64	73	32	105	32	103
	48.9%	51.1%	46.7%	53.3%	23.4%	76.6%	23.7%	76.3%
Nonwhite male	30	11	22	19	3	38	22	19
	73.2%	26.8%	53.7%	46.3%	7.3%	92.7%	53.7%	46.3%
White female	15	11	4	22	8	18	11	15
	57.7%	42.3%	15.4%	84.6%	30.8%	69.2%	42.3%	57.7%
Nonwhite female	4	3	4	3	1	6	3	4
	57.1%	42.9%	57.1%	42.9%	14.3%	85.7%	42.9%	57.1%

1. Contingency coefficient=0.19, S=0.05
2. Contingency coefficient=0.22, S=0.01
3. Contingency coefficient=0.18, S=0.08
4. Contingency coefficient=0.26, S=0.00

volved in criminal litigation than their white male counterparts. (Tau C=0.14, S=0.02)

As Table 11 makes clear, nonwhite nominees are relatively most likely to have attained sufficient prominence to be considered for a federal judgeship in practices marked by a substantial criminal law component. White females, on the other hand, emerge as most likely to have engaged in a primarily civil law practice with 71.4 per cent asserting that over 90 per cent of their cases were civil in nature. Returning to the nominee's case studies for further elaboration of this finding, 94.2 per cent of the white women designated at least 70 per cent civil cases as among their most important as compared to only 62.5 per cent of the nonwhite males. More than twice as many (47.1 per cent) white women designated all civil cases than was the case for nonwhite males (21.9 per cent).

Finally, it should be noted, nontraditional nominees were more likely than white males to have been recruited from what we have operationalized as a nontraditional legal practice on the basis of coding the subject matter of the 10 volunteered case studies. (Tau B=0.14, S=0.03) Thus, a solid majority (55.7 per cent) of the nontraditional nominees (57.9 per cent of the nonwhites and 60.6 per cent of the nonwhite males) were classified in this fashion as compared to 40.2 per cent of the white males (and 41.5 per cent of all whites).

In sum, the data clearly demonstrate that white male candidates and what we have labeled " nontraditional" nominees travel different routes to the federal bench. As importantly, significant differences existed among the career patterns evidenced by different categories of nontraditional nominees.

Stark differences

That stark career differences would appear among our categories of nominees was suggested by their widely divergent aggregate ABA ratings. White male candidates were generally recruited for judgeships after having traveled a well-worn path established by a time honored selection process. They enjoyed long years of legal experience, prestigious courtroom admissions and, for the most part, highly successful private practices.

Such prominent and successful private practices were not likely to be fertile grounds for locating viable nontraditional judgeship candidates. Nonwhites, however, were recruited from sitting judgeships or, more generally, from among those who had gained some public prominence in their legal careers through their judicial experience. Nonwhites, particularly males, were most likely to have had legal aid backgrounds and to have served in predominantly criminal practices.

While women nominees appeared less likely to be among the heaviest litigators, their litigation tended to disproportionately occur in civil law cases found in the federal court system. In seeking women for the bench, recruitment authorities turned disproportionately to the law schools where several women attorneys had gained prominence as academicians. Their scholarly achievements were also evidenced in their greater likelihood to have served in prominent law clerkships than other candidates.

These findings are of much interest, suggesting that "exceptional" women attorneys became prominent candidates for judgeships by escaping their stereotyped legal roles and, perhaps, by being at the forefront of professional developments which were altering those very roles during the decade of the 1970s. Indeed, commenting on women attorneys during the 1950s, Ginsburg's characterization only partially captures the professional world of

Table 10 Court frequency and nominee status

Nominee status	Regularly	Occasionally	Not at all
White male	112	21	2
	83.0%	15.6%	1.5%
Nonwhite male	38	3	0
	92.7%	7.3%	0.0%
White female	15	6	0
	71.4%	28.6%	0.0%
Nonwhite female	6	0	1
	85.7%	0.0%	14.3%

Contingency coefficient=0.26, S=0.02

Table 11 Percentage civil litigation and nominee status

Nominee status	90-100%	51-89%	11-50%	0-10%
White male	73	44	14	2
	54.9%	33.1%	10.5%	1.5%
Nonwhite male	12	15	11	2
	30.0%	37.5%	27.5%	5.0%
White female	15	5	1	0
	71.4%	23.8%	4.8%	0.0%
Nonwhite female	2	2	1	1
	33.3%	33.3%	16.7%	16.7%

Contingency coefficient=0.31, S=0.01

women federal judgeship candidates during the late 1970s:

Surely there was a chill wind for women in the law schools of the 1950's . . . . Although women were long accepted as criminal defenders at legal aid, where salaries were low, United States Attorneys offices would not assign women to the criminal division. Pace setting law firms wanted no women lawyers, prestigious judicial clerkships were off limits to females. With only a handful of exceptions, women did not teach in law schools.[37]

Yet as Ginsburg herself notes, much change has been occurring. Thus, for example, while only three women had served as Supreme Court clerks in the history of the Court prior to 1971, between 1971 and 1976, 14 additional women had so served.[38] Our data indicate that while women have made less substantial inroads in lucrative private practices, the doors to several other arenas of professional status and success have begun to open. At bottom, however, it should be stressed that nontraditional candidates tended to emerge disproportionately from what we have identified as nontraditional legal practices.

Some concluding thoughts

Our data on the demographic, educational, political, and legal career backgrounds of judicial nominees during the 96th Congress have clearly revealed diverse patterns of recruitment to the federal bench. Such diversity, however, is not random, and distinctive paths to federal judgeships distinguish among candidates along racial and gender lines. It is quite evident that the road to the bench predominantly exhibited by white male nominees—with its inclusion of many traditional measures of personal and professional success—is not widely shared by nontraditional (that is, those who are nonwhite or female) judgeship nominees.

Major differences in paths to the federal bench are directly related to the different social, economic, and political roles played in the aggregate by the groups to which nontraditional candidates belong in American society and to the opportunities available to members of these groups. Perhaps of equal importance, nontraditional candidates differ substantially from each other as well. Recruitment strategies aimed at increasing the representativeness of the federal judiciary must begin with the recognition that different avenues of prominence may predominate in the life experiences of white males, nonwhite males, white women, and nonwhite women.

Representativeness in the judicial branch is difficult to come by and, if an administration chooses to pursue it, can only be realized by a commitment to a broad search for qualified candidates in nontraditional settings, thus overcoming the bias inherent in longstanding judicial selection norms and traditions. The qualities which go into the making of a "good" judge are, perhaps, even more elusive than achieving representation on the bench. While differences abounded among the candidates examined, they did not in any sense appear to underlie the inherent superiority of the backgrounds or the path to the bench traveled by white male nominees. Clearly, candidates demonstrated different means of attaining the prominence and stature which resulted in their being seriously considered for a federal judgeship. While who were the "better" judges may be a judgment analysts are able to make in due course, the judgment of which were the "best" candidates depends largely on whose standards of merit prevail.

The data regarding alternate career paths to the federal bench traveled by the representatives of divergent groups in American society must be considered in a temporal context. That is, while "nontraditional" candidates traveled different paths to the bench than did white males, this is not to suggest that the differences observed must, of necessity, continue unabated. It is possible that as the number of nontraditional attorneys increases on the bench and in the legal profession writ large, barriers will be broken down and distinctive nontraditional legal career patterns will begin to disappear as the former "outsiders" take their place in the established legal order.

A second scenario would suggest that if nontraditional paths to the federal bench continue to be accepted and, to some degree, rewarded, white male candidates may begin to emerge from these recruitment patterns in significant numbers as well, and a reassessment of just what constitutes a "traditional" path to the bench would be called for. Finally, the possibility exists that the distinctive career paths leading to the bench exhibited by the different groups among our candidates will continue to distinguish among their recruitment patterns. What mix of scenarios is controlling must await the judgment of future recruitment patterns and scholarly analysis.[39]

Finally, while representativeness on the bench may be of great symbolic importance for the public which the judiciary serves, many of the important questions concerning judicial recruitment are behavioral in nature. At bottom, does it really make a difference how representative the American bench is for the decisions reached by American courts? With regard to the men and women appointed to the federal bench during the 96th Congress our knowledge about this behavioral dimension remains somewhat sketchy and exploratory in nature.[40] Indeed, focus on the decisional propensities among our categories of nominees is a priority for future research in this area.

NOTES

This article originally appeared in Volume 67, Number 8, March 1984, pages 370-388.

This research was generously supported with grants-in-aid from the Social and Behavioral Science Research Committee and the Graduate School of the Ohio State University. Thanks are owed to Professor Richard Lempert of the University of Michigan Law School and to several anonymous reviewers whose thinking and suggestions about my research led to the formulation and refinement of this manuscript.

1. For an early "pathbreaking" study in this area focusing on U.S. Supreme Court justices see Schmidhauser, *The Justices of the Supreme Court: A Collective Portrait*, 3 MIDWEST J. OF POL. SCI. 49 (1959).

2. *See, generally*, the work of Sheldon Goldman including Goldman, *Characteristics of Eisenhower and Kennedy Appointees to the Lower Federal Courts*, 18 WESTERN POLITICAL Q. 755 (1965); Goldman, *Johnson and Nixon Appointees to the Federal Lower Courts: Some Socio-Political Perspectives*, 34 J. OF POL. 934 (1972); and Goldman, *Reagan's judicial appointments at mid-term: shaping the bench in his own image*, 66 JUDICATURE 334 (1983).

3. *See, for example*, Barrow and Walker, "Racial Diversity on the Federal Bench," paper presented at the 1983 meeting of the Southwestern Political Science Association; Goldman, *Voting Behavior on the United States Courts of Appeals 1961-1964*, 60 AM. POL. SCI. REV. 375 (1966); Goldman, *Backgrounds, Attitudes, and the Voting Behavior of Judges: A Comment on Grossman*, 31 J. OF POL. 214 (1969); Goldman, *Voting Behavior on the United States Court of Appeals, Revisited*, 69 AM. POL. SCI. REV. 491 (1975); Grossman, *Social Backgrounds and Judicial Decision-Making*, 79 HARV. L. REV. 1551 (1966); Grossman, *Social Backgrounds and Judicial Decisions: Notes for a Theory*, 29 J. OF POL. 336 (1967); Tate, *Personal Attribute Models of the Voting Behavior of U.S. Supreme Court Justices: Liberalism in Civil Liberties and Economic Decisions, 1946-1978*, 75 AM. POL. SCI. REV. 335 (1981); Ulmer, *Social Background as an Indicator to the Votes of Supreme Court Justices in Criminal Cases: 1947-1956 Terms*, 17 AM. J. OF POL. SCI. 622 (1973); Vines, *Federal District Judges and Race Relations Cases in the South*, 26 J. OF PUB. L. 338 (1964); Walker, "Affirmative Action in Federal Judicial Selection: Policy and Process Ramifications," paper presented at the 1982 meeting of the Southern Political Science Association.

4. Grossman, *Social Backgrounds and Judicial Decision-Making*, *supra* n. 3.

5. Carbon, *Women in the judiciary: an introduction*, 65 JUDICATURE 285 (1982). To illustrate Carbon's point, in 1910 women constituted only one per cent of all lawyers. In 1930 women constituted 2.1 per cent, in 1963 the figure was 2.7 per cent and in 1970 the figure was 2.8 per cent. By 1980, however, women constituted approximately 13 per cent of all practicing lawyers. It is projected that women will comprise a full third of the legal profession by the year 2000. Berkson, *Women on the bench: a brief history*, 65 JUDICATURE 289-290 (1982).

6. *See, for example*, Cook, "Women's Issues Before Women Judges in State Trial Courts," paper presented at the 1978 meeting of the Law and Society Association; Cook, *Political Culture and Selection of Women Judges in Trial Courts*, in Stewart, ed., WOMEN IN LOCAL POLITICS 42-60 (New Jersey: Scarecrow Press, 1980). *Women Judges and Public Policy in Sex Integration*, in Stewart, ed., WOMEN IN LOCAL POLITICS 130-148 (New Jersey: Scarecrow Press, 1980); Kritzer and Uhlman, *Sisterhood in the Courtroom: Sex of Judge and Defendant in Criminal Case Disposition*, 14 SOC. SCI. J. 77 (1977); Uhlman, *Race, Recruitment and Representation: Background Differences Between Black and White Trial Court Judges*, 30 WESTERN POL. Q. 457 (1977); and Uhlman, *Black Elite Decision-Making: The Case of Trial Judges*, 22 AM. J. OF POL. SCI. 884 (1978).

More recently, however, work has begun to be focused on nontraditional federal judges. *See, for example*, Martin, *Women on the federal bench: a comparative profile*, 65 JUDICATURE 306 (1982); Walker, *supra* n. 3; Barrow and Walker, *supra* n. 3; and Gottschall, *Carter's judicial appointments: the influence of affirmative action and merit selection on voting on the U.S. Courts of Appeals*, 67 JUDICATURE 164 (1983).

7. Kritzer and Uhlman, *supra* n. 6, at 86.

8. Uhlman, *Race, Recruitment and Representation*, *supra* n. 6, at 470.

9. *Id.* at 458.

10. Cook, "Political Culture and Selection of Women Judges in Trial Courts," *supra* n. 6, at 49-50.

11. Uhlman, *Black Elite Decision-Making: The Case of Trial Judges*, *supra* n. 6, at 892-893.

12. Lipschutz and Huron, *Achieving a more representative federal judiciary*, 62 JUDICATURE 483 (1979).

13. For consideration of the scope and implications of the president's affirmative action program in judicial selection see Walker, *supra* n. 3; and Slotnick, *Lowering the Bench or Raising it Higher?: Affirmative Action and Judicial Selection During the Carter Administration*, 1 YALE L. & POLICY REV. 270 (1983).

14. Goldman, *Carter's judicial appointments: a lasting legacy*, 64 JUDICATURE 344 (1981).

15. *Id.* at 349.

16. For a preliminary exploratory studies of the behavior of the nonwhite and women judges appointed by Carter see Walker, *supra* n. 3; Barow and Walker, *supra* n. 3 and Gotschall, *supra* n. 6.

17. The data base for this research consists primarily of the responses to a Senate Judiciary Committee questionnaire administered to all judicial nominees during the 96th Congress. Completion of the questionnaire was required before a nomination hearing would be held on a candidate and, therefore, before any appointment could be finalized on the Senate floor. The detailed questionnaires contain a wealth of comparable data on nominees of a kind previously difficult if not impossible to obtain. Questionnaire responses are likely to result in an unusually valid data source on appointees since they constituted a record, submitted under oath, on which members of the Judiciary Committee, the Senate, the press, other interested parties, and the general public would scrutinize a nominee. Questionnaire data were supplemented by information concerning nominee race, political party affiliation, religion and ABA rating graciously provided by Professor Sheldon Goldman. Data drawn from the 96th Congress questionnaires provides information on more than 80 per cent of all judicial nominations made during the Carter presidency.

18. For all relationships discussed, $p \leq 0.05$ will be treated as statistically significant. Contingency coefficients are utilized when the variables are measured at the nominal level. For ordinally measured variables, Tau B was utilized for "square" tables with equal numbers of rows and columns. Tau C was used for "rectangular" tables with unequal numbers of rows and columns and ordinal data.

19. It should be noted, however, that Uhlman's data did find racial differences in lineage among his judges. While "early local ties are a hallmark of the entire Metro City bench, . . . An extremely high proportion of the white bench is native to the area . . . By comparison, the black bench is significantly more diverse geographically." Uhlman, *Race, Recruitment and Representation, supra* n. 6, at 460.

20. Law school honors was operationalized as attaining membership on the school's law review or law journal, earning Order of the Coif distinction, graduating at the top of one's class, competing in national moot court competition, etc. "Elite" law schools were operationalized by utilizing several subjective and objective indicators to compile a composite ranking. A school was considered to be "elite" if it was included on three of the following measures:

- The Gourman Report (14 "distinguished" law schools)
- Barron's Guide "Group 1" law schools (14 "high resource" law schools)
- Blau-Margulies Report (top 9 law schools)
- Cartter Report (top 15 law schools)
- Ladd-Lipset Report (top 8 law schools)
- Juris Doctor (top 13 law schools)

21. Uhlman, *Race, Recruitment and Representation, supra* n. 6, at 462.

22. Our aggregate findings are similar to those reported by Martin for women circuit judges. Martin notes that 82 per cent of the women appellate judges received some "special honor" in law school as compared to only 26 per cent of the males appointed between 1933 and 1976. Martin, *supra* n. 6, at 312.

23. Merritt, *Winners and Losers: Sex Differences in Municipal Elections*, 21 AM. J. OF POL. SCI. 731, 736 (1977).

24. Stewart, ed., WOMEN IN LOCAL POLITICS, *supra* n. 6, at 219.

25. Goldman, *supra* n. 14, at 351-52.

26. Martin, *supra* n. 6, at 313.

27. For consideration of the ABA Committee, its evaluative process, and the correlates of its ratings see Slotnick, *The ABA Standing Committee on Federal Judiciary: a contemporary assessment (Parts 1 and 2)*, 66 JUDICATURE 348, 385 (1983).

28. Indeed, even when engaged in private practices in prominent firms women are unlikely to enjoy partnerships which could lend visibility to a judgeship candidacy. Thus, according to Epstein, "Of the 1520 partners distributed among the large New York firms in 1977, 29 were women. This represented almost a tenfold increase since 1971." By 1980, "of the 3,987 partners in the top 50 law firms in the country, 85 were women. This is . . . only about two per cent. . . . As of 1980, . . . more than a quarter of the large firms . . . have no women partners." Epstein, WOMEN IN LAW 179 (New York: Basic Books, 1981).

29. Cook, *supra* n. 6, at 43.

30. Epstein, *supra* n. 28, at 129.

31. Martin, *supra* n. 6, at 312.

32. Epstein, *supra* n. 28, at 38.

33. *Id.* at 120.

34. *Id.* at 99.

35. The subject matter codes used to categorize the case studies were as follows: Business Organization and Management, Contracts, Real Property, Torts, Personal Finances, Family and Estate, Criminal, and several Public Law categories (Governmental Regulatory Powers, Prisoner and Defendant Rights, Equal Protection and Abuse of Governmental Authority). The effort to characterize a "nontraditional legal practice" proceeded from conventional wisdom concerning what types of individuals were generally considered to be "mainstream" attorneys and likely candidates for federal judgeships. Nontraditional legal practice was conceptualized as work in the areas of criminal defense, public law plaintiff (or defendant against governmental regulatory activity), tort plaintiff, personal finances, or family law. When a nominee acted in these capacities in at least four of the 10 case studies developed in the questionnaire he or she was considered to enjoy a nontraditional legal practice.

36. Our data which suggest that women candidates were not among the heaviest litigators is not surprising. Epstein reports on the common conception that "women lawyers did not go to court. Like law students or summer internships, women did research and brief writing . . . . *Time* magazine made it all clear in a March 6, 1964, article that described the legal profession's view of women lawyers as 'unfitted for trial work, suited only for matrimonial cases or such backroom fields as estates and trusts.' " Epstein, *supra* n. 28, at 103-104. While such perspectives have changed and, undoubtedly, continue to do so, their residual effect may be evidence in the litigation records of female attorneys with sufficient legal experience to be judgeship candidates.

37. Ginsburg, *Women at the Bar: A Generation of Change*, 2 U. OF PUGET SOUND L. REV. 1, 4 (1978).

38. *Id.* at 7.

39. I am indebted to Beverly Blair Cook for initially raising the concerns alluded to in this section of the analysis.

40. *See* Walker, *supra* n. 3; Barrow and Walker, *supra* n. 3; and Gottschall, *supra* n. 6.

Trial Courts: Civil and Criminal Justice Processes

INTRODUCTION

Trial courts are tribunals of first instance in the American judiciary, the forum in which civil and criminal justice matters are initially heard. In most instances, the trial court is also the arena in which legal matters are definitively resolved either through pretrial negotiated settlements or actual trial proceedings. The articles in this section consider several aspects of the operation of American trial courts.

Robert Litan's "Speeding up civil justice" presents the recommendations of a recent blue-ribbon task force that considered the issue of how delay and costs could be lessened in civil proceedings. The article underlines the importance of developing appropriate incentives to induce litigants to reduce delay and cost. It also emphasizes that not all cases are alike and that, consequently, generic civil procedures are inappropriate mechanisms for reform. In "Measuring the pace of civil litigation in federal and state trial couts," Joel Grossman, Herbert Kritzer, Kristin Bumiller, and Stephen McDougal argue that delay in the civil courts may be a more complex phenomenon than it appears to be on the surface. Speed and efficiency may not always be desirable in case disposition and their maximization may undermine other important goals.

"Critical issues in the courtroom: exploring a hypothetical case" is a panel discussion that turns our gaze to criminal court proceedings. Panel participants (including judges, prosecutors, defense attorneys, and academics) discuss a wide range of criminal justice concerns including the issues of bail setting, plea bargaining, jail crowding, and alternatives to incarceration. The panel discussion considers many hypothetical case examples. In contrast, Norval Morris's piece on "Race and crime: what evidence is there that race influences results in the criminal justice system?" brings considerable data to bear on the problems he addresses. Morris's data support the argument that the criminal justice system discriminates against blacks at multiple stages in the process including arrest, conviction, and punishment. The author considers remedies for the problems he highlights and concludes, "The whole law and order movement that we have heard so much about is, in operation though not in intent, anti-black and anti-underclass—not in plan, not in desire, not in intent, but in operation."

William McDonald's study of "Judicial supervision of the guilty plea process: a study of six jurisdictions" returns our attention to the actions of judges in the criminal justice arena and their role in assuring fairness in plea-bargaining outcomes. McDonald's research convinces him that pleas are more intelligent than in the past and defendants generally get the deals that they expect. Nevertheless, significant problems remain with reforms that "have left the coercive character of plea bargaining intact. They have not moved plea bargaining much closer to the trial procedure's determination of legal guilt. They do not constitute a means by which an independent third party weighs the evidence against some standard of legal proof."

The final selection in this section, Susanna Barber's article "The problem of prejudice: a new approach to assessing the impact of courtroom cameras" develops an argument that has implications for our consideration of trial courts, jury behavior, and the role of the media in the judicial process. Barber addresses the popular concern of whether cameras inherently bias trial proceedings by distracting jurors and causing other courtroom participants to alter their behavior. She asks, alternatively, whether factors other than cameras are responsible for prejudicing trials and whether, therefore, bans on courtroom cameras can be justified. Ultimately, Barber concludes that much bias in trials is inherent in trial proceedings and that cameras in the courtroom could actually eliminate some of the system's most blatant excesses.

Speeding up civil justice

The Brookings Institution and the Foundation for Change convened a task force of 35 lawyers, law professors, and former judges to consider how delay and costs in the courts can be reduced. Among their recommendations are strict time limits, "staged" discovery, and expanded judicial resources.

by Robert E. Litan

The United States has long been admired throughout the world for its sophisticated and well-developed system of civil justice, which is designed to guarantee all citizens the opportunity to resolve disputes peaceably before a jury of their peers in a court overseen by impartial judicial officers. Indeed, the United States can be proud that it affords legal protections to victims of injustice— protections that are provided through litigation and the court system.

But increasingly, all who participate in the judicial system—litigants, judges, and attorneys—are voicing complaints about both its lack of fairness and its inefficiency. In many courts, litigants must wait for years to resolve their disputes. In the meantime, their attorneys pursue ever more expensive means of preparing for trial, often having to duplicate their preparation when trial dates are postponed. Among the bulk of cases that are never tried but settled, many are overprepared. In short, civil litigation costs too much and takes too long.

The high costs of litigation burden everyone. Our businesses spend too much on legal expenses at a time when they are confronted with increasingly intense international competition. They pass those costs on to consumers, who then pay unnecessarily high prices for the products and services they buy. Individuals who take their cases to court or who must defend themselves against legal actions often face staggering legal bills and years of delay.

Out of frustration with this state of affairs, the chairman of the Senate Judiciary Committee, Joseph R. Biden (D-Del.), asked the Brookings Institution and the Foundation for Change to convene a task force of representatives of the major participants in the civil justice system to consider how delay and costs in the courts can be reduced. The task force was formed in the summer of 1988 and ultimately consisted of 35 leading attorneys, law professors, and former judges throughout the nation. This article summarizes the report the task force has issued.

The problem

The members of the task force were able to agree to a set of recommendations largely because, in spite of their diverse interests outside the courtroom, they all agreed that the problems of delay and cost are too serious to be ignored. To determine whether this sentiment was more widely shared, the Foundation for Change commissioned Louis Harris and Associates to survey over 1,000 participants in the civil justice system—private litigators representing plaintiffs and defendants, "public interest" litigators, corporate counsel and federal district court judges. The survey, conducted in mid-1988 through in-depth telephone interviews, sought the respondents' opinions on a wide range of issues relating to transaction costs and delay. The responses are summarized on page 331.

Several important findings stand out:

• More than half of the federal judges, corporate counsel, and public interest litigators surveyed believe that the costs of litigating civil cases in the United States today are a "major problem." Even 40 per cent of private litigators hold this view. Those who have litigated abroad perceive U.S. litigation costs to be substantially higher than those in foreign countries. And a majority of corporate counsel and federal judges think that litigation costs, corrected for inflation, have increased "greatly" during the past decade.

• A majority of judges and lawyers agree that the high costs of litigating in America unreasonably impede access to the civil justice system by the ordinary citizen. Furthermore, they believe that the civil justice system today gives an unfair advantage to "large interests" with greater resources.

• The respondents agree that the most important cause of high litigation costs or delays is abuse by attorneys of the discovery process, which leads to "over-discovery" of cases rather than to attempts to focus on controlling issues. Both plaintiffs' and defendants' attorneys share in the blame. Corporate counsel and private litigators estimate that 60 per cent of all litigation costs in a typical federal court case arise out of discovery. As Judge William Schwarzer has written elsewhere: "For many lawyers, discovery is a Pavlovian reaction. When the lawsuit is filed, and the filing stamp comes down, the word processor begins to grind out interrogatories and requests for production. Deposition notices drop like autumn leaves."[1]

• A majority of the lawyers and even the judges surveyed also believe that the "failure of judges to control the discovery process" is another important cause of high litigation costs.

Given the widespread dissatisfaction with the current system, one would expect those who participate in it to be pessimistic about the possibilities for implementing meaningful reforms. Surprisingly, the respondents to the Harris survey overwhelmingly agreed that such changes *can* be made and that, if implemented, would *significantly reduce* the costs of litigation.

Specifically, nearly all of the lawyers surveyed, as well as eight out of 10 federal judges, support procedural systems that put cases on different discovery and trial "tracks" based on complexity: the less complex the case, the more accelerated the track. Consistent with this recommendation, almost 80 per cent of the attorneys also favor a 28-month limit on discovery, with provisions for exceptional circumstances. Both lawyers and judges overwhelmingly favor increasing the role of federal judges as active case managers, making greater use of pretrial and status conferences to monitor and limit discovery, and scheduling early and firm trial dates.

To summarize, there is a significant degree of consensus among those who regularly participate in the civil justice system about what reforms are most needed to reduce transactions costs and delays. This consensus was also reflected in the recommendations urged by the task force.

Recommendations for reform

More than 50 years have passed since the Federal Rules of Civil Procedure (FRCP), which govern civil litigation in the federal courts, were drafted and adopted. As expressed in 1938, the core objectives of the Rules are threefold: "the just, speedy and inexpensive determination of every action."

While these objectives have not changed in five decades, the federal courts look very different. Many court dockets are overcrowded, not only with civil cases but with criminal cases, which by law effectively are given priority. In addition, judges must now adjudicate a wide range of highly complex cases not seen 50 years ago: huge class actions, often involving thousands of parties, and frequently presenting complicated legal and scientific questions.

The changes in the numbers and complexity of cases have outpaced attempts to amend the Federal Rules. Former Supreme Court Justice Lewis Powell's dissent from the adoption of the 1980 amendments has been prophetic:

I doubt that many judges or lawyers familiar with the proposed amendments believe they will have an appreciable effect on the acute problems . . . The Court's adoption of these inadequate changes could postpone effective reform for another decade . . . I do not dissent because the modest amendments recommended by the Judicial Conference are undesirable. *I simply believe that Congress' acceptance of these tinkering changes will delay for years the adoption of genuinely effective reforms* [emphasis added].[2]

The members of the task force believe that the time has come to correct the problems Justice Powell saw so clearly nearly a decade ago. In developing the recommendations outlined below, the group was mindful of many past efforts by many distinguished bodies to accomplish the same or similar objectives. Accordingly, every effort was made to avoid "reinventing the wheel" by borrowing freely from ideas that have been in the public domain for some time, as well as from successful experiments by many federal and state courts. In addition, the group was sensitive to the enormous problems facing the federal judiciary, as well as to the views of federal judges themselves, by inviting sitting judges to attend one of the discussion sessions and by circulating its draft report to others throughout the country.

The place to begin, the members agreed, is to reform the procedural rules themselves—not through simple directives, but instead through devices that give litigants the proper *incentives* to reduce delay and cost.

Several important principles run through the recommendations. First, the proposals recognize that the same set of generic procedures need not—and indeed should not—apply to all types of cases. Second, the recommendations give particular emphasis to the setting of early, firm deadlines for all major aspects of a civil case—disposition of key motions, completion of discovery, and trial.

Finally, and perhaps most significantly, the group believes it would be a mistake, given the diversity of caseloads and types of litigation across different federal jurisdictions, for Congress to specify a uniform set of reform suggestions to be applied by all district courts throughout the nation. Instead, reform must come from "the bottom up," or from those in each district who must live with the civil justice system on a regular basis.

District court plans

The core recommendation is that Congress direct each federal district court to develop its own "Civil Justice Reform Plan," a step that certain districts already have undertaken. In developing its plan, each district court should include in its planning group lawyers practicing in law firms and corporations representing each of the major categories of litigants in the district; public representatives; and a representative magistrate in the district. The task force members believe that it is essential for judges to obtain input from those in their districts who use the courts most heavily, not only because such involvement is likely to maximize the prospects that workable plans will be developed, but also to stimulate a much needed dialogue between the bench, the bar, and client communities about methods for streamlining litigation practice.

To ensure that all districts develop a plan, the task force recommends that "backup" plans be readied by the Judicial Council for each federal circuit, drawing on public comments and technical expertise provided by the Federal Judicial Center (FJC). The backups would automatically go into effect in all districts that had not implemented a plan within 12 months. To provide additional incentives for timely compliance, the task force also suggests that those districts that implement plans on time be eligible for federal financial assistance for administrative support staff and facilities.

To assist in the development of the plans, the group urges Congress to make available appropri-

---

The Harris Survey

To determine attitudes toward cost and delay in the civil justice system, the Foundation for Change commissioned Louis Harris and Associates to conduct an in-depth telephone survey, unprecedented in its scope and scale, of roughly 1,000 experts:

150 private litigators who represent plaintiffs; 250 private litigators who represent defendants; 100 "public interest" litigators; 300 corporate general counsel selected from the 6,000 largest corporations in the United States; and 147 current federal district court judges. The interviews were conducted between August and October 1988. The full findings of the survey are reported in Louis Harris and Associates, *Procedural Reform of the Civil Justice System* (1988). Some of the key results, categorized by respondents, are shown below.

	Private litigators Defense	Plaintiff	Public interest litigators	Corporate counsel	Federal judges
% who believe that transactions costs in the federal courts are a "major" problem	38	43	53	52	53
% who believe that high litigation transaction costs "unreasonably" impede the use of the civil justice system by ordinary citizens	52	63	85	69	56
% who believe that the transactions costs of litigating in the U.S. courts are higher than in courts outside the U.S.	61	60	70	79	N/A
% who believe that lawyers who abuse the discovery process are a "major" cause of high litigation transaction costs	62	62	63	80	71
% who believe that inadequate judicial management is a major cause of high litigation transaction costs	40	40	43	57	32
% who believe it is possible to make procedural changes that would significantly reduce transaction costs	68	74	77	87	81

ate funds to the FJC. In addition, the FJC should be directed to collect all information about the plans and report on them to Congress, as well as gather data from the districts on how their plans are working so that the FJC can be in a position to recommend to the districts new procedural suggestions from time to time. Finally, the group urges Congress to fund either the FJC or the Administrative Office of the U.S. Courts to produce a "Manual for Litigation," which would provide commentary on the plans themselves, explain the rationale behind various decisions underlying the plans and discuss how the plans might be implemented effectively as total, integrated packages.[3]

Case tracking

Although the judges in each district are encouraged to experiment with different techniques for reducing delay and cost, the task force members believe that all plans should implement a system of case tracking or, as some have termed it, differentiated case management, whereby cases of different degrees of complexity are placed on different time tracks for discovery and trial. The State of New Jersey has experimented with a three-track system that could serve as a useful model for federal reform:

• Track One applies to "simple" or "expedited" cases—cases that require little or no judicial intervention prior to trial and that can be resolved in fairness to all parties relatively quickly.

• Track Two applies to "complex" cases—cases characterized by the need for early and intense judicial involvement.

• Track Three applies to "standard" cases—cases not falling into the other two categories.[4]

Case tracking can alleviate the problems that arise when a single set of rules is applied indiscriminately to all lawsuits—when, in the words of procedural expert Maurice Rosenberg, "[c]adillac-style procedures" are used to process "bicycle-sized lawsuits." For many cases, the large-scale discovery methods available under the Federal Rules are simply not necessary. Case tracking can give simple cases the quick scheduling they deserve, while reserving more time for complex cases. Significantly, the Harris Survey results reported earlier show overwhelming support among plaintiffs' and defendants' attorneys for case tracking.

Time limits

Case tracking requires that time limits apply to each track. Judges would apply these deadlines in the "typical" case falling within each track to various stages of the litigation.

With the exception of cases categorized as "complex," the task force suggests that trial dates be set at a mandatory scheduling conference that should be held in all but the simplest of cases within at most 45 days following the first responsive pleading to the complaint. For complex cases, whose length and difficulty can often frustrate attempts to provide trial schedules too far in advance, a *discovery cutoff date* can be set at the mandatory initial conference. Thereafter, within some period (say 120 days) before the discovery cutoff, the trial judge could be required to set dates for resolution of dispositive motions and trial. Each district would consider whether trial dates should be set by day, week, or month, depending on the nature of the docket in the district and whether the particular case required a jury trial.[5] Exceptions to these deadlines would be made only in the rarest of circumstances.

The task force recommends that each track within the district's tracking system also provide deadlines for the completion of discovery. Using the example of the three-track system noted previously, the "expedited" track might have a discovery guideline of 50-100 days; the "standard" track might have a guideline of 100-200 days for the completion of discovery; and the "complex" track might have a discovery guideline of six to 18 months (or failing a deadline at the outset, then at least clear intermediate targets for different stages of the litigation short of the completion of discovery).

It is essential that these dates be set at the initial stage of a litigation. As Judge Peckham has observed, a "fairly prompt status conference prods lawyers to prepare themselves and sets the tenor of the entire litigation, by making it clear at the outset that the judge will take an active interest in the management of his case."[6] In less complex cases, this conference could be done by telephone or as a "paper conference."

The task force believes that application of time limits is essential for improving overall case management by attorneys and judges, reducing discovery abuse, and lowering litigation transaction costs. This sentiment is backed by available empirical evidence. For example, a recent study by the National Center for State Courts finds from data across numerous state courts that while time standards are not a panacea, "they can be an important part of a comprehensive program to reduce or prevent delays."[7] The General Accounting Office has confirmed these findings at the federal level based on a review of nearly 800 closed case files that took one year or more to terminate in nine federal district courts.[8]

The task force believes that by far the most important deadline that should be set early in the case is the trial date. Nothing does more to convince the parties and their lawyers to move expeditiously toward resolution of their dispute than knowing at the outset when they are scheduled for trial.[9] In addition, an early firm trial date eliminates costly duplicative preparation of witnesses when trials are rescheduled, requires more serious planning by the courts and is cost-effective for trial attorneys, providing them with efficient and predictable scheduling. Not surprisingly, therefore, strong majorities in the Harris Survey supported the concept.

The conference procedure and time deadlines can also be used by districts to reduce their case backlogs, which in many courts are the principal reason for delay. Each district plan could provide that in all cases of a certain age—say two years—the parties must be called to a status conference where the judge will impose discovery cutoff and trial dates. In addition, courts with significant backlogs are encouraged to experiment with "settlement weeks"—crash court-sponsored settlement efforts—such as those tried successfully in the Superior Court for the District of Columbia.

Staging

Courts can accelerate the disposition of cases by "staging" discovery, which can take a variety of forms. One approach, pioneered by Judge Peckham, limits the parties in the first stage to developing information needed for a realistic assessment of the case, perhaps by inspecting a few documents and taking a few depositions. If the case does not end, a second, more detailed, stage would begin.[10]

Staging the disposition of key issues by judicial rulings can also be productive. For example, it is common in legal disputes for the parties to quarrel over the length and applicability of a relevant statute of limitations or the meaning of certain words in a contract. Often such disputes can be resolved quickly and inexpensively once a core

issue is decided. Courts might also be encouraged, where appropriate, to bifurcate issues for trial— asking the jury to decide liability before damage issues, or vice versa, in torts cases, for example.

Other procedural suggestions

The task force recommends a series of additional procedural measures to reduce delay and cost.

Since a major cause of delay is the failure by judges to decide fully briefed motions on a timely basis, the district plans should also set standard time periods for the disposition of motions. In addition, to prod judges to make these decisions, the districts could develop procedures or obliging judges to report to counsel at a status conference, or otherwise, concerning delays in making such decisions. As a further incentive, the task force urges that the Administrative Office be directed to implement computerization of the docket in each district so that quarterly reports can be made to the public of pending unresolved motions before particular judges. In addition, the courts should report data for each judge indicating the aging of his or her caseload in each of the tracking categories developed by the district.

Traditional litigation may not always be the best way of resolving disputes. Over the past decade, interest has grown in a variety of "alternative dispute resolution" (ADR) techniques, including arbitration, mediation, and nonbinding summary trials in which the attorneys present brief summaries of their cases to juries without live testimony. Although much research remains to be done about the effectiveness of these techniques and about the circumstances to which specific ADR procedures best apply, there is some anecdotal evidence that ADR can help resolve disputes more quickly and at less cost than traditional litigation.

Accordingly, the task force suggests that the district courts experiment with ADR techniques by requiring the parties in all but the simplest, and most routine cases, to attend a conference at the outset of their cases with a neutral court representative to assess the suitability and desirability of ADR procedures. Congress should make funds available to districts to experiment with different ADR mechanisms, with a body designated to administer the funding program.

Finally, the task force members believe that cases would be disposed of more quickly if at court-sponsored settlement conferences, the clients themselves are required to be available in person or by telephone. The presence of the client makes it impossible for the attorney to delay settlement discussions—often for weeks or months—with the time-honored excuse, "Let me get back to you after I've discussed this with my client."

The task force recognizes that there have been criticisms of the kind of active judicial case management or, as some have put it, "managerial judging," that its recommendations reflect. It concluded, however, that judicial case management can be pursued without sacrificing fundamental due process objectives, citing the views of Judge Alvin Rubin:

> The judicial role is not a passive one. A purely adversarial system, uncontrolled by the judiciary, is not an automatic guarantee that justice will be done. It is impossible to consider seriously the vital elements of a fair trial without considering that it is the duty of the judge, and the judge alone, as the sole representative of the public interest, to step in at any stage of the litigation where . . . intervention is necessary in the interest of justice. Judge Learned Hand wrote, "[a] judge is more than a moderator; he is charged to see that the law is properly administered, and it is a duty which he cannot discharge by remaining inert."[11]

Expanding judicial resources

No package of procedural reform proposals can produce meaningful change without the active participation of a modern, well-supported and well-trained judiciary. Yet given the importance and magnitude of their responsibilities, our judges are underpaid and the administrative support they receive is far from sufficient. In addition, computer facilities in many courts lag far behind the equipment and personnel available to the private bar. No case tracking system can work efficiently unless the computer facilities and data base systems are in place to track the progress of all of the cases in each district.

The task force believes that with a relatively modest amount of additional funds—several hundred million dollars, at most—the federal judicial system can be readied for the 21st century. At least three specific measures are required:

Enhanced administrative support: The task force suggests that at the time each district submits its plan to the FJC, it should also transmit to Congress a report indicating both its objectives in reducing cost and delay and what additional resources— including administrative staff, computer facilities and software support—are required to achieve

those objectives. This process should educate Congress, the executive branch, and the public in general about the relatively modest additional resource requirements for making the substantial improvements in the civil justice system that we believe can be made. At the same time, however, Congress also should make available right away some funds for additional staff and computer support and direct those funds to those districts that develop and implement the plans.

Judicial case management training: Given the wide variety of professional backgrounds and experiences of federal district court judges, many judges may find it useful to be familiarized with the case management techniques being used throughout the country. To facilitate the dissemination of this information, current judicial training programs should be expanded to include a new curriculum and emphasis on efficient case management.

Increase judicial salaries: Given the public outcry over the proposed federal pay raise in January 1989, perhaps no subject is more emotional and hotly contested than the question of salaries. However, the task force firmly believes that with respect to judicial salaries, there is no longer any room for debate. Adjusted for inflation, federal judicial salaries have fallen 30 per cent during the past 20 years, and now badly lag behind those for practicing attorneys. Indeed, graduating law students can now earn in law firms in New York City *in their first year* as much as a federal judge. Elsewhere around the country, it takes only several years out of law school for attorneys to do the same.

While lifetime judgeships carry prestige and security, it is shortsighted for society to expect that America's best attorneys will continue to be attracted to the judiciary when, as practicing lawyers, they can earn substantially greater sums. Inadequate judicial salaries have already led some federal district judges to return to the private sector. Members of the task force know of highly qualified lawyers who have turned down potential appointments because of the salary. If this trend continues, this nation faces a real threat that many of its best federal judges will leave the bench for private practice and many more highly qualified potential judges will be discouraged from taking on judicial responsibilities. To prevent such an outcome, the task force recommends that Congress move quickly to provide substantial pay increases to federal judges.

Recommendations for clients and attorneys

Although it is essential that the civil justice system be structured to provide incentives for the participants to resolve their disputes expeditiously and inexpensively, clients and their attorneys must also respond to those incentives. Although the members of the task force did not pretend to have all the answers about how these responses are best made, they singled out several appropriate steps.

For the organized bar, the challenge is to respond to the strong criticism leveled in the Harris Survey against the profession: strong majorities of each respondent group identified "lawyers and litigants who use discovery as an adversarial tool or tactic to raise the stakes for their opponents" as a major cause of litigation costs and delays. Simply put, the professional legal societies must encourage more of the kinds of interchanges the members of the task force have just had. The recommendation that planning groups be formed in each federal district to develop civil justice reform plans, if followed, would stimulate such meetings. In addition, firms and their lawyers can adopt such cost-cutting techniques as providing their clients litigation budgets and strategic plans at the outset of a case to alert them of the expenses ahead and thus to facilitate quicker resolution of disputes. Firms also should underwrite training of attorneys at recognized trial advocacy programs to enhance skills at selecting winning from losing cases and to avoid unnecessary discovery.

With respect to the client community, the group focused almost entirely on measures that large corporations can undertake. The group applauded the trend of corporations bringing their litigation "in house," where the lawyers have no incentive to bill unnecessary hours, but in fact to do the opposite: to move cases expeditiously. For nonroutine, complex litigation that often is not well-suited for in-house representations, corporate clients can and must do a better job of supervising their outside lawyers. Several supervisory techniques that some corporations are now using should be adopted more widely:

• Greater involvement by corporate counsel in case management by specifying guidelines for outside attorneys; developing trial books or manuals for acceptable litigation techniques and tactics; presence of corporate counsel at trial; development of computer-based case tracking systems that allow corporations to follow day-to-day litigation actions.

• Using these computerized systems or other techniques to develop cost data on routine cases and using that data to develop litigation budgets; taking competitive bids for certain work.

• Insisting upon litigation budgets and litigation plans at the outset of a case.

• Encouraging the use of more paralegals and other nonlawyers for reading and summarizing files and documents.

• Appointment of corporate record supervisors to monitor and facilitate record production.

At bottom, companies should evaluate each case to determine whether it is most efficient to be defended or pursued in-house or outside. All cases, however, must be managed and not simply handed off by default to the responsible attorney. This applies to all clients, large or small.

Finally, the task force was frustrated throughout its deliberations by the paucity of adequate data concerning the use and effectiveness of the variety of procedural innovations adopted by different courts (federal and state) and the cost-reduction steps taken by clients and their attorneys. This data deficiency should be rectified. The task force urges Congress to direct the Department of Justice to expand the research agenda of the National Institute of Justice to include civil litigation problems as well as the criminal issues now within its purview. In addition, it hopes that in the future the organized bar and the "client community" will significantly enhance their support for further research in this area.

NOTES

This article originally appeared in Volume 73, Number 3, October-November 1989, pages 162-167. It was adapted from *Justice For All: Reducing Costs and Delay in Civil Litigation*, a task force report published by the Brookings Institution in October 1989.

1. Schwarzer, *Mistakes Lawyers Make in Discovery*, LITIGATION, No. 2, Winter 1989, at 31.

2. Powell, dissenting statement to *Amendments to the Federal Rules of Civil Procedure*, 85 F. R. D. 522-523 (1980).

3. The suggested manual would build upon the success of the Manual for Multi-district Litigation and its successor, the Manual for Complex Litigation (Second Edition).

4. For a further discussion, see Bakke and Solomon, *Case differentiation: an approach to individualized case management*, 73 JUDICATURE 17 (1989).

5. Some courts already set early and firm trial dates. Indeed, subsection (b) of Rule 16, as amended in 1983, authorizes the practice. The task force has concluded, however, that a *system-wide* requirement must be implemented.

6. Peckham, *The Federal Judge as a Case Manager: The New Role in Guiding a Case from Filing to Disposition*, 69 CAL. L. REV. 770 (1981).

7. Mahoney, CHANGING TIMES IN TRIAL COURTS (Williamsburg,

VA: National Center for State Courts, 1988).

8. General Accounting Office, *Better Management Can Ease Federal Civil Case Backlog* (February 24, 1981).

9. This is also well supported in the legal literature. *See* Brazil, *Improving Judicial Controls Over the Development of Civil Action: Model Rules For Case Management and Sanctions*, 4 Am. B. Found. Research J. 875-965 (1981) and Elliott, *Managerial Judging and the Evolution of Procedure*, 53 U. Chi. L. Rev. 306-336 (1986).

10. The Southern District of New York has used another form of staged discovery relating specifically to its interrogatory practice. Under this procedure the parties initially are limited to issuing "identification" interrogatories—requesting the names of individuals with knowledge of the subject matter of the action, information relating to the computation of damages and information regarding the location, custodian, and description of relevant documents. Thereafter, additional interrogatories are permitted only by leave of court. The task force believes that in determining whether to adopt such a two-stage interrogatory procedure, courts should consider both the efficiency gained from such a procedure and the equities in scaling back the availability of interrogatories, which are the least expensive discovery device available to individual plaintiffs.

11. Rubin, *The Managed Calendar: Some Pragmatic Suggestions About Achieving the Just, Speedy and Inexpensive Determination of Civil Cases in Federal Court*, 4 Just. Sys. J. 135 (1979).

Measuring the pace of civil litigation in federal and state trial courts

Using techniques such as survival analysis, we can compare the rate at which courts terminate cases, identify the pace of litigation for different kinds of cases and different courts, and see which stages of the litigation process contribute most to what is often called "delay."

by Joel B. Grossman, Herbert M. Kritzer, Kristin Bumiller, and Stephen McDougal

"Delay breeds cynicism about justice," Maurice Rosenberg has written, echoing the lament of Shakespeare's Hamlet, the words of Roscoe Pound, and the indelible image of Charles Dickens' *Bleak House*.[1] The modernization of courts and court procedures and the constant infusion of new judges may have alleviated the worst abuses. Yet court congestion still exists and eliminating delay remains a priority for reformers.

The intractability of "delay" and its resistance to reform can be interpreted in two ways. It may only be that courts have applied too little effort and inadequate resources to solve a problem constantly compounded by rising litigation rates. But it is also possible that the problem is more rhetorical than real—or really significant. And if delay is truly a problem, it is not self-evident what kind of problem it is, for whom it is a problem, or what its consequences may be.

We recognize the negative consequences of some time lapses in the litigation process—the erosion of evidence before trial, the hardships in waiting for fair compensation, and the increased costs, to name just a few. A litigant whose rights are undercut or who must pay excessive costs because of delay has suffered unnecessary harm. But delay, defined by Church as "excessive case processing time,"[2] is a pejorative term that should not be regarded as synonymous with lack of speed. It may not always be desirable for courts to operate with speed and efficiency.[3] Indeed, we believe it is impossible to say, without qualification, that the "speedy resolution of civil cases is an important social goal."[4]

Church and others whose research we will summarize later have tried to explain the causes of court delay. Our effort, while also theoretical, is not intended to produce a theory of delay. Indeed, we would discard the term delay as vague, inherently subjective, and hopelessly weighted down by speculative normative assumptions. Our focus, alternatively, is on the *pace* of litigation, a term we will define with more precision later.

We are interested in what causes some cases to be processed faster than others. But we are also interested in the impact of *time* and *timing* on litigation interests and strategies, outcomes, and on the behavioral organization of courts. We see the manipulation of time or pace as a key variable in the litigation process.

Theory building has its skeptics, and current "theories" of court delay have attracted more than their share. We share in some of this skepticism, particularly when it reflects a lack of conceptual and definitional clarity. But there is also skepticism about the efficacy of data-based approaches.

Steven Flanders has recently suggested that the uniqueness and "irregular nature" of case processing makes it a poor subject for certain kinds of mathematical modelling techniques.[5] There are, indeed, great difficulties in transforming court records information into meaningful statistics and comparing those statistics across 51 court systems. The error factor is likely to be high, and the difficulty of translating the results of such research into meaningful reforms is well known. Yet the risks of eschewing such research and relying primarily on

Table 1   Views about the efficiency of courts

*Respondents answered this question: "Here is a list of social problems that people are talking about today . . . .
Please tell me how serious is the problem of the efficiency of courts?"*

	"No problem at all"	"Small problem"	"Moderate problem"	"Serious problem"	"Very serious problem"
Lawyers (N=486)	1.4%	15.5%	46.9%	26.1%	10.0%
Judges (N=332)	4.2	19.3	48.8	22.3	5.4
Community leaders (N=377)	0.3	7.4	33.7	34.7	23.9
General public (N=1,868)	3.0	8.4	28.8	30.3	29.5

Source: Law Enforcement Assistance Administration, *The Public Image of Courts: General Public Data and Special Publics Data* (1977). Survey conducted by Yankelovich, Skelly and White, Inc.

strategies derived from purely managerial or bureacratic premises are at least as great.

Before looking at our data, it might be useful to examine briefly the "problem," and then, in more detail, the literature on delay. Doing so will provide a useful perspective on the discussion that follows.

No uniform standards

There are no objective measures of delay or of its impact. The effects of slow or irregular case processing on lawyers' and litigants' interests and satisfactions are not uniform (and certainly not uniformly bad). The same can be said of the interests of justice itself. Without such measures, the case for allocating scarce resources to reducing or eliminating "delay" is weak. The failure of past efforts to bring about uniform reductions of delay merely underscores the ambiguity of reform based on normative expectations of how the adversary process ought to work rather than on demonstrated needs.

Different participants in the system have competing interests that may be satisfied by *either* slower or speedier resolution of cases. Court administrators and judges are concerned with efficient case processing and with the burdens of heavy caseloads—and thus with reducing delay. Lawyers and litigants, however, may have a different perspective. Lawyers—not alone among professionals in taking more business than they can expeditiously handle—may sometimes have to postpone one client's case in order to complete necessary and timely work on another's. Not every case moves—or needs to move—at the same pace. Not every client expects immediate and continuous service.

For lawyers, time is money in the obvious sense of hours billed. But time is also money in a different way—lawyers (in non-contingency fee cases) can maximize profits by "keeping busy" and avoiding

the costs of "dead time." What is important to the self-interest of lawyers is a controlled pace of activity and a relatively predictable flow of new business. The desirability of speedy case resolution to them is, at best, a relative matter.[6]

The interests of clients may also favor deliberation instead of speed. The manipulation of time is often a factor in the settlement process; continuances, postponements, excessive demands for discovery, motions for removal to another court and amended pleadings all consume time but do not necessarily cause client dissatisfaction. Manipulating the pace of case processing is often a deliberate strategy, common to both plaintiff and defendant to shift the balance in their favor. Litigant satisfaction appears to depend mostly upon the outcome of a case; speed itself is unlikely to be the measure of satisfaction.

There is no a priori reason to assume that present patterns of litigation are the cause of serious dissatisfaction. Indeed, Church's study of delay in 21 courts concluded that participants in "slow courts"—those where delay seems endemic—"simply do not regard the existing pace of litigation to be a significant problem; if they address it at all, the response is typically a short term burst of energy followed by a return to business as usual."[7] The duration of case processing may be perceived as a problem (i.e., "delay") only where there are significant departures from local norms.

The public viewpoint

While there is little systematic evidence of litigant views toward the speed and duration of case processing, there is some ambiguous evidence of participant and public views. A 1977 survey asked four groups of respondents—lawyers, judges, community leaders, and the general public—their views on the importance to American society of "efficiency in the courts" (Table 1). About two-thirds of

Table 2 Views about faster case processing

Respondents answered this question: "Please tell me how useful it would be to have your tax dollars spent on . . . trying to make the courts handle their cases faster."

	"Not at all helpful"	"Slightly helpful"	"Somewhat helpful"	"Very helpful"	"Extremely helpful"
Lawyers (N=484)	12.6%	14.0%	23.1%	30.5%	19.7%
Judges (N=332)	11.1	12.0	22.9	32.5	21.4
Community leaders (N=377)	3.4	10.6	13.3	34.7	37.9
General public (N=1,900)	7.7	8.6	19.2	31.3	33.2

Source: Law Enforcement Assistance Administration, *The Public Image of Courts: General Public Data and Special Publics Data* (1977). Survey conducted by Yankelovich, Skelly and White, Inc.

the lawyers and judges believed that court efficiency was a "moderate" or "serious" problem; relatively few regarded it as "very serious." Among community leaders and the general public, who have little contact with the courts, more than 25 per cent believed court efficiency to be a "very serious problem."

A second question asked whether it would be helpful to spend tax dollars to try to "make the courts handle their cases faster." The response pattern was strikingly similar (Table 2). Community leaders and the general public—the non-participants—are substantially more sanguine about the acceleration of case processing than lawyers and judges, about 25 per cent of whom respond that such expenditures would be "not at all helpful" or only "slightly helpful." About half the lawyers and judges would appear to favor allocating resources for this purpose.

These data are difficult to interpret because the questions are vague. What does "efficiency in the courts" mean? What is the baseline from which to measure whether courts should "handle their cases faster?" Faster than what? Moreover, the questions do not distinguish between civil and criminal cases.

Although Church and others argue that similar cultural and structural attributes cause delay in both civil and criminal courts,[8] delay in criminal courts is widely regarded as less tolerable. But we do not know from this data whether respondents thought the questions referred to both civil and criminal cases, or primarily to the latter. Lawyers and judges are about evenly divided; some regard accelerated case processing as desirable, others do not. The stronger favorable views of non-participants means no more than that they believe, *ceteris paribus*, that fast and efficient case disposition is a good thing. In short, we have no evidence here that demonstrates the need—or lack of need—for civil case processing reform.

The ambiguity of delay reform ideology is further revealed when we consider the perspective of the entire system, and not merely that of individual participants. As Engel and Steele have recently observed, ours is a complex civil justice system of interdependent parts.[9] It cannot be merely a question of "reducing delay." What are the marginal costs of processing cases more quickly? What kinds of new cases will be drawn into the system (as inevitably they will) to replace those resolved more rapidly? How many will there be? What will be the effect on disposition patterns?

A single-minded dedication to reducing delay may undermine other, perhaps more important, reform goals such as improving the quality of justice or increasing access to justice by creating alternative dispute processing mechanisms. Scare resources channeled into the fight against delay may be counter-productive or at best yield results of only marginal utility.[10]

The literature on delay

Contemporary social science investigations of court delay flow from the pioneering work of Hans Zeisel and his associates.[11] Zeisel's study conceptualized delay as "a problem of supply and demand."[12] Delay occurred when the parties were ready to take a case to trial, but were "prevented from doing so solely by the unavailability of the court."[13]

Since the causes of delay were presumed to be bad management practices, the focus was on examining those aspects of the litigation process that might be manipulated to reduce delay. "Supply" might be reduced by use of pretrial conferences, providing more judge time, or reducing trial time; "demand" might be manipulated by measures designed to induce early settlements.[14]

Emphasis on the structural characteristics of courts as the major cause of delay has been the dominant theme of research. Rosenberg, examining cases that proceeded to trial, looked at some case-specific characteristics such as amount requested in remedy and the presence of outside attorneys.[15] His recognition in a subsequent study that delay might be caused by attorneys' "own unreadiness to proceed" as much as by court management structures or practices provided a needed corrective, but most of his proposed solutions to the problem fell within Zeisel's supply-and-demand framework: decreasing demand and enlarging available judicial resources.[16]

The same theme pervades current studies, which stress that delay stems from poor court management rather than from the way in which courts are used by the litigants. France, in his 1973 study of Ohio courts, stressed various rule changes concerning pretrial activities and a fixed trial date as two means of handling backlogs. He did chide court reformers for "excessive reliance on structural and administrative changes in the courts as 'cure alls,' " but he seemed to attribute those largely to "insufficient attention to methods of operations."[17]

Likewise, Gillespie's economic analysis of court production attempted little more than a measurement of court behavior in structural terms. He noted that a "court's performance . . . depends significantly upon the characteristics of the private bar and the U.S. attorney practicing in the district," but made no attempt to include some measure of these factors in his analysis.[18]

Flanders' study for the Federal Judicial Center is certainly the most comprehensive effort to focus on court management techniques. Utilizing the concepts of "court management" and "case management" to examine differences in court productivity, he concludes that "the differences [in court productivity] lie in the relative effectiveness of alternative forms of case management."[19] Judge personality is discounted; the pace of litigation is seen as a direct consequence of management techniques such as calendaring, scheduling of trials, use of magistrates, greater reliance on clerks, and levels of judge involvement prior to conclusion of discovery procedures.

The key is management control:

The districts that have an effective administrative structure, effective case management, and adequate internal communication have a resilience and an ability to handle new problems that are sadly lacking elsewhere.[20]

Control means essentially the presence of automatic procedures for monitoring the stages of development in each case to minimize the involvement of the judge until the completion of discovery. A strong governance structure, Flanders argues, can regularize and quicken the pace of litigation: "there is nothing unavoidable about delay. Delay can be controlled and eliminated even by courts suffering from heavy caseloads."[21]

Other perspectives

A second perspective on the causes of delay comes from studies viewing courts as organizations and employing the analytic tools of organization theory. A prime example is Eisenstein and Jacob's study of "courtroom workgroups" in three cities. A workgroup was viewed as a social system of interactive behavior among the judge, counsel, and clerk. Each "player" has a stake in the smooth operation of the workgroup, although each has different interests in the substantive outcome of each case. But they all operate within a framework of shared values and goals that serve to make behavior predictable.[22]

Implicit in this approach is a bargaining model; it is the interaction among the workgroup members, more than the formal rules of procedure, which determines the outcome. Potential reforms, Eisenstein and Jacob conclude, must confront the organizational realities of a court. Reforms that do not alter the organizationally-induced incentives will not result in real reform, but merely in compensating adjustment by workgroup members.

In a variation on this theme, Nardulli argued that court productivity was primarily the result of "the interests of the court's dominant coalition."[23] Like Eisenstein and Jacob, Nardulli was writing about criminal cases, and like other recent scholars, he was concerned with the effects of caseload pressures on the tendency of courts to conclude cases by administrative dispositions. What is important for our purposes is his observation that increases in caseload pressures resulted in corresponding increases in the severity of application of sanctions against those members of the "courtroom elite" who violated existing norms of procedure.

A third perspective has come from increased interest in trial courts as political institutions and consequent efforts to understand and explain the linkages between courts and the local environment in which they operate. The studies by Dolbeare, Glick and Vines, Richardson and Vines, and Gibson suggest that courts respond to local environmental pressures.[24]

Richardson and Vines, for example, coined the term "legal subculture" in attempting to demonstrate the linkages between judicial recruitment and local political cultures. Levin's study of the sentencing practices of criminal courts in Pittsburgh and Minneapolis suggested a cultural explanation for the differences that he found in those cities.[25] Balbus provided a vivid demonstration of how different local courts reacted to the urban ghetto riots of the late 1960s.[26]

None of these studies was directed to the problem of delay, and only Dolbeare's dealt at all with the processing of civil cases. Yet as a group they pointed the way to the probable existence of linkages between courts and political cultures. Jacob's study of bankruptcy and garnishment cases in four Wisconsin cities was the first to postulate and actually test a possible relationship between political culture and the disposition of court cases.[27] But his interest was in who used the courts and in outcomes, not the modes of processing cases. Grossman and Sarat had little success in using the political culture concept to explain propensities to litigate in the federal courts.[28] Use of political culture to explain patterns of case processing and disposition in the court-records data collected by the Civil Litigation Research Project was not notably more successful.[29]

Applying the political culture concept to understanding the organization and operation of urban courts was first suggested by Glick and Vines,[30] and a variant of it was employed in Church's study of delay in trial courts.[31] Church found no clear association between patterns of litigation delay and sundry structural variables such as settlement procedures, incidence of trials, and calendaring systems. What he did find was a relative lack of case management concern and techniques that relegated "control" to attorneys.

Church also observed a similarity of delay propensities in state and federal courts within the same district. Combination of these two findings led to his conclusion that comparative delay patterns were the result of "local legal cultures," which he defined as the "established expectations, practices, and informal rules of behavior of judges and attorneys."[32] Interviews with lawyers and judges seemed to support this explanation, although the few interview statements actually presented in the book do not lead inescapably to this conclusion.[33]

The local legal culture

Culture is an elusive concept, and Church is not alone in treating it as an error factor in explanation of political and legal phenomena. One need only recall invocation of the concept of "claims consciousness" by Zeisel and associates to explain geographic differences in levels of personal injury litigation to recognize the attractiveness of this kind of residual explanation.[34] But the fact of the matter is that "local legal culture" can only "explain" delay at a very high level of abstraction.

If local legal culture is nothing more than "the established practices and informal roles of behavior of judges and attorneys, then it comes close to being a tautology."[35] At the very least we would have to determine if local practitioners actually held these norms and were guided by them. Zeisel also had no evidence that litigants in different locales had differing attitudes toward litigation that resulted in higher litigation rates. And Church's interviews demonstrate the subjectiveness of the concept of local legal culture and of attitudes toward it. In both slow and fast courts, he found complaints about delay as well as expressed satisfaction with the pace of litigation.

Despite these difficulties, Church's local legal culture hypothesis has some intuitive appeal. It nicely complements Flanders' work. Where Flanders emphasized "the normative assertion that judges have a positive responsibility to manage dockets,"[36] Church concluded that "the most important, and the most difficult, change a court should make is in the long-term expectations and practices of civil attorneys practicing in the court."[37]

Taken together, the two studies underscore Nimmer's observation that judicial reform efforts "are typically . . . the product of . . . conscious behavioral choices made both individually and as a group by professionals within the system."[38] In other words, successful reform efforts must be based, in substantial part, on creating different kinds of incentives for the main actors in the system. This conclusion is not at all inconsistent, we might add, with the findings of the organizational theory studies.

Role theory

A fourth perspective utilizes role theory and offers some chance to attain theoretical unity among approaches to the problem of delay. Role theory has only recently been employed in understanding patterns of delay. Carter used the idea in discussing the effect of active versus passive judges on the pace of litigation.[39] Glick and Vines devoted an entire chapter to "self-conceptualization" of role among state court judges.[40]

Central to our concerns is an article by Keith Boyum. Expanding upon Church's idea of local legal culture, Boyum argues that delay is really an "unintended consequence" of institutional activity that can be understood best by "setting goals and motivations in the context of organized groups."[41] Role theory is particularly sensitive to the interaction between the perceptions of officials and institutionalized expectations of how they will fulfill their roles.

Using data from a mail questionnaire and aggregate measures of litigation pace, Boyum was able to show a considerable relationship between the self-defined role of judges concerning "the importance of fulfilling administrative or management related functions of their positions" and the general pace of litigation in their courts. Cases moved quicker in those courts where judges saw their function as facilitating case management. Without formal controls, it is impossible to be certain that positive role perceptions toward strong case management are as strongly related to fast pace as Boyum suggests.[42] Yet his findings are in accord with those of Flanders and certainly not contradictory to Church's conclusions.

The evidence we have reviewed, when taken as a whole, certainly supports the conclusion that "delay in the courts" is a subjective concept not easily amenable to precise and objective measurement. Nevertheless, it is widely regarded as a leading "problem" of the court system requiring the primary attention of court reformers. Clearly, unlocking the "secret" of delay requires a more comprehensive and theoretical approach.

(*Editor's note:* In the remainder of this article the authors extensively analyzed data from the Civil Litigation Research Project that bore directly on the question of the pace of civil litigation. The results and implications of that empirical analysis are broadly summarized in the authors' conclusions printed below.)

Conclusion

Data of the kind we have presented can address a host of questions about the pace of civil litigation. The limits of our sample require that our findings be interpreted with appropriate caution. Nevertheless, they do offer a number of guideposts.

First, there is no single national problem of "delay in the courts." Different courts process cases at different speeds; there appears to be a wide variation in norms about what pace is appropriate. Federal courts differ from state courts and from each other. But the differences appear to be less patterned than idiosyncratic; they are in any case extremely difficult to explain.

Second, "local legal culture" is not an explanation as much as it is a convenient restatement of the problem. It merely applies a label to what is generally accepted: that the practices and attitudes toward court processing of attorneys and court personnel play a significant role in determining the pace of litigation in a particular court. On some dimensions (but not others) there is greater similarity among the federal courts in our sample than among the state courts or between each state court-federal court pair. We have attributed this in part to the commonality of rules and procedures in all federal courts. It may also be that state courts in the same state exhibit similar pace characteristics, but we know of no study that systematically compares the pace of litigation in a number of courts from one state.

Third, more work is required to identify those cases, or case characteristics, that systematically affect the speed of disposition. It may well be that there is not one "pace" of litigation for a particular court, but a complex of patterns that describe the way in which particular kinds of cases are processed. Our data do not directly support this, but do not render it inconceivable.

Our "area of law" categories, for example, were not refined; more precise categorization might well yield stronger associations than we obtained. We did find that certain types of cases were disposed at the same speed regardless of the type of court (state or federal). A more sophisticated breakdown of courts might be especially fruitful in explaining speed of disposition, but this would require a much larger sample of courts.

Fourth, there is probably strong interdependency between the pace of civil and criminal cases where they are handled by the same court. Criminal cases generally are expedited, either by rule or statute. But the disposition pace of criminal cases will have a varying effect on civil cases in different courts.

Particular attention should be paid to the federal courts where criminal cases, which have increased at a more rapid rate than civil cases, must be expedited under provisions of the Speedy Trial Act. But federal courts differ in the number of criminal cases, the ratio of these cases to civil cases, and in the modes of disposing criminal cases; plea bargaining rates may vary, with consequent fluctuations in judge-time available for civil cases.

Fifth, we have just begun to understand the relationship of time to case outcomes. One example is the relationship between levels of discovery activity and the likelihood of settlement. Posner proposed that discovery increases the probability of settlement.[43] Our data did not permit us to test this proposition directly, but they are not inconsistent with it. Nor can we yet say whether other variables—such as uncertainty about case outcome, differential resources among the parties, or the stakes involved—may be more or less important than time in promoting or retarding settlement.

Finally, further research is required to understand the relationship of litigation "stages" to each other and to overall case processing times. Our brief treatment of case stages in part 4 suggests that pleading reforms, whatever other virtues they may have, probably won't do much to systematically reduce case processing times. On the other hand, we were surprised by, and not entirely able to explain, the finding that most trial activity occurs relatively early in the litigation process. Long queues awaiting trial are not the norm; long waits for trial do not account for much of the elapsed time in processing civil cases, at least not in our sample. Horror stories of interminable and costly delays are not hard to find, of course.[44]

This report does not provide definitive answers. But we hope it moves us along in the process of thinking theoretically about the pace of litigation in civil cases. Our goal has been to identify the obvious and the not so obvious pitfalls of this kind of research. There is a lot more to be done.

NOTES

This article originally appeared in Volume 65, Number 2, August 1981, pages 86-113.

Data reported in this paper were collected by the Civil Litigation Research Project, a joint venture of the University of Wisconsin Disputes Processing Research Program and the University of Southern California Program of Disputes Processing Research. Research was funded under Contract No. JAOIA-79-C-0040 with the Federal Justice Research Program, U.S. Department of Justice, with additional assistance provided by the Law School and the Graduate School of the University of Wisconsin, Madison.

The authors wish to thank Judith Hansen, Laura Guy and Richard Miller for their help in collecting and processing the data and David Trubek, William Felstiner, Austin Sarat, Terence Dungworth, Cheryl Martorana, John P. Frank, Jon Newman, Maurice Rosenberg, Tom Church, and Mae Kuykendall, for reading and commenting upon the manuscript. An earlier version was presented at the Rand Corporation's Conference on The Pace of Litigation, May 13-15, 1981, Santa Monica, California.

1. Rosenberg, *Court Congestion: Status, Causes and Proposed Remedies*, in Jones (ed.), THE COURTS, THE PUBLIC, AND THE LAW EXPLOSION 29-59, 232 (Englewood Cliffs: Prentice-Hall, 1965).

2. Church, JUSTICE DELAYED 5 (Williamsburg, VA: National Center for State Courts, 1978).

3. Sarat, *Understanding trial courts: a critique of social science approaches*, 69 JUDICATURE 324 (1978). *See also* Rosenberg, *Civil Justice Research and Civil Justice Reform*, 15 LAW & SOC'Y REV. 473 (1981). Rosenberg and his colleagues were similarly cautious about the efficacy of expediting appeals. *See* Carrington, Meador and Rosenberg, JUSTICE ON APPEAL (St. Paul: West Publishing Co., 1976). *See also* Luskin, *Building a theory of case processing time*, 62 JUDICATURE 116 (1978).

4. Church, *supra* n. 2, at 1.

5. Flanders, *Modeling Court Delay*, 2 LAW AND POL'Y Q. 305 (1980). For an insightful analysis of theories of case processing time, *see* Luskin, *supra* n. 3.

6. Johnson, *Lawyers' Choice: A Theoretical Appraisal of Litigation Investment Decisions*, 15 LAW & SOC'Y REV. 567 (1981). *See also* Rosenthal, LAWYER AND CLIENT: WHO'S IN CHARGE? (New York: Russell Sage Foundation, 1974). We do not argue, of course, that self-interest is the only basis for lawyers' decisions, only that it is a factor.

7. Church, *supra* n. 2, at 83.

8. *Id.*

9. Engel and Steele, *Civil Cases in Society: Legal Process, Social Order and the Civil Justice System*, 1979 AM. BAR FOUNDATION RESEARCH J. 295 (1979).

10. *Id. See also* Rosenberg, *supra* n. 1, and Engel, *Legal Pluralism in an American Community: Perspectives on a Civil Trial Court*, 1980 AM. BAR FOUNDATION RESEARCH J. 425 (1980).

11. Zeisel, Kalven and Buchholz, DELAY IN THE COURT (Westport: Greenwood Press, 1959).

12. *Id.* at 3.

13. *Id.* at 43.

14. *Id.* at chapters 9, 13, 15, 19. *See also* Warren, *Delay and Congestion in the Federal Courts*, 43 J. AM. JUD. SOC'Y 6 (1958).

15. Rosenberg, *supra* n. 1. *See also* Rosenberg and Sovern, *Delay and the Dynamics of Personal Injury Litigation*, 59 COLUM L. REV. 1115 (1959).

16. *Id.* at 32.

17. France, *Order in the Court Revisited: Progress and Prospect of Controlling Delay in the Tory Jury Litigation Process, 1966-1973*, 7 AKRON L. REV. 5 (1973).

18. Gillespie, *The Production of Court Services: An Analysis of Scale Effects and Other Factors*, 5 J. OF LEGAL STUD. 243 (1976).

19. Flanders, *et al.*, CASE MANAGEMENT AND COURT MANAGEMENT IN UNITED STATES DISTRICT COURTS (Washington, D.C.: Federal Judicial Center, 1977).

20. *Id.* at 71.

21. *Id.* at 76.

22. Eisenstein and Jacob, FELONY JUSTICE 35-37 (Boston: Little, Brown, 1977).

23. Nardulli, *The Caseload Controversy and the Study of Criminal Courts*, 70 J. OF CRIME, L. AND CRIMINOLOGY 98 (1979).

24. Dolbeare, TRIAL COURTS IN URBAN POLITICS (New York:

John Wiley, 1967); Glick and Vines, STATE COURT SYSTEMS (Englewood Cliffs: Prentice-Hall, 1973); Richardson and Vines, THE POLITICS OF FEDERAL COURTS: LOWER COURTS IN THE UNITED STATES (Boston: Little, Brown, 1970); Gibson, *Environmental Constraints on the Behavior of Judges: A Representational Model of Factors and Criteria*, 14 LAW & SOC'Y REV. 343 (1980).

25. Levin, URBAN POLITICS AND THE CRIMINAL COURTS (Chicago: University of Chicago Press, 1977).

26. Balbus, THE DIALECTICS OF LEGAL REPRESSION: BLACK REBELS BEFORE THE AMERICAN CRIMINAL COURTS (New Brunswick: Transaction Books, 1973).

27. Jacob, DEBTORS IN COURT: THE CONSUMPTION OF GOVERNMENT SERVICES (Chicago: Rand McNally, 1969).

28. Grossman and Sarat, *Litigation in the Federal Courts: A Comparative Perspective*, 9 LAW & SOC'Y REV. 321 (1975).

29. Grossman, Kritzer, Bumiller, Sarat, Miller, and McDougal, *Dimensions of Institutional Participation: Who Uses the Courts and How?*, 43 J. OF POL. (1981).

30. Glick and Vines, *supra* n. 24.

31. Church, *supra* n. 2.

32. *Id.* at 54.

33. For example, there is no mention in any of his quotations of comparisons between federal and state courts; many of the questions refer specifically either to the Miami or Detroit state courts. There are clear differences between *those* two courts, but no responses suggest directly the existence of a legal culture common to *both* federal and state couts in either city.

34. Zeisel, *et al.*, *supra* n. 11, at 234.

35. Church, *supra* n. 2, at 54.

36. Flanders, *supra* n. 19, at 77.

37. Church, *supra* n. 2, at 192.

38. Nimmer, THE NATURE OF SYSTEM CHANGE—REFORM IMPACT IN THE CRIMINAL COURTS 76 (Chicago: American Bar Foundation, 1978).

39. Carter, *Effective Calendar Control—Objectives and Methods*, 29 F.R.D. 227 (1962).

40. Glick and Vines, *supra* n. 24, chapter 4.

41. Boyum, *A Perspective on Civil Delay in Trial Courts*, 5 JUST. SYS. J. 170 (1979).

42. Thus, Boyum concludes "that courts do what they do primarily because of what the people in them think they ought to do. That means that what we have characterized as elements of structure and procedure within courts are distinctly secondary." *Id.* at 182.

43. Posner, *An Economic Approach to Legal Procedure and Judicial Administration*, 2 J. OF LEGAL STUD. 399 (1973).

44. This finding is contrary to Rosenberg, *supra* n. 1, at 37.

Critical issues in the courtroom: exploring a hypothetical case

Editor's note: One of the highlights of the "Presiding in Criminal Court," the First National Judicial State of the Art Conference, was a session in which Professor Charles Nesson of Harvard Law School led a panel of judges, prosecutors, defense attorneys, and other court and justice system personnel in a spirited exchange about several hypothetical criminal court cases.

The participants wrestled with a wide range of issues, including setting bail, predicting dangerousness of the defendant, plea bargaining, victim input into both the charging and sentencing decisions, jail crowding and alternatives to incarceration, drug testing, and AIDS. Although no definitive answers emerged, the session stimulated much thinking and debate.

Presented here is an edited version of that session.

Professor Charles Nesson: You know Vernon Jones to be the reverend of Zion Baptist Church for 15 or 20 years and he is being arraigned in front of you and when the charges are read, they're very serious. It's rape, attempted rape, and assault. Judge Daffron, you are going to have to set bail. That's the first order of business. Tell me how you are going

to proceed.

Judge John Daffron: The consideration would be the danger to the community, the likelihood that the accused would appear for future proceedings, and if he, in fact, is an established member of the community. On the point of his likelihood to appear, it seems he would be very likely to have bail set and be able to post bond in spite of the fact that the offenses are very serious.

Nesson: Do you want to know any details about the offenses?

Daffron: I would ask the prosecutor or the police officer the facts of the offenses and try to make some determination of the strength of the case, the potential danger to the community, and the effect on the victim.

Nesson: Here is apparently what happened. Mr. Jones has been molesting young women right in his office at the Zion Baptist Church. He apparently has been making a practice of picking out young, impressionable women who were deeply religious, having sex with them in his office and then following it up with the strictest, scariest direction to them not to disclose to anyone or God will punish them and their mothers. By the way, there are

The participants on the panel

Facilitator: Charles Nesson, professor, Harvard Law School.

Panelists: Rusty Burress, U.S. probation officer, U.S. Sentencing Commission; Thomas Coughlin III, commissioner, New York State Department of Correctional Services; John Daffron, judge, Circuit Court, Chesterfield, Virginia; Mercedes Deiz, judge, Circuit Court, Portland, Oregon; Larry Dye, president, National Association of Ex-Offenders; Lucy Friedman, executive director, Victim Services Agency, New York, New York; Stephen Goldsmith,

prosecutor, Marion County, Indianapolis, Indiana; Donald Lumpkins, attorney, Washington, D.C.; Robert Murphy, chief justice, Court of Appeals, Annapolis, Maryland; Thomas O'Toole, presiding criminal court judge, Superior Court of Maricopa County, Phoenix, Arizona; A. Charles Peruto, attorney, Philadelphia, Pennsylvania; Ricardo M. Urbina, presiding judge, Family Division, Superior Court of the District of Columbia; Frances Washington, probation officer, Superior Court of the District of Columbia.

people taking notes out there like mad. Suddenly you see a scurry in the back of the courtroom with people running out and court reporters starting to filter in.

Daffron: If there is a probability that other charges may be placed or that other people were at risk, then it seems to me that it swings toward pretrial confinement.

Nesson: What do you mean it swings towards pretrial confinement? What are you actually going to do now?

Daffron: If these are all the facts, I'm going to lock him up.

Nesson: You're going to lock him up period? No bail, no bond, no nothing?

Daffron: Place him in confinement. I would set a bail. It would be commensurate with what I think the risk is and so far, from what I've heard, there is a significant risk to others.

Nesson: Judge O'Toole, are you right along with him here?

Judge Thomas O'Toole: I just want to make sure that if he is going to be released, the community is assured he is going to abide by the conditions of the release and I would make my decision according to those factors.

Nesson: You don't have any problems at all using the dangerousness of this fellow as the criterion on which you are making the judgment?

Daffron: If there is not a significant risk to the community or individual people, then there should be a moderate amount applied that would be designed to assure his appearances at the proceeding. When you add in the factor of potential risk as it has been presented so far, it comes across as a matter that requires pretrial detention.

Nesson: How are those reporters in the back of the room affecting you?

Daffron: It sounds pompous, but I don't really think I'd be particularly concerned with the fact that it's going to be a news item.

Nesson: Do you want that news item to be "Judge Daffron Releases Jones"?

Daffron: No, I'd rather it say, "Judge Daffron Makes Wise Decision."

Nesson: And it's sounding wiser and wiser to you, at least for the moment, to lock this guy up?

Daffron: From what I've heard so far, yes. My leaning is to confinement.

Nesson: Mr. Peruto, you represent this fellow. Now what do you think you could do for him?

A. Charles Peruto: Well, in the first place, I need a couple of facts that would make me think he's a hell of a man.

Nesson: We should let our audience know that you have in front of you a little sheet that gives some minor details on this fellow. It's got his name and his date of birth (he's 52 years old), his address (Rocky Peak), and telephone number. He was divorced seven years ago and he's employed. It also includes the date of the offense, the charges, possible penalties, and his employment history. His employment history is basically fairly impressive; it amounts to that he's been a minister here for 20 years.

Peruto: In the first place, I'd argue that he's been removed from his position where this was alleged to have occurred and therefore the likelihood of recurrence is remote. I would point out that he has a splendid record. I'm going to say to the judge that there are alternatives. I have to recognize that rape is a very frightening thing in the community, at least to half of the community, and that the judge is in a ticklish position. I also have to recognize that I'm not going to get very far persuading the judge to release this man on a bail that he can make because I've got to understand that he's going to be incurring the wrath of the press. So I think I would start thinking about alternatives, such as daily calling-in, but confined to his own home. In other words, present a program for a man who otherwise had had a splendid record and obviously has been disturbed in some fashion and promise to present him for psychiatric examination; present a program of reporting to the court with regard to any evidence of propensities along the lines of the charges that he faces and suggest alternatives to prison.

Nesson: Ms. Washington, should this fellow be locked up right now or not?

Frances Washington: Yes, he should. He's one of the most trusted members of the community. He molested children, little girls who are probably taught to trust him, and he violated that trust. He inflicted physical and long-lasting psychological damage to these children. He should go to jail. I would not release him back to the community, not to call in. He could be molesting more children while he's calling in. Calling in doesn't have anything to do with this.

Nesson: Judge Murphy, do you have any problem with this reaction? We've got a guy who's got roots in the community that are solid as a rock. He's going to show up on the day of trial and yet the reaction from all of these folks is, "Hey, that's not what counts. What counts is, 'Is he dangerous?'" Is that what counts?

Chief Justice Robert Murphy: I think the fear of those who are opposed to pretrial detention to some extent may be justified by what we're hearing here. I share defense counsel's view on this entirely. He starts with the presumption of innocence. He's probably going to say, "I was in Chicago when all this happened." But this man, based on what I have before me, does not seem to be a candidate for pretrial detention. I don't know how much space you have in the Rocky Peak jail detention center, but I'd save it for someone who's got a track record of dangerousness.

Washington: If this man was a drifter, a drunk, a drug addict, or a burglar who had a history of appearing in court for every hearing, he would still be held with or without bond. I believe that the minister's about to get away with rape because he is "somebody" in the community. Granted, we don't know that he's guilty and I've already found him guilty, but you have to look out for your children and you have an obligation to look out for other people's children.

Nesson: What does the presumption of innocence mean to you?

Washington: That you're innocent until found guilty. But mind you, I work with juveniles and 90 per cent of the juveniles who are caught did what they were accused of doing and that is just the way it is.

Judge Mercedes Deiz: What we are hearing from the probation officer is clearly what we are all concerned about at this conference. The arraigning judge must make a decision as to whether the individual should be released, recognizing the tremendously terrible crime that he is charged with. I have to somehow push that out of my mind and get input from defense counsel and the attorney who is representing this minister. We're lucky enough in my area to have a closed-street supervision outfit and so if the closed-street supervision people will take this man under their regular supervision pending the time of trial then, based upon everything I'm hearing from defense counsel and the district attorney, I think I would release him.

Nesson: Respond to Ms. Washington. She says, "Listen, the presumption of innocence is a very important part of our trial procedure, but let's not set it up as something totally realistic. I've worked day to day for years in the system and I know that 90 per cent of the people that come into the system as arrestees are guilty. If I have to presume that they are innocent, you're asking me to take a totally unrealistic view of the world. And certainly a view of the world that the constituency out there and the reporters scribbling on their pads aren't going to take." What do you say to her?

Deiz: Thank God for the jury system because they listen. The jurors listen to that instruction and literally apply it and recognize that the defendant has to be proven guilty beyond a reasonable doubt on every material aspect of the case. Too often, the DAs goof and forget some material aspect of the case and some guy gets off who is just as guilty and horrible a human being as Ms. Washington is concerned about. But the guy gets off because we have a system that says the person has to be proven guilty.

Judge Ricardo Urbina: You haven't given us the law of the jurisdiction, but I think the judge has to bite the bullet on a case like this. The information you've given us makes it rather clear that there are alternatives to locking this person up before trial. He is presumed innocent and there's any number of reasons that explains the allegations that have been made. It's a heinous crime that he's charged with, but the fact of the matter is that there is a presumption of innocence and that's what the court is required to act on. If there is some danger to the community, there's a number of things the court can do to try to insulate the community from being harmed. The first factor in my mind is going to be whether or not he's going to return to court. The second would be trying to set up some system to assure me, as the judge, the court or the system in the community that they can rest at ease, even based on these allegations about him.

Nesson: Ms. Washington's got a system. Her system to put the people in that church at ease is to lock him up, and that is very reassuring. And in fact all the rest of this stuff, about keeping him at home and checking in with the probation officer once a week, is not very reassuring.

Urbina: I think it's the judge's job to identify the issue and to deal with it directly. It's not the judge's job to make the community feel comfortable with that decision. The judge has got the law to rely on and often that's what the judge has to do—make a decision that's going to make the community uncomfortable.

Lucy Friedman: I think that in this case the judge's job is not to make the community feel comfortable in general terms but to deal with the specifics of this case. From the victim's perspective, this is a troubling case because although we want to presume innocence, we clearly don't want to have this man take advantage and continue doing what he's been doing. I hope the reporters are out there because the more publicity about this case, the better. If he were then released with some kind of supervision, the community would be protected because people would be aware of what he has been accused of doing.

Nesson: Judge Daffron, after considering this very difficult problem, winds up making the judgment that he's going to set a fairly high bond of $150,000. After bond is set, there's quite a bit of action out there in the community. There's a lot of people raising money in support of this fellow to pay off his bond. And you, Mr. Peruto, kind of like the political support that he's getting. You figure you'll have him out in awhile and I want you to think about talking to Mr. Goldsmith about pleading this one out. Mr. Goldsmith, you're willing to talk with him?

Plea bargaining

Stephen Goldsmith: Yes, I think so.

Peruto: I would talk about plea bargaining in the sense of assault and point out that there was no serious injury because I haven't heard anything like that, and that this man obviously has mental difficulty, which I can assure him will be taken care of. Now I would have had him thoroughly examined by people whom I hired that knew how to examine people. You'll always find psychiatrists who you can interest in the efficacy of the problem.

Nesson: You're gonna hire these psychiatrists and you're then going to write the script for them?

Peruto: Absolutely, with all due honesty.

Nesson: Let's assume I'm your psychiatrist. What are your interests in this examination, Mr. Peruto?

Peruto: I want you to examine my client because obviously he has some aberration of mind which has caused this. He's been divorced seven years. He's been very, very morose and he's been very, very depressed. I think it's worked on him to such a point where it's caused him to be a little bit, well, a little careless. He's misinterpreted the smiles of these young ladies. I think that once you've exam-

ined him, you'll agree that this man is not dangerous, but really in dire need of medical attention.

Nesson: Mr. Goldsmith, is this somebody you're gonna press hard with?

Goldsmith: This is a difficult case for the prosecutor, in fact, an unusual case, because the dynamics are against the prosecution. The church has rallied and they're convinced of the man's innocence. It's not a case the prosecutor particularly wishes to test. At the same time, we know there are multiple counts, whether you call them child molesting or rapes. We've gotten your psychiatric report saying he's not a pedophile; he's really a sick person.

The issue is whether this is an aberrational event and he can be treated. We ought to take into consideration whether he is in fact a pedophile who will continue to molest children if he's out. I would say to his attorney, we will not bring the other 16 counts if you will pick one of these counts for which we want a guilty plea. Leave sentencing open to the judge.

Nesson: And what's that going to mean if you take the plea to one count?

Goldsmith: We would require some sort of prison term to be determined by the court.

Nesson: It's going to be up to the judge to sentence?

Goldsmith: I'm assuming that either there's a mandatory imprisonment period or the prosecution requires some imprisonment to be determined by the court.

Nesson: All right, so let me see if I've got this straight. It depends a little bit for you on what the law is in the jurisdiction.

Goldsmith: What the judge's discretion is under the law.

Nesson: If the judge has no discretion, then you are in a total position of power, aren't you? You are going to decide whether this guy does time or not? On the other hand, if the judge has discretion, you have a good deal less power? And you'd respond to that by saying I'm gonna be much less willing to bargain away charges?

Goldsmith: We're trying to get him to plead to something and what I'm giving up is my requirement he goes for a fixed period of time. We're going to kind of roll the dice. He's gonna put his psychiatrist on before the judge; I get a guilty plea out of it. So long as the guy goes to prison, that's good for the state.

Nesson: All right, now here's the situation in the

jurisdiction. The judge has discretion. He could put this fellow on probation. That's possible. And the law in your jurisdiction is that you can't sentence-bargain. You can charge-bargain; you can't sentence-bargain. You go in front of the judge; he pleads guilty; it's up to the judge to sentence. Now, where does that leave you?

Goldsmith: The reason we have a lot less with which to deal is because the sentence ranges from the three counts that have been provided to us are 20-40 years for rape, 15-35 for attempted rape and 8-20 for aggravated assault. If there's no realistic chance the man's ever going to get more than eight years, there's not much advantage for the state to go to trial at all on the top two charges because we know the judges are way to the left of prosecutors and it's going to come down to the minimum sentence. So we say plead guilty to one of the counts, 8-20 years, and we'll forgive the other two counts.

If the judge has a full range of discretion on sentencing, which essentially in this case is 0-40 years, we want a guilty plea which will allow the court—after it hears from you and the probation department, thank goodness, and the other psychiatrist—to come in with a range of penalty that's appropriate. Or we say, "Plead guilty to the 8-20, that's the lowest one, you reduce your risk of going to prison for 40 years, and then let the judge decide."

Nesson: Mr. Goldsmith, is this the discussion between you and Mr. Peruto that's taking place down in your office?

Goldsmith: Right.

Nesson: What happens if Mrs. Robinson wants to be present? She's Darlene's mother. Darlene was the victim of charge number one. Ms. Washington, would you be Mrs. Robinson for me? Talk to Ms. Washington here and discourage her.

Goldsmith: We think, Mrs. Robinson, that if this man is found guilty, the sentence is going to be six or eight years, and there is a chance it could go higher. We could go to trial with your 12-year-old daughter and the chances of an increased sentence are a little bit greater. We can try to get a guilty plea and not put her through it. I'd like your permission to offer a guilty as charged to the count of 8-20 years.

Washington: I don't want my 12 year old to be subjected to a trial after what she has been subjected to by this man. I want him to serve 16 years, not eight, because when he is released, I want my child to be grown, through college, maybe even out of the area and hopefully over this.

Goldsmith: Well, I'm going to have a settlement discussion with his attorney. I'll offer him 15-35 years. I think it would be easier if you weren't there. If he rejects it, then I'll come back to you and talk to you about whether your daughter wants to go through it. But one thing I want you to understand is even if we do go through this trial, the judge could still give the range of sentence that could go all the way down to zero. We can't guarantee a sentence to you, but I'll take your proposal to the defense attorney.

Nesson: You're letting her run your office?

Goldsmith: In this case, the mom has a major say in whether to put her daughter, the victim, through the trial for what could come out of it, much more so than in a robbery or other case that doesn't put her child victim on the stand.

Nesson: Mr. Peruto, what are you going to do about this?

Peruto: Well, I would point out to the district attorney that even with eight years, the man will be 60 so I don't know where she's coming off with the protection of her own child. I would talk to Mr. Goldsmith about things such as considerations of track record. For example, if he has tried cases against me before that he thought were winners and wound up losers, I would say that one of the bits of input has to do with the possibility of success at the trial. I would point out to him that although he gets great sympathetic appeal from the fact that the child is 12, he also has a child that is not going to be able to withstand the kind of cross-examination that I would put the child through. I would suggest that he speak again to Mrs. Robinson and let her know these things and that it might result in serious damage to the child, far greater than the risk she would fear after his release in eight years. It might cause irreparable harm to her. I would throw in all of these things and I would suggest to him that if he wants a plea from me to the extent he wants a plea on the higher charge of rape and leave it to the judge, I could not accept that because he's only passing the buck. I am all too familiar with judges saying, "Well, he's already gotten his break on the reduction of the number of counts," and the judge is on the hot seat because now it's not a question of presumption of innocence. You have a guilty person before you and he's gonna face the press and we all know the way the press came down on that one judge who made that unfortunate comment, "She'll get over it." No judge is going to give him eight years or less than eight years on a plea to the rape charge. It must be the kind of bargain where we have a cap on the sentence; otherwise, I would have to tell my client, "You're a fool—you may as well face a thousand charges than one which exposes you to 95 years total because you can't trust the judge." You gotta put yourself in that judge's position. We just cannot deal under those circumstances on anything higher than the assault charge.

Nesson: What I hear you saying to me, Mr. Peruto, is if you can't make a firm deal that at least caps the sentence, you don't want any deal at all.

Peruto: That's right. I would point out to the DA that I've got my doctors who are going to testify, I've got the great number of parishioners that are going to come in for him; it's going to be a real donnybrook. I'm just going to have to tell my own client you're shooting crap if you come in on a rape plea because then you're defenseless and you're putting the judge in the position that I've previously described and I would advise him to go for broke.

Nesson: Judge O'Toole, should the law permit the prosecutor and defense to make a firm deal on the amount of the sentence? Must it be the law that the prosecution and the defense can make a firm deal on the amount of the sentence?

O'Toole: The answer to that is no, because the judge has to impose sentence and if he has no discretion in accepting or rejecting the deal, they're passing the buck to him whether it's a bad deal. The judge gets the buck from the community so to speak, and they don't suffer from it.

Nesson: Judge Urbina? Do you understand the problem? How should it be?

Urbina: I don't like the idea of having the defense and prosecution dictate what the sentence should be in the case. The judge, as more or less of a neutral person in the situation, has oversight of what's going on and has insight into what should ultimately be appropriate as a sentence. Both the prosecution and defense are coming at the problem with a particular point of view in mind and they've reached a point where they've compromised. I don't think that compromise should really involve the judge.

Nesson: Judge Murphy, how should it be?

Murphy: To a large extent, judges know their prosecutors and their defense counsel and, to some extent, will pay deference to their judgment. They certainly don't have all of the facts before them, but by no means or measure can a trial judge be bound by a bad deal on his judgment. As a practical matter on the plea bargaining process, the bargainers know their judge and I think they ride on the philosophy that what they agree to will in fact be accepted, but they can never be totally assured.

Nesson: What would happen in this case if we were to live in a world with no plea bargaining, no sentence-bargaining, no charge-bargaining?

Murphy: It's a cruel, cruel world and a very unrealistic one. Obviously, the court system would probably break itself very, very shortly if you didn't have the plea-bargaining process.

Goldsmith: It's an unrealistic world that doesn't allow those people closest to the case to negotiate an outcome based on the dynamics of the evidence, the dynamics of the community, and the importance of the charge.

Nesson: So as far as you're concerned, it's part of the prosecutor's job to negotiate outcomes?

Goldsmith: Absolutely.

Nesson: And God help the defense—if they didn't have that to do, what else would they offer their clients?

Goldsmith: Well, I think we arrive together at a decision that more than anything takes the evidence and predicts the judge.

The sentence

Nesson: All right. Let's predict the judge here. Judge O'Toole, just looking for a reaction. What are you going to sentence this man to?

O'Toole: Well, he's gonna go to prison, it's just a question of how long. It's a very serious crime and apparently we have mitigating factors and aggravating factors.

Nesson: He's a distinguished member of the civil liberties movement, civil rights movement, and a pillar in the Baptist Church. Tremendous support from his congregation.

O'Toole: That isn't at the top of my list of priorities for determining sentence.

Nesson: And he's sick.

O'Toole: Is that a factor to consider? That also works the other way because if he's sick, who's to know whether he's going to recover? I would perhaps have a psychiatric examination conducted by a court-appointed expert and you also have the expert input from the probation department. Included in the expert input would be statements of the victims and interested parties. All these players come in line on a sentence.

Mrs. Robinson rings a loud bell when she talks about the concerns of her daughter. I would want to know the impact on the victim. I'd also want to be satisfied as to the length of incarceration this man would serve under the particular sentence. I'd want to know the guidelines for release and what type of parole supervision he's going to have. The man's 52 years old, perhaps it's somewhat pragmatic but I'd want to see him incarcerated until he's 60 and put parole on him. I'd propose a sentence that considers not only punishment and deterrence but community safety and also the interests of the defendant. This is a very serious ongoing pattern of conduct, evident not only by this particular charge, but if I understand the facts, this has been occurring with other young females in the parish.

Nesson: You're going to find out about that during sentencing?

O'Toole: I would think so.

Nesson: Commissioner Coughlin, can you use this man? You've got him now and you've got him for a minimum of eight years. What are you going to do with him?

Thomas Coughlin: Put him to work. I would probably use whatever skills I could get out of him. Not in terms of ministerial skills, but I'd imagine he could read and write pretty good and we'd probably put him in some setting within the prison system where we could use those skills.

Fact pattern

Nesson: All right now, let me introduce you to another character. Judge Thomas O'Toole, you're in the arraignment session and in comes a young man, 19 years old, by the name of James Michael O'Reilly.

He's been charged with armed robbery, assault and battery with a dangerous weapon, unauthorized use and possession with intent to distribute. Jimmy and the co-defendant, who's a 23 year old, much bigger fellow, apparently entered a 7-Eleven convenience store the night before, and Turner, the co-defendant, had a weapon in his hand. They stuck the place up and Jimmy removed $234 from the cash register, and at that point the woman behind the counter apparently made some quick move, and Turner shot and wounded her. She's in the hospital now, in serious condition. They fled,

got into a Ford 4x4, took off and the cops stopped the truck, arrested the two, and there they are before you. Now you are going to set bail for Jimmy. What are you going to do?

O'Toole: He's not going to get out. Looking at the additional information, it doesn't look like he has any substantial means of living. He's single, living with his parents, unemployed. Any bail—reasonable, substantial bail—is going to keep him in jail in fact.

Nesson: So that's what you're gong to do? You're going to keep him in jail? And you're going to do it on the basis that he's a danger to the community?

O'Toole: He's likely to violate the conditions to release if he gets out. He's got an active police record. He's 19 and he's got an active police record . . . juvenile . . . six or seven arrests.

Nesson: So you don't have any problem looking at his juvenile record? None of this business about, "Hey, we seal the record at the point when he's become an adult and we don't look at it after that"?

O'Toole: That's correct.

Nesson: Judge Deiz, does it bother you that he's monkeying around in the juvenile record, making his judgments on the basis of that?

Deiz: I don't look at the juvenile record on whether or not to set bail or whether or not you release a person on personal recognizance because we can't; it's not permitted by statute. However, if someone was looking at it at the time of sentencing, I would like to see this kind of record and I have always wanted to see it, no matter what the charge, in order to assess whether or not an individual should be released. In the practical point of view, the fact that the young man or young woman did something when they were 17 and now that they are 19 is very relevant to how I'm going to assess whether or not they are a good risk to be out pending trial. But I can't have that information.

Nesson: Judge O'Toole, when they arrest this fellow, they tested him for drugs and he comes up dirty. He's apparently high on PCP at the time. How does that affect your judgment?

O'Toole: That obviously would be a factor to consider as to whether that is one of the motives for his committing the offense. Whether it's an indicator of his likelihood to violate conditions of release, I don't know.

Nesson: Mr. Lumpkin, you're representing this fellow. What significance do you think that test is going to have?

Donald Lumpkin: I think the drug test would be negative and as a defense attorney, I have basically two jobs. One is to put my client in the best light. Sometimes it's total darkness. So then I look to my client's best interest. I think it's terribly important which judge I'm going before and I think that a young man, 19 years of age, certainly has some hope. I think with the record before me, he falls within the Youth Act in the District of Columbia.

Nesson: We've got a fellow that's charged as I described and a juvenile record that includes: truancy; another truancy; destruction of property for which he got fined; possession of marijuana, dismissed; possession of marijuana with intent to distribute, for which he was committed to a youth home for six months; petty larceny, for which he's on probation; and a previous adult incident, possession of cocaine, which was not pressed.

Lumpkin: In the District of Columbia, he's still a youth—anyone under 22 years of age. I think this is terribly crucial in this particular case and looking at Mr. O'Reilly's best interest, I would recommend that he undergo detention for 60 days with an intensive psychiatric evaluation. I think it's terribly important that this young man enter a structured environment. I do not wash my hands thinking there isn't hope and I'd certainly ask the judge to give immense weight to the fact that he is only 19. In a properly structured environment, I think there is hope and if there isn't hope, then there's no point even trying.

Nesson: I'm interested in drug testing here. Once he shows up dirty, what does that have to do with anything?

Lumpkin: It shows a couple of things. It shows that we're dealing with a very troubled young man, but it also shows that we're dealing with not such an exceptional person. Thousands and thousands of people, certainly in the District of Columbia, have shown up dirty with PCP. This is not to justify, I'm simply saying that it's not such an exception. It's something to be concerned about, but I would not use him as the single example. Yes he's drugged, it's a matter of great concern, but so are thousands of others.

Nesson: Let me come from a different perspective. Mr. Dye, do you have any problem with this jurisdiction testing everybody that comes through for drugs?

Larry Dye: I do have objections to jurisdictions doing drug tests.

Nesson: Mr. Lumpkin says they're accurate and Judge O'Toole says that's valuable information.

Dye: And there are cases where it is not accurate. There are cases where the drug company doing their testing has made errors. There have been errors made in all kinds of testing so, consequently, I would raise that as a question because potentially you have people who have not used drugs that would turn up dirty.

I'm an offender coming in and when I've been tested, I want my attorney to challenge that test because this jurisdiction has the law that states you're going to take a test. So I'm going to want my attorney to be able to challenge that.

Pretrial release conditions

Nesson: Judge Daffron, we go forward with Jimmy and we put some bail on him and he's been in the can now for some 35 days waiting trial. Let's say he's able to make the bail and it comes up to you now. What kind of pretrial release conditions are you gong to put on him, when you got this drug test and he was dirty when it came in? Are you going to use that test in the context of imposing conditions on him?

Daffron: I'm going to require that he be free from drugs or alcohol. As a condition of bond, he will subject himself to announced and unannounced screenings.

Nesson: Announced and unannounced screenings? How are we going to work the announced screenings?

Daffron: Tell him to come in at a given time.

Nesson: Tell him to come in at a given time and he's going to see Mr. Burress? Mr. Burress, explain it all to me.

Rusty Burress: Essentially they are probably going to put this person in some type of drug program where he will be giving urine samples and then we will have him either reporting to us or we will go out to his home or place of employment, confirm he is still in the community and we'll take urine samples from him at that time.

Nesson: How do you feel about this one? You're going to go to Jimmy's home and you're going to say, "All right, Jimmy, let's go to the bathroom together."

Burress: Yes, I am. It's not a most enjoyable part of the job, but that's one of the regular things you do and particularly if that's the condition of his bond. If he's on the street by remaining drug-free, that's the only way to check it.

Nesson: What happens if he misses an appointment? What's going to happen?

Burress: We'd notify the court. Actually, before we notify the court, we'd probably go out and check on the individual to see if the individual was at home, what reason they had for not coming in, probably take a urine sample at that time just to see if he's reverted to drug use and probably make some judgment as to whether it warranted reporting based upon what this person had told us. If we can't locate them, of course, or if their reason doesn't appear to be a valid one then we'd report it to the court.

Nesson: And suppose he comes in and he tests dirty, what happens?

Burress: We'd report that to the court immediately and then see if the court had any further directions, additional programming.

Nesson: All right, Judge Daffron, you just get a report from Mr. Burress that Jimmy has come up dirty on one of his drug tests three weeks after release?

Daffron: He would be back in court for determination of whether his bond should be revoked.

Nesson: And are you going to revoke his bond?

Daffron: I would say the odds are probable.

Nesson: By the way, I didn't tell you that it isn't in Rocky Peak. This is in a jurisdiction where the jail is chock-a-block full. It's so far over capacity that federal judges have been breathing down the necks of various local administrators and here's Jimmy and he's dirty on his PCP test. You're going to put him back in?

Daffron: He is there until I let him out. This would be a case, it seems to me, for a reasonable bond that Jimmy could make and if he wants to play by the rules of the game he stays out. If he can't, I'm not absolutely convinced right now that he would go back, but I think that the probability is that he will.

Nesson: Mr. Coughlin, just be a jail administrator for me right now, will you? Your jail is just popping at the seams. Do you have any way of letting Judge Daffron know that he really shouldn't be plugging in kids you really don't need just because they come up dirty on their urine test?

Coughlin: Well, if the judge would read the morning newspapers everyday, he'd see all the reasons in the world for not just bringing a guy back for something minor. However, I personally have an opinion on this. You give a guy a bite of the apple,

you put him on bail and he gets out and he comes back dirty. Well that's enough to bring him back in; in my opinion, it shouldn't be the judge's concern whether or not there's room in the jail. That's my concern. That's the executive's concern.

Nesson: Well, it sounds like what should happen is the executive should raise some money and build some new jails, but out in the real world that's pretty tough to make happen.

Coughlin: That's the problem we have with politics. The mayors and the governors around this country don't want to make the hard choice and I'm convinced that they have to make that hard choice.

Nesson: So convinced that you'd be prepared to say it's just not the judge's business to concern themselves with that problem at all?

Coughlin: It's been my experience that they don't concern themselves with that problem and I've been doing this long enough to know. I've talked to judges saying, "It's not your business. You do what you do and I'll do what I do and you use your resources and I'll use my resources." Anything less than that and the system starts to fall apart and you have federal judges stepping in to release people. The top 37 guys on the list are out the door tomorrow. That's not the way it should work.

Nesson: All right, now let me come back to you, Judge Daffron. If you follow the structure, you're going to put a release condition on this kid with respect to drug use and you're going to be under a system where if he's dirty, he's back in the can.

Daffron: Not absolutely, but that would be a likelihood. I don't think it's a bright line rule. You use PCP or heroin or cocaine, you are back in jail and pretrial confinement—the probabilities are certainly higher with that use than it may be with the use of alcohol, marijuana.

Nesson: All right, Mr. Burress, the real rules, aren't they, are that if I use beer or marijuana, I'm not going to get yanked off the street, am I?

Burress: If that's what this judge's criterion is, then that probably is the rule, but I would not tell the defendant that.

Nesson: By the way, if that's the real rule would you bother reporting marijuana use to the judge?

Burress: Yeah, but I probably wouldn't go through a formal procedure. I'd probably just advise the court of this situation and see if the court wanted us to take any action at that time.

Nesson: Let's see it happen. Advise him, advise

him.

Burress: Judge, I've been seeing this Jimmy O'Reilly on a regular basis. He's begun working. He's going to the drug program in general. They have been taking urine samples from him. However, the urine sample we took this week turned up positive for marijuana use. He seems to be basically staying close to the home and at employment. No indications of any other type of activity. The drug program feels that he seems to be making some progress and seems to be trying to profit from attending those sessions. At this point, I think it probably would warrant giving him another shot.

Daffron: Intensify the supervision and leave him on the street.

Nesson: That's it. So you just bought yourself a little more work. Intensify the supervision and when you intensify it, you find out he's smoking marijuana more and more. Are you going to go back again? You're a glutton for punishment, aren't you?

Burress: To some degree, yes sir. Because you do create work for yourself when you report these violations. That's just part of what you do. I could turn a blind eye to the thing, not report it and it would reduce the amount of work but that's not what the function is.

Plea bargaining

Nesson: Mr. Goldsmith, I want Mr. Lumpkin to talk to you for a minute. We want to see if we can deal this one out. We did very well with Vernon. I want to see whether we can deal Jimmy. What do you think just on what you know?

Goldsmith: I just think this conversation is kind of outrageous—a few minor crimes, you're out on bail, no big deal. I'm predisposed against that because he's got a longer history.

Nesson: Mr. Lumpkin?

Lumpkin: If my client is spaced out on drugs, I would explain to him fully he has the responsibility to get off. If he needs help, we'll try to get him help. I cannot see people walking around the city on PCP. If it comes to walking around the city or being in jail, they're safer in jail because then they are not going out to bring harm to society or the community.

I'll tell you an interesting case I had. I had one client who was running down the street in the nude, yelling "liberty for all" on PCP and got shot by a sting gun and was taken to St. Elizabeth's. I talked to five attorneys in Washington, asking if I

should speak to the judge regarding this matter out of the best interest for my client. Absolutely not, they told me. I went to the judge and talked to him. I am not doing any client a favor by not giving him help on drugs.

Nesson: Mr. Peruto, you agree with Mr. Lumpkin here?

Peruto: I am in great pain because I agree with Mr. Goldsmith. You know, the guy that knows more about the condition of the full jail is Jimmy; he knows more about that than anybody. I'm also sick of the judges who say that we have to release people from jail. If they were really concerned with these terribly overcrowded conditions, they would enjoin a man close to the executive to force him to build more institutions. I don't like a judge who says to a guy, "If you use (drugs) while you're out on this bail against my order, you will be recommitted" and then he doesn't recommit, because that promise is the surest way of keeping them in line. If you promise you're going to put them back, put them back. I would have to say to my own client, "Fellow, you're carrying the keys to the jail with you. You got the keys in one pocket and you can put the joint in the other pocket. Don't come crying to me if you're going to smoke the joint." I just don't see my role as defense counsel in the preservation of the presumption of innocence to extend itself to where I'm going to do otherwise in this position.

I think that one of the major causes of crime is the kind of thing you're talking about. I think the system is known much, much better by the offender than it is by the people who administer the system. I think that the newspapers have a lot to do with it. I think we have a bunch of chicken-lily livered people who are in the system who react to newspapers and are scared off by executives for fear of raising taxes and therefore their political party is being defeated.

Nesson: This case looked pretty bad for Jimmy when we first heard about it but there are some details that kind of go his way. There were two witnesses in the 7-Eleven who said in their interviews that Turner was clearly the shooter. Turner seemed to be directing Jimmy during the robbery, telling him what to do and when Turner shot, Jimmy was extremely upset about it and yelled at Turner that he shouldn't have done it. He didn't want anything to do with that shooting and he immediately ran out of the place and hopped into the truck. In fact, when the officers caught up with them, Jimmy stopped the truck and Tuner was yelling, "Why did you stop the truck?" and Jimmy was completely peaceful after that. So it begins to look like maybe Jimmy's not the hardest guy in the world. Could you use that with Mr. Goldsmith?

Lumpkin: Certainly. I see Jimmy as probably a very troubled young man, probably with very poor guidelines, not really having any type of structured environment. What is so frustrating as a defense attorney is representing the best interest of my client and all I have to deal with is incarceration.

Nesson: Mr. Goldsmith, let me make it a little richer. Mr. Lumpkin does a kind of psychiatric look at Jimmy and they find out he's a kid with some learning disabilities, bad self-image on account of it and got himself into some drugs, but really doesn't seem to be such a bad kid. Are you going to hit a point where you're ready to say this kid doesn't have to go away?

Goldsmith: Not for this charge, maybe in 1985 when he stole a leather jacket from the department store but not with the armed robbery with a sawed-off shotgun. We're dealing with how much time, not whether he does time.

Nesson: Suppose he convinces you, in fact, Turner was dragging him along on this one? Still no?

Goldsmith: That's an important factor in reducing the length of the sentence, not in reducing it to zero. Too serious a crime, too long a history. If it's a regular good time two-for-one situation, we'd offer him eight years which means he does four, he testifies and does drug counseling and testing after release from the prison.

Nesson: And what about Mrs. Woods, the lady behind the counter who got shot, now out of the hospital in a wheel chair? Do you consult with her on this one? Ms. Friedman, what do you say if you were representing Mrs. Woods here?

Lucy Friedman: Well, I'd first wish that someone had notified us when Jimmy made bail. I would have liked to have known because my client was getting phone calls from people hanging up. I mean we don't know who it was. It might have been Jimmy, Jimmy's family, it may have been the other guy. So in addition to being injured, perhaps permanently for life, she's been terrified because she's been afraid to go out and got no notice from the courts about what's happening in the case. Then Jimmy went back into jail, we didn't know why.

Nesson: Judge O'Toole, the case comes in front of you for sentence and there is a plea. Clearly the

understanding of Jimmy and his lawyer is that he's going to get a maximum of four years but you're under a guideline system that says, armed robbery, dangerous weapon, minimum eight. Will you go along with the plea bargain?

O'Toole: The plea agreement with the prosecutor is before me and it says he's going to get a maximum of four years. He's obviously not pleading armed robbery to the facts; he's pleading to a less serious offense. I probably would get background information. I prefer not accepting the plea until I read the pre-sentence report. If I didn't like the information, I would reject it. I'd like to have more input from the victim as to what she believes regarding the plea bargain. I'd take the plea, but I wouldn't accept it until I had that information. At the time of sentencing, I'd decide whether or not to accept or reject it.

Sentencing

Nesson: Judge Murphy, here's the situation—your state's adopted sentencing guidelines. Lo and behold, here comes this case in front of you and it's below the guidelines.

Murphy: It's a judgment call. We have hundreds of Jimmys coming into the system every day and they go on a scale of 10 down to 1. There may be a lot to be said for him. If you're a defense lawyer, his juvenile record is really unremarkable.

Deiz: You've made a decision in this case. You're saying that because Jimmy had a troubled childhood and maybe he wasn't of the strongest character with a learning disability, that allowed you to give him a sentence half of what the minimum was.

Murphy: That's what guidelines are all about. You can go above or below. You can get a fellow who looks worse than Jimmy. That sawed-off shotgun is a real loser, although this is a first offense. A sawed-off shotgun just sets off bells in trial judges and if you change the facts a little bit you could go above it.

Nesson: Judge O'Toole, you've got all this information about how Jimmy really was importuned by Turner in this thing and seems to have been dragged along and resisted at every step. He really looks like a salvageable kid in some ways. Tell you something else about Jimmy. He's a small kid. He's about 5'5", long blonde hair, real pretty kid. Does that bother you in sentencing him?

O'Toole: Well it bothers me, but I'm not going to make any decision on the length of incarceration or whether I incarcerate him based upon a likelihood that he may be sexually assaulted in prison.

Nesson: Mr. Coughlin, tell me about your prison system. Have you tested for AIDS in your system?

Coughlin: No, we haven't tested for AIDS, because I wouldn't know what to do if I found someone who tested positive and displayed clinical symptoms of the disease.

Nesson: Here you got Jimmy coming up to your prison and you look at him and you say, "Now there is a pretty kid and I just know what's going to happen to that kid." And your attitude is, "I just don't want to know what the AIDS situation is in my prison."

Coughlin: If you have 42,000 people in prison and a large number, let's say 60 or 70 per cent, have been involved with narcotics use, you're going to have a significant number of people within that prison system who could very well test positive for the virus, not being ill now, but testing positive for the virus. The numbers range anywhere from 20 per cent, depending upon whether the researcher wanted to get his name in the paper, to as high as 80 per cent. If I get a person to test positive, say he shows up at sick call with three or four symptoms and we do the test and we find it positive, we treat him as a medical case. If, however, the guy has a positive test but is not ill, I don't know what to do with him. Do I keep him locked up? Do I start a special prison for him? If I have a prison full of guys who test positive for AIDS, the next step is to lock them all in a cell and not let them out because they're all nasty people; they're going to be doing things to each other, and pretty soon the whole prison will have the actual disease. So, no, I won't test for AIDS unless there's some clinical indication that the person has it.

Nesson: Now, you're not in any doubt about your ability to test for AIDS, that is, there's no legal impediment to your doing this, is there?

Coughlin: No, there's not. We take blood samples when they come into the prison, but we don't run it through the particular screen for the AIDS virus because no one has told me what I'm going to do with the man when I find out that he's got AIDS or been exposed to the AIDS virus. In this whole issue of being exposed to the AIDS virus, nobody has come up with the solid number on conversion—nobody. In the research that we have done—we've had AIDS in our prison system since 1981 and now we've got the largest number in the country today—we have not had a single case of AIDS being

contracted within the prison, not a single case. I'll tell you how we know. We have people who have come to prison, gotten sick and have died of AIDS within six months of coming to prison. You don't die from AIDS within six months, that's how we know. The period of development stretches anywhere from six to seven years before the AIDS virus becomes active enough to kill you. If you've been in prison six months and you die from AIDS or AIDS-related complex issues, it's obvious from medical research that you haven't contracted AIDS within the prison system.

Nesson: All right, Mr. Lumpkin, let's now wind the clock back a moment to the point where you're appearing in front of Judge O'Toole on behalf of Jimmy and you know that Judge O'Toole has got it in his mind that he's going to send Jimmy away for a little bit. Maybe not a long time. He's really kind of wobbly because really this kid doesn't look like he's that bad, maybe salvageable, and he knows that sending him away is extremely serious. Now, do you make an argument to Judge O'Toole based on the AIDS problem?

Lumpkin: I would like to address one issue before getting into that one. I would like to say that studies have shown that blacks and Hispanics generally do die within six to seven months. It is the white gay population that will not die until about two years. And the reason—we're speaking about drug users whose immune system is so low as compared to the white population which is very high among gay males.

Nesson: What you're saying is that generally speaking the gay white population is healthier in terms of the immune system than the narcotic-using population?

Lumpkin: Exactly. Their immune system is much better than the Hispanic or black male who has been using drugs and has no immunity whatsoever, virtually, and they die much, much sooner from the date of diagnosis.

Nesson: All right, so now come back to my question. Do you want to say something to Judge O'Toole about what Jimmy's prognosis is, going off to the prison that Mr. Coughlin runs?

Lumpkin: I would have no problem addressing this issue in the least, but I'm afraid the judge would come back to me and say, "Mr. Lumpkin, that is not my problem as a judge."

O'Toole: I think it's a legitimate concern, especially when the Department of Corrections or the

Bureau of Prisons have decided not to test or sample blood of inmates coming in but, as I understand, the hypothetical isn't so much what his blood condition is when he goes in, it's what it's going to be after he's been there for awhile.

Given the role that I've got in determining a sentence, I could not base any decision on length of incarceration on the possibility that we go to prison and do some testing and this boy's going to be sexually assaulted. I would recommend to the department of corrections that he be placed so that his safety is preserved as much as possible. And I think if he gets to the prison system and he's got a problem, hopefully he's going to be able to file a petition of writ of habeas corpus or something like that.

Daffron: My reaction at the moment on the facts is that Jimmy would go to prison. It seems to me that if there is not a mandatory, minimum period of confinement, that this case may well lend itself to some alternative other than confinement to the penitentiary. For example, it may be a jurisdiction that has a type of youthful offender law that provides confinement but not in the general prison population or adult prison population. But, assuming that doesn't exist, I see a hard time.

Nesson: No, we're perfectly happy to assume we've got house arrest in this state. We could put a little cuff on Jimmy's pants or around his ankle and have him check in once a day though the telephone. We can have intensive probation . . . . Mr. Burress, he's got nothing much to do, now that he's been relieved of all his marijuana work. He can go out on a once-a-day basis and check in on Jimmy to make sure he's staying in the house.

Daffron: Is the first determination either confinement in the penitentiary or something else, or is there an institutional confinement that may be less than the adult prison population? That would make a significant difference to me.

The hardest one is it's either/or, that if there is confinement, he's going to be placed in spite of a classification system within a correctional system in confinement with other adult fellows, and so he is significantly at great risk there. It would be a significant matter whether or not to place this defendant in prison because of the great risk of assault that needs determination without the other facts that I'm waiting for you to give me. I think probably that this defendant, regrettably, would be confined in prison and about the limit of the judge's interven-

tion would be perhaps a letter that we sometimes write to corrections or classifications expressing concern because of evidence presented.

Nesson: What do you do when you get one of those letters, Mr. Coughlin?

Coughlin: Well, we pay pretty close attention. There are a number of options that we have in the prison system to deal with people like this. There are programs within the system. This kid, depending upon what was the final charge—whether it was armed robbery or whether it was less than armed robbery—we would probably put this individual into our shock incarceration program.

You take a young kid who's 19 years old with an on-going juvenile record and this is his first big-time run-in, then you make the assumption the kid is salvageable somehow and you put him into a program designed to test that salvageability, an intensive six-month program, narcotics counseling, disciplined regimen and maybe after six months you can turn somebody out who's not going to come back.

Goldsmith: That's not my deal.

Coughlin: But you don't make that deal.

Goldsmith: Oh no, we made a deal.

Coughlin: It's not yours to determine, it's mine. We're in my statutes.

Nesson: Once you put it in his hands, he says where the kid resides, right? And, if you want it in the maximum security, that's your choice and if you want it in the half-way house, that's your choice.

Let me just change this problem a little bit. Judge Deiz, same kid, Jimmy, in front of you. He's still pretty, but this time things are a little different. Mr. Burress has been talking to Jimmy quite a bit and in fact Mr. Burress has included in the sentence report that he thinks Jimmy makes a little money on the side by being a male prostitute. And, we've come up with information that Jimmy tests positive for AIDS. I want to know if that changes the way you think. Are you going to send Jimmy off to this prison where he's cute, he's available, and he's possibly lethal?

Deiz: All of us in this work know that fashioning appropriate sentences is the most difficult task for all trial judges, and what I've gotten since I'm down here in Phoenix is this new curve of AIDS. This man is now going to the penitentiary because he is involved in drugs and I'm satisfied with the correlation between drugs and continuing criminal activity so, therefore, it isn't so much that he's salvageable as a person that I would put him in an alternative placement in the community, but he would go. The problem now is what you've just thrown at me—how do I get this wonderful commissioner here to really give credence to the strong recommendation that I make that this fellow be followed and somehow kept away from the prison population so that he doesn't spread AIDS. If I'm sending that very kind of potential weapon into your penitentiary knowing about it, I'm not dumping it on you to say that I don't know what to do. I can't understand why you don't know what to do.

Coughlin: Of course I know what to do. If the fact pattern has changed now and you have a male prostitute who tests positive for the AIDS virus, well, that's whole different set of circumstances. I know exactly what to do with this person.

Nesson: Let me do it this way, Mr. Coughlin. This AIDS problem is the big one that's kind of looming over the horizon at everybody and it does kind of wind up with you in the end. The system funnels it towards you and gives it to you in a nice, confined situation where you've got the toughest problems to deal with. Talk to that situation, would you. What are we going to do with this problem?

Coughlin: If he is a male prostitute, tests positive for AIDS, gets convicted, gets sentenced, and comes to prison, the prison system knows what to do with a person like that. Now we have mechanisms within the system that permit us to isolate people like that with equal administrative segregation. I can assure you, he would probably wind up in an administrative protective custody unit very quickly and would stay there until we got some indication of how he was behaving. If his behavior in that administrative protection unit was successful for a period of time, we might try him out in limited contact with the general population where he would go out with everybody knowing that he is a male prostitute and that he tests positive for AIDS. But he's not going to get into the general population until myself or the warden is satisfied that he can handle it and the system can handle him.

Nesson: You'll turn him loose in the general population and you're going to let everybody know that he tests positive?

Coughlin: You said that this AIDS problem is booming on the horizon? At least for my prison system we are beyond the horizon already. Now I'm being very frank with you. We have dealt with the problem of AIDS since 1981. I think we know how

to do it. Remember before we dealt with AIDS, we dealt with a lot of other infectious diseases within a congregated institution and it can be done in a very reasonable way. I have never, in my experience, seen an AIDS patient beat up by other inmates. I have never known an AIDS patient to be murdered by other inmates. Usually other inmates want to stay very far away. Inmates constantly ask, "What can I do? I don't have AIDS and I don't want to catch AIDS." I say the best thing you can do is to "look at the guy living in the cell next to you and say that he's got AIDS and therefore, I'm not going to share a needle with him nor am I going to kiss him." It may sound very simple and it might sound very basic but that's how not to catch AIDS in prison. Prisoners, by and large, are not dumb people and they don't want to catch AIDS and they pay attention to these very simple rules.

Nesson: Ladies and gentlemen on the panel, thank you very much for participating with me.

NOTE

This transcript originally appeared in Volume 72, Number 1, June-July 1988, pages 12-22.

Race and crime: what evidence is there that race influences results in the criminal justice system?

by Norval Morris

I would like to talk about a topic that I find important, yet not much talked about. There is a problem in discussing this topic, and indeed many topics; nowadays, you can't finish framing the question before someone is giving you the answer. That disease is particularly prevalent among my colleagues who study economics and law combined, but I find it increasingly infects lawyers generally and even those people who are referred to as intelligent laymen. As a result, I have turned to fiction. The advantage of fiction is that you can be transported from contemporary society with its knee-jerk reactions to every serious problem; in fiction, you can at least have some hope of framing the question before you get the answer.

Come with me and escape the necessity to avoid talking seriously and quietly about blacks and crime in America. With a teletransporter, we can go to another country and another time to see what conclusions we can draw about that country; what facts we know and what conclusions we might be able to draw from those facts. I've done a lot of work over the years in trying to gather those facts about that country. So let me tell you about that country—not the United States—though it bears a striking resemblance to it. So, "Beam us up, Scottie."

In proportion to the distribution of blacks and whites in that society, let me give you five facts: First, for every one white male in prison, more than seven blacks are in prison. That discrepancy has grown larger, not smaller, over the last 30 years. In 1933, blacks made up less than a quarter of the prison population; now they are nearly a half. Second, although on this "fact" there is some slight doubt, of every 12 black males in their 20s, 1 in every 12 is in prison or jail. That's a fantastic figure. (The Bureau of Justice Statistics says it's not quite that

bad, that it's 1 in 15, but I think they are wrong.) The third fact: Of all black babies born in that distant society today, 1 in 30 will die a victim of intentional or non-negligent homicide. Among black males and females, ages 15 to 44, the leading cause of death is homicide.

Let me give you the fourth fact—a little more encouraging about race and crime and a bit more complicated—a fact that has not been publicized much; blacks are not more likely than whites to be persistent offenders. The return to prison rates differ very little, if at all, between blacks and whites of those in prison, first time, second time, etc. The differential in prison populations between blacks and whites is accounted for by the patterns of first-time criminality within each racial group, rather than by any difference in the patterns of continuing criminality. So the great difference is the function of the percentage of those who commit first-time crimes, not of any unique persistence in crime. That is not an unimportant point.

There is a current belief among people in my trade, interested in sentencing reform, that sentencing should be based in part on incapacitation, on taking high-rate offenders out of circulation, and that we should prolong and adjust sentences according to the threat that the individual prisoner presents. We are good at increasing sentences, but not so good at the reduction. Because blacks are not disproportionately likely to be persistent criminals, sentencing policies that target persistent offenders will not further disadvantage them.

The final, fifth fact about this strange country that I ask you to survey today is that in recent years an increasing number of blacks have moved into the middle class from the underclass, leaving the destroyed inner-city neighborhoods with their astronomical crime rates to those left behind. The crime and delinquency rates of incarceration, and rates of arrest and of victimization of those who move away from these slums, are indistinguishable from whites of the same social class. So much for genetic explanations! That doesn't mean that all human behavior doesn't have a genetic trace, it's all a question of degrees of influence, but that the genes of the blacks play a large part in crime is balderdash.

Professional vs. citizen obligations

So, crime in this country we are visiting, just as in the United States, comes from intense pockets of criminality to be found in the destroyed neighborhoods of the inner-city. Street crime is overwhelmingly intra-racial; it is not inter-racial. On average, the profiles of the criminals and the victim are very similar. In Chicago in the 1970s, for example, 98 per cent of black homicides were committed by other blacks with their ages and social circumstances tending to match. For black males, that mystical country to which we've transported ourselves may not be the land of the free, but it is certainly the home of the brave!

The overwhelming question is this: "Are these racial skewings, in that country, in large part a product of social prejudice, discrimination conscious or unconscious, among the police, the prosecutors, the courts and the correctional agencies of that country, or are they a product of other forces over which those agents of the criminal justice system have little professional control? It's not an unimportant question. Max Weber made the nice distinction between one's obligation professionally and one's obligation as a citizen. If there is substantial racial discriminatory skewing within our system, then the obligations on us as lawyers to do something about it is a very obvious professional duty. If the criminal justice system is less to blame, being merely a barometer of a serious social problem, there may be citizen obligations of high order but they don't happen to be professional obligations.

It's no good going to the legal scholars of this country to answer this question—they don't deal with it, they don't write about it, and they don't discuss it publicly. The first serious legal work on this question seems to me to have been published very recently—on May 19, 1988. The *Harvard Law Review* published a 200-hundred page developments in the law piece in that issue which, if this

topic interests you, you really should read. It's a very well done piece, looking at race in the criminal process. They actually reach rather more extreme conclusions than I will be offering.

Crime reports

So far I have been looking at prison rates in that far country; the ultimate question of discrimination, of course, is whether blacks are imprisoned unfairly in relation to the amount of crime they commit. If you look at the uniform crime reports and the national crime surveys, but particularly the uniform crime reports concerning crimes that are divided into index crimes and other crimes (index crimes are the more serious felonies including homicide, robbery, rape and aggravated assault; others are less serious crimes); the arrest ratio of blacks to whites for index crimes is about 3.6 to 1; for other crimes the ratio is about 2 to 1. But, of course, the prison differential is about 7 to 1. I tried to break those data down into particular crimes and I tried to find a crime in which whites outnumbered blacks proportionately. I thought embezzlement would be right, but it isn't so; I'm afraid the blacks are 2.3 times as frequently arrested as the whites for embezzlement. I couldn't understand that and then I thought about what embezzlement was—it's often a very small purloining of money by a person in a relatively low position of economic trust. The only crime where there was a clear crime report differential adverse to whites was drunk driving, where whites are 1.46 times as likely to be involved in drunk driving as blacks.

There are undoubtedly crimes that whites commit more than blacks, such as insider trading, security fraud, and environmental pollution, but arrest rates don't tell us very much at all about those overwhelmingly white crimes. Many crimes aren't reported to the police and most of those that are reported don't result in arrest. In the inner city, where crimes are highest, a much lower proportion of street crime is reported to the police than is reported in more privileged areas. What we need to know in answer to the question we are addressing is whether there is racial discrimination within the justice system in the differential rates of black and white involvement in crime, as distinct from arrest for crime.

National crime surveys give us some insight into this. There is in every instance some increment of black adversity in the processes that follow commission and arrest for crimes, but nothing like the 7 to 1 differential that is to be found in prison. The starkest prejudice in our system is to be found in the death penalty. Forty-two per cent of the occupants of death row are black and the evidence that racial stereotypes influence the death penalty is powerful. The frequency of exercise of prosecutorial discretion in Georgia adverse to blacks is extraordinary. In matched cases, the prosecutors sought the death penalty in 70 per cent of the cases where there was a black killer and a white victim. The same prosecutor sought it in 15 per cent of the cases when there was a white killer and a black victim, holding constant the gravity of the crime and 200 other matching factors.

To my astonishment, the Supreme Court managed to look at that differential of between 70 per cent and 15 per cent and concluded that it does not rise to the level of being constitutionally objectionable—the McCleskey case is simply a miscarriage of justice, irreconcilable with the rest of the jurisprudence of racial discrimination. It's a scandal and will be seen as such, I'm convinced.

Prejudice in the system

What is one left with? One is left with a situation where some areas seem clear of prejudice within our system and others where the prejudice does not seem to be easily measured, but there is some.

Let me pose four questions arising from this overview of the data and give brief answers to them. Does the criminal justice system discriminate unfairly against blacks at arrest, convictions, and at punishment? Is the death penalty applied unfairly to black killers and yet insufficiently to protect black victims? Do the police disproportionately use deadly force against suspected black felons? If there is injustice in all this, what are the remedies? Justice Harry Blackmun put the point beautifully, and it's an important point: "In order to get beyond racism, we must first take account of race, there is no other way. In order to treat some persons equally, we must treat them differently." Nobody can look responsibly at these data and not agree with that approach.

Well, does the criminal justice system discriminate against blacks in arrest, conviction, and at punishment? The *Harvard Law Review* suggests quite strongly that it does. What I would conclude is that there is a fairly strong case of more vulnerability of the black in relation to the police and

prosecution and in plea bargaining, and at the punishment stage. The studies of Dean Alfred Blumstein of Carnegie-Mellon and of Joan Petersilia of the RAND Corporation conclude that about 80 per cent of the black over-representation in prison can be explained by differential involvement in crime and about 20 per cent by subsequent racially discriminatory processes.

That's probably fair. I think it is as much knowledge as we have. So the answer to the first question is: there appears to be measurable skewing on account of race in the criminal justice system but that skewing is not nearly as dramatic as the figures of differential imprisonment would suggest. That is not at all to say that racial discrimination within the criminal justice system is unimportant; it certainly is important. What is suggested is only that it is relatively less important than other discriminatory pressures.

Now, the second question: is the death penalty applied unfairly to blacks who kill? I won't re-hash the cases and studies on this since I do not think that there is much doubt that the answer to that question is "yes." Why is that important?—after all, capital punishment is largely symbolic. It has no effect on the crime rate generally and it seems to be reasonably well established that it doesn't have much effect on any rates of homicide or attempted homicide, so, why worry? Because it is a centrally important symbol.

Now suppose I am wrong about the death penalty, suppose it is an effective deterrent. Suppose that, as some proponents of that punishment implausibly argue, for every one execution seven or eight lives of potential victims are saved. If that is so, then the *McCleskey* case exhibits something worse than what I've said. If you believe in capital punishment then you must conclude that we are failing to protect black victims—you must, there is no way out of it. So, whatever you believe about capital punishment, whether you approve of it or reject it, the discriminatory effect is profound.

So to question three: Do the police disproportionately use deadly force against black felons? This is an important question because it leads to racial tensions and sometimes to racial riots. Police shoot at about 3,600 people in this country each year. Of these 3,600, about 600 are killed, about 1,200 are wounded and about 1,800 are missed entirely. (Anyone who knows anything about handguns knows that is fairly accurate shooting; the handgun, except at close quarters, is a very inaccurate weapon.)

Police officers in New Orleans are 10 times more likely to kill criminal suspects than police officers in Newark. New Orleans and Newark are both high crime rate areas. The general pattern is typical; Chicago is also fairly typical—70 per cent of the civilians struck by police bullets in the five years that we collected data were black. An additional 20 per cent were white and 10 per cent Hispanic. Philadelphia, Los Angeles, New York have similar figures. The general pattern in most cities where these things have been studied is that minorities being shot by the police are approximately proportional to rates of minorities in street crime, but like earlier figures there is a slight added increment and all you can conclude is the data support what common observation and folk tales make very clear—there is an element of racial prejudice in police shooting at minorities. The *Harvard Law Review* goes much farther than that, but I am content to assert the lesser proposition.

Remedies

Now to the final question. If what I have said about that country we are visiting is true, what are the remedies? First, police can do a lot more to protect the rights of potential victims in a non-discriminatory manner. Some police forces are beginning to do so. The key is to break from the tyranny of the 911-reporting system which disrupts the proper allocation of police resources. Police resources are allocated in the United States by the telephone. There has to be a movement to community-based policing. Black communities have to be mobilized to collaborate with the police. The police have to stop seeing the city's high crime areas as if they were hostile territories. There are people in those areas greatly in need of protection. They can be mobilized and they can be helped. Mini-police stations can be created in inner-city ghettos. It's been demonstrated, it does work. It gives those who have to live there a sense of diminution of fear if not of a diminution of crime.

We need more resourceful police leadership. This hasn't happened much but is happening in a small way. There is a core of younger able administrators coming forward in the police, but there remains a lack of effective leadership in the city police forces. Cities focus on the number of officers in the field and on the budgets, but both are largely irrelevant. They overlook inefficiency and the poor mobilization of resources. There are very many police officers in jobs that could be better done by civilians. We have to change the structure of policing to better protect minorities. There is nothing new in what I've said but the political effort of achieving change when there are no votes in it is challenging.

We have to do better to weed out discrimination in prosecution, plea bargaining and sentencing. The sentencing guideline system has as its greatest virtue the promise of a vehicle which can reduce the current demonstrable adversity to blacks in sentencing.

Changes in the criminal justice system won't do much about the problem of blacks in crime in America. The criminal justice system is a necessary, but limited, system. We've rarely been able to demonstrate any changes in crime rates by making marginal or even relatively substantial changes in policing or in correctional practice. We have got to make these changes because it is the proper thing to do; it's proper to try to diminish unjustified discrimination. But it's not going to make a big difference to the overall crime problem.

Thoughtful scholars now argue that black crime is the symptom, not the disease. The disease, says University of Chicago sociologist William Julius Wilson, the most thoughtful person writing in this field on this problem, is the increasing social isolation of an increasingly concentrated black underclass. University of Chicago political scientist Gary Orfield's study of the schools in Chicago indicates that the problems of the black underclass in the school system of Chicago has grown worse. In family situations today in America, 20 per cent of all children are born to unwed mothers. Unwed mothers account for 15 per cent of all white births, 60 per cent of black births. In Illinois, 64 of each 100 births of black mothers are out of wedlock. I'm not making moralistic propositions, I am speaking of the problems of people being locked in, unable to escape from an inner city underclass. All I've done is underscore an excruciatingly difficult and worsening situation.

To try to sum up, if you look as closely as you can at these data, the bottom line conclusion is: Yes, there is measurable racial discrimination in our police practices, in our prosecutorial practices, in our plea bargaining practices, and in our sentencing, but the bulk of discrimination generating crime lies elsewhere.

I had written a conclusion but a couple of critics I shared these ideas with tell me that I shouldn't say it, since it might be offensive to some. So I have decided not to say it. But, just for your information, the rejected conclusion was: The whole law-and-order movement that we have heard so much about is, in operation though not in intent, anti-black and anti-underclass—not in plan, not in desire, not in intent, but in operation.

NOTE

This article originally appeared in Volume 72, Number 2, August-September 1988, pages 111-113.

Judicial supervision of the guilty plea process: a study of six jurisdictions

Reforms in plea-taking procedures have helped judges ensure a level of fairness. But, because standards remain ambiguous and confusing, many pleas are still coerced and accepted without much assurance of legal guilt.

by William F. McDonald

Judicial supervision of the guilty plea process is regarded by many as a crucial strategy for bringing fairness and legitimacy to the institution of plea bargaining. Numerous nationally recognized groups as well as appellate court decisions have identified the trial judge as the key actor in taming the dragon.[1]

The judge is expected to assure the fairness of the process both to defendants and to the community. For defendants he is to determine that (1) their pleas are "voluntary"—an elusive term which has come to mean not induced by "improper" inducements, such as bribing or physical violence, but not including the inducements normally associated with charge and sentence bargaining (except for inducements involving "overcharging" by prosecutors)[2]; and (2) their pleas are "intelligent"—also an elusive term, meaning that the defendant knows his rights, the nature of the charge to which he is pleading, and the consequences of his plea.

The judge is to establish a record of the plea acceptance as well as the terms of any plea agreement that may have been struck. This procedure has been regarded as not only a protection for defendants by ensuring that they get the deal they thought they had agreed to but also as benefiting the general community by making plea bargaining more visible and efficient (by minimizing appeals on the grounds of broken plea promises).

In addition, the judge is to minimize the possibility of innocent people being convicted by reviewing the evidence and determining that the plea is "accurate," that a "factual basis for the plea" exists—meaning generally that there is reason to believe the defendant committed a crime of equal or greater seriousness than the one to which he is pleading. As for fairness to the community, the judge is expected to check the plea bargaining practices of prosecutors and reject plea agreements that are not appropriate to the total circumstances of the case, including such things as the rehabilitative needs of the defendant, the appearance of justice, and the normal sentencing practices that would apply to similarly situated defendants. The judge is to reject overly lenient and overly severe plea bargains alike.

This article describes the development of standards relating to the judge's supervisory role in the process and describes how that role is performed in six jurisdictions. The analysis is based on interviews with judges and others, plus in-court observations of guilty plea acceptances in a total of 711 felony and misdemeanor cases before 46 felony and misdemeanor courts between July 7, 1977, and August 31, 1977.[3] The majority of observations (72 per cent) were of felony courts.[4] The majority of cases involved pleas to felony charges (70.8 per cent); and in most cases (75.4 per cent) counsel was present.

Plea acceptance standards

As recently as the early 1960s the process of entering a plea of guilty in court was usually brief. The court would ask a few questions, and defendants, often without the advice of counsel, gave one-word answers leading to their convictions—even of serious crimes. The only formal requirement governing the court in accepting guilty pleas in most jurisdictions was that it determine that the plea be voluntarily entered by a competent defendant.[5] Many defendants pleaded guilty after negotiating deals with either the judge, the prosecutor, or the police. But this fact was usually not elicited, much less regarded as having rendered the plea involuntary. On the contrary, such defendants were required to engage in the "pious fraud"[6] of denying for the record that any promises, threats, or inducements had influenced their pleas.

The brevity of the plea acceptance process belied the seriousness of its consequences, a point stressed by the United States Supreme Court:

A plea of guilty differs in purpose and effect from a mere admission or an extra-judicial confession; it is itself a conviction. Like a verdict of a jury it is conclusive. More is not required; the court has nothing to do but give judgment and sentence.[7]

Within a few years the consequences had become even more grave because the plea operated as a waiver of precious constitutional rights newly made applicable to the states, including: the Fifth Amendment privilege against self-incrimination; the Sixth Amendment right to confront one's accusers; and the Sixth Amendment right to a trial by jury.[8]

By the mid-1960s, reforms were underway. In 1966, Rule 11 of the Federal Rules of Criminal Procedure was amended. Now the court would have to personally address the defendant in making its determination that the plea was voluntarily and knowingly made. Also, the court must satisfy itself that there is a factual basis for the plea.[9]

In 1967, the President's Crime Commission[10] recommended that plea agreements should be fully stated for the record and in serious cases reduced to writing and probed by the judge. Also, the judge's guilty plea acceptance decision should be simultaneous with his sentencing decision.

The American Bar Association's 1968 *Standards Relating to Pleas of Guilty* added more requirements that further specified the existing general requirements.[11] The ABA also recommended that the judge satisfy himself that a factual basis for the plea exists, a record be made of the proceedings, and that a defendant not be called upon to plead until he had had aid of counsel and time for deliberation. In addition, the National Advisory Commis-

sion on Criminal Justice Standards and Goals, the American Law Institute, and the National Conference of Commissioners on Uniform State Laws recommended standards for plea acceptance.[12] Each set of standards varies from the other in a few particulars,[13] but they agree on the need for a substantial judicial role in supervising the guilty plea process and the main dimensions along which that role should be performed.

Judicial supervision

Despite reforms, the judge's role in supervising the guilty plea process remains fluid and uncertain. This is for several reasons. The standards are inherently ambiguous,[14] frequently confused with each other by appellate courts,[15] and subject to differing views as to how far the judge should be required to go in fulfilling them.[16] Moreover, although the federal courts developed a set of procedures governing the acceptance of pleas in federal courts,[17] no specific set of procedures has been constitutionally imposed upon the states.[18] The states are only constitutionally obligated to assure that whatever procedures they use satisfy due process. This has meant that state courts may not accept guilty pleas unless defendants enter them knowingly and voluntarily.

Clearly, the minimal plea-taking procedures of former times will no longer meet constitutional muster. The U.S. Supreme Court ruled in *Boykin v. Alabama* that state courts must establish a record sufficient to establish that the defendant is knowingly and voluntarily pleading and that he knows he is relinquishing his constitutional rights, including his privilege against compulsory self-incrimination, his right to trial by jury, and his right to confront his accusers.[19] The courts must assure that the defendant receives adequate notice of the nature of the charge(s) to which he is pleading guilty, meaning that not every element but at least "critical" elements of the charge(s) be explained to the defendant by someone (either the court or defense counsel).[20] The states thus remain free to use different and less stringent procedures for accepting guilty pleas than those required in the federal courts. The variation this has permitted is illustrated by the six states included in this study.

Two states (Arizona and Washington) have revised their rules of criminal procedure, modeling them after many of the provisions of the ABA's standards and the then-anticipated 1975 revisions

Table 1   Setting and nature of guilty plea acceptance by jurisdiction (June-August 1977)

	El Paso (N=106)	New Orleans (N=120)	Seattle (N=138)	Tucson (N=110)	Delaware Co. (N=131)	Norfolk (N=106)	Total* (N=711)**
Setting of proceeding							
Defendant(s) were:							
In group, *without* individualized follow-up	2.9%	0.0%	0.0%	25.5%	0.0%	7.5%	5.5%
In group, *with* individualized follow-up	55.8	1.7	2.9	19.1	4.6	5.7	13.7
Individually addressed	43.3	86.7	97.1	52.7	95.4	85.8	78.2
Other	0.0	11.7	0.0	2.7	0.0	0.9	2.5
Nature of judicial inquiry							
Oral/individualized	77.1	0.0	14.5	91.8	0.8	23.6	31.1
Oral/standardized	1.9	5.0	62.3	5.5	6.1	34.9	20.5
Written inquiry *not* read aloud, signed by defendant	0.0	0.8	18.1	0.0	19.8	0.0	7.3
Oral/plus written inquiry signed by defendant	0.0	89.1	0.7	2.7	71.7	18.9	31.6
No inquiry	21.0	5.0	4.3	0.0	1.5	41.5	11.3

*Percentages that do not total to 100 are due to rounding.
**The sizes of the respective Ns vary slightly due to item non-response.

of FRCP Rule 11. Both states published lengthy forms for recording the terms of plea agreements and to serve as checklists for determining that pleas are knowing, voluntary, and accurate, as required by the U.S. Constitution and their respective state case law.[21] In Washington, judges are required to use special forms.[22] Texas has a somewhat less extensive and different set of required procedures. Similarly, Virginia has even less extensive required guidelines plus a recommended list of questions to guide the judicial inquiry. Pennsylvania's required procedure is minimal, but detailed guidelines are recommended in dicta in a leading case. Louisiana has minimal required guidelines. However, the judges in New Orleans have individually established their own procedures (which vary in certain important respects but generally incorporate many of the guidelines used elsewhere).

How the laws of six states regarding plea taking operate in action and whether they provide the kind of safeguard against defects and abuses of plea bargaining envisioned by their advocates is examined below. The analysis is divided into five parts: the quality of the plea acceptance process; the knowing standard; the voluntary standard; the accuracy standard (factual basis); and the effectiveness of the procedures.

Quality of the process

One of the limits of legally prescribed inquiries is that their purpose can be defeated by the manner in which they are conducted. The most carefully worded, required inquiry can be made into an unintelligible rattle of words when read off like a tobacco auctioneer—as was observed in some courts. Similarly, as Mileski concludes, if defendants are advised of their rights *en masse* rather than individually, they are less likely to comprehend either the meaning or gravity of the advice.[23] Moreover, it is believed by several standard-setting groups that the effectiveness of the warnings and explanations given in the plea acceptance process depends in part on who gives them to whom. It is believed that the most effective procedure is to have the judge personally address the defendant.[24] But, of course, there is a trade-off here. The more painstaking the inquiry, the more time-consuming and the less efficient the guilty plea process becomes. In one place this has led to a search for ways around the new safeguards.[25]

Individualization of the inquiry. Several items in our structured observation of the plea-taking process are related to the quality of the process. As indicated in Table 1, the majority (78 per cent) of guilty pleas (including both felony and misdemeanor charges; and felony and misdemeanor courts) are taken from defendants who are addressed on an individual basis and have the litany of advice and explanations recited to them either in a rote, standardized fashion (20 per cent) or a more individualized fashion (29 per cent); or who, in addition to an individualized inquiry, also have signed a corresponding list of rights, warnings, and understandings (26 per cent); or some combination of the above. Few defendants (11 per cent) have their pleas accepted without any judicial inquiry being made and most of these are in misdemeanor cases (not shown).

Length of the inquiry (by type of charge). One important but not unambiguous indication of the

Table 2   Length of time of plea-taking process by jurisdiction (June-August 1977)

Time for accepting guilty pleas	El Paso (N=106)	New Orleans (N=120)	Seattle (N=138)	Tucson (N=110)	Delaware Co. (N=131)	Norfolk (N=106)	Total* (N=711)**
By type of charge							
Completed within 5 minutes							
Felony	12.5%	77.6%	83.0%	21.7%	1.3%	24.0%	41.6%
Misdemeanor	93.9	84.9	100.0	65.8	3.8	90.3	72.8
All cases	75.4	80.0	87.7	38.2	2.3	43.4	54.7
Completed within 10 minutes							
Felony	25.0	100.0	96.0	71.0	20.5	50.7	65.9
Misdemeanor	96.3	100.0	100.0	95.1	32.1	93.7	85.9
All cases	80.0	100.0	97.1	80.1	25.1	66.2	74.2
Average (mean) time for all cases in minutes (m)							
Felony	17.2m	4.3m	4.2m	10.6m	18.2m	11.0m	9.9m
Misdemeanor	3.4m	3.7m	1.7m	4.9m	14.0m	2.2m	5.2m
All cases	5.9m	4.1m	3.5m	8.5m	16.7m	8.4m	7.8m
By type of court							
Average (mean) time in minutes (m)							
Felony	8.7m	4.3m	4.1m	8.3m	16.7m	8.8m	8.9m
Misdemeanor	3.3m	2.7m	1.7m	3.0m	NA	1.5m	2.6m

*Percentages that do not total to 100 are due to rounding.
**The sizes of the respective Ns vary slightly due to item non-response.

overall quality of the plea-taking process is the length of time it takes. In general, the longer the plea-taking session, the more likely it is to be thorough, individualized, and to accomplish its multiple purposes. But this is not necessarily the case, as the appellate courts themselves have recognized. They allow the scope of the inquiry to vary according to the circumstances of the case. The seriousness of the offense, the defendant's answers, the presence of defense counsel and other factors are supposed to determine the length to which the trial judge goes in supervising the plea.[26] Notwithstanding this imporant qualification, it is still useful to examine the length of time plea acceptances take. This is especially instructive in cross-jurisdictional comparisons. Assuming the mix of cases in the samples is similar, major differences in length of time between jurisdictions cannot be accounted for in terms of the differing needs of individual cases.

The average time for plea acceptance for all crimes (felony and misdemeanor cases combined) in all six jurisdictions is 7.8 minutes (Table 2). The time of accepting pleas to felony charges (9.9 minutes) is almost twice that taken for misdemeanor pleas (5.2 minutes). Most interesting but not easily explicable is the significant difference among the jurisdictions in the length of the plea-taking procedures. Why felony pleas should take four times as long in Delaware County compared to Seattle or New Orleans is unclear. It does not appear to be due to differences in legal requirements. (Seattle has the more extensive list of man-

datory inquiries.) Nor is it apparently due to the efficiency of using prepared lists of inquiries. (The Delaware County judges all use such a list.) No convincing explanation emerges.

With regard to the difference between felonies and misdemeanors, it is clear that in each jurisdiction considerably less time is devoted to supervising pleas to misdemeanors than pleas to felonies. This is not unexpected, given that appellate courts have permitted the scope of the inquiry to be less extensive in less serious crimes. However, those courts have also held that the requirements of *Boykin* apply to misdemeanors as well as to felonies,[27] and they do require judges to widen the scope of the inquiry when defendants are not represented by counsel.[28] Therefore, one would expect some minimal level of judicial inquiry in every misdemeanor plea and a greater level in cases of unrepresented defendants. The differences among the six jurisdictions in the length of plea-taking to misdemeanor charges are not as great as those for felony charges. Most of them average two to five minutes.[29]

Notwithstanding this general similarity, there remains a noteworthy difference. The longest average misdemeanor plea-taking (4.9 minutes in Tucson)[30] is more than twice as long as the shortest (1.7 minutes in Seattle). What accounts for this difference is not clear, but one possible explanation can be discounted—it is not due to differences in the presence of counsel. In New Orleans, where misdemeanors were typically disposed of within 3.7 minutes, all defendants had counsel, whereas in El Paso none of the defendants (pleading to misdemeanors) had counsel yet the pleas took about the same time (3.4 minutes).

Length of the inquiry (misdemeanor courts). The discussion above focused on the difference in plea acceptance between pleas to felony and misdemeanor *charges*. The discussion below focuses on the difference between felony and misdemeanor *courts*. Studies have suggested that the quality of justice is more a function of the level of the court than the level of the charge.[31]

It can be seen that plea acceptances in felony courts average more than three times as long as in misdemeanor courts (Table 2). The two fastest lower courts (Norfolk at 1.5 minutes and Seattle at 1.7 minutes) are worth an additional note because their contrasting practices illustrate an important point. Plea-taking can be swift and yet still have a baseline of consistent warnings and checks built into it. In Seattle, the district courts use a standard, "Statement of Defendant On Pleading Guilty" form modeled after the one used in the superior courts. In contrast, in the Norfolk District Court, defendants are regularly encouraged to waive all rights (including the right to an attorney) and to plead guilty as charged without any inquiry into the plea.[32]

The knowing/intelligent standard

The knowing/intelligent plea standard has three dimensions to it: the waiver of rights, notification of the charges, and notification of the consequences of the plea. In all six jurisdictions the courts are required by virtue of *Boykin* to establish an adequate record showing that the defendant knowingly waived his privilege against self-incrimination, the right to a trial by jury, and the right to confront his accusers.[33] One one of the six jurisdictions (Texas) requires the waiver of anything more than the three rights enumerated in *Boykin*; it requires the defendant be notified of his right to be sentenced by a jury.[34]

Waiver of rights. In 45 per cent of all cases (different types of charges and courts combined) three or more rights were *verbally* mentioned by someone to the defendant (Table 3). The right which is most often mentioned *verbally* in court is the right to trial by jury (70 per cent of all cases). Least frequently mentioned of the three rights which constitutionally must be waived is the right to remain silent (37.9 per cent).

Remember, our data are based on what was *said* in court. Defendants may have been notified of more of their rights than it appears from our in-court observation data. It should also be noted that the use of written forms does not guarantee that all three of the rights which constitutionally must be waived will in fact be covered. The form used in Washington does not mention the privilege against self-incrimination. This omission is rarely remedied by the Seattle courts.

As for who recites the rights, it is clear that in all jurisdictions except Delaware County the judge is more likely to conduct the recitation, if there is one. In 59 per cent of the cases the judge asked the defendant if he understood the right he was waiving. In 56.3 per cent of the cases it was noted for the record that defense counsel had explained to the client the rights being waived.

Explaining the charges. With regard to explaining the charges to the defendant, the issue that has been raised in the appellate courts is how detailed an explanation must be given.[35] Is a mere notification of the charges enough or must the elements of the crime be explained?

The Supreme Court has specifically declined to require a complete enumeration of the elements of the offense to which an accused person pleads. Rather, in *Henderson v. Morgan*,[36] it adopted a "totality of the circumstances" test that permits each case to be judged differently. It also stated its perception as to what typically happens regarding the explanation of charges as follows:

Normally the record contains either an explanation of the charge by the trial judge or at least a representation by defense counsel that the nature of the offense has been explained to the accused. Moreover, even without such an express representation, it may be appropriate to presume that in most cases defense counsel routinely explain the nature of the offense in sufficient detail to give the accused notice of what he is being asked to admit.

We were unable to determine how often defense counsel explain charges to their clients, but our observations provide a more specific and less reassuring view of what "normally" happens regarding the explanation of charges in court. In 31 per cent of all cases (26 per cent of the pleas to felonies) no one in court explained or even read aloud the charges to the defendant. In 41 per cent of all cases, no one asked the accused if he understood the charges to which he was pleading; and in 66 per

Table 3   Methods of establishing the knowing/intelligent nature of guilty pleas by jurisdiction (June–August 1977)

Method/type of charge	El Paso (N=106)	New Orleans (N=120)	Seattle (N=138)	Tucson (N=110)	Delaware Co. (N=131)	Norfolk (N=106)	Total* (N=711)**
Waiver of rights							
One or more rights mentioned as waived?							
Yes	68.2%	95.8%	46.0%	98.2%	87.8%	67.9%	76.8%
Three or more rights?							
Yes	15.1	55.0	29.7	85.5	64.1	16.0	44.7
Five or more rights?							
Yes	0.0	24.2	8.0	0.0	51.1	0.0	15.0
Which rights were verbally specified as being waived?							
Trial by jury	67.9	94.2	46.7	97.3	67.2	56.6	70.0
Remain silent	12.3	0.0	7.2	0.9	0.0	0.0	37.9
Confront witnesses	15.1	50.0	33.3	80.9	64.2	8.6	44.4
Appeal	0.0	81.8	37.0	0.0	78.6	60.9	43.0
Counsel (at no cost)	10.4	0.8	1.4	40.0	68.0	1.3	22.4
Who recited rights waived?							
Judge	22.9	94.1	30.4	98.2	8.5	66.0	51.9
Defense counsel	0.0	0.0	12.3	0.9	73.6	0.0	16.0
None	30.5	5.9	53.6	0.9	14.7	32.1	23.6
Other	46.6	0.0	3.6	0.0	3.1	1.9	8.6
Who asked defendant if he understood rights he was waiving?							
Judge	19.0	96.7	56.5	91.8	24.8	65.1	58.8
Defense counsel	0.0	0.0	0.0	0.9	45.7	0.0	8.5
None	47.6	3.3	42.0	7.3	25.6	33.0	26.6
Other	33.3	0.0	1.4	0.0	3.9	0.9	6.1
Was it noted that defense counsel had explained the defendant's rights to him?							
Yes	8.6	95.0	56.9	18.2	91.5	54.9	56.3
Explaining the charges							
Who explained charges?							
No one							
Felony charge	4.3	59.1	40.0	15.9	3.8	18.7	26.1
Misdemeanor charge	2.4	75.5	68.4	63.4	1.9	45.2	36.6
All cases	2.9	66.4	47.8	33.6	3.1	26.4	30.6
Who asked if defendant understood the charges?							
No one	56.2	19.3	51.1	34.5	46.2	36.8	40.9
Was it noted that counsel had explained charges to defendant?							
Yes	10.5	93.3	18.7	9.1	19.8	55.8	34.4
Explaining the consequences							
Defendant notified of the maximum possible sentence?							
Yes	35.8	75.8	56.6	80.0	6.1	39.1	48.5

*Percentages that do not total to 100 are due to rounding.
**The sizes of the respective Ns vary slightly due to item non-response.

cent of all cases no mention was made as to whether counsel explained the charges to his client. Once again there are wide differences among the jurisdictions in each of these respects.[37]

It is worth noting the difference between what was done in explaining the *charges* compared to how the *rights* were explained. With regard to charges, it was noted for the record that counsel had explained the charges in only 34 per cent of all cases. Yet for the rights, this notation was more likely to be made both for all jurisdictions combined (56 per cent) as well as within each separate jurisdiction. This suggests that greater care is taken in assuring the explanation of rights than of charges. Perhaps this reflects the difference between *Boykin's* requirement that specific rights be enumerated

and the more vague, open-ended requirements of the "totality of the circumstances" test of *Henderson v. Morgan.*

Explaining the consequences. The last component of the knowing/intelligent plea standard is the determination of whether the defendant understands the consequences of his plea. Again, the appellate courts have not made it clear what consequences must be explained.[38] In three of the jurisdictions studied, the defendant must be advised of one or another aspect of the possible sentence he could receive.[39] In the other three states there is either no rule (Virginia), or it is recommended that the defendant be advised of the range of possible sentence, but it is not absolutely required that the defendant be notified of the maximum

Table 4   Methods of establishing the voluntary nature of the plea and the existence of a plea agreement by jurisdiction (June-August 1977)

Method	El Paso (N=106)	New Orleans (N=120)	Seattle (N=138)	Tucson (N=110)	Delaware Co. (N=131)	Norfolk (N=106)	Total* (N=711)**
Who asked if defendant was threatened, coerced or pressured to plead guilty?							
No one	78.6%	6.7%	67.4%	22.7%	42.7%	50.0%	44.7%
Who asked if promises other than plea agreement were made?							
No one	80.2	82.5	73.2	26.4	53.4	91.5	67.7
If other plea agreement reached, what record made?							
Only that an agreement (unspecified) had been reached	0.0	5.8	0.7	0.0	3.8	3.8	2.5
Specific terms of agreement	0.0	43.3	98.6	100.0	96.2	53.8	71.4
No record made	0.0	50.0	0.0	0.0	0.0	0.0	10.3
Unknown if agreement reached	86.8	0.8	0.7	0.0	0.0	2.8	9.5
Other	13.3	0.0	0.0	0.0	0.0	31.1	5.1

*Percentages that do not total to 100 are due to rounding.
**The sizes of the respective Ns vary slightly due to item non-response.

sentence (Pennsylvania);[40] or, it is assumed that defense counsel will advise the defendant of the consequences and therefore the court must do so only in cases of uncounselled defendants.[41]

Notwithstanding these differences in legal requirements, the forms and procedures used by the felony courts in the six jurisdictions all include some specification of the possible sentence—usually the maximum possible. In addition, in 48 per cent of all cases, defendants were advised in court of the maximum possible sentence. But defendants were rarely (2 per cent) told about the possibility of being sentenced as a habitual offender and rarely (4 per cent) told of any collateral consequences of the plea (not shown in Table 3).

The voluntary standard

The concept of voluntariness is exceedingly ambiguous. In defining it as a standard in plea-taking, the courts often confuse it with what would be more accurately classified as the knowing standard. Thus, for example, in Arizona if a defendant has been advised of his rights and the consequences of his plea and states that he still wishes to plead guilty, then it is presumed he is pleading voluntarily. Hence, to the extent that voluntariness is established by a showing that the plea was knowing/intelligent, our findings presented above regarding the knowing standard are applicable as well to the voluntary standard.

Beyond this, there is the matter of whether pleas are involuntary in the sense of being the result of threats, pressures, or promises. The confusion here is that many kinds of pressures, threats, and promises—some with severe consequences—are a regular part of the plea bargaining system and are *not* regarded by the courts as *per se* grounds for declaring pleas involuntary. A prosecutor's promise to dismiss charges and recommend a sentence in exchange for a guilty plea does not make the plea involuntary;[42] nor are pleas presumed to be involuntary even if they are induced by the hope of avoiding the use of a coerced confession;[43] nor because the prosecutor threatened to invoke a habitual offender statute.[44] Rather the courts have adopted a "totality of the circumstances" rule which requires each case to be examined individually. This, of course, leaves the situation without clear guidance. In the six jurisdictions, trial judges are given no further guidance by their respective state laws (excluding the required questions related primarily to whether the plea was knowingly entered).

In the absence of specific direction, judges sometimes include one or more questions in their plea-taking procedures. In 55 per cent of all cases observed the defendant was asked (usually by the judge) if he had been threatened, coerced, or pressured to plead guilty (Table 4). This question, of course, can be confusing to the defendant who is pleading in exchange for some promised deal. It is remarkable that it continues to be asked with any frequency. Unless accompanied by other questions it perpetuates the old hypocrisy of denying that the plea of guilty was induced by the plea agreement. The more accurate phraseology would be to ask whether any promises, threats, or pressures *other than* the plea agreement have been made. This was asked in only 32 per cent of all cases. Where plea agreements were reached, the specific terms of the agreement were usually (71 per cent of all cases) read into the record.[45]

The factual basis standard

Ambiguity of meaning and purpose. Three serious institutional weaknesses of plea bargaining compared to trial as a method of determining guilt are: plea bargaining relies on inducements; in plea bargaining the available evidence may not be assessed against any standard of proof, much less the hallowed legal standard of proof beyond a reasonable doubt; and in plea bargaining the available evidence may not be assessed by an independent, impartial third party. For any or all of these reasons, plea bargaining is regarded as posing a threat of convicting the innocent.[46] A fourth weakness of plea bargaining is that it often destroys the integrity of the criminal justice record system by allowing defendants to appear to be convicted of crimes different from the ones they actually committed.

The efficacy of using plea acceptance standards to offset these four weaknesses in the plea bargaining system differs. Eliminating inducements is not possible without eliminating plea bargaining as such. Hence, the courts have allowed inducements to continue and have relied on the standards relating to the knowing and "voluntary" nature of pleas to offset this inherent weakness of plea bargaining. As for the other three weaknesses, reformers have tried to minimize their danger by requiring that a factual basis for pleas be established. Whether this "accuracy" standard represents a safeguard adequate to such a critical task, whether it assures that persons will not be wrongly convicted, and whether it means that evidence will be tested against some standard of proof similar to the trial standards of either a *prima facie* case or proof beyond a reasonable doubt is problematic.

The difficulty with the accuracy standard is its ambiguity both as to meaning and purpose. The evidentiary standards to be used in determining whether a factual basis exists are unclear, the scope of the inquiry and the methods to be used are ill-defined, and the action to be taken by the judge if it appears that a factual basis does not exist is ambiguous.[47]

When the accuracy standard was added to the Federal Rules of Criminal Procedure Rule 11 in

---

Summary of findings

All felony-level judges in the six jurisdictions studied used some form of check list to guide them at plea-taking. But the check lists do not cover all the same issues among the six jurisdictions or even within them (except in two states where standardized plea-taking forms are required) and do not guarantee that even constitutionally required queries will be made.

The average time for accepting pleas for all cases combined is 7.8 minutes. Pleas to felony *charges* take twice as long as pleas to misdemeanor charges (9.9 minutes compared to 5.2 minutes). Pleas in felony *courts* take over three times longer than pleas in misdemeanor courts (8.9 minutes compared to 2.6 minutes).

The six jurisdictions varied dramatically in the time spent in accepting pleas to felony charges (from 4.2 minutes to 18.2 minutes) and less dramatically in misdemeanor cases (from 1.7 minutes to 4.9 minutes—Delaware County excluded). No convincing explanation could be found for the dramatic differences among the jurisdictions in time spent in accepting pleas.

At the time of entering their pleas defendants were usually (78 per cent) addressed individually before the bench and the plea acceptance inquiry consisted of an oral colloquy (84 per cent) sometimes (32 per cent) supplemented by the submission of a written inquiry signed by the defendant.

The defendants were usually told they had a right to a trial by jury (70 per cent) and sometimes told of their rights to confront witnesses (44 per cent); and remain silent (38 per cent). In many cases (56 per cent) it was noted that the defense counsel had explained the defendants' rights to them. In most cases (73 per cent) the defendants were asked if they understood the rights which they had waived.

In most cases (69 per cent) the defendants had the charges explained to them and were usually (59 per cent) asked if they understood the charges. It was sometimes (34 per cent) noted that defense counsel had explained the charges to their clients.

Defendants were not always (48 per cent) told of the maximum possible sentence; rarely (2 per cent) notified that they were eligible for sentencing as

1966, no probability-of-guilt standard was specified, and the 1974 revision also omitted any such standard. The 1968 ABA standards required a factual basis for pleas but gave no probability-of-guilt standard; nor was one given in the 1980 revised ABA standards. However, two other national groups have specified that certain evidentiary standards be met. The American Law Institute recommended that pleas not be accepted unless reasonable cause exists.[48] The National Advisory Commission went further and recommended that a plea not be accepted if the "admissible evidence is insufficient to support a guilty verdict on the offense" for which the plea is offered, or a related greater offense.[49] This is a higher standard than probable (or reasonable) cause because it requires that the proof be established on *admissible* evidence. Thus, hearsay testimony and illegally obtained evidence would be excluded from establishing the factual basis. If this standard were used and if judges were required to reject guilty pleas whose factual basis could not be established, then plea bargaining would have one of its major weaknesses significantly minimized.

In considering evidentiary standards that might be incorporated into the accuracy standard it should be recognized that there is a tension between the "efficiency" of plea bargaining and high evidentiary standards of proof. The reason many cases are plea bargained is precisely that they are weak. The higher one sets the evidentiary standard for acceptable pleas, the more pleas are going to be unacceptable. Higher rates of plea rejections would necessitate other adjustments in the system. Either cases would have to be made stronger or more would have to be rejected at screening, dismissed, or set for trial.

The policy choice is between two broad alternatives. If evidentiary standards are set low, plea bargaining will continue to have high "efficiency" (dispose of large caseloads) but will represent a wide departure from the traditional beyond-a-reasonable-doubt standard of proof. If evidentiary standards are set high, plea bargaining will more closely approximate the trial system. Innocent defendants will be less likely to be wrongly convicted. But then, plea bargaining will no longer be able to serve as the great laundering machine it often is. Shoddy investigation and prosecution practices

---

habitual offenders; and rarely (4 per cent) notified of any collateral consequences of their pleas.

Defendants were usually (65 per cent) asked if any threats or pressures had caused them to plead guilty. Sometimes (32 per cent) they were asked if promises other than the plea agreement had been made. Usually (71 per cent) the specific terms of any plea agreement were entered into the record.

The method for establishing the factual basis which was most frequently reported by judges (40 per cent) as the one they use is simply to ask the defendant if he committed the offense. This same method was found to be most frequently used in actual plea-taking observed (59 per cent). This inquiry was supplemented in many cases by having the prosecutor show or report some evidence (48 per cent) and by asking the defendant additional questions about the crime (36 per cent).

Defendants rarely (2 per cent) entered equivocal pleas in which they pleaded guilty while maintaining their innocence. Half the judges said they would not accept such pleas.

Overall, judges rarely (2 per cent) rejected any

guilty pleas.

Interviews with non-random samples of defendants who had pleaded guilty suggest that most defendants (91 per cent) had been told of the maximum sentence they might have received; and most (80 per cent) said they understood what was said about the nature of the charges and the rights they waived. But 20 per cent indicated they did not understand or only partially understood what was said. Most defendants (77 per cent) said they felt they had to accept the plea agreement.

Half the defendants reported that their attorneys advised them how to answer the questions at plea taking. In several cases the "advice" was to say "yes" to everything.

A few defendants reported that the police had made promises which apparently did not become part of the required written statement of the plea agreement and were not fulfilled.

—William F. McDonald

Table 5   Methods judges report they use to establish factual bases for guilty pleas by jurisdiction (June-August 1977)

Methods	El Paso (N=9)	New Orleans (N=11)	Seattle (N=23)	Tucson (N=28)	Delaware Co. (N=9)	Norfolk (N=8)	Total (N=88)
Asks defendant if he committed the offense.							
Yes	33%	82%	22%	50%	67%	13%	40%
Asks additional questions about offense.							
Yes	33	0	22	36	0	0	20
Requires DA to produce evidence.							
Yes	33	9	9	21	0	38	17
Requires DA to produce one witness.							
Yes	0	0	4	4	22	25	7
Other							
Yes	0	9	43	0	11	25	15

will no longer come out in the wash. They will either have to be improved or more cases will have to be rejected or dismissed.

Adding to the confusion as to what shall be regarded as an "accurate" plea are the views of appellate courts concerning several common practices which are deemed beneficial to defendants and, hence, not necessarily in their interest to prohibit. Some pleas are to offenses that were not actually committed but which carry lesser sentences (e.g., pleas to daytime rather than nighttime burglary). Some pleas are to offenses which are either not proven by the facts or do not even exist. Sometimes defendants plead guilty but maintain that they are innocent and are only pleading because it is in their best interest to do so. For each of these situations some appellate courts have ruled that the pleas entered were acceptable.[50] Thus, the meaning and purpose of the accuracy standard has been clouded.

One court clarified the standard as follows: "the purpose of the factual basis requirement is to ensure accuracy of the plea, that is, to ensure that the defendant is guilty of a crime at least as serious as that to which he is entering his plea."[51] Thus the "accuracy" standard is not to ensure "accuracy" in the literal sense. It is not to guarantee the integrity of criminal justice records but rather to safeguard against convicting completely innocent persons and against convicting guilty persons of crimes more serious than the ones they actually committed.

Then, there is the question of how a factual basis should be established. Again there is a trade-off between efficiency and protection against false conviction. Plea bargaining can be made to approximate more closely a trial disposition by requiring that evidence and witnesses be produced in court and testimony be taken as to what could be proven if the case went to trial. This might seem to provide courts with a better opportunity to assess case strength (although, as reported below, it does not). But, it would obviously be less efficient.

The legal standard in six jurisdictions. Unlike the knowing and voluntary standards, the accuracy standard was not explicitly imposed upon the states by *Boykin.* Previous studies have reported that very few state court judges inquire into the factual basis for pleas[52] and that only a few states require detailed inquiries into the factual basis for pleas.[53] However, of the six states included in this study three (Texas, Arizona, and Pennsylvania)[54] require a factual basis for pleas.[55]

None of the six states studied has used the factual basis standard to approximate the kind of testing of the evidence that occurs at trial. None has adopted the high evidentiary standard recommended by the NAC, nor for that matter have they even addressed the question of evidentiary standards in familiar legal phrases such as "probable cause" or a *prima facie* case. Rather, they have spoken in the ambiguous and undefined language of "sufficient evidence"[56] or evidence which "negates guilt."[57]

Remarkably, Virginia had what appeared to reformers to be "the greatest protection to defendants pleading guilty."[58] It required a trial by a constitutional provision[59] which was self-executing and could not be waived by the accused. Thus, Virginia's plea bargaining system seemed to closely resemble the trial process in that pleas could not be accepted without sufficient evidence of guilt being presented to a judge. In practice this provision was followed literally by local justice officials. When felony pleas were taken, a witness (usually the principal police officer in the case) would give sworn testimony as to what the state would have

Table 6   Methods of establishing the factual bases for guilty pleas by jurisdiction (June-August 1977)

Method	El Paso (N=106)	New Orleans (N=120)	Seattle (N=138)	Tucson (N=110)	Delaware Co. (N=131)	Norfolk (N=106)	Total* (N=711)**
Who asked if defendant pleading guilty because he was in fact guilty?							
Judge	41.3%	72.5%	47.1%	70.9%	26.9%	53.8%	51.6%
Defense counsel	0.0	0.0	2.2	0.0	28.5	0.0	5.6
Judge & defense counsel	0.0	0.0	0.0	0.0	10.0	0.0	1.8
No one	58.7	27.5	50.7	29.1	34.6	46.2	41.0
Who asked additional questions establishing a factual basis for the plea?							
Judge	42.9	5.8	14.6	75.5	44.5	9.4	31.4
Defense counsel alone or with judge	0.0	0.0	0.0	0.0	2.4	0.0	0.4
Judge & court clerk	33.3	0.0	0.0	0.0	0.0	0.0	5.0
No one	23.6	94.2	85.4	24.5	53.1	90.6	63.6
Did the prosecutor show or report some evidence?							
Yes	100.0	19.2	7.2	5.5	96.2	66.0	48.0
Did the state have available at least one witness (sworn or unsworn)?							
Yes	0.0	2.5	0.0	0.0	13.8	66.0	12.8
Did defendant maintain innocence?							
Yes	0.9	2.5	5.8	0.9	0.8	0.0	2.0

*Percentages that do not total to 100 are due to rounding.
**The sizes of the respective Ns vary slightly due to item non-response.

proven. However, in 1976 the Virginia Supreme Court transformed this provision from one of the nation's strongest to one of the weakest requirements for a factual basis.[60]

The practice in six jurisdictions. The ways in which the factual basis for pleas are established in the six jurisdictions were determined both through interviews and observations. The interviews with judges indicate that no one method is used by a majority of the judges and substantial variations exist both between and within jurisdictions (see Table 5).

The most common method judges (40 per cent) said they use is simply to ask the defendant if he committed the offense. In jurisdictions with plea-taking forms with a place for statements by the defendants, some judges said they have the defendant read the statement and tell whether it is true. This is preferred to having the defendant state the facts orally because it avoids the possibility of a discrepancy between the written and the oral statements. Such discrepancies require additional time to resolve and can necessitate rejecting the plea or can lead to reversal on appeal. Other methods used by judges include asking additional questions about the offense (such as what the defendant was thinking), and requiring the state to show some evidence (e.g., the drug analysis) or to produce one witness. But none of these were used by substantial numbers of judges.

Our in-court observations generally parallel the interview findings (Table 6). The most common method used (59 per cent) was that someone (usually the judge) asked the defendant if he were pleading guilty because he was in fact guilty. But, again, there is considerable variation among the jurisdictions. Additionally, in 48 per cent of the cases the prosecutor either showed or reported evidence. The variation among the jurisdictions here is interesting. In Texas and Pennsylvania, which require both a factual basis and that some evidence be introduced, the rates of introducing evidence are highest. In Arizona, which requires a factual basis but allows it to be established by any part of the record, the rate is lowest. In Virginia, where the formerly high factual basis standard has been emasculated, the former practice of entering some evidence and even having a state witness available continues to operate.

Equivocal (*Alford*) pleas. What it came to the matter of "equivocal" pleas (i.e., defendants pleading guilty but continuing to assert their innocence), judges were evenly split. Although such pleas are constitutionally acceptable,[61] only half the judges said they permit them in their courts—although this position varied among jurisdictions (El Paso, 0 per cent; New Orleans, 100 per cent; Seattle, 78 per cent; Tucson, 44 per cent; Delaware County, 9 per cent; Norfolk, 83 per cent). Judges who refused to accept *Alford* pleas said they distrusted them and worried about the lack of finality. Most of them would agree with the view of the Pennsylvania court which wrote: "Defendant should not be permitted to plead guilty from one side of his mouth and not

Table 7   The knowing and voluntary standards from the defendant's perspective, by jurisdiction (June-August 1977)*

Standard/query	Texas	New Orleans	Tucson	Delaware Co.	Virginia	Total
The knowing standard						
"When you actually pleaded guilty in court did you understand the questions you were asked about the nature of your plea and the rights you gave up?"						
Yes	62%	71%	75%	100%	91%	80%
Not sure; understood somewhat	0	29	10	0	0	7
No	38	0	15	0	9	13
(N)	(8)	(7)	(20)	(9)	(11)	(55)
Did your attorney advise you how to answer these questions?						
Yes	33	57	70	29	45	52
(N)	(9)	(7)	(20)	(7)	(11)	(54)
Did anyone tell you the maximum you could have been sentenced to?						
Yes	67	100	95	89	100	91
(N)	(9)	(9)	(20)	(9)	(11)	(58)
Did the judge tell you the maximum sentence?						
Yes	0	**	26	89	70	45
(N)	(6)		(19)	(9)	(10)	(44)
Did your attorney tell you the maximum sentence?						
Yes	83	**	74	89	80	79
(N)	(6)		(19)	(9)	(10)	(44)
The voluntary standard						
Did you feel you had to accept the plea bargain?						
Yes	**	0	78	89	82	77
No	**	100	22	11	12	23
(N)		(2)	(18)	(9)	(11)	(40)

*Interviews were not done at all in Seattle. Interviews were not done in the local jails at El Paso and Norfolk but rather in state facilities; and most of the defendants interviewed were not from El Paso and Norfolk.
**Data not available.

guilty from the other."[62] Our in-court observations indicate that defendants rarely (2 per cent) maintain their innocence—although again there are substantial differences among the jurisdictions in this respect.

Effectiveness of procedures

Measuring the effectiveness of the plea acceptance procedures cannot be done in any simple, unequivocal way. Given the ambiguity of the standards, the differing purposes behind them and the difficulty of getting valid measures of what defendants actually perceived and believed when they were entering their pleas, it is impossible to obtain anything more than partial and indirect measures.

Plea rejection rates. One indicator that might be assumed to measure effectiveness is the rate at which pleas are rejected. After all, it is through the power to reject pleas that the judge ultimately controls the plea process. If judges were to use that power as the most progressive reformers would have them use it, they would reject pleas whenever the prosecution had "overcharged" or had given away too much or too little, or when other community interests were not properly served by the disposition. Given the frequency with which "overcharg-

ing" and inappropriate plea bargains are alleged to occur, one would anticipate a high rate of rejection from judges who were following such a progressive course. But even if judges were adhering to the minimum requirements imposed by law one might still expect a substantial rate of plea rejection—assuming that there must be many defendants who either are not able to make a knowing plea, or who have been coerced by improper threats or promises, or for whom there is no adequate factual basis.

In any case, it is initially surprising to find that the actual plea rejection rate was as low as 2 per cent overall for all six jurisdictions with a range of from 0 per cent in Norfolk to 5 per cent in Delaware County. However, this finding cannot be taken to mean that judicial supervision of the plea process has failed.

Rejection rates are ambiguous when used either as absolute or comparative measures of the effectiveness of the plea-taking process. Using the rejection rate as a comparative measure, the lack of substantial differences among the six jurisdictions on this measure suggests that the differences in law and practice among them make little difference in the bottom-line of plea-taking, namely, whether the plea is found acceptable. But, on the other hand, it could be argued that differences in the quality of the plea-taking practices do make a difference. The fact that the highest rate of rejection occurred in the jurisdiction with the longest average time for taking pleas (Delaware County) suggests that differences in the "quality" of the procedures (at least, as indicated by length of time consumed) do indeed make a difference in the probability of plea acceptance. Although both interpretations are supportable, we believe the latter is the more plausible.

As an absolute measure, the 2 per cent rejection rate suggests that the tightening of the plea-taking procedures over the last two decades has not met certain goals of some of the reformers. The new plea-taking procedures have not inserted into the guilty plea process a test of evidentiary strength approximating what would occur at trial. The 2 per cent plea rejection rate does not begin to compare with the 22 per cent acquittal rate at bench trials in our sample of robbery and burglary cases from our six jurisdictions or the 16 per cent to 48 per cent acquittal rates at bench trials for all felonies in the four jurisdictions studied by Brosi.[65] Also, those who had hoped judicial supervision would constitute a check on "overcharging" by prosecution must conclude that it has failed in this regard as well. In five of our six jurisdictions there were still complaints about "overcharging." In those five jurisdictions, charge reductions were involved in from 44 per cent to 98 per cent of our sample of 3,383 robbery and burglary cases.

As for whether the community's interest in proper sentencing is being safeguarded, the meaning of the 2 per cent rejection rate is less clear. It suggests that at least in the minds of the judges that interest is being protected. The majority of judges told us they would reject pleas that they thought were inappropriate. But it is difficult to see how some judges make this determination because they do not use presentence reports or take other steps to independently check the appropriateness of the sentence recommended by the prosecutor.

As for the knowing and voluntary criteria of plea acceptability, the 2 per cent rejection rate unequivocally means that as far as the judges are concerned virtually all pleas meet these criteria. Yet our observations on the constitutionally required waiver of constitutional rights strongly suggested that in the *majority* of cases the knowing

standard is *not* being fully met (see Table 3 and related narrative). Moreover, defendants may not really understand the procedure and may be subject to threats or promises which do not get reported in court. Pleas may be entered which meet the legal requirements but in reality are not knowing or voluntary. In short, the rejection rate only measures whether the procedure was followed, not whether the reality which the procedure was intended to assure in fact occurred.

Finally, any use of rejection rates as an indicator of the effectiveness of plea-taking must recognize the powerful incentive among judges to keep rejection rates very low; substantial numbers of rejections would add to the trial docket. Judges are just as concerned, if not more so, as prosecutors in moving the docket. Such an incentive can cause legal standards to be adjusted in practice so that reality is *found* acceptable rather than being *made* acceptable. Reformers must realize that in asking judges to regulate plea bargaining they are not getting a completely disinterested party. Careful and continual scrutiny by appellate courts of the plea-taking practices of trial courts may be necessary to prevent the pressures of the trial docket from reducing plea-taking procedures into mere legal formalities.

The defendants' perspective. To get at the reality behind the plea-taking procedures, we asked defendants who had pleaded guilty to tell us about their decision to plead—why they did it and what occurred at the plea-taking. The samples are small and non-random, so their responses cannot be generalized to any known population of defendants and must be treated with caution. They can only be regarded as at best suggestive and at worst wildly atypical. They imply that while defendants pleading guilty today get a few extra minutes in court, their pleas are not necessarily knowing, not all the promises made are being fulfilled, factually innocent defendants caught up in cases with circumstantial evidence may be just as likely to be convicted as before, and defendants continue to perceive their decisions to plead as "involuntary" (in the layman's sense).

The majority of the defendants indicated that their pleas were "intelligent" in certain respects. Almost all said they were told by someone—usually their attorney—what the maximum sentence could be (Table 7). Most said they understood the rights they had waived and what the charges were. Several added credibility to their responses by reciting for us parts of the plea-taking litany almost verbatim. These findings, of course, are encouraging. But, a substantial minority indicated they did not understand either some or all of what was said. Their limited understanding as well as the difficulty faced by the courts in achieving real understanding with certain defendants was evident in our interviews. Some defendants were slow or unable to grasp the questions we asked or the significance of the decisions which they had made during plea negotiations.

While pleas today appear to be more likely to be "intelligent," they have not lost their coercive character. The majority of the defendants said they felt they had to accept the plea bargain. None of the defendants who said they felt they had to accept the plea agreement reported inducements which courts would regard as *per se* unlawful, namely threats of physical violence. Almost all pleaded for virtually the same reason, namely, to avoid the possibility of a harsher sentence if they went to trial. Some complained about broken promises by the police.

In the only jurisdiction where we asked the question, two of 10 defendants maintained they were innocent but had pleaded guilty anyhow. Both cases involved fact patterns—as told by the defendants—which make it difficult to know whether the defendants actually committed the crimes or not.

The Achilles heel of plea-taking procedures is the fact that defendants can, on their own or as the result of coaching by their attorneys, answer all questions in a way that will be acceptable to the judge. In effect, the same desire for leniency that leads them to plead guilty can emasculate the effectiveness of the plea-taking procedures as a protection of defendants' interest. The majority of our defendants reported that their attorneys had advised them how to answer the plea-taking colloquy. Several indicated that their attorneys had told them exactly what to say and evidently did so without question.

While there is no way of completely protecting plea colloquies from disingenuous but acceptable answers, there are ways of reducing this vulnerability. Repeating and rephrasing questions; requiring more than simple "yes" or "no" answers; asking defendants to explain what a jury trial is before waiving their right to one; having the prosecutor read the state's version of the crime and then asking the defendants to give their version; and

other ways of going beyond a mere recitation of the plea litany can prevent today's plea-taking procedure from being an empty legal ritual. On the other hand, the use of plea-acceptance forms with minimal additional questioning of the defendant; establishing the factual basis in ways designed to minimize the possibility of a discrepancy between what the defendant believes happened and what the state says happened; and the use of other measures designed to meet the mandate of appellate courts in a streamlined manner bring today's plea-taking close to being a new kind of "pious fraud."

Again, the more determined the effort to make the plea acceptance meaningful, the less efficient the guilty plea becomes. Delaware County's average time for taking felony pleas, for example, is four times that of Seattle, where judges rely more on the use of the plea-taking form. Also, in Delaware County there is an increased risk of having pleas rejected.

The state's perspective. While the expansion of the plea-taking procedures since 1966 has not benefited defendants as much as some reformers had hoped, it has come to be recognized as an important benefit to the state. A thorough colloquy does not necessarily reduce the probability of the defendant's appealing the plea,[64] but it does reduce his chance of success. This point has not been lost on either prosecutors or judges.[65]

Several judges emphasized the importance they attach to using the colloquy to prevent reversals. Fortunately, for defendants and reformers who would have the plea-acceptance be as thorough as possible, there is here a happy coincidence of method in achieving a difference in goals. The greater the state's concern about making pleas reversal-proof, the more likely the colloquy is to be thorough and meaningful.

Conclusion

The reforms of the guilty plea acceptance procedures of the last two decades have succeeded in making pleas more intelligent and assuring that defendants get the deals they thought they were going to get. Before their pleas are accepted, the great majority of felony defendants have their constitutional right to trial by jury explained to them, as well as the nature of the charges against them and the maximum possible sentence for which they are eligible. In addition, the terms of the plea agreements are made part of the record. Most defendants appear to understand the explanations of their rights and the charges against them. But a substantial minority of defendants apparently do not understand. Moreover, promises made by the police apparently do not get recorded in plea agreements and are not fulfilled.

The reforms have not made guilty pleas "voluntary" in the sense of uncoerced or free from pressures of inducements. Virtually all defendants still plead guilty because of the inducements offered by the state. But the reforms did not try to eliminate all inducements, only improper inducements such as the threat of violence or bribery and, in the hopes of two national commissions, the use of overcharging. The former two kinds of improper inducements do not appear to be a regular part of plea bargaining but the latter one continues to be.

A factual basis for guilty pleas is now established in the great majority of cases. But this does not guarantee the "accuracy" of the plea in the literal sense (for defendants are allowed to plead to fact patterns which do not accurately reflect their crimes); nor does it mean that innocent defendants are less likely to be wrongly convicted. Contrary to the hopes of some reformers, the factual basis established at plea-taking does not constitute a test of evidentiary strength. However, it does reinforce the informed nature of the plea.

In short, the expanded plea-taking procedures have made guilty pleas far more informed than they once were and have minimized the possibility of broken, misleading, or misconstrued promises. But they have left the coercive character of plea bargaining intact. They have not moved plea bargaining much closer to the trial procedure's determination of legal guilt. They do not constitute a means by which an independent third party weighs the evidence against some standard of legal proof.

The effectiveness of the plea-taking procedures is eroded by three countervailing factors: (1) Defendants are advised by their counsel and willingly agree to give acceptable answers to the litany of queries at plea-taking because of their desire to secure the inducement offered by the state; (2) Judges are just as anxious as prosecutors and defense counsel to dispose of cases as quickly as possible. Hence they are subject to strong pressures to find pleas acceptable, which they almost always do; (3) Except in the occasional case of extraordinarily unusual plea agreements, judges

are not prone to second guess the agreements worked out by prosecutors. To do so on a regular basis would require the judge to assess the evidentiary strength of the case as well as other tactical matters (such as using the defendant as an informer or for state's evidence) that fall within the province of the prosecutor. Hence, the judge's ability to protect the community's interest in seeing defendants sentenced "appropriately" is limited by the judge's not knowing certain information which is a major determinant of what an "appropriate" disposition would be.

If innocent defendants choose to plead guilty today rather than risk a more severe penalty at trial, they will be better informed about their constitutional rights, about the nature of the charges against them, about the consequences of the plea, and about the terms of the agreement than they were in the early 1960s. There is a 50-50 chance they will not be allowed to plead guilty unless they stop asserting their innocence or facts at variance with the state's version of the crime. And, there is an increasing chance that they will be unable to successfully attack their conviction on appeal. Thus the expanded plea-taking procedures have succeeded in bringing a certain kind of fairness to plea bargaining. But, they have not altered the fundamental nature of securing dispositions by inducements nor have they remedied the institutional weakness of plea bargaining—the lack of the weighing of the evidence against a legal standard such as what would be necessary to get a case to the jury.

NOTES

This article originally appeared in Volume 70, Number 4, December-January 1987, pages 203-215.

This research was supported by Grant #77 NI-990-049 and Contract Number 1-0260-J-OJARS to Georgetown University from the National Institute of Justice, U.S. Department of Justice, under the Omnibus Crime Control and Safe Streets Act of 1968, as amended. The following people contributed to the design and collection of the data: W.F. McDonald, H.R. Rossman, V. Kullberg, J. Baker, H. Daudistel, S. Foster, Jeanne Kleyn, J. Connolly, M. Budish, J.A. Cramer, and H.S. Miller. Sam Dash, Cheryl Martorana, and Linda McKay also played important parts in assuring the completion of the study. The points of view and opinions stated herein are solely those of the author.

1. For a review of the case decisions as well as the legal literature see Bond, PLEA BARGAINING AND GUILTY PLEAS (New York: Clark Boardman, 1981). For a review of the recommendations of national standard-setting groups, see Epstein and Austern, UNIFORM RULES OF CRIMINAL PROCEDURE: COMPARISON AND ANALYSIS (Washington, DC: American Bar Association, 1975).

2. Two commissions (President's Commission on Law Enforcement and the Administration of Justice, THE COURTS

(Washington, DC: Government Printing Office, 1967); and National Advisory Commission on Criminal Justice Standards and Goals, COURTS 57 (Washington, DC: Government Printing Office, 1973)) have specifically identified "overcharging" as "improper" inducements which judges should reject.

3. Observations were made of plea acceptances before 5 judges in El Paso, 6 in New Orleans, 8 in Seattle, 11 in Tucson, 9 in Delaware County, and 7 in Norfolk.

4. Except in El Paso where all observations were of misdemeanor courts due to the "no plea bargaining" policy at the felony level.

5. Newman, CONVICTION: THE DETERMINATION OF GUILTY OR INNOCENCE WITHOUT TRIAL 8 (Boston: Little, Brown, 1966); *The Trial Judge's Satisfaction as to The Factual Basis of Guilty Pleas*, Wash. U.L.Q. 306 (1966).

6. Enker, *Perspectives on Plea Bargaining*, in President's Commission on Law Enforcement and Administration of Justice, THE COURTS, *supra* n. 2, at 111.

7. Machibroda v. United States, 368 U.S. 487, 493 (1962), quoting Kercheval v. United States, 274 U.S. 220, 223 (1927).

8. *See* Malloy v. Hogan, 378 U.S. 1 (1964); Pointer v. Texas, 380 U.S. 400 (1965); Duncan v. Louisiana, 391 U.S. 145 (1968).

9. Federal Rules of Criminal Procedure, as amended Feb. 28, 1966, eff. July 1, 1966.

10. *Supra* n. 2, at 12.

11. (New York: Institute for Judicial Administration).

12. National Advisory Commission, *supra* n. 2; American Law Institute, A MODEL CODE OF PRE-ARRAIGNMENT PROCEDURE (Philadelphia: ALI, 1975); National Conference of Commissioners on Uniform State Laws, UNIFORM RULES OF CRIMINAL PROCEDURE (St. Paul: West, 1974).

13. For an itemized comparison of the 1975 FRCP, 1975 ALI, 1968 ABA, NAC, and the 1974 Uniform Rules of Criminal Procedure, see Epstein and Austern, *supra* n. 1.

14. For instance, the criterion of voluntariness has chameleon-like properties—taking on whatever definition best suits it. Bond, *supra* n. 1, at 75.

15. Some pleas are invalidated on the grounds of voluntariness when the fact pattern suggests the more appropriate grounds would have been lack of requisite knowledge. *See, e.g.*, Pilkington v. United States, 315 F.2d 204 (4th Cir. 1963) (defendant was not accurately informed of the maximum sentence he might receive).

16. For instance, in requiring that the judge establish a factual basis for a plea, those reformers who would have the judge serve as a protection against pleas in weak cases and as a mechanism by which an impartial third party assessed the evidence might like to require that the judge determine whether the evidence meets some standard of proof such as probable cause or beyond a reasonable doubt. But others do not agree that such a standard should be required. Bond, *supra* n. 1.

17. FRCP Rule 11, 1975.

18. Bond, *supra* n. 1, at 88.

19. Boykin v. Alabama, 395 U.S. 238 (1969).

20. Henderson v. Morgan, 426 U.S. 637 (1976).

21. *See* McDonald, PLEA BARGAINING: CRITICAL ISSUES AND COMMON PRACTICES (Washington, DC: Government Printing Office, 1985) for full details on the rules and forms used in each of the six jurisdictions.

22. Washington Criminal Rule 4.2(g).

23. Mileski, *Courtroom Encounters: An Observation Study of A Lower Criminal Court*, 5 LAW AND SOC'Y REV. 473 (1971).

24. FRCP Rule 11 (since 1966) requires the judge to personally address the defendant as does the American Bar Association, STANDARDS RELATING TO THE PROSECUTION FUNCTION AND THE DEFENSE FUNCTION (New York: IJA, 1971) and the State of Arizona (Az. R.C.P., Rule 17.2). Pennsylvania law does not require it but does recommend it (Pa. R.C.P. Rule 319).

25. McDonald, *supra* n. 21.

26. Bond, *supra* n. 1, at 280.7; and see, e.g., State v. McKee, 362 N.E.2d 1252 (1976).

27. *See* Whelan v. State, 472 S.W.2d 141 (Tex. 1971).

28. *Accepting the Indigent Defendant's Waiver of Counsel and Plea of Guilty*, 22 FLA. L. REV. 453 (1970).

29. The one exception (Delaware County) with an average of 14 minutes must be regarded as a special case because misdemeanors in Pennsylvania include crimes punishable by up to five years in prison. Thus it is not surprising that they are treated more like felonies.

30. Delaware County is excluded for reasons mentioned above.

31. *See, e.g.*, Robertson, ROUGH JUSTICE (Boston: Little, Brown, 1974).

This hypothesis could not be explored in the preceding analysis because not all the pleas to misdemeanor charges were in misdemeanor courts. In the following analysis, all the cases labeled "misdemeanor courts" are pleas to misdemeanor charges, whereas the cases labeled "felony courts" include pleas to felonies as well as to misdemeanor charges.

32. It should be kept in mind that the workload of the Seattle district judges appears to be considerably less than that of the judge in the Norfolk District Court.

33. 395 U.S. 238 (1969).

34. Texas Code of Criminal Procedure, Article 26.14.

35. Bond, *supra* n. 1.

36. 426 U.S. 637 (1976).

37. Those differences are not related to differences in law in any consistent way. For instance, the two jurisdictions with the highest rates of not explaining the charges (New Orleans, 66 per cent, and Seattle, 48 per cent) are also ones with no special legal requirements regarding such explanations. On the other hand, two of the jurisdictions with the lowest rates of not explaining charges (Delaware County, 3 per cent and Tucson, 16 per cent—for felonies) are ones where such explanations are required.

Arizona requires that the defendant be advised of the nature of the charge (Arizona Rules of Criminal Procedures 17.2(a)), but the nature of the explanation is permitted to vary from case to case as long as the defendant understands what acts are necessary to commit the crime (State v. Duran, 562 P.2d 487 (1973)). In contrast, Pennsylvania's requirements are more rigorous. The defendant must understand every element of the offense. This understanding must be established through an on-the-record colloquy in which the basic legal elements of the crime(s) charged must be outlined in terms understandable to the defendant (Commonwealth v. Ingram, 455 Pa. 198, 316 A.2d 77 (1974)). Merely reading the charges and asking the defendant if he understands them does not meet the requirement (Commonwealth v. Minor, 467 Pa. 230, 356 A.2d 346 (1976)).

Virginia and Texas do not have special requirements regarding explanation of the charges and yet their courts have rates of explaining charges comparable to Arizona and Pennsylvania, where such explanations are required. Thus, while the existence of state requirements beyond federal constitutional requirements does increase concern for this issue, the absence of such requirements does not mean a concomitant lowering of concern.

38. Bond, *supra* n. 1.

39. Texas, Code of Criminal Procedure Art. 26.12(a) "the range of punishment"; Washington, the maximum sentence (In re Vensel, 564 P.2d 326) and any mandatory minimum sentence (Wood v. Morris, 554 P.2d 1032 (1976); Arizona, Rules of Criminal Procedure 17.2(b) "the nature and range of

possible sentence . . . including special conditions regarding sentence, parole, or commutation imposed by statute."

40. Commonwealth v. McNeil, 305 A.2d 51, 54 (1973).

41. Louisiana Code of Criminal Procedure, Article 556.

42. Shelton v. United States, 356 U.S. 26 (1958).

43. McMann v. Richardson, 397 U.S. 759 (1979).

44. Bordenkircher v. Hayes, 343 U.S. 357 (1978).

45. Where written forms are used but not read into the record in court, they would become part of the record but would be coded in our observation as "no record verbally made."

46. See generally, *The Trial Judge's Satisfaction, supra* n. 5; Alschuler, *The Trial Judge's Role in Plea Bargaining, Part I,* 76 COL. L. REV. 1059 (1976); Kipnis, *Criminal Justice and the Negotiated Plea,* 86 ETHICS 93 (1976).

47. See generally, Bond, *supra* n. 1.

48. *Supra* n. 12, at 350.4(3).

49. *Supra* n. 2, at 3.7(8).

50. See generally, Bond, *supra* n. 1, at 159.

51. Beaman v. State, 221 N.W.2d 698, 700 (Minn. 1974).

52. *The Trial Judge's Satisfaction, supra* n. 5.

53. Bond, *supra* n. 1, at 159.

54. Texas Code of Criminal Procedure, Article 1.15; Arizona Rules of Criminal Procedure Rule 17.3; and Pa., Commonwealth v. Maddix, 450 Pa. 406, 409, 300 A.2d 503, 505 (1973).

55. Washington seems to require it by virtue of the fact that one the plea-acceptance form which must be used in Washington there is a section where the defendant is to state the facts which led to his being charged. But case law indicates that the factual basis requirement is recommended but not required (State v. Newton, 87 Wm.2d at 369, 552 P.2d at 686). Louisiana has no law on point—which is reflected in the fact that five of the seven versions of the plea-taking forms developed by the local judges in New Orleans do not address this issue. Virginia does not require courts to establish a factual basis for a plea (Kibert v. Commonwealth, 216 Va. 660, 222 S.E.2d 790 (1976)) but the Virginia Supreme Court suggests that judges ask defendants, "Are you entering the plea of guilty because you are, in fact, guilty of the crime charged?"

56. Texas Code of Criminal Procedure, Article 1.15; Washington, State v. Newton, 87 Wn.2d 363, 372, 1552 P.2d 682, 685 (1976) or evidence which "negates guilt."

57. Commonwealth v. Roundtree, 440 Pa. 199, 202, 269 A.2d 709, 711 (1970).

The states allow the factual basis to be established by a wide variety of means, including police reports, affidavits of witnesses, statements of defendants, and other evidence. An Arizona court ruled that a factual basis was established by a presentence report which the defendant said was "pretty accurate" (State v. Murib, 116 Ariz. 441, 569 P.2d 1339 (1977)). The states do not require that the defendant participate except in Texas where his consent must be obtained to use evidence introduced by stipulation (Texas Code of Criminal Procedure, Article 1.15). There is no requirement that the information used be reliable except in Washington (where, oddly enough, a factual basis, itself, is not required) (Washington, State v. Newton, 552 P.2d 682 (1976)). There is no requirement that the facts established accurately reflect the crime charged or the crime to which the plea is made (except in the latter case for Arizona (State v. McGee, 551 P.2d 568 (1976)); nor is it required that a factual basis be established for each element of the offense except in Arizona (State v. Davis, 112 Ariz. 140, 142, 539 P.2d 897 (1975)).

58. *The Trial Judge's Role, supra* n. 5, at 311.

59. Virginia Constitution Article I, §8.

60. The case involved a defendant who pleaded guilty to first degree murder. The Commonwealth had evidence sufficient to support only second degree murder. Citing Article 8 of the Virginia Constitution as well as Section 19-1166 of the Virginia Code (which provides that the court will "try" a case if the accused pleads guilty) the defendant argued there had been insufficient evidence to convict. But the court held that these laws only require that a judge will *preside* in the event that the accused pleads guilty. They do not imply that evidence will be presented or that the case will be "tried." It explained that a voluntary and intelligent guilty plea is a self-supplied conviction which operates as a waiver of all defenses (other than jurisdictional defects). Included in the waiver is the potential defense of lack of evidence or insufficiency of evidence (Kilbert v. Commonwealth, 216 Va. 6609, 222 S.E.2d 790 (1976)). This decision did not radically change the procedures for accepting pleas in Norfolk, however, as will be shown below.

61. North Carolina v. Alford, 400 U.S. 25 (1970).

62. Commonwealth v. Roundtree, 440 Pa. 199, 202, 269 A.2d 709, 711 (1970).

63. Brosi, A CROSS-CITY COMPARISON OF FELONY CASE PROCESS (Washington, DC: Institute for Law and Social Research, 1979).

64. Pleas to serious crimes are appealed almost routinely in some jurisdiction.

65. Reacting to our finding that in Delaware County much of the plea-taking colloquy is done by defense counsel, this prosecutor expressed concern for such a practice. For one thing, because plea colloquies serve the function of "burying" the defendant he did not think counsel should be the one to do this. But, more importantly, he believes that counsel are increasingly recognizing the litigation value of being ineffective. In order to give their clients a basis for appeal some attorneys are deliberately being ineffective. Allowing counsel to run the plea colloquy increases their opportunity to build in an appeal on the basis of ineffective assistance.

The problem of prejudice: a new approach to assessing the impact of courtroom cameras

As a review of the literature readily shows, the potential for jury bias already exists at all stages of the trial process. If anything, cameras may help make trials fairer.

by Susanna Barber

Careful reading of the majority opinion in *Chandler v. Florida*[1] shows that the whole matter of the prejudicial effects of news cameras in the courtroom remains open to debate.[2] The Supreme Court refused to endorse televised trials in part because the evidence so far compiled has some serious limitations, as Chief Justice Burger explained:

While the data thus far assembled are cause for some optimism about the ability of states to minimize the problems that potentially inhere in electronic coverage of trials, even the Florida Supreme Court conceded that the data were "limited,"... and "non-scientific,"...[3]

The empirical research examined by the Court was based on attitudinal data—perceptions and opinions—not on cause and effect reactions to controlled stimuli, and the researchers drew no conclusions as to how participants might have behaved in the same situations had cameras not been present.[4] It is, of course, impossible to use real trials as laboratory research settings, and the next best type of research environment, simulated trials, has serious limitations. But until such time as new experimental data is compiled, there is another avenue of inquiry that may supplement the courtroom cameras literature produced to date. That avenue is explored here.

It focuses on jury behavior, particularly the impact of trial proceedings and participants on jury verdicts. This approach is taken because probably the most crucial challenge facing courtroom news cameras is their potential impact on the jury.

The problem of prejudice

Opponents of courtroom cameras generally claim that prejudice arises 1) as a direct result of cameras distracting jurors and 2) as an indirect result of cameras causing other trial participants (judges, attorneys, witnesses, and defendants) to behave in ways which, in turn, prejudice the jurors.[5] In short, cameras may prejudice trials by distorting (altering) the courtroom atmosphere in such a way that the jury is "persuaded" to reach a verdict it would not have reached otherwise. Specifically, the appellants in *Chandler* and in *Estes v. Texas*[6]—the two landmark courtroom cameras cases—argued that cameras make a trial notorious, encourage pretrial publicity detrimental to the accused, distract jurors, inhibit witnesses, hinder truthful testimony, encourage judges to grandstand, and turn lawyers into flamboyant actors.

But suppose it can be shown that factors other than cameras are responsible for prejudicing trials, and that consequently, cameras make little or no difference to the fairness of a trial, since the trial process is already loaded with subjectivity and lack of impartiality. An underlying contention here is that to make a fair assessment of the impact of cameras on the trial process and its participants, it is first necessary to identify the factors operating in the trial environment before cameras are introduced. This way it will become clear which prejudices are inherent in the trial process and which are introduced by cameras.

The problem of prejudice is examined in the following literature review. Emphasis is on criminal trial experiences, since cameras have been most hotly contested in the criminal courtroom. The review is organized in three stages, paralleling the sequence of a trial.

Pretrial

Presumed guilt: Prejudice may enter the trial process even before the trial begins. Tans and Chaffee found that a suspect is not always considered innocent until proven guilty—"the mere fact of questioning or arrest may be prejudicing,"[7] and knowledge that a trial has been moved from its original venue may also create juror biases.[8]

Pretrial publicity: Prejudicial pretrial publicity also influences juror opinions, and in some cases prejudices very verdicts, especially in the absence of judicial instructions to ignore non-evidential information. But the role of the judge should be stressed here, because the verdicts of jurors who comply with judicial instructions to ignore prejudicial publicity are the same as those of jurors who have read non-prejudicial information.[9]

Jury selection: In some states, jury selection procedures may be detrimental to the defendant. While a jury is supposed to represent a cross-section of the community, methods of selection such as the key-man system, and even the use of voter registration lists, city directories and tax records, may be inherently biased. Until recently women, blacks, the poor, and the less educated were excluded;[10] hence, the accused may have been tried not by a group of peers, but by a select group of people with contrasting backgrounds and values.

Voir dire: While knowledge of local conditions and contact with trial participants have proven more important than evidence in determining jury verdicts, lawyers and jurors may consciously conceal these facts during *voir dire*.[11] The ineffectiveness of *voir dire* as a tool for eliminating prejudiced jurors has been emphasized by Broeder, who found that some lawyers are reluctant to hold lengthy examinations for fear of irritating the judge and those persons finally chosen as jurors.[12]

On the other hand, *voir dire* is the very vehicle that enables lawyers to introduce bias into the jury. It is no secret that lawyers regard *voir dire* as an opportunity to not only weed out prejudiced jurors, but also to select jurors who will favor their side. Alice Padawer-Singer, a social psychologist and consultant to New York City courts, has described the selection process as a "blend of art, science, and intuition,"[13] an apt description since jurors are chosen on the basis of their "clothing, body language, sex, facial expression, age, occupation, race,

nationality, tone of voice, ability to reason, and preference in books, newspapers, and magazines."[14]

Trial

Juror characteristics: The importance of the jury selection procedure is magnified by the fact that juror characteristics, such as sex, age, race, residence, educational level, social status, occupational status, and level of authoritarianism, rather than trial evidence, determine the verdict. For example, authoritarian jurors tend to evaluate a defendant as responsible and guilty; jurors whose ethnic origins are northern European reach more guilty verdicts than jurors of southern European origins; and jurors with high social status are more likely to vote guilty than jurors with low social status.[15]

Jurors also decide cases on the basis of subjective perceptions about the respectability of a victim in a crime; the character attractiveness of a victim; similarity in attitudes between the defendant and individual jurors; and the social desirability of traits attributed to the defendant.[16]

Defendant characteristics: Defendant characteristics that influence jury verdicts include sex, race, socio-economic status, occupational status, physical attractiveness, character attractiveness, arrogance, and previous criminal record. For example, a defendant may be convicted because of race, even though evidence may not support a conviction. Also arrogant defendants receive more severe sentences, particularly from male jurors; knowledge of a defendant's prior criminal record dramatically affects the likelihood of a guilty verdict; and attractive defendants are likely to receive lighter punishment than unattractive defendants.[17]

Kalven and Zeisel noted two distinct areas of a defendant's characteristics that come to bear on a juror's evaluation: those that affect credibility and those that affect sympathy. Factors affecting sympathy, for example, include handicaps or visible illness, whether the defendant shows remorse or cries, the presence of the defendant's family in court, the defendant's occupation and employment record, and whether the defendant is a veteran.[18]

Two other factors relating to the defendant are important determinants of jury verdicts. First, testifying in one's own defense is reacted to negatively by jurors, because they suspect the defendant is either lying or trying to manipulate them.[19] Second, jurors tend to assess a defendant favorably if there is an escaped accomplice involved in the case, or if an accomplice is not indicted with the defendant.[20]

Adversary process: A very basic but questionable assumption about the fairness of a trial is that the adversary process is an impartial forum for the discovery of truth. Justice Thomas Clark noted optimistically in *Estes* that "(c)ourt proceedings are held for the solemn purpose of endeavoring to ascertain the truth which is the *sine qua non* of a fair trial."[21] But Marvin Frankel, who, when commenting on the trial process in 1975 had been a district judge for nine years, emphasized the apparent inconsistency between the adversary system and the search for truth:

The business of the advocate, simply stated, is to win if possible without violating the law .... His is not the search for truth as such. To put that thought more exactly, the truth and victory are mutually incompatible for some considerable percentage of the attorneys trying cases at any given time .[22]

Mirjan Damaska has also called attention to some of the "shortcomings" of the adversary process:

It may be in the narrow interest of only one party, or in the common interest of both, that some items of information which the witness possesses do not reach the adjudicator—even though their relevancy in the quest for truth is beyond dispute. Evidence unsupportive of one's case has no function in the adversary litigation process, nor do matters which the parties decide to leave out of the disputation. And, as the witness is limited to answering relatively narrow and precise questions, much information may effectively be kept away from the decisionmaker who presumably is responsible for finding the truth within the limits of the charge. Accordingly, the factual basis for the decision may be incomplete.[23]

Presentation of evidence: The fact is, a jury's verdict is rarely the result of impartial consideration of witness testimony. It is more often a function of how evidence is presented than what evidence is presented. For example, jury verdicts are directly related to the number of arguments presented by either side; the order in which they are presented; the introduction of inadmissible evidence; and the vividness of the evidence.[24]

Moreover, few jurors maintain an attitude of doubt about a defendant until all the evidence has been presented. In addition, jurors tend not to base their evaluations on the preponderance of the evidence but, instead, use this term indiscriminately to support their personal judgments, indicating they neither understand the term or its implications, nor base their judgments on the evidence presented.[25]

Behavior of attorneys: Perhaps the most important influences on the jury are the trial attorneys— their skills have more impact on a jury's verdict than either the characteristics of the defendant or the facts of the case.[26] Charles Winick concluded that the key to winning a jury trial case is a lawyer's successful exploitation of jurors' personalities and feelings.[27] Sometimes even the prestige of a lawyer, on its own, is sufficient to persuade jurors to accept an opinion and maintain it as their own.[28] And sometimes jurors feel obligated to vote for a lawyer because he is well known in the local community and has several clients there.[29]

The jury measures not only the attorney's skills of advocacy, but also his appearance and the attractiveness of his personality. Kalven and Zeisel found that jurors are won over by colorful and amusing lawyers who "play" to the jury,[30] and Hoffman and Brodley found that jurors tend to describe the most convincing attorney as "a good actor."[31] In one trial, they observed, the lawyers were very obviously "putting on a show for the jury":

An atmosphere of heated argument, confusion and histrionics prevailed between the two contending sides, as long as the jury was within the room; but as soon as the jury was dismissed for any reason, the argument would be quickly toned down, the facts clarified and the argument became intelligent off-the-record discussion between judge and counsel rather than a fight to the death.[32]

Behavior of trial judges: Another significant influence on the jury is the trial judge. A judge's facial expressions, gestures, and eye movements can destroy or enhance a defendant's case by showing the jury belief or disbelief, annoyance, agreement, or disagreement. In fact, smiles, frowns, head-nodding, and head-shaking can have a greater impact on the jury's assessment of evidence than the testimony of witnesses.[33]

Judicial instructions: A judge's influence is also expressed through judicial instructions to the jury. However, jurors often do not understand judicial instructions, and do not apply them to the facts of a case; some jurors ignore the instructions entirely.[34]

Deliberation

Jury deliberations: The jury deliberation process is yet another stage in the trial in which prejudicial factors, i.e., factors other than trial testimony, determine jurors' opinions and verdicts. Bevan et al. concluded that during deliberations greater respect is shown for the views of high-status people, and that low-status jurors are less active in the deliberation process.[35] Broeder has described the racial prejudice that exists in the jury room and determines jury verdicts,[36] and Reed has pointed out that relatively little of a jury's deliberation time is spent discussing the facts of a case. Instead, jurors discuss topics such as the weather, people on the jury or in the community, the reputation of the parties in the case, the family of the accused, the reputation of the lawyers, and race and racial differences.[37]

But after many trials there may not even be a need for deliberations, since jurors have usually made up their minds before deliberations begin, or even before all the evidence has been presented.[38] Broeder found that in 90 per cent of the cases he studied as part of the Chicago Jury Project, the majority decision on the first ballot was the verdict, even after deliberations.[39] Finally, jury verdicts may also be affected by the size of the jury, by whether the jury must reach a unanimous or majority verdict, by whether or not the jury applies the criterion of "beyond reasonable doubt," by the need for approval of others in attitude formation, and by cognitive and memory processes.[40]

Do cameras increase prejudice?

In the ongoing debate about courtroom cameras, it is worth noting that empirical evidence gathered in Washington, Wisconsin, Florida, California, Louisiana, and Nevada between 1975 and 1979 points to broad but consistent conclusions about the impact of news cameras on trial participants and the trial process.[41] These conclusions refute the arguments against cameras presented in *Chander* and *Estes*, but the Supreme Court did not find enough convincing evidence in the research literature to give broadcasters an unequivocal right to cover trials.

The present study, therefore, has attempted to approach the issue of televised trials from a reversed perspective. A review of the literature shows that whether cameras are present or not, a courtroom is certainly not an impartial forum for the presentation of evidence. It is an environment full of subtle, and sometimes obvious, prejudices, and the fact that cameras may be present will not necessarily alter the criteria used by jurors in reaching a verdict.

A courtroom is simply a microcosm of the society it serves, and jury decisions are inevitably functions of individual jurors' backgrounds and personalities, and the verbal and non-verbal behavior of

other trial participants. A juror cannot be expected to relinquish the human aspect of judgment about fellow human beings; hence, perceptions about a defendant's guilt or innocence will never, it seems, be based solely on impartial consideration of trial testimony. And this, in its most literal sense, rather than the tenuous argument against courtroom news cameras, is trial prejudice.

Sources of prejudice

The discussion does not naively suggest that the empirical evidence examined here remains valid in all circumstances. However, the large quantity of available literature indicates, at a minimum, two very important points. First, that many of the prejudicial behaviors said to result from the presence of cameras in courtrooms are, in fact, operative in the courtroom regardless of the introduction of cameras. Second, that many unfair aspects of trials are not attributable to broadcast news coverage, but to the nature of the trial process in general.

For example, cameras do not make a trial notorious—many trials are inherently notorious by virtue of the issues involved in the case, or because a famous, or infamous, defendant is being tried. Witness he recent trial of famous defense attorney F. Lee Bailey in San Francisco. This trial was televised because it involved a nationally known defendant, and the case would have received widespread print media coverage (as it in fact did) even if news cameras had not been present. Norman Davis of WPLG-TV, Miami, Florida, has skillfully argued the same point about several other notorious trials:

There were no cameras present during the trials of Patty Hearst, Sacco and Vanzetti, John Peter Zenger, the Chicago Seven, the Scottsboro Boys, Murph the Surph, or Joan Little. Even so, all those trials were notorious.[42]

Nor does the fact that a trial may be televised necessarily encourage pretrial publicity. Events leading up to the recent Wayne Williams trial in Atlanta, Georgia, were covered in depth and in detail by both the print and broadcast media, but news cameras were banned from the courtroom during the trial.

The courtroom cameras literature has shown that jurors are rarely distracted by the presence of cameras. But even if a juror's attention were to drift away from the events of the trial from time to time, the verdict would likely remain the same, since jurors seldom decide cases on the basis of trial testimony and often ignore judicial instructions to consider the preponderance of the evidence. As for cameras hindering truthful testimony, studies have implied the contrary,[43] and the present analysis has indicated that, in any event, the adversary process does not lend itself to a search for the truth.

Judges, it would seem, do not always behave prudently even when cameras are not present, and the news cameras studies have not shown that they behave noticeably more imprudently, e.g., by grandstanding, when cameras are present. The same logic applies to an assessment of camera effects on attorneys. Attorneys were playing to the jury long before cameras entered courtrooms, and they will continue to do so even if cameras are banned. In fact, abilities to artfully persuade and interact with jurors are the very skills that distinguish a lawyer as successful and well liked, but studies have not shown that cameras make attorneys more flamboyant.

Making trials more fair

It is interesting to note that of all the trial participants surveyed by the courtroom camera researchers, it was only attorneys, and to a lesser extent judges, who objected to permanent rules allowing news cameras in the courtroom. Might it be that these are the very people who have most to lose if cameras are present? Attorneys, for example, may need to be more cautious about exploiting juror emotions, and judges may need to be more careful to conceal their feelings about a defendant or the case or witness testimony.

It does not seem unreasonable to suggest that news camera coverage has the potential to make trials more rather than less fair: with the added public scrutiny that accompanies the eye of the camera, some of the blatant prejudices discussed earlier might be diffused, if not eliminated. At the very least, it seems that cameras will not measurably alter a courtroom already saturated with prejudice, and which regardless of the presence of cameras, is "a scene of drama, wit, humor and humanity, along with the sorrows and stretches of boredom."[44]

NOTES

This article originally appeared in Volume 66, Number 6, December-January 1983, pages 248-255.

1. Chandler v. Florida, 449 U.S. 560 (January 26, 1981).

2. A clear distinction is made here between news media camera coverage of trials and prerecorded videotaped trial presentations, such as the presentation of witness testimony to jurors. The *Chandler* case concerned possible prejudice to criminal defendants from televising trials, not from showing videotaped testimony to jurors. Neither Chief Justice Warren Burger's majority opinion nor the concurring opinions of Justice Potter Stewart and Justice Byron White mention videotaped trial presentations.

3. Chandler v. Florida, *supra* n. 1, at 576 n. 11.

4. *See,* appendix to the *amicus curiae* brief of the Attorneys General of Alabama, Alaska, Arizona, Iowa, Kentucky, Louisiana, Maryland, Montana, Nevada, New Mexico, Ohio, Rhode Island, Tennessee, Vermont, West Virginia, and Wisconsin, filed with the U.S. Supreme Court in *Chandler v. Florida,* October Term, 1979.

5. *See, for example,* the *amicus curiae* brief of the American College of Trial Lawyers, filed with the U.S. Supreme Court in *Chandler v. Florida,* October Term, 1979.

6. Estes v. Texas, 381 U.S. 532 (1965).

7. Tans and Chaffee, *Pretrial Publicity and Juror Prejudice,* 43 JOURNALISM Q. 654 (1966).

8. Miller and Boster, *Three Images of the Trial: Their Implications for Psychological Research,* in Sales, ed., PSYCHOLOGY IN THE LEGAL PROCESS 21-26 (New York: Spectrum Publications, Inc., 1977).

9. *See, for examples,* Goggin and Hanover, *Fair Trial v. Press: The Psychological Effect of Pretrial Publicity on the Juror's Ability to be Impartial: a Plea for Reform,* 38 S. CAL. L. REV. 672-688 (1965); Simon, *The Effects of Newspapers on the Verdicts of Potential Jurors,* in Simon, ed., THE SOCIOLOGY OF THE LAW (San Francisco: Chandler Publishing Company, 1968); Simon and Eimermann, *The Jury Finds Not Guilty: Another Look at Media Influence on the Jury,* 48 JOURNALISM Q. 343-344 (1971); Hoiberg and Stires, *The Effect of Several Types of Pretrial Publicity on the Guilt Attributions of Simulated Jurors,* 3 J. OF APPLIED PSYCHOLOGY 267-275 (1973); Kline and Jess, *Prejudicial Publicity: Its Effect on Law School Mock Juries,* 43 JOURNALISM Q. 113-116 (1966); and Padawer-Singer, Singer and Singer, *Legal and Psychological Research in the Effects of Pre-Trial Publicity on Juries, Numerical Make-Up of Juries, Non-Unanimous Verdict,* 3 L. AND PSYCHOLOGY REV. 71-79 (1977).

10. *See* Broeder, *The Negro in Court,* DUKE L. J. 19-31 (1965); Hood, *Recent Developments: Trial by Jury,* 20 ALA. L. REV. 76-88 (1967); and Linquist, *An Analysis of Juror Selection Procedures in United States District Courts,* 41 TEMP. L. Q. 32-50 (1967).

11. *See* Broeder, *supra* n. 10; Broeder, *Voir Dire examinations: An Empirical Study,* 38 S. CAL L. REV. 503-528 (1965); Broeder, *The Impact of the Vicinage Requirement: An Empirical Look,* 40 NEB L. REV. 99-118 (1966); and Kalven and Zeisel, THE AMERICAN JURY (Boston: Little, Brown and Company, 1966).

12. Broeder, *Voir Dire, supra* n. 11, at 505-506.

13. Grady, *Picking a Jury,* DISCOVER, January 1981, p. 38.

14. *Id. Also see,* Diamond and Zeisel, *A Courtroom Experiment on Juror Selection and Decision-Making,* PERSONALITY AND SOC. PSYCHOLOGY BULL. 27 (1974); Diamond and Zeisel found that the most frequently mentioned reasons for excusing a juror after *voir dire* were race, demeanor, residence, age, occupation, and sex, and that these variables, in this order, were found to be most frequently correct predictors of a juror's verdict.

15. *See, for example,* Mills and Bohannon, *Juror Characteristics: To What Extent Are they Related to Jury Verdicts?,* 64 JUDICATURE 23-31 (1980); Reed, *Jury Deliberations, Voting, and Verdict Trends,* 45 SW. SOC. SCI. Q. 361-370 (1965); Broeder, *The University of Chicago Jury Project,* 38 NEB. L. REV. 744-760 (1959); Boehm, *Mr. Prejudice, Miss Sympathy, and the Authoritarian Personality: An Application of Psychological Measuring Techniques to the Problem of Jury Bias,* 1968 WIS. L. REV. 734-750; Mitchell and Byrne, *The Defendant's Dilemma: Effects of Jurors' Attitudes and Authoritarianism on Judicial Decisions,* 25 J. OF PESONALITY AND SOC. PSYCHOLOGY 123-129 (1973); Berg and Vidmar, *Authoritarianism and Recall of Evidence About Criminal Behavior,* 9 J. OF RESEARCH IN PERSONALITY 147-157 (1975).

16. *See, for example,* Jones and Aronson, *Attribution of Fault to a Rape Victim as a Function of Respectability of the Victim,* 26 J. OF RESEARCH IN PERSONALITY 415-419 (1973); Landy and Arsonson, *The Influence of the Character of the Criminal and His Victim on the Decision of Simulated Jurors,* 5 J. OF EXPERIMENTAL SOC. PERSONALITY 141-152 (1969); Mitchell and Byrne, *supra* n. 15; and Edwards, *The Relationship Between the Judged Desirability of a Trait and the Probability that the Trait will be Endorsed,* 37 J. OF APPLIED PSYCHOLOGY 90-93 (1953).

17. *See, for example,* Dion, Bersheid, and Walster, *What is Beautiful is Good,* 24 J. OF PERSONALITY and Soc. Psychology 285-290 (1972); Nemeth and Sosis, *A Simulated Jury: Characteristics of the Defendant and Jurors,* 90 J. OF SOC. PSYCHOLOGY 221-229 (1973); Gleason and Harris, *Group Discussion and Defendant's Socio-Economic Status and Determinants of Judgements by Simulated Jurors,* 6 J. OF APPLIED SOC. PSYCHOLOGY 186-191 (1976); Efran, *The Effect of Physical Appearance on the Judgement of Guilt, Interpersonal Attraction, and Severity of Recommended Punishment in a Simulated Jury Task,* 8 J. OF RESEARCH IN PERSONALITY 45-54 (1974); Friend and Vinson, *Leaning Over Backwards: Jurors' Responses to Defendants' Attractiveness,* 24 J. OF COM. 124-129 (1974); Doob, *Evidence, Procedure, and Psychological Research,* in Bermant, Nemeth, and Vidmar (eds.), PSYCHOLOGY AND THE LAW (Lexington, MA: Lexington Books, 1976); and Boone, "The Effects of Race, Arrogance, and Evidence on Simulated Jury Decisions," Ph.D. dissertation, University of Washington, 1972.

18. Kalven and Zeisel, *supra* n. 11, at 200-207.

19. Frankel and Morris, *Testifying in One's Own Defense: The Ingratiator's Dilemma,* 34 J. OF PERSONALITY AND SOC. PSYCHOLOGY 475-480 (1976).

20. *See, for example,* DeJong, Hastorf, and Morris, *Effect of an Escaped Accomplice on the Punishment Assigned to a Criminal Defendant,* 33 J. OF PERSONALITY AND SOC. PSYCHOLOGY 192-198 (1976); and Broeder, *The Importance of a Scapegoat in Jury Trial Cases: Some Preliminary Reflections,* 4 DUQ. L. REV. 513-525 (1965-1966).

21. Estes v. Texas, 381 U.S. 540 (1965).

22. Frankel, *The Search for Truth: An Umpireal View,* 123 U. PA. L. REV. 1037 (1975).

23. Damaska, *Presentation of Evidence and Factfinding Precision,* 123 U. PA. L. REV. 1093 (1975).

24. *See, for example,* Rosenbaum and Levin, *Impression Formation as a Function of Source Credibility and Order of Presentation of Contradictory Information,* 39 J. OF PERSONALITY AND SOC. PSYCHOLOGY 2-12 (1980); Walker, Thibault, and Andreoli, *Order of Presentation at Trial,* 82 YALE L. J. 216-226 (1972); Hoffman and Brodley, *Jurors on Trial,* 17 MO. L. REV. 235-251 (1952); Sue, Smith, and Caldwell, *Effects of Inadmissible Evidence on the Decisions of Simulated Jurors: A Moral Dilemma,* 3 J. OF APPLIED SOC. PSYCHOLOGY 345-353 (1973); and Reyes, Thompson, and Bower, *Judgemental Biases Resulting from Differing Availabilities of Arguments,* 39 J. OF PERSONALITY AND SOC. PSYCHOLOGY 2-12 (1980).

25. *See* Weld and Danzig, *A Study of the Way in Which a Verdict is Reached by a Jury,* 53 AM. J. OF PSYCHOLOGY 518-536 (1940); and Nagel, *Bringing the values of jurors in line with the law,* 63 JUDICATURE 189-195 (1979).

26. *See* Moffat, *As Jurors See a Lawsuit,* 24 OR. L. REV. 199-207 (1945); Hoffman and Brodley, *supra* n. 24; and Kalven and Zeisel, *supra* n. 11.

27. Winick, *The Psychology and Juries,* in Toch, ed., LEGAL AND CRIMINAL PSYCHOLOGY 105-107 (New York: Holt, Rinehart and Winston, 1961).

28. Weld and Danzig, *supra* n. 25.

29. Kalven and Zeisel, *supra* n. 11, at 365.

30. *Id.*

31. Hoffman and Brodley, *supra* n. 24, at 243.

32. *Id.* at 246.

33. Conner, *The Trial Judge's Demeanor: Its Impact on the Jury,* 13 JUDGE's J. 2-4 (1974).

34. *See, for example,* Hervey, *The Jurors Look at Our Judges,* 18 OKLA. B. A. J. 1508-1513 (1947); Strawn and Buchanan, *Jury Confusion: A Threat to Justice,* 59 JUDICATURE 478-483 (1976); Strawn, Buchanan, Pryor and Taylor, *Reaching a verdict, step by step,* 60 JUDICATURE 384-389 (1977); Nagel, *supra* n. 25; and Pryor, Taylor, Buchanan, and Strawn, *An Affective-Cognitive Consistency Explanation for Comprehension of Standard Jury Instructions,* 47 COMMUNICATIONS MONOGRAPHS 68-76 (1980).

35. Bevan et al., *Jury Behavior as a Function of the Prestige of the Foreman and the Nature of His Leadership,* J. OF PUB. L. 419-449 (1958).

36. Broeder, *supra* n. 10.

37. Reed, *supra* n. 15.

38. *See* Weld and Danzig, *supra* n. 25; Kline and Jess, *supra* n. 9; and Nagel, *supra* n. 25.

39. Broeder, *supra* n. 15. This trend of following the majority decision was also strongly apparent in the small-group research conducted by Asch. *See, Effects of Group Pressure Upon Modification and Distortion of Judgements,* in Cartwright and Zander, eds., GROUP DYNAMICS (Evanston, IL: Row, Peterson and Co., 1953).

40. *See, for example,* Kerr et al., *Guilt Beyond a Reasonable Doubt: Effects of Concept Definition and Assigned Decision Rule on the Judgement of Mock Jurors,* 34 J. OF PERSONALITY AND SOC. PSYCHOLOGY 282-294 (1976); Padawer-Singer, Singer and Singer, *supra* n. 9; Nemeth, *Interaction Between Jurors as a Function of Majority vs. Unanimity Decision Rules,* 7 J. OF APPLIED SOC. PSYCHOLOGY 36-56 (1977); and Calder, Insko, and Yandell, *the Relation of Cognitive and Memorial Processes to Persuasion in a Simulated Jury Trial,* 4 J. OF APPLIED SOC. PSYCHOLOGY 62-93 (1974).

41. *See,* WASHINGTON BENCH-BAR-PRESS COMMITTEE, SUBCOMMITTEE ON CANON 35, REPORT, April 5, 1975; Goldman and Larson, *News Cameras in the Courtroom During State v. Solorzano: End to the Estes Mandate?,* 10 SW. U. L. REV. 2001-2067 (1978); Baker, REPORT TO THE SUPREME COURT OF FLORIDA RE: CONDUCT OF AUDIO-VISUAL TRIAL COVERAGE (1978); Sholts, REPORT TO THE SUPREME COURT OF FLORIDA RE: CONDUCT OF AUDIO-VISUAL TRIAL COVERAGE (1978); Mounts, REPORT TO THE SUPREME COURT OF FLORIDA CONCERNING AUDIO-VISUAL TRIAL COVERAGE (1978); Humphries, REPORT ON PILOT PROJECT ON THE PRESENCE OF CAMERAS AND ELECTRONIC EQUIPMENT IN THE COURTROOM, (Louisiana); REPORT OF THE WISCONSIN SUPREME COURT COMMITTEE TO MONITOR AND EVALUATE THE USE OF AUDIO AND VISUAL EQUIPMENT IN THE COURTROOM (April 1, 1979); Florida Conference of Circuit Judges, REPORT IN RE: PETITION OF POST NEWSWEEK STATIONS, FLORIDA, INC., FOR CHANGE IN CODE OF JUDICIAL CONDUCT (1978); Strawn, Buchanan, Meeske, and Pryor, REPORT IN RE: PETITION OF POST NEWSWEEK STATIONS, FLORIDA, INC., FOR CHANGE IN CODE OF JUDICIAL CONDUCT (1978); the Office of the State Courts Administrator, Judicial Planning and Coordination Unit, A SAMPLE SURVEY OF THE ATTITUDES OF INDIVIDUALS ASSOCIATED WITH TRIALS INVOLVING ELECTRONIC MEDIA AND STILL PHOTOGRAPHY COVERAGE IN SELECTED FLORIDA COURTS BETWEEN JULY 5, 1977, AND JUNE 30, 1978; Washington State Superior Court Judges' Association Committee on Courts and Community, CAMERAS IN THE COURTRROM—A TWO YEAR REVIEW IN THE STATE OF WASHINGTON (1978); Netteburg, *Does research support the Estes ban on cameras in the courtroom?,* 63 JUDICATURE 467-475 (1980); Hoyt, *Courtroom Coverage: The Effects of Being Televised,* 21 J. OF BROADCASTING, 487-495 (1977); Ernest H. Short and Associates, Inc., A REPORT TO THE JUDICIAL COUNCIL ON VIDEOTAPE RECORDING IN THE CALIFORNIA CRIMINAL JSUTICE SYSTEM, SECOND YEAR FINDINGS AND RECOMMENDATIONS, 1976.

42. Davis, *Television in our courts: the proven advantages, the unproven dangers,* 64 JUDICATURE 87-88 (1980).

43. *See, in particular,* Hoyt, *supra* n. 41.

44. Frankel, *supra* n. 22, at 1023.

Appellate Court Processes
Access and Docketing Decisions

INTRODUCTION

The lawyer who advises his or her client at their first meeting that "We will fight this case all the way up to the Supreme Court" is usually guilty of overstatement. For one thing, cases ultimately heard by the Supreme Court must implicate a question of federal law. More to the point, as a practical matter only a handful of the cases initiated in the American judicial system ultimately seek Supreme Court review. Further, the Court exercises virtually complete discretion in composing its appellate docket and more than 90 per cent of the cases seeking Supreme Court review are denied that appellate opportunity.

Thus, it is exceedingly unlikely that any one case will be heard by the Supreme Court. At the same time, however, the litigious nature of American society dictates that even if the percentage of cases seeking Supreme Court review is small and the proportion granted such review even smaller, the numbers remain great enough to raise the possibility of a workload crisis of substantial magnitude for the Supreme Court. Indeed, petitions for review by the Supreme Court (certiorari petitions) have increased geometrically during the past half century. Consequently, concerns about the Court's workload and what to do about it have become primary issues for contemplation in the American judicial system.

The articles in this section of readings broadly examine how the Supreme Court determines its docket as well as many suggested reforms for dealing with the Court's burgeoning appellate workload. It is important to keep in mind as you read these selections that the Court's role as a policymaker in the American political system is largely a reflection of the types of cases that it hears. Consequently, reforms that touch upon the accessibility of the Court to cases seeking review may have substantial implications for the Court's policy-making role.

In "Deciding what to decide: how the Supreme Court sets its agenda," D. Marie Provine utilizes a valuable data source, Justice Harold Burton's docket books from 1945 through 1957, to explore the alternative approaches scholars have utilized to understand how the Supreme Court exercises its discretionary docketing jurisdiction. Unlike earlier work, which focused on the collective institutional outcomes of certiorari voting, Provine's database allowed her to focus on the behavior of individual justices in voting for and against the granting of certiorari. Provine's work suggests that the justices' conceptions of the Court's proper role have great implications for their case selection votes. In the time period under study, a broad consensus existed on the Court's role and, consequently, the expression of the policy preferences and political attitudes of individual justices did not appear to be widespread in certiorari voting. In other time frames, however, such as cases seeking review of the constitutionality of the Vietnam War in the 1960s and 1970s and those dealing with capital punishment throughout the 1980s, greater divisiveness existed over the Court's role and, therefore, we would expect considerably more contentious certiorari voting than Provine found. Her article remains quite instructive in highlighting the wide variety of concerns that may enter into certiorari decision making.

Justice John Paul Stevens' offering of "Some thoughts on judicial restraint" was first delivered as an address to the American Judicature Society. In it, he proposed the establishment of a new federal court that would have the authority to decide which cases the Supreme Court would decide on the merits. Such a court, in Stevens' view, would alleviate the Supreme Court's caseload crisis, which he feels has been responsible for the unwise proliferation of per curiam opinions and the increased dismissing of writs of certiorari as improvidently granted. While it is now widely known that most Supreme Court justices rely heavily on their clerks in the certiorari process and that they participate in a certiorari "pool" with their colleagues, Stevens' 1982 public admission that, "I do not even look at the papers in over 80 per cent of the cases that are filed" was quite startling.

Justice William Brennan's 1982 address, "Some thoughts on the Supreme Court's workload," takes issue with Justice Stevens' call for a new tier in the federal judiciary. Indeed, Brennan asserts, the proposal would violate the Constitution's provision calling for "one Supreme Court" and it could only be established by amending the Constitution. Brennan rejects Stevens' basic premise that the Supreme Court's decisions on the merits have been compromised by the pressures of an inflated docket. To reduce the Court's workload, Brennan recommends the exercise of greater care in identifying certworthy cases aided by congressional removal of virtually all of the Court's mandatory appellate jurisdiction, a reform that has largely taken place. Brennan also alludes to various reforms in lower court processes that could alleviate some Supreme Court problems. Brennan argues that the Court's case screening function gets easier for a justice the more it is done and he directly confronts Stevens' confession of delegation. ". . . [M]y view that the screening function is second to none in importance is reflected in my practice of performing the screening function myself."

In "Caseload, conflicts, and decisional capacity: does the Supreme

Court need help?," Arthur Hellman takes the issues discussed by Justices Stevens and Brennan to a more empirical plane and closely examines one particular reform proposal, the creation of an Intercircuit Tribunal of the United States Courts of Appeals. Such a tribunal, unlike the reform most focused on by Stevens and Brennan, which dealt with a court that would screen cases *for* Supreme Court review, this court would decide cases referred to it *by* the Supreme Court. Hellman opposes such a plan, finding it both unnecessary to reduce the Court's workload and unlikely to achieve its stated goal of fostering uniformity in the law. The article highlights the disagreement that exists over the Court's workload problem, even among the justices themselves, regarding its nature and appropriate solutions. Hellman offers a thoughtful analysis that suggests that the workload problem may be a more complex one than first meets the eye. He concludes, "There is simply not enough evidence that the Supreme Court's limited capacity for authoritative decision making has significantly frustrated society's need for uniformity and predictability in the law. Moreover, too little attention has been paid to the possible adverse consequences of creating a new court."

Samuel Estreicher and John Sexton's "Improving the process: case selection by the Supreme Court" offers our final view of this controversial concern. They offer additional evidence that another layer of federal appellate review is not warranted while underscoring several reforms that could help Supreme Court justices manage their scarce resources. Importantly, Estreicher and Sexton's proposals could, in most instances, be effectuated by the justices themselves or through simple congressional action. These would not necessitate the kinds of constitutional changes some argue would be required by more drastic judicial reform measures. Clearly, the questions addressed in this section of readings will continue to be the subject of considerable debate and reform efforts in the foreseeable future.

Deciding what to decide: how the Supreme Court sets its agenda

Justices generally agree about what cases to review largely because they share a concept of the proper business of the Court.

by D. Marie Provine

Since the passage of the 1925 Judiciary Act, the U.S. Supreme Court has enjoyed broad discretion to decide which cases it will resolve on their merits. As dockets have grown more crowded in recent decades, this discretion has become an increasingly significant feature of the Court's institutional power. Currently, for example, the justices refuse review to more than 90 per cent of the cases which come before them, which amounts to approximately 3,500 cases denied review per term.[1] Clearly the criteria the justices use to set their agenda should be of considerable interest to students of the Supreme Court.

Research on the Court, however, remains fixed almost exclusively upon the cases to which the justices have granted review.[2] One explanation for the paucity of research on case selection is lack of data. The Court issues no opinions and releases no votes in denying or granting review. Traditionally, the only exceptions to complete secrecy in case selection have been occasional published dissents from denials of review, sporadic citations of reasons for granting review in opinions on the merits, general statements by justices and their law clerks on the case selection process, and the broadly-stated criteria of the Supreme Court Rules.[3]

Scholars interested in analyzing case selection criteria with statistical tools had only the bare facts of grants and denials to work with until 1965, when the papers of Justice Harold H. Burton became available. Burton's papers, on file at the Library of Congress, include complete docket books recording the case selection votes of each justice for the 13 terms that Burton sat on the Court (1945-1957).

These are the only complete records of case selection votes that are currently available for any period since the advent of discretionary review.

The Burton data make it possible to analyze case selection and its relationship to the more familiar work of the Supreme Court on the merits. Such an analysis suggests that the justices' conceptions of the proper role of the Court have a major impact on their votes to select cases for review. Consensus about the Court's role appears to have channeled and limited the expression of individual policy preferences and political attitudes in review decisions during the Burton period. Even when the justices disagreed in assessing review worthiness, role perceptions seemed to be significant to their decisions. The only case selection records currently available thus suggest that, in agenda setting, judicial sensitivity to the appropriate business of the Court is crucial.

I. Theories of case selection

The case selection process, because of its secrecy, provides the justices with a special opportunity for favoring certain litigants or side-stepping volatile cases, possibilities that have been noted by scholars.[4] Alexander Bickel, for example, suggested that Supreme Court justices should assess the political implications of the merits of cases and use case selection to limit "the occasions of the Court's interventions" in the political process.[5]

Schubert's certiorari game

Theories of how case selection actually proceeds may also take account of the opportunities for politically motivated behavior that the secrecy of the process provides. In the earliest and most provocative analysis, Glendon Schubert used game theory to explore the possibility that in Federal Employers' Liability Act (FELA) cases, a subgroup of justices manipulated others on the Court to gain the outcomes it preferred on the merits.[6] Such manipulation could occur because, by tradition, only four affirmative votes are needed to review, while five are ordinarily necessary to win on the merits. A minority could thus force a reluctant majority to consider minority-selected cases on the merits.

Schubert postulated that the "certiorari bloc," which varied in size and membership over the years, consistently attempted to maximize the number of Supreme Court judgments favorable to worker claims. The object of the bloc was to encourage the lower courts to look more favorably upon worker petitions. To achieve this objective, the bloc would vote against review in all cases brought by railroads, because in those cases the injured worker had been successful below. For worker petitions, the bloc's strategy was to vote for review only when a majority of the whole Court could be expected to reverse on the merits.

Black and Douglas were long-standing members of the "certiorari bloc." Murphy, Rutledge, Clark, Warren, and Brennan were also members during all or almost all of their shorter terms of office. Frankfurter represented an opposing player in the certiorari game. Others on the Court were uncommitted "pawns" to be "coopted" in the conflict between the two sides.

Schubert found that the "certiorari bloc" was not always successful in implementing its goal of achieving a judicial gloss on the FELA most favorable to workers. Its failures to win reversals in as many worker petitions as it might have stemmed in part from its failure to follow what Schubert conceived to be its optimal or "pure" strategy: to vote for review only when the worker won at trial and lost for the first time on appeal.

Schubert's theory is not seriously damaged by the failure of the "certiorari bloc" to adhere to its optimal strategy. Whether or not the justices behaved rationally at all times, the implications of the hypothesis are profound: the behavior of at least some members of the Court in certain cases can be understood in the language of power politics. Schubert's argument, in other words, was that

certain members of the Court, desiring to control the Court's decision making to effectuate preferred policies, made use of the opportunity for subgroup manipulation of the majority afforded by the so-called Rule of Four.

Schubert's analysis cannot be dismissed as a theory of Supreme Court decision making simply because of the limited subject matter it considers. Though the Court received, on the average, fewer than 10 worker-brought FELA cases per term in the period Schubert studied (1942-1960), these cases appear to have been a source of sharp disagreement among the justices. Opinions on the merits in FELA cases reveal deep divisions among the justices about the propriety of plenary, or on-the-merits, review. FELA litigation was, in fact, the most likely locus for outcome-oriented case selection voting on the Supreme Court of that era.

Testing Schubert's theory

The theory of voting behavior Schubert offers is open to criticism, however, on grounds that it does not fit actual voting patterns in FELA cases. Schubert based his research on the pattern of grants and denials in these cases, the only information available when he wrote. The Burton docket books make it possible to check the accuracy of Schubert's suppositions about case selection voting against actual votes.

Burton's records indicate that the "certiorari bloc" Schubert identified did not always vote in the pro-worker direction Schubert hypothesized. Members of the "certiorari bloc," for example, occasionally voted *against* the worker in favor of hearing railroad petitioners. Although no member of the Court did this often, alleged bloc members cast four of the seven pro-railroad votes in the period. The "certiorari bloc" also varied considerably in its support of worker cases; Brennan, for example, voted for only one-third of the cases he should have supported unequivocally. Furthermore, in five cases, the negative vote of one bloc member prevented the review on the merits that the rest of the bloc desired, and in five other cases that did gain review on the merits, the votes of non-bloc members neutralized a negative vote from a bloc member.[7]

Most importantly, the overall voting pattern in worker-brought cases does not match the pattern a theory of power-oriented voting would predict. Schubert's hypothesis implies that certiorari votes in FELA cases should tend to clump around zero and four votes for review. Only during the three-term period when the "certiorari bloc" had a fifth member should five vote grants be common. A consistent pattern of five or more votes would indicate that the bloc had more members than Schubert hypothesized, and frequent instances of fewer than four votes would indicate that conscious manipulation of case selection was absent.[8]

When the worker cases are subdivided by the number of votes they received, however, it is clear that a tight-knit power bloc was not operating during the Burton period. Table 1 indicates the actual pattern in these cases. As this table shows, there were 52 instances in which one, two, three, five, or six votes were cast for review in FELA cases, far too many to suggest the operation of a "certiorari bloc." Table 1 also shows that some justices almost invariably opposed review in FELA cases. Their on-the-merits opinions indicate that Justices Frankfurter, Harlan, and Burton were the members of the Court who consistently opposed review.

Cue theory

Other theories of case selection decision making conceptualize judicial motivation much differently than Schubert did. In an often-cited article, Tanenhaus, Schick, Muraskin, and Rosen hypothesized that Supreme Court justices are concerned with reducing their workload, rather than with competing to get their policy preferences incorporated into decisions on the merits, as Schubert presumed.[9] The authors theorized that the justices cut down case-processing time by summarily eliminating much of the caseload from careful consideration. According to this hypothesis, they use a set of agreed-upon cues to differentiate cases that might be worthy of review from those they know they did not want to hear.

Like Schubert, Tanenhaus and his colleagues wrote before the release of the Burton papers, so they had only the pattern of grants and denials with which to work. Nevertheless, they established an ingenious test of their hypothesis that the Court uses cues to reduce its workload. Relying on the statements of Chief Justice Hughes and others that between 40 per cent and 60 per cent of the petitions filed were clearly without merit, the authors hypothesized that this percentage of the cases contained no cues and was not examined beyond the initial search for cues. The rest of the petitions, which did contain one or more cues, constituted

Table 1 The distribution of votes for review in worker-brought F.E.L.A. cases and overall, 1945-57

Number of votes for review	F.E.L.A.	Overall (appell. dkt.)
1	7 (10%)	762 (24%)
2	12 (17%)	635 (20%)
3	9 (13%)	381 (12%)
4	16 (23%)	317 (10%)
5	16 (23%)	190 (6%)
6	8 (11%)	159 (5%)
7	1 (1%)	159 (5%)
8	0 —	127 (4%)
9	1 (1%)	417 (14%)
	Total=70	Total=3147

the pool from which cases were selected. Because only 5 per cent to 17 per cent of the docket as a whole was reviewed on the merits in the period under analysis, the authors concluded that the grant rate for the pool of cases containing cues must be between 25 per cent and 43 per cent.

The authors named three cues the Court used to select cases for careful scrutiny, and to eliminate summarily the remaining (cueless) 40 per cent to 60 per cent of the caseload:

- the presence of the United States as petitioner;
- the existence of a civil liberties issue;
- disagreement among the lower courts.

Testing cue theory

The accuracy of cue theory can be assessed by examining the fate of cue-containing cases during the Burton period, which matches almost exactly the 1947-1958 period Tanenhaus examined. Burton's papers permit a test of cue theory because his records reveal that a significant proportion of cases were eliminated with only cursory analysis, while the remainder were given more careful attention. The separation was accomplished by special listing, an administrative convenience devised by Chief Justice Hughes before Burton joined the Court.

The practice while Burton sat on the Court was for the chief justice and his staff to prepare a special list, or dead list, of cases deemed unworthy of conference time. The list circulated among the justices each week, and unless one of them put a special-listed case up for conference consideration, it was denied review automatically. Burton filed each week's special lists, and he kept a record of any changes justices requested. These records show that such alterations were rare.

Table 2 indicates the percentage of cue-contain-

Table 2   Disposition of cases containing Tanenhaus cues, 1947-57

Disposition of petitions	U.S. petn'r.	Tanenhaus cues Dissen. below	Civ. libs. Issue	All other appellate cases
Special listed	1%	27%	16%	45%
In conference:				
Denied unan.	8%	23%	22%	21%
Denied nonu.	25%	25%	26%	18%
Gr'ntd nonu.	41%	16%	21%	12%
Gr'ntd unan.	25%	9%	15%	5%
Total cases:	554	131*	629	6323

*Includes data only for 1947 Term.

ing cases that were put on the special list, and the number of votes attracted by those cases with and without cues that survived special listing. As this table shows, cases with cues were significantly more likely to get case selection votes than others on the Appellate Docket. Clearly the cues, especially the U.S. as petitioner, are related to the concerns the justices have in selecting cases for review on the merits. This is not surprising, since Tanenhaus settled upon the cues by examining the statements of Supreme Court justices and others about the types of cases of particular interest to the Court.[10]

Were the authors simply suggesting that some types of cases have a better chance of getting votes for review than others, the Burton data would tend to substantiate the hypothesis. Cue theory, however, purports to explain how the justices reduce the mass of petitions they receive to a more manageable number without actually considering the argument each petitioner makes for review on the merits. As the authors describe the process:

The presence of any one of these cues would warn a justice that a petition deserved scrutiny. If no cue were present, on the other hand, a justice could safely discard a petition without further expenditure of time and energy.[11]

If the cues actually served this short-circuiting purpose, cases containing cues should not appear on the special lists. Yet as Table 2 shows, in all three categories, some cue-containing cases are special listed.

Not a mechanical process

This pattern of voting suggests that the case characteristics that Tanenhaus deemed cues may be significant to the justices in case selection decisions, but that the decision-making process is not as mechanical as the authors suggest. Of course, something differentiates special-listed cases from those discussed in conference. The memos Burton's clerks wrote for him on each case and the case selection

voting patterns suggest that cases with jurisdictional defects, inadequate records, and no clearly presented issues were the most likely to be special listed.[12]

No easily identifiable case characteristics are invariably associated with special listing, however. This suggests that neither the justices nor the clerks rely on a fixed set of cues to separate cases into those worthy of scrutiny and those to be discarded summarily. With the assistance law clerks provide in digesting cases and writing memos, there is little reason to expect Supreme Court justices need such an abbreviated preliminary screening procedure.

It is more likely that the justices reduce the time they spend in evaluating petitions by relying on the clerks' memos. The justices may then reach a decision by engaging in a weighing process in which a few characteristics of cases—including probably the Tanenhaus cues—encourage at least some of the justices to vote for review, while many other characteristics act like demerits, preventing review in the absence of strong reasons in favor. The special-listed cases are those which contain one or more demerits and no countervailing considerations in favor of review.

The pattern of voting in U.S.-brought cases supports this interpretation. Because of the solicitor general's careful screening,[13] these cases seldom contain characteristics strongly discouraging review, so the Court seldom puts them on the special lists. In fact, as Table 2 indicates, U.S. cases are sufficiently impressive that in the Burton period they usually received at least one justice's vote for review. The evidence does not suggest, however, that the justices initially separate U.S. cases from the rest in an attempt to save reading time.

The attitudinal hypothesis

Another approach for understanding how the Court selects cases for plenary review emphasizes judicial predispositions towards litigants and policies.

Sidney Ulmer has actively promoted this perspective, using the Burton papers to test his attitudinal conception of the case selection process.[14]

One of Ulmer's principal findings has been that a justice's votes to review and his later votes on the merits are strongly related to each other.[15] Ulmer was able to show, for example, that for eight of the 11 justices whose votes he examined, a justice's vote to review helped to predict his vote on the merits.[16] Votes to review were associated with votes to reverse on the merits, a pattern which Ulmer explained in terms of judicial attitudes:

Theories of cognitive dissonance and attitudinal stability would lead one to expect some consistency in decisional direction if the factors underlying both decisions are identical or similar. Moreover, if the judge is conditioned to respond in a particular way to the stimulus (S) presented by a case on the first trial (t_1), the conditioned relationship may be reinforced by the mere act of response.[17]

Similarly, in a study limited to cases brought by state and federal prisoners, Ulmer hypothesized that a justice's underlying attitude towards institutional authority explained consistency at both stages of decision.[18]

Recently Ulmer has gone further, arguing that the justices sometimes try to disguise the extent to which they are influenced by their attitudes towards litigants in case selection. According to this hypothesis, when a justice suspects he cannot win review on the merits, he suppresses his ever present desire to vote for the underdog or the upperdog. In so doing, the justices defer to, but do not assimilate, the norm of impartiality in judicial decision making.[19]

Ulmer's emphasis on judicial attitudes in his analysis of case selection raises a question familiar to students of judicial behavior: are broad, pre-existing attitudes toward litigants and the policy issues in which they are entangled the sole or primary determinant of the votes of judges? Or do judges internalize norms that significantly limit the expression of personal preferences in their decisions? This much-debated question is, of course, central to traditional justifications for judicial power in a democracy. It is especially relevant in the context of case selection where, because of the secrecy of the process, external restraints on judicial judgment are absent.[20]

Cross pressures in case selection

While case selection is insulated from the public scrutiny that characterizes decisions on the merits, it is, of course, subject to strictures the justices place on themselves. The Court has consistently articulated one such self-imposed rule: that the justices decide whether a case should be reviewed not on the basis of their agreement or disagreement with the outcome between the parties in the lower court, but on the basis of their assessment of the intrinsic importance of the issues in controversy. A denial of review, therefore, does not mean that the Court agrees with the outcome of the case in the lower court, and a denial carries no significance as a legal precedent. As Frankfurter explained:

It simply means that fewer than four members of the Court deemed it desirable to review a decision of the lower court as a matter "of sound judicial discretion."[21]

The procedure the Court uses to select cases for plenary review, however, ensures that each justice will be well-acquainted with the arguments for relief from the lower court judgment when he decides whether to vote for review. The parties incorporate their views of the proper resolution of the case into their briefs for and against review.[22]

The Burton papers suggest that law clerks respond to these arguments and may even feel competent to pass on the merits at this stage in the proceedings. Burton's clerks typically suggested what they believed to be the correct outcome of the underlying dispute in their memos to the justice. The case selection process thus provides the justices with an easy opportunity to vote for review on the basis of their agreement or disagreement with the lower court result.

Ulmer's finding that votes to review and votes to reverse were correlated suggests that the justices *do* let their assessment of the merits of cases influence their review decisions. This finding does not necessarily mean, however, that the justices simply vote according to their attitudes towards certain types of litigants or policies at each stage of decision. The justices could just as well be responding to litigants in case selection, and later in votes on the merits, in light of general principles that determine the availability of judicial relief.

Ulmer's finding thus suggests two questions for further analysis: whether case selection and voting on the merits are, as a practical matter, indistinguishable; and, to the extent that they are, whether motivation can be persuasively explained in attitudinal terms.

II. An overview of voting patterns

If case selection is functionally equivalent to decision making on the merits, most case selection decisions should be nonunanimous, as most decisions on the merits are. Also, individual decisions to grant review should correlate highly with votes to reverse the lower court on the merits, and votes to reverse should be rare when a justice did not vote for review. Finally, the frequency with which a justice votes for review should be directly related to the level of his overall dissatisfaction with lower court results.

If attitudes towards litigants explain why individual case selection votes correspond with votes in fully considered cases, then the justices generally presumed to be the most politically liberal and the most conservative should seldom vote to review the same case. On the Court as a whole, disagreement among the justices should be parallel at both stages of decision, and this pattern should be consistent with the liberal-conservative spectrum we see in on-the-merits voting.

With the Burton records, we can determine whether or not these patterns existed during a significant portion of the modern Court's history. Analysis of case selection votes can thus contribute to our understanding of the relative significance of role constraints and attitude in judicial decision making.

Unanimity in case selection

Contrary to what one would expect if judicial views of the merits alone determined review decisions, the prevailing pattern in case selection is unanimity. During the Burton period, 82 per cent of case selection decisions were unanimous: 79 per cent were unanimous denials of review and 3 per cent were unanimous grants.[23] Available evidence indicates that the level of unanimity in case selection has remained high since the Burton era.[24] This numerical evidence alone suggests that case selection decisions are not functionally equivalent to decisions on the merits, and that some norm or norms guide the justices in deciding whether to vote for review.

Analysis of the types of cases decided unanimously during the Burton period suggests that the justices shared a conception of the work appropriate to the Court that overshadowed policy preferences and sympathies for certain litigants. Evidence of this is that the types of cases usually

Table 3   Unanimity in favor of review by case type, 1947-57

Case type	N	% granted review unanimously
U.S. petitioner	554	25%
Civil rights/liberties claims	630	14%
Labor claims	593	15%
Federalism issues	578	11%
All criminal petitioners	8572	0%
All other cases not noted above	4311	2%

presumed to tap judicial attitudes most directly were the very types most often denied review unanimously: the petitions of prisoners and suits by business interests seeking relief from government regulation.

This pattern of unanimity in presumably ideologically charged cases cannot be attributed to an unusual period of ideological uniformity on the Supreme Court. The Court's membership in this period included civil libertarians like Black and Douglas as well as nonlibertarians like Reed and Vinson. Yet all of them were in agreement that most of these cases should not be reviewed. In other words, all of the justices seem to have been convinced that certain types of cases were not important enough to review, even if they touched the private sympathies of individual justices.

A review of memos written by Justice Burton's law clerks suggests that this consensus has both procedural and subject-matter aspects. As noted earlier, cases with defective records from below or other weaknesses unrelated to the substance of their claims tended to be denied review unanimously, usually by special listing. Likewise, certain subject matters almost never got votes for review. Contract disputes, common law issues, and real property litigation were prime candidates for unanimous exclusion. Sixty per cent of these cases were special listed.[25]

Unanimity in favor of review

The types of cases in which the justices were most often unanimous in favor of review also suggest the importance of shared views about the proper business of the Court. During the Burton period, as Table 3 indicates, the justices tended to be unanimous in four types of cases which are related to basic areas of responsibility for the court of last resort in a federal system.

• U.S. petitions and labor claims which are similar in frequently raising issues concerning the proper scope of federal law-making authority.

Table 4   The relationship between votes to review and votes to reverse, 1947-57

Justice	*(Nonunanimous cases)*		
	Per cent of votes to reverse in cases he voted to review*	Per cent of votes to reverse in cases he voted against**	Difference between the two columns
Whittaker	93	43	50
Rutledge	85	37	48
Black	80	36	44
Minton	64	25	39
Warren	76	42	34
Vinson	61	31	29
Douglas	75	46	29
Jackson	62	34	28
Frankfurter	67	39	27
Brennan	79	52	27
Reed	58	31	27
Clark	62	35	27
Harlan	62	41	21
Murphy	74	57	17
Burton	56	39	17

*N=100 or more for all except Whittaker (27 votes to reverse in 29 cases favoring review).
**N=100 or more for all except Murphy, Rutledge, Brennan, and Whittaker where instances range from 20 to 50.

• Civil rights and liberties petitions which usually claimed federal constitutional rights against asserted state and local authority.

• Federalism cases, which require the Court to adjust competing jurisdictional claims among governmental and quasi-governmental authorities and which are clearly a central function for the court of last resort in a federal system.

Differences among the justices

When the justices of the Burton era disagreed in case selection, they differed considerably in the extent to which their votes to review paralleled their final votes on the merits, and they differed dramatically in the frequency with which they voted to review. These two measures of differences among the justices appear to be independent of each other.

The association between voting to review and to reverse already noted by Ulmer is evident in Table 4, which ranks the justices according to their tendency to vote for review and then vote to reverse on the merits. As the table shows, although the justices differed in the extent to which considerations favoring review and reversal paralleled each other, all of the justices were more likely to vote to reverse a case they voted to review than one they did not vote to review.

Were the justices considering simply the desired outcome of the dispute in case selection, however, the differences between the two columns in Table 4 would be much closer to 100 per cent. Nor can the failure of these differences to approximate 100 per cent plausibly be attributed to the effect of mis-

taken assessments of the merits at the case selection stage. The inadequacy of transposing the plenary decision to the case selection stage is particularly evident for the justices at the bottom of the table, for whom the relationship between case selection votes and votes for reversal is weakest.

It seems more likely that judicial beliefs concerning the proper work of the Supreme Court explain the imperfect correlations between votes to review and votes to reverse. A justice's failure to vote for reversal in every case he voted to review can be attributed to his belief that the subject was too important to pass over for reasons unrelated to the correctness of the outcome below. Likewise, a justice's vote to reverse a case he voted against reviewing can be attributed to the view that the case was wrongly decided below, but not important enough to review.

Considered in this light, departures from merits-consciousness in nonunanimous votes are consistent with the preponderance of unanimity in case selection: both depend on judicial conceptions of the proper role of the Court which limit the expression of individual sympathies and preferences in case selection votes.

Frequency of votes for review

The significance of role perceptions in case selection decisions is also evident when the Burton period justices are compared according to the frequency with which they voted for review. As Table 5 shows, the justices differed greatly in the frequency with which they voted for review. (This table segments the Burton period into natural

Table 5   Differences in the propensity to vote for review, 1947-57

(Each justice's votes for review//total opportunities to vote for review in pool of cases receiving at least one favorable vote; expressed as percentages)

Justice	1947-48	1949-52	1953-54	1955	1956	1957	Overall	Rank
Murphy	59	—	—	—	—	—	59	1
Douglas	53	61	61	55	59	54	58	2
Black	43	56	54	57	58	54	53	3
Rutledge	49	—	—	—	—	—	49	3
Brennan	—	—	—	—	42	44	43	5
Warren	—	—	31	43	54	38	40	6
Reed	28	38	31	30	—	—	33	7
Harlan	—	—	—	31	36	31	32	8
Jackson	22	30	31	—	—	—	27	9
Burton	22	33	23	29	30	23	27	10
Frankfurter	23	29	26	24	33	28	27	11
Clark	—	25	26	28	32	25	26	12
Vinson	—	21	—	—	—	—	25	13
Whittaker	—	—	—	—	—	21	21	14
Minton	—	10	10	18	—	—	13	15

courts defined by periodic shifts in the membership of the Court.)

Certain justices during the Burton period consistently voted more often for review than their colleagues. The justices often divided into groups on this issue, with 20 percentage points or more separating them in some natural courts. Black and Douglas were the long-standing members of the review-prone group, while Frankfurter and Burton were mainstays of the review-conservative group.

The remaining justices who voted in more than one segment of time also showed consistency in their propensity to vote for review. Generally, when a justice's percentage of votes for review did drop or rise from one natural court to the next, other carryover justices changed in the same direction. The rank order of the justices thus remained fairly constant over the entire period.

Changes in the membership of the Court also did not disrupt voting propensities, even when they affected how a majority of the Court could be expected to vote on the merits. This suggests that those who voted often for review did so with little regard for probable outcome on the merits, and even without regard to marshalling enough votes to gain review. The review-prone justices, in other words, appear to have been unconcerned with the impact of their case selection votes in specific cases.

This pattern raises the question of whether the review-prone justices voted most often for review because they were more dissatisfied with lower court outcomes than the rest of the Court. Such an explanation must assume that, for the more review-prone justices at least, votes to review are motivated primarily by disagreement with lower court outcomes.

Yet the ranking of the justices in Table 4, which estimates the relative tendency to vote to review in order to reverse, does not correlate with the ranking of the justices in their tendency to vote for review (Table 5). The two justices who voted most often for review, for example, were not especially likely to equate case selection and plenary decision making, while the two least review-prone justices were among the most likely to vote the merits in case selection.

In short, the tendency to vote often for review appears to be independent of the tendency to make disagreement with the lower court outcome the primary criterion of review-worthiness. Thus, while disagreement with lower court outcomes almost certainly influences the justices to vote for review, this variable can not by itself account for differences in the tendency to vote for review.

Propensity to vote for review

It seems likely that differences in the frequency with which individual justices voted for review are related to differences in the disposition of the justices to exercise Supreme Court power. Clearly the structure of case selection requires the justices to consider the proper scope of Supreme Court activity in voting for or against review. The identity of the most review-prone and the most review-conservative justices during the Burton period also suggests the relevance of such a concern.

Pritchett's discussion of differences among the justices in plenary decision making is particularly useful in showing this connection. Even though Pritchett restricted his analysis to civil rights and liberties cases, his explanation for voting differ-

Table 6   Justices' propensities to vote for review by case type, 1947-57

(Justice's votes for review/total opportunities to vote for review in pool of cases receiving at least one favorable vote; in percentages)

Justices ranked by overall tendency to vote to review	Criminal rights claims	Civil rights & liberties claims	U.S. claims	Federalism cases
Murphy	77	78	76	61
Douglas	73	76	42	50
Black	67	75	47	39
Rutledge	67	63	60	42
Brennan	68	56	62	56
Warren	42	44	57	34
Reed	23	21	69	27
Harlan	32	38	62	49
Jackson	27	29	33	48
Burton	21	22	54	43
Frankfurter	43	36	21	41
Clark	30	20	53	34
Vinson	12	14	52	47
Whittaker	19	28	23	48
Minton	9	7	35	20
Range:	68	71	41	41
Standard deviations:	26.1	22.9	15.6	10.3

ences is broad, and it seems applicable to Supreme Court decision making generally.

Those men whom Pritchett labeled "libertarian activists" in *Civil Liberties and the Vinson Court* were the most review-prone justices who sat during the entire Burton period.[26] Pritchett's "less libertarians" are among the least review-prone justices. Frankfurter, Pritchett's lone example of libertarian restraint, is somewhere near the middle in case selection, as he is in Pritchett's typology.

Pritchett described the libertarian activist as the judge whose sympathies are aroused by the underdogs in our society and for whom "the result is the test of a decision."[27] A believer in libertarian restraint, on the other hand, emphasizes the process of judicial decision making and the nondemocratic basis of judicial power. For Pritchett, a justice's activism or restraint is a function of the interaction of two variables: his sympathies towards underdogs and "the conception which the justice holds of his judicial role and the obligations imposed on him by his judicial function."[28]

Information about the frequency with which the justices vote for review is consistent with this two-dimensional interpretation of judicial motivation. Sympathy for underdogs and an expansive interpretation of the availability of Court-fashioned relief seemed to play a part in explaining voting frequency.

As Table 6 shows, review-prone justices tended to be willing to go further than their brethren in voting to hear criminal and civil rights and liberties claims. These were the types of cases that raised

new arguments for rights not yet established in precedent or legislation, and they occasioned the greatest disagreement among the justices over review-worthiness. In more established areas of litigation, represented here by U.S.-brought and federalism cases, the review-prone justices were relatively less likely to favor review, although, overall, they still tended to be more likely to vote for review than their colleagues.

The Court's proper workload

Differing convictions among the justices about the workload appropriate to the Court, a question central to the role it should perform, also appear to have been crucial. This is particularly evident when differences in voting frequencies are examined in detail. Table 7 provides such a close-up view of the voting history of the four justices who sat together throughout the Burton period: Douglas, Black, Frankfurter, and, of course, Burton. Douglas and Black, as Table 5 showed, were review prone, while Burton and Frankfurter were not.

Table 7 shows that, had two other justices consistently voted with them, Black and Douglas would have engaged the Court in several times as many cases as either Frankfurter or Burton. The willingness of Black and Douglas to involve the Court in this number of plenary decisions suggests that they placed little value on time-consuming methods of decision making. These men exhibited in their case selection behavior a willingness to reach decisions quickly and to justify them without ado, characteristics that are also evident in their behavior on

Table 7 A comparison of the voting propensities of the four justices who sat together on the Court, 1947-57

(In numbers of votes for review, nonunanimous cases)

	Number of justices voting with justice in left column						
	0	1	2	3	4	5	6 or 7
Burton	47	78	88	95	94	220	
Frankfurter	27	92	109	103	83	81	219
Douglas	243	353	237	186	139	117	216
Black	221	326	198	187	128	107	195

the merits.

Table 7 also shows that Black and Douglas participated in many more four-, five-, and six-vote grants than either Burton or Frankfurter. Only when seven or eight votes were cast were Burton and Frankfurter slightly more likely to have voted for review than Black or Douglas. This pattern indicates that Black and Douglas must have voted for review in many cases without paying much attention to the ideological similarities and differences with their colleagues that were usually in evidence in published decisions. Black and Douglas thus appear to differ from Burton and Frankfurter less in the types of cases they voted to hear than in the numbers they felt competent to decide on the merits.

In the weekly case selection conferences, the contrast between the two approaches must have been continually apparent and frequently irritating. To review-conservative justices like Frankfurter, the more review-prone justices must have seemed insensitive about the workload they were willing to impose on the Court. To the review-prone justices, those who seldom voted for review must sometimes have seemed callous about the plights of petitioners and the development of legal rights.

Conclusion

This analysis suggests that Supreme Court justices during the Burton period shared a powerful conception of the role of their institution, which appears to have sharply limited the level of disagreement that could otherwise have been anticipated in case selection voting. Consensus on the norms of judicial behavior also appears to have discouraged these justices either from combining forces to achieve the results they preferred on the merits or from voting individually in a way that would indicate routine calculation of probable outcomes in the case selection process.

The voting patterns examined here thus suggest that role conceptions serve both a limiting and a liberating function. Judicial conceptions of appropriate behavior help to limit the expression of judicial predispositions towards litigants in voting. Yet role conceptions also operate to free the justices from ideological isolation, permitting them to vote routinely with ideologically dissimilar justices.

The evidence here also suggests that role conceptions can also be a source of disagreement in case selection. The considerable differences among the Burton-period justices in their willingness to vote for review appear to be at least partly attributable to variation in conceptions of the Court's role.

The self-imposed limits of role conceptions, it is important to note, are essentially the only limits upon judicial discretion in case selection. Because of the secrecy of the process, case selection exceeds even plenary decision making in the scope it provides for the exercise of unfettered judicial judgment. The Taft period justices campaigned hard for this broad authority, and until recently, Supreme Court justices were unanimous in their efforts to maximize their agenda-setting power.[29]

Disagreement among the current justices has finally made Court-controlled case selection a public issue, however.[30] The question for policymakers is whether the Court should be permitted to maintain complete control in setting its agenda, limited only by the conceptions the justices hold of the proper way to perform this function.

For students of judicial decision making, the significance of role conceptions in case selection has additional implications. The explanatory power of the concept in this context suggests that role perceptions deserve more attention in analyses of Supreme Court decision making on the merits. Differences in role conceptions have, of course, been the focus of some research,[31] but the phenomenon of consensus among justices has received too little attention.

Preoccupation with voting differences among the justices gives a misleading impression of judicial motivation. Differences in judicial attitudes and role conceptions tend to receive lopsided attention, while the influence of shared norms derived from legal and professional socialization tends to be ignored. This makes it difficult to determine the extent to which judicial decision making parallels political decision making in other contexts. A more accurate picture will emerge only when political scientists acknowledge that the work of Supreme Court justices includes more than nonunanimous decisions on the merits.

NOTES

This article originally appeared in Volume 64, Number 7, February 1981, pages 320-333. It was adapted from the author's book, CASE SELECTION IN THE UNITED STATES SUPREME COURT (Chicago: University of Chicago Press, 1980).

1. *See* ANNUAL REPORT, DIRECTOR OF THE ADMINISTRATIVE OFFICE OF U.S. COURTS. For a brief review of caseload growth, *see* the Federal Judicial Center, REPORT OF THE STUDY GROUP OF THE CASELOAD OF THE SUPREME COURT (Washington, D.C.: Administrative Office of U.S. Courts, 1972).

2. Ulmer, *Selecting Cases for Supreme Court Review: An Underdog Model,* 72 AM. POL. SCI. REV. 902 (1978).

3. The high degree of secrecy the Court has sought to maintain about all its work prior to the release of final decisions was made evident recently by the flurry of interest which greeted *The Brethren,* a journalistic expose of decision making on the Burger Court. Woodward and Armstrong, THE BRETHREN: INSIDE THE SUPREME COURT (New York: Simon and Schuster, 1979).

4. Earp, *Sovereign Immunity in the Supreme Court,* 16 AM. J. OF INT'L L. 903 (1976); and Hanus, *Denial of Certiorari and Supreme Court Policy-Making,* 17 AM. U. L. REV. (1967).

5. Bickel, THE LEAST DANGEROUS BRANCH 128 (Indianapolis: Bobbs-Merrill, 1962).

6. Schubert, QUANTITATIVE ANALYSIS OF JUDICIAL BEHAVIOR (New York: Free Press, 1959); and Schubert, *Policy Without Law: An Extension of the Certiorari Game,* 14 STAN. L. REV. 284 (1962).

7. Provine, CASE SELECTION IN THE UNITED STATES SUPREME COURT 168-169 (Chicago: University of Chicago Press, 1980).

8. Bloc members intent upon persuading the uncommitted members of the Court to vote for workers on the merits would be ill-advised to throw away votes on losing cases because such behavior would expose the true extent of their pro-worker bias. Of course, occasional instances of three votes would be understandable as mistakes, but even these should be rare.

9. Tanenhaus, Schick, Muraskin, and Rosen, *The Supreme Court's Certiorari Jurisdiction: Cue Theory,* in Schubert (ed.), JUDICIAL DECISION-MAKING (New York: Free Press, 1963).

10. *Id.* at 122-125.

11. *Id.* at 118.

12. These were some of the considerations Tanenhaus hypothesized to control the review decision *after* the initial search for cues has occurred. *Id.* at 118.

13. Brigman, "The Office of the Solicitor General of the United States," doctoral dissertation, University of North Carolina, 1966.

14. Ulmer was the first, and for a considerable time, the only scholar to mine the Burton papers for evidence of what Supreme Court justices consider in case selection.

15. Ulmer, *The Decision to Grant Certiorari as an Indicator to Decision 'On the Merits,'* 4 POLITY 429 (1972); and Ulmer, *Supreme Court Justices as Strict and Not-So-Strict Constructionists: Some Implications,* 8 LAW & SOC'Y REV. 13 (1973).

16. Ulmer, *The Decision . . . , supra* n. 15.

17. *Id.*

18. Ulmer, *Supreme Court Justices . . . , supra* n. 15.

19. Ulmer, *supra* n. 2.

20. Of course, assessments of the relative significance of role perceptions are necessarily tentative because available evidence is indirect, and the concepts of role and attitude are too amorphous to operationalize very satisfactorily. *See* Howard, *Role Perceptions and Behavior in Three U.S. Courts of Appeals,* 39 J.

OF POL. 916 (1977); and Gibson, *Judges' Role Orientations, Attitudes, and Decisions,* 72 AM. POL. SCI. REV. 911 (1978).

21. Frankfurter, opinion explaining denial of review in State v. Baltimore Radio Show, 338 U.S. 912 (1950).

22. Prettyman, *Opposing Certiorari in the U.S. Supreme Court,* 61 VA. L. REV. 197 (1975).

23. Provine, *supra* n. 7, at 32

24. Brennan, *Justice Brennan Calls National Court of Appeals Proposal 'Fundamentally Unnecessary and Ill-Advised,'* 59 A.B.A. J. 835 (1973).

25. Provine, *supra* n. 7.

26. Pritchett, CIVIL LIBERTIES AND THE VINSON COURT (Chicago: University of Chicago Press, 1954).

27. *Id.* at 198.

28. *Id.* at 191.

29. Provine, *supra* n. 7, at 10-12 and 72-73.

30. Commission on Revision of the Federal Court Appellate System, STRUCTURE AND INTERNAL PROCEDURES: RECOMMENDATIONS FOR CHANGE (Washington, D.C.: U.S. Government Printing Office, 1975; and REPORT OF THE STUDY GROUP ON THE CASELOAD OF THE SUPREME COURT (Washington, D.C.: Administrative Office of U.S. Courts, 1972).

31. For other research on differences in role conceptions, *see* Pritchett, *supra* n. 26; Grossman, *Role-Playing and the Analysis of Judicial Behavior: The Case of Mr. Justice Frankfurter,* 11 J. OF PUB. L. 285 (1962); and *Dissenting Blocs on the Warren Court: A Study in Judicial Role Behavior,* 30 J. OF POL. 1068 (1968); Howard, *Role Perceptions and Behavior in Three U.S. Courts of Appeals,* 39 J. OF POL. 916 (1977); and Gibson, *supra* n. 20.

Some thoughts on judicial restraint

by John Paul Stevens

**As delivered to the annual meeting and banquet of the
American Judicature Society, August 6, 1982[1]**

During my exceptionally long tenure as the junior justice on the Supreme Court of the United States, I was frequently asked to compare the work on that Court with the work on the Court of Appeals for the Seventh Circuit on which I sat for five years. My answer to that question always made the point that I was much more conscious of the similarities between the two courts than of their differences.

During my brief tenure as one of the eight senior justices on the Court, I have frequently been asked to compare the work on an integrated court with the work on a segregated court. My answer to that question has usually made the point that although every retirement and every new appointment produces a different Court than its predecessor, the similarities between the Court on which Justice Stewart sat, and the Court on which Justice O'Connor sits, far outweigh their differences.

My belief that the common characteristics of the work of judges in a free society are far more significant than their differences has persuaded me that it may be worthwhile to share with you some of my concerns about the way the Supreme Court is presently discharging one of its judicial responsibilities. A frank discussion of our problems may identify some pitfalls that all of us should try to avoid and may uncover some possible solutions that merit further study.

The Supreme Court is now processing more litigation than ever before. The Court is granting more petitions for certiorari; litigants whose petitions are granted next fall may have to wait a full year before their cases are argued.[2] The Court is issuing more pages of written material; opinions for the Court are longer and more numerous, and separate opinions are becoming the norm instead of the exception. The Court is deciding more cases on the merits without the benefit of full briefing and argument, using the currently fashionable technique of explaining its reasons in a "per curiam" opinion—a document generally written for the Court by an anonymous member of its ever increasing administrative staff.[3]

More and more frequently, after a case has been fully argued, the Court finds it appropriate to dismiss the writ of certiorari without making any decision on the merits because it belatedly learns that certiorari was improvidently granted.[4] As is true in so many courts throughout the country, the heavy flow of litigation is having a more serious impact on the administration of justice than is generally recognized.

Some of the consequences of this increased flow are predictable and have already begun to manifest themselves. The problem of delay—which is not yet serious—in a few years will be a matter of national concern. Of even greater importance, however, is what may happen within the Court itself. For when a court is overworked, the judges inevitably will concentrate their principal attention on the most important business at hand. Matters of secondary importance tend to be put to one side for further study or to be delegated to staff assistants for special consideration. Two examples illustrate this point.

At the beginning of our last term, after the Court had processed the list of certiorari petitions that had been filed during the summer recess—if my memory serves me correctly there were about a thousand cases on that list—we agreed that it was essential that we confront the question whether the Court should either support legislation that would increase the appellate capacity of the federal judicial system or try to develop new internal procedures that would ameliorate the impact of the case volume on our own work. As the term developed, however, and we became more and more deeply involved in the merits of a series of difficult cases, our initial recognition of the overriding importance of evaluating our own workload problems—and the desirability of scheduling conferences devoted exclusively to that subject matter—gradually dissipated and no such conference was ever held. We were too busy to decide whether there was anything we could do about the problem of being too busy.

Reviewing approximately 100 certiorari petitions each week and deciding which to grant and which to deny is important work. But it is less important work than studying and actually deciding the merits of cases that have already been accepted for review and writing opinions explaining those decisions. Because there simply is not enough time available to do the more important work with the care it requires and also to read all the certiorari petitions that are filed, I have found it necessary to delegate a great deal of responsibility in the review of certiorari petitions to my law clerks. They examine them all and select a small minority that they believe I should read myself. As a result, I do not even look at the papers in over 80 per cent of the cases that are filed.

I cannot describe the practice of any of my colleagues, but when I compare the quality of their collective efforts at managing the certiorari docket with the high quality of their work on argued cases, I readily conclude that they also must be treating the processing of certiorari petitions as a form of second-class work. My observation of that process during the past seven terms has convinced me that the Court does a poor job of exercising its discretionary power over certiorari petitions. Because we are too busy to give the certiorari docket the attention it deserves, we grant many more cases than we should, thereby making our management problem even more unmanageable.

At this point I should make clear that I am expressing only my own opinion—an opinion that perhaps none of my colleagues may share. Indeed, some of them believe we should be taking many more cases and that our overflow should be decided by a newly created National Court of Appeals.

Under that view, the aggregate lawmaking capacity of the federal judiciary would be enlarged. There would be a significant increase in the number of federal adjudications binding on courts throughout the nation. Moreover, under that view, the management functions performed by the Supreme Court would require a relatively greater portion of the justices' total time. For the justices would not only decide what cases are important enough to justify decision on the merits at a national level, but they would also decide which of the two courts with nationwide jurisdiction should hear those cases. In other words, they would be managing the docket of two courts instead of just one.

The increased national capacity would also make it more difficult for us to resist the temptation to review every case in which we believe the court below has committed an error. Like a new four-lane highway that temporarily relieves traffic congestion, a new national court would also attract greater and greater traffic volumes and create unforeseen traffic problems. In my opinion, it would be unfortunate if the function of the Supreme Court of the United States should become one of primarily—or even largely—correcting errors committed by other courts. It is far better to allow the state supreme courts and federal courts of appeals to have the final say on almost all litigation than to embark on the hopeless task of attempting to correct every judicial error that can be found.

In my opinion, the Court and the nation would be better served by re-examining the doctrine of judicial restraint and by applying its teachings to the problems that confront us. The doctrine of judicial restraint is often misunderstood. It is not a doctrine that relates to the merits of judicial decisions; it is a doctrine that focuses on the process of making judicial decisions. It is a doctrine that teaches judges to ask themselves whether, and if so when, they should decide the merits of questions that litigants press upon them.

It is not a doctrine that denies the judiciary any lawmaking power—our common law heritage and the repeated need to add new stitches in the open fabric of our statutory and constitutional law foreclose the suggestion that judges never make law. But the doctrine of judicial restraint, as explained for example in Justice Brandeis' separate opinion in *Ashwander v. Tennessee Valley Authority*,[5] teaches judges to avoid *unnecessary* lawmaking. When it is necessary to announce a new proposition of law in order to decide an actual case or controversy between adversary litigants, a court has a duty to exercise its lawmaking power. But when no such necessity is present, in my opinion there is an equally strong duty to avoid unnecessary lawmaking.

The fact that the court is granting a larger number of certiorari petitions than ever before raises the question whether it is engaging in unnecessary lawmaking. The answer to that question is suggested by a few examples of the way the Court has exercised its discretionary jurisdiction in recent years. For both in deciding when to review novel questions and in deciding what questions need review, the Court often exhibits an unfortunate lack of judicial restraint.

Thus, the various opinions in our recent case involving a school library plainly disclose that the Court granted certiorari at an interlocutory stage of a case in which further proceedings in the trial court would either have clarified the constitutional issue or perhaps have mooted the entire case.[6] Similar considerations in the case involving a court clerk's claim of immunity prompted the Court to dismiss the writ as improvidently granted.[7] The Court's *timing* in these cases demonstrates that patience is both a virtue and a characteristic of judgment that judges sometimes forget.

In other cases, the Court has displayed a surprising unwillingness to allow other courts to make the final decision in cases that are binding in only a limited geographical area and in which no conflict exists. Thus, in *Watt v. Alaska*, apart from the possibility that error had been committed, there was no reason for our Court to involve itself in a dispute between the State of Alaska and one of its counties over the division of mineral leasing revenues that could only arise in the Ninth Circuit.[8]

In *Oregon v. Kennedy*, the Court elected to review a misapplication of double jeopardy doctrine by the Oregon Court of Appeals even though the particular facts of the case may never be duplicated in other litigation.[9] The fact that the new double jeopardy doctrine pronounced in the opinion of five of my colleagues was totally unnecessary to decide that case adds emphasis to the lack of necessity for granting certiorari at all. Moreover, despite that pronouncement, the Oregon court remained free to reinstate its prior judgment by unambiguously relying on Oregon, rather than federal, law to support its holding.

In *South Dakota v. Opperman*, the state supreme court followed that precise course, thereby proving that our Court had unnecessarily taken jurisdiction of a case in which deference to the state court's judgments would have been appropriate in the first instance.[10] The decision to review (and to reverse summarily without argument) a novel holding by a California intermediate appellate court concerning the burden of proof in an obscenity trial,[11] or an equally novel holding by the Pennsylvania Supreme Court concerning a police officer's order commanding the driver of a vehicle to get out of his car after a traffic violation,[12] are examples of the many cases in which the Court has been unwilling to allow a state court to provide one of its residents more protection than the federal Constitution requires, even though the state decision affected only a limited territory and did not create a conflict with any other decision on a question of federal law, and even though the state court had the power to reinstate its original judgment by relying on state law.[13] A willingness to allow the decisions of other courts to stand until it is *necessary* to review them is not a characteristic of this Court when it believes that error may have been committed.

The Court's lack of judicial restraint is perhaps best illustrated by the procedure it followed in the *Snepp* case.[14] A former CIA agent filed a petition for certiorari seeking review of a Fourth Circuit decision holding that his publication of a book about Viet Nam violated his secrecy agreement with the CIA;[15] he contended that his contract was unenforceable because it abridged his right to free speech. The government opposed his petition and also filed a conditional cross-petition, praying that *if* the Court should grant Snepp's petition, it should also consider whether the remedy ordered by the lower court was adequate.

The Court denied Snepp's petition, but nevertheless granted the cross-petition and, without hearing arguments on the merits, issued a per curiam opinion ordering a constructive trust to be imposed on all of the book's earnings, even though there was neither a statutory nor contractual basis for that novel remedy. Since the government had not even asked the Court to review the remedy issue unless it granted Snepp's petition, it is undeniable that the Court's exercise of law-making power in that case was totally unnecessary.

If you think the *Snepp* case is unique in the revelatory light it casts on the Court's present approach to the doctrine of judicial restraint, I suggest that you read the Court's per curiam opinion in the *McCluskey* case, decided on the last day of this term, in which the Court exercised its majestic power to reinstate the suspension of a high school student who had consumed too much alcohol.[16]

You may think I have wandered away from a discussion of problems created by the mounting tide of litigation that is threatening to engulf our Court. My purpose in discussing the doctrine of judicial restraint, however, is relevant for two quite different reasons. First, it lends support to a possible solution to the problem that I favor; second, it explains why judges who do not share my respect for the doctrine will surely oppose that solution.

Instead of creating a new court to decide more cases on the merits, thereby increasing the aggregate judicial power that the Supreme Court may exercise, I favor the creation of a new court to which the Supreme Court would surrender some of its present power—specifically, the power to decide what cases the Supreme Court should decide on the merits. In essence, this is the proposal that was made by the committee headed by Professor Paul Freund several years ago[17] with one critical difference. I would allow that court to decide—not merely to recommend—that a certiorari petition should be granted or denied. Let me just briefly explain why I believe the creation of a new court with that power would significantly improve the administration of justice.

First, and of greatest importance, I believe an independent tribunal that did not have responsibility for deciding the merits of any case would do a far better job of selecting those relatively few cases that should be decided by the Supreme Court of the United States. As I have already suggested, I think the present Court does a poor job of performing that task. It grants too many cases and far too often we are guilty of voting to grant simply because we believe error has been committed rather than because the question presented is both sufficiently important for decision on a national level and also ripe for decision when action is taken on the certiorari petition. I recognize that a different court might make similar mistakes, but reflection has persuaded me that such a court would be more likely to develop a jurisprudence of its own that properly focused on the factors—other than possible error—that should determine whether or not a certiorari petition should be granted.

Second, if I am correct in my belief that such a court would grant fewer petitions, this Court would be required to decide fewer cases on the merits. Even if that assumption is not correct, if the vast flood of paper and the small army of administrative personnel associated with the processing of our certiorari docket could be entirely removed from the Supreme Court, the time available to the justices for doing their most important work would be dramatically increased.[18] The threat to the quality of that work that is now posed by the flood of certiorari petitions would be entirely removed.

Finally, if the new court were granted the power to control our docket, I believe capable judges would regard membership on that court as worthy of their talent. When the original Freund Committee proposal was made, my initial reaction to it was the same as that of other circuit judges with whom I was serving—it seemed to offer us the opportunity to become law clerks instead of judges. But an important reason for that reaction was the fact that the proposed court was not expected to exercise any real power—it would have done no more than perform a preliminary screening function for the Supreme Court without the actual power of decision.

If the Supreme Court surrendered that power to the new court, the status of that court would indeed be significant. I am firmly convinced that a proper performance of the function of selecting the cases for the Supreme Cout's docket would be rewarding judicial work, requiring a scholarly understanding of new developments in the law and of our democratic institutions that only our ablest judges possess.

Those who question the wisdom of allowing the Supreme Court to relinquish control over its own docket, and who favor the creation of a new National Court of Appeals to decide cases that are referred to it by our Court, rely heavily on the perceived need to enlarge our capacity to resolve conflicts among the circuits. Let me therefore say a word about that asserted need. Again the doctrine of judicial restraint sheds light on the problem.

Putting to one side my own view that the number of unresolved conflicts is exaggerated, I would like to suggest, first, that the existence of differing rules of law in different sections of our great country is not always an intolerable evil and, second, that there are decision makers other than judges who could perform the task of resolving conflicts on questions of statutory construction. As Justice O'Connor noted in her eloquent dissent in the *FERC* case,[19] the fact that many rules of law differ from state to state is at times one of the virtues of our federal system. It would be better, of course, if federal law could be applied uniformly in all federal courts, but experience with conflicting interpretations of federal rules may help to illuminate an issue before it is finally resolved and thus may play a constructive role in the law-making process. The doctrine of judicial restraint teaches us that patience in the judicial resolution of conflicts may sometimes produce the most desirable result.

The doctrine of judicial restraint also raises the question whether the conflict resolution task need always be performed by judges. If the conflict is on a question of constitutional law, it must be resolved by the Supreme Court. But if, as is more frequently the case, the conflict is over the meaning of an ambiguous statutory provision, it may be both more efficient and more appropriate to allow Congress to make the necessary choice between the alternative interpretations of the legislative intent.

If the conflicts problem is—or should become—sufficiently important to justify the creation of an entirely new federal appellate court, I would suppose that the problem would also justify the creation of a standing committee of the Congress to identify conflicts that need resolution and to draft bills to resolve them one way or the other. If the source of the conflict is ambiguity resulting from an omission in a statute, it would seem to make good sense to assign Congress the task of performing the necessary corrective law making.[20]

At the outset, I suggested that a discussion of problems I perceive in our Court might be useful to other judges because the similarities among courts outweigh their differences. Before I close, let me therefore explain why I hope my comments may be relevant to the problems that arise in other courts. First, I would urge you to identify your problems and to discuss them openly and frankly. Disagreements with other judges is a characteristic of our profession that implies no disrespect and no lack of faith in the inherent strength of our institution. We must begin to talk about our problems before we can solve them.

Second, when you are considering possible changes in your procedures—as well as when you are deciding particular cases—keep in mind the teachings of the doctrine of judicial restraint. Consider whether, when, and how the special talent of judges—the thoughtful application of impartial judgment—should play a role in the decision-making process. And finally, I must note that although my remarks have indicated that proper management of a docket requires a court to treat some cases as having a greater importance or priority than others, distinctions that are made for administrative reasons are not applicable to the decisional process itself.

With regard to our primary responsibility, I would urge you to heed the advice of a truly great judge. In an interview a few weeks ago Justice Potter Stewart was asked if there was some opinion of which he was particularly proud. This was his answer:

I worked hard on every opinion. I think they were all satisfactory. I think it's very important for a judge—any judge, anywhere—to remember that every case is the most important case in the world for the people involved in that case, and not to think of a case as a second-class case or a third-class case or an unimportant case. It behooves the judge or justice to apply himself fully to every case and to give it conscientious consideration.

Justice Stewart's example, as well as his written word, is a great teacher.

NOTES

This article originally appeared in Volume 66, Number 5, November 1982, pages 177-183.

1. I wrote these remarks while away from my office and library. Thus, a few of my impressions about our docket have not been borne out by further research. Instead of rewriting the text, I have added a few documentary explanatory footnotes.

2. Of course, cases selected for review under the Court's certiorari jurisdiction are not the only source of backlog. This past year the Court exercised its discretion to grant more petitions for certiorari than ever before, but it also was required to note probable jurisdiction in 25 per cent more cases than in any prior year.

3. This sentence needs elaboration in two ways. First, as a factual matter, I was mistaken. When I say "per curiam," I have in mind an unsigned opinion that decides a case on the merits without argument and does not merely remand for reconsideration in light of a recently decided case. The number of per curiams has oscillated over the past 20 years, and this past term's total of 20 was not unusually large. I should probably have stressed a more disturbing statistic—the number of divisive per curiams, those from which three or more justices dissent. The past term produced 10 divisive per curiams, whereas six prior terms I have examined (1951-52, 1961-62, 1965-66, 1971-72, 1976-77, 1980-81) have produced at most four.

Second, my choice of the phrase "ever increasing administrative staff" was unfortunate. I intended the term "staff" to include the justices' personal law clerks as well as other court employees.

4. Here my memory of this past term failed me. In fact, our dismissal of only two petitions for certiorari as improvidently granted was less than our annual average. The fact that this is a recurring phenomenon, however, provides added support for my central thesis.

5. 297 US. 288, 341-356 (1936).

6. Board of Education, Island Trees Union Free School Dist.

No. 26 v. Pico, 102 S. Ct. 2799 (1982).

7. Finley v. Murray, 102 S. Ct. 1703 (1982).

8. 451 U.S. 259 (1981).

9. 50 U.S.L.W. 4544 (May 24, 1982).

10. 428 U.S. 364 (1976); *on remand*, 247 N.W.2d 673 (S.D. 1976). *See also* Idaho Dep't of Employment v. Smith, 434 U.S. 100 (1977), *on remand*, Smith v. Department of Employment, 100 Idaho 520, 602 P.2d 18 (1979) (state ct. originally finds that state statute violates federal equal protection clause; after reversal, state ct. construes statute to be inapplicable to facts of the case).

11. Cooper v. Mitchell Brothers' Santa Ana Theater, 102 S. Ct. 172 (1981).

12. Pennsylvania v. Mimms, 434 U.S. 106 (1977).

13. *See also* Washington v. Chrisman, 50 U.S.L.W. 4133 (Jan. 13, 1982) (state supreme court held that a police officer violated the Fourth Amendment when, after stopping a student, asking for identification, and accompanying the student back to his room, he entered the room uninvited and without a warrant; U.S. S. Ct. reversed); Minnesota v. Clover Leaf Creamery Co., 449 U.S. 456 (1981) (state supreme court struck down a statute that banned the retail sale of milk in plastic nonreturnable nonrefillable containers, but permitted such sale in other nonreturnable nonrefillable containers such as paperboard cartons; U.S. S. Ct. reversed); Arkansas v. Sanders, 442 U.S. 753 (1979) (state supreme court held that police violated the Fourth Amendment by making a warrantless search of luggage located in an automobile they had lawfully stopped; U.S. S. Ct. affirmed); County Board of Arlington County, Virginia v. Richards, 434 U.S. 5 (1977) (state supreme court struck down a county zoning ordinance prohibiting automobile commuters from parking in designated residential neighborhoods; U.S. S. Ct. reversed).

14. 444 U.S. 507 (1980).

15. 595 F.2d 926 (4th Cir. 1979).

16. Board of Education of Rogers, Ark. v. McCluskey, 50 U.S.L.W. 3998.25 (July 2, 1982).

17. The Freund Committee said: "We recommend creation of a National Court of Appeals which would screen all petitions for review now filed in the Supreme Court.... The great majority, it is to be expected, would be finally denied by that [new] court. Several hundred would be certified annually to the Supreme Court for further screening and choice of cases to be heard and adjudicated there." Federal Judicial Center, REPORT OF THE STUDY GROUP OF THE CASELOAD OF THE SUPREME COURT 18 (Washington, D.C., 1972).

18. Perhaps "dramatically increased" overstates the significance of saving approximately one day each week for work on argued cases instead of certiorari petitions. The more important saving would, I believe, result from the selection of a smaller number of cases for plenary review.

19. Federal Energy Regulatory Comm'n v. Mississippi, 102 S. Ct. 2126, 2145 (1982).

20. In using the word "assign," I do not mean to suggest that the Supreme Court should seek to certify issues of statutory construction to a legislative committee. Rather, I am suggesting that the policymaking branch of the federal government might assign itself that task and an overburdened Court might do well to consider denying certiorari if a case raises only an issue of statutory or regulatory construction—an issue that could be resolved by another branch of the federal government.

Some thoughts on the Supreme Court's workload

by William J. Brennan Jr.

As delivered at the Third Circuit Judicial Conference, September 9, 1982, Philadelphia, Pennsylvania.

Y ou doubtless have read of the concern expressed at the ABA and AJS meetings in San Francisco by Justices White and Stevens that the Supreme Court confronts a calendar crisis so severe as to threaten the Court's ability effectively to discharge its vital responsibility. Justice Powell also addressed the problem but in the broader context of proposals designed to lessen the burdens of the entire federal court system. I should like in these brief remarks to address the problems of the Supreme Court calendar.

First, what is the problem? Justice White identified it:

During last term we granted review in 210 cases, which is 26 more than the term before and 56 more than two terms ago (and I may say parenthetically the largest number of grants in one term during my 26 terms on the Court). Apparently there were just too many petitions for certiorari that we could not conscientiously deny. Our docket is now full through February, next term, and will be completely full (only the March and April sessions remain to be filled) by the end of November if grants next term proceed at the same rate as they did last term.

Of course this means that we shall not be current in our work; cases will be ready for argument and we shall not be ready for them. This is something new and disturbing . . . The [problem thus is] not that the Court [is] not hearing all the cases that it [has] the capacity to hear but that it [does] not have the capacity to review all those cases that the system contemplated would be reviewed at the Supreme Court level.

Justice White asked, "Can or does the Court hear all the cases that must be reviewed and authoritatively decided if the federal law is to survive in the form contemplated by the Constitution?" For now, I think I'd say yes, it does.

It is true, as Justice White said, "that there is a finite limit on the number of cases that the Court can hear and decide with opinion in any one term." For more than 15 of my 26 terms, starting in 1956, the Court averaged about 100 opinions per term plus a few per curiams in argued cases. But since the 1970 term that number has inexorably crept up, first to the high 120, then to the 130s, and last term to 141 signed plus nine per curiam.

That didn't set any record—the 1975 term produced 151 opinions, 138 signed, and 13 per curiam. And since we schedule 160 hours of argument from October through April, it is clear that 150 is the maximum. Of course we could add another month of arguments and theoretically turn out 20 more opinions. But I suggest that the Court, as Justice White says, "should not be expected to produce more than 150 opinions per term in argued cases, including per curiam opinions in such case." There is a limit to human endurance, and with the ever increasing complexity of many of the cases that the Court is reviewing in this modern day, the number 150 taxes that endurance to its limits.

I suppose the solution to the question whether the number of grants can be kept under control and the calendar made manageable without rejection of cases that should be heard and decided depends (a) on what the Court can do for itself to avoid granting cases that should not be granted and (b) on what the Congress and the courts of appeals can do to minimize the necessity for granting review of some cases.

What can we do for ourselves? I must admit frankly that we too often take cases that present no necessity for announcement of a new proposition of law but where we believe only that the court below has committed error. But ever since the

Congress enacted the Judges Bill of 1925, the Supreme Court has not been expected to take on the function of primarily—or even largely—correcting errors committed by other courts. As Justice White reminded us, in 1925 Congress was presented with the proposition that after decision in a trial court and after at least one review in federal or state appellate court, further appeal to the Supreme Court should be permitted only where issues of federal law important to the country were involved, or where further review was essential to resolve conflicts between lower courts on questions of federal constitutional or statutory law, which, by definition was to be equally and uniformly applicable in all parts of the country. "Absent these qualifications, one trial and one appellate review were enough."

It was this history that prompted Justice Stevens to remark, "It is far better to allow the state supreme courts and federal courts of appeals to have the final say on almost all litigation than to embark on the hopeless task of attempting to correct every judicial error that can be found."

And, too, we have made mistakes in granting certiorari at an interlocutory stage of a case when allowing the case to proceed to its final disposition below might produce a result that makes it unnecessary to address an important and difficult constitutional question. Last term's school library case is a paradigm example. It presented the question of whether schools boards were in any wise restrained by the First Amendment in the removal of books from a school library. The district judge held not and granted the school board summary judgment. The Second Circuit reversed on the ground that the case presented a genuine issue of fact as to the school board's motivation and therefore the case should be tried. Obviously, further proceedings in the trial court would either have clarified the constitutional issue or perhaps have mooted the entire case. Yet the Court took the case at the interlocutory stage, disposed of it by an affirmance of the remand for trial, and filed eight separate opinions without producing one that commanded the votes of a majority. Surely we should discipline ourselves to be more faithful to the *Ashwander* principle not to address constitutional issues if there is a way properly to avoid doing so.

Congress could afford the Court substantial assistance by repealing to the maximum extent possible the Court's mandatory appellate jurisdiction and shifting those cases to the discretionary certiorari docket. A bill to this end is pending in the Congress and every member of the Court devoutly hopes it will be adopted. Cases on appeal consume a disproportionate amount of the limited time available for oral argument. That's because time and again a justice who would conscientiously deny review of an issue presented on certiorari cannot conscientiously say that when presented on appeal the issue is insubstantial, the test on appeal. Policy considerations that gave rise to the distinction between review by appeal and review by writ of certiorari have long since lost their force, and abandonment of our appellate jurisdiction (leaving a writ of certiorari as the only means of obtaining Supreme Court review) is simply recognition of reality.

Can we perhaps decide more cases on the merits by denying ourselves the benefit of full briefing and oral argument? There is sentiment among some of my colleagues to do so. Because I wholeheartedly agree with Justice Stevens that "oral argument is a vital component of the appellate process," and have too often witnessed colleagues, who favored summary affirmance at the cert stage, change their minds after oral argument—and because I think further that the Court's favorable image in the eyes of both bar and public rests so heavily on oral audience before us—I have continuously protested against summary dispositions, unless at least all of us believe that the judgment below flatly rejects the controlling authority of one of our decisions. If the losing side commands the agreement of a single justice, it seems to me he's entitled to an opportunity orally to persuade others of us.

One of the Court's important functions of course is the resolution of conflicts in statutory construction or constitutional principles decided by the courts of appeals; a major segment of each term's docket is provided by such cases. Both Justice White and Justice Stevens offered some provocative suggestions for reducing the burden of such cases. "If the resolution of conflicting decisions is at the root of the problem," said Justice White,

there is the option of creating new courts of appeal that would hear appeals from district courts countrywide in certain kinds of cases.

For example, the Court of Appeals for the Federal Circuit, created by the merger of the Court of Customs and Patent Appeals and the Court of Claims, will hear all appeals from district courts in cases arising under the patent laws. Another court that hears all appeals from cases arising under specified statutes is the Emergency Court of Appeals. Courts like these, of course, bypass the regular court of appeals, but they eliminate the possibility of conflicts that normally would have to be heard in the Supreme Court.

That surely is a suggestion worth exploring. It does not foreclose Supreme Court review but removes conflict as the reason for review. No constitutional impediment occurs to me, although doubtless policy considerations might be a reason for congressional opposition.

Justice White offered still another and novel idea for reflection: "That is," he said, "to require a court of appeals to go *en banc* before differing with another court of appeals and to make the first *en banc* decision the nationwide rule." I expect that the court of appeals and district court judges here today might want to mull that one over a bit.

Justice Stevens' contribution is equally imaginative and innovative. If, he says, "as is more frequently the case, the conflict is over the meaning of an ambiguous statutory provision it may be more efficient and more appropriate to allow Congress to make the necessary choice between the alternative interpretations of the legislative intent." This could be accomplished, he suggests, by

the creation of a standing committee of the Congress to identify conflicts that need resolution and to draft bills to resolve them one way or the other. If the source of the conflict is ambiguity resulting from an omission in a statute, it would seem to make good sense to assign Congress the task of performing the necessary corrective law making.

The problem I see with this suggestion is that it overlooks the role of compromise in the legislative process, compromise that often accounts for the studied ambiguity of legislative language, deliberately adopted to let the courts put a gloss on the words that the legislators could not agree upon. If the legislators could not avoid the ambiguity in originally enacting the law it might be no different if they attempted to resolve the conflict.

Justice Stevens also asked whether in any event conflicts of interpretation were necessarily a bad thing. He said,

the existence of different rules of law in different sections of our great country is not always an intolerable evil . . . it would be better, of course, if federal law could be applied uniformly in all federal courts, but experience with conflicting interpretations of federal law may help to illuminate an issue before it is finally resolved and thus may play a constructive role in the law making

process. The doctrine of judicial restraint teaches us that patience in the judicial resolution of conflicts may sometime produce the most desirable result.

I think there is already in place, and has been ever since I joined the Court, a policy of letting tolerable conflicts go unaddressed until more than two courts of appeals have considered a question. Indeed, Justice White has filed opinions in recent terms chiding his colleagues for being too tolerant of conflicts. I confess for myself that I doubt there is much more we can do along those lines.

But suppose, as the Commission on Federal Appellate Revision concluded a few years ago, that these various efforts failed to achieve a manageable calendar and "that at some point the percentage of cases accorded review will have dipped below the minimum necessary for effective monitoring of the nation's courts on issues of federal statutory and constitutional law"—what then? Justice White thought, "There are surely obvious alternatives, particularly if more fundamental structural changes are thought necessary to remedy the problem. Rather than one Supreme Court," he said, "there might be two, one for statutory issues and one for constitutional cases; or one for criminal and one for civil cases." That proposition of course would require a constitutional amendment, but in any event, I cannot see any crisis confronting us that would require so drastic a wrench of our constitutional structure.

Then there is the revival of the proposal originally made a decade ago by the distinguished Freund Commission to create a National Court of Appeals. As Justice White noted, the essence of that proposal was this:

all certioraris and appeals would come to the Court as they do now. The Court would select cases for its own docket as it does now, but if there were other cases deserving of review that it could not hear, it would have the authority to refer those cases to a so-called national court of appeals . . . that court's decisions would be subject to certiorari review, but it was thought that only rarely would certiorari be granted in those cases . . . .

Justice White acknowledged that a bill is now pending in Congress to create such a court but says, "I see no great flurry of activity around it."

Justice Stevens opposes the suggestion of transferring cases for decision by the proposed national court of appeals, but he also opposes the suggestion that that court assist the Supreme Court in selecting the cases that will be set for oral argument and plenary review. This would be done by that court screening out seven-eighths of the cases filed in our Court, leaving us to choose from some 400 to 500 cases the 150 or so that would be heard and decided. Instead of that system, Justice Stevens, in his words,

favors the creation of a new court to which the Supreme Court would surrender some of its present power, specifically the power to decide what cases the Supreme Court should decide on the merits [Unlike the Freund Committee proposal] I would allow that court to decide—not merely to recommend—that a certiorari petition should be granted or denied,

and that court's decision to deny would not be reviewable.

I completely disagree with my respected and distinguished colleague. I dissented from the form in which the Freund Committee made the proposal and feel even more strongly that adoption of Justice Stevens' proposal would destroy the role of the Supreme Court as the framers envisaged it.

Justice Stevens believes that the screening function "is less important work than studying and actually deciding the merits of cases that have already been accepted for review and writing opinions explaining those decisions." Apart from the fact that the plan would clearly violate the constitutional provision establishing "one Supreme Court," and therefore require a constitutional amendment, I reject Justice Stevens' fundamental premise that consideration given to the cases actually decided on the merits is compromised by the pressures of processing the inflated docket of petitions and appeals.

I don't have time to demonstrate here why that premise is unsupportable. Suffice it for present purposes that my view that the screening function is second to none in importance is reflected in my practice of performing the screening function myself. I make an exception only during the summer recess when the initial screening of petitions is invaluable training for next term's new law clerks.

For my own part, I find that I don't need a great deal of time to perform the screening function—certainly not an amount of time that compromises my ability to attend to decisions of argued cases. I should emphasize that the longer one works at the screening function, the less onerous and time-consuming it becomes. Unquestionably the equalizer is experience, and for experience there can be no substitute, not even a second court.

If the screening function were to be farmed out to another court, some enormous values of the Supreme Court decisional process would be lost. Under the present system, a single justice may set a case for discussion at conference, and in many instances that justice succeeds in persuading three or more of his colleagues that the case is worthy of plenary review. Thus the existing procedure provides a forum in which the particular interests or sensitivities of individual justices may be expressed, and therefore has a flexibility that is essential to the effective functioning not only of the screening process but also of the decisional process which is an inseparable part.

Similarly, the artificial construction of the Supreme Court's docket by others than the members of the Court would seriously undermine the important impact dissents from denials of review frequently have had upon the development of the law. Such dissents often herald the appearance on the horizon of possible re-examination of what may seem to the judges of another court doing the screening work to be an established and unimpeachable principle. Indeed, a series of dissents from denials of review played a crucial role in the Court's reevaluation of the reapportionment question, and the question of the applicability of the Fourth Amendment to electronic searches. This history of the role of such dissents on the right to counsel in criminal cases and the application of the Bill of Rights to the states surely is too fresh in mind to ignore.

Moreover, the assumption that the judges of a national court of appeals could accurately select the "most review-worthy" cases wholly ignores the inherently subjective nature of the screening process. The thousands upon thousands of cases docketed each term simply cannot be placed in a computer that will instantaneously identify those that I or any one of my colleagues would agree are "most review-worthy." A question that is "substantial" for me may be wholly insubstantial to some, perhaps all, of my colleagues. As Chief Justice Warren said:

The delegation of the screening process to the National Court of Appeals would mean that the certiorari "feel" of the rotating panels of that Court would begin to play a vital role in the ordering of our legal priorities and control of the Supreme Court docket. More than that, this lower court "feel" would be divorced from any intimate understanding of the concerns and interests and philosophies of the Supreme Court Justices; and that "feel" could reflect none of the other intangible actors and trends within the Supreme Court that often play a role in the certiorari process.

I repeat that a fundamental premise of Justice Stevens' proposal is that the screening function plays only a minor and separable part in the exercise of the Court's fundamental responsibilities. I think that premise is clearly, indeed dangerously, wrong. In my experience over more than a quarter century, the screening process has been, and is today, inextricably linked to the fulfillment of the Court's essential duties and is vital to the effective performance of the Court's unique mission "to define the rights guaranteed by the Constitution, to assure the uniformity of federal law, and to maintain the constitutional distribution of powers in our federal union."

The choice of issues for decision largely determines the image that the American people have of their Supreme Court. The Court's calendar mirrors the ever-changing concerns of this society with every more powerful and smothering government. The calendar is therefore the indispensable source for keeping the Court abreast of these concerns. Our Constitution is a living document and the Court often becomes aware of the necessity for reconsideration of its interpretation only because filed cases reveal the need for new and previously unanticipated applications of constitutional principles. To adopt Justice Stevens' proposal to limit the Court's consideration to a mere handful of the cases selected by others would obviously result in isolating the Court from many nuances and trends of legal change throughout the land.

The point is that the evolution of constitutional doctrine is not merely a matter of hearing arguments and writing opinions in cases granted review. The screening function is an inseparable part of the whole responsibility; to turn over that task to a national court of appeals is to rent a seamless web. And how traumatic and difficult must be the screening task of the judges of a court of appeals required to do major Supreme Court work without being afforded even the slightest glimpse of the whole picture of a justice's function.

It is not only that constitutional principles evolve over long periods and that one must know the history of each before he feels competent to grapple with their application in new contexts never envisioned by the framers. It is also that he must acquire an understanding of the extraordinarily complex factors that enter into the distribution of judicial power between state and federal courts and other problems of "Our Federalism." The screening function is an indispensable and inseparable part of the entire process and it cannot be withdrawn from the Court without grave risk of impairing the very core of the Court's unique and extraordinary functions.

You may rightly ask me then, what would you do to bring about the shrinking of the size of the calendar to manageable numbers? First, I would urge greater care by the Court in the selection of cases for review. Second, I would urge repeal by Congress of virtually all the Court's mandatory appeal jurisdiction. Third, I would urge an immediate study of the feasibility of Justice White's suggestion of creating new courts of appeals that would hear appeals from district courts countrywide in certain kinds of cases, thus obviating conflicts. Fourth, I would urge an immediate study of Justice White's other suggestion for minimizing conflicts—to require a court of appeals to go *en banc* before differing with another court of appeals and make the first *en banc* decision the nationwide rule.

But I would most emphatically reject all proposals for the creation of a national court of appeals, or any other court, to which would be assigned the task of doing the Court's work, whether decisional or screening. Adoption of that proposal would sow the seeds of destruction of the Court's standing as we know it. For remember, Justice Brandeis ascribed the great prestige of the Court with the American public to a single factor, "Because we do our own work."

NOTE

This article originally appeared in Volume 66, Number 6, December-January 1983, pages 230-235.

Caseload, conflicts, and decisional capacity: does the Supreme Court need help?

Examining the Court's work, and workload, suggests we should give more thought to the need for—and structure of—the proposed Intercircuit Tribunal.

by Arthur D. Hellman

Congress is now giving serious consideration to legislation that would effect the most far-reaching change in the structure of the federal judicial system since the creation of intermediate appellate courts nearly a century ago. Bills introduced by Senator Dole and Congressman Kastenmeier, with the apparent support of Chief Justice Burger, would create an "Intercircuit Tribunal of the United States Courts of Appeals" that would hear and decide cases referred to it by the Supreme Court. Unless overruled or modified by the Supreme Court, decisions of the Tribunal would constitute binding precedents in all other federal courts and, with respect to federal issues, in state courts as well.[1]

Proponents argue that creation of the new court is necessary for two reasons: "to relieve the dramatically increased workload of the Supreme Court" and to "provide desperately needed additional decisional capacity for the resolution of disputes where nationwide uniformity is needed."[2] Curiously, although the problems perceived by the sponsors originate in conditions that can hardly be expected to disappear as the years go by, the bills now in committee would create only a temporary court composed of circuit judges who would sit on the Intercircuit Tribunal in ad hoc panels while continuing to serve on their own courts.

The premises underlying this proposal raise fundamental questions about the role of the Supreme Court in the American legal system and the extent to which one tribunal of nine justices can fulfill that role. In this article, I shall address those questions. I conclude that notwithstanding its impressive sponsorship, the legislation should not be enacted, at least in its present form. To the extent that it seeks to reduce the workload of the justices, it is unnecessary. To the extent that it seeks to promote uniformity in the law, it rests on assumptions that have not been proved; but even if those assumptions are correct, creation of a temporary tribunal would do little to foster uniformity, while it would have undesirable consequences for the Supreme Court's performance of the tasks it would not delegate.

One preliminary observation is in order. During the past year, eight of the nine sitting justices have expressed concern about the Court's caseload and the management of its docket. This has led some observers to conclude that the justices agree that the caseload problem has reached crisis proportions and requires immediate legislative reform. However, the more important fact is that the diagnoses offered by the members of the Court are quite different and to some extent contradictory.

Justices White and Rehnquist think that limited decisional capacity is causing the Court to deny review in some cases that require resolution at the national level; Justice Stevens thinks that the Court grants review in more cases than are necessary. Chief Justice Burger finds a plenary docket of 150 cases a term—the current figure—to be so burdensome as to threaten a breakdown of the system; but in the eyes of Justice Rehnquist, it is well within the limits of the tolerable. The chief justice predicts an increase in summary reversals, especially in criminal cases; Justices Brennan, Marshall, and Stevens think that the summary reversal is overused even today. Justices Powell and O'Connor have spoken only in general terms about the Supreme Court's workload; their principal concern has been the proliferation of litigation in the lower federal courts.

This diversity of views provides a poor basis indeed for immediate structural reform. On the contrary, it only emphasizes the need for careful analysis of the Court's functions and practices before any legislation is enacted.

The workload of the justices

In considering whether the justices are overworked, it is necessary to look separately at the two tasks they perform: selecting the cases they will decide, and deciding them. Attention must also be given to the effect of the obligatory jurisdiction on the Court's workload.

Screening cases for plenary review

With the possible exception of Justice Stevens, no member of the present Court has asserted that the process of screening cases for plenary review has become unmanageable.[3] Nor would such an assertion be persuasive. Admittedly, the number of cases to be examined is much greater than it was two decades ago—4,417 in the 1981 term. But a caseload of that size does not impose nearly the burden that it would, for example, at the court of appeals level.

From Taft onward, the justices have emphasized that the function of the Supreme Court is not to correct errors in the lower courts, but to "secur[e] harmony of decision and the appropriate settlement of questions of general importance."[4] Thus, except for the cases that come to the Court on appeal—less than 5 per cent of the total—the purpose of screening is not to determine whether there was error, or even probable error, in the court below. Rather, the Court considers whether the case presents an issue of "wide public importance or governmental interest."[5] Making that determination will usually take very little time, compared with assessing the probable correctness of the decision below.

More important, the vast majority of applications clearly do not meet the standard for "certworthiness" that the justices have articulated. A few years ago, Justice Brennan revealed that 70 per cent of the cases were so obviously unworthy of review that not even one justice requested that they be discussed at the Court's conference.[6] More recently, Chief Justice Burger—who has been in the forefront of those arguing that the Court is overburdened—has said that two-thirds of the new filings are not only unworthy of review but "utterly frivolous."[7]

Perusal of the case summaries in *United States Law Week* confirms these perceptions. In one case after another, the party seeking review asserts only that the lower court abused its discretion or erred in applying well-established rules to particular facts. And those are the paid cases. Almost half of all applications for review are filed by indigent litigants, nearly all of whom are criminal defendants who have nothing to lose by filing petitions whether or not they present an issue appropriate for the Supreme Court.[8]

Deciding cases and writing opinions

The screening process thus constitutes a relatively small part of the justices' total workload. The more time-consuming task is that of reaching decisions and writing opinions in the 140 to 150 cases that do receive plenary consideration each term. Yet is is far from clear that a calendar of that size truly imposes an intolerable burden on the justices.

Under current conditions, each justice is required to write 15 or 16 majority opinions a term—barely two for each month that the Court is in session. Some of the cases will involve intractable social and political issues warranting extended reflection and research, but not all fit this description. In particular, by the time the Court resolves a statutory issue, the competing arguments should have been thoroughly ventilated in the lower courts and the law reviews, and the justices should be able to reach a decision and write their opinions with a minimum of agonizing.

This is not to deprecate the amount of time and effort required for the process of reaching and justifying decisions in the cases on the plenary docket. After all, the justices not only have their own opinions to write; they should also be giving careful scrutiny to the drafts prepared by their colleagues. And if caseload pressures become too great, review of other justices' opinions is likely to be the first casualty, thus reducing the opportunities for clarifying the language, sharpening the reasoning, or otherwise improving the final product through collegial consultation.

This analysis suggests that whether or not the workload has begun to overwhelm the justices, creation of a new court might still be desirable on a different theory: that the Supreme Court could then reduce the number of cases that receive plenary consideration and thus be able to produce opinions of higher quality—however one might measure that elusive goal. Indeed, that was a major theme of Chief Justice Burger's speech in New Orleans calling for creation of an intercircuit panel similar to the one contemplated by the pending legislation.

It might seem intuitively obvious that the justices would write better opinions if they had more time. Nevertheless, the available evidence indicates that the matter is not that simple. In the middle and late 1950s the Court was hearing fewer cases than at any other time in this century; but that was also the era when eminent scholars filled the law reviews with devastating criticism of the Court's craftsmanship. Not everyone agreed with those criticisms, but the history provides little comfort for those who see a smaller docket as leading to wiser adjudications or more illuminating opinions. More recently, the abortion decisions of 1973 were handed down only after an extended process of research, reflection, and deliberation; yet those opinions too have been subjected to vehement criticism, even by scholars who sympathize with the results.

In any event, before we can reach any conclusions about the burdens imposed by the plenary docket, we must consider the actions of the justices themselves. If the members of the present Court are truly overworked, they are behaving in some very strange ways. Consider:

• Separate expressions of views have proliferated in recent years to an extent never before known. In the 1981 term alone the justices issued more than 175 separate opinions.[9] It is understandable, and indeed desirable, that a justice would write separately when he or she cannot support the result or rationale of the majority opinion. But more than 20 of these separate opinions were written by justices who had already joined the opinion of the majority. In addition, there were half a dozen dissenting opinions by justices who had already joined another dissent. Strangest of all, there was one case in which the author of the majority opinion also wrote a separate opinion reversing the court below on a second ground, and another case in which two opinions were joined by different majorities of justices.[10]

• In recent terms, a major component of the plenary docket has consisted of criminal cases in which the lower courts had upheld the defendant's constitutional claims. In some of the cases, a state court had arguably rested its judgment on adequate and independent nonfederal grounds.[11] Other decisions appeared to involve little more than the application of established rules to a particular set of facts.[12] While a Supreme Court ruling would add something to the body of nationally binding precedents, the contribution would be marginal enough that an overburdened Court could deny review without concern that it would be missing an opportunity to significantly clarify the law.

• In other cases where lower courts have accepted a litigant's federal constitutional claim, the Court has reversed without hearing oral argument. These reversals have been accompanied by per curiam opinions, a few of which approach the length of many signed opinions.[13] Here, too, some of the cases have involved only the application of established rules to particular facts.[14] For the most part, nothing in the per curiam opinions has suggested that the particular situations are recurring ones, or that the decisions below reflect oft-repeated errors or a consistent disregard of the governing law.[15] Thus consideration on the merits could not be justified either from the standpoint of the Court's lawmaking functions or as a necessary exercise of its supervisory power.

• In the current term the Court ordered reargument on an important issue that had neither been litigated in the court below nor raised in the petition for review. As the dissenting justices pointed out, these circumstances make more work for the Court in deciding the case.[16]

Effect of obligatory jurisdiction

Assessment of the "workload problem" also requires attention to the fact that the Court today does not have an entirely free hand in selecting the cases it will decide. When a case comes to it on appeal rather than by certiorari, the Court has no choice but to decide the merits. The Court need not—and usually does not—give the case plenary consideration or write an opinion, but it cannot avoid the duty of determining whether the lower court committed error. In recent terms, about half of the cases decided on the merits have been appeals.

It might be thought that because most of the appeal cases are disposed of by summary orders without opinion, abolition of the obligatory jurisdiction would not significantly lighten the Supreme Court's workload. Study of the Court's practices, however, indicates that the continuing flow of appeal cases imposes at least three kinds of burdens on the justices.

First, the obligation to decide the merits of a case sometimes leads the Court to grant plenary consideration to appeals that would have been denied review if they had come up by certiorari. As the justices have pointed out, "[t]here is no necessary correlation between the difficulty of the legal questions in a case and its public importance."[17] As a result, the Court often feels obliged to call for full briefing and oral argument in appeal cases that are too difficult to decide summarily but not important enough to warrant review by certiorari standards. In the 1981 term, fully one out of every four cases on the plenary docket came to the Court on appeal. While many of the cases were worthy of review by certiorari standards, some—probably 10 or more— were not.[18]

Second, even if the issue presented by an appeal is one that the Supreme Court would ultimately want to decide, the particular case may raise it prematurely or in a setting inappropriate for a definitive resolution. Either circumstance makes the Court's job harder. If the issue has not yet been thoroughly ventilated in the lower courts, the process of reaching a decision and writing an opinion will be more difficult because the Supreme Court will be deprived of the benefits of "percolation." If the case is not an appropriate vehicle, not only will the opinion be harder to write, but the decision may not settle the issues, so that they will come back in somewhat different form and require additional consideration.

Finally, the obligatory jurisdiction adds to the Court's burdens even in the cases that receive summary treatment. Whatever the practice may have been before the Court announced that summary dispositions are decisions on the merits,[19] the Court today must give every appeal a degree of attention and thought that need not be accorded a certiorari petition. After all, if certiorari is denied improvidently, the issue remains open in all other jurisdictions, and if the question is truly worthy of review, it will return in another case. But if the Court improvidently affirms a case on appeal, the effect is to establish a nationally binding precedent and to discourage if not preclude further litigation of the issue.[20] Thus the justices must examine each jurisdictional statement with at least enough care to assure themselves that affirmance will not settle a question that they prefer to leave open.[21]

☆ ☆ ☆

Two conclusions emerge from this analysis. First, the Court's workload has not yet reached anything resembling crisis proportions. Second, before implementing structural change, Congress should take the uncontroversial and long-overdue step of eliminating the remaining elements of the obligatory jurisdiction.[22] Once that is done, we will have the opportunity to see how the Court manages its docket on a wholly discretionary basis. If, after a few years, the workload is shown to be truly burdensome, there will be no alternative to structural reform; but Congress, the bar, and the public will have had that much more time to consider the merits of various possible solutions.

The problem of disuniformity

To say that the Court's workload does not justify creation of a new tribunal is not to say that the justices could reasonably be expected to increase the number of cases that receive plenary consideration, and indeed no one takes that view. Thus the stronger argument for structural change rests on the assertion that "additional decisional capacity" is needed to secure uniformity and consistency in federal law.

To evaluate this claim, it is necessary to answer four questions. First, to what extent is there disuniformity in the law today as a result of the limited number of cases the Supreme Court can decide on the merits? Second, how has the lack of "appellate capacity" affected those who must conform their conduct to federal precedents—judges deciding cases in the lower courts, lawyers advising clients, and citizens carrying out their everyday activities? Third, how effective would the proposed new court be in reducing the existing uncertainty? Finally, how would the availability of the reference option affect the Supreme Court's performance of the work it would not delegate?

Unresolved intercircuit conflicts

In introducing the bill to create an Intercircuit Tribunal, Senator Dole asserted that the proposed court would "provide desperately needed additional decisional capacity for the resolution of disputes where nationwide uniformity is needed, many of which are now left unresolved because the

Supreme Court cannot make room on its docket." In a similar vein, Congressman Kastenmeier stated that hundreds of petitions from the courts of appeals are denied review even though some "identify serious conflicts between circuits." The clear implication is that the Supreme Court is denying review in such a large number of conflict cases, with such a substantial impact on consistency in the law, that the need for additional decisional capacity has reached the point of desperation.

But where is the evidence? Where is a list of 50 cases in which the Supreme Court, during a recent term, has denied review despite the presence of a conflict? Where are 30 unreviewed conflicts? Where are 20? One searches in vain for any such compilation, either in the record of the hearings on similar legislation held in 1981 and 1982 or in the statements submitted on the Senate bill this spring.[23]

Within the Court, the most persistent advocate of the view that intercircuit conflicts remain unresolved because the Court "cannot make room on its docket" has been Justice White. A casual reader of the weekly order lists might get the impression that Justice White has identified a substantial number of cases in which the Court has denied review despite the presence of a conflict. But careful counting reveals that in the 1981 term Justice White published only 12 opinions dissenting from the denial of review on that ground. Two involved the same issue; two others involved issues that are scheduled to be considered in the 1982 term. And study of all unreviewed cases in the 1980 term in which Justice White filed a dissenting notation of any kind yields no more than 15 in which the decision below appeared to conflict with the ruling of another appellate court.[24]

On the basis of the available evidence, then, it cannot be said that the number of conflicts presented to the Supreme Court has, to any substantial degree, outstripped the Court's capacity to resolve them. At first blush, this may seem rather surprising. After all, during the last few decades Congress has substantially added to the body of federal statutes that require interpretation; the number of circuits has been enlarged; and the volume of appellate litigation has grown enormously.

But these developments do not necessarily bring about a proportionate increase in the number of conflicts. For one thing, the courts of appeals generally attempt to avoid intercircuit disagreements if they can conscientiously do so.[25] More

important, as new issues arise, old ones become settled (through the accumulation of precedents)[26] or irrelevant (through developments in the law or in the activity being regulated).[27] Finally, as will be discussed more fully below, there are many issues that for one reason or another are just not likely to give rise to conflicting decisions. Thus, even though the United States Code may occupy an ever-larger space on the shelf, the number of questions on which the courts of appeals will actually differ may remain relatively stable.

Potential conflicts

Up to this point I have focused on unresolved intercircuit conflicts as a measure of the adequacy of the national appellate capacity. But the more thoughtful supporters of the proposed new court argue that the desirability of obtaining a definitive resolution of a particular issue does not depend on the existence of an actual conflict. They point out that for those who must regulate their activities in accordance with federal precedents, the presence or absence of a conflict is almost irrelevant; the crucial question is whether there is an issue that is doubtful enough that the possibility of conflict exists. If conflict is possible, uncertainty is inevitable. And, as Professor Meador has suggested, "uncertainty about the ultimate meaning to be given statutory provisions can make the work of lawyers and administrators difficult and more costly to citizens and to government."[28]

Yet even when these considerations are taken into account, it does not necessarily follow that the focus on unresolved conflicts has been misdirected. At the least, the further we move away from an actual conflict, the less likely it becomes that a given case warrants a decision by the Supreme Court, and the more likely it is that the Court would deny review even apart from caseload pressures. There are two reasons why this is so.

First, the particular explanation for the absence of a conflict may suggest that a decision by the Court is unlikely to make a significant contribution to uniformity in the law. For example, if there are no other cases on point, the reason may be that the precise problem arises very seldom; if so, no other court is likely to confront the issue in the future. If there are several decisions, all reaching the same result, that may be because the answer is obvious, and any reasonable lawyer would confidently predict that future courts will follow in the same path.[29]

Finally, and perhaps most important, if there are multiple decisions that look in somewhat different directions without actually conflicting, the reason may be that the underlying factual contexts are so numerous, and the relevant legal considerations so varied, that no one decision—or six—could be "definitive." In short, a Supreme Court decision is most likely to make a significant contribution to uniformity in the law when the issue it addresses is both discrete and recurring as well as doubtful. Issues of that kind are probably the exception rather than the rule in a common law system.[30]

But even if an issue is discrete and recurring, the justices will often be well advised, from the standpoint of reaching sound decisions, to wait for an actual conflict before addressing it. A contrary voice—whether or not it is ultimately persuasive—can illuminate a problem in a way that a series of generally harmonious opinions will not. Sometimes the nonconforming decision will reveal flaws in the reasoning of the courts that considered the question initially.[31] At other times the unpersuasiveness of the later decision will provide reassurance that the first cases reached the correct result after all.[32] In either situation, the Court benefits from the judicial system's analogue to the adversary process—though with the additional and crucial element that the opposing perspectives come from two or more disinterested courts, each of which must justify its position through reasoning that will have the force of law. Moreover, by looking at the various decisions applying the competing rules, the Court can get a sense of how each works in practice and thus be in a better position to make an informed choice between them.

Some lawyers appear to assume that the desirability of speedy resolution and the probable gain from additional "percolation" are independent values that compete with and must be weighed against one another. But this is not necessarily so. The certainty that is supposed to come from speedy resolution may prove illusory if a premature decision raises more questions than it answers. At best the Court will forthrightly modify the view it took before the additional considerations were brought to its attention. At worst the Court will retain the rule but hedge it about with so many qualifications and subrules that the law is more confused than it was before. It is no accident that justices with widely differing views of the Court's proper role in the American system of government have lauded the values of percolation in both constitutional and statutory cases.[33]

Uncertainty and interstitial lawmaking

Those who argue that an Intercircuit Tribunal is needed to bring about uniformity and consistency in federal law bear the burden of showing that the Supreme Court's limited capacity for decision making has resulted in disuniformity and inconsistency on a large scale. They have not met that burden. But this failure of proof is not necessarily dispositive on the question of whether some sort of auxiliary court should be created. The Supreme Court may be able to resolve all ripe intercircuit conflicts. What it cannot do, to any substantial extent, is engage in interstitial lawmaking—the task of interpreting and elaborating upon its landmark precedents. But the essence of a common law system is that "no case can have a meaning by itself,"[34] and that legal rules have meaning only as they are applied in a series of cases. From that standpoint, advocates of the new court would be quite correct in arguing that one Court of nine justices can do at best an incomplete job of declaring the law.

The difficulty is that the common law process need not take place within a single court. The job of filling in the interstices of the Supreme Court's landmark rulings will be carried on in the federal courts of appeals and state appellate courts in any event. How much difference does it make that the United States Supreme Court can make only a limited contribution to the process?

Even on its own terms, that question may be unanswerable. But it is made even more problematic by the fact that the lack of a squarely controlling Supreme Court precedent is only one of the sources of uncertainty and unpredictability in the law. For example, the legal consequences of a particular transaction may depend on a well-settled rule that gives the factfinder wide discretion to reach different or even inconsistent results that will not be disturbed on appeal.[35] Administrative agencies not only have wide leeway in determining the "facts" upon which legal obligations will be based;[36] they may also modify or even reverse the governing rules without running afoul of appellate courts' willingness to defer to "expertise" or the lessons of experience.[37] Within a single agency or appellate court, different panels may view a given transaction quite differently while applying the same articulated rule of law.[38] Even when the Supreme Court addresses a recurring issue, its opinion may be so ambiguous as to leave the question little more settled than it was before.[39] Finally, life is too varied to accommodate itself to a necessarily finite number of precedents. Inevitably, there will be situations that do not fall within any existing rule; perhaps more commonly, situations will arise that are arguably governed by more than one rule, each of which may point to a different result.

These sources of uncertainty are magnified by the operation of the adversary system. In structuring a transaction or considering litigation, a lawyer must make an informed guess about the probable responses of the other parties. Those responses in turn will depend on such variables as wealth, aversion to risk, transaction costs, and familiarity with the law.

Taking these and other considerations into account, Professor Anthony D'Amato has recently argued that legal certainty actually decreases over time, and that "[r]ules and principles of law become more and more uncertain in content and in application because legal systems are biased in favor of unraveling those rules and principles."[40] One need not accept this extreme position to recognize that there are numerous forces that produce uncertainty in the law, and that these forces will continue to have a powerful effect even if the number of nationally binding decisions is increased from 150 to 200 or even to 300.[41] And as long as it cannot be said that actual intercircuit conflicts are going unresolved to any substantial extent, there is a real question whether a larger number of interstitial decisions by a national tribunal would contribute more than marginally to certainty and predictability in the law. At the least, Congress should wait for more evidence before creating a new structure to issue those decisions.[42]

Uniformity and the proposed court

If the evidence showed that the Supreme Court's limited capacity for definitive adjudication constituted a significant impediment to the achievement of uniformity in federal law, could the proposed Intercircuit Tribunal be expected to solve or mitigate the problem? There is good reason to believe that it could not.

The legislation now under consideration contemplates a court of 27 judges who would hear and decide cases in randomly composed panels of five.

This is exactly the system that has led lawyers to complain of inconsistency and unpredictability in the decisions of the large circuits.[43] Nor is this surprising. A court that sits in small panels selected by lot from among a much larger number of judges can hardly develop any kind of institutional approach or recognized set of policies. The lack of continuity in the proposed Intercircuit Tribunal would thus make it difficult if not impossible to achieve the predictability and stability in the law that the design is intended to create.

Recognizing the force of these arguments, several witnesses at the Senate hearings have urged that the new court be composed of a smaller number of judges—seven or nine—who would always sit en banc. That would certainly be an improvement over S. 645 as it now stands, but it would leave untouched the more fundamental flaw in the proposed structure: its reliance on a system of ad hoc case referrals prompted by the need to resolve or perhaps forestall an intercircuit conflict. That approach assumes that cases presenting actual or incipient conflicts typically involve self-contained issues that can be shunted off for resolution by a separate court with little or no effect on the development of the law generally.

But federal law is not a body of distinct rules that operate in isolation from one another. Even a narrow, relatively technical question of statutory construction may depend on the application of doctrines such as the "plain meaning" rule, the weight to be given to an agency's interpretation of the statute it administers, or the significance to be accorded the views of a Congress subsequent to the one that enacted the law. By the same token, lower courts confronted with widely divergent statutory questions will look to the entire corpus of Supreme Court opinions for guidance on these matters.[44] At a simpler level, unclear or ambiguous language in one clause or section often must be interpreted in the light of other provisions of the legislation or with a gloss furnished by the language or law of related statutory schemes.[45] In either situation, the result is to broaden the range of precedents that must be taken into account when any of the various issues are litigated.

If a new tribunal were to issue nationally binding decisions in a selection of cases having nothing in common except the fortuity of an intercircuit conflict, the lower courts would be required to harmonize dual lines of authority in a way that might create more uncertainty rather than less. And the more deeply the new court moves into interstitial lawmaking, the greater the likelihood that its decisions will have arguable relevance for superficially unrelated kinds of litigation.[46] On the other hand, if the new court's docket is confined to square conflicts on narrow issues, the available evidence suggests that there would be very little for the Tribunal to do.

Is there any escape from this dilemma? One possible approach would be to have categorical rather than ad hoc referrals. That is, instead of asking the new court to decide a collection of unrelated cases involving actual or potential conflicts, the Supreme Court would announce in advance, preferably through some kind of rulemaking process, that the new court would be given primary responsibility for overseeing the development of the law in particular areas of federal regulation. Thereafter, all cases in those areas would be referred unless the justices found good reason not to do so. The Intercircuit Tribunal would grant or deny review in accordance with what it perceived the needs of the national law to be.

This arrangement would permit a substantial amount of interstitial lawmaking to be carried on at the national level in those areas of the law that the Supreme Court chose to commit to the new tribunal. And while the Supreme Court would be empowered to review the Tribunal's decisions by writ of certiorari, the assumption must be that review would almost never be granted; otherwise the whole system would be pointless. Thus the new court would provide all of the precedential guidance that otherwise would have to come from the Supreme Court, but in limited areas of the law.

What I have described is, in essence, the approach proposed several years ago by Dean Paul Carrington and other members of the Advisory Council for Appellate Justice.[47] On the surface, at least, it would involve a more radical restructuring than the bills now under consideration. But it would be more consistent with the traditions of the common-law lawmaking process; would minimize (though not avoid entirely) the development of inconsistent lines of authority applicable to the same cases; and would permit the performance of a task that clearly cannot be performed by the Supreme Court alone. Whether this kind of reform is necessary is another question; I am not yet convinced that it is.

Risks for the Supreme Court

In giving qualified support to Chief Justice Burger's proposal for a tribunal very much like the one contemplated by the pending legislation, Professor Daniel Meador suggested that creation of the new court "would involve little expense [and] carry virtually no risk of harm to the system or to anyone's interest."[48] I fear that this view is unduly optimistic.

I do not refer to fiscal costs or to the possible effect on the morale of courts of appeals judges who are not chosen for the new tribunal What concerns me, rather, is the effect of creating the Intercircuit Tribunal on the Supreme Court's performance of the responsibilities it would not delegate. In particular, I foresee two undesirable consequences. First, the case selection process would become more complex and perhaps more divisive. Second, the Supreme Court would tend to become, even more than it is today, a court of constitutional adjudication—a result that would pose risks both for the decisional process within the Court and for public acceptance of the Court's role.

The case selection process

The current legislation contemplates that the Supreme Court would select the docket of the new court. For reasons I have set forth elsewhere, that is the only acceptable approach.[49] But there is no blinking the fact that it would entail additional work for the justices.

Admittedly, when seven members of the present Court gave their views on the Hruska Commission's proposal for a National Court of Appeals with reference jurisdiction, none of them—even those who opposed the idea—appeared troubled by the prospect of having to select the new court's docket. But I cannot help wondering whether they fully thought through the implications of this arrangement.

Today, the justices have only three ways of handling the cases that are brought to them for review: they can grant plenary consideration; they can decide the case summarily; or they can deny review altogether. Reference jurisdiction would add a fourth option.[50] It does not take an expert in small-group theory to hypothesize that to expand the number of choices available to a nine-person committee in a large number of decisions would substantially increase the potential for dissension and even deadlock. In particular, the justices are unlikely to share the same view of the appropriate role of the Intercircuit Tribunal in the development of federal law; and even if they do, they will probably differ in the weight that they give to "percolation," both generally and in particular cases.

No doubt the Court could devise procedures or standards that would enable it to handle potentially divisive situations, but it is hard to avoid the conclusion that the availability of an ad hoc reference option would complicate the selection process and thus add to the justices' burdens.[51] A categorical reference system would probably operate more smoothly; to what extent would depend on the nature of the categories used.

Risks of delegating statutory issues

In any event, the more serious cost of creating an Intercircuit Tribunal lies in its effect on the Supreme Court's decisional work. What kinds of cases would the Supreme Court refer to the new court? Surely it would not refer cases involving issues of civil rights or other questions of constitutional law. Almost inevitally, decisions in these cases implicate large questions of social policy or turn on deep-seated ethical judgments about the competing claims of liberty and authority. As a consequence, it is highly unlikely that the justices would be willing to share their jurisdiction with another court, whatever its composition.

Moreover, it is on constitutional issues that differences in language, approach, or emphasis are most likely to convey conflicting messages to litigants and lower courts. For example, Fourth Amendment jurisprudence is confusing enough today with only one Court handing down nationally-binding decisions; to have a separate tribunal participate in the process would invite even greater disarray.[52]

Thus the Court is likely to refer only petitions raising narrow or technical questions of statutory construction. A few such referrals would do no harm, but the temptation would be great to refer all or most cases of this kind. The effect would be to restrict the Court's work largely to great issues of civil rights law, federalism, and the interpretation of statutes such as the Sherman Act or the National Labor Relations Act, which have almost the breadth of a constitutional provision. Indeed, it is quite possible that with a new tribunal to resolve some of the narrow statutory issues that today must be heard by the Supreme Court, the justices would take a larger number of constitutional cases for the purpose of correcting possible error.

For some commentators, a de facto division of the Court's work into constitutional and nonconstitutional issues, with the latter diverted to a new tribunal, would be a welcome solution to the caseload problem. Others will see it as but another step in a process that is already far advanced; in recent terms, only one-third of the Court's plenary decisions have involved pure issues of statutory construction, divorced from constitutional concerns. In my view, however, to move further in that direction would entail grave consequences both for the way in which the Court goes about its work and for the way in which that work is perceived by the citizenry.

Internally, the Court would lose an important source of self-discipline. As Justice Rehnquist has pointed out, "[t]o the extent that the Court must deal with statutory and other nonconstitutional questions, in which the permissible limits of adjudication are narrower, the . . . Court is kept on its toes and pressed to remain a classical court rather than a branch of government largely freed from the necessity for giving closely reasoned explanations for what it does."[53] Statutory cases serve another internal function as well: they remind the justices that the Constitution is not the only source of values and that the decisions of the representative branches of government are entitled to respect.

Routine statutory issues may also play an important role in preserving collegiality within the Court. Voting blocs that persist across a wide range of constitutional issues often tend to break up when less earth-shaking questions of statutory interpretation are presented.[54] The existence of cases in which the Court finds itself unified—or divided along unexpected lines—serves to moderate the tensions that are likely to build up in cases involving the Bill of Rights, the Fourteenth Amendment, and the division of powers between state and federal governments.[55] Conversely, the loss of routine statutory issues might well serve to intensify and make more bitter the divisions that do exist among the justices.[56]

For the Court to cut itself off from narrow statutory questions would pose even greater dangers for the way in which the Court's work is perceived by legislators and other citizens. In a democratic society, the legitimacy of judicial review depends in no small part on a shared recognition that the Court nullifies decisions by the representative branches of government not because it is empowered to second-guess the wisdom or appropriateness of majoritarian determinations, but only, in Justice Harlan's words, "because [it is] a court of law . . . charged with the responsibility of adjudicating cases or controversies according to the law of the land and because the law applicable to any such dispute necessarily includes the Federal Constitution."[57]

The more the Court devotes itself to constitutional adjudication, and the less attention it gives to statutory questions of a more conventionally "legal" kind, the easier it is to lose sight of the underpinnings of the Court's role, and the more difficult it will be to defend the Court's intervention. And because constitutional decision making necessarily involves a large element of policy choice on matters not addressed by the text or contemplated by the framers, it is all the more important that the public be reminded at frequent intervals that the Court does, after all, decide questions of law.

It is true that a conscientious Supreme Court could minimize these dangers by keeping 30 to 40 relatively routine statutory cases for itself each term. Yet the more the Court attempts to retain a representative sample of statutory issues, the greater the danger that the two courts will develop parallel lines of authority that are arguably applicable to the same cases. Here again, categorical reference would reduce, through perhaps not entirely eliminate, the problem.

Some empirical evidence

Inevitably, debate over the desirability of creating an auxiliary court involves a large degree of speculation. We must first make predictions about how the Supreme Court would manage its docket if it had the option of referring cases to the new tribunal, and then, on the basis of those predictions, gauge the probable effects on the Court and on uniformity in the law. The latter inquiry must be almost entirely hypothetical, but as to the former there is one bit of evidence that may provide some clues.

By examining the Court's published order lists, we can identify those cases that, under the present system, came within one vote of the four required for plenary review. The inference can be drawn—though it is far from compelling—that these are the cases that would have been adjudicated at the national level if the Intercircuit Tribunal had been in existence. That is, if the total national decisional capacity had been enlarged through the availability of the reference option, these are the cases that would most likely have received either four votes for review by the Supreme Court or five votes for reference to the new tribunal.

Study of the order lists in the four terms 1977 through 1980 reveals that there were 119 cases in which three justices voted to grant certiorari or note probable jurisdiction but could not persuade a fourth justice to join them; thus, under the Rule of Four, review was denied.[58] The overwhelming majority were civil rights cases, and the largest portion of these involved issues of criminal law and procedure.[59] Only 27 cases in all four terms dealt with questions of federalism, general federal law, or jurisdiction and procedure outside the context of civil rights.

These findings lend at least some support to the views expressed in the preceding pages. They confirm the justices' strong, indeed overriding, interest in constitutional issues. We already know that the Court cannot expand the number of cases that receive plenary consideration, and that some statutory cases reach the plenary docket only because the Court feels obliged to resolve an intercircuit conflict.[60] Putting these facts together, it is quite plausible to suppose that if the reference option had been available, at least some of the three-vote constitutional cases would have received a fourth vote for consideration within the Court, while an equal number of statutory cases would have been routed to the Intercircuit Tribunal. The effect would have been to bring the Court one step closer to having a purely constitutional docket without necessarily increasing the number of nationally binding precedents on statutory issues, where the need for additional guidance exists if it exists anywhere.

Admittedly, these data are far from definitive. For one thing, there may well be cases in which three justices voted at the Court's conference to grant plenary review, but one or more of them chose not to make their position public. More important, the availability of the reference option would itself change the justices' voting behavior in ways we cannot fully anticipate. Nevertheless, at the present time we have no better evidence as to what would happen if the national decisional capacity were to be expanded in the manner proposed by the pending legislation. And that evidence is not reassuring.

Nor is reassurance provided by anything the justices have said. On the contrary, statements by one member of the Court tend to confirm the hypothesis advanced here. In his speech to the American Bar Association, Chief Justice Burger predicted that "if there is not prompt action to give relief [to the Supreme Court], there will be a large increase in summary dispositions, particularly in . . . criminal cases when the lower courts have either misread or ignored our controlling holdings."[61] Presumably the Court would not allow these judgments to stand if the new tribunal were created; instead, it would give them plenary consideration. And if the pattern of recent years were to continue, these would be largely cases in which the lower court had accepted the defendant's constitutional claim.[62]

It would be wrong to read too much into the Chief Justice's comments, but they do suggest a line of inquiry that Congress ought to pursue. There would be no point in creating the Intercircuit Tribunal—or any auxiliary court—unless the members of the Supreme Court were in substantial agreement both as to the need for the new structure and on the use to which it would be put. Thus, at some point in the national debate, the justices will have to speak out. Would it not be desirable to ask them to tell us quite specifically how they would use the reference option—perhaps even to identify the cases that would be sent to the new court?

There would be no need for the justices to submit agreed-on case lists to Congress. Rather, they could provide the information in a series of individual or joint opinions dissenting from—or concurring in—the denial of plenary review. Opinions and notations of this kind are already part of the Court's regular practice; the added burden of specifying the cases that particular justices would send to the new court would be minimal. And only on the basis of such a record can Congress and the public make informed judgments about how the reference option would work and what its consequences would be.[63]

Designing a structure

Further research may well show that there are indeed more cases deserving resolution at the national level than one Supreme Court can comfortably handle. The task then will be to design a structure that will enlarge the national decisional capacity without compromising the values that have given the federal judicial system the stature it has today.

I have already argued that a rotating panel system is unlikely to foster uniformity and certainty in the law. Assuming that that problem can be avoided by having a court of seven or nine judges who would always sit en banc, two questions remain to be addressed. First, how should the judges of the new court be selected? Second, should the tribunal be established on a temporary or on a permanent basis?

Selection of the judges

Under the bill now pending in the Senate, the members of the Intercircuit Tribunal would be designated by the circuit councils of the various circuits. There are several difficulties with this approach. To begin with, it is anomalous at best to decentralize the process of selecting judges for a national court. The incongruity is particularly striking in view of the 1980 legislation that gave the circuits wide leeway in deciding how many judges would serve on the councils and how they would be chosen.

More than a lack of symmetry is at stake. Ordinarily, when new judges are selected for a court, the appointing authority considers, among other factors, the composition of the court apart from the positions to be filled. That kind of coordination would be impossible if the members of the Tribunal were chosen in separate proceedings in the various circuits.[64] Indeed, there is surely some irony in creating a court to promote uniformity, but having the judges selected by 13 separate groups of individuals, each employing its own standards and procedures.

Vesting the appointment power in the circuit councils also runs a substantial risk of fostering dissension and politicization among the judges. To avoid those consequences, many if not all of the circuits are likely to adopt some sort of lottery system for choosing the members of the new tribunal. In this they would be following the procedure used by the Ninth Circuit Court of Appeals to select its "limited en banc" panels. But whatever the merits of that system for declaring the law of the circuit, it would introduce a jarring element of arbitrariness, both in appearance and in reality, if a group of judges selected at random were to be given the power to establish the law of the nation.

For all of these reasons, it would be unwise to

have the members of the auxiliary court chosen within the various circuits. How, then, might they be selected? Some proposals have vested the appointment power in the Supreme Court as a whole; others, in the chief justice alone. However, neither system is desirable. The former would not only add to the burdens of the justices; it would also provide a fertile ground for tension and dissension within the Supreme Court. The latter would give far too much power to one individual.

It is one thing to authorize the chief justice to designate judges for specialized tribunals such as the Temporary Emergency Court of Appeals or the Judicial Panel on Multidistrict Litigation. It is quite another to allow him to select the individuals who will be establishing nationally-binding precedents on a wide variety of recurring issues, subject only to occasional review by the Supreme Court.

Indeed, a more fundamental point is at stake. Recent events have reminded us of the inherent tension between majoritarian power and an independent judiciary. To allow judges—any judges—to select the members of an important court would upset the delicate balance that has been worked out over the years. By eliminating the role of the Senate and the president at the appointment stage, such an arrangement would severely weaken the majoritarian check that makes it possible for a democratic society to accept the exercise of vast lawmaking powers by judges who, once appointed, are not responsive to the political process.

It is no answer to say that because the new court would be dealing only with statutory issues, Congress could always overrule its decisions. Even if the court has misinterpreted the legislative will, forces such as inertia, deadlock, or the pressure of other business will often make it impossible to amend a statute. Nor is it adequate that the members of the panel, as circuit judges, will have previously been nominated and confirmed through the Article III process. Appointments to the circuit bench are generally treated as regional appointments; often they are the prerogative of a single senator. While the quality of the judges has been very high, the candidates simply do not receive the kind of national scrutiny that could be anticipated for appointments to what would be, in effect, an auxiliary Supreme Court.

I conclude, therefore, that the new tribunal should be constituted in the same way as all existing general-function federal courts: its judges should be appointed by the president with the consent of the Senate. That, indeed, was the recommendation of the Hruska Commission, which reached its conclusion after carefully weighing the alternatives. As already noted, however, the legislation now before Congress takes a different approach: the new court would be composed of sitting circuit judges who would be designated to serve for limited periods of time.

Proponents of this system place great emphasis on how little it would cost. And at a time when both political parties are struggling to reduce government spending, there is an obvious attraction in the prospect of increasing the national decisional capacity without creating any new judgeships. However, in the context of a federal budget that now exceeds $800 billion, the amount of money that would be required for an auxiliary court barely rises above the level of the trivial. In fiscal 1983 the budget for the Supreme Court came to about $15 million—less than was authorized for the maintenance, care, and operation of the House office buildings. If disuniformity is truly rampant in federal law, interfering on a large scale with the efficient planning of transactions and the speedy resolution of disputes, the cost of a new national court, smaller and less prestigious than the Supreme Court, would be a small price to pay to set things right.

In any event, it would be shortsighted to consider only fiscal costs. Even now, Congress is considering a recommendation by the Judicial Conference of the United States that 24 new judgeships be created in the courts of appeals to meet the demands imposed by current caseloads. Those caseloads are not likely to diminish in the years to come. Obviously, judges who are deciding cases at the national level can handle correspondingly fewer cases in their own circuits. Something would have to give: either circuit backlogs would grow, or decisional processes would be further truncated. Whatever the outcome, the system and its users incur costs, albeit not ones that would be reflected in the federal budget.

The preference for the designation approach also rests on the feeling that it would be politically unacceptable to give a single president the opportunity to appoint the entire initial membership of the new court. However, as long as at least one house is controlled by a party other than the president's, it should be possible, at the time of establishing the court, to reach an informal understanding that would require diversity and bipartisanship in the first group of appointments.

Last—and emphatically least—the designation approach may be seen as a way of mollifying the feelings of circuit judges who would otherwise perceive the new tribunal as eroding the prestige of their own courts. But if the new court is created on the basis of convincing evidence that the present system is not working, it is unlikely that circuit judges would feel more than a twinge of regret at the passing of the old order. In any event, if the lack of national appellate capacity has reached the point of desperation, the judges' sensitivities surely should not be allowed to stand in the way of necessary reform.

Temporary or permanent?

The legislation now before Congress differs from the Hruska Commission's proposal in a second important respect: it would create only a "temporary" tribunal that would automatically go out of existence if Congress did not re-authorize it. The concerns underlying this approach are certainly understandable. The proponents seek to mute the instinctive opposition of the bar and the judiciary to the creation of additional structures within the judicial system. And what could be more reassuring than to provide that unless the new court has proved its worth, it will simply disappear into oblivion? But notwithstanding its surface appeal, I think that a "sunset" provision would be unwise.

To begin with, it is important to remember that Congress can abolish even a "permanent" court. That is precisely what happened with the Commerce Court: three years after it was created, Congress put an end to its existence, and thereafter the judges continued to serve on other Article III courts.

Of course, it must be conceded that the new court is much less likely to suffer this fate if abolition rather than re-authorization requires affirmative action by Congress. And in any event, proponents of the sunset provision will ask, what's wrong with an experiment? What harm can there be in giving the new court a trial run so that advocates and doubters alike can see how it will actually work?

I see three major drawbacks to the "experimental" approach. First, in the words of the Hruska Commission, a new court "would be significantly handicapped . . . if its decisions lacked the author-

ity and credibility of an independent tribunal, the position of which was secured by a permanent charter."[65] Why so? The court would be exercising the power of review over judges who previously had to answer only to the United States Supreme Court. To make matters worse, under a system of reference jurisdiction the panel would be in the anomalous situation of not being able to enforce its precedents without the intervention of another tribunal. If by law the new court were scheduled to go out of existence on a specified day a few years in the future, the authority of its decisions would be rendered even more precarious. In contrast, if the new court were designed to be permanent, both judges and lawyers would have a much stronger motivation to treat it as a fait accompli and respect its judgments.

Second, a sunset provision would make the new court much more vulnerable to the combined effect of various human weaknesses. Making the tribunal only "temporary" reduces the incentive for its creators to build a solid record showing that the present system is inadequate. The weaker the evidence of need, the more likely it is that lower-court judges will resent the new court as an unjustifiable addition to the hierarchy that reduces the authority of their own decisions. And the more widespread that perception, the greater the difficulty the tribunal will have in securing understanding and absorption of its precedents.

Finally, notwithstanding what I have just said, "temporary" structures have a way of becoming permanent. That fate is particularly likely to befall the proposed new court because it will be impossible to know after five or even seven years whether it is achieving its purpose of reducing something as intangible as disuniformity in the law. Thus, unless the tribunal has proved an utter disaster, Congress is likely to extend its life. And given the pressure of other business, there will be neither time nor inclination to rethink any of the particulars. Unfortunately, a structure that is created for the short term is not likely to be satisfactory in the long run, nor is it likely to receive the same degree of care in its design. But that initial structure is the one that is likely to endure.

Thus, if Congress is convinced that the Supreme Court cannot provide all of the nationally-binding precedents that the legal system needs, it should establish a seven-judge court without a termination date.[66] The legislation could provide for a study commission that would come into existence six years after the new court begins operations, and that would be required, three years later, to make recommendations to Congress and the president as to whether the court should be continued. If the evidence shows that the court is not needed or is working badly, Congress would abolish it and designate the judges to sit on the circuit and district courts.

Finally, if political realities compel the inclusion of a sunset provision, the new court should be given an initial lifespan of 10 years rather than five. Without at least that much time, evaluation would be little more than guesswork. Of greater importance, the limited lifespan need not and should not preclude Congress from providing for appointment of the judges by the president with the consent of the Senate. If, after 10 years, the court is not reestablished, the judges will be able to provide useful service elsewhere in the federal judicial system.

Conclusion

Arguments that the Supreme Court is overworked, or that it cannot resolve all of the issues that deserve resolution at the national level, comport easily with our intuitions. We are a litigious nation of 235 million people, and in an era when the scope and complexity of federal law have expanded far beyond what was contemplated by the framers, it almost strains credulity to suggest that one Court of nine justices does *not* need help in performing the functions assigned to it in our system of government.

Yet all would agree that changes in the structure of the federal judicial system should not be based on intuitions, but on convincing evidence that existing arrangements are not working. Legislation to eliminate the remaining vestiges of the Supreme Court's obligatory jurisdiction meets that test, and should be enacted without further delay. The same cannot be said of proposals to create an auxiliary tribunal to assist the Court in deciding cases. There is simply not enough evidence that the Supreme Court's limited capacity for authoritative decision making has significantly frustrated society's need for uniformity and predictability in the law. Moreover, too little attention has been paid to the possible adverse consequences of creating a new court.

The want of evidence is not less tolerable if the new court is established with a "sunset" provision.

Indeed, the saddest aspect of the current drive for a "temporary" tribunal is that the experimental label can all too easily become a substitute for careful analysis of the need for the new court and the structure that would best satisfy it. And if that analysis is not undertaken before the tribunal is first created, it is unlikely ever to be attempted at a time when it can make a difference. Moreover, the shaky empirical foundation would itself increase the difficulty the new court will have in maintaining the authority of its precedents.

In the end, judgments about the need for an Intercircuit Tribunal or something similar to it may depend as much on one's perception of how legal rules operate as on the results of empirical studies. Thus, if it were shown that actual intercircuit conflicts were going unresolved on a large scale, the case for structural reform would be quite strong; but even then there would still be room for "arguments about how essential it is . . . that . . . particular question[s] be taken up and authoritatively settled at the highest judicial level."[67] And the more meager the numbers, or the larger the proportion that are no more than "sideswipes," the easier it will be to maintain that inaction by the Supreme Court pales into insignificance in the light of other sources of uncertainty in the law.

Nevertheless, it is a necessary first step to find out what the Supreme Court is not doing and how its limited capacity for decision making actually affects people's ability to plan and litigate efficiently. To forgo this inquiry is to run the risk of pursuing mischievous "solutions" to problems that exist only in the mind of the beholder.

NOTES

This article originally appeared in Volume 67, Number 1, June-July 1983, pages 28-48.

1. The Senate bill is S. 645, 98th Cong., 1st Sess. §§601-07 (1983); *see* 129 CONG. REC. S1947-48 (daily ed. Mar. 1, 1983) (remarks of Sen. Dole). The House bill is H.R. 1970, 98th Cong., 1st Sess. (1983); *see* 129 CONG. REC. H1 192-93 (daily ed. Mar. 15, 1983) (remarks of Cong. Kastenmeier). Congressman Kastenmeier stated that Chief Justice Burger, as an individual, had "expressed support" for his proposal, and indeed the chief justice had endorsed a very similar suggestion in his midyear report to the American Bar Association. *See* Burger, *Annual Report on the State of the Judiciary*, 69 A.B.A. J. 442 (1983). In this article, I shall focus primarily on the Senate bill, which has already been the subject of hearings.

2. *See* 129 CONG. REC. at S1947-48 (remarks of Sen. Dole).

3. Although Justice Stevens has argued that the Court is "too busy to give the certiorari docket the attention it deserves," his real complaint is not that the selection process imposes a great burden, but rather that his colleagues are too free in granting review of cases that he believes need not be heard by the

Supreme Court. *See* Stevens, *Some thoughts on judicial restraint*, 66 JUDICATURE 177, 179 & *passim* (1982).

4. Address of Chief Justice Hughes at the American Law Institute Meeting, quoted in 20 A.B.A. J. 341, 341 (1934). Whether the justices always adhere to this principle is of course another question—one that cannot be pursued here.

5. *Supreme Court Jurisdiction Act of 1978: Hearings on S. 3100 Before the Subcomm. on Improvements in Judicial Machinery of the Senate Judiciary Comm.*, 95th Cong., 2d Sess. 40 (1978) (letter signed by all nine sitting justices) [hereinafter cited as *Supreme Court Jurisdiction Hearings*].

6. Brennan, *The National Court of Appeals: Another Dissent*, 40 U. CHI. L. REV. 473, 477-478 (1973).

7. *Chief Justice Burger's Challenge to Congress*, U.S. NEWS & WORLD REPORT, Feb. 14, 1983, at 38, 40 [hereinafter cited as Burger interview].

8. Although the total number of cases on the docket has little significance as a measure of the justices' workload, the figures have been cited so often that two points about them deserve mention here. First, the rate of increase in the overall caseload has declined dramatically from what it was in the 1960s. In the decade preceding the Freund Study Group's report in 1972, the growth rate averaged just under 7 per cent a year. Over the past decade the rate has been only about 2 per cent. Thus, even in the 1981 term, which brought the largest number of new cases in the Court's history, the total was only 21 per cent greater than it was in the 1971 term. In contrast, filings in the federal courts of appeals nearly doubled over the same period. Second, for whatever it is worth, new filings have fallen off in the 1982 term. At this writing it appears that the number of cases docketed will be about 200 under what it was in the 1981 term.

9. This figure does not include concurring and dissenting opinions less than a page in length.

10. *See* Logan v. Zimmerman Brush Co., 455 U.S. 422 (1982); Mills v. Habluetzel, 456 U.S. 91 (1982).

It may be suggested that the proliferation of separate opinions, far from signifying that the justices are not truly overburdened, actually reinforces the conclusion that they are. The premise would be that the pressures of caseload make it impossible for the justices to hammer out consensus opinions, so that the only alternative is the separate expression of views.

But the available evidence does not support this premise. For example, Professor Dennis Hutchinson's study of the Court's decisional practices under Chief Justice Vinson points out that when the Court "was able or willing to debate issues internally at great length, . . . it frequently produced multiple opinions and judgments with no majority opinion." Hutchinson, *Felix Frankfurter and the Business of the Supreme Court, O.T. 1946-O.T. 1961*, 1980 SUP. CT. REV. 143, 208-209. More recently, former Justice Potter Stewart, when asked shortly after his retirement whether he had any regrets about his tenure on the Court, expressed the wish that he had had more time to write his own dissenting opinions instead of joining dissents that "were written not exactly the way I would have written them." *Interview With Justice Potter Stewart*, THIRD BRANCH, Jan. 1982, at 1, 9.

In short, there can be no doubt that the members of the Court have a strong desire to make known their individual views in the cases before them. The evidence suggests that with a smaller plenary docket the justices would satisfy this desire more often, rather than spend the extra time working with the authoring justice to produce a single opinion that embodied the majority's collective wisdom.

11. *See, e.g.*, Oregon v. Kennedy, 102 S. Ct. 2083, 2092 n. 1 (1982) (Stevens, J., concurring in the judgment); People v. Long, 413 Mich. 461, __, 320 N.W.2d 866, 870 (1982), cert.

granted, 103 S. Ct. 205 (1982).

12. *See, e.g.*, Marshall v. Lonberger, 103 S. Ct. 843 (1983); State v. Bradshaw, 54 Or. App. 949, 636 P.2d 1011 (1981), cert. granted, 103 S. Ct. 292 (1982).

13. *See, e.g.*, Harris v. Rivera, 454 U.S. 339 (1981); Jago v. Van Curen, 454 U.S. 14 (1981).

14. *See, e.g.*, Anderson v. Harless, 103 S. Ct. 276 (1982); Board of Educ. v. McCluskey, 102 S. Ct. 3469 (1982). Justice Stevens believes that most of the recent summary reversals fit this description. See *id.*, 102 S. Ct. at 3473 & n. 4 (Stevens, J., dissenting).

15. Cf. Bauman v. United States, 557 F.2d 650 (9th Cir. 1977) (standards for mandamus).

16. Illinois v. Gates, 103 S. Ct. 436 (1982) (Stevens, J., dissenting).

17. *Supreme Court Jurisdiction Hearings, supra* n. 5, at 40.

18. *See, e.g.*, Blum v. Bacon, 102 S. Ct. 2355 (1982); Rodriguez v. Popular Democratic Party, 102 S. Ct. 2194 (1982); Greene v. Lindsay, 102 S. Ct. 1874 (1982). In three other appeal cases, the Court unanimously reversed decisions by single district judges holding federal statutes unconstitutional. If the obligatory jurisdiction had been abolished, these cases would have gone to the courts of appeals, which in all likelihood would have upheld the statutes. In that posture it is questionable whether the cases would have merited Supreme Court review.

19. Hicks v. Miranda, 422 U.S. 332 (1975). *See* Hellman, *The Business of the Supreme Court Under the Judiciary Act of 1925: The Plenary Docket in the 1970s*, 91 HARV. L. REV. 1709, 1722-1723 (1978).

20. *See* Sidle v. Majors, 429 U.S. 945, 949-950 (1976) (Brennan, J., dissenting from denial of certiorari). Here and elsewhere I shall refer to dismissals for want of a substantial federal question as affirmances; certainly they are in effect. *See* Hellman, *supra* n. 19, at 1722 n. 57.

21. The obligatory jurisdiction also imposes another kind of burden: that of determining whether cases have properly been brought as appeals. Particularly in cases from state courts, the scope of the appeal jurisdiction depends on rules that are not always easy to apply. In the 1980 term, 80 state-court appeals were decided summarily on the merits; 47 others were found to have been improperly brought as appeals. Determining which cases fell into each category took time and effort that would not have been necessary if the obligatory jurisdiction had been abolished.

22. I recognize that the legislation would not eliminate every vestige of the obligatory jurisdiction, but the remaining fragments would be of such small moment, from the standpoint of workload, that for the sake of convenience I use the term without qualification.

23. The two most comprehensive empirical studies, both conducted nearly a decade ago, came to very different conclusions. Compare COMMISSION ON REVISION OF THE FEDERAL COURT APPELLATE SYSTEM, STRUCTURE AND INTERNAL PROCEDURES: RECOMMENDATIONS FOR CHANGE 93-109 (1975) [hereinafter cited as Hruska Commission Report], with Casper & Posner, THE WORKLOAD OF THE SUPREME COURT 87-92 (Chicago: American Bar Foundation, 1976).

24. There were only five cases in which a dissent by Justice White explicitly adverted to the existence of a conflict. Another dozen or so cases involved recurring issues, and in perhaps half of those there appears to have been a conflict of some sort.

25. *See, e.g.*, Nygaard v. Peter Pan Seafoods, Inc., 701 F.2d 77, 80 (9th Cir. 1983); Aldens, Inc. v. Miller, 610 F.2d 538, 541 (8th Cir. 1979), cert. denied, 446 U.S. 919 (1980).

26. *See, e.g.*, Copper Liquor, Inc. v. Adolph Coors Co., 701 F.2d 542 (5th Cir. 1983) (en banc court overrules case that created intercircuit conflict); United States v. Adamson, 700

F.2d 953, 956-965 (5th Cir. 1983) (en banc court, overruling prior decisions, adopts rule followed in eight other circuits that had considered the question).

27. *See, e.g.,* United States v. Gelb, 700 F.2d 875 (2d Cir. 1983) (circuits divided on scope of 1970 legislation; 1982 law eliminated ambiguity).

28. Meador, *A Comment on the Chief Justice's Proposals,* 69 A.B.A. J. 448, 449 (1983).

29. I put to one side the very serious problems raised by the federal government's practice of relitigating an issue without seeking certiorari even after its position has been rejected in several circuits. In this situation a Supreme Court decision would certainly make a significant contribution to uniformity in the law, but because of the government's litigation policy the Court does not get a chance to address the issue. *See, e.g.,* May Dep't Stores Co. v. Williamson, 549 F.2d 1147, 1149-1150 (8th Cir. 1977) (Lay, J., concurring). It is true that the solicitor general, in deciding whether to seek review, probably takes into account the fact that the Court can hear only a limited number of cases; on the other hand, these issues do seem to reach the Court eventually. Compare Hruska Commission Report, *supra* n. 23, at 133-143, with NLRB v. Enterprise Ass'n of Steam Pipefitters, 429 U.S. 507 (1977), and Bayside Enterprises, Inc. v. NLRB, 429 U.S. 298 (1977). Thus it is not clear whether the problem (apart from government intransigence) is truly one of inadequate decisional capacity or is more a matter of timing.

30. Thus it is somewhat ironic that United States v. Cartwright, 411 U.S. 546 (1973), has so often been cited as exemplifying the kind of question that should be settled at the earliest possible time without necessarily waiting for an intercircuit conflict. Perhaps it is, but the issue presented by that case—whether mutual funds shares in a decedent's estate are to be valued, for federal tax purposes, at the "bid" or the "asked" price—is of a kind that is relatively rare in the law: there are no shades of gray, but only black and white; and once the issue is decided in one case, that ruling will immediately resolve, without further inquiry, all disputes of a similar nature. Compare, e.g., Florida v. Royer, 103 S. Ct. 1319, 1329 (1983) (plurality opinion); Hillsboro Nat'l. Bank v. Commissioner, 103 S. Ct. 1134, 1144 (1983), discussed *infra* n. 39.

31. *See, e.g.,* Illinois v. Abbott & Assocs., 103 S. Ct. 1356 (1983) (Court unanimously affirms decision that rejected holdings by first two circuits to address issue); Bayside Enterprises, Inc. v. NLRB, 429 U.S. 298 (1977) (same); Otte v. United States, 419 U.S. 43 (1974) (Court unanimously affirms decision rejecting both of the two alternate positions taken by the circuits that initially addressed the issue).

32. *See, e.g.,* Coffy v. Republic Steel Corp., 447 U.S. 191 (1980) (Court unanimously reverses decision that declined to follow earlier holdings by two other circuits).

33. *See, e.g.,* Colorado Springs Amusements, Ltd. v. Rizzo, 428 U.S. 913, 917-918 (1976) (Brennan, J., dissenting from denial of certiorari); Maryland v. Baltimore Radio Show, Inc., 338 U.S. 912, 918 (1950) (opinion of Frankfurter, J., respecting the denial of certiorari); Burger interview, *supra* n. 7, at 39. It is particularly important to note that in the justices' eyes the value of the process is not limited to constitutional cases. *See, e.g.,* E. I. du Pont de Nemours & Co. v. Train, 430 U.S. 112, 135 n. 26 (1977): "This litigation exemplifies the wisdom of allowing difficult issues to mature through full consideration by the courts of appeals. By eliminating the many subsidiary, but still troubling, arguments raised by industry, these courts have vastly simplified our task, as well as having underscored the reasonableness of the agency view."

34. Llewellyn, THE BRAMBLE BUSH 48 (Dobbs Ferry, New York: Oceana, 1951).

35. *See, e.g.,* Pullman-Standard v. Swint, 102 S. Ct. 1781, 1788-1791 (1982); Commissioner v. Duberstein, 363 U.S. 278, 287-291 (1960).

36. *See, e.g.,* Herman Bros., Inc. v. NLRB, 658 F.2d 201, 209 (3rd Cir. 1981).

37. *See, e.g.,* NLRB v. J. Weingarten, Inc., 420 U.S. 251, 265-267 (1975); Permian Basin Area Rate Cases, 390 U.S. 747, 784 (1968); Texaco, Inc. v. NLRB, 700 F.2d 1039, 1042-1043 (5th Cir. 1983); Melrose-Wakefield Hospital Ass'n v. NLRB, 615 F.2d 563, 567 (1st Cir. 1980).

38. *See, e.g.,* Friendly, *Adverting the Flood by Lessening the Flow,* 59 CORNELL L. REV. 634, 655 (1974).

39. For example, in Hillsboro Nat'l. Bank v. Commissioner, 103 S. Ct. 1134, 1144-1145 (1983), the taxpayers and the government proposed competing formulations of the tax benefit rule. The Court rejected both formulations and concluded instead that the rule "must be applied on a case-by-case basis."

40. D'Amato, *Legal Uncertainty,* 71 CALIF. L. REV. 1, 1 (1983).

41. Chief Justice Burger envisaged a temporary panel that would decide about 50 cases a year. A full-time, seven-judge National Court of Appeals could probably be expected to hand down about 150 decisions annually.

42. Much has been made of the fact that in the 1981 term, for the first time in recent history, the Court granted review in more cases than it could hear in a single term. However, even putting aside the question whether all of the cases truly deserved consideration at the national level, the significance of this development should not be overstated. In the preceding term—1980—the Court had granted review in so few cases that it was unable to fill its argument calendar for the April session. (The figures for the 1977 through 1979 terms were also below the level of the 1971-1976 period.) The justices may well have responded by moving somewhat too far toward the other extreme. In the current term the number of cases granted review has again decreased. In any event, it would be shortsighted to place great reliance on year-to-year fluctuations in the number of cases heard rather than trying to assess the needs of the national law.

43. *See* Hellman, *Legal Problems of Dividing a State Between Federal Judicial Circuits,* 122 PA. L. REV. 1188, 1208-1209 (1974) (citing lawyers' statements).

44. *See, e.g.,* Mid-Louisiana Gas Co. v. FERC, 664 F.2d 530, 534-535 (5th Cir. 1981) (in assessing degree of deference due to agency order under Natural Gas Policy Act, court cites cases involving, inter alia, securities regulation, welfare, and truth in lending), cert. granted, 103 S. Ct. 49 (1982); Montana Wilderness Ass'n v. United States Forest Service, 655 F.2d 951, 957 (9th Cir. 1981) (in construing Alaska Lands Act, court relies on Supreme Court decision interpreting Freedom of Information Act), cert. denied, 455 U.S. 989 (1982); Leist v. Simplot, 638 F.2d 283, 319, 327 (2d Cir. 1980) (majority and dissent differ on implications to be drawn from Supreme Court decision interpreting different statute), aff'd, 102 S. Ct. 1825 (1982).

45. *See, e.g.,* United States v. Stauffer Chemical Co., 684 F.2d 1174, 1187-1188 (6th Cir. 1982) (Clean Air Act and Clean Water Act), cert. granted, 51 U.S.L.W. 3756 (U.S. Apr. 18, 1983).

46. *Compare, e.g.,* Coffy v. Republic Steel Corp., 447 U.S. 191 (1980) (resolving conflict in interpretation of Vietnam Era Veterans' Readjustment Assistance Act; decision has been cited almost exclusively in cases involving veterans' reemployment rights), with Vermont Yankee Nuclear Power Corp. v. Natural Resources Defense Council, Inc., 435 U.S. 519 (1978) (reaffirming and applying precedents on scope of review of agency action; decision cited in wide variety of administrative law cases).

47. *See* Carrington, Meador & Rosenberg, JUSTICE ON APPEAL

215-216 (St. Paul: West, 1976); Hufstedler, *Courtship and Other Legal Arts*, 60 A.B.A. J. 545, 547 (1974).

48. Meador, *supra* n. 28, at 449.

49. Hellman, *How Not to Help the Supreme Court*, 69 A.B.A. J. 750 (1983).

50. In fact, the pending legislation would actually add two new options: referring the case with directions to decide it, or referring the case and giving the new court discretion whether to decide it.

51. Some of the potential complications could be avoided if cases could be referred to the new tribunal only on the affirmative vote of six justices, rather than the five contemplated by the current Senate bill.

52. For this reason, not only disarray but chaos would likely result if the Intercircuit Tribunal (or any other auxiliary court) were given direct jurisdiction to review state-court judgments resting on federal law, as some have suggested. Under a system of reference jurisdiction, the Supreme Court at least has the ability to limit the issues the new court would address; if direct appeals were permitted, the only safeguard against inconsistency would be Supreme Court review of the new court's decisions—an additional burden that would defeat one of the purposes of the enterprise.

53. Rehnquist, *Whither the Courts*, 60 A.B.A. J. 787, 790 (1974). Dean Terrance Sandalow of the University of Michigan Law School has expressed similar concerns. *See* 2 Commission on Revision of the Federal Court Appellate System, Hearings Second Phase 739-740 (1975).

54. For example, in the 1981 term, Chief Justice Burger and Justice Brennan invariably took opposing positions when the Court divided 5-4 on civil rights issues, but they found themselves on the same side in two cases where matters of general federal law were resolved by 5-4 votes.

55. In the 1981 term, the Court was unanimous in only 25 per cent of the civil rights cases decided on the merits, but in the general federal law segment of the docket the figure was 40 per cent.

56. I am indebted to Professor David L. Shapiro for bringing this point to my attention.

57. Mackey v. United States, 401 U.S. 667, 678 (1971) (Harlan, J., concurring and dissenting).

58. This figure excludes cases in which Justices Brennan, Stewart, and Marshall would have reversed obscenity convictions, along with a few cases in which the dissenting justices would have vacated the judgment below for reconsideration in light of an intervening Supreme Court decision or other development.

Of the 119 cases, 28 came before the Court on appeal, thus the dissents might well have rested on an unwillingness to affirm rulings of dubious correctness, rather than a belief that the cases warranted consideration by the Supreme Court. This interpretation is supported by the fact that in 15 of the appeal cases, one of the three votes for plenary consideration came from Justice Stevens, who takes a very narrow view of the Court's certiorari function and never notes his dissent from the denial of discretionary review.

59. In two-thirds of the cases in which the lower court had rejected a civil rights claim, Justices Brennan and Marshall provided two of the three votes for review. In two-thirds of the cases upholding the claim, Chief Justice Burger and Justice Rehnquist were among the three dissenters.

60. *See* Hruska Commission Report, *supra* n. 23, at 182 (letter from Justice White).

61. Burger, *supra* n. 1, at 455.

62. *See also* Massachusetts v. Podgurski, 103 S. Ct. 1167 (1983) (Burger, C.J., dissenting from denial of certiorari): "In my view, only the finite limitations of the Court's time preclude our granting review of this case. I would grant certiorari and summarily reverse the judgment of the Supreme Judicial Court of Massachusetts [upholding the defendant's Fourth Amendment claim]." *See also* Stevens, *supra* n. 3, at 179-180.

63. The need for this information is underscored by consideration of the differing views expressed by Chief Justice Burger and Justice Rehnquist. Both have endorsed the idea of an intercircuit tribunal, and both envision sending 35 to 50 cases a year to the new court. However, the chief justice would use the reference option to reduce the Supreme Court's own docket to about 100 cases a year, while Justice Rehnquist would retain the present level of 150. Since a plenary docket of 100 cases would be just about filled by the civil rights and federalism caseloads of recent years, the chief justice's approach would almost certainly bring about the results hypothesized in the text: a Supreme Court devoted almost entirely to constitutional litigation, and little if any increase in the number of nationally binding decisions on statutory issues. Justice Rehnquist's approach might or might not have those consequences; that would depend on how many constitutional cases were heard by the Supreme Court in the place of statutory cases sent to the new tribunal. What the full Court would do, we do not know. But of the 55 cases in which Justice Rehnquist dissented from the denial of plenary review in the 1977-1980 terms, 41 involved constitutional issues.

64. For example, as Professor A. Leo Levin pointed out in his statement to a Senate subcommittee, it would probably be a good idea to have some senior judges on the new court, but it would not be desirable if all of the members of the court had senior status. Under the system contemplated by the pending legislation it would be impossible to assure an appropriate balance.

65. Hruska Commission Report, *supra* n. 23, at 31.

66. Seven is preferable to nine because it distinguishes the new tribunal from the Supreme Court, and because a smaller number of judges can work together more easily. Certainly no showing has been made that the volume of work destined for the court would require more than seven full-time judges.

67. *National Court of Appeals Act: Hearings Before the Subcomm. on Improvements in Judicial Machinery of the Senate Comm. on the Judiciary*, 94th Cong., 2d Sess. 190-191 (1976) (statement of Prof. Rosenberg).

Improving the process: case selection by the Supreme Court

A national court of appeals has been suggested to relieve a perceived "caseload problem" at the Supreme Court. The authors suggest that before that step is taken, some less drastic measures might alleviate whatever problem exists.

by Samuel Estreicher and John Sexton

We have produced elsewhere our empirical assessment of the case for a new national court of appeals or intercircuit tribunal, concluding on the basis of a study of all the cases granted and denied review by the Supreme Court during the 1982 term that the data do not support creation of a new tier of appellate review interposed between the present courts of appeals and the Supreme Court.[1] We do not propose to retrace that ground here. We do believe, however, that whether or not new courts are ultimately established, there are several reforms that should be put in place to enable the justices to manage better their scarce decisional resources. Most of the reforms we propose here could be effected by the justices themselves; one or two would require congressional action. Each would enable the Court to perform its managerial functions better and to fulfill its role as articulator of authoritative and uniform federal law.

Abolish mandatory jurisdiction

All the justices and virtually all commentators endorse the proposal to abolish mandatory jurisdiction. The Court's mandatory appellate docket accounts for somewhere between 25 and 35 per cent of the Court's caseload (21 per cent in the 1982 term).[2] In our view, however, commentators have overstated the significance of abolition, inasmuch as most cases currently treated as appeals—other than state rulings of statutory validity under 28 U.S.C. §1257(2)—would require the Supreme Court's attention even if styled as *certiorari* petitions.[3] Nevertheless, an appreciable number of cases—in our study, 12 of 164, or 7 per cent of the plenary docket[4]—would not merit review if obligatory jurisdiction were abolished. More importantly, abolition would relieve the Court of the burden of acting on all cases denominated as appeals, and thus eliminate the nettlesome question of the precedential effect of summary dispositions. Where summary dispositions present hurdles to a desired outcome, the Court often attempts to deprecate their precedential effect.[5] Yet, even dismissals of appeals, though not fully deliberated,[6] are deemed judgments on the merits.[7] The confusion thus created requires the Court to grant review on occasion for the purpose of dispelling the supposed precedential force of a prior dismissal.[8]

The mandatory appellate docket is a remnant of the outdated view that the Court ought to hear any case a disappointed litigant has the resources and determination to carry to the highest level of review. The abolition of mandatory appellate jurisdiction would give the Court full control over its docket and endow the Court with the flexibility necessary to carry out its managerial responsibilities.[9]

Develop specific criteria

We urge the Court to develop more specific criteria for selecting cases for review. Supreme Court Rule 17, we submit, offers no guidance to the bar and unnecessarily exacerbates the Court's difficulties in managing its docket.[10]

Rule 17 reflects the tension between the promise that the Court may hear all important federal questions and the reality that it cannot do so:

A review on writ of *certiorari* is not a matter of right, but of judicial discretion, and will be granted only when there are special and important reasons therefor. The following, while neither controlling nor fully measuring the Court's discretion, indicate the character of reasons that will be considered.

(a) When a federal court of appeals has rendered a decision in conflict with the decision of another federal court of appeals on the same matter; or has decided a federal question in a way in conflict with a state court of last resort; or has so far departed from the accepted and usual course of judicial proceedings, or so far sanctioned such a departure by a lower court, as to call for an exercise of this Court's power of supervision.

(b) When a state court of last resort has decided a federal question in a way in conflict with the decision of another state court of last resort or of a federal court of appeals.

(c) When a state court or a federal court of appeals has decided an important question of federal law which has not been, but should be, settled by this Court, or has decided a federal question in a way in conflict with applicable decisions of this Court.

Presumably, conflicts—whether among the federal courts of appeals or the state courts of last resort, or between federal courts of appeals and state courts of last resort—presents a strong claim for review. But in our study period, "conflict" appeared as a justification for a grant of *certiorari* in only about 35 per cent of the cases.[11]

Rule 17 is indeterminate with respect to the other potential grounds for review. Conflict with Supreme Court precedent, if viewed in the narrow sense of head-on clash with prior rulings, would clearly warrant a grant of *certiorari*, but such cases are few and far between: we identified only five such cases out of the 164 on the docket during the 1982 term.[12] We are told that review is also appropriate in cases calling for "an extraordinary exercise" of the Court's power of supervision, but the very language used suggests that this is a narrow category of cases. Thus, Rule 17 accounts for most of the nonconflict cases heard by the Court under the open-ended residual category of "important question[s] of federal law which [have] not been, but should be, settled by this Court."

It is, of course, vaguely comforting that the Court is free to grant *certiorari* whenever a particular petition strikes it as meritorious, thus making the Court potentially available for all significant questions of federal law. But for the Court to assume, and for students of the Court to insist upon, an unrealistic set of responsibilities is to ensure dissatisfaction and, more importantly, to forestall careful thinking about what the Court should be doing with its limited decisional capacity—an inquiry that must be undertaken whether or not new courts are to be created.

Although the criteria advanced in our study are not the final word,[13] we think it is possible to improve upon the generalities of Rule 17 and provide a more useful guide to the Court's exercise of discretion in handling its *certiorari* docket. Simply as a matter of national policy, it is important that various conceptions of the role of the Supreme Court in our judicial system be subjected to a process of public debate, in the hope that a clearer definition of the justices' responsibilities might emerge. Moreover, more precise criteria for case selection would probably reduce the Court's screening burden by reducing the number of petitions filed. A system that encourages the filing of petitions that would not be filed if the Supreme Court's review criteria were clearly articulated unnecessarily inflicts costs on both litigants and the Court.

A principled set of case selection criteria would send clearer signals to the bar. Definite criteria for "certworthiness" would enable practitioners to self-censor many petitions filed in full compliance with Supreme Court Rule 17 as presently written, but that clearly do not merit review.[14] Moreover, the tendency to construe a denial of review as a judgment on the merits would be significantly diminished.

Link petitions to the criteria

The rules governing petitions for *certiorari* should require petitioners to file a short supplemental statement—possibly on a checklist form developed by the Court—setting forth procedural information to facilitate the Court's evaluation of the certworthiness of each petition. This statement should indicate whether the petition is from a final judgment of the court below and should explicitly link the petitioner's request for review to the Court's articulated criteria. When the basis of the request for review is an alleged conflict among the circuits, the statement should provide three additional pieces of information.

First, the petitioner should identify the precise issue on which a conflict is alleged. Second, the petitioner should cite, say, at least three, but no more than six, cases presenting the conflict. Third, the petitioner should aver that the alleged conflict was brought to the attention of the court below.

This proposed statement should require no more than a few marks on a checklist, coupled with a paragraph or two of citations (for allegations of intercourt conflicts). Many petitions would not survive a *prima facie* examination. For others, the checklist would highlight the purported basis for requesting the Court's intervention. In many cases, the Court would no longer need to wade through prolix petitions and string cites; in all, litigants would be compelled to focus their arguments for Supreme Court review.

Alert lower court to conflicts

In order to promote intercircuit reconciliation, we recommend that a petitioner who alleges a conflict among the circuits be required to demonstrate that the conflict was considered by the lower court.[15] The petitioner should be required to bring the conflict to the attention of the court of appeals. If the appeals panel does not acknowledge the existence of the alleged conflict in its opinion, the petitioner must again raise the issue in the petition for rehearing or suggestion for rehearing *en banc.* In the rare case in which a conflict arises after the petition for rehearing is filed, but before the last date for filing with the Supreme Court, the petitioner should be permitted—indeed, encouraged—to return to the court of appeals for reconsideration based on the allegedly conflicting decision.

Penalize frivolous petitions

We urge that the Supreme Court, on the model of Rule 11 of the Federal Rules of Civil Procedure, require certification that the petition for review is not frivolous under the Court's criteria. Costs or other sanctions should be imposed on attorneys who violate this procedure. Certification could take various forms. Professors Kurland and Hutchinson suggest that the Court publish separately denials of review for petitions that do not merit discussion, list the names of counsel who file meritless petitions, and impose substantial costs for doing so.[16] Milton Handler proposes that the courts of appeals certify that a particular decision presents an issue meriting the Court's review. If a litigant seeks review of an uncertified case and the petition is unanimously denied, Professor Handler suggests, the costs borne by the respondents should be imposed on the petitioner.[17]

We favor the adoption of a version of Federal Rule 11 modified to fit the special conditions of Supreme Court practice. An attorney would certify that he has examined the case selection criteria articulated by the Court and that he has in good faith a reasonable basis for urging Supreme Court review in a particular case. The Court could then impose sanctions (costs and attorney's fees involved in opposing the petition) if, under the Court's criteria, the attorney filed a frivolous petition.

This approach would achieve its intended goal with less risk of undesirable and unintended consequences than the other certification proposals. Professors Kurland and Hutchinson concede that they have not fully worked out their proposal.[18] Professor Handler's suggestion would require that lower court judges re-evaluate decisions they have already rendered, this time as a screen for the Supreme Court. Our certification proposal would not require the courts of appeals to second-guess themselves and would keep the decision to seek Court review within the discretion of the litigants.

A second look

Under present procedures, once four justices vote to hear a case (the Rule of Four), review is granted. Usually the announcement is made by the Court on the Monday following the conference. The case is not studied again until the Court considers it on the merits.

Occasionally the justices dismiss a writ of *certiorari* as having been improvidently granted. As recently illustrated by *Gillette Co. v. Miner,*[19] *Westinghouse Electric Corp. v. Vaughn,*[20] and *Illinois v. Gates,*[21] this practice wastes the Court's time and damages its credibility. Moreover, we suspect that the incidence of overt dismissals understates the justices' own tally of improvident grants, because the Court tends to decide a case once *certiorari* has been granted.

Relatively modest procedural changes could reduce the number of improvident grants. The justices at the initial conference should vote on each petition to grant or deny review, as they do now. However, the results of that vote should not be announced. Instead, petitions that receive at least four votes should be submitted to an independent staff of the caliber of the justices' clerks, headed by a leading member of the Supreme Court bar. The staff would evaluate each proposed grant under the Court's criteria to determine whether the case merited review. They would also inquire whether there were any procedural obstacles to consideration of the merits, such as the absence of a final judgment, and evaluate the state of the record to determine whether the case provided a suitable vehicle for review. Then the petitions, accompanied by the staff reports, would be returned to the justices for reconsideration and a final vote at a second conference. If the case still received at least four votes, review would be granted and the result announced.

We recognize that some critics will view this suggestion as a further step toward "bureaucratic justice," whereby the justices do not make the decisions themselves but merely manage a bureaucratic machine.[22] Our proposal, in fact, involves no delegation of decision making or loss of accountability, because the function of our proposed staff is purely advisory; its members would simply highlight difficulties with the tentatively granted petition, in light of the Court's case selection criteria, the state of the record, and the suitability of the case as a proposed vehicle. The justices would receive and act on the staff's recommendations, but they would not be bound by them in any way.

We urge that the screening process include another preliminary step when a petition is to be granted as a possible vehicle for announcing a major doctrinal shift or innovation. There is no point in a vehicle grant that will yield only a plurality opinion and a splintered Court. As former Secretary of Transportation William T. Coleman recently suggested, fragmented opinions encourage later litigants to seek review on the chance that a plurality or concurring opinion might presage a shift in the Court's position.[23] Therefore, to better identify appropriate vehicles, the justices should take a straw vote or in some other way determine whether they will be able to unite on an opinion that authoritatively sets forth clear and easily applied rules and legal principles. Naturally, this straw vote would not (and should not) preclude a change of mind after briefs and argument. But if the justices' straw vote determines that there is no consensus on the structure or substance of an eventual Court opinion, then the justices will have had an advance notice that the case may prove to be an unsuitable vehicle.

Less frequent conferences

The justices presently vote on requests for review as part of their weekly conference. Consequently, most of the cases the Court selects come from relatively small and unrepresentative samples of the annual pool of filed cases. During these weekly conferences, case selection is conducted without any real sense of how the docket is evolving. By contrast, the justices' major conference each September, at which they have before them approximately one-fifth of the cases filed in a year, provides a striking lesson in how case selection might differ if the weekly conferences were dropped in favor of less frequent deliberations. Presumably, the cases at the September conference are representative of those filed throughout the year. Yet, over the last four terms, the ratio of cases granted *certiorari* to petitions considered at the September conference has been significantly lower than that for the rest of the year.[24]

If by contrast, the justices were to review petitions on a monthly or semi-monthly rather than weekly basis, they could gain a more accurate overview of the developing docket and the work of the lower courts. By locating each decision to grant or deny review in the context of a larger sample of the docket, monthly or semi-monthly review would reduce the incidence of improvident grants.

We also urge consideration of the suggestion of Judges Feinberg[25] and Friendly[26] that petitions be screened by panels of three justices, with only one vote necessary to bring a petition before all nine justices for review. This proposal would reduce substantially the screening burden; each justice would consider only the one-third of all petitions handled by his or her panel and those cases referred to the full Court by the other two panels.

Facilitate further research

The Court should facilitate empirical research by publishing the justices' votes on decisions to grant or deny review. Publication need not be simultaneous with the actual vote; records on votes to grant or deny review could be made available several years after the actual vote. Such information would be extraordinarily useful in discussing proposals for reform. For example, it would provide a data base for assessing the operation of the Rule of Four, and for evaluating proposals for a Rule of Five. Similarly, publication of these votes would permit students of the Court to evaluate the contribution, if any, of the *cert* pool practice to the overgranting phenomenon.

We do not suggest that the clerks' bench memoranda on each case be published or otherwise made available.[27] First, these memoranda are not final decisions or even well-considered resolutions. They are written solely to familiarize individual justices with the issues presented by the petitions, and should not be used for any other purpose. Second, there is no need to give disappointed litigants possible grounds for urging reconsideration by publicizing a clerk's necessarily preliminary recommendations to his or her justice.

Modify transfer and venue rules

In our view, the mere fact that two circuits are in conflict presents no pressing reason for Supreme Court intervention, unless a party can take advantage of the conflict by forum shopping or unless the conflict stymies the planning of multicircuit actors.[28] Much can be done, however, to minimize these undesirable features of conflicts while preserving the benefits of intercircuit percolation and reducing significantly the number of conflict cases requiring the Court's attention.

The most promising approach, in our view, would be for Congress generally to restrict federal venue to the district or circuit where the claim or cause of action arose.[29] Under a restrictive venue regime, parties would know with certainty the law that would govern their affairs. Moreover, they would be unable to bring themselves under a different set of legal rules by forum choice. We recognize that this approach raises difficult questions, such as the assignment of a *situs* to multidistrict or multicircuit transactions. Special rules might also be needed for cases involving challenges to government regulations or other decisions of national applicability; for example, venue could be restricted to the District of Columbia Circuit or to the principal place of business or the residence of the challenger. For actions originating at the district court level, provision for transfer of venue for reasons of litigation convenience would be necessary, but, by analogy to the rules governing transfer in federal diversity cases,[30] the law of the transferor circuit would apply.[31]

Other proposals

In our view, the proposals that follow should be adopted only as a last resort before the creation of a new intermediate appellate court. These cures pose difficulties or undermine important values and practices, yet are distinctly preferable to creation of a new national court of appeals or intercircuit tribunal.

Modification of the Rule of Four. Several commentators and at least one justice have suggested that the Rule of Four be replaced by a Rule of Five.[32] This proposal's drawback is that it would enable an entrenched majority to foreclose even threshold consideration of issues of concern to a significant minority of justices. Moreover, although a Rule of Five might increase the reversal rate for cases on the *certiorari* docket, or reduce the aggregate number of grants per term, adoption of the proposal would provide no additional assurance of appropriate case selection.

Giving nationally binding effect to certain *en banc* circuit court decisions. Justice White and several commentators have proposed a novel way of addressing intercircuit conflicts. If, after a panel of one circuit decides a legal issue, a panel of a second circuit decides the same issue differently, the second circuit court must convene *en banc* to reconsider the issue. The resulting *en banc* decision would become a nationally binding rule that could be overturned only by the Supreme Court.[33]

Although this proposal appears at first glance to be an attractive way to dispose of intercircuit conflicts, we do not support it for several reasons. First, and foremost, it does not give sufficient weight to the value of percolation. For example, legal issues are susceptible of more than two polar resolutions; the Court should have the benefit of intermediate approaches. Second, this proposal would permit a circuit with little experience and knowledge in an area of law to overrule a circuit with widely acknowledged expertise (for example, the Second Circuit on securities regulation law or the District of Columbia on administrative law). Third, this proposal shares some of the difficulties that would beset an intercircuit tribunal. Because the *en banc* decision would purport to bind the nation yet be authoritative only if not overturned by the Supreme Court, litigants still would press further their claims, and the Court would be under considerable pressure to review the *en banc* ruling.

In any event, adoption of this proposal would be premature at this point. It would be wiser to implement less radical reforms and see whether they work. Still, whatever its faults, the "binding *en banc* decision" remedy does not involve the severe systemic problems and destabilizing effects that would result from the creation of a new tier of appellate review.

Another proposal for resolving intercircuit conflicts is set forth in a recent article by former Secretary of Transportation Coleman.[34] Essentially, it calls for special panels to rehear cases in which a circuit court has rendered a decision that conflicts with the law of another circuit. Each special panel would be composed of three judges from each of the two conflicting circuits and a seventh judge from another circuit, assigned by the chief justice. This panel's decision would be binding on all circuits, subject only to discretionary Supreme Court review. However, "[s]hould a third circuit fail to follow the precedent established by the intercircuit *en banc* hearing, the petitioner [in the third case] could request an *en banc* hearing by seven judges, two from each of the three circuits that had addressed the issue and one assigned by the chief justice." Presumably, the seventh judge would be from a fourth circuit, and this new panel's decision would have nationally binding effect, subject only to Supreme Court review.

Aside from obvious problems of unwieldiness, the unacceptable extent to which serendipity would control which judges served on each proposed intercircuit *en banc* panel is bound to frustrate hopes for coherence in national law. Further, it is not clear how designation of judges from conflicting circuits would necessarily produce decisive conflict resolution. Presumably the judges from each circuit will already have considered these questions with their colleagues. Especially in cases that provoke dissents from the original circuit decisions, it is far from certain that the intercircuit panel would be able to provide an authoritative final judgment. As long as there was an opportunity to appeal, disappointed litigants would continue to seek a truly authoritative resolution of the conflict from the Supreme Court, irrespective of the number of intervening *en banc* intercircuit panel decisions. Surely the "binding *en banc* decision" rule proposed by Justice White is preferable to this cumbersome proposal.

Referring "trivial" conflicts to disinterested circuits or to Congress for binding resolution. Two variants of the "binding *en banc* decision" proposal deserve further discussion. Some commentators contend that many of the conflicts the Court hears involve relatively narrow issues of statutory construction in areas of federal law that are not of general interest and are too insignificant to merit the Court's attention.[35] There are, of course, reasons to be skeptical of this contention. A conflict

among three or more circuit courts or state courts of last resort suggests that the issue is at least difficult and recurring. We invite the reader to peruse our study of the Court's docket and to identify the "trivial" conflicts resolved during the 1982 term.

Even if one assumes, for the sake of argument, the existence of trivial conflicts, a statute authorizing the Court to refer them to a randomly chosen circuit court is still preferable to creation of an intercircuit tribunal. Such a statute might authorize the circuit court to issue a nationally binding resolution reviewable at the discretion of the Supreme Court, thereby freeing up docket capacity without sacrificing the benefits of lower court percolation or creating a new tribunal whose only ostensible task would be handling parochial, relatively insignificant cases.

Instead of creating new courts, Congress might also consider proposals to establish the creation of a National Law Revision Commission designed to identify, on a continuing basis, conflicts on statutory question for legislative resolution.[36] The National Law Revision proposal has the advantage of involving Congress in the clarification of statutory law while liberating docket capacity.

Significant number of trivial conflicts or no, our study raises doubt about the alleged pressing need to free up additional docket capacity. According to our criteria, the cases requiring the Court's attention during the 1982 term (what we call the "priority docket") accounted for only 48 per cent of the overall grants, and nearly one in four decisions to grant review was improvident.[37] Any referral function makes the case selection process more complex and time consuming. We doubt that the justices will agree readily on which conflicts are trivial. Moreover, trivial conflicts may quickly be decided without substantial expenditure of the Court's decisional resources, and the Court may well benefit institutionally from the occasional easy case in which the justices can reach agreement without a proliferation of separate opinions or rancor.[38]

Specialized appellate courts. Some commentators have suggested the creation of specialized appellate courts, on the model of the Court of Appeals for the Federal Circuit.[39] These courts would eliminate intercircuit conflicts in areas over which they had exclusive jurisdiction. A specialized court for tax appeals is the most frequently suggested new tribunal.[40] Critics of this proposal argue that a judge familiar with the full range of legal questions potentially implicated in a federal case will decide cases more soundly and creatively than a specialist judge, and that a court that deals exclusively with a governmental agency might become too deferential to the views of either the agency or a specialized segment of the bar.[41] We doubt that specialized appellate courts can effectively reduce the Court's caseload. Such courts would sacrifice the benefits of percolation, are vulnerable to capture by special interests, and, if given responsibility over controversial subjects, would require greater Supreme Court supervision.

Courts of exclusive jurisdiction, if established, should be confined to areas that are not likely to generate wide controversy, to areas in which certainty and predictability in the law are paramount.[42] Patent litigation is one such area, and thus assignment of patent cases to the Court of Appeals for the Federal Circuit was appropriate.[43] We do not expect litigants in patent cases to seek Supreme Court review regularly. Similarly, we do not expect the justices to feel any strong temptation to intervene. Tax litigation might be another such area. To avoid the "captive court" problem, tax cases should also be assigned to the Court of Appeals for the Federal Circuit. This practice would expand the subject-matter responsibilities of that court, and, correspondingly, the breadth of perspective of its judges.

We do not at present urge the creation of additional specialized tribunals. Even in the tax area, the case has yet to be made with convincing clarity that such a change is needed.[44] Forum shopping in tax cases could be eliminated by restricting the role of the Claims Court and codifying the policy by which the Tax Court follows the law of the circuit in which the dispute arises. Moreover, our study does not identify any significant number of conflicts in the tax area that are left unresolved by the Court (only one two-court conflict was found).[45] It is true that the tax area may be one where planning by the parties may be imperiled as much by "incoherence" in the law as by conflicts. If that be the case, however, assignment of tax cases to the Court of Appeals for the Federal Circuit might be the answer.

Conclusion

We, of course, urge the reader to consider in full the empirical study we have undertaken of the Supreme Court's 1982 term and our proposed criteria for case selection by the Supreme Court.

We do not believe that the case for a new national appeals court has been made to date. However, whatever one's view on that question, there are steps that should be taken—most capable of being implemented by the justices themselves, only a few requiring new legislation—that would measurably alleviate the Court's burden and enable it better to direct the national lawmaking process.

NOTES

This article originally appeared in Volume 70, Number 1, June/July 1986, pages 41-47. It is based upon the penultimate chapter of Estreicher and Sexton, *A Managerial Theory of the Supreme Court's Responsibilities: An Empirical Study*, 50 N.Y.U. L. Rev. 681 (1984). The subject is also treated in the authors' book, REDEFINING THE SUPREME COURT'S ROLE: A THEORY OF MANAGING THE FEDERAL COURT SYSTEM (New Haven: Yale University Press, 1986).

1. *See* Estreicher and Sexton, *A Managerial Theory of the Supreme Court's Responsibilities: An Empirical Study*, 50 N.Y.U. L. Rev. 681 (1984); *see generally*, *The New York University Supreme Court Project*, 59 N.Y.U. L. Rev., Nos. 4-6 (1984).

2. *See* Estreicher and Sexton, *supra* n. 1, at 746-747, 799; Coleman, *The Supreme Court of the United States: Managing Its Caseload to Achieve Its Constitutional Purpose*, 52 FORDHAM L. REV. 1, 17 & n. 88 (1983).

3. *See* Estreicher and Sexton, *supra* n. 1, at 722 & n. 153, 728-730.

4. *See id.* at 746, 799.

5. *See, e.g.*, Anderson v. Celebreeze, 460 U.S. 780, 784 & n. 5 (1983) (summary dispositions by Court should be accorded "limited precedential effect"); Sporhase v. Nebraska *ex rel.* Douglas, 458 U.S. 941, 949 (1982) (affirmance indicates only Court's agreement with result reached by lower court).

6. *See, e.g.*, Hicks v. Miranda, 422 U.S. 332, 344 (1975) (describing summary dismissal of appeal in Miller v. California, 418 U.S. 915 (1974), as decision on merits); *see also* Mandel v. Bradley, 432 U.S. 173, 176 (1977) (*per curiam*).

7. *See, e.g.*, 16 Wright, Miller, Cooper and Gressman, FEDERAL PRACTICE AND PROCEDURE: Jurisdiction Section 4003 (St. Paul, MN: West, 1977).

8. *See, e.g.*, Edelman v. Jordan, 415 U.S. 651 (1974).

9. *See generally*, *Supreme Court Jurisdiction Act of 1978: Hearings on S. 3100 Before the Sub-comm. on Improvements in Judicial Machinery of the Senate Comm. on the Judiciary*, 95th Cong., 2d Sess. 40 (1978) (letter signed by all nine sitting justices); *id.* at 2 (statement of Solicitor General McCree, quoting Justice Stevens); *id.* at 32 (statement of Professor Hellman).

10. *See, e.g.*, Gunther, CASES AND MATERIALS ON CONSTITUTIONAL LAW 71 (St. Paul, MN: Foundation Press, 10th ed. 1980) (Court's unpredictable grants of *certiorari* encourage filing of petitions); Handler, *What To Do With the Supreme Court's Burgeoning Calendars?*, 5 CARDOZO L. REV. 249, 261 (1984) ("The Court's *certiorari* rule is itself partly responsible for encouraging the filing of groundless petitions.").

11. Sixty-nine cases (or 42 per cent) presented intercourt conflicts, only 57 of which (or 34 per cent) were properly granted on a conflict rationale under the criteria of this study. *See* Estreicher and Sexton, *supra* n. 1, at 748; *also* Posner, THE FEDERAL COURTS: CRISIS AND REFORM 59-77 (Cambridge, MA: Harvard University Press, 1985).

12. *See* Estreicher and Sexton, *supra* n. 1, at 747.

13. *See id.* at 720-739.

14. Professors Kurland and Hutchinson have suggested that the large number of unmeritorious claims is the product of an

irresponsible bar: attorneys can rarely bill clients for unwritten *certiorari* petitions. Kurland and Hutchinson, *The Business of the Supreme Court, O.T. 1982*, 50 U. CHI. L. REV. 628, 646 (1983). Similarly, some unscrupulous petitioners may draw out the appellate process solely to delay execution of a money judgment. A stay of judgment of execution pending an application for *certiorari* may be granted either by a judge of the court rendering judgment or by a justice of the Supreme Court. 28 U.S.C. Section 2101(f) (1982); 11 Wright and Miller, FEDERAL PRACTICE AND PROCEDURE: Civil section 2908 (1973). Naturally, the development of clear case selection criteria is at best half the battle. To enforce those criteria, the Court should fine attorneys who consistently file frivolous petitions. *See also* Sup. Ct. R. 56(4) (authorizing award of "reasonable damages").

15. *See* Thomas v. Arn, 106 S. Ct. 466, 470-471 (1975), in which the Court approved an analogous procedure involving review of magistrates' reports.

16. Kurland & Hutchinson, *supra* n. 14, at 646.

17. Handler, *supra* n. 10, at 266-267.

18. Kurland & Hutchinson, *supra* n. 14, at 628.

19. 459 U.S. 86 (1982); *see* Note, *Procedural Law*, 59 N.Y.U. L. REV. 1343, 1388 (1984).

20. 104 S. Ct. 2163 (1984).

21. 462 U.S. 213, 217 (1983) (Rehnquist, J.) ("We decide today, with apologies to all, that the issue we framed for the parties was not presented to the Illinois courts and, accordingly, [we] do not address it.").

22. *See, e.g.*, Edwards, *The Rising Work Load and Perceived "Bureaucracy" of the Federal Courts: A Causation-Based Approach to the Search for Appropriate Remedies*, 68 IOWA L. REV. 871, 879-889 (1983); Higginbotham, *Bureaucracy—The Carcinoma of the Federal Judiciary*, 31 ALA. L. REV. 261 (1980); Hoffman, *The bureaucratic spectre: newest challenge to the courts*, 66 JUDICATURE 60 (1982); McCree, *Bureaucratic Justice: An Early Warning*, 129 U. PA. L. REV. 777 (1981); Rubin, *Bureaucratization of the Federal Courts: The Tension Between Justice and Efficiency*, 55 NOTRE DAME L. REV. 648 (1980); Vining, *Justice, Bureaucracy, and Legal Method*, 80 MICH. L. REV. 248 (1981).

23. Coleman, *supra* n. 2, at 27; *see also* Handler, *supra* n. 10, at 277-285.

24. During the 1979 term, for example, the ratio of granted cases to cases considered at the September conference was only 1 in 20 (22 of 391), whereas for the rest of the year it was 1 in 12 (110 of 1,385). During the 1980 term, the ratio was 1 in 23 at the September conference (21 of 458), 1 in 11 for the rest of the year (146 of 1,541). During the 1981 term, the ratio was 1 in 14 at the September conference (26 of 373), 1 in 10 for the rest of the year (177 of 1727). During the 1982 term, the ratio was 1 in 24 at the September conference (16 of 412), and 1 in 10 for the rest of the year (153 of 1480). (Figures compiled from data in U.S.L.W. vols. 47-50.)

25. Feinberg, *A National Court of Appeals?*, 42 BROOKLYN L. REV. 611, 626 (1976).

26. Friendly, *Averting the Flood by Lessening the Flow*, 59 CORNELL L. REV. 634, 656 n. 77 (1974).

27. *Contra*, Handler, *supra* n. 10, at 263-264.

28. *See* Estreicher & Sexton, *supra* n. 1, at 725-726.

29. For useful discussion of venue proposals to reduce forum shopping, see McGarity, *Multi-Party Forum Shopping for Appellate Review of Administrative Action*, 129 U. PA. L. REV. 302 (1980); Sunstein, *Participation, Public Law, and Venue Reform*, 49 U. CHI. L. REV. 976 (1982); Note, *Venue for Judicial Review of Administrative Actions: A New Approach*, 93 HARV. L. REV. 1735 (1980).

30. Van Dusen v. Barrack, 376 U.S. 612 (1964).

31. For a contrary view, see Marcus, *Conflicts Among Circuits and Transfers within the Federal Judicial System*, 93 YALE L. J. 677 (1984).

32. *See, e.g.*, Handler, *supra* n. 10, at 269; Kurland and Hutchinson, *supra* n. 14, at 645-646; Stevens, *The Life Span of a Judge-Made Rule*, 58 N.Y.U. L. REV. 1, 10-21 (1983).

33. *See* White, *Challenges for the U.S. Supreme Court and the Bar: Contemporary Reflections*, 51 ANTITRUST L. J. 275 (1982); *accord*, Note, *Securing Uniformity in National Law: A Proposal for National Stare Decisis in the Courts of Appeals*, 87 YALE L. J. 1219, 1238-1240 (1978); *see also* Handler, *supra* n. 17, at 273 & nn. 80-82. Walter Schaefer would go even further. He argues that the first *panel* decision of a circuit court should bind all other circuit courts unless it is overruled by any circuit court sitting *en banc* or by the Supreme Court. *See* Schaefer, *Reducing Circuit Conflicts*, 69 A.B.A. J. 452, 455 (1983).

34. Coleman, *supra* n. 2, at 18-20.

35. *See, e.g.*, Griswold, *Rationing Justice—The Supreme Court's Caseload and What the Court Does Not Do*, 60 CORNELL L. REV. 335, 350-351 (1975).

36. Feinberg, *supra* n. 25, at 627; Friendly, *The Gap in Lawmaking—Judges Who Can't and Legislators Who Won't*, 63 COLUM. L. REV. 787, 802-807 (1963).

37. *See* Estreicher and Sexton, *supra* n. 1, at 745-747, 757-758.

38. *See* Hellman, *Error Correcting, Lawmaking, and the Supreme Court's Exercise of Discretionary Review*, 44 U. PITT. L. REV. 795, 801-802 (1983); Hellman, *The Business of the Supreme Court Under the Judiciary Act of 1925: The Plenary Docket in the 1970's*, 91 HARV. L. REV. 1709, 1800 (1978).

39. *See, e.g.*, Griswold, *The Need for a Court of Tax Appeals*, 57 HARV. L. REV. 1153 (1944); Handler, *supra* n. 10, at 274-275; Jordan, *Should litigants have a choice between specialized courts and courts of general jurisdiction?*, 66 JUDICATURE 14 (1982); Rifkind, *A Special Court for Patent Litigation? The Danger of a Specialized Judiciary*, 37 A.B.A. J. 425 (1951); Wald, *Judicial Review of Complex Administrative Agency Decisions*, 462 ANNALS 72, 74-75 (1982).

40. *See, e.g.*, Ginsburg, *Making Tax Law Through the Judicial Process*, 70 A.B.A. J. 74 (1984); Griswold, *supra* n. 39; Handler, *supra* n. 10, at 275.

41. E.g., Rifkind, *supra* n. 39; *see also* Edwards, *supra* n. 22, at 919 (arguing that such proposals might result in segregation of disfavored classes of litigation).

42. The difficulties that the District of Columbia Circuit (which is the exclusive or alternative venue in many federal regulatory cases) has had in recent years with the Supreme Court suggest that creation of a court of exclusive jurisdiction over controversial areas of federal law may well exacerbate the justices' workload. *See* Estreicher and Sexton, *supra* n. 1, at 795; Note, *Disagreement in D.C.: The Relationship Between the Supreme Court and the D.C. Circuit and Its Implications for a National Court of Appeals*, 59 N.Y.U. L. REV. 1048 (1984).

43. *See* Federal Courts Improvement Act of 1982, 29 U.S.C. Section 1295 (1982). The Federal Courts Improvement Act provides for the merger of the Court of Customs and Patent Appeals and the Court of Claims into the 12-judge United States Court of Appeals for the Federal Circuit. Section 127 of the Act provides that the new court shall retain substantially all of the jurisdiction of the two courts abolished in the merger. This includes jurisdiction over such matters as appeals in suits against the government and appeals from the Patent and Trademark office, the Court of International Trade, the Merit Systems Protection Board, and the boards of contract appeals. It also includes jurisdiction over patent appeals from the district courts, appeals from final determinations of the United States International Trade Commission relating to unfair practices in import trade, appeals from certain findings of the Secretary of Commerce, and appeals arising under the Plant Variety Protection Act, 28 U.S.C. Section 1245 (1982). The legislative history indicates that the Act was intended to create an appellate forum capable of exercising nationwide jurisdic-

tion over appeals in areas of the law in which there was a particular need for nationwide uniformity. *See* S. Rep. No. 275, 97th Cong., 2d Sess. 2, reprinted in 1982 U.S. CODE CONG. & AD. NEWS 11, 12. Of particular concern was the practice of forum shopping in patent litigation, which often resulted in different appellate courts reaching diametrically opposed conclusions from identical or nearly identical facts. *Id.* at 15.

44. The Court granted *certiorari* in 16 tax cases in the 1982 term, although not all addressed technical aspects of the Internal Revenue Code. *See, e.g.*, Allen v. Wright, 104 S. Ct. 3315 (1984) (black parents of school-age children lack standing to challenge IRS procedures that determine tax-exempt status for racially discriminatory private schools). *See generally* Note, *Tax Law*, 59 N.Y.U. L. REV. 1394 (1984).

45. Note, *supra* n. 44, at 1395-1401.

Appellate Court Processes
Internal Court Processes and Decisions on the Merits

INTRODUCTION

Many of the efforts of social scientists studying appellate courts have focused on judicial decision making. In particular, scholars have utilized several theoretical perspectives in an effort to understand why judges decide cases the way they do. At times, academic research has even resulted in the successful prediction of outcomes in pending cases. Among the concerns researchers have focused on to understand judicial behavior have been factors such as the social background characteristics of judges, their ideological preferences, their interrelationships in a collegial appellate court setting, their judicial philosophies, their concerns about the "proper" judicial role, and, moving beyond factors intrinsic to the individual judge, the fact patterns present in cases before the court.

While these concerns are not exhaustive of the variables that can enter into a judge's decisional equation, and while none of them acting alone are likely to be the exclusive basis for judges deciding cases the way they do, social science research has demonstrated clearly that such factors *do* matter and that judicial decisions do not emanate solely from the law itself. The articles in this section all focus on internal processes of appellate courts and shed some light on how such courts reach their decisions on the merits in cases before them.

Stephen Wasby's piece, "The functions and importance of appellate oral argument," utilizes data from interviews with lawyers and judges to explore this underexamined area of the judicial process. While examining oral argument in an intermediate appellate court setting, the Ninth Circuit, Wasby's observations have clear relevance for all appellate courts, including the U.S. Supreme Court. The article examines two alternative perspectives on the value of oral argument. On one end of the spectrum some contend that oral argumentation facilitates the development of information and clarification of issues and helps focus case proceedings. Face to face contact among the actors in the judicial process also provides real and symbolic benefits. Others contend, however, that oral argument is often unnecessary and exacerbates delay in an already overloaded system. Wasby finds a degree of truth in both perspectives as well as an inherent tension between them. "On the one hand is the desire to maintain a practice that is not merely an 'amenity' but is also thought to have considerable importance for both appellate judges and appellate lawyers. On the other hand is a feeling of the need to adjust to substantial appellate caseloads by recognizing that different types of cases can be treated differently."

Dennis Dorin's study of "Social leadership, humor, and Supreme Court decision making" focuses on the day-to-day workings of the Court and the importance of effective personal relationships, often accompanied by humor, for facilitating efficient decision making through "relieving tension and promoting harmony." The article underlines the importance of social leadership for managing judicial conflict and suggests that in its absence institutional disintegration and incapacitation could result.

Dorin's article takes a "small groups" perspective to judicial decision making, which suggests that collegial behavior is more than simply the sum of its individual parts. Small groups analysts have often suggested that in the Supreme Court's social system newly seated justices serve an apprenticeship period during which time they do not align themselves in the Court's ideological fray; they are seen but not often heard through opinion writing, and they are somewhat bewildered by their new job. In "Revisiting the freshman effect hypothesis," Albert Melone presents findings on some recently seated Supreme Court justices and, in particular, Anthony Kennedy, which raise substantial questions about the various "freshman effect" hypotheses. Melone concludes that organizational developments in the Court, such as increased staffing and improved management techniques, lessen the need for the socialization to the Court that the "freshman effect" may have served in an earlier era. The article also serves to add additional perspectives to the dynamics of Supreme Court recruitment and the Court's decisional processes.

Jeffrey Segal and Harold Spaeth's article, "Decisional trends on the Warren and Burger Courts," lies in the mainstream of social scientific work on judicial decision making. The study reports results from a massive and recently collected data base on Supreme Court cases that will be a major resource to scholars in the years to come. The analysis centers on civil liberties and economics cases and demonstrates that decisions in these areas are related, albeit imperfectly so. Segal and Spaeth document the rise of civil liberties support during the Warren Court's tenure in the early 1960s as well as the dramatic drop of such support after 1968 caused, in part, by personnel changes. The authors demonstrate considerable variation among justices in their voting, a central concern in judicial behavior research, as well as change in the voting patterns of individual justices over time.

All Supreme Court justices may not be created equal when it comes to consideration of their power on the Court in relationship to their colleagues, and, in fact, there are several institutional prerogatives of the chief justice that offer the occupant of the Court's center chair considerable opportunity to be first among equals, "primus inter pares." Sue Davis's article, "Power on the Court: Chief Justice Rehnquist's opinion assignments," examines one facet of the chief's power, his ability to designate the author of majority opinions in those instances when he is a part of the Court's majority. Davis reports on the first three years (1986-1988) of the Rehnquist Court and finds that the new chief distributed opinions among his colleagues with considerable equity in the broad universe of case assignment opportunities. Rehnquist, like earlier chiefs, reserved an overabundance of the Court's most "important" cases for his own pen. Overall, Rehnquist pursued a somewhat mixed strategy in his opinion assignment behavior and clearly did not maximize all the potential power of his institutional role. Davis suggests, however, that given the congenial conservative majority that Rehnquist enjoyed on his Court, little strategic behavior on his part was necessary to prod the Court towards decisions that he favored. For the most part, the Court arrived at such holdings as a matter of course.

Finally, in "The spirit of dissent," J. Louis Campbell III considers the role played by dissenting opinions on the Supreme Court and underlines their importance. He finds dissent to be analogous to civil disobedience and characterizes it as "institutional disobedience" that offers protest and seeks systemic change. At bottom, dissents are seen as "sources of energy and cogency in the law." Campbell's article includes consideration of the history of dissent while also offering examples of famous dissenting opinions and their impact.

The articles in this section of readings underline the considerable diversity in subject matter and methodology that characterizes social scientific research on internal court processes and decisions on the merits. Indeed, the questions asked in this domain and the manner in which they are addressed are subject only to the limits of the imagination and resources of the researcher. Eclectic and interesting research efforts should continue to be found in future writing on judicial decision making.

The functions and importance of appellate oral argument: some views of lawyers and federal judges

Although some critics have proposed curtailing or eliminating oral argument in certain cases, both judges and lawyers believe it plays a vital role in the appellate process, a recent survey shows.

by Stephen L. Wasby

One of the most traditional and important elements of deciding cases on appeal is oral argument, an element of advocacy older than written briefs in this country. Briefs originally were not required in appeals, and oral argument continued without time limits even when briefs were submitted. Eventually briefs did begin to displace argument: the Supreme Court first waived oral argument when written arguments were submitted, then mandated briefs prior to argument, and finally both reserved argument for the most important cases and reduced the time granted each party.[1]

Curtailment of oral argument in other appellate courts, partly the result of caseload pressure, has attracted continued attention. Various sources have warned that eliminating oral argument in all cases would harm the appellate process.[2] Most recently, the Devitt Committee (the Committee to Consider Standards for Admission to Practice in the Federal Courts of the Judicial Conference of the United States) brought further attention to legal advocacy at both trial and appellate levels. The "substantially divided" committee, however, made no recommendations concerning appellate advocacy because it found "the problems presented . . . not sufficiently serious to call for the recommending of remedies"[3]—at least by comparison with trial advocacy, to which the committee devoted the bulk of its attention. Despite the Devitt Committee's view, appellate advocacy remains of considerable importance.

Recent literature shows tension between two divergent tendencies: to retain an essential practice, part of the "procedural amenities" through which courts are "seen to be obeying and enforcing the law,"[4] and to curtail its use in some types of cases to facilitate its retention in others, where it is thought more useful.[5] This article looks at the opinions of the two groups most immediately concerned with appellate argument: lawyers and judges. It is based on interviews with circuit and district judges in the Ninth U.S. Circuit Court of Appeals and with attorneys who had argued before that court.[6]

All the circuit judges and most of the district judges, in their careers as lawyers, had argued appellate cases, but only a few had done so extensively. The experience of the surveyed lawyers is disproportionate to that of most lawyers because not many lawyers engage frequently in appellate work and still fewer argue appellate cases. Two of the attorneys had argued more than 200 state and federal appellate cases each, two others had argued more than 100, and two more had argued between 50 and 100. The least experienced attorneys, by contrast, had argued fewer than 20.

Half the circuit judges said their views of oral argument had changed since their days as practicing lawyers, also true of most of the district judges responding; the other half of the circuit judges said their views had not changed. Those whose views had changed used to feel that as lawyers they could help judges or could "guide the judges" with their knowledge and that "there was something I could add."[7] Now, observed one, he had found as a judge that a "strong minority" of cases was so deficient in merit that "if John Davis argued, it wouldn't make a difference." Other judges now realized that the court's caseload prevented oral argument in every case. Moreover, one noted, judges' preparation—

consistently high, unlike the situation in some state appellate courts—made argument less useful, as did the short time allowed for it.

Almost two-thirds of the lawyers had changed their views of appellate argument from prior to participating in it; most now saw it as less important. They found that "brilliance" had little effect on the court, that argument was not "the highly persuasive medium for the judges" they had thought it would be, and that the judges asked fewer questions than they had anticipated. Indeed, some said that at times argument seemed superfluous. This did not, however, stem from any dissatisfaction with the Ninth Circuit. On the whole, the lawyers were satisfied with oral argument in that court—"by and large, an agreeable court to argue to," "prepared," and "open," with the judges asking "intelligent questions."

In the remainder of this article, we examine first whether appellate oral argument is thought more important for judges or for lawyers. Then we turn to discuss ways in which oral argument helps judges and attorneys and the functions oral argument is thought to perform. We follow this by a look at whether judges and lawyers believe oral argument significant or determinative, as well as the types of cases in which oral argument is thought to be most and least helpful. We draw on Ninth Circuit interviews and on comments from other studies, particularly Federal Judicial Center surveys of judges and of attorneys in the Second, Fifth, and Sixth Circuits.[8]

How oral argument helps

"A great many appellate judges . . . strongly believe that the arguments are a major help," Marvell has noted.[9] The chief judges of the U.S. courts of appeals, responding to Judge Myron Bright's queries, generally found oral argument valuable—"sometimes when least expected," according to First Circuit Judge Frank Coffin,[10] but generally "only in some cases." Screening out cases thought not worthy of argument, the practice in most circuits, has made argument valuable more often when it takes place. Some feel, however, that when judges have long thought about a problem, oral argument is not likely to add much to the resolution of a case.

Both circuit and district judges and lawyers in the Ninth Circuit were almost unanimous in finding appellate oral argument helpful. An interesting difference does occur, however, between judges'

and lawyers' opinions on whether argument is more important for lawyers or judges or is equally important for both. Roughly half the circuit judges felt oral argument equally important for both groups; the other half was divided between those who thought it more important for judges and those who thought it more important for lawyers.[11] However, *no* lawyers believed oral argument more important for themselves, except perhaps as a way of impressing clients; two-thirds said it was equally important for the two groups, with the remainder finding it more important for the judges. The lawyers' position may be explained by a circuit judge's observation that "at the appellate stage, the case is no longer the lawyer's but the court's."

A retired state supreme court justice has written that the functions of oral argument are, in descending important:

(1) to persuade judges, (2) to focus on one important matter only, (3) to reiterate most major points in the brief, (4) to clarify facts, (5) to counter opposition's arguments, (6) to appeal to "justice," "right," and "fairness," (7) to legitimate the legal process by a public confrontation of issues, (8) to urge judges to read (or reread) briefs, (9) to prepare judges for conference deliberations, (10) to force judges to communicate with each other.[12]

Ninth Circuit judges and attorneys differed in the emphasis each group placed on ways that appellate argument helped.[13] Judges found principally that argument helped them clarify matters and focus on important issues, with the opportunity to communicate with lawyers and ask questions only slightly less important. Judges also suggested that oral argument provided information and aided in disposing of cases. Least frequently noted was argument's assistance in increasing the visibility of the court.

For attorneys, clarification and an opportunity for communication with judges were mentioned more than other functions of argument for the judges, with neither function predominant. Attorneys gave far less attention to providing information, assisting in disposition of cases, giving judges an opportunity to ask questions, and helping to save judges' time.

Judges' and lawyers' comments on argument's functions for lawyers also revealed differences. Most frequently mentioned by judges were argument's functions of assisting lawyers in clarifying matters, persuading judges, and generally in communicating with the judges. Least frequently noted were providing information to judges, answering judges' questions, and making the lawyer's case more visible.

Lawyers spoke about the usefulness of argument for themselves in persuading and prodding judges. They also gave considerable weight to argument's help in clarifying issues. Lawyers also found of moderate importance that oral argument helped them learn about judges. Least frequently mentioned as a function of appellate argument for lawyers were the opportunities to answer questions or to help facilitate disposition of cases.

Assisting the judge

Public relations. There is a "public relations" reason for oral argument—so that lawyers and their clients will feel that their cases have been heard. As one judge observed, lawyers need the satisfaction of knowing they have presented their cases well. The other side of this "P.R." coin is that oral argument assists in legitimating the court's judicial function.[14] The Federal Judicial Center's lawyer survey showed that slightly more than half the lawyers in each circuit studied agreed that "when a litigant is denied the right to have his lawyer argue his appeal, the litigant will feel that he has not had his day in court."[15] Submission of briefs is not thought sufficient to assure lawyers and litigants that judges have focused on the case, because one could not be sure the briefs were read.

As Marvell notes, the "public relations function" of contact between attorneys and judges during argument "is especially important when attorneys suspect that not all judges read the briefs or that the court's staff plays a major role in the decision process."[16] An observer of the First Circuit adds that "by demonstrating the openness and the balanced presentation of all material issues in an individual case, the court assures the public that each action is being given their personal and undivided attention in order to reach a reasoned solution."[17] The Hruska Commission echoed this perspective in pointing out that oral argument "assures the litigant that his case has been given consideration by those charged with deciding it."[18]

Communication. Oral argument is valuable for "establish[ing] a human connection between bench and bar" because it is the only face-to-face communication between attorneys and judges during a case's appellate course. As a Ninth Circuit judge noted, argument assists lawyers by "help[ing]

the judges to know who the attorneys are" as well as giving lawyers "a notion of the orientation of the court" and the way it is thinking.

The crucial role of the judge-attorney communication has often been stressed. According to the late Third Circuit Judge William Hastie, "The oral argument is the court's one chance to invite counsel to meet head on what seemed to be the strongest opposing contentions."[19] In the Federal Judicial Center survey, there was extremely high agreement among lawyers that "oral argument permits the attorney to address himself to those issues which the judges believe are crucial to the case."[20]

In addition to the above considerations, the process and "mechanics" of conducting argument help Ninth Circuit judges, particularly because argument comes after a judge has read the briefs. The judge thus hears counsel "against the generalized background of the case." Some judges found this particularly so when a lawyer is "a better talker than a writer"—and some judges simply hear better than they read, as one judge commented. (Oral argument also allows judges to criticize an incompetent lawyer without having to reduce the criticism to writing.)

A less-well-noted aspect of oral argument is communication *among* judges. Questions ostensibly directed to an attorney may be intended for a judicial colleague, to sway that judge or at least to warn of the need to face certain issues.[21] As one lawyer noted, judges "may use the attorney's mouth to convince his colleagues." Appellate argument thus provides judges an "opportunity to respond to each other's questions" and to communicate the "key points of a case" to other members of the panel. If this is effective, at argument's conclusion judges "will have an excellent idea of the key points of a case" and of a problem's "soft underbelly" as well as a sense of other judges' views. Concessions may be more important to judges when a lawyer makes them than if they heard the same argument from a colleague during their collective consideration of the case in conference.

Questions. Central to communication during appellate argument are the judges' questions. Ninth Circuit judges emphasized the opportunity that oral argument provides for exploring doubts they had about the record and "items not entirely clear." A lawyer's response may emphasize a point differently from the emphasis conveyed by the briefs. As a result, "Sometimes we can't understand until we ask questions." (Ninety per cent of attorneys in the Federal Judicial Center survey agreed that "by asking questions of counsel, the judges are better able to avoid erroneous interpretations of the facts or issues in the case.")[22]

Questions also allow judges to test attorneys' positions, particularly to see whether the lawyer can help the judge "decide the case his way easily." A lawyer unable to answer effectively will not carry the court. In a complex case, an attorney's responses may provide a judge with necessary "reinforcement" for tentatively adopted positions.

Ninth Circuit attorneys found it easier to argue to judges who asked more questions. They disliked "passive judges," "who stare at you or over your head" or "just smile or go to sleep." Indeed, one lawyer said he didn't object to a judge "disposed against him" if the judge asked questions. The lawyers were, however, concerned about the quality as well as about the frequency of questions; judges who merely "interrogated" were not appreciated, but lawyers generally preferred "tough" or "perceptive" questions.

Despite lawyers' general preference for judges who asked (good) questions, some lawyers felt that judges' questioning cut into the time needed to argue their cases. This is like the conflict Marvell found: several attorneys he interviewed "said they liked questions; yet they complained that the questions cut into their allotted time so much that they had to abandon some of the points they had wished to emphasize."[23]

Information, clarification, and focus

Questioning allows judges to obtain information and to clarify elements of a case. Appellate argument brings to their attention matters not evident in the briefs or not available earlier.[24] Finding out about matters the last brief left unresolved is of some importance when much time has elapsed between filing of the last brief and oral argument. Information conveyed to the judges through argument includes factual and procedural items as well as new legal arguments. Argument is particularly likely to provide judges new information when a lawyer " 'lays back' and doesn't put everything in the briefs." Argument also allows judges to "learn where new cases would go if unleashed in this case" as well as to learn about the "practical effect" unique cases might have.

Oral argument "allows the judges . . . to clear up any doubts that the court might have about the case or the lawyer's approach to it," observes Eighth Circuit Judge Myron Bright;[25] many Ninth Circuit judges agreed that clarification was a salient function of appellate argument. Clarification occurs not only when briefs are "ambiguous" or even poor, but also when they are of high quality, especially in extremely complex cases.

Argument can lead to clarification when it prompts judges to return to the record, but a lawyer can also "straighten out" a judge at argument before the judge engages in such research. Clarification involves the correction of errors, but it also includes "cast[ing] new light" on important aspects of cases that are vague in the briefs when the court requires the lawyer to clarify his position through a "good, logical analysis of the briefs" during argument.

Part of clarification is a focus on issues. Several federal judges have testified to argument's importance in this regard.[26] At least a majority of judges surveyed by the Federal Judicial Center favored oral argument in part because it "focuses the court's attention on the issues [and] provides the needed impetus to get the 'tough' thinking done efficiently."[27] The late Judge Frederick Hamley of the Ninth Circuit commented that judges found argument helpful because of its "tendency to narrow and pinpoint the question to be decided and the points of law to be reviewed," with "the exact point of disagreement which must be resolved" emerging during argument.[28] The Ninth Circuit judges interviewed concurred. They noted argument's function of narrowing issues, allowing judges to "determine what counsel thinks most salient," and permitting worthless arguments to be swept away.

Disposition. Both clarification and focus assist with disposition of a case; focus is essential before the court can bring a case to resolution. The argument process assists in this regard by setting some issues aside as peripheral, so that the judges can deal with the key issues more directly and quickly. By sharpening judges' thinking, argument provides an "opportunity to formulate a judgment." Even if argument does not itself speed disposition, judges' preparation for it does so.[29]

Improving assistance to judges. Before appellate argument takes place, judges must engage in some communication, among themselves and with the attorneys who are to present argument, if argument is to be most helpful both to the court and the attorneys. A preargument conference of the judges can serve this purpose; it can result in questions to be asked to help guide argument in ways that will assist the judges without the attorney having to cover ground of little (or less) interest to them.

More helpful would be communication before the argument session, where judges could indicate points from the briefs on which they wished lawyers to concentrate, those they wished developed further, and questions they wanted answered. Of course, judges need not pose all their questions prior to argument. They could, however, provide some guidance while reserving further questions for argument itself. Judges often object to such suggestions either because their heavy caseload makes it difficult to consider briefs or the record in advance or because they feel it interferes with the adversary process. Yet argument would be more useful for the judges even if attorneys received questions—perhaps developed from staff attorneys' bench memoranda—only a couple of days before argument.

A further and more extreme suggestion is to hold argument *after* the judges have written and circulated a tentative opinion. Marvell made such a suggestion because of his concern about "the lack of communication back and forth between counsel and the court to iron out exactly what points interest the court so that the counsel can give information the court needs."[30] A natural objection is that judges' views would tend to become frozen. However, if judges could keep their opinions tentative, such a procedure would certainly communicate to attorneys the issues the judges wanted addressed. To be effective, however, the procedure does require judges to put "a good deal of work into a case early, in time to tell counsel of their concerns and to give counsel a chance to prepare answers."[31]

Assisting the lawyers

Communication. Judges, we have noted, find that appellate argument assists them in establishing communication with lawyers. Lawyers find it similarly helpful in establishing communication with judges. Argument provides a lawyer "the opportunity to discourse with the court, and to argue and discuss with the court, or share ideas," as well as to get "points firmly lodged in the judicial mind."[32] For Ninth Circuit attorneys, appellate argument "allows face-to-face contact between an attorney and the court," thus permitting a lawyer "to grapple

with a mind which has already come to grips with the problem" in a case and work through problems bothering the judges.

Appellate argument also allows indirect communication of certain messages. If an attorney tells judges at argument that the attorney's client is present, judges, who appreciate such candor, "understand that some of the things he says are for the benefit of the client, who came to hear them said." An important part of what is communicated at appellate argument is information. This includes "background details," material not covered in briefs, and information about cases decided since the briefs were filed. (Argument may also serve to warn lawyers that they should file supplemental briefs to provide more information on specific points.)

Lawyers also use appellate argument to persuade judges. One senior circuit judge observed that it is the "forcefulness, preparation, and dedication" of particular lawyers that made argument helpful. Part of persuasion for the lawyers was catching the judges' attention or "stimulat[ing] their minds into active thought processes." Another part was to "challenge the judges' concept of a case" and to make them "re-examine their positions."

Clarification and focus. Clarification is a particular significant function of oral argument for attorneys, just as it is for judges. Argument is "enormously beneficial in illuminating . . . precisely what the issues are as counsel sees them."[33] In addition, argument can "cure factual misapprehensions and legal misconceptions," "the two areas than can be met only by oral argument."[34]

Also involved in clarification is the "opportunity to explain seeming contradictions, inconsistencies, or weaknesses in the client's position." When argument allows a lawyer to sense the court's problems with a case, the lawyer can "develop a new theory" to help resolve them. As roughly three-fifths of the attorneys surveyed by the Federal Judicial Center responded, oral argument "allows counsel to gauge the feelings of the judges and to couch his arguments accordingly."[35]

The most crucial element involved in focusing a case at argument is the direct emphasis that can be placed on the most important issues in the case: the lawyer can provide "the crystallized oral statement of the 'gut issue.' "[36] Focusing may entail discarding certain issues as well as stressing others. When flaws in a lawyer's position are revealed at argument, the court does not have to deal with those matters. A lawyer may also use argument to "signal . . . that one or more points in his brief are not well taken"; the judges, realizing that the points were included "to satisfy his client," can then "apply more attention to what he says about his important points" and the lawyer also gains "a little extra credit for his candor."

Oral argument's importance

Relative importance and significance. A large majority of both Ninth Circuit judges and lawyers felt oral argument not of equal importance in all cases. Moreover, no Ninth Circuit appellate judge and only two district judges believed that all cases required the same amount of argument time. Their position is like that of judges surveyed by the Federal Judicial Center, who stressed "varied sets of criteria" for determining appropriate time length for argument and indicated "that a case-by-case method is mandatory with an examination of issue complexity and nature of record and briefs as a starting point."[37]

Ninth Circuit judges felt that complex cases—those with either legal or factual complexity or cases with multiple issues or multiple-defendant criminal cases—required more extended argument. However, they noted only a few specific areas of law in which longer argument was thought necessary, although antitrust, patent, and securities were mentioned by several judges.

Asked to estimate the proportion of cases where appellate argument was "significant," Ninth Circuit judges gave opinions ranging from 5 per cent to 85 per cent. However, only five judges gave estimates of over 10 per cent. Several judges commented specifically that argument was helpful in greater proportions of cases if criminal cases were excluded, because so many of those cases were thought not to raise important issues. Several judges, however, were especially sensitive about eliminating oral argument in criminal appeals; they thought retaining it necessary for the appearance of justice. All the circuit judges and most district judges responding also thought oral argument "determinative"[38] in at least some cases, but, as expected, the proportion of cases in which argument was thought determinative was much smaller than the proportion in which it was considered significant; most estimated the proportion of cases to be "relatively small" or "minimal."

Where most helpful? In what types of cases is

appellate argument thought most helpful? In the Federal Judicial Center study, a majority of circuit judges thought oral argument "essential" in "cases that involve matters of great public interest despite the absence of substantial legal issues" and in only one other category—cases involving the constitutionality of a state statute or state action. By contrast, in civil appeals based on sufficiency of the evidence, only 9 per cent thought argument essential.[39]

In the present study, Ninth Circuit judges defined helpfulness in terms of both legal subject-matter and case characteristics. All but a couple of the judges stressed that appellate oral argument helped most in government regulation cases, particularly those involving new statutes or new administrative agencies. *No* judge found appellate argument more helpful in criminal appeals. Ninth Circuit lawyers primarily found appellate argument most helpful when cases were complex or novel. They cited "novel or undeveloped legal issues," "issues of first impression," or "changing fields of law," as well as "sensitive, complicated, political issues" where a lawyer's views tended to differ from prevailing judicial sentiment or where a lawyer was trying to move the law in a new direction.

Lawyers form the Second, Fifth, and Sixth Circuits considered oral argument essential in "cases which involve matters of great public interest (despite the absence of substantial legal issues) [and] cases involving the constitutionality of a state statute or a state action."[40] Half of the Sixth Circuit lawyers and a clear majority of those from the Second Circuit also thought oral argument essential in direct criminal appeals.[41] Generally, lawyers were more likely than judges to find appellate argument essential than were judges, although "the essentiality of oral argument varies from case-type to case-type for [both] judges and lawyers, with order of preference almost the same from the perspective of bench and bar."[42]

Where least helpful? Ninth Circuit judges tended to find argument least helpful in cases where the circuit had controlling precedent. Resolution of such cases was "largely mechanical." Otherwise, they found argument least helpful in "frivolous cases" or "factual, run-of-the-mill" cases. Not surprising in view of their other comments, argument commonly was felt least helpful in criminal cases. The lawyers also suggested that argument was least helpful in cases where briefs were short and the issue simple (a simple fact pattern), particularly if the law were "static." However, in a comment counter to the typical views, one attorney found oral argument not helpful "when the lawyer was trying to overturn old legal principles and establish new rules of law." Such matters, he believed, were best argued in the briefs.[43]

Some judges said oral argument was not needed when briefs are adequate and "address the issues and are cogent" or when judges and lawyers agree as to what the principal argument is. Thus, ironically, for these judges, good briefing makes argument of less help. Others thought a lawyer might make his point better orally when briefs were poor, but some colleagues felt poor briefs usually meant poor argument.

Most judges, however, focused on lawyers' deficiencies at argument; lawyers agreed that deficiencies in attorney skills detracted from oral argument. (Some attorneys also suggested that certain characteristics of judges interfere with the effectiveness of argument, for example, when judges were "not inclined to listen" or were "impatient," appearing to "have made up their minds." Only one circuit judge blamed judges—when they preempt argument time—for detracting from argument.)

Judges thought that in a number of cases lawyers' argument was of little help because the lawyers were "not well prepared," not "up to" argument, or were "not good on their feet when asked questions." Lawyers agree that "boring, incompetent presentations" by lawyers can cause damage. Just as important is that lawyers not "take too rigid a position" or adopt a stance they know is not valid—something that will produce a loss of credibility.

Judges noted and lawyers also frequently mentioned as less than helpful situations in which attorneys read their presentations or "simply repeated the briefs." Recitation of facts not woven into the law were also thought not helpful. Lawyers who made speeches, engaged in fancy rhetoric, or made "impassioned jury pleas to an appellate judge" were also thought ineffective. However, comments about the need for a "just result" in a case are thought appropriate if they are related to the law—not made in isolation from the law.

Attorneys may not make most effective use of appellate argument because relatively few of them have tried appellate cases. Still fewer have handled appeals in the federal courts. The skills of a trial lawyer and an appellate attorney can differ markedly, and attorney specialization decreases the likelihood that an individual attorney will possess both. Ability to make an effective jury argument is not the same as being able to focus succinctly on often rapid-fire questions from a "hot" bench of three appellate judges, well-prepared from having read the briefs.

A Federal Judicial Center survey of lawyer competence casts some light on types of lawyers judges think least effective in appellate argument. A majority "believe there is a serious problem among lawyers employed by state or local governments," but less than 10 per cent thought such a problem existed among "public or community defenders, Justice Department lawyers other than those in U.S. attorneys' offices and on strike forces, and private practitioners representing corporate clients in civil cases."[44] Age, size of a lawyer's office, previous courtroom experience, and a lawyer's educational background were all found not to be related to judges' ratings.

Curtailing and eliminating oral argument

The Hruska Commission stated in 1975 that "to mandate oral argument in every case would clearly be unwarranted." The Commission also thought it inappropriate to ignore "risks to the process of appellate adjudication inherent in too-ready a denial of the opportunity to present a litigant's case."[45] At about the same time, the Advisory Council on Appellate Justice recommended that "oral argument should be allowed in most cases" but also conceded "it may be curtailed or eliminated in certain instances."[46] The American Bar Association's position was most direct. In 1974, the ABA's House of Delegates opposed "the rules of certain United States courts of appeals which drastically curtail or entirely eliminate oral argument in a substantial proportion of non-frivolous appeals . . ."[47]

Federal Judicial Center surveys show agreement between judges and lawyers on limiting oral argument but definite disagreement on situations in which it might be eliminated. *All* circuit judges found it acceptable to limit argument to 15-20 minutes per side and over 98 per cent of the lawyers agreed.[48] Continuing their agreement, both judges and lawyers were less willing to limit oral argument to 15-20 minutes per side and to deny argument completely when the reason was "avoidance of extreme delay" than they were to do so either when an appeal was close to "frivolous" or where clear issues could be decided by circuit precedent.

Moreover, "approximately 90 per cent of the judges recognized occasions when elimination of oral argument is an acceptable procedure." Eighty-eight per cent of the circuit judges agreed that denying oral argument was "ever acceptable." However, the percentages of lawyers agreeing with such a proposition ranged from 84 per cent (Fifth Circuit) to only 67 per cent (Second Circuit).[49]

Roughly 95 per cent of judges were willing either to limit or eliminate oral argument in frivolous cases, and similarly high percentages were willing to do so in cases governed by precedent. When the reason was to avoid extreme delay, the proportions declined (86 per cent for limiting argument, only 62 per cent for denying it).[50] Lawyers showed a similar pattern of differences between cases types, with ranking parallel to the judges'. By comparison with the judges, however, proportionately far more lawyers objected to eliminating argument than were willing to accede to time limitations.

Lawyers' objections to time limits on argument can be seen in the Hruska Commission testimony of Moses Lasky, "dean" of Ninth Circuit appellate attorneys. Lasky argued against any "official limitation on the time for arguments." Arguments, he felt, should take as much time as necessary for the judges "to squeeze all the values out of it that they can get out." Endless argument would not be the result, said Lasky, citing the comment attributed to Abe Lincoln: "When asked how long should a man's legs be, he replied, 'Long enough to reach the ground.'" Some arguments would take no longer than 15 minutes, while some might profitably extend for hours.[51]

A clear majority of judges in the Federal Judicial Center survey saw oral argument as dispensable in two types of cases: prisoner petitions seeking alteration of prison conditions, and collateral attacks on federal and state convictions. Almost half the judges also thought oral argument could be eliminated in sufficiency-of-evidence cases. However, only 7 per cent of circuit judges thought that courts court dispense with argument in "cases which involve matters of great public interest despite the absence of substantial legal issues."[52]

Not surprisingly, a greater proportion of judges than attorneys thought oral argument was dispensable for each type of case.[53] In no case category did a majority of attorneys agree that oral argument was dispensable, although the proportion reached 30 per cent for challenges to prison conditions and

diversity-of-citizenship cases raising only state law questions.[54] Furthermore, faced with limitations on traditional procedures, including argument, lawyers were less willing to accept limitations—"to the extent that they accept [them] at all"—for "administrative reasons" than for "substantive legal reasons."[55]

All Ninth Circuit circuit and district judges interviewed believed that oral argument could be eliminated in some cases. Four of 12 circuit judges thought, however, that eliminating oral argument would not "assist the court in completing its business." Despite the repeated concerns about the need to allow argument in criminal cases for the sake of the appearance of justice, criminal cases were most frequently mentioned as the type where argument could be eliminated. However, some judges distinguished between direct criminal appeals, in which they were reluctant to eliminate argument, and habeas corpus cases, where they would do so, particularly in pro se appeals.

At least some judges found some civil cases—particularly simple ones—to require "no oral argument," especially if all members of a panel agreed that all problems were already presented in the briefs. Even if a case contained more than one issue, argument might not be necessary if all issues were simple. Some judges also did not find argument helpful in administrative agency cases, where their task was a limited review of the record. Similarly, argument was not thought to aid the judges in agency cases involving the "abuse of discretion" standard.

Only a bare majority of Ninth Circuit attorneys agreed that the court could dispense with argument in even some cases. Other than an occasional mention of criminal cases and a suggestion of cases involving ineffective counsel or misjoinder of offenses, lawyers seldom mentioned specific subject-matter areas for eliminating oral argument. They instead focused on cases where "it is perfectly obvious how it would go," and noted as well cases that had been dispositively handled by the circuit, particularly if the briefs indicated agreement on the issues.

Oral argument versus written opinion

Reduction or elimination of oral argument is only one way of reducing appellate court workloads. Both judges and lawyers in the Federal Judicial Center surveys were more willing to accept limitations on oral argument than to approve limitations on written opinions. However, judges, faced with a choice between argument and full written opinions, clearly preferred retaining argument and making greater use of memorandum opinions or "reasoned oral disposition" in most categories of cases. A majority of judges also agreed on the importance of issuing at least memoranda, so the courts "do not give the appearance to litigants of acting arbitrarily." However, only one-third of the circuit judges thought that "the absence of a reasoned disposition" would provide "no guidance to . . . district judges or the bar in future cases."[56] Conversely, in terms of the courts' legitimacy, "nearly half the circuit judges agreed that in the absence of a reasoned disposition, members of the bar may infer that the court has acted arbitrarily, yet little more than a quarter of the district judges concurred."[57]

Fifty-six per cent of attorneys from the Second Circuit preferred oral argument and memorandum opinions or reasoned oral disposition rather than full opinion and limited or no oral argument, a preference consistent with practice in their circuit. Attorneys from the Fifth and Sixth Circuits had the reverse preference.[58] Ninth Circuit attorneys in the present study were closely divided in their preferences.[59] Among those preferring oral argument, one attorney found "bad results without it" but thought written opinions were "needed for development of the law." The value of a written opinion, said another attorney, was the "proper check" placed on "the court's superficiality and discretion"; an opinion forced the court to express its views in ways "credible to the bar."

Willingness to accept delay in order to obtain certain practices is a measure of support for those practices. A "large proportion" of judges surveyed by the Federal Judicial Center felt that retaining both argument and written opinions was worth waiting longer than the current time to disposition. Judges were, however, "more concerned about avoiding extreme delay" than were attorneys.[60] Lawyers also wanted both argument and written opinions even if more time would be consumed in the process.

Indeed, "the speed with which opinions are rendered is a matter of relatively low priority" for the attorneys; few felt that eliminating argument or limiting opinions is "the most acceptable way to avoid long delays in the court's calendar when the docket becomes crowded."[61] In no category of cases were more than one-fifth of the attorneys willing to give up both oral argument and written opinions to reduce time to disposition. Conversely, slightly over three-fourths would accept longer disposition times to obtain traditional practices.[62]

Conclusion

Although trial advocacy has received more attention than appellate argument in recent years, the latter also is significant and deserves attention. Efforts by both federal and state appellate courts to "streamline" proceedings require an understanding of the functions appellate oral argument is expected to perform. Lawyers need a better grasp of judges' views concerning the types of cases for which reduced oral argument or elimination of argument is considered appropriate and vice versa. The view of Ninth Circuit judges and lawyers and data from Federal Judicial Center surveys should make clear that the range of opinions about appellate argument is wide. It should also be clear that appellate oral argument is expected, by both attorneys and judges, to serve multiple functions.

Beneath all these views runs a recurrent theme of tension between perspectives, a tension that shows little sign of abating. On the one hand is the desire to maintain a practice that is not merely an "amenity" but is also thought to have considerable importance for both appellate judges and appellate lawyers. On the other hand is a feeling of the need to adjust to substantial appellate caseloads by recognizing that different types of cases can be treated differently. Despite "inroads" some feel have been made in appellate argument, neither element in the tension has ousted the other, and appellate argument is in no danger of being extinguished as a significant part of appellate practice.

NOTES

This article originally appeared in Volume 65, Number 7, February 1982, pages 340-353. It is drawn from a more extensive report, Wasby, *Oral Argument in the Ninth Circuit: The View from Bench and Bar*, 11 GOLDEN GATE L. REV. 21 (1981). Financial assistance for the research came from the Office of Research and Projects, Southern Illinois University at Carbondale, and from the Penrose Fund of the American Philosophical Society.

1. *See generally* Wasby, D'Amato and Mertrailer, *The Function of Oral Argument in the U.S. Supreme Court*, 62 Q. J. SPEECH 410, particularly at 412 (1976).

2. *See* Commission on Revision of the Federal Court Appellate System, STRUCTURE AND INTERNAL PROCEDURES: RECOMMENDATIONS FOR CHANGE 106, 107 (1975).

3. Judicial Conference of the United States, Committee to Consider Standards for Admission to Practice in the Federal Courts, Report and Tentative Recommendations 30-31 (1978).

4. Carrington, *Ceremony and Realism: Demise of Appellate Proce-*

dure, 66 A.B.A. J. 860 (1980).

5. Godbold, *Improvements in Appellate Procedure: Better Use of Available Facilities*, 66 A.B.A. J. 863 (1980).

6. In the spring of 1977, all but one of 11 active-duty circuit judges and five of the seven senior circuit judges were interviewed as were a dozen district judges, primarily from California and Oregon, chosen from those who had sat frequently on the appellate court "by designation." To provide some comparison with the judges' responses and a different perspective, 13 San Francisco lawyers (all those contacted) were also interviewed, and responses to mail questionnaires were obtained from six Los Angeles lawyers (roughly one-third of those contacted). All the lawyers had argued more than one case before the Ninth Circuit in the previous year. Lawyers and judges were, for the most part, asked parallel questions.

7. Material appearing in quotation marks without attribution is drawn from the author's interviews.

8. Goldman, ATTITUDES OF UNITED STATES JUDGES TOWARD LIMITATION OF ORAL ARGUMENT AND OPINION-WRITING IN THE UNITED STATES COURTS OF APPEALS (Washington, D.C.: Federal Judicial Center, 1975); Drury, Goodman, and Stevenson, ATTORNEY ATTITUDES TOWARD LIMITATION OF ORAL ARGUMENT AND WRITTEN OPINION IN THREE U.S. COURTS OF APPEALS (Washington, D.C.: Bureau of Social Science Research, 1974).

9. Marvell, APPELLATE COURTS AND LAWYERS: INFORMATION GATHERING IN THE ADVERSARY SYSTEM 75 (Westport, CT: Greenwood Press, 1978).

10. Bright, *The Changing Nature of the Federal Appeals Process in the 1970s: A Challenge to the Bar*, 65 F.R.D. 496, 505 n. 8 (1975).

11. Both one senior district judge and two lawyers thought argument equally unimportant for both lawyers and judges.

12. Weaver, quoted in Sheldon and Weaver, POLITICIANS, JUDGES, AND THE PEOPLE: A STUDY IN CITIZENS' PARTICIPATION 86 (Westport, CT: Greenwood Press, 1980).

13. In discussing oral argument's functions as viewed from the Ninth Circuit, we draw primarily on judges' comments about why oral argument is helpful to them, and on lawyers' responses as to why they find argument helpful. Although a high proportion of lawyers found oral argument more important for judges than for themselves, they made few specific comments as to how it helped the judges. Perhaps they simply found reasons why oral argument was helpful to judges to be the complement of reasons why it assisted lawyers.

14. *See* Wasby et al., *supra* n. 1, at 418.

15. Drury, *supra* n. 8, at 306 n. 13.

16. Marvell, *supra* n. 9, at 306 n. 13.

17. Corey, *Some Aspects of Oral Argument in the United States Court of Appeals for the First Circuit*, 21 BOSTON B. J. 21, 32 (1977).

18. STRUCTURE AND INTERNAL PROCEDURES, *supra* n. 2, at 106.

19. Quoted in Maris, *In the Matter of Oral Argument*, 1 PRACTICAL LAWYER (1955), quoted in Commission on Revision of Federal Appellate System, FIRST PHASE: HEARINGS 67 (Washington, D.C.: 1973).

20. Drury, *supra* n. 8, at 38 (Table 26).

21. *See* Wasby et al., *supra* n. 1, at 418; Wasby, *Communication Within the Ninth Circuit Court of Appeals*, 8 GOLDEN GATE L. REV. 1, 5 (1977).

22. Drury, *supra* n. 8, at 38 (Table 26).

23. Marvell, *supra* n. 9, at 79.

24. However, less than half the attorneys in federal appellate practice surveyed by the Federal Judicial Center felt oral argument the *only* way to inform judges effectively of facts and issues in a case. Drury, *supra* n. 8, at 38 (Table 26).

25. Bright, *supra* n. 10, at 506.

26. See Commission, 2 HEARINGS: SECOND PHASE 1974-1975, 408, 826 (Washington, D.C.: 1975).

27. Sutcliffe, addendum to Goldman, *supra* n. 8, at 2 (1975).

28. Quoted at FIRST PHASE, *supra* n. 19, at 777.

29. For examination of judges' preparation for argument, *see* Wasby, *Oral Argument in the Ninth Circuit: The View from Bench and Bar*, 11 GOLDEN GATE L. REV. 21, 74-78 (1981).

30. Marvell, *supra* n. 9, at 247.

31. *Id.* at 248.

32. FIRST PHASE, *supra* n. 19, at 66, 322.

33. 1 SECOND PHASE, *supra* n. 26, at 350.

34. FIRST PHASE, *supra* n. 19, at 804.

35. Drury, *supra* n. 8, at 38 (Table 26).

36. FIRST PHASE, *supra* n. 19, at 794.

37. Sutcliffe, *supra* n. 27, at 1.

38. Like "significant," "determinative" was not further defined when the question was asked. When a judge inquired as to its meaning, the interviewer said he was interested in cases in which oral argument made the judge change his mind or made the essential difference in the case.

39. Goldman, *supra* n. 8, at 8 (Table V). The only other categories where substantial proportions of circuit judges found oral argument essential were direct criminal appeals (38 per cent) and en banc cases previously heard by a panel (35 per cent). For the views of Ninth Circuit judges on the latter, *see* Wasby, *supra* n. 9, at 69-71.

40. Drury, *supra* n. 8, at 22.

41. Intercircuit differences in responses could be explained in part by intercircuit differences in argument practices. Goldman, *supra* n. 8, at 20-21. The Second Circuit had oral argument in every case, but decided a number of cases from the bench without opinion; the Fifth Circuit made "extensive use of truncated procedures," *id.* at 3, with "no oral argument" in a high percentage of cases; and the Sixth Circuit, by contrast, had retained a relatively traditional oral argument arrangement.

42. *Id.* at 8-10.

43. *See also* comments by Hruska Commission Executive Director A. Leo Levin, FIRST PHASE, *supra* n. 19, at 503-504.

44. Partridge and Bermant, THE QUALITY OF ADVOCACY IN THE FEDERAL COURTS 25 (Washington, D.C.: Federal Judicial Center, 1978).

45. STRUCTURE AND INTERNAL PROCEDURE, *supra* n. 2, at 107.

46. Advisory Council on Appellate Justice, Recommendations, summarized in 7 THIRD BRANCH (November 1975).

47. *See* 60 A.B.A. J. 1214 (1974).

48. Goldman, *supra* n. 8, at 13 (Table III).

49. *Id.* at 5; *id.* at 13 (Table III); Drury, *supra* n. 8, at 19 (Table 13).

50. Goldman, *supra* n. 8, at 7a (Table IV).

51. FIRST PHASE, *supra* n. 19, at 932.

52. Goldman, *supra* n. 8, at 11 (Table IV).

53. Drury, *supra* n. 8, at 16; Goldman, *supra* n. 8, at 12.

54. Drury, *supra* n. 8, at 24 (Table 16). The difference among the three circuits were less severe for judgments about dispensability of argument than for judgments that argument was essential. However, "in the Second and Sixth Circuits, where oral argument is generally allowed, the idea that oral argument should always be accorded unless the appeal is frivolous received the greatest support." *Id.* at 47.

55. *Id.* at 19.

56. Goldman, *supra* n. 8, at 12, 17 (Table IX).

57. *Id.* at 20 (Table XII).

58. Drury, *supra* n. 8, at 26 (Table 17).

59. The judges were not asked about their preference between oral argument and full written opinions.

60. Goldman, *supra* n. 8, at 7, 14.

61. Drury, *supra* n. 8, at 32, 34.

62. *Id.* at 33 (Table 22) and 34 (Table 24). *See also id.* at 35-36 (Table 25), indicating the median number of months attorneys perceive required to obtain a final disposition and median number of months they are willing to wait to have both oral argument and written opinion.

Social leadership, humor, and Supreme Court decision making

The justices frequently find themselves at the "storm center" of far-reaching controversies, but members of the Court often have been able to use humor to relieve the tension that could lead to incapacitation or disintegration.

by Dennis D. Dorin

The justices of the United States Supreme Court have been characterized, on more than one occasion, as "nine scorpions in a bottle,"[1] and no wonder! Rumors about their purportedly fierce policy and personality conflicts have been rampant throughout a large part of the Court's history. Few Courts have been blessed with an overriding ideological consensus. Their members have often found themselves in what Justice Holmes called the "storm center" of many of the nation's most far-reaching controversies. Buffeted by all sorts of conflicting societal interests, struggling with an arduous workload, colliding with and attempting to accommodate each other within a potentially explosive small group setting, they could be expected to spend a major portion of their time locked in bitter conflict.

Yet, even given the increased dissent rates of the justices in recent years, their degree of personal rancor may well have been exaggerated. The media, as just one example, have probably distorted the picture by reporting, at face value, the often very strong condemnations of each other's positions that the justices convey to "the outside world" through their opinions. Such argumentation, however, is, to a considerable extent, simply part of the adversarial process to which a justice tends to resort after he or she has crystallized his or her position.[2] Intense rhetoric may, in such instances, be merely an acceptable part of the game.

And, of course, constitutional law professors and political scientists join their journalistic colleagues in emphasizing dissension. Their focus tends to be upon contrasting jurisprudential perspectives, such as those of justices Black and Frankfurter or chief justices Warren and Burger. They stress the battles between the "activists" and the "restraintists" or the "liberal" and "conservative" blocs or factions.

Such focal points, however, tend to ignore the relatively high degree of cohesion that characterizes not only the Court, but most of our appellate tribunals. Indeed, from this perspective, the recent public expression of hostility among members of the California Supreme Court is remarkable in its rarity.[3] Somehow most of our appellate benches manage to contain personality conflicts that otherwise might lead to incapacitation or disintegration.

Social leadership on the Court

How personality conflict is contained might prove an interesting lesson in judicial administration. Social leadership may be at least part of the explanation. One or more justices, depending on the situation, tend to take the lead in relieving tension and promoting harmony. They attend to the emotional needs of their colleagues, affirming their "value as individuals and as Court members . . . ,"[4] and through warmth, sensitivity, and responsiveness, help make the Court socially cohesive. Chief Justice Taft, according to political scientist David Danelski, was just such a leader during the Court's conferences. Cheerful, warm, and understanding, he encouraged the justices with whom he served to think of themselves as "team players."[5]

We may miss much that is relevant, however, if we simply search for the social leaders of recent Courts.

At times, they may be discernible. But when they are not, their absence may suggest much about the Court in question. We might, for example, expect the Court to be seriously divided with significant implications for its decisions.[6] Yet, this outcome is hardly guaranteed, since social leadership may still be exercised. It simply may be diffused among a number of justices whose social acumen puts them on a relative parity.

Social leaders and humor

That humor[7] can be an important tool for such social leaders should hardly be surprising. When tactfully employed, it has served, since prehistoric times, to diffuse tense situations. Sharing a joke with someone is an age-old way of affirming his or her importance. Joking about common burdens is often an integral part of colleagueship. Recalling their years with Chief Justice Vinson, his clerks noted that his "sense of humor and boundless fund of homely anecdotes and tall stories served many times to take the edge off heated discussion."[8] And looking back upon his service as a law clerk with Justice Powell, J. Harvie Wilkinson III remarked that a "good laugh" was often "the best and sometimes the only escape from a hard day."[9]

There are, indeed, a number of reasons why Supreme Court justices, in particular, might be expected to resort to humor when attempting social leadership. First, as John Schmidhauser has observed, many of the justices come from families and careers that are unusually politically active.[10] Such socialization might well involve myriad opportunities to develop the sensitivity and timing necessary to effectively employ humor.[11]

Second, for all but a few of them, service on the Court is the culmination of their careers. They are part of a historic group; they share an *esprit de corps* not found elsewhere. This sense of being "brethren," or a "sister," can be a strong catalyst for inside jokes and anecdotes that are socially cohesive. The justices get to know each other well. Their foibles, eccentricities, and tribulations, if treated sympathetically, can be the stuff of a gentle and amiable humor.

Justice Potter Stewart has recalled, for example, that his colleague, Felix Frankfurter, "loved debate and disputation the way other men liked tennis, golf, or bridge; it was his joy and avocation." But Chief Justice Warren, Stewart recalled, "the solver of great policy problems," never understood this. For him, Frankfurter was the sower of discord. Warren seemed to be constantly befuddled by him. "It was," Stewart exclaimed, "like the mouse and the elephant!"[12]

Recourses to humor may be encouraged by a third factor—the justices' maxim that they can disagree without being disagreeable. "Lawyers," Stewart tells us, "learn early in the game that professional differences are not personal ones." This understanding, he maintains, stays with them when they become jurists: "This case we may vehemently disagree. The next one you may be the only one brilliant enough to join my dissent." There will constantly be "shifting alliances." When a case is over, "you go on to the next." There is no time to "sit around and brood" or nourish rancors. "There's the crush of the docket; the next case is waiting."[13]

Humor can be an important complement to such an attitude. Tom Clark, for example, was perusing Volume 357 of *The United States Reports* during an interview, searching for a case concerning prejudicial influences upon juries. He happened to turn to *Crooker v. California* (1958),[14] however. Clark's holding in *Crooker* had been decimated over his strong opposition in *Escobedo v. Illinois* (1964)[15] and *Miranda v. Arizona* (1966).[16] "*Crooker*," he chuckled good naturedly, "they sure whittled that one down on me!"[17]

A fourth way in which humor might help in social leadership is suggested by the doctrine of *Chaplinsky v. New Hampshire* (1942).[18] In *Chaplinsky*, Justice Murphy was quoting the New Hampshire Supreme Court's description of those "fighting words" not protected by the First and Fourteenth Amendments. Their very utterance, he related, inflicted injury and tended to incite a breach of the peace "when said without a disarming smile."[19]

The Court has been the scene of many disarming smiles! Its members vent considerable aggression toward each other. Doing so in a serious manner can irreparably disrupt relationships. Recourses to humor are safer. Pressure valves may be released, and strong and pointed messages sent in ways that mute conflict. Justice Stewart, for example, apparently resorted to the "disarming smile" to convey to Frankfurter the broadly shared view that he was monopolizing the conference's precious discussion time. "I used to tell him," Stewart remembered, "that he held forth for exactly fifty minutes, the length of a law school class period at Harvard."[20]

Humor may also make it possible for justices not to take themselves, and even the Court, too seriously. Mental health may depend upon a realistic sense of perspective. This orientation may well express itself through a humor that is self-effacing—one that is a medium for a becoming humility. "I agreed with all you say and some of it I understand," Sutherland wrote Stone on the draft of one of Stone's more complex patent case opinions![21]

A few humorous examples

The recently opened papers of justices such as Harold Burton and Tom Clark,[22] *The Brethren*,[23] and a number of other sources[24] have suggested strongly that humor pervades the justices' decision making. Members of the Court, of course, are hardly stand-up comics. Their jokes are seldom of the sideslapping variety. They are, by contrast, more the witticisms of individuals working very hard, and under heavy pressures, together. As might be expected, they have a distinctly lawyer's cast; some may not seem the least bit funny to laymen. But, for the justices, they appear to punctuate important stages in their decision of cases. Invoked by would-be social leaders at crucial points in the Court's processes, they may frequently serve as both a major lubricant and as a powerful cohesive force in its decision making.

The stage at which the Court selects its cases, for example, may be especially crucial. Contemporary justices are, of course, inundated with requests for review. Agenda-setting through the acceptance of only a tiny percentage of proffered controversies is thus of far-reaching importance.[25] Votes can sometimes be very close. High stakes and substantial tensions can prevail. Attempts at social leadership through humor can consequently be expected.

Consider, as one instance, Justice Jackson's recourse to humor in *Sutton v. Leib* (1951).[26] Jackson very much wanted the Court to hear this case. But he fell one short of the required four votes. His medium to try to persuade a brother to join him was a memorandum filled with humor. *Sutton v. Leib*, Jackson concluded, was a natural for such a treatment. A woman's three marriages and two divorces had created a massive legal tangle involving the courts of three states and the federal system. Her former and present husbands, Jackson noted, must have been dumbfounded. After all,

Nevada told Mr. Henzel that he was free of wife No. 1 and could take on No. 2. But then New York told him he was still married to No. 2 . . . Now the [federal courts tell] him he is still stuck with No. 2, who meanwhile has found another nearer to her heart's desire. Mr. Sutton, on the other hand, finds that in New York he is married to [the woman involved] while in Illinois, and perhaps in Nevada, [she] is a bigamist and their marriage is void. No one can tell how the other forty-five states and [D.C.] would act upon the thing. It may be unsafe for them to get outside of New York State, even to visit the Nation's capital.

"Perhaps the only safe thing" for all of these people to do, Jackson mused, would be "to scurry around to the remaining states that have not yet been drawn into this squabble" to obtain rulings from them as to whom they consider each to be married![27]

Jackson succeeded in obtaining his fourth vote, and, in this sense, his employment of humor may be more indicative of task, than social, leadership. For he used it primarily as an intellectual weapon to convince at least one of his colleagues to join him.[28] But it is difficult to believe that any member of the Court had not been amused by his tongue-in-cheek account of Mrs. Sutton's (or was it Mrs. Leib's or Mrs. Henzel's?) marital and legal vicissitudes. To the extent that it brought the justices together to laugh at the law's absurdities, it played a significant social leadership role.

Oral arguments are yet another potential trouble spot in the justices' decision making. Counsel and Court work under strict time parameters. The justices may argue with each other through questions and comments to the attorneys. A large number of the lawyers are experiencing the nervousness of appearing before the Court for the first time and their arguments may well fall below the Court's standards. No wonder that such sessions are often punctuated with tension-reducing laughter!

It should thus come as no surprise that justices such as William Douglas sought release through humor during such intervals. "When some incompetent soul was wasting our time trying to present a case," Douglas recalled in his autobiography, "I often sent a note to Felix Frankfurter. Sometimes it read: 'I understand this chap led your class at Harvard Law School.' Sometimes it read: 'Rumor has it that this lawyer got the highest grade at Harvard Law School you ever awarded a student.' Almost always," Douglas remembered, "Felix would be ignited, just like a match."[29]

The Court's conference discussion and vote on the merits may be the most potentially explosive phase of its decision making. The justices deliberate face-to-face with even more severe time constraints and higher stakes than during the oral arguments. The chances for sensitive egos to clash seem especially high.

Perhaps this is one of the reasons why the justices' rare public reminiscences about the conference tend to be humorous. Justice Clark, among others, has related the classic story of this genre. The strong-willed first John Harlan was presenting a view of a case with which Holmes vehemently disagreed. "That won't wash!" Holmes interjected. The two men glared at each other. But the diminutive Chief Justice Fuller quickly intervened. Fuller, sharing Harlan's views, turned to Holmes. "Well," he laughed, "I'm scrubbing away, anyhow." "A tense situation passed over," Clark concluded, "during the ensuing laughter."[30]

A feel for the pervasive role of humor in the Court's social leadership might best be conveyed through the justices' written communications during the opinion-writing stage. A perusal of this higly creative and stressful phase of the process shows that the witticisms are not only plentiful, but purposeful.

Justice Clark, for example, delighted in using his returns of other justices' opinions for satire. In *Spano v. New York* (1959),[31] as one instance, he received a draft opinion from Warren arguing that Spano had made a coerced confession. He had confessed to murder, Warren asserted, due to the lies and entreaties of a childhood friend who had become a police officer. Spano, he concluded, was apparently unaware of John Gay's famous couplet:

"An open foe may prove a curse, but a pretended friend is worse, . . ."

Clark, enjoying the opportunity to make light of his own voting record, which showed that he almost never accepted a defendant's coerced confession claim, as well as Warren's sentimentality, communicated the news that he was joining Warren's opinion in the following fashion:

"Dear Chief: You've got even hard-hearted me crying. OK TCC"[32]

A "join-me" letter such as Clark's, however, is a pleasure. And a bit of humor with it is simply icing. The pain comes in the communication stating that the other justice will *not* be joining one's opinion. It is fascinating that justices frequently accompany such negative declarations with a touch of soften-

ing humor. This form of social leadership is reminiscent of Stewart's orientation, saying "I must part with you at this important instance, but I trust we still are friends."

Consider, as just one of many examples, Hugo Black's response to Clark's draft opinion in *Briethaupt v. Abram* (1957).[33] In this case, Clark would permit into evidence against a defendant a blood sample extracted from him, without his prior approval, as he lay unconscious. A skilled professional, Clark noted, took the sample at the request of the law enforcement authorities. It was thus a minor intrusion upon the defendant's privacy, hardly one that was forbidden by the Constitution. The Due Process Clause, he declared, was not to be measured by the "yardstick of personal reaction on the sphygmograph[34] of the most sensitive person, but by [the] whole community sense of 'decency and fairness' . . . ."[35]

Black could scarcely have found another approach more repugnant. He would later join Douglas in an opinion that described the taking of the blood sample as an assault on a helpless man. Clark's draft was legitimating what, for Black, was a blatant violation of the Fifth and Fourteenth Amendments. And, he must have guessed, rightly, that Clark's allusion to "the whole community sense of 'decency and fairness' " had been added to his opinion at Frankfurter's suggestion, thus representing an approach to the interpretation of the Due Process Clause that Black loathed. Clark and Black were unalterably on a collision course. Yet, Black chose to respond with a dose of humor. "As you may suspect," he wrote Clark at this tense juncture, "I am going to dissent in this case." "This may be conditional, however," he added, "What is a 'sphygmograph'? This may change my whole viewpoint."[36]

☆ ☆ ☆

Humor's role in Supreme Court social leadership hardly lends itself to precise measurement. It cannot be quantified. It is subject to all of the pitfalls of subtle communication. A justice's attempt at a harmless joke might well be interpreted by his or her colleague as demeaning sarcasm.[37] Students of judicial administration would thus be hard put to place the justices' recourses to humor in neat typologies. And yet, they might be wrong to ignore them. Something induces a relatively high level of cohesiveness into our appellate judiciaries. The socialization of our jurists, their career experiences, their conceptions of their roles, their interactions within the constraints of their courts' rules and customs may all play extremely important parts. But so does a form of social leadership that relies upon the human need for laughter.

NOTES

This article originally appeared in Volume 66, Number 10, May 1983, pages 462-468.

1. Epstein, *Is Internal Dissent Hobbling U.S. Supreme Court?*, THE CHARLOTTE OBSERVER, October 4, 1982, at 7A.

2. Howard, *On the Fluidity of Judicial Choice*, 62 AM. POL. SCI. REV. 47-49 (March, 1968).

3. Lewis, *Unveiling the Courts*, THE N.Y. TIMES, September 6, 1969, at A21.

4. Danelski, *The Influence of the Chief Justice in the Decisional Process*, in Murphy and Pritchett (eds.), COURTS, JUDGES, AND POLITICS 498 (New York: Random House, 1961).

5. *Id.* at 499-500.

6. *See*, for example, Epstein, *supra* n. 1.

7. *Webster's* first definition of humor would seem suitable for our purposes: "that quality which appeals to a sense of the ludicrous or absurdly incongruous...." *See* WEBSTER'S SEVENTH NEW COLLEGIATE DICTIONARY 405 (Springfield, Massachusetts: G. and C. Merriam Company, 1963).

8. *Chief Justice Vinson and His Law Clerks*, 49 Nw. U. L. REV. 34 (1954).

9. Wilkinson, SERVING JUSTICE 78 (New York: Charterhouse, 1974).

10. Schmidhauser, *The Justices of the Supreme Court: A Collective Portrait*, 3 MIDWEST J. OF POL. SCI. 13-16 (February 1959).

11. As attorney general, a position he held directly before his appointment to the Court, for example, Tom Clark never hesitated to include humorous anecdotes, many self-deprecating, in his addresses to bar associations. Typical of many of these was one he told to the Nebraska Bar Association in the mid-1940s. As attorney general, he was counselled by protocol people, he was supposed to deport himself with a new dignity. "I began to hold my shoulders up—my chin—what's left of it—out," he related. Then the Clarks found themselves entertaining an ambassador and his wife and other high dignitaries at their home. "There was much dignity present," he noted, "the maid had served some refreshments; we were all sitting up like statues; the conversation was on a high plane. We were, as I would say in Texas, in tall cotton. Then my little girl entered. She curtsied rather stiffly, looked over the guests and then ran to me calling out, 'Get off your high horse, let's piggy back, Pop.' " *See* Clark, *Administrative Law*, 25 NEB. L. REV. 79-80 (March 1946).

12. Personal interview with retired Justice Potter Stewart, United States Supreme Court Building, Washington, D.C., November 13, 1981.

Justice Clark, as another example, particularly appreciated stories featuring the wilderness adventures of his colleague, William Douglas. In one instance, he kept in his files for a quarter of a century a jingle that Douglas sent him in 1951. It was written by one of Douglas's fellow travelers in the Himalayas after Douglas had suffered minor injuries attempting to ride a yak: The Justice after his whack,/Said ruefully, straightening his back:/Well, the Court that sits high/Is often upset by/A dissenting opinion! Yak! Yak! *See* Clark, *Bill Douglas—A Portrait*, 28 BAYLOR L. REV. 217 (Spring, 1976).

13. Stewart, *supra* n. 12.

14. 357 U.S. 433 (1958).

15. 378 U.S. 478 (1964).

16. 384 U.S. 436 (1966).

17. Personal interview with retired Justice Tom C. Clark,

United States Supreme Court Building, Washington, D.C., August 15, 1973.

18. 315 U.S. 568 (1942).

19. *Id.* at 573.

20. Stewart, *supra* n. 12.

21. Mason, HARLAN FISKE STONE: PILLAR OF THE LAW 248 (New York: Viking Press, 1956).

22. Justice Tom Clark's, one of the most recently opened collections, is on file at the Tarleton Library, University of Texas Law School, Austin, Texas.

23. Woodward and Armstrong, THE BRETHREN (New York: Simon and Schuster, 1979).

24. *See*, for example, Mason, *supra* n. 21 and Howard, MR. JUSTICE MURPHY: A POLITICAL BIOGRAPHY (Princeton, NJ: Princeton University Press, 1968).

25. Provine, CASE SELECTION IN THE UNITED STATES SUPREME COURT 1-3 (Chicago: University of Chicago Press, 1980).

26. 342 U.S. 402 (1951).

27. Memorandum to the Conference in No. 143 Sutton v. Leib, October Term 1951 (circulated October 5, 1951), the Supreme Court Papers of Justice Tom C. Clark, Tarleton Library, The University of Texas Law School, Austin, Texas.

28. Danelski, *supra* n. 4, at 498.

Jackson's memorandum also demonstrates how a justice may resort to humor in attempts to employ one, or all, of the tactics delineated by Walter Murphy in his ELEMENTS OF JUDICIAL STRATEGY. Jackson's communication was an obvious attempt "to persuade his colleagues on the merits." And, by also brightening their day and enhancing their positive feelings towards him, it might have helped him "increase their personal regard." But, he circulated it as a draft of a dissent from a denial of certiorari. It might have also been perceived as a threat "to employ sanctions." By publishing it, Jackson may have made his colleagues look ridiculous for not hearing *Sutton v. Leib*. Hence, it might have presented an implicit but clear "bargain." A decision to hear the case would, obviously, necessitate Jackson's "burying" it. Indeed, the present article is apparently the first publication to reveal it. *See* Murphy, ELEMENTS OF JUDICIAL STRATEGY 43-49, 49-54, 54-56, and 56-58 (Chicago: University of Chicago Press, 1964).

29. Douglas, THE COURT YEARS, 1939-1975 (New York: Random House, 1980).

30. Clark, *The Supreme Court Conference*, address before the Section of Judicial Administration of the American Bar Association, Dallas, Texas, August 27, 1956, published in 19 F.R.D. 303 at 306.

31. 360 U.S. 315 (1959).

32. Circulate of June 10, 1959, in No. 582 Spano v. New York, October Term, 1958, "Spano Case File, the Supreme Court Papers of Justice Tom C. Clark," Tarleton Library, The University of Texas Law School, Austin, Texas.

33. 352 U.S. 432 (1957).

34. *Webster's* defines "sphygmograph" as an "instrument that records graphically the movements or character of the pulse." *See* WEBSTER'S SEVENTH NEW COLLEGIATE DICTIONARY, *supra* n. 7, at 841.

35. This phrase can be found at 352 U.S. at 436.

36. February 21, 1956, memorandum from Black to Clark in No. 69 *Briethaupt v. Abram*, October Term, 1956, "Briethaupt Case File, the Supreme Court Papers of Justice Tom C. Clark," Tarleton Library, The University of Texas Law School, Austin, Texas.

37. Consider, for example, Justice Frankfurter's unsuccessful attempt to persuade Justice Clark to change his views in *Irvine v. California*, 347 U.S. 128 (1954). At the early stages of *Irvine*, Clark had taken the position that the old case of *Wolf v. Colorado*, 338 U.S. 25 (1949)—which he detested—compelled him to affirm Irvine's conviction, even though the California

police had blatantly violated Irvine's rights. Frankfurter, the author of *Wolf*, read it as requiring no such thing. He thus sent the following message to Clark: "Because one does not like a decision but feels he must respect it, is hardly a reason for enlarging what one does not [like]. I know there are some Catholics who are more Catholic than the Pope. You do not have to be more *Wolfish* than *Wolf*." (*See* December, 1953 memorandum from Frankfurter to Clark, No. 12, "Irvine v. California File, October Term, 1953, U.S. Supreme Court Papers of Justice Tom C. Clark," Tarleton Library, The University of Texas Law School, Austin, Texas.)

My tendency, given that this memorandum was sent during a period when Frankfurter and Clark were apparently on excellent terms, is to interpret Frankfurter's "more *Wolfish* than *Wolf*" comment as an attempt to exploit a delight in humor that he knew was shared by his colleague. Some of my colleagues, however, have interpreted it as sarcasm reflecting Frankfurter's contempt for Clark's position.

Revisiting the freshman effect hypothesis: the first two terms of Justice Anthony Kennedy

Kennedy's behavior during his first two terms on the Court cannot be described as disoriented, uncertain, or vacillating—characteristics of the "freshman effect." In fact, reports indicate he settled nicely into his new job within a short period.

by Albert P. Melone

Many believe that newly-appointed justices to the United States Supreme Court exhibit behavioral patterns collectively known as the "freshman effect." Three factors characterize this phenomenon. First, these justices are bewildered by their new duties and responsibilities. They are awed by the office and need several years to become psychologically adjusted before they perform their duties with confidence. Second, in an attempt to ease newly-appointed members into the demands of the small group setting, senior justices do not assign their junior colleagues an equal share of opinion writing chores. Third, freshmen fail to align themselves immediately with the Court's established voting blocs. Instead, they take time to investigate their political and interpersonal environment.[1]

We need to ascertain whether, and to what extent, freshmen behave in this way so that we can better understand Supreme Court small group dynamics. The ability of the Court to conduct its task effectively and efficiently is profoundly affected by the integration of new members, each contributing their fair share to the workload. Moreover, the ability of presidents to affect immediately the decisional outputs of the Supreme Court may be adversely affected by the timeliness and extent to which new appointees join existing voting coalitions.

Recent research casts doubt on the ubiquitous nature of the so-called freshman effect. Independent studies focusing on Sandra Day O'Connor and Antonin Scalia suggest that the freshman effect hypothesis may be incorrect or time bound.[2] The accession of Anthony Kennedy to the high Court provides an opportunity to test the proposition once again.

Initial bewilderment

Late in their careers some justices acknowledged that they were bewildered when they came to the Supreme Court. Justice Frankfurter commented that even those justices who had prior judicial experience ". . . do not find the demands of their new task familiar."[3] Justice Brennan observed that ". . . One enters a new and wholly unfamiliar world when he joins the Supreme Court . . . ."[4] In Justice Murphy's case one scholar reported that " a minimum of three terms was required before he was assimilated confidently into the life and work of the court."[5]

Early in their Court tenure, neither O'Connor nor Scalia exhibited signs of bewilderment.[6] The fact that they both had prior judicial experience and each possessed established formulations of the judicial role probably operated to socialize them to the tasks ahead. The impact of anticipatory socialization upon Kennedy may have been similar, no doubt closer to Scalia's federal court of appeals experience than to O'Connor's Arizona trial and appellate court background. Yet, the extraordinary circumstances surrounding his appointment suggest that the manifest freshman sense of bewilderment might be at work.

Kennedy joined the Court in February 1988, four months after the beginning of the October 1987 Court term. As the third choice of President Reagan to fill the position vacated by Justice Powell, Kennedy

Table 1   Number of opinions authored, 1987 Supreme Court term

	Majority opinions	Majority votes[1]	OAR	Concurring opinion	Dissenting opinion[2]	Total opinion author[3]
Rehnquist	15	115	13.04%	4	7	26
Brennan	16	108	14.81	12	13	41
White	20	124	16.13	17	11	48
Marshall	15	106	14.15	1	11	27
Blackmun	15	114	13.16	11	10	36
Stevens	19	115	16.52	9	19	47
O'Connor	17	110	15.45	13	12	42
Scalia	16	115	13.91	16	10	42
Kennedy	7	56	12.50	4	2	13
Mean	15.56	107.00	14.41	9.67	10.56	35.78
Std. Dev.	3.47	18.68	1.34	5.29	4.30	10.91

1. The number of times a justice voted in the majority (including concurring votes).
2. Opinions are counted as dissents whether the justice dissented in part or in whole.
3. Majority opinions+Concurring opinions+Dissenting opinions.

did not undergo the intense public interrogation of the president's first choice, Robert Bork, or the personal scrutiny of Douglas Ginsburg, the administration's second choice. Yet, the White House failure to win senatorial confirmation for Robert Bork probably served to intensify Mr. Kennedy's prenomination interrogation at the hands of President Reagan's advisors. Kennedy was one of three finalists interviewed at the White House. Attorney General Meese, along with his predecessor William French Smith, favored Douglas Ginsburg; Kennedy was championed by Howard Baker, the White House chief of staff. A third candidate, William Wilkins Jr., was favored by South Carolina Senator and ranking minority member of the Judiciary Committee, Strom Thurmond. It was not until the Ginsburg nomination was withdrawn that Kennedy got the presidential nod.[7]

In light of these circumstances, only the most unusual personalities could fail to experience any feelings of bewilderment. In an interview just a week after his accession, Kennedy revealed he was awed by his new surroundings. In that early interview conducted by Supreme Court public information officers, Kennedy said he was "impressed with the tremendous volume of work that is required of a Justice."[8] At the same time he found equally impressive the "dispatch" with which justices dispose of their work.[9] He was impressed that his water goblet is the same used by a favorite former justice, Hugo Black. The thought that some day his name would be engraved on the very same pewter cup alongside the names of Black and his successor Powell made Kennedy feel proud.[10] Expressions of awe may be associated with feelings of bewilderment, but the two are not necessarily one and the same. Personal modesty and genuine humility may affect an individual's sense of reverence without resulting in personal disorientation. Even if one is willing to accept the dubious conclusion that expressions of awe equal bewilderment, the record also indicates that any such period was short.

Senior colleague Justice Blackmun, and others, report that Kennedy settled into the job quickly. By the end of the 1987 term and midway through the 1988 term, reports surfaced indicating that the easy-going Kennedy was settling in at the Marble Palace. He was poised to make a positive contribution to the task functions of the Court and to fulfill his promise as a member of the conservative coalition.[11] It is not possible to write authoritatively about Justice Kennedy's subjective feelings until such time as he comments more publicly about his early Supreme Court experiences. However, if Kennedy did experience feelings of bafflement, it could not have lasted long, and there is no evidence suggesting that it interfered with his job performance. On balance, then, the totality of the existing evidence lends little support for the bewilderment dimension of the freshman effect hypothesis. Rather, it tends to support similarly negative findings as do the O'Connor and Scalia studies.

Opinion writing

The chief justice and senior justices are institutionally situated to assign opinions to junior colleagues when both of them vote with the majority. If the chief justice votes with the majority, then he may assign the opinion either to himself or to one of the other justices voting with the majority. If the chief does not cast his lot with the majority, then the most senior justice in the majority makes the opinion

Table 2   Number of opinions authored, 1988 Supreme Court term

	Majority opinions	Majority votes[1]	OAR	Concurring opinion	Dissenting opinion[2]	Total opinion author[3]
Rehnquist	16	120	13.33%	2	8	26
Brennan	17	88	19.32	12	17	46
White	19	125	15.20	9	7	35
Marshall	15	85	17.65	0	14	29
Blackmun	14	100	14.00	13	22	49
Stevens	15	103	14.56	19	23	57
O'Connor	13	114	11.40	16	9	38
Scalia	12	124	9.68	24	9	45
Kennedy	16	126	12.70	11	4	31
Mean	15.22	109.44	14.20	11.78	12.56	39.56
Std. Dev.	1.99	15.09	2.80	7.18	6.41	9.751.

1. The number of times a justice voted in the majority (including concurring votes).
2. Opinions are counted as dissents whether the justice dissented in part or in whole.
3. Majority opinions+Concurring opinions+Dissenting opinions.

writing assignment. A second postulate of the freshman effect hypothesis is that newly appointed justices write less than their fair share of opinions. Further, the opinions assigned by senior colleagues to neophyte justices are deemed to be routine and not particularly difficult.[12]

There is ample reason to question the apprenticeship notion. One study finds that during the period of the Taft Court through the early years of the Burger Court (1921-1973), newly appointed justices were among the most prolific opinion writers.[13] Recent studies analyzing the behavior of O'Connor and Scalia tend to confirm this conclusion.[14] However, evidence from Kennedy's first two years points to the operation of a freshman effect in this one but limited respect. Nevertheless, even this modest conclusion needs to be qualified.

Tables 1 and 2 indicate the number of opinions authored by each justice during the 1987 and 1988 terms. Data for the October 1987 term support the freshman effect hypothesis: Kennedy wrote only seven opinions, the fewest number written by any justice. Justice White proved most prolific, authoring 20 majority opinions. This disparity should not be overstated. Because Kennedy acceded to the Court months after the opening of the 1987 term, he did not participate in the consideration of all the cases. The absolute number of opinions written by Kennedy is misleading because he was available to write majority opinions only when he cast his vote with the majority: a total of only 56 times as compared, for example, to White's 125 opinion writing opportunities. The Opinion Assignment Ratio (OAR) compensates for this distortion. It is calculated by dividing the number of times a justice is assigned the majority opinion by the number of

times the justice votes with the Court's majority, multiplied by 100 to yield a percentage.[15]

For the October 1987 term, Kennedy's OAR is 12.50, placing him at the lowest end of the ratio rankings; that is, he is last among all the justices. However, this figure is only slightly in excess of 1 standard deviation below the Court mean of 14.41, and just behind Chief Justice Rehnquist's ratio of 13.04. Although they are not exceedingly indulgent, the senior justices do respect the tradition of assigning new justices relatively few majority opinions; this pattern is consistent with the data for Scalia's first term.[16] Unlike Scalia, however, Kennedy wrote during his initial term relatively few concurring and dissenting opinions. On the one hand, the fact that he wrote only four concurring and two dissenting opinions may be solely a function of his participation in only 77 of the Court's 140 signed opinions. On the other hand, there is modest evidence based on his own statements that Kennedy's low total may be a faint reflection of a freshman's sense of bewilderment. A third explanation, which is idiosyncratic to the political situation, seems preferable. Kennedy may have viewed his role during his first term as an opportunity to calm the political waters surrounding the Supreme Court caused by the intense and unsettling battle over the ill-fated Bork nomination. He avoided interviews during the 1987 term, and his maiden speech before the American Bar Association was characterized as a "bland bafflement to many who listened."[17] Moreover, John Marshall's admonition to his colleagues to speak with one voice was particularly appropriate after President Reagan's defeat over the Bork nomination in the Senate. There he lost the battle, but with Kennedy's confirmation he may have ultimately won the war.

Table 2 contains information on the number of opinions authored in the October 1988 term, the first full term in which Kennedy was seated. He wrote 16 opinions, almost one more than the Court average, but he joined with the majority 126 times, more often than any other justice. The result is an OAR of 12.70, within 1 standard deviation below the Court mean. Both the absolute number of majority opinions he wrote and his OAR figure are considerably higher than Scalia's[18] and slightly higher than O'Connor's figures for their initial court terms.[19]

It appears, then, that the light opinion load intended for neophytes lasted in Kennedy's case for only a brief period, that is, during the extraordinary October 1987 term. By the end of the October 1988 term, Kennedy was clearly pulling his own weight.

Judging from his opinion writing conduct, Kennedy does not appear to be a person driven to have his views heavily represented in print. During the 1988 term he wrote 11 concurring opinions, a number almost identical to the Court mean—11.78 opinions. Further, he had fewer dissenting opinions than any other justice, namely four compared with the Court mean of 12.56 dissenting opinions. Although it is hardly a complete explanation, the fact that he cast more majority votes than any other justice is probably one reason for his relatively modest writing output. Then, too, he exhibits this reticence despite the reality that other justices feel a need to write concurring and dissenting opinions.

It is not enough to know how many opinions a new justice has written. How significant the assigned opinions are is an indication of how quickly neophyte justices become fully-fledged institutional members. If new justices must craft difficult and important opinions, then it matters little that they write fewer opinions than their colleagues. Writing an important opinion may require more legal and political skill than writing many routine ones. Was Kennedy assigned routine and less important opinions to write, thereby following the traditional pattern for freshmen justices, or did he write a share of important decisions?

Consistent with the method employed in some earlier studies, an "important decision" is operationally defined as one that is headlined on the cover of the Advance Sheets of the United States Supreme Court Reports, Lawyers' Edition. Head-

lining opinions is a way for the editors to alert readers to noteworthy judicial decisions that are likely to interest many attorneys. The headlining method is not faultless, but neither are other methods. The headlining method uses an independent authority to judge importance without waiting years for expert opinion to form a consensus.[20]

During the October 1987 term, which was Kennedy's first, there were 10 cases headlined on the cover of the Advance Sheets. Of these 10, White wrote three, Rehnquist and Scalia wrote two each, Brennan, O'Connor, and Kennedy wrote one apiece, and Marshall, Blackmun and Stevens wrote none. For the October 1988 term, there were 23 important opinions. Rehnquist and White wrote six each, Kennedy followed with three opinions, Brennan, Blackmun, O'Connor, and Scalia authored two opinions each, and Marshall and Stevens authored no important opinions.

Not only did Kennedy write close to his fair share of opinions during his first two terms of service, he also authored four important ones. The first important decision came during his first term, within four months of his accession to the high bench. Thus, senior colleagues in the position to observe Kennedy's abilities expressed confidence in him by integrating him quickly into the Court's decision-making mix. It is also true that a junior member of the Court may not write majority opinions unless there is evident agreement with the views of senior colleagues.

In summary, the data confirm the expectation that freshmen justices write fewer majority opinions than their senior colleagues. However, by the end of his second term, Kennedy wrote close to the Court's average number of opinions. Unlike other recent neophytes, he wrote several important decisions. Such behavior is inconsistent with the expectations of the freshman effect hypothesis.

Approach to the judicial role

Kennedy's opinions reveal an ideological perspective essentially consistent with the other Reagan appointees. His integration into the flow of the Court's work may have been facilitated by a compatible world view coupled with a similar approach to the judicial function.

Kennedy's first reported majority opinion, which, according to the Court's tradition, he probably selected himself, was for an unanimous Court in *Bethesda Hospital Association v. Bowen*.[21] It involved a matter of statutory interpretation where Kennedy applied the plain-meaning rule. He concluded that the secretary of health and human services must honor the request of a Medicare provider to claim dissatisfaction with amounts of reimbursement allowable under departmental regulations. Because all members of the Court could agree with the final case disposition and with Kennedy's literal statutory interpretation, there is support for a key freshman effect postulate; specifically, newly-appointed justices are assigned relatively easy or routine cases for their maiden writing assignment.

Kennedy's easy assignment load was short-lived, however. *K Mart Corp. v. Cartier, Inc.*, was first argued October 6, 1987, but, after Kennedy joined the Court in February, it was reargued on April 26, 1988.[22] Marked by intra-Court disagreements, it was a noteworthy opinion because it was an "important" and very complicated one. It was not the type of opinion one might anticipate if one accepts the premises of the freshman effect hypothesis. Relying on the plain-meaning rule of statutory interpretation, Kennedy found that a Customs Service regulation concerning gray market commerce was consistent with the letter of the law. This is the case insofar as the law exempts from a ban on importation of goods manufactured abroad by the same parties holding a U.S. trademark or by a person who is subject to common control with the U.S. trademark holder. However, he found that the authorized-use exception of the Customs Service regulation conflicted with the plain language of the operative congressional statute. Thus, by employing the plain-meaning rule of statutory interpretation, Kennedy upheld one regulation and voided another.

Although Kennedy's mode of analysis in *K Mart* was remarkably similar to his approach just weeks earlier in *Bethesda Hospital*, there was nonetheless in *K Mart* an absence of intra-Court agreement. Justice Brennan wrote an opinion concurring in part and dissenting in part in which Marshall and Stevens joined, and White joined in part. Scalia filed an opinion concurring in part and dissenting in part in which Rehnquist, Blackmun, and O'Connor joined. Obviously, Kennedy had great difficulty crafting an opinion which minimized the extent of the disagreement on the Court. If one accepts the freshman effect hypothesis, then the *K Mart* case was hardly the type that a neophyte might author.

During his initial Court term, one in which he joined the majority in 56 of only 77 participating decisions, the freshman Kennedy authored seven majority opinions. The first, *Bethesda Hospital Association v. Bowen*, was straightforward and non-controversial. Kennedy's second majority opinion, *K Mart v. Cartier*, was operationally defined as an "important decision." Scalia did not author any such noteworthy opinions during his first term, nor is such behavior anticipated by the freshman effect hypothesis. This may be an indicator of the high esteem his senior colleagues have for Kennedy. Yet, it may also reflect the practical needs of an understaffed Court, a body operated with only eight justices for four months. Because of a pressing docket, it cut short the traditional year-long hiatus in which new justices ease into their awe-inspiring jobs. Both explanations are compatible because as Justice Blackmun and Court commentators have attested, Kennedy was quickly assimilated as a task master, and as a congenial social group member.[23]

Whatever his status may have been during his first term, there is no doubt that Kennedy became a fully integrated member of the Court during his second year, the October 1988 term. His written opinions for the majority reflect a close alignment with the ideological agenda of the president who appointed him. Of Kennedy's 16 opinions, three are "important." Two of the three were companion Fourth Amendment drug testing cases: *National Treasury Employees Union v. Von Raab*,[24] and *Skinner v. Railway Labor Executives' Association.*[25] Using a balancing of interests test, Kennedy found that the Fourth Amendment does not require a warrant, probable cause, or a reasonable suspicion test. The use of drug testing on railroad employees and certain employees of the United States Customs Service serves compelling governmental interests that outweigh employees' privacy rights. These nonunanimous decisions, 5-4 and 7-2 respectively, not only raised predictable opposition from the most cohesive liberal duo, Brennan and Marshall, but also one opinion induced opposition from one of the Court's most conservative members, and Kennedy's most consistent voting ally. Justice Scalia eloquently dissented in *National Treasury Employees*, arguing that the majority failed to demonstrate by sufficient evidence that the Customs Service drug testing program is a reasonable means of protecting society. Scalia also concluded that the symbolism of a drug-free government ser-

Table 3 Interagreement in split decisions¹ of the full Supreme Court, 1987 term (per cent)

	RE	SC	O'C	KE	WH	BL	ST	BR	MA
Rehnquist	—	75.8	81.8	66.7	63.6	33.3	33.3	18.2	18.2
Scalia	75.8	—	75.8	84.8	69.7	39.4	33.3	30.3	24.2
O'Connor	81.8	75.8	—	72.7	75.8	45.5	39.4	24.2	24.2
Kennedy	66.7	84.8	72.7	—	78.8	54.5	48.5	45.5	39.4
White	63.6	69.7	75.8	78.8	—	57.6	57.6	48.5	42.4
Blackmun	33.3	39.4	45.5	54.5	57.6	—	69.7	78.8	78.8
Stevens	33.3	33.3	39.4	48.5	57.6	69.7	—	78.8	72.7
Brennan	18.2	30.3	24.2	45.5	48.5	78.8	78.8	—	87.9
Marshall	18.2	24.2	24.2	39.4	42.4	78.8	72.7	87.9	—

1. Includes only those 33 nonunanimous cases where all nine justices participated.
Indicies of Interagreement:

Rehnquist, Scalia, O'Connor, Kennedy, White	=.75
Rehnquist, Scalia, O'Connor, Kennedy	=.76
Marshall, Brennan, Stevens, Blackmun	=.78
Marshall, Brennan, Stevens	=.80

vice is an insufficient justification for the unacceptable impairment of individual liberties.²⁶

Kennedy's opinion for the Court in *Patterson v. McLean Credit Union*²⁷ is further evidence of his commitment to the Reagan agenda. He accomplishes this feat within a framework of judicial self-restraint made operational in this case through a literal approach to statutory interpretation. This case raises the issues of (a) whether section 1981 of the 1866 Civil Rights Act applies to claims of racial harassment on the job or is a limit to the establishment and enforcement of contract obligations only; and, (b) whether the district court erred when it instructed the jury that the black employee petitioner had to prove that she was better qualified than a white employee who received a promotion instead of her. The civil rights community held its breath when the justices requested of the parties that they brief and argue in addition to the issues already before the Court whether the landmark decision in *Runyon v. McCrary* should be reconsidered.²⁸

Resolving the *Runyon* issue first, Kennedy concluded for the Court that this 1976 decision should not be overruled. He touted the doctrine of stare decisis as ". . . fundamental to the rule of law" and although ". . . precedents are not sacrosanct . . ." deviation from stare decisis demands special justification.²⁹ Kennedy found no special justification for overruling *Runyon*. However, in the words of the dissenting Brennan, "what the Court declines to snatch away with one hand, it takes with the other."³⁰ Kennedy found that racial harassment relating to employment is not actionable under section 1981 because that statutory provision applies only to making and enforcing contracts. However, the district court did err in its jury instructions

concerning a white employee's relative qualifications. Significantly, Kennedy ignored historical evidence surrounding the passage of the 19th century civil rights acts as well as contemporary legislation. Instead, he read section 1981 narrowly, thereby employing, once again, a literal or plain-meaning approach to statutory interpretation.

Justice Kennedy's opinions for his first two terms show him to be one of the most conservative justices on the contemporary Court. He is a person committed to judicial self-restraint rooted in a conception of the judicial role best characterized as judicial absolutism or mechanical jurisprudence. It is a view that may explain his choice of Hugo Black as a favorite predecessor,³¹ although it is doubtful the two would share the same policy preferences today. Kennedy avoids an expansive reading of the Constitution and prefers to decide matters on statutory, rather than on constitutional, grounds. He exhibits a well-defined literal approach to statutory matters. When Kennedy engages in constitutional interest balancing, the result favors the interests of the many over the rights of the few. While interest balancing is not consistent with absolutism, it is nonetheless compatible with the exercise of judicial self-restraint. Writing a separate concurring opinion in the controversial flag desecration case, *Texas v. Johnson*,³² Kennedy exhibited his approach to the judicial function. He wrote:

The case before us illustrates better than most that the judicial power is often difficult in its exercise. We cannot here ask another branch to share responsibility, as when the argument is made that a statute is flawed or incomplete. For we are presented with a clear and simple statute to be judged against a pure command of the Constitution. The outcome can be laid at no door but ours.

The hard fact is that sometimes we must make deci-

Table 4   Interagreement in split decisions¹ of the full Supreme Court, 1988 term (per cent)

	RE	KE	WH	O'C	SC	ST	BL	BR	MA
Rehnquist	—	87.3	84.8	84.4	82.2	52.6	38.0	25.3	21.8
Kennedy	87.3	—	79.7	74.0	89.9	52.6	45.6	32.9	27.8
White	84.8	79.7	—	81.8	77.2	50.0	45.6	32.9	28.2
O'Connor	84.4	74.0	81.8	—	74.0	53.9	44.2	31.2	30.3
Scalia	82.2	89.9	77.2	74.0	—	52.6	43.0	38.0	34.6
Stevens	52.6	52.6	50.0	53.9	52.6	—	61.5	60.2	61.0
Blackmun	38.0	45.6	45.6	44.2	43.0	61.5	—	72.2	70.5
Brennan	25.3	32.9	32.9	31.2	38.0	60.2	72.2	—	96.2
Marshall	21.8	27.8	28.2	30.3	34.6	61.0	70.5	96.2	—

1. Includes only those 79 non-unanimous cases where all nine justices participated.
Indicies of Interagreement:

Rehnquist, Kennedy, White, O'Connor, Scalia	=.82
Rehnquist, Kennedy, White, Scalia	=.84
Rehnquist, Kennedy, White, O'Connor	=.82
Marshall, Brennan, Blackmun, Stevens	=.70
Marshall, Brennan, Blackmun	=.80

sions we do not like. We make them because they are right, right in the sense that the law and the Constitution, as we see them, compel the result. And so great is our commitment to the process that, except in the rare case, we do not pause to express distaste for the result, perhaps for fear of undermining a valued principle that dictates the decision. This is one of those rare cases.[33]

This explanation for judicial activism, "the Constitution made me do it," may be interpreted by some as the immature reflections of a freshman faced with the necessity to decide. To the contrary, I think it is more likely that Kennedy's statement epitomizes a mechanical view of jurisprudence reminiscent of Justice Owen Roberts' classic formulation in *United States v. Butler.*[34] Given an act clearly at variance with the basic document, Kennedy agreed to declare a legislative act unconstitutional, but he did so only after appropriate genuflections toward the altar of self-restraint. Kennedy's views may change over time and it may be premature to write with confidence about whether he possesses a fixed conception of the judicial role. We can conclude, however, that although Kennedy's current view of the judicial function need not necessarily lead to politically conservative results in all cases, it is compatible with the immediate goals of the president who appointed him. Whether, and to what extent, Kennedy has aligned with other Reagan appointees is an important test of that proposition.

Voting alignment

Recent studies contradict earlier findings that freshmen justices align initially with pivotal cliques and do not align with discernible blocs of interagreeing colleagues. Research findings focusing on both O'Connor's and Scalia's initial tenure are consis-

tent with those studies investigating patterns for most other freshmen justices appointed during the Warren and Burger Court eras. Several newly-appointed justices aligned immediately with one or more senior justices, most often the chief justice.[35] The data for Kennedy are supportive of the conclusion that the freshman effect does not operate in this, the third aspect of the test. However, the data reveal interesting exceptions worth noting.

Tables 3 and 4 are interagreement matrices based upon nonunanimous decisions for the 1987 and 1988 Supreme Court terms. Each table contains cell entries representing the number of times two justices vote together. It is derived by dividing the number of times a pair of justices vote together (in either the majority or the minority) by the total number of cases in which they jointly vote. Indices of Interagreement measure the strength of the blocs and are the mean of the percentages of the included pairs of justices. Convention dictates that an Index of Interagreement of .70 or greater is deemed high, .60 to .69 is moderate, and .60 or less is low.[36]

During his initial term, Kennedy participated in only 33 split decisions. He is part of what most observers call the majority conservative bloc; it consists of Rehnquist, Scalia, O'Connor, White, and himself. Though the interagreement index of .75 is high for the October 1987 term, the index for the October 1988 term is even greater: the Index of Interagreement for the same majority bloc increases to .82.

Interestingly, Kennedy does not exhibit the closest interagreement score with the chief justice. His coalition behavior is unlike Scalia's during his first term[37] but like O'Connor's during her first term.[38]

Instead, Kennedy is in highest agreement with Scalia (84.8), followed by White (78.8), O'Connor (72.2), and then by the chief justice (66.7). The data for the 1988 term indicate that the Scalia/Kennedy relationship remains Kennedy's strongest (89.9). The Kennedy/Rehnquist dyad improves to 87 per cent, just behind the Scalia/Kennedy agreement score, followed by White/Kennedy (79.2), and O'Connor/Kennedy (73.3).

The strength of the Scalia/Kennedy relationship is second only to that of Brennan/Marshall (87.9 in 1987 and 96.1 in 1988). This pattern calls into question the observation that in recent decades newly appointed justices have aligned immediately with one or more senior justices, most often the chief justice.[39] Instead, Kennedy is most closely aligned with the most junior member of the Court. Why?

Although Kennedy, Scalia, and Rehnquist are President Reagan's appointees, Rehnquist had been a member of the Supreme Court for many years before his elevation to the chief justiceship. He is also considerably older than both Kennedy and Scalia. Unlike the chief justice, both Scalia and Kennedy had prior service on the court of appeals. Although both Scalia and Kennedy share Chief Justice Rehnquist's general ideological outlook, it may be that Kennedy's most natural ally is age and background cohort Antonin Scalia. This may be a significant factor in future terms as changes take place in the Court's personnel. Leadership of the conservative bloc may not necessarily fall to the chief justice. In terms of interagreement among all of the justices, Kennedy is second only to Rehnquist in his alignment during the October 1988 term with what is widely understood as the Court's conservative majority and against the liberal bloc.[40]

Conclusion

The case of Anthony Kennedy does not support the freshman effect hypothesis. Considering the exceptional circumstances surrounding his accession, Kennedy's behavior during his first two terms on the Supreme Court cannot be characterized as disoriented, uncertain, or vacillating. There are interesting differences between Kennedy's behavior and that of those justices who joined the Court immediately preceding him. However, the collective evidence points to the conclusion that the hypothesis is either incorrect or time-bound. Although it may be possible to interpret Kennedy's

initial expressions as signs of bewilderment, empirical evidence confirms that any disorienting period, if it existed at all, was short. His appointment came after two nominees failed to run the confirmation gauntlet successfully. As a result, Kennedy took his seat in February 1988, several months after the beginning of the October 1987 term. Reports indicate that Kennedy settled nicely into his new job within a short period. As was true for O'Connor and Scalia, it is reasonable to assume that Kennedy's prior bench experience (in his case; the U.S. court of appeals) provided him with a measure of expectation about his new job as did his experience as a constitutional law professor. In short, the process of anticipatory socialization may have prepared Kennedy for the tasks ahead, and may have operated to ease his sudden but foretold passage from the prestigious appeals bench to the highest court in the land.

The relative paucity of majority opinion writing assignments remains the one freshman effect characteristic providing some support to the general hypothesis. However, even here the evidence is not unambiguous. Consistent with the data for O'Connor's and Scalia's initial terms, Kennedy wrote fewer majority opinions during his first term than any other justice. Moreover, consistent with the O'Connor and Scalia data, by the end of his second term Kennedy no longer wrote the least number of opinions. In fact, the opinion assignment ratio for his second term is within one standard deviation of the Court mean. Significantly, however, Kennedy, unlike Scalia,[41] was called upon to be the author of an important decision during his first term, and of three more the following year. This fact contradicts the expectation that freshmen write only routine opinions. Furthermore, unlike Scalia's and O'Connor's behavior during their initial terms, Kennedy clearly eschews writing concurring and dissenting opinions in what may be a sign of respect for the judgments of others. So Kennedy's senior colleagues may have been solicitous toward their new colleague by giving him relatively few writing assignments during that extraordinary October 1987 term. Yet they also exhibited confidence by asking him to write a relatively important and difficult opinion.

There are several plausible explanations why the Kennedy case does not fulfill expected freshman writing patterns. First, when Kennedy was finally seated, the Court had been hearing cases for several months and it was shorthanded. Senior justices probably assigned Kennedy relatively few opinions out of respect for past practice and good manners. But because they needed help in expediting the docket, he was assigned an "important" decision to write. Second, Kennedy's prior judicial experience and familiarity with constitutional issues, coupled with what is reputed as a winsome personality, made it possible to integrate him rapidly into the Court's opinion writing task functions. Third, Kennedy wrote fewer concurring and dissenting opinions than both O'Connor and Scalia during their first terms because he probably understood that the Court is now firmly in conservative hands. Following the acrimonious national debate surrounding the Bork nomination, it may be more important for Justice Kennedy to calm the political waters by maintaining a low profile than to demonstrate independence or to impress the legal community with intellectual prowess.

The final characteristic of the so-called freshman effect is unsupported by any recent study. Eloise Snyder was the first to argue that new justices are absorbed by first joining a pivotal clique, but at some later date they move into distinct ideological blocs. She believed that this may occur because neophytes may lack self-confidence and therefore respond in a neutral manner.[42] Researchers Heck and Hall found, to the contrary, that new justices are absorbed quickly because they have about the same policy commitments as the justices already on the Court;[43] the findings for O'Connor and Scalia support this conclusion.[44] Although his behavior is not precisely the same, Kennedy immediately aligned himself with the Court's conservative majority bloc. Thus, in recent years at any rate, newly-appointed justices are not timid about joining preexisting voting blocs.

Why is it that for the current era there is so little empirical support for the so-called freshman effect hypothesis? Besides the idiosyncratic factors already discussed for Kennedy and for the other Reagan appointees, there are several additional conditions that require special mention. First, recent Court appointees were carefully screened by President Reagan for their ideological commitment to his judicial agenda, including a view of the judicial function that in the contemporary context is supportive of present conservative ideals. These appointees do not need time to figure out what the great issues facing the Court might be, or where

they stand on those issues. They bring to the Court pre-existing and self-conscious attitudes on the great constitutional issues of the day. The politics of appointment demand that all potential federal judicial personnel have carefully considered constitutional policy positions. Indeed, President Reagan and his staff went to considerable lengths to insure that persons with the correct ideological outlooks were named to the entire federal judiciary.[45] Knowing their minds, the Reagan appointees immediately joined with their ideological confreres. Second, prior judicial experience, particularly in the cases of courts of appeals judges Scalia and Kennedy, provides detailed knowledge of many issues facing the Supreme Court. It prepares judges for the challenges ahead and provides them with socializing experiences in anticipation of high court service.

Finally, organizational developments within the institution itself encourage justices to go their own ideological way. Increased staff and improved management tools create the opportunity for a Court composed of nine separate mini-firms, each chamber competing to accomplish individualistic goals.[46] Small group influences assumed to be important in explaining a freshman effect are not as salient today as they once were. Bureaucracy always has consequences. For better or for worse, the diminution of a freshman effect may be one of them. Therefore, if the so-called freshman effect exists at all it is a matter of degree, and its operation as a small group dynamic is modest at best.

NOTES

This article originally appeared in Volume 74, Number 1, June-July 1990, pages 6-13. It is a revision of a paper first presented at the Midwest Political Science Association 48th Annual Meeting, April 5-7, 1990. I want to thank panel discussants Richard A. Brisbin, Jr., and Robert Dudley for their perceptive insights. Scott Myers, my research assistant at Southern Illinois University, put in many hours helping to collect and to process the data for this study. Marc George Pufong also provided assistance. Finally, my helpful colleague, Richard Dale, read the manuscript for clarity and provided useful suggestions for final revision.

1. Snyder, *The Supreme Court as a Small Group*, 36 Soc. Forces 232 (1958); Howard, *Mr. Justice Murphy: The Freshman Years*, 18 Vand. L. Rev. 474 (1965); Ulmer, *Toward a Theory of Sub-Group Formation in the Supreme Court*, 27 J. Pol. 133 (1965).

2. Slotnick, *Judicial Career Patterns and Majority Opinion Assignments on the Supreme Court*, 41 J. Pol. 640 (1979); Heck, *The Socialization of a Freshman Justice: The Early Years of Justice Brennan*, 10 Pacific L. J. 707 (1979); Heck and Hall, *Bloc Voting and the Freshman Justice Revisited*, 43 J. Pol. 852 (1981); Brenner, *Another Look at Freshman Indecisiveness on the United States Supreme Court*, 16 Polity 320 (1983); Scheb and Ailshie, *Justice Sandra Day O'Connor and the "Freshman Effect,"* 69 Judicature 9

(1985); Rubin and Melone, *Justice Antonin Scalia: a first year freshman effect?* 72 JUDICATURE 98 (1988).

3. Frankfurter, *The Supreme Court in the Mirror of the Justices*, 105 U. PA. L. REV. 789 (1957).

4. Brennan, *National Court of Appeals: Another Dissent*, 40 U. CHI. L. REV. 484 (1983).

5. Howard, *supra* n. 1, at 477.

6. Scheb and Ailshie, *supra* n. 2, at 10; Rubin and Melone, *supra* n. 2, at 99.

7. Barnes, *White House Watch: Round II*, THE NEW REPUBLIC 9-11 (Nov. 23, 1987).

8. 24 The Docket Sheet of the Supreme Court of the United States, Winter 1988, at 1, col. 1.

9. *Id.*

10. *Id.* at 7, col. 2.

11. N. Y. TIMES, July 18, 1988, at A10; Taylor, *Blackmun Provides a Peek at the People Under Those Robes*, N. Y. TIMES, July 25, 1988, at B6; Mauro, *Kennedy Lunches High on the Hogs*, LEGAL TIMES, February 20, 1989, at 15.

12. Heck and Hall, *supra* n. 2, at 853; Scheb and Ailshie, *supra* n. 2, at 10.

13. Slotnick, *supra* n. 2, at 648.

14. Scheb and Ailshie, *supra* n. 2, at 10-11; Rubin and Melone, *supra* n. 2, at 99-100.

15. Rubin and Melone, *supra* n. 2, at 99.

16. *Id.*

17. Mauro, *supra* n. 10.

18. Rubin and Melone, *supra* n. 2, at 99 (Table 1).

19. Scheb and Ailshie, *supra* n. 2, at 10 (Table 1).

20. *See* Spaeth, *Distributive justice: majority opinion assignments in the Burger Court*, 67 JUDICATURE 301, 302 (1984); Rubin and Melone, *supra* n. 2, at 100.

21. 108 S. Ct. 1255 (1988). It is possible that Kennedy may have been assigned a majority opinion prior to this one that is reported at a later date. Presently, I have no way to verify my assumption that *Bethesda Hospital Association v. Bowen* is a case Kennedy selected himself.

22. 108 S. Ct. 1811 (1988).

23. *Supra* n. 10.

24. 109 S. Ct. 1384 (1989).

25. 109 S. Ct. 1402 (1989).

26. 109 S.Ct. 1398-1402.

27. 109 S. Ct. 2363 (1989).

28. 96 S. Ct. 2586 (1976).

29. 109 S.Ct. 2370.

30. 109 S.Ct. 2379.

31. *Supra* n. 8, at 7, col. 1

32. 109 S. Ct. 2533 (1989).

33. 109 S.Ct. 2548.

34. 56 U.S. 312 (1936).

35. Heck and Hall, *supra* n. 2, at 858.

36. Schubert, QUANTITATIVE ANALYSIS OF JUDICIAL BEHAVIOR 91 (Glencoe, IL: The Free Press, 1959); For a detailed analysis of bloc voting, see also Sprague, VOTING PATTERNS OF THE UNITED STATES SUPREME COURT 21-25 (Indianapolis: Bobbs-Merrill Co., 1968.

37. Rubin and Melone, *supra* n. 2, at 101.

38. Scheb and Ailshie, *supra* n. 2, at 11 (Table 2).

39. Heck and Hall, *supra* n. 2, at 858.

40. For determining the relative position of each justice in Tables 3 and 4, I used methods described by Schubert, *supra* n. 36, at 84-85.

41. Scalia authored no "important opinion" during his first term (October 1986 term), two during his second term (October 1987 term), and two more in his third term (October 1988 term).

42. Snyder, *supra* n. 1, at 232.

43. Heck and Hall, *supra* n. 2, at 860.

44. Scheb and Ailshie, *supra* n. 2, at 12; Rubin and Melone, *supra* n. 2, at 101.

45. Goldman, *Reaganizing the judiciary: the first term appointments*, 68 JUDICATURE 313-329 (1985).

46. Morris, "Can the Supreme Court be Led? A Re-evaluation of the Role of Chief Justices," (Paper presented at the 1986 Annual Meeting of the American Political Science Association, August 28-31, 1986), at 63.

Decisional trends on the Warren and Burger Courts: results from the Supreme Court Data Base Project

The U.S. Supreme Court Judicial Data Base is providing a wealth of new information, enabling students of the Court to gain new insight and understanding.

by Jeffrey A. Segal and Harold J. Spaeth

This article presents findings on decision making in the Warren and Burger Courts from data collected and compiled for the first phase of the Supreme Court Data Base Project. In particular, it examines the decisions of the Court, the votes of the justices, and the dissents of the justices in civil liberties and economic cases for the purpose of documenting some theoretical and empirical concerns that scholars have previously addressed. In the process, it provides highlights of the data base and suggestions for using the data for those who have access to it.

The United States Supreme Court Judicial Data Base is a multi-year project funded by the Law and Social Science Program of the National Science Foundation. The data for Phase I of the project have been gathered and the documentation prepared. It is designed for multi-investigator use and the final version should be available from the Inter-University Consortium for Political and Social Research in Ann Arbor by 1990. An oversight committee, composed of productive scholars from the law and social sciences community with experience in the judicial process area advised in the selection of the endogenous and exogenous variables that the data base should include, as well as in the operationalization, coding, and formatting of the data.

The Supreme Court data base allows for flexibility in the counting and analysis of cases. For example, one can count cases by docket number, by case citation or, if one desires, by legal provision or issue being adjudicated. Similarly, one can include or exclude formally decided cases, cases decided without oral argument, memorandum cases, de-

crees, cases decided by equally divided votes and per curiam cases. In the analysis that follows, we use docket number as our unit of analysis. If a case citation has two docketed cases, one of which produces a conservative outcome and the other a liberal result, then we count the citation as two decisions: one conservative and the other liberal. To include only the first docketed case from a single citation would result, for the purposes of this article, in an arbitrary counting of cases.[1]

We do not include all docketed cases in our analysis. We limit ourselves to those that the Court formally decided; i.e., orally argued, whether the opinions are signed or per curiam.

We also limit our study to two broad issue areas, civil liberties and economic cases. Civil liberties issues include cases involving criminal procedure, civil rights, the First Amendment, due process, and privacy. Economic issues include cases involving unions and general economic activity. Liberal decisions in the area of civil liberties are pro-person accused or convicted of crime, pro-civil liberties or civil rights claimant, pro-indigent, pro-Indian, and anti-government in due process and privacy. In economic cases, we define liberal votes as pro-union, anti-business, anti-employer, pro-competition, pro-liability, pro-injured person, pro-indigent, pro-small business vis-a-vis large business, pro-debtor, pro-bankrupt, pro-environmental protection, pro-economic underdog, pro-consumer, and pro-accountability in governmental corruption.[2]

Results

We begin by examining the per cent of liberal and

conservative decisions in the areas of civil liberties and economics by term of the Court. These results are presented in Table 1.[3] The Court Earl Warren inherited from Fred Vinson at the beginning of the 1953 term was not liberal in the realm of civil liberties. Despite historic advances in racial equality, the early Warren Court was indifferent to the rights of the accused in state courts[4] and inconsistent in its protections of First Amendment rights.[5]

From the beginning of the Warren Court until the 1961 term, the Court's percentage of liberal civil rights and liberties decisions ranged from a low of 47.5 (1953) to a high of 62.5 (1954). Following the 1960 term, in which 54.3 per cent of these cases were decided liberally, the proportion jumped to 79.6 per cent in the 1961 term and remained in the seventies or above for six of the remaining seven years of the Warren Court. This dramatic shift in the early 1960s is almost universally recognized, but explanations for it are not entirely accurate. The conventional wisdom ascribes the shift to the appointment of Goldberg at the beginning of the 1962 term.[6] In fact, the shift occurred before Goldberg joined the Court, and probably would have occurred even if he had never been nominated and confirmed.

The 1960 term was one of the most closely divided in the Court's history. According to the data, a vote of 5-4 decided 23 of the 52 nonunanimous civil liberties decisions. Three factors shifted this delicate balance from moderation to liberalism during the succeeding (1961) term. First, Whittaker's mid-term retirement prevented him from voting in 32 of the Court's 49 civil liberties cases. Second, because of a stroke, Frankfurter voted in only 24 of these 49 cases. Third, Stewart, who supported the liberal side 41.5 per cent and 52.2 per cent of the time in the 1959 and 1960 terms, jumped to 71.4 per cent in 1961. White, Whittaker's replacement, voted in only two civil liberties cases of the 1961 term; thus, he could not have been a factor in the liberal shift.

Goldberg was crucial to the Court's liberal majority in the 1962 term, but not in the 1963 or 1964 terms. In 1962, a single vote determined the outcome of 13 civil liberties cases. Twelve produced a liberal result, and Goldberg voted with the majority in every one. In the 1963 term, however, Stewart voted liberally in 68.3 per cent of the cases, with the result that only three liberal decisions were minimum-winning. In the 1964 term the liberal majority was again sufficiently entrenched to result in only six close votes.

Table 1   Warren and Burger Courts' liberal decisions, by term

Term	Civil liberties % Liberal	n	Economic cases % Liberal	n
53	47.5	40	34.6	52
54	62.5	40	77.4	31
55	57.6	33	82.0	50
56	55.0	60	80.9	47
57	52.2	69	70.6	51
58	58.3	48	70.0	60
59	53.8	39	75.0	44
60	54.3	70	65.2	46
61	79.6	49	78.3	46
62	81.8	55	71.4	56
63	83.6	61	75.0	40
64	79.2	48	74.1	27
65	73.2	56	77.5	40
66	61.4	70	86.1	36
67	73.6	72	69.1	68
68	80.3	76	78.3	23
69	54.5	66	52.2	23
70	51.1	94	56.5	23
71	53.8	104	52.4	42
72	46.3	108	64.3	42
73	43.0	100	55.9	34
74	53.7	82	47.6	42
75	42.5	106	40.0	35
76	39.4	109	40.6	32
77	48.8	82	75.0	48
78	41.1	95	40.5	37
79	45.1	91	47.5	40
80	35.6	73	54.8	42
81	46.2	91	53.8	39
82	40.5	84	48.9	47
83	33.7	104	35.0	40
84	42.3	97	47.4	38
85	33.7	101	42.9	21

ity was again sufficiently entrenched to result in only six close votes.

Had President Kennedy appointed a more moderate justice, one who voted liberally in half of the close votes, the difference would have been felt only in the 1962 term. Identification of major cases confirms these findings. *Mapp v. Ohio*[7] and *Baker v. Carr*[8] were decided before Goldberg joined the Court; *Miranda v. Arizona*[9] was decided after he left. Several crucial cases were decided during his tenure, including *Gideon v. Wainwright,*[10] *Heart of Atlanta Motel v. United States,*[11] *Katzenbach v. McClung,*[12] *Reynolds v. Sims,*[13] *Griswold v. Connecticut,*[14] and *Escobedo v. Illinois.*[15] Of these, only *Escobedo* received more than two conservative votes. The liberal reputation of the 1961 through 1968 Warren Court would be unchanged had Goldberg never served on the Court.

The resignations of Earl Warren and Abe Fortas had a strong and immediate impact on the Court's civil liberties decisions. The per cent liberal dropped from 80.3 per cent in the 1968 term to 54.5 per cent in the 1969 term. The effect of the replacement of

Table 2   Justices' support for civil liberties in the Warren Court

Justice	All cases % Liberal	n	Nonunanimous cases % Liberal	n
Black	76.1	877	74.7	582
Reed	33.3	123	12.2	74
Frankfurter	49.5	412	37.1	278
Douglas	90.4	876	96.1	583
Jackson	46.2	39	38.9	18
Burton	35.5	242	21.4	159
Clark	43.1	729	24.7	485
Minton	36.3	113	17.5	63
Warren	78.1	866	77.6	576
Harlan	41.7	811	22.1	551
Brennan	78.1	757	76.0	509
Whittaker	43.4	265	26.1	184
Stewart	54.6	635	39.6	424
White	57.8	424	44.2	278
Goldberg	89.6	164	87.3	102
Fortas	80.4	230	81.1	159
Marshall	81.8	121	83.5	79

Table 3   Justices' support for economic cases in the Warren Court

Justice	All cases % Liberal	n	Nonunanimous cases % Liberal	n
Black	82.5	704	83.6	450
Reed	54.0	150	40.7	86
Frankfurter	39.5	377	20.2	247
Douglas	84.7	704	86.4	455
Jackson	31.8	44	20.8	24
Burton	52.0	229	38.6	145
Clark	73.5	601	70.3	380
Minton	60.4	134	53.3	75
Warren	79.7	710	79.2	457
Harlan	43.0	616	20.9	402
Brennan	75.8	578	71.5	382
Whittaker	37.3	236	17.5	166
Stewart	51.5	462	33.8	299
White	71.9	285	62.9	175
Goldberg	67.3	113	58.3	72
Fortas	64.7	136	51.1	90
Marshall	60.0	35	56.0	25

Black and Harlan with Powell and Rehnquist during the 1971 term was not felt until the 1972 term. The per cent liberal dropped from 53.8 per cent to 46.3, and rose to the 50 per cent level only once in the remaining 14 terms of the Burger Court (1974).

The correlation between the per cent liberal in civil liberties cases and the per cent liberal in economic cases is .73 for the two Courts combined. This coincides with previous findings that these two areas have related, but distinct, dimensions.[16] Unlike civil liberties, the Warren Court was extremely liberal economically almost from the beginning. In the 1953 term, the Court voted in a liberal direction in but 34.6 per cent of its economic cases. The very next term the figure jumped to 77.4 per cent and remained above the 65 per cent mark through the 1968 term. Analysis indicates that the lower liberal percentage of the 1953 term results in part from our use of docket number rather than case citation as the unit of analysis. All 16 of the multiple docket numbers were conservatively decided.[17] Their exclusion increases the liberal proportion to 50 per cent. The other factor explaining the 1953 term is Justice Jackson. As Table 7 shows, Jackson never dissented from a conservative economic decision during his single term on the Warren Court. In seven conservatively decided cases, his vote was outcome determinative; it never was in a liberally decided case. If we exclude these seven cases, the liberal proportion exceeds 62 per cent.

We next examine the mix of cases the Court chooses to place on its agenda each term. Previous research suggests that requests by the solicitor general for review, disapproval of lower court decisions and the filing of briefs by amicus groups affect the likelihood of particular cases being heard.[18] With the exception of Pacelle's recent work, there has been far less systematic analysis of the Court's aggregate agenda.[19] The data presented here indicate a persistent increase in the number of civil liberties cases heard per term. An ordinary least squares regression analysis reveals an increase of two cases per term to the Court's agenda, on average, over the 33 years of the study. On the other hand, the decrease in the number of economic cases per term is but .39. The predicted drop in economic cases for each unit increase in the number of civil liberties cases, -.16, supports the hypotheses that the increase in civil liberties cases did not, for the most part, come at the expense of the Court's economic agenda.[20]

Voting behavior and the justices

The Warren Court. Great variation exists among Warren Court justices in their support for civil liberties. (See Table 2.) Examining all cases, unanimous and nonunanimous, Douglas emerges as the most liberal (90.4 per cent), followed closely by Goldberg (89.6 per cent). Slightly less liberal are Marshall (81.8), Fortas (80.4 per cent), Warren and Brennan (78.1 per cent) and Black (76.1 per cent). After Black, a large drop-off occurs until we get to those with a moderate proportion: White (57.8 per cent), Stewart (54.61 per cent), Frankfurter (49.5 per cent), Jackson (46.2 per cent),

Table 4 Support for civil liberties in the Burger Court

Justice	All cases % Liberal	n	Nonunanimous cases % Liberal	n
Black	54.1	159	43.9	107
Douglas	90.6	540	94.1	374
Harlan	43.0	158	27.6	105
Brennan	77.2	1,556	85.5	1,086
Stewart	49.6	1,104	43.6	782
White	41.0	1,577	33.7	1,103
Marshall	79.3	1,543	88.5	1,078
Burger	29.7	1,575	17.6	1,099
Blackmun	40.9	1,397	39.5	1,056
Powell	37.7	1,317	31.2	940
Rehnquist	19.6	1,350	5.6	959
Stevens	56.3	963	61.4	676
O'Connor	30.6	477	24.5	318

Table 5 Support for economic cases in the Burger Court

Justice	All cases % Liberal	n	Nonunanimous cases % Liberal	n
Black	63.6	44	65.4	26
Douglas	75.6	192	78.4	111
Harlan	42.2	45	29.6	27
Brennan	67.1	605	74.2	329
Stewart	45.6	412	32.1	234
White	55.3	617	50.6	328
Marshall	64.7	607	68.2	321
Burger	41.3	620	25.0	328
Blackmun	53.1	589	46.5	310
Powell	42.5	478	29.7	256
Rehnquist	40.6	544	22.8	285
Stevens	54.3	398	52.6	211
O'Connor	39.6	177	31.0	87

Whittaker (43.4 per cent), Clark (43.1 per cent) and Harlan (41.7 per cent). Anchoring the conservative end are Minton (36.3 per cent), Burton (35.5 per cent), and Reed (33.3 per cent).

While the earliest behavioral research in public law examined nonunanimous decisions only,[21] this limitation is occasionally inappropriate.[22] But methodological and theoretical reasons sometimes exist for relying on nonunanimous decisions only. Many of the early behavioral studies in public law relied upon techniques borrowed from social psychology, such as cumulative scaling.[23] Unanimous decisions are inappropriate for such analyses because they artificially inflate relevant summary statistics, such as the coefficient of reproducibility.

For theoretical reasons, unanimous cases have been excluded from studies that do not require their exclusion on methodological grounds.[24] The theoretical argument against using unanimously decided cases draws from legal models of decision making. According to Sheldon Goldman, "in general a consensually decided case indicates that 'objectively' the case situation (either because of clear cut precedent, or the straight-forward applicability of the statute, or constitutional provision to the facts of the case) offered little leeway for the judge and that institutional pressures inhibited an outcome other than that achieved."[25] While this may be true in part, unanimous decisions also represent the ideological make-up of the court in question. In separate analyses of the U.S. courts of appeals, Burt Atkins and Donald Songer demonstrate that the direction of unanimous decisions correlated with the ideology of panel members.[26] We observe similar results from the Warren and Burger Courts. During the liberal terms of the Warren Court (1961-

68), 88.7 per cent of the unanimous decisions were liberal. After the appointments of Powell and Rehnquist, only 52.2 per cent of the Burger Court's unanimous decisions were liberal. If the legal model were solely responsible for unanimous decisions, this would not be the case. Empirically, however, there appears to be little difference between cases with and without unanimous decisions. While excluding unanimous cases tends to make liberals appear more liberal and conservatives more conservative, the correlation between the two sets of scores in Table 2 is .99.[27]

In Table 3 we examine ideological voting in economic cases during the Warren Court. Douglas is again the most liberal (84.7 per cent), but this time he is followed by fellow Roosevelt appointee, Hugo Black (82.5 per cent). Warren (79.7 per cent) and Brennan (75.8 per cent) retain their liberal patterns, while Goldberg (67.3 per cent), Fortas (64.7 per cent), and Marshall (60.0 per cent) drop considerably. They are passed by two justices who are moderate in civil liberties but liberal here: Clark (73.5 per cent) and White (71.9 per cent). The conservative end of the spectrum consists of Frankfurter (39.5 per cent), Whittaker (37.3 per cent), and Jackson (31.8 per cent).

The Burger Court. Republican presidential candidate Richard Nixon campaigned in 1968 on the promise to appoint "strict constructionists" (read "conservatives"; he gave no indication of wanting strict constructionists on First Amendment questions) to the Supreme Court. Nixon eventually had the opportunity to select four justices. Three of them, Burger, Powell, and Rehnquist, can be considered solid conservatives on questions of civil liberties (29.7, 37.7, and 19.6 per cent liberal,

Table 6   Dissent behavior of justices, civil liberties, 1953-1986

Justice	% Dissent from Liberal majority	(n)	Conservative majority	(n)
Black	14.1	668	48.6	368
Reed	43.1	72	0.0	51
Frankfurter	19.7	233	9.5	179
Douglas	1.3	861	77.7	555
Jackson	16.7	18	14.3	21
Burton	36.1	133	0.9	109
Clark	33.8	474	0.0	255
Minton	38.1	63	4.0	50
Warren	3.3	577	40.8	289
Harlan	38.8	637	4.8	332
Brennan	2.1	1,204	55.4	1,109
Whittaker	22.9	144	3.3	121
Stewart	17.5	956	13.5	783
White	20.8	1,020	8.6	981
Goldberg	0.0	134	43.3	30
Fortas	4.7	170	38.3	60
Marshall	1.2	782	62.4	882
Burger	34.0	695	1.0	880
Blackmun	17.9	552	14.0	845
Powell	18.0	556	5.3	761
Rehnquist	54.8	568	0.9	782
Stevens	10.7	391	33.7	572
O'Connor	26.9	186	3.4	291

Table 7   Dissent behavior of justices, economic cases, 1953-1986

Justice	% Dissent from Liberal majority	(n)	Conservative majority	(n)
Black	3.6	534	43.9	214
Reed	22.2	99	7.8	51
Frankfurter	43.3	254	4.1	123
Douglas	7.6	618	62.6	278
Jackson	17.6	17	0.0	27
Burton	20.6	157	13.9	72
Clark	3.4	440	10.6	161
Minton	11.9	84	14.0	50
Warren	0.4	510	29.0	200
Harlan	42.3	487	1.7	174
Brennan	3.3	730	30.5	453
Whittaker	49.4	172	1.6	64
Stewart	26.6	548	7.4	326
White	8.5	529	16.6	373
Goldberg	12.8	86	3.7	27
Fortas	15.7	102	5.9	34
Marshall	3.3	333	29.8	309
Burger	20.2	312	2.3	308
Blackmun	11.7	298	17.2	291
Powell	16.5	230	4.4	248
Rehnquist	26.0	277	6.0	267
Stevens	16.8	197	25.9	201
O'Connor	26.5	83	9.6	94

respectively. See Table 4.) The fourth, Blackmun (40.9 per cent), is closer to the moderates but nevertheless has been quite conservative in criminal procedure cases (32.6 per cent), which were most important to President Nixon.

Nixon enhanced his fortunes not only by selecting four justices who voted conservatively to replace three who did not, but by the changing behavior of sitting justices as well. Justice Black voted much more conservatively as his tenure on the Court continued.[28] While he supported the liberal side in 76.1 per cent of the Warren Court's civil liberties cases, he did so only 54.1 per cent of the time in the Burger Court. To a lesser extent, White also became more conservative. His civil liberties score dropped 16.8 points to 41.0 per cent. The appointment of the moderate Stevens (56.3 per cent) to replace the liberal Douglas (90.6 per cent) did little to change the Court's aggregate output (See Table 1), for a conservative majority was already ensconced. Similarly, little aggregate change can be detected from O'Connor's (30.6 per cent) replacement of the moderate Stewart (49.6 per cent).

The economic cases produce similar results (See Table 5). Black and White voted substantially more conservatively than they did during the Warren Court, with drop-offs of 18.9 and 16.6 points, respectively. The Nixon appointees are conservative, but only in a relative sense: none of their percent-ages fall below 40 per cent when unanimous and nonunanimous cases are considered, Douglas is, by far, the most liberal (75.6 per cent), followed by Brennan (67.1 per cent), Marshall (64.7 per cent), and Black (63.6 per cent). O'Connor anchors the conservative side at 39.6 per cent.

Dissent behavior

During much of the Court's history, dissents occurred infrequently. But beginning with the chief justiceship of Harlan Fiske Stone in 1941, dissents have proven to be almost as much the rule as the exception. Between the 1939 and 1942 terms, the proportion of cases in which dissent occurred jumped from .15 to .54.[29] Scholars have since sought to explain the variance in dissent rates among the justices. Schmidhauser found that conservative justices of humble origin and those from the Northeast were most likely to dissent,[30] while Ulmer reported that Catholicism, rural birth, and academic or corporate law practice correlated with dissent.[31] These findings will be discussed in the light of the data presented below. First we specify the dissent rates of the Warren and Burger Court justices in civil liberties (Table 6) and economic cases (Table 7).

As in their voting behavior, the justices vary their rates of dissent greatly. Douglas dissented from only 1.3 per cent of the liberal decisions in civil liberties, but from 77.7 per cent of the conservative decisions. Rehnquist, on the other hand, dissented from 54.8 per cent of the liberal decisions, but only 0.9 per cent of the conservative decisions. Goldberg never dissented from a liberal civil liberties decision, and Clark never dissented from a conservative one during the years under investigation. In the economic cases, we note in particular that Goldberg dissented from only one of 23 conservative decisions while he was on the Court.

In evaluating these data, it is useful to consider two distinct models of dissent behavior, the attitudinal model[32] and the social background model.[33] The attitudinal model simply holds that justices will dissent when the majority's position is further from their ideal point than a dissenting vote would be. The social background model argues that in addition to policy concerns, justices dissent due to psychological predispositions that can be traced to definable background characteristics.

If the background model is correct, some justices should frequently dissent regardless of the issue area or direction of the Court's decision. If justices dissent only from liberal decisions or only in certain types of cases, then dissent would appear to be a function of policy attitudes, not psychological predispositions. (Note that lack of dissent across all issues and direction cannot be used to demonstrate predispositions against dissent: such justices might simply be in the median position.) We define frequent dissent rather loosely—as dissent in 10 per cent or more of the relevant cases. A frequent dissenter is one who dissents in more than 10 per cent of the liberal and conservative economic and civil liberties cases. Use of this criterion shows that only two justices demonstrate a generalized tendency to dissent, Blackmun and Stevens. Correlating the frequency with which the various justices dissent across issue categories provides further evidence that dissent behavior is almost entirely policy based. The correlations (Pearson r) between liberal and conservative dissent rates in civil liberties and economics are -.62 and -.60, respectively, despite the fact that median justices will be low on both liberal and conservative dissents. This, of course, does not demonstrate that dissent behavior is a function of the justices' attitudes, for we have not independently measured those attitudes. Rather, we demonstrate that dissent behavior is consistent with the attitudinal model, while it is inconsistent with social background models that predict psychological predispositions as the bases for dissent.[34]

Conclusion

We have used data from the United States Supreme Court Judicial Data Base to show that: 1) conventional explanations for the Court's dramatic shift in support of civil liberties in the early 1960s lack accuracy; 2) the increase in the number of civil liberties cases decided by the Warren and Burger Courts did not occur at the expense of the Cout's economic agenda; 3) theoretical reasons for excluding unanimous decisions from consideration lack validity even though empirical evidence shows little ideological difference between unanimous and nonunanimous decisions; and 4) attitudinal, rather than the social background, model is consistent with the justices' dissent behavior.

Although these findings do not begin to mine the wealth of data Phase 1 of the data base contains (almost 9,000 case records covering 57 separate fields of data, with each field containing at least one, and as many as several hundred, variables), we hope they illustrate its utility for students and scholars of the Supreme Court.

NOTES

This article originally appeared in Volume 73, Number 2, August-September 1989, pages 103-107.

1. *See, for example*, Western Air Lines v. Civil Aeronautics Board, 347 U.S. 67 (1954).

2. We excluded from analysis suits between unions and union members, as the "liberal" side is by no means apparent. Data base users may easily redefine the scope of civil liberties and economic cases, along with the other issue areas, as they see fit. Over 260 policy oriented issues are identified; these are organized into 13 major groupings. Users may also easily respecify the directionality (i.e., support or opposition) of such issues as they choose. The default setting for affirmative action, for example, defines support of the issue as pro-affirmative action. A user, however, may prefer to alter directionality to view support for affirmative action as antithetical to civil rights—as "conservative" rather than "liberal."

3. We clerically changed the 29 cases in the data set in which the only difference between the majority and the dissenters is that the dissenters would go further than the majority; *e.g.*, the majority might reverse and remand a petitioner's conviction while the dissenters would simply reverse. In such cases, the majority was coded conservative in the data base to signify that it was more conservative than the dissent. Nevertheless, as both parties supported the defendant in such a case, we count the position of the majority and the dissent as liberal. Additionally, we clerically deleted duplicates of docket numbers that appeared in the data base because the case contained multiple issues, as well as those that were duplicated because they contained a combination of multiple issues and legal provisions.

4. Breithaupt v. Abram, 352 U.S. 432 (1957).

5. Watkins v. United States, 354 U.S. 178 (1957); Barenblatt v. United States, 360 U.S. 109 (1959).

6. *E.g.*, Wasby, THE SUPREME COURT IN THE FEDERAL JUDICIAL SYSTEM 11 (Chicago: Nelson Hall, 1988); Baum, THE SUPREME COURT 2d ed. 143 (Washington: Congressional Quarterly,

1985).

7. 367 U.S. 643 (1961).

8. 369 U.S. 186 (1962).

9. 384 U.S. 436 (1966).

10. 372 U.S. 335 (1963).

11. 379 U.S. 241 (1964).

12. 379 U.S. 294 (1964).

13. 377 U.S. 533 (1964).

14. 381 U.S. 479 (1965).

15. 378 U.S. 478 (1964).

16. Rohde and Spaeth, Supreme Court Decision Making 137-140 (San Francisco: W.H. Freeman, 1976).

17. In no other term does the liberal proportion differ substantially between docket number and case citation.

18. Tanenhaus et al. *The Supreme Court's Certiorari Jurisdiction: Cue Theory* in Schubert (ed.) Judicial Decision-Making (Glencoe, IL: Free Press, 1963); Ulmer, *The Supreme Court's Certiorari Decisions: Conflict as a Predictive Variable*, 78 Am. Pol. Sci. Rev. 901 (1984); Caldeira and Wright, *Organized Interests and Agenda Setting in the U.S. Supreme Court*, 82 Am. Pol. Sci. Rev. 1109 (1988).

19. *See* Pacelle, "The Supreme Court's Agenda Across Time: Dynamics and Determinants of Change," Unpublished Ph.D. dissertation, Ohio State, 1985.

20. The models are Civ = -60.5 + 1.96 * Term, Econ = 67.4 - .39 * Term, and Econ = 52.6 - .16 * Term, where Civ is the number of civil liberties cases per term, Econ is the number of economic cases per term and Term is the two-digit term of the Court, running from 53 to 85. The models used here are for descriptive purposes only. The term of the Court does not cause an increase or decrease in the types of cases heard. Rather, the term of the Court is associated with an increase or decrease in the types of cases heard. The regressions reported here rely on the assumption of no autocorrelation. The Durbin-Watson D statistics, which measure first order autocorrelation, are 1.29, 1.93 and 1.89 respectively, suggesting autocorrelation for the first model only. Where autocorrelation exists t-statistics and R^2s are overestimated, but slope coefficients, such as the ones we report, remain unbiased. *See* Wannacott and Wannacott, Introductory Statistics for Business and Economics, 3d ed., ch. 24 (New York: Wiley, 1984).

21. Pritchett, The Roosevelt Court (New York: Macmillan, 1948); Schubert, Quantitative Analysis of Judicial Behavior (Glencoe, IL: The Free Press, 1959); Goldman, *Voting Behavior on the U.S. Courts of Appeals*, 60 Am. Pol. Sci. Rev. 374 (1966).

22. Atkins and Green, *Consensus on the United States Courts of Appeals: Illusion or Reality?*, 20 Am. J. of Pol. Sci. 735 (1976). Songer, *Consensual and Nonconsensual Decisions in Unanimous Opinions of the United States Courts of Appeals*, 26 Am. J. of Pol. Sci. 225 (1982).

23. Schubert, *supra* n. 21; Spaeth, *Warren Court Attitudes Toward Business: The "B" Scale*, in Schubert (ed.) Judicial Decision Making (New York: Free Press, 1982).

24. Goldman, *supra* n. 21; Tate, *Personal Attribute Models of the Voting Behavior of U.S. Supreme Court Justices*, 75 Am. Pol. Sci. Rev. 355 (1981).

25. Goldman, *Backgrounds, Attitudes and the Voting Behavior of Judges*, 39 J. of Pol. 214 at 219 (1969). *Cf.* Spaeth, *Consensus in the unanimous decisions of the U.S. Supreme Court*, 72 Judicature 274 (1989).

26. Atkins, *Decision-Making Rules and Judicial Strategy on the United States Courts of Appeals*, 25 West. Pol. Q. 626 (1972); Songer, *supra* n. 22. *Cf.* Spaeth, *supra* n. 25.

27. The correlation coefficient used is the simple Pearson r, which is widely used for interval level data. The comparable correlations for Tables 3, 4 and 5 are .98, .98, and .99, respectively.

28. Ulmer, *The Longitudinal Behavior of Hugo Lafayette Black:*

Parabolic Support for Civil Liberties, 1 Fla. St. L. Rev. 131 (1973). More sophisticated attempts to measure change overtime control for the types of cases being heard. *See* Segal, *Measuring Change on the Supreme Court*, 29 Am. J. of Pol. 461 (1985), and Baum, *Measuring Policy Change in the U.S. Supreme Court*, 82 Am. Pol. Sci. Rev. 905 (1988). Fortunately, the correlation between corrected scores (scores controlled for the types of cases being heard) and uncorrected scores in Baum's data, .88, is high enough that little information is lost by not controlling for the types of cases being heard.

29. Walker, Epstein and Dixon, *On the Mysterious Demise of Consensual Norms in the United States Supreme Court*, 50 J. of Pol. 361 (1988).

30. Schmidhauser, *Stare Decisis, Dissent, and the Background of the Justices of the Supreme Court of the United States*, 14 U. of Tor. L. J. 194 (1962).

31. Ulmer, *Dissent Behavior and the Social Background of Supreme Court Justices*, 32 J. of Pol. 580 (1970).

32. Schubert, The Judicial Mind (Evanston, IL: Northwestern Univ. Press, 1965); Schubert, The Judicial Mind Revisited (New York: Oxford Univ. Press, 1974); Rohde and Spaeth, *supra* n. 16.

33. Schmidhauser, *supra* n. 30; Ulmer, *supra* n. 31.

34. Our finding receives independent support from Segal and Cover, *Ideological Values and the Votes of Supreme Court Justices*, 83 Am. Pol. Sci. Rev. (1989), which uses an independent and reliable measure of the justices' values to establish the validity of the attitudinal model to explain the votes of all Supreme Court justices from Warren to Kennedy.

Power on the Court: Chief Justice Rehnquist's opinion assignments

An analysis of his first three terms suggests that Rehnquist has not fully utilized his opinion assignment prerogative as an instrument to shape the decisions of the Court. Thus, his leadership has not been crucial to the emergence of a conservative majority.

by Sue Davis

By the spring of 1989 it was clear that the Supreme Court had shifted to the right.[1] As observers proclaimed the arrival of a genuine Rehnquist Court,[2] they seemed to take as a matter of faith that the leadership of the chief justice was instrumental in cementing the conservative majority. Although his clearly established record for fourteen-and-a-half years as the Burger Court's most conservative member made William H. Rehnquist seem to be the ideal choice to carry out the legacy of Ronald Reagan's presidency, a chief justice's ability to shape the Court's decisions is always constrained by the other members of the Court. By 1988, the replacement of Lewis Powell by Anthony Kennedy and the presence of two other justices appointed by Ronald Reagan,[3] combined with Justice White made the emergence of a cohesive conservative majority quite likely. Indeed, the dynamic of the eight associate justices could have been as crucial to building a conservative majority to fulfill the goals of the Reagan Administration as the chief justiceship of William Rehnquist. This article examines the role that Rehnquist, in his capacity as chief justice, has played in the Supreme Court's turn to the right. How effectively has he used the powers of chief justice to shape the Court's decisions? Has his leadership been essential? Or would the "musicians . . . play the same notes without him"?[4]

As chief justice, Rehnquist holds the potential power to shape the decisions of the Court by persuading "others to vote in ways (in the short and long run) favorable to his policy goals."[5] The chief justice is often described as primus inter pares, "first among equals." Although he has one vote as do each of the eight associate justices, the chief justice who wishes to maximize his position as a policy leader has a number of devices. He has the opportunity to influence the outcome of cases in the leadership roles and strategies he adopts in conference,[6] the strategy he uses in opinion assignments, in circulating the "discuss list" for petitions for certiorari,[7] in the crafting of his own opinions, in the image he presents to the public, and in his personal interaction among the other justices.

In this article I examine one instrument of the chief justice's power—the assignment of majority opinions—in order to begin to assess the extent to which Rehnquist is acting as a policy leader. In cases in which the chief justice votes with the majority, the rules of the Court provide that he assign the writing of the opinion either to himself or to one of the other justices who voted with him. David J. Danelski explained that the selection of the author of the majority opinion is important because the opinion determines not only the value of a decision as a precedent, but also how acceptable it will be to the public.[8] The author of the opinion, moreover, may be responsible for holding the majority together in a close case, and may persuade would-be dissenters to join the majority.

David W. Rohde underlined the importance of the assignment of majority opinions by identifying two sets of concerns: intra-Court and extra-Court factors.[9] The first set of concerns includes holding together a tenuous majority, increasing the size of a solid majority, and promoting harmony among the justices. Walter F. Murphy pointed to an intra-Court factor when he reflected that a chief justice might reward his coalition within the Court by assigning the interesting and important cases to those "who tend to vote with him, leaving the dregs for those who vote against him on issues he thinks important."[10]

Extra-Court factors include those that involve the relationship between the Court and the rest of the political system. The chief should be sensitive to "public relations" in assigning opinions, particularly those that will be unpopular to a large segment of the public. Further, as Elliot Slotnick noted, the chief justice may be the most appropriate member of the Court to author the majority opinion in critical cases because of his symbolic status.[11] Rohde also pointed to a third factor that "has to do with the personal policy preference of the assigner"[12] The chief justice can make assignments strategically to members of the Court whose views are most similar to his own in order to maximize the likelihood that the majority opinion will further his objectives.

Assignment strategies

Seeking to further an understanding of the Supreme Court as a collegial decision-making body, scholars have formulated and tested a number of hypotheses concerned with the strategies used by the assigners of majority opinions. Danelski formulated two assignment rules that a chief justice might use to influence others to join the majority.[13] First, he might assign the opinion to the justice whose views are the closest to the dissenters in the belief that the justice would take an approach upon which both majority and minority could agree. Second, where there are blocs on the Court and a bloc splits, the chief justice might assign the case to a majority member of the dissenters' bloc. Danelski found that of the three chief justices he studied, only Hughes appeared to follow such rules. A number of scholars, attempting to determine whether assigners followed Danelski's first rule, have found a pattern of overassignment to the justice closest to the dissenters in cases in which a change in one vote would have altered the outcome.[14] Saul Brenner and Harold J. Spaeth found that assigning the majority opinion to the marginal justice did not actually help maintain an original minimum winning coalition.[15] Thus, it is not clear

what an assigner accomplishes by favoring the justice closest to the dissenters over the other members of the majority.

Rohde hypothesized that the justice who assigns the majority opinion will either write the opinion himself or assign it to the justice whose position is closest to his own on the issue in question. Analyzing civil liberties cases decided during the Warren era, he found that the pattern of opinion assignments supported his hypothesis.[16] Moreover, the assigner's tendency to give opinions to the justice closest to him increased in important cases and as the size of the majority increased.

When Gregory Rathjen replicated Rohde's study using economics rather than civil liberties cases, he found that the pattern of assigning opinions to the closest justice disappeared.[17] While Rathjen endorsed the theory that justices assign opinions on the basis of policy preferences, he suggested that Rohde's hypothesis was most viable in cases that involved issues of primary concern to the chief. He surmised that the issues presented in economics cases were less salient to Warren than those of individual rights, so that the chief justice may have placed policy concerns aside in those cases in order to assign in a manner that would help to equalize the workload.

Slotnick explored an alternative to ideological concerns in assigning opinions: equality of workload.[18] Examining two models of opinion assignment—the opinion assignment ratio (OAR), which is conditioned on the frequency with which each justice is a member of the majority, and the model of absolute equality of caseloads, whereby all justices would have substantially the same number of majority opinions regardless of how often they agreed with the majority—he found that the six chief justices from Taft through Burger followed a norm of absolute equality rather than the OAR model. Moreover, it was Chief Justice Burger's behavior that most closely approximated the model of absolute equality. Likewise, Spaeth found that Burger practiced equal distribution to an extent that was unmatched by any of his five predecessors.[19]

Slotnick discovered that chief justices departed from the norm of equality in important cases, assigning opinions to themselves at a substantially higher rate than they did for the universe of cases. That pattern of self-assignment in important cases was most pronounced in highly cohesive cases—in cases where the Court was divided the chief tended to avoid writing the opinion. Slotnick found those who most often voted with the chief justice were favored in the assignment of opinions in important cases. Spaeth's analysis of Burger's assignments revealed the same pattern.[20]

Hypotheses

The theory and methods developed in previous judicial research provided the basis for the four hypotheses tested here. The hypotheses reflect the two expectations that Rehnquist has assigned opinions with a goal of equal distribution of workload and that he has also attempted to assign opinions so as to further his policy preferences.

Rehnquist can be expected to continue the tradition of distributing opinions on the basis of absolute equality that Slotnick found to be the norm for chief justices from Taft through Burger. By the chief justice's own account:

[Assigning opinions] is an important responsibility, and it is desirable that it be discharged carefully and fairly. The chief justice is expected to retain for himself some opinions that he regards as of great significance, but he is also expected to pass around to his colleagues some of this kind of opinion. I think it also pleases the other members of the Court if the chief justice occasionally takes for himself a rather routine and uninteresting case, just as they are expected to do as a result of the assignment process. At the start of the October 1986 term I tried to be as evenhanded as possible as far as numbers of cases assigned to each justice, but as the term goes on I take into consideration the extent to which the various justices are current in writing and circulating opinions that have previously been assigned.[21]

The chief justice's comments suggest that "evenhandedness" rather than ideology would be the dominant factor in his assignments. Accordingly, Hypothesis 1 states that the opinions have been evenly distributed among the nine justices.

Studies of opinion assignment decision making by previous chief justices have revealed a departure from the norm of equality in important cases.[22] Thus, Hypothesis 2 posits that in important cases the chief justice has overassigned opinions to himself but that evenhandedness has prevailed to the extent that he has not kept the important cases for himself at a significantly higher rate than his predecessors.

Rohde's theory, based on the assumption that "justices are rational and that their primary motivation in making decisions is their own personal preferences about what is good public policy," is considered in Hypothesis 3.[23] If the chief's goal is to keep the majority and to have the opinion written in a way that is compatible with his preferences, he should assign opinions to the justice whose views most resemble his own. Thus, according to Hypothesis 3, Rehnquist has overassigned opinions to himself or to the justice whose position is closest to his on the issue in question.

Finally, I address the question of whether the chief justice uses his authority to assign opinions to hold a minimum winning coalition together by assigning the majority opinion to the justice closest to the dissenters. Specifically, Hypothesis 4 states that in cases decided by a minimum majority coalition Rehnquist has overassigned to the justice closest to the dissenters.

Analysis and results

The data used here are comprised of all cases decided with full opinion during the terms 1986 through 1988—a total of 445 cases.[24] To test Hypothesis 1, the total number of opinions assigned to each justice were determined and OAR's for each justice for each of the three terms were calculated.[25] The results are displayed in Table 1.

The table includes the opinions written by each justice regardless of who made the assignment. The results suggest that Rehnquist has taken the assignments made by others into account in order to achieve an equal distribution of opinions. Table 1 indicates that Rehnquist has continued the tradition of absolute equality in opinion assignments. The standard deviation was highest for 1986—but still only 2.39—when Scalia served his "freshman" term.[26] When the three years are considered together each justice wrote an average of 15.35 opinions per term with a standard deviation of only 1.57.

The coefficient of relative variation (CRV), which is calculated by taking the ratio of a standard deviation to its mean, standardizes a series of standard deviations based on means of varying size so that distribution of assignments can be compared for different years and equality of assignment can be compared for different assigners.[27] For the terms 1986 through 1988 the CRV was 0.149, 0.116, and 0.118 respectively—only slightly higher than Spaeth found for the Burger Court through the 1980 term. Spaeth also found Burger's overall CRV for the terms 1969 through 1980 to be 0.179.[28] As Table 2 shows, Rehnquist's CRV for the terms 1986 through 1988 was only slightly higher at 0.187.[29]

The data support Hypothesis 1. Rehnquist ap-

Table 1   Distribution of opinions on the Rehnquist Court, 1986-1988

1986 Term

Justice	Majority opinions	Majority votes	OAR	Expected OAR
Powell	20	127	15.75	15.01
O'Connor	18	109	16.51	14.92
Rehnquist	17	109	15.60	15.21
White	16	118	13.55	14.16
Brennan	16	89	17.97	14.44
Marshall	16	90	17.77	14.44
Stevens	16	96	16.66	14.92
Blackmun	13	105	12.38	14.65
Scalia	12	114	10.52	15.23

mean=16
standard deviation=2.39
CRV=s.d./mean 2.39/16=0.149

1987 Term

Justice	Majority opinions	Majority votes	OAR	Expected OAR
White	20	121	16.52	14.96
Stevens	19	112	16.96	14.57
Brennan	16	106	15.09	14.42
O'Connor	16	108	14.81	14.57
Scalia	16	114	14.03	14.81
Rehnquist	15	114	13.15	14.83
Marshall	15	103	14.56	14.04
Blackmun	15	110	13.66	14.29
Kennedy*	7	54	12.96	14.22

*Kennedy was excluded from the calculations of the mean and standard deviation.
mean=16.5
standard deviation=1.92
CRV=s.d./mean 1.92/16.5=0.116

1988 Term

Justice	Majority opinions	Majority votes	OAR	Expected OAR
White	18	121	14.88	13.77
Stevens	15	93	16.12	14.81
Brennan	16	79	20.25	13.16
O'Connor	13	108	12.04	14.57
Scalia	12	115	10.43	14.77
Rehnquist	15	115	13.04	15.00
Marshall	14	78	17.95	13.08
Blackmun	14	93	15.05	13.83
Kennedy	15	121	12.40	15.10

mean=14.66
standard deviation=1.73
CRV=s.d./mean 1.73/14.66=0.118

Table 2   Chief Justice Rehnquist's overall CRV 1986-1988 (based on OAR)

Assignee	Number of opinions	Votes w/majority	OAR
Rehnquist	47	338	13.91
Powell	18	103	17.47
White	49	316	15.51
Stevens	40	238	16.81
Brennan	22	201	10.95
O'Connor	44	296	14.86
Scalia	35	311	11.25
Marshall	35	199	17.59
Blackmun	31	238	13.03
Kennedy	17	158	10.75

mean=14.21
Standard deviation=2.66
CRV=2.66/14.21=0.187

constitutional law texts.[30] All the methods share an element of arbitrariness and none of them take into account the importance of the cases to the chief justice at the time they were decided. I have chosen to utilize the method devised by Spaeth whereby the cases headlined in the *Lawyers' Edition of the United States Reports* are classified as "important cases."[31] Spaeth's method has the advantage that it eliminates bias in favor of constitutional cases and makes it possible to classify cases that have been decided so recently that they have not been included in any of the casebooks.

Table 3 displays Rehnquist's distribution of assignments in important cases. The *Lawyer's Edition* identified 48 such cases for the terms 1986 through 1988. Rehnquist assigned opinions in 36 of those cases, nine of which he assigned to himself (25 per cent). Both Spaeth and Slotnick found that chief justice Burger assigned about 25 per cent of the important cases to himself. Slotnick found the average self-assignment ratio for chief justices from Taft through the first five years of the Burger Court to be 24.8.[32] Rehnquist's CRV for the important cases was .77, considerably higher than that of all of the chief justices in Slotnick's study except for Taft (.95) and Hughes (.93). Rehnquist's CRV for the important cases was notably higher than the .47 that Spaeth found for Burger,[33] which suggests that chief justice Rehnquist has assigned opinions in important cases less evenhandedly than his predecessor. The data support Hypothesis 2 insofar as Rehnquist clearly overassigned opinions to himself. The unexpected finding was that he did so at a rate exceeding that of his predecessors.

The most interesting finding with regard to important cases was that Rehnquist assigned more opinions to Justice White than he did to himself.

pears to be adhering to the norm of equality of workload in assigning opinions. The tests of the remaining three hypotheses should shed light on the extent to which he also uses policy considerations as a basis for allocating opinion assignments.

"Important cases"

Hypothesis 2 requires a definition of "important cases." Several methods of identifying such cases have been utilized in judicial research. For example, important cases may be identified as those that were cited most often by the Court in subsequent decisions, or those included in the leading

Table 3 Rehnquist's assignments in important cases, 1986-1988

Assignee	Number of opinions	Times available	OAR
Marshall	0	14	0.0
Brennan	1	14	7.14
Blackmun	1	18	5.56
Stevens	0	19	0.0
White	11	33	33.33
Scalia	4	33	12.12
O'Connor	4	31	12.90
Powell	3	7	42.86*
Kennedy	3	24	12.50
Rehnquist	9	36	25.00

*Powell was excluded from the calculations of the mean and standard deviation. Using Slotnick's rule (see footnote 11, at 68, n.7) that a justice be available for assignment in at least 10 important cases, Kennedy was included.
mean=12.06
Standard deviationJ9.26
CRV=s.d./mean=9.26/12.06=0.77

The chief justice's apparent preference for White may be a result of the latter's increasing alignment with Rehnquist. During the last five terms of the Burger Court White and Rehnquist voted together in 65.6 per cent of the cases in which they both participated. During the first three years of the Rehnquist Court, however, their percentage of interagreement rose to 74.6 per cent. It is possible, therefore, that Rehnquist assigned opinions to White with the goal of maximizing the prospects of cementing the alliance between them and, thus, of drawing White closer to the conservatives.

Agreement

Tests of Hypotheses 3 and 4 mandate a technique to measure agreement between the chief justice and the other members of the majority. Following the example of previous studies,[34] I used cumulative scaling to identify the "closest" justice to the opinion assigner.[35] Because the analysis included only three terms, the possibility of constructing a scale for each issue was precluded. Still, "semi-refined" scales seemed to be preferable to a simple civil liberties scale. Therefore, I constructed separate scales for the three issues of criminal procedure, civil rights, and the First Amendment and used the scale scores of the justices to determine their "closeness" to the chief justice. That is, in a given case the justice in the majority with the scale score nearest to Rehnquist's was considered to be the justice in the position closest to that of the chief justice.[36]

For Hypothesis 3 to be supported, Rehnquist's assignment of opinions should reveal a pattern of overassignment to himself (position 1) and to the justice in the majority with the scale score closest to his own (position 2). The distribution of opinions for the 1986 term (see Table 1), as well as previous research,[37] suggests the existence of a "freshman effect" in opinion assignments. Accordingly, I excluded justices serving a first term on the Court from the analysis. Specifically, the pattern of assignment to the closest justice was analyzed excluding Scalia for cases decided during the 1986 term and excluding Kennedy for cases decided during the 1987 term.

In order to measure "overassignment," I began with the assumption that in any case each justice in the majority has an equal probability of being assigned the opinion. That made it possible to compare the actual proportion of majority opinions Rehnquist assigned to a position to the proportion that could be expected if he were assigning randomly.[38] Thus, for the hypothesis to be supported, the comparisons would have to reveal a substantially greater proportion of opinions Rehnquist assigned to Positions 1 and 2. The results are shown in Table 4.

The difference between the actual and expected proportion of opinions assigned is in the predicted direction but the difference is not great enough to be statistically significant. Thus, the hypothesis that Rehnquist has assigned opinions to the justices whose views are most compatible with his own failed to be supported.

The chief justice's goal of maintaining an equal workload may have acted as a constraint on his ability to assign opinions ideologically. Additionally, as Rathjen suggested,[39] an opinion assigner may utilize his discretion to assign opinions to the justices most likely to further his policy goals in areas that are most salient to him and in other areas concentrate on equality of workload, thereby conserving his resources. If one of the three issues is more important to the chief justice than the others, he might assign opinions accordingly. But the pattern of Rehnquist's assignments in each of the three areas does not suggest that to be the case.

As Table 5 shows, the difference between the actual and expected proportion of assignments to positions 1 and 2 was in the predicted direction when criminal procedure, civil rights, and the First Amendment were considered separately, but was not statistically significant for any of the three issues.

Table 4   Rehnquist's majority opinion assignments in criminal procedure, civil rights, and First Amendment cases, 1986-1988[1]

Total assigned	Number to closest	Proportion to closest	Expected	Difference	Z*	Prob.
161	55	.342	.299	.043	1.19	.1170

1. Both Scalia and Kennedy were excluded from the analysis during their first terms on the Court (1986 and 1987 respectively).
*One-tailed difference of proportions test.

Table 5   Rehnquist's majority opinion assignments, three issue areas considered separately[1]

Issue	Number to closest/total	Proportion to closest	Expected	Difference	Z*	Prob.
Criminal procedure	26/86	.302	.299	.003	.060	.4761
First Amendment	10/25	.400	.299	.101	1.10	.1357
Civil rights	19/50	.380	.298	.082	1.27	.1020

1. Both Scalia and Kennedy were excluded from the analysis during their first terms on the Court (1986 and 1987 respectively).
*One-tailed difference of proportions test.

Table 6   Rehnquist's assignments in criminal procedure, civil rights, First Amendment cases decided by one-vote margin, 1986-1988

Position	Number assigned	Actual proportion	Expected	Difference	Z*	Prob.
1	11	.200	.202	-.002		
2	10	.200	.202	-.002		
3**	10	.182	.202	-.020		
4	11	.200	.202	-.002		
5	14	.254	.202	-.052	.96	.1685

N=55
*One-tailed difference of proportions test.
**In the two cases decided by a vote of 4-3 Rehnquist assigned one to position 2 and one to position 3.

Rathjen's assertion concerning the importance of the issue to the assigner, Rehnquist's own statements regarding the importance of federalism,[40] along with the lack of support for Hypothesis 3 lend credibility to the possibility that neither criminal procedure, civil rights, nor the First Amendment are particularly salient to Rehnquist. If federalism and/or economic issues are more important to Rehnquist than any sub-category of civil liberties, analysis may reveal a pattern of overassignment to the justice in the position closest to his in those areas. Unfortunately, attempts to scale both economics and federalism cases proved unsuccessful, rendering any identification of the closest justice to Rehnquist unreliable.

Hypothesis 4 predicts that in cases decided by a margin of one vote Rehnquist will assign the opinion to the justice in the majority whose scale score places him/her closest to the dissenters (the marginal position) in order to maintain the majority coalition. Thus, the data will support Hypothesis 4 if the results show that Position 5 received the assignment in a substantially greater proportion of cases than would have been expected by chance. It should be emphasized that the justice who occu-

pies Position 5 varies according to the composition of the majority coalition—that is, Position 5 is not an individual justice. As Table 6 shows, Position 5 received a greater proportion of assignments then the other positions and at a greater rate than was expected. Still, the difference between the actual and expected proportion was not statistically significant. Thus, Hypothesis 4 failed to be supported.

The lack of support for Hypotheses 3 and 4 indicates that Rehnquist did not favor the justice whom he believed would write an opinion that would further the chief justice's own policy goals, nor did he show a preference for the marginal justice in close cases. The failure of the analysis to reveal either that Rehnquist overassigned majority opinions to the justice closest to him or to the justice closest to the dissenters in close cases suggests that the chief justice has not used his discretion to assign opinions in order to advance his policy goals.

Conclusion

The results of the analysis of opinion assignments during the first three terms of the Rehnquist Court show that if the chief justice's goal has been to distribute the workload evenly he has been successful except with respect to the important cases. His assignments in important cases suggest that he combined a goal of equal workload with one of advancing his policy preferences by keeping opinions for himself and by assigning to White, thereby courting an increasingly close ally. But the assertion that he assigned opinions with an eye to advancing his policy preferences is not otherwise supported by the data. In short, the results suggest that Rehnquist has not fully utilized his opinion assigning prerogative as an instrument to shape the decisions of the Court.

This article, because it examines only one aspect of the chief justice's leadership, reveals nothing about Rehnquist's use of other resources that a chief justice may use to maximize his power. Moreover, it is important for the reader to be aware that the analysis, by necessity, is based only on the final vote of the Court, as conference votes are not available. Thus, it is impossible to take into account that in any given case Rehnquist may have voted with the minority in conference and then switched or that the members of a winning coalition in the final vote may not be the same as the original majority.

Still, the results are consistent with the assertion that Rehnquist's leadership has not been crucial to the emergence of a solid conservative majority. It is possible that the chief justice has not exercized the prerogatives of his office to their full extent simply because he has not needed to do so. The membership of the Court is such that opinion assignments may rarely make any difference to the outcome of the cases. If so, the chief justice has no need to act as a strong leader. The dynamic of a Court whose members consist of four conservatives in addition to the chief justice may have rendered it unnecessary for Rehnquist to draw on all the resources of his power.

NOTES

This article originally appeared in Volume 74, Number 2, August-September 1990, pages 66-72.

The author wishes to thank Harold J. Spaeth not only for providing a copy of the Data Base, but also for reading an earlier version of this paper and providing a number of helpful suggestions. The author also wishes to thank Donald R. Songer for his helpful comments.

1. *See for example*, Patterson v McLean, 109 S.Ct. 2363 (1989) (narrowing the application of civil rights laws that prohibit discrimination in employment) Wards Cove Packing Co. v Atonio, 109 S.Ct. 2115 (1989); Richmond v Croson, 109 S.Ct. 706 (1989) Martin v Wilks, 109 S.Ct. 2180 (1989) (curtailing affirmative action); National Treasury Employees Union v Von Raab, 109 S.Ct. 1384 (1989); Skinner v Railway Labor Executives' Association, 109 S.Ct. 1402 (1989) (upholding drug testing for federal employees); Duckworth v Eagan, 109 S.Ct. 2875 (1989), Arizona v Youngblood, 109 S.Ct. 333 1988; U.S. v Sokolow, 109 S.Ct. 1581 1989; Florida v Riley, 109 S.Ct. 693 (1989) (making further exceptions to the rules established by the Warren Court that protect the rights of the accused); Penry v Lynaugh, 109 S.Ct. 2934 1989; Stanford v Kentucky 109 S.Ct. 2969 (1989) (upholding the death penalty for convicted murderers who committed the crime at the age of sixteen and convicted murderers who are mentally retarded); Webster v Reproductive Health Services, 109 S.Ct. 3040 (1989) (approving state restrictions on abortion).

2. *See, for example*, Wermiel, *Rehnquist Emerges as a Skillful Leader of the Court's Majority*, WALL STREET JOURNAL June 29, 1989, at 1.

3. Sandra Day O'Connor joined the Court in 1981. Antonin Scalia filled the vacancy left by Rehnquist's elevation to chief justice in 1986. Anthony Kennedy, who replaced Lewis Powell, took his position on the Court in February of 1988.

4. Wermiel, *supra* n. 2.

5. O'Brien, STORM CENTER: THE SUPREME COURT IN AMERICAN POLITICS 233 (New York: W.W. Norton, 1986).

6. Danelski, *The Influence of the Chief Justice in the Decisional Process of the Supreme Court*, in Goldman and Sarat, AMERICAN COURT SYSTEMS: READINGS IN JUDICIAL PROCESS AND BEHAVIOR 506-519 (San Francisco: W.H. Freeman and Company, 1978); Murphy, ELEMENTS OF JUDICIAL STRATEGY (Chicago: University of Chicago Press. 1964).

7. The Court grants certiorari when four members vote to accept the case for review. The chief justice circulates a "discuss list"—a list of cases that he considers worthy of discussion in the conference. Each of the other members of the Court may add cases to that list. A case is not discussed unless it is placed on that list. Stevens, *Deciding What to Decide: The Docket and the Rule of Four*, in Cannon and O'Brien, THE JUDICIARY AND CONSTITUTIONAL POLITICS: VIEWS FROM THE BENCH 79-86 (Chatham, NJ: Chatham House Publishers, Inc., 1985).

8. Danelski, *supra* n. 6.

9. Rohde, *Policy Goals, Strategic Choice and Majority Opinion Assignments in the U.S. Supreme Court*, 16 MIDWEST J. OF POL. SCI. 652-682, 679 (1972).

10. Murphy, *supra* n. 6, at 84.

11. Slotnick, *Who Speaks for the Court? Majority Opinion Assignment from Taft to Burger*, 23 AM. J. OF POL. SCI. 60-77, at 75 (1979).

12. Rohde, *supra* n. 9, at 658.

13. Danelski, *supra* n. 6.

14. Ulmer, *The Use of Power in the Supreme Court*, 30 J. PUB. L. 49-67 (1970); McLauchlan, *Ideology and Conflict in Supreme Court Opinion Assignment, 1946-1962*, 25 W. POL. Q. 16-27 (1972). McLauchlan found a pattern of overassignment to justices occupying the position closest to the minority in close cases (the pattern was more pronounced in civil liberties than in economic cases), which he construed as evidence of a strategy to reduce conflict among the members of the Court. Although Rohde found that there was some advantage to being closest to the dissenters and concluded that the "marginality hypothesis does, at one point, add to our understanding of the process" he actually found only limited support for the hypothesis. The marginal justice had an advantage only where he was both marginal and a member of the group closest to the assigner. Rohde, *supra* n. 9. Brenner also questioned the argument that the opinion assigner favors the marginal justice in order to prevent defection in *Strategic Choice and Opinion Assignment on the U.S. Supreme Court: A Reexamination*, 35 W. POL. Q. 204-211 (1982).

15. Brenner and Spaeth, *Majority Opinion Assignments and the*

Maintenance of the Original Coalition on the Warren Court, 32 AM. J. OF POL. SCI. 72-81,77-78 (1988). Brenner and Spaeth compared original coalitions with final votes using the docket books of three members of the Warren Court. Although they found that the marginal justice in minimum winning original coalitions was assigned more opinions than could have been expected by chance, their analysis also revealed that the assignment of the majority opinion to the marginal justice did not increase the probability that the minimum winning original coalition would survive.

16. Rohde, *supra* n. 9. Ulmer found that closeness in terms of policy preferences of the assigner and the assignee was an influence on the assignments of Chief Justice Warren. *The Use of Power in the Supreme Court*, 30 J. PUB. L. 49-67 (1970).

17. *Policy Goals, Strategic Choices, and Majority Opinion Assignments in the U.S. Supreme Court: A Replication*, 18 AM. J. POL. SCI. 713-724 (1974).

18. Slotnick, *supra* n. 11.

19. Spaeth, *Distributive justice: majority opinion assignments in the Burger Court*, 67 JUDICATURE 299-304 (1984).

20. *Id.* at 303-304.

21. Rehnquist, THE SUPREME COURT: HOW IT WAS HOW IT IS 297 (New York: William Morrow and Company, Inc. 1987).

22. Slotnick, *supra* n. 11; Spaeth, *supra* n. 19.

23. Rohde, *supra* n. 9, at 681.

24. I used Harold Spaeth's United States Supreme Court Judicial Data Base, Phase I.

25. A justice's OAR is calculated by dividing the number of majority opinions by the number of his or her votes with the majority and multiplying the result by 100 to obtain a percentage. Slotnick, who devised the OAR, pointed out that it is a measure that is sensitive to a justice's availability for assignment of majority opinions. A justice who was in the majority infrequently would not be likely to write as many majority opinions as a justice who voted with the chief a great deal of the time. Slotnick, *supra* n. 11, at 63, n. 4. It was for that reason that I elected to use OARs in addition to the absolute number of opinions assigned.

26. Rubin and Melone, *Justice Antonin Scalia: a First Year Freshman Effect?*, 72 JUDICATURE 98-102 (1988).

27. *See*, Slotnick, *supra* n. 11, at 66, n. 6; Spaeth, *supra* n. 19, at 302.

28. Spaeth, *supra* n. 19, at 302.

29. The OAR was used to determine Rehnquist's CRV.

30. *See* Slotnick, *supra* n. 11, at 62, n. 2.

31. Spaeth, *supra* n. 19, at 303.

32. Slotnick, *supra* n. 11, at 69, Table 3.

33. Spaeth, *supra* n. 19, at 304.

34. Rohde, *supra* n. 9; McLauchlan, *supra* n. 14; Rathjen, *supra* n. 17.

35. I have used the conventions that scholars of judicial behavior have developed for scalogram analysis. *See*, Rohde and Spaeth, SUPREME COURT DECISION MAKING ch. 4 (San Francisco, CA: W.H. Freeman, 1976); Goldman and Jahnige, THE FEDERAL COURTS AS A POLITICAL SYSTEM. Third Edition ch. 5 (New York: Harper and Row, 1985); Murphy and Tanenhaus, THE STUDY OF PUBLIC LAW ch. 5 (New York: Random House. 1972).

36. The scale scores of the justices for each of the scales were as follows.

Criminal Procedure

1986 Term		1987&88 Terms	
Rehnquist	-1.000	Rehnquist	-.953
White	-.939	Kennedy	-1.000
O'Connor	-.878	O'Connor	-.867
Scalia	-.758	White	-.767
Powell	-.575	Scalia	-.767
Stevens	.152	Blackmun	.023
Blackmun	.697	Stevens	.349
Marshall	.939	Brennan	.809
Brennan	1.000	Marshall	.907

Civil Rights

1986 Term		1987&88 Terms	
Rehnquist	-.900	Rehnquist	-1.000
Scalia	-.900	Kennedy	-.826
White	-.800	Scalia	-.533
O'Connor	-.500	White	-.354
Powell	.300	O'Connor	-.333
Stevens	.263	Stevens	.290
Blackmun	.700	Blackmun	.806
Brennan	.900	Brennan	.935
Marshall	1.000	Marshall	.935

First Amendment

1986 Term		1987&88 Terms	
Rehnquist	-1.000	Rehnquist	-1.000
Scalia	-.556	O'Connor	-1.000
White	-.333	White	-.684
Stevens	-.111	Kennedy	-.333
O'Connor	.111	Scalia	-.158
Powell	.111	Stevens	-.053
Blackmun	1.000	Blackmun	.368
Brennan	1.000	Brennan	1.000
Marshall	1.000	Marshall	1.000

37. See, for example, Howard, *Mr. Justice Murphy: The Freshmen Years*, 18 VAND. L. REV. 473-505, 476 (1965) and Rubin and Melone, *supra* n. 26, at 99. But see Slotnick, supra n. 11, at 72, finding no apprenticeship period in opinion assignments.

38. The expected proportion of opinions was determined in the following way. The total number of assignments made by the chief justice in the three issue areas was 161. 39 of those were decided by a vote of 9 (Rehnquist had 9 choices in 39 cases) 19 were decided by a vote of 8, 13 by a vote of 7, 35 by a vote of 6, 53 by a vote of 5, and 2 by a vote of 4. Thus, 9(39/161)+8(19/161)+7(13/161)+6(35/161)+5 (53/161)+4(2/161)=6.68. The chief justice had 6.68 opinion writers available per case. The probability that he would assign to any two: 2/6.68'.299. Thus, the expected proportion of opinions assigned to either Position 1 or 2 was .299.

39. Rathjen, *supra* n. 9.

40. *See, for example*, National League of Cities v Usery, 426 U.S. 833 (1976); Davis, JUSTICE REHNQUIST AND THE CONSTITUTION (Princeton, NJ: Princeton University Press, 1989).

The spirit of dissent

Although there is a bias in the legal community against judicial dissent, dissenting opinions function analogously to acts of civil disobedience in bringing about needed legal and political changes.

by J. Louis Campbell III

Since the advent of collegial courts minority-view judges have used published dissents to register their objections and reservations to majority judgments.[1] This has been particularly true of the U.S. Supreme Court, where, in fact, the first reported opinion of a justice was a dissent, coming as the justices delivered their opinions *seriatim*.[2] Chief Justice Marshall, though highly regarded for his dissent in *Ogden v. Saunders*,[3] fostered a preference against dissents and secured the Court tradition of one majority opinion standing as the last word on the law.

Marshall's leadership and a rather homogeneous tribunal militated against dissents for some time.[4] Then with Marshall's death and the ascendency of Chief Justice Taney (1836), the era of dissent began. The great dissenters in the Court's history have since included some of our most illustrious justices, such as Holmes, Brandeis, and Douglas.

Notwithstanding, there remains a bias in the legal community against dissent. There seems in particular to be some question about its efficacy. Prominent legal philosopher H. L. A. Hart has written that "A supreme tribunal has the last word in saying what the law is, and when it has said it, the statement that the Court was 'wrong' has no consequence within the system: no one's rights are thereby altered."[5]

Nevertheless, statements that the Court was wrong, I propose, do have important consequences apart from direct and immediate alteration of rights and duties, and these consequences may be found within the system. Dissenting opinions function analogously to acts of civil disobedience in offering protest and securing systemic change. "Institutional disobedience" is a good term to characterize

dissents and their authors. That is, in writing and publishing dissents, judges are protesting as authorities within institutional roles, analogous to civilians in non-institutional roles who physically enact their protest. Dissent can influence change in both the judicial system and the larger political milieu, and many legal professionals have provided corroborative evidence for this theory of dissent.

The roots of civil disobedience

First, what is "civil disobedience"? Civil disobedience is an appeal to controlling authorities and to the general public "to alter certain laws or policies that the minority takes to be incompatible with the fundamental principles of morality, principles to which it believes the majority is committed,"[6] according to Marshall Cohen. In self-governing communities its essence is:

... propositional, stipulative, suggestive. Discovery, harangue, advocacy are its instruments of corrective persuasion of the beliefs and desires of others ... Its central function is not directly to change the law ... by forcing new policy ... its function is to *locate* wrong, *inform* the public of such wrong, and *persuade* the electorate to reconsider.[7]

Perception, identification, criticism, persuasion—these are the mechanisms of civil disobedience as a means of social change, influence, and coordination toward a point of view. It is not purposeless, reckless, or anarchistic. On the contrary, the civil disobedient has chosen to participate in democratically sanctioned processes for democratically praiseworthy ends.

A civil disobedient person serves two such democratic ends: First, the reinforcement of the ideal of self-choice, the freedom to arrive at one's own perspective, "a fundamental condition of free government and of all moral judgment;" and second, persuasion of others to join the cause celebre.[8] The cause of the disobedient is:

concerned with improving the existing legal system. He envisions his role as therapeutic rather than destructive. He believes that the ideal of justice is being violated in some way in the existing laws . . . He therefore makes of himself a martyr, bearing witness to the truth, and hoping thereby to educate and enlighten and to move men of good will.[9]

The civilly disobedient person appeals to the democratic ethos:

[He is] a man who defies that law out of conscience or moral belief . . . If he acts out of conscience it is important to remember that he appeals to it as well . . . . It is to protest the fact that the majority has violated these principles that the disobedient undertakes his disobedience.[10]

The form of civil disobedience need not, and indeed some would argue that it must not, be violent. It is a "quiet, symbolic act . . . aimed at peaceful revision of attitude."[11] Acts that run counter to the majority can be justified as civil disobedience only when they are acts of political speech, appeals, a form of persuasion as opposed to coercion.[12]

Institutional disobedience

It is this nonviolent quality of civil disobedience that has allowed modern democracies to provide *institutional* means of protest to minorities in recognition of their prerogative to oppose majority viewpoints.[13] This type of dissension can "observe, or follow, lines of political 'due process.'"[14] In fact, contemporary scholars suggest that instead of perceiving civil disobedience as essentially contrary to the ideas of authority and obligation, "we might consider building into the very idea of authority and obligation in a democracy a conception of allowable civil disobedience."[15] Dissenting opinions, indeed, may be seen in just this kind of light, as inherent, disparate, due process "acts" allowed to system authorities on behalf of minority viewpoints, or in other words, as institutional disobedience.

Dissents are protestual, propositional, stipulative, and suggestive in appealing to the authority of conscience, with the hope of a future remedy for a present wrong. Thus they militate against monolithic solidarity in the judiciary, reflecting the innate nature and exigence of law in contemporary society as a mosaic. Dissents offer an avenue of representation for perceptions at variance with the dominant vision. They locate wrong in the majority, inform the audience of such wrong, and persuade the audience to reconsider.[16] Thus in this respect dissents function analogously to civil disobedience in our society.

Further, as the world changes so must the law. And the dissenting opinion is "one of the processes that aids that development as the law meets and solves new situations."[17] The dissent initiates and presses change in the system, again analogous to civil disobedience. Without the judicial dissent, "boulders which are fused together with time-defying cement form a wall which could some day obstruct the passage of a needed road to the City of the Realized Hope of Man."[18]

Though there may be various bases for dissent, many dissents are grounded in moral or ethical terms, just as is civil disobedience. These subsets of judicial opinion move beyond the purely legal world "by placing the imprimatur of respectable moral leadership upon controversial social or economic reforms."[19] The appeal is to conscience. Justice Douglas wrote that dissents "may salvage for tomorrow the principle that was sacrificed or forgotten today. Their discussion and propagation of the great principles of our Charter may keep the democratic ideal alive in the days of regressions, uncertainty, despair."[20]

Contesting the imprimatur of infallibility for majority opinions, dissents are foresighted.[21] Chief Justice Hughes pointed to the conscience inherent in minority opinions, regardless of specific rationale, when he wrote, "The dissent is an appeal to the brooding spirit of the law, to the intelligence of a future day . . . ."[22] Advocacy is the instrument of this corrective persuasion. Dissents are evidence that the minority view has been heard—the wrong located, the public informed and persuaded. Though the minority view has not triumphed, it has been endowed with a quality of permanence for constant review by sympathetic advocates and system authorities.

The symbolic means of protest is an area of difference between civil and institutional disobedients. Civil disobedients use acts to oppose, such as sit-ins. Judges, on the other hand, use rhetoric. This difference does not make either civil or institutional disobedience inherently more effective. Rather, it reflects a strategic awareness of which symbols, acts or words, can best facilitate protest given the different contexts.

Civil disobedients resort to action because language has failed to effectively oppose. "Mere speech may fail to produce change in many situations because it does not demand a response."[23] In order to elicit a response, protesters act. In the civil context, this works well as a tool of opposition.

Language and the law

It is fitting that institutionally disobedient persons oppose through rhetoric the majority encroachment of their values. Law and language are inherently related. By stressing conflict resolution through procedure, ceremony, and rhetoric, "legal institutions provide the methods both for symbolically encouraging change while preserving continuity, and for symbolically assuring stability while fostering change."[24] Specifically, it has been argued that "language is the greatest instrument of social control . . . . law is only a division of language."[25] Why is it that language has such power?

In part, the answer lies in the nature of rhetoric. "words are important as words in that they represent symbolically and artificially an order which exists nowhere in the actual daily lives of persons."[26] Words are able to represent a sense of order because they continuously interact with the human psyche. We naturally experience a need for order, for structure. This need arises out of our normal experience of life, its vastness, complexity, variety. Words organize our thoughts, feelings, responses. They are therefore able to produce a sense of satisfaction, a reduction of the psychological tension arising from our need for order in the face of massive quantities and qualities of stimuli. Language acts as a screen through which our inherent needs, particularly for order, can be filtered. This essential nature of language is of critical significance in law, and makes words appropriate tools of protesting an order imposed by the majority, and designing an alternative order.

A second reason why rhetoric is appropriate deals with its communicative advantage. Laws, as rules and guidelines, must be persuasively communicated to those for whom they will serve as frameworks, and they must be communicated in such a way that the person absorbing them understands that they apply to a variety of situations.[27] The two main devices available for communicating are the example and rhetoric.[28]

H. L. A. Hart argues that examples are imprecise

means of communication. While they may be couched in explicit or implicit "do as I do" directives, they still "may leave open ranges of possibilities, and hence of doubt, as to what is intended."[29] Walter Probert agrees that examples are too indeterminant left embedded in concrete with the actor. Others then must speculate on intent, on what will be approved, and on the extent to which one's behavior must trace that of the actor in order to rightly follow the guidelines.[30]

In contrast, language may offer a clearer, more dependable means of communicating standards. The rules are no longer embedded within the confines of a single actor. They are contained in words and language structures about which there is broad agreement as to meaning. The observer, the respondent, can know what he or she must do in the future and at what time. "He has only to recognize instances of clear verbal terms to 'subsume' particular facts under general classificatory heads and draw a simple syllogistic conclusion."[31]

The power of judicial dissent

This theory of dissent sounds rather romantic, relying on such supporting phrases as "the brooding spirit of the law," "the City of the Realized Hope of Man," and other idealized references. But beyond the romance of dissent are important, substantive, systemic effects. The primary persuasive objective of disobedience is remedy—the remedy of a perceived wrong. And the remedy has been applied successfully in numerous cases. The dissent of a Supreme Court justice avoids the civil disobedient's scorn as "mere speech" that does not demand a response, and it can "heavily influence the allocation of values among relevant competing interests . . . In broader social terms [it] may modify or enhance the legitimacy that relevant publics in the larger social system accord a decision, a policy, or a law."[32] Three major examples in the area of civil and human rights alone, where dissents eventually became the majority viewpont, add substance to the romance.[33]

In *Plessy v. Ferguson,*[34] the Supreme Court upheld the East Louisiana Railway's right to require Homer Plessy to ride in the "separate but equal" Colored" car of the train, contrary to Plessy's wish. Justice John Marshall Harlan dissented, describing "the thin disguise of 'equal' accommodations" for what it really was, a veil of racism. Fifty-six years later, in 1952, the Court began hearing the series of cases known as *Brown v. Board of Education.*[35] And the core premise of Harlan's dissent became law—separate was no longer to be considered equal. Justice Harlan's view of segregation as unconstitutional and a social evil became the majority position.

In December 1938 Smith Belts, an unemployed farm worker on relief, was charged with armed robbery and assault. At arraignment, Belts, unable to afford a private counsel, asked Judge Forsythe to appoint an attorney for him. The judge informed him that attorneys were appointed only for indigent defendants charged with murder or rape. Declaring his innocence, Belts saw no possibility of conducting a jury trial himself, so he waived his right to trial by jury. The court found Belts guilty and handed down a prison sentence. From prison Belts sought a writ of habeas corpus, the denial of which he appealed to the Supreme Court. In *Belts v. Brady,*[36] the Court found no violation of due process. Justice Hugo Black dissented, supported by justices Douglas and Murphy, arguing for the right of counsel for the poor as a safeguard of freedom. Twenty-one years later, in *Gideon v. Wainwright,*[37] analogous circumstances saw Mr. Black's dissent become a majority position, and the right to counsel became a cornerstone in American law.

A final example from the many available is Justice Douglas' dissent in *Dennis v. United States.*[38] Here 11 persons were convicted under an extremely broad Smith Act for conspiring to organize a Communist Party and to advocate the forcible overthrow of the U.S. government. The Supreme Court upheld the conviction of the 11 with justices Black and Douglas dissenting. While Mr. Black's opinion was brief, revolving around an absolute view of the First Amendment, Mr. Douglas wrote a more detailed argument on the clear and present danger test. Six years later, after the close of the McCarthy Era, a similar case reached the Supreme Court. In *Yates v. United States,*[39] however, the Court moved largely within Mr. Douglas' preview. Mr. Douglas concurred in part and dissented in part. Notwithstanding, the guarantee of freedom of advocacy had been substantially restored.

Courts are not alone in accepting the persuasion of non-majority opinions. Legislatures frequently accept remedial measures advocated therein.[40] Justice Iredell's dissent in *Chisolm v. Georgia,*[41] became part of the Constitution as the Eleventh Amendment.[42] The Dred Scott dissenters' arguments became the foundations for the Thirteenth, Four-

teenth, and Fifteenth Amendments to the Constitution.[43] Justice Story's dissent in *Cary v. Curtis*[44] was enacted into law by Congress in 36 days—before the publication of the volume containing his opinion.[45]

Judicial dissents may also influence lawyers. Advocates note not only the majority opinions and the ratio therein, but also the non-controlling, non-majority messages.[46] "Essentially retrospective, [lawyers] search for a comforting precedent, whether it be in a majority or dissenting opinion."[47] Prospectively, lawyers may draw lines of difference among majority and minority opinions and justices, and anticipate future results and alignments under changed facts.[48] Thus, judicial history has shown that non-majority opinions have "exercised a corrective and reforming influence upon the law."[49]

Dissent has potential effects outside the judicial system, as well, in a larger political context. Public allies of the ideology embodied in the dissent find image enhancement in this form of due process disobedience a positive step in resolving discord. Rehetoric from authorities with status also tends to defuse more violent acts of civil disobedience, and to calm those who must be persuaded.

Official support of one group's claim acts as a positive statement of the stature of that group's subculture . . . . The use of supportive rhetoric . . . would allow opponents of the functioning ideology to strive for and occasionally gain official support while reducing the overt threat to the governmentally sanctioned value set.[50]

Perceptions of dissent

What the dissenter intends to do by dissenting may be identified in part by what he or she says. But another crucial element in recognizing intent is what members of the legal community believe about the dissents. What are mutual beliefs about the genre of judicial opinion labeled, "dissent"?

The metaphors used when discussing dissents are important clues to perception. More than a literary device, the metaphor represents a way of seeing, a way of believing. It symbolizes inferences the thinker has made through comparison or analogy regarding the subject.

For example, Richard Stephens, writing in the *Florida Law Review,* perceived authors of dissents "acting" as advocates.[51] Here, the metaphor is "acting," and Stephens sees dissenters as engaging in physical behavior, with the implicit comparison to civil disobedients who enact their protest.

Justice Douglas conjured images of civil disobedience when he wrote:

It is the right of dissent, not the right or duty to conform, which gives dignity, worth, and individuality to man. As Carl Sandburg recently said, 'There always ought to be beatniks in a culture, hollering about the respectables.'[52]

Thus we have judicial dissenters analogyzed to non-conformity, individualistic "beatniks hollering about the respectables." Mr. Douglas' view of dissent must surely have flowed from his view of the Supreme Court's role in our cultural lives. He wrote, "The Court that *raises its hand against the mob* may be temporarily unpopular; but it soon wins the confidence of the nation. The court that fails to *stand before the mob* is not worthy of the great tradition."[53]

Significantly, there are others who share Mr. Douglas' point of view on dissent while avoiding his reputation as a maverick. Benjamin Cardozo used metaphor to characterize judicial dissent:

The voice of the majority may be that of force triumphant, content with the plaudits of the hour, and recking little of the morrow. The dissenter speaks to the future, and his voice is pitched to a key that will carry through the years. Read some of the great dissents . . . and feel after the cooling time of the better part of a century, the glow and fire of a faith that was content to bide its hour. The prophet and martyr do not see the hooting throng. Their eyes are fixed on the eternities.[54]

Again, the dissenter is painted in colors of civil disobedience.

A final example comes from prominent legal philosopher Karl Llewellyn. Though he prefers the quantity of dissents kept at a minimum, as indicated below, he nevertheless acknowledges the quality of dissent in terms familiar to civil disobedients. He writes, "the dissent, by forcing or suggesting full publicity, rides herd on the majority."[55] Thus, from scholars, attorneys, and dissenters we have seen a mutual belief about dissents. These beliefs seem to confirm the analogy of dissent as civil disobedience.

A second mutual belief that lends support to dissent as civil disobedience concerns the reception of dissents. Dissents do not have to be received as illegitimate to be versions of disobedience. On the contrary, due process is at the core of civil disobedience. And judicial dissent is the institutional due process equivalent to civil disobedience. However, acknowledgment of the disparate nature of the act or opinion, its contraction of the mainstream or authoritative will, would seem necessary to warrant the characterization, "disobedience."

And there is evidence of such a belief about dissent.

Though dissents have been published since the earliest cases and are common today, they remain eschewed. Justice Douglas alluded to the controversy surrounding dissents when he wrote, "All of us in recent years have heard and read many criticisms of dissenting . . . opinions. Separate opinions have often been deplored. Courts have been criticized for tolerating them."[56]

Justice Edward White declared that the only purpose a dissent could serve is to weaken the Court.[57] Chief Justice Hughes deprecated "persistent expressions of opinions that do not command the agreement of the Court."[58] Philosopher Llewellyn prefers dissents to be few in number because they tend to diminish a "single way of seeing."[59]

Conclusion

The issue of the importance of judicial dissent has been debated for years. A school of thought represented by H.L.A. Hart has argued that dissents have no system-wide consequences because they do not alter rights in immediate cases. Here, I have disagreed. To the goal of system-wide change is dissent, its effects, and supporting perceptions deployed.

The conclusion that dissents are sources of energy and cogency in law is important in order to understand how and why we carry on the ideals of our system of justice. Knowledge enhances our effectiveness. The makers of dissent need not question the efficacy of their effort, and the audiences of dissent can appreciate the value of the message. They are both engaged in a significant expression of the legal process.

More generally, analysis of any function of that process can offer insight into the process itself, and ease the identification of essential characteristics. The analysis of dissent here points to the conclusion that the law is far more complex than the status of rights in immediate cases. First, law is transcendent—it lives not only within a particular set of facts and determines a particular set of rights, but also rises to a more universal plane of consciousness. It encompasses more than the present in its spread.

Second, and related to the first, law is enduring rather than ephemeral. It lives beyond the cases that animated it; it is progenerative. Its participation in the historical process into which all humans are born gives even aged or overturned law a role in contemporary dynamics. And third, law is infused with humanity, and thus is inherently concerned with symbolizing human yearnings and the persuasion of humans by means of the quintessential human process, the power of language. Dissent calls forth these characteristics of the judicial system, and helps illumine Chief Justice Hughes' perception that the dissent appeals to the "brooding spirit" of the law.

NOTES

This article originally appeared in Volume 66, Number 7, February 1983, pages 304-312.

1. Evans, *The Dissenting Opinion—Its Use and Abuse*, 3 MO. L. REV. 120 (1938).

2. McWhinney, *Judicial Concurrences and Dissents: A Comparative View of Opinion-Writing in Final Appellate Tribunals*, 31 CANADIAN B. REV. 609-610 (1953).

3. 12 Wheat 22, 331 (1827).

4. Ganoe, *The Passing of the Old Dissent*, 21 OR. L. REV. 286 (1942).

5. THE CONCEPT OF LAW 138 (New York: Oxford University Press, 1961).

6. *Civil Disobedience in a Constitutional Democracy*, PHILOSOPHIC EXCHANGE 104 (1970). "Morality" here broadly refers to that which is considered "good" or "valuable." Additional discussions may be found in Power, *Civil Disobedience as Functional Opposition*, 34 J. POL. 37 (1972); and *On Civil Disobedience in Recent American Democratic Thought*, 64 AM. POL. SCI. REV. 35 (1970); Spitz, *Democracy and the Problem of Civil Disobedience*, 48 AM. POL. SCI. REV. 386 (1954).

7. Black, *The Two Faces of Civil Disobedience*, 1 SOC. THEORY & PRAC. 21 (1970).

8. *Id.* at 22.

9. Morano, *Civil Disobedience and Legal Responsibility*, 5 J. VALUE INQUIRY 193 (1971).

10. Cohen, *supra* n. 6, at 99.

11. Black, *supra* n. 7, at 22.

12. Frazier, *Between Obedience and Revolution*, 1 PHIL. & PUB. AFF. 316 (1972).

13. Endres, *Civil Disobedience and Modern Democracy*, 43 THOUGHT 503 (1968).

14. Martin, *Civil Disobedience*, 80 ETHICS 136 (1970).

15. *Id.*

16. "Persuade" here refers to the process of influencing, not necessarily the result.

17. Simmons, *Use and Abuse of Dissenting Opinions*, 16 LA. L. REV. 498 (1956).

18. Musmanno, *Dissenting Opinions*, 6 KAN. L. REV. 411 (1958).

19. Davis and Reynolds, *Juridical Cripples: Plurality Opinions in the Supreme Court*, 1974 DUKE L. J. 63 (1974).

21. Carter, *Dissenting Opinions*, 4 HASTINGS L. J. 121 (1953).

22. Hughes, as quoted in Edwards, *Dissenting Opinions of Mr. Justice Smith*, 34 U. DET. L. J. 82 (1956).

23. Frazier, *supra* n. 12, at 317.

24. Ingber, *Procedure, Ceremony and Rhetoric: The Minimization of Ideological Conflict in Deviance Control*, 56 B. U. L. REV. 321 (1976).

25. Williams, *Language and the Law*, 62 L. Q. REV. 71 (1945).

26. Pranger, *An Explanation for Why Final Political Authority is Necessary*, 60 AM. POL. SCI. REV. 996 (1966).

27. Probert, *Law Through the Looking Glass of Language and Communicative Behavior*, 20 J. LEGAL EDUC. 51 (1968).

28. Hart, *supra* n. 5, at 121.

29. *Id.* at 220.

30. Probert, *supra* n. 27, at 51.

31. *Id.*

32. Ulmer, *Dissent Behavior and the Social Background of Supreme Court Justices*, 32 J. POL. 581 (1970).

33. These examples, along with others, are discussed in detail in Barth, PROPHETS WITH HONOR: GREAT DISSENTS AND GREAT DISSENTERS IN THE SUPREME COURT (New York: Random House, 1974, 1975). For additional examples *see* Carter, *supra* n. 21; Brown, *A Dissenting Opinion of Mr. Justice Story Enacted as Law Within Thirty-Six Days*, 26 VA. L. REV. 759 (1940); Ganoe, *supra* n. 4, at 295; Lashly and Rava, *The Supreme Court Dissents*, 28 WASH. U. L. Q. 191 (1943); Sanders, *The Role of Dissenting Opinions in Louisiana*, 23 LA. L. REV. 676 (1963); and McWhinney, *supra* n. 2, at 611.

34. 163 U.S. 537 (1896).

35. 347 U.S. 483 (1954).

36. 316 U.S. 455 (1942).

37. 372 U.S. 335 (1963).

38. 341 U.S. 494 (1951).

39. 354 U.S. 298 (1957).

40. Brown, *supra* n. 33, at 759.

41. 2 U.S. 419 (1793).

42. Carter, *supra* n. 21, at 119.

43. Musmanno, *supra* n. 18, at 140.

44. 3 Howard 236, 252 (1845).

45. Brown, *supra* n. 33, at 760. For additional examples *see* Fuld, *Voices of Dissent*, 62 COL. L. REV. 927 (1962).

46. Freedman, *Dissenting Opinions and Justice Musmanno*, 30 TEMP. L. Q. 253 (1957).

47. Sanders, *supra* n. 33, at 675.

48. Jackson, *Dissenting Opinions*, 100 PITTSBURGH L. J. 3 (1952).

49. Carter, *supra* n. 21, at 118.

50. Ingber, *supra* n. 24, at 269.

51. Stephens, *Function of Concurring and Dissenting Opinions in Courts of Last Resort*, 5 U. FLA. L. REV. 404 (1952).

52. Douglas, AMERICA CHALLENGED 4-5 (Princeton, NJ: Princeton University Press, 1960).

53. Douglas, WE THE JUDGES 443 (Garden City, NY: Doubleday, 1956).

54. Cardozo, LAW AND LITERATURE AND OTHER ESSAYS AND ADDRESSES 36 (New York: Harcourt, Brace & Co., 1931).

55. Llewellyn, THE COMMON LAW TRADITION: DECIDING APPEALS 26 (Boston: Little, Brown & Co., 1960).

56. Douglas, *supra* n. 20, at 104.

57. Pollack v. Farmers Loan and Trust Co., 157 U.S. 429, 608.

58. Federal Trade Comm'n v. Beechnut Co., 257 U.S. 441, 456 (1922).

59. Llewellyn, *supra* n. 55, at 463. For a discussion of non-majority opinions as anathema to Continental European jurists, *see* Dumbauld, *Dissenting Opinions in International Adjudication*, 90 U. PA. L. REV. 929 (1943); *see also* Fuld, *supra* n. 45, at 924-925.

The Courts and Their Publics
Public Opinion and the Media

INTRODUCTION

The judiciary is the most invisible branch of American government and the branch about which the public knows the least. Since that is the case, the media have a uniquely important informational role in this domain and, indeed, they may be the exclusive source of information about the courts for most Americans. In this section of readings we focus on the complex of relationships among the courts, public opinion, and the media.

In "Public opinion and the Rehnquist Court," Thomas Marshall explores many facets of the interface between the Court and the public. Supporters of the Rehnquist Court have asserted that it is properly majoritarian—that is, it tends to defer to the legislative choices of elected legislatures. Marshall argues, however, that legislative choices do not necessarily reflect majoritarianism if what we really mean by that elusive concept is the public will. Indeed, utilizing public opinion polls that measure attitudes on issues analogous to those decided by Supreme Court cases, Marshall finds the Rehnquist Court to be slightly *less* majoritarian than its predecessors for which similar data is available. Only slightly more than half of the Rehnquist Court's rulings on issues analogous to public opinion questions appear to be majoritarian. Like other analysts of public opinion and the Court, Marshall examines the ability of judicial rulings to alter public views. Here again, his findings are sobering. "The Rehnquist Court can no more influence American public opinion than could earlier Courts. As other studies have also suggested, the Court's rulings typically either produce no significant poll swings . . . or . . . small shifts away from the Court's position."

Marshall's analysis also notes a modest drop in public confidence in the Court and its maintenance of a middling position vis-a-vis the confidence levels enjoyed by other institutions. The lack of importance the Court places on public opinion is also documented. The ultimate irony of this interesting study is, of course, the picture it draws of a Court that often praises majoritarian democracy while its very decisions often violate majority sentiment.

The nature of public opinion about the courts is, in large measure, a reflection of what information the public receives through media coverage. In "Media coverage of the courts: improving but still not adequate," journalist David Shaw surveys some of the major criticisms of press coverage based on interviews with attorneys, judges, academics, and other journalists. Among the problems highlighted are inadequate followup of stories, neglect of the broad issues underlying specific cases, inconsistency, and inadequacy in the scope of media attention. At bottom, the press pursues a result orientation, who wins and who loses, but does not pay appropriate attention to the legal system and the larger judicial process per se. Shaw sees coverage improving but finds a great deal still lacking.

Among the media covering the Court, as in other domains, television has emerged as the public's most utilized and trusted source of information. Ethan Katsh's study, "The Supreme Court beat: how television covers the Court," summarizes the nature of TV coverage during a five-year period of Supreme Court decision making. Large gaps exist in television coverage that Katsh attributes, in part, to the visual nature and needs of the medium. Indeed, only about one in five Supreme Court decisions received some mention during the period under study, with television's emphasis placed on cases involving individual rights, including coverage of *every* abortion decision rendered. Katsh utilizes a measure of case importance to demonstrate that newsworthiness and importance are not necessarily the same thing. Interestingly, Katsh found no significant differences among the three major networks in their Supreme Court coverage.

ABC News' Tim O'Brien offers a rejoinder to Katsh in "Yes, but . . . ," and he demonstrates that the evening newscasts, Katsh's sole focus, represent but a small slice of the television coverage the Court receives from the networks' news divisions. For the most part, however, O'Brien shares Katsh's concerns about media coverage. He underlines, however, that the problems are not all the fault of the network but, rather, reflect institutional obstacles that stand in the way of the press doing a better job. According to O'Brien, "Today . . . the justices seem more intent on closing their doors than on opening them. The Supreme Court remains the most secretive and inaccessible of governmental institutions."

In "Best kept secrets of the judiciary" O'Brien discusses further numerous issues residing at the media/court interface. In a prospective vein he underlines the necessity for enhancement of public awareness and understanding of the work and importance of courts and judges. "My premise . . . is that the more people know about courts, the more they will appreciate and respect them."

Public opinion and the Rehnquist Court

Although often viewed as a majoritarian Court, a comparison of recent Rehnquist Court rulings with nationwide polls suggests that it has no more often reflected American public opinion than did earlier Courts.

by Thomas R. Marshall

A s the Rehnquist Court begins its fifth term, judicial scholars have already begun to pay serious attention to the new Court. Different accounts have examined the Rehnquist Court's voting patterns,[1] opinion assignment patterns,[2] increasing conservativism,[3] and renewed reliance on judicial restraint and deference to the popularly elected branches.[4]

With the retirement of Justice William Brennan and the confirmation of Justice David Souter, the Rehnquist Court's focus on issues of federalism, its tendency toward judicial restraint, and its ideological conservatism seem likely to accelerate. As one observer has noted, the Court's interest in minority rights and equality may well be waning.[5]

But is the Rehnquist Court a majoritarian Court? That question may be answered in two different ways. The first approach focuses on whether the Court typically defers to the decisions of popularly elected branches, such as state legislatures, local agencies, and the Congress. The second approach focuses instead on whether the Court's rulings reflect American public opinion, as measured by scientific nationwide polls.[6]

Most judicial scholars agree that the early Rehnquist Court moved strongly—if unevenly[7]—toward deference to state legislatures and local laws. An examination of nationwide public opinion polls, however, suggests that the early Rehnquist Court has not been a particularly majoritarian Court, compared with other Courts since the mid-1930s.

This article takes a preliminary look at public opinion and the early Rehnquist Court, in part, based on specific Court rulings which can be compared with scientific, random-sampling national polls. Pollsters often write questions to tap attitudes on important Supreme Court cases.[8] During the Rehnquist Court's first four terms, 14 rulings can be directly compared or matched with comparable poll items.

The available polling evidence on the Rehnquist Court goes well beyond simply comparing individual Court rulings with public opinion poll items. Polling organizations have also tapped attitudes toward the Supreme Court in several other ways. Pollsters have measured public approval toward the Court, compared with other American institutions such as Congress or the military. Available polls also measure public awareness of Supreme Court rulings. Less frequently, pollsters have asked an identically worded question, both before and after a Court ruling, or else several times after a ruling. These repeat questions permit attitude changes to be tracked over time in order to see if Court rulings appear to influence public opinion.[9]

Public opinion analysis has been used increasingly in judicial research, particularly in analyzing the U.S. Supreme Court. Since modern polls first appeared during the mid-1930s, polls have provided a methodology for examining public attitudes toward the Supreme Court and its rulings and to explore public awareness of and reactions to Court rulings.[10]

Representing public opinion

Overall, the early Rehnquist Court was consistent with American public opinion in slightly over half—57 per cent, or 8 of 14—of the rulings which could be matched with nationwide polls. In the remaining six (of 14) rulings, the Court's ruling contra-

Figure 1   Rehnquist Court rulings, by public opinion poll approval

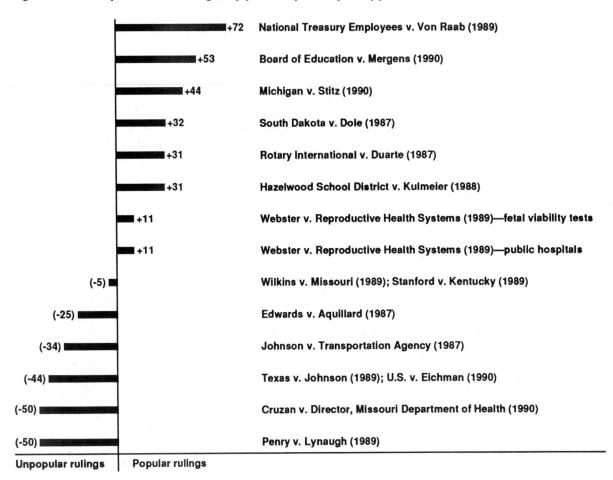

| Unpopular rulings | Popular rulings |

dicted available polls. This 57 per cent consistent figure for the Rehnquist Court's first four terms is slightly lower than the 63 per cent consistent figure observed for the 1934/35-1985/86 Court terms, or the 62 per cent consistent observed for the Burger Court alone.[11]

The 14 rulings examined here ranged the full gamut from very unpopular rulings to equally popular rulings. Several of these rulings rank among the Supreme Court's historically least popular ones—such as the flag-burning dispute, in *Texas v. Johnson* (1989) and *U.S. v. Eichman* (1990); the death penalty for mentally retarded convicts, in *Penry v. Lynaugh* (1989); or discontinued medical treatment for terminally ill patients, in *Cruzan v. Director, Missouri Department of Health* (1990).[12] By contrast, equally large poll majorities agreed with the Supreme Court's decision concerning student religious groups' use of school facilities, in *Board of*

Education v. Mergens (1990); drug testing for safety employees, in *National Treasury Employees Union v. Von Raab* (1989); or random police searches for drunk drivers, in *Michigan v. Stitz* (1990). Figure 1 illustrates the striking diversity in how well, or how poorly, these 14 Rehnquist Court rulings agreed with nationwide polls.

Of the 10 justices who served during these four terms, some agreed with nationwide public opinion more often than others. Individually, justices Rehnquist and White most often agreed with available polls—79 per cent or 71 per cent consistent, respectively. Justices Brennan and Marshall least often reflected nationwide public opinion majorities (or pluralities)—doing so in only 36 per cent or 43 per cent of their votes, respectively.

Because so few decisions can as yet be matched with polls for the Rehnquist Court, it may be more meaningful to examine blocs of justices' votes collectively rather than the separate votes of individual justices. Five justices (Rehnquist, Kennedy, White, Scalia, and O'Connor) all cast ideologically conservative votes in three-fourths or more of their votes on the 14 rulings counted here, forming the Court's "conservative bloc." The remaining five justices (Brennan, Marshall, Stevens, Blackmun, and Powell) all cast ideologically liberal votes in four-fifths or more of the votes examined here, forming the Court's "liberal bloc."[13]

When the two opposing blocs' votes are combined and compared, a significant difference appears. The early Rehnquist Court's conservative bloc was more likely to agree with nationwide polls than the Court's liberal bloc (see Table 1).

Perhaps surprisingly, the early Rehnquist Court represented the attitudes of different demographic or social groups about equally well. As earlier research has suggested, American social and demographic groups are seldom sharply polarized on Supreme Court cases. As a result, the Court seldom confronts disputes in which it must agree with some social or demographic groups but disagree with others.[14]

In the single clearest case of conflicting group attitudes, the Court agreed with black majorities and disagreed with white majorities. The 5-4 decision in *Johnson v. Transportation Agency* (1987) agreed with a 56-to-34 per cent majority of American blacks, but disagreed with a 67-to-25 per cent majority of whites, as well as with majorities of all other identified social and demographic groups.[15] Overall, however, the early Rehnquist Court agreed nearly equally as often with majorities or pluralities of different racial, religious, educational, income, gender, age, regional, or political party groups. The Court's rate of agreement ranged from 64 per cent consistency with men, to 50 per cent consistency with college-educated or high-income groups.

Public opinion toward the Rehnquist Court

Available Gallup, Times Mirror, and National Opinion Research Center polls also provide evidence of changing public attitudes toward the early Rehnquist Court. Two of three available over-time polls suggested that the Rehnquist Court suffered drops in public confidence and public approval during its first four years. Deteriorating approval ratings, however, were typical of declining public approval toward most major American institutions during the late 1980s and are not

Table 1 Conservative and liberal blocs' agreement with polls

	Conservative bloc	Liberal bloc
Per cent consistent with nationwide polls	66%	46%
Per cent inconsistent with nationwide polls	34%	54%
Total	100%	100%
Total votes	65	59

A chi-square would be significant at .05.

unique to the Supreme Court alone.

Between July 1986 and August 1990, the Rehnquist Court's confidence ratings dropped by 7 per cent—from 54 per cent confidence to 47 per cent confidence in the annual Gallup Poll survey (combining the responses of those with "a great deal" or "quite a lot" of confidence in the Court). By comparison, public confidence in most American institutions also declined. Public confidence declined for churches and organized religion (by 1 per cent), for banks (by 13 per cent), for public schools (by 4 per cent), for big business (by 3 per cent), for television (by 2 per cent), and most dramatically, for Congress (by 17 per cent). Public confidence improved only for newspapers (by 2 per cent) and for the military (by 5 per cent).

How does the Supreme Court compare with other institutions in public confidence? In the 1990 Gallup Poll item, the Court's 47 per cent approval rating ranked third among 10 major U.S. institutions. The Court's 47 per cent confidence rating was lower than the military (at 68 per cent approval) or the church (56 per cent approval)—but higher than public schools (45 per cent), newspapers, (39 per cent), banks (36 per cent), organized labor (27 per cent), big business (25 per cent), television (25 per cent), or Congress (24 per cent). The Court's middling popularity ranking has not changed since the last Burger Court term—when the Court also ranked third among the same listing of 10 institutions.

The Times Mirror ratings for 1990 reflect similar findings. The Supreme Court won a 65 per cent approval rating (combined "very" or "mostly favorable"). Rating higher than the Court were network TV news (82 per cent), George Bush (at 76 per cent), the reader's daily newspaper (76 per cent), the military (73 per cent), or the UN (70 per cent). By contrast, the Rehnquist Court rated higher than Gorbachev (at 62 per cent), Congress (61 per cent), or the CIA (48 per cent).

The Rehnquist Court's approval ratings varied only slightly for most of America's largest demographic or social groups. The Court was rated most favorably by Republicans (54 per cent combined confidence in the Gallup Poll) and by high income groups (52 per cent confidence). The Rehnquist Court was ranked less favorably by Democrats (only 41 per cent confidence) or Independents (42 per cent), or by low income groups (only 39 per cent confidence).

The poll results

Following is a list of 14 cases decided by the Rehnquist Court. Listed with each case is a question from a public opinion poll and the accompanying results. All the numbers after "approve," "disapprove," "no opinion" or similar categories represent percentages.

Johnson v. Transportation Agency of Santa Clara County, 480 U.S. 616 (March 25, 1987); Gallup: "The U.S. Supreme Court recently ruled that employers may sometimes favor women and members of minorities over better qualified men and whites in hiring and promoting to achieve better balance in their work forces. Do you approve or disapprove of this decision?" Approve—29; Disapprove—63; No opinion—8 (April 10-13, 1987).

Board of Directors of Rotary International v. Rotary Club of Duarte, 481 U.S. 537 (May 4, 1987); and **Roberts v. U.S. Jaycees,** 468 U.S. 609 (July 3, 1984); Gallup: "Do you think that private clubs should or should not have the right to exclude prospective members on the basis of their sex?" Should—32; Should not—63; No opinion—5 (June 8-14, 1987).

Edwards v. Aguillard, 482 U.S. 578 (June 19, 1987); Roper: (Favor or oppose . . .) "requiring that public schools teach the creation theory if they also teach Darwin's theory of evolution?" Favor—55; Oppose—30; Don't know—16 (February 13-27, 1983).

South Dakota v. Dole, 97 L Ed 2d 171 (June 23, 1987); Gallup: "In 1984 a law was passed requiring all states to raise their legal drinking age to 21 or face reductions in federal highway funds. At present, nine states and the District of Columbia permit legal drinking under age 21. Would you favor or oppose having the Federal government start withholding funds from these states if they fail to raise their drinking age to 21 by October first?" Favor—64; Oppose—32; No opinion—4 (June 9-16, 1988).

Hazelwood School District v. Kuhlmeier, 98 L Ed 2d 592 (Jan. 13, 1988); Gallup: "The U.S. Supreme Court recently ruled in favor of more authority for high school principals to censor school-sponsored student publications. Do you believe that this was a good ruling or a bad ruling?" Good ruling—59; Bad ruling—28; Don't know—13 (April 8-10, 1988).

National Treasury Employees Union v. Von Raab, 103 L Ed 2d 685 (March 21, 1989); CBS/New York Times: "Would you favor (such a drug testing policy) for those responsible for the safety of others, such as surgeons, airplane pilots, and police officers, or would that be an unfair invasion of privacy?" Yes, favor—83; No, unfair—11; Depends (vol.)—3; No opinion—3 (August 18-21, 1986).

Texas v. Gregory Lee Johnson, 105 L Ed 2d 342 (June 21, 1989), and **U.S. v. Eichman,** 110 L Ed 2d 287 (June 11, 1990); Los Angeles Times Poll: "Do you approve or disapprove of the recent Supreme Court decision which says that burning the American flag is protected by the U.S. Constitution because it is freedom of speech?" (combined) Approve—26; (combined) Disapprove—70; Not sure—4 (July 3, 1989); see also Gallup: "Do you think we should pass a constitutional amendment to make flag burning illegal or not?" Should pass—68; Should not pass—27; No opinion—5 (June 1989, Gallup for *Newsweek* magazine).

Penry v. Lynaugh, 106 L Ed 2d 256 (June 26, 1989); Harris: "Some people think that persons convicted of murder who have a mental age of less than 18 (or the 'retarded') should not be executed. Other people think that 'retarded' persons should be subject to the death penalty like anyone else. Which is closer to the way you feel, that 'retarded' persons should not be executed, or that 'retarded' persons should be subject to the death penalty like anyone else?" Should not be executed—71; Should be—21; Depends, other—7 (June 3-September 12, 1988); see also Yankelovich: "Do you favor or oppose the death penalty for mentally retarded individuals convicted of serious crimes, such as murder?" Favor—27; Oppose—61; Not sure—12 (June 28, 1989).

Wilkins v. Missouri and **Stanford v. Kentucky,** 106 L Ed 2d 306 (June 26, 1989); Harris: "In many

The Rehnquist Court was also perceived less favorably by nonwhites (only 36 per cent confidence) than by whites (47 per cent confidence). These results reverse the often-noted earlier pattern from the Warren Court era. During the 1950s and 1960s, blacks consistently rated the Warren Court much more favorably than whites, and Southern whites were especially negative toward the Warren Court. Perhaps because of the late Burger and early Rehnquist Courts' less sympathetic rul-

---

states, one of the criminal punishments that is available is the death penalty. Some people think that persons convicted of murder committed when they are under 18 years old should never be executed, while other people think it is right to execute those who are under the age of 18 at the time the crime was committed. Which is closer to the way you think, that young people who are convicted of murder, committed when they are younger than 18, should never be executed, or it is right to execute young people for a murder they committed before they were 18?" Never be executed—49; Right to execute—44; Not sure, refused—7 (June 3-Sept. 12, 1988).

Webster v. Reproductive Health Services, 106 L Ed 2d 410 (July 3, 1989), re: fetal viability tests; Gallup: "(favor or oppose . . .) in cases where the mother is five months pregnant, requiring a test to see if the fetus might survive outside the womb before allowing the abortion?" Favor—52; Oppose—41; No opinion—7 (July 6-9, 1989); see also Los Angeles Times Poll: "The Supreme Court also allowed states to require a test of viability to protect the unborn child. If it should be determined that the fetus could survive, then the abortion could not be performed. Are you in favor of that part of the decision, or are you opposed to it?" Favor—57; Oppose—32; Not sure—11 (July 3, 1989); see also CBS/New York Times: "Here are some possible restrictions on abortion that are being debated in some states. Would you favor or oppose . . . requiring a test to make sure that the fetus is not developed enough to live outside the womb before a woman could have an abortion?" Favor—60; Oppose—28; Depends (vol.)—3; Don't know—9 (July 25-30, 1989).

Webster v. Reproductive Health Services, 106 L Ed 2d 410 (July 3, 1989), re: public hospital restrictions; Gallup: "(favor or oppose . . .) not allowing abortions to be performed in public hospitals unless the abortion is required to save a woman's life?" Favor—54; Oppose—43; No opinion—3 (July 6-9, 1989); see also Los Angeles Times Poll: "The

Court today also gave any state the right to prohibit public employees or public hospitals from performing abortions, except to save the mother's life. Are you in favor of that part of the decision, or are you opposed to it?" Favor—56; Oppose—40; Not sure—4 (July 3, 1989).

Board of Education of Westside Community Schools v. Mergens, 110 L Ed 2d 191 (June 4, 1990); Gallup: (Would or would not object to . . .) "making facilities available after school hours for use by student religious groups or organizations?" Would object—21; Would not object—74; No opinion—5 (October 24-27, 1986).

Michigan Department of State Police v. Stitz, 110 L Ed 2d 412 (June 14, 1990); Roper: "(The United States Constitution guarantees U.S. citizens the right to privacy and protection against unreasonable search. Here is a list of measures being proposed as laws around the country. I want to ask you both whether you approve or disapprove of those measures, and whether you think they are invasions of privacy.) Now for each one of those measures would you tell me whether you approve or disapprove of it, even though it may be an invasion of privacy? . . . Police roadblocks to stop cars and check for drunk drivers?" Approve—71; Disapprove—27; Don't know—2 (February 4-23, 1990); see also Harris: "Do you favor or oppose the use of random police checks at toll booths to check drivers for signs of alcohol and drug intoxication?" Favor—74; Oppose—25; Not sure—1 (January 11-February 11, 1990).

Cruzan v. Director, Missouri Department of Health, 111 L Ed 2d 224 (June 25, 1990); Times Mirror: "If a patient with a terminal disease is unable to communicate and has not made his or her own wishes known in advance, should the closest family member be allowed to decide whether to continue medical treatment, or should a family member not be allowed to make this decision?" Allowed—71; Not allowed—16; Depends (vol.)—5; Don't know—8 (May 1-5, 1990).

ings toward minority claims, however, the earlier pattern of greater approval of the Court by nonwhites had, by the late 1980s, been reversed.[16]

The National Opinion Research Center (NORC) ratings present the most favorable assessment of the Rehnquist Court. In the 1990 NORC ratings, some 37 per cent of Americans expressed "a great deal" of confidence in the Court, while 50 per cent expressed "only some" confidence, and 13 per cent expressed "hardly any" confidence. The 1990 figure of 37 per cent with "a great deal" of confidence was up 6 per cent from the last pre-Rehnquist Court poll in 1986. In the 1990 NORC poll the Court ranked second of 12 institutions rated— behind only the scientific community (with 41 per cent expressing a "great deal" of approval).

Persuading the public

Political scientists have long debated whether Supreme Court decisions can influence (or "manipulate") public opinion. Earlier studies often suggested that the Court's prestige could legitimize its rulings and favorably influence public opinion.[17] More recent empirical studies, however, suggest that while Supreme Court decisions may polarize public attitudes,[18] or influence public approval toward the Court itself,[19] the Court's rulings typically have very little effect on aggregate poll attitudes toward specific issues.[20]

Efforts to untangle the Supreme Court's impact on American public opinion are unusually difficult, in part because of the very small number of identically worded pre- and post-decision polls available for Court rulings. For the early Rehnquist Court, however, some polling evidence is available that reinforces earlier findings that the Court's rulings cannot influence American public opinion favorably. Indeed, in each available instance the polls moved away from the Supreme Court's ruling, not toward it.

Three poll soundings tap attitudes toward the Court's highly visible and controversial abortion rulings in *Webster v. Reproductive Health Services* (1989) and other restrictive abortion rulings.[21] Each of these three polls asked an identical question both before and after the *Webster* ruling, which permitted states to require fetal viability tests and to limit abortions at public hospitals except to save the life of the mother.

The Supreme Court's abortion and flag-burning rulings present the best opportunity to test the Court's impact on American public opinion because these rulings were unusually highly visible. The Supreme Court's 1989 *Webster* and *Johnson* rulings ranked among the top 10 most closely followed news stories from 1986 through 1989, according to a July 12, 1989, Times Mirror report. Fifty-one per cent of the American public followed "very closely" the flag-burning ruling, while 47 percent followed "very closely" the *Webster* abortion ruling. In 1990, some 72 per cent of Americans reported that they had discussed the flag-burning ruling, while 69 per cent reported discussing the abortion ruling.[22]

High awareness, however, failed to ensure that the Court's flag-burning or abortion rulings were always accurately perceived. When asked, "(d)o you happen to know . . . did the Supreme Court rule that laws banning flag burning are constitutional, or did they rule that such laws are unconstitutional?" 52 per cent (correctly) responded unconstitutional, 31 per cent responded constitutional, and 17 per cent did not know. On the Court's 1990 abortion rulings, *Hodgson v. Minnesota* and *Ohio v. Akron Center for Reproductive Health,* 66 per cent of Americans (correctly) reported that the Court had allowed states to require that minors seeking an abortion notify their parents, while the remaining 34 per cent had either inaccurate views or no knowledge of the Court's 1990 abortion rulings.[23]

A Times Mirror Poll asked whether the respondent favored or opposed "changing the laws to make it more difficult for a woman to get an abortion?" In May 1987 (before *Webster*), some 41 per cent favored more restrictive laws. In May 1990 (after *Webster*), 38 per cent favored more restrictive laws—a drop of 3 per cent in support of the Court's position.

Similar evidence appears in other polls. A Gallup Poll in fall 1988 (pre-*Webster*) asked whether "abortions should be legal under any circumstances, legal only under certain circumstances, or illegal in all circumstances?" In fall 1988, 24 per cent answered "in all circumstances"; by April 1990 (post-*Webster*), that figure had risen to 31 per cent— a shift of 7 per cent away from the Court's ruling.

A third Gallup Poll tapped the Court's restrictive abortion rulings less directly, asking whether or not respondents favored overturning the first-trimester right to an abortion.[24] In December 1988 (pre-*Webster*), 37 per cent favored overturning the right to first trimester abortions. By July 1989 (post-*Webster*) only 34 per cent favored restricting first trimester abortions—a shift of 3 per cent away from the Court's restrictive rulings.

Polls on the Rehnquist Court's 1989 *Webster* ruling provide another puzzle concerning the Court's ability to influence public opinion. Shortly after the *Webster* ruling, the *Los Angeles Times* poll reported that majorities approved of both the fetal viability test (57 per cent approved) and the public hospital restriction (56 per cent approved). However, when the same poll sample was asked, "Overall, do you approve or disapprove of the Supreme Court's decision today?", only 47 per cent approved.

Similarly, the Gallup Poll reported that 54 per cent of respondents approved of the public hospital restriction and 52 per cent approved of the fetal viability test restriction. However, only 37 per cent approved of "this week's Supreme Court decision allowing states to pass laws that restrict abortions." In both polls, approval of the decision was significantly lower than approval of the decision's two major parts.[25]

In two other instances, poll items were available shortly after a Supreme Court ruling and then again even later. These two instances—on the flag-burning controversy and on a private club's right to sexually discriminate in membership—tap the Court's ability to sway public opinion after its rulings.

In the flag-burning case, a post-*Texas v. Johnson* Gallup Poll in June 1989 reported support for the Court's decision at only 27 per cent. One year later, however, support for the Court's ruling dropped to 24 per cent—a drop of 3 per cent.

Finally, the Court's *Rotary International v. Duarte* (1987) ruling held that private clubs should not have the right to exclude potential members on the basis of sex. In June 1987, shortly after *Duarte*, some 63 per cent agreed with the Court's ruling. By July 1988, the percentage agreeing with the Court declined to 56 per cent. Once again, the shift (of 7 per cent) was away from the Court's ruling.

To be sure, the evidence is quite limited but uniformly points to the same conclusion: The Rehnquist Court can no more influence American public opinion than could earlier Courts. As other studies have also suggested, the Court's rulings typically either produce no significant poll swings at all,[26] or else produce small shifts away from the Court's position.[27]

Table 2 Direct mentions of public opinion, by type of opinion

	1792–1859	1860–1933	1934–1986	Rehnquist Court
Direct mention occurs in:				
majority opinion	76%	79%	52%	42%
concurring opinion	5	0	13	8
dissenting opinion	9	21	35	50
Total mentions	100%	100%	100%	100%

Evolving doctrine

The early Rehnquist Court's opinions, on the average, directly mentioned "public opinion" nearly five times (4.8) per term. Although five direct mentions of public opinion per term may not seem strikingly high, it is higher than the number of direct mentions of public opinion in earlier historical periods. Before 1933 the Court directly mentioned public opinion less than one time per term. Between 1934 and 1986 the Court mentioned public opinion on the average nearly three times a term.

The Rehnquist Court's direct mentions of public opinion were also more likely to appear in dissenting opinions, compared with earlier Court periods. This trend reflects both the post-New Deal trend toward more frequent (and longer) dissenting opinions and especially the sharp increase in dissenting opinions during the Rehnquist Court's first four terms[28] (see Table 2).

In other areas, however, there were only slight variations in the Rehnquist Court's usage of public opinion, compared with earlier Courts. About two-fifths of direct mentions reflected the judicial theory that some speech or action informs public opinion and is entitled to First Amendment protection no matter how unpopular. About one-fifth of the Court's direct mentions of public opinion reflect the theory that law and policy should reflect evolving public opinion, or that public opinion may threaten rights and should be restrained. As in earlier Courts, more direct mentions of public opinion occur in criminal process and trial rights disputes—most notably, in death penalty cases—than in any other single area (see Tables 3 and 4).

The Rehnquist Court's most explicit consideration of public opinion came in its death penalty decisions, especially *Penry v. Lynaugh* (1989), on mentally retarded prisoners, and in *Stanford v. Kentucky* (1989) and *Wilkins v. Missouri* (1989), on 16- or 17-year-old convicted murderers.[29] In *Penry, Stanford,* and *Wilkins* the Court's liberal and conser-

Table 3 Frequency of four judicial theories in direct mentions of public opinion, over time

	1792–1859	1860–1933	1934–1986	Rehnquist Court
Judicial theory:				
Speech or action influences or informs public opinion, merits protection	0%	6%	41%	37%
Public opinion is an adequate check on policy-making	24	50	21	5
Law and policy should reflect evolving public opinion	43	29	21	21
Public opinion is a threat to rights, should be restrained	29	18	19	21
All other usages	5	3	6	16

Note: Percentages may exceed 100% since multiple usages appear in some decisions.

Table 4 Type of case involved in direct mentions of public opinion, over time

	1792–1859	1860–1933	1934–1986	Rehnquist Court
Type of case				
Criminal process	19%	24%	35%	42%
Press, media	0	6	21	16
Dissent	0	0	18	16
Labor	0	6	14	0
Elections	0	6	8	5
Business regulation	48	50	8	16
Foreign & military policy	33	9	5	0
Civil rights, race	5	12	4	0
Privacy, sex	0	0	3	5
All others	0	3	6	0

Note: Percentages sum down, by column, and may exceed 100% due to multiple issues raised in a single decision.

vative blocs debated the question of what constitutes a national consensus and the evolving contemporary standards of public opinion on the death penalty.

The Court's five-member conservative bloc (O'Connor, Scalia, Rehnquist, Kennedy, and White) explicitly asked whether an "emerging national consensus" prohibited the death penalty execution for murder of a mentally retarded convict or of a 16- or 17-year-old. In finding that no such consensus exists, the five-member majority pointed to state legislation, federal laws, and jury convictions as the appropriate tests of modern society's attitudes on the death penalty. Public opinion polls, along with professional associations' positions and scientific ("socioscientific") evidence regarding deterrence effects were all discounted as "uncertain foundations" for measuring a modern societal consensus:

... (P)etitioners seek to demonstrate (a consensus against capital punishment for 16- and 17-year-old offenders) through other indicia, including public opinion polls, the views of interest groups and the positions adopted by various professional associations. We decline the invitation to rest constitutional law upon such uncertain foundations.[30]

Similarly, in *Penry*, Justice O'Connor, for the majority, discounted public opinion polls—even state polls in the specific state (Texas) where the death penalty for a mentally retarded convicted murderer was to be administered:

Penry does not offer any evidence of the general behavior of juries with respect to sentencing mentally retarded defendants, nor of decisions of prosecutors. He

points instead to several public opinion surveys that indicate strong public opposition to execution of the retarded .... The public sentiment expressed in these and other polls and resolutions may ultimately find expression in legislation, which is an objective indicator of contemporary values upon which we can rely. But at present there is insufficient evidence of a national consensus against executing mentally retarded people convicted of capital offenses for us to conclude that it is categorically prohibited by the Eighth Amendment.[31]

The majority's opinion closely reflects the views expressed in another celebrated death penalty case, *Furman v. Georgia* (1972), nearly two decades earlier. There, Justice Powell, dissenting, wrote that "(p)ublic opinion polls (have) little probative relevance."[32] Chief Justice Burger, also dissenting, wrote that state and federal statutes were the most reliable indicia of contemporary attitudes.[33]

By contrast, the four liberal dissenters in *Penry*, *Stanford*, and *Wilkins* argued that the majority misinterprets and miscounts existing state laws, and also argued that an assessment of contemporary attitudes should take a broader view than state or federal laws or jury actions alone.[34] The dissenters would also have included international treaties, other countries' laws and practices, and opinions of respected groups, organizations, and commissions.

Surprisingly, though, the dissenters nowhere cited public opinion polls among their lengthy list of indicators for evolving or contemporary public attitudes. This may seem yet more surprising since all the available polls in *Penry* suggested that an overwhelming majority of Americans opposed the death penalty for mentally retarded convicts.[35]

Why should the four dissenters have cast such a broad net in searching for contemporary attitudes and a modern societal consensus on the death penalty, but completely ignore available polls—even overwhelmingly one-sided polls from those states (Georgia, Texas, Florida) that employ the death penalty most widely? Part of the answer may be that at least one of the dissenters, Justice Thurgood Marshall, had earlier written to disparage polls as an indicator of public acceptance in the death penalty:

While a public opinion poll obviously is of some assistance in indicating public acceptance or rejection of a specific penalty, its utility cannot be very great.[56]

The Rehnquist Court's two blocs, then, have agreed upon at least one answer to the question: What constitutes modern American attitudes or an emerging national consensus? To the Court, public opinion polls do not merit serious attention. Instead, the Rehnquist Court may look to (and dispute the meaning of) state laws, federal laws, and jury actions—held to be "objective" evidence of attitudes. The liberal bloc may also look even more broadly—even overseas, to laws of foreign countries—but not, apparently, to available American public opinion polls.

Conclusion

The Rehnquist Court's increasing conservatism has been widely noted. In its death penalty rulings, its restrictive abortion decisions, and its use of judicial restraint, the Rehnquist Court's first four terms have already marked an important transition away from a Court focused on rights and equality and toward a Court focused on issues of federalism, separation of powers, and judicial restraint.[57] With Justice Brennan's retirement and his replacement by Justice Souter in October 1990, the Rehnquist Court's post-equality jurisprudence may be accelerated further.

Whether the Rehnquist Court will reflect American public opinion any more often than did previous Courts, however, remains in doubt. To date, the limited available polling evidence suggests that the Rehnquist Court has no more often agreed with nationwide public opinion than did earlier Courts. Its individual decisions have run the full gamut from widely popular rulings to widely unpopular rulings.

Neither of the Rehnquist Court's two ideological blocs has demonstrated any great attention to public opinion polls. When the Court's emerging conservative majority speaks of deferring to politi-

cal majorities, it means deference to the popularly elected branches—state legislatures, local governments, and the Congress. Nationwide public opinion polls appear to be of little concern to the Court's conservative majority, who dismiss polling evidence out of hand.

This version of majoritarianism, however, does not ensure that the Court will reflect nationwide public opinion particularly often. Historically, nearly half of the state or local laws which came before the Supreme Court (and which could be matched with public opinion polls) have been inconsistent with nationwide public opinion.[58] Of the 13 state and local laws or policies considered here during the early Rehnquist Court, seven (or 57 per cent) were inconsistent with nationwide public opinion.[39]

These results should give pause to those who would describe the Rehnquist Court as a "majoritarian" Court. A Supreme Court whose jurisprudence is based on judicial restraint and deference to state or locally determined policies is not, ipso facto, a majoritarian Court in the sense of reflecting nationwide American public opinion.

The Court's dwindling liberal bloc pays no more attention to polling evidence of nationwide public opinion. As the *Penry* ruling demonstrates, the Court's remaining liberal bloc will disregard polling evidence, even when American attitudes are overwhelmingly one-sided, and provide evidence of an emerging national consensus in agreement with the justices' own views. Further, as the admittedly limited evidence above suggests, the Court's remaining liberals have less often reflected public opinion in their votes than have the Court's more conservative justices.

The Rehnquist Court's relationship to American public opinion is complex—and ironic. It is a Court that praises majoritarian democracy, but no more often agrees with American public opinion than earlier Courts did. It is a Court that is dedicated to judicial deference toward the decisions of popularly elected officials, but this will inevitably lead the Court to uphold many state or local laws and policies that are unpopular nationally (and, as *Penry* illustrates, unpopular even in the state where the law originated). It is a Court that defers to popularly elected institutions, but that faces sagging public approval. It is a Court that cannot influence or "manipulate" American public opinion through its rulings. And, finally, it is a Court whose justices entirely disregard available polls in favor of more "objective" evidence of attitudes on which meaning they cannot agree.[40]

NOTES

This article originally appeared in Volume 74, Number 6, April-May 1991, pages 322-329.

1. *Supreme Court Moves Sharply to Right*, CQ ALMANAC 293 (1990).

2. Davis, *Power on the Court: Chief Justice Rehnquist's opinion assignments*, 74 JUDICATURE 65 (1990).

3. Rohde and Spaeth, *Ideology, strategy and Supreme Court decisions: William Rehnquist as chief justice*, 72 JUDICATURE 247 (1989); *Solid New Majority Evident As 1988-89 Term Ends*, CONG. Q. W. REP. 1694 (July 8, 1989).

4. Segal and Spaeth, *Rehnquist Court disposition of lower court decisions: affirmation not reversal*, 74 JUDICATURE 84 (1990); *Justices Show a Propensity for Letting Others Decide*, CONG. Q. W. REP. 2130 (July 7, 1990); Chemerinsky, *The Vanishing Constitution*, 103 HARV. L. REV. 44 (1989).

5. Brisbin, "Justice Antonin Scalia, the Separation of Powers, and the Legalistic State" (presented at the Annual Meeting of the American Political Science Association, San Francisco, CA 1990).

6. Marshall, PUBLIC OPINION AND THE SUPREME COURT 4-7 (Boston: Unwin Hyman, 1989). The use of scientific nationwide polls as a method of testing the Supreme Court's representation of mass public opinion was first suggested by Robert Dahl. See Dahl, *Decisionmaking In a Democracy: The Supreme Court as a National Policymaker*, 6 J. PUB. L. 279 (1957). Because few polls were then available, Dahl instead relied on congressional laws signed by the president ("legislative majorities") as indirect evidence of public attitudes ("national majorities").

7. Prominent examples of Rehnquist Court-era rulings which overturned state, local, or federal laws and policies include Texas v. Gregory Lee Johnson, 105 L Ed 2d 342 (1989), U.S. v. Eichman, 110 L Ed 2d 287 (1990), Edwards v. Aguillard, 482 U.S. 578 (1987), and City of Richmond v. Croson, 102 L Ed 2d 854 (January 23, 1989).

8. Marshall, *supra* n. 6, at 68-77.

9. *Id.* at 145-156.

10. For an examination of early polls and the New Deal-era Court, see Caldeira, *Public Opinion and the U.S. Supreme Court: FDR's Court-Packing Plan*, 81 AM. POL. SCI. REV. 1139 (1987); see also Barnum, *The Supreme Court and Public Opinion: Judicial Decision Making in the Post-New Deal Period*, 47 J. POL. 652 (1985).

11. Marshall, *supra* n. 6, at 78-80.

12. Earlier rulings which were as unpopular in the polls as *Penry*, *Cruzan*, and *Gregory Lee Johnson* would include *Abington School District v. Schempp*, 374 U.S. 203 (1963) and *Engel v. Vitale*, 370 U.S. 421 (1962); *Swann v. Charlotte-Mecklenberg Board of Education*, 402 U.S. 1 (1971); *U.S. v. Rutherford*, 442 U.S. 544 (1979); *Smith v. Maryland*, 442 U.S. 735 (1979); and *Moore v. Duckworth, Warden*, 443 U.S. 713 (1979).

13. For a discussion of liberal-versus-conservative definitions, see Goldman, *Voting Behavior on the United States Courts of Appeals Revisited*, 69 AM. POL. SCI. REV. 491 (June 1975). For a discussion of voting blocs during the Rehnquist Court era, see *The Statistics*, 102 HARV. L. REV. 350 (1988), and 103 HARV. L. REV. 394 (1989).

14. Marshall, "Who Does the Supreme Court Represent Best?" (presented at the Annual Meeting of the Midwest Political Science Association, Chicago, IL, 1990).

15. Gallup, April 10-13, 1987.

16. Hirsh and Donohew, *A Note on Negro-White Differences on Attitudes Toward the Supreme Court*, 49 SOC SCI. Q. 557 (1968). For evidence and an explanation of declining black confidence in the Court, see Gibson and Caldeira, "Black Support for the American Supreme Court" (paper presented at the Annual Meeting of the Midwest Political Science Association, Chicago, IL, 1990).

17. Frank, LAW AND THE MODERN MIND 13-21 (New York: Brentano, 1930); Corwin, *The Constitution as Instrument and as Symbol*, 30 AM. POL. SCI. REV. 1071 (1936); and Arnold, THE SYMBOLS OF GOVERNMENT 196-197 (New Haven: Yale, 1935).

18. Franklin and Kosaki, *Republican Schoolmaster: The U.S. Supreme Court, Public Opinion, and Abortion*, 83 AM. POL. SCI. REV. 751 (1989).

19. Caldeira, *Neither the Purse Nor the Sword: The Dynamics of Public Confidence in the United States Supreme Court*, 80 AM. POL. SCI. REV. 1209 (1986).

20. Hyde, *The Concept of Legitimation in the Sociology of Law*, 1983 WIS. L. REV. 379 (1983); Marshall, *supra* n. 6, at 145-156; Page, Shapiro, and Dempsey, *What Moves Public Opinion?*, 81 AM. POL. SCI. REV. 23 (1987).

21. For other restrictive abortion rulings during the 1988/89 term, see *Hodgson v. Minnesota* (June 25, 1990) and *Ohio v. Akron Center for Reproductive Health* (June 25, 1990). See also *New Limits on Abortion Rights Are Upheld by 5-4 Majority*, CONG. Q. W. REP. 1698 (July 8, 1989).

22. Times Mirror Poll, July 6-9, 1989.

23. Times Mirror Poll, July 5-8, 1990.

24. Gallup, July 6-9, 1989, and Dec. 27-29, 1988: "In 1973 the Supreme Court ruled that states cannot place restrictions on a woman's right to an abortion during the first three months of her pregnancy. Would you like to see this ruling overturned, or not?"

25. Gallup, July 6-8, 1989, and Los Angeles Times Poll, July 3, 1989.

26. Marshall, *supra* n. 6, at 145-156.

27. Page, Shapiro, and Dempsey, *supra* n. 20.

28. For historical trends in dissents, see O'Brien, STORM CENTER (New York: W.W. Norton, 1986); for the Rehnquist Court, see *Justices Show A Propensity For Letting Others Decide*, CONG. Q. W. REP. 2130 (July 7, 1990).

29. See also Thompson v. Oklahoma, 101 L Ed 2d 702 (June 29, 1988); and McCleskey v. Kemp, 481 U.S. 279 (April 22, 1987).

30. Stanford v. Kentucky (1989), at 323, (Justice Scalia).

31. Penry v. Lynaugh (1989), at 288-289, (Justice O'Connor).

32. Furman v. Georgia (1972), at 441, 442.

33. *Id.* at 385.

34. Penry v. Lynaugh, at 326-341.

35. *Id.*

36. Furman v. Georgia (1972), at 361, (Justice Marshall).

37. Brisbin, *supra* n. 5.

38. Marshall, *supra* n. 6, at 95, 97.

39. Of the 14 poll-to-ruling matches here, only *National Treasury Employees Union v. Von Raab* (1989) did not involve a state or local law or policy.

40. For the conservative bloc's interpretation of the meaning of state statutes ("objective indicia that reflect the public attitude . . .") toward the death penalty for teenagers, see *Stanford v. Kentucky* (1989), at 318-320.

Media coverage of the courts: improving but still not adequate

The major problem, says one reporter, is that the media "focus largely on the result—who won or lost—and not on the system, the process."

by David Shaw

Fifteen years ago, Fred Graham was a lawyer in Washington, working for the secretary of labor. Then—"out of the blue," as Graham recalls it—he was offered one of the most prestigious jobs in American journalism: covering the U.S. Supreme Court for *The New York Times*. The last man to have that job won a Pulitzer Prize, and—as Graham says now—"I was amazed they offered me the job. I hadn't done any reporting since I worked my way through law school as a reporter for the *Nashville Tennessean*."

But Graham had a couple of powerful sponsors at the *New York Times*—Washington bureau chief Tom Wicker and reporter David Halberstam, both of whom had also worked at the *Nashville Tennessean*. Moreover, in 1965, attorneys with journalistic experience—or journalists with law degrees—were a very rare breed. "If that same job opened up today," Graham said, "there would be 300 qualified applicants."

That is a considerable exaggeration. But there would probably be at least half a dozen—maybe two dozen—which is a lot more than there were in 1965. All three television networks—including CBS, where Graham himself has worked since 1972—now have reporters who are also lawyers covering the legal beat. Two *Los Angeles Times* reporters who cover the courts are also lawyers. *The New York Times* recently hired two lawyers with journalistic experience to write about legal affairs.

Even reporters with no formal legal training—and they are still the vast majority—are becoming increasingly sophisticated about the law. As their sophistication grows, once-common complaints from the legal profession about inaccuracies, irresponsibility, and sensationalism in media coverage of the courts are diminishing. "The media is doing a much better job than it used to," says Miami attorney Paul Levine. District Attorney Cecil Hicks of Orange County calls this improvement "remarkable." Twenty years ago, Hicks says, "There was often very little similarity between what actually happened in court and what I read in the papers. That seldom happens now."

Inadequate coverage

Despite this improvement, however, media coverage of the nation's legal system is still largely inadequate, according to *Times* interviews over the last month with almost 100 attorneys, judges, legal scholars, reporters, editors, and journalism professors in more than a dozen American cities. Only five newspapers have full-time reporters covering the U.S. Supreme Court. No general circulation paper has a reporter covering its state supreme court full time. Even at the trial court level, many newspapers provide only part-time, hit-or-miss coverage.

Too often, critics say, reporters still make serious mistakes, miss good stories, overlook important legal issues, misinterpret major court decisions, and fail to follow up their stories. The last charge was the most oft-voiced complaint in this *Times* study—"My most serious criticism, the most troublesome thing the press does," in the words of Robert Morgenthau, district attorney for the borough of Manhattan in New York.

There are countless examples in virtually every city of the many ways in which the press fails to follow up stories on the law:

• A newspaper will publish a story on an arrest or an indictment but—through oversight or lack of space or interest—will never publish the result of the case, especially if there is a dismissal or acquittal. ("You leave a guy hanging out there, forever guilty in the public's mind," complains one Los Angeles attorney.)

• In civil suits, the press often publishes a story about a multimillion-dollar lawsuit, then fails to publish the final judgment or out-of-court settlement, especially if it involves little or no money. ("If a guy sues for $10 million and the courts gives him $1.98, you ought to print it," one Chicago lawyer said. "Otherwise, the public gets a mistaken, inflated impression of the value of even the most frivolous lawsuits and they file bigger and bigger lawsuits and the spiral of costs goes up and up for everyone.")

• Controversial court decisions often trigger angry forecasts of doom and disruption—which are duly reported by the press. But there is little subsequent effort to re-examine the situation and see if, in fact, the "landmark decision" actually changed anything. ("I think I and my colleagues ought to do a lot more of this sort of follow-up," said one reporter who covers the Supreme Court.)

Neglect of larger issues

But the most significant criticism of press coverage of the legal system today is not so much neglect (or inaccuracy) *inside* the courtroom as it is neglect and superficiality *outside* the courtroom—an overemphasis on day-to-day, case-by-case coverage and a concomitant laxity in the coverage of the larger issues confronting the legal system (and, ultimately, society at large).

This is especially true of television because of limitations on time and format. But newspapers also devote too little attention to the inner workings and ultimate impact of the legal system—to what one lawyer calls "the 99 per cent of lawyering that never get to court." "Press coverage of the really important issues is somewhere between lousy and abysmal," said George Edwards, chief judge of the 6th U.S. Circuit Court of Appeals in Michigan, Ohio, Kentucky, and Tennessee.

Many journalists agree. "I've been in the business since 1948," said Lyle Denniston, who covers the U.S. Supreme Court for the *Washington Star*, "and I know of no beat where reporters are lazier and do less to penetrate the process they're supposed to cover than legal reporting."

Although a few papers generally do a better job than most in covering legal affairs, critics say the press too often:

• Fails to write about incompetent (or unethical) lawyers or abusive, tyrannical, incompetent judges, unless a formal, investigative proceeding is already under way.

• Ignores or covers superficially and sporadically many important subjects, issues, problems, and developments in the law. Among these are legal clinics, increased prosecution of white-collar crimes, lawyers' fees and billing procedures, the quality of legal representation given the poor, unaccredited law schools, lawyers' trial strategies, experiments in nonjudicial forums for dispute resolutions, the burgeoning costs of litigation, procedural complexities that delay cases, regulatory agency law, and multimillion-dollar awards in personal injury cases.

• Misunderstands the role of the judge and the function of the courts as a co-equal, independent branch of government. ("Judges are generally bound by legal precedents," says one judge, "but the press sometimes gives the impression that our rulings are personal preferences, and they criticize us for 'thwarting the will' of the people or the legislature.")

• Virtually ignores the intermediate appellate courts (all the courts above the trial level and below the U.S. Supreme Court), where many interesting cases are resolved and many important principles of law are enunciated. Four reporters who cover the U.S. Supreme Court all told the *Times* they come across significant stories virtually every day that should have been covered—but were not—before they reached Washington. Says one appellate judge: "We make a lot of controversial decisions, but we're almost completely invisible."

The *Baltimore Sun* does have a reporter assigned full-time to the Maryland state appellate courts, and the *Philadelphia Inquirer* recently created a similar beat. "It's become glaringly clear that we're blowing it at the appellate level," said Gene Roberts, executive editor of the *Inquirer*. "We are convinced that we'll never have a responsible court unless we cover them responsibly."

Preble Stolz, a law professor at the University of

California, says he wishes newspapers in California would also cover the intermediate appellate courts—especially the California Supreme Court—full-time. "A reporter who just shows up (at the Supreme Court) on decision day can't read the briefs and the lower-court opinions and get the necessary background to cover the court intelligently," Stolz said.

Inconsistent coverage

Not surprisingly, coverage of the legal system is generally poorest at smaller papers with fewer resources. Nor is it surprising that the best big-city papers generally do the best job. The *Wall Street Journal, The New York Times* and the *Los Angeles Times* were the most widely praised in interviews for this story.

But most papers of any size—including these three and other generally respected metropolitan dailies—do not consistently provide the kind of legal coverage that even many editors say they should offer their readers. "We just don't do very well on either day-to-day court coverage or looking at the larger legal issues," editor Bill Burleigh of the *Cincinnati Post* says of his own paper's coverage. "I'm often let down personally by all the press on this, though. I want to know a lot that the press just neglects to cover."

The press can never, of course, cover the legal system as comprehensively as those involved in the system would like—any more than it can cover any other area (medicine, business, literature) as well as people involved in those areas would like. There simply is not enough time, space, or manpower to cover every subject exhaustively in a daily newspaper. Nor is there any indication that the average reader wants his paper to become a legal (or medical or business or literary) journal.

"It is somewhat unreasonable . . . to blame the press for not printing a daily civics textbook or law book," said Joseph Mandel, president of the Los Angeles County Bar Association. "That really isn't their function."

Moreover, some attorneys and judges contribute to superficial and inaccurate coverage of the legal system by their attitude toward the press. But there is a great deal more the press could be doing (and should be doing) to cover the legal system. Especially now.

A litigation explosion

The courts today have become the ultimate forum for resolving not only personal, commercial, and criminal matters but also for a whole range of public policy decisions on the air we breathe, the food we eat, the books we read, the people we marry.

In California alone, Superior Court filings have increased more than 50 per cent in the last decade, creating a whole series of interrelated problems—massive court backlogs, an increasingly complex body of procedures and case law, litigation so expensive than many Americans can no longer afford a legal redress of their grievances. Critics say that despite the increased staff, time, and space devoted to legal matters in the press—especially in the best newspapers—the press just has not kept pace with the growing phenomenon (and the accompanying problems) of the law as a social, political, and governmental institution.

"The only two questions really worth asking about the courts are 'Is there justice?' and 'How do they [the courts] operate as a political institution?' " said Bob Woodward, metropolitan editor of the *Washington Post.* "The press doesn't do a very good job of trying to answer either [of those questions]. The courts are a political institution, and we don't cover them as such," Woodward says. "Anyone who thinks differently has his head in the sand."

Woodward—co-author of *The Brethren,* a best-selling book on the Supreme Court—is particularly interested in the personal and political relationships among judges on appellate courts and other collegial courts and also in the politics of judicial promotions and case assignments. "My father was an appellate judge in Illinois," he said, "and the courthouse politics he used to tell me about—which you just never see in the press—is highly relevant to how judges are elevated . . . and (how) cases are assigned and decided and whether there really is justice in America."

Many in Washington and elsewhere are critical of the *Post's* own coverage of the legal system—especially its erratic Supreme Court coverage of late. One reporter who covers the court says he does not even bother to read the *Post's* coverage any more.

Woodward and other journalists—especially in Washington and New York—say the press must also do more stories on the legal establishment, the network of high-priced, well-connected lawyers who often dominate the upper echelons of government and private enterprise. "Every time I see a big Washington law firm, I realize that's a whole area of

American power we don't cover at all," said Jim Mann, who reports on the U.S. Supreme Court for the *Los Angeles Times*.

The *Los Angeles Times* has more reporters covering the legal system than any other newspaper in the country—seven reporters covering various courts full time, several others who routinely cover suburban courts as part of other beats and one full-time specialist who is not usually assigned to any specific court and is free to write the kind of general pieces on legal affairs that critics say is so often missing from the press. (The paper also plans to hire a second specialist.) But critics say there are still too few stories in the *Times* (and other papers) like the insightful series it published last March on the changing power and responsibility of the judiciary.

"The *Times* rarely has the kind of think piece . . . on the courts that we see there on other institutions of government," said Robert Thompson, a former federal judge now teaching law at the University of Southern California. "Some stories nibble around the edges of that, but very little is really in depth." Dennis Britton, national editor of the *Times*, has another complaint. "In the *Times* . . . you never get the feeling that the courts are peopled by human beings. Our coverage of state and local courts is just too 'police-blotterish' for that."

Roderic Duncan, a reporter for two years before he went to law school and now a municipal court judge in Oakland, said he is continually astounded by the number of "people stories, human interest stories, that come through the court and are never covered by any newspaper. I almost OD on them," Duncan says, "and I keep wondering, Jesus Christ, where are the reporters?"

The principal players

More important, the press rarely writes about the principal players in the courtroom—the judges and lawyers. Three years ago, Chief Justice Warren Burger of the U.S. Supreme Court made a speech about the incompetence of a great many lawyers. But except for reporting the resultant attempts by some in the American Bar Association to rebuke Burger, the press made little effort to pursue or evaluate Burger's charges.

Similarly, although journalists and lawyers in virtually every big city know of judges who abuse lawyers, fall asleep on the bench, drink heavily, make racist remarks in court, or act incompetently,

stories are rarely written about them unless formal disciplinary proceedings are invoked. Carol Benfell, a reporter for the *Oakland Tribune*, said she once had first-hand evidence of a judge's incompetence but failed to write the story for reasons that "even now, I'm not sure I know." "I was inexperienced, I guess. And chicken. I was afraid I'd lose the other judges as potential news souces. And I really didn't have the time to do the job right."

No time. That is the biggest complaint most court reporters have—especially those who cover the courts for the wire services. Dick Carelli, who covers the U.S. Supreme Court for the Associated Press, often has to write about 20 or 30 different cases in one day. Not only does that leave virtually no time to probe the deeper issues involved in significant decisions, but—inevitably—Carelli concedes, he makes mistakes. "There have only been a few cases in four years where I figured, 'Hey, Carelli, you better get it right the first time.' Most often, my initial screw-up isn't going to change the course of history. I can fix it (when I file subsequent stories that same day.)"

But two years ago, when Carelli was covering the Court's controversial decision in the Allan Bakke affirmative action case, he realized, "It could affect race relations in this country for years to come if the press gives the wrong initial impression (of the court ruling)." So how much time did Carelli spend studying the decision before he filed his "initial impression"—what the wire services call a "bulletin lead"? "Three minutes," he says. Within 30 minutes, he had filed his entire story.

Television moves even more quickly. NBC went live with the *Bakke* decision 90 seconds after it was handed down. Since most people learn about Supreme Court decisions either from network television or from wire service reports on the radio or in their local papers, it is obvious that the vast majority of Americans receive only the most superficial—and sometimes distorted— accounts of these decisions.

But the pace is hectic for reporters covering local courthouses in big cities, too. Reporter Dave Racher says he turned in 1,800 local court stories to the *Philadelphia Daily News* last year. Reporter Myrna Oliver says she spends so much time—three or four hours a day—just checking the daily court calendar and daily filings and keeping track of potentially newsworthy cases in her card file that her job covering the downtown civil courts for the *Los Angeles Times* is little more than a "bookkeeping nightmare," with little time for actual reporting.

Specialized coverage

That is why some newspapers are increasingly hiring reporters to cover the legal system from outside the courthouse, with no responsibility for daily case coverage. *The New York Times* recently hired Stuart Taylor Jr. to travel around the country, writing about the law under the broad rubric of "Justice in America."

Taylor, who graduated first in his Harvard law school class and was working for a prestigious Washington, D.C., law firm when he was hired, had been a reporter for the *Baltimore Sun* for three years before he went to law school. When he decided he preferred journalism to law, he gave *New York Times* editors a nine-page memo on what he would like to do for the paper. "The *Times* and other daily newspapers do not cover the law as insightfully or as comprehensively as they could," Taylor said, and he listed almost 30 possible stories in a variety of subject areas that now "receive only occasional and sporadic attention and little in the way of informed analysis."

Taylor said he wanted to probe "beneath the surface of events to identify underlying issues, problems, and trends and explain their significance," and to provide insights into "some of the more fundamental issues and problems that characterize our system of justice."

Must a reporter be a lawyer, like Taylor, to do that well? In early years, the courthouse beat—like the police beat—was routinely given on most newspapers to young, inexperienced reporters. On many smaller papers, that is still true. But as editors have come to realize the growing significance of the legal beat, they have increasingly assigned better, more experienced reporters—especially to write about legal affairs beyond day-to-day case coverage.

Although few would insist that a reporter must be a lawyer to write intelligently about the law, there are many who say some formal legal training is advisable, perhaps essential. "You just can't cover the legal system in depth, the way it has to be covered today, if you don't have legal training," says Bernard Witkin, the author of several books on the California legal system. Witkin thinks a six- to 12-month law course designed specifically for journalists would contribute immeasurably toward more enlightened press coverage of the legal system.

There are other alternatives as well. Since 1976, the Ford Foundation has sponsored a program for five journalists a year to attend the first year of Yale Law School—not a special course, just the regular first-year law school curriculum. But many editors are reluctant to send reporters to law school, for fear that they will be tempted to abandon journalism for the more lucrative field of law—as several participants in the Yale/Ford program seem to be doing.

Formal training

There are also some editors and reporters who think formal legal training may be more damaging than beneficial for reporters. "Every reporter I know who went through law school wound up thinking like a lawyer, not a journalist," said Lyle Denniston of the *Washington Star* and author of the book *The Reporter and the Law*. "I think it was Dean Acheson who once said, 'The law sharpens the mind by narrowing it,' and that's true. A reporter with a law degree starts looking on the law as theory . . . . He loses some of his skepticism, too. He becomes part of the system . . . too respectful of lawyers and judges, too obligated to courtroom procedures . . . too likely to write for other lawyers, not the general audience."

The New York Times is particularly guilty of that in its Supreme Court coverage, Denniston says. Linda Greenhouse, who attended the Yale/Ford program and now covers the Supreme Court for *The New York Times*, does, indeed, occasionally become too enmeshed in legalese—as in a long story she wrote last year that involved little more than a legal dispute over "the meaning of the word 'accrues' in the Federal Tort Claims Act.'" But Greenhouse, who generally does a good job covering the Court, says of her legal training, "The more you know about anything, the better reporter you are, no matter what you cover."

Most journalists and attorneys concur. They say some legal training is helpful; it enables a reporter to speak the same, often arcane language as the people he covers, and it also enables him to invite confidence not easily given to nonlawyers—and to provide historical perspective to his daily reportage. Steven Brill, editor of *The American Lawyer* magazine and a graduate of Yale Law School, says legal training simply enables a journalist to "avoid being buffaloed . . . intimidated. When a lawyer says he's going to file a motion to blah-blah-blah, you don't draw a blank or have to ask a question . . . or maybe make a mistake."

Intimidation seems to be a major problem for many reporters covering legal affairs. The formal panoply of the courtroom and the stilted language of the lawyers and judges cow some reporters into silence and acquiescence. Several lawyers told the *Times* they were astounded by the number of reporters who accepted what they said—or did not say—without either question or challenge, either out of laziness, ignorance, or a fear of being perceived as ignorant.

"If you ask some prolix, wordy guy like me a few questions, you might learn something," said attorney John Martzell of New Orleans, "but most reporters never bother to ask . . . . They don't even bother to ask to look at the actual physical evidence in a trial most of the time, and I can think of a couple of trials when I've put some of the damndest things in evidence." Presumably, a reporter with legal training would be less likely to overlook such potentially newsworthy material—or to refrain from asking a pointed question or two.

But Brill thinks that debates over legal training for reporters miss the main point—the main shortcoming—of the coverage of legal affairs. "You don't have to be a lawyer to cover the law any more than you have to be a . . . cop to work the police beat," Brill said. "What you have to be is a good reporter, and there are too few of them covering the law. The law is the only beat I know of where the attention is focused almost exclusively on the result—who won or lost the case—not on the system, the process."

Perpetuating myths

When reporters do write about the process, Brill says, they too often accept and perpetuate inaccurate myths and stereotypes. "Look at all the stories over the years about plea-bargaining—so-called 'revolving door justice'—with maniacal murderers let loose after they're permitted to plead guilty to lesser charges . . . by lenient judges and bleeding heart [lawyers] who give the courthouse away. Well, I was involved in a study of more than 1,000 cases a few years ago, and we found it was a lot more complicated than that," Brill says. "We found out that a lot of defendants who plea-bargain actually wind up with more jail time than the average defendant who goes to trial. But I didn't see any real follow-up media coverage of that." So the "myth" endures.

The press bears a special burden—and responsi-

bility—where myths involving the judiciary are concerned because of what one judge terms the "unique . . . constitutional predicament'" of the judiciary. People in the executive and legislative branches of government may—indeed must—explain their actions to the public, but the courts must rely almost exclusively on the press to do that job for them.

"The force of judicial decisions depends . . . on a fragile constitutional chemistry, and it flows directly from popular knowledge and acceptance of their decisions," said Irving R. Kaufman, chief judge of the 2nd U.S. Circuit Court of Appeals in New York. "Courts cannot publicize; they cannot broadcast, they must set forth their reasoning in accessible language and logic, and then look to the press to spread the word."

Too often, critics say, the word that is spread is inaccurate. Or oversimplified. Or distorted. Or sensationalized. Or, worse, the right word—the important word—is not spread at all.

For all the criticism of the press, some good stories are occasionally published on various aspects of the legal system. In fact, says attorney Robert Meserve of Boston, a former president of the American Bar Association, "Some stories explaining complex, emotional legal issues have been helpful not only in enlightening the public but in defusing unfair criticism of the courts."

Even some newspapers not normally associated with the first rank of American journalism have recently published insightful stories on the law from time to time. The *Pittsburgh Post-Gazette* ran a story on proposals to regulate specialization among lawyers. The *Cincinnati Enquirer* ran a series on juvenile court problems. The *San Francisco Examiner* has been running periodic articles on life in the courtroom of Municipal Judge Perker Meeks Jr.

But such articles are the exception to the rule, critics say, and sometimes even these good articles do not get the display they deserve. The September 1 *San Francisco Examiner* article on Meeks's courtroom, for example, was published on the fifth page of the third section—next to the classified ads for massage parlors and lost and found.

NOTE

This article originally appeared in Volume 65, Number 1, June-July 1981, pages 18-24.

The Supreme Court beat: how television covers the U.S. Supreme Court

This study found no significant differences in Supreme Court coverage among the three major networks—each gave some air time to about one out of five of the Court's decisions. But are the quantity and quality of coverage adequate?

by Ethan Katsh

Justice Felix Frankfurter was fond of asking why the news media did not cover the Supreme Court as well as it did the World Series.[1] In 1956, journalist Max Freedman commented that the Supreme Court is "the worst reported and worst judged institution in the American system of government."[2] Since the 1950s there have been significant changes and improvements in television news and each network now has a well-known correspondent assigned to cover legal affairs on a full-time basis. Yet Justice Frankfurter would probably still not be satisfied. Although television is the primary source of news for the majority of the American public, television coverage of the Supreme Court is limited, and some important legal issues are consistently neglected. There is, it is fair to say, more taking place at the Court than meets the television eye.

This conclusion results from an analysis of all Supreme Court cases which were reported on the three national network news programs from October 1976 to July 1981, a period of five court terms. Among the findings were the following:

• Each network gave some coverage to approximately one out of five Supreme Court decisions.

• One in 10 Supreme Court decisions was reported or analyzed by the network's legal affairs correspondent.

• There were no significant differences among the networks.

• The Supreme Court itself, by the way it schedules cases, is a large impediment to more frequent reporting of its decisions.

• Cases involving corporate and business issues are much less likely to be reported than cases involving individual rights.

The importance of law-related reporting

Before describing these findings in detail and exploring their meaning, it is important to understand the significance of law-related news reporting and its relationship to public trust in law and legal institutions. Frankfurter's dream was based on a belief that public faith in law and the legal system depends on how they are perceived, and how they are perceived depends on how they are portrayed by the media. It is not only what courts do that is important, but what they are perceived to be doing. "The force of judicial decisions," Judge Irving Kaufman has stated, "depends on a fragile constitutional chemistry, and it flows directly from popular knowledge and acceptance of their decisions. Courts cannot publicize; they cannot broadcast. They must set forth their reasoning in accessible language and logic, and then look to the press to spread the word."[3]

Spreading the word about law affects the public in two ways. First, specific factual information is provided to citizens about legal issues—about what a court has ruled and about what consequences might flow from the decision—with the hope that consumers of legal news will become more informed and knowledgeable about law. Second, there is communicated a sense of how important law is in our society and what functions it performs. Whether or not the viewer learns something specific about legal rules or procedures, he or she will have been told that our culture relies on law to resolve important disputes and social problems. As a counterweight to news reporting of the executive and legislative branches, which suggest that we are a society governed by politics, coverage of the Supreme Court promotes the idea of a society ruled by law.

Although there have been a few studies of newspaper coverage of the Supreme Court, television reporting of the Court has been almost totally neglected.[4] Yet the importance of television as a source of news has been documented repeatedly by researchers. Television is the major source of news about national affairs. A majority of the public relies on television more than on any other medium and a plurality cite television as the "most thorough" source of national news.[5] A study in the mid-1970s of 111 individuals from 11 occupational groups found that 71 per cent believed that they usually obtained reliable information about Supreme Court decisions from television.[6]

These findings are particularly interesting since general public knowledge about law is at a disappointing level. A 1978 study concluded that "public knowledge of and direct experience with courts is low."[7] Three out of four persons surveyed admitted that they knew very little or nothing at all about state and local courts. More than half believed that the burden of proving innocence is on the accused and 72 per cent believed that every decision made by a state court could be reviewed by the U.S. Supreme Court.

Television has been found to be a source of both information and misinformation about law. Research on prime time police programs found that the "officers of the law" on such shows regularly violated the constitutional rights of citizens.[8] A study of news reporting of crime revealed that "crime news distorts the reality of crime commission by disproportionate emphasis on street crime as compared to white-collar crime."[9]

Reporting the Court

During the five-year period studied, the Court handed down a total of 663 written decisions. Using the *Television News Index and Abstracts*, prepared by the Vanderbilt University Television News Archives, as well as videotapes of some broadcasts, it was determined that 20 per cent of these decisions received some mention on ABC and NBC

and 23 per cent on CBS.[10] Thus, fewer than one in four decisions is likely to receive mention. For other kinds of Supreme Court actions, the odds of a case being reported are very much lower. In the years covered, for example, an average of only 11 review denials and five oral arguments were reported on each network each year.

In considering the number of cases covered, it is important to distinguish between cases reported by the anchorperson alone and cases covered by the network's legal affairs correspondent. Correspondent reports are longer, frequently contain interviews, always have pictures, and generally provide more details about the nature of the judge's reasoning and the significance of the case. These reports are one to three minutes in length compared with 10 to 30 seconds for anchor stories. If the public is to learn anything meaningful about the Court, it will probably be from these reports. Of the 663 decisions handed down, 10.4 per cent received correspondent coverage on ABC, 10.7 per cent on CBS, and 11.6 per cent on NBC. Thus, approximately half of the decisions which were reported on these programs were covered by a correspondent.

Network differences

Although CBS did carry more reports of cases than the other networks, the margin of difference was not statistically significant. Other analyses also did not reveal important differences in coverage among the networks. In fact, what was revealed was a pattern of striking similarity. For example, during the five-year period, the total number of decisions and non-decisions covered by a correspondent was 115 for ABC, 114 for CBS, and 116 for NBC.

This indicates that the pattern of news reporting described here is probably not due to the particular qualities of the correspondent assigned to the Supreme Court or to the editors and producers at a particular network. Rather, as will be suggested later, why the Supreme Court is covered the way it is is more likely due to institutional factors inherent in broadcast news or to the special qualities of the medium of television.

What issues are covered?

Figure 1 reveals a bias in network news coverage of Supreme Court decisions. Individual rights cases are almost twice as likely to be reported than cases involving an economic issue. Criminal cases and

Figure 1   Per cent of decisions reported by average network, 1976-1981

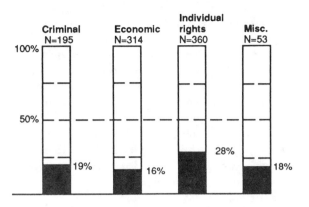

miscellaneous decisions (foreign affairs, elections, etc.) fall in between. This pattern of reporting occurs on all of the networks.

Comparing more specific issues also reveals wide disparities in coverage. The most likely issue to be covered was abortion, with every decision handed down during the five-year period covered by at least one of the networks. Also receiving coverage more than 50 per cent of the time on at least one network were decisions involving free press, free speech, and freedom of religion. Cases involving antitrust, individual and corporate taxation, patents, copyrights, and trademarks were much less likely to be covered. Criminal cases also seem somewhat neglected. While capital punishment cases were often reported, no other criminal areas were reported more than half of the time.

Do important cases go unreported? This is a particularly difficult question to answer because there is no objective standard for determining importance. It could be argued that, by the mere fact that it has been selected for review by the Court, there is something noteworthy about every case. Yet it can also be persuasively argued that legal importance and public importance are not synonymous.

Even admitting the problem of rating the significance of cases, it is still interesting to take two frequently used legal summaries of the Supreme Court term and compare them with network coverage. Each summer, *U.S. Law Week* publishes a summary of the previous term's decisions that its editors consider to be the most significant; and each fall, the *Harvard Law Review* publishes a more detailed but narrower analysis of the previous year's term. Figure 2 uses cases which were included on either list and analyzes by subject area how many were covered, on average, by each network.

The pattern of selective reporting that was noted earlier is present here as well. Even among these cases, which can be assumed to be the most legally important decisions, significantly fewer cases with economic issues were reported than individual rights cases. Interestingly, cases with criminal issues fared even worse. What is most important is that even with these legally significant cases, no network reported more than 50 per cent of the cases in any category. Newsworthiness and legal significance, therefore, do not seem to be equivalent terms.

Figure 2   Per cent of decisions in *U.S. Law Week* or *Harvard Law Review* reported on each network, 1976-1981

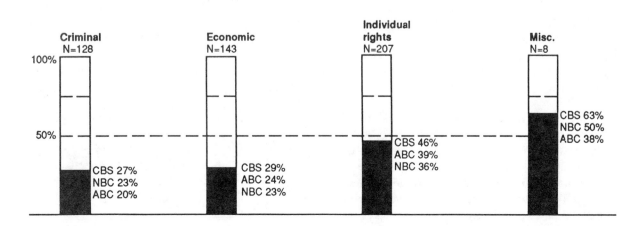

Law and television

It should not be surprising that relatively few Supreme Court decisions make the network news programs. These programs average 22 minutes in length, with 10 to 15 stories reported each evening. Competition for air time is fierce. To get a Supreme Court story on the air, one network correspondent has stated, the case must be "both interesting and important" and capable of being made meaningful to viewers in a minute and a half.[11] The exclusionary rule and the elimination of diversity jurisdiction in the federal courts were given as examples of issues that are important but that would probably fail the "interesting" standard and thus not be covered on the national news.[12]

The small number of reported decisions is also partly a function of the Court's schedule of handing down decisions. Announcing decisions in clusters on one or two days during a week makes it less likely that all will be covered. Similarly, the practice of announcing more than a third of the yearly decisions in June reduces the number than can practically be reported. If public reporting of court decisions is considered important, some study should be given to modifying the Court's calendar.

While it is debatable whether the Supreme Court receives its fair share of attention on the national news programs, the uneven reporting of different issues is more clearly open to criticism. Rulings involving important subjects like collective bargaining are almost totally ignored and court decisions involving large economic institutions are underreported. Those in academia, for example, would probably be interested to learn that *NLRB v. Yeshiva*, 444 U.S. 672 (1980), which limited the right of private college faculty to unionize, received no mention on any news program the day it was decided. It would not be surprising if public understanding of legal responses to concentrations of economic power was negligible.

One plausible explanation for the bias in reporting and not reporting certain issues concerns the nature of the television medium. In general, television tends to emphasize the visual and the concrete, and to neglect the abstract. As University of California sociologist Todd Gitlin has written, "television news stories are built around images of particular personages and dramatic conflict. Stories are personified; they issue forth from sanctioned politicians and certified authorities. Stories include visual images that will secure the flickering attention of the mass audience. Other things being equal, the dramatic image—a burning flag, a raging fire, a battle—gets priority, especially the image that lies on the surface, immediately visible to the camera."[13] It is at least arguable, therefore, that individual rights cases are covered more frequently, not because they are more newsworthy or important but because they are more easily made interesting to viewers. Individual plaintiffs are live human beings with whom viewers can identify much more readily than with corporate spokesmen. In other words, individual rights cases are also often human interest stories, can be dealt with in a visual manner, and therefore appear on the air more often.

This study reveals only a small part of the information we should try to gather about the television image of law. How, for example, are other legal institutions covered? What appears on local news programs? Do public attitudes toward the law and courts parallel the television image? The ABA's invitation to actress Veronica Hammel of "Hill Street Blues" to speak at its 1982 annual meeting illustrates the fact that it is often difficult to draw a line between television reality and what exists in real life. It is clear that television plays an influential role in modern life and what this implies for the law has not yet been fully determined.

NOTES

This article originally appeared in Volume 67, Number 1, June-July 1983, pages 6-12. The research described was supported by a grant from the University of Massachusetts Research Council.

1. Baker, FELIX FRANKFURTER 218 (New York: Coward-McCann, 1969).

2. Freedman, *Worst Reported Institution*, 8 NIEMAN REPORTS 2 (April 1956).

3. Quoted in Shaw, *Media coverage of the courts: improving but still not adequate*, 65 JUDICATURE 24 (1981).

4. Newspaper coverage of the Supreme Court is discussed in Grey, THE SUPREME COURT AND THE NEWS MEDIA (Evanston: Northwestern University Press, 1968); Goldschlager, "The Law and the News Media" (unpublished thesis, Yale Law School, 1971); Dennis, *Another Look at Press Coverage of the Supreme Court*, 20 VILL. L. REV. 765 (1975); Newland, *Press Coverage of the United States Supreme Court*, 17 W. POL. Q. 15 (1964); Ericson, *Newspaper Coverage of the Supreme Court: A Case Study*, 54 JOURNALISM Q. 605 (177); MacKenzie, *The Warren Court and the Press*, 67 MICH. L. REV. 303 (1968); Sobel, *News Coverage of the Supreme Court*, 56 A.B.A. J. 547 (1970); Cranberg, *What Did The Supreme Court Say*, SATURDAY REVIEW 90, April 8, 1967; Lewis, *Problems of a Washington Correspondent*, 33 CONN. B. J. 363 (1959); Hess, THE WASHINGTON REPORTERS (Washington: The Brookings Institution, 1981).

5. Roper Organization, CHANGING PUBLIC ATTITUDES TOWARD TELEVISION AND OTHER MASS MEDIA, 1959-1977 (New York: Television Information Office, 1977).

6. Berkson, THE SUPREME COURT AND ITS PUBLICS 64 (Lexington: D.C. Heath and Co., 1978).

7. Yankelovich, Skelly and White, *Highlights of a National Survey of the General Public, Judges, Lawyers and Community Leaders*, in Fetter, ed., STATE COURTS: A BLUEPRINT FOR THE FUTURE 5-69 (Williamsburg, VA: National Center for State Courts, 1978).

8. Arons and Katsh, *How TV Cops Flout the Law*, SATURDAY REVIEW 11, March 19, 1977.

9. Graber, CRIME NEWS AND THE PUBLIC 42 (New York: Pantheon, 1980).

10. The programs studied included all of the early evening weekday network news programs, and all of the early evening weekend broadcasts after November 1978. From October 1976 to November 1978 the only weekend data in THE TELEVISION NEWS INDEX AND ABSTRACTS was for the CBS and NBC early evening programs.

11. Katsh, *Law in the Lens: An Interview With Tim O'Brien*, 5 AM. LEG. STUD. FORUM 37 (Fall, 1980).

12. *Id.*

13. Gitlin, *Television's Screens: Hegemony in Transition*, in Apple, ed., CULTURAL AND ECONOMIC REPRODUCTION IN EDUCATION 209 (Boston: Routledge and Kegan Paul, 1982).

Yes, but . . .

by Tim O'Brien

Ethan Katsh should be commended for his valuable contribution in a much neglected area of inquiry. His statistics show conclusively what many who cover the Court must concede, however unhappily: many legal issues confronting the Supreme Court fail to get the attention they deserve from television news.

I regret, however, that Katsh chose to confine his inquiry to the early evening news broadcasts,[1] a misleadingly narrow focus. Thee was a time when the evening news was the only regularly scheduled news programming on the air. Today, however, it accounts for less than 10 per cent of the networks' regularly scheduled news and public affairs programming.[2]

Limiting the study to the evening news broadcasts obscures not just the *frequency* of court coverage, but also the *depth*. Last term, for example, ABC's "Nightline" program devoted 30 minutes to exploring the issues confronting the Supreme Court in *Bob Jones University v. United States* (federal tax exemptions for private schools with racially discriminatory policies); another "Nightline" broadcast was devoted, in its entirety, to *Rogers v. Lodge* (voting rights).

ABC's "Good Morning America" devoted segments, running seven to ten minutes, to a number of Supreme Court cases, including *Bob Jones, Murphy v. Hunt* (preventive detention), and *Youngberg v. Romeo* (rights of involuntarily committed mental patients). A dozen Supreme Court cases[3] were explored on the ABC Sunday News last term—some in reports that ran twice as long as the weekday broadcasts would allow—thus permitting substantially greater analysis.[4]

All of these broadcasts would seem worthy of at least some consideration in any evaluation of the networks' overall performance in covering the Court. Yet they are not even mentioned in Katsh's survey. Would Katsh evaluate a newspaper's coverage of the Court by examining only the front page, or even the first news section of the newspaper?

Katsh's conclusion that cases raising certain kinds of issues are more likely to get reported is, of course, true. I submit, however, the selection may be less the result of the visual needs of television—as Katsh suggests—than a reflection of editors' perceptions of the needs and interests of the audience.

Are there surveys comparing the networks' selection of cases with that of middle America's leading newspapers?[5] I am aware of none, but I suspect any difference in cases reported between the newspapers and television would be negligible. In fact, getting the "dramatic image" for a Supreme Court story is seldom a problem. Behind every Supreme Court case, not just individual rights cases, is some person or persons with a very large stake. They tend to give us all the dramatic image we need—personalizing what (to a layman) might appear as abstruse legalisms. This technique has helped us to illustrate many issues that would not ordinarily be regarded as "television fare."[6]

Incidentally, I must assume some personal responsibility if Katsh exaggerated the reluctance of the networks to tackle such esoterica as diversity jurisdiction of the federal courts and the exclusionary rule. I made that indictment myself in an interview with Mr. Katsh[7] and now am duty bound to report that I was at least partly mistaken. All three networks discussed the exclusionary rule in connection with their coverage of *Illinois v. Gates*.[8] ABC News also addressed the exclusionary rule in the context of a 10-part series on crime and the criminal justice system.

Institutional obstacles

None of the above points, however, can lessen the central thrust of Ethan Katsh's study. Insofar as the evening news programs are concerned, important cases do go unreported. Two major institutional factors did not escape Katsh's attention: the limited amount of time available for news in a half hour evening broadcast (roughly 22 minutes) and the Court's tendency to announce a third of its decisions in the last three weeks of the term. The annual, unyielding nightmare created by the interaction of these two factors should not be glossed over.

Last term, for example, the justices announced major rulings on the death penalty (*Enmond v. Florida*), obscenity (*Ferber v. New York*), and liability for civil rights boycotts (*NAACP v. Claiborne Hardware*) all on the same day. ABC News had spent considerable time and thousands of dollars researching these stories and taping background material on them in Florida, Mississippi, and New York. But very little of our efforts made it on the air when the cases were decided.[9] There were simply too many other developments in the world competing for that limited air time on the same day those cases were decided. Too little time was left for us to give *any* of these decisions the attention we would have preferred.

Among the obvious solutions to the problem of inadequate Court coverage would be for the networks to expand their evening broadcasts to a full hour. The news divisions of all three networks have been trying for years to accomplish this but resistance from local affiliates has been overwhelming. We are no closer to expanding our early evening news broadcasts now than we were five years ago.

Another possibility would be for the justices to abandon their self-imposed Fourth of July deadline for decisions. There is, of course, much more at stake here than media convenience and improved public information. Can anyone presume these major cases get the same careful thought and deliberation in the June deluge that they might get in the comparative tranquility of the rest of the term? The decision-making process suffers as well as reporting. The words the justices write live for generations; they ought not be written in haste. Each Supreme Court opinion requires scholarship, craftsmanship, and even art. But the eleventh hour manifestos we end up with in June may often obfuscate issues, rather than resolve them.[10]

Ethan Katsh is a respected authority in legal research. His conclusions about the relationship between media coverage of the courts and public

confidence in the legal system must be taken seriously. (As, of course, must the concurring views of Felix Frankfurter and Irving Kaufman.) If the electronic media is as influential as Katsh suggests, one might think the Supreme Court would find it in its own interests to better accommodate their needs. As an institution the Court functions well, arguably more in keeping with what the Founders had in mind than any other branch of government.[11] The justices' commitment to interpreting the Constitution and the laws of the nation is often inspiring. But I fear that no matter how hard we try, what Supreme Court justices actually *do* (and their devotion to doing it well) will be largely lost on the American public until our cameras are allowed in their courtroom.

Today, however, the justices seem more intent on closing their doors than on opening them. The Supreme Court remains the most secretive and inaccessible of government institutions.[12] Reporters get no advance word of what decisions are likely to be announced on a given day, although considering the complexity of the cases, that would be enormously helpful in the effort to explain them. What the Court plans to say about a case, and when it plans to say it, are among the most closely held secrets in Washington. Most reporters are never given any guidance on what an opinion means. Most justices avoid reporters like lepers.

Some isolation at the Court may be desirable, perhaps even necessary. But the justices should consider whether they may have taken a good idea to an unnecessary, and dangerous, extreme.[13]

Competition among the networks at the Court is intense. I believe my colleagues work diligently to explain the Court's work in the most effective way that we are able. We would, of course, reject any notion that, in our coverage, we have failed to promote the idea that ours is a society ruled by law. Nor is there anything "unreal" about our portrayal of what the Court does.

Katsh concluded by stating, as fact, "that it is often difficult to drawn a line between television reality [sic] and what exists in real life," which Katsh says is illustrated by the ABA's invitation to the actress Veronica Hamel of "Hill Street Blues" to speak at its 1982 convention. Perhaps he may take some solace that, although Ms. Hamel was a smash hit with all the lawyers at the ABA,[14] no network news executives have yet invited her to report on Supreme Court decisions.

NOTES

This article originally appeared in Volume 67, Number 1, June-July 1983, pages 12-15.

1. Katsh's research only partially considered weekend broadcasts and failed to take into account any of the networks' morning and late night broadcasts. The surveys showing Americans get most of their news from *television* (the premise of Katsh's piece) do not distinguish newscasts, morning from evening or daily from weekend.

2. Katsh's figures, for example, show that ". . . of the 663 decisions handed down [by the Supreme Court between 1976 and 1981], 10.4 per cent received correspondent coverage on ABC." Had Katsh gone beyond the *evening* newscast, however, he would have found the numbers much higher. Last term, for example, of 141 signed decisions, the network had "correspondent coverage" of 29 cases, or 20.6 per cent—nearly twice Katsh's average.

In fact, even Felix Frankfurter might have been pleased. Despite the network's legendary emphasis on sports, in 1982 the Supreme Court got much more attention from ABC News than the World Series!

3. *Widmer v. Vincent* (campus prayer), *Hoffman Estates v. Flipside* (drug paraphernalia), *Mesquite v. Alladin's Castle* (video arcades), *Nixon v. Fitzgerald* (immunity), *New York v. Ferber* (child pornography), *Rogers v. Lodge* (voting rights), *Doe v. Plyler* (illegal aliens), *Washington v. Seattle School Board*, together with *Crawford v. Los Angeles* (busing), *U.S. v. MacDonald* (speedy trial), *Emmond v. Florida* and *Eddings v. Oklahoma* (both death penalty).

4. CBS and NBC, similarly, do not limit their examination of Supreme Court issues to their evening newscasts.

5. Because Katsh is of course correct that legal significance and newsworthiness are not synonymous, comparisons with the *Harvard Law Review* and *Law Week* are not totally relevant. The Supreme Court's *cert.* denial in *Hearst v. U.S.*, for example, was devoid of any *legal* significance whatsoever. The *practical* significance, however, was that newspaper heiress Patricia Hearst was finally going to prison—a newsworthy development that was broadcast on all three networks.

6. Business cases that made compelling television stories include *Teamsters v. Daniel* (application of the 1934 Securities and Exchange Act to pension funds), *Diamond v. Chakrabarty* (patents), *Sony v. Universal Studios,* (copyright infringement).

Other important Supreme Court cases involving issues thought by some "too ethereal for television" but that were broadcast might include: *Cannon v. University of Chicago* (standing to sue), *Stump v. Sparkman* (judicial immunity), *Marshall v. Barlow's Inc.* (OSHA safety inspections, *Coker v. Georgia* (proportionality analysis in capital cases), *Merrion v. Jicarila* (mineral rights).

7. Katsh, *Law in the Lens: An Interview With Tim O'Brien,* 5 Am. Leg. Stud. Forum 37 (Fall, 1980).

8. Argued in the Supreme Court, March 1, 1983; #81-430.

9. The networks did give these cases some exposure earlier in the year, when they were argued.

10. Associate Justice Lewis F. Powell Jr., addressing the Eleventh Circuit Conference in Savannah, Georgia, stated: "Today, the 9th of May, we have more than a hundred argued cases not yet disposed of. The crunch for the remainder of the Term is likely to result in opinions of inferior quality, even though the judgments will have been maturely considered."

11. For reassuring insights, see: Easterbrook, *Ways of Criticizing the Court,* Harv. L. Rev. 803-832 (1982); and Goldberg, *Reflections About the U.S. Supreme Court,* 5 Nova L. J. 159-166 (1981).

12. For impartial discussion, *see The Court and the Press* in Guide to the U.S. Supreme Court 721-724 (Washington, D.C.: Congressional Quarterly, 1979).

13. "Everything secret degenerates, even the Administration of Justice." Lord Acton.

14. Margolick, *A.B.A. Blends Inspiration and Adoration at its Parley,* The N.Y. Times, Sec. 1, P. 9, August 14, 1982.

Best kept secrets of the judiciary

ABC News' law correspondent reflects on our judicial system and the need to enhance public awareness and understanding of the work of courts and judges.

by Tim O'Brien

Covering the Supreme Court, and the law generally, has been an enjoyable experience for me. The job has turned out pretty much as I had expected, but I have learned more than I thought I would. And I now realize that in my views on journalism, as in my views on the law, I have labored under many misconceptions.

I always used to think, for example, that the great lawyers win a lot, never recognizing that they always get the most hopeless cases; that the Supreme Court was SO supreme it could do whatever it wanted to do, without regard to rules of jurisdiction, standing, that there be a federal question or a real case or controversy.

I had some misconceptions about network news too. I used to believe that network news was the top of the mountain where mistakes just don't happen. Many of the people I work with today—producers and editors in Washington and New York—I am absolutely convinced are among the best in the profession. But looking back over the years, you do see occasional lapses.

I recall when I joined ABC News years ago, one of my first stories had to do with a sharp drop in unemployment. I dutifully got all of my statistics together and brought them to our graphics department. The idea was to have a graph created which would illustrate how dramatic this drop in unemployment was. At ABC, once you have script approval, the producers and correspondents get together with a director in a studio, and they put together all the visual effects that will go into the spot.

As my piece was being assembled, I recall remarking to the people in the control room that the graphics department must have made a mistake, that the drop in unemployment was much sharper than the graph indicated. The director stopped everything and, over the headsets, I heard him call to one of the cameramen: "Camera two . . . you got that art card with the line graph on it? Yeah . . . you want to tilt that card a little to the right please! Hey Tim . . . how's that?" Today, all the graphs, and other visuals, are produced electronically and are guaranteed for accuracy. Thank goodness. Accuracy is, of course, key.

One time-honored tradition in journalism is the so-called "scoop"—being first with a big story. It's always nice to be first, to have an exclusive, so long as you're right. There can be no greater nightmare for a reporter than the "exclusive" that remains forever, "exclusive." Merely being first has never been the first priority, not at ABC and not among my colleagues at the Supreme Court. Getting the decision correct, and presenting it in a comprehensible way is universally regarded as a much more important objective. But from time to time, you may have a senior producer who asks, "Why can't we be correct, comprehensible, and still be first?" After all, someone has to be first. This conjures up memories of the important Alan Bakke case, and the efforts of each of the three networks to be the first on the air with the decision.

You may recall the case of *The University of California v. Alan Bakke,* the first real Supreme Court test of affirmative action. The question is: is it unconstitutional for the state to award a preference, based on race, in order to remedy lingering effects of past discrimination? The Supreme Court of California ruled that it was . . . were the Supreme Court of the United States to affirm, it would likely be the death knell for affirmative action. On the other hand, should the decision be reversed, that might well be the green light for affirmative action. We all prepared accordingly, recognizing that whichever way the Court went, we had a news story of exceptional dimensions.

Starting in April, one news organization had a live camera outside the Court every day the Court was announcing decisions. A correspondent was with the camera, and a courier was inside the Court, in track shoes, ready to sprint outside with the decision. When it finally was announced on June 28, they were ready.

The courier races out, hands over the decision, red light on the camera goes on . . . and, on national television, the reporter reads:

The decision of the Supreme Court of California is affirmed . . . in part, and reversed in part.
Justice Powell announced the Court's judgment and filed an opinion expressing his views in the case of Parts I, II-A and V-C, in which Justice White joined; and in Parts I, and V-C in which Brennan, Marshall, and Blackmun joined.
Brennan, White, Marshall, and Blackmun filed an opinion concurring in the judgment in part and dissenting in part.
White, Marshall, and Blackmun filed separate opinions.
Stevens filed an opinion concurring in the judgment in part and dissenting in part in which Burger and Stewart, and Rehnquist joined.
Film at 11!

There are other difficulties we have in reporting the news that are more serious. We are frequently asked about BIAS on the evening news. Is there a bias? There's not just one bias, there are lots of them. In most of the interviews we put on the air, for example, there is usually a bias in favor of the person being interviewed. We may speak to someone for an hour, but it's the person's most persuasive, most articulate statement, that more often than not gets on the air.

Is there a LIBERAL bias? If there is, I personally don't believe it to be significant. Most reporters share average, middle-American values—a perception, I suspect, some may disagree with. Is there an institutional bias in favor of reporting negative news? Of course there is! As Walter Cronkite, the former CBS News anchorman put it a few years back, "It simply isn't our job to report on every cat that isn't caught up a tree." This is the bias that most affects government generally and certainly the legal profession. Every failing seems to be magnified, every success seems to be minimized or ignored.

Public misconceptions

Sadly, the American people don't seem to know very much about our legal system . . . and much of what they think they know is incorrect. In a 1983 Hearst survey, half the respondents said that, in a criminal trial, it is up to the accused to prove his innocence. Remarkably, half of those who believed that had served on a jury. Fifty per cent of those polled believed that when a criminal defendant is acquitted, the state can appeal; 45 per cent said the district attorney's job was to defend accused criminals who cannot afford counsel.

For me, closer to home and equally revealing, the tour guides at the Supreme Court tell me that among the most frequently asked questions are:
• Where does the jury sit?
• How come there's no witness stand?
People just don't understand how our court system works, and, in my view even more unfortunate, they don't understand how well it works.

Justice Antonin Scalia alluded to this in a recent lecture before the American Enterprise Institute in Washington. Scalia said judges have no need to respond to criticism, nor should they suffer the sting of it, but he did offer that much of it is ill-informed. Most public officials are rated by how acceptable their performance is to the public—do they like the "results."

Scalia, quite correctly, points out that it's different with judges. The nature of the job compels them to make unpopular decisions, decisions that often have unfair or unwise results. Scalia makes the point that the critics don't always understand that judges, of all people, must be faithful to the Constitution and the law, without regard to what he or she may subjectively believe to be the "right" result. Take last June's flag burning decision. Many people thought the Court had condoned flag burning. What does that tell us? I think it tells us that, collectively, in getting the work of the Court across to the public we've screwed up.

If I have a disagreement with Scalia, it's that he seems to accept this as an inevitable way of life. I do not. It's going to happen, sure, but I think we can all agree that we can minimize this kind of misunderstanding with a more interested, and better informed, public. How do we get it?

Reaching out

An ABA Task Force on Outreach to the Public suggested two parallel campaigns—one directed at the news media, the other at the nation's school system. Why is it that our schools don't teach courses in how the legal system works? Why is it that our children seem to learn more about criminal law from cop shows on television than they do from their teachers in the public schools?

This is an area where the state bar associations can, and in many cases have, taken a leadership role. Courses should be available about the law and the legal system at every level. In my own Montgomery County, Maryland, the county, with the assistance of the local bar, offers courses on the legal system that are available to anyone—and they are quite popular.

Courtrooms are fascinating places. Leaders of the bar should get together with educators and work out field trips for high school students to visit the county courthouse and watch a trial. The most important message they can get is to come back. This is your courtroom, and you have a right to sit in on any trial that interests you.

And then there is the media, where I have a little more expertise. The courts should try to use the media to their own advantage. Everone else does! There's nothing unseemly about it; it's the American way.

My premise today is that the more people know about our courts, the more they will appreciate and respect them. The American Judicature Society has, for many years, been part of the solution with its publication of the journal, *Judicature.* Since joining AJS several years ago, I've stolen countless story ideas from this fine publication. (Giving appropriate credit of course.) *Judicature* is on the cutting edge, and AJS should consider making it available to the managing editor of every major newspaper—and the assignment editor of every major television station.

Government can help

George Bush wants to be the "Education President." He can help too! Some of the best cases, the most interesting cases affecting the most people, are those selected for review by the Supreme Court. The solicitor general files amicus briefs in many of these cases "on behalf of the United States." The United States ought to know about it. This year, the U.S. has filed briefs in cases on abortion, the right to die, prayer in the schools, and many other issues.

When the solicitor general files a brief in these tantalizing cases, he should hold a news confer-

ence to explain and defend his position. For one, the American people are entitled to know what their government is arguing. And there is the ancillary benefit of focusing public attention on the work of the courts, and the difficult balancing act facing the justices in so many of these cases.

There are ways the courts themselves can help the media to educate the public about their work. There is no court in the country that gets the media attention that the Supreme Court gets; nor does any other court have greater influence on the public perception of the legal system. The Court should consider giving reporters advance notice of what decisions it plans to announce. A number of state supreme courts do this and it helps. It allows us time to do research, to have the right people in the right place at the right time for reaction, it gives us time for more thoughtful analysis.

We would also do a better job of reporting the decisions of the Supreme Court if they didn't announce the most significant ones on the same day. Last year, the Court had a major religion decision—whether cities may erect nativity scenes and menorahs in observance of religious holidays. It was all but obscured by an abortion decision that came down on the same day. The year before, the Court announced 10 decisions on the last day of the term, including six of the most closely watched of the year.

The scenario gets a bit ridiculous. The Court is quiet all year long. We know they're working but no one else does. Then, in June, you get this monumental deluge of opinions, and then silence. All you hear is someone calling for an intermediate court of appeals to help with the workload, and a call for a pay increase for judges; the judges themselves are nowhere to be found—they're on vacation until October. This is not effective use of the media.

The Court seems to feel that it doesn't need media attention and that it should not do anything that could be perceived as seeking attention. That's short-sighted. It isn't that the Court needs the attention, it is that the public needs to know what the Court is doing.

Cameras in the Court

The late Justice Felix Frankfurter lamented that the Supreme Court doesn't get the attention that the World Series gets. But there is an obvious, transparent difference between the Supreme Court and baseball. Baseball is on television. Can you imagine what would happen if they banned cameras from the ballpark? Baseball would become an endangered species. Television has done nothing to diminish the majesty of the game.

Our legal system is, arguably, more important to our survival as a free nation than baseball, all the more reason why cameras should be even more welcome in a courtroom than in a ballpark. This sounds self-serving, but I don't believe it is. My greatest problem as a network correspondent is that I rarely have enough time to tell my story as thoroughly as I would like and, quite frankly, I'm not enthusiastic about sharing precious seconds with justices who, from time to time, speak a language that our viewers might not readily identify as English.

On a day to day basis, maybe it wouldn't make that much difference. But think of the documentaries we could do. The value to the schools, not just law schools, but education at every level, would be incalculable. Think of the historical record that is being denied future generations. If by some miracle we had a tape of the great Chief Justice John Marshall, and his questions in *Marbury v. Madison*, or tape of Daniel Webster and the other great Supreme Court advocates, would we lock it up so no one could see it? That may be the practical effect of the Court's refusal today to make a video record of its proceedings.

Historians, educators and most importantly, the millions of Americans who care deeply about what the Court does, should not be denied the right to see the Court do its work simply because they can't get to Washington in person.

If the American people could see the Supreme Court from my vantage point, I believe they would be as impressed—and proud—as I am. When I joined ABC News, I fully expected that I would be doing a lot of traveling, and covering the Supreme Court has now taken me to 48 states. It seems I've been everywhere, but the job has also taken me to some exciting places you don't see on a map—to the traditions of our country and the conscience of our law: Those words "due process" and "fair trial" and "free speech" and "Equal Protection"; the historic national commitment that all people, "being created equal," shall remain equal in the eyes of the law.

What have I learned in 13 years covering the courts? I have learned that our legal system is genuinely committed to these principles and I am inspired by it. Our courts are beset by many problems. But I believe the best kept secret of the judiciary is how well they work. Like that cat that doesn't get caught up the tree, that's not news. And we don't report it. But it's not a secret we should be keeping.

Keeping it secret undermines confidence in, and respect for, the courts. It deprives those who have dedicated themselves to making the system work of the appreciation they deserve. The media can help, but the bar and the bench may have to take the initiative. When you feel we have failed you, I would only refer you to that sign in the old country-western saloon: "Please Don't Shoot the Piano Player—He's Doing The Best He Can."

And, I might add to it, "If you don't care for the melody, he'd welcome a helping hand."

NOTE

This article originally appeared in Volume 73, Number 6, April-May 1990, pages 341-343. It is adapted from Mr. O'Brien's address to the joint luncheon of the American Judicature Society and the National Conference of Bar Presidents on February 10, 1990, in Los Angeles.

The Courts and Their Publics
Courts, Congress, and the Presidency

INTRODUCTION

We have already seen that the judicial recruitment process is the most public setting for the carrying out of the relationship between the courts, Congress, and the presidency. Additional perspectives on that interface are offered in the first two articles in this section of readings. It is useful to recognize, however, that there are many other matters that have importance to the courts and other institutions of American government in tandem. Thus, for example, judicial decisions based on constitutional or statutory interpretation may be the start of a continuing and heated substantive dialogue between the Court and Congress that is marked by additional legislation, public posturing by legislators, and, perhaps, additional decisions by courts. In the areas of greatest controversy, Congress may even initiate measures under its constitutionally defined jurisdictional powers to alter the nature of the cases that federal courts can hear. This is the subject matter of the final selection in this section of readings.

Paul Simon's article, "The Senate's role in judicial appointments," is a thoughtful and provocative essay written by a major participant in federal judicial selection processes, a senator serving on the Judiciary Committee. Simon admits to great concern about the quality and ideological bent of judicial appointments in recent years and considers how the Senate ought to go about fulfilling its advice and consent responsibilities. Simon favors an active institutional role in which senators evaluate a nominee's qualifications and open-mindedness. Judges constitute an independent branch of government and are not members of any president's team. Consequently, senators are not compelled to allow presidents full freedom of choice in their selections. The substantive views of nominees can be explored by senators, albeit not so far as to seek their specific views on pending or likely future litigation. Interestingly, Simon concludes, "The Senate's willingness to play a more active role may, in fact, be the best strategy for ultimately reducing the role of ideology in the process . . . . The Senate's willingness to counter the president's nominations that are too ideological could well induce the president to propose fewer such nominations. The Senate's failure to play that role leaves today's appointments process ideological, but solely on the president's terms."

It is interesting to note that Senator Simon's remarks were written before President Reagan's ill-fated nomination of Robert Bork to the Supreme Court and the recent confirmation battle over the seating of Justice Clarence Thomas.

In "Supreme Court confirmation hearings: a view from the Senate," George Watson and John Stookey offer a broad view of the functions of such hearings and stress that even those that lack great controversy warrant public interest and attention. Based on interview data and the public records of the confirmation hearings of Justice O'Connor, Chief Justice Rehnquist, and Justice Scalia, the authors demonstrate that senators pursue numerous roles (evaluator, validator, partisan, educator, and advertiser) in both controversial and noncontroversial hearings, although different roles predominate in different settings. In an addendum on the Bork nomination's confirmation process, Watson and Stookey develop and illustrate a model of Senate hearings based on their degree of situational and nominee controversy that helps "make sense" out of the outcome of the Bork and other nomination battles.

The final selection in this section of readings is Kenneth Kay's exploration of "Limiting federal court jurisdiction: the unforeseen impact on courts and Congress." Kay documents the increasing tendency for members of Congress to react to their unhappiness with judicial rulings by initiating efforts to alter the Court's jurisdiction so as to remove the ability to hear future cases in the offending area of legal development. Kay contends that, too often, such action has been "an emotional response to a particular decision of the Supreme Court" rather than a considered judgment of the larger impact of withdrawing jurisdiction from the Court and Congress. For one thing, jurisdictional removal "freezes" the very decision Congress may be reacting against, possibly giving the Court the "last word." More broadly, in addition to raising vexing constitutional questions about Congress' powers, jurisdictional removal threatens judicial independence and the separation of powers. From the perspective of Congress, the public's perception of the jurisdictional weapon could make the halls of the legislature a haven for those unhappy with any and every judicial ruling. Kay concludes that ample protections exist in several facets of our governmental system that offer protection against judicial tyranny without the necessity of removing the Court's jurisdiction. It is clear, however, that congressional power over the Court's jurisdiction will remain an important subject of controversy in any discussion of the proper scope of judicial power for the foreseeable future.

The Senate's role in judicial appointments

While the president "nominates" people for the federal courts, the Senate must "advise and consent." Here, a member of the Judiciary Committee suggests how the Senate should go about fulfilling its responsibility.

by Paul Simon

The Senate's role in the appointment of federal judges is receiving more attention. Since the Senate has been involved in these appointments from the beginning of the republic, this is obviously not a new question, but it presses today with special urgency. We are witnessing an enormous turnover on the federal bench. A majority of the federal judiciary will have changed membership during President Reagan's service in office—and on our most important court, the United States Supreme Court, a substantial turnover in membership is possible. Since federal judges are lifetime appointments, what is at stake in all these changes is the character of our judicial branch for a generation, and the real-world meaning of our Constitution and federal law.

I have concerns about the judicial nominations that have been made since I joined the Senate: I am concerned about their quality, and I am concerned about their ideological bent, and we in the Senate must think harder about how we can try to assure that judicial appointments are the best possible. I am especially concerned that we lay the groundwork now for considering future nominees to the Supreme Court—that we think about our standards and processes before people are nominated and before the debate turns to specific personalities. I hope that these remarks will begin to lay that groundwork.

I start with the general view that the Senate should play an active role in the appointment of federal judges. In contrast to presidential nominations to executive departments, there should be no automatic presumption that the president gets the judges he wants. The Constitution provides that the president shall "nominate" people for the federal courts, but it also provides that the Senate must give its "advice and consent" to any appointment. I have recently reread the relevant records surrounding the adoption of this provision at the Constitutional Convention, and they are instructive. Far from supporting any idea that the president essentially controls judicial appointments, they clearly establish that the framers expected the Senate to be an active partner in the appointment process. The convention records establish that the current provision was a compromise between those who wanted judicial appointments solely in the hands of the Senate—the prevailing position until the end of the convention—and those who thought the president should have a greater role. By tradition the Senate has played a prominent role in the district court nominations when the senator or senators are of the same political party as the president. But nominees for the circuit courts of appeals have by recent tradition had significantly less Senate input.

There is a reason judicial nominees should receive the special scrutiny of the Senate. In contrast to the president's nominations to positions within his own executive branch, appointments to the judiciary are to a branch of government that is supposed to be independent of the president and for a duration exceeding his own term of office. For the president to control such appointments unilaterally would be inappropriate, especially in a political system where checks and balances are so important. The Senate is an institution in some ways not as broadly representative as it should be; we have only two women; there are no blacks; no Hispanics.

But the Senate is broadly representative of the country's political diversity. It does not defer to the president when it thinks his proposed budget or legislation will be bad for the country, and the same should be true with respect to his judicial nominees. While the law is more likely to have national impact than most judicial nominees, the law usually can be changed with greater ease than you can change judges.

Taken as a whole, the federal court system is another institution that is not as broadly representative as it should be. Under the Reagan administration the representation of women and minorities in the judicial branch has worsened. In my first year on the Judiciary Committee, we reviewed 92 nominees; 70 for district courts and 22 for the appellate level. Of the 70 district nominees, five were women, two were black, three were Hispanic, and none were Asian. Among the 22 circuit nominees, three were women. Not a single circuit judge nominee was black, Hispanic, or Asian. The impact of federal judges is so enduring that we cannot view approval of these appointees as a clerical or routine duty of the Senate.

Above all: quality

Given that basic perspective, what criteria should the Senate use in evaluating judicial nominees as part of its advice and consent role? A central feature of the Senate's role must be to evaluate the nominees' quality. By "quality" I mean several things. First, we must be concerned about a nominee's professional competence, which includes intellectual capacity and legal skills, as well as the nominee's experience—a factor which bears on the nominee's practical wisdom about people and the world as well as more narrow professional skills. Second, we must be concerned about the nominee's integrity and moral character. Third, we must be concerned about the nominee's temperament: his or her openmindedness, judgment, evenhanded consistency, and sense of fair play.

Few, if any, of my Senate colleagues would disagree in the abstract with the notion that the Senate should evaluate "quality" factors. But we need to be more demanding than we have been in actually insisting that nominees be of high quality. The American Bar Association's Standing Committee on Federal Judiciary uses four categories to rate nominees: "Exceptionally Well Qualified," "Well Qualified," "Qualified," and "Not Qualified." The

next-to-the-bottom rating, "Qualified," in fact applies to nominees with only minimally acceptable qualifications. Since I have been on the Senate Judiciary Committee, a full 50 per cent of the U.S. courts of appeals nominees have received only this "Qualified" rating. About three-fourths of these were found "Not Qualified" by a minority of the ABA Committee. During this same period, 48.6 per cent of the district court nominees also received only a "Qualified" rating, of whom approximately 20 per cent were found "Not Qualified" by a minority of the ABA Committee.

These numbers are disturbing. For years, my image of federal judges was of people who are really stellar members of the bar. That image, unfortunately, is changing, for me and for many others. Those appointed to our federal bench for life should be the best the legal profession has to offer. Too many clearly are not. Federal judges resolve matters that are of extraordinary importance not only to individual litigants but to the country as a whole. Their work is complex, and, as we are so often reminded, court dockets are extremely heavy. Competence and efficiency, along with wisdom, are absolutely essential job requirements. I know the contending political forces that can surround judicial nominations, but the plain fact is that the job of a federal judge is so important today that our country cannot afford nominees of borderline qualifications; we need the best. When we lower standards, we lower the prestige of the bench, and when that is lowered the desirability to serve for the really fine minds and experienced barristers wanes. It is a downward spiral we are on, and we must inaugurate an upward spiral. Having said that, it is still true that federal judgeships remain among the most honored and sought-after positions in American life; we need not settle for borderline qualifications. We can have the best, if only we have the will to insist upon it. This we have not done.

Substantive legal views

A more difficult question is whether senators should limit themselves to matters of professional quality or should also consider nominees' substantive legal views, particularly their views about the meaning of the Constitution and the role of federal courts. This may be the most significant issue about the confirmation process facing a senator today— and it has broad implications for the judiciary and for the country. President Reagan has candidly stated his intention to try to shape the substantive direction of our constitutional law by nominating judges who share his constitutional views and who seem likely to decide cases in accordance with them. Like many others, I have become troubled by the ideological bent of the president's nominees; so it becomes important to know in what situations, if any, a senator should withhold "consent" to a judicial nomination because of disagreement with the nominee's legal views.

My thoughts on this difficult issue, I acknowledge, are still evolving, and I do not presume to set out the definitive answers. What I want to do instead is offer some comments and raise some questions with the goal of inviting the broader debate on this subject that is needed.

I see three separate aspects to this issue that should be kept somewhat distinct:

• Are a nominee's substantive legal views altogether irrelevant to the Senate's confirmation decision?

• If not, what standard should a senator use in evaluating a nominee's views?

• In light of the standard, how should a senator go about finding out what a nominee's views are—in particular, what can a senator properly ask a nominee?

You often see reference to the supposedly conventional wisdom that a nominee's legal views should be altogether irrelevant to the Senate's confirmation decision. In actuality, though, it is hard to believe that many people really believe this as an absolute, since most senators would probably vote against a nominee who believed that racial apartheid would be constitutional or who held similarly outlandish views. In fact, the so-called conventional wisdom has not actually been the convention. Time and again over the past two centuries, senators have voted against judicial nominees whose views they deemed unacceptable. Examples of this span as far back as the Senate's rejection of John Rutledge's nomination by George Washington as chief justice in 1795, and include such recent examples as the Senate's rejection of G. Harold Carswell's nomination to the Supreme Court in 1969, a rejection based on "quality" grounds and on the fact that his segregationist views on civil rights matters were deemed unacceptable.

But there are two fundamental reasons that nominees' legal views should not be altogether off-limits to the Senate. One is that just as we know that a nominee's competence and integrity will affect his views as a judge, we know that the nominee's individual views about legal matters will in some measure affect decisions the nominee makes as a judge. The reason is that judges inevitably have leeway. They must fill in gaps in the law and must resolve ambiguities about what the law is, and in doing so a judge inevitably draws upon his or her views and outlook. This is true of all judges, and it is especially true of Supreme Court justices, whose leeway in giving meaning to the majestic general commands of the Constitution is particularly great, and who must resolve conflicts among lower courts on a daily basis. A senator who considers only whether a judicial nominee will "follow the law" is ignoring the fact that the law to be followed is often not clear, and that judicial decisions are often affected by a judge's individual legal views. To contend that a senator may not properly consider those views amounts to a contention that things highly relevant to the job—things that make a good or bad judge—may not be considered. Here we must remind ourselves that the constitutional mandate for the Senate is to "advise and consent," not merely to consent. How should we fulfill that advising role in the case of federal judicial nominees?

A second reason a nominee's views may be relevant to the current Senate is that they were relevant to the president's own decision to nominate. As an active partner in the judicial appointment process, as the authority that must "advise and consent" to nominations in our system of checks and balances, should the Senate evaluate any factor the president does? And if the president is trying to shape future judicial decisions by self-consciously nominating people with particular legal views, should the Senate—at least to some extent—consider whether those views are appropriate ones and good for the country?

But if a nominee's legal views should not be altogether irrelevant to the Senate, what standard should a senator use in evaluating a nominee's views? This, for me, is the harder question. The choice, as I see it, is between two basic possibilities. One is for a senator only to determine whether the nominee's views are within the outer boundaries of reasonableness. Under this standard, a senator would disapprove only those nominees holding unreasonably extreme views—for example, nominees who think *Brown v. Board of Education* was wrongly decided. Different senators, of course, would place the boundary of reasonableness at different places. But, under this standard, the senator would be willing to approve any nominee holding views within some broadly defined "reasonable" range, even if the senator thought those views to be wrong and bad for the country. And this suggests a problem with this standard: it allows this president or any president to systematically appoint people whose views fall at one end within the broadly tolerable range, even though that unilateral presidential action could have serious consequences for the country. Why should the Senate acquiesce in this deliberate skewing of our judges and our fundamental law?

An alternative standard is more comprehensive and demanding: Are the nominees' views about the meaning of the Constitution and the role of federal courts views which, at least in their broad outlines, the senator believes are correct ones? What are the nominee's views on key elements: majority and minority rights, presidential and congressional authority, federal power and state and local authority, and the meaning of the First Amendment? These standards, of course, could not mean that a senator would actually vote against every nominee with whom the senator disagrees. If a president tries to appoint too many judges whose ideological slant a senator opposes, political compromise on both sides would be necessary to avoid deadlock. Moreover, a senator might choose to apply this standard only in limited situations—for example, where the nominee's other qualifications are borderline. The danger in applying a more ideological standard is that the Senate should not be the abuser of ideological rigidities any more than the president should be. Some of those who criticize the rigidities of right-wing ideology would impose rigidities of the left. Both rigidities should be rejected.

Whatever standard is used, each senator has to decide for himself or herself which particular matters are most relevant in deciding whether the nominee's views are acceptable. And the question of what is relevant to each senator is related to the final issue: How should a senator go about learning what the nominee's relevant views really are?

What yardsticks?

The easiest sources are those in the public record—the nominee's prior judicial opinions, articles, speeches and statements. The more difficult issue is what questions a senator may properly ask nominees about their views. Asking a nominee's general views about the Constitution and constitutional interpretation is clearly appropriate. Judicial nominees should all demonstrate their understanding that our constitutional system not only gives scope to majority rule but also guarantees minority and individual rights; that federal courts have traditionally played a critical role in protecting those rights. Middle-range questions—for example, asking the nominee, "How do you assess the legacy of the Warren Court?"—can also uncover relevant information without being objectionable. And the same is true of general questions concerning particular provisions of the Constitution—for example, asking the nominee, "What do you think the Establishment Clause means?"

The problem with these relatively general questions is that they can easily generate responses that are unhelpfully fuzzy or cliched. To get answers that provide more useful information, a senator may be inclined to ask more specific questions. But specific questions can pose more sensitive problems. For example, asking how a nominee would decide some pending or future issue improperly puts the nominee in a compromised position, even though it may well seek relevant information. These future-oriented questions ask the nominee to prejudge a matter that might come before him or her as a judge and to give an "advisory opinion" abstracted from concrete facts. These questions also create the unseemly appearance that a binding commitment about certain future cases is a *quid pro quo* for Senate confirmation. Such questions should be avoided.

Specific questions about prior cases or about specific issues already decided by the courts do not necessarily pose these problems, but they suggest difficulties of their own. For example, to use a nominee's views on any single issue as a "litmus test" ordinarily would be unfair and inappropriate and is an unreliable way to predict the nominee's overall future performance. Specifics should be probed to provide illustrations of the nominee's views about the enduring great themes of American law—federalism, free speech, equal protection, separation of powers—but not as a checklist for special-interest groups. It does not seem inappropriate to question a nominee as to his or her understanding and commitment to the First Amendment. Or what does the phrase "cruel and unusual punishment" mean to the nominee? Or what is there in the nominee's background to suggest that there is some sensitivity to minorities so that the Equal Protection Clause will have real meaning to that person?

There is much to be said for a rather comprehensive Senate consideration of nominees' views when the president is considering them, particularly the views of nominees to the Supreme Court and the U.S. circuit courts of appeals. But we should have a fuller public debate, addressing the full range of possible objections and concerns, including those that I can mention here only briefly. I hope these remarks will help inaugurate this fuller public discussion.

An active Senate role

Some have already objected to questioning nominees about issues, because, they say, this path would be a new one for the Senate, and they are uneasy for that reason. Even if that objection were factually accurate, it needs to be evaluated in light of the way the president is systematically making ideological nominations, more so than any president since Franklin D. Roosevelt.

Another concern is that a more active Senate role will produce confrontation and deadlock. But this body, which is accustomed to working out practical compromises, can work out compromises with the president in such a way that the quality of the federal judiciary will not be reduced.

Another possible objection, this one from members of my own party, is that Democrats will be hurt by an active Senate role when we recapture the White House. It is true that a Senate that restrains a Republican president from making appointments that are too ideological or lacking in quality will also restrain a Democratic president from doing that. But we should welcome that restraint. It will both improve the quality of the judiciary and keep the law from being some huge pendulum, swinging whichever way the current political winds blow. There should be a stability and certitude in the law, and ideological swings erode that. In the *Federalist Papers*, Alexander Hamilton describes the Senate's role as being "an efficacious source of stability." A president will be thwarted only when he holds significantly more extreme views than the Senate, and seeks to use judicial appointments to impose those views.

And finally, we need to consider whether an active Senate role will make the appointments process more political and ideological, thereby undercutting the courts' authority and stature. The Senate's willingness to play a more active role may, in fact, be the best strategy for ultimately reducing the role of ideology in the process. That is particularly needed for nominees to the circuit court and the Supreme Court. Senate passivity itself can allow the law to become that pendulum swinging back and forth, simply following ideological changes at the White House. The Senate's willingness to counter the president's nominations that are too ideological could well induce the president to propose fewer such nominees. The Senate's failure to play that role leaves today's appointments process ideological, but solely on the president's terms.

To more effectively evaluate all of this, I have discussed with Senator Joseph Biden, the ranking Democrat on the Judiciary Committee, the possibility of asking our distinguished colleague from South Carolina who heads the Judiciary Committee, Senator Strom Thurmond, that hearings be held on the fundamental questions: What should the role of the Senate be in judicial nominations? There is an implied subsidiary question: How can we through this process improve the quality of the nominations? And we should ask: What is the role of this administration in the nomination process, and how does that compare to previous administrations?

If we should make such a request and it is not granted, we could hold our own independent *ad hoc* hearings on this important issue. Congress plays another role in the quality of the judiciary. The pay for federal judges is not adequate. It is good enough for mediocre judges, and if that is our goal, the pay scale helps achieve it. Our goal obviously should be significantly different. But within the present pay framework, there still could be a marked improvement in the quality of appointments to the federal bench.

NOTE

This article originally appeared in Volume 70, Number 1, June-July 1986, pages 55-58. It is adapted from an address Senator Simon delivered to the National Press Club on March 10, 1986.

Supreme Court confirmation hearings: a view from the Senate

Through the adoption of certain roles, senators pursue distinct goals throughout Supreme Court confirmation hearings, one of which includes influencing future nominations.

by George Watson and John Stookey

Editor's note. The following article was prepared prior to the nomination and subsequent defeat by the Senate of Judge Robert Bork. The authors discuss the unique nature of the Bork hearing in "The Bork hearing: rocks and roles," page 547.

With the exception of the initial announcement of a nominee's name by the president, public attention to the Supreme Court nomination process is focused mostly on the Senate confirmation hearings. They represent the most visible and formal evaluation of the nominee's suitability and qualifications. With the consideration of Justices Rehnquist and Scalia behind us and with the expectation of others to come in the not too distant future, it is a good time to examine the role of such hearings in the nomination process.

Drama or theatrics

At a common-sense level the significance of a confirmation hearing depends upon how controversial the nomination is. For example, in a relatively controversial nomination, like that of Justice Rehnquist, the hearings of the Judiciary Committee often rate as high drama in the media and are considered a significant part of the confirmation process. Conversely, the hearings in noncontroversial nominations are often dismissed as theatrics, a mere formality of going through the motions.

The conclusion that the high degree of confirmation certainty associated with a noncontroversial nominee precludes interesting and important questions about the hearing process, however, is uninformed. It is based on the limited views that these hearings are worthy of attention only if the voting is expected to be close or if a significant proportion of the legislators are playing what might be called an "evaluator role," namely, seeking information at the hearings to help them decide whether to support or oppose the nominee. From this perspective, the hearings of two of the last three nominees (O'Connor and Scalia) can be ignored as inconsequential, mere theatrical events devoid of any genuine drama or substantive value to judicial or legislative scholars. There was little doubt the decisions to confirm O'Connor or Scalia were assured before the hearings.[1] Nor are such hearings uncommon, as reflected by two scholars who noted that the hearings are ". . . essentially a pro-forma part of the decision process."[2]

Among the last three hearings, only the Rehnquist one provided the drama that attracts public and scholarly attention. Such interest springs primarily from the uncertainty of the outcome, which derives from a division of opinion among the senators or from an apparent indecision by senators concerning which way to vote. Because scholars have focused primarily on the outcome of hearings, their attention has been on variation in voting behavior and the factors that affect vote decision. While outcome is clearly a significant concern, we believe that a more complete understanding of the confirmation process is desirable. A perspective that helps to make sense of both controversial and noncontroversial nomination hearings is both possible and fruitful.

Such an alternative perspective focuses not on how controversial the nomination is, nor on the impact of the hearings on the outcome, but rather on the individual perceptions and goals of the senators involved. What is each senator trying to accomplish, and how does the configuration of the senators' goals change depending upon the level of controversy involved? Rather than a filter that determines whether the hearings are even worth our attention, level of controversy becomes a variable that affects the goals and behaviors of the senators involved.

Senatorial roles

The concept of legislative role has a long tradition. For example, representation roles, such as delegate and trustee, are often discussed by political scientists.[3] A delegate is a legislator who sees his role as reflecting the wishes of his or her district. On the other hand, the trustee role suggests that the legislator should rely on his or her own judgment about issues, rather than attempt to directly reflect home district opinion on each vote.

These generic types of roles are useful in explaining the behavior of a legislator in the confirmation setting, as well as other legislative decision making. For our discussion here, however, the term "role" is used as a convenient and common sense label to describe what a legislator is trying to accomplish in a given setting. We call these purposive situational roles, because they reveal the purpose or intent of the senator, and they are specific to a particular setting or situation, in this instance, a confirmation hearing. For example, in a Supreme Court confirmation hearing, a senator seeking to gather information and insight concerning the nominee in order to decide about his vote is playing the role of evaluator. The evaluator role provides the normative model of the open-minded senator who uses the hearings to gather and evaluate information in making a decision on how to vote.[4] It is the nature of virtually all nominations, however, that this role is assumed by a distinct minority of the committee membership, whether the nomination be controversial or noncontroversial. The question arises, then, what other roles are adopted by senators in these nomination hearings? If their vote is not at stake, just what *is* happening at these hearings?

Our effort to establish the various roles that senators may play during confirmation hearings, as well as the factors that affect role selection, began with the O'Connor hearings in September 1981. For this initial effort, it seemed important to gather

information concerning role selection contemporaneous with the hearing itself. The narrow time frame available, however, provided an obvious problem of access to the senators. As an alternative, we suspected and confirmed that the key people to interview in the attempt to identify roles were the staff members responsible to the various senators for developing information and formulating statements and questions for the hearings.[5] Each senator assigned this responsibility to his chief staff member serving on the Judiciary Committee or, more often, on one of the Judiciary subcommittees.

While the use of staff to measure senator role conceptions may be second-best to interviewing each senator directly, it seems that little measurement error occurs. This is due to the fact that the interaction between senator and staff member actually produces an articulation of role conception as the senator directs staff members to develop an opening statement and subsequent questions that will reflect the objectives sought by the senator. In those four instances in which both senators and staff were interviewed separately, we found no difference in the role conceptions articulated by the senator and his staff member. In the O'Connor nomination, interviews were conducted with the appropriate staff members for 16 of the 18 senators.[6] One senator was not included in the analysis because of his virtual absence from the proceedings. We were unsuccessful in repeated efforts to gain interviews with staff members for another senator.

In the Rehnquist and Scalia hearings, a different approach was used. Although motivations and behaviors are best understood by talking with the senators or with the staff members responsible for developing the opening statements and questions, such opportunities for "insider information" are rare. Since one purpose of this article is to provide insight that would permit outside observers to interpret the behavior and actions of the senators, we decided to examine the Rehnquist and Scalia hearings by analyzing only the information that would be available to any careful observer, namely, normal press coverage along with the opening statements and subsequent questioning by the senators.

News accounts serve to provide an understanding of the political milieu and an assessment of the nominee's qualification, background, and ideology. They also may serve to provide some sense about senatorial reaction to the nomination. Moreover, we observed a reasonably close adherence in the O'Connor hearings between what senators and staff told us in private and the comments made in the opening statements by these senators in the confirmation hearings. These statements often provide a clue to the senators' intentions and role predispositions.

On the basis of this combination of interviews in the O'Connor hearings, along with the opening statements from all three hearings, we identified various roles that appear to characterize the intentions and goals of senators during these Senate confirmation hearings. The behaviors determined by these roles are the questions and statements made by the senators during the question-and-answer part of the hearings. A specification of these roles and examples of behaviors they engender should prove most helpful in providing insight to the significance of these Senate confirmation hearings.

The prelude to role selection

The fact that many or most senators do not play an evaluator role in Supreme Court nomination hearings is perhaps more easily understood if one realizes that the hearings represent not the first, but the fourth step of the information gathering process for the Judiciary Committee members. Moreover, senatorial role selections are affected by the political environment in which the hearings occur, as well as the personal attitudes and attributes of the senators.

The information gathering process. The first step involves the collection of information by each senator's staff once the nominee is known. Each staff member becomes an independent collector of considerable printed material concerning the nominee and the nomination, in addition to letters and calls that come into the senator's office. At the same time, staffers make telephone calls to friends and associates of the senator in the nominee's home state and elsewhere in an effort to secure overviews and evaluations of the nominee. Almost without exception, special attention is paid to any known liabilities or problems concerning the nominee, such as past memberships in segregated clubs or suspect financial dealings. Because of some presumption by the senators in favor of the president's choice,[7] attention focuses on any negative factors that might alter that presumption. In fact, Wayne Sulfridge posits as virtually a necessary condition for opposition to a nominee "strong emotional issues

which can excite the public imagination."[8]

The second step in this process is the collection of information from official sources. FBI reports on nominees, once considered provocative, are now commonplace, but access to them is strictly limited to the senator only, not his staff. The chief counsel, with cooperation from the minority counsel, is responsible for gathering information for the committee as a whole. A questionnaire submitted to the nominee gathers basic biographical information, financial data, conflict of interest statements, and responses to some general interest questions. In the cases of these three justices, questions asked their response to a short criticism of "judicial activism" and to specify actions in their professional and personal lives that demonstrated their concern for "equal justice under the law."

The third part of the pre-hearing process involves a private meeting with the nominee by each of the senators on the committee. This is an important part of the process for both the nominee and the senator. From the nominee and administration's perspective, it provides insights into the concerns of the committee members and permits a preview of questions that are likely to be put to the nominee during the formal hearings. Each senator, in turn, is able to evaluate various aspects of the nominee and check out certain reservations he may possess.

By the time of the hearings, senators have acquired and evaluated substantial information concerning the nominee. They tend to assume that the information gathered is fairly exhaustive and that the nominee's strong and weak points have been identified. Since the senators presume that any important negative information concerning the nominee will be discovered before the hearings, it is further assumed that those who will testify against the confirmation will reveal no startling new information that will alter their assessment of the nominee.

The political and personal environment. While the information gathering process is critical to the individual decisions of senators concerning their vote, there are also many political and personal factors that structure the nature of the hearings. In turn, we may distinguish between those political factors that deal with the political situation in which the nomination occurs and those that involve the specific nominee to the Court. Among those situational variables of importance are presidential power and popularity; partisan and ideological distribution in the Senate; the president's party and ideology; the current make-up of the Court with respect to ideology, race, sex, and other dimensions; and public opinion. Characteristics of the nominee that may assume prominence are ideology, race or ethnicity, sex, religion, character, experience, and other such factors. For an individual senator, factors include, but are not limited to, his general legislative role orientation, sense of loyalty to party and president, personality, constituency consideration, and personal agenda in the Senate.

While any one or more of these factors may play a significant role in one nomination or another, there are two factors, more than any others, that serve to structure the hearings of the modern era: the presumption in favor of the president's nominee and political ideology. As articulated by Senator Simpson in the Rehnquist hearings:

President Reagan was elected by a large majority . . . . He has the right and the obligation to nominate qualified men and women who share the philosophy of this president.[9]

This presumption exists not from respect for the president's wisdom, although there is an assumption that some initial screening will have produced a nominee without severe moral, ethical, or legal liabilities; rather, the presumption is a recognition of his power. A president willing to "go to the wall" on an issue is a formidable opponent indeed. When that power is augmented by a compatible Senate Judiciary Committee and/or Senate, then the minority must conserve its effort for those situations in which it can appeal beyond ideology. Senator Biden's attempt to place the burden of proof on the supporters of Justice Rehnquist to the contrary,[10] Grossman and Wasby have correctly noted that

. . . the confirmation process has been based on the assumption that the president should be allowed to make any reasonable choice and that the "burden of proof" as to a nominee's lack of qualifications must be sustained by the opposition.[11]

As Biden's effort demonstrates, however, such a presumption is less likely to be respected by those in ideological opposition to the nominee. There seems little doubt that the ideological match between senator and nominee serves as the primary source of a senator's disposition concerning the nomination. Where ideological congruence exists, the qualifications and background of the nominee

are simply less important. The positive elements emerge as great strengths and the negative elements as relatively minor problems. However, where the ideologies of senator and nominee are in conflict, a very careful scrutiny of the qualifications and background is typically pursued by the senator. Positive elements tend to be reduced to a presumptive minimum, and negative items assume considerable prominence.

The significance of ideology on predispositions to the nominees is clearly evident in Table 1. Support for the three Reagan nominees was explicitly forthcoming from committee conservatives in their opening statements in all but four instances. In one of those four, Simpson engaged in a rambling, introspective presentation in which his support for Scalia seemed apparent, but which avoided an explicit statement of it.[12] The other three, occurring in the O'Connor nomination, actually reinforce the importance of ideological congruence rather than refute it. For senators East, Grassley, and Denton, the so-called "right-to-life" principle was a critical component of their conservative ideology. O'Connor's stand on this dimension was unclear. In other words, ideological congruence was precisely the question here. To the extent that they found her in step with them, their support would be forthcoming. On the other hand, to find her in ideological opposition on this principle would likely prompt their opposition.

Examination of the moderates and liberals on the committee confirms that those not in ideological "sync" with the nominees were more likely to withhold support. There are two exceptions. Senator DeConcini qualifies as a moderate based on his voting record, yet he explicitly supported all three nominees. His is an unusual case, however, because of his position as home state senator for both O'Connor and Rehnquist. For DeConcini, the political milieu and his own agenda as an Arizona senator seem to have played a role in his explicit support. The other exception comes in the explicit support for O'Connor from three of the five committee liberals and implicit support from a fourth. Once again, however, the apparent exception to the importance of ideology is actually in accord with it. There is no doubt that O'Connor's status as the first female appointee to the Court overshadowed the concerns of liberals and moderates about her conservative ideology. Committee liberals could hardly place themselves in a position of opposing

Table 1 Political ideology and pre-hearing commitment to the nominee

Senator	Party	Ideology	O'Connor	Rehnquist	Scalia
Thurmond	Rep.	Conservative	ex. sup.	ex. sup.	ex. sup.
Mathias	Rep.	Moderate	ex. sup.	noncom.	im. sup.
Laxalt	Rep.	Conservative	ex. sup.	ex. sup.	ex. sup.
Hatch	Rep.	Conservative	ex. sup.	ex. sup.	ex. sup.
Dole	Rep.	Conservative	ex. sup.	ex. sup.	ex. sup.
Simpson	Rep.	Conservative	ex. sup.	ex. sup.	im. sup.
East	Rep.	Conservative	noncom.	n.a.	n.a.
Grassley	Rep.	Conservative	mixed	ex. sup.	ex. sup.
Denton	Rep.	Conservative	uncertain	ex. sup.	ex. sup.
Specter	Rep.	Moderate	noncom.	noncom.	im. sup.
McConnell	Rep.	Conservative	n.a.	ex. sup.	ex. sup.
Broyhill	Rep.	Conservative	n.a.	ex. sup.	ex. sup.
Biden	Dem.	Liberal	im. sup.	uncertain	noncom.
Kennedy	Dem.	Liberal	ex. sup.	ex. opp.	mixed
Metzenbaum	Dem.	Liberal	ex. sup.	uncertain	mixed
DeConcini	Dem.	Moderate	ex. sup.	ex. sup.	ex. sup.
Leahy	Dem.	Liberal	ex. sup.	uncertain	noncom.
Baucus	Dem.	Liberal	noncom.	n.a.	n.a.
Heflin	Dem.	Conservative	ex. sup.	ex. sup.	ex. sup.
Simon	Dem.	Liberal	n.a.	uncertain	im. sup.

1. The levels of commitment for the last three columns in this table use the following labels: ex. sup.—support for the nominee was stated in the senator's opening remarks: im. sup.—support for the nominee seemed apparent from the senator's positive statements, but a specific commitment of support was not given; uncertain—indecision concerning how one might vote was explicitly stated; noncom.—statement was noncommittal, containing no positive or negative statements concerning the nominee nor any statement of indecision; mixed—both positive traits and negative bases for concern were mentioned, but no explicit support nor opposition was provided; ex. opp.—opposition to rather than support for the nominee was indicated; n.a.—not applicable, the senator was not on the committee for those particular hearings.

2. Political ideology was established using the ratings of the Conservative Caucus and Americans for Democratic Action. Scores between 25 and 75 were assigned a "moderate rating" while scores of 75 and above or 25 and below were assigned the appropriate "conservative" or "liberal" label. The 1981 scores were drawn from the "Congressional Voting Scores" data file made available by the Interuniversity Consortium for Political and Social Research. The 1986 scores were assessed from the November 15th and 22nd issues of *Congressional Quarterly Weekly Report*, 1986. Of course, neither the ICPSR nor *Congressional Quarterly* bears responsibility for the interpretation of the data.

3. With pre-hearing commitment reduced to three categories—support; uncertain/mixed/noncommittal; and opposition—gamma=.80, P<.01, indicating a relationship between ideological congruence and support for the nominee.

4. Denton abstained in the Committee vote on O'Connor. All others voted "Yes." For Rehnquist, the vote was 13-5. The "No" votes came from Biden, Kennedy, Metzenbaum, Leahy and Simon. The Scalia vote was a unanimous "Yes" one.

the first woman, especially in the absence of any considerable negative factors about her. In a real sense, liberal opposition to O'Connor was pre-empted by the liberals' own claims in support of women's rights.

The presumption of confirmation clearly worked to the benefit of nominees O'Connor and Scalia, both of whom were perceived as politically conservative nominees. In the absence of negative findings in any of the pre-hearing information, no opposition emerged. O'Connor's status as the first female nominee overcame questions of experience and competence. Scalia, on the other hand, was unable to win over his ideological adversaries in advance of the hearings. However, the normal presumption in favor of the nominee was augmented in his case by the fact that his hearings came immediately on the heels of Justice Rehnquist's. Opposition from the liberal minority to both of these back-to-back nominations surely seemed unwise, so Justice Rehnquist was targeted as the more vulnerable of the two, precisely because of the presence of certain negative factors on

which to base an opposition.[13] Thus, while Scalia failed to gain the prior support of the liberal faction, he at least avoided their opposition.

While one might consider that Justice Rehnquist had a double presumption in his favor, being a sitting justice as well as the president's choice, Justice Fortas' problems in a similar setting in 1968 demonstrate the potential difficulty with being a sitting justice. There is no doubt that Rehnquist's record of conservative judgments bothered committee liberals. While Scalia appeared to be as conservative as Rehnquist in many areas, there were simply no negative emotional issues associated with Scalia over which the ideological opposition could muster an attack. With Rehnquist, however, there seemed to be several, none of which by itself constituted a sufficient cause, but the cumulative effect of which just might. As we shall see, this ultimately laid the foundation for certain role selections by various senators.

Role types

Given the amount of pre-hearing information and

the usual context of the political and personal milieu, it is hardly surprising that by the time of the hearings most senators have already made up their minds and therefore do not pursue an evaluator role. Our concern here is with what alternative roles might be played by the non-evaluators. In these three hearings, we isolated four additional distinct situationally specific roles: validator, partisan, advertiser, and educator.

Each of these roles is a function of the senator's certainty of support for or opposition to the nominee, strategic considerations in light of the senator's political agenda and personal predispositions to act in a certain way. Thus, one who is uncertain about the nominee will almost surely pursue an evaluator role. On the other hand, strategic considerations are significant for those who are certain about their votes. The hearings may be expected to be controversial by virtue of a close or uncertain voting outcome or by a conscious decision by opponents to stir up controversy over the nominee; then the likelihood of a "certain" supporter playing a partisan role to help ensure approval is much more likely. Noncontroversial nominations permit a wider choice of roles. In the absence of uncertainty, which promotes the evaluator role, and controversy, which stimulates partisan roles, senators pursue other objectives. Some of these will become manifest as we describe each of the roles in turn.

The evaluator. The evaluator role is one designed to help a senator make up his mind concerning his vote on the nominee. The archetypical evaluator is probably one who carefully evaluates the nominee's responses to all questions, listens to all the evidence, and poses carefully framed questions designed to determine the fitness of the nominee. In reality, the evaluator is more likely to be one who is uncertain or unsettled about the nominee on some one or just a few issues. It is also likely that any such issue is pivotal, virtually a necessary condition for the senator's consent or opposition to the nomination. The pivotal nature of such an issue usually means that it is a very prominent issue or that it strikes at that senator's "core requirements" for a Supreme Court justice. The evaluator is best characterized as one who will ask serious questions of the nominee that are designed to resolve those doubts in the senator's mind. Such a role is exemplified by the opening statement of Denton to Judge O'Connor:

Your answers at this hearing . . . will determine my esti-

mate of your position . . . . It is my earnest hope that your responses will be neither broad nor bland, because I will base my single vote on those responses.[14]

Evaluators do not appear to be all that common in confirmation hearings, because so many of the factors that affect the voting decision have already made their impact. Evaluators are often recognizable, however, because of their forthrightness in an opening statement, as with Denton above. However, alternative opening styles for an evaluator are the noncommittal approach, used by East, which often simply notes the significance of the occasion, and the mixed approach of Grassley, who both praised and expressed reservations concerning nominee O'Connor.

Since the evaluator seeks to resolve doubts of a particular nature, he typically displays a very direct style of questioning that relates to those issues deemed so pertinent. For two of the three evaluators we observed in the O'Connor hearings, the issue of abortion was clearly pivotal. East asked eight questions during the hearings, seven of which dealt specifically with abortion. Denton managed 23 questions, 17 of which dealt specifically with abortion, two of which dealt with parents' rights concerning a young daughter's abortion and three of which concerned the role of women in the military. The abortion issue presented precisely the type of strong emotional issue Sulfridge asserts as essential for opposition to a nominee.[15] Had O'Connor given responses that indicated a pro-abortion stance, there seems little doubt that opposition would have resulted.

What makes life particularly difficult for an evaluator in a Supreme Court nomination hearing is the problem of getting straightforward answers from the nominee on any particular issue. Nominees typically are unwilling to comment on particular cases that have come before the Supreme Court or on specific issues that could conceivably come before the Court. After two dozen or so questions dealing with abortion, Denton lamented, "I do not feel I have made any progress personally in determining where you stand on the issue of abortion . . . ."[16] When asked by the chair whether another 15 minutes to question the nominee would be helpful, Denton responded, "I do not know whether another month would do, Mr. Chairman."[17]

Grassley did not pursue the same line of questioning on abortion as the other two, although his questions did support their efforts. His initial round of questions for the most part did not deal with substantive questions designed to assist his evaluation of O'Connor. Rather he attempted to surmount O'Connor's earlier evasiveness with East's questions on abortion and her refusal to comment on *Roe v. Wade* on the grounds that it was an issue that might again confront the Court.[18] The nature of his questioning reminds us that there is more to the evaluator's role than just asking substantive questions with respect to the issues of concern. There may also be "sparring time" in which the evaluator must try to elicit responses from the nominee with an acceptable degree of specificity.

The validator. The validator role is often played by a senator who has made a preliminary decision on the nominee and who wishes to use the hearings to confirm or validate that opinion. Typically, such a role involves one who is inclined to vote "yes" on the confirmation, but who remains sufficiently open-minded to change his mind in the event that some serious shortcoming or flaw in the nominee arises. Such a position was expressed by Senator Metzenbaum in his opening statement in the Scalia hearings, in which he praised the nominee's integrity but proceeded to note that he retained an "open mind on this nomination."[19]

Empirically, we observed no validators who were leaning against the confirmation in any of the three nominations, and it seems probable that an individual leaning in opposition is likely to pursue a more active role in revealing the negative aspects of the nominee's credentials, a role different from that of validator. This assumption stems from the premise of the presumption in favor of the nominee. Since those who oppose carry the burden of establishing the nominee's "unfitness," those who lean in opposition must pursue the negative traits of the nominee to establish certainty of opinion in functionally the same way a negative partisan might carry the battle.

While the evaluator seeks to resolve for himself some very fundamental concerns regarding the fitness of the nominee to serve, the validator usually has resolved such basic questions. There is no need, then, for the validator to ask questions that will reveal the position of the nominee on a fundamental issue that relates to the necessary conditions of fitness for the senator. More commonly expressed is a desire to evaluate the quality of the nominee's mind and to assess the nominee's ability to function in pressure situations. The validator's

goal, in effect, is to reassure himself concerning his vote, as exemplified by Biden's "relief" when Scalia affirmed that free speech can encompass physical actions and his overall "feeling better" about Scalia at the conclusion of his questioning.[20]

An analogy to doctoral dissertation defenses comes to mind here. Just as professors engage a doctoral student in mental gymnastics, the validating senator seeks to gain insight into the mental capacities of the nominee. It is conceivable that questions posed by the doctoral committee may reveal an unanticipated weakness that leads to failure of the exam. However, the norm is that the exam is passed, just as it is also the norm that validating senators do indeed validate their prior notions concerning the nominee.

The types of questions that provide such insight will vary widely, according to the knowledge, experience, and characteristics of each individual senator, as well as the order in which the senator is permitted to question. A staff member of one junior senator noted the problem of assuring that the senator would have good questions to ask even after his 15 colleagues had preceded him. Thus, Senator Baucus' so-called "tombstone question" ("How do you want to be remembered?") is an effort to be creative, clever and, at the same time, provide some psychological insight into the nominee.

More often than not, the validator assumes a somewhat benign approach in his questioning. Just as in a dissertation defense, however, senators will not hesitate to pursue certain points where the nominee betrays a weakness. For example, O'Connor responded inadequately on a question dealing with *Brown v. Board*, which prompted further probing by two validating senators on the Republican side.[21] Also similar to dissertation defenses in which the basic subject and approach of the dissertation is accepted, questions tend to focus on procedural matters and questions of interpretation. Among the 100 questions asked O'Connor by presumably validating senators, 85 per cent dealt with legal principles and procedures as opposed to substantive policy issues like abortion or school prayer. Thus, O'Connor was quizzed on *stare decisis*, federal-state jurisdictions, federal court jurisdiction, legislative-judicial relationships, constitutional revision, and other topics of judicial relevance, but not on topics one would think sufficient to prompt a negative decision concerning the nominee.

Partisan. A partisan is one who has already decided how to vote on the nominee and uses the hearings to press the partisan view. A partisan may be either positive or negative toward the nominee. The positive partisan will use the hearings as an opportunity to assist the nominee. This is done through praise of the nominee, by posing questions that permit the nominee to look as good as possible and by defending the nominee against attacks of opponents. On the other hand, the negative partisan will use the hearings to call the fitness of the nominee into question.

pos.= assist nominee

neg.= quest. nominee

Senator Thurmond provides an interesting profile of a positive partisan for the Reagan nominations and, by way of contrast, a negative partisan in the Thurgood Marshall and Abe Fortas (nomination to be chief justice) hearings. In the O'Connor, Rehnquist, and Scalia hearings, Thurmond's opening statements were supportive of the nominees. His lead-off questions to each of the justices provided them with the opportunity to confront major issues of their nominations in a relatively unthreatening way. As the initial interrogator, Thurmond was able to pose questions in a very open-ended fashion that dealt with what was perceived to be the concern of potential opponents. In this way the nominee was able to make initial statements about these issues in a nonconfrontational way. This is exemplified by the following questions to O'Connor, each of which was not followed with further probes by Thurmond, but was simply dropped after O'Connor made what appeared to be virtually a prepared statement.

> . . . would you state your views on the proper role of the Supreme Court in our system of government?[22]
>
> Would you discuss your philosophy on abortion, both personal and judicial, and explain your actions as a state senator in Arizona on certain specific matters?[23]

In more controversial nominations, the positive partisan may find it necessary to play a more vigorous role in defense of the nominee and in counterattacking the negative partisans. In the Rehnquist hearings, Senator Hatch displayed this vigorous aspect of the positive partisan. For example, he defended Rehnquist's lone dissent in the "Bob Jones" case, arguing there were legitimately two sides to the question involved and that Rehnquist's dissent was indeed rational and not a function of racial prejudice. He presented detailed data concerning the frequency of Rehnquist's dissents to demonstrate how his tendency to dissent on his own had declined in more recent years. Even though

the Scalia nomination was less controversial, Hatch pursued the positive partisan role there as well, defending certain decisions by Scalia to allay fears that he might be anti-press with respect to the First Amendment.

For negative partisans, the hope is to persuade others to oppose the nomination and to make the nominee look bad. In the Abe Fortas hearings, Thurmond also played the partisan role with cunning and vigor, but in that instance as a negative partisan. His questions were of a type that Fortas, as would have most any other nominee, refused to answer as inappropriate. However, whereas Thurmond invited O'Connor to decline to answer if she felt her answers ". . . would impinge upon (her) responsibilities as an Associate Justice of the Supreme Court . . . ,"[24] Thurmond rifled question after question at Fortas, chiding each refusal to answer with ". . . and you refuse to answer that?"[25] In the Marshall hearings, Thurmond took the nominee through questions of legal technicalities and historical occurrences that proved difficult to answer in an effort to embarrass the nominee and perhaps gain support for the opposition effort.[26]

In the Rehnquist hearings, some Democrats tried to make Rehnquist look bad with respect to certain legal, moral, and ethical questions. For example, they raised questions concerning Rehnquist's accession to restrictive housing covenants, whether he had participated in intimidating minority voters, whether he supported maintaining the "separate but equal" doctrine at the time of *Brown v. Board*, and other issues. They argued that his frequency of lone dissents placed him out of the mainstream of legal thought in the country. In the absence of a single major negative issue, the opponents tried to construct a basis for opposition on an accumulation of negative elements over a period of 32 years. In the end, their failure to rally enough opposition may have been due in part to the absence of a sufficiently strong emotional issue, and certainly in part to the fact that political liberals constituted a distinct minority of senators both on the committee and in the Senate.

Educator. Senators who have made up their minds before the hearings have the most flexibility in their role selection. Unencumbered by a need to establish information on which their decision will be based, they are free to pursue a wide range of objectives. This is particularly true in a noncontroversial nomination in which the role of partisan seems relatively unnecessary. One additional role that surfaced in the O'Connor and Scalia hearings is that of "educator." This is a broad role that may have different targets for educational improvement. Senators may wish to educate the nominee, fellow committee members, fellow senators, the president, the public, and perhaps specific population subgroups as well. The educator, then, is one who wishes to use the hearings as an opportunity to inform and perhaps influence one or more of these targets.

In the Scalia hearing, Senator Kennedy was explicit about his role as he expressed in his opening statement the ". . . hope that, as a result of these hearings . . . he (Scalia) will look with greater sensitivity on (the) critical issues . . ." of race discrimination and women's rights.[27] While it might seem futile to "educate" the nominee, more than one senator thought it worth the effort. As Metzenbaum, an educator in the O'Connor hearings told us, "You just might get her to think or re-think about points that you have made and, at some point down the line, perhaps something positive will happen." Biden also played the educator with nominee O'Connor as the target:

Would it be, in your opinion, inappropriate for you as the first and only woman at this point on the Supreme Court . . . to for example be involved in national efforts to promote the ERA?

It is your right, if it were your desire, to go out and campaign like the devil for the ERA. It is your right to go out and make speeches across the country about inequality for women, if you believe it. Don't wall yourself off.[28]

Other targets of the educator also surfaced. One Democratic senator commented privately on the need to educate the president to the fact that he should be concerned with more than pleasing conservative Republicans by his appointments, that liberal senators in both parties were concerned about and would scrutinize the views of Supreme Court nominees. Another senator commented on the opportunity provided by the hearings to raise an issue concerning legislation that he was backing and to obtain publicity for it, targeted at both senatorial colleagues and the general public. In one such instance, a senator proceeded to describe the legislation that was pending, provide his justification for the legislation, and secure the nominee's somewhat passive assent that the legislation probably posed no constitutional problems.[29]

Advertiser. Closely akin to the role of educator is that of advertiser. Like the educator, the advertiser may have a variety of targets. Behaviorally, the difference between trying to educate and simply advertise is rather obscure, at best. At this initial stage of inquiry, however, we think there is an important conceptual distinction that relates to the intentions of senators. The intent of the educator is to develop the target's mind and perhaps to persuade to some point of view, while the intent of the advertiser is to inform or publicize some point without the developmental or persuasive component. One example of advertiser behavior is the line of questioning pursued by Kennedy in the O'Connor hearing.

From your own knowledge and perception how would you characterize the level of discrimination on the basis of sex today?[30]

I wonder if you briefly would discuss your perception of the degree to which black Americans or Hispanic Americans are denied equality in our society.[31]

Such a line of questioning could come from either an educator or an advertiser. This illustrates the inappropriateness of trying to classify role type from the behavioral enactment of that role. Our interview with Kennedy's staff during the O'Connor hearing led us to conclude that he wished to use this opportunity to demonstrate his concern about what he believed to be the persistent discrimination in our society.

In still other instances, questions asked by the advertiser may not differ much from questions asked by an evaluator, to the extent that both may be reflecting concerns that are relevant to their constituents. For example, Senator Dole's question concerning O'Connor's interpretation of the term "strict constructionist" and whether or not she felt that concept described her might come from an evaluator who thought the concept was particularly pertinent. In this case, however, it came form a senator who perceived a home constituency would be reassured by the nominee's anticipated answer. He sought to advertise to his constituency that she was a "strict constructionist" and he was safeguarding the Court by making that determination. These examples suggest that, quite often, the advertising senator is also advertising himself by advertising an issue.

Conclusion

With respect to Supreme Court nomination hearings, it seems a fact of political and scholarly life that only controversial nominations offer any interest and insight regarding the confirmation process. Such a view tends to focus only on the outcome of the nomination as being significant. From that perspective, the most recent three hearings were merely theatrics. As Table 1 shows, the vast majority of senators in each of the three hearings had already made up their minds how to vote even before the hearings had begun. Table 1 reveals that those who expressed "uncertainty" concerning their votes ended up opposing the nominee in committee. On the other hand, those whose statements were best characterized as "mixed" or "noncommittal" always favored the nominee in the committee vote. If one is interested only in outcome, the hearings offered little in drama or significance.

It is our contention, however, that outcome is not the only relevant question for hearings. Senators pursue important goals in both controversial and noncontroversial nominations, as reflected by the efforts of negative partisans, educators and advertisers. Not the least of these goals is to influence the next nomination even before it is made. We do hope that our discussion of several situationally specific roles, along with an explanation of factors that foster these roles, will contribute not only to an understanding of the last three confirmation hearings, but will enhance our comprehension of future hearings—controversial or noncontroversial.

NOTES

This article originally appeared in Volume 71, Number 4, December-January 1988, pages 186-196.

1. In the O'Connor nomination, 13 of the 18 committee members made opening statements that voiced satisfaction with the nominee, while only three explicitly expressed any reservations. NOMINATION OF SANDRA DAY O'CONNOR: HEARINGS BEFORE CONGRESS, FIRST SESSION Serial No. J-97-51, 1-31, 34-36, *passim*. (Washington: U.S. Government Printing Office, 1982). For Scalia, 13 of the 18 also voiced satisfaction in opening statements, while none of the Senators expressed explicit reservations. TRANSCRIPT OF PROCEEDINGS; UNITED STATES SENATE; COMMITTEE ON THE JUDICIARY; NOMINATION OF ANTONIN SCALIA, TO BE ASSOCIATE JUSTICE OF THE SUPREME COURT 2-3, 11-64, *passim*. (Washington, DC: Miller Reporting Co., 1986).

2. Grossman and Wasby, *The Senate and Supreme Court Nominations*, 1972 DUKE L. J. 563.

3. Jewell, *Attitudinal Determinants of Legislative Behavior: The Utility of Role Analysis*, in Kornberg and Musolf, (eds.), LEGISLATURES IN DEVELOPMENTAL PERSPECTIVE 491 (Durham, NC: Duke University Press, 1970).

4. The myth of the hearings as a meeting of open-minded senators seeking information for their decisions is poignantly illustrated during the testimony of Reverand Carl McIntire in the O'Connor hearing. In providing testimony against nominee O'Connor, the Rev. McIntire finds himself addressing

only the chair, Senator Thurmond. All other senators are absent. "Senator, I want to protest it. I want to protest coming down to the end of this hearing and only having you to talk to. I sat here and listened at every Senator here on the bench . . . and a majority have already said they are going to vote for her . . . ." O'CONNOR HEARINGS, *supra* n. 1, at 345.

5. The role of the staff in interacting with and preparing senators for their committee presentations is noted in Jones and Woll, THE PRIVATE WORLD OF CONGRESS 154-171 (New York: Free Press, 1979); and in Mackenzie, THE POLITICS OF PRESIDENTIAL APPOINTMENTS 182 (New York: Free Press, 1981).

6. The research design is best described as field research involving an unstructured interview, but one that consistently sought answers to a basic set of concerns, namely:

• the criteria considered important in Supreme Court nominations;

• the techniques and sources for gathering information concerning the nominee;

• the sources of efforts to influence a senator's decision regarding the confirmation;

• the importance of the nominee's gender in this particular nomination;

• the purposes or functions of the senator's questions during the hearings.

7. Grossman and Wasby, *supra* n. 2, at 588.

8. Sulfridge, *Ideology as a Factor in Senate Consideration of Supreme Court Nominations*, 42 J. OF POL. 566 (May 1980).

9. REHNQUIST HEARINGS (C-Span televised hearings, July 30, 1986).

10. In his opening statement of the Rehnquist hearings, Senator Biden, the ranking Democratic member of the committee, asserted that ". . . as the framers of the Constitution intended, the burden is upon the nominee and his proponents to make the case for confirmation of Chief Justice." REHNQUIST HEARINGS, *supra* n. 9.

11. Grossman and Wasby, *supra* n. 2, at 588.

12. SCALIA PROCEEDINGS, *supra* n. 1, at 36-40.

13. For newspaper coverage of Rehnquist, see especially, THE NEW YORK TIMES July 27, 1986, at A18, and July 29, 1986, at A14. For a report on Scalia, see THE NEW YORK TIMES, August 6, 1986, at A13.

14. O'CONNOR HEARINGS, *supra* n. 1, at 29.

15. Sulfridge, *supra* n. 8, at 566.

16. O'CONNOR HEARINGS, *supra* n. 1, at 249.

17. *Id.* at 248.

18. *Id.* at 116-118.

19. SCALIA HEARINGS, *supra* n. 1, at 29.

20. *Id.* at 118, 121.

21. O'CONNOR HEARINGS, *supra* n. 1, at 102-103, 131-132.

22. *Id.* at 60.

23. *Id.* at 60.

24. *Id.* at 132.

25. NOMINATIONS OF ABE FORTAS AND HOMER THORNBERRY; HEARINGS BEFORE THE COMMITTEE OF THE JUDICIARY, UNITED STATES SENATE, NINETIETH CONGRESS, SECOND SESSION 183-184 (Washington, DC: U.S. Government Printing Office, 1968).

26. NOMINATION OF THURGOOD MARSHALL; HEARINGS BEFORE THE COMMITTEE OF THE JUDICIARY, UNITED STATES SENATE, NINETIETH CONGRESS, FIRST SESSION 183-184 (Washington, DC: U.S. Government Printing Office, 1968).

27. SCALIA PROCEEDINGS, *supra* n. 1, at 25.

28. The written transcript deviates somewhat from Biden's actual comments as revealed by a videotape playback. We provide a quote from the videotape.

29. O'CONNOR HEARINGS, *supra* n. 1, at 153-154.

30. *Id.* at 76.

31. *Id.* at 77.

The Bork hearing: rocks and roles

From the day the president nominated Robert Bork, it was apparent this hearing would be different from those of Reagan's other three nominations. Senator Kennedy sounded immediate opposition that grew to include the five liberal Democrats pitted in a partisan battle against the five conservative Republicans[1] for the hearts and votes of the committee moderates (Specter, Deconcini, Byrd) and the conservative Democrat Heflin. As undecided decision makers, these latter four would pursue evaluator roles in an effort to make up their respective minds concerning their votes. Given the uncertainty of the outcome, no one had the luxury of pursuing the validator, educator, and advertiser roles discussed in our accompanying article.

Not only was the configuration of role playing different from the previous hearings, the level of hostility was considerably greater. Partisans on both sides hurled verbal rocks at each other, the president, various groups and individuals lobbying the hearing, and the nominee himself. These differences from previous hearings stimulated our interest in two directions. First, we wanted to see if our approach in the accompanying article could help make sense of these events. Second, we wanted to determine if a more generalized model of the role playing process could be suggested to incorporate the different hearings of the four Reagan nominees.

Hearing controversy

Clearly, what was different about the Bork hearings was their level of controversy. The O'Connor and Scalia hearings lacked any real drama. The Rehnquist elevation to chief justice had stirred some controversy because the relatively small group of Democratic liberals on the Judiciary Committee chose to play negative partisan roles. The Bork nomination added the essential defining characteristic of a controversial nomination, namely, the potential for actually defeating the nomination. For the first time among the Reagan nominees, the outcome was genuinely in doubt.

The controversy stemmed from two of the basic components that structure the nature of the hearings: the political situation at the time of the nomination and the nominee himself.[2] Three aspects of the political situation seem especially significant:

First, the partisan and ideological opposition to the nominee no longer constituted a distinct mi-

Table 1 Political ideology and pre-hearing commitment to Judge Bork

Senator	Party	Ideology[1]	Pre-hearing commitment
Biden	Dem.	liberal	explicit opposition
Kennedy	Dem.	liberal	explicit opposition
Byrd	Dem.	moderate	uncertain
Metzenbaum	Dem.	liberal	explicit opposition
DeConcini	Dem.	moderate	uncertain
Leahy	Dem.	liberal	explicit opposition
Heflin	Dem.	conservative	uncertain
Simon	Dem.	liberal	implicit opposition
Thurmond	Rep.	conservative	explicit support
Hatch	Rep.	conservative	explicit support
Simpson	Rep.	conservative	explicit support
Grassley[2]	Rep.	moderate	explicit support
Specter	Rep.	moderate	uncertain
Humphrey	Rep.	conservative	explicit support

1. Political ideology was established by averaging the ratings of the Conservative Coalition and Americans for Democratic Action (ADA). Scores between 25 and 75 were assigned a "moderate" rating, while scores of 75 and above and 25 and below were assigned the appropriate "conservative" or "liberal" label. The ADA scores were drawn from the *Congressional Quarterly Weekly Report*, August 22, 1987, at 1968. The Conservative Coalition scores were kindly provided by the *Congressional Quarterly* research staff (Michael Amin and Andrew Taylor) and covered 23 votes in 1987 up to the August recess.

2. Senator Grassley's classification reflects a departure from previous, more conservative ratings. With scores of 30 on the ADA index and 61 on the Conservative Coalition, he remains closer to his conservative colleagues than to the other moderates. Given his initial support for Bork and his consistent conservative stance in the Reagan nominations, we have continued to characterize him in the text as one of the five conservative Republicans on the committee.

nority who faced certain defeat. The 1986 election produced a substantial Democratic majority (54 to 46) to replace the Republican majority that had considered the president's previous nominees. On the Judiciary Committee, the Republican majority of 11 members, containing 9 conservatives, was reduced to only 5 conservatives (plus the moderate Specter). On the other hand, the Democrats retained their five liberals, two moderates, and one conservative (see Table 1).

Second, the president's power had waned. Combined with the electoral resurgence of the Democratic opposition in 1986 were the facts that the president had now entered the "lame duck" period, the last two years in office, and had suffered prestige and credibility drops due to the Iran-contra hearings and other political setbacks. At the time of the Rehnquist and Scalia hearings, the president's approval rating hovered around 67 per cent. When the Bork hearings took place, these ratings had dropped to about 52 per cent.[3] The presumption in favor of a president's nominee, based on the president's power, was seriously eroded.

Third, the ideological balance of the Court

Figure 1. Interplay of situation and nominee controversy in the Reagan nominations

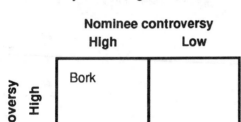

seemed to be at stake. The retiring Justice Powell had been on the winning side of more 5 to 4 decisions than any other justice.[4] His apparently pivotal role on the Court upped the ante for this particular nomination.

In addition to the inherently controversial situation, Bork proved to be a nominee who provided several negative emotional issues around which to rally an opposition. In prior nominations, negative emotional issues more commonly involved questions of ethics, incompetence, or racism. The nomination of Bork, an academician with nearly impeccable ethical and intellectual credentials, might normally have provoked little excitement. Instead the hearings provided a rare sight in judicial nomination proceedings, a controversy stirred by emotions about legal concepts. It was Bork's own intellectual passion, as represented in a career of provocative conservative writings, that roused the opposition, which articulated concerns over the nominee's apparent lack of commitment to a variety of civil rights and liberties.

Controversy, it seems, can arise as a result of an interplay of factors that constitute the political situation or as a result of factors that relate to an individual nominee; however, these are not independent factors. Whether the nominee's sex, ethnicity, religion, or ideology are potentially controversial matters depends, in part, on the political atmosphere of the times. In turn, these factors may help structure the political situation.

In Justice O'Connor's case, gender played a major role in creating a noncontroversial nomination. In Judge Bork's case, his ideology, portrayed by opponents and even some supporters as an ardent, almost reactionary, conservatism, assured his status as a controversial nominee to liberals and eventually to moderates and southern Democratic conservatives as well. Of course, Justice Rehnquist attained a certain controversiality among liberals by virtue of his conservative record. Yet his initial nomination and his more recent elevation to chief justice did not reach the level of controversy surrounding the Bork nomination. Why?

The answer lies with those aspects of the political system and environment in which Judge Bork found himself, as highlighted by the three factors specified at the beginning of this note. In short, the situation was highly charged. Contrast this with Scalia and Rehnquist, both of whom were perceived as quite conservative nominees. Those hearings, however, occurred with a stronger president, prior to the next congressional election, with a more conservative dominated Republican majority in the Senate, and at a time when the ideological make-up of the Court did not rest in the balance. Conservative Scalia replaced the equally conservative Burger. Rehnquist, of course, was already on the Court.

Figure 1 models the interplay of these two areas. We place the O'Connor and Scalia nominations in the cell that denotes a relatively low level of controversy with respect to both the nominee and the situation. Rehnquist presents a controversial nominee, but in a political situation devoid of so many of the potential conflicts that beset Bork. Of course, Bork falls in the cell of high controversy for both situation and nominee, which helps to visualize why the hearings were so controversial. We shall return to this model later to discuss some implications that derive from it.

Controversy and role playing

Given the controversy surrounding the Bork nomination, we may ask whether the types of roles differed from those played in the less controversial hearings of the three previous nominees. Implicit in our article is a model of individual role selection, presented in Figure 2.

We have identified a considerable number of situational, nominee, and personal factors that affect whether or not a senator will make a decision concerning his vote by the commencement of the

Figure 2. A model of individual role selection

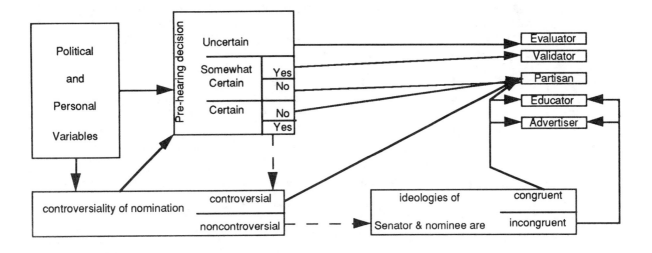

hearings.[5] These factors determine the level of controversy surrounding the nomination and they affect the pre-hearing disposition of the senator's confirmation decision. The model also suggests that the level of controversy may influence a senator's pre-hearing decision status. For example, it is our perception that controversy tends to reduce the likelihood of a "somewhat certain" position. Controversy is partly generated by firmly held opposing opinions, which, in turn, induces those holding less firm opinions into one or another of the two camps.

The role adopted by a senator at the hearings will depend most directly on his pre-hearing disposition. The model asserts that those senators who are uncertain about their vote will pursue an evaluator role. They must ask questions designed to address their uncertainties. In the Bork nomination senators Specter, DeConcini, and Heflin seem to have done just that.[6] All other votes on the committee were already certain, as evidenced by pre-hearing and/or opening statements. Because the opposition carries the burden of establishing the unfitness of the nominee, they tend to adopt partisan roles in an aggressive effort to discredit the nominee. The "certain Yes" senators can pursue a variety of strategies unless the nomination is controversial. In such circumstances, they too must pursue a partisan role in an effort to combat the opposition. This clearly occurred in the Bork hearing, with the partisan efforts reaching spectacular heights (or depths) that were, in turn, deplored by both sides.

In less controversial hearings, those who still are uncertain about the nominee as the hearings begin will adopt the evaluator role. We are also likely to see the re-emergence of a few who are somewhat certain supporters, in which case the validator role will be pursued. Any opposition will play the negative partisan role.[7] The biggest change in less controversial hearings is that those whose votes are certain for confirmation are free to pursue the educator and advertiser roles, as well as a somewhat less intense positive partisan role.

Implications

The two models and the ensuing discussions have implications for assessing the character of future hearings, the individual roles that are pursued in those hearings, and even the outcome. The model of situation/nominee controversy provides one way of characterizing hearings. In conjunction with the individual role selection model, one may seek the presence, absence, or predominance of certain roles in particular types of hearings. Thus, partisan and evaluator roles are most likely in instances of high situation and high nominee controversy. Conversely, in a nomination that is low on both dimensions of controversy, senators are able to play educator, advertiser, and validator roles, in addition to the evaluator and partisan ones.

In mixed nominations, where there is controversy on one dimension but not on the other, the partisan and evaluator roles are also quite likely to surface. The other roles may be played as well, but

Figure 3. Interplay of situation and nominee controversy on Committee confirmation

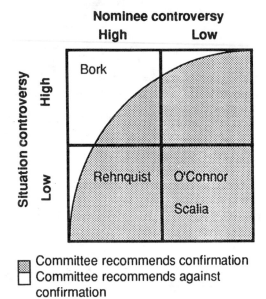

Committee recommends confirmation
Committee recommends against confirmation

We think a more certain route towards confirmation is another strategy offered by the model. A simple appointment of a noncontroversial individual, even if quite conservative, can still gain confirmation to the Court.

—*John Stookey and George Watson*

NOTES

This article originally appeared in Volume 71, Number 4, December-January 1988, pages 194-196.

1. See note 2 in Table 1.

2. Watson and Stookey, *Supreme Court confirmation hearings: a view from the Senate*, 71 JUDICATURE 188-189 (1988).

3. As communicated to us by Richard Morin, polling editor, *Washington Post*, from data collected through the ABC/Washington Post surveys of September 1986, and September 1987, respectively.

4. Goldman, CONSTITUTIONAL LAW: CASES AND ESSAYS 157 (New York: Harper and Row, 1987).

5. Watson and Stookey, *supra* n. 2, at 188-189.

6. Senator Byrd did not participate fully in asking questions due to his other commitments as majority leader. While he did exhibit uncertainty in his opening statement of the Bork hearing, his diminished or lack of participation in all of the Reagan nominee hearings has led us to omit him from the analysis.

7. Watson and Stookey, *supra* n. 2, at 191-192.

predicting their appearance depends in part on the degrees of controversy presented by the nominee or situation. We save a fuller exploration of such specification for another time.

Another interesting aspect of the situation/nominee controversy model is the implication for predicting outcome. For example, in instances of low situation and low nominee controversy, confirmation is a certainty. Where either the situation or nominee is controversial, but not both, the odds still favor confirmation, depending on the location of the nominee in that particular cell. Finally, in highly charged situations with a controversial nominee, the outcome can go either way. These implications are diagrammed in Figure 3.

An interesting aspect of this model is an implication that, had the Bork and Scalia nominations been reversed in order, both would likely have gained seats on the Court. A Bork nomination in a less controversial situation should have succeeded. Scalia's noncontroversial status as an individual presumably would have produced confirmation even in a more volatile political situation.

Whether the failure of the Bork nomination serves to defuse an inherently controversial political situation remains to be seen at this writing. That seemed clearly to be the administration's strategy in pursuing the Bork nomination to a Senate vote.

Limiting federal court jurisdiction: the unforeseen impact on courts *and* Congress

Limiting jurisdiction will not change past Supreme Court decisions. In fact, it will leave American rights and liberties vulnerable to the whims of future Congresses and the states.

by Kenneth R. Kay

Congressional attempts to remove the jurisdiction of the federal courts over specific controversial issues are not new or unique to the 97th Congress. In the last 25 years, there have been isolated efforts to remove the Supreme Court's jurisdiction over specific subjects in response to Court opinions.[1] However, in the last two years, the incidence of such attempts by Congress has increased dramatically.

• In April 1979, the then Democrat-controlled Senate voted 51 to 40 in favor of an amendment, offered by Senator Jesse Helms of North Carolina, to a Supreme Court jurisdiction bill.[2] The amendment would have eliminated Supreme Court and lower federal court jurisdiction over the issue of school prayer.

• This year, subcommittees of both the House and Senate judiciary committees have held hearings on the overall issue of congressional attempts to limit the federal courts, and on July 9 the Senate Separation of Powers Subcommittee favorably reported legislation that would eliminate lower federal court jurisdiction in certain abortion cases.[3]

• The Senate recently engaged in a lengthy filibuster because of an amendment to the Department of Justice authorization bill, which would limit those instances in which a federal court could issue a busing order.[4] This same issue is currently under active consideration in the Senate Judiciary Committee.[5]

• There are approximately 20 separate pieces of legislation pending in the House and the Senate that would limit the jurisdiction of the federal courts.[6]

Clearly, congressional attempts to remove federal court jurisdiction are no longer limited to isolated occurrences. Nor are the bills introduced merely to serve as vehicles for congressional hearings or to send a "message" to the courts. Rather, the jurisdiction bills are beginning to serve as the legislative centerpieces of the lobbying efforts of several constituencies. Single-interest groups that until now have failed to mobilize sufficient support for constitutional amendments have shifted their focus to court jurisdiction proposals. The issue of court jurisdiction is likely to be the battlefield on which the struggles over the nation's most controversial social issues will be fought. The court jurisdiction proposals represent a profound and substantial assault on the federal judiciary.

It is in this context that the emphasis of the current congressional dialogue is most disturbing. The focus on each piece of court jurisdiction legislation has been an emotional response to a particular decision of the Supreme Court, rather than on the substantive impact of withdrawing court jurisdiction. For example, when the full Senate voted on the Helms amendment in April 1979, the vote was perceived as a vote on school prayer. Congressional consideration of these bills continues to be in the context of school prayer, abortion, or busing, and not in the context of the role of the federal courts in the American system of government.

The constitutional debate

Equally disturbing has been the congressional preoccupation with whether or not the proposals to withdraw court jurisdiction are constitutional. The debate, thus far, has progressed on the premise that if the Constitution gives the Congress the *authority* to do it, then the Congress *ought* to do it.

There are credible constitutional arguments on both sides. In the case of Supreme Court jurisdiction, the "exceptions clause" in Article III, Section 2, clearly gives Congress some meaningful power to withdraw jurisdiction in certain cases. This power was upheld by the Supreme Court in *McCardle.*[7] However, the Supreme Court has recognized that the power does not include the power to determine how the court shall decide cases.[8] Equally significant is the fact that the Supreme Court does not exist at the discretion of Congress, but is created by Article III of the Constitution. Therefore, the "exceptions" clause cannot be read as including in it the power to virtually eliminate the Court as a branch of government.

Congressional power to remove the jurisdiction of lower federal courts is a less complicated matter. Under Article III, Congress has the power to create the inferior federal courts and from that flows the power to reduce or eliminate their jurisdiction. However, even this power of Congress cannot be exercised in violation of other provisions of the Constitution.

For example, Congress could not restrict lower federal court jurisdiction on the basis of race. Such a statute would blatantly violate the equal protection clause. It is also plausible to argue that in other specific areas where there is a recognized constitutional right, removal of lower federal court jurisdiction over that subject would violate the corresponding constitutional provision. This analysis is strongest where it can be demonstrated that Congress has removed the jurisdiction for the very purpose of weakening the ability of citizens to vindicate a particular right.

In the final analysis, however, the fascinating constitutional dialogue is simply that—a fascinating dialogue. Even if we could resolve the question of whether Congress has the power, the more critical question is whether Congress ought to exercise it. Rather than constitutionality or emotion, what we need to do is pay far more attention to the public policy considerations of the various proposals.

The public policy debate

The argument in favor of the proposals to remove court jurisdiction goes something like this: The Supreme Court has acted unconstitutionally in reaching decisions—it has usurped the legislative function by expanding its own power under the Fourteenth Amendment. The school prayer cases are just one example of such court conduct.[9] When the court so acts, it is not only permissible, but appropriate, for the Congress to take the court out of the business of acting unconstitutionally.

The argument is based on the everyday analogy that if a child has used his BB gun to put a hole through a window at the Jones' house, then the parents should take the gun away. If he doesn't have a gun, he can't do any more damage.

The analogy breaks down immediately because the Congress and the courts are involved in something more akin to a marriage than a parental relationship. But even if one stays with the analogy, pending proposals amount to much more than the parents simply taking the gun away. The proposals amount to telling the child that he can never go over to the Jones' house again, even for some positive purpose like helping them mow their lawn. And it's important to note that keeping the child from ever going to the Jones' again does not replace the broken window.

Removal of court jurisdiction over specific subject matter does not repair any damage. The simple fact is that withdrawing the Supreme Court's jurisdiction over school prayer does not return prayer to the schools. Withdrawing court jurisdiction over abortion does not outlaw abortion. While this may seem obvious, it is a point that has escaped many who have engaged in the dialogue over this issue.

In fact, one can plausibly argue that not only do these jurisdictional bills not alter the substantive state of the law, but that they actually elevate Supreme Court decisions to the status of the "permanent" law of the land. The Court's school prayer decisions would not only be the law of the land today, but would be locked in stone as the last word from the Supreme Court.

Also possible is the situation where state courts might further restrict the scope of current Supreme Court rulings. For example, it is generally agreed that current Supreme Court rulings do not preclude school periods of silent meditation. If Supreme Court jurisdiction over school prayer were removed, individual state supreme courts would be free to declare periods of silent meditation in schools unconstitutional. In those states, citizens who support school prayer would have to live with an even more unacceptable state of the law than that which the Supreme Court has already declared.

Similarly, the opponents of abortion would have

substantially damaged their own cause if they had attempted and succeeded in removing Supreme Court jurisdiction over abortion in the wake of *Roe v. Wade*.[10] The Court would have been unable to render its decision in the *McRae* case in which it held that Congress and state legislatures can constitutionally prohibit federal and state funding of abortions.[11] State supreme courts would have been free to declare that a state's funding of abortions was constitutionally required in that state.

Finally, consider the confusion created by a scheme where federal funding of abortions is constitutionally required in some states, not constitutionally required in others, and not reviewable by the Supreme Court. In such a situation, the removal of Supreme Court jurisdiction over abortion would have have aided those who opposed the Court's ruling in *Roe v. Wade*.

Impact on the judicial system

Not only do these proposals do so little to promote the cause of their proponents, they do much to upset many basic principles upon which our judicial system currently operates. Two of the primary principles at stake are those of judicial independence and the separation of powers. These proposals undermine the essential function of the courts to serve as the final protector and arbiter of the terms of the U.S. Constitution. As Alexander Hamilton stated in Federalist 78, it is the duty of the courts "to declare all acts contrary to the manifest tenor of the Constitution void. Without this, all reservations of particular rights or privileges would amount to nothing."[12] The court jurisdiction proposals envision a system of government in which the judicial branch's ability to protect constitutional rights and privileges can be removed by a simple majority of Congress.

The proponents argue that judicial usurpation of the legislative function is ample justification for their proposals. But they have clearly prescribed the legislative usurpation of the judicial function as the antidote. The end result of their proposals is that constitutional protections become illusory. If Congress can determine which rights and privileges are to be reviewed, Congress has, in effect, decided which rights and privileges exist. The protections of the Constitution will only be what 51 per cent of the House and 51 per cent of the Senate say they are. This is not what was intended by the framers of our Constitution.

President Andrew Johnson made this exact point in his message of veto of the legislation that became the subject of the *McCardle* decision.

The legislation proposed (to foreclose constitutional review in the Supreme Court) is not in harmony with the spirit and intention of the Constitution . . . it establishes a precedent which, if followed, may eventually sweep away every check on arbitrary and unconstitutional legislation.

Thus far, during the existence of the government, the Supreme Court of the United States has been viewed by the people as the true expounder of their Constitution, and in the most violent party conflicts, its judgments and decrees have always been sought and deferred to with confidence and respect . . . any act which may be construed into or mistaken for an attempt to prevent or evade its decisions on a question which affects the liberty of the citizens and agitates the country cannot fail to be attended with unpropitious consequences.[13]

A third principle profoundly affected by such legislation is that of *stare decisis*. One of the most unfortunate aspects of these jurisdictional bills is that at their heart they depend on an erosion of the principle. The congressional sponsors of the legislation realize that they cannot directly reverse the Supreme Court school prayer decision, so instead they want to withdraw the Supreme Court's jurisdiction and give the state courts a knowing wink and say, "go ahead—they can't touch you now." This congressional wink is, in my view, not responsible legislation. It is an open invitation to the states to overrule decisions of the Supreme Court. Likewise it is an open invitation for the general disrespect of the rule of law.

A fourth principle that would be affected is that of uniformity of constitutional interpretation. Regardless of the intentions of the framers of the Constitution, Congress can, and should, make the judgment that today, in 1981, the First Amendment in Montana will offer the same protections as the First Amendment in North Carolina. The definition of the term "person" under the Fourteenth Amendment should be the same in Louisiana as it is in Illinois. Permitting 50 state courts to engage in setting 50 different definitions of constitutional terms destroys the ability of the Constitution to serve as a meaningful national document.

Impact on Congress

Many members of Congress have not only underestimated the impact of these bills on the basic principles of our judicial system, but have also underestimated the impact on the Congress itself.

If Congress decides to enter this arena, the pressure to respond to a wider range of constitutional issues will grow. Every constituency that feels victimized by an adverse constitutional ruling will come running to Congress for a jurisdiction withdrawal bill.

Anyone who argues that this jurisdiction removal approach would only be used in the most flagrant cases of "excessive" judicial decision making ought to examine the record created thus far in the 97th Congress. One bill was introduced to remove Supreme Court jurisdiction over sex bias in the Selective Service system.[14] This legislation was introduced prior to the Court's recent decision on the subject.[15] Now that the Court has ruled that a male-only military registration is not a denial of the equal protection clause, the need for removing the subject from the Court's jurisdiction no longer exists. Another court jurisdiction bill would go so far as to remove jurisdiction over "any order of a court of a state if such order is, will be, or was, subject to review by the highest court of the state."[16]

After reviewing all the bills introduced in this Congress, it is not wholly implausible to predict that jurisdiction withdrawal language will become a boiler-plate provision of much legislation. Any time a member of Congress was unsure whether the Supreme Court would uphold legislation, he or she could tack on a section denying the Court jurisdiction over that issue. This could apply to taxation and personal property as well as to social issues.

If the Supreme Court ever upheld legislation to withdraw jurisdiction over the issue of school prayer or abortion, there is no area of constitutional law which would be immune from congressional action. If one accepts the desirability of even a partial removal of substantive constitutional jurisdiction, then one is condoning the possibility of the removal of the entire Supreme Court appellate jurisdiction.

The proponents of these measures ought to contemplate future Congresses, who may have significantly different views on substantive issues, playing the jurisdictional withdrawal game as well. They should consider carefully whether we would like a pro-gun-control Congress to preclude the Supreme Court from interpreting the meaning of the right to bear arms.

Current restraints on the judiciary

Many in Congress are not concerned about these effects. They believe that without the enactment of these proposals, the Congress and the nation are defenseless against an "imperial" judiciary. I would suggest that our system of government does permit us to respond to fundamentally wrong or "unconstitutional" decisions of the Supreme Court. The framers of our Constitution wisely provided within Article 5 a mechanism for Congress and our citizenry to respond to such decisions. The Eleventh, Fourteenth, Sixteenth, and Twenty-Sixth Amendments were all responses to Supreme Court decisions. This country has had a long and consistent history of actively responding to constitutional decisions of the Supreme Court.

Furthermore, the president of the United States and 100 members of the U.S. Senate have been able to change the philosophical composition of the federal judiciary to respond to changes in public positions on major constitutional issues. Additionally, partial remedies are often available to those in Congress who want to respond to constitutional decisions of the Supreme Court. For example, many of those in Congress who opposed the court's ruling in *Roe v. Wade* exercised their constitutional power to eliminate federal funding over most abortions.

The Congress also has the power to fashion judicial remedies as long as it does not preclude the courts from vindicating constitutional rights. Finally, the court itself has the ability to review its own decisions, which has often served as a significant self-correcting mechanism.

It is my view that our constitutional amendment process, congressional control over the federal pocketbook, and congressional power to fashion judicial remedies gives Congress and our citizenry adequate tools with which to deal with controversial decisions of the Supreme Court. It would be unfortunate if in an effort to promote a specific social agenda, basic principles of governance that have served this country well for 200 years would be undermined.

The issue of federal court jurisdiction may be the single most important item on our nation's noneconomic agenda in the 1980s. The outcome of this debate will determine the status of individual rights and liberties in this country for decades to come. It is my hope that future dialogue will help the Congress and the nation to re-examine what is really at stake in the court jurisdiction proposals.

NOTES

This article originally appeared in Volume 65, Number 4,

October 1981, pages 185-189. It was adapted from an address delivered at the annual meeting of the American Judicature Society Board of Directors in New Orleans on August 8, 1981.

1. In 1957, Senator William E. Jenner introduced S. 2646, a bill designed to forbid the Supreme Court from reviewing cases that questioned any action of a congressional committee or any action of Congress against a witness charged with contempt of Congress or any state laws or regulations that combated subversive activities. A similar effort to remove the Court's jurisdiction occurred in 1968 when an amendment to the Omnibus Crime Control and Safe Streets Act proposed that the Supreme Court be restricted from reviewing state criminal proceedings involving *Miranda* issues. None of these efforts were successful. *See* S. 2646, 85th Cong., 1st Sess. (1957) and Title II of S. 917, 90th Cong., 2nd Sess. (1968), as amended in S. REP. No. 1097, 90th Cong., 2nd Sess. (1968).

2. *See* 125 CONG. REC. S. 4128-S. 4132 (April 5, 1979) and S. 4138-S. 4165 (April 9, 1979). S. 450 as amended passed the Senate but was never formally considered in the House.

3. *See* S. 158, 97th Cong.

4. *See* Johnston Amendment to S. 951, 97th Cong.

5. *See* S. 528, S. 1147, S. 1005, 97th Cong.

6. *See also* S. 481, H.R. 72, 73, 114, 326, 408, 761, 865, 867, 869, 989, 1079, 1180, 1335, 2347, 2365, 2791, 97th Cong.

7. 74 U.S., 7 Wall. 506 (1868).

8. United States v. Klein, 80 U.S., 13 Wall. 128 (1872).

9. *See* Engle v. Vitale, 370 U.S. 421 (1962) and Abbington School Dist. v. Schempp, 374 U.S. 203 (1963).

10. 410 U.S. 113 (1973).

11. Harris v. McPae, 448 U.S. 297 (1980).

12. *See* Hamilton, THE FEDERALIST, No. 78.

13. *See* Message of Veto, President Andrew Johnson, CONG. GLOBE, 40th Cong., 2nd Sess., 2165, (1868).

14. *See* H.R. 2365, 97th Cong.

15. Rosther v. Goldberg, U.S. 80-251 (June 25, 1981).

16. *See* H.R. 114, 97th Cong.

The Courts and Their Publics
States and State Courts

INTRODUCTION

The United States is a federal system in which national supremacy was established over the state governments by the U.S. Constitution and its interpretation by John Marshall for the Supreme Court in the classic case of *McCulloch v. Maryland* in 1819. The American judiciary, too, is organized on a federal model with federal courts coexisting with their state court counterparts. The development of constitutional law has also established federal judicial supremacy as the rule for the relationships among American courts. Consequently, when examining the relationships between the Supreme Court and its "public," much attention must be paid to the interface of the Supreme Court, the states, and state courts.

Thomas Morris' article, "States before the U.S. Supreme Court: state attorneys general as amicus curiae," studies the underresearched role of the states' attorneys general, acting through amicus curiae briefs, before the U.S. Supreme Court. Morris examines the period between 1974 and 1983 and finds that only the U.S. solicitor general is involved in more cases than the states' attorneys general. State amicus activity is shown to be increasing on many measures, including the number of cases per year, the percentage of cases per year, and the number of joinings per year in which states are playing an amicus role. Morris underlines the environment of cooperation and the general absence of conflict that characterizes states in their amicus activity, while also demonstrating why states are at a disadvantage, relative to the U.S. solicitor general, in influencing the Supreme Court. He finds that states are rarely involved as amici in cases where private parties have challenged governmental action, while they are often pitted against the solicitor general in cases dealing with federalism issues. Given the increased importance of federalism for the contemporary court, Morris' subject matter clearly warrants further study. Lee Epstein and Karen O'Connor's piece, "States before the U.S. Supreme Court: direct representation in cases involving criminal rights," supplements Morris' study through an examination of direct representation by the states in criminal rights cases through a decade and a half of Supreme Court litigation. They explore the relative success of appellant and appellee states, while also finding regional differences in state success before the Supreme Court.

In the wake of the increasing conservatism of the Burger and Rehnquist courts in the rights and liberties domain in the past decades, many voices (including that of Justice Brennan) have called for the active pursuit of "new judicial federalism," a phenomenon in which state courts rely increasingly on their own laws and constitutions to decide cases wherever possible. It was hoped by many that such an approach to adjudication could protect and, perhaps, expand upon the rights and liberties legacy of the Warren Court. Shirley Abrahamson and Diane Gutman offer us our first view of this topic in, "The new federalism: state constitutions and state courts." The article develops the historical foundation of the relationship between federal and state courts while emphasizing the greater role that the state courts could play in the wake of the Supreme Court's 1983 decision in *Michigan v. Long*. In that case Justice O'Connor stated for the Court's majority that, "State courts will be presumed to be acting as 'federal forums,' unless they plainly state that they are not so acting . . . . If a state court plainly says that it is relying on state law, the Supreme Court will not review its decision."

Abrahamson and Gutman's analysis of *Michigan v. Long* emphasizes the case's potential for giving state courts "substantial freedom in determining the extent of their autonomy as long as their decisions do not violate federal law." If this suggests, however, that such "freedom" and the "new judicial federalism" are destined to expand the scope of citizen rights, the two empirical analyses by Barry Latzer ("The hidden conservatism of the state court 'revolution' ") and Harold Spaeth, ("Burger Court review of state court civil liberties decisions"), which close out this section of readings, seriously question that view.

Latzer's study of two decades of state supreme court decisions reveals that the adoption of Burger/Rehnquist court doctrines for state law far outweighs their rejection. Latzer does not find a trend whereby state courts expound individual state constitutional doctrine independent of Supreme Court constitutional interpretation. Rather, "The dominant approach is active incorporation of conservative Supreme Court doctrines." Latzer's analysis explores why the new judicial federalism has not been the "liberating" rights vehicle some had expected.

> The conservatism of state constitutional law ratifies the Supreme Court whose doctrines are being endorsed. It satisfies state law-and-order forces, because these doctrines favor the prosecution. And it gives state high courts the satisfaction of being in the judicial mainstream of the state law movement.

In a similar vein, Spaeth utilizes data covering the same period as the Latzer study and argues that the Burger Court did not inhibit liberal state court decision making on civil rights. Rather, the Supreme Court overturned two out of three state court decisions decided by it on review, the majority of which states had decided antithetically to civil liberties and civil rights claims.

All of the articles in this section underline that federalism is a dynamic process in the American system that is always in a state of "becoming." It is clear that federalism issues and the relationship between the Supreme Court, states, and state courts will remain high on the list of the American judiciary's concerns in the years to come.

States before the U.S. Supreme Court: state attorneys general as amicus curiae

State legal offices have not been nearly as successful in influencing the Supreme Court as the U.S. solicitor general, but amicus participation by and coordination among the states is increasing, especially in cases involving federalism issues.

by Thomas R. Morris

Governmental actors, like private interest groups, normally have two ways to lobby the U.S. Supreme Court: direct involvement in cases and participation as amicus curiae. An extensive body of literature exists on the litigation activities of private interest groups.[1] The success of the Office of U.S. solicitor general in using both litigation strategies to defend national policy objectives has also been well documented.[2] The other primary governmental actor before the court, namely the states individually and as a group, has not been examined nearly as much. Furthermore, studies of the litigation record of states have been primarily in terms of the states as direct litigants before the court.[3]

Needless to say, any evaluation of governmental representation before the U.S. Supreme Court is incomplete without consideration of the litigation activities of state attorneys general and their staff attorneys. As a group, their rate of participation both as direct parties and amicus curiae in Supreme Court cases is second only to the solicitor general's office. The reappearance of federalism as a dominant constitutional value makes the period of the Burger Court an appropriate one for examining representation of state interests.

For this study, the Lexis computer-based legal research system was utilized to scan the legal counsel for all cases argued before the U.S. Supreme Court from the 1974 through 1983 terms of the Court. State attorneys general or their staff attorneys participated as a direct party or as amicus curiae in 551 cases, which constituted 32 per cent of the total cases published with full or per curiam opinions in the *U.S. Reports* during that time period. By way of comparison, the U.S. solicitor general's office participated in 1,089 cases (63 per cent) or almost twice as often as the state attorneys general.

The proportion of national to state participation drops well below the two-to-one ratio when only amicus activity is examined. The solicitor general's office submitted amicus briefs in 20 per cent of the cases argued before the Supreme Court during the 1974 through 1983 terms of the Court; state attorneys general, by comparison, participated as amicus curiae in 13 per cent of the cases during that time period. During the 10-term period of this study, state attorneys general participated as amici in 234 (42 per cent) of the cases in which they participated overall; the federal office was involved as amicus in 351 (32 per cent) of the cases in which it participated before the court. Table 1 reveals that in one term, 1977, state attorneys general actually participated as amicus curiae in five more cases than did the Office of solicitor general. Unlike the federal government, of course, states regularly participate as both direct parties and amici in the same case.

This article examines the amicus participation of the states before the nation's highest court for a 10-year period of the Burger Court era. State amicus activity is evaluated in light of the amicus record of the solicitor general's office. Comparisons between the federal and state offices are made in terms of their independence, case selection, and success

Table 1   Comparison of amicus participation by state attorneys general and the solicitor general's office, 1974-1983 terms

Term	State attorneys general No.	Per cent*	Solicitor general No.	Per cent*
1974	14	27	22	20
1975	23	40	45	37
1976	20	33	34	35
1977	27	52	22	23
1978	18	30	36	37
1979	17	43	30	28
1980	26	60	33	33
1981	28	44	47	45
1982	25	41	43	33
1983	36	58	39	33
Totals	234	42	351	32

Data for the Solicitor General is taken from Annual Reports of the Attorney General of the United States, 1978 and 1984.
*Percentage is based on total cases in which the respective offices participated before the Supreme Court.

before the Court. The policy areas most likely to attract the attention of the states are also analyzed, along with the patterns of state involvement and the extent to which amicus participation has changed over time.

The role of state attorneys general

The position of state attorneys general is unique in American government. It operates in the interstices of law and politics, on the front line of federal-state relations, and at the conjunction of the executive, legislative, and judicial processes. Prior to the 1970s, state attorneys general tended to look upon their role as being merely ministerial functionaries of the state administration; they were in office to do the bidding of other political executives and defend the state establishment from legal attacks. The size and responsibilities of state attorneys general's offices expanded in the 1970s to include public advocacy roles in such areas as consumer protection, antitrust enforcement, utility rate intervention, and environmental protection.[4] Largely passive attorneys general's offices were transformed into activist ones. A new breed of state attorneys general, younger and better educated than their predecessors, increasingly exploited the political advantages of their offices. Popularly elected in 43 states, state attorneys general supplemented the traditional legal defense roles of the office with public advocacy activities that contributed to the growing perception of the office as a political stepping stone to higher elective office.

Initially appointed to the Minnesota attorney generalship in 1961 at the age of 32, Walter Mondale was one of the earliest of the new breed of state attorneys general. Declaring himself an "activist," Mondale sought "ways of using the office not in the old traditional passive way, but in an affirmative public protection role."[5] Confronted with complaints of a furnace-repair hoax and initially stymied by the absence of a consumer fraud statute, Mondale's consumer protection unit took action against the company based on a public nuisance law originally written to protect citizens from barking dogs.

Mondale's service as attorney general is also remembered for his involvement in the landmark decision of the U.S. Supreme Court in *Gideon v. Wainwright* (1963). In the early summer of 1962, Florida attorney general Richard W. Ervin mailed a letter to his counterparts in the other states inviting them to submit amicus briefs supporting the 1942 precedent of *Betts v. Brady* on which Florida's restrictive right-to-counsel policy for indigents was based. His letter carried the familiar appeal to states as states by invoking "the right of states to determine their own rules of criminal procedure."[6]

Mondale's surprising response detailed his support of the policy followed by Minnesota and 34 other states to provide for the appointment of counsel for indigents in all felony cases. He sent a copy of his letter to Massachusetts attorney general Edward J. McCormick Jr., whose office took on the responsibility of drafting an amicus brief arguing for a change of the *Betts* precedent. Mondale and McCormick enlisted 21 other attorneys general, including three from states which had no such requirement for counsel, to join them in filing a brief with the Court opposing the existing policy in Florida. Only two states—North Carolina and Alabama—supported Florida's position. In his opinion for the Court, Justice Black took notice of the unexpected position of the states: "Twenty-two states as friends of the Court argue that *Betts* was an anachronism when handed down and that it should be overruled. We agree."[7]

The division of state opinion in the *Gideon* case is a reminder there can be more than one state position on Supreme Court litigation. One of the elements of state representation to be examined in this article is the frequency and nature of such differences among the states. Unanimity of state legal positions, of course, does not assure supportive decisions by the Supreme Court. When the Court was faced with the extension of *Gideon* in *Argersinger v. Hamlin* (1972) nine years later, for example, all state participation supported the position taken by Florida, but the outcome was the same as before—the Court ruled against Florida's policy. The attorneys general of 10 states joined the respondent state of Florida and separate amicus briefs were filed by three states supporting Florida's practice of restricting right to counsel to offenses punishable by more than six months imprisonment.

Comparisons with solicitor general

The U.S. solicitor general is appointed by the president and answers formally to the U.S. attorney general. As a matter of practice, however, occupants of the solicitor general's post have rarely sought the approval of the attorney general in carrying out their responsibilities as the chief advocate of the federal government in the U.S. Supreme Court.[8] The solicitor general's office routinely seeks review by the Supreme Court of only a small percentage of the potentially appealable cases under its control. By selectively making a "confession of error" rather than defending the government's position, the office has acquired a favorable reputation that increases the likelihood of securing review and ultimately winning cases when it does choose to take them to the high court.[9]

For complex political reasons, state attorneys general have not generally enjoyed the same degree of independence as the solicitor general in deciding which cases to take to the Supreme Court. They interact with a wide array of officials at both the state and local levels of government, and most of them participate in campaigns for re-election or election to other offices in which litigation records (especially the failure to appeal cases) can become an issue. In 1984, for example, Dennis Roberts, attorney general of Rhode Island, was locked in a close re-election contest with Arlene Violet, who had challenged him two years earlier. His decision to petition the U.S. Supreme Court for review of his state supreme court's decision to grant Claus von Bulow a new trial was dismissed by the accused's attorney as "political" and by Justice Stevens as "frivolous."[10] Roberts ultimately lost both the appeal and the election. A 1985 *National Law Journal* article also reported a sudden upsurge in petitions to the Supreme Court from Missouri during the period when the state's attorney general, John

Ashcroft, was running for governor.[11]

In the 1970s, the states were generally criticized by scholars and justices alike as poor litigators in the Supreme Court. In a 1975 address to the Fifth Circuit Judicial Conference, Justice Powell noted that "some of the weakest briefs and arguments came from . . ." assistant state attorneys general, especially when compared with the lawyers representing the advocacy groups most likely to oppose state governments.[12] The National Association of Attorneys General (NAAG) responded to the criticisms of state performance in the nation's highest court by designating a lawyer to work full-time as the Supreme Court counsel to the attorneys general. Prior to the fall of 1982, states participating as direct parties or considering an amicus brief would write other state offices they thought might be interested or occasionally put a notice in the NAAG's monthly newsletter. The counsel now arranges moot courts several days prior to scheduled arguments for attorneys general and their staff attorneys before the Court. The counsel also orchestrates a communications network among the state offices that informs them about pending litigation and amicus activity in other states. The network has been credited with more "effective coordination " of amicus curiae briefs filed by the states in some 100 cases.[13]

The effort to provide more centralized coordination of state litigation since 1982 is an important development, but it cannot expect to match the tight control of the solicitor general's office. NAAG's effort can operate only as a support structure for the independent state offices. Varying political considerations and legal authority among the states can substantially shape appellate policy before the Supreme Court. Despite the modern trend encouraged by NAAG toward consolidation of all state legal authority in a centralized attorney general's office, some states permit local government attorneys and state agencies to initiate and appeal cases impacting on statewide interests without the approval, or even over the objection, of the state's chief legal officer.

In Texas, the attorney general decided it was in the best interests of the state not to appeal a federal trial court's decision invalidating a state sodomy statute. After unsuccessfully trying to have the state supreme court order the attorney general to pursue an appeal, a local prosecutor succeeded in his effort to have the U.S. Court of Appeals for the

Fifth Circuit permit him to intervene and appeal the case over the objections of the attorney general. Texas' petition for certiorari to the Supreme Court was supported by the attorney general of Oregon, who filed an amicus brief joined by 25 other states requesting reversal of the Fifth Circuit's inappropriate and potentially disastrous signal to lower echelon and nonlegal state policymakers: If you disagree with the attorney general's legal advice and litigation strategy, you may be treated as a spokesperson for the state in the federal courts.[14]

The high Court denied certiorari on July 2, 1986, but an earlier case provided some support for the position of the amici states. When a New York district attorney appealed a decision by the state high court invalidating a state statute regulating deviant sexual behavior, the Supreme Court indicated that the determination of what state officials should represent the state is "wholly a matter of state concern." The New York attorney general submitted an amicus brief in the case arguing that the statute as applied in the case violated free speech and privacy rights, but that it should not have been struck down on its face. The conflict in the positions taken by the attorney general and the district attorney was cited as one reason for dismissing the writ of certiorari as improvidently granted. In the process of explaining its decision, however, the Court did concede that "in addressing the constitutionality of a statute with statewide application we consider highly relevant the views of the State's chief law enforcement official."[15]

The amicus briefs filed with the Supreme Court by the solicitor general's office have long been held in high regard. Studies examining the solicitor general as amicus curiae from 1920 through the 1983 term of the Supreme Court report a success rate of 70 to 75 per cent, with a somewhat higher figure in civil liberties cases.[16] The rate for Rex Lee, the first solicitor general in the Reagan administration, was a respectable 65 per cent for all amicus cases; however, it dropped to 45 per cent for civil liberties cases. A controversial amicus brief filed in a 1983 abortion case became the focal point of charges that Lee's office had become excessively political and might have contributed to the difficulty his office encountered from the Court in civil liberties cases.[17] Whatever the explanations for Lee's won/loss record, the offices of state attorneys general, given the highly political environment in which they operate, will always be susceptible to the types of criticisms leveled against Lee.

The status of amicus briefs

Rule 36.4 of the Supreme Court facilitates the filing of "friend of the court" briefs. States represented by their attorneys general, as well as any other public agency at any level of government represented by its appropriate legal representative, are exempt from the requirement imposed on private groups to secure the consent of other parties to the litigation or the approval of the Court before filing amicus briefs. In most instances, state officials merely file briefs with the Court, although on rare occasions they argue as amici curiae. For the 10 terms of the Court examined in this study, state attorneys general or their staff attorneys argued as amicus curiae in only 14 cases, and five of those were the death penalty cases heard on March 30 and 31, 1976.[18]

Representation of states when they are direct parties to litigation has traditionally been considered one of the primary responsibilities of the offices of state attorneys general. Participation as amicus curiae, on the other hand, is more likely to be determined by office resources and the personal interest and discretion of the state attorney general. The availability of attorneys otherwise committed to representing traditional clients in state legal offices becomes an important factor in amicus activity. Attorney general Dave Frohnmayer of Oregon estimated that five hours per case are necessary for the approximately eight requests each month for his office to write or join in an amicus curiae brief. Even though the briefs usually address the most important issues of the day, he notes that there is no way to charge the cost of the screening time to any particular client-agency. Finally, assuming the office files two major amicus briefs in the U.S. Supreme Court at 150 hours per case, 780 attorney hours would be necessary each year for amicus activity.[19]

While it is difficult to determine how much effect amicus briefs have on Supreme Court decisions, the large number of amicus briefs submitted to the Court by government officials and private groups provides some indication of the importance attributed to them. Developments during the oral arguments in the short-lived precedent of *National League of Cities v. Usery* (1976) is instructive in this regard. Four states—Alabama, Colorado, Michigan, and Minnesota—filed amicus briefs in opposition to the state position taken by California and 19 other states. The position of the four states was cited by the solicitor general during oral argument as an indication that state sovereignty was not threatened, as the majority maintained, by the extension of the Fair Labor Standards Act to all state and local employees. The attorney for the majority state position replied that he had a letter from the governor of Colorado instructing the attorney general of his state to withdraw his name from the brief referred to by the solicitor general. Upon hearing about the solicitor general's comment, Governor George Wallace of Alabama responded by immediately sending a telegram to the Supreme Court indicating his state supported the position taken by the majority of states participating in the case.[20]

Opposing positions by the states before the Court was a rarity during the period of this study. Not counting original jurisdiction cases, where conflict among the states is much more likely, splits took place in only about 2 per cent of the cases. There were no instances comparable to *Gideon* whereby minimal state support was forthcoming for the respondent state even as large numbers of states joined together to file an amicus brief in opposition. Regional opposition patterns, such as southern versus non-southern states, were not evident. Most of the divisions did not consist of a significant number of states on either side, but rather one or two states on either side or one or two dissenters from an otherwise large number of states.

Commerce clause cases were most frequently the source of divisions among the states. In *Commonwealth Edison Co. v. Montana* (1981), Montana's 30 per cent severance tax on coal precipitated seven amicus briefs addressing the question of whether the tax constituted an unconstitutional burden on interstate commerce. Support for the tax came from states rich in energy resources—New Mexico, North Dakota, West Virginia, Wyoming, Colorado, Nevada, Idaho, Washington, and Oregon. Meanwhile, the existence of half of the nation's low-sulphur coal reserves within Montana's borders prompted energy-consuming states to complain that the state was unfairly exploiting its strategic advantage over the other states; amicus briefs opposing the tax were filed by Kansas, New Jersey, Michigan, Minnesota, Iowa, and Wisconsin. Texas filed a separate brief declaring that while it did not oppose severance taxes per se, no state should be able to benefit inordinately from Congress' decision to substitute coal for increasingly scarce oil and natural gas.

Local disputes were also the source of state conflicts.[21] A commuter tax pitted Maine and Vermont against New Hampshire, which attracted the amicus support of New Jersey. Disagreement over the legal basis for abating a nuisance caused by interstate water pollution resulted in Wisconsin's filing an amicus brief against the respondent states of Illinois and Michigan. The issue of whether a state could prohibit the exportation of hydroelectric energy produced within its borders by a federally licensed facility resulted in Massachusetts and Rhode Island challenging New Hampshire. One final example can be cited when a single state took it upon itself to challenge a respondent state. New Jersey filed an amicus brief opposing the position on the public's right of access to criminal trials argued by Virginia's attorney general in *Richmond Newspapers, Inc. v. Virginia* (1980).

Nature and extent of participation

State amicus activity has steadily increased over the past 25 years. An earlier study of amicus participation by state attorneys general in all decisions reaching the merits in the 1960 through 1973 terms of the Supreme Court identified 164 cases (4 per cent of the total cases decided on the merits).[22] State amicus activity by attorneys general in this study for three fewer terms of the Court amounted to 234 cases (13 per cent of the total cases argued). Prior to the 1970 term, the total number of cases attracting state amici had never exceeded 15. Table 1 reveals that the total number of cases for the 1980 through 1983 terms has never been fewer than 25, and virtually half of the amicus participation occurred in the last four years of the 10-year period.

One measure of the importance attached to amicus activity is the number of states joining such briefs. Twenty-four cases in this study attracted more than half of the states as amici. The states won all five of the criminal cases falling into that category; three of those cases were decided in the 1983 term when the states enjoyed the amicus support of the solicitor general's office.[23] In one-third of the noncriminal cases, the states joined together as amici in important antitrust cases before the Court.

Given the rapid growth of state antitrust enforcement in the 1970s, the high level of cooperation is not surprising. Whereas only nine states assigned attorneys to antitrust activities on a full-time basis in 1970, 40 states had antitrust divisions, collectively employing more than 300 attorneys, by the end of the decade.[24] The states suffered three major setbacks in antitrust enforcement despite the amicus support of the solicitor general.[25] *Illinois Brick Co. v. Illinois* (1977) restricted antitrust actions to direct purchasers, thereby limiting the effectiveness of state attorneys general acting as parens patriae on behalf of state consumers because most such suits are indirect purchaser actions. In *Illinois v. Abbott and Associates* (1983), the states also failed in their effort to convince the Court that federal law should be interpreted to permit state attorneys general access to grand jury files pertaining to federal antitrust violations without having to demonstrate a "particularized need." Finally, in a 1984 decision, the Court rejected the states' argument on the standard of proof to find a vertical price-fixing conspiracy.

Unanimous state support was forthcoming for Maryland's position of categorically denying in-state status to domiciled nonimmigrant aliens holding G-4 visas. Nevertheless, the state policy was held invalid under the Supremacy Clause of the United States Constitution.[26] Other cases attracting large numbers of state amici dealt with the award of attorney's fees for plaintiffs prevailing in civil rights actions (three cases), Indian ownership of land, and the preemption of California's food labeling statute by federal laws.[27]

Noticeably missing from the category of large-scale state amici participation were the major decisions of the Burger Court during the period of this study in such controversial areas as race and sex discrimination, abortion, freedom of speech and press, and church-state relations. Only two cases of those involving half the states could be classified as civil liberties cases.[28] Thirty-three states filed two amicus briefs supporting Florida's challenge to an interpretation of the Rehabilitation Act of 1973 requiring "affirmative conduct" by states in the admission of handicapped persons to clinical training programs. The Court agreed with the states' position even though opposing amicus briefs were filed by the solicitor general and the attorney general of California. Similarly, in 1982, 31 states joined in a brief amicus curiae where the petitioner alleged that her state employer had denied her employment opportunities solely on the basis of her race and sex. The Court rejected the states' argument that state administrative remedies must

be exhausted as a prerequisite to the petitioner's action under federal law.

Whereas the solicitor general has generally been active in civil liberties and civil rights cases, states seldom choose in either large or small groups to participate as amici in cases litigating First and Fourteenth Amendment issues. Individual states, of course, are involved as direct parties defending challenged state policies, but rarely is there amicus participation in such cases and, if it does occur, it almost always consists of one or two states supporting another state's position.[29] A case in which states take a "pro-rights" or "pro-individual" stance as amici against another state, as occurred in *Gideon*, is truly exceptional.

Past research has demonstrated that amicus activity is significantly less likely to occur in criminal cases.[30] The results of this study largely confirm that research. Prior to the 1983 term, the states participated as amici in only 30 criminal cases, representing 16 per cent of the state amicus activity, and five of those were the death penalty cases argued by an assistant attorney general of California in 1976. Furthermore, 20 cases consisted of only one state submitting an amicus brief. The 1983 term, however, provided evidence of increased cooperation among the states in criminal cases. In that term alone, amicus briefs were filed by the states in 11 criminal cases. Single state filings occurred in only four of the cases, and, in three cases, 32 or more states signed on as amici.

Not surprisingly, the cases most likely to attract significant state amici are those dealing with federalism issues. Twenty-six (38 per cent) of the noncriminal cases involving more than 10 states fell into this category. Federalism cases are classified as those concerned with the constitutionality and interpretation of federal statutes and regulations affecting the states, including federal preemption issues, but excluding the construction of Section 1983 of the Civil Rights Act of 1871. The solicitor general's office participated in opposition to the state position in all but three of the cases. The states, not surprisingly, were only half as likely to be in agreement with the Court as was the solicitor general.[31] In the Section 1983 cases, only one of which attracted federal participation, the states fared better, agreeing with the Court three out of five times. In a related category of cases dealing with water rights and land ownership, the solicitor general opposed the state attorneys general in five of the seven cases, including two original jurisdiction cases in which 12 eastern seaboard states unsuccessfully challenged federal control and definition of offshore seabeds.[32]

Practically no federal opposition was encountered in the other noncriminal cases in which more than 10 states were involved as amici. The solicitor general did not participate in the seven cases pertaining to state taxation issues or the two cases in which in-state student status was litigated. In seven of the 10 antitrust cases, the solicitor general took similar positions to those assumed by the states. Likewise, the federal office was supportive of the state position in two challenges to municipal zoning ordinances as constituting a taking of private property without just compensation in violation of the Fifth and Fourteenth Amendments.[33]

Patterns and success

The California attorney general's office participated in one-third of the cases attracting state amicus briefs. It earned the top ranking for the states by filing more separate briefs than any other state and by participating in well over half of the criminal cases in this study. The New York office was also a leader in drafting briefs and was involved in 28 per cent of the state amicus cases. After the top two states, the rate of participation did not vary dramatically; three-fourths of the states were involved in from 15 to 25 per cent of the cases, and no state participated in fewer than 10 per cent of the state amicus cases. While all states filed at least one amicus brief, in some cases the states are simply listed in alphabetical order with no indication as to which state was primarily responsible for writing the brief. Extensive interviewing in the state legal offices would be necessary to learn more about the collaborative efforts among the states in drafting certain briefs. Nevertheless, a review of the record of briefs filed indicates that as many as half the states supplemented the efforts of California and New York at one time or another by taking primary responsibility for preparing a brief joined in by a significant number of states.

The dominant role played by the California and New York offices is not surprising when you consider that each employs more than 450 attorneys while more than half the state legal offices have fewer than 100 lawyers on their staffs. California and New York also lead the states as direct parties in Supreme Court litigation. States with few cases

Table 2　Amici groupings of state attorneys general, 1974-1983 terms

Number of state attorneys general filing amicus	Number of of cases	Per cent
One state only	81	35
2 to 3 states	40	17
4 to 10 states	33	14
11 to 18 states	30	13
19 to 25 states	26	11
26 to 50 states	24	10

before the high Court and small legal staffs can, nevertheless, magnify their impact by choosing to participate as a friend of the Court. Interviews by this author with selected attorneys general revealed that they take seriously the decision as to whether to join amicus briefs submitted to their offices. They recognized that whether they like it or not, a U.S. Supreme Court decision adverse to the interests of another state may very well apply to their state. Camaraderie among the attorneys general is another factor influencing support of sister states. On the other hand, professional norms and limited personnel require attorneys general to consider carefully both the quality and relevance for their state of amicus briefs before agreeing to have their names listed.

Interestingly, California achieved its top ranking in amicus participation despite George Deukmejian's aversion to filing or joining amicus briefs during his four years as attorney general (1979-1983). He believed the state should conserve its resources unless no one else was in a position to file such a brief. A smaller state rarely before the high court as a direct party, however, might actually welcome amicus opportunities. The absence of direct party cases can actually permit states the luxury of writing amicus briefs. The Wyoming office, for example, appeared in only one case as a direct party before the Supreme Court during the period of this study, and yet it argued as amicus in one of 14 cases so argued by the states, wrote or contributed to the drafting of a number of amicus briefs, and participated overall in 21 per cent of the state amicus cases.[34]

Table 2 shows that more than one-third of the amicus activity by states involves only one state and slightly over one-half of the participation is by three or fewer states. The number of briefs filed by the states per case has not changed appreciably from the norm of one or two. If anything, movement toward grater cooperation among the states has reduced the number of cases in which more than two state briefs are filed. What has changed, in addition to the greater number of cases in which states are participating, is the number of states involved in each case. There are almost as many instances, for example, when more than 10 states participated as amici during the 1981, 1982, and 1983 terms of the Court as there were in the preceding seven terms.

The range of state amici in individual cases from one to 49 states makes it difficult to evaluate the success of state cooperation. The significance of an amicus brief filed by one state might be greater than one with unanimous state support, depending on the quality and persuasiveness of the argument. Nevertheless, by examining the record of the one-third of the cases in which more than 10 states participated as amici, a clearer picture of state cooperation emerges than would be reflected if all cases were considered.

The won/loss record for the state legal officials in noncriminal cases was somewhat higher (56 per cent) than when they participated as direct parties in such cases (49 per cent).[35] A phenomenal record of 11 wins in 12 criminal cases attracting more than 10 states increases the overall success rate for the states to 63 per cent. In 10 of the criminal cases won by the states in this category, they submitted amicus briefs in support of the appealing party. Given the Supreme Court's record over the past 30 years of reversing the lower court in two out of three certiorari cases, it is generally advantageous to be supporting the appealing party.[36] Another significant variable in determining success before the Court in light of the solicitor general's record in advocacy of a position consistent with the one advanced by the federal office. Not surprisingly, therefore, the success rate in all cases attracting more than 10 states as amici went up when they were supportive of the position taken by either the solicitor general (75 per cent) or the appealing party (77 per cent).

Conclusion

State attorneys general have received minimal scholarly attention despite their importance as litigators in the U.S. Supreme Court. This article examined the rate of participation of states as amici and the types of cases attracting the attention of large groups of states. State amicus activity was found to be increasing both in terms of the number and percentage of cases entered each term as well as the number of states choosing to join amicus briefs. The general absence of conflict among the states in Supreme Court litigation, excluding original jurisdiction cases, makes an environment of greater cooperation possible. The states are fairly active in significant numbers as amici in cases involving federalism issues, where they are most likely to be opposed by the solicitor general, and in antitrust cases, where the support of that federal official is much more likely. On the other hand, unlike the solicitor general, state attorneys general are scarcely involved as amici at all when private parties challenge governmental policies on the basis of the First and Fourteenth Amendments.

State legal offices are at a distinct disadvantage in influencing the Supreme Court in comparison with the solicitor general's office. The relative independence and centralized control traditionally enjoyed by the solicitor general have permitted that office to screen its cases carefully in order to maximize its influence on the Court. Individual state offices, by contrast, are confronted with few cases as direct parties and find it more difficult to screen their cases for the ones most promising of success. Amicus opportunities permit the states some discretion in deciding which state cases to support, but even then, limited office resources confine them most of the time to cases in which another state is a direct party. The state legal offices are regularly confronted with the reality of defending existing state practices and policies rather than selectively deciding how best to influence the policy formation of the high court.

Nevertheless, the record of state amici when more than 10 states participate is considerably higher than when the states appear as direct parties. Increased coordination of state amicus activity as part of an overall effort to improve state advocacy has apparently been successful in increasing state participation. Not all state cases are "winnable," of course, but amicus briefs can contribute to narrowing the legal or constitutional basis for a decision in hopes of avoiding a sweeping ruling that might adversely affect all states. After all, an amicus brief joined by a good number of states provides the Court with an excellent impact analysis in state litigation.

NOTES

This article originally appeared in Volume 70, Number 5, February-March 1987, pages 298-305. The research was funded by a grant from the University of Richmond Faculty Research

Committee. An earlier version of the article was delivered at the 1985 annual meeting of the American Political Science Association.

1. Vose, CAUCASIANS ONLY (Berkeley: Univ. of Calif. Press, 1959); O'Connor, WOMEN'S ORGANIZATIONS' USE OF THE COURTS (Lexington, MA: D.C. Heath and Co., 1980); Epstein, CONSERVATIVES IN COURT (Knoxville: Univ. of Tenn. Press, 1985).

2. Puro, *The United States as* Amicus Curiae in Ulmer (ed.), COURTS, LAW AND JUDICIAL PROCESSES (New York: The Free Press, 1981); O'Connor, *The* amicus curiae *role of the U.S. solicitor general in Supreme Court litigation*, 66 JUDICATURE 256 (1983); Ulmer and Willison, "The solicitor general of the United States as Amicus Curiae in the U.S. Supreme Court, 1969-1983 Terms," paper presented to American Political Science Association (1985).

3. O'Connor and Epstein, "States as Litigants," paper presented to Southern Political Science Association (1985); Jordan, "U.S. Supreme Court Litigation Activities of State Attorneys General," paper presented to Midwest Political Science Association (1985).

4. Morris and Thompson, "The State attorney general as Public Advocate," paper presented to Western Political Science Association (1985).

5. Lewis, MONDALE: PORTRAIT OF AN AMERICAN POLITICIAN 105 (New York: Harper and Row, 1980).

6. Lewis, GIDEON'S TRUMPET 142 (New York: Vintage Books, 1964).

7. 372 U.S. 335, 345 (1963). Justice Black referred to 22 states rather than 23 because the New Jersey attorney general's name had inadvertently been omitted from the brief and the correction was not made until the final U.S. REPORTS was printed. See Lewis, *supra* n. 6, at 148.

8. Jenkins, *The Solicitor General's Winning Ways*, 63 A.B.A. J. 734-738 (June 1983).

9. Wasby, THE SUPREME COURT IN THE FEDERAL JUDICIAL SYSTEM, 2nd edition, 106 (New York: Holt, Rinehart and Winston, 1984).

10. Dershowitz, REVERSAL OF FORTUNE: INSIDE THE VON BULOW CASE 160-162 (New York: Random House, 1986); California v. Carney, 471 U.S. 386, 396, n. 4 (1985); the attorneys general of Connecticut and Arizona filed amicus briefs supporting Roberts' petition for review, but Professor Dershowitz indicates that several other attorneys general thought the Supreme Court had no power to review the case and so indicated to attorney general Roberts. Dershowitz, p. 161.

11. THE NATIONAL LAW JOURNAL, January 28, 1985, at 30.

12. Quoted in Baker and Asperger, *Foreword: Toward A Center for State and Local Advocacy*, 31 CATH. U. L. REV. 368 (1982).

13. Ross, *Safeguarding Our Federalism: Lessons for the States from the Supreme Court*, 45 PUB. AD. REV. 727 (1985).

14. Brief Amici Curiae for the States, Texas v. Hill (No. 85-1251), Oct. Term, 1985, p. 2. On the issue of whether state attorneys general may appeal cases against the wishes of their state clients, state court precedents are divided. See Feeney v. Commonwealth, 373 Mass. 359, 366 N.E.2d 1262 (1977) for an example permitting such appeals and Santa Rita Mining Co. v. Department of Property Valuation, 111 Ariz. 368, 530 P.2d 260 (1975) denying that discretion.

15. New York v. Uplinger, 467 U.S. 246, 247, n. 1 (1984).

16. Ulmer and Willison, *supra* n. 2, at 8-10, 16-17.

17. *Id.* at 12; NEW YORK TIMES, July 18, 1985 at A-18; see also politicization charges leveled at Lee's successor, Fried, THE WASHINGTON POST, July 7, 1986, at A-7.

18. Gregg v. Georgia, 428 U.S. 153 (1976); Proffitt v. Florida, 428 U.S. 242 (1976); Jurek v. Texas, 428 U.S. 262 (1976); Woodson v. California, 428 U.S. 280 (1976); Roberts v. Louisiana, 428 U.S. 325 (1976).

19. Office of attorney general of Oregon, Agency Budget Request, 1985-87 biennium, pp. 71-72.

20. Kurland and Casper (eds.), LANDMARK BRIEFS AND ARGUMENTS OF THE SUPREME COURT OF THE UNITED STATES, vol. 86, 853, 873 (Washington, DC: University Publications of America, Inc., 1977); copies of the gubernatorial correspondence are in appellate case file No. 74-878 at the National Archives, Washington, DC.

21. Austin v. New Hampshire, 420 U.S. 656 (1975); Milwaukee v. Illinois, 451 U.S. 304 (1981); New England Power Co. v. New Hampshire, 455 U.S. 331 (1982).

22. Johnson, "State Attorneys General as Amici Curiae in Supreme Court Litigation," paper presented to Southern Political Science Association (1975); even assuming all of the amicus briefs for the 1960-1973 terms were submitted just in cases argued, they still would represent only 8 per cent of the total.

23. Nix v. Williams, 467 U.S. 431 (1984); Strickland v. Washington, 466 U.S. 668 (1984); Massachusetts v. Sheppard, 468 U.S. 981 (1984).

24. Marvin, *Settlement of Government and Private Cases: The States*, 50 ANTITRUST L. J. 36 (1981).

25. Illinois Brick Co. v. Ill., 431 U.S. 720 (1977); Ill. v. Abbott and Associates, 460 U.S. 557 (1983); Monsanto Co. v. Spray-Rite Service Corp., 465 U.S. 752 (1984).

26. Toll v. Moreno, 458 U.S. 1 (1982).

27. Hensley v. Eckerhart, 461 U.S. 424 (1983); Patsy v. Board of Regents, 457 U.S. 496 (1982); Blum v. Stenson, 465 U.S. 886 (1984); Wilson v. Omaha Indian Tribe, 442 U.S. 653 (1979); and Jones v. Rath Packing Co., 430 U.S. 519 (1977).

28. Southern Community College v. Davis, 442 U.S. 397 (1979); Patsy v. Board of Regents, 457 U.S. 496 (1982).

29. Amicus briefs were filed by Delaware in Columbus Board of Education v. Penick, 443 U.S. 449 (1979); Washington in Regents of Univ. of Calif. v. Bakke, 438 U.S. 265 (1978); Pennsylvania and Texas in Milliken v. Bradley, 433 U.S. 267 (1977); New York and Ohio in Heffron v. International Society for Krishna Consciousness, 452 U.S. 640 (1981); and New York and California in Roberts v. U.S. Jaycees, 468 U.S. 609 (1984).

30. Hakman, *The Supreme Court's Political Environment: The Processing of Noncommercial Litigation* in Grossman and Tanenhaus, FRONTIERS OF JUDICIAL RESEARCH (New York: Wiley, 1969); Casper, LAWYERS BEFORE THE WARREN COURT (Urbana: University of Illinois Press, 1972).

31. The examples of state agreement with the Court over the opposition of the solicitor general are as follows: Train, Admin., EPA v. City of New York, 420 U.S. 35 (1975); Colorado River Water Conservation District v. U.S., 424 U.S. 800 (1976); National League of Cities v. Usery, 426 U.S. 833 (1976); Southeastern Community College v. Davis, 442 U.S. 397 (1979); Pennhurst State School and Hospital v. Halderman, 451 U.S. 1 (1981); Pacific Gas and Electric Co. v. State Energy Resources Conservation and Development Commission, 461 U.S. 190 (1983); Silkwood v. Kerr-McGee Corp., 464 U.S. 238 (1984).

32. U.S. v. Fla., 420 U.S. 531 (1975); U.S. v. Me., 420 U.S. 515 (1975).

33. Agins v. City of Tiburon, 447 U.S. 255 (1980); San Diego Gas and Electric Co. v. City of San Diego, 450 U.S. 621 (1981).

34. Brown v. Thomson, 462 U.S. 835 (1983); Kleppe v. Sierra Club, 427 U.S. 390 (1976).

35. Jordan, *supra* n. 3, at 5; the success rate for the states in criminal cases for the 1969 through 1981 terms was 54 per cent, O'Connor and Epstein, "States Rights or Criminal Rights: An Analysis of State Performance in U.S. Supreme Court Litigation," paper presented to Northeastern Political Science Association (1983).

36. Wasby, *supra* n. 9, at 166.

States before the U.S. Supreme Court: direct representation in cases involving criminal rights, 1969-1984

by Lee Epstein and Karen O'Connor

How do states fare before the U.S. Supreme Court when they bring or "sponsor" cases involving criminal rights?[1] As shown in Table 1, the mean success rate[2] of the 22 states participating in more than five cases was 59 per cent. This compares favorably with that reported by Thomas Morris for amicus curiae participation. Tremendous variation exists, however, among state success rates; for example, compare Oregon's 10 out of 11 victories with Arizona's meager 29 per cent success score.

How can we explain such variation among the states? One plausible argument is that states differ in terms of the centralization of their efforts: some states have specialized litigation offices or allow only their attorneys general to handle U.S. Supreme Court litigation, while others permit local attorneys to bring cases before the high Court. Based on the literature analyzing the success of the U.S. solicitor general, who operates a tight, centralized litigating office, and of other parties, we would expect that states maintaining a high degree of control over their court efforts may perform better than their counterparts.[3]

In a survey sent to state attorneys general, we attempted to discern how they routinely handled criminal cases at the level of the U.S. Supreme Court. Sixty-eight per cent of the 22 states included for analysis here either possess a centralized litigation department (of the sort run by the solicitor general) or generally permit only the attorney general's office to bring cases to the Supreme Court; the remaining 32 per cent typically allow local district attorneys to litigate cases they handled at lower court levels. But are such disparate means of handling cases associated with success before the

Table 1   States and the Supreme Court, 1969-1984 terms*

State	Prop. of success	N of participation
Alabama	.50	6
Arizona	.29	7
Arkansas	.29	7
California	.78	32
Connecticut	.83	6
Florida	.63	30
Georgia	.33	18
Illinois	.55	22
Kentucky	.57	14
Louisiana	.25	12
Massachusetts	1.00	9
Michigan	.90	10
Missouri	.50	10
New York	.67	21
New Jersey	.60	5
North Carolina	.50	12
Ohio	.62	13
Oregon	.91	11
Pennsylvania	.50	8
Tennessee	.77	9
Texas	.56	16
Virginia	.50	6

*Data collected by the authors. Only states participating in five or more criminal cases are listed.

high Court? Table 2 addresses this question by cross-tabulating success (dichotimized as high—above the mean of 59 per cent—and low—below the mean) with the presence or absence of "litigation control" (also dichotimized as high—state litigation is conducted almost exclusively by a centralized office by the attorney general—and low—litigation may be conducted by local prosecutors).

As Table 2 indicates, no apparent association exists between state success in criminal litigation and "control." Of the 15 states possessing a "high" degree of control, success was almost equally divided, with eight falling below and seven above the 59 per cent success mark. In fact, the only support for the proposition that centralization alone is related to increased success for all states is that seven of the 10 states achieving success rates of over 59 per cent were categorized as having high litigation control.[4]

More specific examples reinforce the finding that litigation "control" and success of states generally are unrelated. Consider the example of New York, a state with a 67 per cent success score. According to the deputy solicitor general of the state, "The handling of criminal issues, unless there is a direct challenge to the constitutionality of a state statute, rests with the district attorneys." Hence, New York possesses no centralized apparatus, yet its success score is seven points above the mean. Arizona, on the other hand, claims that its criminal division in the attorney general's office handles 99 per cent of all U.S. Supreme Court cases, but its success rate of 29 per cent is well below the 59 per cent mark.

Other explanations

If the presence of a specialized office alone does not provide a useful indicator of state success, what other explanations may be more helpful? Scholars have argued that at least two other factors may explain variations among parties, including states. S. Sidney Ulmer, among others, has noted that the Court holds negative perceptions of states in the South and Southwestern regions of the country.[5] Researchers have based such a claim on a number of factors; during the 1960s, for example, the justices perceived the South as thwarting their authority in the areas of civil rights, liberties, and criminal justice.

Table 3, which presents a cross-tabulation of success by region (southern versus nonsouthern),[6] tests this proposition for the Burger Court era. As is clearly indicated, assumptions about the Court's negative perception of Southern litigators remain valid. The lambda statistic suggests that knowledge of a state's region reduces error in predicting its success category by 40 per cent. Put in other terms, 80 per cent of the Southern states had success rates lower than 59 per cent, compared with only 33 per cent of the nonsouthern states. Hence, we can conclude that regional differences are certainly related to success rates before the Court, a finding that reinforces Ulmer's conclusion that "some sections of the country appear consistently more prone to Constitutional Turpitude than others."[7]

Table 2   Litigation control and state success

	Low control	High control
Low success	57.1%	53.3%
	(4)	(8)
High success	42.9	46.7
	(3)	(7)
Totals	100.0	100.0
(N)	(7)	(15)

Lambda=0.0

Table 3   Region and state success

	South	Non-south
Low success	80.0%	33.3%
	(8)	(4)
High success	20.0	66.7
	(2)	(8)
Totals	100.0	100.0
(N)	(10)	(12)

Lambda=.40

Table 4   Appellate rates and state success

	Low appeal	High appeal
Low success	72.7%	36.4%
	(8)	(4)
High success	27.3	63.6
	(3)	(7)
Totals	100.0	100.0
(N)	(11)	(11)

Lambda=.30

Another explanation for variation among parties in Supreme Court litigation emanates from the literature on the judicial process. Scholars have argued that "appellants" have advantages over their "appellee" counterparts because the Court usually takes cases to reverse.[8] Table 4 examines the relationship between appellate rates[9] and success. Here, we simply defined appeal rates as "high" (above the mean of 51 per cent) and "low" (below the mean of 51 per cent) and cross-tabulated those with state success. Once again, our analysis in Table 4 seems to confirm scholarly suspicions concerning appellants. Eight of the 11 states appealing fewer than 51 per cent of their total cases had success rates lower than 59 per cent. In contrast, only three of the 10 states with high success scores appealed fewer than 51 per cent of their cases. Finally, consider two extreme examples: the state of Massachusetts, which won all of its cases during the period under analysis, appealed eight of its nine cases (89 per cent), while one of the least successful states, Georgia, appealed only four of its 18 cases (22 per cent).

In this brief note, we attempted to draw a descriptive picture of states as sponsors of criminal litigation. Although our analysis provides an examination of several explanations for variations among the states, we encourage more systematic research efforts, of the sort conducted by Thomas Morris, exploring these important litigators and their efforts as sponsors and *amicus curiae* before the Supreme Court.

NOTES

This article originally appeared in Volume 70, Number 5, February-March 1987, pages 305-306.

1. The data reported in this note were collected from the *U.S. Reports*. We defined criminal cases as those involving rights under the Fourth, Fifth, Sixth, and Eighth Amendments.

2. We operationally defined success as the number of wins/number of participations.

3. *See* Puro, "The Role of Amicus Curiae in the United States Supreme Court: 1920-1966," unpublished Ph.D. dissertation, SUNY Buffalo (1971); Scigliano, THE SUPREME COURT AND THE PRESIDENCY (New York: The Free Press, 1971); Wasby, *Interest Groups in Court: Race Relations Litigation*, in Cigler and Loomis, eds., INTEREST GROUP POLITICS (1st Edition) 251-274 (Washington, DC: CQ Press, 1983).

4. A multivariate mode of state success also found centralization to be an insignificant determinant of success. When we looked exclusively at success of southern versus nonsouthern states and controlled for a range of other variables, however, centralization adds to our understanding of the success of southern states, but not to that of their nonsouthern counterparts. *See* Epstein and O'Connor, "States and the Court: An Examination of Litigation Success," unpublished manuscript (1986).

5. Ulmer, *The Discriminant Function and a Theoretical Context for its use in Estimating the Votes of Judges*, in Grossman and Tanenhaus, eds., FRONTIERS OF JUDICIAL RESEARCH 335-369 (New York: John Wiley and Sons, 1969); Ulmer, "The Sectional Impact of Judicial Review: Another Look," paper delivered at the annual meeting of the American Political Science Association, Washington, DC, 1986.

6. "Southern" states included for analysis were: Alabama, Arkansas, Florida, Georgia, Kentucky, Louisiana, North Carolina, Tennessee, Texas, and Virginia.

7. Ulmer, "Section Impact," *supra* n. 4, at 16.

8. Provine, CASE SELECTION IN THE UNITED STATES SUPREME COURT (Chicago: University of Chicago Press, 1980); Wasby, THE SUPREME COURT IN THE FEDERAL JUDICAL SYSTEM (2nd Edition) (New York: Holt, Rinehart and Winston, 1984).

We use the terms "appellees" and "appellants" to represent winners and losers at lower court levels. As such, we also included "respondents" and "petitioners" to represent the same concepts.

9. We operationalized appealing party as the proportion of cases that a state appealed (number of appeals/number of participants).

The new federalism: state constitutions and state courts

The "perplexing" idea of federalism has a long and complex history in the United States; jurists and commentators have grappled with its application to the state and federal court systems. The U.S. Supreme Court's Michigan v. Long *decision has opened up a new chapter in this struggle.*

by Shirley S. Abrahamson and Diane S. Gutmann

In 1984, Judge John Minor Wisdom, senior judge, U.S. Court of Appeals for the Fifth Circuit, commented, "It is striking indeed that so many . . . [who] write on the subject of 'Civil Rights and Federalism' have focused on the growing role of the *states* in protecting civil rights, in some cases going beyond Supreme Court guidelines."[1]

For a long time, few people seemed aware that protection of individual liberties could lie in the state constitution—and not solely in the U.S. Constitution. In the 1970s, state courts gradually reawakened to their legitimate authority to construe the rights that their state constitutions provide independently of the U.S. Supreme Court's construction of analogous rights in the federal Constitution. When a state court construes the state constitution in the same way that the U.S. Supreme Court construes the federal Constitution, or when a state court goes beyond the Supreme Court in the protection of human rights, there is no inherent conflict between nation and state. Conflict does arise when state standards fall short of federal standards.

Federal court of appeals Senior Judge J. Skelly Wright recently declared himself an "enthusiastic new convert to 'federalism'" and applauded "state judges who have resumed their historic role as the primary defenders of civil liberties and equal rights."[2]

Federalism has been a perplexing idea from its very inception. At the Constitutional Convention one of the framers expressed his confusion with the as yet not fully developed idea of federalism when he said, "I cannot conceive of a government in which there exist two supremes."[3] Although the Constitution explicitly makes the federal government supreme, the idea that the states remain in some sense sovereign or autonomous has retained vitality throughout our history.

As James Madison recognized in *Federalist 37*, no mathematical formula can tell us how to allocate power between the national government and the state governments. History shows that the allocation of authority between the states and the national government shifts over time. The tension between pressures for state autonomy and pressures for national supremacy is fundamental to federalism. This tension has led at times to conflict and at other times to dialogue and accommodation.

Some commentators use the term *new federalism* to refer to a new relationship between federal and state courts and between the federal and state constitutions. New federalism refers to the renewed willingness of state courts to rely on their own law, especially state constitutional law, in order to decide questions involving individual rights. In new federalism, the federal Constitution establishes minimum rather than maximum guarantees of individual rights, and the state courts determine, according to their own law (generally their own state constitutions), the nature of the protection against state government. New federalism also includes the potential for greater deference by federal courts to state court proceedings and decisions.

Federal and state courts work out their relationship with each other as they work out the relationship between the federal and state constitutions.

The balance between state autonomy and national supremacy is vividly illustrated in the context of the protection of civil liberties.

In this article we examine, first, the historical background of the relationship between federal and state courts. Then, we turn to the experience of both court systems in the protection of civil liberties. Finally, we attempt to assess the impact on both court systems of incorporation, that is, applying many portions of the federal Bill of Rights to the states through the Fourteenth Amendment. We look at the U.S. Supreme Court reaction in *Michigan v. Long* (1983)[4] to the increased role of the state courts in the interpretation and application of the state and federal bills of rights.

Dual governments

The states predate the Constitution and its predecessor, the Articles of Confederation. Before the Declaration of Independence, members of the Continental Congress suggested that each colony form an independent state government. During the months preceding independence, colonists debated the uniformity of state constitutions but rejected such uniformity in favor of each state's calling a convention to draw up a constitution of its own. This individuality reflected a political reality that manifested itself in such incidents as the response of New Jersey soldiers to George Washington's attempt to get them to swear allegiance to the United States: "New Jersey is our country."[5]

At the time of the Constitutional Convention of 1787 in Philadelphia, the states were an independent and somewhat fractious lot loosely bound together by a central "government" backed only by the force of persuasion. Protective of state autonomy, the people waited nervously for the results of the convention, unaware that the delegates were laboring over an entirely new Constitution in apparent disregard of the mandate to meet "for the sole and express purpose of revising the Articles of Confederation."

The idea of unqualified state "sovereignty" lost some of its luster under the Articles of Confederation, but state sovereignty was to survive—albeit somewhat redefined—the framing and ratification of the Constitution.

A proposal at the convention that the existing governmental foundations be swept away in favor of a purely national government was not well received. The framers built the Constitution on the foundation of the states, rather than attempting to lay an entirely new foundation. The Constitution assumes the existence of states (mentioning them at least 50 times), state judiciaries (at least three times), and state constitutions (at least once). In structure and conception, the Constitution drew heavily on the constitutions of the states. As John Adams declared, "What is the Constitution of the United States, but that of Massachusetts, New York, and Maryland! There is not a feature in it which cannot be found in one or the other."[6]

Thus the document that emerged at Philadelphia presupposed two levels of government, each with its own constitution and governmental structure, each existing simultaneously in the same geographic territory, and each deriving its powers from and governing the same people. The states remained autonomous entities under the Constitution, instead of being reduced to mere administrative subdivisions of the central government. Like the people, the states retained whatever powers were not delegated to the central government. James Madison wrote in *Federalist 45*:

The powers delegated by the proposed Constitution to the federal government are few and defined. Those which are to remain in the State governments are numerous and indefinite . . . . The powers reserved to the several States will extend to all the objects which, in the ordinary course of affairs, concern the lives, liberties, and properties of the people, and the internal order, improvement, and prosperity of the State.

Although the states retained autonomous status, the United States was constituted as more than a federation, more than a league or an alliance between nations. The government established by the new Constitution acted on the people directly as well as on the states, in contrast to the Articles of Confederation, which were concerned only with relations between the states.

As Madison described it, the Constitution "is, in strictness, neither a national nor a federal Constitution, but a composition of both."[7] Alexis de Tocqueville put it aptly many years later: "Evidently this is no longer a federal government, but an incomplete national government, which is neither exactly national nor exactly federal; but the new word which ought to express this novel thing does not yet exist."[8] The Constitution established a hybrid national-federal government in which the national government was not to swallow up the states and the states were not to undermine the national government. The Constitution encased two political communities within one system, creating the potential for conflict as well as the potential for fruitful collaboration and dialogue.

A classic description of our federalism in this century comes from Justice Hugo Black. He described it as "a proper respect for state functions, a recognition of the fact that the entire country is made up of a Union of separate state governments, and a continuance of the belief that the National Government will fare best if the States and their institutions are left free to perform their separate functions in their separate ways."[9] The concept of federalism, observed Justice Black, requires neither "blind deference to States' Rights" nor the centralization of control over every important issue. Rather, each government must be sensitive to the legitimate interests of the other. Anxious though the national government may be to vindicate and protect national rights and national interests, it must do so in ways that will not impede legitimate state activities.

Federalism and individual rights have been intertwined in American constitutional history from the very beginning. The framers strove to bestow upon the national government authority to deal with national problems, while safeguarding state autonomy and individual liberty. As Madison wrote in *Federalist 51*, "In the compound republic of America, the power surrendered by the people is first divided between two distinct governments, and then the portion allotted to each subdivided among distinct and separate departments. Hence, a double security arises to the rights of the people. The different governments will control each other, at the same time that each will be controlled by itself."

With the division of powers between the national and state governments and the separation of powers, the framers of the Constitution, according to John Quincy Adams, gave us "the most complicated government on the face of the globe."[10]

Dual courts

In attempting to tell the story of the dual court system in condensed form, we begin with the ending. This country has two independent but interrelated judicial schemes: state and federal. The framers and Congress provided for a complex and intricate system of two sets of courts with overlapping jurisdiction. They did not attempt to simplify the dual judicial scheme by apportioning federal

adjudicative powers solely to the federal courts and state adjudicative powers solely to the state courts. Rather, both the federal and state courts apply federal and state law.

Before exploring the interaction between state and federal courts as an aspect of our federalism, we will trace the origins of the dual system of courts. The dual judicial system grows out of the tension between two contending principles: national supremacy and state autonomy.

The federal judiciary seems so natural and inevitable now that it may be difficult to imagine a time when its establishment and existence were controversial. We have been schooled to think of constitutional governments as necessarily composed of three branches: the legislative, the executive, and the judicial. Our government would seem unbalanced without a judiciary.

Yet in order to comprehend the original understanding of the role of the federal judiciary, we must realize that a federal judiciary was not at all inevitable. There was no national judiciary under the Articles of Confederation. While not very controversial during the drafting process, the establishment of a federal judiciary became intensely controversial during the ratification process. The establishment of the federal judiciary was perceived as a threat to state autonomy. The resistance to this perceived threat did not succeed in blocking the establishment of a federal judiciary, but it did succeed in influencing its structure and jurisdiction.

The cornerstones of the present-day federal judicial system are Article III of the Constitution and the Judiciary Act of 1789.

The Convention: Article III. If we were to look to the records of the Constitutional Convention for information on the original understanding of the role of the federal judiciary and its relationship to the states, we would find surprisingly little on the subject. What controversy there was concerning the federal judiciary centered on the form it would take, not on whether it should exist at all.

The Convention quickly decided to establish a federal judiciary separate from the existing state judicial systems, adopting Edmund Randolph's resolution "that a National Judiciary be established." The reason for this quick assent, Alexander Hamilton later explained, was that the framers were convinced that a national judiciary was an essential part of a government. This conviction must have rested in part on the belief that all properly formed governments have three branches. The national government would rely on the national judicial system to uphold federal laws (especially when the national and local policy were at variance) and to provide a more uniform system of justice than the state courts could. As Tocqueville later put it, "The object of creating a Federal tribunal was to prevent the state courts from deciding, each after its own fashion, questions affecting the national interests, and so to form a uniform body of jurisprudence for the interpretation of the laws of the Union."[11]

Although the framers were willing to limit state autonomy in order to ensure that the laws and the Constitution of the national government would be fairly and uniformly applied, they balked at setting up any federal courts other than the Supreme Court. Many feared that lower federal tribunals would unacceptably infringe on state autonomy and the integrity of the state judicial system. John Rutledge urged that "the State tribunals might and ought to be left in all cases to decide in the first instance, the right of appeal to the supreme national tribunal being sufficient to secure national rights & uniformity of Judgments: that it was making an unnecessary encroachment on the jurisdiction of the States and creating unnecessary obstacles to their adoption of the new system."[12] Some delegates viewed creating a national system of courts as expensive and as a possible impediment to the states' ratification of the Constitution if the states feared that lower federal courts would encroach on the jurisdiction of the state courts. Madison and other delegates, however, favored a provision in the Constitution creating lower federal courts with final jurisdiction.

After Rutledge's motion against lower federal courts carried, James Wilson and Madison urged that "there is a distinction between establishing such tribunals absolutely and giving a discretion to the Legislature to establish or not establish them."[13] They proposed the compromise that the convention adopted: The national legislature would be empowered to institute lower federal courts. Thus, because the framers were unable to reach a conclusion on the issue of lower federal courts, they decided to leave the matter to Congress.

To summarize what emerged from the convention concerning the judiciary, Article III of the Constitution expressly provides that the federal judicial power encompasses both the states and individuals as litigants. Furthermore, the federal judicial power, like the legislative and executive powers, is an enumerated power. The listed categories of cases that federal courts could hear may be viewed as restrictions on federal invasion of state judicial power. The federal judicial power of the United States extends to "all cases in law and equity arising under the Constitution," a broadly worded grant of jurisdiction, and to laws of the United States and to diversity jurisdiction, that is, to suits between citizens of different states.[14] Diversity jurisdiction was accepted without debate at the convention and without explanation of its purpose, although debate on this provision was extensive during ratification and has been intermittent ever since. Hamilton explained in *The Federalist* that because state courts could not be supposed to be impartial in cases pitting a citizen of their state against a citizen of another state, diversity jurisdiction was properly in the federal courts.[15]

The text of the Constitution clearly evinces concern for the independence of the federal judiciary, perhaps because the framers were aware that many state judges depended on state legislatures. This concern is evident in the method of judicial appointment (the president with the advice and consent of the Senate), the protection of judicial tenure (during good behavior), and the prohibition on diminishing judicial salary during continuance in office.

One issue the Constitution did not address directly, however, is the relation of the federal courts to the state courts.

The supremacy clause. A mechanism was needed to settle disputes over the respective spheres of state and federal judicial power, i.e., to ensure that the states did not undermine the national government and that the national government did not usurp state powers. To address that need, the framers adopted Article VI of the Constitution, the supremacy clause. The supremacy clause provides that the Constitution, laws, and treaties of the United States are the supreme law of the land, superior to state constitutions and state laws. State judges are bound by oath to support the Constitution and are "bound [by the Constitution], any thing in the Constitution or Laws of any State to the Contrary notwithstanding." The supremacy clause makes the Constitution enforceable in all the courts in the land.

Madison, in *Federalist 44*, vividly portrayed the

need for the supremacy clause, stating that without it, "the world would have seen, for the first time, a system of government founded on an inversion of the fundamental principles of all government; it would have seen the authority of the whole society everywhere subordinate to the authority of the parts; it would have seen a monster, in which the head was under the direction of the members." In contrast to the constitutional mechanism to prevent the states from undermining the national government, the Constitution did not expressly provide a mechanism to thwart a central government's "natural tendency" to destroy state governments. Although scholars still debate the original understanding of the framers, the federal judiciary has had this power since *Marbury v. Madison* (1803).[16]

The framers did not try to resolve with finality the tension they had set up between national supremacy and state autonomy in the judicial sphere. Future generations would have to work that out by adjusting and readjusting the relationship between state and federal courts. As Hamilton said in *Federalist 82*, "Time only can mature and perfect so compound a system, liquidate the meaning of all the parts, and adjust them to each other in a harmonious and consistent WHOLE."

Ratification. The need for a federal judiciary, which had seemed so self-evident to the framers at the convention, became the center of controversy during the ratification debates. Some antifederalists feared the breadth of federal judicial power and argued that state courts were adequate. In fact, the antifederalists prophesied the demise of the state tribunals should the Constitution be ratified. According to George Mason, "the Judiciary of the United States is so constructed and extended, as to absorb and destroy the Judiciaries of the several States."[17]

In contrast to the gloomy picture painted by the antifederalists, some passages of *The Federalist Papers* paint a rosy picture in which the state and federal courts function as kindred systems and parts of a whole. Hamilton interpreted the Constitution as permitting state and federal courts concurrent jurisdiction, with both state courts and federal courts deciding questions of state and federal law arising in cases within their respective judicial powers.

According to Hamilton, the state courts would retain the jurisdiction they had, except where state jurisdiction was expressly prohibited. The state courts were not, according to Hamilton, divested of their "primitive jurisdiction" except for appeals.[18] Furthermore, except where expressly prohibited, the state courts would have concurrent jurisdiction in all cases arising under the laws of the union. Hamilton reasoned that the supremacy clause demonstrates the framers' assumption that state courts could adjudicate issues of federal law.

Hamilton concluded, however, that in instances of concurrent jurisdiction, the Supreme Court's appellate jurisdiction would extend to decisions of the state courts as well as the federal courts. Indeed, Hamilton saw a need for federal appellate jurisdiction over state courts. He claimed in *Federalist 81* that state judges could not be "relied upon for an inflexible execution of national laws" because, in all states, judges were to some degree dependent on the state legislatures through selection, salary, or term, and might not stand up to them. Hamilton found no impediment to permitting appeals from state courts to inferior federal courts. "The evident aim of the plan of the convention is," wrote Hamilton, "that all the causes of the specific classes shall, for weighty public reasons, receive their original *or* final determination in the courts of the union.

The prospect of a national court with ultimate authority to determine the final meaning of the supremacy clause was a frightening one for the antifederalists. Not only was the federal government deemed supreme, it was also empowered to decide what this supremacy meant. Federal courts were charged with the important responsibility of limiting the supremacy of the federal government and protecting state autonomy.

The Judiciary Act of 1789. Article III was not self-executing, and on September 24, 1789, the first Congress adopted "An Act to establish the Judicial Courts of the United States." The Judiciary Act of 1789 is weighty evidence of the true meaning of the Constitution, according to the U.S. Supreme Court, because it was passed by the first Congress assembled under the Constitution, many of whose members had taken part in the convention. Furthermore, the act set forth, to a large extent, the basic structure of the federal courts as we know it.

The Judiciary Act of 1789 established the Supreme Court, which has existed continuously ever since, although the number of associate justices has changed. More significantly, the act resolved the controversy over lower courts: Congress approved them. After a vigorous debate reminiscent of ratification, Congress decided that federal trial courts were necessary. The act set up two tiers of trial courts: district courts (at least one per state) and three circuit courts. The circuit courts, composed of two Supreme Court justices and one district court judge, were the weak spots in the system and were later abolished; separately constituted circuit courts of appeals were ultimately established.

Congress did not confer on the federal courts the full judicial power granted by the Constitution. Surprisingly, the act did not grant the federal trial courts jurisdiction over "federal question cases," that is, cases arising under the Constitution or laws of the United States in private civil litigation. The prevailing view was that state courts were the appropriate forum for the enforcement of federal law and that federal courts should be available to citizens who might be victims of bias in sister state courts. Accordingly, Congress granted diversity jurisdiction to the lower courts, concurrent with state courts, and authorized the removal of diversity actions from state court to federal court.

Federal district courts did not obtain "federal question" jurisdiction until 1875. Until that time, federal question cases, in the absence of diversity jurisdiction, could only be brought in state courts.

To ensure state court autonomy and a final determination by a federal court for all cases raising federal issues, the 1789 act provided for Supreme Court review of state courts' final judgments or decrees in matters of federal concern in three categories of cases in which the state court held *against* a federal claim:

• where the validity of a treaty, statute, or authority of the United States is drawn into question, and the state court decides against its validity;

• where the validity of a state statute or authority is challenged on the basis of federal law, and the state court decides in favor of the validity of the state statutory authority;

• where a state court construes the U.S. Constitution, a U.S. treaty, statute, or commission and decides against a title, right, privilege, or exemption under any of them.[19]

The Supreme Court could not review state court decisions favorable to a claim of federal right until 1914, when Congress granted this review power to the Supreme Court. This amendment was prompted largely by a New York Court of Appeals decision holding a state workers' compensation law in conflict with the due process guarantees of both the federal and state constitutions.

During Reconstruction and thereafter, Congress broadened federal jurisdiction largely at the expense of state courts. Federal removal jurisdiction was expanded. The writ of *habeas corpus* empowered lower federal courts to test the legality of confinements by reviewing the judgments of state courts, even after they had been affirmed by the state's highest court. Thus, state criminal defendants could challenge their convictions in lower federal court and ultimately in the U.S. Supreme Court. Within this scheme, federal courts have a significant impact on state courts and cases.

The United States still has the dual system of courts it had initially. State courts retain the authority they possessed before the Constitution, plus the power to hear questions of federal law. In the Constitution and the Judiciary Act, the state courts appeared to be the primary guarantors of federal constitutional rights and in many instances actually have been the ultimate ones. Congress gave federal courts, existing side by side with their state counterparts, limited jurisdiction. The ability of federal courts to decide matters of state law was restricted to state law issues arising in cases in which federal jurisdiction was independently established. Thus, only the basic outline of the relationship between federal and state courts was set by the Constitution and the Judiciary Act. Much was left to be worked out in practice.

Protection of liberties

Although it initially lacked a bill of rights, the Constitution did not ignore the subject of individual liberties altogether. It guaranteed jury trial in criminal cases, freedom from both federal and state *ex post facto* laws and bills of attainder, and freedom from state laws impairing the obligation of contract. Missing, however, were the traditional clauses of a bill of rights, found in many state constitutions, protecting such individual liberties as freedom of religion, freedom of speech and press, and freedom from unreasonable searches and seizures or compulsory self-incrimination. Thomas Jefferson viewed the absence of a bill of rights securing the people's liberties against governmental power as a major obstacle to the acceptance of the Constitution. The champions of ratification, recognizing their political error, promised to amend the Constitution. The first session of the first Congress drafted a bill of rights in the form of a series of amendments, 10 of which were approved by the required number of states by December 15, 1791.

The federal Bill of Rights now protects individual liberties against the federal and state governments, while the state constitutions protect against the state government and sometimes against action by private persons. It has not always been so.

The federal Bill of Rights. Despite the presence of bills of rights in so many state constitutions, the delegates, with the notable exception of George Mason, seemed uninterested in appending a bill of rights to the Constitution. Mason objected: "There is no Declaration of Rights, and the laws of the general government being paramount to the laws and constitution[s] of the several states, the Declaration of Rights in the separate states are no security."[20] Until Mason raised it, James Wilson said, the issue of a bill of rights had never "struck the minds" of the delegates.[21]

To many of the delegates, the guarantees of individual liberty in the state constitutions appeared to be enough, in part because the Constitution, unlike the state constitutions, was a government of limited, enumerated powers. Roger Sherman apparently expressed the consensus of the convention when, in response to a question about the need to preserve the right to trial by jury, he said, "The State Declarations of Rights are not repealed by the Constitution; and being in force are sufficient."[22] Sherman's argument was that the Constitution could not be interpreted to authorize the federal government to violate rights that the states could not violate.

During the ratification process, the people were unpersuaded by federalist arguments against inclusion of a federal bill of rights in the Constitution: the state declarations of rights would adequately protect individual liberty; the state declarations of rights would wither away if a federal bill of rights were established; and the enumeration of rights in a federal declaration of rights might prejudice those rights not enumerated. The popular clamor for a bill of rights was so great that several states agreed to ratify the Constitution only on the understanding that a bill of rights would be added. The Constitution was ratified without a bill of rights, but Congress immediately took up the issue.

Abiding by promises made during ratification, James Madison, initially a staunch opponent of a federal bill of rights, supported the Bill of Rights in Congress. Arguing before Congress that fundamental rights should not depend on the "too uncertain" hope that the limited powers of the national government enumerated in the Constitution would be interpreted to protect individual liberties, Madison claimed that state declarations of rights would not be sufficient. Echoing Mason's argument at the convention, Madison noted that while a state bill of rights might protect an individual's rights from state interference, it might not prevent the national government from interfering with those same rights. Besides, some states had no bill of rights and bills of other states were defective.[23]

Although Madison's arguments in favor of a bill of rights restraining the national government prevailed, his proposal to have the federal bill of rights impose specific restraints on the state governments failed. Madison's proposed amendment no. XIV provided: "No State shall infringe the right of trial by Jury in criminal cases, nor the right of conscience, nor the freedom of speech or of the press." Although some states had no bill of rights, and although Madison reasonably argued that "if there were any reason to restrain the Government of the United States from infringing upon these essential rights, it was equally necessary that they should be secured against the State Governments,"[24] amendment no. XIV did not pass. A federal constitutional protection against state infringement of individual rights would have to wait until well after the adoption of the Fourteenth Amendment after the Civil War.

Separate and distinct spheres. The challenge after the ratification of the Bill of Rights was to reconcile its existence with the existence of state bills of rights. The Supreme Court responded to this challenge by confining the Bill of Rights to national governmental action. In *Barron v. Baltimore* (1833),[25] an owner of a wharf sought compensation from the City of Baltimore under the Fifth Amendment to the Constitution for destroying the commercial use of his property in making street improvements. The Supreme Court concluded that the owner had no Fifth Amendment protection, calling the issue a matter "of great importance, but not of much difficulty."

Overlapping spheres of the two constitutions. Reconstruction dramatically changed the scope of the Bill of Rights and changed the relations between the court systems. Adopted in 1868, the Fourteenth Amendment expressly limits states' interference with civil liberties. It is reminiscent of Madison's proposed amendment no. XIV, but Madison's proposal was restricted to certain specific rights; the language of the Fourteenth Amendment is more open-textured.

Section 1 of the Fourteenth Amendment prohibits the state from making or enforcing any law that abridges the privileges or immunities of citizens of the United States; deprives any person of life, liberty, or property without due process of law; or denies any person within its jurisdiction the equal protection of law. The last section of the amendment empowers Congress to enforce the amendment by appropriate legislation.

Between 1866 and 1877 Congress took steps to enforce the Fourteenth Amendment by adopting several major civil rights statutes that created new federal rights and remedies modifying existing state law. Congress also increased federal judicial jurisdiction. It opened the lower federal courts to civil rights claims, and, in 1875, to all cases founded on federal law. Thus, litigants could bypass state courts in federal question cases. Finally, Congress authorized the lower federal courts—as opposed only to the Supreme Court—to supervise or supersede the state courts in their implementation of federal law by *habeas corpus*, removal, and injunction.

The first test of the limits of the postwar restructuring of federal-state relationships came in the *Slaughterhouse Cases* (1873).[26] The Fourteenth Amendment provides that no state shall abridge "the privileges and immunities" of citizens of the United States. In the *Slaughterhouse Cases* a group of butchers challenged as a denial of one of the protected privileges and immunities a Louisiana statute granting a monopoly of the slaughtering trade to a private corporation. The Court declared that the claim was not a federal right or privilege but rather a state right or privilege not within the ambit of the Fourteenth Amendment.

The Supreme Court construed the Fourteenth Amendment as extending against the states only those rights that were national in character: the right to travel, the right to petition for redress of grievances, the right to use the navigable waters of the United States, and other similar rights. This list of national rights remained short, because the Supreme Court refused to hold that the other guarantees enumerated in the Bill of Rights were

among the privileges and immunities of citizens of the United States.

Although the Supreme Court read the privileges and immunities clause of the Fourteenth Amendment narrowly in the *Slaughterhouse Cases*, the Court later applied many of the first eight amendments to the states through the Fourteenth Amendment's due process clause, rather than the privileges or immunities clause. This application of the first eight amendments to the states through the Fourteenth Amendment is known as incorporation.

In 1897, the Court held that the Fourteenth Amendment proscribed the taking of private property for public use without payment of just compensation.[27] It was not until 1925, in *Gitlow v. New York*,[28] that the Court suggested in *dictum* that the rights guaranteed by the First Amendment are among the fundamental personal rights and liberties protected by the due process clause of the Fourteenth Amendment against the state government.

Thus, from 1787 to 1925, the Bill of Rights offered individuals little or no protection in their relations with state and local governments. The state constitutions provided those protection. During that period, however, the states' records in preserving individual rights were uneven within a state and among the states. For example, the states' records were good in appointing counsel for indigent criminal defendants at public expense. In 1859, the Wisconsin Supreme Court, as a matter of its own state constitutional law, required counties to appoint counsel for indigent felony defendants at county expense. It was not until 1963, 104 years after the Wisconsin Supreme Court had acted, that the U.S. Supreme Court required states, as a matter of Fourteenth Amendment due process, to provide counsel in state felony trials. By the time the U.S. Supreme Court imposed this requirement, most states appointed counsel at public expense, as called for by state constitutions, state laws, or state practice. In *Gideon v. Wainwright* (1963)[29] the U.S. Supreme Court brought only a few laggard states into line.

In other areas of individual rights, the states' records were poor. Many have argued that the failure of the states to provide better protection for individual rights created a void—one that the Supreme Court felt compelled to fill.

Incorporation after 1925. After 1925, the incorporation of the enumerated guarantees of the first eight amendments into the Fourteenth gained momentum, and the pace accelerated during the 1960s. The incorporation doctrine partly nationalized individual liberties and the doctrine coincided with technological, economic, and social changes that tended also toward nationalization.

Because many of the first eight amendments deal with the criminal process, the incorporation doctrine involves, to a large extent but not exclusively, a defendant's criminal procedural rights. The Fourteenth Amendment, for instance, now applies to the states the guarantees of the Sixth Amendment, including the rights to obtain a speedy trial, to have a public trial, to have an impartial jury, to confront one's accusers, to have compulsory process for obtaining witnesses in one's behalf, and to have the assistance of counsel. The Fourth Amendment right of freedom from unreasonable searches and seizures, including the federal exclusionary rule, which since 1914 has required federal judges to exclude illegally seized evidence from the trial, has been fully binding on the states since 1961. The Court made the Fifth Amendment prohibition of double jeopardy and the rule against compulsory self-incrimination fully binding upon the states as well. This privilege against self-incrimination became the basis of *Miranda v. Arizona* (1966),[30] requiring police to give warnings before custodial interrogation. Those rights in the federal Bill of Rights that are not incorporated in the Fourteenth Amendment remain dependent on state law.

The Supreme Court also expanded certain rights afforded by the Constitution as it was extending them against the states through the Fourteenth Amendment. The Court expanded not only the procedural rights of the criminal defendants but also other civil liberties. For example, several decisions of the 1960s expanded First Amendment protections, thereby barring state-required prayers in public schools and limiting the extent to which public officials and public figures could avail themselves of state libel laws.

The incorporation doctrine gave prominence to the Constitution as a protection against invasions of individual liberties by either the state or national government. The combination of incorporation and expansion of rights increased state judges' obligations to apply federal law in state cases.

State courts, of course, were not total strangers to federal law. The two systems have always influenced each other, both directly and indirectly. Federal courts had always applied and developed state law, and state courts had always applied and developed federal law. As Justice John Harlan wrote in the 1884 *Robb v. Connolly* decision, "Upon the State courts, equally with the courts of the Union, rests the obligation to guard, enforce, and protect every right granted by the Constitution of the United States . . ."[31]

Nevertheless, the incorporation of much of the Bill of Rights through the Fourteenth Amendment, as well as the extension of the reach of federal law in general, made the state courts partners with the federal courts in the enforcement of federal law to an unprecedented extent. Working out the terms of this new partnership is one of the main challenges in adjusting federal-state court relations in the post-incorporation period.

Independent state grounds

The U.S. Supreme Court does not have a responsibility to review a state court interpretation of state law and will not do so unless an interpretation somehow implicates issues of federal law. In other words, if a state judgment rests on adequate and independent state grounds, the Supreme Court will not reach either the state or the federal issues in the case. While some commentators assert that neither the Constitution nor federal statutes requires this position, the adequate and independent state grounds doctrine is the generally accepted and traditional test for reconciling the respective claims of the state for independence of state law and of the national government for review of interpretations of federal law.

The genesis of the adequate and independent state grounds test as a way of determining which state court decisions are subject to Supreme Court review lies in *Murdock v. City of Memphis* (1875).[32] Seventy years later, the Supreme Court more clearly explained its position in *Herb v. Pitcairn* (1945).[33] The doctrine is premised on the Court's respect for the independence of state courts and the Court's desire to avoid issuing advisory opinions, that is, opinions that discuss and answer legal questions unnecessary to the resolution of the case. The Court explained:

This Court from the time of its foundation has adhered to the principle that it will not review judgments of state courts that rest on adequate and independent state grounds. The reason is so obvious that it has rarely been thought to warrant statement. It is found in the partitioning of power between the state and federal judicial systems and in the limitations of our own jurisdiction. Our only power over state judgments is to correct them to the extent that they incorrectly adjudge federal rights. And our power is to correct wrong judgments, not to revise opinions. We are not permitted to render an advisory opinion, and if the same judgment would be rendered by the state court after we corrected its views of federal laws, our review could amount to nothing more than an advisory opinion.[34]

Complications arise when the state court opinion is ambiguous about whether the court relied on federal or state law. Determining whether an independent and adequate state ground exists is no easy task. Until 1983, when presented with an ambiguous state court decision, the Supreme Court could exercise one of several options. It could dismiss the case. It could vacate the decision and send the case back to the state court to clarify the grounds. It could order a continuance and direct the petitioner to obtain clarification from the state court. Finally, the Court itself could determine which constitution the state court relied upon.

In 1983, in *Michigan v. Long,* the Court admitted that it "had not developed a satisfying and consistent approach for resolving this vexing issue" and adopted a new approach to the independent and adequate state grounds test, concluding that its prior "ad hoc method of dealing with cases that involve possible adequate and independent state grounds is antithetical to the doctrinal consistency that is required when sensitive issues of federal-state relations are involved."

Michigan v. Long

Michigan v. Long involved the constitutionality of a protective police search of an automobile for weapons. During the search of the trunk, the police found 75 pounds of marijuana; the defendant moved to suppress the evidence. Citing the Michigan Constitution twice, but otherwise relying exclusively on federal law, the Michigan Supreme Court held "that the deputies' search of the vehicle was proscribed by the Fourth Amendment to the United States Constitution and art. I, sec. 11 of the Michigan Constitution."[35]

Writing for the five-member majority, Justice Sandra Day O'Connor stated that the Court was unconvinced that the Michigan decision rested upon independent state grounds. More important, the Court announced a new approach to its use of the adequate and independent state grounds doc-

trine in state cases in which the grounds for the decision are ambiguous. The Court would "accept as the most reasonable explanation that the state court decided the case the way it did because it believed that federal law required it to do so."

In other words, the Court set forth a presumption that the state decision rested on federal grounds. If the state court wanted to avoid this presumption, it

need only make clear by a plain statement in its judgment or opinion that the federal cases are being used only for the purpose of guidance, and do not themselves compel the result that the court has reached . . . . If the state court decision indicates clearly and expressly that it is alternatively based on bona fide separate, adequate, and independent grounds, we, of course, will not undertake to review the decision.[36]

The Court's justification for imposing the plain statement requirement was to protect the integrity of both federal and state law making. To the extent that a state court decision is based on federal law, federal review is required for doctrinal coherence, and for uniformity of federal constitutional law. State court systems and the federal courts develop and interpret federal constitutional law. Indeed, state courts turn out a larger body of criminal law cases than the federal courts. Justice O'Connor viewed the mixed federal-state opinions as threatening the federal system with a deluge of unauthoritative elaboration on federal law. The *Michigan v. Long* rule promotes uniformity by enabling the Court to review more state court decisions, because the Court now reviews decisions that are or *may* be based on federal law. The Supreme Court thus fulfills its role as the final arbiter of federal constitutional law.

Commentators assert that the *Michigan v. Long* presumption apparently rests on the Court's belief that the Constitution is the primary law in the state courts for protecting civil liberties. They say that the presumption relegates state constitutional law to a marginal role such that state judges may ignore it altogether and render judgment exclusively under federal law. The effect of the presumption is that the U.S. Supreme Court treats state courts as functional equivalents of federal courts unless the state courts expressly deny equivalency in a particular case.

In this sense, *Michigan v. Long* nationalizes state courts when their decisions are based on federal and state grounds. The Court will presume that state court decisions resolving federal and state issues rest on the resolution of the federal issues in the case. State courts will be presumed to be acting as "federal forums," unless they plainly state that they are not so acting.

In summary, in the interests of "efficiency," "uniformity," and "justice," and out of "respect for independence of state courts," the Court requires that state court opinions contain a "plain statement" that their judgments rest on adequate and independent state grounds if they do not wish to invite Supreme Court review. The judicial presumption, therefore, is that a state court's decision does *not* rest on adequate and independent state grounds, and a state court must clearly rebut that presumption if it wishes to insulate its decision from federal review.

Michigan v. Long also seeks to protect the integrity of the state. If a state court plainly says that it is relying on state law, the Supreme Court will not review its decision. The Court reaffirms the state court's opportunity to be the final arbiter of its own law and to divest the U.S. Supreme Court of jurisdiction to review. As Justice O'Connor explained in a speech, a state determines whether to "grant or withhold jurisdiction to the Supreme Court by the choice and articulation of the grounds for the state court decisions."[37] Furthermore, *Michigan v. Long* appears to encourage state courts to function more effectively by considering separately their functions as "federal courts" and as state courts. As author of the majority opinion, Justice O'Connor stated the goal as facilitating justice and judicial administration, not thwarting state constitutional development.

One effect of *Michigan v. Long*, therefore, is to shift the burden to the state courts to decide just how far they are going to be nationalized. If a state court feels it important to assert the state's autonomy by interpreting its constitution independently—not necessarily differently, just independently—then the court itself must ensure that its decisions are based on adequate and independent state grounds. Essentially, state courts must begin to develop their own philosophy of federalism from the state perspective.

Nonreviewability is the U.S. Supreme Court's acknowledgment of state autonomy. Reviewability is the affirmation of national supremacy.

The dissent

Justice John Paul Stevens viewed the case as raising "profoundly significant questions concerning the relationship between two sovereigns—the State of Michigan and the United States of America." He argued that historically the presumption was that adequate state grounds are independent unless it clearly appears otherwise. He favored retaining this policy of federal judicial restraint, thereby husbanding the limited resources of the Supreme Court. Justice Stevens expressed the belief that "a policy of judicial restraint—one that allows other decisional bodies to have the last word in legal interpretation until it is truly necessary for this Court to intervene—enables this Court to make its most effective contribution to our federal system of government."

Moreover, Justice Stevens reasoned, the Court has an interest in a case only when state standards fall short of federal standards and an individual has been deprived of a federal right. He believed the Court should not be concerned when the state court interprets federal rights too broadly and overprotects the individual. Justice Stevens complained of a "docket swollen with requests by States to reverse judgments that their courts have rendered in favor of their citizens."

Some commentators take issue with Stevens' contention that the majority's presumption of reviewability is not supported by any significant federal interest. They point out that cases that grant rights to the citizen against the state government affect important government functions that protect all of us and that Supreme Court review ensures that state courts will not hamper state officials by imposing erroneous federal constitutional requirements on them. Other commentators assert that the majority's presumption serves the federal interest in having effectively functioning states, because it eliminates a "dysfunction" caused by incorporation.[38] According to this dysfunction viewpoint, where a state court decision that erroneously relies on federal law to restrain state action goes unreviewed, because a state ground was also cited for the decision, there would be an error in the system that everyone would seem powerless to correct. The Supreme Court could not correct it because it could not review it. It would be beyond the reach of the state legislature as well.

The majority and dissent in *Michigan v. Long* agree that state courts may constitutionally develop an independent body of civil liberties law and that if no federally guaranteed rights are abridged in the process, state courts may apply state law to the exclusion of federal law. *Michigan v. Long* does not signal a change in the rule that state constitutions may provide more protections for the individual than those provided in the federal Constitution. It does remind the states that when they act like federal courts and interpret federal rights, they are potentially subject to review as a federal court.

The disagreement between Justice Stevens and Justice O'Connor is thus not whether to adopt a clear rule for determining whether a state decision is independent, but what that rule should be.

The aftermath

Michigan v. Long has engendered a large body of literature that ranges from praise for the decision to condemnation of the "plain statement" rule to questioning the constitutional, theoretical, and functional bases of the adequate and independent state grounds doctrine. The proponents of the decision support it as a workable, practical way for handling state decisions that fail to state clearly whether they rest on federal grounds or independent and adequate state grounds. They conclude that the U.S. Supreme Court ought to promote its federal lawmaking role and ought not to renounce its power to interpret federal law in favor of the nonauthoritative state court readings of federal law. They view *Michigan v. Long* as promoting the U.S. Supreme Court's maintaining uniformity and supremacy of federal law.

To its admirers, *Michigan v. Long* furthers federalism because it delineates clearly the respective spheres of state and federal law and possibly enhances the ability of state courts to experiment in developing principles of constitutional law suitable for that state's constitution and that state's people. They see the case as attempting to encourage states to construct their own inviolable sphere of state law. Some commentators conclude that the plain statement will be a burden only to those state courts that were purposely ambiguous in grounding their decision in federal and state law to evade Supreme Court review and to insulate the decision from the state political process.

Other commentators are more skeptical. They question whether *Michigan v. Long*, which was decided in the name of federalism, really encourages federal judicial interference with state courts' constitutional discretion. The detractors of *Michigan v. Long* view it as an artificial attempt to impose

federal law on state courts. They suspect the case is not based on a natural principle of federalism but rather is a means of constraining civil liberties protection. They view *Michigan v. Long* as masking the Court's substantive goal of keeping state courts from interpreting their constitutions generously.

These commentators conclude that although, in theory, *Michigan v. Long* preserves the state court's ability to interpret its own constitution, in the real world the decision hinders state courts from developing state law. These writers argue that the state political climate might prevent state judges from interpreting state law more broadly than federal law. They say that a state court opinion that benefits a minority or runs against majoritarian preferences places a state judge, who is often an elected official, at risk. The detractors reason that a state judge who holds that state and federal law together compel an unpopular result is taking a safer political course than a judge who holds that state law gives greater rights than federal law. Moreover, these commentators point out that the people of the state can respond to an unpopular state court interpretation by amending the state constitution. Indeed, some states have amended their constitutions to require state courts to harmonize their interpretation of the state constitution with federal precedents. Putting a new twist on the old fear that state judges are "dependent" rather than independent and are not on a par with federal judges, some argue that state courts whose interpretations of the state constitutions will be subject to review by state legislators and the electorate will not be as receptive to claims that a constitutional right has been denied as would be a federal court that is independent from other branches of government and from the electorate at large. Thus, the argument goes, state courts will either interpret their constitutions restrictively or risk Supreme Court review so that the Court will take the blame for the increased protection of civil liberties.

Regardless of which view one takes of *Michigan v. Long*, the U.S. Supreme Court has itself made a plain statement. If a state court wishes to insulate its decision from Supreme Court review, it must express clearly the state law grounds for its decision and must, of course, not deny any federal right.

The advent of incorporation has required a readjustment of the relations between federal and state courts. Incorporation affects each system. It threatens the federal system with a loss of control over federal law, and it threatens the state system with nationalization. In *Michigan v. Long*, the Supreme Court apparently tried to stave off both these threats. The measure of its success will be seen in future state and federal court decisions involving civil liberties.

The impact

Michigan v. Long will be felt in federal district courts and circuit courts of appeals as well as in state courts. As we said earlier, federal courts may apply state law and thus function as state courts. In *City of Mesquite v. Aladdin's Castle, Inc.* (1982),[39] for example, the U.S. Supreme Court remanded a case to the Fifth Circuit to decide whether its opinion declaring a city ordinance violative of the constitutional guarantees of due process and equal protection rested on Texas law or federal law. The Supreme Court held that it would not decide this novel federal constitutional question if Texas law provided independent support for the courts of appeals judgment.

Similarly, in 1985 the Ninth Circuit set aside a city ordinance prohibiting the solicitation of donations in public areas used by a municipal stadium. The court began its analysis by stating that the challenge was based on both the federal and California constitutions and that if the California Constitution provides independent support for the claim, there is no need for a decision of the federal issue. There is no certification procedure in California for the federal court to ask the state supreme court to declare the state law issue. The Ninth Circuit decided the state law question, holding the ordinance violative of the California Constitution, and did not reach the federal question.

It is too early to judge the long-term impact of *Michigan v. Long* on state and federal courts. We can say, however, that many state courts remain unaffected by *Michigan v. Long*, and their decisions are like their pre-1983 decisions. Many still do not refer to state constitutions. Those that do often make no effort to separate the state and federal grounds upon which the decision is based. At the same time, a growing number of state high courts have been relying on their own constitutions. If a state court adopts federal interpretations as the interpretation of the state constitution, however, the state ground may not be sufficiently independent of federal law to insulate the decision from review.

If federal and state courts respond to *Michigan v.*

Long in the future by increased reliance on state law, the number of cases in which the Court can articulate its views of federal constitutional law may be decreased. In this eventuality, *Michigan v. Long* may achieve disparity between federal and state interpretations of similar constitutional provisions.

Michigan v. Long does not mandate any particular approach to federal and state constitutional claims, although scholars are divided on whether Justice O'Connor's and Justice Stevens's opinions represent a debate over the interstitial and primacy approaches, which in turn represent different views toward federalism. For the present, however, hopes and fears will abound with regard to *Michigan v. Long*. Some will continue to fear that federal review of state court decisions that do not make clear whether they rest on federal or state grounds will become "advisory" in a new sense—that the U.S. Supreme Court will be advising the states how to construe their state constitutions. Such advice is not unprecedented. In a case predating *Michigan v. Long*, Chief Justice Burger criticized the Florida Supreme Court's construction of the Florida Constitution, saying that it was not rational law enforcement and suggesting that the people amend the state's laws or constitution to override state court opinions that extend individual rights.

Others will continue to hope that the presumption of reviewability will force state courts to make clear the grounds of their decisions and interpret their state constitutions. In that case, the Supreme Court may also receive some unsolicited commentary, favorable or unfavorable, on its own opinions, such as that found in some recent state court opinions.

Perhaps such spirited mutual advice is not totally unwelcome in a federal system of which one of the chief virtues is the dialogue between the national and the state governments.

Conclusion

Federalism will continue to mean different things to different people. From the time the framers adopted the term *federalism*, there was confusion and disagreement about what the term meant. Deriving from *foedus*, meaning treaty or alliance, the term *federal* was, some assert, coopted by the proponents of the Constitution to refer to their quasi-national form of government. As Garry Wills puts it, "By a kind of pre-emptive verbal strike, the centralizers seized the word and cast the original federalists in the role of antifederalists."[40]

The term was born through a process of redefinition, and it has been continually redefined since that time. The genus federalism already includes a wide variety of species: dual federalism, cooperative federalism, interactive federalism, classical federalism, and dialectical federalism, to name just a few. We will not attempt to classify "new federalism" within any of these categories.

New federalism represents an attempt to reinvigorate the idea of federalism by reviewing the idea of state autonomy, an idea that some had declared dead during the incorporation period. The meaning of state autonomy and the proper role for states remain unsettled: state courts, among other institutions, will play a role in resolving these unsettled issues as they decide whether and how to apply the protections of civil liberties in their state constitutions. In this respect, new federalism is a return to the preference of the framers for a monolithic system tempered by pluralism.

New federalism is not an attempt to return to the nullificationist vision of the role of states. The proponents of new federalism do not suggest that state courts be the sole guardians of individual liberty or that the U.S. Supreme Court retreat from applying the Bill of Rights to state action. As Justice Brennan said, "One of the strengths of our federal system is that it provides a double source of protection for the rights of our citizens. Federalism is not served when the federal half of that protection is crippled."[41] The difficulty is to work out a system in which federal and state protections can coexist. The fundamental puzzle, as Professor Paul Bator notes, is to determine what the appropriate criteria are for deciding which questions the federal Constitution should be deemed to have made a matter of uniform national policy.[42]

State court approaches to the questions of when and how to interpret their state bills of rights will also tend to define their relationship with the federal courts. As *Michigan v. Long* seems to indicate, state courts will have substantial freedom in determining the extent of their autonomy as long as their decisions do not violate federal law. Thus, the great challenge for state courts in the post-incorporation era is to ground their decisions both in the protection of individual liberties and in the principles of federalism.

NOTES

This article originally appeared in Volume 71, Number 2, August-September 1987, pages 88-99. It is adapted from a paper presented at the 73rd American Assembly, Arden House, Harriman, New York, April 23-26, 1987, and which appears in its entirety in A WORKABLE GOVERNMENT?: THE CONSTITUTION AFTER 200 YEARS (New York: W.W. Norton, 1987).

The authors wish to thank Diana Balio, Sharon Ruhly, and Joel R. Wells for their assistance in the preparation of the manuscript.

1. Wisdom, *Foreword: The Ever-Whirling Wheels of American Federalism*, 59 NOTRE DAME L. REV. 1063, 1076 (1984).

2. Wright, *In Praise of State Courts: Confessions of a Federal Judge*, 11 HASTINGS CONST. L.Q. 165, 188 (1984).

3. Gouverneur Morris, quoted in Bowen, MIRACLE AT PHILADELPHIA 40 (1966).

4. 463 U.S. 1032 (1983).

5. Bowen, *supra* n. 3, at 7.

6. *Id.* at 199.

7. THE FEDERALIST PAPERS, No. 39.

8. De Tocqueville, DEMOCRACY IN AMERICA 164 (Henry Reeve Text as Revised by Francis Bowen, 1945).

9. Younger v. Harris, 401 U.S. 37, 44 (1971).

10. John Quincy Adams, "Jubilee of the Constitution: A Discourse Delivered at the Request of the New York Historical Society in the City of New York on Tuesday, the 30th of April, 1839, Being the Fiftieth Anniversary of the Inauguration of George Washington as President of the United States on Thursday, the 30th of April, 1789," p. 115 (1839).

11. De Tocqueville, *supra* n. 8, at 148.

12. 1 Farrand, THE RECORDS OF THE FEDERAL CONVENTION OF 1787, 124 (1966).

13. *Id.* at 125.

14. Art. III, Sec. 2, U.S. Const.

15. THE FEDERALIST PAPERS No. 80.

16. 1 Cranch 137, 2 L.Ed. 60 (1803).

17. 2 Farrand, THE RECORDS OF THE FEDERAL CONVNENTION OF 1787, 638 (1966).

18. FEDERALIST PAPERS No. 82.

19. Act of Sept. 24, 1789, 1 Stat. 73.

20. 2 Farrand, *supra* n. 17, at 637.

21. Wood, THE CREATION OF THE AMERICAN REPUBLIC 536 (1969).

22. 2 Farrand, *supra* n. 17, at 588.

23. 1 Kurland & Lerner, THE FOUNDERS' CONSTITUTION 479-484 (1987).

24. *Id.* at 492.

25. 32 U.S. (7 Pet.) 243 (1833).

26. 83 U.S. (16 Wall.) 36 (1873).

27. Chicago B. & Q.R.R. v. Chicago, 166 U.S. 226, 241 (1897).

28. 268 U.S. 652 (1928).

29. 372 U.S. 335 (1963).

30. 384 U.S. 436 (1966).

31. 111 U.S. 624 (1884).

32. 87 U.S. (20 Wall.) 590 (1875).

33. 324 U.S. 117 (1945).

34. *Id.* at 125-126 [citations omitted].

35. People v. Long, 413 Mich. 461, 320 N.W.2d 866, 870 (1982).

36. 463 U.S. 1032, at 1041 (1983).

37. O'Connor, *Our Judicial Federalism*, 35 CASE WEST RES. L. REV. 1, 5 (1984-85).

38. Althouse, *How to Build a Separate Sphere: Federal Courts and State Power*, 100 HARV. L. REV. 1485 (1987).

39. 455 U.S. 283 (1982).

40. Wills, EXPLAINING AMERICA: THE FEDERALIST 169 (1981).

41. Brennan, *State Constitutions and the Protection of Individual Liberties*, 90 HARV. L. REV. 489, 503 (1977).

42. Bator, *Some Thoughts on Applied Federalism*, 6 HARV. J. L. & PUB. POL'Y 51, 58 (1982).

The hidden conservatism of the state court "revolution"

The image of the New Judicial Federalism is that of a wholly liberal legal movement, but an examination of state court decisions rendered over the past two decades reveals that the adoption of Burger/Rehnquist Court doctrines for state law far outpaces their rejection.

by Barry Latzer

"A study of state constitutional criminal law should include state cases that adopt federal decisions as valid interpretations of state constitutions as well as those that do not. If the state is the laboratory, all experiments must be studied."[1]

—Shirley S. Abrahamson, Justice,
Wisconsin Supreme Court

The last two decades have witnessed a major upsurge in state court decisions predicated upon state, as opposed to federal, constitutional law. As we enter the 1990s there is a sizeable and growing body of case law interpreting state constitutional provisions, especially the state bills of rights. This development has been referred to variously as the "state law revolution," the "state bill of rights movement," and the "New Judicial Federalism." The image of this New Federalism is that of a wholly liberal legal movement. From judges to the mass media to legal scholars, the widespread perception is that state constitutions are being interpreted more favorably to criminal defendants, civil liberties, and civil rights litigants than is the U.S. Constitution. For instance, *The New York Times* declared in a recent front page article: "On Rights, New York Looks to State, Not U.S. Law."[2] California Supreme Court Justice Stanley Mosk announced in a law review that, unlike the old states' rights movement of Orval Faubus and George Wallace, "[t]oday states' rights are associated with increased, not lessened individual guarantees."[3] The *National Law*

Journal recently described the New Federalism as "a forceful reaction to the increasing conservatism of the federal courts," and it quoted Ronald K.L. Collins, a leading authority, to the effect that there are now "more than 600 opinions that go beyond the federal minimum standards on individual rights issues."[4]

This perception is understandable. The New Federalism was born in response to the conservatism of the Burger Court.[5] Former Justice William Brennan, champion of liberal causes on the Court, served as the movement's cheerleader, publishing articles and giving speeches in support.[6] And much publicity is given to state decisions rejecting, on state law grounds, conservative Burger/Rehnquist doctrines.[7] Thus, in the area of criminal procedure law, it has become a commonplace to assume that state bills of rights are being interpreted much more favorably to criminal defendants than the federal Bill of Rights.

However, because the rights-expanding decisions have been the focus of so much of the literature, insufficient attention has been paid to the myriad state constitutional rulings that have not broadened individual rights. When the vast bulk of state constitutional criminal law rulings—both rights-expanding and rights-contracting—are analyzed, the picture that emerges is considerably different than the literature would lead one to believe. This article is part of a study of the state constitutional criminal procedure decisions of the courts of last resort of all 50 states rendered over the last two decades. A thorough examination of these decisions—perhaps as complete an analysis as has been done to date—reveals that the *adoption* of Burger/Rehnquist Court doctrines for state law far outpaces their rejection. Indeed, for every state high court decision repudiating U.S. Supreme Court doctrine there are at least two cases endorsing it. Concededly, there are now hundreds of cases expanding criminal defendants' rights in reliance upon state law, and a one-out-of-three rate of rejection of Supreme Court rulings is a major development deserving all of the attention it has received. However, a balanced assessment of state constitutional law also requires attention to the fact that two-thirds of the criminal rulings are endorsements, not repudiations, of the Supreme Court.

It should be emphasized that this not a situation where the Supreme Court's relatively insignificant doctrines have been approved, and its significant ones rejected; there is a mix of important and not-so-important cases on both sides of the equation. Moreover, any suggestion that the "more important" state courts, the ones that set the trends for the rest, are more rejectionist, and that therefore rejectionism is the wave of the future, is also unsupported by the evidence. As will be seen, while some leadership courts (e.g., New York and Oregon) are fairly rebellious, other vanguard tribunals (e.g., Connecticut, New Hampshire, and New Jersey) have very high rates of approval of the output of the Burger/Rehnquist majority.

Some of the limitations of the study from which these conclusions have been drawn must be noted. First, the data are derived from the decisions of the state high courts and do not include the outputs of the intermediate appeals tribunals, which are the appellate courts of *first* resort in 37 states. Insofar as the intermediate appeals courts also decide cases based upon their respective state constitutions, disregarding their rulings made the study more manageable, if less precise an indicator of the current law of each state. On the other hand, given the largely "clearinghouse" role of these courts, and their relatively secondary and transitory role as expositors of new law, it may be expected that the high courts afford a reasonably accurate picture of state constitutional law.

Another limitation of this study is its confinement to criminal justice cases, omitting state constitutional rulings on such matters as religion, abortion, race discrimination, or free speech. It is possible that if decisions in these other areas were taken into account, the overall picture of the New Federalism would look different. A court may be more liberal in one area of law, say on abortions, and more conservative in another. On the other hand, aside from the interest in criminal cases in their own right, such cases are probably good indicators of the relative activism of the states in developing state constitutional law. Criminal cases make up a sizeable portion of the state appellate court workload, and probably a disproportionately high number of its state constitutional law decisions as well. Even if they do not give the total picture of the New Federalism, the criminal cases are a good measure of state constitutional activism.

With these limitations in mind, we seek to answer the following questions about the scope and nature of the criminal law aspects of the New Federalism. First, as to scope: how extensively do state courts rely upon their state constitutions to decide criminal cases; and how do the states compare on this score? Are some states more active than others in developing state law? Second, as to the nature of this body of law: how different is state constitutional criminal law from its federal counterpart, and how is it different? Is state law more protective of defendants' rights, or no more protective? Do some states interpret their state bills of rights more favorably to defendants than others? Third, we must try to explain the reasons for the response of the state judiciary to the state law movement. Especially, we must ask why the New Federalism has developed as it has, with so many Supreme Court doctrines being incorporated into state law.

Methodology

To answer these questions, the following methodology was used. All of the state high court criminal procedure cases based upon state constitutional law decided from the late 1960s to the end of 1989 were collected.[8] This was made more difficult by the failure of the state courts to make clear, in judicial opinions, whether the decision was based upon an interpretation of the U.S. Constitution, the state constitution, or both. Generally, these "law-ambiguous" cases were excluded and the study was limited to what may be considered "pure" state constitutional law cases.[9] Each case that took the same position as the U.S. Supreme Court in one of its federal Bill of Rights rulings was deemed an "adoption" decision. Each case taking a position contrary to the High Court was treated as a "rejection."[10] The cases were then grouped by state, and within each state, by conformity ("adoption") or nonconformity ("rejection") with the U.S. Supreme Court.[11] This made it possible to compare the extent to which each state court has relied upon its own constitution, as opposed to the U.S. Constitution, in deciding criminal cases. It also facilitated a comparison of the states in terms of the degree of doctrinal conformity/nonconformity with the High Court in Washington.

Florida and California were treated differently from the other states because of recent anti-exclusionary rule amendments to their respective state constitutions.[12] In 1982, both states adopted constitutional amendments designed to reduce the exclusion of evidence on state law grounds. The California amendment, approved in a public referendum (Proposition 8), barred the exclusion of any "relevant evidence," effectively abolishing most state constitutional exclusionary rules.[13] The Florida amendment required that its search and seizure provision be "construed in conformity" with the Fourth Amendment as interpreted by the Supreme Court, apparently compelling the adoption of Burger/Rehnquist search and seizure doctrines for the state constitution. Because these amendments were expected to have a major impact upon the constitutional law of the two states, it was felt that a distinction should be drawn between pre- and post-amendment state court rulings. Therefore, for California and Florida, cases predating the amendments were grouped separately from cases decided thereafter. In addition, post-amendment reaffirmations of earlier decisions were separately counted. This facilitated assessment of the impact of these provisions, and the rather dramatic results are discussed below.

Table 1 covers the collected state constitutional criminal procedure decisions of all 50 states. The percentages in parentheses were derived by dividing the number of adoptions (or rejections) by the sum of each state's adoptions and rejections. In the interest of saving space, references to all of the adopting or rejecting cases have been omitted.[14] Cases on issues never ruled on by the Supreme Court (as of the end of 1989) were not counted.

Actives and inactives

The above data enable us to group the states in terms of their relative reliance upon their state constitutions as a basis for decision making. By

Table 1 Rejection and adoption of U.S. Supreme Court criminal procedure doctrines by state high courts on grounds of state constitutional law

State	Rejections	Adoptions
Alabama	1 (33%)	2 (66%)
Alaska	18 (82%)	4 (18%)
Arizona	3 (37%)	5 (63%)
Arkansas	0 (0%)	1 (100%)
California	9 (47%)[1]	10 (53%)[1]
	20 (83%)[2]	4 (17%)[2]
Colorado	6 (33%)	12 (67%)
Connecticut	2 (8%)	22 (92%)
Delaware	1 (11%)	8 (89%)
Florida	4 (18%)[3]	18 (82%)[3]
	4 (80%)[4]	1 (20%)[4]
Georgia	3 (60%)	2 (40%)
Hawaii	7 (58%)	5 (42%)
Idaho	2 (25%)	6 (75%)
Illinois	0 (0%)	13 (100%)
Indiana	2 (67%)	1 (33%)
Iowa	1 (6%)	17 (94%)
Kansas	1 (14%)	6 (86%)
Kentucky	2 (20%)	8 (80%)
Lousiana	5 (36%)	9 (64%)
Maine	5 (25%)	15 (75%)
Maryland	1 (8%)	11 (92%)
Massachusetts	9 (75%)	3 (25%)
Michigan	3 (21%)	11 (79%)
Minnesota	2 (67%)	1 (33%)
Mississippi	5 (29%)	12 (71%)
Missouri	1 (13%)	7 (87%)
Montana	8 (31%)	18 (69%)
Nebraska	0 (0%)	8 (100%)
Nevada	1 (50%)	1 (50%)
New Hampshire	8 (20%)	33 (80%)
New Jersey	6 (27%)	16 (73%)
New Mexico	0 (0%)	3 (100%)
New York	12 (60%)	8 (40%)
North Carolina	1 (7%)	13 (93%)
North Dakota	1 (20%)	4 (80%)
Ohio	1 (14%)	6 (86%)
Oklahoma	5 (36%)	9 (64%)
Oregon	12 (43%)	16 (57%)
Pennsylvania	14 (52%)	13 (48%)
Rhode Island	5 (38%)	8 (62%)
South Carolina	0 (0%)	0 (0%)
South Dakota	4 (23%)	13 (77%)
Tennessee	3 (27%)	8 (73%)
Texas	4 (19%)	17 (81%)
Utah	4 (23%)	13 (77%)
Vermont	4 (33%)	8 (67%)
Virginia	0 (0%)	3 (100%)
Washington	9 (45%)	11 (55%)
West Virginia	10 (40%)	15 (60%)
Wisconsin	1 (6%)	17 (94%)
Wyoming	2 (12%)	14 (88%)
Totals	232 (32%)	489 (68%)

1. Post-Proposition 8. If the offense was committed before the effective date of the anti-exclusionary amendment the applicable state constitutional law is based upon pre-amendment interpretations—even if the appeal were decided after Proposition 8. People v. Smith, 34 Cal.3d 251, 667 P.2d 149, 193 Cal. Rptr. 692 (1983).
2. Pre-Proposition 8.
3. After 1983 Amendment.
4. Before 1983 Amendment.

simply adding together each state's total number of rejections and adoptions we get an activism score. The higher the score, the more activist the state.[15] The 10 most active states, in order of de-

Table 2   Reliance upon state constitutions by state high courts: 10 most active states

State	Cases
California	43
New Hampshire	41
Oregon	28
Florida	27
Pennsylvania	27
Montana	26
West Virginia	25
Connecticut	24
Alaska	22
New Jersey	22

Table 3   Reliance upon state constitutions by state high courts: 10 least active states

State	Cases
South Carolina	0
Arkansas	1
Nevada	2
Alabama	3
Indiana	3
Minnesota	3
New Mexico	3
Virginia	3
Georgia	5
North Dakota	5

creasing activism, are listed in Table 2.

Using the same scoring system, the 10 least active states, in order of increasing activism, are shown in Table 3.

Before analyzing these results however, we must look to the substance of the state court outputs, i.e., the doctrinal congruence of state decisions with the output of the U.S. Supreme Court. Merely considering state constitutional activity without regard to doctrinal output is potentially misleading: it masks the extent to which the state courts can participate in the state law movement without conflicting with the Supreme Court. Looking at activity in isolation from doctrine gives the false impression that there is greater state court-Supreme Court conflict than there is in fact. In other words, state constitutional activity is not identical with rejection of Supreme Court doctrine. The hypothesis suggested here (and discussed below) is that doctrinal conformity serves as a buffer between the state and U.S. supreme courts, enabling the former to meet both Supreme Court ("vertical") pressures to conform and sister state court ("horizontal") pressures to develop independent state law.

Adopting and rejecting Supreme Court doctrine

It is important to differentiate the states not only in terms of their tendency to rely upon their state constitutions, but also in terms of their willingness to break with the U.S. Supreme Court. Among those states which have rendered five or more state constitutional rulings in criminal cases (five having been chosen because the eight most inactive states each decided fewer than four cases), we may distinguish those which have most frequently and those which have least often repudiated Supreme Court doctrine.

Although the figure is somewhat arbitrary, it was felt that a 75 per cent rate of agreement or disagreement with Supreme Court doctrine was a good indicator of a propensity on the part of a state supreme court to conform with or rebel against its federal counterpart. That is, where at least three-quarters or more of a state's cases were all adoptionist or all rejectionist, the state was considered more of a conformist or rebel than its sister states. The grouping of states in Table 4 is in order of decreasing rates.

The data in Table 4 indicate that 44 per cent of all the states are high adopters of Supreme Court doctrine, while only 8 per cent are high rejecters. The rejectionist category is probably inflated because it counts California and Florida, although since the amendments of their constitutions compelling conformity with federal law, their rejection rates have declined dramatically. California's went from 83 per cent to 47 per cent, and Florida's plummeted from 80 per cent to 18 per cent. The conforming amendment to Florida's constitution was so potent that the state appears on *both* lists, having been a high rejectionist before the amendment and a high adopter since. If these two states were removed from the rejectionist list only two states (4 per cent of the country) could be considered rejectionist.

The adoptionist list would be considerably longer if the many hundreds of "law-ambiguous" decisions were to be counted, as these are overwhelmingly in conformity with Supreme Court dogma. Those states which routinely render law-ambiguous decisions, and have not made five or more "pure" state law rulings over the last 20 years are here considered state constitutional inactives. But if these law-ambiguous cases were to be treated as true state constitutional law, the number of adoptionist cases would increase dramatically, and the list of adoptionist states would include a clear majority, rather than 44 per cent of the states. In short, not only is the rejectionist list inflated, the adoptionist list may also be an underestimate.

Table 4 Highest state adopters and rejecters of U.S. Supreme Court doctrine

Rejectionist states (4) (75% +) (5+ cases)	Adoptionist states (22) (75% +) (5+ cases)
California (pre-Prop. 8) (83%)	Illinois (100%)
Alaska (82%)	Nebraska (100%)
Florida (before '83 Am.) (80%)	Iowa (94%)
Massachusetts (75%)	Wisconsin (94%)
	North Carolina (93%)
	Connecticut (92%)
	Maryland (92%)
	Delaware (89%)
	Wyoming (88%)
	Missouri (87%)
	Kansas (86%)
	Ohio (86%)
	Florida (after '83 Am.) (82%)
	Texas (81%)
	Kentucky (80%)
	New Hampshire (80%)
	North Dakota (80%)
	Michigan (79%)
	South Dakota (77%)
	Utah (77%)
	Idaho (75%)
	Maine (75%)

Reassessing the New Federalism

These figures suggest that there are a number of misconceptions about the New Federalism in need of correction. The high number of states which routinely and invariably incorporate Supreme Court doctrines into their state constitutional law compels reevaluation of the phenomenon. First, considered overall, the state "revolution" is not nearly as liberal as it is generally perceived; the dominant approach is active incorporation of conservative Supreme Court doctrines. "Conservative," in this context, may be defined as a court ruling in favor of the state, whereas a "liberal" ruling is one in favor of the defendant.[16] Measured by these standards, the Burger/Rehnquist Court was and is clearly conservative, especially in Fourth Amendment, *Miranda*, and confrontation clause cases.[17] That is, most of its decisions in those areas have been in favor of the state. Therefore, most state court decisions adopting Burger/Rehnquist doctrines are conservative, and most of the decisions repudiating these doctrines are liberal. Although rejections get the most attention, adoptionism is the dominant feature of state constitutional law. Furthermore, as will be shown, adoptionism is likely to dominate the 1990s, because it enables the state courts to reconcile conflicting pressures upon them.

Second, the conservative Burger/Rehnquist majority is "winning." That is, the New Federalism has not been a repudiation of its approach and an endorsement of the more defendant-oriented

Brennan-Marshall perspective. Two of the most activist states in the country, Connecticut and David Souter's New Hampshire, give the conservative Supreme Court majority approval ratings of, respectively, 92 per cent and 80 per cent. The significant number of inactive states, which can be expected to seldom take a more defendant-protective position than the Supreme Court, and the low number of rejectionist states only strengthen the conclusion.

Third, the trend is not toward independent state constitutional doctrine, if by that is meant doctrines developed without regard to those propounded by the High Court. Some champions of the New Federalism have urged the development of an independent state constitutional jurisprudence.[18] However, there are inherent limitations impeding such development. The vast bulk of significant state constitutional cases deal with issues already decided by the Supreme Court. This is, perhaps, inevitable given the similar wording of the state and federal provisions, and the sizeable number of issues already reached by the Supreme Court.[19] In addition, to avoid supremacy clause violations, the state courts are virtually compelled to give consideration to Supreme Court doctrine to insure that the federal minima are provided.[20]

This study suggests a trend to construe state provisions and their federal parallels alike. In addition to the 22 high adoptionist states, there are 10 inactive states which either do not regularly interpret their state constitutions at all, or gratuitously cite state charters in cases that are doctrinally indistinguishable from Supreme Court rulings. For all practical purposes, these inactive states have bills of rights with no independent meaning. Adding the 10 inactives to the 22 high adoptionists yields 32 states or 64 per cent of the total which either affirmatively or by indecision mimic the Supreme Court.

Although the New Federalism is relatively young, and significant changes toward greater state constitutional independence are certainly possible, there are a number of reasons to believe that such a development is not going to occur. Thus, while it is conceivable that the 10 inactive states could become active rejectionists, this is highly unlikely given the political and legal cultures of the inactive states, half of which are in the South.[21] Moreover, the pressures toward conformity inherent in state constitutional lawmaking, such as the requirements of the supremacy clause, and the threat of Supreme Court review, militate against such a trend. Finally, the "discovery" that the states can develop their constitutions while simultaneously satisfying both the Supreme Court and internal conservative constituencies is likely to be too tempting to resist.

Explaining state court conservatism

There seems little doubt that the state constitutional movement began as a reaction to the Burger Court's attempt to narrow defendants' federal constitutional rights. The early reactions among legal scholars to Burger Court rulings were, to say the least, hostile.[22] Supreme Court Justices Brennan and Marshall gave aid and comfort to the state constitutional movement by directly urging its development and by providing doctrinal weapons in the form of a steady string of dissents.[23] Reliance upon state law was generally accepted as wholly proper in principle, and criticisms of the development were muted.[24] Much attention was paid to the growing list of cases repudiating Burger Court rulings.[25] The atmosphere was right for a state law revolt; the national legal culture was supportive.

Obviously this cannot explain the conservatism of the state law movement: the widespread reliance upon state law along with the adoption of the largely pro-prosecution positions of the Burger/Rehnquist Court. For this explanation we must look to concepts other than legal culture. Most helpful here is the work of political scientists G. Alan Tarr and Mary C. A. Porter.[26] In their study of state supreme courts these authors define the role of these institutions in terms of three sets of relationships:

(1) the state high court's relations with federal courts (vertical judicial federalism) . . . ;

(2) its relations with courts in other states, particularly other state supreme courts (horizontal judicial federalism); and (3) its relations with other institutions of state government . . . .[27]

Vertical judicial federalism describes the relationship between the state high courts and, especially, the U.S. Supreme Court. This relationship is a rather complex and fluid one, the parameters of which are determined by laws and rules found in the Constitution (Article III, establishing Supreme Court jurisdiction, the Tenth Amendment, reserving state court authority over state law, and the supremacy clause, mandating state court conformity on federal constitutional questions), acts of Congress (28 U.S.C. §1257, governing Supreme Court jurisdiction over state courts), and Supreme Court cases (e.g., *Michigan v. Long*, modifying the independent and adequate state law ground doctrine). Moreover, these parameters themselves have been altered in response to nonlegal, and, in part, ideological considerations. Twenty-five years ago, the Warren Court modified the adequate state ground doctrine in order to compel recalcitrant states to conform to liberal (pro-individual rights) decisions based upon the Bill of Rights and the Fourteenth Amendment due process clause.[28] Similarly, *Michigan v. Long*[29] may be seen as a Burger Court effort to keep the state courts from "infecting" federal constitutional law with liberal rulings ambiguously grounded in both state and federal law.

The general thrust of vertical federalism has been to pressure state courts to adopt U.S. Supreme Court doctrines. The Warren, Burger, and Rehnquist Courts have all sought to insure conformity with their interpretations of the U.S. Constitution, whether they were liberal or conservative. The supremacy clause, and other laws governing Supreme Court jurisdiction, as well as the legal concept of stare decisis are the chief legal weapons. The principal sanction is Supreme Court review and reversal of nonconforming state decisions. There are at least three limitations upon this pressure toward doctrinal conformity, one legal, one practical, and one institutional.

First is the legal concept of adequate and independent state law grounds. By resting their decisions on state law the state courts gain immunity from Supreme Court review and can freely reject Supreme Court doctrines. However, *Michigan v. Long* attempts to exact a price for state law independence: the state courts must sharply differentiate their state and federal law decisions, and conform the latter to Supreme Court rulings. *Long* demands a plain statement clarifying the legal basis of decision (i.e., state or federal law), in the absence of which the Supreme Court may review the case. *Long* is an attempt to promote federal doctrinal conformity while tolerating state law doctrinal nonconformity.

But there is mounting evidence that *Long* has been unsuccessful in reducing the number of law-ambiguous state rulings, i.e., the state courts frequently do not differentiate their state and federal law decisions.[30] This failure of *Long* may be attributable to the second—the practical—limitation upon the force of vertical federalism. The Supreme Court is inherently constrained by the sheer number of state cases and the limits on the ability of nine justices to review more than a tiny portion of those cases. Each year the 50 state supreme courts render thousands of decisions, while the one U.S. Supreme Court resolves fewer than 300 on the merits. Thus, vertical federalism's most potent weapon—Supreme Court review—is limited by the vastness of the state court output. (Of course, the Supreme Court also reviews a substantial number of rulings by lower *federal* courts, further reducing the ability of the justices to cope with errant state rulings.)[31]

Furthermore, if, against the odds, the Supreme Court reviews and reverses a state ruling, it almost always *remands* the case back to the state courts for further decision. The state court can then get the last word by reaffirming its previous ruling, only this time, resting unambiguously on state law.[32] Thus, state courts apparently feel free to resist vertical pressures to clarify the law basis of their rulings. If they do not obey the mandate of Long (i.e., they fail to clarify the basis for decision) they are in no worse position than if they ruled on purely federal grounds; the worst that could happen is that the Supreme Court will review, reverse, and remand.[33]

The third factor weakening vertical pressures to conform is the lack of consensus among Supreme Court Justices, and the frequent resort to dissenting and plurality opinions. The dissenting views of Warren era holdovers Brennan and Marshall—in an extraordinarily high proportion of the Burger/Rehnquist rulings against the criminal defendant—have made it appear that the post-Warren majority (or plurality) has been undermining established Warren Court precedent.[34] These dissents have certainly given doctrinal aid and comfort to state judges seeking to reject Burger/Rehnquist rulings. As for plurality opinions, a rather striking example of their impact was provided by a recent Florida Supreme Court ruling. Although that state court is mandated by the amendment to its state constitution to conform to Supreme Court Fourth Amendment doctrine, it announced that it was *not* bound to do so where the doctrine was endorsed by only a plurality of the U.S. Supreme Court![35] While the Florida situation is certainly atypical, it illustrates that plurality opinions may be viewed by state courts as less authoritative than those rendered by a majority.

At this point, one might well have the impression that the vertical pressures on state courts to adopt

Supreme Court doctrines are so attenuated as to be virtually nugatory. Such a conclusion would go too far. The threat of Supreme Court review is certainly effective in preventing the most glaring instances of nonconformity in cases decided on federal constitutional grounds. No state court simply rejects contrary Supreme Court precedent as a matter of U.S. constitutional law. However, as has been noted, the Supreme Court has been far less effective in reducing the number of law-ambiguous cases. *Michigan v. Long's* demand that the state courts sharply compartmentalize their state law and federal law rulings has been honored more in the breach: there has been no great upsurge in "plain statements" since *Long*.[36]

The pressures of vertical federalism may be summarized as follows. The Supreme Court demands that state courts adopt Supreme Court doctrines for decisions based upon the U.S. Constitution, and that they indicate unambiguously when their rulings are intended to rest upon exclusive state law grounds.

Horizontal federalism

We must now examine the supports for state courts to develop their state constitutions in the first instance. The explanation for this is rooted in Tarr and Porter's second category: horizontal judicial federalism. State courts are not legally bound to follow the decisions of sister state courts. Each state is free to interpret its own law independently, and another state court's decision interpreting the foreign state's law is persuasive, not mandatory authority. However, persuasive authority can be very persuasive. Praise from the academy in the law reviews, and a solid lineup of court decisions coming to a similar conclusion surely bolster a court's feeling that its ruling is right. Contrary rulings and scholarly criticism, while sometimes viewed as a badge of independence, probably create pressure on a court to reconsider its position. An alert bar will, in its briefs, encourage attention to sister state rulings. Private interest groups and even the mass media may call a court's attention to out-of-state developments. The fact that California and New York, and other "leadership" courts began resorting to their state charters has undoubtedly encouraged the state law "movement" throughout the nation. No state court wants to be perceived as so "backward" that it does not accept the latest development in state law. Every state court appears to perceive itself as the independent guardian of that state's law. Thus, horizontal federalism encourages reliance upon state law, while leaving each state court free to interpret that law as it wishes.

If the "upward" pull of vertical federalism is toward doctrinal conformity on federal law with doctrinal independence on state law, and if the "outward" pull of horizontal federalism is toward development of state law, should we not expect compliance with *Michigan v. Long*: conforming federal law decisions and independent, nonconforming state law rulings? In a few states—Alaska and Massachusetts—that is precisely what is happening. And over 200 criminal cases have rejected Supreme Court doctrines on state law grounds. But the more common occurrence is *conforming* state law rulings, i.e., state cases incorporating Burger/Rehnquist doctrines into state constitutional law. To account for this we must look at the third of Tarr and Porter's factors: relations with other institutions of state government.

Intrastate pressure

It is the intrastate pressure on the state high court that accounts for this largely overlooked twist in the development of the New Federalism. Conservative (pro-prosecution) state forces in the offices of prosecutors, police and corrections administrators, and among law-and-order state legislators and executives do not object to state constitutional rulings—so long as they favor the state. State courts are continually exposed to "law enforcement" pressures to rule against defendants: prosecutors' briefs, get-tough-on-crime legislative enactments and "lock-'em-up" re-election campaigns by state politicos. The revolt against the liberal state high courts in Florida and California, culminating in the anti-exclusionary rule amendments to those state constitutions, and the removal of some of the judges in California, vividly illustrate the types of pressures that have been and could be brought to bear on "overly liberal" state jurists.[37] In 38 states, high court judges are either elected to their positions or are subject to retention election after initial appointment, and in four states they may be removed by the voters by petition or recall election.[38] Although these elections may not normally arouse much interest on the part of the electorate, the potential for checking the judiciary is there, and, as the recent removal of California Supreme Court justices attests, a mobilized public can be effective.

In short, many, if not most, state courts are under considerable intrastate pressure to *not* expand defendants' rights. Combine this pressure with horizontal inducements to develop state constitutional law as well as vertical pressures to conform to Supreme Court decisions and the result is state constitutional rulings adopting the conservative decisions of the Burger/Rehnquist Court. The conservatism of state constitutional law satisfies the Supreme Court whose doctrines are being endorsed. It satisfies state law-and-order forces, because these doctrines favor the prosecution. And it gives state high courts the satisfaction of being in the judicial mainstream of the state law movement. To state the same thing, adoptionist decisions enable the state high courts to reconcile countervailing pressures upon them.

This is not to say that rejectionist decisions have no support. There are liberal internal forces as well—defense bar, liberal media, civil liberties interest groups, law professors, and some of the judges. However, the mood of the country remains conservative, at least on criminal justice matters, and in some states that sentiment is much stronger than others. Adoptionism is more likely to mute criticism of the state court—from both within and without the state.

There is every reason to expect the state law movement to continue into the foreseeable future. The 1990s will produce more state constitutional rulings, adding to the extraordinary output of the last two decades, an output unprecedented in American history. Judging by that output, the future of state constitutional criminal law is likely to consist of selective rejectionism of Supreme Court doctrines, widespread adoptionism, and a great deal of law-ambiguity with respect to the grounds of the decision. In this way state high courts can continue to satisfy the cross-pressures upon them.

NOTES

This article originally appeared in Volume 74, Number 4, December-January 1991, pages 190-197.

1. Abrahamson, *Criminal Law and State Constitutions: The Emergence of State Constitutional Law*, 63 TEX. L. REV. 1141, 1166 (1985).

2. N.Y. TIMES, Jan. 8, 1990, at A1, col. 2. Similar homage was subsequently paid the New Jersey Supreme Court. Sullivan, *New Jersey Court Seen as Leader on Rights*, N.Y. TIMES, July 18, 1990, at B1, col. 2.

3. Mosk, *The Power of State Constitutions in Protecting Individual Rights*, 8 N. ILL. U. L.J. 651, 662 (1988).

4. Resnick, *This Court's a Backwater No More*, NAT'L L.J., May 28, 1990, at 1, 30.

5. *See, e.g.,* Howard, *State Courts and Constitutional Rights in the Day of the Burger Court,* 62 VA. L. REV. 873 (1976).

6. *See, e.g.,* Brennan, *State Constitutions and the Protection of Individual Rights,* 90 HARV. L. REV. 489 (1977).

7. *The New York Times* articles about the New York and New Jersey high courts, *supra* n. 2, and the *National Law Journal* piece on the Florida Supreme Court, *supra* n. 4, all emphasized the expansion of rights under state law.

8. Criminal procedure cases are defined as cases involving a claim based upon the Fourth Amendment, Fifth Amendment double jeopardy or self-incrimination clauses, Sixth or Eighth Amendments to the U.S. Constitution or their state constitutional equivalents. Cases were collected by use of legal databases (Lexis and Westlaw) and by cross-checking secondary sources, such as the sizeable list of cases collected in the *National Law Journal,* Sept. 29, 1986.

9. If a case merely cited a state constitutional provision along with its federal counterpart and then presented federal constitutional doctrine—treating the state and federal provisions as if they were interpretively indistinguishable—it was excluded from the study. If, however, the lead opinion indicated an intention to independently interpret the state provision, by either a "plain statement" to that effect, such as demanded by the Supreme Court in *Michigan v. Long,* 463 U.S. 1032 (1983), or an exclusive citation to a state constitutional provision, or a citation to a state case which itself clearly rested upon a state provision, that case was included in the study.

10. If a single state case adopted or rejected more than one federal doctrine, and the doctrines concerned distinctive legal issues, the case was counted more than once, as an adoption or rejection of each federal doctrine. Where a state court first rejected or adopted U.S. Supreme Court doctrine, then reversed itself, this was counted as one rejection and one adoption. If the state court ruled on an issue not decided by the Supreme Court at the time of the state case, that case was not counted as either a rejection or adoption. However, once the Supreme Court ruled on the issue, any subsequent state case was counted as an adoption or rejection, as appropriate. Where more than one case decided by a single state court reaffirmed essentially the same doctrine all of the cases were counted as one. (However, Florida and California are treated differently with respect to reaffirmations, for the reasons given below.) If the state court unambiguously adhered to doctrine providing narrower rights than recognized for the U.S. Constitution, this was considered to be a rejection.

11. This study did not include cases on issues not considered by the U.S. Supreme Court, and it generally excluded cases interpreting state provisions without analogue in the federal Bill of Rights.

12. Cal. Const. art. I, §B28(d); Fla. Const. art. I, §12 (effective Jan. 1983).

13. Of course, the California state courts must continue to exclude evidence, relevant or not, as required by federal constitutional law.

14. These citations are available from *Judicature* upon request.

15. The figures do not reflect the total number of cases citing state constitutional provisions because cases on issues not considered by the U.S. Supreme Court, and law-ambiguous cases were excluded from the data. Thus, "inactivism" is taken to mean relatively few "pure" state law cases, but many of the inactive states fairly frequently cited state constitutional provisions.

16. Usually this takes the form of a judgment in the defendant's behalf, but occasionally the judgment is in favor of the prosecution, while the law being established advantages the accused. Consider, for example, *Rhode Island v. Innis,* 446 U.S. 291 (1980), in which the defendant lost the case (his incriminating remarks were admitted), but the pro-defendant Miranda doctrine was liberally construed (broad definition of "interrogation"). Such cases are here counted as liberal rulings, whereas judgments for the defendant coupled with pro-prosecution doctrines are deemed conservative.

17. An examination of all of the major Warren, Burger, and Rehnquist criminal procedure decisions reveals the following. In eight areas (speedy trial, discovery and disclosure, self-incrimination, double jeopardy, due process/trials, entrapment, juveniles, and the constitutionality of penal statutes) the Burger/Rehnquist Court was not distinctly more conservative than its predecessor. In three areas (Fourth Amendment, Miranda, confrontation of witnesses) it was clearly more conservative. And in two (counsel and jury trial), it was in part more liberal, in part less. For comparisons of the Burger and Warren Courts, *see* Israel, *Criminal Procedure, The Burger Court, And The Legacy Of The Warren Court,* 75 MICH. L. REV. 1319 (1977); Kamisar, *The Warren Court (Was It Really So Defense-Minded?), The Burger Court (Is It Really So Prosecution-Oriented?),* and *Police Practices,* in Blasi, ed., THE BURGER COURT: THE COUNTER-REVOLUTION THAT WASN'T 62 (1983); Saltzburg, *Forward: The Flow and Ebb of Constitutional Criminal Procedure in the Warren and Burger Courts,* 69 GEO. L.J. 151 (1980).

18. A notable example is Oregon Supreme Court Justice Hans Linde, who has favored the interpretation of state constitutions independent of U.S. Supreme Court doctrines. *See, e.g.,* Linde, *E Pluribus—Constitutional Theory and State Courts,* 18 GA. L. REV. 165, 179 (1984). "The right question is not whether a state's guarantee is the same as or broader than its federal counterpart as interpreted by the Supreme Court. The right question is what the state's guarantee means and how it applies to the case at hand." However, supporters of the development of independent state law concede that most state constitutional criminal procedure decisions are "reactive," i.e., apply Supreme Court doctrine. Collins & Galie, *Models of Post-Incorporation Judicial Review: 1985 Survey of State Constitutional Individual Rights Decisions,* 55 U. CIN. L. REV. 317, 320 (1986), reprinted in 16 PUBLIUS: THE JOURNAL OF FEDERALISM 111 (Summer, 1986).

19. A comparison of the texts of state and federal criminal justice provisions reveals the following: Thirty-four of the 50 state constitutional search and seizure provisions are substantially identical to the federal Fourth Amendment. 34 out of 45 state double jeopardy provisions mirror the Fifth Amendment. For right to counsel (Sixth Amendment), self-incrimination (Fifth Amendment) and cruel and unusual punishment (Eighth Amendment) the textual similarities are not as great. The figures, respectively, are: 10/49, 16/48, and 20/49. (State figures below 50 reflect the absence of any state provision.)

20. The supremacy clause, art. VI, §2, states: "This Constitution . . . shall be the supreme Law of the Land; and the Judges in every State shall be bound thereby, any Thing in the Constitution or Laws of any State to the Contrary notwithstanding." This compels state courts to enforce valid federal constitutional claims made by litigants. State constitutional rights narrower than the federal are unenforceable if enforcement would deny federal rights.

21. *See supra* Table 3.

22. *E.g.,* Chase, *The Burger Court, The Individual, and the Criminal Process: Directions and Misdirections,* 52 N.Y.U. L. REV. 518 (1977) (Burger Court decisions are a departure of major proportions from animating premises of Warren Court decisions); Dershowitz & Ely, *Harris v. New York: Some Anxious Observations on the Candor and Logic of the Emerging Nixon Majority,* 80 YALE L.J. 1198 (1971) (majority misstates the law and the record in Harris v. New York); George, *From Warren to Burger to Chance: Future Trends in the Administration of Criminal Justice,* 12 CRIM. L. BULL. 253, 258 (1976) ("Even a cursory

review of the Burger Court cases affecting the constitutional status of police investigations clearly reveals the sweeping extent to which the operative principles of the Warren Court era have either been abandoned or are being eroded."); Levy, AGAINST THE LAW (1974) (Burger Court majority "no damn good as judges;" more like advocates for law enforcement).

23. Of 191 pro-prosecution criminal procedure decisions during the Burger years, Brennan and Marshall dissented or concurred on more rights-expansive grounds 140 times, 73 per cent of the total. In addition to his articles and speeches in behalf of the state law movement, *supra* n. 6, Brennan used his court opinions to openly encourage state rejectionism. *E.g.*, Oregon v. Kennedy, 456 U.S. 667, 680-81 (1982) ("nothing in the holding of the Court today prevents the state courts, on remand, from concluding that respondent's retrial would violate the provision of the Oregon Constitution that prohibits double jeopardy . . . .") (Brennan and Marshall, J.J., concurring).

24. Not only Justice Brennan, but the prestige of Harvard Law School supported the New Federalism, although not uncritically. Project, *Developments in the Law, The Interpretation of State Constitutional Rights*, 95 HARV. L. REV. 1324 (1982). For an early critique, *see* Bice, *Anderson and the Adequate State Ground*, 45 S. CAL. L. REV. 750 (1972).

25. In the criminal procedure area, perhaps the most influential articles were a series by Professor Donald E. Wilkes, who appears to be the first to have used the expression "New Federalism" for the state constitutional law movement. Wilkes, *The New Federalism in Criminal Procedure Revisited*, 64 KY. L.J. 729 (1976); Wilkes, *More on the New Federalism in Criminal Procedure*, 63 KY. L.J. 873 (1975); Wilkes, *The New Federalism in Criminal Procedure*, 62 KY. L.J. 421 (1974).

26. Tarr and Porter, STATE SUPREME COURTS IN STATE AND NATION (1988).

27. *Id.* at 2.

28. Henry v. Mississippi, 379 U.S. 443 (1965) (procedural state law cannot provide adequate state grounds unless it serves a substantial state interest).

29. 463 U.S. 1032 (1983).

30. Notes, *Fulfilling the Goals of Michigan v. Long: The State Court Reaction*, 56 FORDHAM L. REV. 1041 (1988) (authored by Felicia Rosenfeld).

31. In the 1987-88 term, for example, the Supreme Court docketed 4,401 cases, and disposed of 142 of them with full written opinions. Only 13 of the 142 were state criminal cases. 102 HARV. L. REV. 354, 358 (1988).

32. *People v. Class* is a notable example. The New York Court of Appeals initially ruled, on ambiguous state and federal grounds, that a police entry into an automobile to examine the vehicle indentification number (VIN) was unlawful. 63 N.Y.2d 491, 483 N.Y.S.2d 181, 472 N.E.2d 1009 (1984). The U.S. Supreme Court reversed on Fourth Amendment grounds, basing jurisdiction on the absence of a "plain statement," and remanding to the Court of Appeals. 475 U.S. 106 (1986). The New York tribunal then reinstated its earlier judgment, this time relying solely upon the state constitution. 67 N.Y.2d 431, 494 N.E.2d 444, 503 N.Y.S.2d 313 (1986).

33. Furthermore, complying with *Long* could damage the position of the state court in terms of its relations with other state institutions. If the court rests a decision on unambiguous state law grounds that increases its exposure to criticism from internal state forces opposed to the ruling. For instance, if a decision expands the rights of criminal defendants, and the court is attacked by police, prosecutors, and conservative state legislators, it will be unable to defend itself by contending that its ruling was compelled by federal precedent. By forcing the court to rely solely upon state law, *Long* strips away whatever federal law "cover" the court might have used to defend its

decision.

34. *See supra* n. 23.

35. State v. Welker, 536 So.2d 1017, 1019 (Fla. 1988) (adopting United States v. White, 401 U.S. 745 (1971) while denying court bound to do so).

36. *See supra* n. 30.

37. California voters recalled Chief Justice Rose Bird and two liberal associate justices. N.Y. TIMES, Nov. 6, 1986, at A30, col. 1. See Wold & Culver, *The defeat of the California justices: the campaign, the electorate, and the issue of judicial accountability*, 70 JUDICATURE 348 (1987).

38. The Council of State Gov'ts, THE BOOK OF THE STATES 163-73 (1989).

Burger Court review of state court civil liberties decisions

Contrary to popular opinion, an analysis of civil liberties cases decided between 1969 and 1984 indicates that decisions were much more liberal after Supreme Court review than they were before.

by Harold J. Spaeth

As a result of several recent decisions,[1] most dramatically *Michigan v. Long*,[2] the Burger Court is being perceived as inhibiting liberal state court decision making, especially in the area of civil rights and liberties. This article will show that the Burger Court has overturned more than two-thirds of all state court decisions that it accepted for review—the largest proportion of which the state courts decided *antithetically* to civil liberties and civil rights claimants—and that its bias against liberal state court decisions extends only to search-and-seizure and Miranda warning cases, and not to criminal procedure or civil rights and liberties generally.

During the heyday of the Warren Court, the notion of a state court more liberal than the Supreme Court was oxymoronic, but the replacement of Warren and Fortas with Burger and Blackmun ended liberal dominance.[3] Thereafter, federal protection of at least certain individual rights lessened, much to the chagrin of the last of the Warren Court's liberals—Justices Brennan and Marshall—and like-minded commentators.

To counter the Supreme Court's increasing conservatism, Justice Marshall proposed in a dissent in *Oregon v. Hass*, which was joined by Justice Brennan, that the Supreme Court not review state court decisions that reverse convictions on the basis of federal law.[4] Nine months later, Brennan, joined by Marshall, urged the state courts to use state, rather than federal, law to protect civil rights and liberties.[5] The use of state constitutional and statutory provisions for this purpose is unobjectionable, of course, because federal law sets a floor on rights rather than a ceiling. Hence, the states are free to use their own constitutions and laws to supplement or expand federally guaranteed rights.[6]

The availability of state law as a basis for expanded protection of civil rights and liberties appears to have been compromised, however, as a result of the Supreme Court's decision in *Michigan v. Long*.[7] Justice O'Connor, in an opinion joined by four of her colleagues, stated that the Supreme Court will presume jurisdiction over state court decisions absent a clear and express indication that they are based on "bona fide separate, adequate, and independent [nonfederal] grounds."[8] Although *Michigan v. Long* appears to do major violence to considerations of federalism insofar as the autonomy of state courts is concerned,[9] preclusion of liberal decisions is a separate issue, one to which we now turn.

The data

Whether or not the Supreme Court has prevented the state courts from supporting the contentions of civil rights and liberties claimants is an empirical question that depends on whether the states themselves decided such cases liberally or conservatively, and the effect of Supreme Court review on such decisions.

The cases we consider include all the orally argued cases on review from a state court that the Burger Court decided during its first 15 terms: from October 1969 to July 1984.[10] Also considered are the non-orally argued per curiam decisions on review from a state court for which the *Lawyers' Edition* of the *U.S. Reports* provides a summary and headnotes.[11] Docket numbers are counted rather than case citations. It is not uncommon for cases from different states to be combined together under a single opinion of the Court; furthermore, cases so combined are not necessarily resolved in the same fashion: one may be affirmed, another reversed. *Miranda v. Arizona*[12] illustrates both features. Because the local courts of the District of Columbia and Puerto Rico are courts of last resort for the purposes of Supreme Court review, they are treated as *quasi* states[13] and included in this analysis.

In reviewing state court decisions, the Supreme Court may affirm,[14] reverse, or remand the case back to the state court whose decision was reviewed. No distinction is made between decisions vacated and remanded and those reversed and remanded. Four cases that the Supreme Court affirmed in part and reversed in part—one each from Arizona, California, Illinois, and New Mexico—are treated as half affirmed and half reversed.[15] Four additional state cases are excluded from analysis because the Supreme Court's disposition does not fit the affirm-reverse-remand typology. Two requested issuance of writs of mandamus,[16] one involved certification of question,[17] and one a pro se motion for dismissal.[18]

The foregoing decision rules produce 574 cases. As the first column of Table 1 shows, 31.9 per cent were affirmed, 46.5 per cent remanded, and 21.6 per cent reversed. These percentages substantiate the judgment of those who consider error correction and policy formation the major reasons for the Supreme Court's exercise of jurisdiction.[19] Supporting this judgment is the fact that 39 of the 183 affirmations (21.3 per cent) were technically denials or dismissals of the request for review. These typically result when the justices deem jurisdiction deficient or the federal question insufficiently substantial.[20] If they are excluded from consideration, the proportion of state court decisions that the Supreme Court overturned rises to 73.1 per cent (391 of 535).

Civil rights and liberties

In the second and third columns of Table 1, I have separated civil rights and liberties decisions from other state court cases and divided them into those that the Supreme Court liberally decided and those that it conservatively decided. I define civil rights and liberties to include the Bill of Rights, the

Table 1 Supreme Court disposition of state court decisions, 1969-1983 terms

Disposition	Civil rights and liberties cases		All other cases
Affirmed	liberal outcome	15.5	
N=183	conservative outcome	89.5	
(31.9%)		105	78
Reversed	liberal outcome	70.5	
N=123	conservative outcome	11.5	
(21.6%)		82	42
Remanded	liberal outcome	146	
N=267	conservative outcome	66	
(45.5%)		212	55
Total			
574		399	175

Fourteenth and Fifteenth Amendments, liability under federal civil rights statutes, and cases involving Indian claims. Due process cases pertaining to jurisdiction and the takings clause are excluded because they do not fit the liberal-conservative distinction; for the same reason, equal protection challenges to zoning ordinances are omitted. In the included cases, a liberal outcome supports the civil liberties/civil rights claimant. In the context of affirmative action a liberal result upholds the minority; in libel actions, the communicator.[21]

Comparison of the civil rights and liberties decisions with other types of cases shows the Court more inclined to overturn the former and uphold the latter. This results in part because 27 of the non-civil liberties affirmances are dismissals and denials, whereas only 12 pertaining to civil rights are such.[22]

We may parenthetically note that the Court flatly reversed state court decisions in more than one in five of both the civil liberties and the non-civil liberties cases that it reviewed. For a Court that "normally returns (remands) the case to the state court for proceedings 'consistent with this opinion' "[23] when it overturns a decision, these proportions of reversals arguably undermine the system of comity and its abstention doctrine,[24] which, in the words of the Court, enables us to "remain loyal to the ideals and dreams of 'Our Federalism.' "[25]

Assessment of the data in the second column of Table 1 clearly establishes the Burger Court to be hostile not only to liberal state court decisions, but hostile to state court decisions, period. Thus, the Court upheld only 15.5 liberal state court decisions. It reversed 11.5 and remanded 66 that the states had liberally decided. Consequently, the

Table 2 Directionality of state court civil liberties decisions reviewed by the Burger Court

	Prior to review	After review
Liberal	75 (18.8%)	232 (58.1%)
Conservative	324 (81.2%)	167 (41.9%)

Table 3 Proportion of liberal decisions before and after Supreme Court review

Jurisdiction	Before	After	Liberal change
Alabama	0-7	7-0	+7 (1.00)
Alaska	0-3	3-0	+3 (1.00)
Arizona	1-10	10-1	+9 (.82)
Arkansas	1-2	3-0	+2 (.67)
California	11-17	8-20	-3 (-.11)
Colorado	2-0	1-1	-1 (-.50)
Connecticut	2-4	3-3	+1 (.17)
Delaware	1-1	2-0	+1 (.50)
District of Columbia	2-3	1-4	-1 (-.20)
Florida	3-25	13-15	+10 (.36)
Georgia	1-26	20-7	+19 (.70)
Idaho	1-1	1-1	0 (.00)
Illinois	5-21	12-14	+7 (.27)
Indiana	0-6	4-2	+4 (.67)
Kentucky	1-11	6-6	+5 (.42)
Louisiana	0-16	12-4	+12 (.75)
Maine	2-0	1-1	-1 (-.50)
Maryland	1-6	4-3	+3 (.43)
Massachusetts	2-4	2-4	0 (.00)
Michigan	9-1	3-7	-6 (-.60)
Minnesota	2-2	2-2	0 (.00)
Mississippi	0-5	5-0	+5 (1.00)
Missouri	1-13	13-1	+12 (.86)
Montana	0-3	3-0	+3 (1.00)
Nebraska	0-3	2-1	+2 (.67)
North Dakota	0-1	1-0	+1 (1.00)
New Hampshire	0-3	2-1	+2 (.67)
New Jersey	1-8	5-4	+4 (.44)
New Mexico	0-2	1-1	+1 (.50)
New York	4-29	16-17	+12 (.36)
North Carolina	1-7	3-5	+2 (.25)
Ohio	4-18	13-9	+9 (.41)
Oklahoma	0-5	5-0	+5 (1.00)
Oregon	4-5	1-8	-3 (-.33)
Pennsylvania	2-4	3-3	+1 (.17)
Puerto Rico	0-2	1-1	+1 (.50)
Rhode Island	1-0	0-1	-1 (-1.00)
South Carolina	0-3	1-2	+1 (.33)
South Dakota	2-1	0-3	-2 (-.67)
Tennessee	1-8	8-1	+7 (.78)
Texas	2-10	9-3	+7 (.58)
Utah	0-5	3-2	+3 (.60)
Virginia	0-7	5-2	+5 (.71)
Washington	1-11	8-4	+7 (.58)
West Virginia	2-0	1-1	-1 (-.50)
Wisconsin	2-4	5-1	+3 (.50)
Wyoming	0-1	0-1	0 (.00)
Totals	75-324	232-167	+157 (.39)

Court upheld only 16.7 per cent of the liberal state court decisions that it reviewed (15.5 of 93). Of conservative decisions, 89.5 received support. Of those producing a liberal outcome, 70.5 were reversed and 146 remanded—a percentage of 29.2 upheld. These proportions indicate that although the Burger Court has not supported state civil liberties decisions overall (294 overturned, 105 upheld), it supports almost twice as many conservative decisions (29.2 per cent) as it does those that uphold individual rights (16.8 per cent).

These proportions, however, are misleading because 17 of the cases that the Court remanded or reversed and which produced a conservative outcome were also decided antithetically to the civil liberties claimant by the state court.[26] Two additional cases, which the Supreme Court affirmed in part and reversed in part, and which produced a conservative outcome, were also decided conservatively by the state court whose decision the Court reviewed.[27] Accordingly, as Table 2 shows, only 75 (18.8 per cent) of the cases accepted for Supreme Court review were actually decided liberally by the states, rather than the 93 indicated by the middle column of Table 1 (15.5 + 11.5 + 66). Following review, the number of liberal outcomes almost tripled—to 231. Conversely, the 324 conservative outcomes prior to review were reduced by one-half—to 167. Note especially that the bulk of the liberal outcomes resulted from the Burger Court's disregard of considerations of federalism by remanding (146) and reversing (70.5) cases conservatively decided by the states. These remands and reversals produced 93.3 per cent (216.5 of 232) of the liberal outcomes. By contrast, "respect for state functions"[28] in the form of affirming state court decisions produced more than half the conservative decisions (89.5 of 167).

State by state

While the data in Tables 1 and 2 establish the fact that the Burger Court disapproved of more than two-thirds of the state court decisions that it reviewed, these data tell us nothing of the Court's treatment of the individual states' courts. It is quite possible, given the disproportionate number of remands and reversals shown in Table 1, that, as the disapproving commentators assert,[29] the Burger Court has overturned liberal decisions emanating from those state courts that support expansion of individual rights. To this we now turn.

Table 3 alphabetically lists the states, the proportions of their reviewed civil liberties decisions that they decided liberally, the proportion of each state's decisions that were liberally decided as a result of Supreme Court review, and the amount of liberal increase (or decrease) resulting from Supreme Court review. The amount of change can range from 1.00 to -1.00. It is calculated by subtracting the number of liberal decisions before Supreme Court review from those that exist thereafter and dividing this number by the total number of reviewed civil liberties cases decided by the state in question. The maximum amount of liberal change results if the state conservatively decided all its civil liberties questions and the Supreme Court then reversed or remanded them all. The minimum amount (-1.00) results if all reviewed decisions were initially liberal and subsequently reversed or remanded.

Five states do not appear in Table 3. The Burger Court decided no cases from Nevada through the end of the 1983 term and no civil liberties decisions were reviewed from the courts of Hawaii, Iowa, Kansas, or Vermont.

The first column of Table 3 reveals that only six states exceed the proportion of liberal decisions that resulted from Burger Court review—58.1 per cent. (See Table 2.) Colorado, Maine, and West Virginia decided both of their reviewed cases liberally, as did Rhode Island in its single case. Michigan decided nine of its 10 liberally, and South Dakota two of its three. No other state exceeded 50 per cent liberal. At the other extreme, in 16 jurisdictions the Burger Court reviewed only conservative decisions: Louisiana 16; Alabama 7; Indiana and Virginia 6; Mississippi, Oklahoma, and Utah 5; Alaska, Montana, Nebraska, New Hampshire, and South Carolina 3; New Mexico and Puerto Rico 2; and North Dakota and Wyoming 1.

The effect of Burger Court review increased the liberal proportion in 34 jurisdictions, reduced it in nine, and produced no change in four states. Showing the maximum liberal increase as a result of Burger Court review are six of the states which had only conservative decisions reviewed: Alabama 7, Mississippi and Oklahoma 5, Alaska and Montana 3, and North Dakota 1. Indeed, of the 71 decisions from the 16 wholly conservative jurisdictions, the Supreme Court upheld only 17 (23.9 per cent).

In addition to the six states that attained a liberal increase of 1.00, another 13 showed a net liberal improvement exceeding 50 per cent following Burger Court review of their decisions: Missouri from 1-13 to 31-1, Arizona from 1-10 to 10-1, Tennessee 1-8 to 8-1, Louisiana 0-16 to 12-4, Virginia 0-7 to 5-2, Georgia 1-26 to 20-7, Indiana 0-6 to 4-2, Arkansas 1-2 to 3-0, Nebraska and New Hampshire 0-3 to 2-1, Utah 0-5 to 3-2, Washington 1-11 to 8-4, and Texas 2-10 to 9-3.

Table 4 Proportion of liberal decisions before and after Supreme Court review (by term)

Term	Before	After	Liberal change
1969	1-23	14-10	+13 (.54)
1970	3-32	21-14	+18 (.51)
1971	1-43	22-22	+21 (.48)
1972	1-26	13-14	+12 (.44)
1973	2-25	20-7	+18 (.67)
1974	1-14	12-3	+11 (.73)
1975	7-20	13-14	+6 (.22)
1976	4-21	16-9	+12 (.48)
1977	3-16	14-5	+11 (.58)
1978	10-28	23-15	+13 (.34)
1979	5-20	19-6	+14 (.56)
1980	8-17	13-12	+5 (.20)
1981	5-18	13-10	+8 (.35)
1982	13-10	7-16	-6 (-.26)
1983	11-11	12-10	+1 (.05)
Totals	75-324	232-167	+157 (.39)

Of the four states in which review produced no change, a grand total of only eight cases were involved: four from Minnesota, two from Idaho, and one each from Maine and Wyoming.

The nine jurisdictions whose liberal proportion was reduced as a result of Burger Court review include six whose percentage of liberal decisions exceeded that of the Supreme Court (57.9 per cent): Rhode Island from 1-0 to 0-1, Michigan from 9-1 to 3-7, South Dakota 2-1 to 0-3, and Colorado, Maine, and West Virginia 2-0 to 1-1. The other three jurisdictions are California and Oregon, both of which suffered a net loss of three liberal decisions: from 11-17 to 8-20 and 4-5 to 1-8, respectively, and the District of Columbia, with a net loss of one liberal decision. Note, however, that unlike the six states whose liberal proportion the Burger Court reduced, Oregon, California, and the District of Columbia decided more than half their reviewed civil liberties cases conservatively: 5 of 9, 17 of 28, and 3 of 5, respectively.

Finally, commentators[30] disproportionately cite 1982 term cases[31] as evidence of Burger Court hostility toward liberal state court decision making. Analysis of the 23 state civil liberties decisions reviewed by the Court during its 1982 term supports the commentators' concern. (See Table 4.) The states liberally decided 13 of these cases. Following Supreme Court review, liberal outcomes declined to seven, a change of -.26. However, one term does not necessarily establish a trend. In the 1981 term, with personnel identical to those sitting in 1982, the court reviewed 23 state civil liberties decisions, only five of which the state court decided liberally. Following review, 13 cases produced a liberal result, a change of +.35.[32] In the 1983 term, the Court returned to a net liberal change, albeit by a single case.

Issue breakdown

Analysis of the issues in the cases in which the Court overturned a liberal state court decision reveals that 55 per cent of them (33 of 60) concerned search-and-seizure or self-incrimination. Of the 20 search-and-seizure cases, nine involved vehicles, and 11 did not; while all but four of the 13 self-incrimination cases pertained to Miranda warnings.[33] Furthermore, these 33 cases were disproportionately decided during the 1982 and 1983 terms (8 and 6, respectively) and, in addition, 19 of them came from eight of the nine states which show a negative liberal change on Table 3. If these cases are excluded from consideration, these eight states show no change in their proportion of liberal decisions before and after Supreme Court review. Only West Virginia continues to have a lower proportion of liberal decisions after Supreme Court review (1-1) than it had before (2-0). Exclusion of the 14 cases that were decided in the 1982 and 1983 terms also causes these terms—like all of the others—to display a higher number of liberal decisions after Supreme Court review than they did before.

In conclusion, allegations of Burger Court hostility to state civil liberties decisions are sustainable only as applied to those terms (1982 and, marginally, 1983) and to those jurisdictions that disproportionately produced liberal decisions pertaining to search-and-seizure and self-incrimination. Thus, the Burger Court reviewed 10 Michigan decisions during its first 15 terms, 6 of which concerned search-and-seizure or self-incrimination,[34] as did 3 of Oregon's 9,[35] 3 of California's 28,[36] 2 of South Dakota's 3,[37] 1 of Maine's 2,[38] 1 of the District of Columbia's 5,[39] both of Colorado's,[40] and Rhode Island's 1.[41] This limited disapproval of liberal state court decision making should not be allowed to obscure the Burger Court's overall record, however. Out of a total of 399 civil liberties decisions, the state courts decided only 75 liberally. Following Burger Court review, 232 of these cases had a liberal outcome—a net increase of 157. This liberal improvement, moreover, extends to the decisions of 33 states and Puerto Rico out of the 47 jurisdictions whose civil liberties decisions the Burger Court reviewed.

Given the foregoing findings, conservative com-

mentators, rather than their liberal counterparts, should be objecting to the Burger Court's decision making. The former, rather than the latter, should be urging the bench and bar to develop and rely on independent state grounds for decision.

NOTES

This article originally appeared in Volume 68, Numbers 7-8, February-March 1985, pages 285-291. The data on which this research is based are drawn from a preliminary version of the author's U.S. Supreme Court Judicial Data Base, a project funded by the Law and Social Sciences Program of the National Science Foundation, Grant No. SES-8313773.

1. Oregon v. Hass, 420 U.S. 714 (1975); Michigan v. Mosley, 423 U.S. 96 (1975); South Dakota v. Opperman, 428 U.S. 364 (1976); Delaware v. Prouse, 440 U.S. 648 (1979); South Dakota v. Neville, 74 L Ed 2d 748 (1983); Montana v. Jackson, 75 L Ed 2d 782 (1983); Florida v. Casal, 77 L Ed 2d 277 (1983). Note the Chief Justice's concurring opinion at 278.

2. 77 L Ed 2d 1201 (1983).

3. Spaeth, SUPREME COURT POLICYMAKING 128-135 (San Francisco: W.H. Freeman, 1979); Schwartz, SUPER CHIEF: EARL WARREN AND HIS SUPREME COURT 761-772 (New York: New York University Press, 1983).

4. 420 U.S. 714, 726 (1975).

5. 423 U.S. 96, 120 (1975). Brennan elaborated his argument in *State Constitutions and the Protection of Individual Rights*, 90 HARV. L. REV. 489 (1977).

6. Howard, *State Courts and Constitutional Rights in the Day of the Burger Court*, 62 VA. L. REV. 874 (1976); Galie and Galie, *State Constitutional Guarantees and Supreme Court Review: Justice Marshall's Proposal* in Oregon v. Hass, 82 DICK. L. REV. 273 (1977-1978); Note, *Developments in the Law—the Interpretation of State Constitutional Rights*, 95 HARV. L. REV. 1324 (1982); Margolick, *State Judiciaries Are Shaping Law That Goes beyond Supreme Court*, N.Y. TIMES, May 19, 1982, at 1; Collins, *A Fresh Way for the States to View the Exclusionary Rules*, NATL. L. J., July 18, 1983, at 3; Murphy, "State Supreme Courts and Civil Liberties: Nemesis or Nirvana?" paper presented at the Midwest Pol. Sci. Assn. meetings, April 1984. Also see the essays by Porter, Friedelbaum, Tarr, and Kramer and Riga in Porter and Tarr, eds., STATE SUPREME COURTS: POLICY MAKERS IN THE FEDERAL SYSTEM (Westport, CT: Greenwood, 1982).

The states, however, don't necessarily rest their liberal decisions on their own law. *E.g.*, Massachusetts v. Upton, 80 L Ed 2d 721 (1984). Note especially Justice Stevens' sharply worded criticism, at 728, of the Massachusetts Supreme Court for its failure to do so.

7. 77 L Ed 2d 1201 (1983).

8. *Id.* at 1214.

9. Collins, *High Court Asserts Its Authority*, NATL. L. J., August 1, 1983, at 5; Collins and Welsh, *The Court vs. Rights*, N.Y. TIMES, October 7, 1983, at 31; Collins, *Quarrels, Quotas and Darwinism: What's Happening in State Courts*, NATL. L. J., January 2, 1984, at 20; Collins, *Plain Statements: The Supreme Court's New Requirement*, 70 A.B.A. J. 92 (March 1984). Also see the exchange in the concurring opinions in Colorado v. Nunez, 79 L Ed 2d 338 (1984).

10. The Burger Court reviewed decisions from the lower courts of 26 states, in addition to those handed down by state supreme courts. The federal questions contained in the lower court cases were decisions "by the highest court of a State in which a decision could be [or was] had . . ." 28 U.S.C. §1257.

11. Rochester, NY: Lawyers Co-operative Publishing Co., 2d series, vols. 24-81. Summaries and headnotes are routinely provided all such cases that appear in the front section of the

U.S. REPORTS and which were decided since the end of the 1972 term. During the 1969-1972 terms, however, the official REPORTS, paralleled by the LAWYERS' EDITION, included large numbers of cases in the front of each volume that differed from those in the back of each volume only by the presence of the phrase, "per curiam." Compare, for example, those in 396 U.S. at 1-12, 22-27, 39-40, 111-121, 272-281, 373-374, 554-556 with those in the "Order" portion at 801-1066. Because of the similarity of these non-summarized, non-headnoted cases with the memorandum decisions and the orders at the back of each volume of the REPORTS, they are excluded from consideration.

12. 384 U.S. 436 (1966).

13. National Center for State Courts, STATE COURT ORGANIZATION 1980, 489, 499 (Williamsburg, VA: National Court Statistics Project, 1982). The Supreme Court reviewed seven cases from the District of Columbia Court of Appeals and two from the Puerto Rico Supreme Court.

14. Cases in which the petition for certiorari is "denied" or the appeal is "dismissed" are counted as affirmations. Such dispositions obviously approximate affirmations more closely than they do reversals or remands.

15. Bates v. State Bar of Arizona, 433 U.S. 350 (1977); Regents of the University of California v. Bakke, 438 U.S. 265 (1978); Grayned v. City of Rockford, 408 U.S. 104 (1972); Mescalero Apache Tribe v. Jones, 411 U.S. 145 (1973). Each pertains to individual rights.

16. Buscolo v. Adkins, 424 U.S. 641 (1976), and General Atomic Co. v. Felter, 436 U.S. 493 (1978).

17. Massachusetts v. Feeney, 429 U.S. 66 (1976).

18. Hammett v. Texas, 448 U.S. 725 (1980).

19. Spaeth, *Supreme Court disposition of federal circuit court decisions*, 68 JUDICATURE 245 (1985). As evidence that other concerns explain the decision making of subsupreme appellate courts, see the meticulous analysis of Davies, *Affirmed: A Study of Criminal Appeals and Decision-Making Norms in a California Court of Appeal*, 1982 AM. B. FOUNDATION RES. J. 543, 548-549, 583-632.

20. Stern and Gressman, SUPREME COURT PRACTICE 156-245 (5th ed., Washington, DC: Bureau of National Affairs, 1978). If the 39 denials and dismissals are excluded, the Court affirmed only 144 of 535 decisions, 26.9 per cent. My exclusion of the vast bulk of the denials of certiorari petitions and writs of appeal (*supra* n. 11) precludes analysis of an error correction strategy. The justices, for example, may tolerate conservative errors in the state courts to a considerably greater extent than they do decisions producing a liberal outcome. If such be the situation, then a smaller proportion of conservatively decided state court cases should be accepted for Supreme Court review than those in which the state court upheld the civil liberties claimant. Excellent discussions of the strategy of error correction may be found in Baum, *Policy Goals in Judicial Gatekeeping: A Proximity Model of Discretionary Jurisdiction*, 21 AM. J. OF POL. SCI. 13 (1977); Songer, *Concern for Policy Outputs as a Cue for Supreme Court Decisions on Certiorari*, 41 J. OF POL. 1185 (1979); and Armstrong and Johnson, *Certiorari Decisions by the Warren and Burger Courts: Is Cue Theory Time Bound?*, 15 POLITY 141 (1982).

21. The opposite specification of "liberal" in affirmative action and libel cases increases the number of liberal outcomes and reduces conservative decisions by 1.5 each.

In this article, no distinction is made between or among civil rights, civil liberties, or individual rights.

22. Four cases decided by an equally divided vote are included among the 75 non-civil liberties affirmances. These cases, though orally argued, contain neither summaries nor headnotes—only the fact of the equal division and the name of the nonparticipant. Though the Court may have agreed to review these cases because of the civil liberties issue they

presented, the fashion in which they were decided precluded resolution of their merits.

Non-civil rights and liberties cases which the Court resolved on the merits predominantly involve such matters as state taxation, business regulation, national supremacy, and federal pre-emption of state court jurisdiction.

23. Murphy and Prichett, COURTS, JUDGES, AND POLITICS 359 (3rd ed., New York: Random House, 1979).

24. *Id.* at 85. Also see Stone v. Powell, 428 U.S. 465 (1976). *Cf.* Neuborne, *The Myth of Parity*, 90 HARV. L. REV. 1105 (1977).

25. Younger v. Harris, 401 U.S. 37, 44 (1971).

26. These cases are: Brockington v. Rhodes, 396 U.S. 41 (1969); Columbo v. New York, 400 U.S. 16 (1970); Monitor Patriot Co. v. Roy, 401 U.S. 265 (1971); Santobello v. New York, 404 U.S. 257 (1971); Columbo v. New York, 405 U.S. 9 (1972); Moore v. Illinois, 408 U.S. 786 (1972); Ham v. South Carolina, 409 U.S. 524 (1973); Miller v. California, 413 U.S. 15 (1973); Paris Adult Theatre I v. Slaton, 413 U.S. 49 (1973); Kaplan v. California, 413 U.S. 115 (1973); Heller v. New York, 413 U.S. 483 (1973); Roaden v. Kentucky, 413 U.S. 496 (1973); Alexander v. Virginia, 413 U.S. 836 (1973); Menna v. New York, 423 U.S. 61 (1975); Time Inc. v. Firestone, 424 U.S. 448 (1976); Puyallup Tribe v. Dept. of Game of Washington, 433 U.S. 165 (1977); and Wood v. Georgia, 450 U.S. 261 (1981).

Six of the foregoing, those in 413 U.S., are the landmark Burger Court obscenity cases, in all of which the state court had upheld the plaintiff's conviction. In six others, the Court upheld the civil liberties claimant: *Columbo, Santobello, Columbo, Ham, Menna,* and *Wood*. They are classified as conservative decisions, however, because one or more dissenting justices would have provided the claimant more relief than the majority—*e.g.,* reversal of conviction rather than remanding for further proceedings. If these six had been classified in Table 2 as liberal after review, the liberal proportion increases to 59.4 per cent, and the conservative proportion decreases to 40.6 per cent.

27. Grayned v. City of Rockford, 408 U.S. 104 (1972), and Mescalero Apache Tribe v. Jones, 411 U.S. 145 (1973). *Supra* n. 15. Each is counted as half conservative.

28. Younger v. Harris, 401 U.S. 37, 44 (1971).

29. *Supra* n. 9; Galie and Galie, *supra* n. 6.

30. *Supra* n. 9.

31. *Supra* n. 1, 2.

32. Although the Court's production of liberal outcomes on review during the 1982 term declined, its overall disapproval of state court decisions did not. Of the 23 cases reviewed, only seven were affirmed (30.4 per cent). Interestingly, two of the seven decisions in the illiberal 1982 term that produced a liberal outcome resulted form affirmations of state court decisions. By contrast, none of the liberal outcomes on review during the liberal 1981 term resulted from the Court's affirming a liberal state decision. The five affirmations in the 24 cases of the 1981 term (20.8 per cent) all upheld conservative state decisions.

33. The Court also overturned an equal number of conservatively decided non-vehicle search-and-seizure cases (11). Where vehicles were involved, the Court overturned only two that were conservatively decided as opposed to nine that were liberally decided. In self-incrimination cases that pertained to Miranda warnings, the Court overturned four that the states had conservatively decided, as compared with nine that overturned a liberal state decision. In non-Miranda cases, the Court overturned the same number of conservative and liberal decisions (four). The Court also affirmed five liberally decided search-and-seizure cases, five that were conservatively decided, and five conservatively decided self-incrimination cases, one of which involved Miranda.

34. Michigan v. Mosley, 423 U.S. 96 (1975); Michigan v.

Doran, 439 U.S. 282 (1978); Michigan v. DeFillippo, 443 U.S. 31 (1979); Michigan v. Summers, 452 U.S. 692 (1981); Michigan v. Thomas, 458 U.S. 259 (1982); and Michigan v. Long, 77 L Ed 2d 1201 (1983).

35. Oregon v. Hass, 420 U.S. 714 (1975); Oregon v. Mathiason, 429 U.S. 492 (1977); and Oregon v. Bradshaw, 77 L Ed 2d 405 (1983).

36. California v. Byers, 402 U.S. 424 (1971); California v. Prysock, 453 U.S. 355 (1981); and California v. Beheler, 77 L Ed 2d 1275 (1983).

37. South Dakota v. Opperman, 428 U.S. 364 (1976), and South Dakota v. Neville, 74 L Ed 2d 748 (1983).

38. Maine v. Thornton, 80 L Ed 2d 214 (1984).

39. United States v. Washington, 431 U.S. 181 (1977).

40. Air Pollution Variance Board v. Western Alfalfa Corp., 416 U.S. 861 (1974), and Colorado v. Bannister, 449 U.S. 1 (1980).

41. Rhode Island v. Innis, 46 U.S. 291 (1980).

Alternative Forms of Dispute Resolution

INTRODUCTION

It was not too many years ago when the topic of alternative dispute resolution (ADR) would have been considered a frontier concern not worthy of inclusion in a course examining the workings of the American legal system. While ADR has not, in any sense, displaced courts as a mechanism for resolving civil disputes between citizens, clearly multifaceted ADR processes are here to stay and constitute an important component of the American system of justice. Indeed, situations now exist in which ADR mechanisms are not just vehicles of voluntary settlement but are at times ordered by courts to seek, in the words of John Cooley, "swift, inexpensive, simple justice." ADR has clearly become, over time, a more accepted means of dealing with court delay and case management problems in a highly litigious society.

In the first article in this section, John Cooley examines two ADR approaches, "Arbitration vs. mediation—explaining the differences." Cooley demonstrates that the techniques are utilized in different types of disputes and settings. Arbitration involves employment of a third-party decision maker, whereas mediation utilizes a facilitator to foster agreement and/or reconciliation among disputants. Thus, arbitration proceedings are pictured as analogous to a trial, whereas mediation more closely resembles a settlement conference.

In Leslie Ratliff's article, "Civil mediation in Palm Beach," a case study is offered of the operation of an innovative and highly successful mediation program in Florida that relies exclusively on the use of widely available retired judges as mediators. While not the norm, mediation in Palm Beach is even seen to work in the settlement of multimillion dollar cases. As a mark of the Palm Beach program's success, it is shown to be financially solvent and self-sustaining. Although not all settings are marked by the conditions that foster the Palm Beach program's success, the case study is clearly suggestive of some of the elements of a model mediation program.

In "ADR problems and prospects: looking to the future," Stephen Goldberg, Eric Green, and Frank Sander offer our most critical assessment of alternative dispute resolution and ask why ADR has not spread more rapidly given its apparent success when utilized. Among the impediments to ADR that the authors examine are the lack of public knowledge about and acceptance of alternatives to litigation and the role of lawyers for whom litigation is often the path of least resistance. Critiques of ADR, particularly mediation and the "second-class justice" argument often attached to it, are explored as is the emerging concern about the professionalization and institutionalization of ADR mechanisms. The authors are wary of some facets of professional institutionalization, supporting certification and training that serves ADR consumers, while opposing licensure, which they claim only serves professional self-interest. Much of the article is speculative in tone and clearly underlines the need for additional research in the ADR domain. Indeed, as Goldberg, Green, and Sander conclude:

What we need now is a multi-pronged effort to expand our limited present understanding of the field. This will require continued experimentation and research . . . . It will necessitate enhanced public education about the benefits to be derived from alternative modes of dispute settlement . . . . Above all, if the movement is to hold any significant promise of gaining a permanent foothold on the American scene, it will require the broadened involvement and support not only of the legal and legal education establishments but also of the society at large.

Arbitration vs. mediation—explaining the differences

by John W. Cooley

An amazing number of lawyers and business professionals are unaware of the difference between arbitration and mediation. Their confusion is excusable.

In the early development of the English language, the two words were used interchangeably. The *Oxford English Dictionary* provides as one historical definition of arbitration: "to act as formal arbitrator or umpire, to mediate (in a dispute between contending parties)." The Statutes of Edward III (1606) referring to what today obviously would be called a commercial *arbitration* panel, provided: "And two Englishmen, two of Lombardie and two of Almaigne shall (be) chosen to be mediators of questions between sellers and buyers."[1]

Modern labor relations statutes tend to perpetuate this confusion. As one commentator has observed:

Some statutes, referring to a process as "mediation" describe formal hearings, with witnesses testifying under oath and transcripts made, require reports and recommendations for settlement to be made by the neutral within fixed periods, and either state or imply the finality of the "mediator's recommendations." In one statute the neutral third parties are called, interchangeably, mediators, arbitrators and impasse panels.[2]

The Federal Mediation and Conciliation Service (note the absence of "arbitration" in its title) performs a basic arbitration function by maintaining a roster from which the service can nominate arbitrators to the parties and suggest "certain procedures and guides that [the service believes] will enhance the acceptability of arbitration."[3]

The National *Mediation* Board (emphasis added) performs important functions in the promotion of arbitration and the selection of arbitrators for the railroad and airline industries.[4]

Libraries also assist in perpetuating the arbitration/mediation definitional charade. Search under "mediation" and you will invariably be referred

to "arbitration." In the midst of this confusion—even among congressional draftsmen—it is time to explain the differences between the processes.

The most basic difference between the two is that arbitration involves a *decision* by an intervening third party or "neutral"; mediation does not.

Another way to distinguish the two is by describing the processes in terms of the neutral's mental functions. In arbitration, the neutral employs mostly "left brain" or "rational" mental processes—analytical, mathematical, logical, technical, administrative; in mediation, the neutral employs mostly "right brain" or "creative" mental processes—conceptual, intuitive, artistic, holistic, symbolic, emotional.

The arbitrator deals largely with the objective; the mediator, the subjective. The arbitrator is generally a passive functionary who determines right or wrong; the mediator is generally an active functionary who attempts to move the parties to reconciliation and agreement, regardless of who or what is right or wrong.

Because the role of the mediator involves instinctive reactions, intuition, keen interpersonal skills, the ability to perceive subtle psychological and behavioral indicators, in addition to logic and rational thinking, it is much more difficult than the arbitrator's role to perform effectively.[5] It is fair to say that while most mediators can effectively perform the arbitrator's function, the converse is not necessarily true.

Besides these differences the two processes are generally employed to resolve two different types of disputes. Mediation is used where there is a reasonable likelihood that the parties will be able to reach an agreement with the assistance of a neutral. Usually, mediation is used when parties will have an ongoing relationship after resolution of the conflict. Arbitration, on the other hand, is generally appropriate for use when two conditions exist: there is no reasonable likelihood of a negotiated settlement, and there will not be a continuing relationship after resolution.[6]

If the two processes are to be used in sequence, mediation occurs first, and if unsuccessful, resort is made to arbitration.[7] Viewed in terms of the judicial process, arbitration is comparable to a trial and mediation is akin to a judicial settlement conference. They are as different as night and day.[8] The differences can best be understood by discussing them in terms of the processes of arbitration and mediation.

The arbitration process

Arbitration has had a long history in this country, going back to procedures carried over into the colonies from mercantile England. George Washington put an arbitration clause in his last will and testament to resolve disputes among his heirs. Abraham Lincoln urged lawyers to keep their clients out of court and himself arbitrated a boundary dispute between two farmers. Today, arbitration is being used more broadly for dispute settlement both in labor-management relations and in commercial transactions.

Aside from its well-known use in resolving labor disputes, arbitration is now becoming widely used to settle intercompany disputes in various industries, including textile, construction, life and casualty insurance, canning, livestock, air transport, grain and feed, and securities.[9]

Simply defined, arbitration is a process in which a dispute is submitted to a third party or neutral (or sometimes a panel of three arbitrators) to hear arguments, review evidence, and render a decision.[10] Court-annexed arbitration, a relatively new development, is a process in which judges refer civil suits to arbitrators to render prompt, nonbinding decisions. If a particular decision is not accepted by a losing party, a trial *de novo* may be held in the court system. However, adverse decisions sometimes lead to further negotiation and pretrial settlement.[11]

The arbitration process, court-annexed or otherwise, normally consists of six stages: initiation, preparation, prehearing conferences, hearing, decision making, and award.

Initiation. The initiation stage of arbitration consists of two substages: initiating the proceeding, and selecting the arbitrator. An arbitration proceeding may be initiated either by: submission; "demand" or "notice;" or, in the case of a court-annexed proceeding, court rule or court order.

A submission must be signed by both parties and is used where there is no previous agreement to arbitrate. It often names the arbitrator (or method of appointment), contains considerable detail regarding the arbitrator's authority, the procedure to be used at the hearing, statement of the matter in dispute, the amount of money in controversy, the remedy sought, and other matters.

On the other hand, where the description of a dispute is contained in an agreement and the parties have agreed in advance to arbitrate it, arbitration may be initiated unilaterally by one party serving upon the other a written "demand" or "notice" to arbitrate.

However, even where an agreement contains a "demand" or "notice" arbitration clause, parties sometimes choose also to execute a submission after the dispute has materialized. In the court-annexed situation, a lawsuit is mandatorily referred to an arbitration track and the parties must select an arbitrator from a court-maintained roster or otherwise by mutual agreement.[12]

Several types of tribunals and methods of selecting their membership are available to parties who wish to arbitrate. Parties may choose between the use of a "temporary" or "permanent" arbitrator. They can also choose to have single or multiple arbitrators. Since success of the arbitration process often hinges on the expertise of the tribunal, parties generally select a tribunal whose members possess impartiality, integrity, ability and experience in the field in which the dispute arises. Legal training is often helpful but not indispensable.

Information concerning the qualifications of some of the more active arbitrators is contained in the *Directory of Arbitrators*, prepared by the Bureau of National Affairs, Inc., and in *Who's Who* (of arbitrators) published by Prentice-Hall, Inc. Also, the Federal Mediation and Conciliation Service (FMCS), the National Mediation Board (NMB), and the American Arbitration Association (AAA) provide biographical data on arbitrators.[13]

Preparation. The parties must thoroughly prepare cases for arbitration. Obviously, a party must fully understand its own case to communicate effectively to the arbitrator. Depending on the nature of the case, prehearing discovery may be necessary, and its permissible extent is usually determined by the arbitrator. The advantages of simplicity and utility of the arbitration mode normally weigh against extensive discovery. During this stage, the parties also enter into fact stipulations where possible.[14]

Ordinarily, most or all of the arbitrator's knowledge and understanding of a case is based upon evidence and arguments presented at the arbitration hearing. However, the arbitrator does have some "preparation" functions. Generally, where no tribunal administrator (such as AAA) is involved, the arbitrator, after accepting the office, designates the time and place of the hearing, by mutual agreement of the parties if possible. The arbitrator also signs an oath, if required in the particular jurisdiction, and determines whether the parties will have representation, legal or otherwise, at the hearing.[15]

Prehearing conferences. Depending on the complexity of the matter involved, the arbitrator may wish to schedule a prehearing conference, which is normally administrative in nature.[16] Briefing schedules, if necessary, are set on motions attacking the validity of claims or of the proceeding. But generally, briefing is minimized to preserve the efficiency of the process. Discussion of the underlying merits of claims or defenses of the parties are avoided during a prehearing conference. *Ex parte* conferences between the arbitrator and a party are not permitted.[17]

The hearing. Parties may waive oral hearing and have the controversy determined on the basis of documents only. However, an evidentiary-type hearing in the presence of the arbitrator is deemed imperative in virtually all cases. Since arbitration is a private proceeding, the hearing is not open to the public as a rule but all persons having a direct interest in the case are ordinarily entitled to attend.

A formal written record of the hearing is not always necessary; use of a reporter is the exception rather than the general practice. A party requiring an interpreter has the duty to arrange for one. Witnesses testifying at the hearing may also be required to take an oath if required by law, if ordered by the arbitrator, or on demand of any party.[18]

Opening statements are made orally by each party in a brief, generalized format. They are designed to acquaint the arbitrator with each party's view of what the dispute is about and what the party expects to prove by the evidence. Sometimes an arbitrator requests each party to provide a short written opening statement and issue statement prior to the hearing. Occasionally, a respondent opts for making an opening statement immediately prior to presenting initial evidence.[19]

There is no set order by which parties present their cases in arbitration, although in practice the complaining party normally presents evidence first. The parties may offer any evidence they choose, including personal testimony and affidavits of witnesses. They may be required to produce additional evidence the arbitrator deems necessary to determine the dispute. The arbitrator, when authorized by law, may subpoena witnesses or documents upon his or her own initiative or by request of a party. The arbitrator also decides the relevancy and materiality of all evidence offered. Conformity to legal rules of evidence is unnecessary. The arbitrator has a right to make a physical inspection of premises.[20]

The parties make closing arguments, usually limited in duration. Occasionally, the arbitrator requests post-hearing briefs. When this occurs, the parties usually waive oral closing arguments.[21]

Decision making. When the issues are not complex, an arbitrator may render an immediate decision. However, when the evidence presented is voluminous and/or time is needed for the members of an arbitration panel to confer, it might require several weeks to make a decision.

The award is the arbitrator's decision. It may be given orally but is normally written and signed by the arbitrator(s). Awards are normally short, definite, certain, and final as to all matters under submission. Occasionally, they are accompanied by a short, well-reasoned opinion. The award is usually issued no later than 30 days from the closing date of the hearing. When a party fails to appear, a default award may be entered.[22] Depending on the nature of the award (i.e., binding), it may be judicially enforceable and, to some extent, reviewable. The losing party in a court-annexed arbitration is entitled to trial *de novo* in court.

The mediation process

Mediation is a process in which an impartial intervenor assists the disputants to reach a voluntary settlement of their differences through an agreement that defines their future behavior.[23] The process generally consists of eight stages: initiation, preparation, introduction, problem statement, problem clarification, generation and evaluation of alternatives, selection of alternative(s), and agreement.[24]

Initiation. The mediation process may be initiated in two principal ways: parties submit the matter to a public or private dispute resolution organization or to a private neutral; or the dispute is referred to mediation by court order or rule in a court-annexed mediation program.

In the first instance, counsel for one of the parties or, if unrepresented, the party may contact the neutral organization or individual and the neutral will contact the opposing counsel or party (as the case may be) to see if there is interest in attempting to mediate the dispute.

Preparation. As in arbitration, it is of paramount importance that the parties to a dispute in mediation be as well informed as possible on the background of the dispute, the claims or defenses and the remedies they seek. The parties should seek legal advice if necessary, and although a party's lawyer might attend a typical nonjudicial mediation, he or she normally does not take an adversary role but is rather available to render legal advice as needed.

The mediator should also be well-informed about the parties and the features of their dispute and know something about:

• the balance of power;
• the primary sources of pressure exerted on the parties;
• the pressures motivating them toward agreement as well as pressures blocking agreement;
• the economics of the industry or particular company involved;
• political and personal conflicts within and between the parties;
• the extent of the settlement authority of each of the parties.

The mediator sets the date, time and place for the hearing at everyone's convenience.[25]

Introduction. In the mediation process, the introductory stage may be the most important.[26] It is in that phase, particularly the first joint session, that the mediator establishes his or her acceptability, integrity, credibility, and neutrality. The mediator usually has several objectives to achieve initially. They are: establish control of the process; determine issues and positions of the parties; get the agreement-forging process started; and encourage continuation of direct negotiations.[27]

Unlike a judge in a settlement conference or an arbitrator who wields the clout of a decision, a mediator does not, by virtue of position, ordinarily command the parties' immediate trust and respect; the mediator earns them through a carefully orchestrated and delicately executed ritual of rapport-building. Every competent mediator has a personal style. The content of the mediator's opening remarks is generally crucial to establishing rapport with the parties and the respectability of the mediator and the process.

Opening remarks focus on: identifying the mediator and the parties; explaining the procedures to be followed (including caucusing),[28] describing the mediation function (if appropriate) and emphasizing the continued decision-making responsibility of the parties; and reinforcing the confidentiality and integrity of the process.[29] When appropriate, the mediator might invoke the community and public interest in having the dispute resolved quickly and emphasize the interests of the constituents in the successful conclusion of the negotiations.[30]

Finally, the mediator must assess the parties' competence to participate in the process. If either party has severe emotional, drinking, drug, or health problems, the mediator may postpone the proceeding. If the parties are extremely hostile and verbally abusive, the mediator must endeavor to calm them, by preliminary caucusing if necessary.[31]

Problem statement. There are essentially two ways to open a discussion of the dispute by the parties: Both parties give their positions and discuss each issue as it is raised; or all the issues are first briefly identified, with detailed exposition of positions reserved until all the issues have been identified. The second procedure is preferred; the first approach often leads to tedious time-consuming rambling about insignificant matters, sometimes causing the parties to become more entrenched in their positions.[32]

Generally, the complaining party tells his or her "story" first. It may be the first time that the adverse party has heard the full basis for the complaint. The mediator actively and empathically listens, taking notes if helpful, using listening techniques such as restatement, echo and nonverbal responses. Listening is the mediator's most important dispute-resolving tool.[33]

The mediator also:

• asks open-ended and closed-ended questions at the appropriate time and in a neutral fashion;
• obtains important "signals" from the behavior and body movements of the parties;

- calms a party, as necessary;
- clarifies the narration by focused questions;
- objectively summarizes the first party's story;
- defuses tensions by omitting disparaging comments from the summary;
- determines whether the second party understands the first party's story;
- thanks the first party for his or her contribution.

The process is repeated with the second party.[34]

Problem clarification. It is in this stage that the mediator culls out the true underlying issues in the dispute. Often the parties to a dispute intentionally obfuscate the core issues. The mediator pierces this cloud cover through separate caucuses in which he or she asks direct, probing questions to elicit information that one party would not disclose in the presence of the other party. In a subsequent joint session, the mediator summarizes areas of agreement or disagreement, being careful not to disclose matters that the parties shared with the mediator in confidence. They are assisted in grouping and prioritizing issues and demands.[35]

Generation and evaluation of alternatives. In this stage, the mediator employs two fundamental principles of effective mediation: creating doubt in the minds of the parties as to the validity of their positions on issues; and suggesting alternative approaches that may facilitate agreement.[36] These are two functions that parties to a dispute are very often unable to perform by themselves. To carry out these functions, the mediator has the parties separately brainstorm to produce alternatives or options; discusses the workability of each option; encourages the parties by noting the probability of success, where appropriate; suggests alternatives not raised by the parties, and then repeats the three previous steps.[37]

Selection of alternative(s). The mediator may compliment the parties on their progress and use humor, when appropriate, to relieve tensions; assist the parties in eliminating the unworkable options; and help the parties determine which of the remaining workable solutions will produce the optimum results with which each can live.[38]

Agreement. Before the mediation is terminated, the mediator summarizes and clarifies, as necessary, the terms of the agreement reached and secures the assent of each party to those terms; sets a follow-up date, if necessary; and congratulates the parties on their reasonableness.

The mediator does not usually become involved in drafting a settlement agreement. This task is left to the parties themselves or their counsel. The agreement is the parties', not the mediator's.[39]

A mediator's patience, flexibility, and creativity throughout this entire process are necessary keys to a successful resolution.

The "neutral's" functions

To fully appreciate the differences (or the similarities) between the two processs, and to evaluate the appropriate use of either process, it is instructive to focus on considerations that exist at their interface—the function and power of the "neutral." This is a particularly important exercise to acquire a realistic expectation of the result to be obtained from each process.

The arbitrator's function is quasi-judicial in nature and, because of this, an arbitrator is generally exempt from civil liability for failure to exercise care or skill in performing the arbitral function.[40] As a quasi-judicial officer, the arbitrator is guided by ethical norms in the performance of duties. For example, an arbitrator must refrain from having any private (*ex parte*) consultations with a party or with an attorney representing a party without the consent of the opposing party or counsel.[41]

Moreover, unless the parties agree otherwise, the arbitration proceedings are private and arbitrators must take appropriate measures to maintain the confidentiality of the proceedings.[42] It has generally been held that an arbitrator may not testify as to the meaning and construction of the written award.[43]

In contrast, a mediator is not normally considered to be quasi-judicial, unless he or she is appointed by the court as, for example, a special master. Some courts have extended the doctrine of immunity to persons termed "quasi-arbitrators"— persons empowered by agreement of the parties to resolve disputes arising between them.[44] Although the law is far from clear on this point, a very persuasive argument may be advanced that mediators are generally immune from lawsuits relating to the performance of their mediation duties where the agreement under which they perform contains a hold-harmless provision or its equivalent.

In absence of such contractual provision, it would appear that a functionary such as a mediator, selected by parties to perform skilled or professional services, would not ordinarily be immune from charges of negligence but rather is required to work with the same skill and care exercised by an average person engaged in the trade or profession involved.[45]

Of course, weighing heavily against a finding of negligence on the part of a mediator is the intrinsic nature, if not the essence, of the mediation process which invests the parties with the complete power over their destiny; it also guarantees any party the right to withdraw from the process and even to eject the mediator during any pre-agreement stage.[46]

Also, in contrast to arbitrators, certain ethical restrictions do not apply to mediators. Mediators are permitted to have *ex parte* conferences with the parties or counsel. Indeed, such caucuses, as they are called, are the mediator's stock-in-trade. Furthermore, while one of the principal advantages of a privately-conducted mediation is the nonpublic or confidential nature of the proceedings, and although Rule 408 of the Federal Rules of Evidence and public policy considerations argue in favor of confidentiality, the current state of the law does not provide a guarantee of such confidentiality.[47] However, in most cases a strong argument can be made that the injury from disclosure of a confidential settlement proceeding is greater than the benefit to be gained by the public from nondisclosure.[48]

Finally, unlike the arbitrator, the performance of whose function may be enhanced by knowledge, skill, or ability in a particular field or industry, the mediator need not be an expert in the field that encompasses the subject of the dispute. Expertise may, in fact, be a handicap, if the parties look wrongly to the mediator as an advice-giver or adjudicator.[49]

Comparative power

The arbitrator derives power from many sources. The person may be highly respected in a particular field of expertise or widely renowned for fairness. But aside from these attributes, which emanate from personal talents or characteristics, the arbitrator operates within a procedural and enforcement framework that affords considerable power, at least from the perspective of the disputants. Under certain circumstances, arbitrators may possess broad remedy powers, including the power, though rare, to grant injunctive relief.[50] They normally have subpoena power, and generally they have no obligation to anyone, not even "to the court to give reasons for an award."[51]

In general, a valid arbitration award constitutes a full and final adjustment of the controversy.[52] It has all the force and effect of an adjudication, and effectively precludes the parties from again litigating the same subject.[53] The award can be challenged in court only on very narrow grounds. In some states the grounds related to partiality of the arbitrator or to misconduct in the proceedings, such as refusal to allow the production of evidence or to grant postponements, as well as to other misbehavior in conducting the hearings so as to prejudice the interests of a party.[54]

A further ground for challenge in some states is the failure of the arbitrator to observe the limits of authority as fixed by the parties' agreement—such as determining unsubmitted matters or by not dealing definitely and finally with submitted issues.[55] In Illinois, as in most states, a judgment entered on an arbitration award is enforceable "as any other judgment."[56] Thus, from a systemic perspective, the arbitrator is invested with a substantial amount of power.

In striking contrast, with the exception of a special master appointed by the court or a neutral appointed by some governmental body, the mediator has little if any systemic-based power. Most if not all of a mediator's power is derived from experience, demonstrated skills and abilities, and a reputation for successful settlements.

Any particular mediator may wield power by adopting a particular role on what might be described as a continuum representing the range of strengths of intervention: from virtual passivity, to "chairman," to "enunciator," to "prompter," to "leader," to virtual arbitrator.[57] The mediator who can adopt different roles on this continuum, changing strategies to fit changing circumstances and requirements of both the disputants and himself, is inevitably more effective in accumulating and wielding power that is real, yet often not consciously perceptible by the disputants themselves.[58]

Since, in the ordinary case, the result of the mediation process is an agreement or contract not reduced to a court judgment,[59] the result is binding on the parties only to the extent that the law of contracts in the particular jurisdiction requires. And to the same extent, the result is enforceable by one party against another. As a practical matter, where a party breaches an agreement or contract that is the product of mediation and the agreement is not salvageable, prudence would seem to dictate that in most cases the underlying dispute—and not the breach of agreement—should be litigated.

Table 1   A comparison of arbitration/mediation processes

Arbitration	Mediation
1. Initiation Submission Demand or notice Court rules or order Selection of arbitrator	**1. Initiation** Submission Court rule or order Assignment or selection of mediator
2. Preparation Discovery Prehearing conference Motions Stipulations Arbitrator's oath Arbitrator's administrative duties Arbitrator does not seek out information about parties or dispute	**2. Preparation** Usually, no discovery Parties obtain background information on claims, defenses, remedies Mediator obtains information on parties and history of dispute Usually, no mediator oath
3. Prehearing conference Administrative Scheduling No discussion of underlying merits of claims or defenses No *ex parte* conference	**3. Introduction** Mediator: Conduct *ex parte* conferences, if necessary, for calming Gives opening descriptive remarks Develops trust and respect Emphasizes importance of successful negotiations Helps parties separate the people from the problem

4. Hearing
Not generally open to public
Written record, optional
Witnesses and parties testify under oath
  Opening statement
  Made orally
  Sometimes also in writing
  Order of proceedings and evidence
  Complaining party usually presents evidence first
  Arbitrator may subpoena witnesses
  Evidence rules relaxed
  Arbitrator rules on objections to evidence; may reject evidence
  Closing arguments
  Oral arguments normally permitted for clarification and synthesis
  Post-hearing briefs sometimes permitted
	4. Problem statement
	Confidential proceeding, no written record
	Parties do not speak under oath
	Issues identified
	Issues discussed separately, stories told
	Mediator listens; takes notes
	Mediator asks questions; reads behavioral signals
	Mediator calms parties; summarizes stories; defuses tensions
	Mediator determines whether parties understand stories
	Mediator usually has no subpoena power
	
	5. Problem clarification
	Mediator:
	Culls out core issues in caucus
	Asks direct, probing questions
	Summarizes areas of agreement and disagreement
	Assists parties in grouping and prioritizing issues and demands
	Helps parties focus on interests, not positions

5. Decision making If issues non-complex, arbitrator can issue an immediate decision If issues complex, or panel has three members, extra time may be required	**6. Generation and evaluation of alternatives** Mediator: Creates doubts in parties' minds as to validity of their positions Invents options for facilitating agreement Leads "brainstorming;" discusses workability; notes probability of success of options **7. Selection of alternative(s)** Mediator: Compliments parties on progress Assists parties in eliminating unworkable options Helps parties to use objective criteria Helps parties determine which solution will produce optimum results
6. Award Normally in writing, signed by arbitrator(s) Short, definite, certain and final, as to all matters under submission Occasionally a short opinion accompanies award Award may be judicially enforceable or reviewable	**8. Agreement** Mediator: Summarizes and clarifies agreement terms Sets follow-up date, if appropriate Congratulates parties on their reasonableness Usually does not draft or assist in drafting agreement Agreement is enforceable as a contract and subject to later modification by agreement

Summary

It is clear that both the functions and the levels of power of arbitrators and mediators are dramatically different. Counsel must assess the nature of the dispute and the personalities of the disputants prior to determining which process, arbitration or mediation, has the best chance to achieve a successful resolution of the particular conflict.

For example, arbitration would probably prove to be the better dispute resolution choice where the dispute involves highly technical matters; a long-standing feud between the disputants; irrational and high-strung personalities; and no necessity of a continued relationship after resolution of the conflict.

On the other hand, mediation may prove to be the most effective choice where disputants are stubborn but basically sensible; have much to gain from a continued relationship with one another; and conflict resolution is time-critical.

Arbitration and mediation are two separate and distinct processes having a similar overall goal (terminating a dispute), while using totally different methods to obtain dissimilar (decisional vs. contractual) results. These differences are best understood by viewing the processes side-by-side in Table 1.

The benefits of arbitration and mediation to litigants, in terms of cost and time savings, are just beginning to be recognized by lawyers and business professionals alike. It is hoped that this discussion of the arbitration and mediation processes and their differences will help lawyers feel more comfortable with these two methods of dispute resolution and to use them to their clients' advantage in their joint pursuit of swift, inexpensive, simple justice.

NOTES

This article originally appeared in Volume 69, Number 5, February-March 1986, pages 263-269. It is adapted from a version that appeared in the CHICAGO BAR RECORD (January-February, 1985).

1. Robins, A GUIDE FOR LABOR MEDIATORS 6 (Honolulu: University Press of Hawaii, 1976).

2. *Id.*

3. Elkouri and Elkouri, HOW ARBITRATION WORKS 24 (Washington, D.C.: BNA, 3rd ed. 1973).

4. *Id.* at 25.

5. As one American professional mediator put it, the mediator "has no science of navigation, no fund inherited from the experience of others. He is a solitary artist recognizing, at most, a few guiding stars and depending mainly on his personal power of divination." Meyer, *Function of the Mediator in Collective Bargaining,* 13 INDUS. & LAB. REL. REV. 159 (1960).

6. In labor relations arbitration, of course, condition (2) is normally not present. Labor disputes are generally divided into two categories: rights disputes and interest disputes. Disputes as to "rights" involve the interpretation or application of existing laws, agreements, or customary practices; disputes as to "interests" involve controversies over the formation of collective agreements or efforts to secure them where no such agreement is yet in existence. Elkouri and Elkouri, *supra* n. 3, at 47.

7. Because of ethical considerations, the arbitrator and mediator normally are different persons. It should also be noted that mediation is frequently effective when it is attempted, with the concurrence of the parties, during the course of an arbitration with a neutral other than the arbitrator serving as the mediator. Often the unfolding of the opponent's evidence during the course of arbitration leads to a better appreciation of the merits of their respective positions and hence an atmosphere conducive to settlement discussions.

8. The stark distinction between mediation and arbitration was well made by a professional mediator who became chairman of the New York State Mediation Board: "Mediation and arbitration . . . have conceptually nothing in common. The one [mediation] involves helping people to decide for themselves, the other involves helping people by deciding for them." Meyer, *supra* n. 5, at 164, as quoted in Gulliver, DISPUTES AND NEGOTIATIONS, A CROSS-CULTURAL PERSPECTIVE 210 (New York: Academic Press, 1979).

9. Cooley, *Arbitration as an Alternative to Federal Litigation in the Seventh Circuit,* REPORT OF THE SUBCOMMITTEE ON ALTERNATIVES TO THE PRESENT FEDERAL COURT SYSTEM, SEVENTH CIRCUIT AD HOC COMMITTEE TO STUDY THE HIGH COST OF LITIGATION 2 (July 13, 1978).

10. *Paths to Justice: Major Public Policy Issues of Dispute Resolution,* REPORT OF THE AD HOC PANEL ON DISPUTE RESOLUTION AND PUBLIC POLICY, Appendix 2 (Washington, D.C.: National Institute for Dispute Resolution, October, 1983).

11. *Id. See also* EVALUATION OF COURT-ANNEXED ARBITRATION IN THREE FEDERAL DISTRICT COURTS (Washington, D.C.: Federal Judicial Center, 1981).

12. Cooley, *supra* n. 9, at 4, Elkouri and Elkouri, *supra* n. 3, at 183-186. Domke on Commercial Arbitration. §§14:00-14:05 (Rev. Ed. 1984). Arbitrators, if chosen from a list maintained by an arbitration organization or court-maintained roster, are normally compensated at the daily rate fixed by the organization or the court. Arbitrators selected independently by the parties are compensated at the daily or hourly rate at which they mutually agree. In such cases, the parties equally share the expense of the arbitrator's services.

13. Elkouri and Elkouri, *supra* n. 3, at 24-25.

14. Elkouri and Elkouri, *supra* n. 3, at 197; (for preparation checklist *see* pp. 198-199); Domke, *supra* n. 12, §§24:01 and 27:01.

15. *Id.*

16. Some of the matters that might be discussed at a prehearing conference are: whether discovery is needed and, if so, scheduling of same; motions that need to be filed and briefed or orally argued; and the setting of firm oral argument and hearing dates.

17. Cooley, *supra* n. 9, at 4-5; Elkouri and Elkouri, *supra* n. 3, at 186-190.

18. Cooley, *supra* n. 9, at 5.

19. Elkouri and Elkouri, *supra* n. 3, at 224-225.

20. Cooley, *supra* n. 9, at 5; Elkouri and Elkouri, *supra* n. 3, at 223-228.

21. Elkouri and Elkouri, *supra* n. 3, at 225.

22. Cooley, *supra* n. 9, at 6.

23. Salem, *Mediation—The Concept and the Process,* in INSTRUCTORS MANUAL FOR TEACHING CRITICAL ISSUES (1984, unpublished).

See generally Simkin, MEDIATION AND THE DYNAMICS OF COLLECTIVE BARGAINING 25 (BNA, 1971). Court-annexed mediation is a process in which judges refer civil cases to a neutral (mediator or master) for settlement purposes. It also includes in-court programs in which judges perform the settlement function full-time.

24. *See generally* Ray, *The Alternative Dispute Resolution Movement*, 8 PEACE AND CHANGE 117 (Summer 1982). The process of mediation and the roles and strategies of mediators have been generally neglected in studies of negotiation. As one author remarked, "Mediation still remains a poorly understood process." Gulliver, *supra* n. 8.

25. Meagher, "Mediation Procedures and Techniques," 18-19 (unpublished paper on file in the Office of the General Counsel, FMCS, Washington, D.C.). Mr. Meagher is a former commissioner of FMCS.

26. The success of the introductory stage is directly related to two critical factors: (1) the appropriate timing of the mediator's intervention, and (2) the opportunity for mediator preparation. A mediator's sense of timing is the ability to judge the psychological readiness of an individual or group to respond in the desired way to a particular idea, suggestion, or proposal. Meagher, *supra* n. 25, at 5, *see also* Maggiolo, TECHNIQUES OF MEDIATION IN LABOR DISPUTES 62 (Dobbs Ferry, NY: Oceana Publications, 1971). The kinds of preparatory information needed by the mediator are discussed in the text *supra*. In many instances, such information is not available prior to intervention and thus it must be delicately elicited by the mediator during the introductory stage.

27. Meagher, *supra* n. 25, at 26-27. Wall, *Mediation, An Analysis, Review and Proposed Research*, 25 J. CONFLICT RES. 157, 161 (1981).

28. Caucusing is an *ex parte* conference between a mediator and a party.

29. Meagher, *supra* n. 25, at 28; Maggiolo, *supra* n. 26, at 42-44.

30. *Id.*

31. Ray, *supra* n. 24, at 121; Maggiolo, *supra* n. 26, at 52-54.

32. Meagher, *supra* n. 25, at 30; Maggiolo, *supra* n. 26, at 47.

33. Ray, *supra* n. 24, at 121; Salem, *supra* n. 23, at 4-5; Robins, *supra* n. 1, at 27; Maggiolo, *supra* n. 26, at 48-49.

34. Ray, *supra* n. 24, at 121.

35. *Id.* at 121-122; Meagher, *supra* n. 25, at 57-58; Robins, *supra* n. 1, at 43-44; Maggiolo, *supra* n. 26, at 49-50.

36. Maggiolo, *supra* n. 26, at 12. Other basic negotiation principles that some mediators use to advantage throughout the mediation process are found in Fisher and Ury, GETTING TO YES (New York: Penguin Books, 1983). Those principles are: (1) separate the people from the problem; (2) focus on interests, not positions; (3) invent options of mutual gain; (4) insist on using objective criteria.

37. Ray, *supra* n. 24, at 122. Meagher, *supra* n. 25, at 48-49, describes additional techniques of "planting seeds," "conditioning," and "influencing expectations."

38. Ray, *supra* n. 24, at 122.

39. *Id.*

40. Domke, *supra* n. 12, §23:01, at 351-353.

41. *Id.* §24:05, at 380.

42. *Id.*

43. *Id.* §23:02, at 355.

44. See Craviolini v. Scholer & Fuller Associated Architects, 89 Ariz. 24, 357 P.2d 611 (1960), where an architect was deemed to be a "quasi-arbitrator" under an agreement with the parties and therefore entitled to immunity from civil liability in an action brought against him by either party in relation to the architect's dispute-resolving function. *Compare* Gammell v. Ernst & Ernst, 245 Minn. 249, 72 N.W.2d 364 (1955), where certified public accountants, selected for the specific purpose of making an examination and of auditing the books of a corporation to ascertain its earnings, were held not to have acquired the status of arbitrators so as to create immunity for their actions in the performance of such service, simply because the report was to be binding upon the parties.

45. Domke, *supra* n. 12, §23:01, at 352-353.

46. As two professional mediators have poignantly commented: "Unlike arbitration and other means of adjudication, the parties retain complete control . . . If they do not like the mediator, they get another one. If they fail to produce results, they may end the mediation at any time." Phillips and Piazza, *How to Use Mediation*, 10 A.B.A. J. OF SECT. OF LIT. 31 (Spring, 1984).

47. *See* Grumman Aerospace Corp. v. Titanium Metals Corp., 91 F.R.D. 84 (E.D. N.Y. 1981) (court granted a motion to enforce a subpoena *duces tecum* involving a report prepared by a neutral fact-finder on the effects of certain price-fixing activities). *See generally* Restivo and Mangus, *Alternative Dispute Resolution: Confidential Problem-Solving or Every Man's Evidence? Alternatives to the High Cost of Litigation*, 2 LAW & BUS. INC./CTR. FOR PUBLIC RESOURCES 5 (May, 1984). Parties can assist the preservation of confidentiality of their mediation proceedings by reducing to writing any expectations or understanding regarding the confidentiality of the proceedings and by being careful to protect against unnecessary disclosure both within their respective constituencies and the outside world, *id.* at 9.

48. *See, e.g.*, NLRB v. Joseph Macaluso, 618 F.2d 51 (9th Cir. 1980); Pipefitters Local 208 v. Mechanical Contractors Assn. of Colorado, 90 Lab. Cas. (CCH) ¶12,647 (D. Colo. 1980).

49. Phillips and Piazza, *supra* n. 46, at 33.

50. In re Ruppert, 29 LA 775, 777 (N.Y. Ct. App. 1958); In re Griffin, 42 LA 511 (N.Y. Sup. Ct. 1964). *See generally* Elkouri and Elkouri, *supra* n. 3, at 241-251.

51. Domke, *supra* n. 12, §29:06, at 436.

52. Donoghue v. Kohlmeyer & Co., 63 Ill. App. 3d 979, 380 N.E.2d 1003, 20 Ill. Dec. 794 (1978).

53. Borg, Inc. v. Morris Middle School Dist. No. 54, 3 Ill. App. 3d 913, 278 N.E.2d 818 (1972).

54. Domke, *supra* n. 12, §33:00, 463.

55. *Id.* In Illinois, the court's power to vacate or modify arbitration awards is narrowly circumscribed. *See* ILL. REV. STAT. ch. 10, ¶¶112, 113 (1981).

56. ILL. REV. STAT. ch. 10, ¶114 (1981).

57. Gulliver, *supra* n. 8, at 220.

58. *Id.* at 226.

59. Where a settlement agreement is reduced to a judgment, for example, through intervention and assistance of a special master, the "consent judgment" is generally enforceable, if necessary, before the court in which the consent judgment is entered.

Civil mediation in Palm Beach: a "retired" Massachusetts judge pioneers a successful new program

by Leslie C. Ratliff

Just two days after he retired from the Massachusetts bench, Judge Albert S. Silverman left a stark New England winter and headed south to Florida, fully intending to exchange his judicial robes for golfing attire. But things didn't quite work out that way, at least not in the long run. Instead, at age 72, Judge Silverman found himself embarking on a new career—one which was to have a significant impact on the courts of Palm Beach County and ultimately on the administration of justice throughout Florida.

Since 1982, Judge Silverman has served as a circuit court mediator for Florida's Fifteenth Judicial Circuit. He and his colleagues—all retired from the bench—mediated more than 550 cases in 1987.* Their caseload for 1988 more than doubled—1,820 cases. In both years, over 60 per cent of the cases they mediated were settled.

What has grown to be the most extensive circuit court mediation program in Florida began quite by accident, growing out of a chance meeting a long way from Florida. In 1975, Judge Silverman attended classes at the National Judicial College in Reno, Nevada. There, he met Judge Edward Rodgers of Florida's Fifteenth Judicial Circuit. Seeking to renew the acquaintance after his move to Florida, Judge Silverman called on Judge Rodgers and, over lunch, Judge Silverman confessed that he was a miserable failure at being retired. Golf and volunteer work aside, he was, quite simply, tired of retirement.

Apparently, Judge Silverman's confession was taken seriously, for two weeks later he received a call from Judge Rodgers. Could he assist two attorneys experiencing difficulties in completing a series of depositions in a complicated case? Judge Rodgers explained he could no longer spare the time necessary to resolve the numerous objections being generated by questions asked during these depositions. As an alternative, Judge Rodgers suggested that the attorneys consider having him appoint Judge Silverman as a special master to preside at the depositions, to which the attorneys agreed. The appointment was readily accepted by Judge Silverman and, although he was not able to settle the case, the depositions were concluded without further problems. It was out of this initial appointment that Palm Beach County's Circuit Civil Mediation Program would eventually emerge.

Although Judge Silverman continued for a time to be appointed as a "special master," he recalls that from the very beginning he was engaged in mediation, a role in which he was comfortable. He realized there was a connection with his work on the bench, in the sense that Silverman had been a judge who believed in settling cases. He applied the same techniques he had honed on the bench to his work in Palm Beach County—encouraging attorneys and their clients to focus on their common interests and to put realistic offers and counteroffers on the table.

Initially no one, not even Judge Silverman, recognized the case management potential in his activities. During 1985, he was referred no more than 20 cases the entire year. Prior to that, referrals were even more sporadic. The first cases referred to Judge Silverman were primarily complex, long-standing litigation—cases which judges did not want to spend weeks or months trying. It was, more than anything, the nature of the cases he was settling that assured that the judge's mediation work would eventually call attention to itself. Ultimately, it was his role in successfully mediating two multimillion dollar construction defect cases which piqued both public and judicial curiosity. As word spread, Judge Silverman found himself, not only with increasing referrals, but with requests for newspaper interviews and speeches as well.

Growing numbers

By 1986, the number of mediation sessions Judge Silverman conducted per month had grown to between 35 and 40. The increased demands on his time and attention were rapidly transforming what he had initially viewed as a diversion into a full-time job. He often worked past five o'clock and on weekends. Soon, he believed, it would be more than he could handle. At about that time, Judge Silverman met Judge Bernard Snierson at a cocktail party. The two found they had a lot in common. Judge Snierson, a retiree from the New Hampshire bench, had headed south intending, like Judge Silverman, to substitute a relaxed Florida retirement for a hectic judicial calendar. But also like Judge Silverman, he soon found that he was bored and restless. A short time after their initial meeting, he joined Judge Silverman in accepting mediation referrals. A third retired judge, Edward Malmed of the Philadelphia bench, joined their ranks after reading an article about Judge Silverman in the *Miami Herald*. Impressed, he contacted Judge Silverman and soon found himself regularly traveling to the Palm Beach County Courthouse.

Gradually, it became apparent that what had been Judge Silverman's one-man operation was now a de facto court program in need of more formalized structuring. Increased referrals and increased numbers of participating retired judges had made it obvious that it was no longer practical to expect mediators to schedule their own appointments or to operate without any permanently assigned rooms in which to hold their conferences. Court administrators and judges of the Fifteenth Circuit began to explore the usual set of considerations arising whenever any new program is contemplated: how would the mediators be paid? In an already overcrowded courthouse, where would space be found in which to conduct increasing numbers of mediation conferences? Was funding available for support staff and office equipment?

Funding the program

Court budgeting staff was not optimistic that the Board of County Commissioners would vote adequate funding for the program. Finances were tight and mediation was not something that the commissioners had much experience with or any appreciation of. Members of the board were invited to attend mediation sessions, but the general consensus was that even if awareness could be raised significantly, securing funding from the county would still be difficult.

The State of Florida afforded no better prospect for funding. Palm Beach County's proposed Circuit Civil Mediation Program would be the first of its kind in Florida and it was not until 1987 that circuit civil mediation would be recognized in Florida statutes.

As public funding was problematic, the Fifteenth Circuit elected to try a different approach to supporting its pioneer mediation effort. That approach established an essentially self-supporting mediation program which would be court-annexed. Specifically, the retired judges would work as independent contractors and not as employees of the court or county. They would bill parties for their services and remit 20 per cent of their fee to the Board of County Commissioners of Palm Beach County. The board would, in turn, use the remittance to cover the salary of a support person or persons, costs for office equipment, and other overhead including space requirements. Court personnel would supervise program support staff, and court and county personnel would provide other administrative support, *e.g.*, development and implementation of a computer software package to assist in billing and record keeping. After all program expenses were met, the Board of County Commissioners would retain any monies remaining form the mediator's remittance. These funds could be spent as the board chose and were not necessarily earmarked for other mediation or court programs.

This arrangement benefited everyone. Neither the Fifteenth Circuit nor Palm Beach County had to provide funding for mediator salaries. The mediators did not have to worry about administrative details and could spend their time doing what they did best: mediating. Support staff assigned to the program received the fringe benefits associated with county employment, including health and life insurance and retirement benefits. And most significantly, the Fif-

Breakdown of monthly income remitted to Board of County Commissioners, Palm Beach County from 1/1/88 through 12/31/88

January 1988	$4,485.54
February 1988	5,118.76
March 1988	7,751.82
April 1988	5,858.28
May 1988	6,414.62
June 1988	6,484.52
July 1988	6,982.82
August 1988	6,457.22
September 1988	5,986.42
October 1988	6,889.52
November 1988	6,656.76
December 1988	5,146.62
Totals	$74,232.90*

This gives an average of $6,186.08 per month for 1988.

*$65,190.00 was budgeted for the program for fiscal year 1988. Thus the 20 per cent remittance amount resulted in a $9,042.90 surplus for 1988. The surplus is retained by the Board of County Commissioners.

Outcome of mediated cases, by type: April-December 1987

Breakdown by case type:	# Cases	%	Outcome* 1	2	3	Other
Personal injury	268	48%	172	7	71	18
Breach of contract	96	18	62	1	25	8
Equity matters	7	1	5	0	1	1
Divorce (financial)	42	8	32	1	9	0
Malpractice	30	5	19	0	10	1
Product liability	12	2	9	0	3	0
Condo dispute	12	2	6	2	4	0
Construction defect	14	3	9	1	3	1
Other	75	14	43	2	25	3
Totals	556		357	14	151	32

*Outcome code:
1—Completely resolved
2—Partially resolved
3—Impasse reached
Other—Resolution expected pre-trial

teenth Circuit reduced its delay problem.

Fees charged for mediation have changed over time, increasing as the program has proven its utility. Judge Silverman was paid $25 per hour for the first case he mediated, although he says he would have gladly paid $25 for the privilege of being back at work. In the years following, fees rose to $50, then $100, per hour as attorneys and judges began to equate mediation with early settlement of cases and the savings ultimately accruing to parties in legal and witness fees when they were able, with the mediator's assistance and encouragement, to settle their differences. The contract negotiated with the Board of County Commissioners, which formalized the program provided for mediators to remit 20 per cent of a $125 per hour fee to the board. This fee has enabled the program to be self-sustaining. For the two years the contract has been in effect, the remittance has covered the program's budget with a portion remaining to be spent at the board's discretion.

The average circuit civil case referred to mediation takes just short of two hours to mediate and the mediator's fee is split between the parties. Mediators can and do forgo their fees when parties are able to convince them or a circuit judge that payment of the fee would impose undue economic hardship. Billings are handled by program support staff who mail statements to attorneys who, in turn, bill parties. As fees are received, support staff tabulate each judge's earnings and each then remits 20 per cent of those earnings to Palm Beach County's Board of County Commissioners. The $125 per hour fee has, over time, become the standard fee charged by most circuit court mediators working in Florida.

The program today

Although circuit mediators still tackle the complex, long-standing litigation which engendered the program, most referrals are now of more typical cases. For example, in 1988, personal injury cases at 44 per cent made up the bulk of mediation referrals. Contract cases made up an additional 22 per cent of the mediators' caseload that same year. On the other hand, domestic relations cases accounted for only 9 per cent of the referrals in 1988. Family law judges traditionally have referred only very complicated, large dollar domestic relations matters to circuit civil mediation. However, a workload of over 1,100 domestic cases per family law judge has necessitated increased reliance on mediation and a recent administrative order provides for referral to mediation of any domestic case which the attorneys have stipulated will require more than three hours to try. As such, the Circuit Civil Mediation Program will be working hand in hand with the Fifteenth Circuit's Family Mediation Program to expedite resolution of domestic matters.

Judges of the Fifteenth Circuit make referrals to mediation at their discretion. If a judge believes that a matter can be settled or, if not settled, issues beneficially narrowed or clarified, he or she will order the parties and their attorneys to mediation. Many of the circuit's judges are increasingly turning to mediation. As a staff writer for the Fort Lauderdale *Sun-Sentinel* observed in a July 6, 1987, article:

For a sign of a shift in the way civil legal disputes are getting resolved in Palm Beach County, look at Judge

Outcome of mediated cases, by type: January-December 1988

Breakdown by case type:	# Cases	%	1	2	Outcome* 3	4	5	Estimated trial time saved— in days
Personal injury	807	44.0%	440	12	186	139	30	1,234.25
Breach of contract	404	22.0	221	9	101	57	16	494.00
Divorce (financial)	163	9.0	87	16	29	19	12	165.50
Real estate	95	5.2	5.1	2	14	23	5	102.50
Mechanics liens, etc.	53	2.9	37.0	1	8	5	2	62.00
Malpractice	42	2.3	22.0	0	13	7	0	130.00
Construction defect	41	2.3	15.0	3	8	10	5	47.00
Probate	32	1.8	19.0	1	8	2	2	535.00
Equity matters	21	1.2	10.0	1	3	5	2	23.00
Condominium disputes	20	1.1	7.0	1	5	5	2	17.00
Product liability	19	1.0	7.0	0	5	6	1	36.00
Other	123	6.8	5.7	2	37	17	10	131.50
Total	1,820		973.0	48	417	295	87	2,977.75

*Outcome code:
1—Completely resolved
2—Partially resolved
3—Impasse reached
4—Continued for further mediation
5—Other

Mary Lupo's calendar of upcoming jury trials. Scratched under the names of dozens of parties suing each other are the words "Settled by Silverman."

Most circuit civil and all family law judges in Palm Beach County refer at least some of their cases to mediation. Many refer cases routinely. Hoping to avoid litigation entirely, attorneys have themselves, in some instances, submitted matters for mediation before seeking to file them with the court.

The Palm Beach program operates a bit differently from other court mediation programs. Most notably, all of the active mediators are retired judges. Due to the availability of these judges, retired or active attorneys and lay individuals have not been used as mediators at the circuit civil level. Mediators are assigned to cases on a blind rotational basis, except in instances where one or both parties express a preference for a particular mediator. The Palm Beach mediation program also differs from some others in that not only the parties but their attorneys are required to be present at the mediation session, as are insurance company representatives possessing authority to settle in those cases involving insured defendants. If parties or representatives with authority to settle do not attend, judges refuse to conduct mediation. Also, unlike mediators in many other programs, Palm Beach mediators, at the request of the parties, can act also as arbitrators and even as judges in summary jury proceedings.

Prior to Florida's passage of comprehensive mediation and arbitration legislation in 1987, a retired judge could become a mediator in the Fifteenth Circuit if that judge left the bench, wherever he or she served, in good standing and provided that the would-be mediator completed an apprenticeship requirement, observing Judge Silverman mediate for a two-week period. With the enactment of the new legislation, all mediators receiving referrals from circuit, family or county court judges in Florida must be certified. Certification requirements include formal education prerequisites for circuit and family mediators and practice requirements, *i.e.*, the candidate must possess an advanced degree and have practiced for a specified minimum number of years in his or her degree field. In addition, there is now a formal training requirement. For example, circuit court mediators must complete at least 40 hours of formal mediation training and pass a written exam in order to be certified.

There are presently 10 mediators working in the Palm Beach County Circuit Civil Mediation Program. All those currently serving are certified as circuit court mediators. Some are certified as family mediators. About half the mediators who have been associated with the program served on the bench outside Florida. The remainder are judges retired from Florida's Fifteenth Judicial Circuit. Presently, four of the Palm Beach mediators, including Judge Silverman, work an eight-hour day. The six remaining mediators work on a part-time basis, usually two or three days a week. One support person works full-time for the program and a second works part-time.

The program has been extremely successful. In

1988 alone, 973 cases were settled as a result of mediation. It is estimated, based on attorney assessments of how much time would have been involved in trying these cases, that over 2,900 days of trial time were saved, freeing judges to concentrate their energies on their remaining caseload. Although many, if not most, of these cases might have eventually settled prior to trial, the mediation program has by all accounts accelerated that process, substituting early settlements for those which might otherwise have occurred on the morning of trial and only after absorbing many hours of judicial time and energy. Even in those cases where mediation does not produce a settlement, circuit mediators report that the conferences are frequently successful in narrowing or clarifying issues for trial, thus saving the court trial time.

The Palm Beach program has served as a model for other Florida circuits seeking affordable ways of containing or reducing their delay problems. Judge Silverman and his colleagues have traveled across the state mediating cases and speaking to local bar associations and judicial groups. The Palm Beach program served as the prototype for a civil mediation program recently implemented in Florida's Seventeenth Circuit, and Palm Beach mediators routinely travel to Fort Lauderdale to assist that program.

NOTES

This article originally appeared in Volume 73, Number 1, June-July 1989, pages 51-53, 57.

* In 1987, statistics were kept only from April 1 through December 31.

ADR problems and prospects: looking to the future

The alternative dispute resolution movement is at a critical turn in the road. What is needed now is a multipronged effort to expand understanding and promote increased involvement and support among all members of society.

by Stephen B. Goldberg, Eric D. Green, and Frank E.A. Sander

If alternative dispute resolution is an idea whose time has come, why has it not spread more rapidly and widely? Why is it that, although the users of neighborhood justice centers appear satisfied with the process, many of these centers are starving for business? Why is there such an abundance of individuals who want to provide mediation services, yet so few customers? In this article we will explore some of these questions, as well as possible answers. It should be noted at the outset, however, that much of our discussion will be based on speculation, for there is a dearth of reliable data concerning alternative dispute resolution mechanisms. Indeed, the absence of such data is itself a deterrent to the use of alternative processes.

Impediments to ADR use

The reason most frequently given for the failure of disputants to make greater use of mediation and other alterntives to the courts is that they don't know about their existence. Despite increasing publicity given to alternatives, we suspect that if a Gallup poll were taken today asking what an individual should do if he had a dispute with his neighbor which they could not resolve, most citizens would say "go to court" or "see your lawyer," rather than "visit your local neighborhood justice center." The emphasis given to courts and lawyers as the paradigm dispute resolvers in American society is simply too pervasive to be easily disturbed. One need only consider, by way of example, the consistent message conveyed by television—"People's Court," "Miller's Court," and "Perry Mason." We have no programs entitled Perry Mediator, Miller's Neighborhood Justice Center, or People's Ombudsman.

Even if potential disputants are aware of alternatives to the court and live in a community where such mechanisms are available, it is often difficult to locate them because they have not been publicly institutionalized. This segregation of alternatives from the judicial process also has other adverse consequences, such as the common absence of public funding, which sometimes requires disputants to pay for alternative dispute resolution services even as the judicial ones are provided free. More subtle discouragement derives from the distrust that often accompanies processes that are new and unfamiliar and that appear to be unaccompanied by the legal protections that disputants have been taught over the years to value so highly. A related deterrent may be the absence of mechanisms for ensuring high standards in the provision of alternatives.

Psychological factors may also play a part in the gravitational pull of disputants toward the courts. Over 100 years ago de Tocqueville commented on the tendency in the United States of most social problems to devolve eventually into legal problems. Many disputants go to court because they want to challenge their adversaries rather than come to terms with them. In 20th century United States, lawsuits are the socially acceptable form of fighting.

In addition to these general explanations, special considerations may come into play in particular sectors of the disputing universe. For example, large institutional litigants may want a binding precedent to guide future disputes, which they can only get from a court. In bureaucratic organizations, such as the government, there is also the tendency towards following the path of least resistance and minimal risk. This means taking the tried-and-true route of dumping the problem into the court's lap, rather than risking criticism that might come from what some superior views as an unwise settlement.

The role of lawyers

No discussion of the impediments to the use of alternative dispute resolution processes would be complete without considering the role played by lawyers. For all the reasons alluded to above, most disputes that cannot be resolved by the disputants themselves are today presented to lawyers. In most instances, the client will, we suspect, be unaware of the existence of alternative dispute resolution processes. Hence, if such processes are to be utilized, it will typically be as a result of the lawyer's suggestion and encouragement.[1] The fact that alternative dispute resolution processes have not been more widely used suggests that lawyers have not been actively encouraging their use. Why not?

Initially, some of the factors that deter disputants from using alternative processes also deter lawyers from recommending them. While lawyers are more likely than their clients to be aware of the existence of alternatives, a surprising number of lawyers know very little about them, frequently confusing mediation and arbitration.[2] Hence, they are reluctant to suggest their use. The lack of institutionalization also has a deterrent effect. If a lawyer takes a case to court, she knows what she will find—a procedure that is specified by rules and that is familiar in every respect. If she opts for an alternative process, she frequently must decide what rules she wishes to apply and then obtain opposing counsel's agreement to those rules. The path of least resistance is to litigate. Finally, the lawyer is apt to have in common with her client the view that adversary combat in a judicial arena is the normal, socially acceptable, and psychologically satisfying method of resolving disputes. Indeed, most legal education is premised on an adversarial approach to dispute resolution.[3]

There are also psychological factors that discourage an enthusiastic acceptance of alternative processes by lawyers. Like most other professionals, lawyers frequently exert considerable control over their clients, which derives from the lawyer's ability to utilize a complex set of technical rules. This

dominance is jeopardized by the use of dispute resolution methods like negotiation and mediation that place greater emphasis on client control over the outcome. These methods contemplate at times a diminished role for lawyers (e.g., as non-participating advisers in a divorce mediation) and at other times a different conceptualization of their role (e.g., as process facilitators who enable the parties themselves to arrive at the best possible solution). While these new roles may represent an exciting challenge to younger lawyers seeking to integrate their personal values with their professional training, they are regarded as threatening by many older lawyers who have become accustomed to the dominance and control inherent in much traditional legal practice.

Economic considerations may also constitute a significant impediment to the greater use of alternatives. Over the past decade, law firms have built up immense litigation departments. Even though some of the leading litigation practitioners are prominent in the alternatives movement because they see the advantages of accommodative problem-solving in many situations, the very existence of these expanding litigation empires constitutes a self-reinforcing movement towards more and more litigation.

Aside from these institutional forces, there are elements of the typical attorney compensation structure that militate against greater use of alternatives. The lawyer who gets paid on an hourly basis has no short-run economic interest in faster methods of dispute resolution. The plaintiff's lawyer who is paid on a contingent fee basis might, unless he will receive a higher proportion of a jury verdict than of a settlement. Under these circumstances, processes that encourage settlement may not be welcome.

Alternatives may also have an impact on future fees. If mediation, as advertised, deters future disputes so that people do not have to go to a lawyer as often, then lawyers may see the alternatives movement as disadvantageous to their economic interest. On the other hand, lawyers must be concerned about their competitive position vis-a-vis other lawyers; once clients become aware of the benefits of alternatives, they may bring pressure on their attorneys to use these methods or threaten to take their business elsewhere. Inasmuch as attorneys can buttress the case against the use of alternatives by the uncertain results and the absence of legal protections inherent in those processes, it may be only the client with considerable sophistication who will be capable of withstanding the countervailing pressures and insist upon the use of alternatives.

Even those attorneys who support alternative processes in principle, and would encourage their use in specific cases, may encounter difficulties. For example, some lawyers believe that a suggestion to opposing counsel that alternatives to litigation be explored may be taken as a sign of weakness (fear of litigation), which will negatively affect the lawyer's negotiating position. It is also possible that the Code of Professional Responsibility's emphasis on "zealous representation" deters some lawyers from proposing what has been called "a warmer way of disputing."[4] Furthermore, the lawyer who would not only advocate, but engage in, the provision of dispute resolution services must be concerned with the vague prohibitions of the Code against dual representation, which, to some uncertain extent, preclude lawyers from acting in a mediatory role.

There are also barriers to the provision of alternative dispute resolution services by those who are not lawyers. They must first acquire the necessary skills—no easy task at a time when the state of the art is still fairly primitive. Then they must turn these skills into a marketable career, which brings them up against the impediments earlier alluded to—a minimal demand compounded by the absence of institutional structures and public funding. Finally, there is the risk that in providing dispute resolution services they will run afoul of the prohibitions on the unauthorized practice of law. Indeed, there have already been a number of instances in which such prohibitions have been invoked against divorce mediators. To be sure, the extent to which nonlawyers should be free to provide dispute resolution services presents difficult issues. For present purposes, however, the point is that the unauthorized practice rules deter the provision of dispute resolution services by nonlawyers, and thereby to some extent discourage their use.

Needless to say, these barriers to the use of alternatives have crosscutting and interlocking effects. For example, one reason for the shortage of empirical data is the shortage of research funds, but the shortage of persuasive research data in turn makes more difficult the procurement of additional funds to facilitate the enhanced institutionalization of alternative mechanisms.

In subsequent sections of this article, we will explore further some of these barriers and ways of ameliorating them. As regards the overriding goal of the need for enhanced education with respect to alternatives, perhaps the most promising efforts along these lines are presently being made through inclusion of conflict resolution units in the public school curriculum.[5] Only if people learn at an early age about the varied ways of resolving conflict can the prevailing emphasis on adversary dispute settlement be significantly moderated.

Critiques of mediation

The principal thrust of recent criticism of ADR has been aimed primarily at mediation, perhaps because that process blends third-party facilitation with disputant control of outcome, and hence is inherently imprecise and manipulable. In theory, mediation is a voluntary process whereby two or more disputants arrive at a mutually acceptable solution with the help of a neutral third party. In fact, some of these features are often lacking. Because of the not uncommon reluctance of one party to participate in mediation, overt or covert pressure is brought against the reluctant party.

As regards the element of coercion, a distinction should be drawn between coercion "into" and coercion "in" mediation. Although ideally a disputant should be able to make a knowing choice between going to mediation and going to court, a bit of a push towards mediation does not seem too serious, given the general ignorance of that process, as long as the disputants are free to choose any outcome they wish *in* the mediation proceeding.

In a recent piece, Professor Owen Fiss of Yale Law School launched a ringing attack on one of the fundamental premises of the alternatives movement—that settlement as a general rule is a social good.[6] Fiss contends that settlement necessarily involves a compromise of legal entitlements, which is of particular concern when there is a sharp power disparity between the parties.

The case against mediating disputes of the disadvantaged has been articulated with particular fervor by radical critics of the legal system, for they see the alternatives movement as a calculated effort by the establishment to discourage the disadvantaged from asserting their legal rights[7] and hence as simply another form of social control. By way of factual support, these critics point out that the three Neighborhood Justice Centers that were set up by the United States Department of Justice in the late seventies were in fact used predominantly by lower income disputants.[8]

Another argument raised on behalf of the lower income users of alternatives is that they are relegated to "second class" justice while the rich preempt the courts. Like most slogans, the term "second class" justice requires closer analysis. It appears to consist of three distinct ideas.

The first is that the thrust of the mediation process is towards a surrender of legal rights; its goal is settlement, not assertion of principle. This is the thesis that is so forcefully asserted by Fiss, not only from the perspective of the individual disputant but also in terms of the potential harm to society where socially important issues are at stake. To take a common example, if a consumer who has been victimized by a merchant sues in small claims court and then is referred to mediation, the case may be settled by having the vendor make some modest payment, without the consumer ever being apprised of his right to get treble damages under the applicable consumer protection act.

The second concern is that mediation lacks the legal protections associated with the adjudicatory process. Lawyers rarely participate in mediation, there are no evidentiary rules to prevent the introduction of unreliable or even prejudicial evidence, and in criminal-type cases no provision is made for the assertion of constitutional rights, such as the privilege against self-incrimination. In short, there is no guarantee of due process in mediation.

The assumption that underlies both preceding arguments—that many persons "relegated" to alternative processes would prefer to go to court—is dubious at best. When the disputants have an ongoing relationship, or the dispute is polycentric,[9] mediation may be far more responsive to the needs of the disputants than adjudication. Consider, for example, sexual harassment in the work place. While adjudication, if successful, would provide vindication, it might also create such tension that a continuation of the employment relationship might, as a practical matter, be extremely difficult. In such a situation, employees might well prefer mediation to adjudication.

Another assumption of the "second-class" justice argument is that if lower-income disputants were not relegated to alternative processes, they would receive the procedural protections and full-blown trial inherent in the phrase "first-class" justice. In actuality, however, most "minor" disputes are shunted aside or mass-processed by the judicial system in a way that provides very little of the deliberative flavor that is the advertised hallmark of adjudication. Hence, the real choice may often be between mediation and surrogates for true adjudication. In this connection it is crucial to draw a sharp distinction between complex and pathbreaking litigation (such as a desegregation case that receives a disproportionate amount of judicial attention) and run-of-the-mill civil or criminal cases that are far more likely to be thoughtfully considered in the alternative processes.

A third implication of the "second-class" justice argument is that mediation, by focusing on accommodative resolutions of individual disputes, prevents aggregate solutions. For example, using the previous consumer fraud example, if a manufacturer has committed flagrant violations of the consumer protection laws, these wrongs will not be effectively redressed if the perpetrator is allowed to "buy off" individual complainants through settlements that do not address directly the legality of the underlying practice.

Here again the assumption that the asserted deficiency is necessarily avoided in court is open to question. To be sure, a class action may be brought, or an individual case may create a binding precedent, but the vast preponderance of cases in court are settled without addressing any broader recurring issue that may be involved. This is particularly true of the high volume lower-level courts where most of these cases are brought. Hence what may be best is a mechanism (such as a consumer protection bureau in an attorney general's office) that effectively blends redress of individual grievances (perhaps through mediation) with aggregate relief through adjudication for "pattern and practice" violations.

In the final analysis, the question is how best to bring about change by individual or by institutional defendants. Sometimes lawsuits represent the most promising way; at other times, institutional change is brought about best from within, through accommodative processes such as mediation.[10]

A need for empirical research

Notable progress has been made in demonstrating empirically some of the claimed advantages of alternative methods of dispute resolution, such as the greater satisfaction of disputants with mediation.[11] Most of the mediation research, however, has been carried out with disputants who mediated voluntarily. The obvious risk is that those disputants who were willing to mediate were particularly susceptible to a mediatory approach, and that if mediation were compulsory, as may be necessary to bring about its widespread use, its apparent advantages would disappear. For example, settlement rates, compliance, and participant satisfaction might all diminish if mediation were compulsory.

Another risk of compulsory mediation is that disputants who would otherwise resolve their disputes through direct negotiation might take advantage of the easy accessibility of mediation, each hoping to do better in mediation than in negotiation. If that would occur in a substantial proportion of cases, mediation would, as a practical matter, be a substitute for negotiation, and should be compared to it, not adjudication. Hence, research on the effects of compulsory mediation on settlements by negotiation is called for, as is research comparing compulsory mediation with adjudication.

The data on compulsory mediation are slim. McEwen and Maiman found that in the mediation of small claims, neither settlement rates nor compliance varied according to whether mediation was voluntary or compulsory.[12] However, their findings are weakened by the fact that in the small claims courts they studied, the assignment of cases to mediation was not random. Judges in some courts ordered disputants to mediation, while others made mediation voluntary. It is not clear whether those judges who imposed mediation did so in all cases, or only in those cases in which they thought the parties were susceptible to a mediatory approach. If the latter procedure were followed, the data regarding the effectiveness of compulsory mediation would be weakened.[13] A subsequent study, however, in which a six-month period of voluntary mediation of grievances arising under a collective bargaining contract was followed by a six-month period of compulsory mediation, found that settlement rates at mediation were not affected by whether mediation was voluntary or compulsory. The same study found compulsory mediation associated with a decrease in directly negotiated settlements, although the existence of a causal relationship could not be determined.[14]

Considerably more research on the effects of compulsory participation in alternatives to litigation is needed. One opportunity for such research in the mediation context is presented by California's recent change from voluntary to compulsory mediation of child custody disputes. Data comparing mandatory mediation to voluntary mediation or adjudication of child custody disputes on each of the criteria discussed by Pearson would be extremely useful.[15] Obviously, any such study would have to be replicated in other contexts before we could generalize from it.

The spread of compulsory court-annexed arbitration provides ample opportunity for testing the extent to which this process is capable of resolving disputes more satisfactorily than they would be resolved by the traditional route of settlement negotiations followed by trial for those cases that do not settle. It is, of course, important in collecting data on this question that courts which are experimenting with arbitration do so in a truly experimental mode, assigning cases randomly to the arbitration route and the traditional route. Only then will we have a clear comparison of the two approaches. One problem with such research, however, is that it is unclear whether random assignment would constitute constitutionally impermissible disparate treatment.[16]

If the alternatives to adjudication have all the advantages claimed for them, why are they not more widely used? The answers to this question remain a matter of controversy. It is, however, an exceedingly important question. For, until we know why voluntary alternatives are not more used, any response to their underutilization will necessarily be based on speculation, with all the false starts and inefficient expenditure of resources that entails.

Researches have already determined what proportion of disputes result in court filings by tracking disputes from their origin to their final disposition.[17] However, that research does not disclose why those disputants who went to court did not utilize one of the alternatives to litigation. To answer the latter question, one might offer disputants their choice of adjudication or mediation. Those who chose adjudication rather than mediation could be questioned concerning their reasons. Additionally, the characteristics of those who chose mediation could be compared with those who chose adjudication. In conducting research of this type with individuals who accepted and rejected mediation of child custody disputes, Pearson, Thoennes, and Vanderkooi found that the lawyers' attitude toward mediation was the key factor in the choice of processes.[18] Similar research could be conducted in conjunction with the multidoor court-house experiments described by Finkelstein elsewhere in this issue.[19]

Lack of knowledge

It is frequently asserted that a major reason for the failure to use alternatives to adjudication is lack of knowledge. One recent study, however, casts doubt upon this assertion. According to Merry and Silbey, who studied attitudes and behaviors of disputing in three neighborhoods, disputants do not use alternatives to the extent hoped for by their proponents because by the time they are willing to turn to an outsider for help, they do not want what alternatives have to offer.[20] They no longer wish to settle the dispute by discussion and negotiation; rather each wants vindication, protection of his or her rights, an advocate to help in the battle, or a third party who will declare the other party wrong.

Another approach to testing the hypothesis that lack of knowledge is a major barrier to the use of alternatives would be to compare the number of cases submitted to the judicial system and to, for example, the neighborhood justice center, in two closely matched communities, preceding and following an extensive education program, using both the media and the schools in one of those communities. Any significant difference in the proportion of cases submitted to the neighborhood justice center in the "educated" community compared with the control community could (absent other intervening variables) be attributed to the educational campaign; any significant increase in the total volume of cases presented to the neighborhood justice center and the courts combined in the "educated" community compared with the control community might also indicate that an effect of the education campaign was to reduce the frequency of "lumping it" or avoidance as a means of dispute resolution.[21]

Another means to determine the extent to which lack of knowledge regarding alternatives explains their limited use is to provide such knowledge, together with encouragement to try an alternative in appropriate cases, and facilitate access to the alternatives. That is the approach being taken by the multi-door courthouse experiments.

What can research accomplish?

Can we develop a satisfactory taxonomy of dispute resolution processes, matching disputes to appropriate dispute resolution processes? To some extent, the success of the multidoor courthouse will depend on the capacity of its staff to direct disputants to a process that is appropriate for their dispute. However, to the best of our knowledge, there are no empirical data on this question. To generate such data, a laboratory experiment might be conducted in which the same dispute was dealt with in a variety of dispute resolution processes. Measures could then be taken of settlement rate, cost, speed, participant satisfaction with process and outcome, and other relevant variables. If such an experiment were conducted with a number of different types of disputes, varying in such criteria as subject matter, amount at issue, presence or absence of a continuing relationship, presence or absence of a substantial power disparity, etc., one would begin to develop some empirical basis for suggesting that a particular type of dispute might be best handled in a particular process. Laboratory experiments of this nature, in which the same dispute has been subjected to a variety of dispute resolution processes, and participant satisfaction measured in each, have been conducted by Thibaut and Walker, LaTour, et al. and Brett.[22]

Can we develop a sophisticated cost-benefit analysis for the various dispute resolution processes? Doing so presents substantial questions of measurement. Some items can be measured in financial terms, some in psychological terms, some not at all. For example, many of the costs to both the public and the parties of resolving a dispute in one process or another—attorneys' fees, dispute resolvers' salaries—are easily measurable in financial terms. Similarly, some benefits, such as increased compliance and deterrence of future disputes, can be translated into financial terms.

There are, however, some items, such as participant satisfaction, that can be measured only in psychological terms, and others that cannot be measured at all. What, for example, is the cost to the justice system or the parties of a dispute being settled in mediation, but no precedent being set, as it would be in adjudication?[23] Another problem of cost-benefit analysis in this context is the difficulty in determining the appropriate unit of measurement. If mediation does, indeed, lead to greater compliance and deterrence of future disputes, its benefits extend beyond the individual case in which it is used, and treating the case as the appropriate unit of measurement would be misleading. In sum, the most that research may be able to accomplish in this context is to provide a variety of measures on which to compare some of the costs and benefits of the various dispute resolution processes. Still, even those data, limited as they are, are preferable to sheer impressionism as a means for allocating limited funds among these processes.

Is there a danger that in our preoccupation with finding the appropriate dispute resolution *process,* we will lose sight of the need for fair outcomes? While one cannot engage in empirical research bearing directly on this speculative question, it is possible to design research with the aim of minimizing the danger that the need for fair outcomes will be overlooked. For example, in doing the research necessary to develop a taxonomy of dispute resolution processes, one could include among the measures to be examined both objective criteria such as the efficiency of the outcome (the extent to which joint gains have been maximized) and subjective criteria such as the parties' satisfaction with outcome, as distinguished from process. Indeed, considerable research has already been done on participant satisfaction. That research suggests that satisfaction with process is related to satisfaction with outcome—disputants who believe that a dispute resolution process was fair tend also to believe that the outcome was fair.

Is there a danger that the availability of alternatives will shunt low- and middle-income disputants to a form of second-class justice, consisting primarily of semi-coerced compromise settlements, while the so-called first-class justice offered by the courts becomes available only to the rich and powerful? To some extent, this question presents an issue of definition. What is first-class justice? If it is defined as a method of resolving disputes that includes legal representation, formal rules of procedure, and a resolution based upon law, then those alternatives that are mediatory in nature will inevitably be labeled second-class, and the central question essentially answers itself. If, however, first-class justice is defined as that dispute resolution process which most satisfies the participants, research can be conducted by surveying the users of the alternative processes concerning their satisfaction with them, and comparing their responses with those of the users of the courts. Much of that research has been done, and uniformly concludes that participants in the alternative processes are as satisfied or more satisfied with those processes than are partici-

pants in court adjudication.[24]

There are undoubtedly other questions not mentioned here that are important for the future of the dispute resolution movement as a whole or for particular processes. The crucial point is that as such questions are identified they should be scrutinized to determine the extent to which they are susceptible to empirical research. Such research may, to be sure, have a limited effect on the resolution of the underlying legal and policy questions, a phenomenon frequently noted (and bemoaned) by social science researchers.[25] Still, empirical data can be influential in changing policy, particularly to the extent that existing policy is based on factual misconceptions. In a field as comparatively new as dispute resolution, such misconceptions are certain to abound. Hence, the opportunity exists for empirical researchers to make a significant contribution to removing at least some of the impediments to the expanded use of alternative dispute resolution processes.[26]

Creating a coherent scheme

It is implicit in the preceding discussion that dispute resolution mechanisms are dispersed all through the social fabric. Sometimes they are private; sometimes they are public. Sometimes they are mandatory; at other times they are optional. Wherever disputes arise between individuals and organizations, a complex network of possible grievance mechanisms appears to be available for the venting of these grievances.[27]

The question naturally arises what, if any, relationship there should be between the different types of mechanisms. This question assumes importance not only for the disputant who might benefit from some guidance concerning where to take any particular dispute but also from the point of view of society seeking to provide a coherent response to these requests.

One can certainly envision a system in which there is some kind of hierarchy and structure within the formal public dispute resolution system, but where that system is complemented in some vague way by a vast and ill-understood network of indigenous dispute mechanisms. Indeed, that, in essence, is our present system. Disputants may first try to utilize the vast array of informal mechanisms that are provided in the particular universe where the dispute arises, and then, as a last resort, take the dispute to the public forum, the court.[28] At least that is the paradigm. In fact, of course, informal private mechanisms often are not available, or if they are, they are not resorted to, and the typically American habit of taking the case immediately to court often becomes the prevailing practice. The net effect is that many disputes presented to court are not appropriate for court adjudication and could be better handled by some other mechanism.[29]

This situation led to a suggestion by one of the authors in a paper delivered at the Pound Conference in 1976[30] that, in lieu of the courthouse as we now know it, we might envision in years ahead a more comprehensive and diverse mechanism known as a Dispute Resolution Center, which would seek to provide a variety of dispute resolution processes, according to the needs of the particular dispute. Someone subsequently dubbed this concept "the multidoor courthouse."

The multidoor courthouse

What would such an institution look like? A provisional first-step type of multidoor courthouse could consist essentially of a screening and referral clerk who would seek to diagnose incoming cases and refer them to the most suitable process. Depending on the available mechanisms in the particular community, referrals might be made to mediation, arbitration, court adjudication, fact finding, malpractice screening, a media action line, or an ombudsman.[31]

One of the fringe benefits of such an institution is that it would provide an opportunity to learn more about what process is most appropriate for what kinds of disputes; it would also give helpful feedback concerning what "doors" were missing or not working effectively. That information could then be utilized to refine the model.

The potential benefits of such an approach are enhanced responsiveness and effectiveness, possible time and cost savings, and the legitimization of various alternative dispute resolution processes. What should result is less frustration among the populace in dealing with the vagaries of the legal system. An additional benefit would come from a better understanding of the peculiar advantages and disadvantages of particular processes for specific types of disputes.

There are also potential pitfalls. Not only will the success of a multidoor courthouse largely depend on the skill of the intake official, there is also a real danger—as with all administrative innovations— that it will become the genesis of a new bureaucracy

that will result in Kafkaesque shunting of individuals from one "door" to another without any genuine effort to address the problems presented. In addition, there are some difficult questions that must be addressed such as whether the multidoor courthouse should be a centralized institution under one roof, or more akin to a wheel, with a core operation at the center, supplemented by satellite intake and referral offices. Another critical question—whether the referral should be mandatory or voluntary—is discussed below.

Institutionalization

It should be recognized that the multidoor courthouse is but one form of publicly provided alternative dispute resolution. The issues surrounding the public institutionalization of alternatives, or their private provision through public funding, are vital issues that warrant further discussion.

The case for public institutionalization of alternatives rests on a number of propositions. Since courts are publicly provided, why should an alternative process that might be more effective in particular cases not be publicly provided? Unless it is, society creates a financial disincentive to the use of the more effective process. Moreover, for better or worse, the courthouse is where most American citizens ultimately go if they cannot otherwise resolve their disputes. Hence, from the point of view of public education and exposure, as well as enhanced credibility, governmental provision of alternatives in the courthouse itself may be essential.

The question of mandatory use of alternatives raises different issues depending in large part on the effect to be given to the mandated process. As indicated earlier, coercion *into* mediation does not seem objectionable, as long as there is no coercion *in* mediation to accept a particular outcome, and as long as unsuccessful mediation does not serve as a barrier to adjudication. Similarly, we perceive no persuasive objection to mandating nonbinding arbitration as a precondition to litigation for small or middle-size money claims. If, however, participation in mandatory mediation or arbitration were to bar access to the courts, serious constitutional questions would be presented. Inasmuch, however, as no program for the mandatory use of alternatives has this effect, the more realistic question concerns the extent to which the outcome of a mandatory alternative should be allowed to affect the adjudication process (e.g., by financial preconditions on resort to court or use in court of the noncourt result).

Public institutionalization of alternatives involves their public funding; that is a powerful additional argument put forward by the proponents of institutionalization, who are all too mindful of the fact that private foundations are constantly searching for novel experiments, and are usually not interested in facilitating the continuation of successful pilot programs.[32]

But public funding does not necessarily imply public provision of dispute resolution services. Governments might make grants to private organizations; this is the path taken by New York State, which supports more than 30 privately operated community dispute resolution programs in the state. Texas, meanwhile, has developed a novel path for raising public funds for alternative dispute resolution; it has authorized counties to add a surcharge to the civil filing fee, with the accumulated funds to be used to fund alternative programs. The possibility of federal funding for dispute resolution programs was at least temporarily aborted when the Dispute Resolution Act of 1980 was not funded.

Institutionalization, whether public or private, carries with it potent dangers. Any attempt to make an experiment permanent and larger in scale is likely to result in increasing bureaucratization.[33] As the proportion of volunteers declines, the exuberance and excitement that initially pervaded the project may give way to routinization and burnout. Particularly where public funds are involved, bureaucratic job requirements are likely to be imposed, and political influences may come into play. Whether an innovative program can withstand "success" by effectively making the transition to institutionalization may well be the ultimate test of the program.

A final question concerns the competing claims of alternatives and the courts for limited public funds. Ideally, the funds should go to that system which is more cost effective or qualitatively superior. But, as was noted earlier, we are only beginning to accumulate adequate sophisticated data to help make that judgment. Pending obtaining that data, we need to hedge our bets by encouraging experimentation with alternatives, coupled with careful research to determine their effectiveness.

Professionalization

As the practice of dispute resolution outside the courts expands, the question arises how to ensure high standards of practice and ethical behavior. A related question is how prospective users can find high-quality dispute resolution services suited to their needs.

These questions urgently require answers. In recent years, the number of persons and organizations offering mediation and other dispute resolution services has increased significantly. In addition to a dozen or more national and regional organizations that offer a broad range of dispute resolution services,[34] there are over 180 local mediation programs.[35] Further, both lawyers and other professionals are more often offering mediation as one of their services.

Ensuring high standards is also important at this time because the alternatives movement is in the early stages of professional development. According to Wilensky's[36] typology of the steps through which "occupations" pass on the way to becoming "professions," the alternatives movement is in the stage of professionalization in which people work at the occupation full-time, practitioners press for the establishment of training schools, enthusiastic leaders emerge who are the protagonists of some new technique, and activists engage in much soul searching on "whether the occupation is a profession, what the professional tasks are, how to raise the quality of recruits, and so on." As this occurs, there is "a self-conscious effort to define and redefine the core tasks of the occupation,"[37] and a struggle often ensues over whether the occupation will become fully professionalized with specialized degree programs and exclusionary licensing.

There are vigorous advocates of professionalization of mediation. Robert Coulson, president of the American Arbitration Association, has recently issued a call for "a full-fledged profession of Certified Public Mediator."[38] He visualizes a system in which local courts would regulate mediators as they now regulate lawyers, and litigation could not be undertaken without the assurance by a CPM that mediation had been fully utilized in an effort to avoid litigation. Although most CPMs would be lawyers certified by the court, there would be a role for nonlawyers in specialized substantive areas.[39]

Others oppose efforts to professionalize the alternatives movement. They contend that professionalization is inconsistent with the goal of community building through lay dispute resolution. They are also concerned that replacing volunteer mediators with paid professionals will increase costs and restrict the availability of alternatives.[40]

While at present there is no legal regulation of the private practice of dispute resolution, there is an increasing tendency by public agencies to set minimum education and experience requirements for mediators. The California, Connecticut, Nevada, and Oregon courts, for example, require that family mediators employed by them have a master's degree in counseling, social work, or a related field, as well as substantial experience. Other courts require that mediators working in court-established mediation programs be members of the bar or establish their expertise in the subject of the dispute.[41]

The pros and cons of such standards and of greater regulation of private mediation are discussed by Folberg and Taylor.[42] As they point out, some commentators argue that minimum education and experience requirements and licensure of practitioners are necessary to protect an unknowing public from incompetents and charlatans. These commentators point out that the quality of services cannot easily be judged by the results obtained, and that most clients will have little or no experience against which to evaluate the performance of a mediator or other dispute resolution practitioner. Further, the generally private, informal, and interdisciplinary nature of dispute resolution practice increases the danger that "bad" or unfair practices will occur and go undetected.

Codes and standards

A logical conclusion of this reasoning is not only to set minimum educational and experience requirements, but also to establish standards of practice that will enable clients to judge the quality of the services they receive. Such standards can serve as a set of expectations and minimally acceptable common practices for the service offered, thereby protecting both the client and the provider by defining what is "reasonable care."[43] Others, however, argue that alternative dispute resolution is still such a new field that it is difficult if not impossible to set standards of practice with any degree of confidence. In lieu of standards of practice, they would do no more than articulate basic ethical precepts, derived from fundamental notions of fairness, decency, and morality.

We doubt whether this distinction between standards of practice and ethical limitations—between "do's" and "don'ts" in Folberg and Taylor's ter-

minology[44]—is easy to apply in practice or serves much purpose. Codes of ethics for arbitrators have been promulgated by the American Arbitration Association and other arbitration associations.[45] Standards of practice and codes of ethics have also been promulgated by interested and responsible groups in the fields of family and labor mediation. Others will undoubtedly follow. The real question is what use is to be made of such standards and codes. If they are used to educate novice practitioners and inform the public of what is generally considered good practice, and to serve as guidelines for agencies and courts when judging whether a practitioner has used reasonable care, then careful and flexible use of such standards will be beneficial. If, however, they are applied rigidly or for the purpose of protecting the turf of a particular group, then such standards are likely to retard desirable experimentation and growth.

It is therefore important to consider how standards might be enforced. There are four traditional options:

- regulation and licensing by government;
- self-regulation and licensing by a trade or professional organization with expulsion the ultimate sanction;
- liability principles, i.e., suits for malpractice or negligence;
- public disclosure and the operation of the marketplace, coupled, perhaps, with certification of expertise or education.

These options are not mutually exclusive. In most professions (e.g., law, medicine) standards of practice and ethical behavior are enforced in all of these ways. But these professions tend to be well-established, cohesive, and highly developed, as opposed to the emerging dispute resolution profession.

Moreover, even in the older, established professions, critics contend that professionalization, when coupled with standards and licensure, serve more to protect the turf of the powerful than the interests of the public. The tendency of professionals to create a monopoly by employing licensing standards in an economically self-interested manner is well documented.[46] Indeed, the "higher" stages of professionalization are characterized by this development and by the conflicts within the developing profession and with outsiders that this inevitably generates. According to Wilensky[47] and Pipkin and Rifkin,[48] a pecking order emerges that stratifies practitioners and creates conflict and internecine struggles between new and old cohorts of practitioners, and between practitioners of the new occupation and other occupations who claim the same territory. These final stages of professional development typically involve the formation of associations which seek the support of law to impose licensure restrictions on practitioners and thus protect the territory from outsiders and exclude the unqualified and unscrupulous. At some point in this process, the profession codifies its rules of ethics as a basis for self-regulation.

If the alternatives movement develops in the direction of licensure, the impetus is likely to come from public agencies that employ mediators and which must decide, in making employment decisions, who is qualified to be a mediator. California and other states with publicly supported mediation programs chose to specify formal training and degrees. Rather than specify the kind of degree a person had to have to be a mediator—an approach that is bound to engage the agency in a highly charged and broad-based turf battle between lawyers and those in the healing professions—Michigan chose instead to specify the *skills* that a mediator had to possess.

This approach may only serve to camouflage the conflict by specifying skills that go with a certain kind of education. Moreover, the likely result of specifying skills is the establishment of an industry offering to provide eager practitioners with such skills. There is still the problem of ensuring that practitioners actually possess the skills that their degrees advertise for them. Thus, either the teachers that train practitioners in these skills (or their schools) may have to be licensed (the same old problem), or practitioners will have to be tested. This raises the difficult question of whether it is possible at this time to do skills testing of dispute resolution practitioners.

We believe that it is possible to devise and administer a skills test that could effectively screen for basic mediator competency and ethics. Any such test would have to be carefully pretested and administered with flexibility, however, so as not to exclude practitioners on the basis of legitimate differences of theory or style.

Certification and training

A compromise between full-scale professionalization with licensure and no professionalization at all would be the establishment of certification and training programs for dispute resolution practitioners. Certification would indicate that the certified individual met the criteria established by the certifying organization, and so provide potentially useful information to users, but would not bar practice by noncertified persons. Although the same problems of defining good practice and skills testing exist with certification as with licensure, the absence of any occupational exclusionary power minimizes the problem. Many flowers can bloom and the public may learn to identify the flowers and choose among them. This appears to be the approach favored by the Ethics Committee of the Society of Professionals in Dispute Resolution, although the committee took no formal position on licensure, certification, or training.[49]

A form of certification program for arbitrators, pursuant to which lists of arbitrators certified as meeting minimum criteria are made available on request, is currently administered by the American Arbitration Association and the Federal Mediation and Conciliation Service. Similarly, the Center for Public Resources and the American Arbitration Association provide lists of prominent mediators and private judges. But certification or listing by these organizations is based essentially on recommendations or number of cases handled. There is no attempt at testing, and no effort to train those certified or to monitor their performance. Only a serious violation of ethical rules will cause a listed arbitrator to be removed from the AAA or FMCS lists.

A different approach to certification is offered by educational programs that offer training in dispute resolution skills, and certification based on that training. Some of these programs are university-based, others are free-standing. Some last as long as a year, others no longer than a weekend. Many of these programs do not attempt to evaluate the competency of participants, and others certify everyone who completes the program. Hence, there is apt to be little correlation between possessing a certificate from some of these programs and possessing the certified skills.

Despite those shortcomings, certification, together with the operation of market forces and legal liability for malpractice, appears to be a better approach than licensure for the dispute resolution field at the present time. Notwithstanding problems at the edges in defining standards of good practice and ethical limitations, and in ensuring quality training and monitoring of certified practitioners, certification by responsible organizations and well-established and operated training programs may be of some help to the inexperienced consumer. Licensure, on the other hand, adds little to certification in the way of consumer protection, and creates the very real danger that in enforcing licensing rules, professional self-interest will predominate over consumer protection. Whichever approach is taken, given the conceptual ferment in this field, it is important that standards and norms not be viewed as immutable precepts, but as subject to experience, debate, and modification.

Conclusion

The alternative dispute resolution movement is at a critical turn in the road. After 10 years or so of scholarly inquiry and practical experimentation, our knowledge of the field has been substantially enhanced and there is a far greater awareness, both among the general public and in the legal community, of the promise of alternative dispute settlement.

What we need now is a multipronged effort to expand our limited present understanding of the field. This will require continued experimentation and research, as well as further attempts to conceptualize the field. It will necessitate enhanced public education about the benefits to be derived from alternative modes of dispute settlement. Ways must be found to develop career paths and employment opportunties for talented individuals who wish to devote their lives to providing alternative dispute resolution services. This will probably require, at least in the short run, some infusion of public financing. Above all, if the movement is to hold any significant promise of gaining a permanent foothold on the American scene, it will require the broadened involvement and support not only of the legal education establishments but also of the society at large.

NOTES

This article originally appeared in Volume 69, Number 5, February-March 1986, pages 291-299. An initial version was presented by Professor Sander as a paper at a conference at Harvard Law School in October 1982. Portions of the revised paper are adapted from Goldberg, Green and Sander, DISPUTE RESOLUTION (Little, Brown and Co., 1985).

1. Pearson, Thoennes and Vanderkooi, *The Decision to Mediate: Profiles of Individuals Who Accept and Reject the Opportunity to Mediate Contested Child Custody and Visitation Issues*, 6 J. DIVOERCE 17 (1982).

2. *See* Cooley, *Arbitration vs. mediation: explaining the differences*, 69 JUDICATURE 263 (1986).

3. Riskin, *Mediation and Lawyers*, 43 OHIO ST. L.J. 29 (1982).

4. Smith, *A Warmer Way of Disputing: Mediation and Conciliation*, 26 AM. J. COMP. L. (Supp.) 205 (1978).

5. Davis, *Justice Without Judges*, UPDATE ON LAW-RELATED EDUCATION (Chicago: American Bar Association Special Committee on Youth Education For Citizenship, 1984).

6. Fiss, *Against Settlement*, 93 YALE L.J. 1987 (1984).

7. Abel, *The Contradictions of Informal Justice*, in Abel, ed., THE POLITICS OF INFORMAL JUSTICE: THE AMERICAN EXPERIENCE 1 (New York: Academic Press, 1982); Auerbach, JUSTICE WITHOUT LAW? (New York: Oxford, 1983).

8. Cook, Roehl and Shepard, NEIGHBORHOOD JUSTICE CENTER FIELD TEST: FINAL EVALUATION REPORT (Washington, DC: U.S. Government Printing Office, 1980).

9. Fuller, *The Forms and Limits of Adjudication*, 92 HARV. L. REV. 353 (1979).

10. Singer, *Nonjudicial Dispute Resolution Mechanisms: The Effects on Justice for the Poor*, 13 CLEARINGHOUSE REV. 569 (1979); Rowe, *Predicting the Effects of Attorney Fee Shifting*, 47 LAW AND CONTEMP. PROBS. 139 (1984).

11. Pearson, *An Evaluation of Alternatives to Court Adjudication*, 7 JUST. SYS. J. 420 (1982).

12. McEwen and Maiman, *Small Claims Mediation in Maine: An Empirical Assessment*, 33 ME. L. REV. 237 (1981).

13. But see McEwen and Maiman, *Mediation in Small Claims Court: Achieving Compliance Through Consent*, 18 LAW & SOC'Y REV. 11, 22-28 (1984).

14. Brett and Goldberg, *Grievance Mediation in the Coal Industry*, 37 INDUS. AND LAB. REL. REV. 49, 56, 59-60 (1983).

15. Pearson, *supra* n. 11.

16. Federal Judicial Center, EXPERIMENTATION IN THE LAW: REPORT OF THE FEDERAL JUDICIAL CENTER ADVISORY COMMITTEE ON EXPERIMENTATION IN THE LAW (Washington, DC: U.S. Government Printing Office, 1981).

17. Miller and Sarat, *Grievances, Claims and Disputes: Assessing the Adversary Culture*, 15 LAW AND SOC'Y REV. 525 (1981).

18. Pearson, Thoennes and Vanderkooi, *supra* n. 1.

19. Finkelstein, *The D.C. multi-door courthouse*, 69 JUDICATURE 305 (1986).

20. Merry and Silbey, *What Do Plaintiffs Want? Reexamining the Concept of Dispute*, 9 JUST. SYS. J. 151 (1984).

21. Felsteiner, Abel and Sarat, *The Emergence and Transformation of Disputes: Naming, Blaming, Claiming*, 15 LAW AND SOC'Y REV. 631 (1981).

22. Thibaut and Walker, PROCEDURAL JUSTICE: A PSYCHOLOGICAL ANALYSIS (Hillsdale, NJ: Lawrence Erlbaum, 1975); LaTour, Houlden, Walker, and Thibaut, *Procedure: Transnational Perspectives and Preferences*, 86 YALE L.J. 258 (1976); Brett, *Procedural Justice* in Symposium, JUSTICE: BEYOND EQUITY THEORY (Convention, Academy of Management, 1983).

23. Fiss, *supra* n. 6.

24. Pearson, *supra* n. 11.

25. Weiss, USING SOCIAL SCIENCE RESEARCH IN PUBLIC POLICY MAKING (Lexington, MA: Lexington Books, 1977); Lindblom and Cohen, USABLE KNOWLEDGE (New Haven, CT: Yale University Press, 1979).

26. The need for additional empirical data is equaled by the need for careful analysis of both existing and newly-collected data. Galanter, *Reading the Landscape of Disputes: What We Know and Don't Know (and Think We Know) About Our Allegedly Contentious and Litigious Society*, 31 U.C.L.A. L. REV. 4 (1983).

27. Galanter, *Justice in Many Rooms*, 19 J. OF LEG. PLURALISM 1 (1981).

28. "At present, it is almost accidental if community members find their way to an appropriate forum other than the regular courts. Several other modes of dispute resolution already are available in many communities. Still, since they are operated by a hodge-podge of local government agencies, neighborhood organizations, and trade associations, citizens

must be very knowledgeable about community resources to locate the right forum for their particular dispute." Johnson, *Toward a Responsive Justice System* in STATE COURTS: A BLUEPRINT FOR THE FUTURE 122 (Williamsburg, VA: National Center for State Courts, 1978).

29. Sander, *Varieties of Dispute Resolution*, 70 F.R.D. 111 (1976).

30. *Id.*

31. For a description of the way cases are handled in a multidoor courthouse, see Finkelstein, *supra* n. 19.

32. The National Institute for Dispute Resolution appears to be well aware of the problems of institutionalizing successful programs. Lacking the funds to achieve that goal itself, it has attempted to use its limited resources to leverage public-sector and other private-sector funds.

33. Edelman, *Institutionalizing Dispute Resolution Alternatives*, 9 JUST SYS. J. 134 (1984).

34. Marks, Johnson and Szanton, DISPUTE RESOLUTION IN AMERICA: PROCESSES IN EVOLUTION 69-74 (Washington, DC: National Institute for Dispute Resolution, 1984).

35. American Bar Association, DISPUTE RESOLUTION PROGRAM DIRECTORY (Washington, DC: American Bar Association, 1983).

36. Wilensky, *The Professionalization of Everyone?*, 70 AM. J. SOC. 137 (1964).

37. Pipkin and Rifkin, *The Social Organization in Alternative Dispute Resolution: Implications for Professionalization of Mediation*, 9 JUST SYS. J. 204, 205-206 (1984).

38. Coulson, PROFESSIONAL MEDIATION OF CIVIL DISPUTES (New York: American Arbitration Association, 1984).

39. *Id.* at 24-25, 32-33.

40. Pipkin and Rifkin, *supra* n. 37, at 207.

41. The issue also arises in connection with confidentiality statutes that seek to limit the individuals who are entitled to the statutory protections. See e.g., Mass. Ann. Laws c. 233, §23c (1985).

42. Folberg and Taylor, MEDIATION: A COMPREHENSIVE GUIDE TO RESOLVING CONFLICTS WITHOUT LITIGATION 244 (San Francisco, Jossey-Bass, 1984).

43. *Id.* at 250.

44. *Id.*

45. Hay, Carnevale, and Sinicropi, *Professionalization: Selected Ethical Issues in Dispute Resolution*, 9 JUST SYS. J. 228, 236 (1984).

46. Gellhorn, *Abuse of Occupational Licensing*, 44 U. CHI. L. REV. 6, 39 (1976).

47. Wilensky, *supra* n. 36.

48. Pipkin and Rifkin, *supra* n. 37.

49. Hay, Carnevale, and Sinicropi, *supra* n. 45, at 230, 236-240.

Judicial Policy Making in the United States

INTRODUCTION

Throughout this anthology we have presented selections that offer the reader a slice of the American judicial process through pieces examining a single topic or facet of our legal system. This final section of readings includes two selections that take a broader perspective and consider the place of the judiciary in the larger fabric of American democracy.

"The federal courts since 1787: stability and change in 200 years" is an edited transcript of a panel discussion among judges, academicians, and attorneys that examines the relationship of the federal courts, particularly the Supreme Court, with the other components of our governmental system in the light of two centuries of experience. Among the topics considered are judicial review, the appropriate scope of judicial authority, judicial activism, and judicial independence. The panel discussion is a lively and provocative one and brings together many of the concerns raised throughout this volume.

We close with Stephen Wasby's thoughtful exposition in "Arrogation of power or accountability: judicial imperialism revisited." At bottom, Wasby offers a response to the criticism that the judiciary has become an "imperial" branch of American government that too often improperly intervenes in American life and policy formulation. In Wasby's view, judges exercise powers that have been granted to them legitimately, and they are publicly and governmentally accountable in many ways. Further, Wasby asserts, judges have the capacity to deal with policy matters and, indeed, perform comparatively well when held to the standards of other policy makers in our system. Clearly, Wasby's argument is a controversial and challenging one that leaves us a great deal to contemplate as we assess judicial policy making in the United States.

The federal courts since 1787: stability and change in 200 years

At the annual meeting of the American Judicature Society on August 8, 1987, in San Francisco, a panel examined the relationship of the federal courts, and especially the Supreme Court, to the other branches of government in light of 200 years of experience. Here is an edited transcript of their remarks. Although space did not permit publication of the full transcript, every effort has been made to avoid distorting the participants' views.

Justice Christine Durham: I'd like to share with you a little passage that I found recently in an old book that belonged to my father-in-law, who was a political scientist and a university president. In one of the old treatises I found this passage—it was written in 1912. "It is then the consciousness of the American people that law must rest upon justice and reason. But the Constitution is a more ultimate formulation of the fundamental principles of justice and reason . . . . And the judiciary is a better interpreter of those fundamental principles than the legislature. It is this consciousness which has given such authority to the interpretation of the Constitution by the Supreme Court. I would not hesitate to call the government system of the United States the aristocracy of the robe, and I do not hesitate to pronounce this the truest aristocracy for the purposes of government which the world has produced." I suspect that we're here today to discuss the aristocracy of the robe, and the truth thereof.

Professor A.E. Dick Howard: What I want to do this morning is to think about certain features of the American judicial landscape. I want to take the long view and speak primarily of those features of the landscape which appear as you stand back and look over 200 years of American judicial history, especially as fashioned through the eyes and by the hands of the U.S. Supreme Court.

One must begin where law professors always begin, with *Marbury v. Madison* and the principle of judicial review. Without the Supreme Court's power to strike down legislative acts they think unconstitutional, a great deal of the other landscape features would not really make much difference. The striking thing about judicial review is that the Constitution nowhere mentions that power of the courts. Nowhere, in my judgment, is it possible to read the debates in Philadelphia or any diaries, letters, or other documents that came out of that meeting, and make the persuasive case that the founders clearly intended for the Court to have that power. I suppose the best evidence of their intention is found in Article VI's language—the supremacy clause—which says that those laws passed in pursuance of the Constitution shall be the supreme law of the land.

I think it is fair to say that much of the argument in support of *Marbury v. Madison* flows form the long path of Anglo-American constitutional history reaching back certainly to the 17th century to Dr. Bonham's case (1606), back to colonial experiences. It's probably fair to say that the ultimate rationalization for *Marbury* flows from the experience of the founding period—it was really the enactment of the Judiciary Act of 1789, the addition to the Constitution of the Bill of Rights, events of that kind, which began to make much plainer

---

The participants on the panel

Moderator: Honorable Christine M. Durham, associate justice, Utah Supreme Court. *Presenters:* A.E. Dick Howard, professor of law, University of Virginia School of Law; Lawrence Baum, professor of political science, Ohio State University. *Responders:* Honorable Stephen Reinhardt, a judge of the U.S. Court of Appeals for the Ninth Circuit; James J. Brosnahan, Esq., Morrison & Foerster, San Francisco.

the need that the courts had for the power which John Marshall said they should have in *Marbury*.

In my foreign travels, I have found that separation of powers, federalism, and a lot of other things are interesting to foreign audiences. But one feature that I think strikes them as the most important single contribution to American constitutionalism is the power of judicial review.

The second landmark that I observed as I sauntered across this constitutional landscape is the expansive interpretation by the court of national power—it fulfills the expectation of some framers that a national court system would inevitably have a tendency to favor national power. It's a historical trend that begins very early, in cases such as *McCulloch v. Maryland* where John Marshall gives a very generous reading to the "necessary and proper" clause, in effect, reading "necessary" as saying something like "convenient or appropriate."

Soon thereafter, in *Cohens v. Virginia*, Marshall established the Supreme Court's constitutional authority to review state supreme court judgments. That opinion has been called Marshall's great nationalist address. One of his critics was the chief justice of Virginia's supreme court, Spencer Roane. Roane called *Cohens* "a most monstrous and unexampled decision, which may be accounted for only from that love of power which history informs us corrupts all who possess it and from which even the upright and ermined judges are not exempt."

Examples of this expansive interpretation of national power are many—I'll simply remind you of the commerce powers as one example. We, of course, think about the most contemporary commerce clause cases, but you could go back to *Gibbons v. Ogden* in 1824 and read Marshall's description of the commerce power and I don't find modern dictum which describes that power any more broadly than Marshall did in *Gibbons v. Ogden*. The Court, to be sure, later tried to limit the commerce power, for example, by drawing distinctions between "production of goods" and "interstate traffic in goods," but since 1937, the Court has basically gotten out of the business of putting any substantial limitation at all on the commerce power. Indeed, the Court's current posture is that even when the states as states complain of Article I power being used by Congress, that is in effect, though perhaps not technically stipulated, a political question. A few years ago, in the *Garcia* case,

Justice Blackmun, writing for the majority, basically said to the states, "If you have a complaint about Congress' commerce power usage, then go to Congress—that's the forum to address, not the courts."

There is also, finally, a thread that runs through some of the modern Supreme Court cases, and that is an insensitivity to, or more fundamentally, a mistrust of states and their institutions. This phenomenon, I think, is most obvious in the Warren Court era. A great many of the Court's decisions at that time showed an obvious distrust of state courts. It's hard otherwise to explain the imposition upon the states of rules such as *Miranda* and the exclusionary rule. This is still a battleground; we have Brennan on the one hand and Rehnquist on the other currently battling over certain unstated premises about the extent to which state courts can in fact be trusted to enforce federal rights.

The "living" Constitution

Sauntering a bit further, the third landmark is the one that has come to be called the "living" Constitution. Because it does seem to be that in the battle between those who adhere to a very strict construction of the Constitution and those who would show a willingness to adapt and reinterpret constitutional language, at least for the moment, the "living" Constitution theory is the one very much paralleled. Once again, Marshall sets the stage, in the famous line, "We must never forget it is a (here he italicizes the word) *constitution* we are expounding." Yes, it is indeed a constitution. But in Marshall's language, a constitution intended to endure for ages to come and consequently to be adapted to the various crises of human affairs. Marshall obviously has contrasted the Constitution with ordinary legal documents such as contracts and wills.

There are many examples of this phenomenon. I suppose one of the best would be the Court's uses of the Fourteenth Amendment equal protection laws. A good example would be *Brown v. Board of Education* (1954). As you may recall, the Court ordered that case to be reargued in the 1953 term, having first heard the case in the 1952 term. And in the reargument the counsel were asked to investigate, as they did exhaustively, circumstances surrounding the adoption of the Fourteenth Amendment; for example, the fact that the same Congress that approved the Fourteenth Amendment also appropriated funds for segregated schools in the

District of Columbia. But in *Brown*, in the opinion written by Earl Warren, the Court found all this history and investigation, as Warren put it, inconclusive. More to the point, Warren found that education in 1954 was simply not the same as it had been in 1868. In approaching this problem, we cannot turn the clock back to 1868, when the amendment was adopted, or even 1896, when *Plessy v. Ferguson* was decided. We must consider public education in the light of its full development and its present place in American life. This is what I call the adaptation of the Fourteenth Amendment to the circumstances.

A fourth landmark, and this is really a corollary of what I call the "living" Constitution, is the court's ability to discover substantive constitutional rights, even in cases where there is no direct textual support for those rights. The most conspicuous historical example is the use of substantive due process in *Lochner v. New York* (1905), a famous case where Justice Peckham used the due process clause to strike down a New York statute limiting the hours that bakers could work at their trade. Peckham said that statutes "limiting the hours in which grown intelligent men may labor to earn their living are a mere meddlesome interference with the rights of the individual." Substantive use of the due process clause had fallen into ill repute since 1937 since the so-called constitutional revolution. But just as soon as people thought it was dead, it reemerged in a somewhat different context, beginning this time in 1965 with *Griswold v. Connecticut*. This is not the right of contract, but the right of privacy explicitly mentioned in the Constitution.

I'm sure most of you remember reading *Griswold*. And you remember Justice Douglas' painful effort not to admit that he was using substantive due process. He was obviously embarrassed by it. Just eight years later, in *Roe v. Wade*, Justice Blackmun, in talking about the right to privacy, said it comes from the Fourteenth Amendment's due process clause. All of this is familiar debating territory and I'm sure we'll be hearing more about this debate over unenumerated rights when the Senate Judiciary Committee begins its work with Judge Bork.

This dispute over the so-called "living" Constitution reflects, I would think, a tension between two traditions, both of which are very much a part of the American constitutional fabric. It is, on the one hand, looking to the Constitution's text as the ultimate point of reference. On the other hand,

there is the need to adapt the Constitution to changing circumstances. This inevitably creates tension.

The equity power

Another landmark. This would be one that the layman would probably not appreciate as much as the lawyer, and that is the continued expansive use of federal courts' equity powers. The corollary of increasing rights as we all know them is more equity powers as well. This has come into its own in a year in which the class action has become the paradigm lawsuit.

There are those on the court, and I think Rehnquist would be foremost among them, who are battling valiantly to limit what they see as excessive use by federal and district courts of their equity powers. It may not have been a losing battle, but I would say that, by and large, the Supreme Court has been very permissive toward lower courts in their use of their power.

I think one of the features of this increasing use of institutional litigation as an approach to the courts (and the court's response, by the way, is to use more equity powers), has been to a trend away from what might in the framers' eyes have been the negative use of rights—what Hugo Black used to call the "thou shalt nots," which the Bill of Rights says government can't do. But the U.S. Constitution, unlike most foreign constitutions, simply doesn't talk about affirmative rights. You read a Third World country's constitution and you're likely to find rights, including the negative rights such as speech and religion, but you'll also find affirmative rights such as the right to a job. We don't have that in our Constitution's text, but in the work of the courts in these equity cases, there seems to be a slide in that direction, especially in education cases.

Let me add another feature of the landscape, and this is one that probably is more of an outgrowth of the Fourteenth Amendment that it is of the original Constitution. I think there is a fundamental and special concern and preoccupation in the eyes of the Supreme Court with minorities, and in particular with those who are without clout in the political process. You may remember Justice Stone's famous *Carolene Products* case in 1938. Footnote 4 in that case is probably the most famous footnote in the Supreme Court's history. In it, some raised the question of whether there might be more searching judicial inquiry when the Court had reviewed statutes aimed at limiting the rights of minorities.

Well, footnote 4 has proved to be the font of an enormous amount of Supreme Court jurisprudence, especially in the area of race. For example, the first right of association case came out of the State of Virginia's effort to put the NAACP out of business back in the 1950s. The first right to counsel case was *Powell v. Alabama* back in the '30s involving the so-called Scottsboro boys. Think about First Amendment speech in public places in the '60s—I could give you a long list—but I think it fair to say that the doctrine has emerged in areas that don't seem to affect race.

Judicial supremacy

My last feature on the landscape brings me full circle. Having started with judicial review, I think the last feature on the landscape is what some call judicial supremacy. One recalls *Marbury*, in which Marshall left open the question whether the Supreme Court not only has the power to interpret the Constitution, but whether it also is the ultimate arbiter, the ultimate interpreter. It was in *Cooper v. Aaron* in 1958, the Little Rock school case, where state officials claimed that they were not bound by the ground rules, because they weren't parties to it. Well, in *Cooper v. Aaron*, all nine justices signed off on the opinion. That's most unusual on the Supreme Court. In *Aaron*, the Court quoted from *Marbury* that language which is often quoted, "it is emphatically the province and duty of the judicial department to say what the law is." In *Cooper v. Aaron*, the Court reinterpreted that language almost casually to mean, "the Federal Judiciary is supreme in the exposition of the law of the Constitution," as if it were some self-defining proposition. I suppose the lay public would assume that was the way things are, so that you can ask the average nonlawyer who has the final word and he would say the Supreme Court. Our attorney general has reminded us that there may be questions about the reach of Supreme Court authority.

What conclusion does all this lead to? It is interesting in this bicentennial year to recall that at the Philadelphia convention in 1787 the judicial power was the least debated. Most of the time was given to arguing over how powerful the executive should be. What should the respective relationship between the federal and state government be?

Though the judiciary was by no means an afterthought, it simply didn't require the same kind of focused attention. And yet today it is the work of that branch of government which year in and year out stokes the most extensive debate over constitutional questions.

Certainly at no time in the past 200 years have appointments to the Supreme Court occasioned more national attention than in the last year or two. These confirmation hearings, to which we all shall be glued come September, are likely to have all the trappings of some medieval morality play. The forces of good and evil will battle each other while senators mount their horses in Washington. Underlying all of the political issues and all the hype and all the commentary, we'll be reminded again of the very pervasive place in American life of the American judiciary.

The other side

Professor Lawrence Baum: I would like to talk about the other side of what Dick Howard was discussing. Professor Howard outlines a sequence of events in court actions that at the beginning and increasingly over time enhanced the role and power and policy-making significance of the federal courts. My concern is how the other branches of government reacted to that growing role of federal courts.

We know that a good deal of what the federal courts have done over time, beginning even earlier than *Marbury v. Madison*, has aroused a good deal of unhappiness in the other branches of government. We also know that the other branches of government have the power to do a great many bad things to the federal courts should they choose to do so. The question is, how much *have* they chosen to do so? I want to suggest that given this tremendous array of powers held by the other branches, they have been remarkably forebearing in making use of their powers. Whatever we may conclude about the restraint of the courts, the really remarkable restraint is by Congress and the president.

I find the task of trying to talk about a period of 200 years quite impossible. So I want to take a shortcut and focus on a period of approximately the last 35 years in which the federal courts have taken, in many cases, strongly activist positions, primarily as defenders of civil liberties, most dramatically and most visibly in the Supreme Court, but also increasingly in the lower federal courts. This period since the 1950s is certainly not perfectly representative of our history as a whole, but I think it is representative of the general rule—that although the federal courts have often aroused a good deal of unhappiness in the other branches, they have been, I think, given the political power of the other branches, remarkably free and safe to follow their own course as decision makers and as policymakers.

Let me begin by reminding you of something with which you are all familiar, the tremendous activism of the federal courts since the 1950s. There are a lot of different ways in which to measure activism. If we simply look at the number of laws that have been declared unconstitutional, you all know that the numbers since 1960 have been unprecedented, that more than one-third of all the federal and state and local laws that have been struck down by the Supreme Court have come in the last 25 years.

In an even more dramatic way, consider the intervention of the Court in the operation of public institutions, whether it's schools or prisons or mental institutions. None of these things is unprecedented, none of those kinds of activities are new in the last quarter century, but their extent is probably unprecedented. I think it's easy enough to argue that there has been unprecedented activism since the 1950s and particularly the 1960s.

Certainly, we're also familiar with the fact that a great deal of what federal courts have done in this period has been highly unpopular in the country as a whole, but more relevantly in the other branches. Some of the Supreme Court's major civil liberties decisions have been quite popular—the right to counsel in *Gideon*, for example. But others have aroused a good deal of congressional and presidential wrath. Consider the school busing decisions, which have had relatively little support in the other branches. Or the school prayer decisions. The restrictions on police searches and questioning. Protections of people on the political left, particularly in the 1950s. If any of those decisions had come to a vote in Congress, there would have been very few votes for them on the merits. And yet, the other branches have not done a great deal to attack either the decisions or the courts that made them.

Keep in mind all the various things that Congress and the president can do: Structural things, such as restricting the jurisdiction of federal courts; verbal attacks of various sorts which are the one thing that's easiest to do; limiting court size and budgets.

Congress and the president also have a good deal of power over the implementation of court decisions. There is a lot of ammunition that the other branches have. And yet it's striking how little of that has been used since the 1950s. A great deal of verbal attack, some in very strong language; a lot of bills introduced, a lot of proposals made to restrict court jurisdiction. And yet, very little of that has become law. It's probably true that some of the restrictions on budgets and salaries have resulted from unhappiness with court decisions.

There were also symbolic bills on busing; there was a symbolic bill passed in 1968 to restrict *Miranda*. But that's about all. None of the proposed constitutional amendments have been adopted; none of the proposed limits on court jurisdiction have been adopted. Basically, all the unpopular things that the Supreme Court and the lower federal courts have done since the 1960s have been allowed to stand. That to me is more remarkable than the things that the courts themselves have done. It seems to me the question then is "why?" Given all this power, and all the unhappiness they have with so many decisions, why have Congress and the president basically let those decisions stand and left the courts unscathed? I don't think there is any one particularly good answer. But it does seem to me there are several bits and pieces.

Why court decisions stand

First of all, there has been some self-restraint by the courts themselves. It is easy enough to assume that because there has been so much active policymaking by the courts since the 1950s they acted without any sense of restraint at all. Clearly that is not the case. We have some subtle evidence of this from the papers of Supreme Court justices—the judges have recognized that they can push only so far. So, in part, I think the courts protected themselves with some degree of restraint.

Second, let me suggest that as unpopular as some court decisions have been, all of them have enjoyed some support, not only from society at large, but within Congress as well. Even the most unpopular decisions—school busing, school prayer—have enjoyed some basis of support in Congress. And so when the Court has been on the run, when there are strong efforts to overturn its decisions or to limit its jurisdiction, there have always been some members of Congress willing to support the Court.

Third, and this is something that is primarily a

modern development, there has been an increasing acceptance in the other branches of government of the desirability of maintaining the autonomy of the courts. I don't mean to imply there is some awe of the courts. Rather, I think there is general public support for the independence of the courts, that the system requires that the courts be given a degree of autonomy. And this creates some restraint on the part of the president and members of Congress when they are considering curbing the courts.

I think the best example to illustrate this is proposals to restrict the Court's jurisdiction. Although there is some controversy about the extent of Congress' constitutional power to restrict Court jurisdiction, it has a great deal of such power—that much is clear. And all it needs to do is pass bills with simple majorities to restrict the Court's jurisdiction. And yet Congress has not done so since 1868, and certainly has not done so in the modern period of civil liberties support by the Supreme Court. I think this is because there's a feeling that trying to manipulate the Court by restricting its jurisdiction is going to be viewed by people as unacceptable.

In the 19th century it was quite common to increase or decrease the number of Supreme Court justices. And sometimes that was done in order to manipulate the Court. Of course, the effort to do that during the New Deal was defeated. And it's not even considered anymore because, again, I think there is a tinge of illegitimacy to it. I think there is an element of self-restraint based on a feeling that federal courts must be left alone, not because of anything mystical about them, but because the people demand it, and because the system seems to require it.

Finally, and to me the most interesting thing, there is a good deal of evidence that presidents, but even more, members of Congress, are grateful to the Court for taking burdens off themselves. Every controversial issue that is decided by the Court takes a good deal of heat off the Congress to deal with that issue. School integration is a good example. The decisions of the Supreme Court have largely left Congress powerless to deal with the issue in more than a peripheral and symbolic way. I think that for many members of Congress that's a great thing. It keeps them from having to deal with something that's going to make people on one side or the other very unhappy.

The issue of abortion is similar. Certainly many members of Congress feel very strongly that the Supreme Court's decisions on abortion have been quite wrong in both the legal and moral senses. And yet I think members of Congress, and even more state legislators, are grateful that they don't have to deal with the issue. Had *Roe v. Wade* never been decided, in every legislative session at both the national and state levels there would be tremendous battles over abortion. Should the Supreme Court reverse *Roe v. Wade*, we can be guaranteed those battles will be quite bloody. And so however much they disagree with *Roe*, as many legislators strongly do, nonetheless the Court has done them a favor by taking the issue out of their hands. I think there is a certain reluctance to wrest that power away from the Court and take the burdens back onto themselves.

Having emphasized the fact that the other branches have left the courts alone, let me say a couple of things to water that down a bit. First, there is a great deal of power over the courts simply through the appointment power. It's delayed power; it doesn't work perfectly, but it does rein in the courts to some degree. It may be that the Reagan administration has not brought about an overturning of any of the decisions of the Warren Court or even the Burger Court, but it has staffed much of the lower courts, and increasingly the Supreme Court, with judges who are more sympathetic to its point of view. That is an important control and it is one that we shouldn't lose sight of.

Even so, it seems to me that the most striking thing is the relative autonomy of the courts in practice. Despite what would seem to be a tremendous weakness, a tremendous subservience to the other branches, even in a time of great controversy such as the last 30 years, the federal courts have been largely left alone to chart active policymaking paths, paths that were often quite unpopular. Autonomy of the courts, rather than control of the courts, has been the primary feature of the system. And that, given the legal and political subservience of the courts, strikes me as remarkable.

In perspective

Judge Stephen Reinhardt: I think what Professor Howard described as the experience of the courts has been the experience of the nation. In fact, I think it has also been the experience of the executive and legislative branches. We've come from a sleepy, rural society with 13 small states to a national, world power in a very complex, fast-moving society. To the same extent that the courts have become more important, more powerful, so have the president and the Congress. So I think it's important to put this picture of the growing power of the federal judiciary in perspective.

It would be hard for this country to function effectively in modern society if the federal judiciary hadn't, thanks to John Marshall and others such as Earl Warren, understood that this nation and its court system were compelled to keep moving, keep advancing, keep up with contemporary life, deal with different and modern problems, find solutions by adjusting our thoughts, our attitudes, our understanding of all the things that we learned over 200 years. Had this country simply said we won't do anything, or had our federal courts said we won't do anything that we can't find in somebody's notes taken 200 years ago, it would be a sad state of affairs indeed.

Therefore, there is really nothing very surprising about the fact that the powers of the federal courts have expanded. Whether that trend will continue or not is a different question—whether the Constitution will continue to stand for what it has for so long depends on whether we are ready and willing now, after 200 years, to accept that evolutionary development. Some may not be. I think there is a serious view that the Constitution doesn't mean what John Marshall said it meant, what we all grew up understanding it meant. I think there are people in prominent positions these days who think that the Bill of Rights doesn't mean anything, that it was a mistake.

Once you accept the premise that the Constitution means what the Supreme Court says it means, then if you have a Supreme Court that doesn't believe in rights, we're not going to have much of a Constitution and we're not going to have many rights. But it's very hard to resist the idea of evolution; it's very hard to resist the idea of growth. It would be very hard to transform this nation into what it was at a different time and a different era. *Back to the Future* was a nice movie, but it's really hard to believe that this nation can go back to the confederation that some might like it to become.

Distrust of courts

The next general area that Professor Howard mentioned is distrust of state courts. That is a sensitive subject, particularly for a federal judge—why fed-

eral courts are better than state courts. To me it doesn't seem particularly peculiar that federal courts should decide federal rights. It should be the body to decide what the federal Constitution means.

I'm all in favor of state courts determining their state constitutions, and affording broader protection—I think that states should absolutely have the right to do whatever they wish to protect people's rights. On the other hand, they have no business limiting people's rights that are protected under federal law. And to say that states may not limit federal rights, but that state courts should decide whether states have limited federal rights, doesn't make a lot of sense.

It seems to me fairly elementary that federal courts are there to protect federal rights. Historically, there may be some conceptual difficulties with that argument. It may not always have been thus. But as we grow in understanding of what the functions of courts are and the purposes of federalism, I don't have much difficulty with thinking that when you have a question of whether state legislation and state action is in violation of federal law, persons who feel that there is a violation should have the right to go to federal court to protect their federal rights.

It sounds very simple when I say it, but there are many people with a different view. The tension that Professor Howard mentioned between the text of the Constitution and the need to grow is not a problem. One of the nice things about our Constitution is you don't find the answers in the text frequently because it was understood that you can't answer constitutional questions in the text. You can only give general principles in the text, and those principles mean different things at different times as we learn more about life. The conflict is between the need to grow and how judges interpret those principles. One of the problems with the debate over the Constitution is that it is not so clear what the intent was.

The role of judges

Essentially, the real debate over the role of judges and over federal judges is in a basic difference in view over what law is and what a judge is. The extremes are that one of you believes that judges should not have discretion; that judges must act like some form of human computer where a judge can look at a case, look at a statute, and there is a clear answer. Well, sometimes there is and I suppose if you look at the volume of our caseload, you would find there are pretty clear answers to most of the cases.

But they're not as easy to decide as some people think. There are problems with more cases than some of my colleagues seem to think. There are judges who will tell you that 80 per cent of the cases are easy, but I find that very few cases are easy. The ultimate outcome in a majority of cases may be fairly clear. But the cases that come to public attention are usually cases that are not so clear. The reason you have divided votes is because, normally, reasonable people can differ. There isn't an automatic, clear scientific answer to the problem. Law is not a science. It requires judgment, and the most important thing to know about a judge is how he goes about the process of applying judgment and what his values are.

I think President Reagan is absolutely correct in looking for judges who reflect his basic philosophical values. It is impossible to decide the kinds of cases the Supreme Court decides without applying one's values. Of course, there are all kinds of limits, and what the limits are is a matter of great disagreement. And it also happens to depend where you are at any particular time. I participated in a panel discussion like this with a representative from the Justice Department and some of President Reagan's appointees who have a rather broad view of overriding or disregarding precedent. And, rather surprisingly, the concept of precedent means very little to a Supreme Court justice. If you don't like the previous decision, that's enough—you just change it.

Justice Rehnquist said pretty much the same thing in *Garcia*, which one of our speakers alluded to. He made it very clear that the next time there was an appointment, the vote would be 5 to 4 the other way, instead of 5 to 4 the way *Garcia* came out. That was probably the most blatant explanation of how courts reach decisions—"we needed one more vote," is what he said, "and we'll get it."

In any event, I don't understand quite why there is this much debate over judges exercising discretion. Sometimes that is referred to as being activist. Other times, it seems to me at least, it's just simply doing the job you are required to do—you are required to apply judgment, to make decisions involving fundamental powers. It is really the only branch of government that is free to apply the principles that we heard about

earlier of justice and reason, without concern over any other consideration.

At least in the federal judiciary, we have the benefit of lifetime appointment and do not have to be concerned about any other consideration. The Constitution is there in large part to protect minorities against the temporary sentiments of the majority. It's thus quite clear why lifetime appointments are desirable. When a majority doesn't like what officeholders do, the majority throws out officeholders, and that's quite appropriate. It's not quite appropriate to throw out judges who are enforcing people's constitutional rights because you don't happen to like those constitutional rights. And that is a great danger in an electoral system. There is a question about how safe the federal judiciary really is these days, and I certainly agree with Professor Baum that we have been very fortunate. A lot could have been done to the federal judiciary that has not been done.

Free from threats

I think probably Professor Baum's predictions, optimistic as they are, are justified. There was a lot of talk several years ago about limiting the powers of the federal judiciary. There was a lot of talk about constitutional changes. Some of the societies that were established in the recent eight to ten years have published serious treatises on modifying our Constitution to change the federal system. Usually, with a little bit of time, those ideas disappear. A senator from California, who happens to be still sitting in the Senate, proposed when he ran for office the first time that we have direct elections of federal judges. Now that he's a senator and has won the election, I don't think he's likely to repeat that proposal. But there were other proposals seriously made by people who have a great impact on the California Supreme Court and who were very involved, long before the recent bloodbath in California, in an effort to change the basic system of replacing California judges in an orderly manner, when they decided and announced they would like to see the same approach applied on a national scale. I think that one of the things that happens, though, is that people who believe in that kind of change in the court system come to power and stay in power long enough so they take over the courts, and then they don't want to change it. In fact, they become the activists themselves, only they are active for a different social policy—instead of protecting individual rights, they protect property rights.

Either way, the system generally continues to go on free from serious external threats, and I think it likely that it will.

Judicial independence

James J. Brosnahan: Professor Howard started by saying that judicial review, *Marbury v. Madison,* is most important—we all agree with that. Over the last five or six years particularly, I've had some clients who have come from other systems. In the last couple of years, I've been talking to people who have fled other systems, and in all of that it seems to me that there is a great new challenge for us to make known to the world, and some American lawyers are trying to do it, what it is about our system that is good—even if we got it accidentally—even if at the convention in Philadelphia they didn't quite focus on it—nonetheless, we've got it.

The starting point is not judicial review, although that is so terribly important as Professor Howard said. What I've come to believe is that judicial independence is everything. In Africa, when judges are consulted, whether they like it or not, by the chief executive officer, there is no judicial independence. You can't have judicial review unless you have judicial independence. There is much to be learned as to what happened in California last year, because conservative or liberal, left or right, center or whatever, I think we would agree that judicial independence is the starting point.

Federal judges, indeed, are independent and have been all the way through, and as a result we have the system that we have. Looking back over 200 years, Professor Howard mentioned the period of national power. My theory is simply that the federal courts are independent, but society moves through those courts, reflecting whatever is happening in our society. The irony of the debate as to whether judges should ever put a little bit of themselves into what they're doing is that we revere the judges over the last 300 or 400 years who have done exactly that. Consider Lord Mansfield, who invented equity while reading one night a book on Roman law. He found that the Romans had edicts by which they could ameliorate the harshness of the law. Thus was equity born. And we remember Mansfield for that and many other things.

Indeed, when you look back on the federal courts, you find rights, as Professor Howard says, that may not spring right out, but that does not automati-cally mean they're not appropriate. For who will now say that the right to privacy should be struck down? The federal courts have become in recent years a great megaphone out of which rights could be declared, but the country, starting by my notes about April 10, 1973, has become quieter. We have been busy with economic matters, to beat the Japanese productively. Rights are still important, but they are not at the center of our particular thinking, although the equity power in federal courts remains very, very vigorous.

It is interesting to see that a pup fish can be defended with tremendous vigor by the federal courts, even though the lawyers and judges, before the case was filed, did not know, as I did not know, what a pup fish is. But in the Ninth Circuit over the last approximately seven years, in 24 cases, 16 have resulted in an injunction. And some of these judges, I think, could fairly be said to be nonactivist judges. And yet, when dependent Native Americans in Alaska are denied by some government agency the subsistence which they need to live over the next month, the judges move to deal with that.

I must say that one of the things that I have been privileged to see in the federal courts is the advancement of other ideas that have come in, including the representation of the poor, and of course there are now federal public defenders. There are judges of all stripes who participate in making the system what it is.

The legislature, I think, will not come after the federal courts, any more than they seem particularly capable of going after the executive branch. Because somewhere deep down in their hearts, they really know they ought to be doing the job. For example, the most telling point I ever heard was with regard to *Miranda.* Between approximately 1930 and the time that the Warren Court started to decide procedures for arrest, no state legislature passed any statute—good, bad or otherwise—on the subject of how people were to be advised of their rights. The legislature is good, they are well meaning, I like them, but they get terribly confused. And this is the great protector, I think, of our federal courts.

The final point I would like to mention is access to the courts, because every legal system is known for something. The Greeks invented the idea of lawyers. When their society died and their legal system crumbled, nonetheless, they had invented the idea of lawyers and courts, something that could go on. The Romans brought uniformity to it—as they brought it to their roads, to their army—a systemized body of law. And the English began the concept of rights. But only in this country has it been the idea, which we have approached, but not totally achieved, that people of the smallest and weakest position will have access to the courts. We haven't made it, because in the civil field we have no doctrine that a person is entitled to a lawyer in civil cases. Very good lawyers have argued that, but we have never succeeded. Yet, overall, our best thing is that everybody will get a chance to go to court to articulate his or her position. So, when doctrines come down in the federal courts whacking away at access, they are whacking away at our best thing. Access to the courts is what our society will be remembered for.

NOTE

This transcript originally appeared in Volume 71, Number 2, August-September 1987, pages 116-122.

Arrogation of power or accountability: "judicial imperialism" revisited

The "imperial judiciary" is an illusion. Judges only exercise power given them by others and remain accountable both to professional interests and the public.

by Stephen L. Wasby

In the last half-dozen years it has become increasingly popular to argue that judges, particularly federal judges, have become an "imperial judiciary" improperly intervening in American life. Both an intellectual argument, made most notably by Nathan Glazer and Raoul Berger,[1] and political efforts have developed to restrict courts' power, with the former used to bolster the latter. Proposed constitutional amendments would limit federal judges to a single 10-year term[2] or would directly overturn Supreme Court abortion and school desegregation rulings thought to result from improper activism. Methods for reversing the courts' invalidation of federal or state laws have also been proposed.[3]

Complaints come from within as well as outside the judiciary. Justice Rehnquist has asserted that "It is basically unhealthy to have so much authority concentrated in a small group of lawyers who have been appointed to the Supreme Court and enjoy virtual life tenure." And Justice Powell has characterized the lower courts' orders in the 1979 school desegregation cases as "wholesale substitution of judicial legislation for the judgments of elected officials and professional educators" and "social engineering that hardly is appropriate for the federal judiciary."[4]

One can certainly make a strong, but hardly new, case that courts play a large role in American policy making. The question is whether a critic is engaging in dispassionate treatment of judicial policy making capacity or simply arguing against such policy making on the basis of disliked results. As noted by Cavanagh and Sarat, "However cast, argu-ments about failures of competence or capacity tend to be political statements about the desirability of particular court decisions or aspects of legal doctrine."[5] In short, dislike of substantive results fully pervades the discussion of "judicial imperialism" and lack of judicial capacity, both explicitly as in Glazer's work or somewhat more thinly veiled as in Horowitz's oft-cited study.[6]

Arguments supporting a limited role for the judiciary are part of a long, honorable tradition of *normative* argument. Among several legitimate normative positions on the place of judges in the system, however, critics of "judicial imperialism" seem to recognize only passivity—at least when convenient to applaud it. (At other times, they often wish judges to retain a strong hand, for example, so that regulators can be restrained or so that some of their own substantive goals can be attained.)

In the social climate of the last decade, with reduced support for civil rights and endemic disaffection with the social programs of the 1960s, crossing over into result-oriented advocacy is especially easy. Arguments like those by Glazer and Horowitz are certainly legitimate social *criticism*, but one should be cautious about accepting them as neutral or objective accounts. "Judicial imperialism" is a useful rhetorical device, but the assertions accompanying it are seldom supported by hard analysis. As Monti notes, "Critics of judicial activism have not posed their arguments in a way that anticipates, much less permits, the introduction of information that could qualify or contradict their positions."[7]

In this essay, I raise questions about the "judicial imperialism" argument as rhetoric and ideology, maintaining that the argument that judges have arrogated power to themselves is seriously defective. Critics of the "imperial judiciary" ignore the genesis of judicial rulings and blame the messenger—the courts—for others' acts or omissions. Instead, judges exercise power given them by others and are accountable in many ways both to professional interests and the larger political system. Furthermore, despite claims often made along with attacks on "judicial imperialism," judges are not incapable of dealing with policy issues presented to them and, when compared with other institutions, do so well.

Judicial imperialism and incapacity

The "imperial judiciary" argument gives disproportionate attention to certain types of cases, reinforced by result-oriented selection of examples; fails to examine closely the causes of litigation, leading to a strong tendency to blame the messenger rather than the source; lacks systematic *comparative* examination of the capacity of courts and other political institutions to resolve policy disputes; and fails to examine ways in which judges, instead of arrogating power, are both potentially and actually accountable.

Selectivity of cases

The general tone of the "judicial imperialism" argument is set by the critics' selectivity in choosing types of cases to support their argument. Horowitz even dismisses the question of whether the cases in his study are representative by asserting—not showing—that they are not "aberrational" and by arguing that "frequency is not an issue in this study."[8] Yet how is one to know whether cases are "aberrational" without some baseline or idea of the frequency with which they occur?

Repeated emphasis on Judge Garrity's Boston school desegregation rulings and Judge Frank Johnson's Alabama prison and mental hospital decisions, with the former often misrepresented, has led many to expect incorrectly that those decisions are the norm. However, most judges are not "activist" but instead are "narrow-minded lawyers with little stomach for being creative or for second-guessing other government officers."[9]

With respect to school desegregation cases, on which critics often focus, "it is not at all clear that the courts are prepared to assume the responsibility of directing a far-reaching program of institutional reform in the public schools."[10] Concerning prison cases, Justice Brennan has pointed out that "no one familiar with litigation in this area could suggest that the courts have been overeager to usurp the task of running prisons."[11] More generally, "Even in an era in which 'landmark' decisions with broad social implications dominate much of the debate over the role of courts, most court decisions present no arguable infringement on legislative, executive, or electoral prerogatives."[12]

The selectivity of those arguing against "judicial imperialism" extends even further. The pejorative "judicial activism" is applied only to Warren Court decisions and not those of the Burger Court. But certainly, promises to appoint "strict constructionist" judges has not meant that President Nixon's appointees have acted in a consistently "self-restrained" manner when faced with legislation running counter to deeply-held values.

Nor have critics of activism showed concern when judges have acted imperiously in the absence of some large social issue. The critics' concerns would have been more heartening if they had joined dissent from the Supreme Court's ruling in *Stump v. Sparkman* that judges were immune from suit if acting within what appears to be formal jurisdiction.[13] Justice Stewart, objecting to immunity for actions judges have no constitutional or statutory authority to take, certainly has the better of the argument: "A judge is not free, like a loose cannon, to inflict indiscriminate damage whenever he announces that he is acting in his judicial capacity."[14]

Clearly, critics are unable to penetrate the rhetoric of "strict construction," "judicial policy making," an "unaccountable" judiciary, or "judicial imperialism." Certainly political scientists have raised serious questions about accepting at face value a judge's rhetoric on self-restraint;[15] those writing more recently can legitimately be expected to exercise more care in their use of labels. But the critics' inability—or unwillingness—raises the question of how the events leading to 1937, which certainly should have taught us that the courts are policy makers, ever occurred. If "judicial policy making" may still be used pejoratively, chances for serious public discussion of courts' operation are slim. Such a difficulty clearly infects *The Brethren*,[16] where the authors' breathless discussion of bargaining within the Court suggests a failure to accept the Court's role as a policy maker. What else would we expect from a major policy making institution but bargaining and compromise?

An aspect of the critics' biased selectivity is their lack of historical perspective. "Social policy" issues have long been placed in the courts' hands. Contemporary commentators forget that "commercial interests in diversity jurisdiction dominated circuit dockets in the beginning [of the U.S. Courts of Appeals, while] the Great Depression and World War II brought into court continuing relations with powerful social aggregates concerned with labor relations, taxation, and public regulation of basic industries"[17]—all definitely "social policy" matters. Perhaps what discomforts the neoconservatives is that "the deprived have joined the advantaged as users of [the judicial] route of grievance redress."[18] Whatever the reason, the critics confuse differences in substantive content—the presence on the docket of, for example, environmental issues—with differences in procedure and remedy, thus exaggerating changes in the latter.

The "imperial judiciary" critics also demonstrate a lack of historical perspective by failing to remind us of earlier judicial "activism"—interference with governmental regulation of the economy in the 1930s and earlier. Those earlier decisions, in aid of a conservative ideology, are conveniently not seen as activist. Moreover, the critics fail to deal with Dahl's argument that the Supreme Court has seldom been out of line with the nation's dominant political interest.[19] The Court, Dahl argued, has been able to do little without support from Congress and the president, although it could maneuver when the other branches were in disagreement. Neither his posture that the Court conferred legitimacy on the policies developed by the other branches, nor his critics' view that elites legitimize the Court rather than the reverse, support a view of judicial overreaching.[20]

Causes of judicial actions

Although some judicial rulings said to indicate an "imperial judiciary" are based on broad constitutional provisions concerning "equal protection" and "cruel and unusual punishment," many challenged decisions stem from interpretation and enforcement of statutes. Vague and ambiguous constitutional clauses and statutory provisions may allow judges to project their values into decisions.

However, the judges are not to blame for either the existence of the provisions or their lack of clarity.

Justice Powell has reminded us that "Congress' failure to make policy judgments can distort our system of separation of powers by encouraging other branches to make essentially legislative decisions."[21] Yet the critics find it easier to blame courts for decisions based on statutes than to question the legislative action itself. Similarly, it is not the plethora of administrative regulations based on those statutes that are attacked but the greater judicial action necessary to resolve disputes stemming from the regulations.[22]

Critics forget that if judges misread congressional intent, Congress has the power to right the situation, just as it can scrutinize the regulations designed to implement its own statutes. Yet critics seldom question Congress' failure to review such regulations and to strike down those that it disapproves. Failing to acknowledge that oversight has often meant *overlook*, critics continue to attack the courts, not the Congress, for not exercising its responsibilities and delegating substantial policy making authority to the executive.[23]

Decisions attracting critics' particular attention restrain officials or require them to improve substantially the conditions in the facilities they direct. It is, however, the judges' actions rather than events leading to their rulings that are criticized. Perhaps the best example is the attention given Judge Garrity's schools desegregation rulings in Boston rather than the Boston School Board's adamant refusal to obey clear state law. Similarly, rulings ordering improvement in prison conditions get attention, not state officials' unwillingness to correct long-standing, appalling and clearly unconstitutional conditions. Wishing to make judges accountable, critics of judicial imperialism ignore institutional officials' desire to remain unaccountable or to criticize legislators and senior political executives for not keeping the officials accountable.

Intent on ignoring the causes of allegedly unprecedented and improper judicial actions, the critics imply that judges are imposing particular views concerning the prisons or schools rather than responding to complaints brought by others, often as a last resort. It is, after all, the litigants, not the courts, who have the "power to initiate legal action," so that "litigants, not judges, set court agendas."[24] People need not turn to courts to satisfy their claims. Perhaps their doing so is in part a reflection of larger social or cultural trends or of "the oft-noted litigiousness of the American people."[25] Perhaps it is because plaintiffs find the legislature or executive unresponsive and are not content to be denied their due. Such use of the courts "belies the assessment of the courts as somehow being immune to the vagaries of the political process"[26] and indeed shows not their imperious isolation but their *connectedness* to the political process.

The critics also do not realize that most judges act only when conditions have become so atrocious that even the most conservative among them are horrified. Such judicial hesitation results from deference paid the expertise of those administering the institutions, part of the older "hands-off" policy now revived and thoroughly ensconced in the Supreme Court's prisoners' rights rulings.[27] Similarly ignored is the fact that more severe judicial orders are provoked by state resistance to initial judicial action; the critics instead make further complaints about later orders, forgetting that intransigent parties have always had to be forced to comply with decrees.[28]

In any event, when judges do act, dire predictions about the potential consequences of their rulings seldom are borne out.[29] Officials' authority is *not* invariably destroyed by judicially-established monitoring of their activities and judicial action does lead defendant officials to undertake seriously their responsibilities, with resulting improvements in institutional conditions.

Critics of the judiciary also conveniently ignore the fact that some decrees are not judicially-written or imposed but are consent decrees to which the executive branch agrees. If the state later does not fully assume responsibility for the decree,[30] who is to blame if plaintiffs return to court and the judge orders implementation? It is also important to note that administrators may find it politically useful to be hauled into court, so they have a reason for agreeing to carry out politically unpopular actions.[31] As professionals, they may share plaintiffs' standards about proper conditions. More generally, "the interests of officials with direct operating responsibility—for example, institutional superintendents and their deputies—often overlap substantially with those of the plaintiffs."[32] Perhaps all this is but another piece of evidence for the proposition that litigation is not only an end in itself but is part of a continuing disputing process and a wedge to negotiation when nothing else will attract

the other side's serious attention. Indeed, "extended impact litigation does not displace negotiation and compromise but is frequently an essential precondition to it."[33]

The foregoing reinforces the point that judges are embedded in the governmental system, not external to it. Nor is this unusual. Shapiro points out that judging is "an integral part of the mainstream of political authority rather than . . . a separate entity."[34]

What, then, of the norm of "judicial independence" so highly touted in the American political system and so strongly adhered to because of the belief that the costs of a judiciary directly subservient to the political powers-that-be are much too great? At one level it refers to judges not being dependent on one of the parties to a lawsuit; at another level, it entails an institutional separation so that judges are not attached to the same part of the government with whom an individual may be having a dispute.[35] Such a separation, with the judiciary expected to check and balance the other branches, may result in the judiciary acquiring "substantial lawmaking and administering capabilities."[36]

An "independent judiciary" does not, however, mean one completely separate from the political system, and may well indicate a system serving certain broad societal interests, historically the "upper class and nationalizing interests rather than dominant local interests."[37] Among the interests the American federal judiciary has at time served has been the cause of minority rights. The critics forget that the judiciary's very task is to protect civil liberties, a task that, despite public perceptions created by Warren Court decisions, the courts have not often fulfilled. Without such action or "activism," there would be even further erosion of our liberties, "because of the substantial political and bureaucratic obstacles that hinder the implementation of the Court's decisions and blunt their impact." Put differently, "because the statements in the Bill of Rights are only rights in theory, they need all the help they can get if they are to survive in fact" because "pressures in the real world" against them are "substantial"—a consideration favoring the view that courts "lean harder in the direction of emphasizing our nation's constitutional ideals."[38]

Beyond rulings on the merits, judges must also attend to implementation of decrees. Without such "intrusive" implementation, judicial orders are likely to be ineffective, remaining "merely a paper victory for the plaintiffs."[39] If neoconservatives showed greater concern for alternative modes of securing the rights sought and implemented through the courts in this way, their criticism of judicial "activism" would carry more weight. Yet one hears only the criticism, not suggestions of alternative methods of resolving societal disputes.

Judicial incapacity

A last important element of the attack on "judicial imperialism" is the argument that courts lack the capacity to resolve complex social policy issues. (This argument is separate from the position that, regardless of competence, courts in a democracy should not be making decisions about complex social issues.) In making their argument, critics often suffer from indecision about whether to focus only on courts or to compare courts with the other branches of government. They usually settle for the former, taking cheap pot-shots at the courts while ignoring the possibility that the other branches suffer from some of the same defects claimed to affect or infect the judiciary.

An example of the faulty analysis by those claiming judicial incapacity is Horowitz's argument that courts "carve up and . . . treat as separate" related transactions when those transactions "are intertwined in social life."[40] We are also told that judges are preoccupied with individual cases, and thus do not think about whether the cases before them represent a typical situation, from which precedent for later cases might be properly derived, or are extremes and thus to be confined to their facts. Furthermore, attention to individual cases is said to produce piecemeal policy making.

Incremental decision making does characterize the judiciary, but it also characterizes *all* governmental policy making,[41] despite occasional instances of "speculative augmentation."[42] Administrative agencies as well as courts have long been criticized for predominant reliance on a case-by-case approach instead of using rule making—although rule making is also criticized when it produces disliked results.

Nor does reliance on a case-by-case approach always entail ad hoc decision making, as the critics appear to assume. Legislators, administrators, and judges generally begin policy making with a problem presented by particular instances or cases. However, all contemplate to some degree other situations to which their rulings would apply. In particular, courts have regularly grouped cases involving common issues so as not to base decisions too narrowly on the specifics of an individual case. If courts are not self-starters, having to wait for cases to be filed or appealed, we must also remember that most legislative action does not commence until after a series of constituent or interest group complaints.

We are also told that courts cannot effectively make advance estimates of the magnitude or direction of the effects of their decisions. We are not told, of course, that legislatures and executives similarly fail to predict effectively. Judicial correction of policy is said to be intermittent. Yet it is equally the case that agencies charged with enforcing legislation do not continuously monitor many matters under their jurisdiction. The critics also do not recognize that, whatever the courts' difficulties with new subject-matter, other governmental institutions also have trouble processing new material effectively; however, for all institutions, courts included, time and preparation can overcome the problem.

To argue that judges are not prepared by training and experience to supervise administrative agencies like mental health and corrections departments or even to select appropriate masters whose work the judges are to supervise ignores the fact that legislators are generalists sharing problems "of being adequately informed about disputes and in their relations with experts,"[43] as well as in selecting specialist staff. Judges' supervision of agencies can be facilitated by requiring periodic reports and by reliance on complainants' attorneys to return to court if something is amiss. Beyond that, judicial appointment of masters can "compensate for judges' lack of familiarity with organizational routines and procedures in defendant institutions," and their use may be essential in securing compliance with judicial decrees.[44]

To engage in serious analysis of courts' capacity to resolve matters requires a set of well-defined criteria; Carter provides us with one. An institution's policy, to be effective, must "accord with fundamental, widely shared beliefs about acceptable governmental action" and must "carry some plausible hope of alleviating the problem." Moreover, the promulgation and implementation of the policy must not "destroy the position and authority of the position's source."[45] The criteria Carter suggests include technical competence, effective information processing, and political accountability:

(1) *familiarity* with the language in which a policy problem is articulated and an *understanding* about "cause and effect beliefs that define the existence of a problem in the first place";[46]

(2) *reliable access to information* bearing on the problem's causes, on all solutions proposed and their direct and indirect consequences, on targets, and on implementation strategies;

(3) the *ability to reformulate policy* when new information is obtained; and

(4) once there is agreement that a problem exists and on perceptions of the problem, the *public's belief* that the institution's authority and competence match the problem.

Once an institution (legislative, executive, or judicial) is seen to satisfy any one of these criteria, the question arises whether,

regardless of the skill of members of a given policy making institution (PMI), any other PMI is equally or better prepared to proceed, and whether alternative policy sources, even if they may be better equipped technically to proceed, will in fact do so.[47]

Use of the criteria and of this comparative formulation will produce different answers at different times as to the appropriateness of judicial action. What is important is that, by insisting that the second question be asked, Carter has properly focused attention on *comparative* capacity as well as on the crucial *will to proceed*, neither of which is addressed seriously by the "imperial judiciary" critics.

Judicial accountability

Advocates of the "judicial imperialism" position ignore ways in which the judiciary *is* accountable. To remedy this omission, it helps to stress not arrogation of power but accountability, defined to mean "keeping an institution's decisions in line with community political and social values and otherwise imposing constraints on the courts' exercise of discretion."[48] Means of judicial accountability may appear to be few or at times less than fully effective, but that does not mean there is no accountability.

For one thing, despite American emphasis on judicial independence, courts are not fully independent or autonomous institutions. Their structure, jurisdiction, and resources, including their budget and personnel, are determined by the other branches of government. Courts are initially established, and often reorganized, by the legislature. And, as indicated by current debate over limiting the Supreme Court's appellate jurisdiction—or the jurisdiction of all federal courts—the legislature can limit what the courts hear.

Ironically, discussion of judicial imperialism, both by those attacking the judiciary and defenders, has itself contributed to accountability by producing more intellectual soul-searching by judges. In general, accountability of judges is of two principal types—within the legal system and to the broader political system. The former includes judges' socialization; precedent and the public nature of judicial action; reversal of lower court judges' decisions; and constraints imposed by courts' organizational needs. Political accountability derives from selection and removal of judges (also part of accountability within the legal community); the role of public opinion; and resistance to judges' decisions.

The socialization of judges

Given the limited amount of *formal* training of judges as judges, judges' most extensive socialization has been to their earlier role as lawyers. This includes socialization to the norm of judicial independence, the idea that judges ought not be accountable to the other branches of government. Thus, we find judges, as lawyers, socialized to norms about accountability itself. The lack of formal training for judges means that the most important direct socialization of judges is through contact with other judges; reliance on each other is reinforced by norms against consultation with those who are not judges and especially with nonlawyers. All this reinforces accountability within the judicial profession rather than to others.

Part of lawyers' socialization is to precedent. Lawyers also learn that, even when precedent is lacking, they should look to "the law," not popular feelings, as the source of their decisions. Precedent affects the process by which judges arrive at reasoned decisions: "We contain our judges by method, and demand justification of their results by reason."[49] In particular, we wish judges' rulings to be characterized by *formality*. The requirement of written opinions is part of the process of producing accountability. Believers in role theory will agree that judges' beliefs that they *should* follow precedent and that their decisional process *ought* to be a reasoned one, even if the true bases of their decisions are not in fact presented, will affect judges' actions.

Socialization to precedent can lead judges away from legislative and executive branches and toward their own colleagues. That has helped produce a consensus on how to decide many cases. That such a consensus exists in the Supreme Court is evident from the high degree of unanimity on which cases are appropriate for review and on the disposition of many other cases.[50] Such consensus suggests that "judicial role," not personal values about preferred policy goals, drives much judicial activity, although variations exist in the degree to which values and judicial role reinforce or crosscut each other.

Other forms of accountability

Coupled with precedent is the openness of the judicial decision process, at least at the result stage. Although most trial court opinions are not written or published, and despite federal appellate courts' increased use of not-for-publication opinions, people expect that judges will justify their rulings in published (or at least public) documents. However, serving to reduce accountability is the fact that judges' deliberations are private. Moreover, some courts have been slow to explain even their operating procedures, and Freedom of Information Act (FOIA) provisions do not extend to internal court documents. A penchant for secrecy seems apparent in the Administrative Office of the U.S. Courts' practice of masking judges' identities so that they cannot be matched with particular decisions.

If precedent and openness help produce accountability, so does the sanction of reversal by higher courts for not following precedent or for not viewing the law as the higher court does. Higher courts thus limit lower courts' freedom of action. However, appellate court review of lower court decisions is limited in several ways. Not all trial court decisions are appealed, because the decision to appeal is in lawyers', not judges', hands. Moreover, the absence of controlling precedent also reduces appellate courts' ability to control lower courts, particularly in novel or changing areas of law. Similarly, the Supreme Court and other courts with discretionary jurisdiction cannot take all cases. Because of the limited number of cases they decide, they cannot establish controlling doctrine for all issues faced by lower courts.[51] Even lower appel-

late courts hearing a higher volume of cases may be hard pressed to issue controlling precedents for the trial courts.

Certain judicially-established standards—the "abuse of discretion" doctrine, for example—also limit higher courts' propensity to overturn lower courts. Not only are those tests flexible and work to affirm the lower courts' rulings, but high courts also cannot afford to antagonize the lower courts, on which they must rely if their precedential rulings are to be implemented. Frequency of reversal is thus not high, so that the *fear* of reversal—its symbolic effect—must be more important than actual reversal in achieving accountability. And, indeed, most judges do follow law developed by higher courts; at least they "go along" because higher court rulings on most topics fall within their "zone of indifference."[52]

Attention to the criminal trial courts has recently revealed another aspect of judicial accountability— lateral or horizontal accountability to norms of the "courtroom workgroup."[53] Organizational dynamics control many dispositions reached or recorded in the trial courts. Values shared by trial judges, prosecutors, defense attorneys and other court personnel often limit the effect of higher court rulings, particularly in crisis situations, such as major civil disturbances when some judges seem to suspend independent judgment almost completely.

Selection and public opinion

Methods of judicial selection may also help achieve judicial accountability. Although judges, once chosen, might go their own ways, continuing accountability would be less necessary if accountability were "built in" through selection of judges with characteristics and values thought appropriate by those to whom the judges were to be accountable. Which groups play a dominant role in judicial selection is thus quite important, because it is to the values of those groups that accountability will run. Thus the "merit system," in which lawyers play an explicit role, would increase accountability of judges within the legal system, while partisan election systems would increase accountability to political parties and the values represented by party leaders, that is, "political accountability."

Elections, whether in the merit system, which has led to non-retention (removal) of very few judges,[54] or in nonpartisan or partisan elections, do not substantially increase judicial accountability. Use of nonpartisan ballots makes it difficult for voters to tell "good" candidates from "bad" ones, particularly if the candidates lack previous public identity. Moreover, the norm that one should not run against sitting judges often leaves candidates unopposed. Stiff competition occurs infrequently, and voting in judicial elections is generally reduced by comparison with turnout in elections for other positions.[55]

The difficulty of holding judges accountable through methods of selection, coupled with accounts of improper personal or judicial behavior, has led most states to implement methods for judicial discipline, including removal.[56] Serious discussion of means short of impeachment for handling such problems at the federal level has led to proposals for a separate discipline court and to legislation, enacted in 1980, strengthening the role of the circuit councils in the discipline process, but leaving impeachment as the only means of removing a federal judge from office.[57]

Political accountability may also be achieved through public opinion. Despite the high value placed on judicial independence, public opinion does appear to affect judges. Judges politically active before becoming judges had both become familiar with public opinion and accustomed to responding to it. Although judges do differ in how strongly they adhere to local values, the continuing pull of constituency can be seen in numerous cases, for example, in the race relations area.[58]

Public opinion may, however, be less effective in promoting judicial accountability than it is in the legislative arena because the public, accepting the norm of judicial independence, generally leaves judges alone. At least until recently, negative public opinion about judicial decisions has seldom shown up as more than negative responses in public opinion surveys. More recently, however, "single-issue" interest groups have been pressing effectively for legislation to overturn especially disliked decisions or to remove the courts' jurisdiction over controversial areas. However, even without such activity and even in the absence of a high degree of public knowledge about the decisions, public opinion can affect judicial action. The absence of specific mechanisms for transmitting public opinion to the courts indicates not the absence of an effect of public opinion but only the presence of a noncoercive linkage between public opinion and judicial decisions.

If quiescence most often characterizes even negative reaction to the courts' ruling, there *are* notable instances in which the public resists judicial action. Such resistance, while not making judges directly accountable, certainly lessens the claimed effects of "judicial imperialism." Not only are rulings appealed, with reversal or modification producing some accountability, but, more important, they are at times ignored, resisted, attacked, and overturned in other arenas. Such action, whatever it may say about the presence of a "government of laws," is certainly an effective means of holding courts accountable to views of important segments of the public. This is true even if noncompliance may have received attention disproportionate to its occurrence.[59]

In all of this, however, we should be careful not to overestimate the effect of public opinion on judicial accountability. For one thing, as noted above, public knowledge of judicial decisions is limited. For another, if public opinion can produce accountability when it is clear and unidirectional, at many times opinion is confused, fragmented, and weak, thus providing courts considerable room in which to maneuver. When the public's view differs from views held by the organized bar, judges have freedom to choose between competing audiences.

As the above suggests the two basic types of accountability must be seen together. Those mechanisms providing accountability within the legal system and those providing political accountability at times seem to diverge. Within the legal system, judicial accountability is primarily to lawyers or to other judges, while political accountability propels judges toward the broader public or at least the more attentive members of the public. Despite these potentially divergent strains, some overlap exists because lawyers simultaneously play a large role in judicial selection and are members of the political elite.

Perhaps particularly important is that the values and attitudes of the elite constitute a large part of the environment in which judges function. Appellate judges developing legal doctrine base decisions in part on the political environment or "democratic subculture."[60] Lower court judges expected to follow appellate rulings will have absorbed values from that same political and legal culture before taking the bench and will continue to draw from it because of their greater exposure to the local community. This would suggest that, over the long run, important conjoint legal and political system constraints can operate to limit judges' discretion and thus to hold them accountable.

The burden of this essay has been that the "judicial imperialism" and "judicial incapacity" arguments are defective in a number of important ways. One is a failure to use terminology carefully; another is a lack of historical perspective, coupled with a biased selectivity in examples critics choose to make their case. Perhaps most serious is the critics' sole focus on selected judicial acts rather than on the sources of judicial action—in statutes and administrative regulations. Examination of judicial capacity solely in terms of the judiciary rather than through a comparison of differential institutional capacity is another serious weakness in the critics' argument. So is their attention solely to what they see as lack of judicial accountability without attention to the numerous important ways in which judges are accountable.

More, of course, is necessary than a critique of the critics' arguments. These arguments have, however, been so readily accepted that their defects must be exposed. The possibility for evenhanded analysis of the problems of judicial action in a political system and for thorough comparative analysis of institutional capacity has also been pointed to here, but it remains for others to carry such work forward.

NOTES

This article originally appeared in Volume 65, Number 4, October 1981, pages 209-219.

An earlier version of this article was presented at the American Political Science Association meeting in New York on September 4, 1981.

1. Glazer, *Toward an Imperial Judiciary*, 40 PUB. INT. 104-123 (Fall, 1975), and *Should Judges Administer Social Services?*, 50 PUB INT. 64-80 (Winter, 1980); Berger, GOVERNMENT BY JUDICIARY: THE TRANSFORMATION OF THE FOURTEENTH AMENDMENT (Cambridge, MA: Harvard University Press, 1977).

For other, rather different positions on judicial review, *see* Choper, JUDICIAL REVIEW AND THE NATIONAL POLITICAL PROCESS: A FUNCTIONAL RECONSIDERATION OF THE ROLE OF THE SUPREME COURT (Chicago: University of Chicago Press, 1980); and Ely, DEMOCRACY AND DISTRUST: A THEORY OF JUDICIAL REVIEW (Cambridge, MA: Harvard University Press, 1980).

2. S.J. Res. 24, 97th Cong. 1st Sess., CONG. REC. (Jan. 29, 1981) S 787 (Rep. Dornan).

3. H.R. 4111, 96th Cong. 1st Sess., CONG. REC. (Oct. 10, 1979), E 4953 (Rep. Dornan).

4. Richmond Newspapers v. Virginia, 100 S.Ct. 2814, 2843 (1980); Columbus Bd. of Educ. v. Penick, 443 U.S. 229 (1979).

5. Cavanagh and Sarat, *Thinking About Courts: Toward and Beyond a Jurisprudence of Judicial Competence*, 14 LAW & SOC'Y REV. 371, 386 (Winter, 1980).

6. Glazer, *supra* n. 1, and, particularly, AFFIRMATIVE DISCRIMINATION: ETHNIC INEQUALITY AND PUBLIC POLICY (New York: Basic Books, 1975), Horowitz, THE COURTS AND SOCIAL POLICY (Washington, D.C.: The Brookings Institution, 1977).

7. Monti, *Administrative Foxes in Educational Chicken Coops: An Examination of the Critique of Judicial Activism in School Desegregation Cases*, 2 LAW & POL'Y Q. 233, 242 (April, 1980).

8. Horowitz, *supra* n. 6, at 63.

9. Miller, *For Judicial Activism*, N.Y. TIMES, Nov. 10, 1979.

10. Monti, *supra* n. 7, at 252-253.

11. Rhodes v. Chapman, 101 S.Ct. 2392, 2403 (1981).

12. Cavanagh and Sarat, *supra* n. 5, at 372.

13. 435 U.S. 439 (1978). *See* Way, *A call for limits to judicial immunity: must judges be kings in their courts?*, 64 JUDICATURE 390 (April 1981).

14. 435 U.S., at 367.

15. *See, e.g.*, Grossman, *Role-Playing and the Analysis of Judicial Behavior: The Case of Mr. Justice Frankfurter*, 11 J. PUB. L. 285 (1962).

16. Woodward and Armstrong, THE BRETHREN (New York: Simon and Schuster, 1979).

17. Howard, COURTS OF APPEALS IN THE FEDERAL JUDICIAL SYSTEM: A STUDY OF THE SECOND, FIFTH, AND DISTRICT OF COLUMBIA CIRCUITS 17 (Princeton, NJ: Princeton University Press, 1981).

18. Monti, *supra* n. 7, at 236.

19. Dahl, *Decision-Making in a Democracy: The Role of the Supreme Court as a National Policy-Maker*, 6 J. PUB. L. 279 (Fall, 1957).

20. Adamany, *Legitimacy, Realigning Elections, and the Supreme Court*, 1973 WISC L. REV. 790.

21. Schweiker v. Wilson, 101 S.Ct. 1074, 1088 (1981).

22. *See* Greanias and Windsor, *Is judicial restraint possible in an administrative society?*, 64 JUDICATURE 400, 401 (April, 1981).

23. *Id.* at 410-411.

24. Howard, *supra* n. 17, at 13.

25. *Id.* at 17.

26. Monti, *supra* n. 7, at 235-236.

27. Bell v. Wolfish, 99 S.Ct. 1861 (1979); Jones v. North Carolina Prisoners' Labor Union, 433 U.S. 119 (1977).

28. Eisenberg and Yeazell, *The Ordinary and the Extraordinary in Institutional Litigation*, 93 HARV L. REV. 465, 492, 476-481 (January, 1980).

29. Harris and Spiller, AFTER DECISION: IMPLEMENTATION OF JUDICIAL DECREES IN CORRECTIONAL SETTINGS 21 (Washington, D.C.: LEAA, 1977), quoted in Rhodes v. Chapman, *supra* n. 11, at 2405 (Justice Brennan).

30. Hansen, *Willowbrook: Try, Try Again*, 10 SOC. POL'Y 41 (November/December 1979).

31. "Even prison officials have acknowledged that judicial intervention has helped them to obtain support for needed reform." Rhodes v. Chapman, *supra* n. 11, at 2406 (Justice Brennan).

32. Diver, *The Judge as Political Power Broker: Superintending Change in Public Institutions*, 65 VA. L. REV. 43, 71 (February 1979).

33. Cavanagh and Sarat, *supra* n. 5, at 405.

34. Shapiro, COURTS: A COMPARATIVE AND POLITICAL ANALYSIS 20 (Chicago: University of Chicago Press, 1981).

35. *Id.* at 19, 27.

36. *Id.* at 31-32.

37. *Id.* at 24.

38. Wasby, CONTINUITY AND CHANGE: FROM THE WARREN COURT TO THE BURGER COURT 210-211 (Pacific Palisades, CA: Goodyear, 1976).

39. Special Project, *The Remedial Process in Institutional Reform Litigation*, 78 COLUM. L. REV. 785, 815 (May, 1978). See also Monti, *supra* n. 7, at 238, 241; Cavanagh and Sarat, *supra* n. 5, at 408; Rhodes v. Chapman, *supra* n. 11, at 2402.

40. Horowitz, *supra* n. 6, at 260.

41. Shapiro, *Stability and Change in Judicial Decision-Making: Incrementalism and Stare Decisis*, 2 LAW IN TRANS. Q. 134-157 (1965); see Lindblom, *The Science of 'Muddling Through'*, 19 PUB AD. REV. 79 (1959).

42. *See* Jones, *Speculative Augmentation in Federal Air Pollution Policy-Making*, 36 J. POL. 438 (May, 1974); Schulman, *Nonincremental Policy Making: Notes Toward an Alternative Paradigm*, 69 AM. POL. SCI. REV. 1354 (December, 1975).

43. Howard, *Adjudication Considered as a Process of Conflict Resolution: A Variation on the Separation of Powers*, 18 J. PUB. L. 339, 350 (1969).

44. Cavanagh and Sarat, *supra* n. 5, at 406; see also Nathan, *The Use of Masters in Institutional Reform Litigation*, 10 TOLEDO L. REV. 419 (Winter, 1979), and Special Project, *supra* n. 39, at 805-809.

45. Carter, *When Courts Should Make Policy: An Institutional Approach*, in Gardiner (ed.), PUBLIC LAW AND PUBLIC POLICY 145 (New York: Praeger, 1977).

46. *Id.*

47. *Id.* at 146.

48. Wasby, *Accountability of the Courts* 145, in Greer et al. (eds.), ACCOUNTABILITY IN URBAN SOCIETY (Beverly Hills: Sage, 1978). The following material draws on that article.

49. Dixon, *The "New" Substantive Due Process and the Democratic Ethic*, 1977 B.Y.U..L. REV. 43, 73 n. 134.

50. Provine, CASE SELECTION IN THE UNITED STATES SUPREME COURT (Chicago: University of Chicago Press, 1980).

51. See Howard, *supra* n. 17, at 41, 56.

52. Baum, *Lower-Court Response to Supreme Court Decisions: Reconsidering a Negative Picture*, 3 JUST SYS. J. 208, 216 (Spring, 1978).

53. See Eisenstein and Jacob, FELONY JUSTICE: AN ORGANIZATIONAL ANALYSIS OF THE CRIMINAL COURTS (Boston: Little, Brown, 1977).

54. Carbon, *Judicial retention elections: are they serving their intended purpose?*, 64 JUDICATURE 210 (November 1980).

55. Dubois, FROM BALLOT TO BENCH—JUDICAL ELECTIONS AND THE QUEST FOR ACCOUNTABILITY (Austin: University of Texas Press, 1980); Dubois, *Public Participation in Trial Court Elections*, 2 L. & POL'Y. Q. 133 (April, 1980).

56. Hoelzel, *No easy answers: a report on the national conference for judicial conduct organizations*, 64 JUDICATURE 279 (December-January 1981).

57. For a discussion of the new law, *see* Neisser, *The new federal judicial discipline act: some questions Congress didn't answer*, 65 JUDICATURE 142 (September, 1981).

58. See Peltason, FIFTY-EIGHT LONELY MEN (New York: Harcourt, Brace and World, 1961); Vines, *Southern State Supreme Courts and Race Relations*, 13 WEST POL. Q. 5 (March, 1965); Hamilton, THE BENCH AND THE BALLOT: SOUTHERN FEDERAL JUDGES AND BLACK VOTERS (New York: Oxford University Press, 1973).

59. Baum, *supra* n. 52.

60. Richardson and Vines, THE POLITICS OF THE FEDERAL COURTS (Boston: Little, Brown, 1970).

The Contributors

Henry J. Abraham is the James Hart Professor of Government and Foreign Affairs at the University of Virginia.

Shirley S. Abrahamson is a justice of the Supreme Court of Wisconsin.

Arlin N. Adams is a retired judge of the U.S. Court of Appeals for the Third Circuit and a lecturer at the University of Pennsylvania School of Law.

Larry T. Aspin is an associate professor of political science at Bradley University.

Susanna Barber was chair of the Department of Communication at Menlo College, Atherton, California, before beginning law studies at the University of California, Berkeley, in the fall of 1991.

Lawrence Baum is a professor of political science at the Ohio State University.

Susan Behuniak-Long is an associate professor of political science at Le Moyne College, Syracuse, New York.

Larry C. Berkson served as director of educational programs for the American Judicature Society from 1976-1982. He is currently in private business in New Hampshire.

Wayne E. Bohannon is president of Behavioral Science Associates.

William J. Brennan Jr. was an associate justice of the Supreme Court of the United States from 1956-1990.

Kristin Bumiller is an assistant professor of political science at Amherst College.

J. Louis Campbell III was an assistant professor of speech, theater, and the humanities at Missouri Western State College.

Bradley C. Canon is a professor of political science at the University of Kentucky.

John W. Cooley is a former United States magistrate who has served as a settlement master, mediator, and arbitrator.

David Crump is a professor of law at the University of Houston.

John Culver is a professor of political science at California Polytechnic State University.

Sue Davis is an associate professor of political science at the University of Delaware.

Shari S. Diamond is a professor of psychology at the University of Illinois, Chicago, and a senior research fellow at the American Bar Foundation.

Dennis D. Dorin is a professor of political science at the University of North Carolina, Charlotte.

Samuel Estreicher is a professor of law at New York University.

Lee Epstein is an associate professor of political science at Washington University, St. Louis.

Stephen B. Goldberg is a professor of law at Northwestern University School of Law.

Sheldon Goldman is a professor of political science at the Univesity of Massachusetts, Amherst.

Barbara Luck Graham is an associate professor of political science at the University of Missouri, St. Louis.

Eric D. Green is a professor of law at Boston University.

Joel B. Grossman is a professor of political science and law at the University of Wisconsin, Madison.

Diane S. Gutmann is an attorney in Madison, Wisconsin.

William K. Hall is a professor and chairperson of political science at Bradley University.

Howell T. Heflin is a United States senator from Alabama and a member of the Senate Judiciary Committee.

Arthur D. Hellman is a professor of law at the Univesity of Pittsburgh School of Law.

Ethan Katsh is a professor of legal studies at the University of Massachusetts at Amherst.

Kenneth R. Kay is a partner in Preston Gates Ellis & Rouvelas Meeds, Washington, D.C.

Herbert M. Kritzer is a professor of political science at the University of Wisconsin, Madison.

Barry Latzer is an associate professor of government at John Jay College of Criminal Justice, City University of New York.

Susan E. Lawrence is an associate professor of political science at Rugers University.

Robert E. Litan is a senior fellow in the Economic Studies Program of the Brookings Institution.

Bruce Littlejohn (retired) was chief justice of the Supreme Court of South Carolina.

George Mace was an associate professor and vice president at Southern Illinois University, Carbondale. He is currently in private enterprise in Carbondale.

Thomas R. Marshall is a professor of political science at the University of Texas, Arlington.

William F. McDonald is a professor of sociology at Georgetown University.

Stephen McDougal is an assistant professor of political science at Carroll College.

Robert McDuff is an attorney with the Lawyers' Committee for Civil Rights Under Law.

Albert P. Melone is a professor of political science at Southern Illinois University, Carbondale.

Carol J. Mills is director of research at the Johns Hopkins University Center for Talented Youth.

Norval Morris is the Julius Kreeger Professor of Law and Criminology at the University of Chicago.

Thomas R. Morris is a professor of political science at the University of Richmond.

G. Thomas Munsterman is director of the Center for Jury Studies of the National Center for State Courts.

Tim O'Brien is the law correspondent for ABC News.

Karen O'Connor is a professor of political science and adjunct professor of law at Emory University.

Nathan L. Posner was a partner in the Philadelphia law firm of Fox, Rothschild, O'Brien & Frankel and served as chancellor of the Philadelphia Bar Association, 1975-76.

D. Marie Provine is a professor of political science at Syracuse University.

Leslie Ratliff is director of the Alternative Dispute Resolution Office, Palm Beach County, Florida.

Frank E. A. Sander is Bussey Professor and associate dean at the Harvard Law School.

Jeffrey A. Segal is an associate professor of political science at State University of New York, Stony Brook.

John Sexton is a professor of law and dean at the New York University School of Law.

Jeffrey M. Shaman is a professor of law at DePaul University and Senior Fellow of the American Judicature Society.

David Shaw is a reporter for the *Los Angeles Times.*

Paul Simon is a U.S. senator from Illinois and a member of the Senate Judiciary Committee.

Elliot E. Slotnick, editor of *Judicial Politics: Readings from Judicature,* is an associate professor of political science at the Ohio State University.

Christopher E. Smith is an associate professor of political science at the University of Akron.

Harold J. Spaeth is a professor of political science at Michigan State University and a member of the Michigan bar.

Peter W. Sperlich is a professor of political science at the University of California, Berkeley.

John Paul Stevens is an associate justice of the Supreme Court of the United States.

John Stookey is a professor of political science at Arizona State University.

David U. Strawn is president of Dispute Management, Inc., Orlando, Florida.

J. Clifford Wallace is chief judge of the United States Court of Appeals for the Ninth Circuit.

Stephen L. Wasby is a professor of political science at the State University of New York, Albany.

George Watson is a professor of political science at Arizona State University.

Ronald E. Weber is the Wilder Crane Professor of Government at the University of Wisconsin, Milwaukee.

John T. Wold is a professor of political science at California State University, Stanislaus.

aJs The American Judicature Society

Founded in 1913, the American Judicature Society is an independent national organization of more than 20,000 citizens working to improve the courts through research, educational programs, and publications.

Judicature, the Society's refereed bimonthly journal, is a forum for fact and opinion relating to all aspects of the administration of justice and its improvement. The journal has been published continuously since 1917.